A Comprehensive Introduction to Object-Oriented Programming with **Java**™

C. Thomas Wu
Naval Postgraduate School

Higher Education

Boston Burr Ridge, IL Dubuque, IA New York San Francisco St. Louis
Bangkok Bogotá Caracas Kuala Lumpur Lisbon London Madrid Mexico City
Milan Montreal New Delhi Santiago Seoul Singapore Sydney Taipei Toronto

The McGraw-Hill Companies

A COMPREHENSIVE INTRODUCTION TO OBJECT-ORIENTED PROGRAMMING WITH JAVA

Published by McGraw-Hill, a business unit of The McGraw-Hill Companies, Inc., 1221 Avenue of the Americas, New York, NY 10020.

This book is printed on acid-free paper.

1 2 3 4 5 6 7 8 9 0 DOC/DOC 0 9 8 7

ISBN 978–0–07–352339–2
MHID 0–07–352339–9

Publisher: *Alan R. Apt*
Executive Marketing Manager: *Michael Weitz*
Senior Project Manager: *Sheila M. Frank*
Lead Production Supervisor: *Sandy Ludovissy*
Associate Media Producer: *Christina Nelson*
Designer: *Rick D. Noel*
Cover Designer: *Elise Lansdon*
(USE) Cover Image: *breaking wave on foaming ocean surface, ®Ron Dahlquist/Getty Images*
Compositor: *ICC Macmillan Inc.*
Typeface: *10.5/12 Times Roman*
Printer: *R. R. Donnelley Crawfordsville, IN*

Library of Congress Cataloging-in-Publication Data

Wu, C. Thomas.
A comprehensive introduction to object-oriented programming with Java / C. Thomas Wu. – 1st ed.
p. cm.
ISBN 978–0–07–352339–2 — ISBN 0–07–352339–9
1. Object-oriented programming (Computer science) 2. Java (Computer program language) I. Title.

QA76.64.W77 2008
005.1′17–dc22

2006048064

www.mhhe.com

To my family

Contents

17 Generics and Type Safety 945

18 List ADT 981

19 Stack ADT 1035

Preface

This book is an in-depth introduction to object-oriented programming using the Java programming language. In addition to covering traditional topics for a CS1 course, some of the more advanced topics such as recursion and linked lists are included to provide a comprehensive coverage of beginning to intermediate-level materials. There are more materials in the book than what are normally covered in a typical CS1 course. An instructor may want to teach some of the chapters on data structures in an advanced CS1 course. Topics covered in Chapters 16 to 20 are also suitable for use in a CS2 course.

Key Differences from the Standard Edition

This comprehensive edition is based on *An Introduction to Object-Oriented Programming with Java,* Fourth Edition. The key differences between this comprehensive version and the fourth edition standard version are as follows:

1. **Data Structures Chapters.** Chapter 16 covers topics on managing linked nodes. Using this as the foundation, Chapters 18 through 20 present three abstract data types (ADTs) List, Stack, and Queue, respectively. For all three ADTs, both array-based and linked-list implementations are shown, and their relative advantages and disadvantages are discussed.
2. **More Discussion on Java 5.0 Features.** Many of the new Java 5.0 features are explained and used in the sample programs. They include the enumerator type, the for-each loop construct, auto boxing and unboxing, and the generics. One complete chapter (Chapter 17) is dedicated to the generics.
3. **Exclusive Use of Console Input and Output.** All the GUI related topics, including the JOptionPane class, are moved to Chapter 14. Sample programs before Chapter 14 use the standard console input (Scanner) and output (System.out). Those who want to use JOptionPane for simple input and output can do so easily by covering Section 14.1 before Chapter 3.

Book Organization

There are 21 chapters in this book, numbered from 0 to 20. The first 11 chapters cover the core topics that provide the fundamentals of programming. Chapters 11 to 15 cover intermediate-level topics such as sorting, searching, recursion, inheritance, polymorphism, and file I/O. And Chapters 16 to 20 cover topics related to data structures. There are more than enough topics for one semester. After the first 11 chapters (Ch 0 to Ch 10), instructors can mix and match materials from Chapters 11 to 20 to suit their needs. We first show the dependency relationships among the chapters and then provide a brief summary of each chapter.

Chapter Dependency

For the most part, chapters should be read in sequence, but some variations are possible, especially with the optional chapters. Here's a simplified dependency graph:

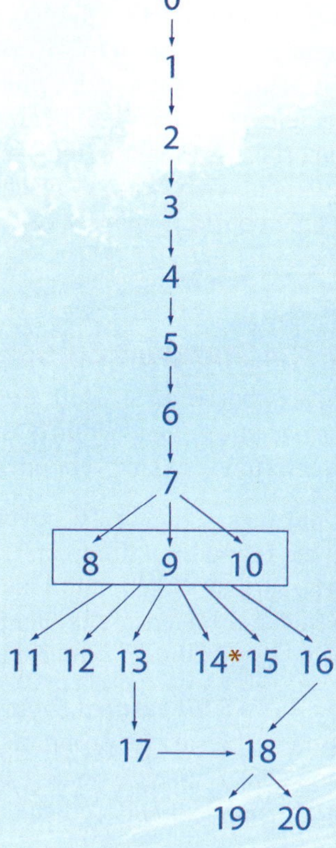

*Note: Some examples use arrays, but the use of arrays is not an integral part of the examples. These examples can be modified to those that do not use arrays. Many topics from the early part of the chapter can be introduced as early as after Chapter 2.

Brief Chapter Summary

Here is a short description of each chapter:

- **Chapter 0** is an optional chapter. We provide background information on computers and programming languages. This chapter can be skipped or assigned as an outside reading if you wish to start with object-oriented programming concepts.
- **Chapter 1** provides a conceptual foundation of object-oriented programming. We describe the key components of object-oriented programming and illustrate each concept with a diagrammatic notation using UML.
- **Chapter 2** covers the basics of Java programming and the process of editing, compiling, and running a program. From the first sample program presented in this chapter, we emphasize object-orientation. We will introduce the standard classes String, Date, and SimpleDateFormat so we can reinforce the notion of object declaration, creation, and usage. Moreover, by using these standard classes, students can immediately start writing practical programs.We describe and illustrate console input with System.in and the new Scanner class and output with System.out.
- **Chapter 3** introduces variables, constants, and expressions for manipulating numerical data. We explain the standard Math class from java.lang and introduce more standard classes (GregorianCalendar and DecimalFormat) to continually reinforce the notion of object-orientation. We describe additional methods of the Scanner class to input numerical values. Random number generation is introduced in this chapter. The optional section explains how the numerical values are represented in memory space.
- **Chapter 4** teaches the basics of creating programmer-defined classes. We keep the chapter accessible by introducting only the fundamentals with illustrative examples. The key topics covered in this chapter are constructors, visibility modifiers (public and private), local variables, and passing data to methods. We provide easy-to-grasp illustrations that capture the essence of the topics so the students will have a clear understanding of them.
- **Chapter 5** explains the selection statements if and switch. We cover boolean expressions and nested-if statements. We explain how objects are compared by using equivalence (==) and equality (the equals and compareTo methods). We use the String and the programmer-defined Fraction classes to make the distinction between the equivalence and equality clear. Drawing 2-D graphics is introduced, and a screensaver sample development program is developed. We describe the new Java 5.0 feature called *enumerated type* in this chapter.
- **Chapter 6** explains the repetition statements while, do–while, and for. Pitfalls in writing repetition statements are explained. One of the pitfalls to avoid is the use of float or double for the data type of a counter variable. We illustrate this pitfall by showing a code that will result in infinite loop. Finding the greatest common divisor of two integers is used as an example of a nontrivial loop statement. We show the difference between the straightforward (brute-force)

and the clever (Euclid's) solutions. We introduce the Formatter class (new to Java 5.0) and show how the output can be aligned nicely. The optional last section of the chapter introduces recursion as another technique for repetition. The recursive version of a method that finds the greatest common divisor of two integers is given.

- **Chapter 7** is the second part of creating programmer-defined classes. We introduce new topics related to the creation of programmer-defined classes and also repeat some of the topics covered in Chapter 4 in more depth. The key topics covered in this chapter are method overloading, the reserved word this, class methods and variables, returning an object from a method, and pass-by-value parameter passing. As in Chapter 4, we provide many lucid illustrations to make these topics accessible to beginners. We use the Fraction class to illustrate many of these topics, such as the use of this and class methods. The complete definition of the Fraction class is presented in this chapter.
- **Chapter 8** teaches exception handling and assertions. The focus of this chapter is the construction of reliable programs. We provide a detailed coverage of exception handling in this chapter. We introduce an assertion and show how it can be used to improve the reliability of finished products by catching logical errors early in the development.
- **Chapter 9** covers nonnumerical data types: characters and strings. Both the String and StringBuffer classes are explained in the chapter. Another string class named StringBuilder (new to Java 5.) is briefly explained in this chapter. An important application of string processing is pattern matching. We describe pattern matching and regular expression in this chapter. We introduce the Pattern and Matcher classes and show how they are used in pattern matching.
- **Chapter 10** teaches arrays. We cover arrays of primitive data types and of objects. An array is a reference data type in Java, and we show how arrays are passed to methods. We describe how to process two-dimensional arrays and explain that a two-dimensional array is really an array of arrays in Java. Lists and maps are introduced as a more general and flexible way to maintain a collection of data. The use of ArrayList and HashMap classes from the java.util package is shown in the sample programs. Also, we show how the WordList helper class used in Chapter 9 sample development program is implemented with another map class called TreeMap.
- **Chapter 11** presents searching and sorting algorithms. Both N^2 and $N\log_2 N$ sorting algorithms are covered. The mathematical analysis of searching and sorting algorithms can be omitted depending on the students' background.
- **Chapter 12** explains the file I/O. Standard classes such as File and JFileChooser are explained. We cover all types of file I/O, from a low-level byte I/O to a high-level object I/O. We show how the file I/O techniques are used to implement the helper classes—Dorm and FileManager—in Chapter 8 and 9 sample development programs. The use of the Scanner class for inputting data from a textfile is also illustrated in this chapter.

- **Chapter 13** discusses inheritance and polymorphism and how to use them effectively in program design. The effect of inheritance for member accessibility and constructors is explained. We also explain the purpose of abstract classes and abstract methods.
- **Chapter 14** covers GUI and event-driven programming. Only the Swing-based GUI components are covered in this chapter. We show how to use the JOptionPane class for a very simple GUI-based input and output. GUI components introduced in this chapter include JButton, JLabel, ImageIcon, JTextField, JTextArea, and menu-related classes. We describe the effective use of nested panels and layout managers. Handling of mouse events is described and illustrated in the sample programs. Those who do not teach GUI can skip this chapter altogether. Those who teach GUI can introduce the beginning part of the chapter as early as after Chapter 2.
- **Chapter 15** covers recursion. Because we want to show the examples where the use of recursion really shines, we did not include any recursive algorithm (other than those used for explanation purposes) that really should be written nonrecursively.
- **Chapter 16** covers contiguous and noncontiguous memory allocation schemes and introduces the concept of linked lists. Ample examples are provided to illustrate the manipulation of linked lists of primitive data types and linked lists of objects. This chapter lays the necessary foundation for the students to learn different techniques for implementing the abstract data types covered in Chapters 18 through 20.
- **Chapter 17** covers new Java 5.0 generics in detail. The chapter describes how generic classes are defined and how the type safety is supported by generics. A concrete example of using generics is shown by defining a simple linked list with generic nodes.
- **Chapter 18** introduces the concept of abstract data types (ADT) and covers the List ADT. Key features of the List ADT are explained and two implementations using an array and a linked list are shown. The iterator pattern to traverse the elements in the List ADT is introduced.
- **Chapter 19** covers the Stack ADT. Key features of the Stack ADT are explained and two implementations using an array and a linked list are shown. Sample applications that use stacks are described.
- **Chapter 20** covers the Queue ADT. Key features of the Stack ADT are explained and two implementations using an array and a linked list are shown. A special type of queue called a *priority queue* is also intoduced in this chapter.

Hallmark Features of the Text

Problem Solving

2.5 Sample Development

Printing the Initials

Now that we have acquired a basic understanding of Java application programs, let's write a new application. We will go through the design, coding, and testing phases of the software life cycle to illustrate the development process. Since the program we develop here is very simple, we can write it without really going through the phases. However, it is extremely important for you to get into a habit of developing a program by following the software life cycle stages. Small programs can be developed in a haphazard manner, but not large programs. We will teach you the development process with small programs first, so you will be ready to use it to create large programs later.

We will develop this program by using an incremental development technique, which will develop the program in small incremental steps. We start out with a bare-bones program and gradually build up the program by adding more and more code to it. At each incremental step, we design, code, and test the program before moving on to the next step. This methodical development of a program allows us to focus our attention on a single task at each step, and this reduces the chance of introducing errors into the program.

Problem Statement

We start our development with a problem statement. The problem statement for our sample programs will be short, ranging from a sentence to a paragraph, but the problem statement for complex and advanced applications may contain many pages. Here's the problem statement for this sample development exercise:

> *Write an application that asks for the user's first, middle, and last names and replies with the user's initials.*

Overall Plan

Our first task is to map out the overall plan for development. We will identify classes necessary for the program and the steps we will follow to implement the program. We begin with the outline of program logic. For a simple program such as this one, it is kind of obvious; but to practice the incremental development, let's put down the outline of program flow explicitly. We can express the program flow as having three tasks:

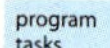

1. Get the user's first, middle, and last names.
2. Extract the initials to formulate the monogram.
3. Output the monogram.

Having identified the three major tasks of the program, we will now identify the classes we can use to implement the three tasks. First, we need an object to handle the input. At this point, we have learned about only the **Scanner** class, so we will use it here. Second, we need an object to display the result. Again, we will use **System.out**, as it is the only one we know at this point for displaying a string value. For the string

Sample Development Programs

Most chapters include a sample development section that describes the process of incremental development.

Development Exercises

give students an opportunity to practice incremental development.

Development Exercises

For the following exercises, use the incremental development methodology to implement the program. For each exercise, identify the program tasks, create a design document with class descriptions, and draw the program diagram. Map out the development steps at the start. Present any design alternatives and justify your selection. Be sure to perform adequate testing at the end of each development step.

8. In the sample development, we developed the user module of the keyless entry system. For this exercise, implement the administrative module that allows the system administrator to add and delete `Resident` objects and modify information on existing `Resident` objects. The module will also allow the user to open a list from a file and save the list to a file. Is it proper to implement the administrative module by using one class? Wouldn't it be a better design if we used multiple classes with each class doing a single, well-defined task?
9. Write an application that maintains the membership lists of five social clubs in a dormitory. The five social clubs are the Computer Science Club, Biology Club, Billiard Club, No Sleep Club, and Wine Tasting Club. Use the `Dorm`

Object-Oriented Approach

We take the object-first approach to teaching object-oriented programming with emphasis on proper object-oriented design. The concept of objects is clearly illustrated from the very first sample program.

```
/*

    Chapter 2 Sample Program: Displaying a Window

    File: Ch2Sample1.java

*/

import javax.swing.*;

class  Ch2Sample1 {

   public static void main(String[] args) {

       JFrame    myWindow;

       myWindow = new JFrame();

       myWindow.setSize(300, 200);
       myWindow.setTitle("My First Java Program");
       myWindow.setVisible(true);
   }
}
```

Good practices on object-oriented design are discussed throughout the book and illustrated through numerous sample programs.

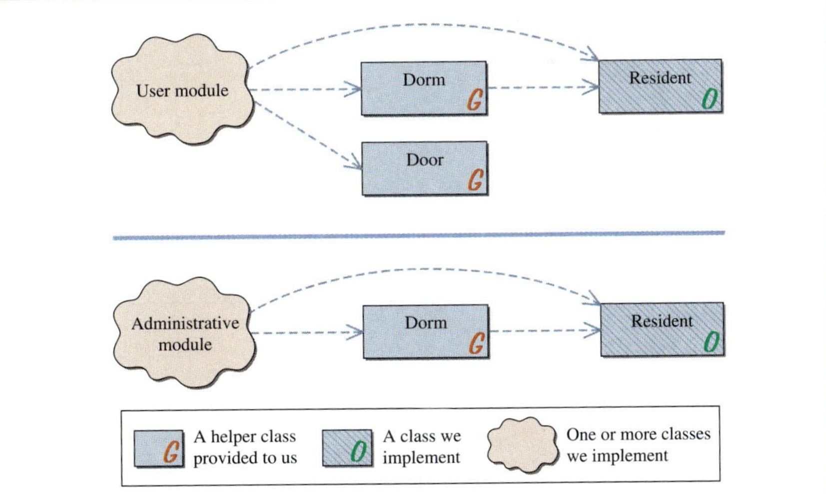

Figure 8.8 Program diagrams for the user and administrative modules. Notice the same **Dorm** and **Resident** classes are used in both programs. User and administrative modules will include one or more classes (at least one is programmer-defined).

Illustrative Diagrams

Illustrative diagrams are used to explain all key concepts of programming such as the difference between object declaration and creation, the distinction between the primitive data type and the reference data type, the call-by-value parameter passing, inheritance, and many others.

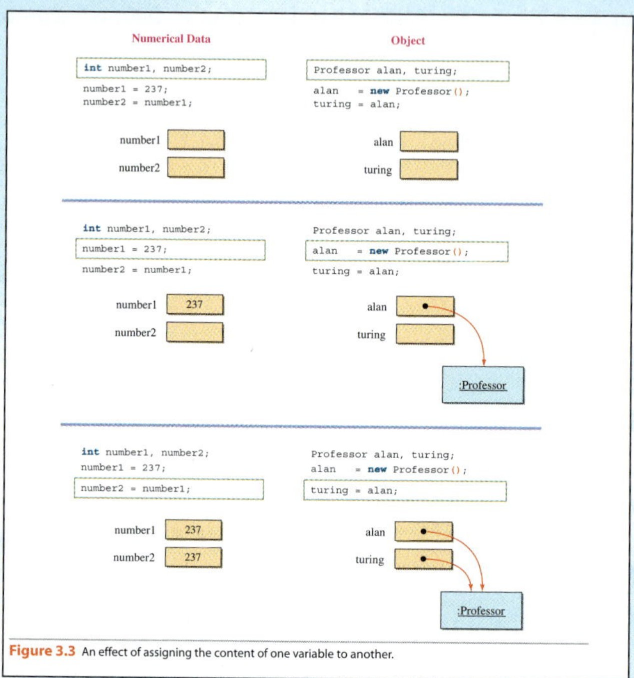

Figure 3.3 An effect of assigning the content of one variable to another.

Lucid diagrams are used effectively to explain data structures and abstract data types.

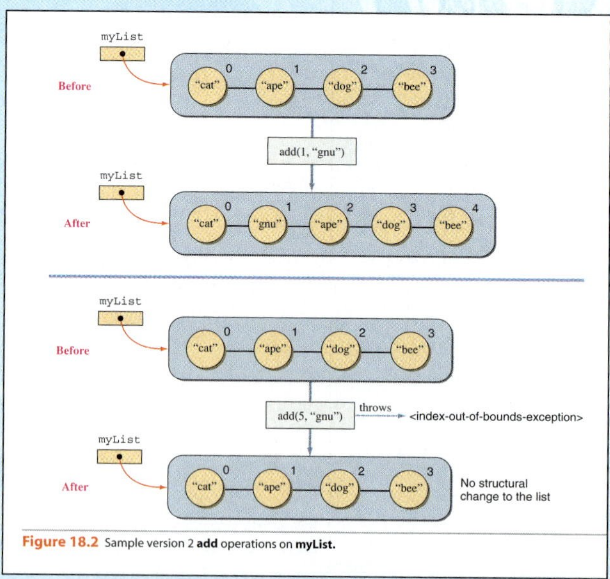

Figure 18.2 Sample version 2 **add** operations on **myList.**

Student Pedagogy

Always define a constructor and initialize data members fully in the constructor so an object will be created in a valid state.

Design Guidelines provide tips on good program design.

Things to Remember boxes provide tips for students to remember key concepts.

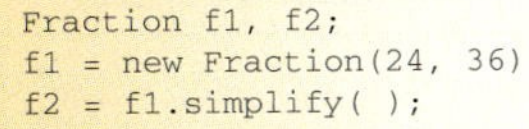

*List the **catch** blocks in the order of specialized to more general exception classes. At most one **catch** block is executed, and all other **catch** blocks are ignored.*

Hints, Tips, & Pitfalls

It is not necessary to create an object for every variable we use. Many novice programmers often make this mistake. For example, we write

```
Fraction f1, f2;
f1 = new Fraction(24, 36);
f2 = f1.simplify( );
```

We didn't write

```
Fraction f1, f2;
f1 = new Fraction(24, 36);
f2 = new Fraction(1, 1); //not necessary

f2 = f1.simplify( );
```

because it is not necessary. The ***simplify*** method returns a ***Fraction*** object, and in the calling program, all we need is a name we can use to refer to this returned ***Fraction*** object. Don't forget that the object name (variable) and the actual object instance are two separate things.

Tips, Hints, and Pitfalls provide important points for which to watch out.

You Might Want to Know boxes give students interesting bits of information.

You Might Want to Know

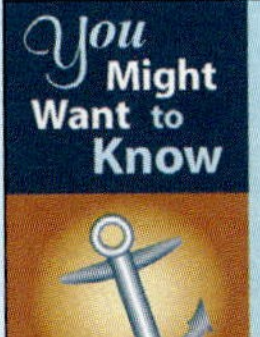

We can turn our simulation program into a real one by replacing the **Door** class with a class that actually controls the door. Java provides a mechanism called Java Native Interface (JNI) which can be used to embed a link to a low-level device driver code, so calling the **open** method actually unlocks the door.

1. What will be displayed on the console window when the following code is executed and the user enters abc123 and 14?

```
Scanner scanner = new Scanner(System.in);
try {
   int num1 = scanner.nextInt();

   System.out.println("Input 1 accepted");

   int num2 = scanner.nextInt();

   System.out.println("Input 2 accepted");

} catch (InputMismatchException e) {

   System.out.println("Invalid Entry");
}
```

Quick Check exercises at the end of the sections allow students to test their comprehension of topics.

Supplements for Instructors and Students

On-Line Learning Center is located at www.mhhe.com/wu

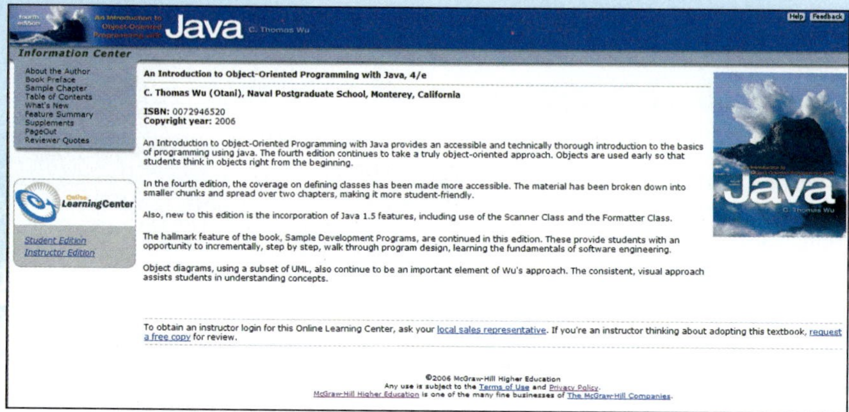

For Instructors

- Complete set of **PowerPoints,** including lecture notes and figures.

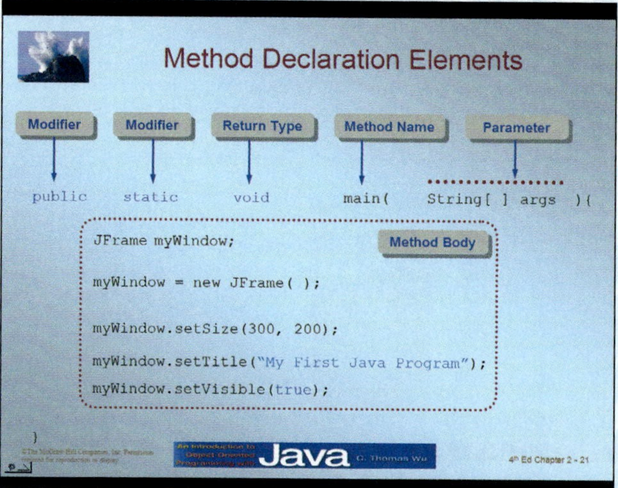

- **Complete solutions** for the exercises
- **Example Bank**—Additional examples, which are searchable by topic, are provided online in a "bank" for instructors.
- **Homework Manager/Test Bank**—Conceptual review questions are stored in this electronic question bank and can be assigned as exam questions or homework.
- **Online labs** which accompany this text, can be used in a closed lab, open lab, or for assigned programming projects.

For Students

- **Compiler How Tos** provide tutorials on how to get up and running on the most popular compilers to aid students in using IDEs.

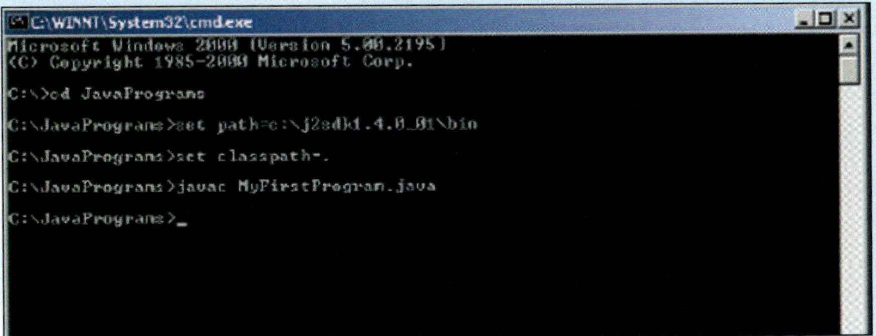

- **Interactive Quizzes** allow students to test what they learn and get immediate feedback.
- **Source code** for all example programs in the book.
- **Answers** to quick check exercises.
- **Glossary** of key terms.
- **Recent News** links relevant to computer science.
- **Additional Topics** such as more on swing and an introduction to data structures.

Acknowledgments

First, I would like to thank the following reviewers for their comments, suggestions, and encouragement.

Wu Focus Group—Jackson Hole, WY
Elizabeth Adams, *James Madison University*
GianMario Besana, *Depaul University*
Michael Buckley, *State University of New York, Buffalo*
James Cross, *Auburn University*
Priscilla Dodds, *Georgia Perimeter College*
Christopher Eliot, *University of Massachusetts-Amherst*
Joanne Houlahan, *John Hopkins University*
Len Myers, *California Polytechnic State University, San Luis Obispo*
Hal Perkins, *University of Washington*
William Shea, *Kansas State University*
Marge Skubic, *University of Missouri, Columbia*
Bill Sverdlik, *Eastern Michigan University*
Suzanne Westbrook, *University of Arizona*

Reviewers

Ajith, Abraham, *Oklahoma State University*
Elizabeth Adams, *James Madison University*
David L. Atkins, *University of Oregon*
GianMario Besana, *DePaul University*
Robert P. Burton, *Brigham Young University*
Michael Buckley, *State University of New York, Buffalo*
Rama Chakrapani, *Tennessee Technological University*
Teresa Cole, *Boise State University*
James Cross, *Auburn University*
Priscilla Dodds, *Georgia Perimeter College*
Kossi Delali Edoh, *Montclair State University*
Christopher Eliot, *University of Massachusetts-Amherst*
Michael Floeser, *Rochester Institute of Technology*
Joanne Houlahan, *John Hopkins University*
Michael N. Huhns, *University of South Carolina*
Eliot Jacobson, *University of California, Santa Barbara*
Martin Kendall, *Montgomery Community College*
Mike Litman, *Western Illinois University*
Len Myers, *California Polytechnic State University, San Luis Obispo*
Jun Ni, *University of Iowa*
Robert Noonan, *College of William and Mary*
Jason S. O'Neal, *Mississippi College*
Hal Perkins, *University of Washington*
Gerald Ross, *Lane Community College*
William Shea, *Kansas State University*
Jason John Schwarz, *North Carolina State University*
Marge Skubic, *University of Missouri, Columbia*
Bill Sverdlik, *Eastern Michigan University*
Peter Stanchev, *Kettering University*
Krishnaprasad Thirunarayan, *Wright State University*
David Vineyard, *Kettering University*
Suzanne Westbrook, *University of Arizona*
Melissa Wiggins, *Mississippi College*
Zhiguang Xu, *Valdosta State University.*

The following reviewers have provided feedback on the chapters new to this comprehensive edition:

Eric Matson, *Wright State University*
Tim Margush, *University of Akron*
Roxanne Canosa, *Rochester Institute of Technology*
Ivan Bajic, *San Diego State University*
Carolyn Miller, *North Carolina State*
Sunil Prabhakar, *Purdue University*
Weining Zhang, *University of Texas, San Antonio*

Personal Story

In September, 2001, I changed my name for personal reasons. Prof C. Thomas Wu is now Prof Thomas W. Otani. To maintain continuity and not to confuse people, we continue to publish the book under my former name. For those who care to find out a little about my personal history can do so by visiting my website (www.drcaffeine.com).

0 Introduction to Computers and Programming Languages

Objectives

After you have read and studied this chapter, you should be able to

- State briefly a history of computers.
- Name and describe five major components of the computer.
- Convert binary numbers to decimal numbers and vice versa.
- State the difference between the low-level and high-level programming languages.

Introduction

Before we embark on our study of computer programming, we will present some background information on computers and programming languages in this optional chapter. We provide a brief history of computers from the early days to present and describe the components found in today's computers. We also present a brief history of programming languages from low-level machine languages to today's object-oriented languages.

0.1 A History of Computers

Humans have evolved from a primitive to a highly advanced society by continually inventing tools. Stone tools, gunpowder, wheels, and other inventions have changed the lives of humans dramatically. In recent history, the computer is arguably the most important invention. In today's highly advanced society, computers affect our lives 24 hours a day: class schedules are formulated by computers, student records are maintained by computers, exams are graded by computers, dorm security systems are monitored by computers, and numerous other functions that affect us are controlled by computers.

Charles Babbage

Difference Engine

Although the first true computer was invented in the 1940s, the concept of a computer is actually more than 160 years old. ***Charles Babbage*** is credited with inventing a precursor to the modern computer. In 1823 he received a grant from the British government to build a mechanical device he called the ***Difference Engine***, intended for computing and printing mathematical tables. The device was based on rotating wheels and was operated by a single crank. Unfortunately, the technology of the time was not advanced enough to build the device. He ran into difficulties and eventually abandoned the project.

Analytical Engine

But an even more grandiose scheme was already with him. In fact, one of the reasons he gave up on the Difference Engine may have been to work on his new concept for a better machine. He called his new device the ***Analytical Engine***. This device, too, was never built. His second device also was ahead of its time; the technology did not yet exist to make the device a reality. Although never built, the Analytical Engine was a remarkable achievement because its design was essentially based on the same fundamental principles of the modern computer. One principle that stands out was its programmability. With the Difference Engine, Babbage would have been able to compute only mathematical tables, but with the Analytical Engine he would have been able to compute any calculation by inputting instructions on punch cards. The method of inputting programs to computers on punch cards was actually adopted for real machines and was still in wide use as late as the 1970s.

Ada Lovelace

The Analytical Engine was never built, but a demonstration program was written by ***Ada Lovelace***, a daughter of the poet Lord Byron. The programming language *Ada* was named in honor of Lady Lovelace, the first computer programmer.

In the late 1930s John Atanasoff of Iowa State University, with his graduate student Clifford Berry, built the prototype of the first automatic electronic calculator.

One innovation of their machine was the use of binary numbers. (We discuss binary numbers in Sec. 0.2.) At around the same time, Howard Aiken of Harvard University was working on the *Automatic Sequence-Controlled Calculator,* known more commonly as ***MARK I***, with support from IBM and the U.S. Navy. MARK I was very similar to the Analytical Engine in design and was described as "Babbage's dream come true."

MARK I

MARK I was an electromechanical computer based on relays. Mechanical relays were not fast enough, and MARK I was quickly replaced by machines based on electronic vacuum tubes. The first completely electronic computer, ***ENIAC I*** (*Electronic Numerical Integrator And Calculator*), was built at the University of Pennsylvania under the supervision of John W. Mauchly and J. Presper Eckert. Their work was influenced by the work of John Atanasoff.

ENIAC I

ENIAC I was programmed laboriously by plugging wires into a control panel that resembled an old telephone switchboard. Programming took an enormous amount of the engineers' time, and even making a simple change to a program was a time-consuming effort. While programming activities were going on, the expensive computer sat idle. To improve its productivity, John von Neumann of Princeton University proposed storing programs in the computer's memory. This ***stored program*** scheme not only improved computation speed but also allowed far more flexible ways of writing programs. For example, because a program is stored in the memory, the computer can change the program instructions to alter the sequence of the execution, thereby making it possible to get different results from a single program.

stored program

generations of computers

We characterized these early computers with vacuum tubes as *first-generation computers. Second-generation computers,* with transistors replacing the vacuum tubes, started appearing in the late 1950s. Improvements in memory devices also increased processing speed further. In the early 1960s, transistors were replaced by integrated circuits, and *third-generation computers* emerged. A single integrated circuit of this period incorporated hundreds of transistors and made the construction of minicomputers possible. Minicomputers are small enough to be placed on desktops in individual offices and labs. The early computers, on the other hand, were so huge that they easily occupied the whole basement of a large building.

Advancement of integrated circuits was phenomenal. Large-scale integrated circuits, commonly known as *computer chips* or *silicon chips,* packed the power equivalent to thousands of transistors and made the notion of a "computer on a single chip" a reality. With large-scale integrated circuits, *microcomputers* emerged in the mid-1970s. The machines we call *personal computers* today are descendants of the microcomputers of the 1970s. The computer chips used in today's personal computers pack the power equivalent to several millions of transistors. Personal computers are *fourth-generation computers.*

Early microcomputers were isolated, stand-alone machines. The word *personal* describes a machine as a personal device intended to be used by an individual. However, it did not take long to realize there was a need to share computer resources. For example, early microcomputers required a dedicated printer. Wouldn't it make more sense to have many computers share a single printer? Wouldn't it also make sense to share data among computers, instead of duplicating the same data on individual machines? Wouldn't it be nice to send electronic messages between the computers? The notion of networked computers arose to meet these needs.

network

LAN

WAN

internet

Computers of all kinds are connected into a ***network***. A network that connects computers in a single building or in several nearby buildings is called a *local-area network* or ***LAN***. A network that connects geographically dispersed computers is called a *wide-area network* or ***WAN***. These individual networks can be connected further to form interconnected networks called ***internets***. The most famous internet is simply called the ***Internet***. The Internet makes the sharing of worldwide information possible and easy. The hottest tool for viewing information on the Internet is a *Web browser*. A Web browser allows you to experience *multimedia information* consisting of text, audio, video, and other types of information. We will describe how Java is related to the Internet and Web browsers in Section 0.4.

If you want to learn more about the history of computing, there is a wealth of information available on the Web. You can start your exploration from

www.yahoo.com/Computers_and_Internet/History

For more information on the pioneers of computers, visit

en.wikipedia.org/wiki/category:Computer_pioneers

1. Who was the first computer programmer?
2. Who designed the Difference Engine and Analytical Engine?
3. How many generations of computers are there?

0.2 Computer Architecture

A typical computer today has five basic components: RAM, CPU, storage devices, I/O (input/output) devices, and communication devices. Figure 0.1 illustrates these five components. Before we describe the components of a computer, we will explain the binary numbering system used in a computer.

Binary Numbers

To understand the binary number system, let's first review the decimal number system in which we use 10 digits: 0, 1, 2, 3, 4, 5, 6, 7, 8, 9. To represent a number in the decimal system, we use a sequence of one or more of these digits. The value that each digit in the sequence represents depends on its position. For example, consider the numbers 234 and 324. The digit 2 in the first number represents 200, whereas the digit 2 in the second number represents 20. A position in a sequence has a value that is an integral power of 10. The following diagram illustrates how the

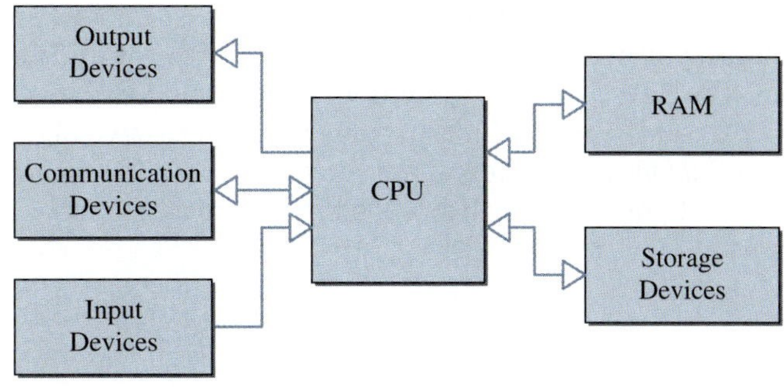

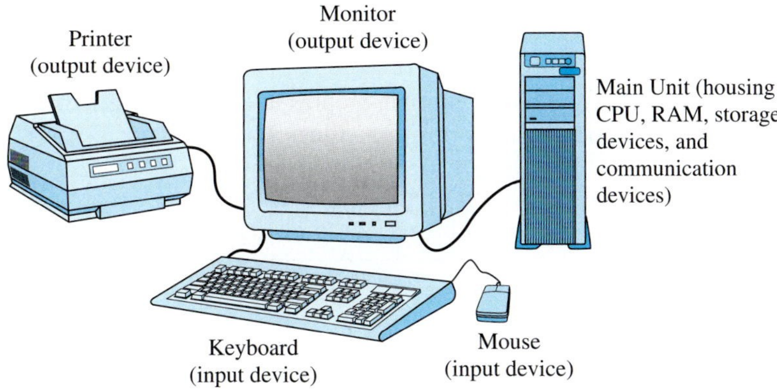

Figure 0.1 A simplified view of an architecture for a typical computer.

values of positions are determined:

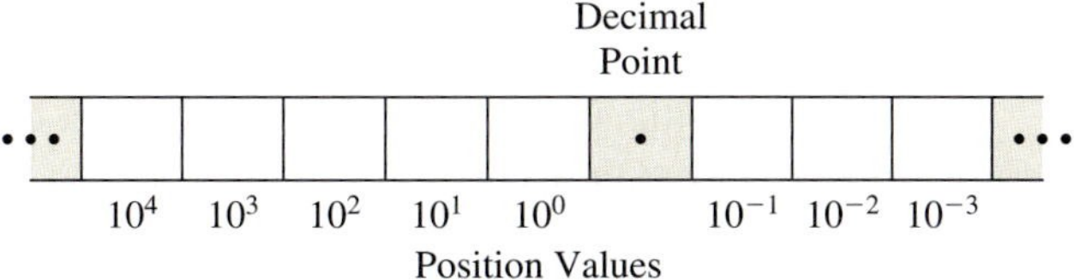

The value of a decimal number (represented as a sequence of digits) is the sum of the digits, multiplied by their position values, as illustrated:

2	4	8	•	7
10^2	10^1	10^0		10^{-1}

$$= 2 \times 10^2 + 4 \times 10^1 + 8 \times 10^0 + 7 \times 10^{-1}$$

$$= 2 \times 100 + 4 \times 10 + 8 \times 1 + 7 \times 1/10$$

$$= 200 \quad + 40 \quad + 8 \quad + 7/10 \quad = 248.7$$

base-2 numbers

binary number

bits

In the decimal number system, we have 10 symbols, and the position values are integral powers of 10. We say that 10 is the *base* or *radix* of the decimal number system. The ***binary number*** system works the same as the decimal number system but uses 2 as its base. The binary number system has two digits (0 and 1) called ***bits***, and position values are integral powers of 2. The following diagram illustrates how the values of positions are determined in the binary system:

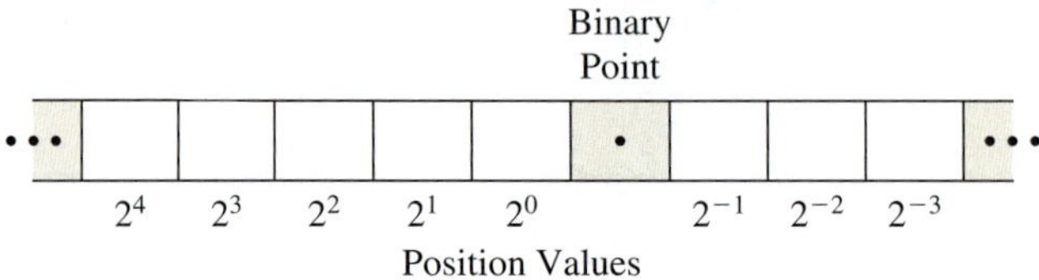

The value of a binary number (represented as a sequence of bits) is the sum of the bits, multiplied by their position values, as illustrated:

1	0	1	•	1
2^2	2^1	2^0		2^{-1}

binary-to-decimal conversion

$$= 1 \times 2^2 + 0 \times 2^1 + 1 \times 2^0 + 1 \times 2^{-1}$$

$$= 1 \times 4 \ + 0 \times 2 \ + 1 \times 1 \ + 1 \times 1/2$$

$$= 4 \quad + 0 \quad + 1 \quad + 1/2 \quad = 5.5$$

So the binary number 101.1 is numerically equivalent to the decimal number 5.5. This illustration shows how to convert a given binary number to the decimal equivalent. How about converting a given decimal number to its binary equivalent?

The following steps show how to convert a decimal number (only the whole numbers) to the equivalent binary number. The basic idea goes something like this:

decimal-to-binary conversion

1. Divide the number by 2.
2. The remainder is the bit value of the 2^0 position.
3. Divide the quotient by 2.
4. The remainder is the bit value of the 2^1 position.
5. Divide the quotient by 2.
6. The remainder is the bit value of the 2^2 position.
7. Repeat the procedure until you cannot divide any further, that is, until the quotient becomes 0.

The following diagram illustrates the conversion of decimal number 25.

Division #5		Division #4		Division #3		Division #2		Division #1	
$2\overline{)1}$ ← quotient 0		$2\overline{)3}$ ← quotient 1		$2\overline{)6}$ ← quotient 3		$2\overline{)12}$ ← quotient 6		$2\overline{)25}$ ← quotient 12	
0		2		6		12		24	
1		**1**		**0**		**0**		**1**	
2^4		2^3		2^2		2^1		2^0	
16	+	8	+	0	+	0	+	1	= 25

The binary system is more suitable for computers than the decimal system because it is far easier to design an electrical device that can distinguish two states (bits 0 and 1) than 10 states (digits 0 through 9). For example, we can represent 1 by turning the switch on and 0 by turning the switch off. In a real computer, 0 is represented by electrical voltage below a certain level and 1 by electrical voltage at or above this level.

When you pay closer attention to the on/off switch on computers and other electronic devices, you should notice an icon like this

This is a stylized representation of binary digits 0 and 1.

RAM

RAM

byte

Random access memory or ***RAM*** is a repository for both program instructions and data manipulated by the program during execution. RAM is divided into *cells,* with each cell having a unique address. Typically, each cell consists of 4 ***bytes*** (B), and a single byte (1 B) in turn consists of 8 *bits.* Each bit, which can be either on or off, represents a single binary digit. RAM is measured by the number of bytes it contains. For example, 128 kilobytes (KB) of RAM contains $128 \times 1024 = 131{,}072$ B because 1 KB is equal to $2^{10} = 1024$ B. Notice that 1 K is not equal to 10^3, although $10^3 = 1000$ is a close approximation to $2^{10} = 1024$. The first IBM PC introduced in 1981 came with 16 KB of RAM, and the first Macintosh computer introduced in 1984 came with 128 KB of RAM. In contrast, a typical PC today has anywhere from 128 MB to 512 MB of RAM. Given that 1 MB is equal to 1024 KB, we know that 256 MB means 256×1024 KB $= 262{,}144$ KB $= 262{,}144 \times 1024$ B $= 268{,}435{,}456$ B.

CPU

CPU

The *central processing unit* or ***CPU*** is the brain of a computer. The CPU is the component that executes program instructions by fetching an instruction (stored in RAM), executing it, fetching the next instruction, executing it, and so on until it encounters an instruction to stop. The CPU contains a small number of ***registers***, which are high-speed devices for storing data or instructions temporarily. The CPU also contains the *arithmetic-logic unit* (ALU), which performs arithmetic operations such as addition and subtraction and logical operations such as comparing two numbers.

register

clock speed

CPUs are characterized by their ***clock speeds***. For example, in the Intel Pentium 200, the CPU has a clock speed of 200 megahertz (MHz). The *hertz* is a unit of frequency equal to 1 cycle per second. A *cycle* is a period of time between two on states or off states. So 200 MHz equals 200,000,000 cycles per second. The fastest CPU for commercially available personal computers was around 200 MHz in 1997 when the first edition of this textbook was published. But by the beginning of 1998, many vendors started selling 300-MHz machines. And in a mere 6 months, by the middle of 1998, the top-of-the-line personal computers were 400-MHz machines. As of this writing in late 2002, we see computers with 2.0-GHz (2000-MHz) CPU being advertised and sold. The increase of the CPU speed in the last two decades is truly astonishing. The clock speed of the Intel 8080, the CPU introduced in 1974 that started the PC revolution, was a mere 2 MHz. In contrast, the clock speed of the Intel Pentium 4 introduced in 2001 was 2 GHz (2000 MHz). Table 0.1 lists some of the Intel processors.

I/O Devices

I/O devices

Input/output or ***I/O devices*** allow communication between the user and the CPU. Input devices such as keyboards and mice are used to enter data, programs, and commands in the CPU. Output devices such as monitors and printers are used to display or print information. Other I/O devices include scanners, bar code readers, magnetic strip readers, digital video cameras, and musical instrument digital interface (MIDI) devices.

Storage Devices

nonvolatile and volatile memory

Storage devices such as disk and tape drives are used to store data and programs. Secondary storage devices are called ***nonvolatile memory***, while RAM is called ***volatile memory.*** *Volatile* means the data stored in a device will be lost when the power to the device is turned off. Being nonvolatile and much cheaper than RAM, secondary storage is an ideal medium for permanent storage of large volumes of data. A secondary storage device cannot replace RAM, though, because secondary storage is far slower in data access (getting data out and writing data in) compared to RAM.

The most common storage device today for personal computers is a disk drive. There are two kinds of disks: hard and floppy (also known as diskettes). Hard disks provide much faster performance and larger capacity, but are normally not removable; that is, a single hard disk is permanently attached to a disk drive. Floppy disks, on the other hand, are removable, but their performance is far slower and their capacity far smaller than those of hard disks. As the standard floppy disks can

Table 0.1 A table of Intel processors. For some CPUs, several types with different clock speeds are possible. In such case, only the fastest clock speed is shown. For more information on Intel CPUs, visit http://www.intel.com.

	CPU	Date Introduced	Clock Speed (MHz)
1970s	4004	11/15/71	0.108
	8008	4/1/72	0.200
	8080	4/1/74	2
	8088	6/1/79	8
1980s	80286	2/1/82	12
	80386SX	6/16/88	16
	80486DX	4/10/89	25
1990s	Pentium	3/22/93	66
	Pentium Pro	11/1/95	200
	Pentium II	5/7/97	300
	Pentium II Xeon	6/29/98	400
	Pentium III	10/25/99	733
2000s	Xeon	9/25/01	2000
	Pentium 4	4/27/01	2000
	Itanium 2	7/8/02	1000
	Pentium 4 Extreme Edition	2/2/04	3400
	Core 2 Extreme	7/27/06	3200

store only up to approximately 1.44 MB, they are becoming less useful in today's world of multimegabyte image and sound files. They are fast becoming obsolete, and hardly anybody uses them anymore. Removable storage media with much higher capacity such as zip disks (capable of holding 100 to 250 MB of data) replaced floppy disks in late 1990s. Computer technology moves so quickly that zip disks themselves are already becoming obsolete. The most common form of portable storage medium today (2006) is a compact USB flash drive, whose capacity ranges from 125 MB to 16 GB.

Hard disks can store a huge amount of data, typically ranging from 20 GB (gigabyte; 1 GB = 1024 MB) to 80 GB for a standard desktop PC in 2002. Portable and removable hard disk drives, with performance and capacity that rival those of nonremovable hard disks, are also available, but their use is not widespread.

Compact disks (CDs) are very popular today for storing massive amounts of data, approximately 700 MB. Many software packages we buy today—computer games, word processors, and others—come with a single CD. Before the CD became a popular storage device for computers, some software came with more than 20 floppy diskettes. Because of the massive storage capacity of the CD, most computer vendors eliminated printed manuals altogether by putting the manuals on the CD.

You Might Want to Know

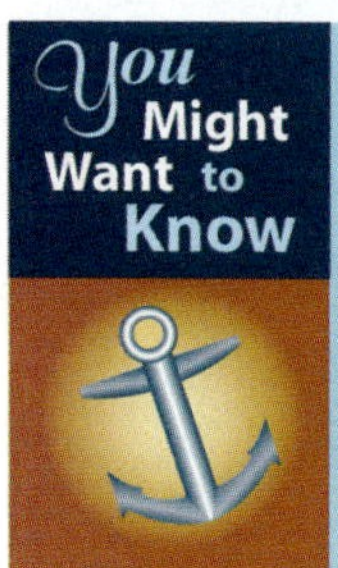

Today we see more and more companies are even eliminating CDs and promoting "boxless" online distribution of software. With this scheme, we go to their websites and download the software, after paying for it with our credit card. Maybe someday we may be able to buy textbooks in the same manner and stop carrying 20 lb of dead trees in our backpacks.

Communication Devices

communication device

A ***communication device*** connects the personal computer to an internet. The most common communication device for computers at home and in small offices is the *modem*. A modem, which stands for *modulator-demodulator*, is a device that converts analog signals to digital and digital signals to analog. By using a modem, a computer can send to and receive data from another computer over the phone line. The most critical characteristic of a modem is its transmission speed, which is measured in *bits per second* (bps). A typical speed for a modem is 56,000 bps, commonly called a 56K modem. Under an ideal condition (no line noise or congestion), a 56K modem can transfer a 1 MB file in about 2½ minutes. Frequently, though, the actual transfer rate is much lower than the possible maximum. So-called DSL and cable modems are not truly modems because they transfer data strictly in digital mode, which allows for much faster connection speeds of 144K or above. High-speed satellite connection to the Internet is also available today.

A communication device for connecting a computer to a LAN is a *network interface card* (NIC). A NIC can transfer data at a much faster rate than the fastest modem. For instance, a type of NIC called *10BaseT* can transfer data at the rate of 10 Mbps over the network. Traditional networks are connected, or wired, by the cables. Increasingly, networks are connected wirelessly, where data are carried over radio waves. Wireless networking is called WiFi or 802.11 networking. Today you will find wireless networking almost universally available at airports and hotels.

Quick CHECK

1. Name five major components of a computer.
2. What is the difference between volatile and nonvolatile memory?
3. What does the acronym *CPU* stand for?
4. How many bytes does the 64 KB RAM have?
5. Which device connects a computer to the Internet using a phone line?

0.3 Programming Languages

machine language

Programming languages are broadly classified into three levels: machine languages, assembly languages, and high-level languages. ***Machine language*** is the only programming language the CPU understands. Each type of CPU has its own machine language. For example, the Intel Pentium and Motorola PowerPC understand different machine languages. Machine-language instructions are binary-coded and very low level—one machine instruction may transfer the contents of one memory location into a CPU register or add numbers in two registers. Thus we must provide many machine-language instructions to accomplish a simple task such as finding the average of 20 numbers. A program written in machine language might look like this:

machine code

```
10110011 00011001
01111010 11010001 10010100
10011111 00011001
01011100 11010001 10010000
10111011 11010001 10010110
```

assembly language

One level above machine language is ***assembly language***, which allows "higher-level" symbolic programming. Instead of writing programs as a sequence of bits, assembly language allows programmers to write programs by using symbolic operation codes. For example, instead of 10110011, we use MV to move the contents of a memory cell into a register. We also can use symbolic, or mnemonic, names for registers and memory cells. A program written in assembly language might look like this:

assembly code

```
MV   0,    SUM
MV   NUM,  AC
ADD  SUM,  AC
STO  SUM,  TOT
```

assembler

Since programs written in assembly language are not recognized by the CPU, we use an ***assembler*** to translate programs written in assembly language into machine-language equivalents. Compared to writing programs in machine language, writing programs in assembly language is much faster, but not fast enough for writing complex programs.

high-level languages

High-level languages were developed to enable programmers to write programs faster than when using assembly languages. For example, FORTRAN (FORmula TRANslator), a programming language intended for mathematical computation, allows programmers to express numerical equations directly as

high-level code

```
X = (Y + Z) / 2
```

COBOL (COmmon Business-Oriented Language) is a programming language intended for business data processing applications. FORTRAN and COBOL were developed in the late 1950s and early 1960s and are still in use. BASIC (Beginners All-purpose Symbolic Instructional Code) was developed specifically as an easy language for students to learn and use. BASIC was the first high-level language available for microcomputers. Another famous high-level language is Pascal, which was designed as an academic language. Since programs written in a high-level language are not recognized by the CPU, we must use a ***compiler*** to translate them to assembly language equivalents.

compiler

The programming language C was developed in the early 1970s at AT&T Bell Labs. The C++ programming language was developed as a successor of C in the early 1980s to add support for object-oriented programming. Object-oriented programming is a style of programming gaining wider acceptance today. Although the concept of object-oriented programming is old (the first object-oriented programming language, Simula, was developed in the late 1960s), its significance wasn't realized until the early 1980s. Smalltalk, developed at Xerox PARC, is another well-known object-oriented programming language. The programming language we use in this book is Java, the newest object-oriented programming language, developed at Sun Microsystems.

0.4 Java

Java

Java is a new object-oriented language that is receiving wide attention from both industry and academia. Java was developed by James Gosling and his team at Sun Microsystems in California. The language was based on C and C++ and was originally intended for writing programs that control consumer appliances such as toasters, microwave ovens, and others. The language was first called Oak, named after the oak tree outside of Gosling's office, but the name was already taken, so the team renamed it Java.

Java is often described as a *Web programming language* because of its use in writing programs called ***applets*** that run within a Web browser. That is, you need a Web browser to execute Java applets. Applets allow more dynamic and flexible dissemination of information on the Internet, and this feature alone makes Java an attractive language to learn. However, we are not limited to writing applets in Java. We can write Java applications also. A Java ***application*** is a complete stand-alone program that does not require a Web browser. A Java application is analogous to a program we write in other programming languages. In this book, we focus on Java applications because our objective is to teach the fundamentals of object-oriented programming that are applicable to all object-oriented programming languages.

applet

application

We chose Java for this textbook mainly for its clean design. The language designers of Java took a minimalist approach; they included only features that are indispensable and eliminated features that they considered excessive or redundant. This minimalist approach makes Java a much easier language to learn than other object-oriented programming languages. Java is an ideal vehicle for teaching the fundamentals of object-oriented programming.

Summary

- Charles Babbage invented the Difference Engine and Analytical Engine, precursors to the modern computer.
- Ada Lovelace is considered the first computer programmer.
- The first two modern computers were MARK I and ENIAC I.

- John von Neumann invented the stored-program approach of executing programs.
- Computers are connected into a network. Interconnected networks are called internets.
- Binary numbers are used in computers.
- A typical computer consists of five components: RAM, CPU, storage devices, I/O devices, and communication devices.
- There are three levels of programming languages: machine, assembly, and high-level.
- Java is one of the newest high-level programming languages in use today. This textbook teaches how to program using Java.

Key Concepts

network
LAN
WAN
internets and Internet
CPU
RAM
I/O devices
communication devices
binary numbers
binary-to-decimal conversion
machine language
assembly language
assembler
high-level language
compiler
Java

Exercises

1. Visit your school's computer lab or a computer store, and identify the different components of the computers you see. Do you notice any unique input or output devices?
2. Visit your school's computer lab and find out the CPU speed, RAM size, and hard disk capacity of its computers.
3. Convert these binary numbers to decimal numbers.

   a. 1010
   b. 110011
   c. 110.01
   d. 111111

4. Convert these decimal numbers to binary numbers.

   a. 35
   b. 125
   c. 567
   d. 98

5. What is the maximum decimal number you can represent in 4 bits? 16 bits? *N* bits?
6. If a computer has 128 MB of RAM, how many bytes are there?
7. How do high-level programming languages differ from low-level programming languages?
8. Consider a hypothetical programming language called *Kona*. Using Kona, you can write a program to compute and print out the sum of 20 integers entered by the user:

```
let sum = 0;

repeat 20 times [
   let X = next input;
   add X to sum;
]

printout sum;
```

Is Kona a high-level language? Why or why not?

1 Introduction to Object-Oriented Programming and Software Development

Objectives

After you have read and studied this chapter, you should be able to

- Name the basic components of object-oriented programming.
- Differentiate classes and objects.
- Differentiate class and instance methods.
- Differentiate class and instance data values.
- Draw program diagrams using icons for classes, objects, and other components of object-oriented programming.
- Describe the significance of inheritance in object-oriented programs.
- Name and explain the stages of the software life cycle.

Introduction

Before we begin to write actual programs, we need to introduce a few basic concepts of ***object-oriented programming*** (OOP), the style of programming we teach in this book. The purpose of this chapter is to give you a feel for object-oriented programming and to introduce a conceptual foundation of object-oriented programming. You may want to refer to this chapter as you progress through the book. What we discuss in the next four sections is independent of any particular programming language.

object-oriented programming

Hints, Tips, & Pitfalls

Those of you who have some experience in programming, whether object-oriented or non-object-oriented, will probably find many similarities between Java and the programming languages you already know. This similarity may accelerate your learning process, but in many cases what seems to be similar at first may turn out to be quite different. So please do not jump to any conclusions about similarity prematurely.

Another purpose of this chapter is to introduce the software development process. To be able to write programs, knowledge of the components of object-oriented programs is not enough. We must learn the process of developing programs. We will present a brief introduction to the software development process in this chapter.

1.1 Classes and Objects

object

The two most important concepts in object-oriented programming are the class and the object. In the broadest term, an ***object*** is a thing, both tangible and intangible, that we can imagine. A program written in object-oriented style will consist of interacting objects. For a program to keep track of student residents of a college dormitory, we may have many Student, Room, and Floor objects. For another program to keep track of customers and inventory for a bicycle shop, we may have Customer, Bicycle, and many other types of objects. An object is comprised of data and operations that manipulate these data. For example, a Student object may consist of data such as name, gender, birth date, home address, phone number, and age and operations for assigning and changing these data values. We will use the notation shown in Figure 1.1 throughout the book to represent an object. The notation we used in the book is based on the industry standard notation called *UML*, which stands for Unified Modeling Language. In some of the illustrations, we relax the rules of UML slightly for pedagogy.

Almost all nontrivial programs will have many objects of the same type. For example, in the bicycle shop program we expect to see many Bicycle and other objects. Figure 1.2 shows two Bicycle objects with the names Moto-1 and Moto-2 and one Customer object with the name Jon Java.

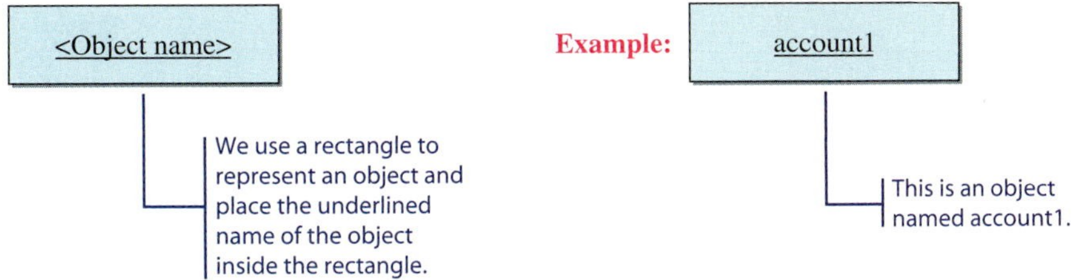

Figure 1.1 A graphical representation of an object.

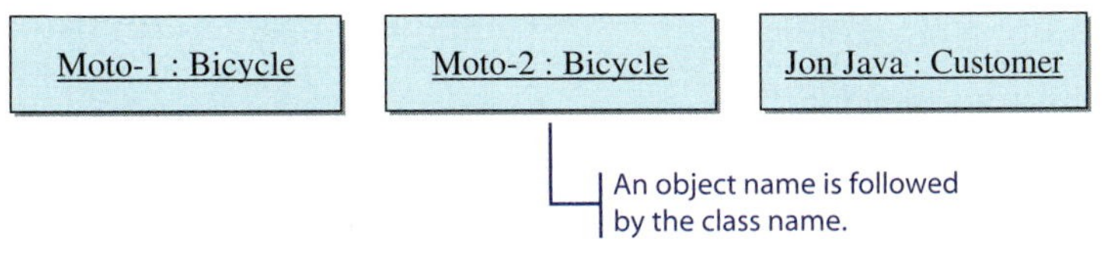

Figure 1.2 Two Bicycle objects with the names Moto-1 and Moto-2 and one Customer object with the name Jon Java.

class

instance

Inside a program we write instructions to create objects. For the computer to be able to create an object, we must provide a definition, called a ***class***. A class is a kind of mold or template that dictates what objects can and cannot do. An object is called an ***instance*** of a class. An object is an instance of exactly one class. An instance of a class *belongs to* the class. The two Bicycle objects Moto-1 and Moto-2 are instances of the Bicycle class. Once a class is defined, we can create as many instances of the class as a program requires.

Things to Remember

A class must be defined before you can create an instance (object) of the class.

Figure 1.3 shows a diagram that we will use throughout the book to represent a class.

Quick CHECK

1. Draw an object diagram for a Person class and two Person objects, Ms. Latte and Mr. Espresso.
2. What must be defined before you can create an object?

Notice the name of a class is not underlined while the name of an object is.

<Class Name>

We use a rectangle to represent a class with its name appearing inside the rectangle.

Example:

Account

Figure 1.3 A graphical representation of a class.

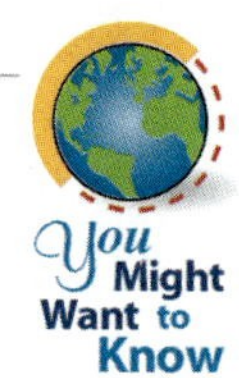

You Might Want to Know

Many beginning programmers may not see the distinction between the class and object as clearly as the more experienced programmers do. It may be helpful to compare the class and object to a woodcut and the prints produced from the woodcut. A woodcut is a block of wood engraved with a design for printing. Once you have a woodcut, you can make as many prints as you wish. Similarly, once you have a class, you can make as many objects from the class. Also, just as you cannot make prints without having a woodcut, you cannot create an object without first defining a class. For sample prints by the 19th-century Japanese artist Hiroshige, visit
http://www.ibiblio.org/wm/paint/auth/hiroshige/

Another helpful analogy is a robot factory. A factory is a class, and the robots produced from the factory are the objects of the class. To create robots (instance), we need the factory (class) first. Those interested in mobile robots can visit
http://www.ai.mit.edu/projects/mobile-robots/robots.html

1.2 Messages and Methods

In writing object-oriented programs we must first define classes, and while the program is running, we use the classes and objects from these classes to accomplish tasks. A task can range from adding two numbers, to computing an interest payment for a college loan, to calculating the reentry angle of a space shuttle. To instruct a class or an object to perform a task, we send a ***message*** to it. For example, we send a message deposit to an Account object to deposit $100.

message

For a class or an object to process the message, it must be programmed accordingly. You cannot just send a message to any class or object. You can send a message only to the classes and objects that understand the message you send. For a class or an object to process the message it receives, it must possess a matching ***method***, which is a sequence of instructions that a class or an object follows to perform a task. A method defined for a class is called a ***class method***, and a method defined for an object is an ***instance method***.

method

class and instance methods

Let's look at an example of an instance method first. Suppose a method called walk is defined for a Robot object and instructs the robot to walk a designated distance. With this method defined, we can send the message walk to a Robot object, along with the distance to be walked. A value we pass to an object is called an *argument* of a message. Notice that the name of the message we send to an object or a class must be the same as the method's name. In Figure 1.4 we represent the sending of a message.

argument

The diagram in Figure 1.4 illustrates one-way communication; that is, an object carries out the requested operation (it walks the designated distance) but does not respond to the message sender. In many situations we need a reply in which an object responds by returning a value to the message sender. For example, suppose we want to know the distance from a robot to its nearest obstacle. The designer of a robot may include a method getObstacleDistance that returns the desired value. The diagram in Figure 1.5 shows a method that returns a value to the message sender. Instead of returning a numerical value, a method can report back the status of the requested operation. For example, a method walk can be defined to return the status success/fail to indicate whether the specified distance was covered successfully or not (e.g., it fails when the robot bumps into an obstacle).

Now let's look at an example of class methods. The class method getMaximumSpeed shown in Figure 1.6 returns the maximum possible speed of all Robot objects. A method such as getMaximumSpeed that deals with collective information about the instances of a class is usually defined as a class method. So we define an instance method for a task that pertains to an individual instance and a class method for a task that pertains to all instances.

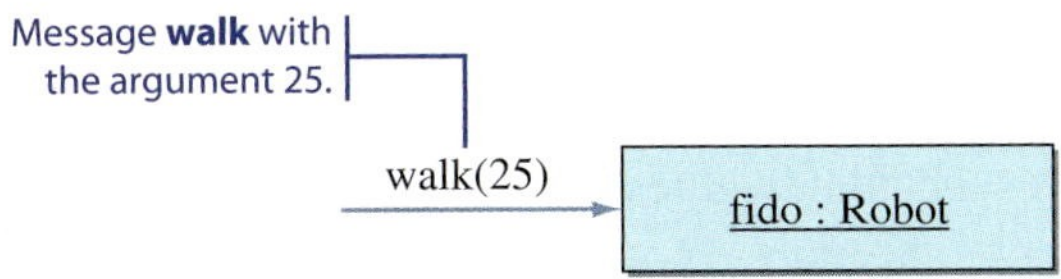

Figure 1.4 Sending the message **walk** to a **Robot** object.

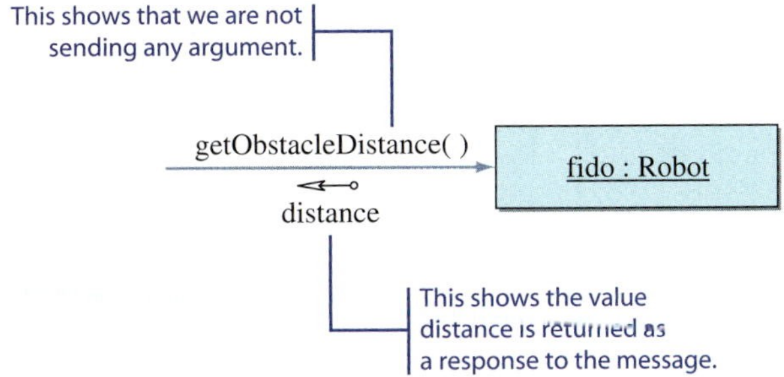

Figure 1.5 The result **distance** is returned to the sender of the message.

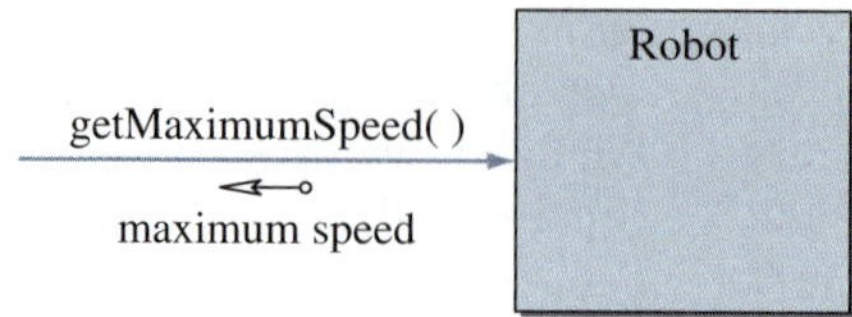

Figure 1.6 The maximum possible speed of all **Robot** objects is returned by the class method **getMaximumSpeed.**

1. Draw an object diagram of an Account object with instance methods deposit and withdraw.
2. Is the getObstacleDistance method an instance or a class method?

1.3 Class and Instance Data Values

instance data value

class data value

Suppose the method deposit of an Account object instructs the object to add a given amount to the current balance. Where does the object keep the current balance? Remember that an object is comprised of data values and methods. Analogous to defining class and instance methods, we can define class and instance data values. For example, we define an ***instance data value*** current balance for Account objects to record the current balance. Figure 1.7 shows three Account objects with their data values current balance. Notice that they all have the same data value current balance. All instances of the same class will possess the same set of data values. The actual dollar amounts for current balance, as the diagram illustrates, differ from one instance to another. Items such as opening balance and account number are other possible instance data values for Account objects.

A ***class data value*** is used to represent information shared by all instances or to represent collective information about the instances. For example, if every account must maintain a minimum balance of, say, $100, we can define a class data value minimum balance. An instance can access the class data values of the class to which it belongs, so every Account object can access the class data value minimum balance.

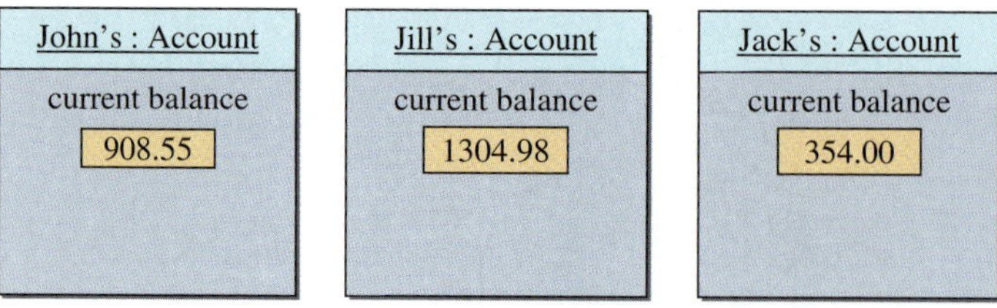

Figure 1.7 Three **Account** objects possess the same data value **current balance,** but the actual dollar amounts differ.

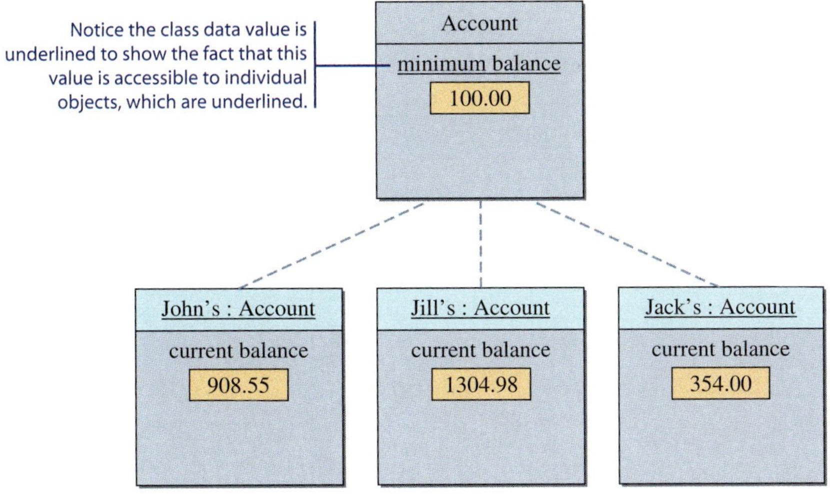

Figure 1.8 Three **Account** objects sharing information (**minimum balance** = $100) stored as a class data value.

Figure 1.8 shows how we represent a class data value. Notice that we underline the class data value. Because the objects of a class are underlined, and the class data values are accessible to all objects of the class, we likewise underline the class data value to show this relationship. Data values are also called ***data members*** because they belong to a class or instance of the class.

data member

To appreciate the significance of a class data value, let's see what happens if we represent minimum balance as an instance data value. Figure 1.9 shows three Account objects having different dollar amounts for the current balance but the same dollar amount for the minimum balance. Obviously, this duplication of minimum balance is redundant and wastes space. Consider, for example, what happens if the bank raises the minimum balance to $200. If there are 100 Account objects, then all 100 copies of minimum balance must be updated. We can avoid this by defining minimum balance as a class data value. Figure 1.10 shows another example where the opening and closing times are shared by all cafeterias on campus.

There are two types of data values: those that can change over time and those that cannot. A data value that can change is called a ***variable***, and one that cannot

variable

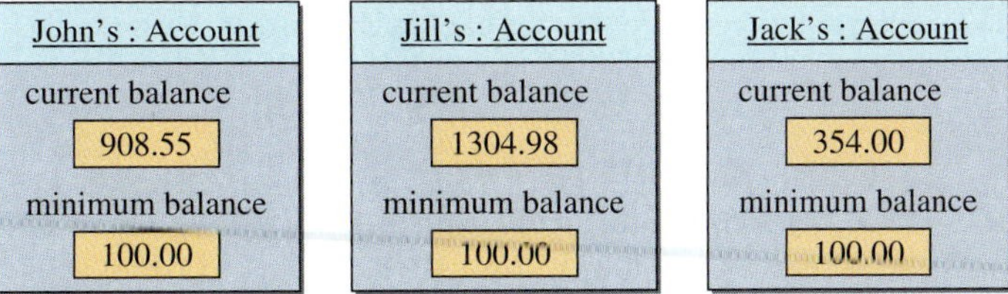

Figure 1.9 Three **Account** objects duplicating information (**minimum balance** = $100) in instance data values.

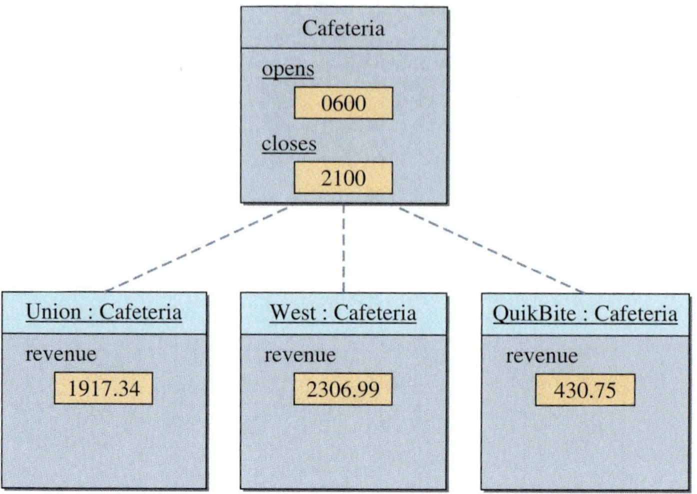

Figure 1.10 Three **Cafeteria** objects sharing the same opening and closing times, stored as class data values.

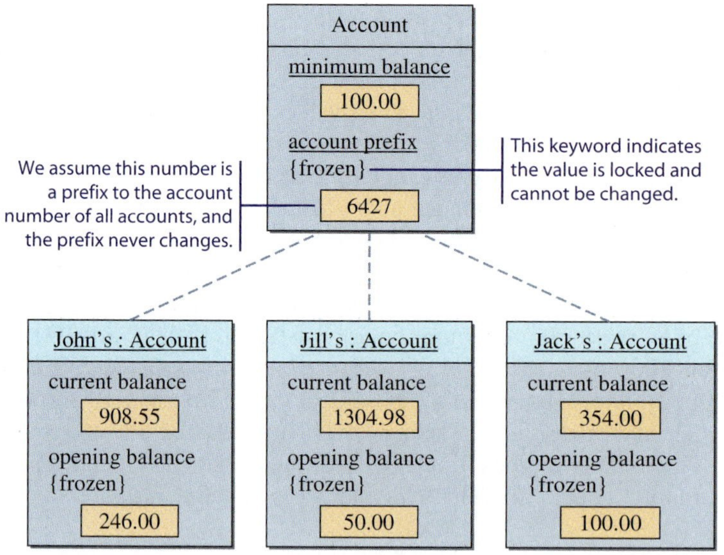

Figure 1.11 Graphical representations for four types of data values: class variable, class constant, instance variable, and instance constant.

constant

change is a ***constant***. Figure 1.11 illustrates how we represent and distinguish between variables and constants. We use the keyword `frozen` for constants to indicate that they cannot change. Notice that we now have four kinds of data values: class variables, class constants, instance variables, and instance constants.

1. What is the difference between a constant and a variable?
2. Draw an object diagram of a Person object with the three instance variables name, age, and gender.

1.4 Inheritance

When we used the Account class and its instances to illustrate object-oriented concepts, some of you were probably thinking about checking accounts, while others may have been thinking about savings accounts. We did not distinguish between the two in the examples. But when we look at the problem a little more carefully, we will realize that in fact these two types of accounts are different, even though they share many features.

inheritance

In general, using only a single class to model two or more entities that are similar but different is not good design. In object-oriented programming, we use a mechanism called ***inheritance*** to design two or more entities that are different but share many common features. First we define a class that contains the common features of the entities. Then we define classes as an extension of the common class inheriting everything from the common class. We call the common class the ***superclass*** and all classes that inherit from it ***subclasses***. We also call the superclass an *ancestor* and the subclass a *descendant*. Other names for superclass and subclass are *base class* and *derived class,* respectively. For the bank example, we can define a superclass Account and then define Savings and Checking as subclasses of Account. We represent the superclass and its subclasses as shown in Figure 1.12. Notice that we draw arrows from each subclass to its superclass because a subclass can refer to items defined in its superclass, but not vice versa.

superclass and subclass

Inheritance is not limited to one level. A subclass can be a superclass of other classes, forming an inheritance hierarchy. Consider the example shown in Figure 1.13. Inheritance is very powerful, and if it is used properly, we can develop

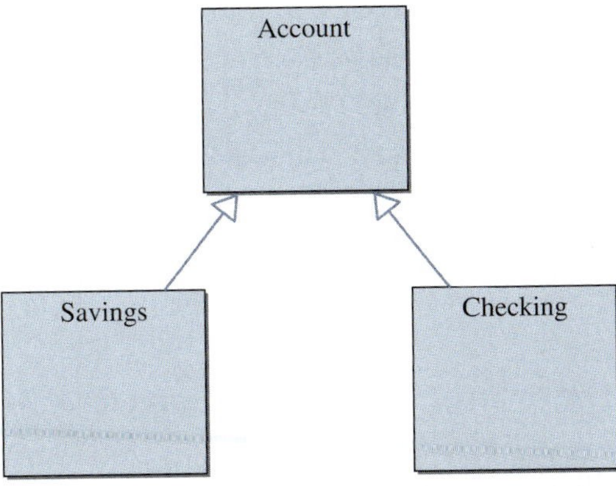

Figure 1.12 A superclass **Account** and its subclasses **Savings** and **Checking.**

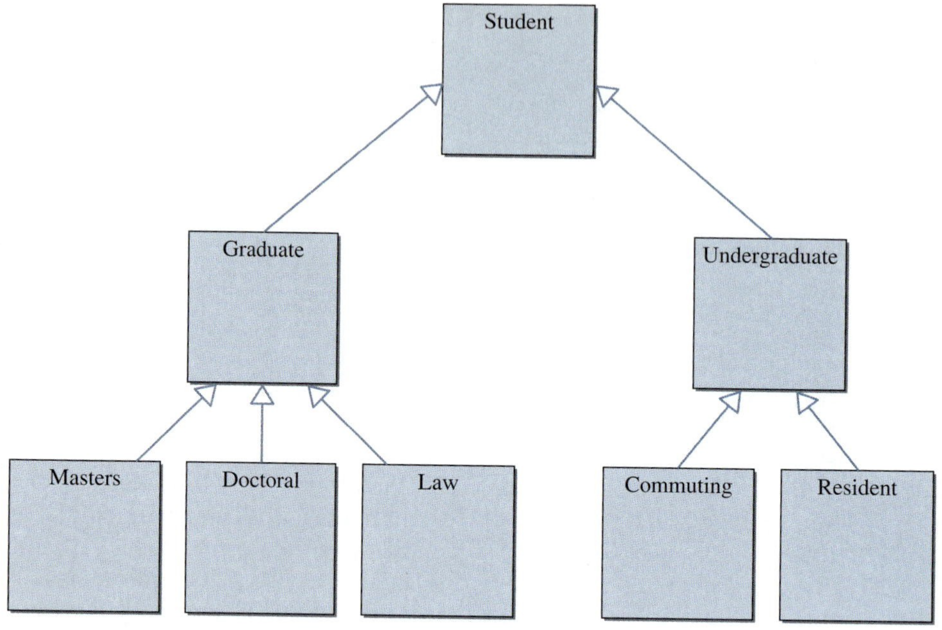

Figure 1.13 An example of inheritance hierarchy among different types of students.

complex programs very efficiently and elegantly. The flip side of using a very powerful tool is that if we do not use it correctly, we could end up in a far worse situation than if we did not use it. We will be seeing many examples of inheritance throughout this book. In Chapter 2, for example, we will introduce many classes that come with the Java system. Most of these classes are defined using inheritance. We will provide an in-depth discussion of inheritance and related topics in Chapter 13.

1. If Class A inherits from Class B, which is a superclass? Which is a subclass?
2. Draw a diagram that shows Class A is inheriting from Class B.
3. What are the other names for superclass and subclass?
4. If we have Animal, Insect, and Mammal classes, which one will be a superclass?
5. Model different types of vehicles, using inheritance. Include Vehicle, Automobile, Motorcycle, Sports Car, Sedan, and Bicycle.

1.5 Software Engineering and Software Life Cycle

When we say *computer programming,* we are referring not only to writing Java commands, but also to a whole process of software development. Knowing a programming language alone is not enough to become a proficient software developer.

You must know how to design a program. This book will teach you how to design programs in an object-oriented manner.

We construct a house in well-defined stages and apply the engineering principles in all stages. Similarly, we build a program in stages and apply disciplined methodology in all stages of program development. The sequence of stages from conception to operation of a program is called the ***software life cycle***, and ***software engineering*** is the application of a systematic and disciplined approach to the development, testing, and maintenance of a program.

software life cycle

software engineering

There are five major phases in the software life cycle: analysis, design, coding, testing, and operation. Software starts its life from the needs of a customer. A person wants an online address book, for example. In the ***analysis*** phase, we perform a feasibility study. We analyze the problem and determine whether a solution is possible. Provided that a solution is possible, the result of this phase is a *requirements specification* that describes the features of a program. The features must be stated in a manner that is testable. One of the features for the address book program may be the capability to search for a person by giving his or her first name. We can test this feature by running the program and actually searching for a person. We verify that the program behaves as specified when the first name of a person in the address book and the first name of a person not in the address book are entered as a search condition. We do this testing in the testing phase, which we will explain shortly.

analysis

In the ***design*** phase, we turn a requirements specification into a detailed design of the program. For an object-oriented design, the output from this phase will be a set of classes that fulfill the requirements. For the address book program, we may design classes such as `Person`, `Phone`, and others.

design

In the ***coding*** phase, we implement the design into an actual program, in our case, a Java program. Once we have a well-constructed design, implementing it into actual code is really not that difficult. The difficult part is the creation of the design, and in this book, we place greater emphasis on the design aspect of the software construction.

coding

When the implementation is completed, we move to the ***testing*** phase. In this phase, we run the program, using different sets of data to verify that the program runs according to the specification. Two types of testing are possible for object-oriented programs: *unit testing* and *integration testing*. With unit testing, we test classes individually. With integration testing, we test that the classes work together correctly. Activity to eliminate programming error is called ***debugging***. An error could be a result of faulty implementation or design. When there's an error, we need to backtrack to earlier phases to eliminate the error.

testing

debugging

Finally, after the testing is successfully concluded, we enter the ***operation*** phase, in which the program will be put into actual use. The most important and time-consuming activity during the operation phase is ***software maintenance***. After the software is put into use, we almost always have to make changes to it. For example, the customer may request additional features, or previously undetected errors may be found. Software maintenance means making changes to software. It is estimated that close to 70 percent of the cost of software is related to software maintenance. So naturally, when we develop software, we should aim for software that is easy to maintain. We must not develop a piece of software hastily to reduce the

operation

software maintenance

software development cost. We should take time and care to design and code software correctly even if it takes longer and costs more to develop initially. In the long run, carefully crafted software will have a lower total cost because of the reduced maintenance cost. Here's an important point to remember:

Things to Remember

Well-designed and -constructed software is easy to maintain.

In this book, we will focus on the design, coding, and testing phases. We will present a requirements specification in the form of a problem statement for the sample programs we will develop in this book. We present the first sample program developed by following the design, coding, and testing phases in Chapter 2. We will come back to the discussion of software engineering and the software life cycle throughout the book and provide more details.

1. Name the stages of the software life cycle.
2. How does the quality of design affect the software maintenance cost?
3. What is debugging?

Summary

- The style of programming we teach in this book is called object-oriented programming.
- An object is an instance of a class. Many instances can be created from a single class.
- There are class and instance methods. We can send messages to objects and classes if they possess matching methods.
- There are class and instance data values. Data values are also called data members.
- Inheritance is a powerful mechanism to model two or more entities that are different but share common features.
- The sequence of software development stages from conception to operation is called the software life cycle.

- Five major phases of the software life cycle are analysis, design, coding, testing, and operation.
- Software engineering is the application of a systematic and disciplined approach to the development, testing, and maintenance of a program.

Key Concepts

object-oriented programming
class
object
message
class and instance methods
instance and class data values
variable
constant
inheritance
superclass (ancestor, base class)
subclass (descendant, derived class)
software life cycle
software engineering
analysis
design
coding
testing
operation

Exercises

1. Graphically represent a Vehicle class and three Vehicle objects named car1, car2, and car3.
2. Graphically represent a Person class with the following components:
   - Instance variables name, age, and gender.
   - Instance methods setName, getName, and getAge.
   - Class method getAverageAge.
3. Design a CD class where a CD object represents a single music CD. What kinds of information (artist, genre, total playing time, etc.) do you want to know about a CD? Among the information in which you are interested, which are instance variables? Are there any class variables or class constants?
4. Suppose the Vehicle class in Exercise 1 is used in a program that keeps track of vehicle registration for the Department of Motor Vehicles. What kinds of instance variables would you define for such Vehicle objects? Can you think of any useful class variables for the Vehicle class?
5. Suppose the following formulas are used to compute the annual vehicle registration fee for the vehicle registration program of Exercise 4:
   - For cars, the annual fee is 2 percent of the value of the car.
   - For trucks, the annual fee is 5 percent of the loading capacity (in pounds) of the truck.

   Define two new classes Car and Truck as subclasses of Vehicle. *Hint:* Associate class and instance variables common to both Car and Truck to Vehicle.

6. Consider a student registration program used by the registrar's office. The program keeps track of students who are registered for a given semester. For each student registered, the program maintains the student's name, address, and phone number; the number of classes in which the student is enrolled; and the student's total credit hours. The program also keeps track of the total number of registered students. Define instance and class variables of a Student class that is suitable for this program.
7. Suppose the minimum number and maximum number of courses for which a student can register are different depending on whether the student is a graduate, undergraduate, or work/study student. Redo Exercise 6 by defining classes for different types of students. Relate the classes, using inheritance.
8. Imagine you are given the task of designing an airline reservation system that keeps track of flights for a commuter airline. List the classes you think would be necessary for designing such a system. Describe the data values and methods you would associate with each class you identify. *Note:* For this exercise and Exercises 9 through 12, we are not expecting you to design the system in complete detail. The objective of these exercises is to give you a taste of thinking about a program at a very high level. Try to identify about a half dozen or so classes, and for each class, describe several methods and data members.
9. Repeat Exercise 8, designing a university course scheduling system. The system keeps track of classes offered in a given quarter, the number of sections offered, and the number of students enrolled in each section.
10. Repeat Exercise 8, designing the state Department of Motor Vehicles registration system. The system keeps track of all licensed vehicles and drivers. How would you design objects representing different types of vehicles (e.g., motorcycles and trucks) and drivers (e.g., class A for commercial licenses and class B for towing vehicles)?
11. Repeat Exercise 8, designing a sales tracking system for a fast-food restaurant. The system keeps track of all menu items offered by the restaurant and the number of daily sales per menu item.
12. When you write a term paper, you have to consult many references: books, journal articles, newspaper articles, and so forth. Repeat Exercise 8, designing a bibliography organizer that keeps track of all references you used in writing a term paper.
13. Consider the inheritance hierarchy given in Figure 1.12. List the features common to all classes and the features unique to individual classes. Propose a new inheritance hierarchy based on the types of accounts your bank offers.
14. Consider a program that maintains an address book. Design an inheritance hierarchy for the classes such as Person, ProfessionalContact, Friend, and Student that can be used in implementing such a program.
15. Do you think the design phase is more important than the coding phase? Why or why not?
16. How does the quality of design affect the total cost of developing and maintaining software?

2 Getting Started with Java

Objectives

After you have read and studied this chapter, you should be able to

- Identify the basic components of Java programs.
- Write simple Java programs.
- Describe the difference between object declaration and object creation.
- Describe the process of creating and running Java programs.
- Use the **Date, SimpleDateFormat, String,** and **Scanner** classes from the standard Java packages.
- Develop Java programs, using the incremental development approach.

Introduction

We will describe the basic structure of simple Java programs in this chapter. We will also describe the steps you follow to run Java programs. We expect you to actually run these sample programs to verify that your computer (either your own or the one at the school's computer center) is set up properly to run the sample programs presented in the book. It is important to verify this now. Otherwise, if you encounter a problem later, you won't be able to determine whether the problem is the result of a bad program or a bad setup. Please check Appendix A for information on how to run the textbook's sample programs.

We will develop a sample application program in Section 2.4 following the design, coding, and testing phases of the software life cycle. We stress here again that our objective in this book is to teach object-oriented programming and how to apply object-oriented thinking in program development. The Java language is merely a means to implement a design into an executable program. We chose Java for this book because Java is a much easier language than other object-oriented programming languages to use to translate a design into an actual code. Beginning students often get lost in the language details and forget the main objective of learning the development process, but the use of Java should minimize this problem.

2.1 The First Java Program

pixel

Our first Java application program displays a window on the screen, as shown in Figure 2.1. The size of the window is set to 300 pixels wide and 200 pixels high. A ***pixel*** is a shorthand for *picture element,* and it is the standard unit of measurement for the screen resolution. A common resolution for a 17-in screen, for example, is 1024 pixels wide and 768 pixels high. The title of the window is set to My First Java Program.

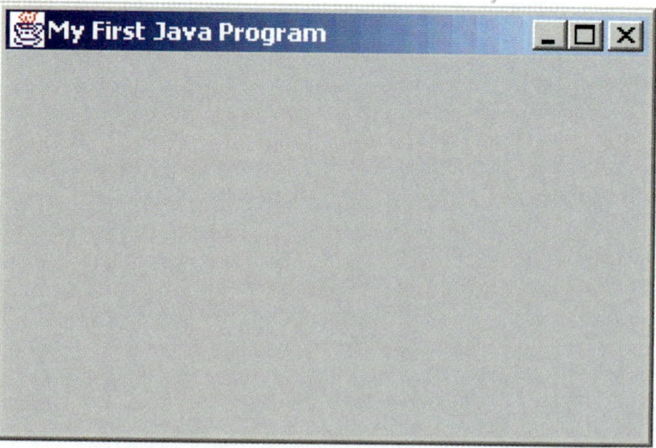

Figure 2.1 Result of running the **Ch2Sample1** program. The window size is 300 by 200 pixels and has the title **My First Java Program**.

Although this program is very simple, it still illustrates the fundamental structure of an object-oriented program, which is as follows:

Things to Remember

An object-oriented program uses objects.

It may sound too obvious, but let's begin our study of object-oriented programming with this obvious notion. Here's the program code:

```
/*

    Chapter 2 Sample Program: Displaying a Window

    File: Ch2Sample1.java

*/

import javax.swing.*;

class  Ch2Sample1 {

   public static void main(String[] args) {

       JFrame    myWindow;

       myWindow = new JFrame();

       myWindow.setSize(300, 200);
       myWindow.setTitle("My First Java Program");
       myWindow.setVisible(true);
   }
}
```

This will not concern the majority of you, but if you are using a Java development tool that does not let you stop a running program easily, then insert the statement

```
myWindow.setDefaultCloseOperation(JFrame.EXIT_ON_CLOSE);
```

after

```
myWindow.setVisible(true);
```

so the program terminates automatically when the frame window is closed. Please read Appendix A for more information.

This program declares one class called Ch2Sample1, and the class includes one method called main. From this main method, the Ch2Sample1 class creates and uses a JFrame object named myWindow by sending the three messages setSize, setTitle, and setVisible to the object. The JFrame class is one of many classes that come with the Java system. An instance of this JFrame class is used to represent a single window on the computer screen. To differentiate the classes that programmers define, including ourselves, and the predefined classes that come with the Java system, we will call the first ***programmer-defined classes*** and the latter *Java standard classes,* or simply, ***standard classes***. We also use the term *system classes* to refer to the standard classes.

programmer-defined classes

standard classes

Expressing this program visually results in the ***program diagram*** shown in Figure 2.2. In this diagram, we draw individual messages, but doing so would easily clutter a diagram when we have more than a handful of messages. Instead of drawing messages individually, we can draw one arrow to represent a ***dependency relationship***. For this program, we say the Ch2Sample1 class is *dependent* on the services provided by a JFrame object, because the Ch2Sample1 class sends messages to the MyWindow object. We draw a dotted arrow from Ch2Sample1 to myWindow to indicate the dependency relationship, as shown in Figure 2.3

program diagram

dependency relationship

We begin the explanation of the program from the following core five lines of code:

```
JFrame    myWindow;

myWindow = new JFrame();

myWindow.setSize(300, 200);
myWindow.setTitle("My First Java Program");
myWindow.setVisible(true);
```

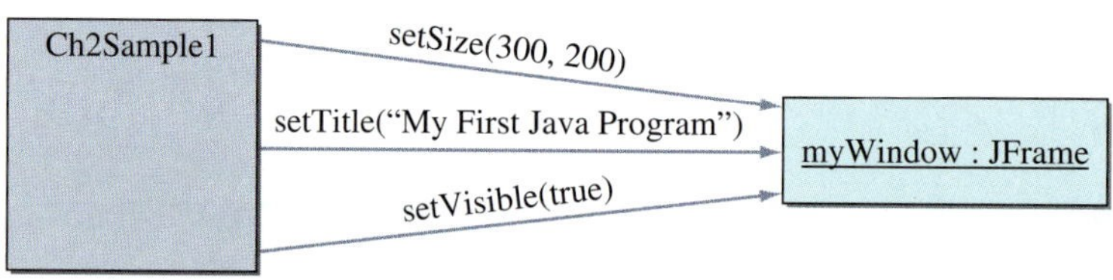

Figure 2.2 The program diagram for the **Ch2Sample1** program.

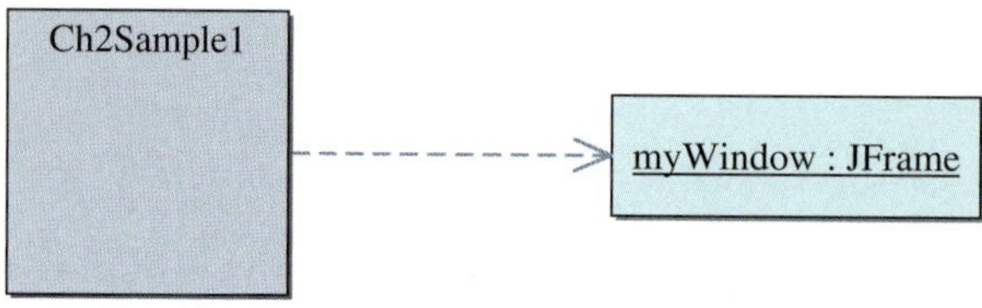

Figure 2.3 The program diagram for the **Ch2Sample1** program that shows the dependency relationship.

We will explain the rest of the program in Section 2.2. These five lines of code represent the crux of the program, namely, an object-oriented program that uses objects. The rule to remember in using objects is as follows:

Things to Remember

To use an object in a program, first we declare and create an object, and then we send messages to it.

In the remainder of this section, we will describe how to declare an object, create an object, and use an object by sending messages to the object.

Object Declaration

Every object we use in a program must be declared. An object declaration designates the name of an object and the class to which the object belongs. Its syntax is

object declaration syntax

```
<class name>  <object names>  ;
```

where <object names> is a sequence of object names separated by commas and <class name> is the name of a class to which these objects belong. Here's how the general syntax is matched to the object declaration of the program:

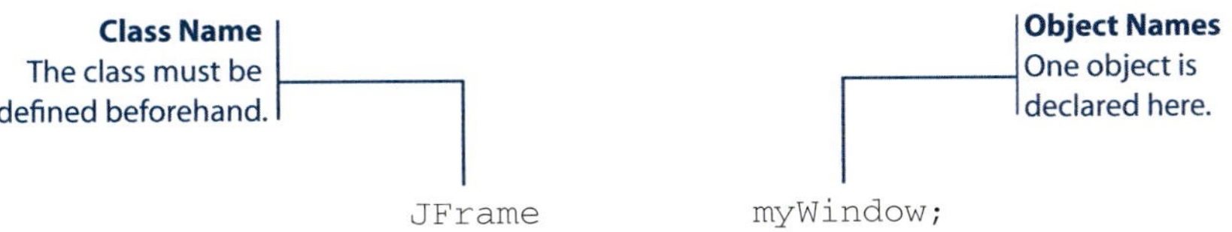
Class Name
The class must be defined beforehand.
Object Names
One object is declared here.
JFrame
myWindow;

Here are more examples:

```
Account    checking;
Customer   john, jack, jill;
```

The first declaration declares an Account object named checking, and the second declaration declares three Customer objects.

To declare an object as an instance of some class, the class must be defined already. First we will study how to use objects from system classes. Later in the book, we will show you how to define your own classes, from which you can create instances.

identifier

When we declare an object, we must give it a name. Any valid identifier that is not reserved for other uses can be used as an object name. A Java ***identifier*** is a sequence of letters, digits, underscores (_), and dollar signs ($) with the first one being a letter. We use an identifier to name a class, object, method, and others. The following words are all valid identifiers:

```
MyFirstApplication
FunTime
ComputeArea
DEFAULT_VALUE
```

Upper- and lowercase letters are distinguished, so the following four identifiers are distinct:

```
myWindow          mywindow
MYwindow          MYWINDOW
```

No spaces are allowed in an identifier, and therefore, the three lines

```
Sample Program
My First Application
Program FunTime
```

are all invalid identifiers.

Since upper- and lowercase letters are distinguished, you can use robot as the name for an object of the class Robot. We name objects in this manner whenever possible in this book so we can easily tell to which class the object belongs. We follow the Java ***standard naming convention*** of using an uppercase letter for the first letter of the class names and a lowercase letter for the first letter of the object names in this book. It is important to follow the standard naming convention so others who read your program can easily distinguish the purposes of identifiers. Programs that follow the standard naming convention are easier to read than those that do not. And remember that software maintenance is easier with easy-to-understand programs.

standard naming convention

When an identifier consists of multiple words, the Java naming convention dictates the first letter from every word, except the first word, will be capitalized, for example, myMainWindow, not mymainwindow.

Design Guidelines

Follow the standard naming convention in writing your Java programs to make them easier to read.

Table 2.2 in the Summary section summarizes the naming convention.

Object Creation

No objects are actually created by the declaration. An object declaration simply declares the name (identifier) that we use to refer to an object. For example, the declaration

```
JFrame     myWindow;
```

new operator

designates that the name myWindow is used to refer to a JFrame object, but the actual JFrame object is not yet created. We create an object by invoking the new *operator*. The syntax for new is

object creation syntax

```
<object name> = new <class name> ( <arguments> ) ;
```

where <object name> is the name of a declared object, <class name> is the name of the class to which the object belongs, and <arguments> is a sequence of values passed to the new operation. Let's match the syntax to the actual statement in the sample program:

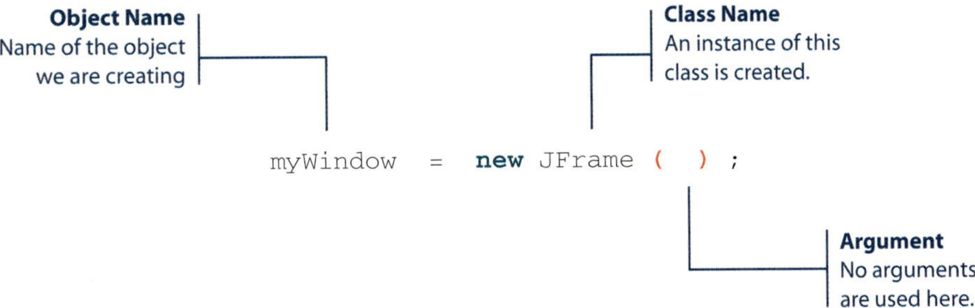

Figure 2.4 shows the distinction between object declaration and creation. Figure 2.5 shows the relationship between the UML-based program diagram and the state-of-memory diagram. The state-of-memory diagram borrows the notation from UML for consistency, but it is not a true UML diagram because it uses symbols and notations not found in UML.

Now, consider the following object declaration and two statements of object creation:

```
Customer  customer;
customer = new Customer( );
customer = new Customer( );
```

What do you think will happen? An error? No. It is permissible to use the same name to refer to different objects of the same class at different times. Figure 2.6

Instead of writing statements for object declaration and creation separately, we can combine them into one statement. We can write, for example,

```
Student john = new Student();
```

instead of

```
Student john;
john = new Student();
```

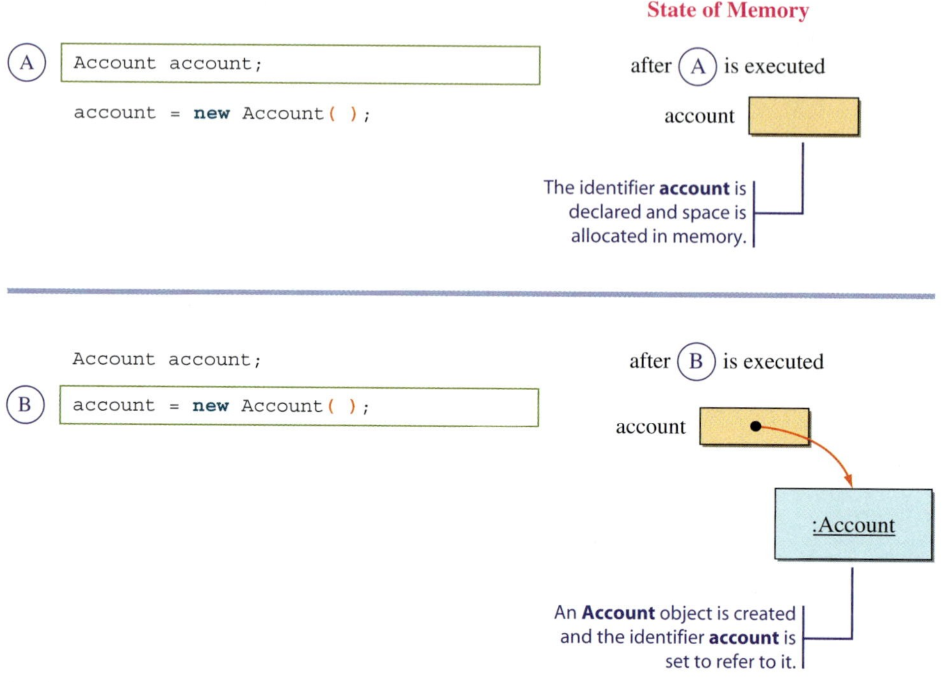

Figure 2.4 Distinction between object declaration and object creation.

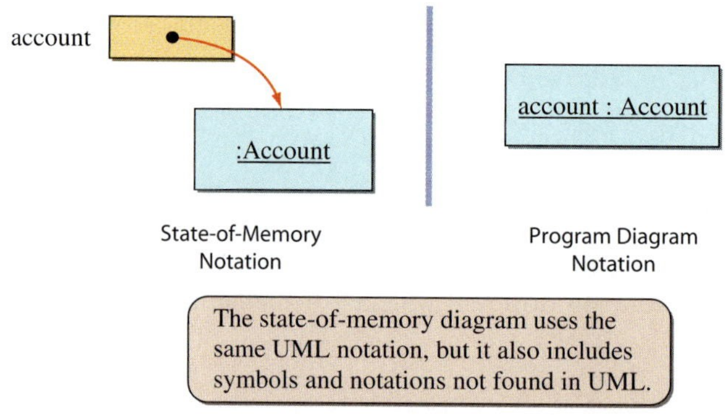

Figure 2.5 Relationship between the state-of-memory diagram and the program diagram notation.

shows the state-of-memory diagram after the second new is executed. Since there is no reference to the first Customer object anymore, eventually it will be erased and returned to the system. Remember that when an object is created, a certain amount of memory space is allocated for storing this object. If this allocated but unused space is not returned to the system for other uses, the space gets wasted. This

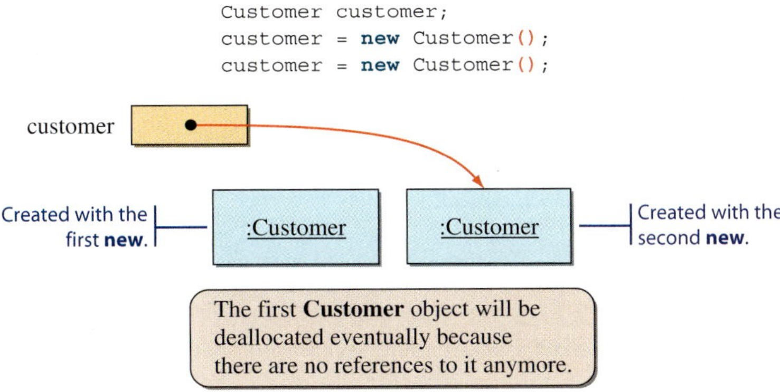

Figure 2.6 The state after two **new** commands are executed.

garbage collection

returning of space to the system is called *deallocation,* and the mechanism to deallocate unused space is called ***garbage collection***.

Message Sending

After the object is created, we can start sending messages to it. The syntax for sending a message to an object is

message-sending syntax

```
<object name> . <method name> ( <arguments> ) ;
```

where <object name> is an object name, <method name> is the name of a method of the object, and <arguments> is a sequence of values passed to the method. In the sample program, we send the setVisible message with the argument true to the mainWindow object to make it appear on the screen. Once again, let's match the components in the general syntax to the actual statement:

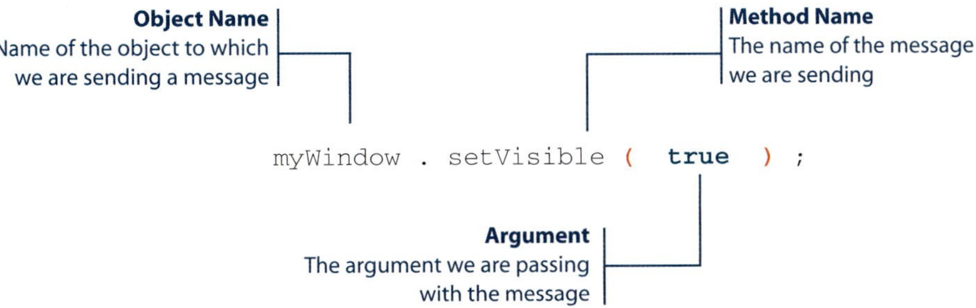

Figure 2.7 shows the correspondence between message sending as represented in the program diagram and in the Java statement. Because the object that receives a message must possess a corresponding method, we often substitute the expression *sending a message* with *calling a method*. We will use these expressions interchangeably.

Note: We can place method icons on either side of a class or instance icon.
Program Diagram
myWindow:JFrame
setVisible(true)
Corresponding Java Statement
myWindow . setVisible (true) ;

Figure 2.7 Correspondence between message sending as represented in the program diagram and in the actual Java statement.

Things to Remember

The expression calling object O's method M *is synonymous with* sending message M to object O.

Notice the argument for the setVisible message does not include double quotes as did the one for the setTitle message in the example shown on page 32. The argument true is one of the two possible logical values (the other is false) used in Java programs. We will study more about the use of logical values later in the book, starting from Chapter 5. For now, it suffices to remember that there are two logical values— true and false—used for certain specific purposes.

Passing true in the setVisible message makes the receiving object appear on the screen. Passing false makes the object disappear from the screen. So, for example, if we write

```
myWindow.setVisible(true);
myWindow.setVisible(false);
myWindow.setVisible(true);
```

then myWindow will appear once, disappear, and then appear on the screen again. (*Note:* Because the computer will execute these statements so quickly, you may not notice any difference from the original program. See Exercise 22 on page 77.)

reserved word

The word true (and false) is called a ***reserved word***. It is an identifier that is used for a specific purpose and cannot be used for any other purpose, such as for the name of an object.

1. Which of the following are invalid identifiers?
   a. one
   b. my Window
   c. 1234

d. DecafeLattePlease
e. hello
f. JAVA
g. hello, there
h. acct122

2. What's wrong with the following code?

```
JFrame myWindow();
myWindow.setVisible(true);
```

3. Is there anything wrong with the following declarations?

```
mainWindow              MainWindow;
Account, Customer       account, customer;
```

4. Which of the following statements is valid?

a. `myFirstWindow.setVisible( "true" );`
b. `myFirstWindow.setVisible( true );`

2.2 Program Components

Now that we have covered the crux of the first sample program, let's examine the rest of the program. The first sample application program Ch2Sample1 is composed of three parts: comment, import statement, and class declaration. These three parts are included universally in Java programs.

Things to Remember

*A Java program is composed of comments, **import** statements, and class declarations.*

You can write a Java program that includes only a single class declaration, but that is not the norm. In any nontrivial program, you will see these three components. We explain the three components and their subparts in this section.

Comments

comments

In addition to the instructions for computers to follow, programs contain ***comments*** in which we state the purpose of the program, explain the meaning of code, and provide any other descriptions to help programmers understand the program. Here's the comment in the sample Ch2Sample1 program:

```
/*
    Chapter 2 Sample Program: Displaying a Window

    File: Ch2Sample1.java

*/

import javax.swing.*;

class Ch2Sample1 {

    public static void main(String[] args) {

        JFrame    myWindow;

        myWindow = new JFrame();

        myWindow.setSize(300, 200);
        myWindow.setTitle("My First Java Program");
        myWindow.setVisible(true);
    }
}
```

Comment

comment markers

A comment is any sequence of text that begins with the marker /* and terminates with another marker */. The beginning and ending ***comment markers*** are matched in pairs; that is, every beginning marker must have a matching ending marker. A beginning marker is matched with the next ending marker that appears. Any beginning markers that appear between the beginning marker and its matching ending marker are treated as part of the comment. In other words, you cannot put a comment inside another comment. The examples in Figure 2.8 illustrate how the matching is done.

single-line comment marker

Another marker for a comment is double slashes //. This marker is used for a ***single-line comment marker***. Any text between the double-slash marker and the end of a line is a comment. The following example shows the difference between multiline and single-line comments:

```
/*
   This is a comment with
   three lines of
   text.
*/

// This is a comment
// This is another comment
// This is a third comment
```

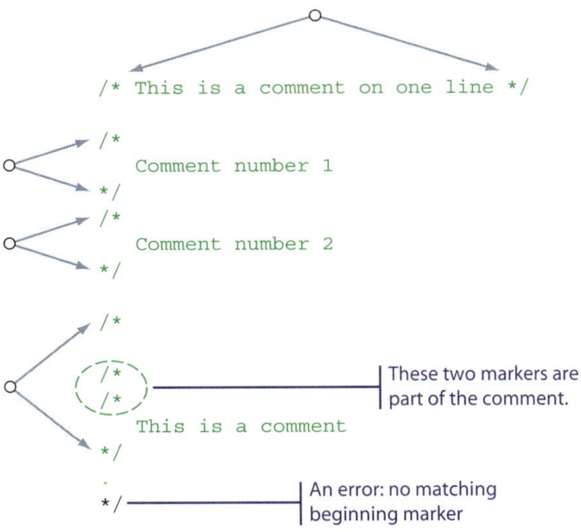

Figure 2.8 How the beginning and ending comment markers are matched.

Things to Remember

Although not required to run the program, comments are indispensable in writing easy-to-understand code.

javadoc comment

The third type of comment is called a ***javadoc comment***. It is a specialized comment that can appear before the class declaration and other program elements yet to be described in the book. We will explain more about javadoc comments in Chapter 7.

Comments are intended for the programmers only and are ignored by the computer. Therefore, comments are really not necessary in making a program executable, but they are an important aspect of documenting the program. It is not enough to write a program that executes correctly. We need to document the program, and commenting the program is an important part of program documentation. Other parts of program documentation include program diagrams, programmers' work logs, design documents, and user manuals. If you can write a program once and use it forever without ever modifying it, then writing a program with no comments may be tolerable. However, in the real world, using programs without ever making any changes almost never happens. For example, you may decide to add new features and capabilities or modify the way the user interacts with the program. Even if you don't improve the program, you still have to modify the program when you detect some errors in it. Also, for commercial programs, those who change the programs are most often not the ones who developed them. When the time comes for a programmer to modify his own or someone else's program, the programmer must first understand the program, and program documentation is an indispensable aid to understanding the program.

header comment

typical header comment for a beginning programming class

There are several different uses of comments. The first is the header comment. At the beginning of a program, we place a comment to describe the program. We characterize such a comment as a ***header comment***. We also may include header comments at the beginning of methods to describe their purposes. Depending on the length and complexity of programs, the description may range from short and simple to long and very detailed. A typical header comment for a beginning programming class may look something like this:

```
/*
 * Program:          TextEditor
 *
 * Author:           Decafe Latte
 *                   decafe@latte.com
 *
 * Written:          May 1, 2006
 *
 * Course:           Comp Sci 101
 *                   Spring 2006
 *                   Program Assignment No. 7
 *
 * Compiler:         JDK 1.5
 * Platform:         Windows XP
 *
 * Description:
 *   This is a simple text editor. The editor allows the user
 *   to save text to a file and read text from a file. The
 *   editor displays text using Courier font only and does not
 *   allow formatting (e.g., bold, italic, etc.). The editor
 *   supports standard editing functions Cut, Copy, and
 *   Paste, but does not support Undo. For more details,
 *   please refer to the TxEditReadme file.
 */
```

Note: The use of the asterisks is in the style of javadoc, but this is not a javadoc comment.

For your own programs, you should write header comments following the guideline provided by your instructor. For listing the sample programs in the book, we will include only the program name and a short description in the header comment, mainly for reference purposes. The header comment in the actual programs, available from our website, includes additional information.

Another use of comments is to explain code whose purpose may not be obvious. Your aim is always to write easily understandable, self-explanatory program code. But at times this is not possible, and you should attach comment to code that is not so easy to understand. There also are times when the original code may not work as intended, and as a temporary measure, you modify the code slightly so the program will continue to work. You should clearly mark such modification with a comment, so you remember what you have done. If you did not put in an appropriate comment and later read your code without remembering about the modification, you would have no idea why you wrote such code. If you cannot understand your own code, imagine the frustration of other programmers (or your T.A. or instructor) trying to understand your modified code.

Yet another use of comments is to identify or summarize a block of code. Suppose a program is divided into three major parts: getting input values from the user, performing computation by using those values, and displaying the computation results. You can place comments at the top of each part to delineate the three major parts clearly.

Remember that adding comments to a poorly designed program will not make it a better program. Your foremost goal is to develop a well-designed program that runs efficiently and is easy to understand. Commenting a program is only a means toward that goal, not a goal itself. In fact, excessive use of comments makes it harder to follow and understand a program.

Design Guidelines

Always aim for self-explanatory code. Do not attempt to make poorly written code easier to read by comments. Good comments are not a substitute for good code. Bad code is bad, no matter how well your comments are written.

Hints, & Tips, Pitfalls

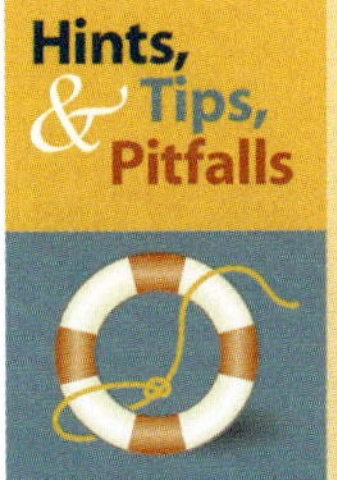

Comment markers are useful in disabling a portion of a program. Let's say you find a portion that may be causing the program to crash, and you want to try out different code for the problem portion. Instead of replacing the whole problem portion with new code, you can leave the questionable code in the program by converting it into a "comment" with comment markers. You can remove the comment markers if you need this code later.

Import **Statement**

We develop object-oriented programs by using predefined classes, both system- and programmer-defined, whenever possible and defining our own classes when no suitable predefined classes are available. In Java, classes are grouped into ***packages***, and the Java system comes with numerous packages. We also can logically group our own classes into a package so they can be reused conveniently by other programs.

package

To use a class from a package, we refer to the class in our program by using the following format:

```
<package name> . <class name>
```

For example, to use the Resident class in the dorm package, we refer to it as

```
dorm.Resident
```

dot notation

which we read as "dorm dot Resident." This notation is called ***dot notation***.

A package can include subpackages, forming a hierarchy of packages. In referring to a class in a deeply nested package, we use multiple dots. For example, we write

```
javax.swing.JFrame
```

fully qualified name

to refer to the class JFrame in the javax.swing package; that is, the swing package is inside the javax package. Dot notation with the names of all packages to which a class belongs is called the class's ***fully qualified name***. Using the fully qualified name of a class is frequently too cumbersome, especially when we have to refer to the same class many times in a program. We can use the import statement to avoid this problem. Here's the original Ch2Sample1 program that uses the import statement:

```
/*

   Chapter 2 Sample Program: Displaying a Window

   File: Ch2Sample1.java
*/

import javax.swing.*;

class Ch2Sample1 {

    public static void main(String[] args) {

        JFrame    myWindow;

        myWindow = new JFrame();

        myWindow.setSize(300, 200);
        myWindow.setTitle("My First Java Program");
        myWindow.setVisible(true);
    }

}
```

Import **Statement**
The **import** statement allows the program to refer to classes defined in the designated package without using the fully qualified class name.

And here's the same Ch2Sample1 program without the import statement:

```
/*
   Chapter 2 Sample Program: Displaying a Window

   File: Ch2Sample1.java
*/

class Ch2Sample1 {

    public static void main(String[] args) {

        javax.swing.JFrame    myWindow;

        myWindow = new javax.swing.JFrame ();

        myWindow.setSize(300, 200);
        myWindow.setTitle("My First Java Program");
        myWindow.setVisible(true);
    }

}
```

No import statement

Fully qualified names

Instead of using the expression javax.swing.JFrame to refer to the class, we can refer to it simply as

```
JFrame
```

by including the import statement

```
import javax.swing.JFrame;
```

at the beginning of the program. Notice that the import statement is terminated by a semicolon. If we need to import more than one class from the same package, then instead of using an import statement for every class, we can import them all by using asterisk notation:

```
import  <package name> . * ;
```

For example, if we state

```
import javax.swing.*;
```

then we are importing all classes from the javax.swing package. We use this asterisk notation in our sample program, even when we use only one of the many classes available in the javax.swing package. We could have used

```
import javax.swing.JFrame;
```

but it is more conventional to use asterisk notation. Notice that the package names are all in lowercase letters. This is another standard Java naming convention. Chapter 4 includes greater discussion of packages.

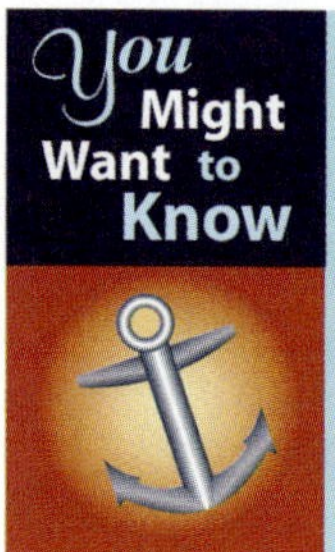

When we say "import a package," it sounds as if we are copying all those classes into our programs. That is not the case. Importing a package is only a shorthand notation for referencing classes. The only effect of importing a package is the elimination of the requirement to use the fully qualified name. No classes are physically copied into our programs.

Class Declaration

class declaration

A Java program is composed of one or more classes; some are predefined classes, while others are defined by us. In the first sample program, there are two classes—JFrame and Ch2Sample1. The JFrame class is one of the standard classes, and the Ch2Sample1 class is the class we define ourselves. To define a new class, we must *declare* it in the program, or make a ***class declaration***. The syntax for declaring the class is

```
class <class name> {

   <class member declarations>

}
```

where <class name> is the name of the class and <class member declarations> is a sequence of class member declarations. The word class is a reserved word used to mark the beginning of a class declaration. A class member is either a data value or a method. We can use any valid identifier that is not reserved to name the class. Here's the class declaration in the sample Ch2Sample1 program:

```
/*

    Chapter 2 Sample Program: Displaying a Window

    File: Ch2Sample1.java

*/

import javax.swing.*;
```

```
class Ch2Sample1 {

    public static void main(String[] args) {

        JFrame     myWindow;

        myWindow = new JFrame();

        myWindow.setSize(300, 200);
        myWindow.setTitle("My First Java Program");
        myWindow.setVisible(true);
    }

}
```

Class Declaration
Every program must include at least one class.

main class

One of the classes in a program must be designated as the ***main class***. The main class of the sample program is Ch2Sample1. Exactly how you designate a class as the main class of the program depends on which Java program development tool you use. We will use the name of a main class to refer to a whole application. For example, we say the Ch2Sample1 *class* when we refer to the class itself, and we say the Ch2Sample1 *application* when we refer to the whole application.

If we designate a class as the main class, then we must define a method called main, because when a Java program is executed, the main method of a main class is executed first. To define a method, we must declare it in a class.

Method Declaration

method declaration

The syntax for ***method declaration*** is

```
<modifiers> <return type> <method name> ( <parameters> ) {

    <method body>
}
```

where <modifiers> is a sequence of terms designating different kinds of methods, <return type> is the type of data value returned by a method, <method name> is the name of a method, <parameters> is a sequence of values passed to a method, and <method body> is a sequence of instructions. Here's the method declaration for the main method:

```
/*

    Chapter 2 Sample Program: Displaying a Window

    File: Ch2Sample1.java

*/
```

```
import javax.swing.*;

class Ch2Sample1 {

    public static void main(String[] args) {

        JFrame    myWindow;

        myWindow = new JFrame();

        myWindow.setSize(300, 200);
        myWindow.setTitle("My First Java Program");
        myWindow.setVisible(true);
    }

}
```

Method Declaration
This declaration declares the **main** method.

Let's match these components to the actual method declaration of the sample program:

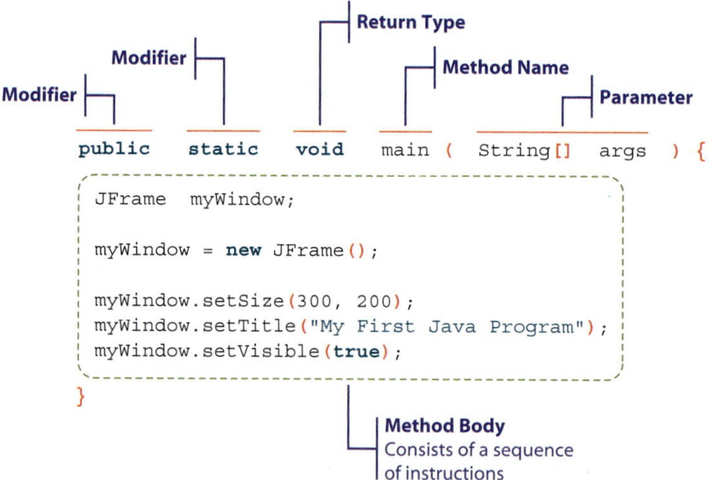

We do not explain the meanings of modifiers, return types, and parameters here. We will explain them in detail gradually as we progress through the book. For now, we ask you to follow a program template that we present next.

A Program Template for Simple Java Applications

The diagram in Figure 2.9 shows a program template for simple Java applications. You can follow this program template to write very simple Java applications. The structure of the sample program Ch2Sample1 follows this template.

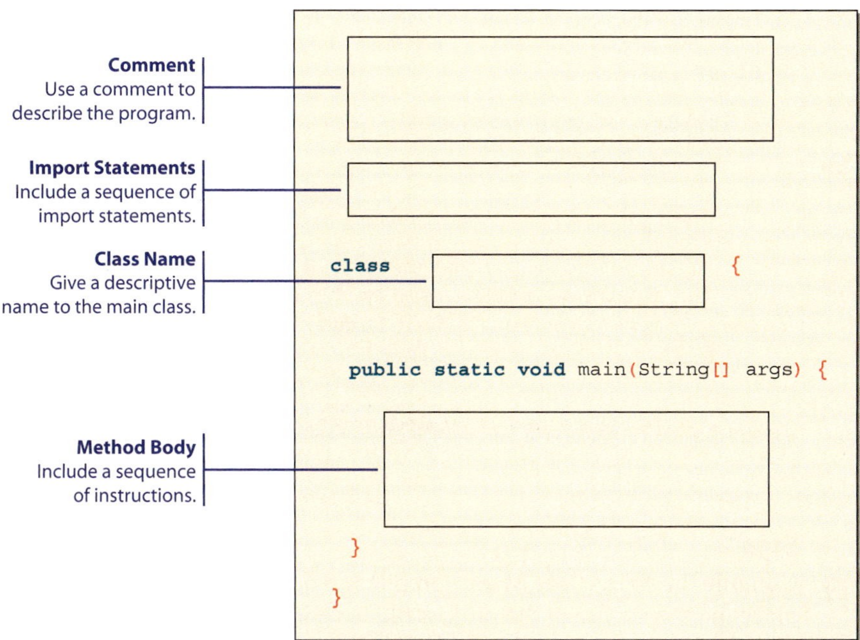

Figure 2.9 A program template for simple Java applications.

2.3 Edit-Compile-Run Cycle

edit-compile-run cycle

We will walk through the steps involved in executing the first sample program. What we outline here are the overall steps in the ***edit-compile-run cycle*** common to any Java development tool you use. You need to get detailed instructions on how to use your chosen development tool to actually run programs. The steps we present in this section should serve as a guideline for more detailed instructions specific to your program development tool. Additional information on how to run Java programs can be found in Appendix A.

Step 1

source file

Type in the program, using an editor, and save the program to a file. Use the name of the main class and the suffix .java for the filename. This file, in which the program is in a human-readable form, is called a ***source file***.

Ch2Sample1.java

```
/*
   Chapter 2 Sample Program: Displaying a Window

   File: Ch2Sample1.java
*/
```

Editor

```
import javax.swing.*;

class Ch2Sample1 {

   public static void main( String[] args ) {

      JFrame    myWindow;

      myWindow = new JFrame();

      myWindow.setSize(300, 200);
      myWindow.setTitle("My First Java Program");
      myWindow.setVisible(true);
   }
}
```

(source file)

Step 2

project file

bytecode

bytecode file

Compile the source file. Many compilers require you to create a ***project file*** and then place the source file in the project file in order to compile the source file. When the compilation is successful, the compiled version of the source file is created. This compiled version is called ***bytecode***, and the file that contains bytecode is called a ***bytecode file***. The name of the compiler-generated bytecode file will have the suffix .class while its prefix is the same as the one for the source file.

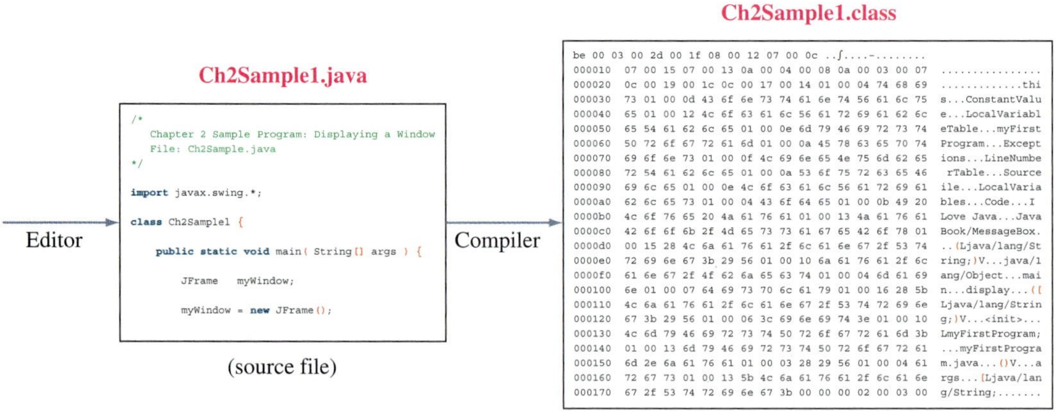

Editor → **Ch2Sample1.java**

```
/*
   Chapter 2 Sample Program: Displaying a Window
   File: Ch2Sample.java
*/

import javax.swing.*;

class Ch2Sample1 {

   public static void main( String[] args ) {

      JFrame   myWindow;

      myWindow = new JFrame();
```

(source file)

Compiler → **Ch2Sample1.class**

```
be 00 03 00 2d 00 1f 08 00 12 07 00 0c ..∫....-........
000010  07 00 15 07 00 13 0a 00 04 00 08 0a 00 03 00 07  ................
000020  0c 00 19 00 1c 0c 00 17 00 14 01 00 04 74 68 69  .............thi
000030  73 01 00 0d 43 6f 6e 73 74 61 6e 74 56 61 6c 75  s...ConstantValu
000040  65 01 00 12 4c 6f 63 61 6c 56 61 72 69 61 62 6c  e...LocalVariabl
000050  65 54 61 62 6c 65 01 00 0e 6d 79 46 69 72 73 74  eTable...myFirst
000060  50 72 6f 67 72 61 6d 01 00 0a 45 78 63 65 70 74  Program...Except
000070  69 6f 6e 73 01 00 0f 4c 69 6e 65 4e 75 6d 62 65  ions...LineNumbe
000080  72 54 61 62 6c 65 01 00 0a 53 6f 75 72 63 65 46   rTable...Source
000090  69 6c 65 01 00 0e 4c 6f 63 61 6c 56 61 72 69 61  ile...LocalVaria
0000a0  62 6c 65 73 01 00 04 43 6f 64 65 01 00 0b 49 20  bles...Code...I
0000b0  4c 6f 76 65 20 4a 61 76 61 01 00 13 4a 61 76 61  Love Java...Java
0000c0  42 6f 6f 6b 2f 4d 65 73 73 61 67 65 42 6f 78 01  Book/MessageBox.
0000d0  00 15 28 4c 6a 61 76 61 2f 6c 61 6e 67 2f 53 74  ..(Ljava/lang/St
0000e0  72 69 6e 67 3b 29 56 01 00 10 6a 61 76 61 2f 6c  ring;)V...java/l
0000f0  61 6e 67 2f 4f 62 6a 65 63 74 01 00 04 6d 61 69  ang/Object...mai
000100  6e 01 00 07 64 69 73 70 6c 61 79 01 00 16 28 5b  n...display...([
000110  4c 6a 61 76 61 2f 6c 61 6e 67 2f 53 74 72 69 6e  Ljava/lang/Strin
000120  67 3b 29 56 01 00 06 3c 69 6e 69 74 3e 01 00 10  g;)V...<init>...
000130  4c 6d 79 46 69 72 73 74 50 72 6f 67 72 61 6d 3b  LmyFirstProgram;
000140  01 00 13 6d 79 46 69 72 73 74 50 72 6f 67 72 61  ...myFirstProgra
000150  6d 2e 6a 61 76 61 01 00 03 28 29 56 01 00 04 61  m.java...()V...a
000160  72 67 73 01 00 13 5b 4c 6a 61 76 61 2f 6c 61 6e  rgs...[Ljava/lan
000170  67 2f 53 74 72 69 6e 67 3b 00 00 00 02 00 03 00  g/String;.......
```

(bytecode file)

When any error occurs in a program, an error message will be displayed. If the sample program contains no errors in syntax, then instead of an error message, you will get nothing or a message stating something like "Compiled successfully." To see what kind of error messages are displayed, try compiling the following program. We purposely introduced three errors. Can you find them? Make sure to compile the correct Ch2Sample1 again before you proceed to the next step.

Bad Version

```
import javax.swing.*;

class Ch2Sample1 {

    public static void main( String[]args ) {

        myWindow = new JFrame();

        myWindow.setSize( );
        myWindow.setTitle("My First Java Program");
        myWindow.setVisible(true)
    }
}
```

compilation error

Errors detected by the compiler are called ***compilation errors***. Compilation errors are actually the easiest type of errors to correct. Most compilation errors are due to the violation of syntax rules.

Step 3

Execute the bytecode file. A Java interpreter will go through the bytecode file and execute the instructions in it. If your program is error-free, a window will appear on the screen.

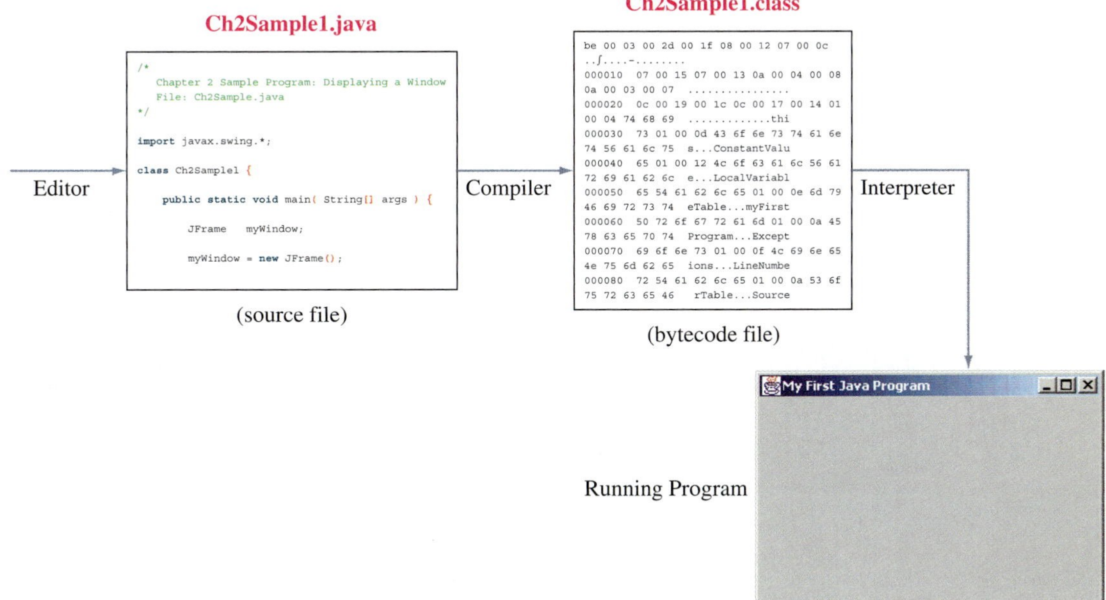

execution error

If an error occurs in running the program, the interpreter will catch it and stop its execution. Errors detected by the interpreter are called ***execution errors***. If you did not see the expected results, go back to the previous steps and verify that your program is entered correctly. If you still do not see the expected results, then most likely your development environment is not set up correctly. Please refer to other sources of information for further help.

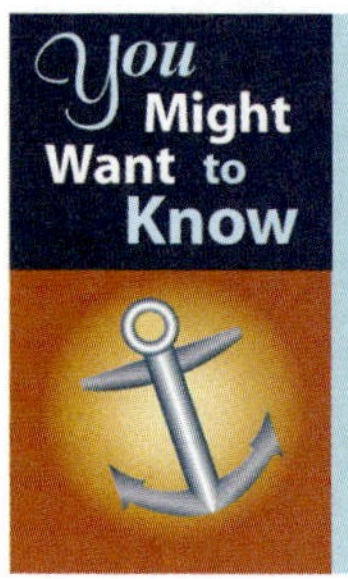

Unlike machine-language instructions, or machine code, Java bytecode is not tied to any particular operating system or CPU. All we need to run the same Java programs on different operating systems is the Java interpreters for the desired operating systems. Currently, there are Java interpreters for Windows, Mac, Unix, and other operating systems. A Java interpreter is also called a Java Virtual Machine (JVM) because it is like a virtual machine that executes bytecode, whereas a CPU is a real machine that executes machine code.

2.4 Sample Java Standard Classes

Eventually, you must learn how to define your own classes, the classes you will reuse in writing programs. But before you can become adept at defining your own classes, you must learn how to use existing classes. In this section, we will introduce standard classes. Sample code using these classes helps us reinforce the core object-oriented programming (OOP) concepts introduced in Chapter 1 with the actual Java statements. Five standard classes we introduce here are JOptionPane, System, Scanner String, Date, and SimpleDateFormat. It is not our objective here to explain these classes fully. Rather, our objective is to get you started in writing practical Java programs with a minimal explanation of some of the useful standard classes. We will introduce additional capabilities of these classes as we progress through the textbook. Although we will scratch only the surface of these classes in this section, what we provide here should serve as a foundation for you to delve more deeply into these classes. For a more detailed description, please consult the documentation for the standard classes. The documentation for the standard classes is commonly called Java API documentation, where API stands for *application programming interface*.

Things to Remember

To become a good object-oriented programmer, first you must learn how to use predefined classes.

Please do not get alarmed by the number of standard classes we introduce here. Although we cover five standard classes at once, we limit ourselves to the most basic operations, so we won't overwhelm you with too much information. Their documentation can be located online at
http://java.sun.com/j2se/1.5.0/docs/api/index.html

2.4.1 Standard Output

console window

System.out

standard output

When a program computes a result, we need a way to display this result to the user of the program. One of the most common ways to do this in Java is to use the ***console window***. The console window is also called the ***standard output window***. We output data such as the computation results or messages to the console window via System.out. The System class includes a number of useful class data values. One is an instance of the PrintStream class named out. Since this is a class data value, we refer to it through the class name as System.out, and this PrintStream object is tied to the console window (there's exactly one console window per program). Every data item we send to System.out will appear on this console window. We call the technique to output data by using System.out the ***standard output***.

We use the print method to output a value. For example, executing the code

```
System.out.print("Hello, Dr. Caffeine.");
```

will result in the console window shown in Figure 2.10. The actual appearance of the console window will differ depending on which Java development tool we use. Despite the difference in the actual appearance, its functionality of displaying data is the same among different Java tools.

Things to Remember

***System.out** refers to a precreated **PrintStream** object we use to output data to the console window. The actual appearance of the console window depends on which Java tool we use.*

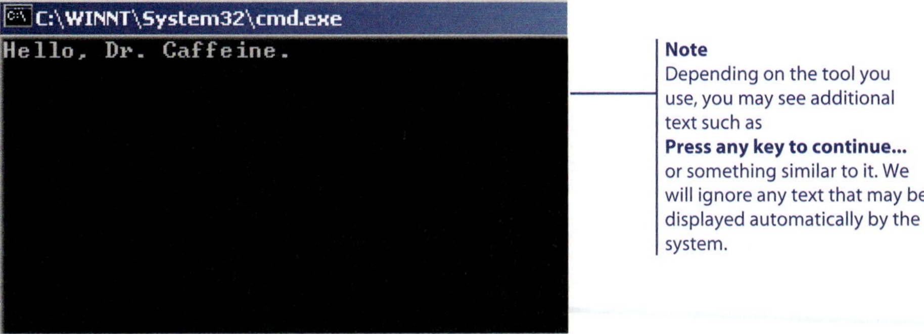

Note
Depending on the tool you use, you may see additional text such as
Press any key to continue...
or something similar to it. We will ignore any text that may be displayed automatically by the system.

Figure 2.10 Result of executing **System.out.print("Hello, Dr. Caffeine.")**.

Code

```
System.out.print("How do you do? ");
System.out.print("My name is ");
System.out.print("Seattle Slew.");
```

Output

```
How do you do? My name is Seattle Slew.
```

Note: Because the actual appearance of the console window is different depending on the Java development tool you use, we use a generic picture for the console window in the diagrams.

Figure 2.11 Result of executing three consecutive **print** methods. The **print** method continues the printing from the currently displayed output.

The print method will continue printing from the end of the currently displayed output. Executing the following statements will result in the console window shown in Figure 2.11.

```
System.out.print("How do you do? ");
System.out.print("My name is ");
System.out.print("Seattle Slew.");
```

Notice that they all appear on the same line. If we want them to appear on individual lines, we can use the println method instead of print. The word *println* is a shorthand for "print line." Figure 2.12 shows the effect of the println method.

This concludes our quick introduction to System.out. We will be gradually introducing additional techniques of outputting to the console window as they are needed.

Code

```
System.out.println("How do you do? ");
System.out.println("My name is ");
System.out.println("Seattle Slew.");
```

Output

```
How do you do?
My name is
Seattle Slew.
```

Figure 2.12 Result of executing three consecutive **println** methods. The **println** method will skip to the next line after printing out its argument.

1. Write a Java statement to display the text I Love Java in the console window.
2. Write statements to display the following shopping list in the console window. Don't forget to include blank spaces so the item names appear indented.

```
Shopping List:
       Apple
       Banana
       Low-fat Milk
```

2.4.2 String

The textual values we passed to the print method or the constructor of the JFrame class are instances of the String class. A sequence of characters separated by double quotes is String constants. As String is a class, we can create an instance and give it a name. For example,

```
String name;
name = new String("Jon Java");
```

will result in a situation as follows:

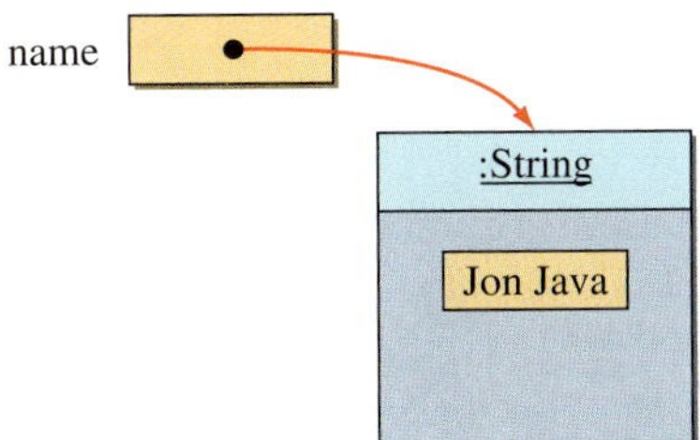

Unlike in other classes, the explicit use of new to create an instance is optional for the String class. We can create a new String object, for example, in this way:

```
String name;
name = "Decafe Latte";
```

substring

There are close to 50 methods defined in the String class. We will introduce three of them here: substring, length, and indexOf. We can extract a ***substring*** from a given string by specifying the beginning and ending positions. For example,

```
String text;
text = "Espresso";
System.out.print(text.substring(2, 7));
```

will display the dialog shown in Figure 2.13.

Code

```
String text;
text = "Espresso";
System.out.print(text.substring(2,7));
```

Output

```
press
```

Figure 2.13 Result of extracting and displaying the substring of **"Expresso"** from index position's 2 to 6. The index position of the first character in a string is 0.

method composition

Notice the use of ***method composition*** in the last statement, where the result of a method call is used as an argument in another method call. In the statement

```
System.out.print (text.substring(2,7));
```

the result of method call

```
text.substring(2,7)
```

is passed as an argument when calling the showMessageDialog method. The sample statement is equivalent to

```
String tempStr;

tempStr = text.substring(2,7);
System.out.print(tempStr);
```

Individual characters in a String object are indexed from 0, as illustrated in Figure 2.14. The first argument of the substring method specifies the position of the first character, and the second argument specifies the value that is 1 more than the

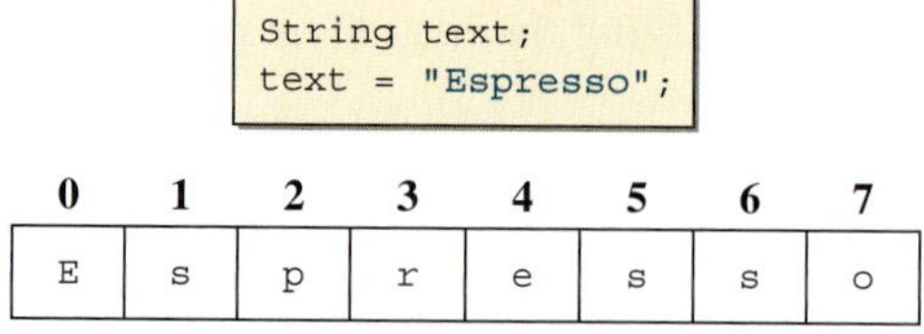

Figure 2.14 Individual characters in a string are numbered from 0.

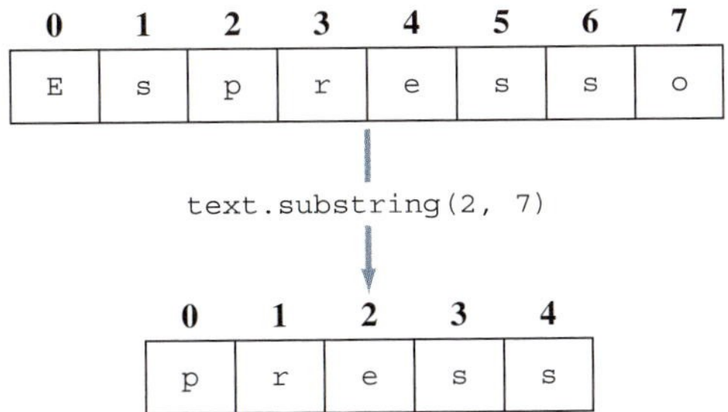

Figure 2.15 The effect of the **substring** method is shown. Notice that a new string is created, and the original string remains intact.

position of the last character. Figure 2.15 shows how the substring method works. Here are some more examples:

```
text.substring( 6, 8 )      ──►     "so"

text.substring( 0, 8 )      ──►     "Espresso"

text.substring( 1, 5 )      ──►     "spre"
```

An error will result if you pass invalid arguments, such as negative values, the second argument larger than the number of characters in a string, or the first argument larger than the second argument.

length

We can find out the number of characters in a String object by using the length method. For example, if the name text refers to a string Espresso, then

```
text.length()
```

will return the value 8, because there are eight characters in the string. Here are some more examples:

```
text1 = "";            //empty string
text2 = "Hello";
text3 = "Java";

text1.length( )     ──►   0

text2.length( )     ──►   5

text3.length( )     ──►   4
```

indexOf

To locate the index position of a substring within another string, we use the ***indexOf*** method. For example, if the name `text` refers to a string `I Love Java`, then

```
text.indexOf("Love")
```

will return the value 2, the index position of the first character of the designated string `Love`. If the searched substring is not located in the string, then −1 is returned. Notice that the search is done in a case-sensitive manner. Thus,

```
text.indexOf("java")
```

will return −1. If there is more than one occurrence of the same substring, the index position of the first character of the first matching substring is returned. Here are some more examples:

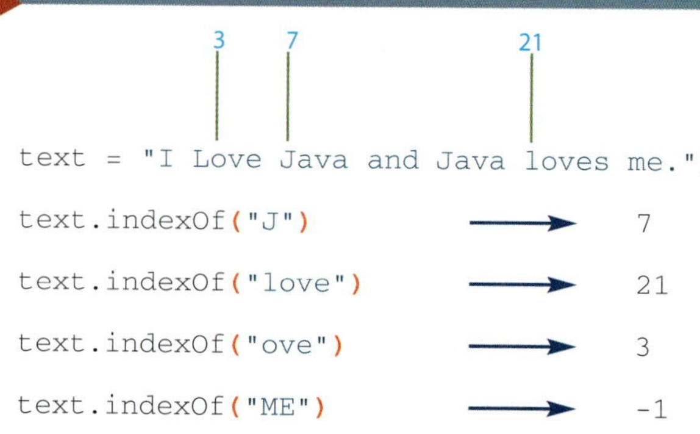
3
7
21
text = "I Love Java and Java loves me.";
text.indexOf("J") → 7
text.indexOf("love") → 21
text.indexOf("ove") → 3
text.indexOf("ME") → -1

string concatenation

Beyond the three methods we cover here and the remaining methods of the `String` class, we have one very useful string operation in Java called ***string concatenation***. We can create a new string from two strings by concatenating the two strings. We use the plus symbol (+) for string concatenation. Here are the examples:

```
text1 = "Jon";
text2 = "Java";

text1 + text2                  →   "JonJava"

text1 + " " + text2            →   "Jon Java"

"How are you, " + text1 + "?"

                               →   "How are you, Jon?"
```

The sample class Ch2StringProcessing divides the given full name into the first and last names and displays the number of letters in the last name.

```
/*
    Chapter 2 Sample Program: Simple String Processing

    File: Ch2StringProcessing.java
*/

class Ch2StringProcessing {

    public static void main( String[] args ) {

        String fullName, firstName, lastName, space;

        fullName  = new String("Decafe Latte");
        space     = new String(" ");

        firstName = fullName.substring(0, fullName.indexOf(space));
        lastName  = fullName.substring(fullName.indexOf(space) + 1,
                                       fullName.length());

        System.out.println("Full Name: " + fullName);

        System.out.println("First: " + firstName);

        System.out.println("Last: " + lastName);

        System.out.println("Your last name has " + lastName.length( )
                                                 + " characters.");
    }
}
```

1. What will be the value of mystery when the following code is executed?

```
String text, mystery;

text    = "mocha chai latte";
mystery = text.substring(1,5);
```

2. What will be displayed on the message dialog when the following code is executed?

```
String text = "I, Claudius";

System.out.println(text.indexOf("I") );
```

3. What will be displayed on the message dialog when the following code is executed?

```
String text = "Augustus";

System.out.println(text.length());
```

4. What will be the value of text3 when the following code is executed?

```
String text1 = "a" + "b";
String text2 = "c";

String text3 = text1 + text2 + text1;
```

2.4.3 Date and SimpleDateFormat

The Date class is used to represent a time instance to a millisecond (one-thousandth of a second) precision. This class is in the java.util package. When a new Date object is created, it is set to the time it is created (the current time is determined by reading the time maintained by the operating system on your machine). The Date class includes the toString method that converts its internal format to a string representation, which we can use to display the time. For example, executing the code

```
Date today;

today = new Date( );
System.out.println(today.toString());
```

will display the current time in this format:

```
Wed Jan 28 15:05:18 PDT 2006
```

Notice that the current time, when converted to a string format, includes the date information also. Internally, the time is kept as an elapsed time in milliseconds since the standard base time known as the epoch, which is January 1, 1970, 00:00:00 GMT (Greenwich Mean Time).

You Might Want to Know

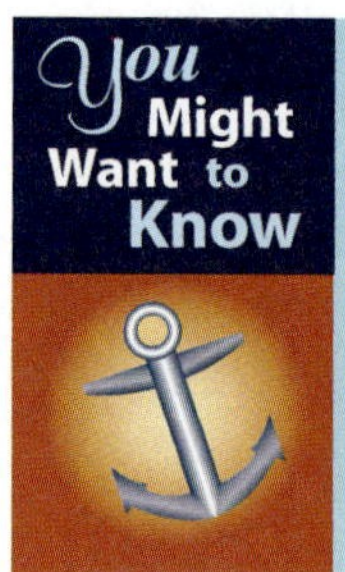

Why is the class called **Date** when its purpose is to keep track of time? The reason is historical. In the older versions of Java, prior to JDK 1.1, the **Date** class was indeed used to manipulate the year, month, and day components of the current time. However, the way they are implemented was not amenable to internationalization. With the newer versions of Java, we use the **GregorianCalendar** class for date manipulation. The **GregorianCalendar** class is explained in Chapter 3.

If we do not like the default format, say we want to display only the month and year or only the hours and minutes in the AM/PM designation, then we can use the SimpleDateFormat class. This class is in the java.text package. For example, if we want to display the month, day, and year in the MM/dd/yy shorthand format, such as 07/04/03, we write

```
Date             today;
SimpleDateFormat sdf;

today = new Date( );
sdf   = new SimpleDateFormat("MM/dd/yy");

System.out.println(sdf.format(today));
```

If today is June 28, 2006, the code will display the date as

```
06/28/06
```

Notice the format designation is done by passing the formatting string when a new SimpleDateFormat object is created. The letters in the formatting string are case-sensitive. The formatting string in this example must be MM/dd/yy, and the letters d and y must be in lowercase. By increasing the number of formatting letters, we can change the length of the information, say, 2006 instead of 06. In case of the month, we change it from the number to a name. For example, when we change sdf to

```
sdf = new SimpleDateFormat("MMMM dd, yyyy");
```

the dialog will display

```
June 28, 2006
```

If we want to display which day of the week today is, we can use the letter E as in

```
Date             today;
SimpleDateFormat sdf;

today = new Date( );
sdf   = new SimpleDateFormat("EEEE");

System.out.println("Today is " + sdf.format(today));
```

Table 2.1 lists the common letters used in the formatting for SimpleDate-Format. For more details, please consult the Java API documentation.

Table 2.1 is provided solely for the purpose of quick reference when you start using the class in real programs. Nobody expects you to remember all those symbols. What is important here is for you to grasp the key OOP concepts and the fundamental way in which objects and classes are used, not to memorize minute details that nobody remembers.

Table 2.1 Some common formatting symbols for *SimpleDateFormat* and their meanings. Please check the Java API documentation for full details.

Symbol	Meaning	Value	Sample
y	Year	Number	yyyy → 2002
M	Month in year	Text or number	MM → 10 MMM → Oct MMMM → October
d	Day in month	Number	dd → 20
D	Day in year	Number	DDD → 289
h	Hour in AM/PM	Number	hh → 09
H	Hour in day (0–23)	Number	HH → 17
a	AM/PM marker	Text	a → AM
m	Minutes in hour	Number	mm → 35
s	Seconds in minute	Number	ss → 54
S	Millisecond	Number	mmm → 897
E	Day in week	Text	E → Sat EEEE → Saturday

If you do not pass any string when creating a new SimpleDataFormat object, the default formatting is used. The sample Ch2DateDisplay class displays today's date, using the default and programmer-designated format.

```
/*
    Chapter 2 Sample Program: Displays Formatted Date Information

    File: Ch2DateDisplay.java
*/

import java.util.*; //for Date
import java.text.*; //for SimpleDateFormat

class Ch2DateDisplay {

    public static void main( String[] args ) {

        Date             today;

        SimpleDateFormat simpleDF1,
                         simpleDF2;

        today      = new Date();
```

```
        simpleDF1 = new SimpleDateFormat( );
        simpleDF2 = new SimpleDateFormat ("EEEE MMMM dd, yyyy");

        //Default short format display
        System.out.println("Today is " + simpleDF1.format(today) );

        //Programmer-designated long format display
        System.out.println("Today is " + simpleDF2.format(today) );
    }
}
```

1. Write a code fragment to display today's date in the 07-04-2002 format.
2. What will be displayed on the message dialog when the following code is executed if today is July 4, 1776?

```
Date              today;
SimpleDateFormat  sdf;

today = new Date( );
sdf   = new SimpleDateFormat("MMM dd, yyyy");

System.out.println("Today is " + sdf.format(today));
```

2.4.4 Standard Input

System.in
standard input
console input

Analogous to System.out for output, we have System.in for input. We call the technique to input data using System.in ***standard input***. System.in accepts input from the keyboard. We also use the term ***console input*** to refer to standard input. Using System.in for input is slightly more complicated than using System.out for output. System.in is an instance of the InputStream class that provides only a facility to input 1 byte at a time with its read method. However, multiple bytes are required to represent common types of data such as strings. The Scanner class from the java.util package provides a necessary input facility to accommodate various input routines. We limit our discussion here to input of string values. We extend our discussion to input of numerical values in Chapter 3.

Scanner

To input data from the standard input by using a Scanner object, we first create it by passing System.in as follows:

```
import java.util.*;
...
Scanner scanner;

scanner = new Scanner(System.in);
```

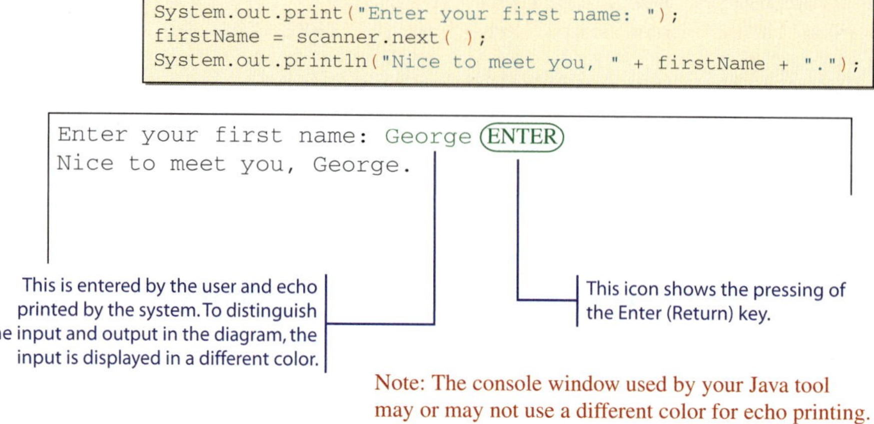
System.out.print("Enter your first name: ");
firstName = scanner.next( );
System.out.println("Nice to meet you, " + firstName + ".");
Enter your first name: George ENTER
Nice to meet you, George.
This is entered by the user and echo printed by the system. To distinguish the input and output in the diagram, the input is displayed in a different color.
This icon shows the pressing of the Enter (Return) key.
Note: The console window used by your Java tool may or may not use a different color for echo printing.

Figure 2.16 Sample interaction using **System.in** with **Scanner** and **System.out.** Keyboard input is echo-printed in the console window.

Once we have a Scanner object, then we can input a single word by using its next method. Here's code to input the first name of a person:

```
Scanner scanner = new Scanner(System.in);

String firstName;

//prompt the user for input
System.out.print("Enter your first name: ");

firstName = scanner.next( );

System.out.println("Nice to meet you, " + firstName + ".");
```

The user interaction of this sample code is shown in Figure 2.16. In the diagram, the characters entered by the user are displayed in the console window as they are typed in, so the user can see what's been entered. Printing out the values just entered is called ***echo printing.*** The string input is processed until the Enter (or Return) key is pressed, so we can erase the characters by pressing the Backspace key while entering the data.

echo printing

Now let's consider the case in which we want to input both the first name and the last name. We can follow the sample code and input them one by one as follows:

```
Scanner scanner = new Scanner(System.in);

String firstName, lastName;

System.out.print("Enter your first name: ");
firstName = scanner.next( );
```

```
System.out.print("Enter your last name: ");
lastName = scanner.next( );

System.out.println("Your name is " + firstName +
                   " " + lastName + ".");
```

```
Enter your first name: George ENTER
Enter your last name: Washington ENTER
Your name is George Washington.
```

What can we do if we want input both the first name and the last name together as a single input? Consider the following (wrong) code:

Bad Version

```
Scanner scanner = new Scanner(System.in);

String fullName;

System.out.print("Enter your first and last names: ");
fullName = scanner.next( );

System.out.println("Your name is " + fullName + ".");
```

Here's a sample interaction of a user entering both the first name and the last name on a single line:

```
Enter your first and last name: George Washington ENTER
Your name is George.
```

What happened to the last name? The blank space between the first name and the last name is treated as a delimiter. So the system has accepted the characters up to, but not including, the blank space as the input value. Because we know there are first and last names, we can input them individually as follows:

```
Scanner scanner = new Scanner(System.in);

String first, last;

System.out.print("Enter your first and last name: ");
first = scanner.next( );
last  = scanner.next( );

System.out.println("Your name is " + first + " "
                                   + last + ".");
```

```
Enter your first and last name: George Washington ENTER
Your name is George Washington.
```

Instead of treating each word individually, it is possible to enter a set of words as a single input. To do so, we must reset the delimiter to other than the blank space. Any character can be set as a delimiter, but since we want to input the whole line as a single input, it is most reasonable to set the delimiter to the Enter key. Here's how we change the delimiter to the Enter key and accept the complete line as a single input:

```
Scanner scanner = new Scanner(System.in);

String lineSeparator
             = System.getProperty("line.separator");

scanner.useDelimiter(lineSeparator);

String quote;

System.out.println("Enter your favorite quote: ");
quote = scanner.next( );

System.out.println("You entered: " + quote);
```

Note we're using **println** here.

```
Enter your favorite quote:
There never was a good war or a bad peace. ENTER
You entered: There never was a good war or a bad peace.
```

We override the default delimiter by calling the useDelimiter method and pass the appropriate argument. We use the class method getProperty of the System class to retrieve the actual sequence of characters for the Enter key that is specific to the platform which our program is running. For the Windows platform, for instance, we can call the useDelimiter method as

```
scanner.useDelimiter("\r\n");
```

But such code is guaranteed only to work on the Windows platform. It may or may not work on other platforms. To make the code general enough to work on all platforms, we use System.getProperty. Incidentally, the backslash character (\) is called a *control character* or an *escape character*. We'll examine the use of control characters later in the book.

1. Write a code to input the last name of a user.
2. Show the content of the console window when the following code is executed and the text Barbaro is entered:

```
Scanner scanner = new Scanner(System.in);

String winner;

System.out.print(
                 "Enter the name of the derby winner: ");
winner = scanner.next( );

System.out.println("2006 Kentucky Derby Winner is "
                       + name + ".");
```

2.5 Sample Development

Printing the Initials

Now that we have acquired a basic understanding of Java application programs, let's write a new application. We will go through the design, coding, and testing phases of the software life cycle to illustrate the development process. Since the program we develop here is very simple, we can write it without really going through the phases. However, it is extremely important for you to get into a habit of developing a program by following the software life cycle stages. Small programs can be developed in a haphazard manner, but not large programs. We will teach you the development process with small programs first, so you will be ready to use it to create large programs later.

We will develop this program by using an incremental development technique, which will develop the program in small incremental steps. We start out with a bare-bones program and gradually build up the program by adding more and more code to it. At each incremental step, we design, code, and test the program before moving on to the next step. This methodical development of a program allows us to focus our attention on a single task at each step, and this reduces the chance of introducing errors into the program.

Problem Statement

We start our development with a problem statement. The problem statement for our sample programs will be short, ranging from a sentence to a paragraph, but the problem statement for complex and advanced applications may contain many pages. Here's the problem statement for this sample development exercise:

Write an application that asks for the user's first, middle, and last names and replies with the user's initials.

Overall Plan

Our first task is to map out the overall plan for development. We will identify classes necessary for the program and the steps we will follow to implement the program. We begin with the outline of program logic. For a simple program such as this one, it is kind of obvious; but to practice the incremental development, let's put down the outline of program flow explicitly. We can express the program flow as having three tasks:

program tasks

1. Get the user's first, middle, and last names.
2. Extract the initials to formulate the monogram.
3. Output the monogram.

Having identified the three major tasks of the program, we will now identify the classes we can use to implement the three tasks. First, we need an object to handle the input. At this point, we have learned about only the **Scanner** class, so we will use it here. Second, we need an object to display the result. Again, we will use **System.out**, as it is the only one we know at this point for displaying a string value. For the string

2.5 Sample Development—*continued*

manipulation, we will use the **String** class. Finally, we will use these classes from the main class, which we will call **Ch2Monogram**. Let's summarize these in a design document:

program classes

Design Document: Monogram

Class	Purpose
`Ch2Monogram`	The main class of the program.
`Scanner`	The next method is used for getting the full name.
`String`	The class is used for string manipulation, extracting initials from the first, middle, and last names.
`(PrintStream) System.out`	The standard output window is used for displaying the resulting monogram.

The program diagram of **Ch2Monogram** is shown in Figure 2.17. Keep in mind that this is only a preliminary design. Although we are not going to see any changes made to this design document because this sample application is very simple, changes to the design document are expected as the programs we develop become larger and more complex. The preliminary document is really a working document that we will modify and expand as we progress through the development steps.

Before we can actually start our development, we must sketch the steps we will follow to develop the program. There is more than one possible sequence of steps to develop

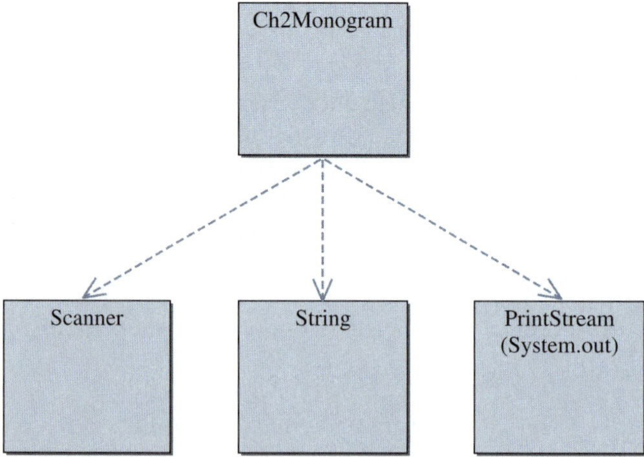

Figure 2.17 The program diagram for **Ch2Monogram.**

a program, and the number of possible sequences will increase as the program becomes more complex. For this program, we will develop the program in two steps:

develop-ment steps

1. Start with the program template and add code to get input.
2. Add code to compute and display the monogram.

Step 1 Development: Getting Input

step 1 design

The problem states that the program is to input the user's name and display its initials. It does not specify how, so in the design stage, we will decide how to do this. Since, at this point, we know only one way to input data, that is, using the **Scanner** class, we will use it here. But in which form shall we input three pieces of data? There are two possible design alternatives.

alternative design 1

In the first design, we will input them separately:

```
String firstName, middleName, lastName;

Scanner scanner = new Scanner(System.in);

System.out.print("First Name: ");
firstName = scanner.next( );

System.out.print("Middle Name: ");
middleName = scanner.next( );

System.out.print("Last Name: ");
lastName = scanner.next( );
```

alternative design 2

In the second design, we will input them together:

```
String fullName;

Scanner scanner = new Scanner(System.in);

scanner.useDelimiter(System.getProperty("line.separator"));

System.out.print("Full Name: ");
fullName = scanner.next( );
```

Which design is better? There is never "one correct answer" to the design problems. We have to select the one from the possible alternatives that satisfies the different criteria most effectively in a given situation. The criteria may include the user's needs and preferences, faster performance, development costs, time contraints, and other factors. For example, in one situation, we may decide to forgo some great user interface features so the development can be completed under budget.

In this sample development, we will consider the alternative designs from the overall quality of the program's user interface. In other words, we want to make our program as user-friendly as possible. We want our users to have a pleasant experience using our program. The program should not be cumbersome to use, or else the users will get very frustrated in using the program. Which design would give the better user experience? In the first approach, the user enters the information separately with three dialogs,

2.5 Sample Development—*continued*

while in the second approach, the user enters the information together with one dialog. We choose the second approach because it allows quicker data entry, and in general, it is more natural to treat the name as a single entity than as three separate entitites. If we were to enter the name, address, and phone number, then we would use three dialogs as they are three separate entities. In this situation, we consider the first, middle, and last names as part of a single entity.

Notice that the decision to enter the full name by using one dialog makes our task as the programmer slightly more difficult because we need to extract the first, middle, and last names from a single string. In the first approach, as we get the first, middle, and last names separately, there's no such need. So, if we consider strictly the ease of development, the first approach is better. It is important to remember, however, that we are developing the program for the sake of the users, not for ourselves.

Things to Remember

We develop programs for the sake of users, not for ourselves. Ease of use has higher priority than ease of development.

step 1 code

Let's implement the second design alternative. In the code, notice the use of the output statement that prints the string entered by the user. This printing of the input is another form of echo printing (introduced in Section 2.4.4). By echo printing, we verify that the input value is indeed read in correctly.

```
/*
    Chapter 2 Sample Program: Displays the Monogram

    File: Step1/Ch2Monogram.java

/*
import java.util.*;

class Ch2Monogram {

   public static void main(String[] args) {

      String name;

      Scanner scanner = new Scanner(System.in);
```

```
        scanner.useDelimiter(System.getProperty("line.separator"));

        System.out.print("Enter your full name (first, middle, last):");

        name = scanner.next( );

        System.out.println("Name entered: " + name);

    }
}
```

step 1 test

After the program is written, we test the program to verify that the program runs as intended. The step 1 program may seem so trivial and not so useful, but it does serve a very useful purpose. Successful execution of this program verifies that the program setup is okay, the necessary packages are imported, and the objects are declared correctly. Since this program is very simple, there's not much testing strategy we can employ other than simply running it. For subsequent sample programs, however, the testing strategy will be more involved. After the step 1 program is compiled and executed correctly, we move on to step 2.

Step 2 Development: Computing and Displaying the Monogram

step 2 design

The next task is to extract initials from the input string. First, because of our limited knowledge of programming at this point, we will assume the input is correct. That is, the input string contains first, middle, and last names, and they are separated by single blank spaces. Second, there are many possible solutions, but we will solve this problem by using only the methods covered in this chapter. Reviewing the string methods we covered in this chapter and the **Ch2String Processing** class, we know that a sequence of **indexOf** and **substring** methods can divide a string (full name) into two substrings (first and last names). How can we adapt this technique to now divide a string (full name) into three substrings (first, middle, and last names)? Aha! We apply the sequence one more time, as shown in Figure 2.18.

Once we divide the input name into first, middle, and last names, extracting the initials is a fairly straightforward application of the **indexOf** method. We can extract the first letter of a string as

```
str.substring(0, 1)
```

And the monogram can be formulated by concatenating three initials as

```
first.substring(0, 1)
  + middle.substring(0, 1)
      + last.substring(0, 1)
```

2.5 Sample Development—*continued*

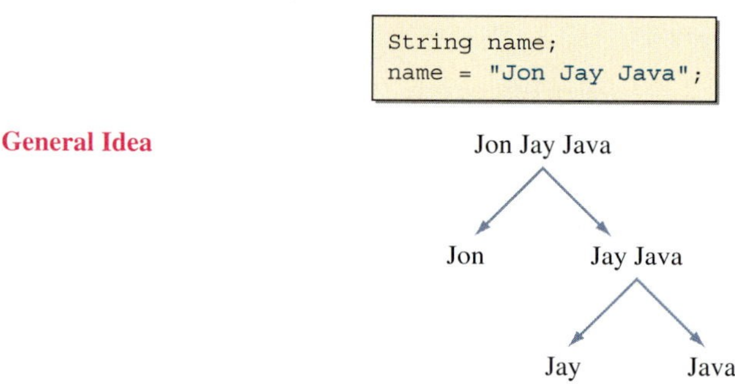

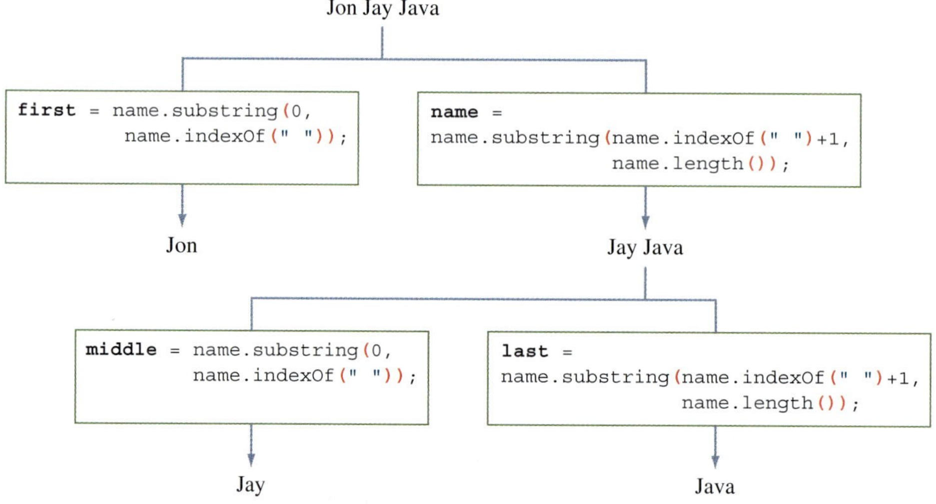

Figure 2.18 Apply the two sequences of **indexOf** and **substring** methods to extract three substrings from a given string.

step 2 code

Here's our step 2 code:

```
/*
    Chapter 2 Sample Program: Displays the Monogram
    File: Step2/Ch2Monogram.java
*/
```

```
import java.util.*;

class Ch2Monogram {

    public static void main(String[] args) {

        String name;

        Scanner scanner = new Scanner(System.in);

        scanner.useDelimiter(System.getProperty("line.separator"));

        System.out.print("Enter your full name (first, middle, last):");

        name = scanner.next( );

        System.out.println("Name entered: " + name);

    }
}
```

step 2 test

To verify the computation is working correctly, we run the program multiple times and enter different names. Remember that we are assuming there is no error in input; that is, first, middle, and last names are separated by single blank spaces. Since there are two subtasks involved in this step, it is important to test them separately. To verify that the input string is divided into three substrings correctly, we place the following temporary test output statements.

```
System.out.println("First:"  + first);
System.out.println("Middle:" + middle);
System.out.println("Last:"   + last);
```

These statements are not shown in the step 2 program listing, but they are included in the actual sample code.

Summary

- The three basic components of a Java program are comments, import statements, and class declarations.
- A Java program must have one class designated as the main class. The designated main class must have the main method.
- An object must be declared and created before we can use it.
- To command an object or a class to perform a task, we send a message to it. We use the expression *calling a method* synonymously with *sending a message*.
- A single name can be used to refer to different objects (of the same class) at different times. An object with no reference will be returned to a system.

- We follow the edit-compile-run cycle to execute programs.
- A source file is compiled into a bytecode file by a Java compiler.
- A Java interpreter (also called a Java Virtual Machine) executes the bytecode.
- The standard classes introduced in this chapter are

```
JFrame          SimpleDateFormat
Scanner         String
Date            System.out
                System.in
```

- Table 2.2 lists the Java naming convention.

Table 2.2 Standard naming convention for Java

Category	Convention	Example

Class	Use an uppercase letter for the first letter of the class names. If the name consists of multiple words, the first letter of every word is capitalized.	`Customer`
		`MainWindow`
		`MyInputHandler`

Instance	Use a lowercase letter for the first letter of the object names. If the name consists of multiple words, the first letter of every word (except the first word) is capitalized.	`customer`
		`inputHandler`
		`myFirstApplication`

Constant	(Note: Sample use of a constant will appear in Chap. 4. We include it here for completeness and easy reference later.) Use all uppercase letters. If the constant consists of multiple words, the underscore characters are used to separate the words.	`DEFAULT_RATE`
		`DEG_TO_RAD`
		`CANCEL`

Package	Use all lowercase letters.	`java`
		`game`
		`finance`

Key Concepts

standard classes
program diagram
identifier
standard naming convention
new operator
garbage collection
comments
packages
dot notation
class declaration
method declaration
edit-compile-run cycle
source file
bytecode file

Exercises

1. Identify all errors in the following program (color highlighting is disabled):

```
/*

   Program Exercise1

   Attempting to display a frame window

//
import swing.JFrame;

class Exercise 1 {
   public void Main() {
      JFrame frame;
      frame.setVisible(TRUE)
   }
}
```

2. Identify all errors in the following program (color highlighting is disabled):

```
//

   Program Exercise2

   Attempting to display a frame of size 300 by 200 pixels

//

import    Javax.Swing.*;

class two {

   public static void main method() {
      myFrame JFrame;
      myFrame = new JFrame();
      myFrame.setSize(300, 200);
      myFrame.setVisible();
   }
}
```

3. Identify all the errors in the following program (color highlighting is disabled):

```
/*

   Program Exercise3

   Attempting to display the number of characters
   in a given input.
*/

class three {
   public static void main( ) {
      String input;
      input = JOptionPane("input:");
```

```
            System.out.print ("Input has " +
                        input.length() + " characters");
        }
    }
```

4. Describe the purpose of comments. Name the types of comments available. Can you include comment markers inside a comment?
5. What is the purpose of the import statement? Does a Java program always have to include an import statement?
6. Show the syntax for importing one class and all classes in a package.
7. Describe the class that must be included in any Java application.
8. What is a reserved word? List all the Java reserved words mentioned in this chapter.
9. Which of the following are invalid Java identifiers?

    a. R2D2
    b. Whatchamacallit
    c. HowAboutThis?
    d. Java
    e. GoodChoice
    f. 12345
    g. 3CPO
    h. This is okay.
    i. thisIsReallyOkay
    j. DEFAULT_AMT
    k. Bad-Choice
    l. A12345

10. Describe the steps you take to run a Java application and the tools you use in each step. What are source files and bytecode files? What different types of errors are detected at each step?
11. Describe the difference between object declaration and object creation. Use a state-of-memory diagram to illustrate the difference.
12. Show a state-of-memory diagram after each of these statements is executed:

```
JFrame      window1;
Resident    res1, res2;

window1     = new JFrame();
res1        = new Resident( );
res2        = new Resident( );
```

13. Show a state-of-memory diagram after each of these statements is executed:

```
Person     person1, person2;

person1     = new Person();
person2     = new Person();
person2     = new Person();
```

14. Which of these identifiers violate the naming convention for class names?

    a. r2D2
    b. whatchamacallit
    c. Java
    d. GoodName
    e. CPO
    f. ThisIsReallyOkay
    g. java
    h. badName

15. Which of these identifiers violate the naming convention for object names?

a. R2D2
b. isthisokay?
c. Java
d. goodName
e. 3CPO
f. ThisIsReallyOkay
g. java
h. anotherbadone

16. For each of these expressions, determine its result. Assume the value of text is a string Java Programming.

```
String text = "Java Programming";
```

a. `text.substring(0, 4)`
b. `text.length( )`
c. `text.substring(8, 12)`
d. `text.substring(0, 1) + text.substring(7, 9)`
e. `text.substring(5,6)`
```
        + text.substring(text.length()-3, text.length())
```

17. Write a Java application that displays today's date in this format: Sunday November 10, 2002.

18. Write a Java application that displays a frame window 300 pixels wide and 200 pixels high with the title My First Frame. Place the frame so that its top left corner is at a position 50 pixels from the top of the screen and 100 pixels from the left of the screen. To position a window at a specified location, you use the setLocation method, as in

```
//assume mainWindow is declared and created
frame.setLocation( 50, 50 );
```

Through experimentation, determine how the two arguments in the setLocation method affect the positioning of the window.

19. Write a Java application that displays the two messages I Can Design and And I Can Program, using two separate dialogs.

20. Write a Java application that displays the two messages I Can Design and And I Can Program, using one dialog but in two separate lines.

21. Write a Java application that displays a very long message. Try a message that is wider than the display of your computer screen, and see what happens.

22. Because today's computers are very fast, you will probably not notice any discernible difference on the screen between the code

```
JFrame myWindow;
myWindow = new JFrame( );
myWindow.setVisible( true );
```

and

```
JFrame myWindow;
myWindow = new JFrame( );
myWindow.setVisible( true );
myWindow.setVisible( false );
myWindow.setVisible( true );
```

One way to see the disappearance and reappearance of the window is to put a delay between the successive setVisible messages. Here's the magic code that puts a delay of 0.5 s:

```
try {Thread.sleep(500);} catch(Exception e) { }
```

The argument we pass to the sleep method specifies the amount of delay in milliseconds [*note:* 1000 milliseconds (ms) = 1 second (s)]. We will not explain this magic code.

23. At the author's website, you will find a Java package called galapagos. The galapagos package includes a Turtle class that is modeled after Seymour Papert's logo. This Turtle has a pen, and when you move the Turtle, its pen will trace the movement. So by moving a Turtle object, you can draw many different kinds of geometric shapes. For example, this program commands a Turtle to draw a square:

```
import galapagos.*;

class Square {
   public static void main( String[] arg ) {
      Turtle turtle;
      turtle = new Turtle( );

      turtle.move( 50 ); //move 50 pixels
      turtle.turn( 90 ); //turn 90 deg counterclockwise

      turtle.move( 50 );
      turtle.turn( 90 );

      turtle.move( 50 );
      turtle.turn( 90 );

      turtle.move( 50 );
   }
}
```

Write a program to draw a triangle. Read the documentation and see if you can find a way to draw the square in a different color and line thickness.

24. Write a program to draw a star, using a Turtle from Exercise 23.

25. Write a program to draw a big letter J, using a Turtle from Exercise 23.

26. Using a Turtle from Exercise 23, write a Java application that displays the text Hello as illustrated here:

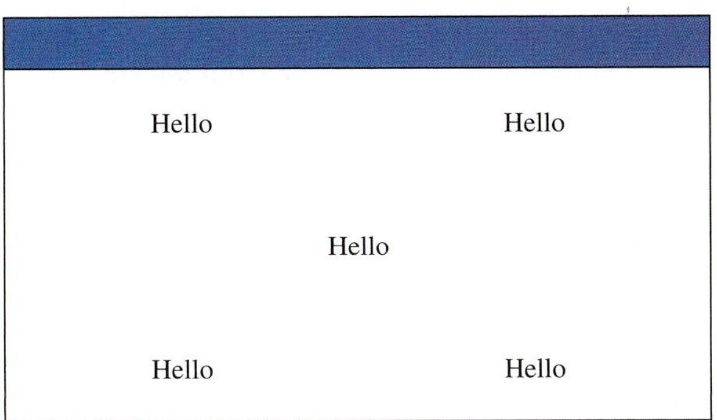

27. Using a Turtle from Exercise 23 and employing the incremental development steps, build a Java application that draws a house.

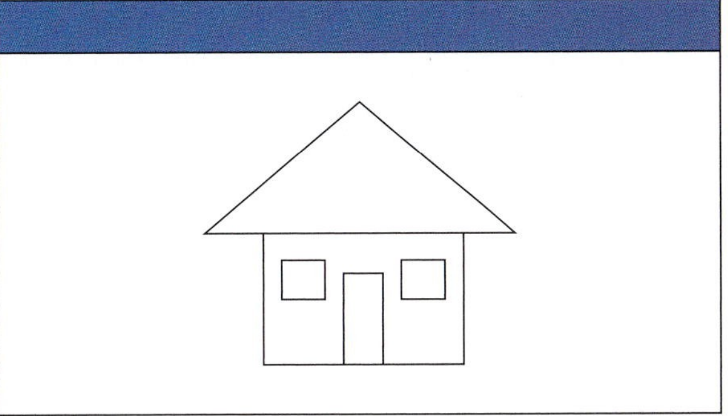

28. Add the moon and a tree to the house you drew in Exercise 27.

29. Follow the incremental development methodology explained in this chapter to implement a program for the following problem statement. You must clearly write down the program tasks, create a design document with class descriptions, and draw the program diagram. Identify the development steps. State any assumptions you must make about the input. Articulate any design alternatives and justify your selection. Be sure to perform adequate testing at the end of each development step.

Problem Statement: Write an application that asks the user for his or her birth date and replies with the day of the week on which he or she was born.

We learned in this chapter that we can create a Date object for today's date by writing

```
import java.util.*;
...
Date today = new Date();
```

To create a Date object for a date other than today, we can use the Date class from the java.sql package. (A more general and flexible way to deal with a date by using the GregorianCalendar class is introduced in Chap. 3.) Notice that there are two distinct classes with the same name Date, but from different packages—one from java.util and another from java.sql. To distinguish the two, we will use the fully qualified names. To create a new java.util.Date object, we can call the class method valueOf of the java.sql.Date class with the string representation of a date. The string representation must be in the format yyyy-MM-dd. For example, to create a java.util.Date object for July 4, 1776, we write

```
java.util.Date bdate = java.sql.Date.valueOf("1776-07-04");
```

Notice that valueOf is a class method of the Date class in the java.sql package. Calling it with a correct argument will return a java.util.Date object for the specified date.

30. Repeat Exercise 29 for this problem statement:

Problem Statement: Write an application that asks the user for her or his full name in the format

first middle last

and replies with the name in the format

last , first middle-initial.

where the last name is followed by comma and the middle initial is followed by period.

For example, if the input is

```
Decafe Chai Latte
```

then the output is

```
Latte, Decafe C.
```

3 Numerical Data

Objectives

After you have read and studied this chapter, you should be able to

- Select proper types for numerical data.
- Write arithmetic expressions in Java.
- Evaluate arithmetic expressions, following the precedence rules.
- Describe how the memory allocation works for objects and primitive data values.
- Write mathematical expressions, using methods in the **Math** class.
- Use the **GregorianCalendar** class in manipulating date information such as year, month, and day.
- Use the **DecimalFormat** class to format numerical data.
- Convert input string values to numerical data.
- Input numerical data by using **System.in** and output numerical data by using **System.out**.
- Apply the incremental development technique in writing programs.
- (*Optional*) Describe how the integers and real numbers are represented in memory.

Introduction

When we review the Ch2Monogram sample program, we can visualize three tasks: input, computation, and output. We view computer programs as getting input, performing computation on the input data, and outputting the results of the computations. The type of computation we performed in Chapter 2 is string processing. In this chapter, we will study another type of computation, the one that deals with numerical data. Consider, for example, a metric converter program that accepts measurements in U.S. units (input), converts the measurements (computation), and displays their metric equivalents (output). The three tasks are not limited to numerical or string values, though. An input could be a mouse movement. A drawing program may accept mouse dragging (input), remember the points of mouse positions (computation), and draw lines connecting the points (output). Selecting a menu item is yet another form of input. For beginners, however, it is easiest to start writing programs that accept numerical or string values as input and display the result of computation as output.

We will introduce more standard classes to reinforce the object-oriented style of programming. The Math class includes methods we can use to express mathematical formulas. The DecimalFormat class includes a method to format numerical data so we can display the data in a desired precision. The GregorianCalendar class includes methods to manipulate the date. In Chapter 2, we performed String input and output by using the standard input (Scanner) and output (System.out). We will describe the input and output routines for numerical data in this chapter.

Finally, we will continue to employ the incremental development technique introduced in Chapter 2 in developing the sample application, a loan calculator program. As the sample program gets more complex, well-planned development steps will smooth the development effort.

3.1 Variables

Suppose we want to compute the sum and difference of two numbers. Let's call the two numbers x and y. In mathematics, we say

```
x + y
```

and

```
x - y
```

To compute the sum and the difference of x and y in a program, we must first declare what kind of data will be assigned to them. After we assign values to them, we can compute their sum and difference.

Let's say x and y are integers. To declare that the type of data assigned to them is an integer, we write

```
int    x, y;
```

variable

When this declaration is made, memory locations to store data values for x and y are allocated. These memory locations are called ***variables***, and x and y are the names we associate with the memory locations. Any valid identifier can be used as a variable name. After the declaration is made, we can assign only integers to x and y. We cannot, for example, assign real numbers to them.

Things to Remember

A variable has three properties: a memory location to store the value, the type of data stored in the memory location, and the name used to refer to the memory location.

Although we must say "x and y are variable names" to be precise, we will use the abbreviated form "x and y are variables" or "x and y are integer variables" whenever appropriate.

The general syntax for declaring variables is

variable declaration syntax

```
<data type>    <variables> ;
```

where <variables> is a sequence of identifiers separated by commas. Every variable we use in a program must be declared. We may have as many declarations as we wish. For example, we can declare x and y separately as

```
int    x;
int    y;
```

However, we cannot declare the same variable more than once; therefore, the second declaration below is invalid because y is declared twice:

```
int    x, y, z;
int    y;
```

six numerical data types

There are ***six numerical data types*** in Java: byte, short, int, long, float, and double. The data types byte, short, int, and long are for integers; and the data types float and double are for real numbers. The data type names byte, short, and others are all reserved words. The difference among these six numerical data types is in the range of values they can represent, as shown in Table 3.1.

higher precision

A data type with a larger range of values is said to have a ***higher precision***. For example, the data type double has a higher precision than the data type float. The tradeoff for higher precision is memory space—to store a number with higher precision, you need more space. A variable of type short requires 2 bytes and a variable of type int requires 4 bytes, for example. If your program does not use many integers, then whether you declare them as short or int is really not that critical. The

Table 3.1 Java numerical data types and their precisions

Data Type	Content	Default Value[†]	Minimum Value	Maximum Value
byte	Integer	0	−128	127
short	Integer	0	−32768	32767
int	Integer	0	−2147483648	2147483647
long	Integer	0	−9223372036854775808	9223372036854775807
float	Real	0.0	−3.40282347E+38[‡]	3.40282347E+38
double	Real	0.0	−1.79769313486231570E+308	1.79769313486231570E+308

[†] No default value is assigned to a local variable. A local variable is explained on page 184 in Section 4.8.
[‡]The character E indicates a number is expressed in scientific notation. This notation is explained on page 96.

difference in memory usage is very small and not a deciding factor in the program design. The storage difference becomes significant only when your program uses thousands of integers. Therefore, we will almost always use the data type int for integers. We use long when we need to process very large integers that are outside the range of values int can represent. For real numbers, it is more common to use double. Although it requires more memory space than float, we prefer double because of its higher precision in representing real numbers. We will describe how the numbers are stored in memory in Section 3.10.

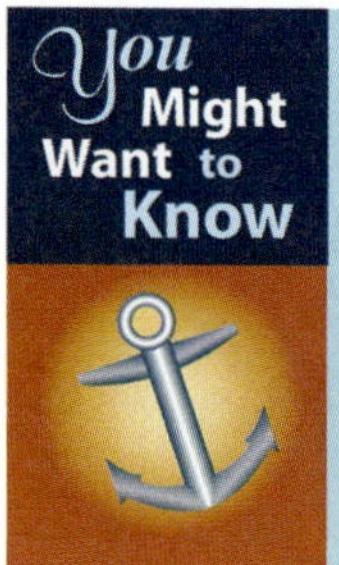

You Might Want to Know

Application programs we develop in this book are intended for computers with a large amount of memory (such as desktops or laptops), so the storage space is not normally a major concern because we have more than enough. However, when we develop applications for embedded or specialized devices with a very limited amount of memory, such as PDAs, cellular phones, mobile robots for Mars exploration, and others, reducing the memory usage becomes a major concern.

Here is an example of declaring variables of different data types:

```
int      i, j, k;
float    numberOne, numberTwo;
long     bigInteger;
double   bigNumber;
```

At the time a variable is declared, it also can be initialized. For example, we may initialize the integer variables count and height to 10 and 34 as in

```
int count = 10, height = 34;
```

As we mentioned in Chapter 2, you can declare and create an object just as you can initialize variables at the time you declare them. For example, the declaration

```
Date today = new Date();
```

is equivalent to

```
Date today;
today = new Date();
```

assignment statement

We assign a value to a variable by using an ***assignment statement***. To assign the value 234 to the variable named firstNumber, for example, we write

```
firstNumber = 234;
```

Be careful not to confuse mathematical equality and assignment. For example, the following are not valid Java code:

```
4 + 5 = x;
x + y = y + x;
```

assignment statement syntax

The syntax for the assignment statement is

```
<variable> = <expression> ;
```

where <expression> is an arithmetic expression, and the value of <expression> is assigned to the <variable>. The following are sample assignment statements:

```
sum        = firstNumber + secondNumber;
solution   = x * x - 2 * x + 1;
average    = (x + y + z) / 3.0;
```

We will present a detailed discussion of arithmetic expressions in Section 3.2. One key point we need to remember about variables is the following:

Things to Remember

Before using a variable, first we must declare and assign a value to it.

The diagram in Figure 3.1 illustrates the effect of variable declaration and assignment. Notice the similarity with this and memory allocation for object declaration and creation, illustrated in Figure 2.4 on page 36. Figure 3.2 compares the two.

State of Memory

(A)
```
int firstNumber, secondNumber;

firstNumber  = 234;
secondNumber = 87;
```

after (A) is executed

firstNumber [ ]

secondNumber [ ]

The variables **firstNumber** and **secondNumber** are declared and set in memory.

```
int firstNumber, secondNumber;
```

(B)
```
firstNumber  = 234;
secondNumber = 87;
```

after (B) is executed

firstNumber [234]

secondNumber [87]

Values are assigned to the variables **firstNumber** and **secondNumber**.

Figure 3.1 A diagram showing how two memory locations (variables) with names **firstNumber** and **secondNumber** are declared, and values are assigned to them.

What we have been calling object names are really variables. The only difference between a variable for numbers and a variable for objects is the contents in the memory locations. For numbers, a variable contains the numerical value itself; and for objects, a variable contains an address where the object is stored. We use an arrow in the diagram to indicate that the content is an address, not the value itself.

Things to Remember

Object names are synonymous with variables whose contents are references to objects (i.e., memory addresses).

Figure 3.3 contrasts the effect of assigning the content of one variable to another variable for numerical data values and for objects. Because the content of a variable for objects is an address, assigning the content of a variable to another makes two variables that refer to the same object. Assignment does not create a new object. Without executing the new command, no new object is created. We can view the situation in which two variables refer to the same object as the object having two distinct names.

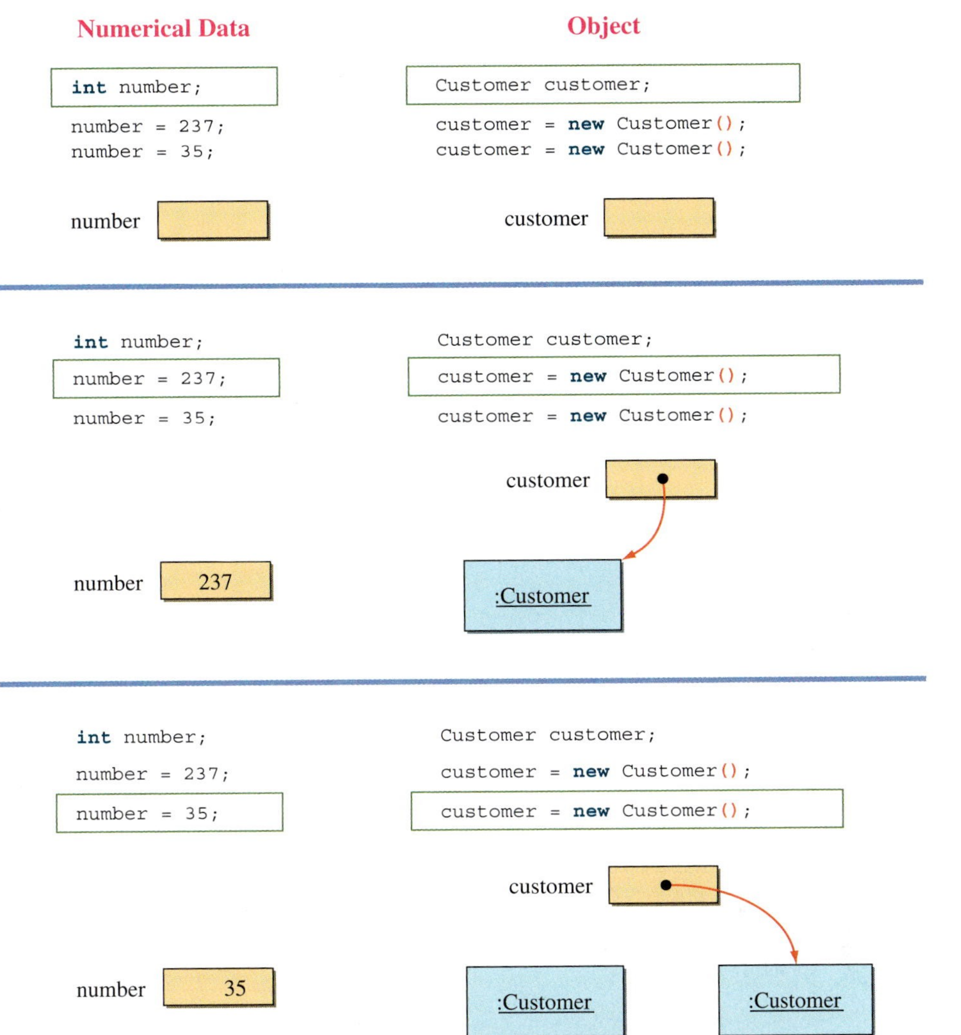

Figure 3.2 A difference between object declaration and numerical data declaration.

For numbers, the amount of memory space required is fixed. The values for data type int require 4 bytes, for example, and this won't change. However, with objects, the amount of memory space required is not constant. One instance of the Account class may require 120 bytes, while another instance of the same class may require 140 bytes. The difference in space usage for the account objects would occur if we had to keep track of checks written against the accounts. If one account has 15 checks written and the second account has 25 checks written, then we need more memory space for the second account than for the first account.

We use the new command to actually create an object. Remember that declaring an object only allocates the variable whose content will be an address. On the

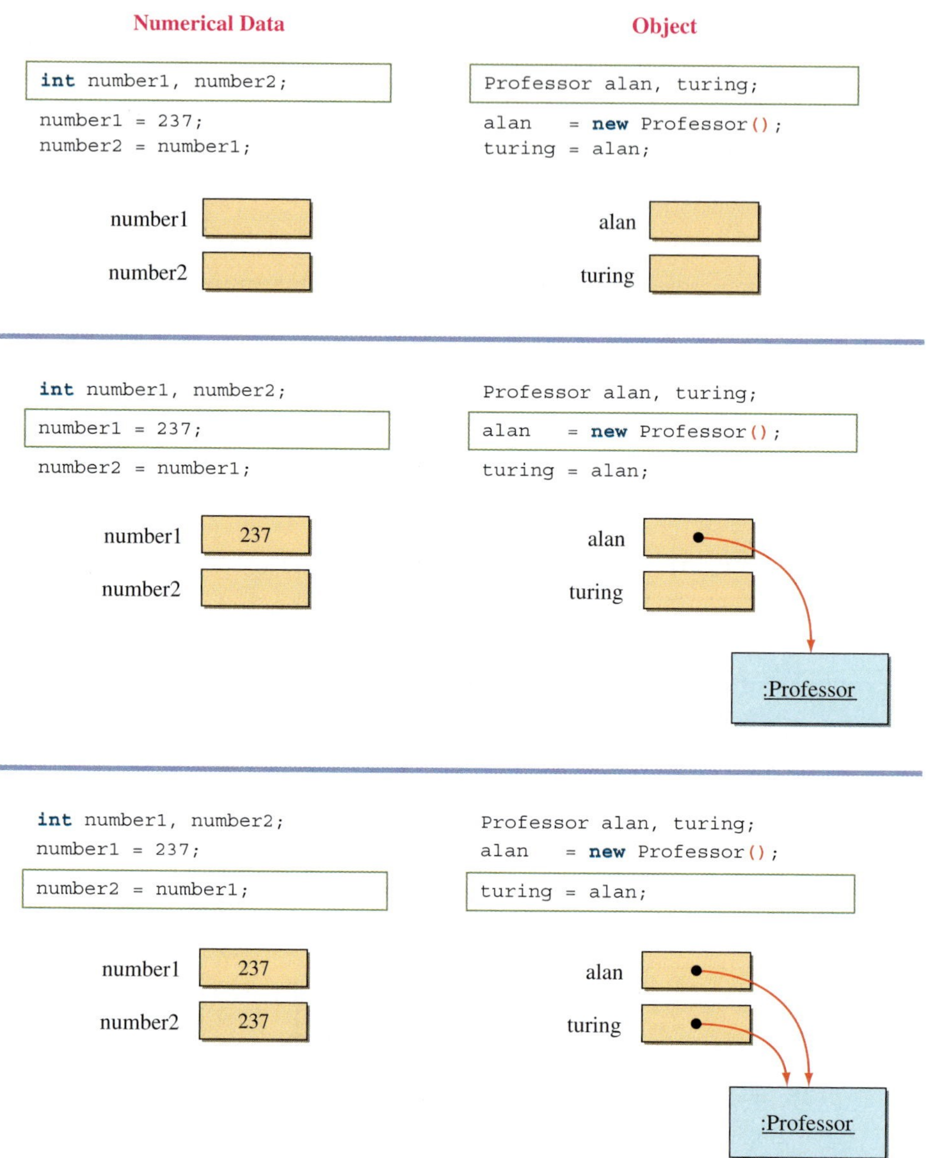

Figure 3.3 An effect of assigning the content of one variable to another.

reference versus primitive data types

other hand, we don't "create" an integer because the space to store the value is already allocated at the time the integer variable is declared. Because the contents are addresses that refer to memory locations where the objects are actually stored, objects are called ***reference data types***. In contrast, numerical data types are called ***primitive data types***.

In addition to the six numerical data types, there are two nonnumerical primitive data types. The data type **boolean** is used to represent two logical values **true** and **false.** For example, the statements

```
boolean raining;
raining = true;
```

assign the value **true** to a boolean variable raining. We will explain and start using boolean variables beginning in Chapter 5. The second nonnumerical primitive data type is **char** (for character). It is used to represent a single character (letter, digit, punctuation marks, and others). The following example assigns the uppercase letter **A** to a **char** variable **letter:**

```
char letter;
letter = 'A';
```

A **char** constant is designated by single quotes. We will study the **char** data type in Chapter 9 on string processing.

1. Why are the following declarations all invalid (color highlighting is disabled)?

```
int       a, b, a;
float     x, int;
float     w, int x;
bigNumber double;
```

2. Assuming the following declarations are executed in sequence, why are the second and third declarations invalid?

```
int       a, b;
int       a;
float     b;
```

3. Name six data types for numerical values.

4. Which of the following are valid assignment statements (assuming the variables are properly declared)?

```
x      =  12;
12     =  x;
y + y  =  x;
y      =  x + 12;
```

5. Draw the state-of-memory diagram for the following code.

```
Account latteAcct, espressoAcct;

latteAcct    = new Account();
espressoAcct = new Account();
latteAcct    = espressoAcct;
```

3.2 Arithmetic Expressions

An expression involving numerical values such as

```
23 + 45
```

arithmetic operator

is called an *arithmetic expression,* because it consists of arithmetic operators and operands. An ***arithmetic operator***, such as + in the example, designates numerical computation. Table 3.2 summarizes the arithmetic operators available in Java.

integer division

Notice how the division operator works in Java. When both numbers are integers, the result is an integer quotient. That is, any fractional part is truncated. Division between two integers is called ***integer division***. When either or both numbers are float or double, the result is a real number. Here are some division examples:

Division Operation	Result
`23 / 5`	`4`
`23 / 5.0`	`4.6`
`25.0 / 5.0`	`5.0`

The modulo operator returns the remainder of a division. Although real numbers can be used with the modulo operator, the most common use of the modulo operator involves only integers. Here are some examples:

Modulo Operation	Result
`23 % 5`	`3`
`23 % 25`	`23`
`16 % 2`	`0`

Table 3.2 Arithmetic operators

Operation	Java Operator	Example	Value (x = 10, y = 7, z = 2.5)
Addition	+	`x + y`	`17`
Subtraction	−	`x - y`	`3`
Multiplication	*	`x * y`	`70`
Division	/	`x / y`	`1`
		`x / z`	`4.0`
Modulo division (remainder)	%	`x % y`	`3`

The expression 23 % 5 results in 3 because 23 divided by 5 is 4 with remainder 3. Notice that x % y = 0 when y divides x perfectly; for example, 16 % 2 = 0. Also notice that x % y = x when y is larger than x; for example, 23 % 25 = 23.

operand

An ***operand*** in arithmetic expressions can be a constant, a variable, a method call, or another arithmetic expression, possibly surrounded by parentheses. Let's look at examples. In the expression

```
x + 4
```

binary operator

we have one addition operator and two operands—a variable x and a constant 4. The addition operator is called a ***binary operator*** because it operates on two operands. All other arithmetic operators except the minus are also binary. The minus and plus operators can be both binary and unary. A unary operator operates on one operand as in

```
-x
```

In the expression

```
x + 3 * y
```

subexpression

the addition operator acts on operands x and 3 * y. The right operand for the addition operator is itself an expression. Often a nested expression is called a ***subexpression***. The subexpression 3 * y has operands 3 and y. The following diagram illustrates this relationship:

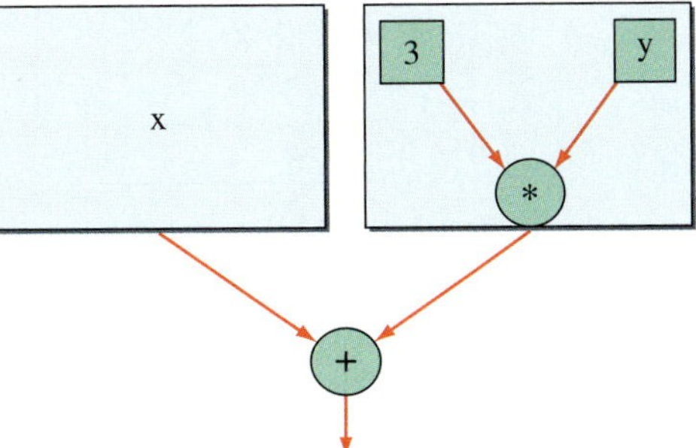

precedence rules

When two or more operators are present in an expression, we determine the order of evaluation by following the ***precedence rules***. For example, multiplication has a higher precedence than addition. Therefore, in the expression x + 3 * y, the multiplication operation is evaluated first, and the addition operation is evaluated next. Table 3.3 summarizes the precedence rules for arithmetic operators.

Table 3.3 Precedence rules for arithmetic operators and parentheses

Order	Group	Operator	Rule
High	Subexpression	( )	Subexpressions are evaluated first. If parentheses are nested, the innermost subexpression is evaluated first. If two or more pairs of parentheses are on the same level, then they are evaluated from left to right.
	Unary operator	-, +	Unary minuses and pluses are evaluated second.
	Multiplicative operator	*, /, %	Multiplicative operators are evaluated third. If two or more multiplicative operators are in an expression, then they are evaluated from left to right.
Low	Additive operator	+, -	Additive operators are evaluated last. If two or more additive operators are in an expression, then they are evaluated from left to right.

The following example illustrates the precedence rules applied to a complex arithmetic expression:

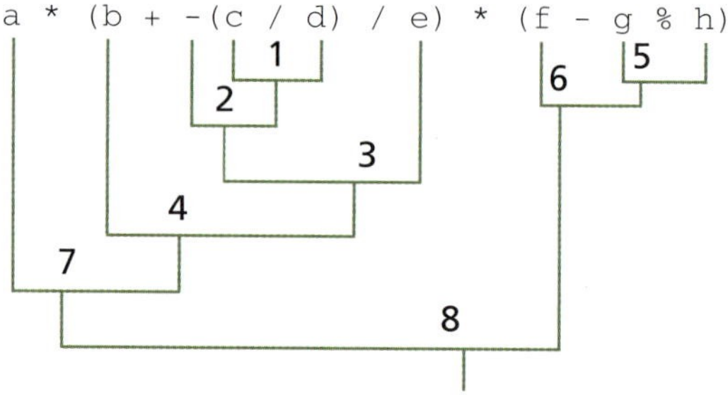

When an arithmetic expression consists of variables and constants of the same data type, then the result of the expression will be that data type also. For example, if the data type of a and b is int, then the result of the expression

```
a * b + 23
```

implicit and explicit type-casting

is also an int. When the data types of variables and constants in an arithmetic expression are different data types, then a casting conversion will take place. A *casting conversion,* or ***typecasting***, is a process that converts a value of one data type to another data type. Two types of casting conversions in Java are ***implicit*** and ***explicit***.

Table 3.4 Rules for arithmetic promotion

Operator Type	Promotion Rule
Unary	**1.** If the operand is of type `byte` or `short`, then it is converted to `int`. **2.** Otherwise, the operand remains the same type.
Binary	**1.** If either operand is of type `double`, then the other operand is converted to `double`. **2.** Otherwise, if either operand is of type `float`, then the other operand is converted to `float`. **3.** Otherwise, if either operand is of type `long`, then the other operand is converted to `long`. **4.** Otherwise, both operands are converted to `int`.

numeric promotion

An implicit conversion called ***numeric promotion*** is applied to the operands of an arithmetic operator. The promotion is based on the rules stated in Table 3.4. This conversion is called *promotion* because the operand is converted from a lower to a higher precision.

typecast operator

Instead of relying on implicit conversion, we can use explicit conversion to convert an operand from one data type to another. Explicit conversion is applied to an operand by using a ***typecast operator***. For example, to convert the int variable x in the expression

```
x / 3
```

to float so the result will not be truncated, we apply the typecast operator (float) as

```
(float) x / 3
```

The syntax is

typecasting syntax

```
( <data type> ) <expression>
```

The typecast operator is a unary operator and has a precedence higher than that of any binary operator. You must use parentheses to typecast a subexpression; for example, the expression

```
a + (double) (x + y * z)
```

will result in the subexpression x + y * z typecast to double.

Assuming the variable x is an int, then the assignment statement

```
x = 2 * (14343 / 2344);
```

will assign the integer result of the expression to the variable x. However, if the data type of x is other than int, then an implicit conversion will occur so that the

assignment conversion

data type of the expression becomes the same as the data type of the variable. An ***assignment conversion*** is another implicit conversion that occurs when the variable and the value of an expression in an assignment statement are not of the same data type. An assignment conversion occurs only if the data type of the variable has a higher precision than the data type of the expression's value. For example,

```
double number;
number = 25;
```

is valid, but

```
int number;
number = 234.56;   <—— INVALID
```

is not.

In writing programs, we often have to increment or decrement the value of a variable by a certain amount. For example, to increase the value of sum by 5, we write

```
sum = sum + 5;
```

shorthand assignment operator

We can rewrite this statement witout repeating the same variable on the left- and right-hand sides of the assignment symbol by using the ***shorthand assignment operator***:

```
sum += number;
```

Table 3.5 lists five shorthand assignment operators available in Java.

These shorthand assignment operators have precedence lower than that of any other arithmetic operators; so, for example, the statement

```
sum *= a + b;
```

is equivalent to

```
sum = sum * (a + b);
```

Table 3.5 Shorthand assignment operators

Operator	Usage	Meaning
+=	a += b;	a = a + b;
-=	a -= b;	a = a - b;
*=	a *= b;	a = a * b;
/=	a /= b;	a = a / b;
%=	a %= b;	a = a % b;

If we wish to assign a value to multiple variables, we can cascade the assignment operations as

```
x = y = 1;
```

which is equivalent to saying

```
y = 1;
x = 1;
```

The assignment symbol = is actually an operator, and its precedence order is lower than that of any other operators. Assignment operators are evaluated right to left.

1. Evaluate the following expressions.

   a. `3 + 5 / 7`
   b. `3 * 3 + 3 % 2`
   c. `3 + 2 / 5 + -2 * 4`
   d. `2 * (1 + -(3/4) / 2) * (2 - 6 % 3)`

2. What is the data type of the result of the following expressions?

   a. `(3 + 5) / 7`
   b. `(3 + 5) / (float) 7`
   c. `(float) ( (3 + 5) / 7 )`

3. Which of the following expressions is equivalent to $-b(c + 34)/(2a)$?

   a. `-b * (c + 34) /  2 * a`
   b. `-b * (c + 34) / (2 * a)`
   c. `-b *  c + 34  / (2 * a)`

4. Rewrite the following statements without using the shorthand operators.

   a. `x += y;`
   b. `x *= v + w;`
   c. `x /= y;`

3.3 Constants

While a program is running, different values may be assigned to a variable at different times (thus the name *variable,* since the values it contains can *vary*), but in some cases we do not want this to happen. In other words, we want to "lock" the assigned value so that no changes can take place. If we want a value to remain fixed, then we use a ***constant***. A constant is declared in a manner similar to a variable but

constant

with the additional reserved word final. A constant must be assigned a value at the time of its declaration. Here's an example of declaring four constants:

```
final double  PI = 3.14159;
final short   FARADAY_CONSTANT = 23060; // unit is cal/volt
final double  CM_PER_INCH = 2.54;
final int     MONTHS_IN_YEAR = 12;
```

We follow the standard Java convention to name a constant, using only capital letters and underscores. Judicious use of constants makes programs more readable. You will be seeing many uses of constants later in the book, beginning with the sample program in this chapter.

named constant

literal constant

The constant PI is called a ***named constant*** or *symbolic constant*. We refer to symbolic constants with identifiers such as PI and FARADAY_CONSTANT. The second type of constant is called a ***literal constant***, and we refer to it by using an actual value. For example, the following statements contain three literal constants:

```
final double  PI   = 3.14159 ;
double area;
area = 2 * PI * 345.79 ;
```

Literal constants

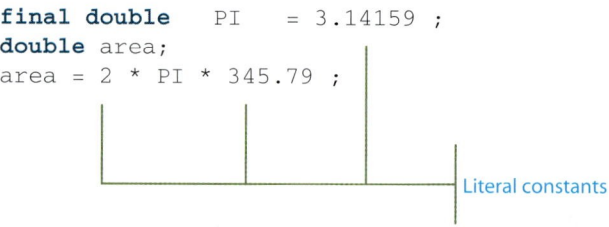

When we use the literal constant 2, the data type of the constant is set to int by default. Then how can we specify a literal constant of type long?[1] We append the constant with an l (a lowercase letter L) or L as in

```
2L * PI * 345.79
```

How about the literal constant 345.79? Since the literal constant contains a decimal point, its data type can be only float or double. But which one? The answer is double. If a literal constant contains a decimal point, then it is of type double by default. To designate a literal constant of type float, we must append the letter f or F. For example,

```
2 * PI * 345.79F
```

To represent a double literal constant, we may optionally append a d or D. So the following two constants are equivalent:

`2 * PI * 345.79` is equivalent to `2 * PI * 345.79D`

We also can express float and double literal constants in scientific notation as

$$\text{Number} \times 10^{\text{exponent}}$$

[1] In most cases, it is not significant to distinguish the two because of automatic type conversion; see Section 3.2.

exponential notation in Java

which in Java is expressed as

```
<number> E <exponent>
```

Hints, Tips, & Pitfalls

Since a numerical constant such as 345.79 represents a **double** value, these statements

```
float number;
number = 345.79;
```

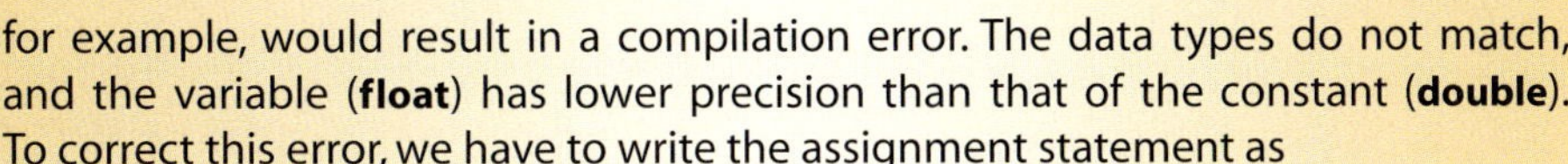

for example, would result in a compilation error. The data types do not match, and the variable (**float**) has lower precision than that of the constant (**double**). To correct this error, we have to write the assignment statement as

```
number = 345.79f;
```

or

```
number = (float) 345.79;
```

This is one of the common errors that people make in writing Java programs, especially those with prior programming experience.

where <number> is a literal constant that may or may not contain a decimal point and <exponent> is a signed or an unsigned integer. Lowercase e may be substituted for the exponent symbol E. The whole expression may be suffixed by f, F, d, or D. The <number> itself cannot be suffixed with symbols f, F, d, or D. Here are some examples:

```
12.40e+209
23E33
29.0098e-102
234e+5D
4.45e2
```

Here are some additional examples of constant declarations:

```
final double SPEED_OF_LIGHT = 3.0E+10D; // unit is cm/s
final short  MAX_WGT_ALLOWED = 400;
```

3.4 Displaying Numerical Values

In Chapter 2, we learned how to output string values to the console window by using System.out. We can easily output numerical values to the console window as well. We will use the same print and println methods to output numerical values. Here's a simple example that outputs the values of a constant and a variable:

```
int num = 15;

System.out.print(num); //print a variable
System.out.print(" "); //print a blank space
System.out.print(10);  //print a constant
```

Executing the code will result in the following console window:

Console Window

```
15 10
```

We can use the println method to skip a line after printing out the value. Executing

```
int num = 15;
System.out.println(num);
System.out.println(10);
```

will result in

Console Window

```
15
10
```

By using the concatenation operation, it is possible to output multiple values with a single print or println method. For example, the statement

```
System.out.print(30 + " " + 40);
```

is equivalent to

```
System.out.print(30);
System.out.print(" ");
System.out.print(40);
```

Notice that the expression

```
30 + " " + 40
```

mixes numerical values and a string. We learned in Chapter 2 that the plus symbol is used to concatenate strings, for example,

```
"Benjamin" + " " + "Franklin"
```

And, in this chapter, we learned the same plus symbol is used to add numerical values, for example,

```
4 + 36
```

The plus symbol, therefore, could mean two different things: string concatenation or numerical addition. When a symbol is used to represent more than one operation, this is called ***operator overloading***.

operator overloading

What happens when the plus symbol appears in a mixed expression? When the Java compiler encounters an overloaded operator, the compiler determines the meaning of a symbol by its context. If the left operand and the right operand of the plus symbol are both numerical values, then the compiler will treat the symbol as addition; otherwise, it will treat the symbol as concatenation. The plus symbol operator is evaluated from left to right, and the result of concatenation is a string, so the code

```
int x = 1;
int y = 2;
String output = "test" + x + y;
```

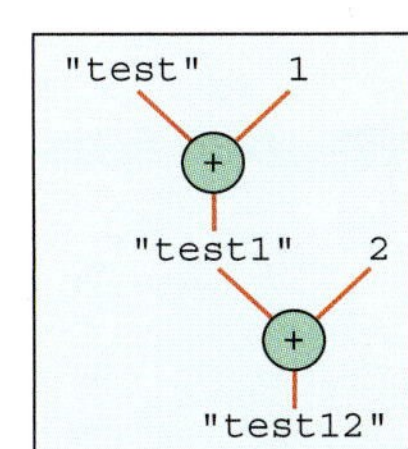

will result in output being set to

```
test12
```

while the statement

```
String output = x + y + "test";
```

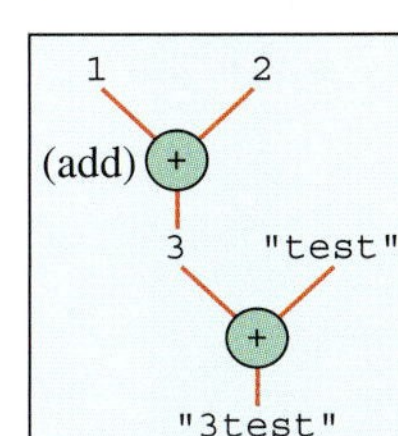

will result in output being set to

```
3test
```

To get the result of test3, we have to write the statement as

```
String output = "test" + (x + y);
```

so the arithmetic addition is performed first.

Now let's look at a small sample program that illustrates a typical use of string concatenation in displaying computation results. In this sample program, we compute the circumference and the area of a circle with a given radius. The value for the radius is assigned in the program (we will discuss how to input this value in Section 3.5). Here's the program:

```
/*
    Chapter 3 Sample Program: Compute Area and Circumference

    File: Ch3Circle.java

*/
```

```
class Ch3Circle {
    public static void main(String[] args) {

        final double PI = 3.14159;

        double radius, area, circumference;

        radius = 2.35;

        //compute the area and circumference
        area          = PI * radius * radius;
        circumference = 2.0 * PI * radius;

        System.out.println("Given Radius: " + radius);
        System.out.println("Area: " + area);
        System.out.println("Circumference: " + circumference);
    }
}
```

When we run this program, we get the following output:

Console Window

```
Given Radius: 2.35
Area: 17.349430775000002
Circumference: 14.765473
```

Notice the precision of decimal places displayed for the results, especially the one for the circumference. Although we desire such a high level of precision provided by double values during the computation, we may not when displaying the result. We can restrict the number of decimal places to display by using the DecimalFormat class from the java.text package.

Although the full use of the DecimalFormat class can be fairly complicated, it is very straightforward if all we want is to limit the number of decimal places to be displayed. To limit the decimal places to three, for example, we create a DecimalFormat object as

```
DecimalFormat df = new DecimalFormat("0.000");
```

and use it to format the number as

```
double num = 234.5698709;
System.out.println("Num: " + df.format(num));
```

When we add an instance of the DecimalFormat class named df and change the output statement of the Ch3Circle class to

```
System.out.println("Given Radius: " + df.format(radius));
System.out.println("Area: " + df.format(area));
System.out.println("Circumference: "
                          + df.format(circumference));
```

we produce the following result:

Console Window

```
Given Radius:  2.350
Area: 17.349
Circumference: 14.765
```

The modified class is named Ch3Circle2 (not shown here).

new-line control character

Instead of using one println method per line of output, it is possible to output multiple lines with a single println or print method by embedding a new-line control character in the output. We briefly mentioned a control character in Section 2.4.4. A control character is for controlling the output, and we use the backslash symbol to denote a control character. The new-line control character is denoted as \n and has the effect of pressing the Enter key in the output. For example, the statements

```
System.out.println("Given Radius:  " + radius);
System.out.println("Area: " + area);
System.out.println("Circumference: " + circumference);
```

can be written by using only one println statement as

```
System.out.println("Given Radius: "  + radius + "\n" +
                   "Area: " + area   + "\n" +
                   "Circumference: " + circumference);
```

There is no limit to the number of new-line control characters you can embed, so we can easily skip two lines, for example, by putting two new-line control characters as follows:

```
System.out.println("Number 1: " + num1 + "\n\n" +
                   "Number 2: " + num2);
```

tab control character

Another useful control character is a ***tab***, which is denoted as \t. We can use the tab ***control character*** to output the labels, and this results in two columns as follows:

```
System.out.println("Given Radius:  " + "\t" + radius + "\n" +
                   "Area: " + "\t\t" + area + "\n" +
                   "Circumference: " + "\t" + circumference);
```

Notice there are two tabs before we output the area. You need to experiment with the actual number of tabs to get the right output (the actual number of spaces used for each tab could be different depending on your Java IDE). The resulting output will be

Console Window

```
Given Radius:  2.35
Area:          17.349430775000002
Circumference: 14.765473
```

You can also adjust the output format by appending blank spaces in the label. For example, you can rewrite the sample statement as

```
System.out.println("Given Radius:   " + "\t" + radius + "\n" +
                   "Area:           " + "\t" + area + "\n" +
                   "Circumference: " + "\t" + circumference);
```

And, as always, the use of symbolic constants will clean up the code:

```
...
final String TAB = "\t";
final String NEWLINE = "\n";
...
System.out.println(
          "Given Radius:  " + TAB + radius + NEWLINE +
          "Area:          " + TAB + area   + NEWLINE +
          "Circumference: " + TAB + circumference);
```

The new program that illustrates the use of both DecimalFormat and control characters is named Ch3Circle3. Here's the program:

```
/*

    Chapter 3 Sample Program: Compute Area and Circumference

    File: Ch3Circle3.java

*/

import java.text.*;

class Ch3Circle3 {

    public static void main(String[] args) {

        final double PI = 3.14159;
        final String TAB = "\t";
        final String NEWLINE = "\n";

        double radius, area, circumference;

        DecimalFormat df = new DecimalFormat("0.000");

        radius = 2.35;

        //compute the area and circumference
        area          = PI * radius * radius;
        circumference = 2.0 * PI * radius;
        //Display the results
        System.out.println(
           "Given Radius:  " + TAB + df.format(radius) + NEWLINE +
```

```
            "Area:          " + TAB + df.format(area)    + NEWLINE +
           "Circumference: " + TAB + df.format(circumference));
    }
}
```

1. What is the purpose of the control characters?
2. Which control character is used for a new line?
3. Using one print statement, output the following:

```
Hello, world!
    My favorite Ben Franklin quote:

        An investment in knowledge
        always pays the best interest.
```

3.5 Getting Numerical Input

We learned how to input string values by using the Scanner class in Chapter 2. We study how to input numerical values with the Scanner class in this section. To input strings, we use the next method of the Scanner class. For the numerical input values, we use an equivalent method that corresponds to the data type of the value we try to input. For instance, to input an int value, we use the nextInt method. Here's an example of inputting a person's age:

```
Scanner scanner = new Scanner(System.in);

int age;

System.out.print("Enter your age: ");

age = scanner.nextInt( );
```

In addition to the int data type, we have five input methods that correspond to the other numerical data types. The six input methods for the primitive numerical data types are listed in Table 3.6.

Table 3.6 Methods to input six numerical data types

Method	Example
nextByte( )	byte b = scanner.nextByte( );
nextDouble( )	double d = scanner.nextDouble( );
nextFloat( )	float f = scanner.nextFloat( );
nextInt( )	int i = scanner.nextInt( );
nextLong( )	long l = scanner.nextLong( );
nextShort( )	short s = scanner.nextShort( );

The following example inputs a person's height in inches (int) and GPA (float):

```
Scanner scanner = new Scanner(System.in);

int height;
float gpa;

System.out.print("Enter your height in inches: ");

height = scanner.nextInt( );

System.out.print("Enter your gpa: ");

gpa = scanner.nextFloat( );
```

Remember that the default delimiter between the input values is a white space (such as the blank space or a tab); it is possible to input more than one value on a single line. The following code inputs two integers:

```
Scanner scanner = new Scanner(System.in);

int num1, num2;

System.out.print("Enter two integers: ");

num1 = scanner.nextInt( );
num2 = scanner.nextInt( );

System.out.print("num1 = " + num1 + " num2 = " + num2);
```

And here's a sample interaction:

Space separates the two input values.

```
Enter two integers: 12 8 ENTER
num1 = 12 and num2 = 87
```

Since the new-line character (when we press the Enter key, this new-line character is entered into the system) is also treated as white space, we can enter the two integers by pressing the Enter key after each number. Here's a sample:

```
Enter two integers:  12 ENTER
87 ENTER
num1 = 12 and num2 = 87
```

input buffer

When we enter data using System.in, they are placed in ***input buffer.*** And the next available data in the input buffer are processed when one of the input methods is called. This means that the actual processing of input data does not necessarily correspond to the display timing of the prompts. Let's look at an example. Consider the following code:

```
Scanner scanner = new Scanner(System.in);

int num1, num2, num3;
```

```
System.out.print("Enter Number 1: ");
num1 = scanner.nextInt( );

System.out.print("Enter Number 2: ");
num2 = scanner.nextInt( );

System.out.print("Enter Number 3: ");
num3 = scanner.nextInt( );

System.out.print("Values entered are " +
                  num1 + " " + num2 + " " + num3);
```

We expect the majority of users will input three integers, one at a time, as requested by the prompts:

```
Enter Number 1: 10 ENTER
Enter Number 2: 20 ENTER
Enter Number 3: 30 ENTER
Values entered are 10 20 30
```

However, users do not really have to enter the values one at a time. It is possible to enter all three values on a single line without waiting for prompts, for example. This will result in an awkward display in the console window. Here's an example:

```
Enter Number 1: 10, 20, 30 ENTER
Enter Number 2: Enter Number 3: Values entered are 10 20 30
```

Although the display is awkward, the input values are assigned to the respective variables correctly. This is so because the three input values are placed in the input buffer, and when the second and third nextInt methods are called, the corresponding values are in the input buffer, so there's no problem inputting them.

In Section 3.2, we explained the assignment conversion that allows us to assign a value to a higher-precision variable (e.g., assigning an int value to a double variable). This type of implicit conversion also occurs with the Scanner class. For example, the nextDouble method works without a problem as long as the user enters a value that is assignable to a double variable. Here's an example:

```
Scanner scanner = new Scanner(System.in);

double num;

System.out.print("Enter a double: ");
num = scanner.nextDouble( );

System.out.print("You entered " + num);
```

```
Enter a double:  35 ENTER
You entered 35.0
```

The nextDouble method accepts the value 35 and then converts it to a double data type. The method returns a double value, so even if the user enters an integer, you cannot assign the input to an int variable. The following code is therefore invalid:

```
Scanner scanner = new Scanner(System.in);

int num;

System.out.print("Enter an integer: ");
num = scanner.nextDouble( );          Type mismatch

System.out.print("You entered " + num);
```

Bad Version

Now let's study how we can mix the input of strings and numerical values. We begin with an example. Consider inputting a racehorse's name and age. Here are a proposed code and a sample of expected interaction:

```
Scanner scanner = new Scanner(System.in);

String horseName;
int age;

System.out.print("Enter the horse name: ");
horseName = scanner.next( );

System.out.print("Enter the age: ");
age = scanner.nextInt( );

System.out.print(horseName + " is " + age + "years old." );
```

```
Enter the horse name: Barbaro ENTER
Enter the age: 3 ENTER
Barbaro is 3 years old.
```

Everything seems to be working okay. What will happen if the name of a horse has more than one word, such as Sea Biscuit? The code will not work because only the first word is assigned to the String variable horseName. Remember that the default delimiter is the white space, so the blank space after the first word is treated as the end of the first input. Here's the result when you enter Sea Biscuit:

```
Enter the horse name: Sea Biscuit ENTER
Enter the age: java.util.InputMismatchException
      at java.util.Scanner.throwFor(Scanner.java:819)
      at java.util.Scanner.next(Scanner.java:1431)
      at java.util.Scanner.nextInt(Scanner.java:2040)
      ...
```

Only the first four lines of error messages are shown here.

The most reasonable solution here is to change the delimiter to the line separator, as described in Section 2.4.4. Here's how:

```
Scanner scanner = new Scanner(System.in);
scanner.useDelimiter(System.getProperty("line.separator"));

 //the rest is the same
```

```
Enter the horse name: Sea Biscuit ENTER
Enter the age: 3 ENTER
Sea Biscuit is 3 years old.
```

For most situations, using the line separator as the delimiter and inputting one value per input line are the best approach. We can, however, use any string for the delimiter. So, for example, we can delimit the input values with a character such as the pound sign (#), provided, of course, that the pound sign does not occur in the actual input values.

Things to Remember

To input more than one string and primitive numerical data, set the line separator as the delimiter and input one value per input line.

Instead of using the data type specific methods such as nextInt, nextDouble, and others of the Scanner class, we can input a numerical value in a string format and convert it to an appropriate data type by ourselves. For example, we can use the class method parseInt of the Integer class to convert a string to an int. Here's a statement that converts "14" to an int value 14:

```
int num = Integer.parseInt("14");
```

So, the statement

```
int num = Integer.parseInt(scanner.next( ));
```

is equivalent to

```
int num = scanner.nextInt( );
```

Passing a string that cannot be converted to an int (e.g., "12b") will result in an error. The conversion method is not particularly useful or necessary with the scanner, but it can be when the input source is different from the scanner. Other common conversion methods are parseDouble, parseFloat, and parseLong of the Double, Float, and Long classes, respectively.

We close this section by presenting a sample program that extends the Ch3Circle3 class by accepting the radius of a circle as an input. Here's the program:

```
/*
   Chapter 3 Sample Program: Compute Area and Circumference with
                             formatting and standard I/O

   File: Ch3Circle4.java
*/

import java.text.*;
import java.util.*;

class Ch3Circle4 {

   public static void main(String[] args) {

       final double PI = 3.14159;
       final String TAB = "\t";
       final String NEWLINE = "\n";

       double radius, area, circumference;

       Scanner scanner  = new Scanner(System.in);

       DecimalFormat df = new DecimalFormat("0.000");

       System.out.println("Enter radius: ");
       radius = scanner.nextDouble( );

       //compute the area and circumference
       area          = PI * radius * radius;
       circumference      = 2.0 * PI * radius;

       //Display the results
       System.out.println(
                 "Given Radius:  " + TAB + df.format(radius) + NEWLINE +
                 "Area:          " + TAB + df.format(area) + NEWLINE +
                 "Circumference: " + TAB + df.format(circumference));
   }
}
```

1. Write a code to input the height of a user in feet (int) and inches (int).
2. Write a code to input the full name of a person and his or her age. The full name of a person includes the first name and the last name.
3. Write a code that creates a Scanner object and sets its delimiter to the pound sign.

3.6 The Math Class

Using only the arithmetic operators to express numerical computations is very limiting. Many computations require the use of mathematical functions. For example, to express the mathematical formula

$$\frac{1}{2}\sin\left(x - \frac{\pi}{\sqrt{y}}\right)$$

we need the trigonometric sine and square root functions. The Math class in the java.lang package contains class methods for commonly used mathematical functions. Table 3.7 is a partial list of class methods available in the Math class. The class also has two class constants PI and E for π and the natural number e, respectively. Using the Math class constant and methods, we can express the preceding formula as

```
(1.0 /2.0) * Math.sin( x - Math.PI / Math.sqrt(y) )
```

Table 3.7 `Math` **class methods for commonly used mathematical functions**

Class Method	Argument Type	Result Type	Description	Example
`abs( a )`	`int`	`int`	Returns the absolute `int` value of `a`.	abs(10) → 10 abs(−5) → 5
	`long`	`long`	Returns the absolute `long` value of `a`.	
	`float`	`float`	Returns the absolute `float` value of `a`.	
	`double`	`double`	Returns the absolute `double` value of `a`.	
`acos( a )`[†]	`double`	`double`	Returns the arccosine of `a`.	acos(−1) → 3.14159
`asin( a )`[†]	`double`	`double`	Returns the arcsine of `a`.	asin(1) → 1.57079
`atan( a )`[†]	`double`	`double`	Returns the arctangent of `a`.	atan(1) → 0.785398
`ceil( a )`	`double`	`double`	Returns the smallest whole number greater than or equal to `a`.	ceil(5.6) → 6.0 ceil(5.0) → 5.0 ceil(−5.6) → −5.0
`cos( a )`[†]	`double`	`double`	Returns the trigonometric cosine of `a`.	cos(π/2) → 0.0
`exp( a )`	`double`	`double`	Returns the natural number e (2.718 . . .) raised to the power of `a`.	exp(2) → 7.389056099

Table 3.7 Math **class methods for commonly used mathematical functions** *(Continued)*

Class Method	Argument Type	Result Type	Description	Example
`floor( a )`	double	double	Returns the largest whole number less than or equal to a.	floor(5.6) → 5.0 floor(5.0) → 5.0 floor(−5.6) → −6.0
`log( a )`	double	double	Returns the natural logarithm (base *e*) of a.	log(2.7183) → 1.0
`max( a, b )`	int	int	Returns the larger of a and b.	max(10, 20) → 20
	long	long	Same as above.	
	float	float	Same as above.	
`min(a, b)`	int	int	Returns the smaller of a and b.	min(10, 20) → 10
	long	long	Same as above.	
	float	float	Same as above.	
`pow(a, b)`	double	double	Returns the number a raised to the power of b.	pow(2.0, 3.0) → 8.0
`random( )`	<none>	double	Generates a random number greater than or equal to 0.0 and less than 1.0.	Examples given in Chapter 5
`round( a )`	float	int	Returns the int value of a rounded to the nearest whole number.	round(5.6) → 6 round(5.4) → 5 round(−5.6) → −6
	double	long	Returns the float value of a rounded to the nearest whole number.	
`sin( a )`[†]	double	double	Returns the trigonometric sine of a.	sin(π/2) → 1.0
`sqrt( a )`	double	double	Returns the square root of a.	sqrt(9.0) → 3.0
`tan( a )`[†]	double	double	Returns the trigonometric tangent of a.	tan(π/4) → 1.0
`toDegrees`	double	double	Converts the given angle in radians to degrees.	toDegrees(π/4) → 45.0
`toRadians`	double	double	Reverse of toDegrees.	toRadians(90.0) → 1.5707963

[†]All trigonometric functions are computed in radians.

Notice how the class methods and class constants are referred to in the expression. The syntax is

```
<class name> . <method name> ( <arguments> )
```

or

```
<class name> . <class constant>
```

Let's conclude this section with a sample program. Today is the final meet of the women's rowing team against the arch rival university before the upcoming Division I NCAA championship. The cheerleaders of the rival team hoisted their school flag on the other shore of the river to boost their moral. Not to be outdone, we want to hoist our school flag, too. To bring the Goddess of Victory to our side, we want our pole to be taller than theirs. Since they won't let us, we can't find the height of their pole by actually measuring it. We can, however, determine the height without actually measuring it if we know the distance b to their flagpole. We can use the tangent of angle to determine the pole's height h as follows:

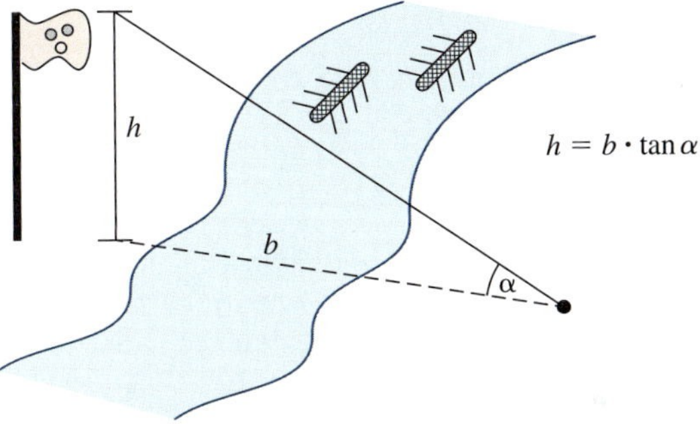

Unfortunately, there's no means for us to go across the river to find out the distance b. After a moment of deep meditation, it hits us that there's no need to go across the river. We can determine the pole's height by measuring angles from two points on this side of the riverbank, as shown below:

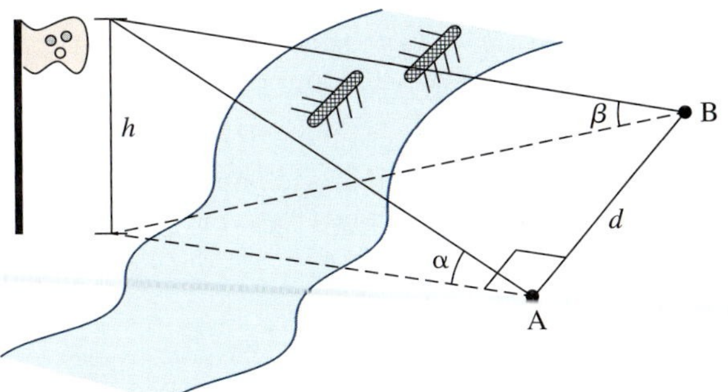

And the equation to compute the height h is

$$h = \frac{d \sin \alpha \sin \beta}{\sqrt{\sin(\alpha + \beta) \sin(\alpha - \beta)}}$$

Once we have this equation, all that's left is to put together a Java program. Here's the program:

```
/*

    Chapter 3 Sample Program: Estimate the Pole Height

    File: Ch3PoleHeight.java

*/

import java.text.*;
import java.util.*;

class Ch3PoleHeight {

    public static void main( String[] args ) {

        double height;          //height of the pole
        double distance;        //distance between points A and B
        double alpha;           //angle measured at point A
        double beta;            //angle measured at point B
        double alphaRad;        //angle alpha in radians
        double betaRad;         //angle beta in radians

        Scanner scanner = new Scanner(System.in);
        scanner.useDelimiter(System.getProperty("line.separator"));

        //Get three input values
        System.out.print("Angle alpha (in degrees):");
        alpha = scanner.nextDouble();

        System.out.print("Angle beta (in degree):");
        beta = scanner.nextDouble();

        System.out.print("Distance between points A and B (ft):");
        distance = scanner.nextDouble();

        //compute the height of the tower
        alphaRad = Math.toRadians(alpha);
        betaRad = Math.toRadians(beta);

        height = ( distance * Math.sin(alphaRad) * Math.sin(betaRad) )
                    /
               Math.sqrt( Math.sin(alphaRad + betaRad) *
                          Math.sin(alphaRad - betaRad) );
```

```
        DecimalFormat df = new DecimalFormat("0.000");

        System.out.println("lnln Estimating the height of the pole"
            + "\n\n"
            + "Angle at point A (deg):          " + df.format(alpha)    + "\n"
            + "Angle at point B (deg):          " + df.format(beta)     + "\n"
            + "Distance between A and B (ft): " + df.format(distance)+ "\n"
            + "Estimated height (ft):           " + df.format(height));
    }
}
```

1. What's wrong with the following?

   a. `y = (1/2) * Math.sqrt( X );`
   b. `y = sqrt(38.0);`
   c. `y = Math.exp(2, 3);`
   d. `y = math.sqrt( b*b - 4*a*c) / ( 2 * a );`

2. If another programmer writes the following statements, do you suspect any misunderstanding on the part of this programmer? What will be the value of `y`?

   a. `y = Math.sin( 360 ) ;`
   b. `y = Math.cos( 45 );`

3.7 Random Number Generation

In many computer applications, especially in simulation and games, we need to generate random numbers. For example, to simulate a roll of dice, we can generate an integer between 1 and 6. In this section, we explain how to generate random numbers using the random method of the Math class. (Alternatively, you can use the Random class. We refer you to the Java API documentation for information on this class.)

pseudorandom number generator

The method random is called a ***pseudorandom number generator*** and returns a number (type double) that is greater than or equal to 0.0 but less than 1.0, that is, $0.0 \leq X < 1.0$. The generated number is called a *pseudorandom number* because the number is not truly random. When we call this method repeatedly, eventually the numbers generated will repeat themselves. Therefore, theoretically the generated numbers are not random; but for all practical purposes, they are random enough.

The random numbers we want to generate for most applications are integers. For example, to simulate the draw of a card, we need to generate an integer between 1 and 4 for the suit and an integer between 1 and 13 for the number. Since the number returned from the random method ranges from 0.0 up to but not including 1.0, we need to perform some form of conversion so the converted number will fall in our desired range. Let's assume the range of integer values we want is [min, max]. If X is a number returned by random, then we can convert it into a number Y such that Y is in the range [min, max] that is, min $\leq Y \leq$ max by applying the following fourmula:

$$Y = \lfloor X \times (\max - \min + 1) \rfloor + \min$$

For many applications, the value for min is 1, so the formula is simplified to

$$Y = \lfloor X \times \max \rfloor + 1$$

Expressing the general formula in Java will result in the following statement:

```
//assume correct values are assigned to 'max' and 'min'
int randomNumber
      = (int) (Math.floor(Math.random() * ( max-min+1))
                + min);
```

Notice that we have to typecast the result of Math.floor to int because the data type of the result is double.

Let's write a short program that selects a winner among the party goers of the annual spring fraternity dance. The party goers will receive numbers $M + 1$, $M + 2$, $M + 3$, and so on, as they enter the house. The starting value M is selected by the chairperson of the party committee. The last number assigned is $M + N$ if there are N party goers. At the end of the party, we run the program that will randomly select the winning number from the range of $M + 1$ and $M + N$. Here's the program:

```
/*

    Chapter 3 Sample Program: Select the Winning Number

    File: Ch3SelectWinner.java
*/

import java.util.*;

class Ch3SelectWinner {

    public static void main(String[] args) {

        int startingNumber; //the starting number
        int count;          //the number of party goers
        int winningNumber;  //the winner
        int min, max;       //the range of random numbers to generate

        Scanner scan = new Scanner(System.in);

        //Get two input values
        System.out.print("Enter the starting number M:      ");
        startingNumber = scan.nextInt();

        System.out.print("Enter the number of party goers: ");
        count = scan.nextInt();
```

```
            //select the winner
            min = startingNumber + 1;
            max = startingNumber + count;
            winningNumber = (int) ( Math.floor(Math.random() * (max - min + 1))
                                                + min);
            System.out.println("\nThe Winning Number is " + winningNumber);
        }
    }
```

3.8 The GregorianCalendar Class

In Chapter 2, we introduced the java.util.Date class to represent a specific instant in time. Notice that we are using here the more concise expression "the java.util.Date class" to refer to a class from a specific package instead of the longer expression "the Date class from the java.util package." This shorter version is our preferred way of notation when we need or want to identify the package to which the class belongs.

Things to Remember

*When we need to identify the specific package to which a class belongs, we will commonly use the concise expression with the full path name, such as **java.util.Date,** instead of writing "the **Date** class from the **java.util** package."*

In addition to this class, we have a very useful class named java.util.GregorianCalendar in manipulating calendar information such as year, month, and day. We can create a new GregorianCalendar object that represents today as

Gregorian-Calendar

```
GregorianCalendar today = new GregorianCalendar( );
```

or a specific day, say, July 4, 1776, by passing year, month, and day as the parameters as

The value of 6 means July.

```
GregorianCalendar independenceDay =
                 new GregorianCalendar(1776, 6, 4);
```

No, the value of 6 as the second parameter is not an error. The first month of a year, January, is represented by 0, the second month by 1, and so forth. To avoid confusion, we can use constants defined for months in the superclass Calendar (GregorianCalendar is a subclass of Calendar). Instead of remembering that the value 6 represents July, we can use the defined constant Calendar.JULY as

```
GregorianCalendar independenceDay =
            new GregorianCalendar(1776, Calendar.JULY, 4);
```

Table 3.8 explains the use of some of the more common constants defined in the Calendar class.

When the date and time are November 11, 2002, 6:13 p.m. and we run the Ch3TestCalendar program, we will see the result shown in Figure 3.4.

Table 3.8 Constants defined in the Calendar class for retrieved different pieces of calendar/time information

Constant	Description
YEAR	The year portion of the calendar date
MONTH	The month portion of the calendar date
DATE	The day of the month
DAY_OF_MONTH	Same as DATE
DAY_OF_YEAR	The day number within the year
DAY_OF_MONTH	The day number within the month
DAY_OF_WEEK	The day of the week (Sun—1, Mon—2, etc.)
WEEK_OF_YEAR	The week number within the year
WEEK_OF_MONTH	The week number within the month
AM_PM	The indicator for AM or PM (AM—0 and PM—1)
HOUR	The hour in 12-hour notation
HOUR_OF_DAY	The hour in 24-hour notation
MINUTE	The minute within the hour

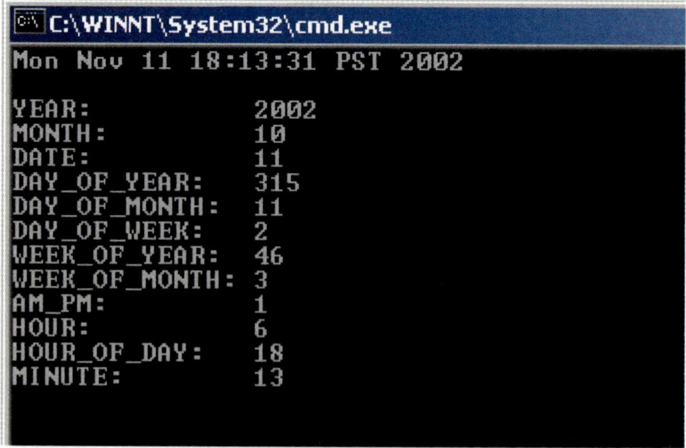

Figure 3.4 Result of running the **Ch3TestCalender** program at November 11, 2002, 6:13 p.m.

```
/*
    Chapter 3 Sample Program: Display Calendar Info

    File: Ch3TestCalendar.java
*/

import java.util.*;

class Ch3TestCalendar {

    public static void main(String[] args) {

        GregorianCalendar cal = new GregorianCalendar();

        System.out.println(cal.getTime());
        System.out.println("");

        System.out.println("YEAR:           " + cal.get(Calendar.YEAR));
        System.out.println("MONTH:          " + cal.get(Calendar.MONTH));
        System.out.println("DATE:           " + cal.get(Calendar.DATE));

        System.out.println("DAY_OF_YEAR:    "
                             + cal.get(Calendar.DAY_OF_YEAR));
        System.out.println("DAY_OF_MONTH:   "
                             + cal.get(Calendar.DAY_OF_MONTH));
        System.out.println("DAY_OF_WEEK:    "
                             + cal.get(Calendar.DAY_OF_WEEK));
        System.out.println("WEEK_OF_YEAR:   "
                             + cal.get(Calendar.WEEK_OF_YEAR));
        System.out.println("WEEK_OF_MONTH:  "
                             + cal.get(Calendar.WEEK_OF_MONTH));

        System.out.println("AM_PM:          " + cal.get(Calendar.AM_PM));
        System.out.println("HOUR:           " + cal.get(Calendar.HOUR));
        System.out.println("HOUR_OF_DAY:    "
                             + cal.get(Calendar.HOUR_OF_DAY));
        System.out.println("MINUTE:         " + cal.get(Calendar.MINUTE));
    }
}
```

getTime

Notice that the first line in the output shows the full date and time information. The full date and time information can be accessed by calling the calendar object's getTime method. This method returns the same information as a Date object.

Notice also that we get only the numerical values when we retrieve the day of the week or month information. We can spell out the information by using the SimpleDateFormat class. Since the constructor of the SimpleDateFormat class accepts only the Date object, first we need to convert a GregorianCalendar object to an equivalent Date object by calling its getTime method. For example, here's how we can display the day of the week on which our Declaration of Independence was adopted in Philadelphia:

```
/*
    Chapter 3 Sample Program: Day of the week the Declaration of
                              Independence was adopted

    File: Ch3IndependenceDay.java
*/

import java.util.*;
import java.text.*;

class Ch3IndependenceDay {

    public static void main(String[] args) {

        GregorianCalendar independenceDay
          = new GregorianCalendar(1776, Calendar.JULY, 4);

        SimpleDateFormat sdf = new SimpleDateFormat("EEEE");

        System.out.println("It was adopted on "
                    + sdf.format(independenceDay.getTime()));
    }
}
```

Let's finish the section with a sample program that extends the Ch3IndependenceDay program. We will allow the user to enter the year, month, and day; and we will reply with the day of the week of the given date (our birthday, grandparent's wedding day, and so on). Here's the program:

```
/*
    Chapter 3 Sample Program: Find the Day of Week of a Given Date

    File: Ch3FindDayOfWeek.java
*/

import java.util.*;
import java.text.*;

class Ch3FindDayOfWeek {

    public static void main(String[] args) {

        int      year, month, day;

        GregorianCalendar cal;
        SimpleDateFormat  sdf;
```

```
        Scanner scanner = new Scanner(System.in);
        scanner.useDelimiter(System.getProperty("line.separator"));

        System.out.print("Year (yyyy): ");
        year      = scanner.nextInt();

        System.out.print("Month (1-12): ");
        month     = scanner.nextInt();

        System.out.print("Day (1-31): ");
        day       = scanner.nextInt();

        cal = new GregorianCalendar(year, month-1, day);
        sdf = new SimpleDateFormat("EEEE");

        System.out.println("");
        System.out.println("Day of Week: " + sdf.format(cal.getTime()));
    }
}
```

Notice that we are allowing the user to enter the month as an integer between 1 and 12, so we need to subtract 1 from the entered data in creating a new GregorianCalendar object.

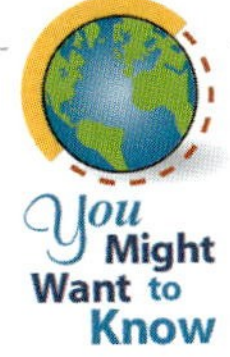

The Gregorian calendar system was adopted by England and its colonies, including the colonial United States, in 1752. So the technique shown here works only after this adoption. For a fascinating story about calendars, visit
http://webexhibits.org/calendars/year-countries.html

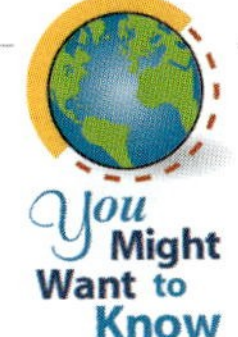

Running **Ch3IndpendenceDay** will tell you that our venerable document was signed on Thursday. History textbooks will say something like "the document was formally adopted July 4, 1776, on a bright, but cool Philadelphia day" but never the day of the week. Well, now you know. See how useful Java is? By the way, the document was adopted by the Second Continental Congress on July 4, but the actual signing did not take place until August 2 (it was Friday—what a great reason for a TGIF party) after the approval of all 13 colonies. For more stories behind the Declaration of Independence, visit
http://www.ushistory.org/declaration/

3.9 Sample Development

Loan Calculator

In this section, we develop a simple loan calculator program. We develop this program by using an incremental development technique, which develops the program in small incremental steps. We start out with a bare-bones program and gradually build up the program by adding more and more code to it. At each incremental step, we design, code, and test the program before moving on to the next step. This methodical development of a program allows us to focus our attention on a single task at each step, and this reduces the chance of introducing errors into the program.

Problem Statement

The next time you buy a new TV or a stereo, watch out for those "0% down, 0% interest until next July" deals. Read the fine print, and you'll notice that if you don't make the full payment by the end of a certain date, hefty interest will start accruing. You may be better off to get an ordinary loan from the beginning with a cheaper interest rate. What matters most is the total payment (loan amount plus total interest) you'll have to make. To compare different loan deals, let's develop a loan calculator. Here's the problem statement:

> *Write a loan calculator program that computes both monthly and total payments for a given loan amount, annual interest rate, and loan period.*

Overall Plan

Our first task is to map out the overall plan for development. We will identify classes necessary for the program and the steps we will follow to implement the program. We begin with the outline of program logic. For a simple program such as this one, it is kind of obvious; but to practice the incremental development, let's put down the outline of program flow explicitly. We can express the program flow as having three tasks:

program tasks

1. Get three input values: **loanAmount, interestRate,** and **loanPeriod.**
2. Compute the monthly and total payments.
3. Output the results.

Having identified the three major tasks of the program, we now identify the classes we can use to implement the three tasks. For input and output, we continue to use the **Scanner** class and **System.out (PrintStream).** For computing the monthly and total payments, there are no standard classes that will provide such computation, so we have to write our own code.

The formula for computing the monthly payment can be found in any mathematics book that covers geometric sequences. It is

$$\text{Monthly payment} = \frac{L \times R}{1 - [1/(1 + R)]^N}$$

where *L* is the loan amount, *R* is the monthly interest rate, and *N* is the number of payments. The monthly rate *R is* expressed in a fractional value, for example, 0.01 for 1 percent monthly rate. Once the monthly payment is derived, the total payment can be determined by multiplying the monthly payment by the number of months the payment is made. Since the formula includes exponentiation, we will have to use the **pow** method of the **Math** class.

Let's summarize what we have decided so far in a design document:

program classes

Design Document: `LoanCalculator`

Class	Purpose
`LoanCalculator`	The main class of the program.
`Scanner`	The class is used to get three input values: loan amount, annual interest rate, and loan period.
`PrintStream` (`System.out`)	`System.out` is used to display the input values and two computed results: monthly payment and total payment.
`Math`	The `pow` method is used to evaluate exponentiation in the formula for computing the monthly payment. This class is from `java.lang`. *Note:* You don't have to import `java.lang`. The classes in `java.lang` are available to a program without importing.

The program diagram based on the classes listed in the design document is shown in Figure 3.5. Keep in mind that this is only a preliminary design. The preliminary document is really a working document that we will modify and expand as we progress through the development steps.

Before we can actually start our development, we must sketch the steps we will follow to implement the program. There is more than one possible sequence of steps to implement a program, and the number of possible sequences will increase as the program becomes more complex. For this program, we will implement the program in four steps:

development steps

1. Start with code to accept three input values.
2. Add code to output the results.
3. Add code to compute the monthly and total payments.
4. Update or modify code and tie up any loose ends.

Notice how the first three steps are ordered. Other orders are possible to develop this program. So why did we choose this particular order? The main reason is our desire to defer the most difficult task until the end. It's possible, but if we implement the computation part in the second incremental step, then we need to code some temporary output routines to verify that the computation is done correctly. However, if we implement the real output routines before implementing the computation routines, then there is no

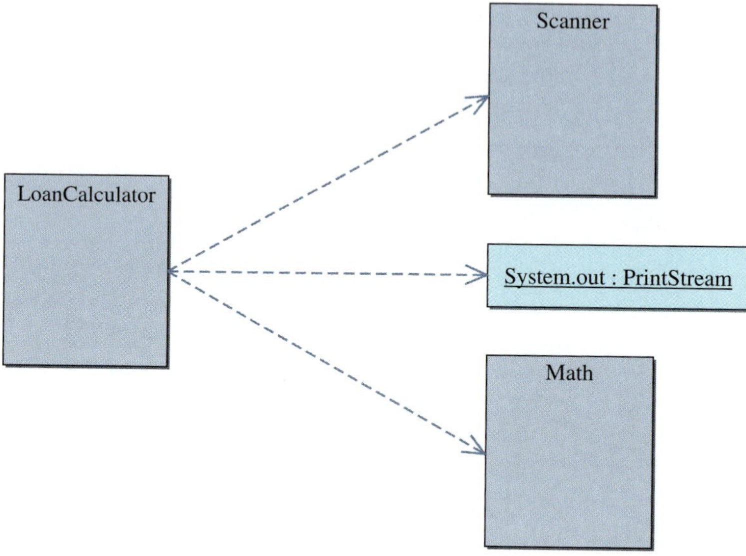

Figure 3.5 The object diagram for the program **LoanCalculator.**

need for us to worry about temporary output routines. As for step 1 and step 2, their relative order does not matter much. We simply chose to implement the input routine before the output routine because input comes before output in the program.

Step 1 Development: Input Three Data Values

step 1 design

The next task is to determine how we will accept the input values. The problem statement does not specify the exact format of input, so we will decide that now. Based on how people normally refer to loans, the input values will be accepted in the following format:

Input	Format	Data Type
Loan amount	In dollars and cents (for example, 15000.00)	`double`
Annual interest rate	In percent (for example, 12.5)	`double`
Loan period	In years (for example, 30)	`int`

Be aware that we need to convert the annual interest rate to the monthly interest rate and the input value loan period to the number of monthly payments, to use the given formula. In this case, the conversion is very simple, but even if the conversion routines were more complicated, we must do the conversion. It is not acceptable to ask users to enter an input value that is unnatural to them. For example, people do not think of interest rates in fractional values such as 0.07. They think of interest in terms of percentages such as 7 percent. Computer programs work for humans, not the other way round. Programs we develop should not support an interface that is difficult and awkward for humans to use.

When the user inputs an invalid value, for example, an input string value that cannot be converted to a numerical value or that converts to a negative number, the program should respond accordingly, such as by printing an error message. We do not possess enough skills to implement such a robust program yet, so we will make the following assumptions: (1) The input values are nonnegative numbers, and (2) the loan period is a whole number.

One important objective of this step is to verify that the input values are read in correctly by the program. To verify this, we will echo-print the input values to **System.out.**

step 1 code

Here's our step 1 program:

```
/*
    Chapter 3 Sample Development: Loan Calculator  (Step 1)

    File: Step1/Ch3LoanCalculator.java

    Step 1: Input Data Values
*/

import java.util.*;

class Ch3LoanCalculator {

    public static void main(String[] args) {

        double  loanAmount,
                annualInterestRate;

        int     loanPeriod;

        Scanner scanner = new Scanner(System.in);
        scanner.useDelimiter(System.getProperty("line.separator"));

        //get input values
        System.out.print("Loan Amount (Dollars+Cents): ");
        loanAmount = scanner.nextDouble();

        System.out.print("Annual Interest Rate (e.g., 9.5): ");
        annualInterestRate = scanner.nextDouble();

        System.out.print("Loan Period - # of years: ");
        loanPeriod = scanner.nextInt();
```

3.9 Sample Development—*continued*

```
            //echo print the input values
            System.out.println ("");
            System.out.println("Loan Amount:          $" + loanAmount);
            System.out.println("Annual Interest Rate: "
                                         + annualInterestRate + "%");
            System.out.println("Loan Period (years):  " + loanPeriod);
        }
    }
```

step 1 test

To verify the input routine is working correctly, we run the program multiple times and enter different sets of data. We make sure the values are displayed in the standard output window as entered.

Step 2 Development: Output Values

step 2 design

The second step is to add code to display the output values. We will use the standard output window for displaying output values. We need to display the result in a layout that is meaningful and easy to read. Just displaying numbers such as the following is totally unacceptable.

```
132.151.15858.1
```

We must label the output values so the user can tell what the numbers represent. In addition, we must display the input values with the computed result so it will not be meaningless. Which of the two shown in Figure 3.6 do you think is more meaningful? The output format of this program will be

```
For
Loan Amount:               $ <amount>
Annual Interest Rate:        <annual interest rate> %
Loan Period (years):         <year>

Monthly payment is $ <monthly payment>
  TOTAL payment is $ <total payment>
```

with **<amount>, <annual interest rate>,** and others replaced by the actual figures.

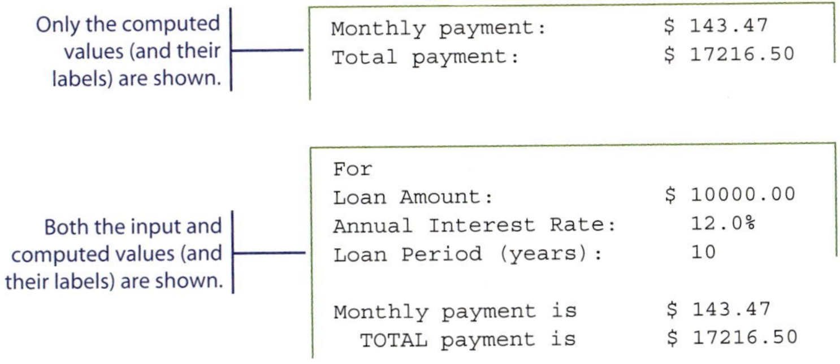

Only the computed values (and their labels) are shown.
Monthly payment: $ 143.47
Total payment: $ 17216.50
Both the input and computed values (and their labels) are shown.
For
Loan Amount: $ 10000.00
Annual Interest Rate: 12.0%
Loan Period (years): 10
Monthly payment is $ 143.47
TOTAL payment is $ 17216.50

Figure 3.6 Two different display formats, one with input values displayed and the other with only the computed values displayed.

Since the computations for the monthly and total payments are not yet implemented, we will use the following dummy assignment statements:

```
monthlyPayment = 135.15;
totalPayment   = 15858.10;
```

We will replace these statements with the real ones in the next step.

step 2 code

Here's our step 2 program with the newly added portion surrounded by a rectangle and white background:

```
/*

   Chapter 3 Sample Development: Loan Calculator (Step 2)

   File: Step2/Ch3LoanCalculator.java

   Step 2: Display the Results

*/

import java.util.*;

class Ch3LoanCalculator {

   public static void main(String[] args) {

         double   loanAmount,
                  annualInterestRate;

         double   monthlyPayment,
                  totalPayment;

         int      loanPeriod;
```

3.9 Sample Development—*continued*

```
        Scanner scanner = new Scanner(System.in);
        scanner.useDelimiter(System.getProperty("line.separator"));

        //get input values
        System.out.print("Loan Amount (Dollars+Cents): ");
        loanAmount = scanner.nextDouble();

        System.out.print("Annual Interest Rate (e.g., 9.5): ");
        annualInterestRate = scanner.nextDouble();

        System.out.print("Loan Period - # of years: ");
        loanPeriod = scanner.nextInt();

        //compute the monthly and total payments
        monthlyPayment = 132.15;
        totalPayment = 15858.10;

        //display the result
        System.out.println("");
        System.out.println("Loan Amount:          $" + loanAmount);
        System.out.println("Annual Interest Rate:"
                                      + annualInterestRate + "%");
        System.out.println("Loan Period (years): " + loanPeriod);

        System.out.println("\n"); //skip two lines
        System.out.println("Monthly payment is    $ " + monthlyPayment);
        System.out.println("  TOTAL payment is    $ " + totalPayment);
    }
}
```

step 2 test

To verify the output routine is working correctly, we run the program and verify the layout. Most likely, we have to run the program several times to fine-tune the arguments for the **println** methods until we get the layout that looks clean and nice on the screen.

Step 3 Development: Compute Loan Amount

step 3 design

We are now ready to complete the program by implementing the formula derived in the design phase. The formula requires the monthly interest rate and the number of monthly payments. The input values to the program, however, are the annual interest rate and the loan period in years. So we need to convert the annual interest rate to a monthly interest rate and the loan period to the number of monthly payments. The two input values are converted as

```
monthlyInterestRate = annualInterestRate / 100.0 / MONTHS_IN_YEAR;

numberOfPayments     = loanPeriod * MONTHS_IN_YEAR;
```

where **MONTHS_IN_YEAR** is a symbolic constant with value **12.** Notice that we need to divide the input annual interest rate by 100 first because the formula for loan computation requires that the interest rate be a fractional value, for example, 0.01, but the input annual interest rate is entered as a percentage point, for example, 12.0. Please read Exercise 23 on page 142 for information on how the monthly interest rate is derived from a given annual interest rate.

The formula for computing the monthly and total payments can be expressed as

```
monthlyPayment = (loanAmount * monthlyInterestRate)
                 /
                 (1 - Math.pow( 1 /(1 + monthlyInterestRate),
                                numberOfPayments) );

totalPayment = monthlyPayment * numberOfPayments;
```

step 3 code

Let's put in the necessary code for the computations and complete the program. Here's our program:

```
/*
   Chapter 3 Sample Development: Loan Calculator (Step 3)

   File: Step3/Ch3LoanCalculator.java

   Step 3: Display the Results

*/

import java.util.*;

class Ch3LoanCalculator {

   public static void main(String[] args) {

      final int MONTHS_IN_YEAR = 12;

      double  loanAmount,
              annualInterestRate;

      double  monthlyPayment,
              totalPayment;

      double  monthlyInterestRate;

      int     loanPeriod;

      int     numberOfPayments;
```

3.9 Sample Development—*continued*

```
        Scanner scanner = new Scanner(System.in);
        scanner.useDelimiter(System.getProperty("line.separator"));

        //get input values
        System.out.print("Loan Amount (Dollars+Cents): ");
        loanAmount = scanner.nextDouble();

        System.out.print("Annual Interest Rate (e.g., 9.5): ");
        annualInterestRate = scanner.nextDouble();

        System.out.print("Loan Period - # of years: ");
        loanPeriod = scanner.nextInt();

        //compute the monthly and total payments
        monthlyInterestRate = annualInterestRate / MONTHS_IN_YEAR / 100;
        numberOfPayments    = loanPeriod * MONTHS_IN_YEAR;

        monthlyPayment = (loanAmount * monthlyInterestRate)/
                            (1 - Math.pow(1/(1 + monthlyInterestRate),
                                          numberOfPayments ) );

        totalPayment = monthlyPayment * numberOfPayments;

        //display the result
        System.out.println("");
        System.out.println("Loan Amount:          $" + loanAmount);
        System.out.println("Annual Interest Rate: "
                                  + annualInterestRate + "%");
        System.out.println("Loan Period (years):  " + loanPeriod);

        System.out.println("\n"); //skip two lines
        System.out.println("Monthly payment is    $ " + monthlyPayment);
        System.out.println("  TOTAL payment is    $ " + totalPayment);
    }
}
```

step 3 test

After the program is coded, we need to run the program through a number of tests. Since we made the assumption that the input values must be valid, we will test the program only for valid input values. If we don't make that assumption, then we need to test that the program will respond correctly when invalid values are entered. We will perform such testing beginning in Chapter 5. To check that this program produces correct results, we can run the program with the following input values. The right two columns show the correct results. Try other input values as well.

Input			Output (shown up to three decimal places only)	
Loan Amount	**Annual Interest Rate**	**Loan Period (Years)**	**Monthly Payment**	**Total Payment**
10000	10	10	132.151	15858.088
15000	7	15	134.824	24268.363
10000	12	10	143.471	17216.514
0	10	5	0.000	0.000
30	8.5	50	0.216	129.373

Step 4 Development: Finishing Up

step 4 design

We finalize the program in the last step by making any necessary modifications or additions. We will make two additions to the program. The first is necessary while the second is optional but desirable. The first addition is the inclusion of a program description. One of the necessary features of any nontrivial program is the description of what the program does for the user. We will print out a description at the beginning of the program to **System.out.** The second addition is the formatting of the output values. We will format the monthly and total payments to two decimal places, using a **DecimalFormat** object.

step 4 code

Here is our final program:

```
/*
   Chapter 3 Sample Development: Loan Calculator (Step 4)

   File: Step4/Ch3LoanCalculator.java

   Step 4: Finalize the program
*/

import java.util.*;

import java.text.*;

class Ch3LoanCalculator {

   public static void main(String[] args) {

      final int MONTHS_IN_YEAR = 12;
```

3.9 Sample Development—*continued*

```
double    loanAmount,
          annualInterestRate;

double    monthlyPayment,
          totalPayment;

double    monthlyInterestRate;

int       loanPeriod;

int       numberOfPayments;

Scanner scanner = new Scanner(System.in);
scanner.useDelimiter(System.getProperty("line.separator"));

DecimalFormat df = new DecimalFormat("0.00");

//describe the program
System.out.println("This program computes the monthly and total");
System.out.println("payments for a given loan amount, annual ");
System.out.println("interest rate, and loan period.");
System.out.println("Loan amount in dollars and cents,
                                          e.g., 12345.50");
System.out.println("Annual interest rate in percentage,
                                          e.g., 12.75");
System.out.println("Loan period in number of years, e.g., 15");
System.out.println("\n"); //skip two lines

//get input values
System.out.print("Loan Amount (Dollars+Cents): ");
loanAmount = scanner.nextDouble( );

System.out.print("Annual Interest Rate (e.g., 9.5): ");
annualInterestRate = scanner.nextDouble( );

System.out.print("Loan Period - # of years: ");
loanPeriod = scanner.nextInt( );

//compute the monthly and total payments
monthlyInterestRate = annualInterestRate / MONTHS_IN_YEAR / 100;
numberOfPayments    = loanPeriod * MONTHS_IN_YEAR;

monthlyPayment = (loanAmount * monthlyInterestRate) /
                    (1 - Math.pow(1/(1 + monthlyInterestRate),
                                    numberOfPayments ) );

totalPayment = monthlyPayment * numberOfPayments;
```

```
        //display the result
        System.out.println("");
        System.out.println("Loan Amount:           $" + loanAmount);
        System.out.println("Annual Interest Rate: "
                                        + annualInterestRate + "%");
        System.out.println("Loan Period (years):   " + loanPeriod);

        System.out.println("\n"); //skip two lines

        System.out.println("Monthly payment is   $ "
                                        + df.format(monthlyPayment));
        System.out.println("  TOTAL payment is   $ "
                                        + df.format(totalPayment));

    }
}
```

step 4 test

We repeat the test runs from step 3 and confirm the modified program still runs correctly. Since we have not made any substantial additions or modifications, we fully expect the program to work correctly. However, it is very easy to introduce errors in coding, so even if we think the changes are trivial, we should never skip the testing after even a slight modification.

Things to Remember

Always test after making any additions or modifications to a program, no matter how trivial you think the changes are.

3.10 Numerical Representation (*Optional*)

twos complement

In this section we explain how integers and real numbers are stored in memory. Although computer manufacturers have used various formats for storing numerical values, today's standard is to use the ***twos complement*** format for storing integers and the *floating-point* format for real numbers. We describe these formats in this section.

An integer can occupy 1, 2, 4, or 8 bytes depending on which data type (i.e., byte, short, int, or long) is declared. To make the examples easy to follow, we will use 1 byte (= 8 bits) to explain twos complement form. The same principle applies to 2, 4, and 8 bytes. (They just utilize more bits.)

The following table shows the first five and the last four of the 256 positive binary numbers using 8 bits. The right column lists their decimal equivalents.

8-Bit Binary Number	Decimal Equivalent
00000000	0
00000001	1
00000010	2
00000011	3
00000100	4
. . .	
11111100	252
11111101	253
11111110	254
11111111	255

Using 8 bits, we can represent positive integers from 0 to 255. Now let's see the possible range of negative and positive numbers that we can represent, using 8 bits. We can designate the leftmost bit as a ***sign bit***: 0 means positive and 1 means negative. Using this scheme, we can represent integers from −127 to +127 as shown in the following table:

sign bit

8-Bit Binary Number (with a Sign Bit)	Decimal Equivalent
0 0000000	+0
0 0000001	+1
0 0000010	+2
. . .	
0 1111111	+127
1 0000000	−0
1 0000001	−1
. . .	
1 1111110	−126
1 1111111	−127

Notice that zero has two distinct representations (+0 = 00000000 and −0 = 10000000), which adds complexity in hardware design. Twos complement format avoids this problem of duplicate representations for zero. In twos complement format, all positive numbers have zero in their leftmost bit. The representation of a negative number is derived by first inverting all the bits (changing 1s to 0s and 0s to

1s) in the representation of the positive number and then adding 1. The following diagram illustrates the process:

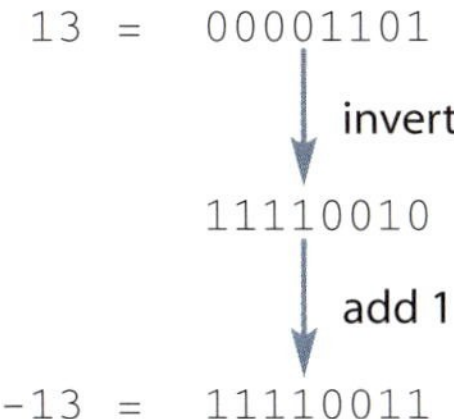

The following table shows the decimal equivalents of 8-bit binary numbers by using twos complement representation. Notice that zero has only one representation.

8-Bit Binary Number (Twos Complement)	Decimal Equivalent
00000000	+0
00000001	+1
00000010	+2
...	
01111111	+127
10000000	−128
10000001	−127
...	
11111110	−2
11111111	−1

floating-point

Now let's see how real numbers are stored in memory in *floating-point* format. We present only the basic ideas of storing real numbers in computer memory here. We omit the precise details of the Institute of Electronics and Electrical Engineers (IEEE) Standard 754 that Java uses to store real numbers.

Real numbers are represented in the computer by using scientific notation. In base-10 scientific notation, a real number is expressed as

$$A \times 10^N$$

where A is a real number and N is an integral exponent. For example, the mass of a hydrogen atom (in grams) is expressed in decimal scientific notation as 1.67339×10^{-24}, which is equal to 0.00000000000000000000000167339.

We use base-2 scientific notation to store real numbers in computer memory. Base-2 scientific notation represents a real number as follows:

$$A \times 2^N$$

The float and double data types use 32 and 64 bits, respectively, with the number A and exponent N stored as follows:

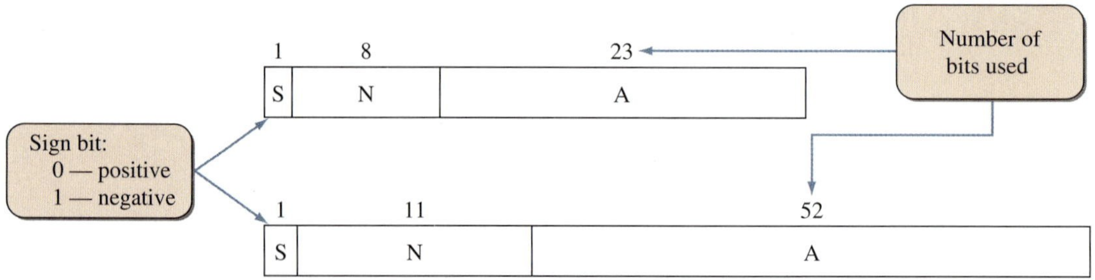

normalized fraction

The value A is a ***normalized fraction***, where the fraction begins with a binary point, followed by a 1 bit and the rest of the fraction. (*Note:* A decimal number has a decimal point; a binary number has a binary point.) The following numbers are sample normalized and unnormalized binary fractions:

Normalized	Unnormalized
1.1010100	1.100111
1.100011	.0000000001
1.101110011	.0001010110

Since a normalized number always start with a 1, this bit does not actually have to be stored. The following diagram illustrates how the A value is stored.

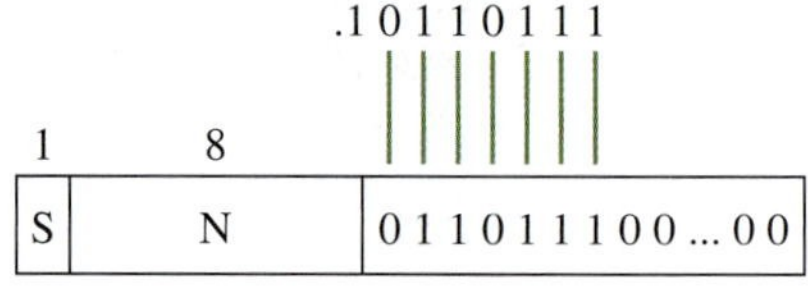

excess format

The sign bit S indicates the sign of a number, so A is stored in memory as an unsigned number. The integral exponent N can be negative or positive. Instead of using twos complement for storing N, we use a format called ***excess format***. The 8-bit exponent uses the excess-127 format, and the 11-bit exponent uses the excess-1023 format. We will explain the excess-127 format here. The excess-1023 works similarly. With the excess-127 format, the actual exponent is computed as

$$N - 127$$

Therefore, the number 127 represents an exponent of zero. Numbers less than 127 represent negative exponents, and numbers greater than 127 represent positive exponents. The following diagram illustrates that the number 125 in the exponent field represents $2^{125-127} = 2^{-2}$.

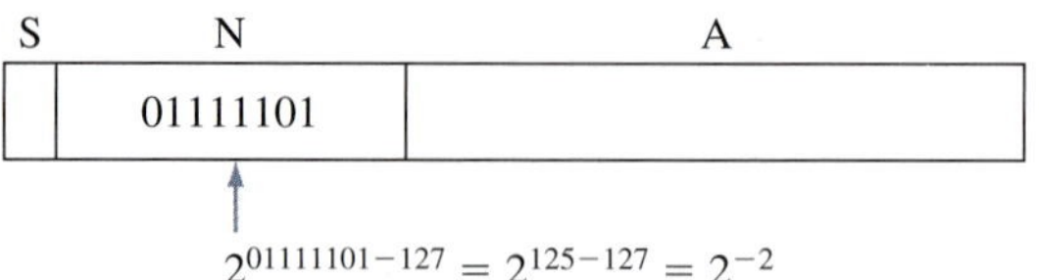

Summary

- A variable is a memory location in which to store a value.
- A variable has a name and a data type.
- A variable must be declared before we can assign a value to it.
- There are six numerical data types in Java: byte, short, int, long, float, and double.
- Object names are synonymous with variables whose contents are memory addresses.
- Numerical data types are called primitive data types, and objects are called reference data types.
- Precedence rules determine the order of evaluating arithemetic expressions.
- Symbolic constants hold values just as variables do, but we cannot change their values.
- The standard classes introduced in this chapter are

  Math
  GregorianCalendar
  DecimalFormat
  PrintStream

- System.out is used to output multiple lines of text to the standard output window.
- System.in is used to input a stream of bytes. We associate a Scanner object to System.in to input primitive data type.
- The Math class contains many class methods for mathematical functions.
- The GregorianCalendar class is used in the manipulation of calendar information.
- The DecimalFormat class is used to format numerical data.
- (*Optional*) Twos complement format is used for storing integers, and floating-pointing format is used for storing real numbers.

Key Concepts

variables
primitive data types
reference data types
arithmetic expression
arithmetic operators
precedence rules
typecasting
implicit and explicit casting
assignment conversion
constants
standard output
standard input
echo printing
twos complement (*optional*)
floating point (*optional*)

Exercises

1. Suppose we have the following declarations:

```
int i = 3, j = 4, k = 5;
float x = 34.5f, y = 12.25f;
```

   Determine the value for each of the following expressions, or explain why it is not a valid expression.

   a. `(x + 1.5) / (250.0 * (i/j))`
   b. `x + 1.5 / 250.0 * i / j`
   c. `-x * -y * (i + j) / k`
   d. `(i / 5) * y`
   e. `Math.min(i, Math.min(j,k))`
   f. `Math.exp(3, 2)`
   g. `y % x`
   h. `Math.pow(3, 2)`
   i. `(int)y % k`
   j. `i / 5 * y`

2. Suppose we have the following declarations:

```
int m, n, i = 3, j = 4, k = 5;
float v, w, x = 34.5f, y = 12.25f;
```

   Determine the value assigned to the variable in each of the following assignment statements, or explain why it is not a valid assignment.

   a. `w = Math.pow(3,Math.pow(i,j));`
   b. `v = x / i;`
   c. `w = Math.ceil(y) % k;`
   d. `n = (int) x / y * i / 2;`
   e. `x = Math.sqrt(i*i - 4*j*k);`
   f. `m = n + i * j;`
   g. `n = k /(j * i) * x + y;`
   h. `i = i + 1;`
   i. `w = float(x + i);`
   j. `x = x / i / y / j;`

3. Suppose we have the following declarations:

```
int    i, j;
float  x, y;
double u, v;
```

   Which of the following assignments are valid?

   a. `i = x;`
   b. `x = u + y;`
   c. `x = 23.4 + j * y;`
   d. `v = (int) x;`
   e. `y = j / i * x;`

4. Write Java expressions to compute each of the following.

   a. The square root of $B^2 + 4AC$ (A and C are distinct variables)
   b. The square root of $X + 4Y^3$
   c. The cube root of the product of X and Y
   d. The area πR^2 of a circle

5. Determine the output of the following program without running it.

```
class TestOutputBox {
    public static void main(String[] args) {

        System.out.println("One");
        System.out.print("Two");
        System.out.print("\n");

        System.out.print("Three");
        System.out.println("Four");
        System.out.print("\n");

        System.out.print("Five");
        System.out.println("Six");
    }
}
```

6. Determine the output of the following code.

```
int x, y;
x = 1;
y = 2;
System.out.println("The output is " + x + y );
System.out.println("The output is " + ( x + y) );
```

7. Write an application that displays the following pattern in the standard output window.

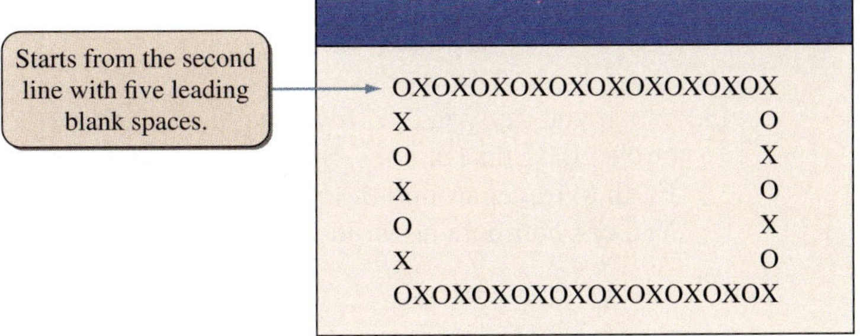

Note: The output window is not drawn to scale.

8. Write an application to convert centimeters (input) to feet and inches (output). 1 in = 2.54 cm.

9. Write an application that inputs temperature in degrees Celsius and prints out the temperature in degrees Fahrenheit. The formula to convert degrees Celsius to equivalent degrees Fahrenheit is

$$\text{Fahrenheit} = 1.8 \times \text{Celsius} + 32$$

10. Write an application that accepts a person's weight and displays the number of calories the person needs in one day. A person needs 19 calories per pound of body weight, so the formula expressed in Java is

```
calories = bodyWeight * 19;
```

(*Note:* We are not distinguishing between genders.)

11. A quantity known as the *body mass index* (BMI) is used to calculate the risk of weight-related health problems. BMI is computed by the formula

$$\text{BMI} = \frac{w}{(h/100.0)^2}$$

where w is weight in kilograms and h is height in centimeters. A BMI of about 20 to 25 is considered "normal." Write an application that accepts weight and height (both integers) and outputs the BMI.

12. Your weight is actually the amount of gravitational attraction exerted on you by the Earth. Since the Moon's gravity is only one-sixth of the Earth's gravity, on the Moon you would weigh only one-sixth of what you weigh on Earth. Write an application that inputs the user's Earth weight and outputs her or his weight on Mercury, Venus, Jupiter, and Saturn. Use the values in this table.

Planet	**Multiply the Earth Weight by**
Mercury	0.4
Venus	0.9
Jupiter	2.5
Saturn	1.1

13. When you say you are 18 years old, you are really saying that the Earth has circled the Sun 18 times. Since other planets take fewer or more days than Earth to travel around the Sun, your age would be different on other planets. You can compute how old you are on other planets by the formula

$$y = \frac{x \times 365}{d}$$

where x is the age on Earth, y is the age on planet Y, and d is the number of Earth days the planet Y takes to travel around the Sun. Write an application that inputs the user's Earth age and print outs his or her age on Mercury, Venus, Jupiter, and Saturn. The values for d are listed in the table.

Planet	d = Approximate Number of Earth Days for This Planet to Travel around the Sun
Mercury	88
Venus	225
Jupiter	4,380
Saturn	10,767

14. Write an application to solve quadratic equations of the form

$$Ax^2 + Bx + C = 0$$

where the coefficients A, B, and C are real numbers. The two real number solutions are derived by the formula

$$x = \frac{-B \pm \sqrt{B^2 - 4AC}}{2A}$$

For this exercise, you may assume that $A \neq 0$ and the relationship

$$B^2 \geq 4AC$$

holds, so there will be real number solutions for x.

15. Write an application that determines the number of days in a given semester. Input to the program is the year, month, and day information of the first and the last days of a semester. *Hint:* Create GregorianCalendar objects for the start and end dates of a semester and manipulate their DAY_OF_YEAR data.

16. Modify the Ch3FindDayOfWeek program by accepting the date information as a single string instead of accepting the year, month, and day information separately. The input string must be in the MM/dd/yyyy format. For example, July 4, 1776, is entered as 07/04/1776. There will be exactly two digits for the month and day and four digits for the year.

17. Write an application that accepts the unit weight of a bag of coffee in pounds and the number of bags sold and displays the total price of the sale, computed as

```
totalPrice        = unitWeight * numberOfUnits * 5.99;
totalPriceWithTax = totalPrice + totalPrice * 0.0725;
```

where 5.99 is the cost per pound and 0.0725 is the sales tax. Display the result in the following manner:

```
Number of bags sold:   32
     Weight per bag:   5 lb
    Price per pound:   $5.99
          Sales tax:   7.25%

        Total price:   $ 1027.884
```

Draw the program diagram.

18. If you invest P dollars at R percent interest rate compounded annually, in N years, your investment will grow to

$$P(1 + R/100)^N$$

dollars. Write an application that accepts P, R, and N and computes the amount of money earned after N years.

19. Leonardo Fibonacci of Pisa was one of the greatest mathematicians of the Middle Ages. He is perhaps most famous for the Fibonacci sequence, which can be applied to many diverse problems. One amusing application of the Fibonacci sequence is in finding the growth rate of rabbits. Suppose a pair of rabbits matures in 2 months and is capable of reproducing another pair every month after maturity. If every new pair has the same capability, how many pairs will there be after 1 year? (We assume here that no pairs die.) The table below shows the sequence for the first 7 months. Notice that at the end of the second month, the first pair matures and bears its first offspring in the third month, making the total two pairs.

Month No.	Number of Pairs
1	1
2	1
3	2
4	3
5	5
6	8
7	13

The Nth Fibonacci number in the sequence can be evaluated with the formula

$$F_N = \frac{1}{\sqrt{5}}\left[\left(\frac{1+\sqrt{5}}{2}\right)^N - \left(\frac{1-\sqrt{5}}{2}\right)^N\right]$$

Write an application that accepts N and displays F_N. Note that the result of computation using the Math class is double. You need to display it as an integer.

20. According to Newton's universal law of gravitation, the force F between two bodies with masses M_1 and M_2 is computed as

$$F = k\left(\frac{M_1 M_2}{d^2}\right)$$

where d is the distance between the two bodies and k is a positive real number called the *gravitational constant*. The gravitational constant k is approximately equal to 6.67E-8 dyn $\cdot$ cm^2/g^2. Write an application that

(1) accepts the mass for two bodies in grams and the distance between the two bodies in centimeters and (2) computes the force F. Use the standard input and output, and format the output appropriately. For your information, the force between the Earth and the Moon is 1.984E25 dyn. The mass of the earth is 5.983E27 g, the mass of the moon is 7.347E25 g, and the distance between the two is 3.844E10 cm.

21. Dr. Caffeine's Law of Program Readability states that the degree of program readability R (whose unit is *mocha*) is determined as

$$R = k \cdot \frac{CT^2}{V^3}$$

where k is Ms. Latte's constant, C is the number of lines in the program that contain comments, T is the time spent (in minutes) by the programmer developing the program, and V is the number of lines in the program that contain nondescriptive variable names. Write an application to compute the program readability R. Ms. Latte's constant is 2.5E2 mocha $\text{lines}^2/\text{min}^2$. (*Note:* This is just for fun. Develop your own law, using various functions from the Math class.)

22. If the population of a country grows according to the formula

$$y = ce^{kx}$$

where y is the population after x years from the reference year, then we can determine the population of a country for a given year from two census figures. For example, given that a country with a population of 1,000,000 in 1970 grows to 2,000,000 by 1990, we can predict the country's population in the year 2000. Here's how we do the computation. Letting x be the number of years after 1970, we obtain the constant c as 1,000,000 because

$$1{,}000{,}000 = ce^{k0} = c$$

Then we determine the value of k as

$$y = 1{,}000{,}000e^{kx}$$

$$\frac{2{,}000{,}000}{1{,}000{,}000} = e^{20k}$$

$$k = \frac{1}{20} \ln \frac{2{,}000{,}000}{1{,}000{,}000} \approx 0.03466$$

Finally we can predict the population in the year 2000 by substituting 0.03466 for k and 30 for x (2000 − 1970 = 30). Thus, we predict

$$y = 1{,}000{,}000e^{0.03466(30)} \approx 2{,}828{,}651$$

as the population of the country for the year 2000. Write an application that accepts five input values—year A, population in year A, year B, population in year B, and year C—and predict the population for year C.

23. In Section 3.9, we use the formula

$$MR = \frac{AR}{12}$$

to derive the monthly interest rate from a given annual interest rate, where MR is the monthly interest rate and AR is the annual interest rate (expressed in a fractional value such as 0.083). This annual interest rate AR is called the *stated annual interest rate* to distinguish it from the *effective annual interest rate,* which is the true cost of a loan. If the stated annual interest rate is 9 percent, for example, then the effective annual interest rate is actually 9.38 percent. Naturally, the rate that the financial institutions advertise more prominently is the stated interest rate. The loan calculator program in Section 3.9 treats the annual interest rate that the user enters as the stated annual interest rate. If the input is the effective annual interest rate, then we compute the monthly rate as

$$MR = (1 + EAR)^{1/12} - 1$$

where EAR is the effective annual interest rate. The difference between the stated and effective annual interest rates is negligible only when the loan amount is small or the loan period is short. Modify the loan calculator program so that the interest rate that the user enters is treated as the effective annual interest rate. Run the original and modified loan calculator programs, and compare the differences in the monthly and total payments. Use loan amounts of 1, 10, and 50 million dollars with loan periods of 10, 20, and 30 years and annual interest rates of 0.07, 0.10, and 0.18 percent, respectively. Try other combinations also.

Visit several websites that provide a loan calculator for computing a monthly mortgage payment (one such site is the financial page at **www.cnn.com**). Compare your results to the values computed by the websites you visited. Determine whether the websites treat the input annual interest rate as stated or effective.

Development Exercises

For the following exercises, use the incremental development methodology to implement the program. For each exercise, identify the program tasks, create a design document with class descriptions, and draw the program diagram. Map out the development steps at the start. State any assumptions you must make about the input. Present any design alternatives and justify your selection. Be sure to perform adequate testing at the end of each development step.

24. Develop an application that reads a purchase price and an amount tendered and then displays the change in dollars, quarters, dimes, nickels, and pennies. Two input values are entered in cents, for example, 3480 for $34.80 and 70 for $0.70. Display the output in the following format:

```
 Purchase Price:     $ 34.80
Amount Tendered:     $ 40.00

 Your change is:     $ 5.20

                     5 one-dollar bill(s)
                     0 quarter(s)
                     2 dime(s)
                     0 nickel(s)
                     0 penn(y/ies)

Thank you for your business. Come back soon.
```

Notice the input values are to be entered in cents (int data type), but the echo printed values must be displayed with decimal points (float data type).

25. MyJava Coffee Outlet runs a catalog business. It sells only one type of coffee beans, harvested exclusively in the remote area of Irian Jaya. The company sells the coffee in 2-lb bags only, and the price of a single 2-lb bag is $5.50. When a customer places an order, the company ships the order in boxes. The boxes come in three sizes: the large box holds 20 bags of 2 lb, the medium 10 bags, and the small 5 bags. The cost of a large box is $1.80; a medium box, $1.00; and a small box, $0.60. The order is shipped using the least number of boxes. For example, the order of 52 bags will be shipped in two boxes, one large and one small. Develop an application that computes the total cost of an order. Display the output in the following format:

```
Number of Bags Ordered: 52 - $ 286.00

Boxes Used:
            2 Large  - $3.60
            1 Medium - $1.00
            1 Small  - $0.60

Your total cost is: $ 291.20
```

26. Repeat Exercise 25, but this time, accept the date when the order is placed and display the expected date of arrival. The expected date of arrival is two weeks (14 days) from the date of order. The order date is entered as a single string in the MM/dd/yyyy format. For example, November 1, 2004 is entered as 11/01/2004. There will be exactly two digits each for the

month and day and four digits for the year. Display the output in the following format:

```
Number of Bags Ordered: 52 - $ 286.00

Boxes Used:
            2 Large  - $3.60
            1 Medium - $1.00
            1 Small  - $0.60

Your total cost is: $ 291.20

Date of Order:                 November 1, 2004
Expected Date of Arrival:      November 15, 2004
```

27. Using a Turtle object from the galapagos package, draw three rectangles. Accept the width and the length of the smallest rectangle from the user. The middle and the largest rectangles are 40 and 80 percent larger, respectively, than the smallest rectangle. The galapagos package and its documentation are available at **www.drcaffeine.com.**

28. Develop a program that draws a bar chart using a Turtle object. Input five int values, and draw the vertical bars that represent the entered values in the following manner:

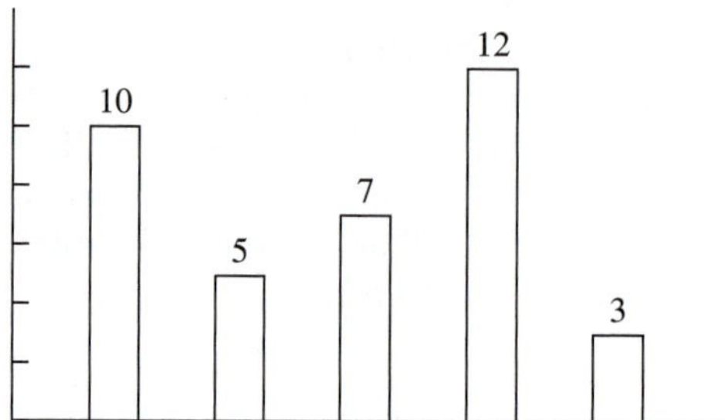

Your Turtle must draw everything shown in the diagram, including the axes and numbers.

4 Defining Your Own Classes—Part 1

Objectives

After you have read and studied this chapter, you should be able to

- Define a class with multiple methods and data members.
- Differentiate the local and instance variables.
- Define and use value-returning methods.
- Distinguish private and public methods.
- Distinguish private and public data members.
- Pass both primitive data and objects to a method.

Introduction

So far we have been using only standard classes such as System, String, and others when we wrote programs. For a basic program, that is fine. However, we need to to learn how to write programs using our own classes (in addition to using the standard classes) when the programs become large and complex. In this chapter, we learn the basics of how to define our own classes. And, in Chapter 7, we will cover more advanced topics on defining classes.

4.1 First Example: Defining and Using a Class

The most economical and effective means of on-campus transportation is without doubt a bicycle. Suppose we want to develop a program that tracks the bicycles by assigning to them some form of identification number along with the relevant information, such the owner's name and phone number. To develop such a Java program, we need to design many different types of objects. For example, we need objects to handle input, output, data storage, and other computational tasks. Among the many types of objects necessary for this program, we will design a core class that models a bicycle. There's no such Bicycle class among the standard classes, of course, so we need to define one ourselves. We will learn how to define the Bicycle class in this section. We will start with a very simplistic Bicycle class. Using this class, we can only assign and retrieve the owner's name. Before we look inside the Bicycle class and explain how the class is defined, let's first look at how we might use it in our program. The following sample program creates two Bicycle objects, assigns the owners' names to them, and displays the information:

```
class BicycleRegistration {

    public static void main(String[] args) {

        Bicycle bike1, bike2;
        String owner1, owner2;

        bike1 = new Bicycle( );   //Create and assign values to bike1
        bike1.setOwnerName("Adam Smith");

        bike2 = new Bicycle( );   //Create and assign values to bike2
        bike2.setOwnerName("Ben Jones");

        //Output the information
        owner1 = bike1.getOwnerName( );
        owner2 = bike2.getOwnerName( );

        System.out.println(owner1 + " owns a bicycle.");
        System.out.println(owner2 + " also owns a bicycle.");
    }
}
```

programmer-defined classes

Here's the definition of the Bicycle class. To distinguish it from the standard classes, we call the Bicycle and other classes we define ***programmer-defined classes***.

```
class Bicycle {

    // Data Member
    private String ownerName;

    //Constructor: Initialzes the data member
    public Bicycle( ) {
        ownerName = "Unknown";
    }

    //Returns the name of this bicycle's owner
    public String getOwnerName( ) {
        return ownerName;
    }

    //Assigns the name of this bicycle's owner
    public void setOwnerName(String name) {

        ownerName = name:
    }
}
```

The dependency diagram between the two classes is as follows:

When this program is executed, we get the following output on the standard output window:

```
Adam Smith owns a bicycle.
Ben Jones also owns a bicycle.
```

This main class should look very familiar to all of us. The key difference lies in the use of the Bicycle class instead of the standard classes we have been using so far. The way we use the Bicycle class is the same. For example, we create a Bicycle object bike2 by calling the new operator, and we assign the name of its owner by executing

```
bike2 = new Bicycle( );
bike2.setOwnerName("Ben Jones");
```

To get the name of the owner of bike2, we write

```
bike2.getOwnerName()
```

And we can assign the returned value to a variable if we write

```
String owner2;
...
owner2 = bike2.getOwnerName();
```

Although it is not a requirement, we will save one class definition per file to keep things simple. For the file name, we will use the name of the class followed by the java suffix. So, we save the Bicycle class in a file named Bicycle.java.

Things to Remember

Save one class definition per file. Use the name of the class followed by the suffix java as the file name. Follow this rule to avoid any unnecessary complications.

For this sample program, we have created two classes—BicycleRegistration (the main class) and Bicycle. So there are two source files for this program.

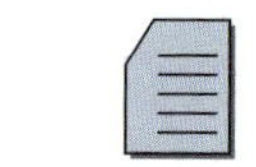

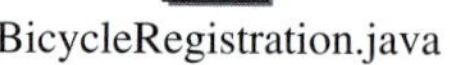

BicycleRegistration.java Bicycle.java

The Bicycle Class

Now let's study the Bicycle class. Table 4.1 lists the three methods of the Bicycle class and their description.

Here's a template for the Bicycle class declaration:

```
class Bicycle {

    //data members

    //methods

}
```

Table 4.1 The three methods of the Bicycle class. The first method is called a constructor

Method	Parameter	Description
Bicycle	None	Initializes the owner's name to Unassigned.
getOwnerName	None	Returns the owner's name.
setOwnerName	Name of the owner (string)	Assigns the bicycle owner's name to the passed value.

The class declaration begins with the reserved word class followed by the name. Any valid identifier that is not a reserved word can be used as the class name.

We define the three methods inside the class declaration. But before we can provide the method definitions, we need to consider the data members of the Bicycle class. Remember, in Section 1.3, we stated that data members of a class are the data values associated with the class or instances of the class, such as the current balance of an Account object. What would be the data members of Bicycle objects? We need to know the owner's name of every Bicycle object, so we'll define one data member to store the owner's name. The data members of a class are declared within the class declaration. Here's how we define the data member ownerName of the Bicycle class:

```
class Bicycle {

    private String ownerName;

    //definitions for the constructor,
    //getOwnerName, and setOwnerName methods come here
}
```

The ownerName data member is an instance variable (we will learn how to declare class constants later in this chapter and class variables in Chap. 7). Remember that, in Section 1.3, we defined an instance variable as the data member we associate to an individual instance and whose value can change over time. In other words, each instance of the class will have its own copy. After the two Bicycle objects are created and assigned their respective names by program, we have the following memory state:

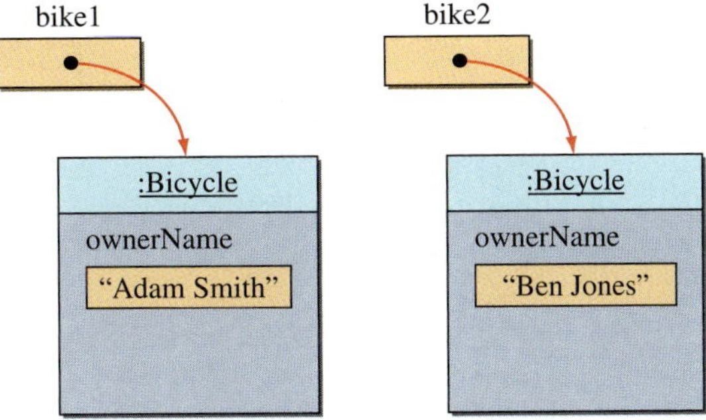

The syntax for the data member declaration is

```
<modifier-list> <data type> <name> ;
```

where <modifier-list> designates different characteristics of the data member, <data type> the class name or primitive data type, and <name> the name of the data member. Here's how the general syntax corresponds to the actual declaration:

Data Type

Modifier **Name**

```
private   String   ownerName ;
```

accessibility modifier

In this example, the data member has one modifier named private. This modifier is called an ***accessibility modifier***, or a *visibility modifier*, and it restricts who can have a direct access to the data member. If the modifier is private, then only the methods defined in the class can access it directly. We will provide a more detailed discussion of the accessibility modifiers in Section 4.6. For now, it suffices to remember that data members are declared private for the most part.

Now that the necessary data member is taken care of, we are ready to define the three methods. We start with the setOwnerName method, which is declared as

```
public void setOwnerName(String name) {

   ownerName = name;

}
```

The syntax for defining a method, as given in Chapter 2, is

```
<modifiers> <return type> <method name> ( <parameters> ) {

  <statements>

}
```

The following diagram shows how the components in the general syntax correspond to the actual elements in the setOwnerName method:

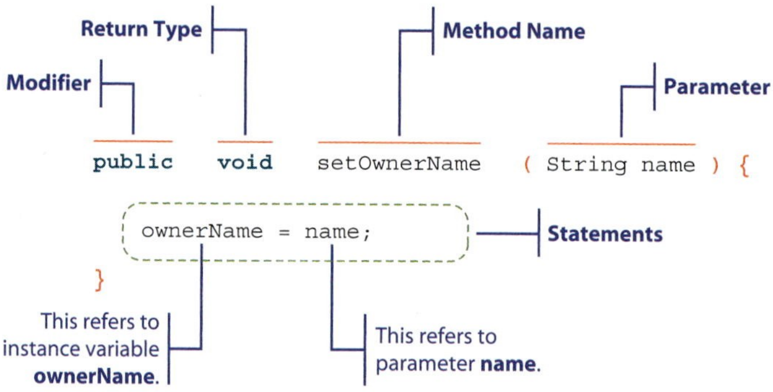

void method

We explained in Chapter 1 that methods may or may not return a value. A method that does not return a value, such as this setOwnerName method, is declared as void. It is called a ***void method***. The accessibility modifier for the setOwnerName method is declared as public. This means the program that uses the Bicycle class can access, or call, this method. It is possible (and could be useful) to declare a method as private. If a method is declared as private, then it cannot be called from the program that uses the class. It can only be called from the other methods of the same class. For now we will limit our discussion to public methods. Here we declare all methods as public because we want the programs that use the Bicycle class to be able to call them. We will go over the use of private methods later in the chapter.

The getOwnerName method is defined as follows:

```
public String getOwnerName( ) {

    return ownerName;

}
```

The following diagram shows how the components in the general syntax correspond to the actual elements in the getOwnerName method:

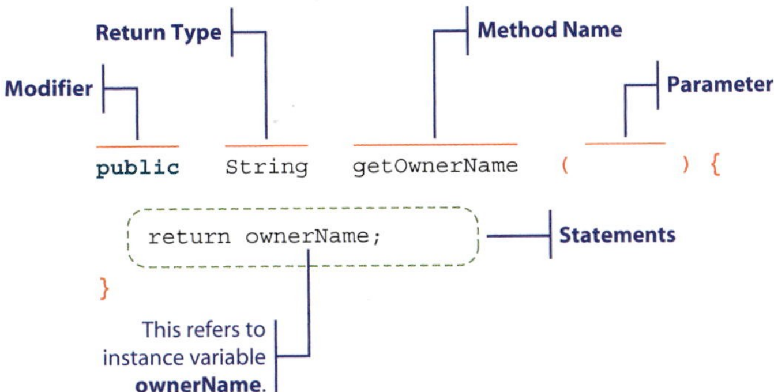

value-returning method

This is a ***value-returning method***. When this method is called, it returns a value to the caller. The getOwnerName method returns a string value—the value of instance variable ownerName—so its return type is declared as String. A value-returning method must include a return statement of the format

return statement syntax

```
return <expression> ;
```

The data type of <expression> must be compatible with the declared return type of the method. For example, if the return type is int, then the data type of the returned value must be compatible with int (data types int, short, and byte are all compatible with int). Data type compatibilites are explained in Section 3.2.

If a method returns a value, then we can include a call to the method in an expression itself. For example, instead of writing

```
Bicycle bike;
...

String owner = bike.getOwnerName( );
System.out.println(owner + "owns a bike.");
```

we can write

```
Bicycle bike;
...

System.out.println(bike.getOwnerName( ) + "owns a bike.");
```

accessor

mutator

A method that returns information about an object (such as who is the owner of a bicycle) is called an ***accessor***. The getOwnerName method is an accessor. An inverse of an accessor that sets a property of an object is called a ***mutator***. The setOwnerName method is a mutator. Accessors and mutators are commonly called *get* and *set methods,* respectively.

A value-returning method can include more than one return statement. The use of multiple return statements make sense only in the context of the control statements, which we will discuss in Chapters 5 and 6. We will be seeing examples of multiple return statements in these chapters.

constructor

The first method defined in the Bicycle class is a special method called a constructor. A ***constructor*** is a special method that is executed when a new instance of the class is created, that is, when the new operator is called. Here's the constructor for the Bicycle class:

```
public Bicycle( ) {

    ownerName = "Unassigned";
}
```

It follows the general syntax

```
public <class name> ( <parameters> ) {
   <statements>
}
```

where <class name> is the name of the class to which this constructor belongs. The following diagram shows how the components in the general syntax correspond to the actual elements in the constructor of the Bicycle class:

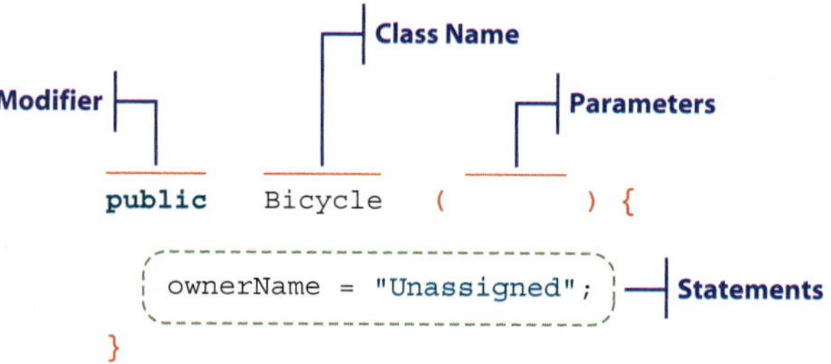

Notice that a constructor does not have a return type and, consequently, will never include a return statement. The modifier of a constructor does not have to be public, but non-public constructors are rarely used. This example shows no parameters, but it is very common to define a constructor with two or three parameters. We will see an example of a constructor that accepts two parameters in Section 4.5. Until then, we will define only a zero-parameter constructor.

The purpose of the Bicycle constructor is to initialize the data member to a value that reflects the state to which the real name is not yet assigned. Since a constructor is executed when a new instance is created, it is the most logical place

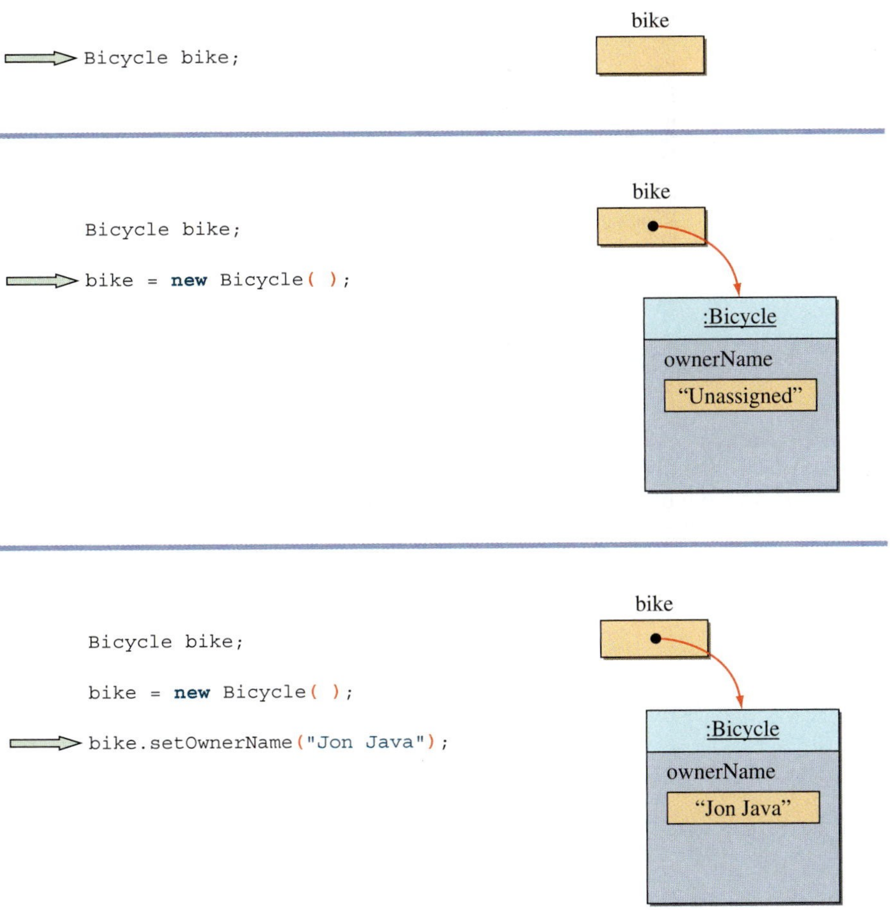

```
Bicycle bike;
```



```
Bicycle bike;

bike = new Bicycle( );
```



```
Bicycle bike;

bike = new Bicycle( );

bike.setOwnerName("Jon Java");
```


Figure 4.1 A sequence of state-of-memory diagrams that illustrate the effects of executing the constructor and the **setOwnerName** method of the **Bicycle** class.

to initialize the data members and perform any other initialization tasks. Figure 4.1 shows a sequence of state-of-memory diagrams illustrating the effects of executing the constructor and the setOwnerName method of the Bicycle class.

We stated earlier that the Bicycle class has three methods, of which one is a constructor. However, a constructor is distinct from other "regular" methods, so it is more common to state that the Bicycle class has one constructor and two methods.

Things to Remember

Instead of saying "a class has three methods including one constructor," it is more common to say "a class has one constructor and two methods." We will use the later expression in this book.

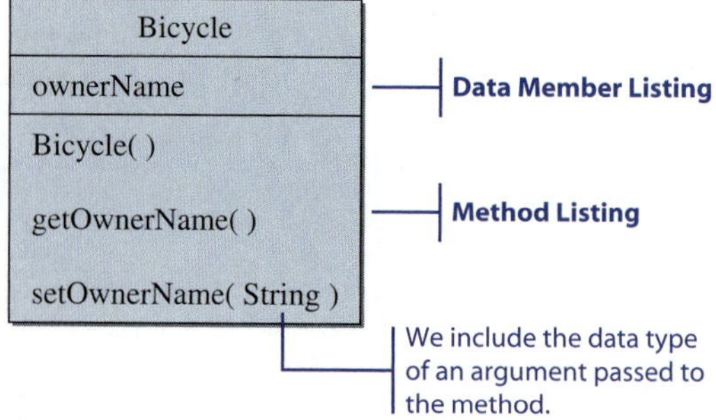

Figure 4.2 A class diagram of the **Bicycle** class with two methods and one data member.

We will provide a more detailed discussion on constructors in Section 4.5.

The class diagram that lists the data member, the constructor, and two methods of the Bicycle class is shown in Figure 4.2.

In listing the data members and methods of a class, we will use the following convention:

class listing convention

```
class <class name>  {

    // data members

    // constructor

    // methods

}
```

We list the data members first, then the constructor, and finally the methods. Within each group, we list elements in alphabetical order. Keep in mind that this convention for grouping elements and ordering them within a group is for our convenience. The Java compiler does not care how we list the data members and methods.

Things to Remember

The Java compiler does not care how we order the methods and data members in the class declaration. We adopt the listing convention to make the class declaration easier for us to follow.

Compiling and Running BicycleRegistration

Up until now, when we ran the sample programs, we simply compiled and executed the main class. That's all we need to do because the main class is the only class we created for the sample programs. But for this sample program, we have created two classes—BicycleRegistration (the main class) and Bicycle. So there are two source files for this program.

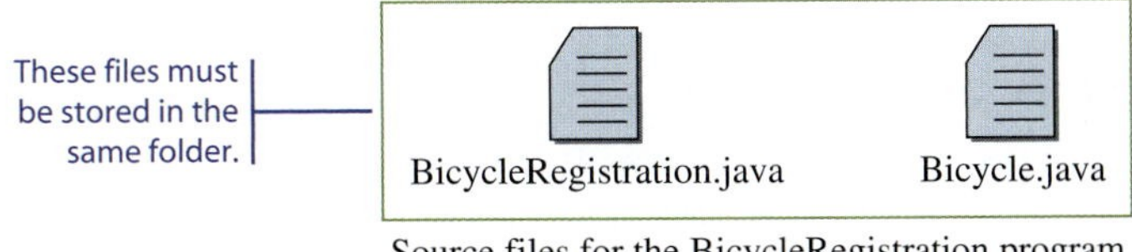
These files must be stored in the same folder.
BicycleRegistration.java
Bicycle.java
Source files for the BicycleRegistration program

From now on, we will use the name of the main class to refer the whole program. To run the BicycleRegistration program, we must first compile the two source files and then run the main class. Here are the steps we follow to run this sample program (we will illustrate the steps using the minimalist approach, see App. A):

1. Compile the Bicycle class.

```
javac Bicycle.java
```

2. Compile the BicycleRegistration class.

```
javac BicycleRegistration.java
```

3. Run the BicycleRegistration class.

```
java BicycleRegistration
```

There is one last thing to remember. The way the classes are written now, the easiest way to manage a program that includes multiple programmer-defined classes is to save the source files in the same folder (directory). We will learn how to organize classes into a package in Chapter 7 so we can manage the organization of classes in a more effective manner. Until then, just remember to place all sources files for a program in the same folder. If you don't do this, the Java compiler and interpreter may not be able to compile and run the program.

Things to Remember

Place all source files for a program in the same folder (directory).

It is not necessary to create a separate folder for each program, though. In other words, one folder can contain source files for multiple programs. For example, we could create one folder to place all source files for this chapter's sample code. However, we recommend that students create a separate folder for each programming assignment or lab project for easy management.

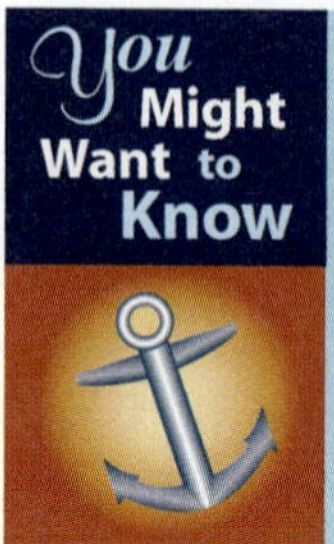

The class declaration can be preceded with the accessibility modifier **public** or **private.** For now, we do not use any accessibility modifier for the class declaration. We will discuss the issue when we discuss a package organization in Chapter 7.

1. Extend the Bicycle class by adding the second data member tagNo of type String. Declare this data member as private.
2. Add a new method to the Bicycle class that assigns a tag number. This method will be called as follows:

```
Bicycle bike;
bike = new Bicycle( );
...
bike.setTagNo("2004-134R");
```

3. Add a another method to the Bicycle class that returns the bicycle's tag number. This method will be called as follows:

```
Bicycle bike;
bike = new Bicycle( );
...
String tag = bike.getTagNo( );
```

4.2 Second Example: Defining and Using Multiple Classes

Let's write a second sample program to get more practice in defining classes. In this example, we will define a new class named Account. An Account object has the name of the owner (String) and the balance (double). We have two methods—add and deduct—to deposit to and withdraw money from the account. There are methods to set the initial balance and retrieve the current balance. These two methods are named setInitialBalance and getCurrentBalance. Finally, we have an accessor and mutator for the account owner's name—getOwnerName and setOwnerName.

The second sample program uses the Bicycle class from Section 4.1 and the Account class we define shortly in this section. Here's the second sample program:

```
class SecondMain {
    //This sample program uses both the Bicycle and Account classes

    public static void main(String[] args) {

        Bicycle bike;
        Account acct;

        String  myName = "Jon Java";

        bike = new Bicycle( );
        bike.setOwnerName(myName);

        acct = new Account( );
        acct.setOwnerName(myName);
        acct.setInitialBalance(250.00);

        acct.add(25.00);
        acct.deduct(50);

        //Output some information
        System.out.println(bike.getOwnerName() + " owns a bicycle and");
        System.out.println("has $ " + acct.getCurrentBalance() +
                                                    " left in the bank");

    }
}
```

This program creates one Bicycle object and one Account object, sets their owner name to Jon Java, initializes the account balance to $250.00, adds $25.00 to the account, deducts $50.00 from the account, and finally prints out some information of bike and acct objects. The program diagram is as follows:

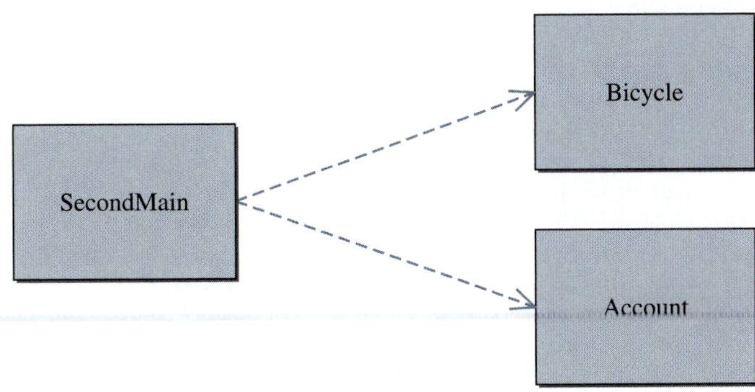

We are using the Bicycle class from Section 4.1 without modification, so we only have to consider defining the Account class. There are two data members for the class, one to store the owner's name and another to maintain the account balance. We have the following declaration for the two data members:

```
class Account {

    private String ownerName;

    private double balance;

    //constructor and method declarations come here

}
```

The set and get methods for the owner's name are identical to those defined for the Bicycle class. The add and deduct methods modifiy the balance by adding or deducting the passed amount. They are defined as follows:

```
public void add(double amt) {
    balance = balance + amt;
}

public void deduct(double amt) {
    balance = balance - amt;
}
```

The setInitialBalance and getCurrentBalance methods are similarly defined as the other set and get methods. Here's the complete definition of the Account class:

```
class Account {

    // Data Members
    private String ownerName;

    private double balance;

    //Constructor
    public Account( ) {
        ownerName = "Unassigned";
        balance = 0.0;
    }

    //Adds the passed amount to the balance
    public void add(double amt) {
        balance = balance + amt;
    }

    //Deducts the passed amount from the balance
    public void deduct(double amt) {
        balance = balance - amt;
    }
```

```
    //Returns the current balance of this account
    public double getCurrentBalance( ) {
        return balance;
    }

    //Returns the name of this account's owner
    public String getOwnerName( ) {

        return ownerName;
    }

    //Sets the initial balance of this account
    public void setInitialBalance(double bal) {
        balance = bal;
    }

    //Assigns the name of this account's owner
    public void setOwnerName(String name) {

        ownerName = name;
    }
}
```

Figure 4.3 shows a class diagram of the Account class.

The second sample program is composed of three classes (we are not counting the standard classes).

SecondMain Program

We need to compile the three classes before we can run the program. However, we do not have to compile all three classes every time we want to run the program. For example, if the Bicycle class is already compiled and we are not making any changes to it, then there's no need to compile the class again. (*Note:* We are assuming here that both programs are placed in the same directory. If the second program is in a separate folder, then you need to copy the bytecode file Bicycle.class to this folder.)

Notice the second call to the deduct method from the main method of SecondMain, which is

```
acct.deduct(10);
```

but the parameter for the deduct method is declared as type double. This call is valid because we are passing a value that is assignment-compatible to the double data type. We will elaborate on this topic in Section 4.3.

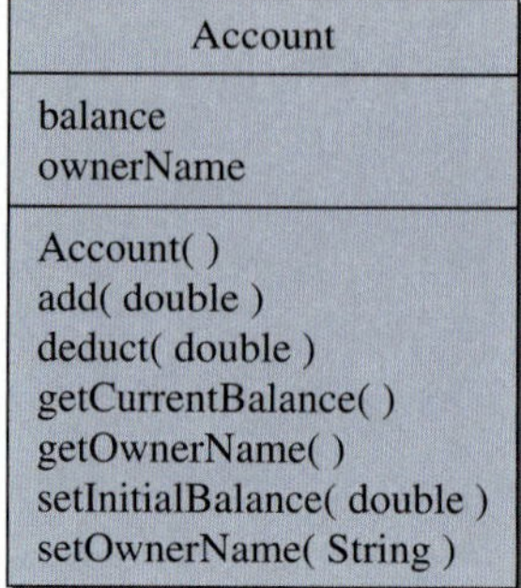

Figure 4.3 A class diagram of the **Account** class with two data members, one constructor, and six methods.

1. What is the output from the following code fragment?

```
Account acct;
acct = new Account( );
acct.setInitialBalance(250);
acct.add(20);

System.out.println("Balance: "
                   + acct.getCurrentBalance());
```

2. Write a code fragment to declare and create two Account objects named acc1 and acct2. Initialize the balance to $300 and $500, respectively. Set the name of owner for both accounts to John Doe.

4.3 Matching Arguments and Parameters

Consider the following sample class that includes a method named compute. This method has three parameters—two int and one double.

```
class Demo {
   . . .

   public void compute(int i, int j, double x) {

      //method body
      //the actual statements in the body
      //are irrelevant to the discussion

   }

   . . .
}
```

When we call the compute method, we must pass three values. The values we pass must be assignment-compatible with the corresponding parameters. For example, it is not okay to pass a double value to an int parameter. Here are some valid calls from the main method:

```
class MyMain {

    public static void main(String[] arg) {

        Demo demo = new Demo();

        int i, k, m;

        i = 12;
        k = 10;
        m = 14;

        demo.compute(3, 4, 5.5);

        demo.compute(i, k, m);

        demo.compute(m, 20, 40);
    }
}
```

In the statement

```
demo.compute(m, 20, 40);
```

argument

parameter

the values m, 20, and 40 are called arguments. An ***argument*** is a value we pass to a method, and the value is assigned to the corresponding parameters. A ***parameter*** is a placeholder in the called method to hold the value of a passed argument. The arguments and parameters are matched in left-to-right order. As long as the data type of an argument is assignment-compatible to the corresponding parameter, the call is valid.

The identifier we use for an argument has no relation to the identifier used for the corresponding parameter. In the statement

```
demo.compute(i, k, m);
```

the fact that the same identifier i is used for both the first parameter and the first argument has no significance. They are two distinct and separate variables, as shown in Figure 4.4. The figure also shows how the matching is done.

Things to Remember

A parameter receives the value of a corresponding argument. Because a parameter is like a placeholder that will not hold a value until an argument is passed to it, a parameter is called a formal parameter and an argument an actual parameter.

```
Demo demo = new Demo( );

int i = 5;
int k = 14;

demo.compute( i, k, 20 );
```

Passing side

```
class Demo {

  public void compute(int i, int j, double x) {
    ...
  }
}
```

Receiving side

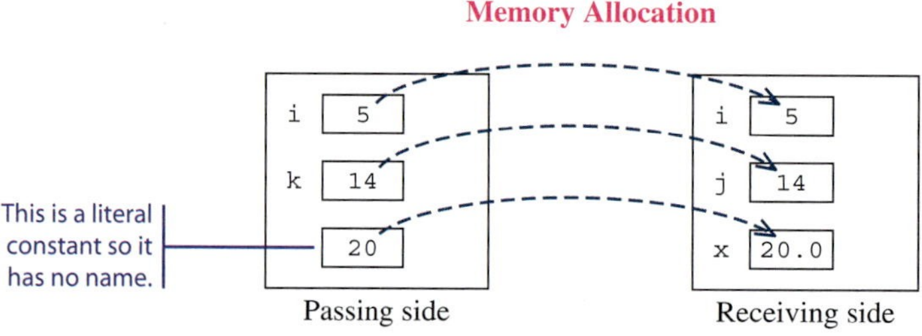

Figure 4.4 This diagram illustrates how the argument values are assigned, or passed, to the matching parameters.

4.4 Passing Objects to a Method

When calling the methods of the Bicycle and Account classes, we passed a numerical value or a String. In this section, we study how to pass an object when calling a method. Since a String is an object, in a sense, we actually know to pass an object as an argument to a method. However, a String is treated much as a primitive datum for the most part, so we will cover this topic using instances of our own class.

First, we define the Student class. A Student object has a name (String) and an email (String). Here's the definition:

```
class Student {

    //Data Members
    private String name;

    private string email;
```

```
    //Constructor
    public Student( ) {
        name = "Unassigned";
        email = "Unassigned";
    }

    //Returns the email of this student
    public String getEmail( ) {

        return email;
    }

    //Returns the name of this student
    public String getName( ) {

        return name;
    }

    //Assigns the email of this student
    public void setEmail(String address) {

        email = address;
    }

    //Assigns the name of this student
    public void setName(String studentName) {

        name = studentName;
    }
}
```

Student
name email
Student( ) getEmail( ) getName( ) setEmail(String) setName(String)

Then we define the LibraryCard class. A LibraryCard object is owned by a Student, and it records the number of books being checked out. Here's the definition:

```
class LibraryCard {

    // Data Members

    //student owner of this card
    private Student owner;

    //number of books borrowed
    private int borrowCnt;

    //Constructor
    public LibraryCard( ) {
        owner = null;
        borrowCnt = 0;
    }
```

LibraryCard
owner borrowCnt
LibraryCard( ) checkOut(int) getNumberOfBooks( ) getOwnerName( ) setOwner(Student) toString( )

```
    //numOfBooks are checked out
    public void checkOut(int numOfBooks) {
        borrowCnt = borrowCnt + numOfBooks;
    }

    //Returns the number of books borrowed
    public int getNumberOfBooks( ) {
        return borrowCnt;
    }

    //Returns the name of the owner of this card
    public String getOwnerName( ) {
        return owner.getName( );
    }

    //Sets owner of this card to student
    public void setOwner(Student student) {
        owner = student;
    }

    //Returns the string representation of this card
    public String toString( ) {
        return  "Owner Name:     " + owner.getName( ) + "\n" +
                "      Email:    " + owner.getEmail( ) + "\n" +
                "Books Borrowed: " + borrowCnt;
    }
}
```

Notice that we initialize the data member owner to null in the constructor. The value of null means that owner is pointing to no object. The setOwner method must be called to assign a Student object. The method accepts a Student object as its parameter and sets the data member owner to this Student object.

The getOwnerName method returns the name of the owner. It is defined as

```
public String getOwnerName( ) {

   return owner.getName( );
}
```

Because the data member owner refers to a Student object, we can get the name of this student by calling its getName method.

The toString method is a method that returns a string representation of an object. Because an object can have a nested structure (e.g., an object's data member points to an instance of another class, the data members of this instance point to instances of other classes, and so forth), it is convenient for those who use the class to have a quick way to get printable information of an instance. Without such a toString method, the programmer who uses the class must write a code to fetch the values of the data members individually. This can be quite tedious. With the toString method, she can display information of an instance by calling just one method toString.

The power of being able to pass an object to a method comes in handy when we want multiple objects to share the same object. For example, suppose a single student owns two library cards (say, one for the general library and another for the engineering library). Then we can make the data member owner of two LibraryCard objects to refer to the same Student object. Here's one such program:

```
class Librarian {

    public static void main(String[] args) {

        Student     student;
        LibraryCard card1, card2;

        student = new Student( );
        student.setName("Jon Java");
        student.setEmail("jj@javauniv.edu");

        card1 = new LibraryCard( );
        card1.setOwner(student);
        card1.checkOut(3);

        card2 = new LibraryCard( );
        card2.setOwner(student); //the same student is the owner
                                 //of the second card, too

        System.out.println("Card1 Info:");
        System.out.println(card1.toString() + "\n");

        System.out.println("Card2 Info:");
        System.out.println(card2.toString() + "\n");
    }
}
```

In this program, we create one Student object. Then we create two LibraryCard objects. For each of these LibraryCard objects, we pass the same student when calling their setOwner methods:

```
card1.setOwner(student);
...
card2.setOwner(student);
```

After the setOwner method of card2 is called in the main method, we have the state of memory as shown in Figure 4.5.

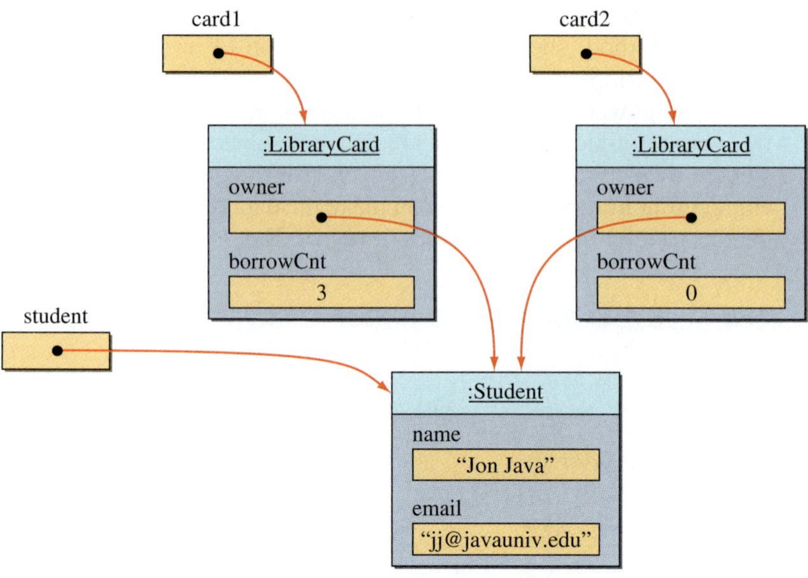

Figure 4.5 The state where the data members of two objects (of **LibraryCard**) are pointing to the same object (of **Student**).

It is critical to realize that when we say *pass an object to a method,* we are not sending a copy of an object, but rather a reference to the object. Figure 4.6 shows how the passing of an object is done.

Things to Remember

When we pass an object to a method, we are actually passing the address, or reference, of an object to the method.

You Might Want to Know

It is possible to return the *Student* object itself by defining the following method:

```
public Student getOwner( ) {

   return owner;
}
```

We will discuss such a method that returns an instance of a programmer-defined class in Chapter 7.

```
LibraryCard card2;

card2 = new LibraryCard( );

card2.setOwner(student);
```

Passing side

```
class LibraryCard {

 public void setOwner(Student student) {
     owner = student;
 }
}
```

Receiving side

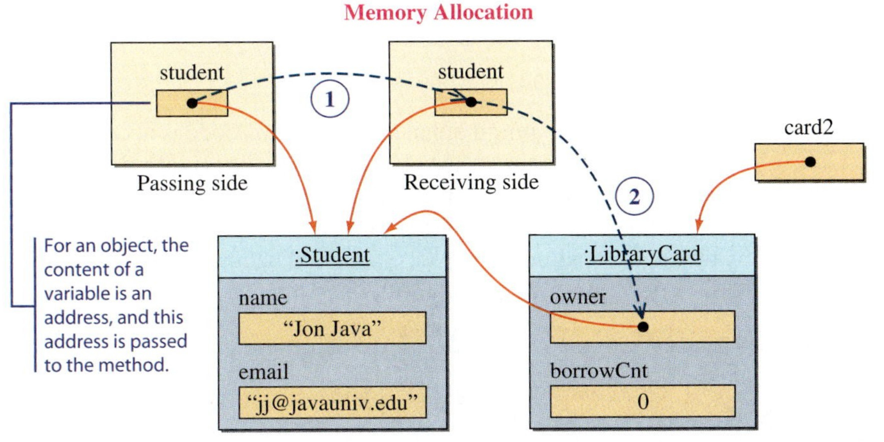

Figure 4.6 This diagram illustrates how an object is passed as an argument to a method.

4.5 Constructors

We provide more detailed coverage of the constructors in this section. The constructors we have defined so far accept no arguments. These constructors set the data members to some initial values. For example, the constructor for the Bicycle class in Section 4.1 initializes the value of owner (String) to Unassigned. For this particular Bicycle class, such a simplistic constructor is adequate. However, most cases require the constructors that accept one or more arguments. In fact, the way we defined the constructor for the Account class in Section 4.2 could lead to potential problems. In this section, we describe the use of constructors that accept one or more arguments, and we show how this solves the potential problems of the Account class.

Let's begin by reviewing the Account class from Section 4.2. We will identify some potential problems and present a new constructor as a solution to rectify them.

Consider the following code:

```
Account acct;
acct = new Account( );

acct.setInitialBalance(500);
acct.setInitialBalance(300);
```

What is the effect of such code? It is logically inconsistent to initialize the starting balance more than once. It should be called exactly one, but there is no such Java language feature that puts constraints on the number of times the setInitialBalance method can be called. The existence of this method is a problem, and we can remove it from the Account class by defining a constructor that sets the initial balance to a specified amount.

Now consider the following code:

```
Account acct;
acct = new Account( );

acct.add(200.00);
```

If an account can have the initial balance of zero, this code is acceptable. But if there is a rule that says, for example, an account must have the initial balance of $25 or more, then the setInitialBalance method must be called first to initialize the balance to 25.00 or more before any transactions (add or deduct) take place. This problem can also be solved by the same constructor that sets the initial balance to a specified amount.

Here's a new constructor that eliminates the two problems in one stroke:

```
public Account(double startingBalance) {

    ownerName = "Unassigned";
    balance = startingBalance;
}
```

Once this constructor is defined, there is no longer a need for the setInitialBalance method, so we can safely remove it from the class defintion. Only the add and deduct methods affect the balance after an object is created.

After the old constructor is replaced by this new constructor, we must create an instance by passing one argument when calling the new operator. For example, the code

```
Account acct;

acct = new Account(500.00);
```

will create a new Account object with its starting balance set to $500. We can no longer create an instance by writing

```
Account acct;

acct = new Account( );
```

because there is no matching constructor anymore.

Instead of this one-parameter constructor, we can define a constructor that accepts the name of the owner also, so that it, too, can be initialized at the time of object creation. Here's how we define the two-parameter constructor:

```
public Account(String name, double startingBalance) {

   ownerName = name;
   balance = startingBalance;
}
```

This is the constructor we will include in the modified Account class. With this two-parameter constructor, here's how we create an Account object:

```
Account acct;

acct = new Account("John Smith", 500.00);
```

Notice that, even with this new constructor, we will keep the setOwnerName method in the class because we want to be able to change the name of the owner after the account is created.

From the three different constructors possible for the Account class, we have selected the two-parameter constructor to include in the class. Actually, it is possible to include all three constructors in the definition of the Account class. But until we learn how to define multiple constructors in Chapter 7, we will define exactly one constructor for our programmer-defined classes.

Hints, & Tips, Pitfalls

It is possible to define more than one constructor to a class. Multiple contructors are called *overloaded constructors*. It is almost always a good idea to define multiple constructors to a class. But to keep things simple, we will manage with one constructor per class until Chapter 7.

We are now ready to list the complete definition. Here's the second version of the Account class (for the actual class name we will use AccountVer2 to avoid confusion when discussing different versions of the class definition):

```
class AccountVer2 {

   // Data Members
   private String ownerName;

   private double balance;

   //Constructor
   public AccountVer2(String name, double startingBalance) {
```

```
            ownerName = name;
            balance = startingBalance;
        }

        //Adds the passed amount to the balance
        public void add(double amt) {
            balance = balance + amt;
        }

        //Deducts the passed amount from the balance
        public void deduct(double amt) {
            balance = balance - amt;
        }

        //Returns the current balance of this account
        public double getCurrentBalance( ) {
            return balance;
        }

        //Returns the name of this account's owner
        public String getOwnerName( ) {

            return ownerName;
        }

        //Assigns the name of this account's owner
        public void setOwnerName(String name) {

            ownerName = name;
        }
    }
```

Default Constructor

As a design guideline, we strongly recommend to include constructors to programmer-defined classes, as we have been doing from the beginning of the chapter. However, it is not a requirement to define a constructor explicitly in a class. If no constructor is defined for a class, then the Java compiler will automatically include a default constructor. A ***default constructor*** is a constructor that accepts no arguments and has no statements in its body. For example, if we omit a constructor from the Bicycle class, a default constructor

default constructor

```
public Bicycle( ) {

}
```

will be added to the class by the compiler to ensure its instances can be created.

Even though a default constructor is automatically added by the compiler, we should never rely on it. We should always define our own constructor so that we can initialize the data members properly and carry out any other initialization tasks. This ensures an object is created in a valid state (such as setting the balance of an account to more than the minimum).

Design Guidelines

Always define a constructor and initialize data members fully in the constructor so an object will be created in a valid state.

Once we define our own constructor, no default constructor is added. This means that once the constructor, such as

```
public Account(String name, double startingBalance ) {

    ownerName = name;
    balance = startingBalance;
}
```

is added to the Account class, we will no longer be able to create a Account object anymore by executing

```
Account acct;
acct = new Account( );
```

because no matching constructor can be found in the class.

Things to Remember

Once a programmer has added an explicitly defined constructor to a class, no default constructor will be added to the class by the compiler.

1. Which of the following constructors are invalid?

```
public int ClassA(int one) {
    ...
}
public ClassB(int one, int two) {
    ...
}
void ClassC( ) {
    ...
}
```

2. What is the main purpose of a constructor?
3. Complete the following constructor.

```
class Test {
   private double score;

   public Test(double val) {
      //assign the value of parameter to
      //the data member
   }
}
```

4.6 Information Hiding and Visibility Modifiers

The modifiers public and private designate the accessibility, or visibility, of data members and methods. Although it is valid in Java, we do not recommend that programmers, especially beginners, leave out the visibility modifier in declaring data members and methods. From the object-oriented design standpoint, we recommend that you always designate the data members and methods as private or public. We explain how to use these modifiers in this section. But before we get into the details, we first discuss the object-oriented design philosophy behind these modifiers.

Consider a mobile robot as an example. What kind of behavior do we expect from a mobile robot? Behaviors such as moving forward, turning, stopping, and changing speed come to mind easily. When we define a class, say, MobileRobot, we will include public methods such as move, turn, stop, and changeSpeed. These methods are declared public so the programmers who use a MobileRobot object can call these methods from their programs. We call these programmers ***client programmers*** and their programs *client programs*.

client programmers

Now let's assume that the move method accepts an integer argument as a distance to travel in meters. Suppose this mobile robot has three wheels with a motor attached to each of the left and right rear wheels. The robot has no steering mechanism, so the turning is done by rotating the left and right rear wheels at different speeds. For example, by rotating the left wheel faster than the right wheel, the robot will make a gradual left turn. To move forward, the robot must send the same amount of power to the two motors. While the motors are rotating, the robot must constantly monitor the distance traveled and stop the motors when the designated distance is traveled.

The MobileRobot class includes methods such as rotate to rotate the motor and readDistance to read the distance traveled. These methods are declared private because they are internal details that need to be hidden from the client programmers. From our perspective as a client programmer, all we care is that the mobile robot exhibits the behavior of moving the desired distance when we call its move method. We do not care what's going on inside. This is called ***information hiding***. It is not our concern how many motors the robot has or what type of mechanism is employed to move the robot. We say the mobile robot ***encapsulates*** the internal workings.

information hiding

encapsulation

This encapsulation mechanism allows easier modification of program code. For example, suppose the motion mechanism of a mobile robot is modified to a single motor and rack-and-pinion steering. Both wheels are now connected to a single axle, and the motor turns this axle (via gears). The internal mechanism has changed, but this will not affect the client programs. Calling the move method still exhibits the same behavior.

To implement its methods (both public and private), the MobileRobot class will necessarily include many data members, such as current speed, current direction, power levels of the motors, and so forth. These data members are internal details of the class because it is not a concern of the client programmers to know which and how many of them are defined in the class. As such, data members are declared as private.

In summary, behavior of the instances is implemented by public methods, while the internal details that must be hidden from the client programmers are implemented by private methods and private data members.

Design Guidelines

Public methods of a class determine the behavior of its instances. Internal details are implemented by private methods and private data members.

Now let's go through a concrete example to see what would happen if something that should be an internal detail is declared public. To illustrate why declaring data members public is considered a bad design, let's consider the AccountVer2 class. Suppose its data member balance is declared as public:

```
class AccountVer2 {
   public double balance;
   //the rest is the same
}
```

You Might Want to Know

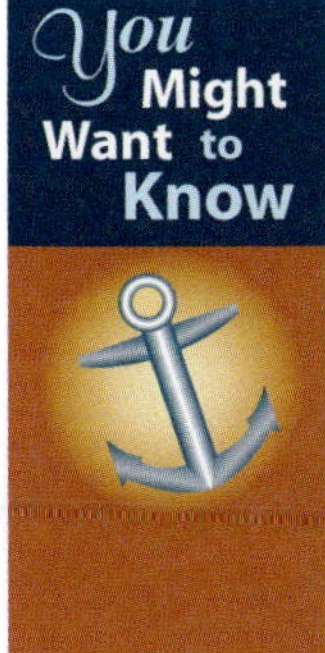

Moving a mobile robot forward in reality is actually a far more difficult task than described in the text. First, applying the same power to the two motors does not guarantee the straight movement due to the difference in the motor characteristics and the floor condition. Second, the robot needs to carry out some form of obstacle avoidance, using a device such as a sonar or infrared sensor, because we normally do not want a robot to crash into a wall. Third, stopping is not achieved by abruptly shutting off the power to the motors. This will make the stopping too sudden. We want to gradually reduce the power level so the robot comes to a smooth stop. And there are other complexities involved in actually moving a physical robot.

If this were the class definition, we could not prohibit client programmers from writing code such as

```
AccountVer2 myAcct;

myAcct = new AccountVer2("John Smith", 300.00);

myAcct.balance = 670.00;
```

This breaks the AccountVer2 class because the balance can be modified directly by the client programmers. The purpose of removing the setInitialBalance method is defeated because the client programmers will have direct access to the data member balance. They can change its value as they wish. If the instance variable balance is properly hidden by declaring it private, then the client programmers cannot modify its value directly. They can update the value indirectly only via the add and deduct methods. This maintains the integrity of the class, because the values of the data members are changed only via the public methods the class designer provides. The client programmers cannot access or modify the data members through the back door.

Design Guidelines

Declaring the data members* private *ensures the integrity of the class.

To distingush the private and public components of a class in the program diagram, we use the plus symbol (+) for public and the minus symbol (−) for private. Using these symbols, the diagram that shows both data members and methods for the AccountVer2 class becomes

AccountVer2
− balance − ownerName
+ AccountVer2(String, double) + add(double) + deduct(double) + getCurrentBalance( ) + getOwnerName( ) + setOwnerName(String)

1. If the data member speed is private, is the following statement valid in a client program?

```
Robot aibo;
aibo = new Robot();
double currentSpeed = aibo.speed;
```

2. Suppose you wrote down important information, such as your bank account number, student registration ID, and so forth, on a single sheet of paper. Will this sheet be declared private and kept in your desk drawer, or public and placed next to the dorm's public telephone?
3. Identify the private methods from the following diagram.

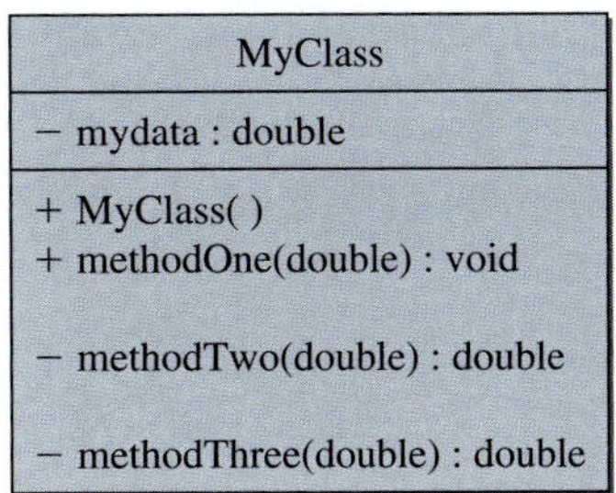

4.7 Class Constants

We introduced the use of the reserved final in declaring constants in Section 3.3. The constants we declared there were used by only one method—the main method. In this section we will show how a class constant is declared. A class constant will be shared by all methods of the class.

Let's define another version of the Account class (the actual name will be AccountVer3). This time we will charge a fixed fee whenever a deduction is made. Here's how the class is declared (we will not list the unchanged methods here):

```
class AccountVer3 {

    // Data Members
    private static final double FEE = 0.50;      Class constant declaration

    private String ownerName;

    private double balance;

    //Constructor
    public AccountVer3(String name, double startingBalance) {

        ownerName = name;
        balance = startingBalance;
    }

    //Deducts the passed amount from the balance
    public void deduct(double amt) {
        balance = balance - amt - FEE;           Fee is charged every time
    }
```

```
    //other methods are exactly the same as before, so
    //we will omit them here

}
```

The following sample program shows that the fee of $1.50 is charged after three deductions.

```
import java.text.*;

class DeductionWithFee {
   //This sample program deducts money three times
   //from the account

   public static void main(String[] args) {

        DecimalFormat df = new DecimalFormat("0.00");

        AccountVer3 acct;

        acct = new AccountVer3("Carl Smith", 50.00);

        acct.deduct(10);
        acct.deduct(10);
        acct.deduct(10);
        System.out.println("Owner: " + acct.getOwnerName());
        System.out.println("Bal   : $"
                             + df.format(acct.getCurrentBalance()));
    }
}
```

This is the output we get when we run the program:

```
Owner: Carl Smith
Bal  : $18.50
```

Notice the use of a DecimalFormat object to display the result to two decimal places. Here is the dependency relationship diagram (standard classes are not included)

and the source files for the program are

The class constant FEE is declared as

```
private static final double FEE = 0.50;
```

The modifier final designates that the identifier FEE is a constant, and the modifier static designates that it is a class constant. The reserved word static is used to declare class components, such as class variables and class methods. The inclusion of the reserved word static in the declaration of the main method indicates that it is a class method. It is not so frequent that we use class variables and class methods (except, of course, the main method), and we will not be seeing their examples until later in the book.

Before we move to another example, consider the following (problematic) declaration:

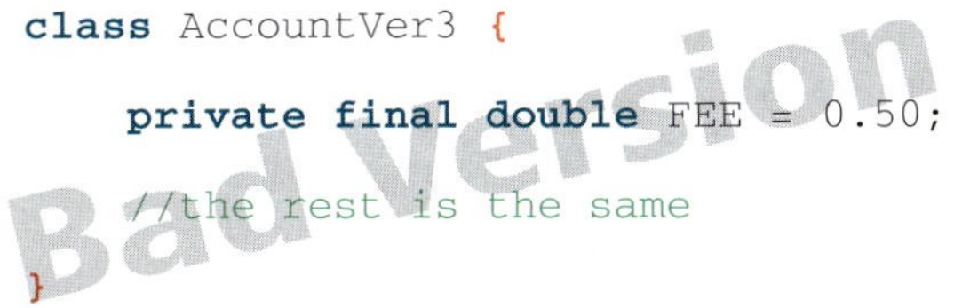


```
class AccountVer3 {

    private final double FEE = 0.50;

    //the rest is the same
}
```

This declaration is not an error, but it is inefficient. If FEE is declared as a class constant, then there will be one copy for the class, and this single copy is shared by all instances of the class. If FEE is declared without the static modifier, then it is an instance constant. This means every instance of the class will have its own copy of the same value. For example, instead of one copy of the value 0.50, there will be 100 copies of the same value 0.50 if there are 100 instances of the class. So, to make effective use of a memory, when we declare a data member as a constant, it should be declared as a class constant. This problem was introduced in Chapter 1, and Figure 1.9 illustrates the problem.

Things to Remember

If a data member is a constant, declare it as a class constant.

Let's try another sample program. This time we will write a class that models a die. Notice how the constants are used in the following Die class:

```
class Die {

    //Data Members

    //the largest number on a die
    private static final int MAX_NUMBER = 6;

    //the smallest number on a die
    private static final int MIN_NUMBER = 1;

    //To represent a die that is not yet rolled
    private static final int NO_NUMBER = 0;

    private int number;

    //Constructor
    public Die( ) {

        number = NO_NUMBER;
    }

    //Rolls the die
    public void roll( ) {
        number = (int) (Math.floor(Math.random() *
                        (MAX_NUMBER - MIN_NUMBER + 1)) + MIN_NUMBER);
    }

    //Returns the number on this die
    public int getNumber( ) {
        return number;
    }
}
```

We use the instance variable number to store the value of a die after it is rolled. Inside the constructor, we initialize number to the constant NO_NUMBER to represent the state before the die is rolled. The roll method uses the formula for random number generation described in Chapter 3. The minimum and the maximum numbers on a die are kept as the class constants. By changing their values, our software die can be made to represent any range of values, not just 1 to 6. (*Note:* Yes, we can change their values when we edit the class. A Java constant only means that we cannot change its value while the program is running.)

Here's a program that uses three Die objects to simulate a roll of three dice:

```
class RollDice {

    //Simulates the rolling of three dice
    public static void main(String[] args) {

        Die one, two, three;

        one   = new Die( );
        two   = new Die( );
        three = new Die( );

        one.roll();
        two.roll();
        three.roll();

        System.out.println("Results are " + one.getNumber( ) + " " +
                                            two.getNumber( ) + " " +
                                            three.getNumber( ) );
    }
}
```

The dependency diagram and a sample output are as follows:

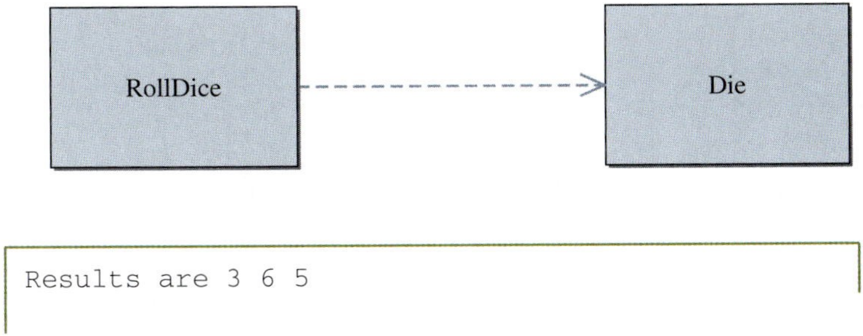


```
Results are 3 6 5
```

The output of this program is rather primitive, but it still conveys the necessary information. We will learn some drawing techniques in Chapter 5, so we can really draw the image of three dice.

Let's adapt the implemention of the Die class to write another program. Here's the scenario for our next program. Getting a single-occupancy room in a dormitory is very tough because of high demand. There's one especially large and comfortable single-occupancy room in your dorm that everybody covets. The housing office runs a lottery at the beginning of a quarter. Students must submit their entries before the lottery (if there's no winner, then the room will be auctioned off at eBay). The result of the lottery will consist of three cards. The numbers on a card range from 10 to 15, and the color of a card can be red, green, or blue. Here are some possible outcomes:

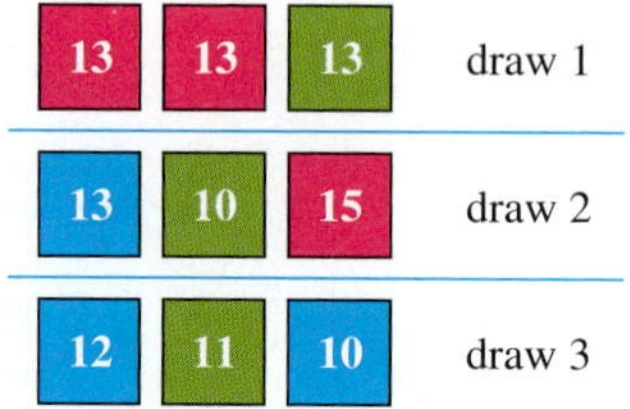

We will write a program that will select a winning combination of lottery cards. Following the implementation style of the Die class, we will define a class that models the lottery card. There will be two instance variables, one for color and another for the number. We will use a random number generator to select a color and a number for each lottery card. To represent a color, we will use a simple coding: 1 for red, 2 for green, and 3 for blue.

Here's the LotteryCard class:

```
class LotteryCard {

    // Data Members

    //the largest number on a card
    private static final int MAX_NUMBER = 15;

    //the smallest number on a card
    private static final int MIN_NUMBER = 10;

    //to represent a card before drawing
    private static final int NO_NUMBER = 0;

    //the 'largest' color for a card
    private static final int MAX_COLOR = 3;

    //the 'smallest' color for a card
    private static final int MIN_COLOR = 1;

    //to represent a card before drawing
    private static final int NO_COLOR = 0;

    //selected number on this card
    private int number;

    //selected color of this card
    private int color;
```

```
    //Constructor
    public LotteryCard( ) {

        number = NO_NUMBER;
        color = NO_COLOR;
    }

    //spin the card
    public void spin( ) {
        number = (int) (Math.floor(Math.random()
                          * (MAX_NUMBER - MIN_NUMBER + 1)) + MIN_NUMBER);

        color = (int) (Math.floor(Math.random()
                          * (MAX_COLOR - MIN_COLOR + 1)) + MIN_COLOR);
    }

    //Returns the number on this card
    public int getNumber( ) {
        return number;
    }

    //Returns the color of this card
    public int getColor( ) {
        return color;
    }
}
```

And here's the main class that draws the winning card combination:

```
class RoomWinner {

    //Simulates the rolling of three dice
    public static void main(String[] args) {

        LotteryCard one, two, three;

        one   = new LotteryCard( );
        two   = new LotteryCard( );
        three = new LotteryCard( );

        one.spin();
        two.spin();
        three.spin();

        System.out.println("Winning Card Combination: ");
        System.out.println("1 - red; 2 - green; 3 - blue");
        System.out.println(" ");
```

```
        System.out.println("             color     number");
        System.out.println("Card 1:          " +   one.getColor( )
                                 + "           " +    one.getNumber( ));
        System.out.println("Card 2:          " +   two.getColor( )
                                 + "           " +    two.getNumber( ));
        System.out.println("Card 3:          " + three.getColor( )
                                 + "           " + three.getNumber( ));
    }
}
```

The dependency diagram is as follows:

When this program is executed, output similar to the following is displayed:

```
Winning Card Combination:
1 - red; 2 - green; 3 - blue

            Color     number
Card 1:       2         13
Card 2:       2         12
Card 3:       1         14
```

Again, the output is rather primitive. We will learn some drawing techniques in Chapter 5 so we can draw the image of a card in the appropriate color.

Public Constants

We stated in Section 4.6 that data members should be declared private to ensure the integrity of a class. Following this guideline, we declared the class constant data members in both sample programs as private. But there is an exception. We may want to declare certain types of class constants as public. Here are the reasons for this exception. First, a constant is "read only" by its nature, so it won't have a negative impact if we declare it as public. Second, a constant is a clean way to make certain characteristics of the instances known to the client programs.

For example, if we want to make the amount of a fee public knowledge (which is a good idea, because consumers need to know such information), we make the class constant public as follows:

```
class AccountVer3 {

      public static final double FEE = 0.50;

      ...
}
```

A client program can then access this information directly as

```
System.out.println("Fee charged per deduction is $ "
                                    + AccountVer3.FEE);
```

Notice that the class data members are accessed by the syntax

```
<class name> . <class data members>
```

The use of public class constants is quite common in Java, and we will be seeing many examples of it in the later sample programs.

1. Declare two class constants named MIN_BALANCE and MAX_BALANCE whose data types are double.
2. Is there any problem with the following declarations?

```
class Question {

   private final int MAX = 20;
   ...
}
```

3. Modify the Die class so its instances will generate a number between 5 and 15, inclusively.

4.8 Local Variables

We often need to use temporary variables while completing a task in a method. Consider the deduct method of the Account class:

```
public void deduct(double amt) {

      balance = balance - amt;
}
```

We can rewrite the method, using a local variable, as follows:

```
public void deduct(double amt) {

   double newBalance;
```

This is a **local variable**

```
        newBalance = balance - amt;
        balance = newBalance;
    }
```

local variable

The variable newBalance is called a ***local variable***. They are declared within the method declaration and used for temporary purposes, such as storing intermediate results of a computation.

Such two-step assignment to update the current balance may not seem so useful here, but consider a situation in which we need to check for certain conditions before actually changing the value of currentBalance. For example, we may want to disallow the purchase if the balance goes below a preset minimum balance. So if newBalance becomes lower than the set minimum, then we'll leave balance unchanged. If we don't use any local variable, then we have to deduct the amount from balance (temporarily) and change it back to the previous amount. Use of a temporary local variable will result in a much cleaner code. We will see how such checking is done in Chapter 5 using a selection statement.

The methods in the sample classes from this chapter are still very short, so the use of local variables may not be clear-cut. However, we will witness an increase in the use of local variables in the coming chapters when the methods become complex.

While the data members of a class are accessible from all instance methods of the class, local variables and parameters are accessible only from the method in which they are declared, and they are available only while the method is being executed. Memory space for local variables and parameters is allocated upon declaration and at the beginning of the method, respectively, and erased upon exiting from the method.

Things to Remember

Local variables and parameters are erased when the execution of a method is completed.

When you declare a local variable, make sure the identifier you use for it does not conflict with the data members of a class. Consider the following hypothetical class declaration:

```
class Sample {
    private int number;
    ...
    public void doSomething( ) {
        int number;
        number = 15;
    }
    ...
}
```

The same identifier is used for both the local variable and the instance variable.

This changes the value of the local variable, not the instance variable.

This class declaration is not an error. It is acceptable to use the same identifier for a local variable, but it is not advisable. The following association rules are used:

Things to Remember

Rules for associating an identifier to a local variable, a parameter, and a data member:

1. *If there's a matching local variable declaration or a parameter, then the identifier refers to the local variable or the parameter.*
2. *Otherwise, if there's a matching data member declaration, then the identifier refers to the data member.*
3. *Otherwise, it is an error because there's no matching declaration.*

So the assignment

```
number = 15;
```

will change the value of the local variable. This may or may not be the intent of the programmer. Even if this is the programmer's intention, it is cleaner and easier to read, especially to other programmers, to use different identifiers for local variables.

Things to Remember

Avoid using the same identifier for the local variables and the data members of a class.

1. How is a local variable different from an instance variable?
2. Rewrite the following method, using local variables.

```
public int totalCharge(int amt) {

    return (balance -
              (int) Math.round(amt * 1.5));

}
```

4.9 Calling Methods of the Same Class

Up until now, whenever we called a method of some object, we used dot notation, such as acct.deduct(12). Just as we can call a method of another object, it is possible to call a method from a method of the same object. Figure 4.7 illustrates the

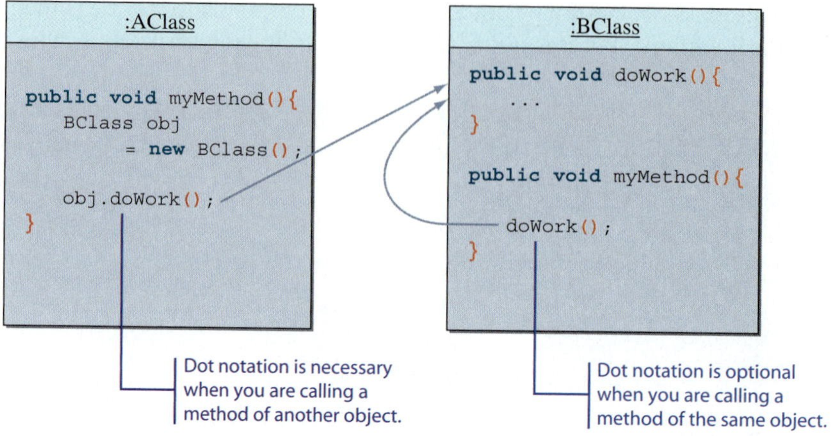

Figure 4.7 The difference between calling a method belonging to the same object and a method belonging to a different object.

difference between calling another method of the same object and calling a method of a different object.

Let's look at a few examples. In the first example, we modify the AccountVer3 class so the add and deduct methods call the private method adjust. Here's how the modified class is declared (the actual class name is AccountVer4, and only the relevant portion is listed here):

```
class AccountVer4 {
    ...

    //Adds the passed amount to the balance
    public void add(double amt) {
        adjust(amt);
    }

    //Deducts the passed amount from the balance
    public void deduct(double amt) {
        adjust( -(amt+FEE) );
    }
    ...

    //Adjusts the account balance
    private void adjust(double adjustAmt) {
        balance = balance + adjustAmt;
    }
}
```

The add and deduct methods differ only in whether you add to or subtract the amount from the balance. In the modified class, we redefine the two methods so they call the common private method adjust. This method adds the passed amount to the balance (in the case for the deduct method, we pass the negative amount because adding a negative value $-X$ is equivalent to subtracting a positive value X). Here's how the add method is defined:

```
public void add(double amt) {

  adjust(amt);

}
```

Notice there is no dot notation. This is calling another method that belongs to the same class.

When we call a method that belongs to the same class, we just include the method name, as follows:

```
adjust(amt);
```

No dot notation is necessary.

Things to Remember

No dot notation is necessary when you call a method from another method of the same class.

Let's look at the second example. In the original Die class, when a new instance was created, we set its number to NO_NUMBER. This means if a programmer calls the getNumber method of a Die object before calling its roll method, she will get NO_NUMBER as a result. For a real die, there's no such NO_NUMBER state, so instead of instantiating a new Die object in such a state, we'll redefine the class so a die gets rolled when it is first created. The trick here is to call the roll method from the constructor. Here's how the modified Die class is declared (the class name is DieVer2):

```
class DieVer2 {

    //Data Members

    //the largest number on a die
    private static final int MAX_NUMBER = 6;
```

```
    //the smallest number on a die
    private static final int MIN_NUMBER = 1;

    private int number;

    //Constructor
    public DieVer2( ) {

        roll();
    }

    //Rolls the die
    public void roll( ) {
        number = (int) (Math.floor(Math.random()
                        * (MAX_NUMBER - MIN_NUMBER + 1)) + MIN_NUMBER);
    }

    //Returns the number on this die
    public int getNumber( ) {
        return number;
    }
}
```

The constructor simply calls the roll method. So when a new Die object is created, a number is already preselected. Notice that it is possible to declare the constructor as

```
public DieVer2( ) {
    number = (int) (Math.floor(Math.random()
                    * (MAX_NUMBER - MIN_NUMBER + 1))
                      + MIN_NUMBER);
}
```

But this ends up duplicating the same code. Instead of repeating the same code in the class, it is much better organizationally to define a single method and call this method from multiple places. Duplication of code, in general, makes the modification of code tedious and error-prone. Imagine the situation in which the same code is repeated at 10 different locations. It is so easy to miss one or two of them at the modification time.

Things to Remember

Avoid duplicating the same code. Duplication of code often means tedious and error-prone activities when you modify the code.

1. Suppose a class Alpha includes a method called compute that accepts no arguments. Define another method of Alpha named myMethod that calls the compute method.
2. Why should duplication of code be avoided?

4.10 Changing Any Class to a Main Class

In this section, we will show you a simple way to make any class (such as Bicycle) also the main class of a program. Instead of defining a separate main class, as we have done so far, it is possible to define the main method to a class so the class becomes the main class of a program also. There are a number of advantages in doing this. First, we have one less class to manage if we don't have to define a separate main class. This advantage may not be seem so substantial. However, when we write numerous classes (e.g., writing solutions to the chapter exercises), writing a separate main class for all those classes so they become executable becomes tedious. Second, when we develop reusable classes (such as Die and Account) for other programmers, we often want to include a simple example on how to use the classes. Instead of providing a separate sample main class, it is more convenient to add the main method to these classes.

We illustrate the procedure, using the Bicycle class from Section 4.1. Suppose we want to show a sample use of this class. Instead of creating a separate sample main class, we can define the main method to the Bicycle class. Here's the Bicycle class that is also a main class:

```
class Bicycle {

    // Data Member
    private String ownerName;

    //Returns the name of this bicycle's owner
    public String getOwnerName( ) {

        return ownerName;

    }

    //Assigns the name of this bicycle's owner
    public void setOwnerName(String name) {

        ownerName = name;

    }

    //The main method that shows a sample
    //use of the Bicycle class
    public static void main(String[] args) {

        Bicycle myBike;

        myBike = new Bicycle( );
```

```
            myBike.setOwnerName("Jon Java");

            System.out.println(myBike.getOwnerName() +
                                        "owns a bicycle");
        }

    }
```

Remember that the new Bicycle class having the main method does not prohibit us from defining a separate main class. All Java requires us to do is to include the main method to the classes we designate as the main class of the program. So it is possible (although not likely) that every class in the program has the main method, and we can select one of them to be the main class when we execute the program. We will use this technique whenever appropriate in the textbook, beginning with this chapter's sample development section.

Things to Remember

Any class can include the main *method. For a program to be executable, the designated main class must include the* main *method. Other classes in the program may or may not include the* main *method. It is irrelevant to the execution of the program.*

4.11 Sample Development

Loan Calculator

In Chapter 3, we wrote a loan calculator program that computes the monthly and total payments for a given loan amount, loan period, and interest rate. We wrote the program using the simplified program structure in which we had one main class with one method (**main**). We will implement the program again, but this time we use classes called **Loan** and **LoanCalculator.**

Problem Statement

The problem statement is the same as that in Chapter 3. We repeat the statement to refresh your memory:

> *Write a loan calculator program that computes both monthly and total payments for a given loan amount, annual interest rate, and loan period.*

Overall Plan

program tasks

The tasks we identified in Chapter 3 for the program are still the same:

1. Get three input values: **loanAmount, interestRate,** and **loanPeriod.**
2. Compute the monthly and total payments.
3. Output the results.

The main difference in this implementation lies in the use of additional classes. Instead of building the program by using only the main class and performing all the tasks in one big **main** method, we will define two classes **Loan** and **LoanCalculator.** An instance of the **LoanCalculator** class acts as a top-level agent that manages all other objects in the program, such as **Loan** and **Scanner.** The **Loan** class captures the logic of loan calculation. A single instance of the **Loan** class represents a loan, so if the program deals with five loans, for example, then five **Loan** objects will be created in the program. We will make the **LoanCalculator** class the main class of the program by adding the **main** method to it. Figure 4.8 shows the program diagram.

Notice that the roles that **LoanCalculator** and **Loan** play in the program are quite different. The **Loan** class is a generic class that provides a service (i.e., loan computation and currency conversion) and is intended to be reused by different programs. The **LoanCalculator** class, on the other hand, is a class designed specifically for this program, so the class is not intended for reuse by other programs. It is important to recognize this distinction because the way we design reusable and nonreusable classes is quite different. We call the class that provides some type of service a ***service provider*** and the class that manages other classes and objects in a program a ***controller***. In general, a service provider is designed as a reusable class, while a controller is designed as a nonreusable class.

service provider

controller

What would be the development steps for this program? If we have multiple classes to implement, we can develop the program in either a top-down or a bottom-up manner. With the ***top-down development***, we develop in a kind of outside-in fashion. We develop the top-level controller class first. But to test its functionalities fully, we need the service objects it uses. In a top-down development, we use temporary dummy service objects that return a fake value from their methods. After we verify that the controller class is working correctly, we then complete the service class with the real methods. The top-down development for this program will implement the **LoanCalculator** class first with the dummy **Loan** class and then the real **Loan** class.

top-down development

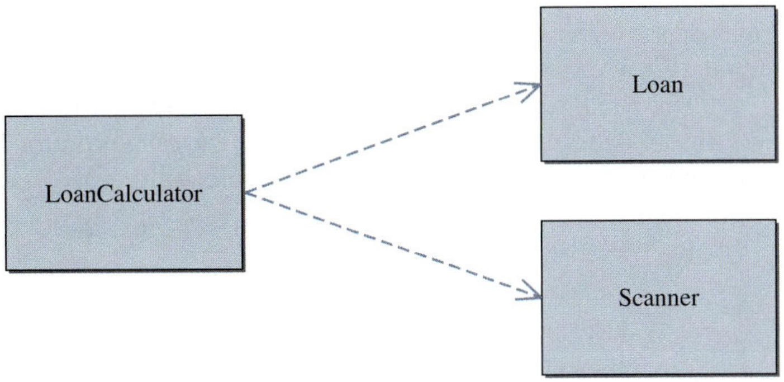

Figure 4.8 The program diagram for the **LoanCalculator** program.

4.11 Sample Development—*continued*

bottom-up development

With the ***bottom-up development***, we develop in the reverse inside-out fashion; that is, we develop the service classes first. To test the service classes, we write a temporary dummy main class. After the service classes are done, we complete the top-level class that uses these service classes. The bottom-up development for this program implements the **Loan** class first fully and then the **LoanCalculator** class. For both approaches, the classes are developed incrementally as usual.

For this sample development, we will adopt the top-down development. We will leave the bottom-up development for this program as an exercise. For some sample applications in the later chapters, we will adopt the bottom-up development. We implement this program in five steps:

development steps

1. Start a skeleton of the **LoanCalculator** class. The skeleton **LoanCalculator** class will include only an object/variable declaration and a constructor to create objects. Define a temporary placeholder **Loan** class.
2. Implement the input routine to accept three input values.
3. Implement the output routine to display the results.
4. Implement the computation routine to compute the monthly and total payments.
5. Finalize the program, implementing any remaining temporary methods and adding necessary methods as appropriate.

Step 1 Development: Program Skeleton

step 1 design

Since the **LoanCalculator** object is the top-level agent of the program that manages other objects, we need a method to create these objects. We do this in the constructor. We define separate methods for input, computation, and output to organize the class more logically. Designing a set of single-task methods is more manageable and easier to understand than having one method that performs all three tasks of input, computation, and output. We will call the methods **getInput, computePayment,** and **displayOutput.** We will also include one method called **describeProgram** that describes the purpose of the program to the user.

Since an instance of the class is the top-level agent, much as a general contractor, we will provide one method the programmer can call to control the whole operation. We will name the method **start** and define it as follows:

```
public void start( ) {

    describeProgram();
    getInput();
    computerPayment();
    displayOutput();
}
```

With this method, we can then call the **main** method as follows:

```
public static void main(String[] args){

    LoanCalculator calculator = new LoanCalculator();

    calculator.start();

}
```

It is possible to define the **main** method to make it call the four operation methods (**describeProgram, computePayment, getInput,** and **displayOutput**) directly, eliminating the need to define the **start** method. However, such organization limits the flexibility and usability of the class. By defining the **start** method, if other programmers want to use the **LoanCalculator** class in their programs, they need only call the **start** method. Without the **start** method, they have to call the four methods and remember to call them in the correct order. Although the difference is not dramatic in this particular case, it can be in the cases when the classes are more complex and the number of classes in a program is large.

Let's summarize the methods we will define for the **LoanCalculator** class:

Design Document: The `LoanCalculator` Class

Method	Visibility	Purpose
`start`	`public`	Carries out the loan calculation by calling the other private methods.
`computePayment`	`private`	Given three parameters—loan amount, loan period, and interest rate—it computes monthly and total payments. The actual computation is done by a `Loan` object.
`describeProgram`	`private`	Displays a short description of the program.
`displayOutput`	`private`	Displays the result—monthly and total payments.
`getInput`	`private`	Uses `Scanner` to get three input values—loan amount, loan period, and interest rate.

Notice that only the **start** method is **public.** We declare all other methods as **private** because we do not want any client programmers to use them directly; we want the client programmers to be able to call only the **start** method.

stub

In this step, we define the four private methods with only a temporary output statement inside the method body to verify that the methods are called correctly. A method that has no "real" statements inside the method body is called a ***stub***. The four

4.11 Sample Development—*continued*

methods are defined as follows:

```
private void describeProgram() {
    System.out.println("inside describeProgram"); //TEMP
}

private void getInput() {
    System.out.println("inside getInput");         //TEMP
}

private void computePayment() {
    System.out.println("inside computePayment");   //TEMP
}

private void displayOutput() {
    System.out.println("inside displayOutput");    //TEMP
}
```

Notice the comment marker **//TEMP** after the output statements. It is our convention to attach this comment marker so we can easily and quickly locate temporary statements. We use **System.out** for temporary output.

The purpose of the skeleton **LoanCalculator** class is to declare and create all the necessary data members. At this step, we know of only one object that will be used by **LoanCalculator,** namely, a **Loan** object. The declaration part of the **LoanCalculator** class will be as follows:

```
class LoanCalculator {

    private Loan loan;

    . . .
}
```

At this point, the constructor for the **LoanCalculator** class is very simple. The only data member is a **Loan** object, so we will create it in the constructor as follows:

```
public LoanCalculator( ) {
    loan = new Loan( );
}
```

For this constructor to work properly, we need the definition for the **Loan** class. We begin with the minimalist skeleton code for the **Loan** class:

```
class Loan {

    public Loan( ) {

    }
}
```

step 1 code

Let's put our design in an actual code. The skeleton **LoanCalculator** class is defined as follows.

```
/*
   Chapter 4 Sample Development: Loan Calculation (Step 1)

   File: Step1/LoanCalculator.java
 */

class LoanCalculator {

    //Data members
    private Loan loan;

    //Main method
    public static void main(String[] arg) {
        LoanCalculator calculator = new LoanCalculator();
        calculator.start();
    }

    //Constructor
    public LoanCalculator() {

        loan = new Loan();
    }

    // Top-level method that calls other private methods
    public void start() {

        describeProgram();  //tell what the program does
        getInput();         //get three input values
        computePayment();   //compute the monthly payment and total
        displayOutput();    //display the results
    }

    // Computes the monthly and total loan payments
    private void computePayment() {

        System.out.println("inside computePayment");     //TEMP
    }

    // Provides a brief explanation of the program to the user
    private void describeProgram() {

        System.out.println("inside describeProgram");    //TEMP
    }

    // Displays the input values and monthly and total payments
    private void displayOutput() {

        System.out.println("inside displayOutput");      //TEMP
    }
```

4.11 Sample Development—*continued*

```
    // Gets three input values—loan amount, interest rate, and
    // loan period—using an InputBox object
    private void getInput() {

        System.out.println("inside getInput"); //TEMP
    }
}
```

And finally the skeleton **Loan** class is defined as follows.

```
/*

    Chapter 4 Sample Development: Loan Calculation (Step 1)

    File: Step1/Loan.java

 */
class Loan {
    public Loan( ) {

    }
}
```

step 1 test

We run the step 1 program and verify that the following text appears in the standard output window:

```
inside describeProgram
inside getInput
inside computePayment
inside displayOutput
```

After the step 1 program is compiled and executed correctly, we move on to step 2.

Step 2 Development: Accept Input Values

step 2 design

In the second step of coding, we implement the **getInput** method. We will reuse the input routine we derived in Chapter 3. When we receive three input values, we must pass these values to the **Loan** object **loan.** We will add three data members to keep track of the three input values and one constant to aid the conversion:

```
class Loan {

    private static final int MONTHS_IN_YEAR = 12;

    private double loanAmount;
    private double monthlyInterestRate;
    private int    numberOfPayments;

    . . .
}
```

Notice that the annual interest rate and loan period expressed in the number of years are the input, but we are keeping monthly interest rate and the number of monthly payments for the loan period to make them more compatible to the loan calculation formula we are using. We need to define three set methods (mutators) for interest rate, loan period, and loan amount. A set method for the number of payments, for example, can be defined as follows:

```
public void setPeriod(int periodInYear) {
    numberOfPayments = periodInYear * MONTHS_IN_YEAR;
}
```

We define a complementary set of accessor methods. The **getPeriod** method, for example, is defined as

```
public int getPeriod( ) {
    return (numberOfPayments / MONTHS_IN_YEAR);
}
```

Notice that the value returned by an accessor may or may not be the data member. It is possible that the value returned is derived from the data member, as was the case with the **getLoanPeriod** method.

We mentioned in Section 4.4 the importance of a constructor initializing an object properly. Now that we have associated data members to the **Loan** class, let's define a constructor that accepts arguments:

```
public Loan(double amount, double rate, int period) {
    setAmount(amount);
    setRate  (rate  );
    setPeriod(period);
}
```

Having this updated **Loan** class, we are now ready to tackle the **getInput** method of the **LoanCalculator** class. We perform the input routine as we did in the sample program from Chapter 3:

```
Scanner scanner = new Scanner(System.in);

System.out.print("Loan Amount (Dollars+Cents): ");
loanAmount = scanner.nextDouble();
```

4.11 Sample Development—*continued*

```
System.out.print("Annual Interest Rate (e.g., 9.5): ");
annualInterestRate = scanner.nextDouble();

System.out.print("Loan Period - # of years: ");
loanPeriod = scanner.nextInt();
```

After getting three input values, we create a new **Loan** object as

```
loan = new Loan(loanAmount,
                annualInterestRate,
                loanPeriod);
```

Finally, we include test output statements to verify that the values are read in and assigned to loan correctly:

```
System.out.println("Loan Amount: $"
                                + loan.getAmount());
System.out.println("Annual Interest Rate:"
                                + loan.getRate() + "%");
System.out.println("Loan Period (years):"
                                + loan.getPeriod());
```

step 2 code

From this point on, to maintain a focus on the changes we are making, we show only the portion where we made modifications or additions. Unchanged portions are represented by three dots (. . .). Please refer to the actual source file for the viewing of complete source code. Here's the step 2 **LoanCalculator** class:

```
/*
    Chapter 4 Sample Development: Loan Calculation (Step 2)

    File: Step2/LoanCalculator.java
 */

import java.util.*;

class LoanCalculator {
    . . .

    public LoanCalculator() {

    }

    . . .

    private void getInput(){
        double loanAmount, annualInterestRate;
```

```
        int       loanPeriod;

        Scanner scanner = new Scanner(System.in);

        System.out.print("Loan Amount (Dollars+Cents):");
        loanAmount = scanner.nextDouble();

        System.out.print("Annual Interest Rate (e.g., 9.5):");
        annualInterestRate = scanner.nextDouble();

        System.out.print("Loan Period - # of years:");
        loanPeriod = scanner.nextInt();

        //create a new loan with the input values
        loan = new Loan(loanAmount, annualInterestRate,loanPeriod);

        //TEMP
        System.out.println("Loan Amount: $" + loan.getAmount());
        System.out.println("Annual Interest Rate:"
                              + loan.getRate() + "%");

        System.out.println("Loan Period (years):" + loan.getPeriod());

        //TEMP
    }
    . . .
}
```

The step 2 **Loan** class is as follows:

```
/*
   Chapter 4 Sample Development: Loan Calculation (Step 2)

   File: Step2/Loan.java

 */

class Loan {

    private final int MONTHS_IN_YEAR = 12;

    private double    loanAmount;

    private double    monthlyInterestRate;

    private int       numberOfPayments;
```

4.11 Sample Development—*continued*

```
    //Constructor
    public Loan(double amount, double rate, int period) {
        setAmount(amount);
        setRate  (rate  );
        setPeriod(period);
    }

    //Returns the loan amount
    public double getAmount( ) {
        return loanAmount;
    }

    //Returns the loan period in number of years
    public int getPeriod( ) {
        return numberOfPayments / MONTHS_IN_YEAR;
    }

    //Returns the loan's annual interest rate
    public double getRate( ) {
        return monthlyInterestRate * 100.0 * MONTHS_IN_YEAR;
    }

    //Sets the loan amount
    public void setAmount(double amount) {
        loanAmount = amount;
    }

    //Sets the annual interest rate
    public void setRate(double annualRate) {
        monthlyInterestRate = annualRate / 100.0 / MONTHS_IN_YEAR;
    }

    //Sets the loan period
    public void setPeriod(int periodInYears) {
        numberOfPayments = periodInYears * MONTHS_IN_YEAR;
    }
}
```

step 2 test

As before, to verify the input routine is working correctly, we run the program multiple times. For each run, we enter a different set of data to verify that the values entered are displayed correctly.

Step 3 Development: Output Values

step 3 design

In the third step of development, we implement the **displayOutput** method. We will reuse the design of output layout from Chapter 3. The actual task of computing the monthly and total payments is now delegated to the **Loan** class, so we will add two methods—**getMonthlyPayment** and **getTotalPayment**—to the **Loan** class. The focus in step 3 is the layout for output, so we will define a temporary dummy code for these two methods in the following manner:

```
public double getMonthlyPayment( ) {
    return 132.15; //TEMP
}

public double getTotalPayment( ) {
    return 15858.10; //TEMP
}
```

To display the monthly and total payments, we add the following code in the **displayOutput** method:

```
private void displayOutput( ) {

    //echo print the input values here

    System.out.println("Monthly payment is $ " +
                        loan.getMonthlyPayment() );
    System.out.println(" TOTAL payment is $ " +
                        loan.getTotalPayment() );
}
```

Notice that by defining the **getMonthlyPayment** and **getTotalPayment** methods in the **Loan** class, the **computePayment** method of **LoanCalculator** becomes redundant and no longer needed. So we will remove it in this step.

step 3 code

Here are the modified **LoanCalculator** and **Loan** classes:

```
/*
   Chapter 4 Sample Development: Loan Calculation (Step 3)

   File: Step3/LoanCalculator.java
 */

import java.util.*;

class LoanCalculator {
   ...
   // computePayment method is removed from the source file

   private void displayOutput() {

      System.out.println("Loan Amount: $" + loan.getAmount());
```

4.11 Sample Development—*continued*

```
        System.out.println("Annual Interest Rate:"
                            + loan.getRate() + "%");
        System.out.println("Loan Period (years): " + loan.getPeriod());

        System.out.println("Monthly payment is $ " +
                                             loan.getMonthlyPayment());
        System.out.println("  TOTAL payment is $ " +
                                              loan.getTotalPayment());

    }

    private void getInput() {

        //same code but the temporary echo print statements
        //are removed
    }
}
```

```
/*
   Chapter 4 Sample Development: Loan Calculation (Step 3)

   File: Step3/Loan.java
*/

class Loan {

     ...

     public double getMonthlyPayment( ) {
         return 132.15; //TEMP
     }

     public double getTotalPayment( ) {
         return 15858.10; //TEMP
     }

    ...
}
```

step 3 test

To verify the output routine is working correctly, we run the program multiple times and verify that the layout looks okay for different values. It is common for a programmer to run the program several times before the layout looks clean on the screen.

Step 4 Development: Compute Loan Amount

step 4 design

In the fourth step of development,we replace the temporary **getMonthlyPayment** and **getTotalPayment** methods with the final version. The changes are made only to the **Loan** class.The other two classes remain the same.

Here's one possible way to define the two methods:

```
private double monthlyPayment;

public double getMonthlyPayment( ) {
   monthlyPayment = ...;
   return monthlyPayment;
}

public double getTotalPayment( ) {
   return monthlyPayment * numberOfPayments;
}
```

Bad Version

The idea is to use the value of the data member **monthlyPayment** set by the **getMonthlyPayment** method in computing the total payment.This setup is problematic because the **getTotalPayment** method will not work correctly unless **getMonthlyPayment** is called first. It is considered a very poor design, and generally unacceptable, to require the client programmer to call a collection of methods in a certain order. We must define the two methods so they can be called in any order, not necessarily in the order of **getMonthlyPayment** and **getTotalPayment.** The correct way here is to call **getMonthlyPayment** from the **getTotalPayment** method:

```
private double getTotalPayment( ) {
   double totalPayment;

   totalPayment = getMonthlyPayment() * numberOfPayments;

   return totalPayment;
}
```

step 4 code

With this approach the data member **monthlyPayment** is not necessary.

Here's the updated **Loan** class:

```
/*
   Chapter 4 Sample Development: Loan Calculation (Step 4)

   File: Step4/Loan.java
 */

class Loan {

   ...
   public double getMonthlyPayment( ) {
       double monthlyPayment;
```

4.11 Sample Development—*continued*

```
        monthlyPayment = (loanAmount * monthlyInterestRate)
                                /
                         (1 - Math.pow(1/(1 + monthlyInterestRate),
                                            numberOfPayments ) );
        return monthlyPayment;
    }

    public double getTotalPayment( ) {
        double totalPayment;

        totalPayment = getMonthlyPayment( ) * numberOfPayments;

        return totalPayment;
    }
        . . .
}
```

step 4 test

After the method is added to the class, we need to run the program through a number of test data. As in Chapter 3,we made the assumption that the input values must be valid, so we will only test the program for valid input values. For sample test data, we repeat the table from Chapter 3.The right two columns show the correct results. Remember that these input values are only suggestions, not a complete list of test data.You must try other input values as well.

Input			Output (shown up to three decimal places only)	
Loan Amount	**Annual Interest Rate**	**Loan Period (in Years)**	**Monthly Payment**	**Total Payment**
10000	10	10	132.151	15858.088
15000	7	15	134.824	24268.363
10000	12	10	143.471	17216.514
0	10	5	0.000	0.000
30	8.5	50	0.216	129.373

Step 5 Development: Finalize

step 5 design

Now in the last step of development, we finalize the class declaration by completing the **describeProgram** method, the only method still undefined. We may give a very long description or a very terse one. An ideal program will let the user decide. We do not know how to write such code yet, so we will display a short description of the program using **System.out.**

Another improvement is the display of monetary values in two decimal places. We can format the display to two decimal places by using the **DecimalFormat** class as explained in Chapter 3.

step 5 code

Here's the **describeProgram** method;

```
private void describeProgram() {
    System.out.println
          ("This program computes the monthly and total");
    System.out.println
          ("payments for a given loan amount, annual ");
    System.out.println
          ("interest rate, and loan period (# of years).");
    System.out.println("\n");
}
```

step 5 test

You may feel that there's not much testing we can do in this step. After all, we add only a single method that carries out a simple output routine. However, many things can go wrong between step 4 and step 5. You may have deleted some lines of code inadvertently. You may have deleted a necessary file by mistake. Anything could happen. The point is to test after every step of development to make sure everything is in order.

Summary

- Data members of a class refer to the instance and class variables and constants of the class.
- An object's properties are maintained by a set of data members.
- Class methods can access only the class variables and class constants.
- Instance methods can access all types of data members of the class.
- Public methods define the behavior of an object.
- Private methods and data members (except certain class constants) are considered internal details of the class.
- Components (data members and methods) of a class with the visibility modifier private cannot be accessed by the client programs.
- Components of a class with the visibility modifier public can be accessed by the client programs.
- A method may or may not return a value. One that does not return a value is called a void method.

- A *constructor* is a special method that is executed when a new object is created. Its purpose is to initialize the object into a valid state.
- Memory space for local variables and parameters is allocated when a method is called and deallocated when the method terminates.
- A public method that changes a property of an object is called a *mutator*.
- A public method that retrieves a property of an object is called an *accessor*.
- Dot notation is not used when you call a method from another method of the same class.
- Any class can be set as the main class of a program by adding the main method to it. In the main method, an instance of this class is created.

Key Concepts

programmer-defined classes
accessibility (visibility) modifiers
void methods
value-returning methods
accessors
mutators
constructors
arguments
parameters
client programmers
information hiding
encapsulation
local variables
service providers
controllers
stub

Exercises

1. Consider the following class declaration.

```
class QuestionOne {
   public  final int   A = 345;
   public  int         b;
   private float       c;

   private void methodOne( int a) {
      b = a;
   }

   public float methodTwo( ) {
      return 23;
   }
}
```

Identify invalid statements in the following main class. For each invalid statement, state why it is invalid.

```
class Q1Main {
   public static void main(String[] args) {
      QuestionOne q1;
      q1 = new QuestionOne( );

      q1.A = 12;
      q1.b = 12;
      q1.c = 12;

      q1.methodOne(12);
      q1.methodOne( );
      System.out.println(q1.methodTwo(12));
      q1.c = q1.methodTwo( );
   }
}
```

2. What will be the output from the following code?

```
class Q2Main {
   public static void main(String[] args) {
      QuestionTwo q2;
      q2 = new QuestionTwo( );
      q2.init();

      q2.increment();
      q2.increment();

      System.out.println(q2.getCount());
   }
}

class QuestionTwo {
   private int count;

   public void init( ) {
      count = 1;
   }

   public void increment( ) {
      count = count + 1;
   }

   public int getCount( ) {
      return count;
   }
}
```

3. What will be the output from the following code? Q3Main and QuestionThree classes are the slightly modified version of Q2Main and QuestionTwo.

```
class Q3Main {
   public static void main(String[] args) {
      QuestionThree q3;
      q3 = new QuestionThree( );
      q3.init();

      q3.count = q3.increment() + q3.increment();

      System.out.println(q3.increment());
   }
}

class QuestionThree {
   public int count;

   public void init( ) {
      count = 1;
   }

   public int increment( ) {
      count = count + 1;
      return count;
   }
}
```

4. Is there any problem with the following class? Is the passing of an argument to the private methods appropriate? Are the data members appropriate? Explain.

```
/*
   Problem Question4
*/
class MyText {

   private String word;
   private String temp;
   private int    idx;

   public String firstLetter( ) {
      idx = 0;
      return getLetter(word);
   }

   public String lastLetter( ) {
      idx = word.length() - 1;
      return getLetter(word);
   }
```

```
    private String getLetter(String str) {
        temp = str.substring(idx, idx+1);
        return temp;
    }
}
```

5. In the RollDice program, we created three Die objects and rolled them once. Rewrite the program so you will create only one Die object and roll it three times.
6. Modify the Bicycle class so instead of assigning the name of an owner (Student), you can assign the owner object itself. Model this new Bicycle class after the LibraryCard class.
7. Extend the LibraryCard class by adding the expiration date as a new property of a library card. Define the following four methods:

```
//sets the expiration date
public void setExpDate(GregorianCalendar date) {...}

//returns the expiration year
public int getExpYear( ) { ... }

//returns the expiration month
public int getExpMonth( ) { ... }

//returns the expiration day
public int getExpDay( ) { ... }
```

8. Write a program that displays the recommended weight (kg), given the user's age and height (cm). The formula for calculating the recommended weight is

```
recommendedWeight = (height - 100 + age / 10) * 0.90
```

Define a service class named Height and include an appropriate method for getting a recommended weight of a designated height.

9. Write a program that computes the total ticket sales of a concert. There are three types of seatings: A, B, and C. The program accepts the number of tickets sold and the price of a ticket for each of the three types of seats. The total sales are computed as follows:

```
totalSales = numberOfA_Seats * pricePerA_Seat +
             numberOfB_Seats * pricePerB_Seat +
             numberOfC_Seats * pricePerC_Seat;
```

Write this program, using only one class, the main class of the program.

10. Redo Exercise 9 by using a Seat class. An instance of the Seat class keeps track of the ticket price for a given type of seat (A, B, or C).

11. Write a program that computes the area of a circular region (the shaded area in the diagram), given the radii of the inner and the outer circles, r_i and r_o, respectively.

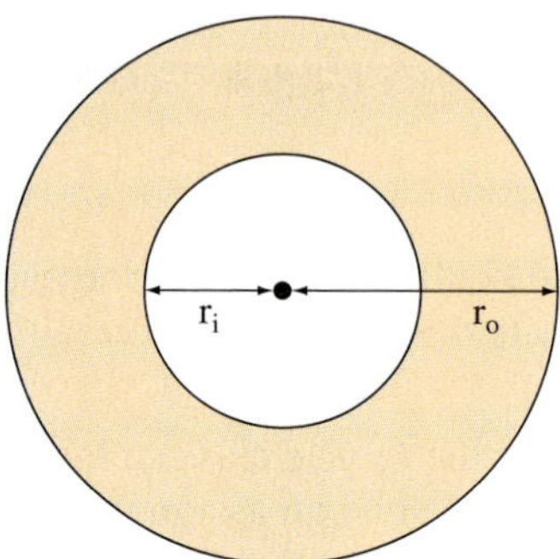

We compute the area of the circular region by subtracting the area of the inner circle from the area of the outer circle. Define a Circle class that has methods to compute the area and circumference. You set the circle's radius with the setRadius method or via a constructor.

12. Write a WeightConverter class. An instance of this class is created by passing the gravity of an object relative to the Earth's gravity (see Exercise 12 on page 138). For example, the Moon's gravity is approximately 0.167 of the Earth's gravity, so we create a WeightConverter instance for the Moon as

```
WeightConverter  moonWeight;
moonWeight = new WeightConverter( 0.167 );
```

To compute how much you weigh on the Moon, you pass your weight on Earth to the convert method as

```
yourMoonWeight = moonWeight.convert( 160 );
```

Use this class and redo Exercise 12 on page 138.

Development Exercises

For the following exercises, use the incremental development methodology to implement the program. For each exercise, identify the program tasks, create a design document with class descriptions, and draw the program diagram. Map out the development steps at the start. Present any design alternatives and justify your selection. Be sure to perform adequate testing at the end of each development step.

13. Redo Exercise 26 on page 143, but this time define and use programmer-defined classes.

14. Write a program that accepts the unit weight of a bag of coffee in pounds and the number of bags sold and displays the total price of the sale, computed as follows:

```
totalPrice        = bagWeight * numberOfBags * pricePerLb;
totalPriceWithTax = totalPrice + totalPrice * taxrate;
```

Display the result in the following manner:

```
Number of bags sold: 32
      Weight per bag: 5 lb
     Price per pound: $5.99
           Sales tax: 7.25%

         Total price: $ 1027.88
```

Format to two decimal places.

Define and use a programmer-defined CoffeeBag class. Include class constants for the price per pound and tax rate with the values $5.99 per pound and 7.25 percent, respectively.

15. In the Turtle exercises from the earlier chapters, we dealt with only one Turtle (e.g., see Exercise 28 on page 144). It is possible, however, to let multiple turtles draw on a single drawing window. To associate multiple turtles to a single drawing, we create an instance of TurtleDrawingWindow and add turtles to it as follows:

```
TurtleDrawingWindow canvas = new TurtleDrawingWindow( );
Turtle winky, pinky, tinky;

//create turtles;
//pass Turtle.NO_DEFAULT_WINDOW as an argument so
//no default drawing window is attached to a turtle.
winky = new Turtle(Turtle.NO_DEFAULT_WINDOW);
pinky = new Turtle(Turtle.NO_DEFAULT_WINDOW);
tinky = new Turtle(Turtle.NO_DEFAULT_WINDOW);

//now add turtles to the drawing window
canvas.add( winky );
canvas.add( pinky );
canvas.add( tinky );
```

Ordinarily, when you start sending messages such as turn and move to a Turtle, it will begin moving immediately. When you have only one Turtle, this is fine. However, if you have multiple turtles and want them to start moving at the same time, you have to first pause them, then give instructions, and finally command them to start moving. Here's the basic idea:

```
winky.pause( );
pinky.pause( );
tinky.pause( );
```

```
//give instructions to turtles here,
//e.g., pinky.move(50); etc.

//now let the turtles start moving
winky.start( );
pinky.start( );
tinky.start( );
```

Using these Turtle objects, draw the following three triangles:

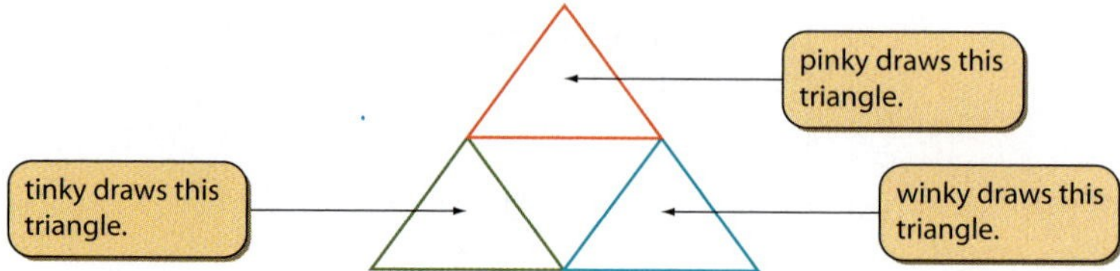

Use a different pen color for each triangle. Run the same program without pausing and describe what happens.

5 Selection Statements

Objectives

After you have read and studied this chapter, you should be able to

- Implement selection control in a program using **if** statements.
- Implement selection control in a program using **switch** statements.
- Write boolean expressions using relational and boolean operators.
- Evaluate given boolean expressions correctly.
- Nest an **if** statement inside another **if** statement's **then** or **else** part correctly.
- Describe how objects are compared.
- Choose the appropriate selection control statement for a given task.
- Define and use enumerated constants.
- Draw geometric shapes on a window.

Introduction

Decisions, decisions, decisions. From the moment we are awake until the time we go to sleep, we are making decisions. Should I eat cereal or toast? What should I wear to school today? Should I eat at the cafeteria today? And so forth. We make many of these decisions by evaluating some criteria. If the number of students in line for registration seems long, then come back tomorrow for another try. If today is Monday, Wednesday, or Friday, then eat lunch at the cafeteria.

Computer programs are no different. Any practical computer program contains many statements that make decisions. Often a course of action is determined by evaluating some kind of a test (e.g., Is the remaining balance of a meal card below the minimum?). Statements in programs are executed in sequence, which is called ***sequential execution*** or ***sequential control flow***. However, we can add decision-making statements to a program to alter this control flow. For example, we can add a statement that causes a portion of a program to be skipped if an input value is greater than 100. Or we can add a statement to disallow the purchase of food items if the balance of a meal card goes below a certain minimum. The statement that alters the control flow is called a ***control statement***. In this chapter we describe some important control statements, called *selection statements*. In Chapter 6 we will describe other control statements, called *repetition statements*.

sequential execution

control statement

5.1 The if Statement

if statement

There are two versions of the if ***statement***, called *if–then–else* and *if–then*. We begin with the first version. Suppose we wish to enter a student's test score and print out the message You did not pass if the score is less than 70 and You did pass if the score is 70 or higher. Here's how we express this logic in Java:

```
Scanner scanner = new Scanner(System.in);

System.out.print("Enter test score: ");

int testScore = scanner.nextInt();

if (testScore < 70)

   System.out.println("You did not pass");

else

   System.out.println("You did pass");
```

This statement is executed if **testScore** is less than 70.

This statement is executed if **testScore** is 70 or higher.

We use an if statement to specify which block of code to execute. A block of code may contain zero or more statements. Which block is executed depends on the

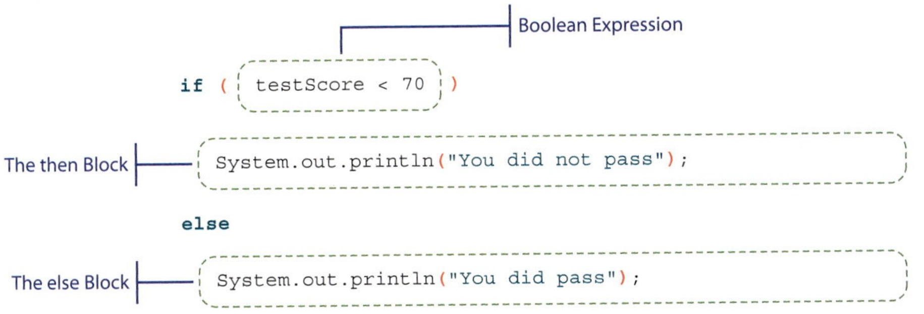

Figure 5.1 Mapping of the sample if–then–else statement to the general format.

boolean expression

result of evaluating a test condition, called a ***boolean expression***. The if–then–else statement follows this general format:

if-then-else syntax

```
if ( <boolean expression> )
   <then block>

else
   <else block>
```

Figure 5.1 illustrates the correspondence between the if–then–else statement we wrote and the general format.

The <boolean expression> is a conditional expression that is evaluated to either true or false. For example, the following three expressions are all conditional:

```
testScore < 80
testScore * 2 > 350
30 < w / (h * h)
```

relational operators

The six ***relational operators*** we can use in conditional expressions are:

```
<      // less than
<=     // less than or equal to
==     // equal to
!=     // not equal to
>      // greater than
>=     // greater than or equal to
```

Here are some more examples:

```
a * a <= c        //true if a * a is less than or equal to c
x + y != z        //true if x + y is not equal to z
a == b            //true if a is equal to b
```

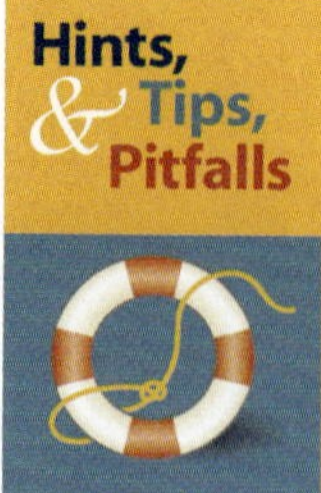

One very common error in writing programs is to mix up the assignment and equality operators. We frequently make the mistake of writing

```
if (x = 5) ...
```

when we actually wanted to say

```
if (x == 5) ...
```

If the boolean expression evaluates to true, then the statements in the <then block> are executed. Otherwise, the statements in the <else block> are executed. We will cover more complex boolean expressions in Section 5.2. Notice that we can reverse the relational operator and switch the then and else blocks to derive the equivalent code, for example,

```
if (testScore >= 70)
   System.out.println("You did pass");

else
   System.out.println("You did not pass");
```

Notice that the reverse of < is >=, not >.

selection statement

The if statement is called a ***selection*** or ***branching statement*** because it selects (or branches to) one of the alternative blocks for execution. In our example, either

```
System.out.println("You did not pass");
```

or

```
System.out.println("You did pass");
```

is executed depending on the value of the boolean expression. We can illustrate a branching path of execution with the diagram shown in Figure 5.2.

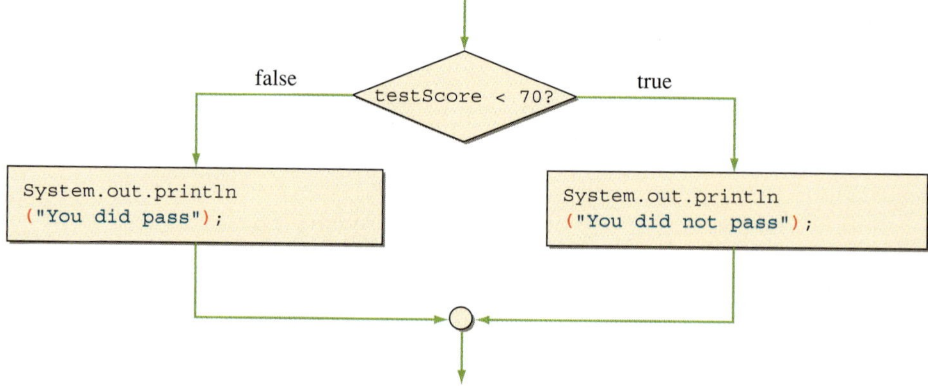

Figure 5.2 The diagram showing the control flow of the sample if–then–else statement.

In the preceding if statement, both blocks contain only one statement. The then or else block can contain more than one statement. The general format for both the <then block> and the <else block> is either a

```
<single statement>
```

or a

```
<compound statement>
```

where <single statement> is a Java statement and <compound statement> is a sequence of Java statements surrounded by braces, as shown below with $n \geq 0$ statements:

```
{
    <statement 1>
    <statement 2>
    ...
    <statement n>
}
```

If multiple statements are needed in the <then block> or the <else block>, they must be surrounded by braces { and }. For example, suppose we want to print out additional messages for each case. Let's say we also want to print Keep up the good work when the student passes and print Try harder next time when the student fails. Here's how:

```
if (testScore < 70)
{
    System.out.println("You did not pass");
    System.out.println("Try harder next time");
}
else
{
    System.out.println("You did pass");
    System.out.println("Keep up the good work");
}
```

Compound Statements

The braces are necessary to delineate the statements inside the block. Without the braces, the compiler will not be able to tell whether a statement is part of the block or part of the statement that follows the If statement.

Notice the absence of semicolons after the right braces. A semicolon is never necessary immediately after a right brace. A compound statement may contain zero or more statements, so it is perfectly valid for a compound statement to include only one statement. Indeed, we can write the sample if statement as

```
if (testScore < 70)
{
  System.out.println("You did not pass");
}

else

{
  System.out.println("You did pass");
}
```

Although it is not required, many programmers prefer to use the syntax for the compound statement even if the then or else block includes only one statement. In this textbook, we use the syntax for the compound statement regardless of the number of statements inside the then and else blocks. Following this policy is beneficial for a number of reasons. One is the ease of adding temporary output statements inside the blocks. Frequently, we want to include a temporary output statement to verify that the boolean expression is written correctly. Suppose we add output statements such as these:

```
if (testScore < 70)
{
   System.out.println("inside then:  " + testScore);
   System.out.println("You did not pass");
}
else
{
   System.out.println("inside else:  " + testScore);
   System.out.println("You did pass");
}
```

If we always use the syntax for the compound statement, we just add and delete the temporary output statements. However, if we use the syntax of the single statement, then we have to remember to add the braces when we want to include a temporary output statement. Another reason for using the compound statement syntax exclusively is to avoid the dangling else problem. We discuss this problem in Section 5.2.

The placement of left and right braces does not matter to the compiler. The compiler will not complain if you write the earlier if statement as

```
if (testScore < 70)
{ System.out.println("You did not pass");
  System.out.println("Try harder next time");} else
{
  System.out.println("You did pass");
  System.out.println("Keep up the good work");}
```

However, to keep your code readable and easy to follow, you should format your if statements using one of the two most common styles:

Style 1

```
if ( <boolean expression> ) {
    ...
} else {
    ...
}
```

Style 2

```
if ( <boolean expression> )
{
    ...
}
else
{
    ...
}
```

In this book, we will use style 1, mainly because this style adheres to the code conventions for the Java programming language. If you prefer style 2, then go ahead and use it. Whichever style you choose, be consistent, because a consistent look and feel is very important to make your code readable.

The document that provides the details of code conventions for Java can be found at **http://java.sun.com/docs/codeconv/html/CodeConvTOC.doc.html**
This document describes the Java language coding standards dictated in the Java Language Specification. It is important to follow the code conventions as closely as possible to increase the readability of the software.

There is a second variation of style 1 in which we place the reserved word else on a new line as

Style 3

```
if ( <boolean expression> ) {
    ...
}
else {
    ...
}
```

Many programmers prefer this variation of style 1 because the reserved word else aligns with the matching if. However, if we nitpick, style 3 goes against the logic behind the recommended style 1 format, which is to begin a new statement at one position with a reserved word. The reserved word **else** is a part of the if statement, not the beginning of a new statement. Thus style 1 places the reserved word else to the right of the matching if.

Again, the actual format is not that important. Consistent use of the same format is. So, whichever style you use, use it consistently. To promote consistency among all programmers, we recommend that everybody to adopt the code conventions. Even though the recommended format may look peculiar at first, with some repeated use, the format becomes natural in no time.

Let's summarize the key points to remember:

Things to Remember

*Rules for writing the **then** and **else** blocks:*

1. *Left and right braces are necessary to surround the statements if the **then** or else **block** contains multiple statements.*
2. *Braces are not necessary if the **then** or **else** block contains only one statement.*
3. *A semicolon is not necessary after a right brace.*

Now let's study a second version of the if statement called *if–then*. Suppose we want to print out the message You are an honor student if the test score is 95 or above and print out nothing otherwise. For this type of testing, we use the second version of the if statement, whose general format is

if-then syntax

```
if ( <boolean expression> )
   <then block>
```

The second version contains only the <then block>. Using this version and the compound statement syntax, we express the selection control as

```
if (testScore >= 95)  {
   System.out.println("You are an honor student");
}
```

Figure 5.3 shows the diagram that illustrates the control flow for this if–then statement. We will refer collectively to both versions as the *if* statement.

Notice that the if–then statement is not necessary, because we can write any if–then statement using if–then–else by including no statement in the else block. For instance, the sample if–then statement can be written as

```
if (testScore >= 95) {

   System.out.println("You are an honor student");

} else { }
```

In this book, we use if–then statements whenever appropriate.

Let's conclude this section with a sample class that models a circle. We will name the class Ch5Circle, and its instances are capable of computing the

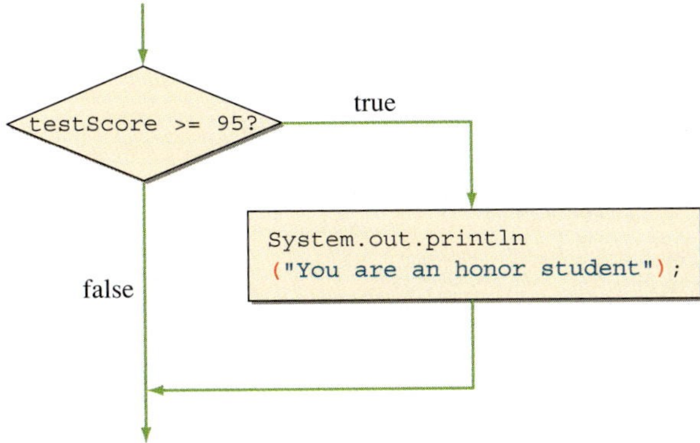

Figure 5.3 The diagram showing the control flow of the second version of the **if** statement.

circumference and area. We will include a test in this class so the methods such as getArea and getCircumference return the constant INVALID_DIMENSION when the dimension of the radius is invalid. Here's the Ch5Circle class (most comments are removed for the sake of brevity):

As the number of methods gets larger, we will use this marker to quickly locate the program components. Shaded icon is used for a private element.

```
/*
    Chapter 5 The Circle class

    File: Ch5Circle.java
*/

class Ch5Circle {

    public static final int INVALID_DIMENSION = -1;

    private double radius;

    public Ch5Circle(double r) {
        setRadius(r);
    }

    public double getArea( ) {

        double result = INVALID_DIMENSION;

        if (isRadiusValid())  {

            result = Math.PI * radius * radius;

        }

        return result;
    }
```

Data Members

getArea

```
    public double getCircumference( ) {

        double result = INVALID_DIMENSION;

        if (isRadiusValid()) {

            result = 2.0 * Math.PI * radius;
        }

        return result;
    }

    public double getDiameter( ) {

        double diameter = INVALID_DIMENSION;

        if (isRadiusValid()) {

            diameter = 2.0 * radius;
        }

        return diameter;
    }

    public double getRadius( ) {
        return radius;
    }

    public void setDiameter(double d) {

        if (d > 0) {
            setRadius(d/2.0);
        } else {
            setRadius(INVALID_DIMENSION);
        }
    }

    public void setRadius(double r) {

        if (r > 0) {
            radius = r;
        } else {
            radius = INVALID_DIMENSION;
        }
    }

    private boolean isRadiusValid( ) {

        return radius != INVALID_DIMENSION;
    }

}
```

getCircumference

getDiameter

getRadius

setDiameter

setRadius

isRadiusValid

Notice the if statement in the getArea method is written as

```
if (isRadiusValid()) {
    ...
}
```

The <boolean expression> in the if statement can be any expression that evaluates to true or false, including a call to a method whose return type is boolean, such as the isRadiusValid method. The use of such a boolean method often makes the code easier to read, and easier to modify if the boolean method is called from many methods (e.g., there are three methods calling the isRadiusValid method).

Here's a short main class to test the functionality of the Ch5Circle class:

```
/*
    Chapter 5 Sample Program: Computing Circle Dimensions

    File: Ch5Sample1.java
*/

import java.util.*;

class Ch5Sample1 {

    public static void main(String[] args) {

        double    radius, circumference, area;

        Ch5Circle circle;

        Scanner scanner = new Scanner(System.in);

        System.out.print("Enter radius: ");
        radius = scanner.nextDouble();

        circle = new Ch5Circle(radius);

        circumference = circle.getCircumference();

        area          = circle.getArea();

        System.out.println("Input radius:  " + radius);
        System.out.println("Circumference: " + circumference);
        System.out.println("Area:          " + area);
    }
}
```

Notice that the program will display -1.0 when the input radius is invalid. We can improve the display by adding an if test in the main program as follows:

```
System.out.print("Circumference: ");
if (circumference == Ch5Circle.INVALID_DIMENSION) {
   System.out.println("Cannot compute. Input invalid");
} else {
   System.out.println(circumference);
}
```

Another possible improvement in the main program is to check the input value first. For instance,

```
radius = ... ;
if (radius > 0) {
   //do the computation as the sample main method
} else {
   //print out the error message
}
```

Even when a client programmer does not include appropriate tests in his program, we must define a reusable class in a robust manner so it will not crash or produce erroneous results. For the Ch5Circle class, we add a test so the data member radius is set to either a valid datum or a specially designated value (INVALID_DIMENSION) for any invalid data. By designing the class in this manner, we protect the class from a possible misuse (e.g., attempting to assign a negative radius) and producing meaningless results, such as –5.88. We always strive for a reliable and robust reusable class that will withstand the abuse and misuse of client programmers.

1. Identify the invalid if statements:

a.
```
if ( a < b ) then
   x = y;
else
   x = z;
```

b.
```
if ( a < b )
   else x = y;
```

c.
```
if ( a < b )
   x = y;
   else {
   x = z;
   };
```

d.
```
if ( a < b ) {
   x = y;  } else
   x = z;
```

2. Are the following two if statements equivalent?

```
/*A*/ if ( x < y )
          System.out.println("Hello");
       else
          System.out.println("Bye");

/*B*/ if ( x > y )
          System.out.println("Bye");
       else
          System.out.println("Hello");
```

5.2 Nested if Statements

nested **if** statement

The then and else blocks of an if statement can contain any statement including another if statement. An if statement that contains another if statement in either its then or else block is called a ***nested if*** statement. Let's look at an example. In the earlier example, we printed out the messages You did pass or You did not pass depending on the test score. Let's modify the code to print out three possible messages. If the test score is lower than 70, then we print You did not pass, as before. If the test score is 70 or higher, then we will check the student's age. If the age is less than 10, we will print You did a great job. Otherwise, we will print You did pass, as before. Figure 5.4 is a diagram showing the logic of this nested test. The code is written as follows:

```
if (testScore >= 70) {
   if (studentAge < 10) {
      System.out.println("You did a great job");
   } else {

      System.out.println("You did pass");//test score >= 70
   }                                     //and age >= 10
} else { //test score < 70

   System.out.println("You did not pass");
}
```

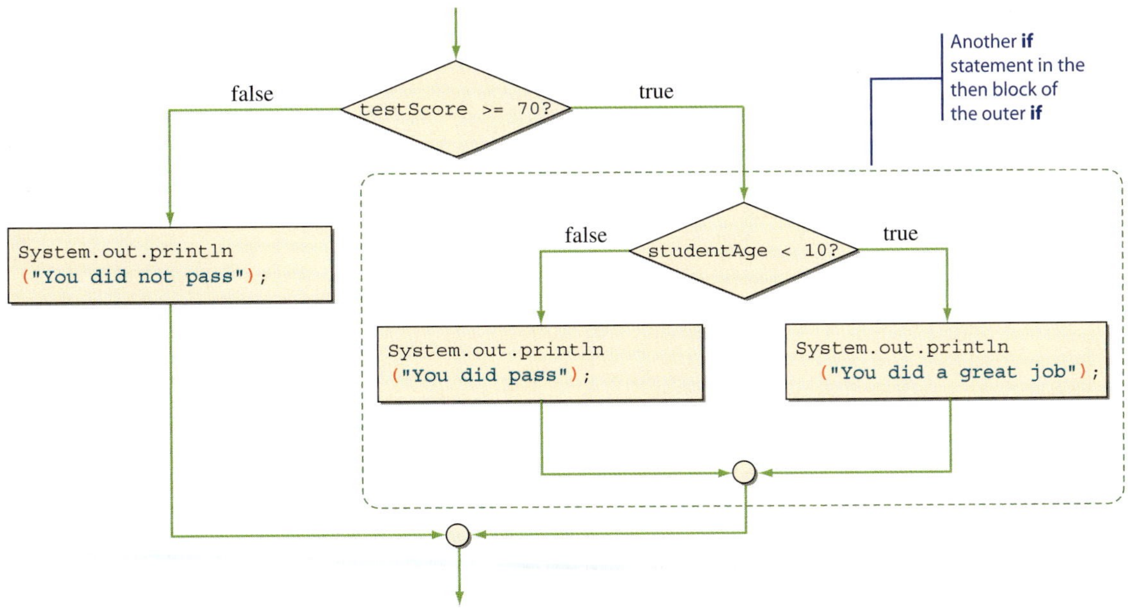

Figure 5.4 A diagram showing the control flow of the example nested **if** statement.

Since the then block of the outer if contains another if statement, the outer if is called a nested if statement. It is possible to write if tests in different ways to achieve the same result. For example, the preceding code can also be expressed as

```
if (testScore >= 70 && studentAge < 10) {
    System.out.println("You did a great job");
} else {
    //either testScore < 70 OR studentAge >= 10

    if (testScore >= 70) {
       System.out.println("You did pass");
    } else {
       System.out.println("You did not pass");
    }
}
```

Several other variations can also achieve the same result. As a general rule, we strive to select the one that is most readable (i.e., most easily understood) and most efficient. Often no one variation stands out, and the one you choose depends on your preferred style of programming.

Here's an example in which one variation is clearly a better choice. Suppose we input three integers and determine how many of them are negative. Here's the first variation. To show the structure more clearly, we purposely do not use the braces in the then and else blocks.

In this and the following examples, we purposely do not use the braces so we can provide a better illustration of the topics we are presenting.

```
if (num1 < 0)
   if (num2 < 0)
      if (num3 < 0)
         negativeCount = 3; //all three are negative
      else
         negativeCount = 2; //num1 and num2 are negative
   else
      if (num3 < 0)
         negativeCount = 2; //num1 and num3 are negative
      else
         negativeCount = 1; //num1 is negative
else
   if (num2 < 0)
      if (num3 < 0)
         negativeCount = 2; //num2 and num3 are negative
      else
         negativeCount = 1; //num2 is negative
   else
      if (num3 < 0)
         negativeCount = 1; //num3 is negative
      else
         negativeCount = 0; //no negative numbers
```

It certainly did the job. But elegantly? Here's the second variation:

```
negativeCount = 0;

if (num1 < 0)
        negativeCount = negativeCount + 1;
if (num2 < 0)
        negativeCount = negativeCount + 1;
if (num3 < 0)
        negativeCount = negativeCount + 1;
```

Which version should we use? The second variation is the only reasonable way to go. The first variation is not a viable option because it is very inefficient and very difficult to read. We apply the nested if structure if we have to test conditions in some required order. In this example these three tests are independent of one another, so they can be executed in any order. In other words, it doesn't matter whether we test num1 first or last.

The statement

```
negativeCount = negativeCount + 1;
```

increments the variable by 1. This type of statement that changes the value of a variable by adding a fixed number occurs frequently in programs. Instead of repeating the same variable name twice, we can write it succinctly as

```
negativeCount++;
```

Similarly, a statement such as

```
count = count - 1;
```

can be written as

```
count--;
```

increment and decrement operators

The double plus operator (++) is called the ***increment operator***, and the double minus operator (−−) is the ***decrement operator*** (which decrements the variable by 1). The increment and decrement operators have higher precedence than unary operators. See Table 5.3 on page 235. *Note:* There are prefix and postfix increment/decrement operators in which the operators come before and after the variable (or an expression), respectively. We only use the postfix operators in this book, and the precedence rules presented in the table apply to the postfix operators only.

Notice that we indent the then and else blocks to show the nested structure clearly. Indentation is used as a visual guide for the readers. It makes no difference to a Java compiler. For example, we make our intent clear by writing the statement as

```
if (x < y)
   if (z != w)
      a = b + 1;
   else
      a = c + 1;
else
   a = b * c;
```

It takes some practice before you can write well-formed **if** statements. Here are some rules to help you write the **if** statements.

Rule 1: Minimize the number of nestings.
Rule 2: Avoid complex boolean expressions. Make them as simple as possible. Don't include many ANDs and ORs.
Rule 3: Eliminate any unnecessary comparisons.
Rule 4: Don't be satisfied with the first correct statement. Always look for improvement.
Rule 5: Read your code again. Can you follow the statement easily? If not, try to improve it.

But to the Java compiler, it does not matter if we write the same code as

```
if (x < y)if (z != w)a = b + 1;else a = c + 1; else a = b * c;
```

Although indentation is not required to run the program, using proper indentation is an important aspect of good programming style. Since the goal is to make your code readable, not to follow any one style of indentation, you are free to choose your own style. We recommend style 1 shown on page 219.

The next example shows a style of indentation accepted as standard for a nested if statement in which nesting occurs only in the else block. Instead of determining whether a student passes or not, we will now display a letter grade based on the following formula:

Test Score	Grade
$90 \le$ score	A
$80 \le$ score < 90	B
$70 \le$ score < 80	C
$60 \le$ score < 70	D
score < 60	F

The statement can be written as

```
if (score >= 90)
   System.out.println("Your grade is A");
else
   if (score >= 80)
      System.out.println("Your grade is B");
   else
      if (score >= 70)
         System.out.println("Your grade is C");
```

```
      else
         if (score >= 60)
            System.out.println("Your grade is D");
         else
            System.out.println("Your grade is F");
```

However, the standard way to indent the statement is as follows:

```
if (score >= 90)
   System.out.println("Your grade is A");

else if (score >= 80)
   System.out.println("Your grade is B");

else if (score >= 70)
   System.out.println("Your grade is C");

else if (score >= 60)
   System.out.println("Your grade is D");

else
   System.out.println("Your grade is F");
```

We mentioned that indentation is meant for human eyes only. For example, we can clearly see the intent of a programmer just by looking at the indentation when we read

```
if (x < y)
   if (x < z)
      System.out.println("Hello");
else
   System.out.println("Good bye");
```

Indentation style A

A Java compiler, however, will interpret the above as

```
if (x < y)
   if (x < z)
      System.out.println("Hello");
   else
      System.out.println("Good bye");
```

Indentation style B

dangling **else** problem

This example has a ***dangling else problem***. The Java compiler matches an else with the previous unmatched if, so the compiler will interpret the statement by matching the else with the inner if (if (x < z)), whether you use indentation style A or B. If you want to express the logic of indentation style A, you have to express it as

```
if (x < y) {
   if (x < z)
      System.out.println("Hello");
} else
   System.out.println("Good bye");
```

This dangling else problem is another reason why we recommend that beginners use the syntax for <compound statement> in the then and else blocks. In other words, always use the braces in the then and else blocks.

Let's conclude this section by including tests inside the add and deduct methods of the Account class from Chapter 4. For both methods, we will update the balance only when the amount passed is positive. Furthermore, for the deduct method, we will update the balance only if it does not become a negative number after the deduction. This will require the use of a nested if statement. The following is the class declaration. The name is Ch5Account, and this class is based on AccountVer2 from Chapter 4. We only list the two methods here because other parts are the same as in AccountVer2.

add

```
class Ch5Account {

    . . .

    //Adds the passed amount to the balance
    public void add(double amt) {

        //add if amt is positive; otherwise, do nothing
        if (amt > 0) {
            balance = balance + amt;
        }
    }
```

deduct

```
    //Deducts the passed amount from the balance
    public void deduct(double amt) {

        //deduct if amt is positive; do nothing otherwise
        if (amt > 0) {
            double newbalance = balance - amt;

            if (newbalance >= 0) {    //if a new balance is positive, then
                balance = newbalance; //update the balance; otherwise,
            }                         //do nothing.
        }
    }
    . . .
}
```

1. Rewrite the following nested if statements without using any nesting.

a.
```
if ( a < c )
    if ( b < c )
        x = y;
    else
        x = z;
```

```
   else
      x = z;
b. if ( a == b )
      x = y;
   else
      if ( a > b )
         x = y;
      else
         x = z;
c. if ( a < b )
      if ( a >= b )
         x = z;
      else
         x = y;
   else
      x = z;
```

2. Format the following if statements with indentation.

```
a. if ( a < b  ) if ( c > d ) x = y;
   else x = z;
b. if ( a < b ) { if ( c > d ) x = y; }
   else x = z;
c. if ( a < b ) x = y; if ( a < c ) x = z;
   else if ( c < d ) z = y;
```

5.3 Boolean Expressions and Variables

In addition to the arithmetic operators introduced in Chapter 3 and relational operators introduced in Section 5.2, boolean expressions can contain conditional and boolean operators. A ***boolean operator***, also called a *logical operator,* takes boolean values as its operands and returns a boolean value. Three boolean operators are AND, OR, and NOT. In Java, the symbols &&, ||, and ! represent the AND, OR, and NOT operators, respectively. Table 5.1 explains how these operators work.

boolean operator

The AND operation results in true only if both P and Q are true. The OR operation results in true if either P or Q is true. The NOT operation is true if A is false and is false if P is true. Combining boolean operators with relational and arithmetic operators, we can come up with long boolean expressions such as

```
(x + 150) == y || x < y && !(y < z && z < x)
(x < y) && (a == b || a == c)
a != 0 && b != 0 && (a + b < 10)
```

In Section 5.1 we stated that we can reverse the relational operator and switch the then and else blocks to derive the equivalent code. For example,

```
if (age < 0) {
   System.out.println("Invalid age is entered");
} else {
   System.out.println("Valid age is entered");
}
```

Table 5.1 Boolean operators and their meanings

P	Q	P && Q	P || Q	!P
false	false	false	false	true
false	true	false	true	true
true	false	false	true	false
true	true	true	true	false

is equivalent to

```
if ( !(age < 0) ) {
   System.out.println("Valid age is entered");
} else {
   System.out.println("Invalid age is entered");
}
```

which can be written more naturally as

```
if (age >= 0) {
   System.out.println("Valid age is entered");
} else {
   System.out.println("Invalid age is entered");
}
```

Reversing the relational operator means negating the boolean expression. In other words, !(age < 0) is equivalent to (age >= 0). Now, consider the following if-then-else statement:

```
if (temperature >= 65 && distanceToDestination < 2) {
   System.out.println("Let's walk");
} else {
   System.out.println("Let's drive");
}
```

If the temperature is greater than or equal to 65 degrees and the distance to the destination is less than 2 mi., we walk. Otherwise (it's too cold or too far away), we drive. How do we reverse the if-then-else statement? We can rewrite the statement by negating the boolean expression and switching the then and else blocks as

```
if ( !(temperature >= 65 && distanceToDestination < 2) ) {
   System.out.println("Let's drive");
} else {
   System.out.println("Let's walk");
}
```

or more directly and naturally as

```
if (temperature < 65 || distanceToDestination >= 2) {
   System.out.println("Let's drive");
} else {
   System.out.println("Let's walk");
}
```

The expression

```
!(temperature >= 65 && distanceToDestination < 2)
```

is equivalent to

```
!(temperature >= 65) || !(distanceToDestination < 2)
```

which, in turn, is equivalent to

```
(temperature < 65 || distanceToDestination >= 2)
```

The logical equivalence is derived by applying the following DeMorgan's law:

Rule 1: `!(P && Q)` ⟺ `!P || !Q`

Rule 2: `!(P || Q)` ⟺ `!P && !Q`

Equivalence symbol

Table 5.2 shows their equivalence.

Now consider the following expression:

```
x / y > z || y == 0
```

arithmetic exception

What will be the result if y is equal to 0? Easy, the result is true, many of you might say. Actually a runtime error called an ***arithmetic exception*** will result, because the expression

```
x / y
```

Table 5.2 The truth table illustrating DeMorgan's law

P	Q	!(P && Q)	!P || !Q	!(P || Q)	!P && !Q
false	false	true	true	true	true
false	true	true	true	false	false
true	false	true	true	false	false
true	true	false	false	false	false

divide-by-zero error

causes a problem known as a ***divide-by-zero error***. Remember that you cannot divide a number by zero.

However, if we reverse the order to

```
y == 0 || x / y > z
```

then no arithmetic exception will occur because the test x / y > z will not be evaluated. For the OR operator ||, if the left operand is evaluated to true, then the right operand will not be evaluated, because the whole expression is true, whether the value of the right operand is true or false. We call such an evaluation method a ***short-circuit evaluation***. For the AND operator &&, the right operand need not be evaluated if the left operand is evaluated to false, because the result will then be false whether the value of the right operand is true or false.

short-circuit evaluation

Just as the operator precedence rules are necessary to evaluate arithmetic expressions unambiguously, they are required for evaluating boolean expressions. Table 5.3 expands Table 3.3 by including all operators introduced so far.

In mathematics, we specify the range of values for a variable as

```
80  ≤ x < 90
```

In Java, to test that the value for x is within the specified lower and upper bounds, we express it as

```
80 <= x && x < 90
```

You cannot specify it as

```
80 <= x < 90
```

Wrong

This is a syntax error because the relational operators (<, <=, etc.) are binary operators whose operands must be numerical values. Notice that the result of the subexpression

```
80 <= x
```

is a boolean value, which cannot be compared to the numerical value 90. Their data types are not compatible.

The result of a boolean expression is either true or false, which are the two values of data type boolean. As is the case with other data types, a value of a data type can be assigned to a variable of the same data type. In other words, we can declare a variable of data type boolean and assign a boolean value to it. Here are examples:

```
boolean pass, done;

pass = 70 < x;
done = true;
```

One possible use of boolean variables is to keep track of the program settings or user preferences. A variable (of any data type, not just boolean) used for this

Table 5.3 Operator precedence rules. Groups are listed in descending order of precedence. An operator with a higher precedence will be evaluated first. If two operators have the same precedence, then the associativity rule is applied

Group	Operator	Precedence	Associativity
Subexpression	( )	10 (If parentheses are nested, then innermost subexpression is evaluated first.)	Left to right
Postfix increment and decrement operators	++ --	9	Right to left
Unary operators	- !	8	Right to left
Multiplicative operators	* / %	7	Left to right
Additive operators	+ -	6	Left to right
Relational operators	< <= > >=	5	Left to right
Equality operators	== !=	4	Left to right
Boolean AND	&&	3	Left to right
Boolean OR	||	2	Left to right
Assignment	=	1	Right to left

flag

purpose is called a ***flag***. Suppose we want to allow the user to display either short or long messages. Many people, when using a new program, prefer to see long messages, such as Enter a person's age and press the Enter key to continue. But once they are familiar with the program, many users prefer to see short messages, such as Enter age. We can use a boolean flag to remember the user's preference. We can set the flag longMessageFormat at the beginning of the program to true or false depending on the user's choice. Once this boolean flag is set, we can refer to the flag at different points in the program as follows:

```
if (longMessageFormat) {
   //display the message in long format
```

```
} else {

   //display the message in short format
}
```

Notice the value of a boolean variable is true or false, so even though it is valid, we do not write a boolean expression as

```
if (isRaining == true) {
   System.out.println("Store is open");
} else {
   System.out.println("Store is closed");
}
```

but more succinctly as

```
if (isRaining) {
   System.out.println("Store is open");
} else {
   System.out.println("Store is closed");
}
```

Another point that we have to be careful about in using boolean variables is the choice of identifier. Instead of using a boolean variable such as motionStatus, it is more meaningful and descriptive to use the variable isMoving. For example, the statement

```
if (isMoving) {
   //the mobile robot is moving
} else {
   //the mobile robot is not moving
}
```

is much clearer than the statement

```
if (motionStatus) {
   //the mobile robot is moving
} else {
   //the mobile robot is not moving
}
```

When we define a boolean data member for a class, it is a Java convention to use the prefix is instead of get for the accessor.

We again conclude the section with a sample class. Let's improve the Ch5Account class by adding a boolean data member active to represent the state of an account. When an account is first open, it is set to an active state. Deposits and withdrawals can be made only when the account is active. If the account is inactive, then the requested opertion is ignored. Here's how the class is defined (the actual class name is Ch5AccountVer2):

```
class Ch5AccountVer2 {

    // Data Members
    private String ownerName;

    private double balance;

    private boolean active;

    //Constructor
    public Ch5AccountVer2(String name, double startingBalance ) {

        ownerName = name;
        balance = startingBalance;

        setActive(true);
    }

    //Adds the passed amount to the balance
    public void add(double amt) {
        //add if amt is positive; do nothing otherwise
        if (isActive() && amt > 0) {
            balance = balance + amt;
        }
    }

    //Closes the account; set 'active' to false
    public void close( ) {

        setActive(false);
    }

    //Deducts the passed amount from the balance
    public void deduct(double amt) {

        //deduct if amt is positive; do nothing otherwise
        if (isActive() && amt > 0) {
            double newbalance = balance - amt;

            if (newbalance >= 0) { //don't let the balance become negative
                balance = newbalance;
            }
        }
    }
```

Data Members

add

close

deduct

getCurrentBalance

```
    //Returns the current balance of this account
    public double getCurrentBalance( ) {
        return balance;
    }
```

getOwnerName

```
    //Returns the name of this account's owner
    public String getOwnerName( ) {

        return ownerName;
    }
```

isActive

```
    //Is the account active?
    public boolean isActive( ) {
        return active;
    }
```

setOwnerName

```
    //Assigns the name of this account's owner
    public void setOwnerName(String name) {

        ownerName = name;
    }
```

setActive

```
    //Sets 'active' to true or false
    private void setActive(boolean state) {

        active = state;
    }
}
```

1. Evaluate the following boolean expressions. Assume x, y, and z have some numerical values.

   a. `4 < 5 || 6 == 6`
   b. `2 < 4 && (false || 5 <= 4)`
   c. `x <= y && !(z != z) || x > y`
   d. `x < y || z < y && y <= z`

2. Identify errors in the following boolean expressions and assignments. Assume x and y have some numerical values.

   a.
   ```
   boolean done;
   done = x = y;
   ```
   b. `2 < 4 && (3 < 5) + 1 == 3`
   c.
   ```
   boolean quit;
   quit = true;
   quit == ( 34 == 20 ) && quit;
   ```

We introduced the logical AND and OR operations using the symbols **&&** and **||**. In Java, there are single ampersand and single vertical bar operations. For example, if we write an **if** statement as

```
if ( 70 <= x & x < 90 )
```

it will compile and run. Unlike the double ampersand, the single ampersand will not do a short-circuit evaluation. It will evaluate both left and right operands. The single vertical bar works in an analogous manner. So, which one should we use? Use double ampersand for AND and double vertical bars for OR. We will most likely never encounter a situation where we cannot use the double ampersand or the double vertical bars.

5.4 Comparing Objects

With primitive data types, we have only one way to compare them, but with objects (reference data type), we have two ways to compare them. We discuss the ways the objects can be compared in this section. First, let's review how we compare primitive data types. What would be the output of the following code?

```
int num1, num2;

num1 = 15;
num2 = 15;

if (num1 == num2) {
   System.out.println("They are equal");
} else {
   System.out.println("They are not equal");
}
```

Because the two variables hold the same value, the output is

```
They are equal
```

Now, let's see how the objects can be compared. We will use String objects for illustration. Since we use string data all the time in our programs, it is very important for us to understand perfectly how String objects can be compared.

Consider the following code that attempts to compare two String objects:

```
String str1, str2;

str1 = new String("Java");
str2 = new String("Java");

if (str1 == str2) {
   System.out.println("They are equal");
```

```
} else {
   System.out.println("They are not equal");
}
```

What would be an output? The answer is

```
They are not equal
```

The two objects are constructed with the same sequence of characters, but the result of comparison came back that they were not equal. Why?

When two variables are compared, we are comparing their contents. In the case of primitive data types, the content is the actual value. In case of reference data types, the content is the address where the object is stored. Since there are two distinct String objects, stored at different addresses, the contents of str1 and str2 are different, and therefore, the equality testing results in false. If we change the code to

```
String str1, str2;

str1 = new String("Java");
str2 = str1;

if (str1 == str2) {
   System.out.println("They are equal");
} else {
   System.out.println("They are not equal");
}
```

No new object is created here. The content (address) of **str1** is copied to **str2**, making them both point to the same object.

then the output would be

```
They are equal
```

because now we have one String object and both variables str1 and str2 point to this object. This means the contents of str1 and str2 are the same because they refer to the same address. Figure 5.5 shows the distinction.

What can we do if we need to check whether two distinct String objects have the same sequence of characters? Many standard classes include different types of comparison methods. The String class, for example, includes the equals and equalsIgnoreCase comparison methods. The equals method returns true if two String objects have the exact same sequence of characters. The equalsIgnoreCase method does the same as the equals method, but the comparison is done in a case-insensitive manner. Using the equals method, we can rewrite the first sample code as

```
String str1, str2;

str1 = new String("Java");
str2 = new String("Java");

if (str1.equals(str2)) {
   System.out.println("They are equal");
} else {
   System.out.println("They are not equal");
}
```

Use the **equals** method.

Case A: Two variables refer to two different objects.

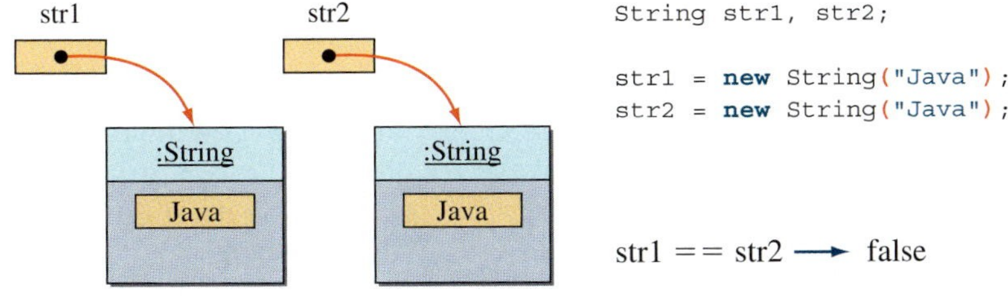

Case B: Two variables refer to the same object.

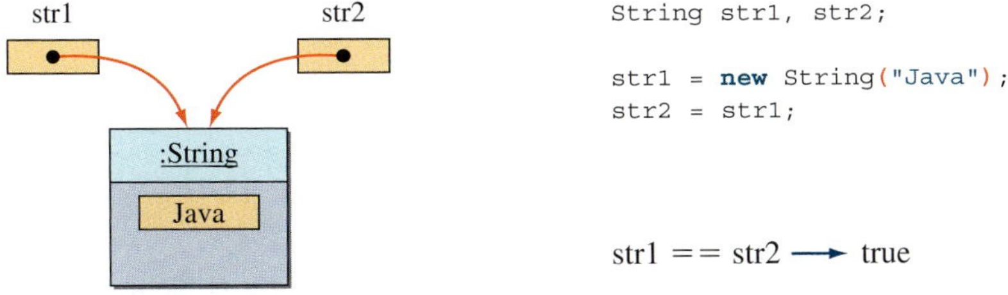

Figure 5.5 How the equality == testing works with the objects.

and get the result

```
They are equal
```

Just as the String and many standard classes provide the equals method, it is common to include such an equals method in programmer-defined classes also. Consider a Fraction class. We say two Fraction objects are equal if they have the same value for the numerator and the denominator. Here's how we can define the equals method for the Fraction class:

```
class Fraction {

   private int numerator;

   private int denominator;

   ...

   //constructor and other methods

   ...

   public int getNumerator( ) {
      return numerator;
   }
```

```
    public int getDenominator( ) {
        return denominator;
    }

    public boolean equals(Fraction number) {
        return (numerator == number.getNumerator()
                && denominator == number.getDenominator());
    }
}
```

Compare this object's values to the values of **number**

Notice that the body of the equals method is a concise version of

```
if (numerator == number.getNumerator( )
        && denominator == number.getDenominator()) {

    return true;

} else {

    return false;
}
```

Using the equals method, we can compare two Fraction objects in the following manner:

```
Fraction frac1, frac2;

//create frac1 and frac2 objects
...

if (frac1.equals(frac2)) {
    ...
}
```

or equivalently as

```
if (frac2.equals(frac1)) {
    ...
}
```

Note that the equals method as defined is incomplete. For example, if we compare fractions 4/8 and 3/6, using this equals method, we get false as the result because the method does not compare the fractions in their simplified form. The method should have reduced both 4/8 and 3/6 to 1/2 and then compared. To implement a method that reduces a fraction to its simplest form, we need to use a repetition control statement. We will revisit this problem when we learn how to write repetition control statements in Chapter 6. Also, we will provide the complete definition of the Fraction class in Chapter 7.

We conclude this section by presenting an exception to the rule for comparing objects. This exception applies to the String class only. We already mentioned in

Chapter 2 that for the String class only, we do not have to use the new operator to create an instance. In other words, instead of writing

```
String str = new String("Java");
```

we can write

```
String str = "Java";
```

which is a more common form. These two statements are not identical in terms of memory allocation, which in turn affects how the string comparisons work. Figure 5.6 shows the difference in assigning a String object to a variable. If we do not use the new operator, then string data are treated as if they are a primitive data type. When we use the same literal String constants in a program, there will be exactly one String object.

This means we can use the equal symbol == to compare String objects when no new operators are used. However, regardless of how the String objects are created, it is always correct and safe to use the equals and other comparison methods to compare two strings.

Things to Remember

*Always use the **equals** and other comparison methods to compare **String** objects. Do not use == even though it may work correctly in certain cases.*

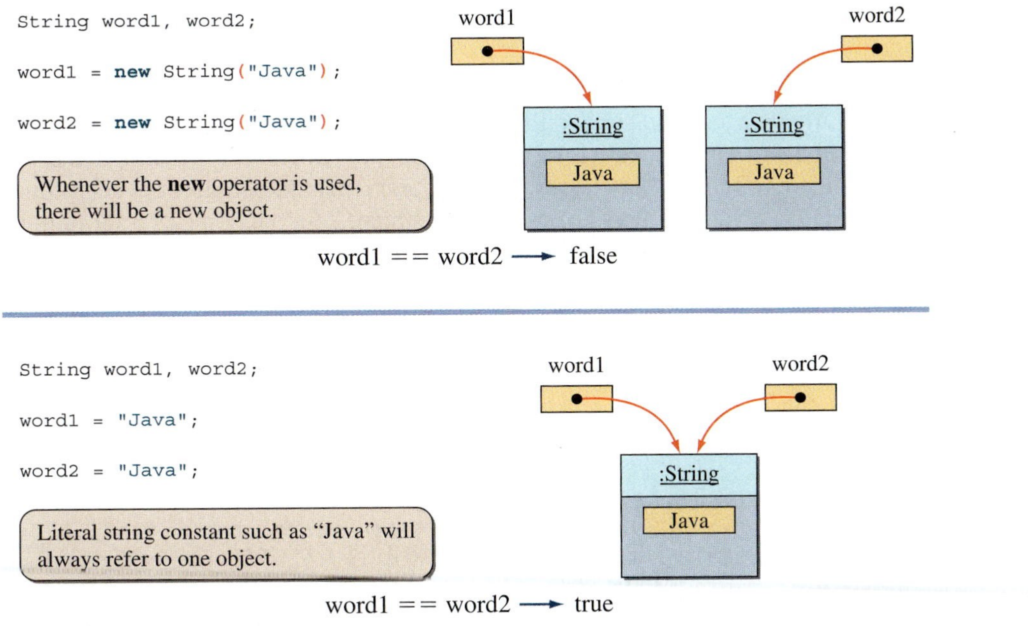

```
String word1, word2;

word1 = new String("Java");

word2 = new String("Java");
```

Whenever the **new** operator is used, there will be a new object.
word1
word2
:String
Java
:String
Java
word1 == word2 → false

```
String word1, word2;

word1 = "Java";

word2 = "Java";
```

Literal string constant such as "Java" will always refer to one object.
word1
word2
:String
Java
word1 == word2 → true

Figure 5.6 Difference between using and not using the **new** operator for **String.**

1. Determine the output of the following code.

```
String str1 = "Java";
String str2 = "Java";

boolean result1 = str1 == str2;
boolean result2 = str1.equals(str2);

System.out.println(result1);
System.out.println(result2);
```

2. Determine the output of the following code.

```
String str1 = new String("latte");
String str2 = new String("LATTE");

boolean result1 = str1 == str2;
boolean result2 = str1.equals(str2);

System.out.println(result1);
System.out.println(result2);
```

3. Show the state of memory after the following statements are executed.

```
String str1, str2, str3;
str1 = "Jasmine";
str2 = "Oolong";
str3 = str2;
str2 = str1;
```

5.5 The switch Statement

switch statement

Another Java statement that implements a selection control flow is the switch *statement*. Suppose we want to direct the students to the designated location for them to register for classes. The location where they register is determined by their grade level. The user enters 1 for freshman, 2 for sophomore, 3 for junior, and 4 for senior. Using the switch statement, we can write the code as

```
int gradeLevel;

Scanner scanner = new Scanner(System.in);

System.out.print("Grade (Frosh-1,Soph-2,...): ");

gradeLevel = scanner.nextInt();

switch (gradeLevel) {

   case 1: System.out.println("Go to the Gymnasium");
           break;

   case 2: System.out.println("Go to the Science Auditorium");
           break;
```

```
        case 3: System.out.println("Go to Halligan Hall Rm 104");
                break;

        case 4: System.out.println("Go to Root Hall Rm 101");
                break;
    }
```

The syntax for the switch statement is

switch statement syntax

```
switch ( <integer expression> ) {

    <case label 1> : <case body 1>
    ...
    <case label n> : <case body n>
}
```

Figure 5.7 illustrates the correspondence between the switch statement we wrote and the general format.

The <case label i> has the form

default reserved word

```
case <integer constant>   or   default
```

and <case body i> is a sequence of zero or more statements. Notice that <case body i> is not surrounded by left and right braces. The <constant> can be either a named or literal constant.

The data type of <arithmetic expression> must be char, byte, short, or int. (*Note:* We will cover the data type char in Chap. 9.) The value of <arithmetic expression> is compared against the constant value i of <case label i>. If there is a

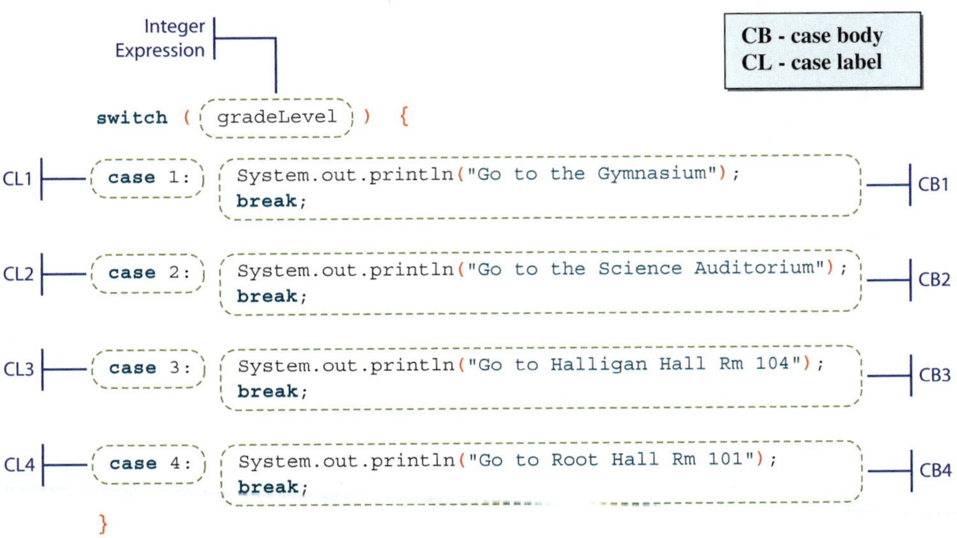

Figure 5.7 Mapping of the sample **switch** statement to the general format.

matching case, then its case body is executed. If there is no matching case, then the execution continues to the statement that follows the switch statement. No two cases are allowed to have the same value for <constant>, and the cases can be listed in any order.

break statement

Notice that each case in the sample switch statement is terminated with the break ***statement***. The break statement causes execution to continue from the statement following this switch statement, skipping the remaining portion of the switch statement. The following example illustrates how the break statement works:

```
//Assume necessary declaration and object creation are done

selection = 1;

switch (selection) {
   case 0: System.out.println(0);
   case 1: System.out.println(1);
   case 2: System.out.println(2);
   case 3: System.out.println(3);
}
```

When this code is executed, the output is

```
1
2
3
```

because after the statement in case 1 is executed, statements in the remaining cases will be executed also. To execute statements in one and only one case, we need to include the break statement at the end of each case, as we have done in the first example. Figure 5.8 shows the effect of the break statement.

The break statement is not necessary in the last case, but for consistency we place it in every case. Also, by doing so we don't have to remember to include the break statement in the last case when we add more cases to the end of the switch statement.

Individual cases do not have to include a statement, so we can write something like this:

```
Scanner scanner = new Scanner(System.in);

System.out.print("Input: ");

int ranking = scanner.nextInt();

switch (ranking) {
   case 10:
   case  9:
   case  8: System.out.println("Master");
            break;
   case  7:
   case  6: System.out.println("Journeyman");
            break;
```

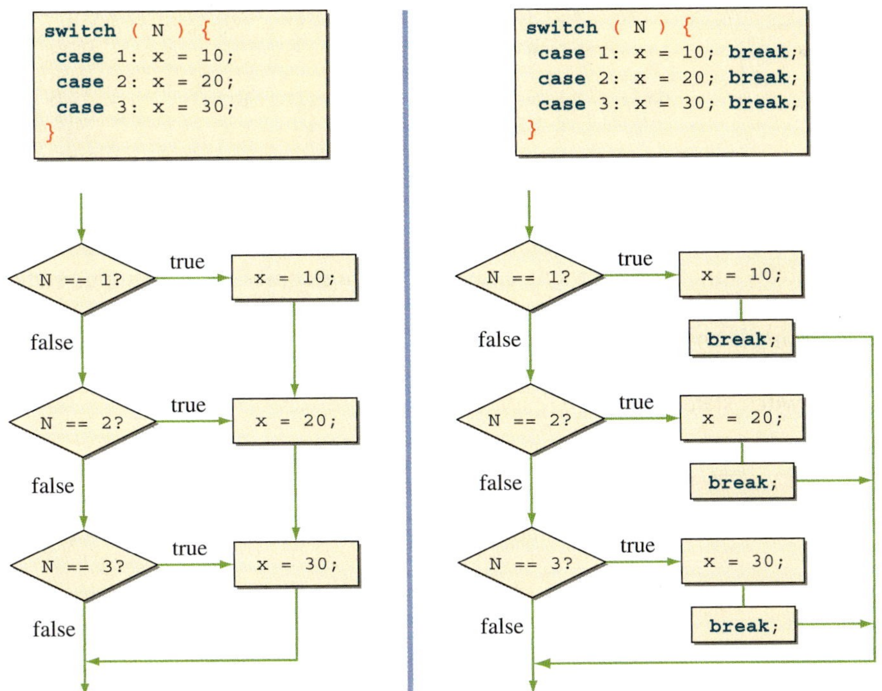

Figure 5.8 A diagram showing the control flow of the **switch** statement with and without the **break** statements.

```
    case  5:
    case  4: System.out.println("Apprentice");
             break;
}
```

The code will print Master if the value of ranking is 10, 9, or 8; Journeyman if the value of ranking is either 7 or 6; or Apprentice if the value of ranking is either 5 or 4.

We may include a default case that will always be executed if there is no matching case. For example, we can add a default case to print out an error message if any invalid value for ranking is entered.

```
switch (ranking) {

    case 10:
    case  9:
    case  8: System.out.println("Master");
             break;

    case  7:
    case  6: System.out.println("Journeyman");
             break;

    case  5:
```

```
        case    4: System.out.println("Apprentice");
                   break;

        default: System.out.println("Error: Invalid Data");
                 break;
    }
```

There can be at most one default case. Since the execution continues to the next statement if there is no matching case (and no default case is specified), it is safer to always include a default case. By placing some kind of output statement in the default case, we can detect an unexpected switch value. Such a style of programming is characterized as ***defensive programming***. Although the default case does not have to be placed as the last case, we recommend you do so, in order to make the switch statement more readable.

defensive programming

1. What's wrong with the following switch statement?

```
switch ( N ) {
   case   0:
   case   1:   x = 11;
               break;
   default:   System.out.println("Switch Error");
               break;
   case   2:   x = 22;
               break;
   case   1:   x = 33;
               break;
}
```

2. What's wrong with the following switch statement?

```
switch ( ranking ) {
   case   >4.55:   pay = pay * 0.20;
                   break;

   case   =4.55:   pay = pay * 0.15;
                   break;

   default:        pay = pay * 0.05;
                   break;
}
```

5.6 Drawing Graphics

We introduce four standard classes related to drawing geometric shapes on a window. These four standard classes will be used in Section 5.7 on the sample development. We describe their core features here. More details can be found in the online Java API documentation.

java.awt.Graphics

java.awt. Graphics

We can draw geometric shapes on a frame window by calling appropriate methods of the Graphics object. For example, if g is a Graphics object, then we can write

```
g.drawRect(50, 50, 100, 30);
```

to display a rectangle 100 pixels wide and 30 pixels high at the specified position (50, 50). The position is determined as illustrated in Figure 5.9. The complete program is shown below. The top left corner, just below the window title bar, is position (0, 0), and the x value increases from left to right and the y value increases from top to bottom. Notice that the direction in which the y value increases is opposite to the normal two-dimensional graph.

content pane of a frame

The area of a frame which we can draw is called the ***content pane of a frame***. The content pane excludes the area of a frame that excludes the regions such as the border, scroll bars, the title bar, the menu bar, and others. To draw on the content pane of a frame window, first we must get the content pane's Graphic object. Then we call this Graphics method to draw geometric shapes. Here's a sample:

```
/*
    Chapter 5 Sample Program: Draw a rectangle on a frame
                              window's content pane

    File: Ch5SampleGraphics.java
*/

import javax.swing.*; //for JFrame
import java.awt.*; //for Graphics and Container

class Ch5SampleGraphics {

    public static void main( String[] args ) {

        JFrame    win;
        Container contentPane;
        Graphics  g;

        win = new JFrame("My First Rectangle");
        win.setSize(300, 200);
        win.setLocation(100,100);
        win.setVisible(true);

        contentPane = win.getContentPane();
        g = contentPane.getGraphics();
        g.drawRect(50,50,100,30);
    }
}
```

win must be visible on the screen before you get its content pane.

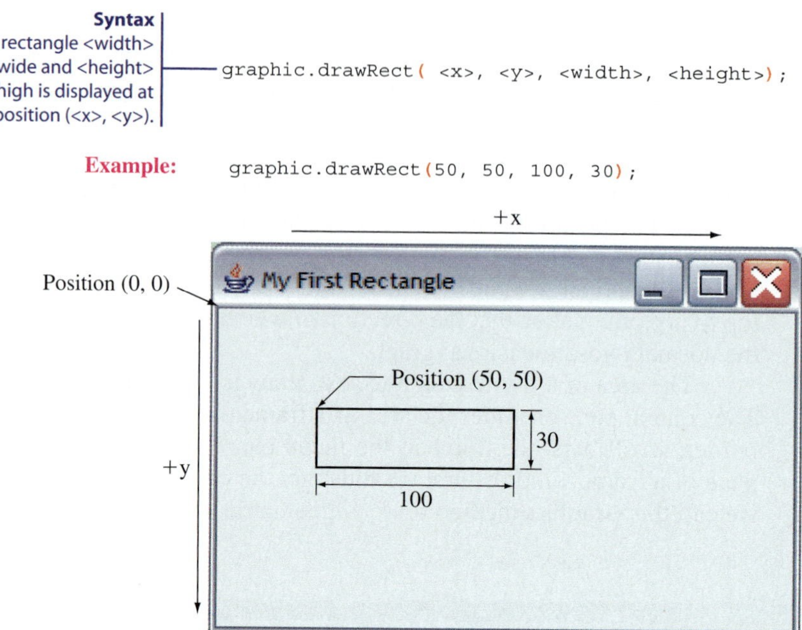
Syntax
A rectangle <width> wide and <height> high is displayed at position (<x>, <y>).
graphic.drawRect(<x>, <y>, <width>, <height>);
Example:
graphic.drawRect(50, 50, 100, 30);
+x
Position (0, 0)
My First Rectangle
Position (50, 50)
30
+y
100

Figure 5.9 The diagram illustrates how the position of the rectangle is determined by the **drawRect** method.

Here are the key points to remember in drawing geometric shapes on the content pane of a frame window.

Things to Remember

To draw geometric shapes on the content pane of a frame window:

1. *The content pane is declared as a* **Container,** *for example,*

   ```
   Container contentPane;
   ```

2. *The frame window must be visible on the screen before we can get its content pane and the content pane's* **Graphics** *object.*

Hints,
& Tips,
Pitfalls

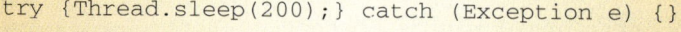

Depending on the speed of your PC, you may have to include the following **try** statement

```
try {Thread.sleep(200);} catch (Exception e) {}
```

to put a delay before drawing the rectangle. Place this **try** statement before the last statement. The argument in the **sleep** method specifies the amount of delay in milliseconds (1000 ms = 1 s). If you still do not see a rectangle drawn in the window after including the delay statement, increase the amount of delay until you see the rectangle drawn. We will describe the **try** statement in Chapter 8.

If there is a window that covers the area in which the drawing takes place or the drawing window is minimized and restored to its normal size, the drawn shape (or portion of it, in the case of the overlapping windows) gets erased. The **DrawingBoard** class used in the sample development (Sec. 5.7) eliminates this problem. For information on the technique to avoid the disappearance of the drawn shape, please check our website at **www.drcaffeine.com**

Table 5.4 lists some of the available graphic drawing methods.

Table 5.4 A partial list of drawing methods defined for the `Graphics` class

Method	Meaning
`drawLine(x1,y1,x2,y2)`	Draws a line between `(x1,y1)` and `(x2,y2)`. (x1,y1) (x2,y2)
`drawRect(x,y,w,h)`	Draws a rectangle with width `w` and height `h` at `(x,y)`. (x,y) h w
`drawRoundRect(x,y,w,h,aw,ah)`	Draws a rounded-corner rectangle with width `w` and height `h` at `(x,y)`. Parameters aw and `ah` determine the angle for the rounded corners. (x,y) h ah aw w

Table 5.4 A partial list of drawing methods defined for the `Graphics` class *(Continued)*

Method	Meaning
`drawOval(x,y,w,h)`	Draws an oval with width `w` and height `h` at `(x,y)`. (x,y) h w
`drawString("text",x,y)`	Draws the string `text` at `(x,y)`. text (x,y)
`fillRect(x,y,w,h)`	Same as the `drawRect` method but fills the region with the currently set color.
`fillRoundRect(x,y,w,h,aw,ah)`	Same as the `drawRoundRect` method but fills the region with the currently set color.
`fillOval(x,y,w,h)`	Same as the `drawOval` method but fills the region with the currently set color.

Notice the distinction between the draw and fill methods. The draw method will draw the boundary only, while the fill method fills the designated area with the currently selected color. Figure 5.10 illustrates the difference.

java.awt.Color

java.awt.Color

To designate the color for drawing, we will use the Color class from the standard java.awt package. A Color object uses a coloring scheme called the *RGB scheme,* which specifies a color by combining three values, ranging from 0 to 255, for red, green, and blue. For example, the color black is expressed by setting red, green, and blue to 0, and the color white by setting all three values to 255. We create, for example, a Color object for the pink color by executing

```
Color pinkColor;
pinkColor = new Color(255,175,175);
```

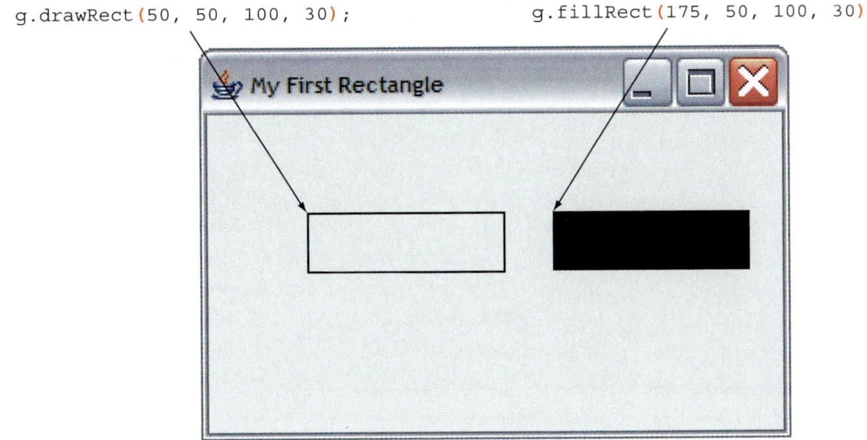

Figure 5.10 The diagram illustrates the distinction between the **draw** and **fill** methods. We assume the currently selected color is black (default).

Instead of dealing with the three numerical values, we can use the public class constants defined in the Color class. The class constants for common colors are

```
Color.BLACK          Color.MAGENTA
Color.BLUE           Color.ORANGE
Color.CYAN           Color.PINK
Color.DARK_GRAY      Color.RED
Color.GRAY           Color.WHITE
Color.GREEN          Color.YELLOW
Color.LIGHT_GRAY
```

The class constants in lowercase letters are also defined (such as Color.black, Color.blue, and so forth). In the older versions of Java, only the constants in lowercase letters were defined. But the Java convention is to name constants using only the uppercase letters, so the uppercase color constants are added to the class definition.

Each of the above is a Color object with its RGB values correctly set up. We will pass a Color object as an argument to the setColor method of the Graphics class to change the color. To draw a blue rectangle, for example, we write

```
//Assume g is set correctly
g.setColor(Color.BLUE);
g.drawRect(50, 50, 100, 30);
```

We can also change the background color of a content pane by using the setBackground method of Container as

```
contentPane.setBackground(Color.LIGHT_GRAY);
```

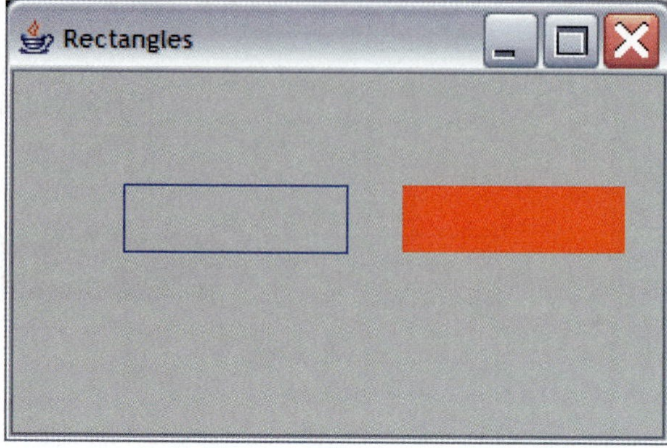

Figure 5.11 A frame with a white background content pane and two rectangles.

Running the following program will result in the frame shown in Figure 5.11.

```
/*
    Chapter 5 Sample Program: Draw one blue rectangle and
                              one filled red rectangle on light gray
                              background content pane

    File: Ch5SampleGraphics2.java
*/

import javax.swing.*;
import java.awt.*;

class Ch5SampleGraphics2 {

    public static void main( String[] args ) {

        JFrame    win;
        Container contentPane;
        Graphics  g;

        win = new JFrame("Rectangles");
        win.setSize(300, 200);
        win.setLocation(100,100);
        win.setVisible(true);

        contentPane = win.getContentPane();
        contentPane.setBackground(Color.LIGHT_GRAY);

        g = contentPane.getGraphics();
        g.setColor(Color.BLUE);
        g.drawRect(50,50,100,30);
```

```
        g.setColor(Color.RED);
        g.fillRect(175,50,100,30);
    }
}
```

java.awt.Point

A Point object is used to represent a point in two-dimensional space. It contains *x* and *y* values, and we can access these values via its public data member x and y. Here's an example to assign a position (10, 20):

```
Point pt = new Point();
pt.x = 10;
pt.y = 20;
```

It is also possible to set the position at the creation time as follows:

```
Point pt = new Point(10, 20);
```

java.awt.Dimension

In manipulating shapes, such as moving them around a frame's content pane, the concept of the bounding rectangle becomes important. A *bounding rectangle* is a rectangle that completely surrounds the shape. Figure 5.12 shows some examples of bounding rectangles.

Just as the (x, y) values are stored as a single Point object, we can store the width and height of a bounding rectangle as a single Dimension object. The Dimension class has the two public data members width and height to maintain the width and height of a bounding rectangle. Here's an example to create a 40 pixels by 70 pixels high bounding rectangle:

```
Dimension dim = new Dimension();
dim.width  = 40;
dim.height = 70;
```

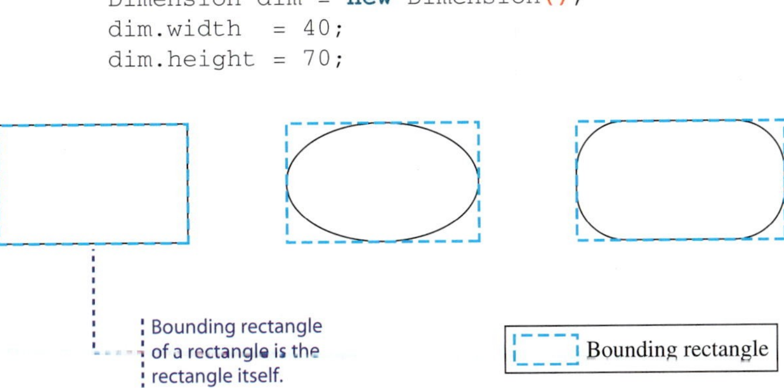

Figure 5.12 Bounding rectangles of various shapes.

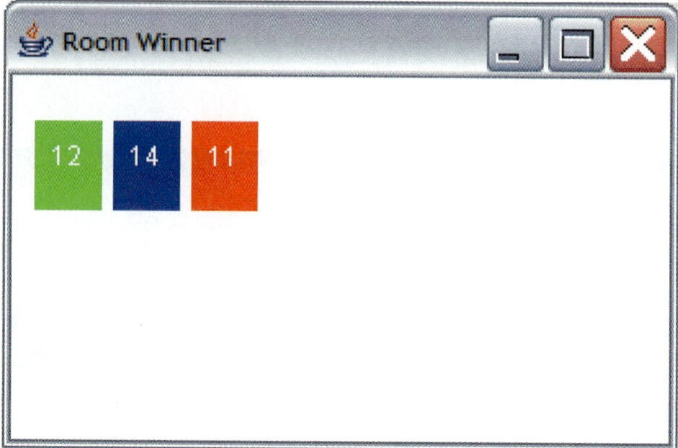

Figure 5.13 Sample output of **Ch5RoomWinner** program.

It is also possible to set the values at the creation time as follows:

```
Dimension dim = new Dimension(40, 70);
```

Let's apply the drawing techniques to an early sample program. In Chapter 4, we wrote the RoomWinner program that randomly selects and displays the dorm room lottery cards. The display was only in text, something like this:

```
Winning Card Combination:
1 - red; 2 - green; 3 - blue

            color    number
Card 1:       2        13
Card 2:       2        12
Card 3:       1        14
```

We will make a graphical version of the program. Figure 5.13 shows a sample output.

Here's the main class Ch5RoomWinner, which has a structure similar to the one for Ch5SampleGraphics2.

```
import java.awt.*;
import javax.swing.*;

class Ch5RoomWinner {

    public static void main( String[] args ) {

        JFrame    win;
        Container contentPane;
        Graphics  g;
```

```
        GraphicLotteryCard one, two, three;

        win = new JFrame("Room Winner");
        win.setSize(300, 200);
        win.setLocation(100,100);
        win.setVisible(true);

        contentPane = win.getContentPane();
        contentPane.setBackground(Color.WHITE);

        g = contentPane.getGraphics();

        one   = new GraphicLotteryCard( );
        two   = new GraphicLotteryCard( );
        three = new GraphicLotteryCard( );

        one.spin();
        two.spin();
        three.spin();

        one.draw(g, 10, 20);
        two.draw(g, 50, 20);
        three.draw(g, 90, 20);
    }
}
```

These objects will draw themselves on **g** at the specified positions.

We modify the LotteryCard class from Chapter 4 by adding code that will draw a card on a given Graphics context. The name of the new class is GraphicLotteryCard. Here's the class definition (we list only the portions that are new):

```
import java.awt.*;

class GraphicLotteryCard {

    // Data Members

    //width of this card for drawing
    public static final int WIDTH = 30;

    //height of this card for drawing
    public static final int HEIGHT = 40;

    //the other data members and methods are the same as before

    public void draw(Graphics g, int xOrigin, int yOrigin) {

        switch (color) {
            case 1: g.setColor(Color.RED);
                    break;
```

```
            case 2: g.setColor(Color.GREEN);
                    break;

            case 3: g.setColor(Color.BLUE);
                    break;
        }

        g.fillRect(xOrigin, yOrigin, WIDTH, HEIGHT);

        g.setColor(Color.WHITE); //draw text in white

        g.drawString( "" + number, xOrigin + WIDTH/4, yOrigin + HEIGHT/2);
    }
}
```

This is a quick way to convert a numerical value to **String**

Notice that the statements in Ch5RoomWinner

```
one.draw(g, 10, 20);
two.draw(g, 50, 20);
three.draw(g, 90, 20);
```

are not as flexible as they can be. If the values for the constant WIDTH and HEIGHT in the GraphicLotteryCard class are changed, these three statements could result in drawing the card inadequately (such as overlapping cards). The two constants are declared public for a reason. Using the WIDTH constant, for example, we can rewrite the three statements as

```
int cardWidth = GraphicLotteryCard.WIDTH;
one.draw(g, 10, 20);
two.draw(g, 10 + cardWidth + 5, 20);
three.draw(g, 10 + 2*(cardWidth+ 5), 20);
```

The statements will draw cards with a 5-pixel interval between cards. This code will continue to work correctly even after the value of WIDTH is modified.

5.7 Enumerated Constants

enumerated constants

We learned in Section 3.3 how to define numerical constants and the benefits of using them in writing readable programs. In this section, we will introduce an additional type of constant called ***enumerated constants*** that were added to the Java language from Version 5.0. Let's start with an example. Suppose we want to define a Student class and define constants to distinguish four undergraduate grade levels—freshman, sophomore, junior, and senior. Using the numerical constants, we can define the grade levels as such:

```
class Student {
   public static final int FRESHMAN = 0;
   public static final int SOPHOMORE = 1;
   public static final int JUNIOR = 2;
   public static final int SENIOR = 3;

   ...
}
```

With the new enumerated constants, this is how we can define the grade levels in the Student class:

```
class Student {
   public static enum GradeLevel
          {FRESHMAN, SOPHOMORE, JUNIOR, SENIOR}

   ...
}
```

The word enum is a new reserved word, and the basic syntax for defining enumerated constants is

```
enum <enumerated type> { <constant values> }
```

where <enumerated type> is an identifier and <constant values> is a list of identifiers separated by commas. Notice that for the most common usage of enumerated constants, we append the modifiers public and static; but they are not a required part of defining enumerated constants. Here are more examples:

```
enum Month {JANUARY, FEBRUARY, MARCH, APRIL,
            MAY, JUNE, JULY, AUGUST,
            SEPTEMBER, OCTOBER, NOVEMBER, DECEMBER}

enum Gender {MALE, FEMALE}

enum SkillLevel {NOVICE, INTERMEDIATE, ADVANCED, EXPERT}
```

One restriction when declaring an enumerated type is that it cannot be a local declaration. In other words, we must declare it outside of any method, just as for the other data members of a class.

enumerated type

Unlike numerical constants, which are simply identifiers with fixed numerical values, enumerated constants do not have any assigned numerical values. They are said to belong to, or be members of, the associated ***enumerated type***. For example, two enumerated constants MALE and FEMALE belong to the enumerated type Gender. (*Note:* We keep the discussion of the enumerated type to its simplest form here. It is beyond the scope of an introductory programming textbook to discuss Java's enumerated type in full detail.)

Just as with any other data types, we can declare variables of an enumerated type and assign values to them. Here is an example (for the sake of brevity, we list the enum declaration and its usage together, but remember that the declaration in the actual use cannot be a local declaration):

```
enum Fruit {APPLE, ORANGE, BANANA}

Fruit f1, f2, f3;

f1 = Fruit.APPLE;

f2 = Fruit.BANANA;

f3 = f1;
```

NOTE: The constant value is prefixed by the name of the enumerated type.

Because variables f1, f2, and f3 are declared to be of the type Fruit, we can only assign one of the associated enumerated constants to them. This restriction supports a desired feature called ***type safety***. So what is the big deal? Consider the following numerical constants and assignment statements:

type safety

```
final int APPLE  = 1;
final int ORANGE = 2;
final int BANANA = 3;

int fOne, fTwo, fThree;

fOne = APPLE;

fTwo = ORANGE;

fThree = fOne;
```

The code may look comparable to the one that uses enumerated constants, but what will happen if we write the following?

```
fOne = 45;
```

The assignment is logically wrong. It does not make any sense to assign meaningless value such as 45 to the variable fOne if it is supposed to represent one of the defined fruit. However, no compiler error will result because the data type of fOne is int. The statement may or may not cause the runtime error depending on how the variable fOne is used in the rest of the program. In either case, the program cannot be expected to produce a correct result because of the logical error.

By defining an enumerated type, a variable of that type can only accept the associated enumerated constants. Any violation will be detected by the compiler. This will eliminate the possibility of assigning a nonsensical value as seen in the case for the numerical constants. Type safety means that we can assign only meaningful values to a declared variable.

Another benefit of the enumerated type is the informative output values. Assuming the variables fTwo and f2 retain the values assigned to them in the sample code, the statement

```
System.out.println("Favorite fruit is " + fTwo);
```

will produce a cryptic output:

```
Favorite fruit is 2
```

In contrast, the statement

```
System.out.println("Favorite fruit is " + f2);
```

will produce a more informative output:

```
Favorite fruit is BANANA
```

We will describe other advantages of using enumerated types later in the book.

As shown, when referring to an enumerated constant in the code, we must prefix it with its enumerated type name, for example,

```
Fruit f = Fruit.APPLE;

. . .

if (f == Fruit.ORANGE) {
   System.out.println("I like orange, too.");
}

. . .
```

A case label for a switch statement is the only exception to this rule. Instead of writing, for example,

```
Fruit fruit;

fruit = ... ;

switch (fruit) {
   case Fruit.APPLE: . . .;
                    break;
   case Fruit.ORANGE: . . .;
                    break;
   case Fruit.BANANA: . . .;
                    break;
}
```

we can specify the case labels without the prefix as in

```
Fruit fruit;

fruit = ...;

switch (fruit) {

   case APPLE: . . .;
              break;
```

```
   case ORANGE: . . .;
              break;

   case BANANA: . . .;
              break;
}
```

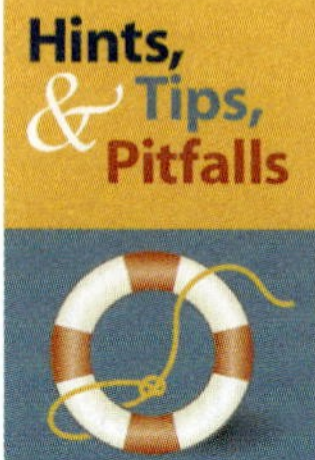

It is not necessary to prefix the enumerated constant with its enumerated type name when it is used as a **case** label in a **switch** statement.

The enumerated type supports a useful method named valueOf. The method accepts one String argument and returns the enumerated constant whose value matches the given argument. For example, the following statement assigns the enumerated constant APPLE to the variable fruit:

```
Fruit fruit = Fruit.valueOf("APPLE");
```

In which situations could the valueOf method be useful? One is the input routine. Consider the following:

```
Scanner scanner = new Scanner(System.in);

System.out.print("Enter your favorite fruit " +
                 "(APPLE, ORANGE, BANANA): ");

String fruitName = scanner.next( );

Fruit favoriteFruit = Fruit.valueOf(fruitName);
```

Be aware, however, that if you pass a String value that does not match any of the defined constants, it will result in a runtime error. This means if the user enters Orange, for example, it will result in an error (the input has to be all capital letters to match). We will discuss how to handle such runtime errors without causing the program to terminate abruptly in Chapter 8.

To access the enumerated constants in a programmer-defined class from outside the class, we must reference them through the associated enumerated type (assuming, of course, the visibility modifier is public). Consider the following Faculty class:

```
class Faculty {

   public static enum Rank
         {LECTURER, ASSISTANT, ASSOCIATE, FULL}

   private Rank rank;

   . . .
```

```
    public void setRank(Rank r) {
        rank = r;
    }

    public Rank getRank( ) {
        return rank;
    }

    . . .
}
```

Notice how the enumerate type Rank is used in the setRank and getRank methods. It is treated just as any other types are. To access the Rank constants from outside of the Faculty class, we write

```
Faculty.Rank.ASSISTANT

Faculty.Rank.FULL
```

and so forth. Here's an example that assigns the rank of ASSISTANT to a Faculty object:

```
Faculty prof = new Faculty(...);

prof.setRank(Faculty.Rank.ASSISTANT);
```

And here's an example to retrieve the rank of a Faculty object:

```
Faculty teacher;

//assume 'teacher' is properly created

Faculty.Rank rank;

rank = teacher.getRank();
```

1. Define an enumerated type Day that includes the constants SUNDAY through SATURDAY.
2. What is the method that returns an enumerated constant, given the matching String value?
3. Detect the error(s) in the following code:

```
enum Fruit {APPLE, ORANGE, BANANA}

Fruit f1, f2;
int f3;

f1 = 1;

f2 = ORANGE;

f3 = f1;

f1 = "BANANA";
```

5.8 Sample Development

Drawing Shapes

When a certain period of time passes without any activity on a computer, a screensaver becomes active and draws different types of geometric patterns or textual messages. In this section we will develop an application that simulates a screensaver. We will learn a development skill very commonly used in object-oriented programming. Whether we develop alone or as a project team member, we often find ourselves writing a class that needs to behave in a specific way so that it works correctly with other classes. The other classes may come from standard Java packages or could be developed by the other team members.

In this particular case, we use the **DrawingBoard** class (written by the author). This is a helper class that takes care of programming aspects we have not yet mastered, such as moving multiple geometric shapes in a smooth motion across the screen. It is not an issue of whether we can develop this class by ourselves, because no matter how good we become as programmers, we would rarely develop an application completely on our own.

We already used many predefined classes from the Java standard libraries, but the way we will use the predefined class here is different. When we developed programs before, the classes we wrote called the methods of predefined classes. Our main method creating a **GregorianCalendar** object and calling its methods is one example. Here, for us to use a predefined class, we must define another class that provides necessary services to this predefined class. Figure 5.14 differentiates the two types of predefined classes. The first type does not place any restriction other than calling the methods correctly, while the second type requires us to implement helper classes in a specific manner to support it.

In our case, the predefined class **DrawingBoard** will require another class named **DrawableShape** that will assume the responsibility of drawing individual geometric shapes. So, to use the **DrawingBoard** class in our program, we must implement the class named **DrawableShape.** And we must implement the **DrawableShape** class in a specific way. The use of the **DrawingBoard** class dictates that we define a set of fixed methods in the **DrawableShape** class. We can add more, but we must at the minimum provide the specified set of fixed methods because the **DrawingBoard** class will need to call these methods. The methods are "fixed" in the method signature—method name, the number of parameters and their types, and return type—but the method body can be defined in any way we like. This is how the flexibility is achieved. For example, the **DrawableShape** class we define must include a method named **draw** with the dictated signature. But it's up to us to decide what we put in the method body. So we can choose, for example, to implement the method to draw a circle, rectangle, or any other geometric shape of our choosing.

As always, we will develop this program following incremental development steps. The incremental development steps we will take here are slightly different in character from those we have seen so far. In the previous incremental developments, we knew all the ingredients, so to speak. Here we have to include a step to explore the **DrawingBoard** class. We will find out shortly that to use the **DrawingBoard** class, we will have to deal with some Java standard classes we have not seen yet. Pedagogically, a textbook may try to

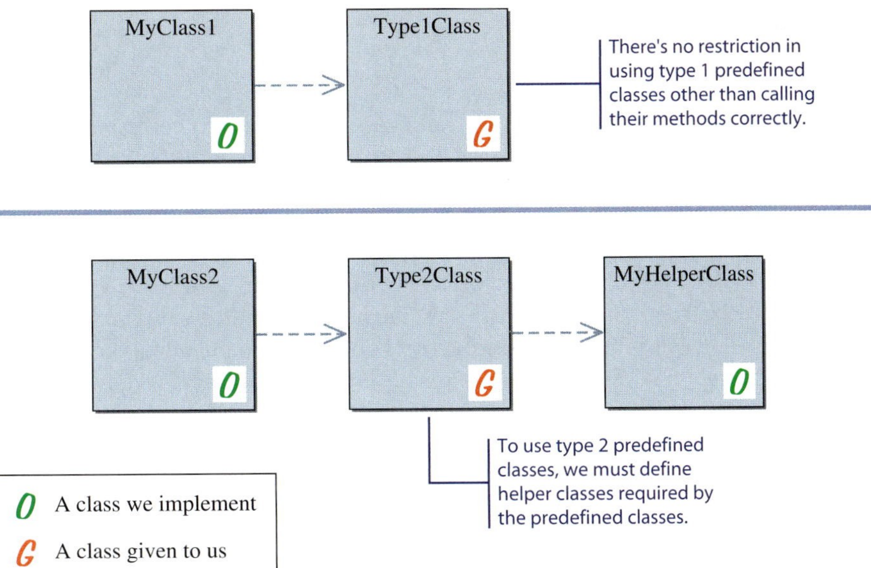

Figure 5.14 Two types of predefined classes. The first type does not require us to do anything more than use the predefined classes by calling their methods. The second type requires us to define helper classes for the predefined classes we want to use.

explain beforehand everything that is necessary to understand the sample programs. But no textbook can explain everything. When we develop programs, there will always be a time when we encounter some unknown classes. We need to learn how to deal with such a situation in our development steps.

Problem Statement

Write an application that simulates a screensaver by drawing various geometric shapes in different colors. The user has the option of choosing a type (ellipse or rectangle), color, and movement (stationary, smooth, or random).

Overall Plan

We will begin with our overall plan for the development. Let's begin with the outline of program logic. We first let the user select the shape, its movement, and its color, and we then start drawing. We express the program flow as having four tasks:

program tasks

1. Get the shape the user wants to draw.
2. Get the color of the chosen shape.
3. Get the type of movement the user wants to use.
4. Start the drawing.

5.8 Sample Development—*continued*

Let's look at each task and determine an object that will be responsible for handling the task. For the first three tasks, we can use our old friend **Scanner.** We will get into the details of exactly how we ask the users to input those values in the later incremental steps. For the last task of actually drawing the selected shape, we need to define our own class. The task is too specific to the program, and there is no suitable object in the standard packages that does the job. As discussed earlier, we will use a given predefined class **DrawingBoard** and define the required helper class **DrawableShape.**

We will define a top-level control object that manages all these objects. We will call this class **Ch5DrawShape.** As explained in Section 4.10, we will make this control object the main class. Here's our working design document:

program classes

Design Document: `Ch5DrawShape`

Class	Purpose
`Ch5DrawShape`	The top-level control object that manages other objects in the program. This is the main class, as explained in Section 4.10.
`DrawingBoard`	The given predefined class that handles the movement of `DrawableShape` objects.
`DrawableShape`	The class for handling the drawing of individual shapes.
`Scanner`	The standard class for handling input routines.

Figure 5.15 is the program diagram for this program.

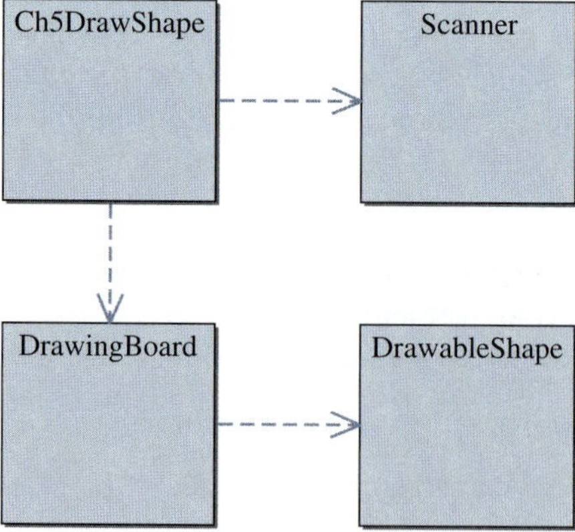

Figure 5.15 The program diagram for the **Ch5DrawShape** program.

We will implement this program in the following six major steps:

development steps

1. Start with a program skeleton. Explore the **DrawingBoard** class.
2. Define an experimental **DrawableShape** class that draws a dummy shape.
3. Add code to allow the user to select a shape. Extend the **DrawableShape** and other classes as necessary.
4. Add code to allow the user to specify the color. Extend the **DrawableShape** and other classes as necessary.
5. Add code to allow the user to specify the motion type. Extend the **DrawableShape** and other classes as necessary.
6. Finalize the code by tying up loose ends.

Our first task is to find out about the given class. We could have designed the input routines first, but without knowing much about the given class, it would be difficult to design suitable input routines. When we use an unknown class, it is most appropriate to find out more about this given class before we plan any input or output routines. Just as the development steps are incremental, our exploration of the given class will be incremental. Instead of trying to find out everything about the class at once, we begin with the basic features and skeleton code. As we learn more about the given class incrementally, we extend our code correspondingly.

Step 1 Development: Program Skeleton

step 1 design

We begin the development with the skeleton main class. The main purpose in step 1 is to use the **DrawingBoard** class in the simplest manner to establish the launch pad for the development. To do so, we must first learn a bit about the given **DrawingBoard** class. Here's a brief description of the **DrawingBoard** class. In a real-world situation, we would be finding out about the given class by reading its accompanying documentation or some other external sources. The documentation may come in form of online javadoc documents or reference manuals.

DrawingBoard

An instance of this class will support the drawing of `DrawableShape` objects. Shapes can be drawn at fixed stationary positions, at random positions, or in a smooth motion at the specified speed. The actual drawing of the individual shapes is done inside the `DrawableShape` class. The client programmer decides which shape to draw.

```
public void addShape ( DrawableShape shape )
```

Adds shape to this `DrawingBoard` object. You can add an unlimited number of `DrawableShape` objects.

(Continued)

5.8 Sample Development—*continued*

DrawingBoard *(Continued)*
`public void setBackground( java.awt.Color color )` Sets the background color of this `DrawingBoard` object to the designated color. The default background color is black.
`public void setDelayTime( double delay )` Sets the delay time between drawings to `delay` seconds. The smaller the delay time, the faster the shapes move. If the movement type is other than `SMOOTH`, then setting the delay time has no visual effect.
`public void setMovement( Movement type )` Sets the movement type to `type`. Class constants for three types of motion are `Movement.STATIONARY`—draw shapes at fixed positions, `Movement.RANDOM`—draw shapes at random positions, and `Movement.SMOOTH`—draw shapes in a smooth motion.
`public void setVisible( boolean state )` Makes this `DrawingBoard` object appear on or disappear from the screen if `state` is `true` or `false`, respectively. To simulate the screensaver, setting it visible will cause a maximized window to appear on the screen.
`public void start( )` Starts the drawing. If the window is not visible yet, it will be made visible before the drawing begins.

Among the defined methods, we see the **setVisible** method is the one to make it appear on the screen. All other methods pertain to adding **DrawableShape** objects and setting the properties of a **DrawingBoard** object. We will explain the standard **java.awt.Color** class when we use the **setBackground** method in the later step. In this step, we will keep the code very simple by only making it appear on the screen. We will deal with other methods in the later steps.

Our working design document for the **Ch5DrawShape** class is as follows:

Design Document: The `Ch5DrawShape` Class

Method	Visibility	Purpose
`<constructor>`	`public`	Creates a `DrawingBoard` object.
`main`	`public`	This is main method of the class.
`start`	`public`	Starts the program by opening a `DrawingBoard` object.

step 1 code

Since this is a skeleton code, it is very basic. Here's the code:

```
/*
        Chapter 5 Sample Development: Drawing Shapes (Step 1)

        The main class of the program.
 */

class Ch5DrawShape {

    private DrawingBoard canvas;

    public Ch5DrawShape( ) {

        canvas = new DrawingBoard( );
    }

    public void start( ) {

        canvas.setVisible(true);

    }

    public static void main(String[] args) {

        Ch5DrawShape screensaver = new Ch5DrawShape( );

        screensaver.start();
    }
}
```

step 1 test

The purpose of step 1 testing is to verify that a **DrawingBoard** object appears correctly on the screen. Since this is our first encounter with the **DrawingBoard** class, it is probable that we are not understanding its documentation fully and completely. We need to verify this in this step. When a maximized window with the black background appears on the screen, we know the main class was executed properly. After we verify the correct execution of the step 1 program, we will proceed to implement additional methods of **Ch5DrawShape** and gradually build up the required **DrawableShape** class.

Step 2 Development: Draw a Shape

step 2 design

In the second development step, we will implement a preliminary **DrawableShape** class and make some shapes appear on a **DrawingBoard** window. To draw shapes, we need to add them to a **DrawingBoard** window. And to do so, we need to define the

5.8 Sample Development—*continued*

DrawableShape class with the specified set of methods. Here are the required methods and a brief description of what to accomplish in them:

Required Methods of `DrawableShape`

`public void draw(java.awt.Graphics)`
Draw a geometric shape on the `java.awt.Graphics`. The `DrawingBoard` window calls the `draw` method of `DrawableShape` objects added to it.

`public java.awt.Point getCenterPoint( )`
Return the center point of this shape.

`public java.awt.Dimension getDimension( )`
Return the bounding rectangle of this shape as a `Dimension`.

`public void setCenterPoint( java.awt.Point )`
Set the center point of this shape. The `DrawingBoard` window calls the `setCenterPoint` method of `DrawableShape` objects to update their positions in the `SMOOTH` movement type.

At this stage, the main task is for us to confirm our understanding of the requirements in implementing the **DrawableShape** class. Once we get this confirmation, we can get into the details of the full-blown **DrawableShape** class.

To keep the preliminary class simple, we draw three filled circles of a fixed size and color. The **DrawableShape** class includes a single data member **centerPoint** to keep track of the shape's center point. If we fix the radius of the circles to 100 pixels, that is, the bounding rectangle is 200 pixels by 200 pixels, and the color to blue, then the **draw** method can be written as follows:

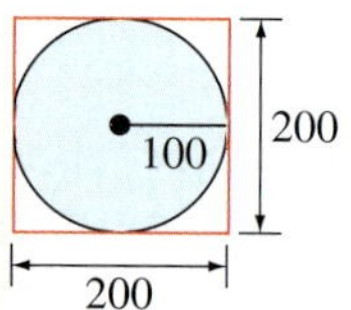


```
public void draw(Graphics g) {

   g.setColor(Color.blue);
   g.fillOval(centerPoint.x-100, centerPoint.y-100, 200, 200);
}
```

Since the size is fixed, we simply return a new **Dimension** object for the **getDimension** method:

```
public Dimension getDimension( ) {

   return new Dimension(200, 200);
}
```

For the **setCenterPoint** and **getCenterPoint** methods, we assign the passed parameter to the data member **centerPoint** and return the current value of the data member **centerPoint,** respectively.

We are now ready to modify the **Ch5DrawShape** class to draw three filled circles. We will implement this by modifying the **start** method. First we need to create three **DrawableShape** objects and add them to the **DrawingBoard** object **canvas:**

```
DrawableShape shape1 = new DrawableShape();
DrawableShape shape2 = new DrawableShape();
DrawableShape shape3 = new DrawableShape();

shape1.setCenterPoint(new Point(250,300));
shape2.setCenterPoint(new Point(500,300));
shape3.setCenterPoint(new Point(750,300));

canvas.addShape(shape1);
canvas.addShape(shape2);
canvas.addShape(shape3);
```

Then we set the motion type to **SMOOTH** movement, make the window appear on the screen, and start the drawing:

```
canvas.setMovement(DrawingBoard.Movement.SMOOTH);
canvas.setVisible(true);
canvas.start();
```

step 2 code

Here's the code for the preliminary **DrawableShape** class:

```
import java.awt.*;

/*
   Step 2: Add a preliminary DrawableShape class

   A class whose instances know how to draw themselves.
 */
class DrawableShape {

    private Point  centerPoint;

    public DrawableShape( ) {

       centerPoint = null;
    }

    public void draw(Graphics g) {

        g.setColor(Color.blue);
        g.fillOval(centerPoint.x-100, centerPoint.y-100, 200, 200);
    }
```

Data Members

Constructors

draw

5.8 Sample Development—*continued*

```
    public Point getCenterPoint( ) {                      getCenterPoint

        return centerPoint;
    }

    public Dimension getDimension( ) {                    getDimension

        return new Dimension(200, 200);
    }

    public void setCenterPoint(Point point) {             setCenterPoint

        centerPoint = point;
    }
}
```

The **Ch5DrawShape** class now has the modified **start** method as designed (the rest of the class remains the same):

```
import java.awt.*;

/*
   Chapter 5 Sample Development: Start drawing shapes (Step 2)

   The main class of the program.
 */

class Ch5DrawShape {

    . . .

    public void start( ) {                                start

        DrawableShape shape1 = new DrawableShape();
        DrawableShape shape2 = new DrawableShape();
        DrawableShape shape3 = new DrawableShape();

        shape1.setCenterPoint(new Point(250,300));
        shape2.setCenterPoint(new Point(500,300));
        shape3.setCenterPoint(new Point(750,300));

        canvas.addShape(shape1);
        canvas.addShape(shape2);
        canvas.addShape(shape3);
```

```
        canvas.setMovement(DrawingBoard.Movement.SMOOTH);

        canvas.setVisible(true);
        canvas.start();
    }
    . . .
}
```

step 2 test

Now we run the program and verify the three bouncing circles moving around. To test other options of the **DrawingBoard** class, we will try the other methods with different parameters:

Method	Test Parameter
`setMovement`	Try both `DrawingBoard.STATIONARY` and `DrawingBoard.RANDOM`.
`setDelayTime`	Try values ranging from 0.1 to 3.0.
`setBackground`	Try several different `Color` constants such as `Color.white`, `Color.red`, and `Color.green`.

We insert these testing statements before the statement

```
canvas.setVisible(true);
```

in the **start** method.

Another testing option we should try is the drawing of different geometric shapes. We can replace the drawing statement inside the **draw** method from

```
g.fillOval(centerPoint.x-100, centerPoint.y-100,
           200, 200);
```

to

```
g.fillRect(centerPoint.x-100, centerPoint.y-100,
           200, 200);
```

or

```
g.fillRoundRect(centerPoint.x-100, centerPoint.y-100,
                200, 200, 50, 50);
```

to draw a filled rectangle or a filled rounded rectangle, respectively.

5.8 Sample Development—*continued*

step 3 design

Step 3 Development: Allow the User to Select a Shape

Now that we know how to interact with the **DrawingBoard** class, we can proceed to develop the user interface portion of the program. There are three categories in which the user can select an option: shape, color, and motion. We will work on the shape selection here and on the color and motion selection in the next two steps. Once we are done with this step, the next two steps are fairly straightforward because the idea is essentially the same.

Let's allow the user to select one of three shapes—ellipse, rectangle, and rounded rectangle—the shapes we know how to draw at this point. We can add more fancy shapes later. In what ways should we allow the user to input the shape? There are two possible alternatives: The first would ask the user to enter the text and spell out the shape, and the second would ask the user to enter a number that corresponds to the shape (1 for ellipse, 2 for rectangle, 3 for rounded rectangle, e.g.). Which is the better alternative?

design alternative 1

We anticipate at least two problems with the first input style. When we need to get a user's name, for example, there's no good alternative other than asking the user to enter his or her name. But when we want the user to select one of the few available choices, it is cumbersome and too much of a burden for the user. Moreover, it is prone to mistyping.

design alternative 2

To allow the user to make a selection quickly and easily, we can let the user select one of the available choices by entering a corresponding number. We will list the choices with numbers 1, 2, and 3 and get the user's selection as follows:

```
System.out.print("Selection: Enter the Shape number\n" +
                 "    1 - Ellipse \n" +
                 "    2 - Rectangle \n" +
                 "    3 - Rounded Rectangle \n");

int selection = scanner.nextInt();
```

For getting the dimension of the shape, we accept the width and height values from the user. The values cannot be negative, for sure, but we also want to restrict the values to a certain range. We do not want the shape to be too small or too large. Let's set the minimum to 100 pixels and the maximum to 500 pixels. If the user enters a value outside the acceptable range, we will set the value to 100. The input routine for the width can be written as follows:

```
System.out.print("Enter the width of the shape\n" +
                 "between 100 and 500 inclusive: ");

int width = scanner.nextInt();

if (width < 100 || width > 500) {
    width = 100;
}
```

The input routine for the height will work in the same manner.

For getting the **x** and **y** values of the shape's center point, we follow the pattern of getting the width and height values. We will set the acceptable range for the **x** value to 200 and 800, inclusive, and the **y** value to 100 and 600, inclusive.

Our next task is to modify the **DrawableShape** class so it will be able to draw three different geometric shapes. First we change the constructor to accept the three input values:

```
public DrawableShape(Type sType, Dimension sDim,
                     Point sCenter) {

    type        = sType;
    dimension   = sDim;
    centerPoint = sCenter;
}
```

The variables **type, dimension,** and **centerPoint** are data members for keeping track of necessary information.

Next, we define the data member constants as follows:

```
public static enum Type {ELLIPSE, RECTANGLE, ROUNDED_RECTANGLE}

private static final Dimension DEFAULT_DIMENSION
                                   = new Dimension(200, 200);

private static final Point DEFAULT_CENTER_PT
                                   = new Point(350, 350);
```

In the previous step, the **draw** method drew a fixed-size circle. We need to modify it to draw three different geometric shapes based on the value of the data member **type.** We can modify the method to

```
public void draw(Graphics g) {

    g.setColor(Color.blue);

    drawShape(g);

}
```

with the private method **drawShape** defined as

```
private void drawShape(Graphics g) {

   switch (type) {

      case ELLIPSE:
            //code to draw a filled oval comes here
            break;

      case RECTANGLE:
            //code to draw a filled rectangle comes here
            break;
```

5.8 Sample Development—*continued*

```
                case ROUNDED_RECTANGLE:
                        //code to draw a filled rounded rectangle
                        //comes here
                        break;
            }
        }
```

step 3 code

Here's the modified main class **Ch5DrawShape:**

```
import java.awt.*;
import java.util.*;

/*
   Chapter 5 Sample Development: Handle User Input for Shape Type (Step 3)

   The main class of the program.
 */

class Ch5DrawShape {

    . . .

    public void start( ) {

        DrawableShape shape1 = getShape();

        canvas.addShape(shape1);

        canvas.setMovement(DrawingBoard.SMOOTH);

        canvas.setVisible(true);
        canvas.start();

    }

    private DrawableShape getShape( ) {

        DrawableShape.Type type = inputShapeType();

        Dimension dim = inputDimension();

        Point centerPt = inputCenterPoint();

        DrawableShape shape = new DrawableShape(type, dim, centerPt);

        return shape;
    }
```

start

getShape

inputShapeType

```
private DrawableShape.Type inputShapeType( ) {

    System.out.print("Selection: Enter the Shape number\n" +
                     "   1 - Ellipse \n" +
                     "   2 - Rectangle \n" +
                     "   3 - Rounded Rectangle \n");

    int selection = scanner.nextInt();

    DrawableShape.Type type;

    switch (selection) {

        case 1:  type = DrawableShape.Type.ELLIPSE;
                 break;

        case 2:  type = DrawableShape.Type.RECTANGLE;
                 break;

        case 3:  type = DrawableShape.Type.ROUNDED_RECTANGLE;
                 break;

        default: type = DrawableShape.Type.ELLIPSE;
                 break;
    }

    return type;
}
```

inputDimension

```
private Dimension inputDimension( ) {

    System.out.print("Enter the width of the shape\n" +
                     "between 100 and 500 inclusive: ");

    int width = scanner.nextInt();

    if (width < 100 || width > 500) {
        width = 100;
    }

    System.out.print("Enter the height of the shape\n" +
                     "between 100 and 500 inclusive: ");

    int height = scanner.nextInt();

    if (height < 100 || height > 500) {
        height = 100;
    }

    return new Dimension(width, height);
}
```

5.8 Sample Development—*continued*

inputCenterPoint

```
    private Point inputCenterPoint( ) {

        System.out.print("Enter the x value of the center point\n" +
                         "between 200 and 800 inclusive: ");

        int x = scanner.nextInt();

        if (x < 200 || x > 800) {
            x = 200;
        }

        System.out.print("Enter the y value of the center point\n" +
                         "between 100 and 500 inclusive: ");

        int y = scanner.nextInt();

        if (y < 100 || y > 500) {
            y = 100;
        }

        return new Point(x, y);
    }
    . . .
}
```

The **DrawableShape** class is now modified to this:

Data Members

```
import java.awt.*;

/*
   Step 3: Draw different shapes

   A class whose instances know how to draw themselves.
 */

class DrawableShape {

    public static enum Type {ELLIPSE, RECTANGLE, ROUNDED_RECTANGLE}

    private static final Dimension DEFAULT_DIMENSION
                                        = new Dimension(200, 200);
```

```
private static final Point DEFAULT_CENTER_PT = new Point(350, 350);

private Point     centerPoint;

private Dimension dimension;

private Type      type;

public DrawableShape(Type sType, Dimension sDim, Point sCenter) {

    type        = sType;
    dimension   = sDim;
    centerPoint = sCenter;
}

public void draw(Graphics g) {

    g.setColor(Color.blue);

    drawShape(g);
}

. . .

public void setType(Type shapeType) {

    type = shapeType;
}

private void drawShape(Graphics g) {
    switch (type) {
        case ELLIPSE:
                g.fillOval(centerPoint.x - dimension.width/2,
                           centerPoint.y - dimension.height/2,
                           dimension.width,
                           dimension.height);
                break;

        case RECTANGLE:
                g.fillRect(centerPoint.x - dimension.width/2,
                           centerPoint.y - dimension.height/2,
                           dimension.width,
                           dimension.height);
                break;

        case ROUNDED_RECTANGLE:
                g.fillRoundRect(centerPoint.x - dimension.width/2,
                                centerPoint.y - dimension.height/2,
                                dimension.width,
                                dimension.height,
```

Constructor

draw

setType

drawShape

```
                                        (int) (dimension.width * 0.3),
                                        (int) (dimension.height * 0.3));
                        break;
            }
        }
    }
```

Notice how we add code for handling the case when an invalid number is entered in the **inputShapeType** method. We use the **default** case to set the shape type to **ELLIPSE** if an invalid value is entered. In addition to handling the invalid entries, it is critical for us to make sure that all valid entries are handled correctly. For example, we cannot leave the type undefined or assigned to a wrong value when one of the valid data is entered.

Things to Remember

When we write a selection control statement, we must make sure that all possible cases are handled correctly.

step 3 test

Now we run the program multiple times, trying various shape types, dimensions, and center points. After we verify that everything is working as expected, we proceed to the next step.

Step 4 Development: Allow the User to Select a Color

step 4 design

In the fourth development step, we add a routine that allows the user to specify the color of the selected shape. We adopt the same input style for accepting the shape type as in step 3. We list five different color choices and let the user select one of them by entering the corresponding number. We use a default color when an invalid number is entered. Analogous to the shape selection routine, we will add a method named **inputColor** to the **Ch5DrawShape** class. The structure of this method is identical to that of the input methods, except the return type is **Color.** Using the **inputColor** method, we can define the **getShape** method as follows:

```
private DrawableShape getShape( ) {

    DrawableShape.Type type = inputShapeType();

    Dimension dim = inputDimension();
```

```
    Point centerPt = inputCenterPoint();

    Color color = inputColor();

    DrawableShape shape

          = new DrawableShape(type, dim, centerPt, color);

    return shape;
}
```

We make a small extension to the **DrawableShape** class by changing the constructor to accept a color as its fourth argument and adding a data member to keep track of the selected color.

step 4 code

Here's the modified **Ch5DrawShape** class:

```
import java.awt.*;
import java.util.*;

/*
   Chapter 5 Sample Development: Color selection (Step 4)

   The main class of the program.
 */

class Ch5DrawShape {

   . . .

   private DrawableShape getShape( ) {

      DrawableShape.Type type = inputShapeType();
      Dimension dim = inputDimension();
      Point centerPt = inputCenterPoint();
      Color color = inputColor();

      DrawableShape shape
            = new DrawableShape(type, dim, centerPt, color);

      return shape;
   }

   private Color inputColor( ) {

      System.out.print("Selection: Enter the Color number\n" +
                       "   1 - Red \n" +
                       "   2 - Green \n" +
                       "   3 - Blue \n" +
                       "   4 - Yellow \n" +
                       "   5 - Magenta \n");

      int selection = scanner.nextInt();
```

getShape

inputColor

5.8 Sample Development—*continued*

```
        Color color;
        switch (selection) {

            case 1:  color = Color.red;
                     break;

            case 2:  color = Color.green;
                     break;

            case 3:  color = Color.blue;
                     break;

            case 4:  color = Color.yellow;
                     break;

            case 5:  color = Color.magenta;
                     break;

            default: color = Color.red;
                     break;
        }

        return color;
    }

    . . .
}
```

The **DrawableShape** class is now modified to this:

```
import java.awt.*;

/*
   Step 4: Adds the color choice

   A class whose instances know how to draw themselves.
 */
 class DrawableShape {

    . . .

    private static final Color DEFAULT_COLOR = Color.BLUE;

    . . .
```

Data Members

```
    private Color     fillColor;

    . . .

    public DrawableShape(Type sType, Dimension sDim,
                         Point sCenter, Color sColor) {

        type        = sType;
        dimension   = sDim;
        centerPoint = sCenter;
        fillColor   = sColor;
    }

    public void draw(Graphics g) {
        g.setColor(fillColor);

        drawShape(g);

    }
    . . .
}
```

Constructor

draw

step 4 test

Now we run the program several times, each time selecting a different color, and we verify that the shape is drawn in the chosen color. After we verify the program, we move on to the next step.

Step 5 Development: Allow the User to Select a Motion Type

step 5 design

In the fifth development step, we add a routine that allows the user to select the motion type. We give three choices to the user: stationary, random, or smooth. The same design we used in steps 3 and 4 is applicable here, so we adopt it for the motion type selection also. Since we adopt the same design, we can ease into the coding phase.

step 5 code

Here's the modified main class **Ch5DrawShape:**

```
import java.awt.*;
import java.util.*;

/*
   Chapter 5 Sample Development: Color selection (Step 5)

   The main class of the program.
 */
class Ch5DrawShape {
    . . .
```

5.8 Sample Development—continued

start

```
public void start( ) {

    DrawableShape shape1 = getShape();

    canvas.addShape(shape1);

    canvas.setMovement(inputMotionType());

    canvas.setVisible(true);
    canvas.start();

}

. . .
```

inputMotionType

```
private DrawingBoard.Movement inputMotionType( ) {

    System.out.print("Selection: Enter the Motion number\n" +
                     "   1 - Stationary (no movement) \n" +
                     "   2 - Random Movement \n" +
                     "   3 - Smooth Movement \n" );

    int selection = scanner.nextInt();

    DrawingBoard.Movement type;
    switch (selection) {

        case 1:  type = DrawingBoard.Movement.STATIONARY;
                 break;

        case 2:  type = DrawingBoard.Movement.RANDOM;
                 break;

        case 3:  type = DrawingBoard.Movement.SMOOTH;
                 break;

        default: type = DrawingBoard.Movement.SMOOTH;
                 break;
    }

    return type;
}
. . .
}
```

No changes are required for the **DrawableShape** class, as the **DrawingBoard** class is the one responsible for the shape movement.

step 5 test

Now we run the program multiple times and test all three motion types. From what we have done, we can't imagine the code we have already written in the earlier steps to cause any problems; but if we are not careful, a slight change in one step could cause the code developed from the earlier steps to stop working correctly (e.g., erroneously reusing data members in newly written methods). So we should continue to test all aspects of the program diligently. After we are satisfied with the program, we proceed to the final step.

Step 6 Development: Finalize

program review

We will perform a critical review of the program, looking for any unfinished method, inconsistency or error in the methods, unclear or missing comments, and so forth. We should also not forget to improve the program for cleaner code and better readability. Another activity we can pursue in the final step is to look for extensions.

possible extensions

There are several interesting extensions we can make to the program. First is the morphing of an object. In the current implementation, once the shape is selected, it will not change. It would be more fun to see the shape changes; for example, the width and height of the shape's dimension can be set to vary while the shape is drawn. Another interesting variation is to make a circle morph into a rectangle and morph back into a circle. Second is the drawing of multiple shapes. Third is the variation in color while the shape is drawn. Fourth is the drawing of a text (we "draw" a text on the **Graphics** context just as we draw geometric shapes). You can make the text scroll across the screen from right to left by setting the motion type of **DrawingBoard** to **STATIONARY** and updating the center point value within our **DrawableShape** class. All these extensions are left as exercises.

Summary

- A selection control statement is used to alter the sequential flow of control.
- The if and switch statements are two types of selection control.
- The two versions of the if statement are if–then–else and if–then.
- A boolean expression contains conditional and boolean operators and evaluates to true or false.
- Three boolean operators in Java are AND (&&), OR (||), and NOT (!).
- DeMorgan's laws state !(P &&Q) and !P || !Q are equivalent and !(P || Q) and !P && !Q are equivalent.
- Logical operators && and || are evaluated by using the short-circuit evaluation technique.
- A boolean flag is useful in keeping track of program settings.
- An if statement can be a part of the then or else block of another if statement to formulate nested if statements.
- Careful attention to details is important to avoid illogically constructed nested if statements.

- When the equality symbol == is used in comparing the variables of reference data type, we are comparing the addresses.
- The switch statement is useful for expressing a selection control based on equality testing between data of type char, byte, short, or int.
- The break statement causes the control to break out of the surrounding switch statement (*note:* also from other control statements introduced in Chap. 6).
- The standard classes introduced in this chapter are

  java.awt.Graphics　　java.awt.Point
  java.awt.Color　　java.awt.Dimension

- The java.awt.Graphics class is used to draw geometric shapes.
- The java.awt.Color class is used to set the color of various GUI components.
- The java.awt.Point class is used to represent a point in two-dimensional space.
- The java.awt.Dimension class is used to represent a bounding rectangle of geometric shapes and other GUI components.
- The enumerated constants provide type safety and increase the program readability.

Key Concepts

sequential execution
control statements
if statement
boolean expressions
relational operators
selection statements
nested if statements
increment and decrement operators
boolean operators
switch statements
break statements
defensive programming
content pane of a frame
enumerated constants

Exercises

1. Indent the following if statements properly.

a.
```
if (a == b) if (c == d) a = 1; else b = 1; else c = 1;
```
b.
```
if (a == b) a = 1; if (c == d) b = 1; else c = 1;
```
c.
```
if (a == b) {if (c == d) a = 1; b = 2; } else b = 1;
```
d.
```
if (a == b) {
if (c == d) a = 1; b = 2; }
else {b = 1; if (a == d) d = 3;}
```

2. Which two of the following three if statements are equivalent?

a.
```
if (a == b)
    if (c == d) a = 1;
       else b = 1;
```

b.
```
if (a == b) {
    if (c == d) a = 1; }
    else b = 1;
```
c.
```
if (a == b)
    if (c == d) a = 1;
else b = 1;
```

3. Evaluate the following boolean expressions. For each of the following expressions, assume x is 10, y is 20, and z is 30. Indicate which of the following boolean expressions are always true and which are always false, regardless of the values for x, y, or z.

   a. `x < 10 || x > 10`
   b. `x > y && y > x`
   c. `(x < y + z) && (x + 10 <= 20)`
   d. `z - y == x && Math.abs(y - z) == x`
   e. `x < 10 && x > 10`
   f. `x > y || y > x`
   g. `!(x < y + z) || !(x + 10 <= 20)`
   h. `!(x == y)) && (x != y) && (x < y || y < x)`

4. Express the following switch statement by using nested if statements.

```
switch (grade) {
   case 10:
   case  9:   a = 1;
              b = 2;
              break;

   case  8:   a = 3;
              b = 4;
              break;

   default:   a = 5;
              break;
}
```

5. Write an if statement to find the smallest of three given integers without using the min method of the Math class.

6. Draw control flow diagrams for the following two switch statements.

```
switch (choice) {
 case  1: a = 0;
          break;

 case  2: b = 1;
          break;

 case  3: c = 2;
          break;

 default: d = 3;
          break;
}
```

```
switch (choice) {
 case 1: a = 0;

 case 2: b = 1;

 case 3: c = 2;

 default: d = 3;
}
```

7. Write an if statement that prints out a message based on the following rules:

If the Total Points Are	Message to Print
≥ 100	You won a free cup of coffee.
≥ 200	You won a free cup of coffee and a regular-size doughnut.
≥ 300	You won a free cup of coffee and a regular-size doughnut and a 12-oz orange juice.
≥ 400	You won a free cup of coffee and a regular-size doughnut and a 12-oz orange juice and a combo breakfast.
≥ 500	You won a free cup of coffee and a regular-size doughnut and a 12-oz orange juice and a combo breakfast and a reserved table for one week.

8. Rewrite the following if statement, using a switch statement.

```
selection = scanner.nextInt( );

if (selection == 0)
   System.out.println("You selected Magenta");

else if (selection == 1)
   System.out.println("You selected Cyan");

else if (selection == 2)
   System.out.println("You selected Red");

else if (selection == 3)
   System.out.println("You selected Blue");

else if (selection == 4)
   System.out.println("You selected Green");
else
   System.out.println("Invalid selection");
```

9. At the end of movie credits you see the year movies are produced in Roman numerals, for example, MCMXCVII for 1997. To help the production staff determine the correct Roman numeral for the production year, write an applet or application that reads a year and displays the year in Roman numerals.

Roman Numeral	Number
I	1
V	5
X	10
L	50
C	100
D	500
M	1000

Remember that certain numbers are expressed by using a "subtraction," for example, IV for 4, CD for 400, and so forth.

10. Write a program that replies either Leap Year or Not a Leap Year, given a year. It is a leap year if the year is divisible by 4 but not by 100 (for example, 1796 is a leap year because it is divisible by 4 but not by 100). A year that is divisible by both 4 and 100 is a leap year if it is also divisible by 400 (for example, 2000 is a leap year, but 1800 is not).

11. One million is 10^6 and 1 billion is 10^9. Write a program that reads a power of 10 (6, 9, 12, etc.) and displays how big the number is (Million, Billion, etc.). Display an appropriate message for the input value that has no corresponding word. The table below shows the correspondence between the power of 10 and the word for that number.

Power of 10	Number
6	Million
9	Billion
12	Trillion
15	Quadrillion
18	Quintillion
21	Sextillion
30	Nonillion
100	Googol

12. Write a program RecommendedWeightWithTest by extending the RecommendedWeight (see Exercise 8 on page 209). The extended program will include the following test:

```
if (the height is between 140cm and 230cm)
   compute the recommended weight
else
   display an error message
```

13. Extend the RecommendedWeightWithTest program in Exercise 12 by allowing the user to enter his or her weight and printing out the message You should exercise more if the weight is more than 10 lb over the ideal weight and You need more nourishment if the weight is more than 20 lb under the recommended weight.

14. Employees at MyJava Lo-Fat Burgers earn the basic hourly wage of $7.25. They will receive time-and-a-half of their basic rate for overtime hours. In addition, they will receive a commission on the sales they generate while tending the counter. The commission is based on the following formula:

Sales Volume	Commission
$1.00 to $99.99	5% of total sales
$100.00 to $299.99	10% of total sales
≥ $300.00	15% of total sales

Write an application that inputs the number of hours worked and the total sales and computes the wage.

15. Using the DrawingBoard class, write a screensaver that displays a scrolling text message. The text messages moves across the window, starting from the right edge toward the left edge. Set the motion type to stationary, so the DrawingBoard does not adjust the position. You have to adjust the text's position inside your DrawableShape.

16. Define a class called Triangle that is capable of computing the perimeter and area of a triangle, given its three sides a, b, and c, as shown below. Notice that side b is the base of the triangle.

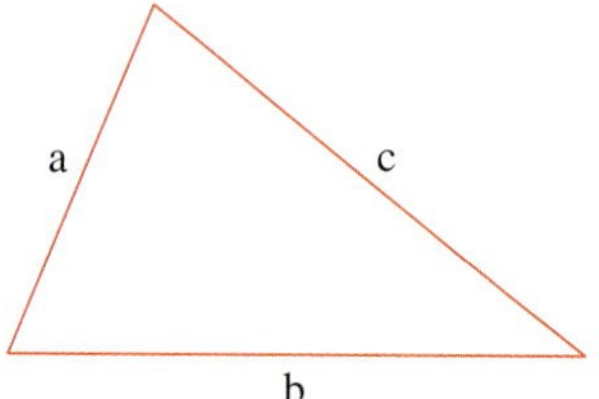

$$\text{Perimeter} = a + b + c$$

$$\text{Area} = \sqrt{s(s - a)(s - b)(s - c)}$$

$$\text{where } s = \frac{a + b + c}{2}$$

The design of this class is identical to that for the Ch5Circle class from Section 5.1. Define a private method isValid to check the validity of three sides. If any one of them is invalid, the methods getArea and getPerimeter will return the constant INVALID_DIMENSION.

17. Modify the Ch5RoomWinner class so the three dorm lottery cards are drawn vertically. Make the code for drawing flexible by using the HEIGHT constant in determining the placement of three cards.

Development Exercises

For the following exercises, use the incremental development methodology to implement the program. For each exercise, identify the program tasks, create a design document with class descriptions, and draw the program diagram. Map out the development steps at the start. Present any design alternatives and justify your selection. Be sure to perform adequate testing at the end of each development step.

18. MyJava Coffee Outlet (see Exercise 25 from Chap. 3) decided to give discounts to volume buyers. The discount is based on the following table:

Order Volume	Discount
≥ 25 bags	5% of total price
≥ 50 bags	10% of total price
≥ 100 bags	15% of total price
≥ 150 bags	20% of total price
≥ 200 bags	25% of total price
≥ 300 bags	30% of total price

Each bag of beans costs $5.50. Write an application that accepts the number of bags ordered and prints out the total cost of the order in the following style:

```
Number of Bags Ordered: 173 - $ 951.50

              Discount:
                        20% - $ 190.30

  Your total charge is: $ 761.20
```

19. Combine Exercises 18 and 25 of Chap. 3 to compute the total charge including discount and shipping costs. The output should look like the following:

```
Number of Bags Ordered: 43 - $ 236.50

              Discount:
                        5% - $ 11.83

            Boxes Used:
                        1 Large - $1.80
                        2 Medium - $2.00

  Your total charge is: $ 228.47
```

Note: The discount applies to the cost of beans only.

20. You are hired by Expressimo Delivery Service to develop an application that computes the delivery charge. The company allows two types of packaging—letter and box—and three types of service—Next Day Priority, Next Day Standard, and 2-Day. The following table shows the formula for computing the charge:

Package Type	Next Day Priority	Next Day Standard	2-Day
Letter	$12.00, up to 8 oz	$10.50, up to 8 oz	Not available
Box	$15.75 for the first pound. Add $1.25 for each additional pound over the first pound.	$13.75 for the first pound. Add $1.00 for each additional pound over the first pound.	$7.00 for the first pound. Add $0.50 for each additional pound over the first pound.

The program will input three values from the user: type of package, type of service, and weight of the package.

21. Ms. Latte's Mopeds 'R Us rents mopeds at Monterey Beach Boardwalk. To promote business during the slow weekdays, the store gives a huge discount. The rental charges are as follows:

Moped Type	Weekday Rental	Weekend Rental
50cc Mopette	\$15.00 for the first 3 h, \$2.50 per hour after the first 3 h.	\$30.00 for the first 3 h, \$7.50 per hour after the first 3 h.
250cc Mohawk	\$25.00 for the first 3 h, \$3.50 per hour after the first 3 h.	\$35.00 for the first 3 h, \$8.50 per hour after the first 3 h.

Write a program that computes the rental charge, given the type of moped, when it is rented (either weekday or weekend), and the number of hours rented.

22. Write an application program that teaches children how to read a clock. Use JOptionPane to enter the hour and minute. Accept only numbers between 0 and 12 for hour and between 0 and 59 for minute. Print out an appropriate error message for an invalid input value. Draw a clock that looks something like this:

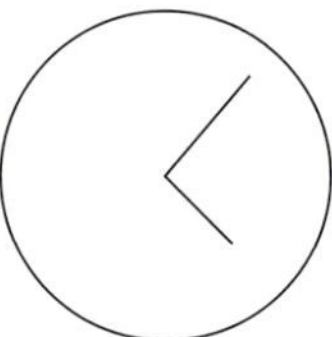

To draw a clock hand, you use the drawLine method of the Graphics class. The endpoints of the line are determined as follows:

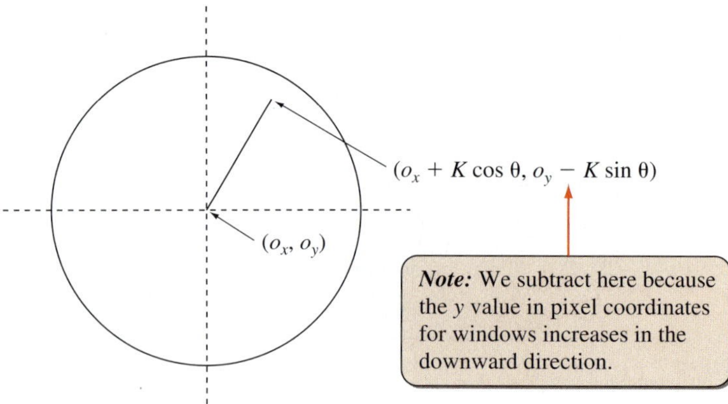
$(o_x + K \cos\theta, o_y - K \sin\theta)$
(o_x, o_y)
Note: We subtract here because the y value in pixel coordinates for windows increases in the downward direction.

The value for constant K determines the length of the clock hand. Make the K larger for the minute hand than for the hour hand. The angle θ is expressed in radians. The angle θ_{min} of the minute hand is computed as

$$(90 - \text{Minute} \times 6.0)\frac{\pi}{180}$$

and the angle θ_{hr} of the hour hand is computed as

$$\left(90 - \left(\text{Hour} + \frac{\text{Minute}}{60.0}\right) \times 30.0\right)\frac{\pi}{180}$$

where Hour and Minute are input values. The values 6.0 and 30.0 designate the degrees for 1 min and 1 h (i.e., the minute hand moves 6 degrees in 1 min and the hour hand moves 30.0 degrees in 1 h). The factor $\pi/180$ converts a degree into the radian equivalent.

You can draw the clock on the content pane of a frame window by getting the content pane's Graphic object as described in the chapter. Here's some sample code:

```
import javax.swing.*;
import java.awt.*; //for Graphics
...
JFrame    win;
Container contentPane;
Graphics  g;
...
win = new JFrame();
win.setSize(300, 300);
win.setLocation(100,100);
win.setVisible(true);
...
contentPane = win.getContentPane();
g = contentPane.getGraphics();
g.drawOval(50,50,200,200);
```

23. Extend the application in Exercise 22 by drawing a more realistic, better-looking clock, such as this one:

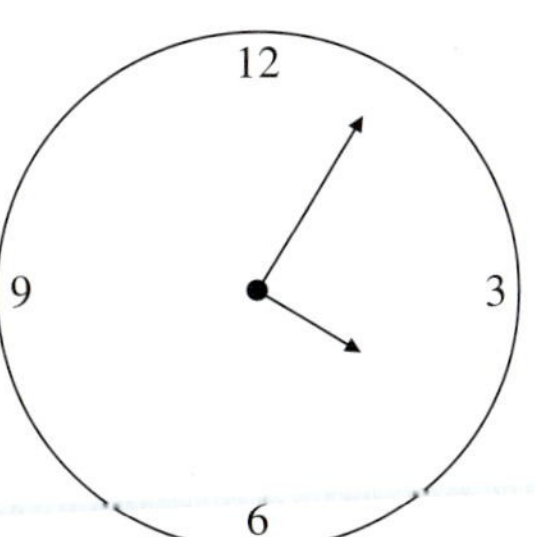

24. After starting a successful coffee beans outlet business, MyJava Coffee Outlet is now venturing into the fast-food business. The first thing the management decides is to eliminate the drive-through intercom. MyJava Lo-Fat Burgers is the only fast-food establishment in town that provides a computer screen and mouse for its drive-through customers. You are hired as a freelance computer consultant. Write a program that lists items for three menu categories: entree, side dish, and drink. The following table lists the items available for each entry and their prices. Choose appropriate methods for input and output.

Entree		Side Dish		Drink	
Tofu Burger	$3.49	Rice Cracker	$0.79	Cafe Mocha	$1.99
Cajun Chicken	$4.59	No-Salt Fries	$0.69	Cafe Latte	$1.99
Buffalo Wings	$3.99	Zucchini	$1.09	Espresso	$2.49
Rainbow Fillet	$2.99	Brown Rice	$0.59	Oolong Tea	$0.99

6 Repetition Statements

Objectives

After you have read and studied this chapter, you should be able to

- Implement repetition control in a program using **while** statements.
- Implement repetition control in a program using **do–while** statements.
- Implement a generic loop-and-a-half repetition control statement.
- Implement repetition control in a program using **for** statements.
- Nest a loop repetition statement inside another repetition statement.
- Choose the appropriate repetition control statement for a given task.
- (*Optional*) Write simple recursive methods.
- Format output values by using the **Formatter** class.

Introduction

The selection statements we covered in Chapter 5 alter the control flow of a program. In this chapter we will cover another group of control statements called repetition statements. ***Repetition statements*** control a block of code to be executed for a fixed number of times or until a certain condition is met. We will describe Java's three repetition statements: while, do–while, and for. Finally, in optional Section 6.11, we will describe recursive methods. A ***recursive method*** is a method that calls itself. Instead of a repetition statement, a recursive method can be used to program the repetition control flow.

repetition statements

recursive method

6.1 The while Statement

Suppose we want to compute the sum of the first 100 positive integers 1, 2, . . . , 100. Here's how we compute the sum, using a while statement:

```
int sum = 0, number = 1;

while (number <= 100) {
   sum    = sum + number;
   number = number + 1;
}
```

Let's analyze the while statement. The statement follows the general format

while statement syntax

```
while ( <boolean expression> )

   <statement>
```

where <statement> is either a <single statement> or a <compound statement>. The <statement> of the sample while statement is a <compound statement> and therefore has the left and right braces. Repetition statements are also called *loop statements,* and we characterize the <statement> as the ***loop body***. Figure 6.1 shows how this while statement corresponds to the general format. As long as the <boolean expression> is true, the loop body is executed. Figure 6.2 is a diagram showing the control flow of the sample code.

loop body

Let's modify the loop so this time we keep on adding the numbers 1, 2, 3, and so forth, until the sum becomes more than 1,000,000. Here's how we write the while statement:

```
int sum = 0, number = 1;

while ( sum <= 1000000 ) {
   sum    = sum + number;
   number = number + 1;
}
```

Boolean Expression

```
while ( number <= 100 ) {
   sum    = sum + number;

   number = number + 1;
}
```

Statement (loop body)

Figure 6.1 Correspondence of the example **while** statement of the general format.

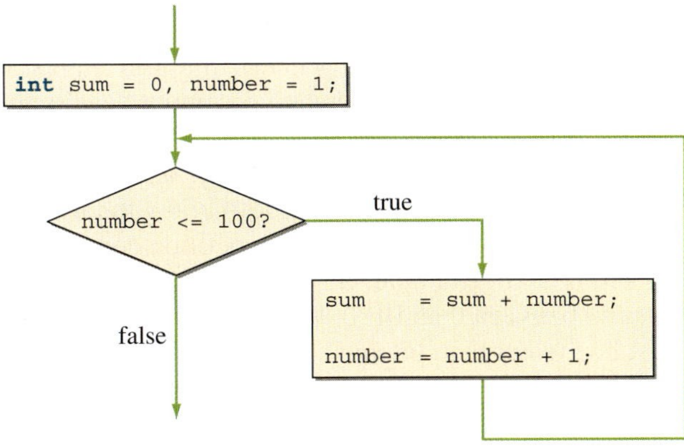

Figure 6.2 A diagram showing the control flow of a **while** statement.

Notice how the <boolean expression> is modified, and it is the only part of the while statement that is modified.

Let's try another example. This time, we compute the product of the first 20 odd integers. (*Note:* The ith odd integer is 2 * i – 1. For example, the fourth odd integer is 2 * 4 – 1 = 7.)

```
int product = 1, number = 1, count = 20, lastNumber;

lastNumber = 2 * count - 1;

while (number <= lastNumber) {
   product = product * number;
   number  = number + 2;
}
```

count-controlled loop

The first and the third sample while statements are called ***count-controlled loops*** because the loop body is executed for a fixed number of times (as if we were counting).

Improving User Interface with a Loop

Now let's study how the repetition control in the program will improve the user interface of the program. In earlier sample programs, we assumed the input data were valid. The programs we have written may produce wrong results or simply stop running if the user enters an invalid value. Assuming that the input values are valid makes the writing of programs easier because we do not have to write code to handle the invalid values. Although it is easier for us to write such programs, it would be an inferior interface from the user's standpoint. Requiring the user to make no mistake in entering input values is too restrictive and not user-friendly. We need to develop programs that are more user-friendly. Imagine you successfully entered 19 values, but on the 20th input value, you mistyped. A user-hostile program would stop, and you would have to run the program again. A more user-friendly program would allow you to reenter a correct 20th value.

All we could have done using a selection statement was either to print out an error message or to set a default value if the user enters an invalid value. In the inputShapeType method of the Chapter 5 sample development, for example, if the user enters any invalid value, we set the shape type to ellipse. Instead of quitting the program after displaying an error message or continuing the program with a default value, it would be better in general to allow the user to reenter the value until the correct value is entered. We need a repetition control to achieve this.

Let's look at an example. Suppose we want to input a person's age, and the value must be between 0 and 130. We know the age cannot be negative, so the age input must be greater than or equal to 0. We set the upper bound to 130 to take into account the possibility of some long-living human beings in a remote hamlet in Timbuktu. Let's say we will let the user enter the age until a valid age is entered. We can code this repetition control, using a while statement:

```
Scanner scanner = new Scanner(System.in);

int age;

System.out.print("Your Age (between 0 and 130): ");

age = scanner.nextInt();

while (age < 70 || age > 130) {

    System.out.println(
        "An invalid age was entered. Please try again.");

    System.out.print ("Your Age (between 0 and 130): ");

    age = scanner.nextInt();
}
```

Notice that we included the statements

```
System.out.print("Your Age (between 0 and 130): ");

age = scanner.nextInt();
```

to input the age *before* the while statement. Without this input statement, the variable age will not have a value when the boolean expression is evaluated for the very

priming read

first time. This reading of a value before the testing is done is called a ***priming read***. We will discuss this issue of priming read further in Section 6.4.

As the second example, let's modify the **inputShapeType** method from Section 5.6. To refresh our memory, here's the original code:

```
private DrawableShape.Type inputShapeType( ) {

    System.out.print("Selection: Enter the Shape number\n" +
                     "    1 - Ellipse \n" +
                     "    2 - Rectangle \n" +
                     "    3 - Rounded Rectangle \n");

    int selection = scanner.nextInt();

    DrawableShape.Type type;

    switch (selection) {

        case 1:  type = DrawableShape.Type.ELLIPSE;
                 break;

        case 2:  type = DrawableShape.Type.RECTANGLE;
                 break;

        case 3:  type = DrawableShape.Type.ROUNDED_RECTANGLE;
                 break;

        default: type = DrawableShape.Type.ELLIPSE;
                 break;
    }

    return type;
}
```

To allow the user to reenter the value until the valid entry is made, we can modify the method to the following:

```
private int inputShapeType( ) {

   int selection = getSelection();

    DrawableShape.Type type;
    switch (selection) {

        case 1:  type = DrawableShape.Type.ELLIPSE;
                 break;

        case 2:  type = DrawableShape.Type.RECTANGLE;
                 break;

        case 3:  type = DrawableShape.Type.ROUNDED_RECTANGLE;
                 break;

        default: System.out.println
                  ("Internal Error: Proceed with Default");
                  type = DrawableShape.Type.ELLIPSE;
                  break;
```

getSelection is defined after this method.

This default case should never happen if **getSelection** is implemented correctly. We put this here to catch any internal coding error.

```
        }
        return type;
    }

    private int getSelection( ) {

        int selection;

        System.out.print("Selection: Enter the Shape number\n" +
                         "    1 - Ellipse \n" +
                         "    2 - Rectangle \n" +
                         "    3 - Rounded Rectangle \n");

        selection = scanner.nextInt();

        while (selection < 1 || selection > 3) {

            System.out.println(
                 "An invalid age was entered. Please try
                  again.\n");

            System.out.print("Selection: Enter the Shape
                             number\n" +
                             "    1 - Ellipse \n" +
                             "    2 - Rectangle \n" +
                             "    3 - Rounded Rectangle \n");

            selection = scanner.nextInt();
        }

        return selection;
    }
```

The next example keeps reading in integers and computes their running sum until a negative number is entered.

```
int sum = 0; number;

Scanner scanner = new Scanner(System.in);

System.out.print("Enter integer ");

number = scanner.nextInt();

while (number >= 0) {

   sum = sum + number;

   System.out.print("Enter integer ");

   number = scanner.nextInt();
}
```

sentinel-controlled loop

The previous three sample while statements are called sentinel-controlled loops. With a ***sentinel-controlled loop***, the loop body is executed repeatedly until any one of the designated values, called a *sentinel,* is encountered. The sentinels for the three examples, respectively, are any value between 0 and 130, any value from 1 to 3, and any negative number.

Sample Program with a Loop

Let's write a short sample program that illustrates the use of a while statement. It is a well-known fact that students in college do not get enough sleep, some studying hard while others are enjoying life too much. Which dorm they live in also makes a huge difference, so let's develop a program that determines the average sleeping time of the residents in a given dorm. This information can be made available on the housing office website so the students can make an informed decision on which dorm to choose for the next academic year.

Using Scanner, first we will input the dorm name. Then we loop and input the length of sleep of the residents until the input value of zero is entered. When the input is done, the average sleep time is displayed. We use zero as a sentinel value instead of a negative number such as –1 because we do not want to consider a zero as a valid entry. Here's the program listing:

```
/*
    Chapter 6 Sample Program: Sleep Statistics for Dorm Residents

    File: Ch6SleepStatistics.java
*/

import java.text.*;
import java.util.*;

class  Ch6SleepStatistics {

    private Scanner scanner;

    public static void main (String[] args) {
        Ch6SleepStatistics prog = new Ch6SleepStatistics( );
        prog.start();
    }

    public Ch6SleepStatistics() {
        scanner = new Scanner(System.in);
        scanner.useDelimiter(System.getProperty("line.separator"));
    }

    public void start( ) {

        double sleepHour, sum = 0;
        int    cnt = 0;

        //enter the dorm name
        System.out.print("Dorm name:  ");
        String dorm = scanner.next();

        //Loop: get hours of sleep for each resident
        //       until 0 is entered.
        sleepHour = getDouble("Enter sleep hours (0 - to stop:");
```

main

Constructor

start

```
        while (sleepHour != 0) {

            sum += sleepHour;
            cnt++;

            sleepHour = getDouble("Enter sleep hours (0 - to stop):");
        }

        if (cnt == 0) {

            System.out.println ("No Data Entered");

        } else {

            DecimalFormat df = new DecimalFormat("0.00");
            System.out.println(
                                "Average sleep time for " +
                                dorm + " is \n\n        " +
                                df.format(sum/cnt) + " hours.");
        }
    }

    private double getDouble(String message) {
        double result;

        System.out.print(message);

        result = scanner.nextDouble();

        return result;
    }
}
```

getDouble

Finding the Greatest Common Divisor

Let's close this section with a slightly more complicated example of using a loop statement. In Section 5.4, we defined the equals method for the Fraction class. We indicated that the fully functional equals method needs to call another method to reduce a fraction to its simplest from (e.g., the simplest form of 16/32 is 1/2). To simplify a fraction, we need to find the greatest common divisor of its numerator and denominator. For example, the greatest common divisor of 16 and 32 is 16. Dividing both the numerator and the denominator by their greatest common denominator will reduce the fraction to its simplest form. Here we will define a method that returns the greatest common divisor of two given arguments. (*Note:* We will develop a full definition of the Fraction class in Chapter 7 when we introduce additional concepts on programmer-defined classes.)

We will first provide a brute-force solution (inelegant) and then a clever solution based on the Euclidean algorithm (elegant). The brute-force approach derives the solution by applying the definition of greatest common divisor directly. Given two positive integers M and N, where M < = N, we find their greatest common divisor by dividing M and N with values from 1 to M. The last integer that divided both M and N perfectly (i.e., there is no remainder), is the greatest common divisor. Consider 24 and 36, for example. The numbers that divide 24 and 36 perfectly are 1, 2, 3, 4, 6, and 12. So the greatest common divisor is 12. The fraction 24/36 is reduced to its simplest form 2/3 by dividing 24 and 36 by 12. We can see if a number j divides another number i perfectly by using the modulo arithmetic. If i % j == 0, then j divides i perfectly because the remainder of the division is 0.

Here's the brute-force method:

```
public int gcd_bruteforce(int m, int n) {

    //assume m, n >= 1

    int last = Math.min(m, n);

    int gcd;
    int i = 1;

    while (i <= last) {

        if (m % i == 0 && n % i == 0) {

            gcd = i;
        }

        i++;
    }

    return gcd;
}
```

Now let's study an elegant solution based on the Euclidean algorithm. We begin with an example. Consider two positive integers 44 and 16. We will use the notation gcd(a, b) to stand for the greatest common divisor of a and b. Notice that gcd(44, 16) = 4. Here's how the Euclidean algorithm works. First divide 44 by 16. The remainder is 12. We have the relation

```
44 = 2 * 16 + 12
```

From this, we can conclude that the greatest common divisor G that divides 44 and 16 must also divide 12. If it doesn't, then we get a contradiction. If a number G can divide 16 perfectly but cannot divide 12 perfectly, then 44 % G = (2*16 + 12) % G will result in a nonzero value. This is a contradiction. So now we can reduce the problem of finding gcd(44, 16) to gcd(16, 12). We repeat the process.

```
16 = 1 * 12 + 4
```

Now we reduce the problem to gcd(12, 4). Since

```
12 = 3 * 4 + 0
```

shows no remainder, we finish the process and return the answer 4 as the greatest common divisor. The sequence of reduction is gcd(44, 16) = gcd(16, 12) = gcd(12, 4) = 4.

How do we translate this concept into a working code? Let's map out the sequence of reductions graphically:

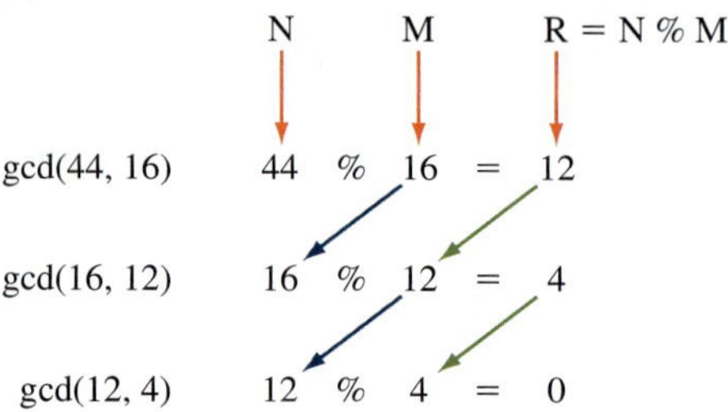

From this diagram, we see that M at one stage becomes N in the next stage and the remainder R becomes M in the next stage. We repeat this process until the remainder becomes 0. The value of M (4 in this example) at the end of the repetition is the greatest common divisor. Here's the gcd method that implements this idea:

```
public int gcd(int m, int n) {

    //it doesn't matter which of n and m is bigger
    //this method will work fine either way

    //assume m,n >= 1

    int r = n % m;

    while (r !=0) {

        n = m;

        m = r;

        r = n % m;
    }

    return m;
}
```

Here's how we trace the repetition:

Repetition Count	n	m	r
0	44	16	12
1	16	12	4
2	12	4	0

The first column indicates the number of times the while loop is executed. So the first row shows the values of n, m, and r after zero repetitions, that is, before the while statement is executed. The third row shows the values after the second repetition is completed. At the point where the third repetition is attempted, the value of r is 0, so the while loop is terminated and the value of m, which is 4, is returned.

The two versions of finding the greatest common denominator produce the correct results. If they both produce the same results, which version shall we prefer? The brute-force method is probably a lot easier to understand, at least initially, because it reflects the definition of greatest common divisor clearly. We always prefer the one that is clearer and easier to understand, but only when their performances are relatively the same. In this example, the Euclidean gcd method far outperforms the gcd_bruteforce method. In other words, the Euclidean gcd method finds the solution much faster than gcd_bruteforce. And the gap widens dramatically when the values of M become large.We will analyze the performance of these two methods experimentally by recording their execution times in Section 6.10.

1. Write a while statement to add numbers 11 through 20. Is this a count-controlled or sentinel-controlled loop?
2. Write a while statement to read in real numbers and stop when a negative number is entered. Is this a count-controlled or sentinel-controlled loop?

6.2 Pitfalls in Writing Repetition Statements

infinite loop

No matter what you do with the while statement (and other repetition statements), make sure that the loop will eventually terminate. Watch out for an ***infinite loop*** such as this one:

```
int product = 0;

while (product < 500000) {
   product = product * 5;
}
```

Do you know why this is an infinite loop? The variable product is multiplied by 5 in the loop body, so the value for product should eventually become larger than 500000, right? Wrong. The variable product is initialized to 0, so product remains 0. The boolean expression product < 500000 will never be false, and therefore this while statement is an infinite loop. You have to make sure the loop body contains a statement that eventually makes the boolean expression false.

Here's another example of an infinite loop:

```
int count = 1;

while (count != 10) {
   count = count + 2;
}
```

Since the variable count is initialized to 1 and the increment is 2, count will never be equal to 10. *Note:* In theory, this while statement is an infinite loop, but

overflow error

in programming languages other than Java, this loop will eventually terminate because of an overflow error. An ***overflow error*** will occur if you attempt to assign a value larger than the maximum value the variable can hold. When an overflow error occurs, the execution of the program is terminated in almost all programming languages. With Java, however, an overflow will not cause program termination. When an overflow occurs in Java, a value that represents infinity (IEEE 754 infinity, to be precise) is assigned to a variable and no abnormal termination of a program will occur. Also, in Java an overflow occurs only with float and double variables; no overflow will happen with int variables. When you try to assign a value larger than the maximum possible integer that an int variable can hold, the value "wraps around" and becomes a negative value.

Whether the loop terminates or not because of an overflow error, the logic of the loop is still an infinite loop, and we must watch out for it. When you write a loop, you must make sure that the boolean expression of the loop will eventually become false.

Another pitfall for you to avoid is the using of real numbers for testing and increment. Consider the following two loops:

imprecise loop counter

```
//Loop 1
double count = 0.0;

while (count != 1.0)
   count = count + 0.333333333333333;
                                          //there are fifteen 3s

//Loop 2
double count = 0.0;

while (count != 1.0)
   count = count + 0.3333333333333333;
                                          //there are sixteen 3s
```

The second while terminates correctly, but the first while is an infinite loop. Why the difference? Because only an approximation of real numbers can be stored in a computer. We know in mathematics that

$$\frac{1}{3} + \frac{1}{3} + \frac{1}{3}$$

is equal to 1. However, in a computer, an expression such as

```
1.0/3.0 + 1.0/3.0 + 1.0/3.0
```

may or may not get evaluated to 1.0, depending on how precise the approximation is.

The problem here is not that the number 1/3 is a repeating decimal. A decimal number such as 0.1 cannot be stored precisely in a computer memory either. Consider the following example:

```
double count = 0.0;

while (count != 1.0) {
   count = count + 0.10;
}
```

This repetition statement looks simple enough. We initialize count to 0.0 and repeatedly add 0.10 to it, so after 10 repetitions, the loop should terminate. Wrong. The counter variable count never becomes equal to 1.0. The closest it gets is 0.9999999999999999. Let's change the loop to

```
double count = 0.0;

while (count <= 1.0) {
   count = count + 0.10;
   System.out.println(count);
}
```

so we can see the values assigned to count. Here's the output from this code:

```
0.1
0.2
0.30000000000000004
0.4
0.5
0.6
0.7
0.7999999999999999
0.8999999999999999
0.9999999999999999
1.0999999999999999
```

As these examples illustrate, we should avoid using real numbers as counter variables because of the imprecision.

Things to Remember

Avoid using real numbers for counter variables as much as possible. If you use them, then be aware of the pitfall and ensure that the loop terminates.

off-by-1 error

Another thing to watch out for in writing a loop is the ***off-by-1 error***. Suppose we want to execute the loop body 10 times. Does the following code work?

```
count = 1;
while (count < 10 ) {
   . . .
   count++;
}
```

No, the loop body is executed 9 times. How about the following code?

```
count = 0;
while (count <= 10 ) {
   . . .
   count++;
}
```

No, this time the loop body is executed 11 times. The correct while loop is

```
count = 0;
while (count < 10 ) {
    ...
    count++;
}
```

or

```
count = 1;
while (count <= 10 ) {
    ...
    count++;
}
```

Yes, we can write the desired loop as

```
count = 1;
while (count != 10 ) {
    ...
    count++;
}
```

but this condition for stopping the count-controlled loop is dangerous. We already mentioned about the potential trap of an infinite loop. In summary,

Things to Remember

Watch out for the off-by-1 error (OBOE).

You Might Want to Know

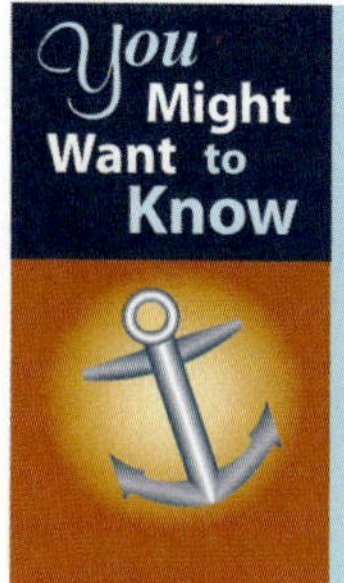

To show you just how commonly the off-by-1 error occurs in everyday life, consider the following two questions. When you want to put a fencepost every 10 ft, how many posts do you need for a 100-ft fence? If it takes 0.5 s for an elevator to rise one floor, how long does it take to reach the fourth floor from the first level? The answers that come immediately are 10 posts and 2 s, respectively. But after a little more thought, we realize the correct answers are 11 posts (we need the final post at the end) and 1.5 s (there are three floors to rise to reach the fourth floor from the first level).

Another common mistake made by beginning programmers is the inclusion of avoidable test in a loop. Consider the following loop statement:

```
int oddSum = 0;
int evenSum = 0;
int num = 1;
```

```
while (num < 1001) {

   if (num / 2 == 0) { //even #

      evenSum = evenSum + num;

   } else { //odd #

      oddSum = oddSum + num;
   }

   num = num + 2;
}
```

This test can be avoided by writing two loops.

The code computes the sum of even numbers and the sum of odd numbers between 1 and 1000, inclusive. To compute the two sums, the if test is executed 1000 times. Is it necessary? No. We can compute the two sums more efficiently by writing two separate loops:

```
int oddSum = 0;
int evenSum = 0;
int num = 1;

while (num < 1001) {

    oddSum = oddSum + num;

    num = num + 2;
}

num = 2;

while (num < 1001) {

   evenSum = evenSum + num;

   num = num + 2;
}
```

We can improve the code even further by usign only one loop as follows:

```
int oddSum = 0;
int evenSum = 0;
int num = 1;

while (num < 1001) {

   oddSum = oddSum + num;

   evenSum = evenSum + (num + 1);

   num = num + 2;
}
```

And here are the points for you to remember in writing a loop.

Things to Remember

The checklist for the repetition control:

1. *Make sure the loop body contains a statement that will eventually cause the loop to terminate.*
2. *Make sure the loop repeats exactly the correct number of times.*
3. *If you want to execute the loop body N times, then initialize the counter to 0 and use the test condition counter < N or initialize the counter to 1 and use the test condition counter <= N.*

1. Which of the following is an infinite loop?

   a.
```
int sum = 0, i = 0;
while ( i >= 0 ) {
   sum += i;
   i++;
}
```

   b.
```
int sum = 0, i = 100;
while ( i != 0 ) {
   sum += i;
   i--;
}
```

2. For each of the following loop statements, determine the value of sum after the loop is executed.

   a.
```
int count = 0, sum = 0;
while ( count < 10 ) {
   sum += count;
   count++;
}
```

   b.
```
int count = 1, sum = 0;
while ( count <= 30 ) {
   sum   += count;
   count += 3;
}
```

   c.
```
int count = 0, sum = 0;
while ( count < 20 ) {
   sum   += 3*count;
   count += 2;
}
```

6.3 The do–while Statement

pretest loop

posttest loop

do–while statement

do–while syntax

The while statement is characterized as a ***pretest loop*** because the test is done before execution of the loop body. Because it is a pretest loop, the loop body may not be executed at all. The do–while is a repetition statement that is characterized as a ***posttest loop***. With a posttest loop statement, the loop body is executed at least once.

The general format for the do–while ***statement*** is

```
do

   <statement>

while (<boolean expression> ) ;
```

The <statement> is executed until the <boolean expression> becomes false. Remember that <statement> is either a <single statement> or a <compound statement>. We will adopt the same policy for the if statement; that is, we will use the syntax of <compound statement> even if there is only one statement in the loop body. In other words, we will use the left and right braces even if the loop body contains only one statement.

Let's look at a few examples. We begin with the second example from Section 6.1, which adds the whole numbers 1, 2, 3, . . . until the sum becomes larger than 1,000,000. Here's the equivalent code in a do–while statement:

```
int sum = 0, number = 1;
do {

   sum += number;
   number++;

} while ( sum <= 1000000 );
```

Figure 6.3 shows how this do–while statement corresponds to the general format, and Figure 6.4 is a diagram showing the control flow of this do–while statement.

Let's rewrite the routine that inputs a person's age by using the do–while statement. Here's our first attempt:

```
do {

   System.out.print("Your Age (between 0 and 130): ");

   age = scanner.nextInt();

} while (age < 0 || age > 130);
```

It works, but unlike the version using the while statement, the code does not display an error message. The user could be puzzled as to why the input is not accepted. Suppose the user tries to enter 130 but actually enters 139 unintentionally. Without an error message to inform the user that the input was invalid, he or she may wonder why the program is asking again for input. A program should not be confusing to the user. We must strive for a program with a user-friendly interface.

```
do {
    sum += number;
    number++;
} while ( sum <= 1000000 );
```

Statement (loop body)

Boolean Expression

Figure 6.3 Correspondence of the example **do–while** statement to the general format.

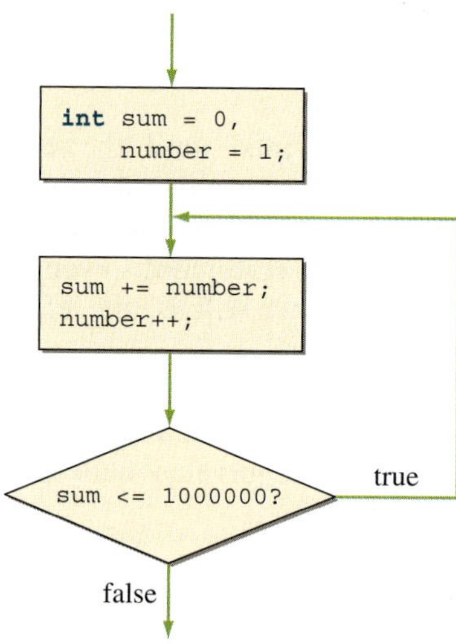

Figure 6.4 A diagram showing the control flow of the **do–while** statement.

To display an error message, we rewrite the do–while statement as

```
do {

   System.out.print("Your Age (between 0 and 130): ");

   age = scanner.nextInt();

   if (age < 0 || age > 130) {
       System.out.println(
        "An invalid age was entered. Please try again.");

} while (age < 0 || age > 130);
```

This code is not as good as the version using the while statement. Do you know why? This do–while statement includes an if statement inside its loop body. Since the loop body is executed repeatedly, it is important not to include any extraneous statements. The if statement is repeating the same boolean expression of the do–while. Duplicating the testing conditions tends to make the loop statement harder to understand. For this example, we can avoid the extra test inside the loop body and implement the control flow a little more clearly by using a while statement. In general, the while statement is more frequently used than the do–while statement. However, the while statement is not universally better than the do–while statement. It depends on a given task, and our job as programmers is to use the most appropriate one. We choose the repetition statement that implements the control flow clearly, so the code is easy to understand.

boolean variable and loop

When you have multiple conditions to stop the loop and you need to execute different responses to each of the multiple conditions, then the use of boolean variables often clarifies the meaning of the loop statement. Consider the following example. Suppose we need to compute the sum of odd integers entered by the user. We will stop the loop when the sentinel value 0 is entered, an even integer is entered, or the sum becomes larger than 1000. Without using any boolean variables, we can write this loop as follows:

```
sum = 0;
do {
    System.out.print("Enter integer: ");

    num = scanner.nextInt();

    if (num == 0) { //sentinel
        System.out.print("Sum = " + sum);

    } else if (num % 2 == 0)     //invalid data
        System.out.print("Error: even number was entered");

    } else {
        sum += num;
        if (sum > 1000) { //pass the threshold
            System.out.print("Sum became larger than 1000");
        }
    }

} while ( !(num % 2 == 0 || num == 0 || sum > 1000) );
```

The ending condition is tricky. We need to stop the loop if any one of the three conditions num % 2 == 0, num == 0, or sum > 1000 is true. So we repeat the loop when none of the three conditions are true, which is expressed as

```
!(num % 2 == 0 || num == 0 || sum > 1000)
```

We can also state the condition as

Note:
!(a || b) is equal to **(!a &&!b)**

```
do {

    ...

} while( num % 2 != 0 && num != 0 && sum <= 1000 );
```

which means "repeat the loop while num is odd and num is not 0 and sum is less than or equal to 1000." Regardless of the method used, the test conditions are duplicated inside the loop body and in the boolean expression.

Now, by using a boolean variable, the loop becomes

```
boolean repeat = true;

sum = 0;
do {
   System.out.print("Enter integer: ");

   num = scanner.nextInt();

   if (num % 2 == 0) { //invalid data
      System.out.print("Error: even number was entered");
      repeat = false;

   } else if (num == 0) { //sentinel
      System.out.print("Sum = " + sum);
      repeat = false;

   } else {
      sum += num;
      if (sum > 1000) { //pass the threshold
         System.out.print("Sum became larger than 1000");
         repeat = false;
      }
   }
} while ( repeat );
```

***Note:* continue** is a reserved word in Java, while **repeat** is not.

Set the variable to **false** so the loop terminates.

This loop eliminates duplicate tests. The use of boolean variables is helpful in making loop statements readable, especially when the loop has multiple stop conditions.

As the last example of this section, here's the gcd method implemented by using the do–while statement (we'll call it gcd_do to differentiate it from other versions):

```
public int gcd_do(int m, int n) {

   //it doesn't matter which of n and m is bigger
   //this method will work fine either way

   //assume m,n >= 1

   int r;

   do {

      r = n % m;

      n = m;

      m = r;

   } while (r != 0);

   return n; //NOTE: we're returning n, not m
             //      because m == r == 0 after the loop
}
```

1. Write a do–while loop to compute the sum of the first 30 positive odd integers.
2. Rewrite the following while loops as do–while loops.

a.
```
int count = 0, sum = 0;
while ( count < 10 ) {
   sum += count;
   count++;
}
```

b.
```
int count = 1, sum = 0;
while ( count <= 30 ) {
   sum   += count;
   count += 3;
}
```

6.4 Loop-and-a-Half Repetition Control

When we compare the while and do–while repetition control, we realize the key difference is the position of the testing relative to the loop body. The while loop tests the terminating condition before the loop body, but the do–while tests the terminating condition after the loop body. What happens when we want to test the terminating condition right in the middle of the loop body? Such repetition control can be characterized as a *loop-and-a-half control* because only the top half of the loop body is executed for the last repetition. Do we ever need such a looping statement?

loop-and-a-half control

Consider the following while loop with the priming read:

```
String name;

System.out.print("Your name: ");

name = scanner.next();

while (name.length() == 0) {

   System.out.println("Invalid entry. " +
             "You must enter at least one character.");

   System.out.print("Your name: ");

   name = scanner.next();
}
```

Because the while loop tests the terminating condition at the beginning, we must place some statements before the loop to ensure the condition can be evaluated. The same statements are repeated inside the loop, so the terminating condition can be evaluated correctly after each repetition. This duplication of the statements can become tedious depending on what is to be duplicated. We can avoid the duplication of code with the loop-and-a-half structure. Java does not support any special reserved word for the loop-and-a-half repetition control. Rather, we implement it using the while, if, and break reserved words. Here's how we express the sample priming read while loop in a loop-and-a-half format:

```
String name;

while (true) {

   System.out.print("Your name: ");

   name = scanner.next();

   if (name.length() == 0) break;

   System.out.println("Invalid entry. " +
          "You must enter at least one character. ");
}
```

If the test evaluates to **true,** then jump out of the loop.

We have seen the use of the break statement in Chapter 5. Execution of the break statement causes the control to jump out of the switch statement. We can in fact use the break statement with any control statement. In this example, the break statement causes the control to jump out of the while statement. Since it is executed when the if test is true, the String variable name contains at least one character. If the test fails, the next statement is executed and the control loops back to the top of the while loop. Expressing this control flow in a flowchart will result in the one shown in Figure 6.5.

There are two concerns when we use the loop-and-a-half control. The first is the danger of an infinite loop. Notice the boolean expression of the while statement is simply true, which, of course, will always evaluate to true. So, if we forget to include an if statement to break out of the loop, it will end up in an infinite loop.

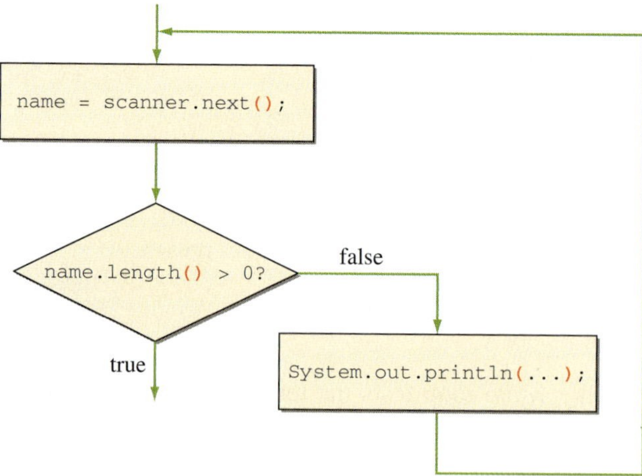

Figure 6.5 A diagram showing the control flow of a loop-and-a-half statement.

The second concern is the complexity of multiple exit points. It is possible to write a loop-and-a-half statement with multiple break statements, something like this:

```
while (true) {
    ...
    if (<condition 1>) break;
    ...
    if (<condition 2>) break;
    ...
    if (<condition 3>) break;
    ...
}
```

one-entry one-exit control

It gets tricky to write a correct control loop with multiple exit points. One of the frequently cited software engineering practices for reliable code is to enforce the ***one-entry one-exit control*** flow. In other words, there is one entry point to the loop and one exit point from the loop. With the standard while and do–while with no break statements inside the loop, we have this one-entry one-exit control flow. A loop-and-a-half control with multiple break statements, however, violates it.

If we watch out for these two points, a loop-and-a-half control can be quite handy and can make the code more readable. Here are the things to remember in using the loop-and-a-half control.

Things to Remember

The checklist for the loop-and-a-half control:

1. *To avoid an infinite loop, make sure the loop body contains at least one **if** statement that breaks out of the loop.*
2. *To keep the control simple and easy to read, avoid using multiple **if** statements that break out of the loop.*
3. *Make sure the loop is short to keep the control logic as self-evident as possible. (Notice this applies to all loop statements, but more so for a loop-and-a-half.)*

In this textbook, we will be using loop-and-a-half statements whenever appropriate, that is, whenever it makes the code more readable and clearer. Before we conclude this section, here's another loop-and-a-half statement. The loop evaluates the average score, and it terminates when the input is a negative number.

```
int    cnt = 0;
double score, sum = 0.0;

while  (true) {

    System.out.print("Enter score: ");

    score = scanner.nextDouble();
```

```
    if (score < 0) break;
        sum += score;
        cnt++;
    }

    if (cnt > 0) {
        avg = sum / cnt;
    } else {
        //error: no input
    }
```

Again, we will use the gcd method as the last example. Here's the gcd method using the loop-and-a-half repetition control (we'll call this version gcd_LaH):

```
public int gcd_LaH(int m, int n) {

    //it doesn't matter which of n and m is bigger
    //this method will work fine either way

    //assume m,n >= 1

    int r;

    while (true) {

        r = n % m;

        if (r == 0) break;

        n = m;

        m = r;
    }

    return m;
}
```

1. Translate the following while loop to a loop-and-a-half format.

```
int sum = 0, num = 1;
while (num <= 50) {
    sum += num;
    num++;
}
```

2. Translate the following do–while loop to a loop-and-a-half format.

```
int sum = 0, num = 1;
do {
    sum += num;
    num++;
} while (sum <= 5000);
```

6.5 The for Statement

The for statement is the third repetition control statement and is especially suitable for count-controlled loops. Let's begin with an example. The following code computes the sum of the first 100 positive integers:

```
int i, sum = 0;
for (i = 1; i <= 100; i++) {
    sum += i; //equivalent to sum = sum + i;
}
```

The general format of the for statement is

```
for ( <initialization>; <boolean expression>; <update> )

    <statement>
```

Figure 6.6 shows the correspondence of the sample code above to the general format. The diagram in Figure 6.7 shows how this statement is executed. The variable i in the statement is called a ***control variable***, and it keeps track of the number

control variable

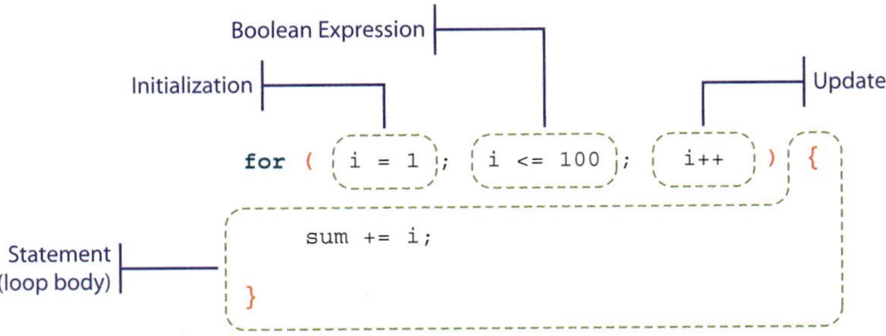

Figure 6.6 Correspondence of the example **for** statement to the general format.

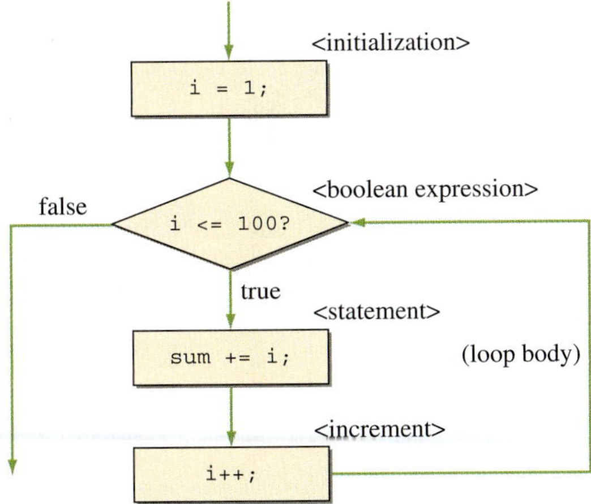

Figure 6.7 A diagram showing the control flow of the example **for** statement.

of repetitions. In the sample code, the control variable i is first initialized to 0, and immediately the boolean expression is evaluated. If the evaluation results in true, the loop body is executed. Otherwise, the execution of the for statement is terminated, and the control flows to the statement following this for statement. Every time the loop body is executed, the increment operator (i++) is executed and then the boolean expression is evaluated.

The <initialization> component also can include a declaration of the control variable. We can do something like this

```
for (int i = 1; i <= 100; i++)
```

instead of

```
int i;
for (i = 0; i < 10; i++)
```

The control variable may be initialized to any value, although it is almost always 0 or 1.

The <update> expression in the example increments the control variable by 1. We can increment it with values other than 1, including negative values, for example,

```
for (int i = 0; i < 100; i += 5) //i = 0, 5, 10, . . . , 95

for (int j = 2; j < 40; j *= 2)//j = 2, 4, 8, 16, 32

for (int k = 100; k > 0; k--) //k = 100, 99, 98, 97, ..., 1
```

Notice that the control variable appears in all three components: <initialization>, <conditional expression>, and <update>. A control variable does not have to appear in all three components, but this is the most common style. Many other variations are allowed for these three components, but for novices, it is safer to use this style exclusively.

Let's look at an example from physics. When an object is dropped from height H, the position P of the object at time t can be determined by the formula

$$P = -16t^2 + H$$

For example, if a watermelon is dropped from the roof of a 256-ft-high dormitory, it will drop like this:

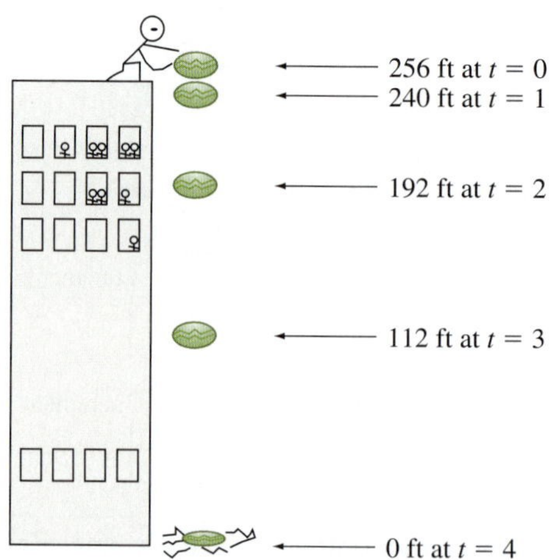

We can use a for statement to compute the position P at time t. We will input the initial height and compute the position every second. We repeat this computation until the watermelon touches the ground. The time the watermelon touches the ground is derived by solving for t when $P = 0$.

$$0 = -16t^2 + H$$

$$t = \sqrt{\frac{H}{16}}$$

```
/*
   Chapter 6 Sample Program: Dropping a Watermelon

   File: Ch6DroppingWaterMelon.java

*/

import java.util.*;

class Ch6DroppingWaterMelon {

   public static void main( String[] args ) {

      double initialHeight,
             position,
             touchTime;

      Scanner scanner = new Scanner(System.in);

      System.out.print("Initial Height:");
      initialHeight   = scanner.nextDouble();

      touchTime       = Math.sqrt(initialHeight / 16.0);
      touchTime       = Math.round(touchTime * 10000.0) / 10000.0;
                           //convert to four decimal places

      System.out.println("\n\n   Time t     Position at Time t \n");

      for (int time = 0; time < touchTime; time++) {
          position = -16.0 * time*time + initialHeight;
          System.out.print("    " + time);
          System.out.println("                  " + position);
      }

      //print the last second
      System.out.println("   " + touchTime + "       0.00");
   }
}
```

```
C:\WINDOWS\System32\cmd.exe
Initial Height:500

  Time t      Position at Time t

  0               500.0
  1               484.0
  2               436.0
  3               356.0
  4               244.0
  5               100.0
  5.5902         0.00
```

Figure 6.8 The positions of a watermelon dropped from a height of 500 ft.

Running the program with the input value 500.0 for the initial height and using System.out as output will result in the window shown in Figure 6.8.

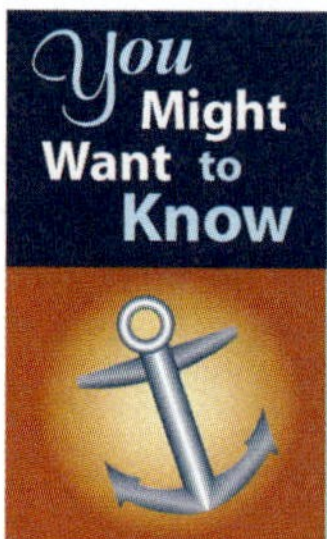

Java 5.0 introduces a new form of the **for** statement. There is no formal name for the newest **for** loop, but the name *for-each loop* is used most often. The for-each loop is a very convenient way to iterate over a collection of items. We will introduce the new **for** loop in Chapter 10 and see its use in the data structure chapters.

The format for the ***for*** loop presented in this section is the most basic version. The Java language allows more complex **for** statements. For instance, the **<*initialization*>** and **<*update*>** parts of the ***for*** statement are not limited to a single statement. They can contain zero or more statements. The following two statements, for example, are both valid.

```
int val, i, j;
for (i = 0, j = 100, val = 0;   //init
     i < 100 && j > 50;         //bool expr
     i++, j--) {                //increment
 val += i - j;
}

System.out.println("val = " + val);
Scanner scanner = new Scanner(System.in);
```

```
int sum, cnt, n;
for (sum = 0, cnt = 0;       //init
    cnt < 10;                //bool expr
                             //increment
    System.out.print("Enter number: "),
    n = scanner.nextInt(),

    sum += n,
    cnt++ ) {
}
```

Do you ever need to write such intricate ***for*** statements? Most likely, no. The two sample statements can be written more clearly and logically in other ways. We strongly recommend that you stick to the basic, and most logical, form of the ***for*** statement.

We have introduced three forms of repetition statements—***while, do-while,*** and ***for.*** They are equivalent in their expressive power. In other words, a loop written in one form of repetition statement can be written by using the other two forms of repetition statement. Although they are equivalent, in many cases one form would express the repetition control in a more natural and direct manner. It is your responsibility as a programmer to implement the repetition control using the most appropriate form.

1. Write a for loop to compute the following.

   a. Sum of 1, 2, . . . , 100
   b. Sum of 2, 4, . . . , 500
   c. Product of 5, 10, . . . , 50

2. Rewrite the following while loops as for statements.

   a.
   ```
   int count = 0, sum = 0;
   while ( count < 10 ) {
      sum += count;
      count++;
   }
   ```

   b.
   ```
   int count = 1, sum = 0;
   while ( count <= 30 ) {
      sum   += count;
      count += 3;
   }
   ```

6.6 Nested for Statements

In many processing tasks, we need to place a for statement inside another for statement. In this section, we introduce a simple nested for statement. We will see more examples of nested for statements later in the book, especially in Chapter 10 on array processing.

Suppose we want to display a quick reference table for clerks at the Rugs-R-Us carpet store. The table in Figure 6.9 lists the prices of carpets ranging in size from 11 × 5 ft to 20 × 25 ft (using System.out for output). The width of a carpet ranges from 11 to 20 ft with an increment of 1 ft. The length of a carpet ranges from 5 to 25 ft with an increment of 5 ft. The unit price of a carpet is $19 per square foot.

We use a nested for statement to print out the table. Let's concentrate first on printing out prices. We'll worry about printing out length and width values later. The following nested for statement will print out the prices:

```
int           price;

for (int width = 11; width <= 20; width++) {

    for (int length = 5; length <= 25; length += 5) {
        price = width * length * 19; //$19 per sq ft.
        System.out.print("  " + price);
    }

    //finished one row; now move on to the next row
    System.out.println("");
}
```

outer for

inner for

Length

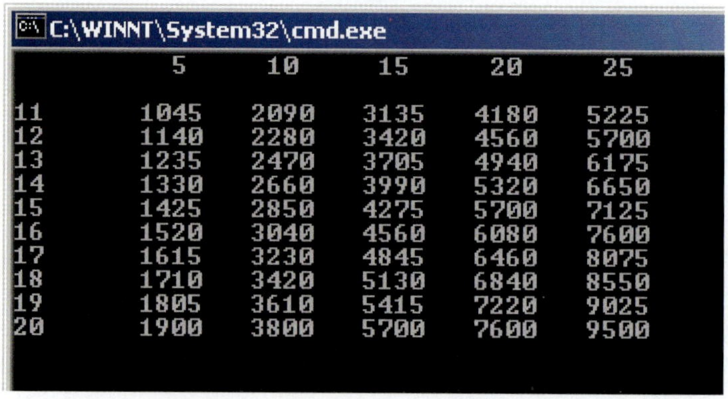

C:\WINNT\System32\cmd.exe

Width

```
             5      10      15      20      25

11        1045    2090    3135    4180    5225
12        1140    2280    3420    4560    5700
13        1235    2470    3705    4940    6175
14        1330    2660    3990    5320    6650
15        1425    2850    4275    5700    7125
16        1520    3040    4560    6080    7600
17        1615    3230    4845    6460    8075
18        1710    3420    5130    6840    8550
19        1805    3610    5415    7220    9025
20        1900    3800    5700    7600    9500
```

Figure 6.9 The price table for carpets ranging in size from 11 × 5 ft to 20 × 25 ft whose unit price is $19 per square foot.

The outer for statement is set to range from the first row (width = 11) to the last row (width = 20). For each repetition of the outer for, the inner for statement is executed, which ranges from the first column (length = 5) to the fifth column (length = 25). The loop body of the inner for computes the price of a single carpet size and prints out this price. So the complete execution of the inner for, which causes its loop body to be executed 5 times, completes the output of one row. The following shows the sequence of values for the two control variables.

width	length	
11		
	5	
	10	
	15	
	20	
	25	Completes the printing of the first row
12		
	5	
	10	
	15	
	20	
	25	Completes the printing of the second row
13		
	5	
	10	
⋮		

Now let's add the code to print out the row and column index values for width and length.

```
int             price;

System.out.print("    5   10   15   20   25");
System.out.print("\n\n");

for (int width = 11; width <= 20; width++) {

   System.out.print(width + "    ");

   for (int length = 5; length <= 25; length += 5) {
     price = width * length * 19; //$19 per sq ft.
     System.out.print("     " + price);

   }

   //finished one row; now move on to the next row
   System.out.print("\n");
}
```

Added statements

The next improvement is to include the labels Width and Length in the output. This enhancement is left as Exercise 19 at the end of the chapter. Also, in the example, literal constants are used for the carpet sizes and the increment value on length (11, 20, 5, 25, and 5), but in a real program, named constants should be used.

1. What will be the value of sum after the following nested for loops are executed?

a.
```
int sum = 0;
for (int i = 0; i < 5; i++) {
   sum = sum + i;
   for (int j = 0; j < 5; j++) {
      sum = sum + j;
   }
}
```

b.
```
int sum = 0;
for (int i = 0; i < 5; i++) {
   sum = sum + i;
   for (int j = i; j < 5; j++) {
     sum = sum + j;
   }
}
```

2. What is wrong with the following nested for loop?

```
int sum = 0;
for (int i = 0; i < 5; i++) {
   sum = sum + i;
   for (int i = 5; i > 0; i--) {
      sum = sum + j;
   }
}
```

6.7 Formatting Output

In the table shown in Figure 6.10, the values are aligned very nicely. We purposely selected the unit price and the ranges of width and length so that the table output would look good. Notice that the output values are all four-digit numbers. Realistically, we cannot expect output values to be so uniform. Let's change the unit price to $15 and the range of widths to 5 through 14 ft and see what happens. The result is shown in Figure 6.10, which is not as neat as the previous output. What we need is a way to format the output so the values are printed out with the proper alignment.

In the code, we used the fixed number of spaces between the values, and it worked because the output values have the same number of digits. To align the values with a varying number of digits, we must vary the number of spaces in front of the values, as shown in Figure 6.11.

The basic idea of formatted output is to allocate the same amount of space for the output values and align the values within the allocated space. We call the space

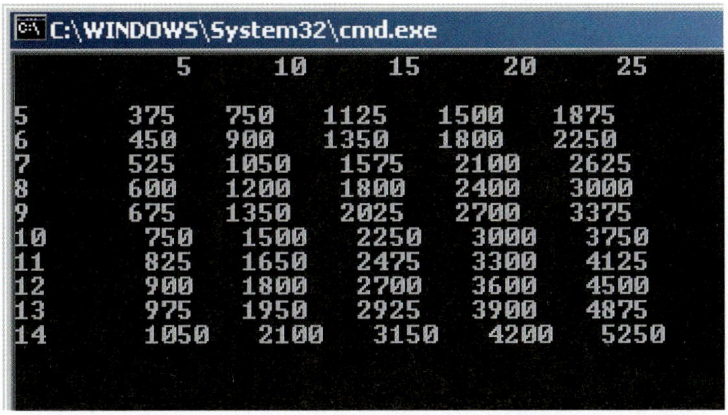

```
C:\WINDOWS\System32\cmd.exe
          5      10      15      20      25

5       375     750    1125    1500    1875
6       450     900    1350    1800    2250
7       525    1050    1575    2100    2625
8       600    1200    1800    2400    3000
9       675    1350    2025    2700    3375
10      750    1500    2250    3000    3750
11      825    1650    2475    3300    4125
12      900    1800    2700    3600    4500
13      975    1950    2925    3900    4875
14     1050    2100    3150    4200    5250
```

Figure 6.10 The price table for carpets with $15 per square foot and width ranging from 5 through 14 ft.

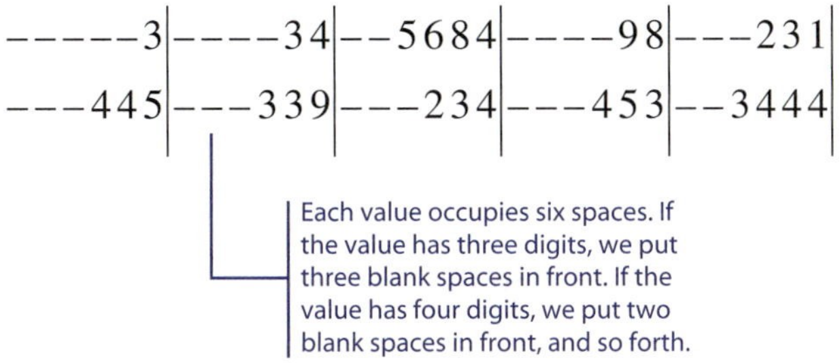

```
-----3|----34|--5684|----98|---231|
---445|---339|---234|---453|--3444|
```

Each value occupies six spaces. If the value has three digits, we put three blank spaces in front. If the value has four digits, we put two blank spaces in front, and so forth.

Figure 6.11 How to place a varying number of spaces to align the output values. Hyphen is used here to indicate the blank space.

field

occupied by an output value the ***field*** and the number of characters allocated to a field its *field width.* In Figure 6.11, the field width is 6.

We have already used two formatting classes—DecimalFormat and Simple-DateFormat—introduced in Chapters 2 and 3. The most recent version of Java SDK 1.5 has a new general-purpose formatting class called Formatter that includes the functionalities of DecimalFormat and SimpleDateFormat. For its power, using the Formatter class is slightly more complicated than using the DecimalFormat and SimpleDateFormat classes.

To format output using Formatter, first we create its instance by passing the destination of the output as an argument. Suppose we want to send the formatted output to System.out; then we create a Formatter object as follows:

```
Formatter formatter = new Formatter(System.out);
```

Next we call its format method to output the formatted values. For example, to output an integer with the field width of 6, we write

```
int num = 467;
formatter.format("%6d", num);
```

control string

The string %6d is called a ***control string***, and it directs how the formatting will take place. The value 6 specifies the field width, and the control character d indicates the output value is a decimal integer.

The general syntax for the format method is as follows:

```
format(<control string>, <expr1>, <expr2>, ...)
```

The first argument is the control string, and it is followed by zero or more expressions. The control string may include the actual output string in addition to control values. For example, the statement

```
int num1, num2, num3;

num1 = 34;
num2 = 9;
num3 = num1 + num2;

formatter.format("%3d + %3d = %5d", num1, num2, num3);
```

will output

```
34 +   9 =    43
```

Figure 6.12 shows how the control values are matched left to right against the arguments. The figure also illustrates how the noncontrol values (such as + and = symbols) are output to the destination.

We can change the default left-to-right argument matching by including the argument index in the control string. The arguments can be indexed as 1$, 2$, and so forth. For example, the output of

```
formatter.format("%3$3d is the sum of %2$3d and %1$3d",
                 num1, num2, num3);
```

will be

```
43 is the sum of   9 and  34
```

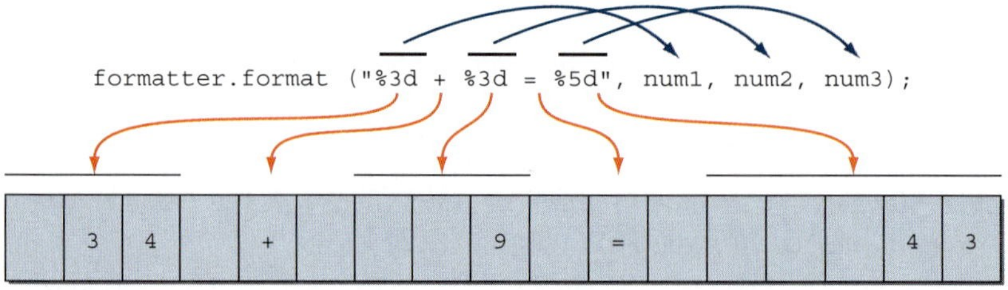

```
formatter.format ("%3d + %3d = %5d", num1, num2, num3);
```

	3	4		+			9		=					4	3

Figure 6.12 The control values are matched left to right.

To format real numbers, we include the number of decimal places along with the field width in the following format:

```
%<field width> . <decimal places> f
```

The control letter f designates formatting a floating-point number. Here's an example to format 345.9867 using a field of width 15 and two decimal places:

```
formatter.format("%15.3f", 345.9867);
```

To format a string, we use the control letter s. Here's an example:

```
String name = "John";

formatter.format("Hello, %s. Nice to meet you.", name);
```

The output will be

```
Hello, John. Nice to meet you.
```

We can also use the format method to format the date information. We use the control letter t for formatting an instance of GregorianCalendar or Date. The control letter t must be followed by another control letter that designates the formatting of the components of the date information, such as month, day, or year. For example, if we write

```
GregorianCalendar day = new GregorianCalendar(1776, 6, 4);

formatter.format("%1$tB %1$te, %1$tY", day);
```

the output will be

```
July 4, 1776
```

The date control letter B designates the full month name, e designates the day in two digits, and Y designates the year in four digits. For other data control letters, please consult the documentation. Notice that there is only one output argument, and it is referred to as 1$ three times in the control string.

The use of the Formatter class gives us the most control over the formatting, but for common output formatting, we can do it by using the format method of System.out or the String class instead. (In this section, we presented only a subset of common formatting.) For example, the following code

```
System.out.format("%5s is %3d years old", "Bill", 20);
```

is equivalent to

```
Formatter formatter = new Formatter(System.out);
formatter.format("%5s is %3d years old", "Bill", 20);
```

```
C:\WINDOWS\System32\cmd.exe
          5      10      15      20      25

  5     375     750    1125    1500    1875
  6     450     900    1350    1800    2250
  7     525    1050    1575    2100    2625
  8     600    1200    1800    2400    3000
  9     675    1350    2025    2700    3375
 10     750    1500    2250    3000    3750
 11     825    1650    2475    3300    4125
 12     900    1800    2700    3600    4500
 13     975    1950    2925    3900    4875
 14    1050    2100    3150    4200    5250
```

Figure 6.13 Carpet price table of Figure 6.11 with proper alignment.

(*Note:* For those who are familiar with C or C++, there's a method named printf defined for System.out that works exactly the same as the format method. However, Java's printf is similar but not identical to the one in C or C++.)

Instead of printing out, it is possible to create a formatted string and assign it to a variable with the format method of the String class. Here's an example:

```
String outputStr
   = String.format("%3d + %3d = %5d", num1, num2, num3);
```

We close the section with a program that produces the carpet price table with proper alignment for the range of values used in producing the table in Figure 6.10. Running this program will produce the table shown in Figure 6.13.

```
/*
   Chapter 6 Sample Program: Sample formatting statements

   File: Ch6CarpetPriceTableWithFormat.java

*/

class Ch6CarpetPriceTableWithFormat {

    public static void main (String[] args) {

        int     price;

        //print out the column labels
        System.out.print("   "); //put three blank spaces first

        for (int colLabel = 5; colLabel <=25; colLabel += 5) {
            System.out.format("%8d", colLabel);
        }
```

```
        System.out.println("");
        System.out.println("");

        //print out rows of prices
        for (int width = 5; width <= 14; width++) {

            System.out.format("%3d", width);

            for (int length = 5; length <= 25; length += 5) {
                price = width * length * 15;

                System.out.format("%8d", price);
            }

            //finished one row; now move on to the next row
            System.out.println("");
        }

        System.out.println("");
        System.out.println("");
    }
}
```

1. Determine the output of the following code.

```
System.out.format("%3d + %3d = %3d, 1, 2, 3);
System.out.format("%tY", new Date());
System.out.format("%2$s,%1$s, "John", "Smith");
```

2. What's wrong with the following code?

```
Formatter f = new Formatter( );
f.format("%8.3f", 232.563);
```

6.8 Loan Tables

The LoanCalculator program computed the monthly and total payments for a given loan amount, annual interest rate, and loan period. To see the monthly payment for the same loan amount and loan period but with a different interest rate, we need to repeat the calculation, entering the three values again. To illustrate the use of the concepts introduced in this chapter, let's design a program that generates a loan table (similar to the carpet price table) for a given loan amount so we can compare different monthly payments easily and quickly. The columns of the table are the loan periods in number of years (5, 10, 15, 20, 25, 30), and the rows are interest rates ranging from 6 to 10 percent in increments of 0.25.

In this section, we provide a discussion of the relevant methods only. Let's begin with a design of the topmost start method of the top-level controller class. The start method can be expressed as

```
tell the user what the program does;

prompt the user "Do you want to generate a loan table?";
while (the user says YES) {

   input the loan amount;
   generate the loan table;

   prompt the user "Do you want another loan table?";
}
```

pseudocode

The start method is expressed in pseudocode. ***Pseudocode*** is an informal language we often use to express an algorithm. Pseudocode is useful in expressing an algorithm without being tied down to the rigid syntactic rules of a programming language. We can express a simple algorithm in the actual programming language statements, but for a more complex algorithm, especially those involving nonsequential control flow logic, pseudocode is very helpful in expressing the algorithm concisely and clearly. Whenever appropriate, we will use pseudocode to express more complex algorithms in the remainder of the book.

Translating the pseudocode into Java code will result in

```
private static enum Response {YES, NO}

public void start( ) {

    Response response;

    describeProgram();

    response = prompt("Generate a loan table?");

       while (response == Response.YES) {

       loanAmount = getLoanAmount();  //get input
       generateLoanTable(loanAmount); //generate table

       response = prompt("Generate another loan table?");
    }
}

private Response prompt(String question) {

   String input;

   Response response = Response.NO;

   System.out.print(question + " (Yes - y; No - n): ");

   input = scanner.next(); 
```

scanner is created in a constructor

```
        if (input.equals("Y") || input.equals("y")) {
            response = Response.YES;
        }

        return response;
    }
```

Notice how the actual start method is almost as easy to read as the pseudocode. By using objects and well-designed (sub)methods, we can express methods that are as easy to read as pseudocode.

The describeProgram method tells the user what the program does if the user requests it. The getLoanAmount method gets the loan amount from the user. The method will allow the user to enter the loan amount between 100.0 and 500000.0. The generateLoanTable method generates the loan table, which we explain in detail next.

We use a nested loop to generate the table. Both the inner and outer loops are count-controlled loops. The loop for columns (years) will range from 5 to 30 with an increment of 5 and the loop for rows (rates) will range from 6.0 to 10.0 with an increment of 0.25. So the nested loop can be written as follows:

```
private static final int BEGIN_YEAR =  5;
private static final int END_YEAR   = 30;
private static final int YEAR_INCR  =  5;

private static final double BEGIN_RATE =  6.0;
private static final double END_RATE   = 10.0;
private static final double RATE_INCR  =  0.25;

...

for (double rate = BEGIN_RATE; rate <= END_RATE;
                                   rate += RATE_INCR){

    for (int year = BEGIN_YEAR; year <= END_YEAR;
                                   year += YEAR_INCR){
    ...

      //compute and display the monthly loan payment
      //for a given year and rate
    }
}
```

Notice the outer loop is using double as the loop counter, something we discouraged in Section 6.2. In this particular case, with the increment value of 0.25, there will be no problem because this value can be represented precisely in computer memory. Moreover, the terminating condition rate <= END_RATE guarantees that the loop will terminate eventually if we keep adding RATE_INCR to rate.

To compute the monthly loan payment, we simply reuse the Loan class we defined in Chapter 4 as follows:

```
double amount = ... ;
double rate   = ... ;
int    period = ... ;
```

```
Loan    loan    = new Loan( );

double monthlyPayment
            = loan.getMonthlyPayment(amount, rate, period);
```

This is the power of object-oriented programming. Because a single well-defined task of loan computation and nothing else is coded in the Loan class, we are able to reuse it here easily. What would happen had we not designed the Loan class? It was certainly possible for us to complete the Chapter 4 sample development program with one service class that handles everything: input, output, and computation tasks. The chance of reusing such a class, however, is very low. Just as we do not expect to buy a textbook that teaches all five subject matters of single-variable calculus, introduction to economics, organic chemistry, introduction to programming, and western civilization, we do not want a service class that is overloaded with many different types of tasks. We do not want one class that does everything. Rather, we want many classes, with each class doing one task effectively and efficiently. This will allow us to mix and match the classes easily.

Finally, the output values can be formatted by using the technique introduced in Section 6.7. Overall design is now complete. It is left as an exercise (Exercise 17) to implement the loan table calculation program.

6.9 Estimating the Execution Time

We promised at the end of Section 6.1 to compare the two versions of gcd methods experimentally. Detailed analysis of algorithms is beyond the scope of this book (we provide a little bit of analytical comparisons of sorting algorithms in this book), but experimental analysis is within our realm. We can compare the performance of different methods by actually running them and clocking their execution times.

Here's the basic idea:

```
Start the clock (stopwatch)

Run the method

Stop the clock

Report the elapsed time
```

There is no clock or stopwatch standard class, but we can time the execution by using the Date class from the java.util package. Before we call the method we want to time, we record the start time by creating a Date object. After the method is completed, we record the end time by creating a second Date object. Calling the getTime method of the Date class returns the number of milliseconds (1 ms = 1/1000 s) since January 1, 1970 00:00:00 Greenwich Mean Time. So by subtracting the start time from the end time, we can get the elapsed time in milliseconds. Here's the general idea:

```
Date startTime = new Date();

//the method call comes here
```

```
Date endTime = new Date();

long elapsedTimeInMilliseconds =
        endTime.getTime() - startTime.getTime();
```

Now let's write a short program to time the performance of gcd and gcd_bruteforce. The program includes many of the techniques discussed in this chapter. Here's the program (we do not repeat the method bodies of gcd and gcd_bruteforce here):

```
/*
   Chapter 6 Sample Program: Time the performance of gcd methods

   File: Ch6TimeGcd.java

*/

import java.util.*;

class Ch6TimeGcd {

   private static enum ComputationType {BRUTE_FORCE, EUCLID}

   private Scanner scanner;

   public static void main(String[] args) {

       Ch6TimeGcd tester = new Ch6TimeGcd( );

       tester.start();

       System.exit(0);
   }

   public Ch6TimeGcd() {
       scanner = new Scanner(System.in);
   }

   public void start( ) {

       long bruteForceTime, euclidTime;
       int m, n;

       while (isContinue()) {

           m = getPositiveInteger( );
           n = getPositiveInteger( );

           //Time the brute force method
           bruteForceTime = timeMethod(m, n, ComputationType.BRUTE_FORCE);

           //Time the Euclidean method
           euclidTime = timeMethod(m, n, ComputationType.EUCLID);
```

```
            System.out.println("M:  " + m);
            System.out.println("N:  " + n);
            System.out.println("Brute Force Time: " + bruteForceTime);
            System.out.println("Euclidean Time:   " + euclidTime + "\n");
        }
    }

    private long timeMethod(int m, int n, ComputationType type) {

        Date startTime, endTime;

        startTime = new Date();

        if (type == ComputationType.BRUTE_FORCE) {

            gcd_bruteforce(m, n);

        } else {

            gcd(m, n);
        }

        endTime = new Date();

        return (endTime.getTime() - startTime.getTime());
    }

    private int getPositiveInteger( ) {

        int input;

        while (true) {

            System.out.print("Enter positive integer (0 is okay):");
            input = scanner.nextInt();

            if (input >= 0) break;

            System.out.println("Input must be 0 or more");
        }

        return input;
    }

    private boolean isContinue( ) {

        String input;

        boolean response = false;

        System.out.print("Run test? ");

        input = scanner.next();

        if (input.equals("Y") || input.equals("y")) {
          response = true;
        }
```

```
        return response;
    }

    private int gcd_bruteforce(int m, int n) {

        . . .
    }

    private int gcd(int m, int n) {

        . . .
    }
}
```

Here's a sample interaction:

```
Run test? y
Enter positive integer (0 is okay):4567820
Enter positive integer (0 is okay):2147483640
M: 4567820
N: 2147483640
Brute Force Time: 94
Euclidean Time:   0

Run test? y
Enter positive integer (0 is okay):1457689098
Enter positive integer (0 is okay):2147483640
M: 1457689098
N: 2147483640
Brute Force Time: 31953
Euclidean Time:   0

Run test? n
```

The value of 0 for Euclidean time does not imply that it took no time to compute the result. It means that the time it took was so miniscule, we weren't able to detect it by the technique we used. Notice that, for the brute-force approach, the difference in the running times between the small and large values for M is substantial, while the difference for the Euclidean approach is not discernible. Detailed analysis will actually tell us that the running time for the brute-force approach is linearly proportional to the input size M, while the Euclidean approach is logarithmically proportional to the input size M. So, for the second comparison in the sample run, there will be 1,457,689,098 divisions performed (actually twice this number because we are executing `m % i == 0 && n % i == 0`) in `gcd_bruteforce`, but only log 1,457,689,098 $\cong$ 9 divisions. See how superior the Euclidean approach is?

Keep in mind that the value we get for the elapsed time is a rough estimate. For one thing, the values we get for the elapsed time differ dramatically according to which CPU we run the program on and whether other processes are running at the same time (e.g., if a garbage collection routine kicks in while a method is running, then the runtime estimate can be way off). Also, the granularity is very coarse when timed from a high-level language such as Java. For example, it is not possible to distinguish between the program that runs in 5 ms and the program that runs in 6 ms. Although the value is a rough estimate, it still give us useful information such as the rate of increase in execution time as we increase the size of input values.

Things to Remember

To estimate the running time of a loop statement:

1. *Record the start time by creating a* **Date** *object, say,* **startTime,** *before the loop statement.*
2. *Record the end time by creating another* **Date** *object, say,* **endTime,** *after the loop statement.*
3. *Elapsed time (in milliseconds) is computed as follows:*

```
elapsedTime = endTime.getTime()
                        - startTime.getTime();
```

6.10 Recursive Methods (*Optional*)

recursive method

In addition to the three repetition control statements we introduced in this chapter, there is a fourth way to control the repetition flow of a program by using recursive methods. A ***recursive method*** is a method that contains a statement (or statements) that makes a call to itself. We explain recursive methods briefly in this section. Realistic examples of recursive methods will be given in Chapter 15.

So far, we have seen only methods that call other methods, something like this:

```
methodOne(...) {
   ...
   methodTwo(...); //methodOne called methodTwo
   ...
}

methodTwo(...) {
   ...
}
```

A recursive method calls itself, and it looks something like this:

```
methodOne(...) {
   ...
```

```
        methodOne (...); //calls the method itself
        ...
    }
```

At first glance, it seems as if a recursive call will never end since the call is made to the same method. Indeed, if you do not follow the rules, you could end up with infinite recursive calls. In this section we explain how to write recursive methods correctly.

Suppose we want to compute the factorial of N. The *factorial* of N is the product of the first N positive integers, denoted mathematically as

```
N! = N * (N-1) * (N-2) * ··· * 2 * 1
```

We will write a recursive method to compute the factorial of N. Mathematically, we can define the factorial of N recursively as

```
              ⎧ 1                          if N = 1
factorial(N) =⎨
              ⎩ N * factorial (N-1)        otherwise
```

The definition states that if N is 1, then the function factorial(N) has the value 1. Otherwise, the function factorial(N) is the product of N and factorial(N – 1). For example, the function factorial(4) is evaluated as follows:

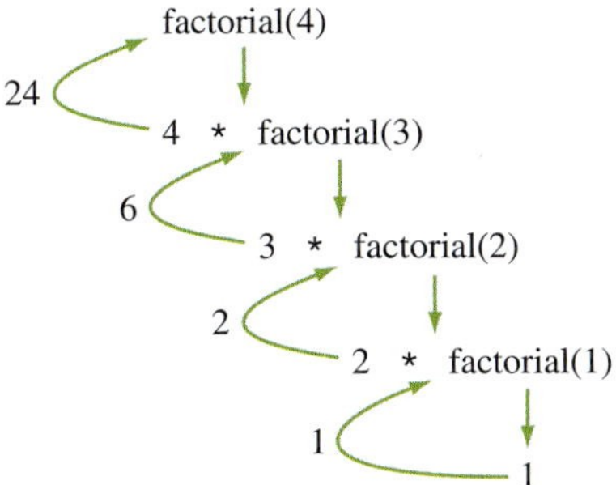

The recursive factorial method parallels the preceding mathematical definition. The method is defined thus:

```
//Assume N is greater than 0
public int factorial(int N) {

    if (N == 1)

        return 1;

    else

        return N * factorial(N-1);
}
```

Test to stop or continue.

End case: recursion stops.

Recursive case: recursion continues with another recursive call.

The diagram in Figure 6.14 illustrates the sequence of calls for the recursive factorial method. Recursive methods will contain three necessary components.

Things to Remember

The three necessary components in a recursive method are

1. *A test to stop or continue the recursion.*
2. *An end case that terminates the recursion.*
3. *A recursive call(s) that continues the recursion.*

To ensure that the recursion will stop eventually, we must pass arguments different from the incoming parameters. In the factorial method, the incoming parameter was N, while the argument passed in the recursive call was N−1. This difference of 1 between the incoming parameter and the argument will eventually make the argument in a recursive call be 1, and the recursion will stop.

Let's implement two more mathematical functions using recursion. The next method computes the sum of the first N positive integers 1, 2, . . ., N. Notice how this method includes the three necessary components of a recursive method.

```
public int sum ( int N ) { //assume N >= 1
   if (N == 1)
      return 1;
   else
      return N + sum( N-1 );
}
```

The last method computes the exponentiation A^N, where A is a real number and N is a positive integer. This time, we have to pass two arguments—A and N. The value of A will not change in the calls, but the value of N is decremented after each recursive call.

```
public double exponent ( double A, int N ) {
   if (N == 1)
      return A;
   else
      return A * exponent( A, N-1 );
}
```

So far we used only mathematical functions to illustrate recursive methods, but recursion is not limited to mathematical functions. Let's look at one example. We know the length method of the String class returns the number characters in a given string. Let's write a recursive method that does the same thing. Here's how we think recursively. The total number of characters in a string is 1 plus the number of characters in the substring from the second position to the end of the string. If the

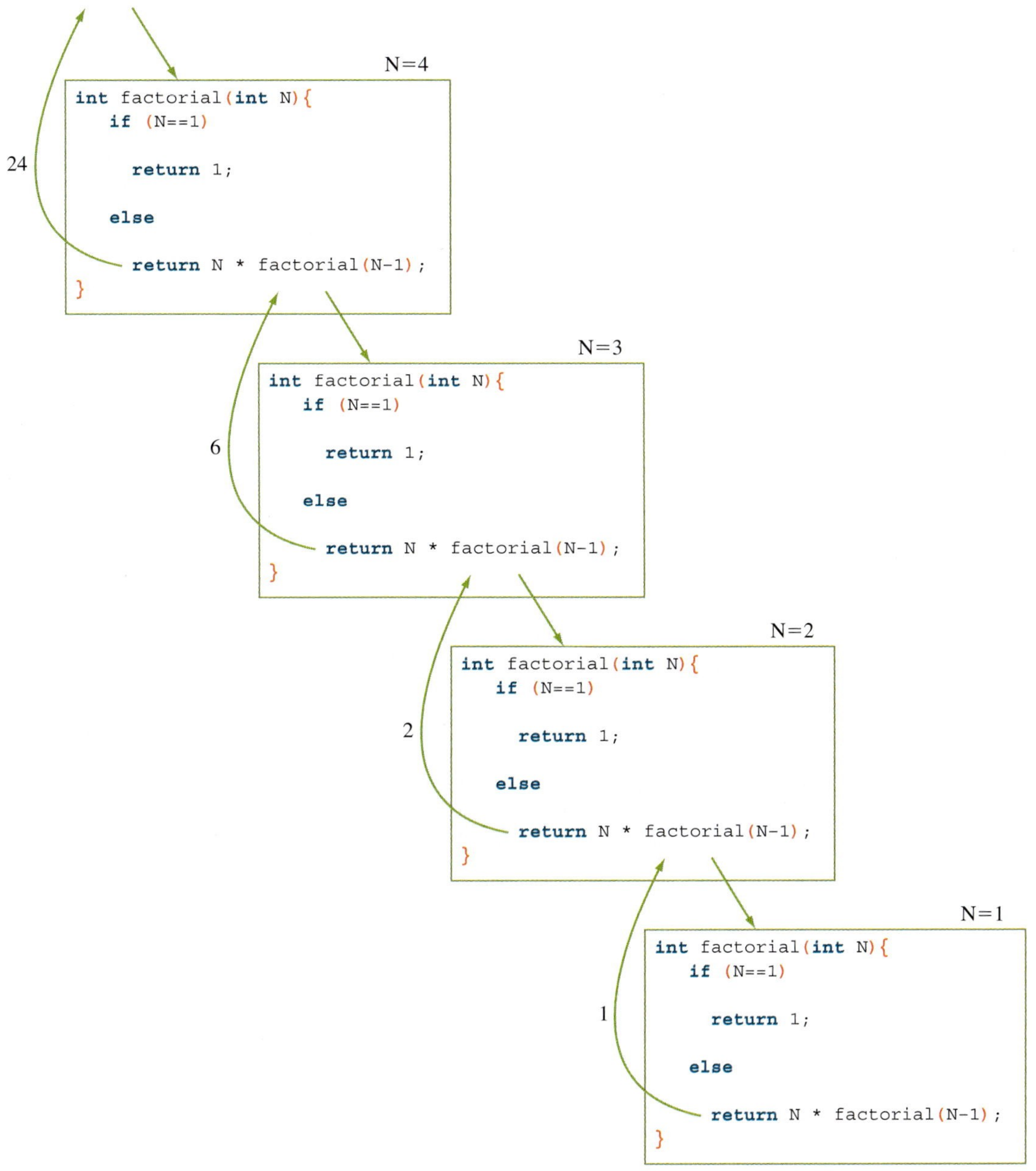

Figure 6.14 The sequence of calls for the recursive **factorial** method.

string has no characters, then the length is zero. Puting this idea into an actual method, we have

```
public int length(String str) {

   if (str.equals("")) { //str has no characters
      return 0;

   } else {

      return 1 + length(str.substring(1));
   }
}
```

Index of the second position is 1.

We will present more examples of recursive methods that implement nonnumerical operations in Chapter 15.

We used factorial, sum, exponentiation, and length as examples to introduce some of the basic concepts of recursion, but we should never actually write these methods using recursion. The methods can be written more efficiently in an iterative (i.e., nonrecursive) manner using a simple for loop. In practice, we use recursion if certain conditions are met.

Things to Remember

Use recursion if

1. *A recursive solution is natural and easy to understand.*
2. *A recursive solution does not result in excessive duplicate computation.*
3. *The equivalent iterative solution is too complex.*

As a final review of the topic, we conclude this section with the recursive version of the Euclidean gcd method. Remember the logic behind the Euclidean gcd method is a sequence of reducing the problem, for example, gcd(48, 16) = gcd(16, 12) = gcd(12, 4) = 4. Here's how we can express this thinking recursively:

```
public int gcd_recursive(int m, int n) {

   int result;

   if (m == 0) { //test

      result = n; //end case

   } else {

      result = gcd_recursive(n % m, m); //recursive case

   }

   return result;
}
```

6.11 Sample Development

Hi-Lo Game

In this section we will develop a program that plays a Hi-Lo game. This program illustrates the use of repetition control, the random number generator, and the testing strategy. The objective of the game is to guess a secret number between 1 and 100. The program will respond with **HI** if the guess is higher than the secret number and **LO** if the guess is lower than the secret number. The maximum number of guesses allowed is six. If we allow up to seven, one can always guess the secret number. Do you know why?

Problem Statement

Write an application that will play Hi-Lo games with the user. The objective of the game is for the user to guess the computer-generated secret number in the least number of tries. The secret number is an integer between 1 and 100, inclusive. When the user makes a guess, the program replies with **HI** *or* **LO** *depending on whether the guess is higher or lower than the secret number. The maximum number of tries allowed for each game is six. The user can play as many games as she wants.*

Overall Plan

We will begin with our overall plan for the development. Let's identify the major tasks of the program. The first task is to generate a secret number every time the game is played, and the second task is to play the game itself. We also need to add a loop to repeat these two tasks every time the user wants to play the Hi-Lo game. We can express this program logic in pseudocode as follows:

program tasks

```
do {

   Task 1: generate a secret number;

   Task 2: play one game;

} while ( the user wants to play );
```

Let's look at the two tasks and determine objects that will be responsible for handling the tasks. For the first task, we will use the **random** method of the **Math** class. We will examine this method in detail later to determine whether it is the one we can use in the program. If this method does not meet our needs, then we will explore further and most likely will have to derive our own random number generator.

For the second task of playing the game itself, we use objects that handle I/O and the logic of repeatedly asking for the next guess until the game is over. For input and output, we use a **Scanner** and **System.out.** We will define a class to handle the logic of playing the game. This class will control the other two classes. We will name this class **Ch6HiLo,** and it will be an instantiable main class.

6.11 Sample Development—*continued*

Here's our working design document:

program classes

Design Document: `Ch6HiLo`	
Class	**Purpose**
`Ch6HiLo`	The top-level control object handles the logic of playing games and manages other objects. This is the instantiable main class.
`Scanner`	This standard class is for inputting user guesses.
`PrintStream` `(System.out)`	This standard class is for displaying hints and other messages.

Figure 6.15 is the program diagram for this program. A keen observer may have noticed that the **Ch6HiLo** class is handling both types of tasks: handling of user interface and controlling the logic of game playing. We will revisit this design in the GUI chapter and provide an alternative. The one-class design we adopt here may not be an ideal design, but may be acceptable for a simplistic game such as this one. The design also provides us with a meaningful comparison when we present an alternative design in the GUI chapter.

We will implement this program using the following four major steps:

development steps

1. Start with a skeleton **Ch6HiLo** class.
2. Add code to the **Ch6HiLo** class to play a game using a dummy secret number.
3. Add code to the **Ch6HiLo** class to generate a random number.
4. Finalize the code by removing temporary statements and tying up loose ends.

Step 1 Development: Program Skeleton

step 1 design

The structure of the **HiLoMain** class is the same as other main classes. All we need to do is to declare, create, and start a **HiLo** object. Instead of forcing the user to play at least one

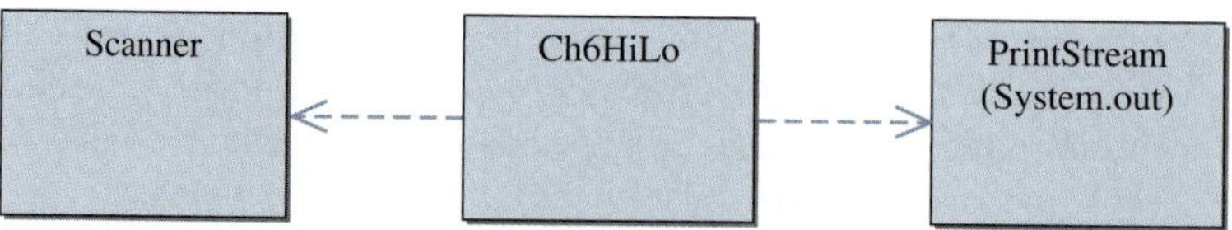

Figure 6.15 The program diagram for the **HiLo** program.

game,we will implement the program so the user has an option of not playing a game at all. In pseudocode we can express this logic as follows:

```
describe the game rules;

prompt the user to play a game or not;

while ( answer is yes ) {

   generate the secret number;

   play one game;

   prompt the user to play another game or not;
}
```

Notice that we use a **while** loop here, so the user can quit the program without playing a game. If we use a **do–while** loop instead, then the user must play at least one game before stopping the program. We opt to use the **while** loop because the user may not want to play the game at all after reading the game rules.

We use a private method **describeRules** to display the game rules. Another private method named **prompt** gets a yes/no reply from the user. We call this method to ask if the user wants to play a game. To generate a secret number, we have the third private method **generateSecretNumber.** Lastly, we define the fourth private method **playGame** to play one game. We declare these four methods **private** because these methods are for internal use. As always, we will use the constructor to perform necessary object creation and initialization.

Our working design document for the **HiLo** class is as follows:

Design Document: The `Ch6HiLo` Class

Method	**Visibility**	**Purpose**
`<constructor>`	`public`	Creates and initializes the objects used by a `HiLo` object.
`start`	`public`	Starts the Hi-Lo game playing. The user has an option of playing a game or not.
`describeRules`	`private`	Displays the game rules in `System.out`.
`generateSecretNumber`	`private`	Generates a secret number for the next Hi-Lo game.
`playGame`	`private`	Plays one Hi-Lo game.
`prompt`	`private`	Prompts the user for a yes/no reply.

6.11 Sample Development—*continued*

step 1 code

For the skeleton program, we include temporary output statements in the private methods to verify that they are called correctly in the right order. Here's the skeleton **Ch6HiLo** class:

```
import java.util.*;

/*

   Chapter 6 Sample Development: Hi-Lo Game (Step 1)

   The instantiable main class of the program.

*/

class Ch6HiLo {

    private static enum Response {YES, NO}

    private Scanner scanner;

    //Main Method
    public static void main (String[] args) {
        Ch6HiLo hiLo = new Ch6HiLo( );
        hiLo.start();
    }

    public Ch6HiLo( ) {

        scanner = new Scanner(System.in);
    }

    public void start( ) {
        Response answer;

        describeRules();

        answer = prompt("Do you want to play a Hi-Lo game?");

        while (answer == Response.YES) {

            generateSecretNumber( );

            playGame();

            answer = prompt("Do you want to play another Hi-Lo game?");
        }

        System.out.println("Thank you for playing Hi-Lo.");
    }
```

main

Constructor

start

describeRules

```
private void describeRules( ) {
    System.out.println("Inside describeRules"); //TEMP
}
```

generateSecretNumber

```
private void generateSecretNumber( ) {
    System.out.println("Inside generateSecretNumber");   //TEMP
}
```

playGame

```
private void playGame( ) {
    System.out.println("Inside playGame"); //TEMP
}
```

prompt

```
private Response prompt(String question) {

    String input;

    Response response = Response.NO;

    System.out.print(question + "  (Yes - y; No - n): ");

    input = scanner.next();

    if (input.equals("Y") || input.equals("y")) {
       response = Response.YES;
    }

    return response;
}
```

step 1 test

We execute the skeleton **Ch6HiLo** class to verify that the class is coded correctly. To verify the correct execution of step 1, we attempt to play the game

1. Zero times
2. One time
3. One or more times

For the first run, we select **No** to the prompt **Do you want to play a Hi-Lo game?** and make sure the program stops without playing a game. For the second run, we select **Yes** to the first prompt and verify that the messages **Inside generateSecretNumber** and **Inside playGame** are shown in the console window. We select **No** to the prompt **Do you want to play another Hi-Lo game?** and make sure the program stops. For the third run, we make sure we can play more than one game. After we verify all the scenarios work correctly, we proceed to the next step.

6.11 Sample Development—*continued*

Step 2 Development: Play a Game with a Dummy Secret Number

step 2 design

In the second development step, we add a routine that plays a Hi-Lo game. Let's begin with the control flow of the **playGame** method. There are two cases to end a Hi-Lo game: The user either guesses the number in less than six tries or uses up all six tries without guessing the number. So we need a counter to keep track of the number of guesses made. Let's call this counter **guessCount.** We stop the game when **guessCount** becomes larger than 6 or the user's guess is equal to the secret number. At the end of the game, we output an appropriate message. Expressing this in pseudocode, we have

```
//Method: playGame

set guessCount to 0;

do {
   get next guess;

   increment guessCount;

   if (guess < secretNumber) {
      print the hint LO;

   } else if (guess > secretNumber) {
      print the hint HI;
   }

} while (guessCount < number of guesses allowed &&
         guess != secretNumber );

if (guess == secretNumber) {

   print the winning message;

} else {
   print the losing message;
}
```

All variables used in this method will be local except **secretNumber**, which will be an instance variable. The value for **secretNumber** is set inside the **generateSecretNumber** method.

To support a better user interface, we will include an input error handling that allows the user to enter only values between **1** and **100**. We will do this input-error-checking routine in a new private method **getNextGuess** because we do want to keep the **playGame** method clean and simple. If we included the code for input error handling directly inside the **playGame** method, the method would become too cluttered and lose the overall clarity of what the method is doing. Pseudocode for the **getNextGuess** method is

```
//Method: getNextGuess

while ( true ) {
   get input value;

   if (valid input) return input value;

   print error message;
}
```

The working design document of the class now includes this new private method:

Design Document: The Ch6HiLo Class		
Method	**Visibility**	**Purpose**
...	...	...
getNextGuess	private	Returns the next guess from the user. Only accepts a guess between **1** and **100.** Prints an appropriate error message when an invalid guess is entered.

step 2 code

In the step 2 coding, we need to implement three methods. In addition to the **playGame** and **getNextGuess** methods, we need to define a temporary **generateSecretNumber** method so we can test the **playGame** method. The temporary **generateSecretNumber** method assigns a dummy secret number to the instance variable **secretNumber.** The temporary method is coded as follows:

```
private void generateSecretNumber( ) {
   secretNumber = 45;     //TEMP
}
```

Any number will do; we simply picked the number **45.** Knowing that the secret number is **45,** we will be able to test whether the **playGame** method is implemented correctly.

We implement the **playGame** method thus:

```
private void playGame( ) {
   int guessCount = 0;
   int guess;

   do {

      //get the next guess
      guess = getNextGuess();

      guessCount++;
```

getNextGuess is a new private method.

6.11 Sample Development—*continued*

```
            //check the guess
            if (guess < secretNumber) {
               System.out.println
                                          "Your guess is LO");

            } else if (guess > secretNumber) {
               System.out.println
                                          "Your guess is HI");
            }
         } while ( guessCount < MAX_GUESS_ALLOWED &&
                   guess != secretNumber );

         //output appropriate message
         if ( guess == secretNumber ) {
            System.out.println
                              "You guessed it in "
                              + guessCount + " tries.");
         } else {
            System.out.println
                              "You lost. Secret No. was "
                              + secretNumber);
         }
      }
```

Repeat the loop if the number of tries is not used up and the correct guess is not made.

This class constant is set to 6.

The **getNextGuess** method will accept an integer between **1** and **100.** The method uses a **while** loop to accomplish this:

```
   private int getNextGuess( ) {

      int  input;

      while (true) {

         System.out.print("Next Guess: ");
         input = scanner.nextInt();

         if (LOWER_BOUND <= input && input <= UPPER_BOUND) {
            return input;
         }

         //invalid input; print error message
         System.out.println("Invalid Input: " +
                              "Must be between " + LOWER_BOUND +
                              "and " + UPPER_BOUND);
      }
   }
```

The necessary constant and instance variable are declared in the data member section of the **HiLo** class as follows:

```
//----------------------------------
// Data Members
//----------------------------------
private final int  MAX_GUESS_ALLOWED  = 6;
private final int  LOWER_BOUND        = 1;
private final int  UPPER_BOUND        = 100;

private int secretNumber;
```

step 2 test

We need to test two methods in this step. To verify the **getNextGuess** method, we input both invalid and valid guesses. We verify the method by running the following tests:

1. Enter a number less than 1.
2. Enter a number greater than 100.
3. Enter a number between 2 and 99.
4. Enter 1.
5. Enter 100.

test cases

The first two ***test cases*** are called *error cases,* the third is called the *normal case,* and the last two are called *end cases*. One of the common errors beginners make is to create a loop statement that does not process the end cases correctly. When our code handles all three types of cases correctly, we will proceed to test the **playGame** method.

To verify the **playGame** method, we need to perform a more elaborate testing. Knowing that the dummy secret number is **45,** we verify the **playGame** method by running the following tests:

1. Enter a number less than **45** and check that the correct hint **LO** is displayed.
2. Enter a number greater than **45** and check that the correct hint **HI** is displayed.
3. Enter the correct guess, and check that the game terminates after displaying the appropriate message.
4. Enter six wrong guesses, and check that the game terminates after displaying the appropriate message.

When all four tests are successfully completed, we proceed to the next step.

Step 3 Development: Generate a Random Number

step 3 design

In step 3,we add a routine that generates a random number between **1** and **100.** As explained in Chapter 3, we can use the method **random** from the **Math** package. Since

6.11 Sample Development—*continued*

the range is between **1** and **100,** we can simplify the formula as

$$\text{secretNumber} = \lfloor X \times 100 \rfloor + 1$$

where **0.0** ≤ **X** < **1.0.**

step 3 code

The **generateSecretNumber** method is defined thus:

```
private void generateSecretNumber( ) {
   double X = Math.random();

   secretNumber = (int) Math.floor( X * 100 ) + 1;

   System.out.println("Secret Number: " + secretNumber);
                                                  // TEMP
}
```

The method includes a temporary statement to output the secret number so we can stop the game anytime we want by entering the correct guess.

step 3 test

To verify that the method generates correct random numbers, we will write a separate test program. If we don't use such a test program and instead include the method immediately in the **Ch6HiLo** class, we have to play the game, say, 100 times to verify that the first 100 generated numbers are valid. The test program generates **N** random numbers and stops whenever an invalid number is generated. We will set **N** to **1000.** Here's the test program:

TestRandom class for testing

```
class TestRandom {
   public static void main (String[] args) {

      int    N = 1000, count = 0, number;
      double X;

      do {

         count++;

         X      = Math.random();
         number = (int) Math.floor( X * 100 ) + 1;

      } while ( count < N &&
                1 <= number && number <= 100 );

      if ( number < 1 || number > 100 ) {
         System.out.println("Error: " + number);
      } else {
         System.out.println("Okay");
      }
   }
}
```

Keep in mind that successfully generating 1000 valid random numbers does not guarantee that the 1001st number is also valid. We did not offer any formal mathematical proof that the routine for the random number generator works correctly. What we are doing here is making an assumption that no user wants to play more than 1000 Hi-Lo games in one session, which we believe is a practical and reasonable assumption. After the **TestRandom** class is executed correctly, we make the necessary changes to the **Ch6HiLo** class and run it. When we verify that the program runs as expected, we proceed to the final step.

Step 4 Development: Finalize

program review

We finalize the program in the last step. We will perform a critical review of the program, looking for any unfinished method, inconsistency, or error in the methods; unclear or missing comments; and so forth. We should also not forget to keep an eye on any improvement we can make to the existing code.

We still have a temporary code inside the **describeRules** method, so we will complete the method by adding code to describe the game rules. This method is left as Exercise 18.

There are still temporary output statements that we used for verification purposes. We can either delete them from the program or comment them out. We will leave them in the program by commenting them out so when the time comes for us to modify, debug, or update the program, we do not have to reenter them.

Summary

- A repetition control statement is used to repeatedly execute a block of code until a certain condition is met.
- Three repetition control statements are while, do–while, and for.
- The count-controlled loop executes the loop body for a fixed number of times.
- The sentinel-controlled loop executes the loop body until any one of the designated values called a *sentinel* is encountered.
- Count-controlled loops can be implemented most naturally with the for statements.
- Sentinel-controlled loops can be implemented most naturally with the while or do–while statements.
- The while statement is called a *pretest loop,* and the do–while statement is called a *posttest loop*. The for statement is also a pretest loop.
- Reading a value before the loop statement is called a *priming read.*
- Off-by-1 error and infinite loop are two common mistakes in writing a loop control.

- The loop-and-a-half repetition control is the most general way of writing a loop. The break statement is used within the loop body to exit the loop when a certain condition is met.
- The nested for statement is used very often because it is ideally suited to process tabular data.
- Output values can be formatted by using the Formatter class.
- Execution time can be estimated by using the Dafe class.

Key Concepts

repetition statements
while statements
do–while statements
for statements
off-by-1 error
infinite loop
priming read
nested for statements
pseudocode
loop-and-a-half control
one-entry-one-exit control
count-controlled loops
sentinel-controlled loops
pretest and posttest loops
formatting output values
recursive methods (optional)

Exercises

1. Identify all the errors in the following repetition statements. Some errors are syntactical while others are logical (e.g., infinite loops).

a.
```
for (int i = 10; i > 0; i++) {
    x = y;
    a = b;
}
```

b.
```
int sum = 0;
Scanner scanner = new Scanner(System.in);
do {
    num = scanner.nextInt();
    sum += num;
} until (sum > 10000);
```

c.
```
while (x < 1 && x > 10) {
    a = b;
}
```

d.
```
while (a == b) ;
{
    a = b;
    x = y;
}
```

e.
```
for (int i = 1.0; i <= 2.0; i += 0.1) {
    x = y;
    a = b;
}
```

2. Write for, do–while, and while statements to compute the following sums and products.

   a. $1 + 2 + 3 + \cdots + 100$
   b. $5 + 10 + 15 + \cdots + 50$
   c. $1 + 3 + 7 + 15 + 31 + \cdots + (2^{20} - 1)$
   d. $1 + \frac{1}{2} + \frac{1}{3} + \frac{1}{4} + \cdots + \frac{1}{15}$
   e. $1 \times 2 \times 3 \times \cdots \times 20$
   f. $1 \times 2 \times 4 \times 8 \times \cdots \times 2^{20}$

3. What will be the value of sum after each of the following nested loops is executed?

a.
```
sum = 0;
for (int i = 0; i <= 10; i++)
     for (int j = 0; j <= 10; j++)
        sum += i ;
```

b.
```
sum = 0;
j = 0;
do {
   j++;
   for (int i = 5; i > j; i--)
      sum = sum + (i+j);
} while (j < 11);
```

c.
```
sum = 0;
i = 0;
while (i < 5) {
   j = 5;
   while (i != j) {
     sum += j;
     j--;
   }
   i++;
}
```

d.
```
sum = 0;
for (int i = 0; i <= 10; i++)
   for (int j = 10; j > 2*i; j--)
        sum = sum + (j - i);
```

4. Determine the output from the following code without actually executing it.

```
System.out.format("%4d", 234);
System.out.format("%5d", 234);

System.out.format("%s", "\n");

System.out.format("$%6.2f", 23.456);
System.out.format("%s", "\n");

System.out.format("%1$3d+%1$3d=%2$5d", 5, (5+5));
```

5. Rewrite the following nested for statements, using nested do–while and while statements.

a.
```
sum = 0;
number = 0;
for (int i = 0; i <= 10; i++)
    for (int j = 10; j >= i; j--) {
        number++;
        sum = sum + (j - i);
    }
```

b.
```
product = 1;
number = 0;
for (int i = 1; i < 5; i++)
    for (int j = 1; j < 5; j++) {
        number++;
        product *= number;
    }
```

6. You can compute sin x and cos x by using the following power series:

$$\sin x = x - \frac{x^3}{3!} + \frac{x^5}{5!} - \frac{x^7}{7!} + \cdots$$

$$\cos x = 1 - \frac{x^2}{2!} + \frac{x^4}{4!} - \frac{x^6}{6!} + \cdots$$

Write a program that evaluates sin x and cos x by using the power series. Use the double data type, and increase the number of terms in the series until the overflow occurs. You can check if the overflow occurs by comparing the value against Double. POSITIVE_INFINITY. Compare the results you obtain to the values returned by the sin and cos methods of the Math class.

7. Write an application to print out the numbers 10 through 49 in the following manner:

```
10 11 12 13 14 15 16 17 18 19
20 21 22 23 24 25 26 27 28 29
30 31 32 33 34 35 36 37 38 39
40 41 42 43 44 45 46 47 48 49
```

How would you do it? Here is an example of poorly written code:

```
for (int i = 10; i < 50; i++) {
   switch (i) {
      case 19:
      case 29:
      case 39: System.out.println(" " + i); //move to the
               break;                       //next line
      default: System.out.print(" " + i);
   }
}
```

This code is not good because it works only for printing 10 through 49. Try to develop the code so that it can be extended easily to handle any range of values. You can do this coding in two ways: with a nested for statement or with modulo arithmetic. (If you divide a number by 10 and the remainder is 9, then the number is 9, 19, 29, or 39, and so forth.)

8. A *prime number* is an integer greater than 1 and divisible by only itself and 1. The first seven prime numbers are 2, 3, 5, 7, 11, 13, and 17. Write a method that returns true if its parameter is a prime number.

9. There are 25 primes between 2 and 100, and there are 1229 primes between 2 and 10,000. Write a program that inputs a positive integer $N > 2$ and displays the number of primes between 2 and N (inclusive). Use the timing technique explained in Section 6.9 to show the amount of time it took to compute the result.

10. Instead of actually computing the number of primes between 2 and N, we can get an estimate by using the Prime Number Theorem, which states that

$$\text{prime}(N) \approx \left\lfloor \frac{N}{\ln(N)} \right\rfloor$$

where prime(N) is the number of primes between 2 and N (inclusive). The function ln is the natural logarithm. Extend the program for Exercise 9 by printing the estimate along with the actual number. You should notice the pattern that the estimate approaches the actual number as the value of N gets larger.

11. A *perfect number* is a positive integer that is equal to the sum of its proper divisors. A proper divisor is a positive integer other than the number itself that divides the number evenly (i.e., no remainder). For example, 6 is a perfect number because the sum of its proper divisors 1, 2, and 3 is equal to 6. Eight is not a perfect number because $1 + 2 + 4 \neq 8$. Write an application that accepts a positive integer and determines whether the number is perfect. Also, display all proper divisors of the number. Try a number between 20 and 30 and another number between 490 and 500.

12. Write an application that lists all perfect numbers between 6 and N, an upper limit entered by the user. After you verify the program with a small number

for *N*, gradually increase the value for *N* and see how long the program takes to generate the perfect numbers. Since there are only a few perfect numbers, you might want to display the numbers that are not perfect so you can easily tell that the program is still running.

13. Write a program that displays all integers between low and high that are the sum of the cube of their digits. In other words, find all numbers *xyz* such that $xyz = x^3 + y^3 + z^3$, for example, $153 = 1^3 + 5^3 + 3^3$. Try 100 for low and 1000 for high.

14. Write a method that returns the number of digits in an integer argument; for example, 23,498 has five digits.

15. Your freelance work with MyJava Lo-Fat Burgers was a success (see Exercise 22 of Chap. 5). The management loved your new drive-through ordering system because the customer had to order an item from each of the three menu categories. As part of a public relations campaign, however, management decided to allow a customer to skip a menu category. Modify the program to handle this option. Before you list items from each category, use a confirmation dialog to ask the customer whether he or she wants to order an item from that category.

16. Extend the program in Exercise 15 so that customers can order more than one item from each menu category. For example, the customer can buy two orders of Tofu Burgers and three orders of Buffalo Wings from the Entree menu category.

17. Complete the loan table program discussed in Section 6.8.

18. Implement the describeRules method of the Ch6HiLo class from Section 6.9. Use a confirmation dialog to ask the user whether or not to display the game rules.

19. The price table for carpet we printed out in Section 6.6 contains index values for width and length, but not labels to identify them. Write an application to generate the table shown next:

C:\WINDOWS\System32\cmd.exe

				LENGTH		
		5	10	15	20	25
	11	1045	2090	3135	4180	5225
	12	1140	2280	3420	4560	5700
	13	1235	2470	3705	4940	6175
	14	1330	2660	3990	5320	6650
WIDTH	15	1425	2850	4275	5700	7125
	16	1520	3040	4560	6080	7600
	17	1615	3230	4845	6460	8075
	18	1710	3420	5130	6840	8550
	19	1805	3610	5415	7220	9025
	20	1900	3800	5700	7600	9500

20. Extend the HiLo class to allow the user to designate the lower and upper bounds of the secret number. In the original HiLo class, the bounds are set to 1 and 100, respectively.

21. A formula to compute the *N*th Fibonacci number was given in Exercise 19 in Chapter 3. The formula is useful in finding a number in the sequence, but a more efficient way to output a series of numbers in the sequence is to use the recurrence relation $F_N = F_{N-1} + F_{N-2}$, with the first two numbers in the sequence F_1 and F_2 both defined as 1. Using this recurrence relation, we can compute the first 10 Fibonacci numbers as follows:

```
F1  = 1
F2  = 1
F3  = F2 + F1 =  1 +  1 =  2
F4  = F3 + F2 =  2 +  1 =  3
F5  = F4 + F3 =  3 +  2 =  5
F6  = F5 + F4 =  5 +  3 =  8
F7  = F6 + F5 =  8 +  5 = 13
F8  = F7 + F6 = 13 +  8 = 21
F9  = F8 + F7 = 21 + 13 = 34
F10 = F9 + F8 = 34 + 21 = 55
```

Write an application that accepts *N*, $N \geq 1$, from the user and displays the first *N* numbers in the Fibonacci sequence. Use appropriate formatting to display the output cleanly.

22. Modify the application of Exercise 21 to generate and display all the numbers in the sequence until a number becomes larger than the value maxNumber entered by the user.

23. Improve the LoanCalculator class from Chapter 4 to accept only the valid input values for loan amount, interest rate, and loan period. The original LoanCalculator class assumed the input values were valid. For the exercise, let the loan amount between $100.00 and $1,000,000.00, the interest rate between 5 and 20 percent, and the loan period between 1 year and 30 years be valid.

24. Extend Exercise 22 on page 292 by drawing a more realistic clock. Instead of drawing a clock like this

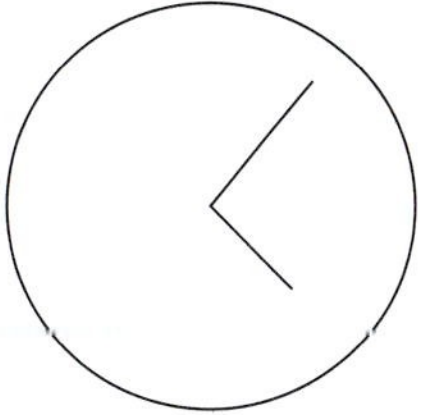

draw a circle at 5-min intervals as follows:

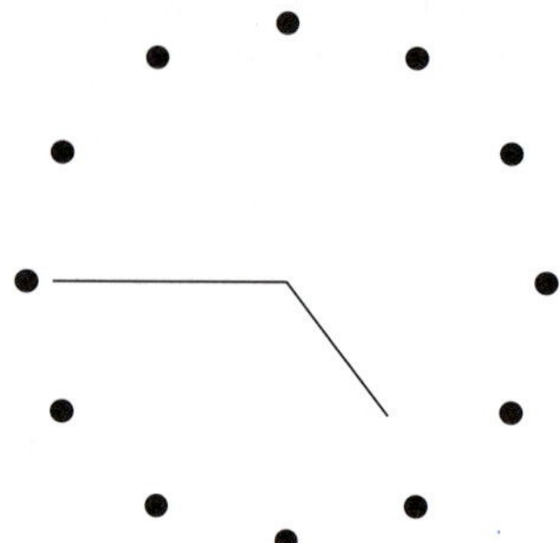

Use a for loop to draw 12 circles.

25. In the formatting examples from the chapter, we always provided a fixed control string, such as

```
System.out.format("%4d", 23);
```

It is possible, however, to dynamically create the control string, as in

```
int i = 4;
System.out.format("%" + i + "d", 23);
```

Using this idea of dynamically creating a control string, write a code fragment that outputs 50 X's, using a separate line for each X. An X on a single line is preceded by two more leading spaces than the X on the previous line. The following figure shows the output for the first five lines.

```
X
  X
    X
      X
        X
```

26. (*Optional*) Write a recursive method to compute the sum of the first *N* positive integers. *Note:* This is strictly for exercise. You should not write the real method recursively.

27. (*Optional*) Write a recursive method to compute the sum of the first *N* positive odd integers. *Note:* This is strictly for exercise. You should not write the real method recursively.

Development Exercises

For the following exercises, use the incremental development methodology to implement the program. For each exercise, identify the program tasks, create a design document with class descriptions, and draw the program diagram. Map out the development steps at the start. Present any design alternatives and justify your selection. Be sure to perform adequate testing at the end of each development step.

28. Write an application that draws nested N squares, where N is an input to the program. The smallest square is 10 pixels wide, and the width of each successive square increases by 10 pixels. The following pattern shows seven squares whose sides are 10, 20, 30, . . . , and 70 pixels wide.

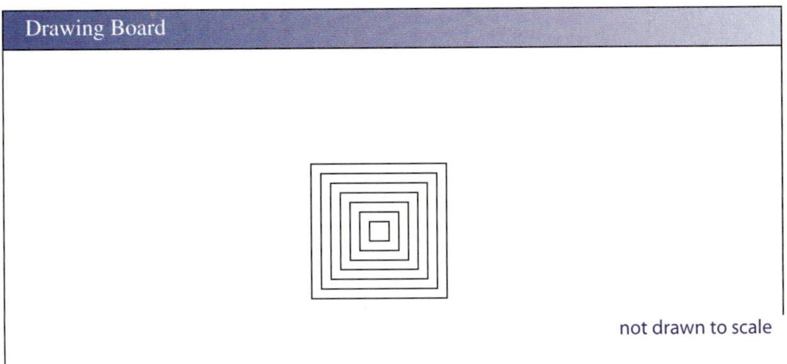

29. The monthly payments for a given loan are divided into amounts that apply to the principal and to the interest. For example, if you make a monthly payment of $500, only a portion of the $500 goes to the principal and the remainder is the interest payment. The monthly interest is computed by multiplying the monthly interest rate by the unpaid balance. The monthly payment minus the monthly interest is the amount applied to the principal. The following table is the sample loan payment schedule for a 1-year loan of $5000 with a 12 percent annual interest rate.

Payment No.	Interest	Principal	Unpaid Balance	Total Interest to Date
1	50.00	394.24	4605.76	50.00
2	46.06	398.19	4207.57	96.06
3	42.08	402.17	3805.40	138.13
4	38.05	406.19	3399.21	176.19
5	33.99	410.25	2988.96	210.18
6	29.89	414.35	2574.61	240.07
7	25.75	418.50	2156.11	265.82
8	21.56	422.68	1733.42	287.38
9	17.33	426.91	1306.51	304.71
10	13.07	431.18	875.34	317.78
11	8.75	435.49	439.85	326.53
12	4.40	439.85	0.00	330.93

Write an application that accepts a loan amount, annual interest rate, and loan period (in number of years) and displays a table with five columns: payment number, the interest and principal paid for that month, the remaining balance after the payment, and the total interest paid to date.

Note: The last payment is generally different from the monthly payment, and your application should print out the correct amount for the last payment. Use the Format class to align the output values neatly.

30. Instead of dropping a watermelon from a building, let's shoot it from a cannon and compute its projectile. The (x, y) coordinates of a watermelon at time t are

$$x = V\cos(\alpha) \cdot t$$

$$y = V\sin(\alpha) \cdot t - \frac{g \cdot t^2}{2}$$

where g is the acceleration of gravity, V is the initial velocity, and α (alpha) is the initial angle. The acceleration of gravity on earth is 9.8 m/s^2.

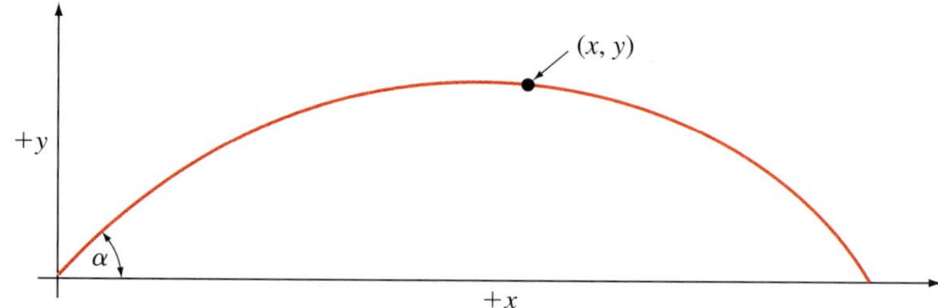

Write an application that inputs an initial velocity V (m/s) and an initial angle alpha (degrees) and computes the projectile of a watermelon cannon ball. The program should repeat the computation until the user wants to quit. The program outputs the (x, y) oordinate value for every second, that is, t = 0, 1, 2, and so forth. The program stops the output when the y value becomes 0 or less. To use the cos and sin methods of the Math class, don't forget that you have to convert the input angle given in degrees to radians. You can convert a degree to equivalent radians by using the following

$$\text{Radian} = \frac{\text{degree} \times \pi}{180}$$

or calling the toRadians method of the Math class. *Note:* Air resistance is not considered in the formula. Also, we assumed the watermelon will not get smashed upon firing.

31. Write an application that simulates a slot machine. The player starts out with M coins. The value for M is an input to the program, and you charge 25 cents per coin. For each play, the player can bet 1 to 4 coins. If the player enters 0 as the number of coins to bet, then the program stops playing. At the end of the game, the program displays the number of coins left and how much the player won or lost in the dollar amount. There are three slots on the machine, and each slot will display one of the three possible pieces: BELL, GRAPE, and CHERRY. When certain combinations appear on the slots, the machine will pay the player. The payoff combinations are as follows:

No.	Combination			Payoff (Times the Betting Amount)
1	BELL	BELL	BELL	10
2	GRAPE	GRAPE	GRAPE	7
3	CHERRY	CHERRY	CHERRY	5
4	CHERRY	CHERRY	-----------	3
5	CHERRY	-----------	CHERRY	3
6	-----------	CHERRY	CHERRY	3
7	CHERRY	-----------	-----------	1
8	-----------	CHERRY	-----------	1
9	-----------	-----------	CHERRY	1

The symbol ----------- means any piece. If the player bets 4 coins and get combination 5, for example, the machine pays the player 12 coins.

7 Defining Your Own Classes—Part 2

Objectives

After you have read and studied this chapter, you should be able to

- Define overloaded methods and constructors.
- Describe the uses of the reserved word **this.**
- Define class methods and variables.
- Describe how the arguments are passed to the parameters in method definitions with the pass-by value scheme.
- Describe how objects are returned from methods.
- Document classes with javadoc comments.
- Organize classes into a package.

Introduction

In Chapter 4, we covered the basics of programmer-defined classes with illustrative examples. There we focused our attention on straightforward cases. After seeing more sample programs in Chapters 5 and 6, we are now ready to attack advanced topics of programmer-defined classes. In addition to introducing several new topics, we will revisit some of the topics from Chapter 4 and provide a more in-depth discussion. In Chapters 5 and 6, we used the Fraction class to illustrate some of the concepts. We will continue to use the Fraction class in this chapter to illustrate the key concepts introduced here. Toward the end of this chapter, we will provide a complete definition of the Fraction class. In addition to this Fraction class, we will go over other sample classes to help students master the key concepts.

7.1 Returning an Object from a Method

return objects from methods

Up until now, when we define a value-returning method, we return either primitive data types, such as int or boolean, or a String. In this section, we learn how to ***return objects from methods***. Again, a String is an object, so in a sense, we know how to return an object from a method. However, a String is treated much as a primitive datum for the most part. Here, we provide a more complete picture of what is going on when we return an object of other standard and programmer-defined classes.

We use the Fraction class to illustrate the returning of an object from a method. Here's the portion of the class definition that includes the constructor, accessors, and mutators (we will add other methods gradually as we cover more topics):

```
class Fraction {

   private int numerator;

   private int denominator;

   public Fraction(int num, int denom) {
       setNumerator(num);
       setDenominator(denom);
   }

   public int getDenominator( ) {

      return denominator;
   }

   public int getNumerator( ) {

      return numerator;
   }
```

We assume both parameters are nonnegative. We remove this assumption when listing the final version in Section 7.8.

```
    public void setDenominator(int denom) {
        if (denom == 0) {
            //Fatal error
            System.err.println("Fatal Error");
            System.exit(1);
        }
        denominator = denom;
    }

    public void setNumerator(int num) {
        numerator = num;
    }

    public String toString( ) {

        return getNumerator() + "/" + getDenominator();
    }

    //other methods come here

}
```

Notice that we do not allow a fraction to have 0 as its denominator. If there is an attempt to assign 0 as a fraction's denominator, we will terminate the whole program. This is quite a draconian measure, but we will do it this way until we learn exception handling in Chapter 8.

Now, let's study the simplify method that reduces a fraction to its simplest form. How about the following?

```
public void simplify( ) {

    int num   = getNumerator();
    int denom = getDenominator();
    int gcd   = gcd(num, denom);

    setNumerator(num/gcd);
    setDenominator(denom/gcd);

}
```

We use the gcd method that returns the greatest common divisor (int) as described in Chapter 6. We get the simplified form by dividing the numerator and the denominator by their greatest common divisor. Here's a sample use of the method:

```
Fraction f1 = new Fraction(24, 36);

f1.simplify( ); //f1 is changed!
```

Notice that the value of f1 is now changed because the method updates the data members of the receiving object (in this example, f1 is a receiving object because we are calling the add method of f1).

Is it acceptable to change the values of the receiving object f1? In this case, is better to keep the values of f1 unchanged and to return a Fraction object that is in the simplified form. This will give flexibility to client programmers. Here's the improved version of the simplify method. (We will make an additional improvement in Section 7.8 to properly handle the case when gcd is zero.)

```
public Fraction simplify( ) {

    int num   = getNumerator();
    int denom = getDenominator();
    int gcd   = gcd(num, denom);

    Fraction simp = new Fraction(num/gcd, denom/gcd);

    return simp;
}
```

The following is the sample use of the improved version:

```
Fraction f1, f2;

f1 = new Fraction(24, 36);

f2 = f1.simplify( );

System.out.println(f1.toString() + "can be reduced to " +
                        f2.toString());
```

The output will be

```
24/36 can be reduced to 2/3
```

Be aware that we can produce such output easily because we did not change the values of f1. Now, if we really want to reduce f1 itself to simplest form, then we just have to assign the result back to f1 as in

```
f1 = f1.simplify( );
```

Let's study the effect of the simplify method when it returns an object. Figure 7.1 shows the state of memory after the simp object is created and assigned the values. Notice that simp is a local variable, but the object itself is created in the heap memory. The return statement at the end of the simplify method returns the value of simp, which is a reference to the Fraction object. Figure 7.2 shows the state after the simplify method is complete. The value of simp is assigned to f2, and now the variable f2 points to this Fraction object. It is critical to realize that when we say *return an object from a method,* we are in fact returning a reference to the object.

Things to Remember

When we say "return an object from a method," we are actually returning the address, or reference, of an object to the caller.

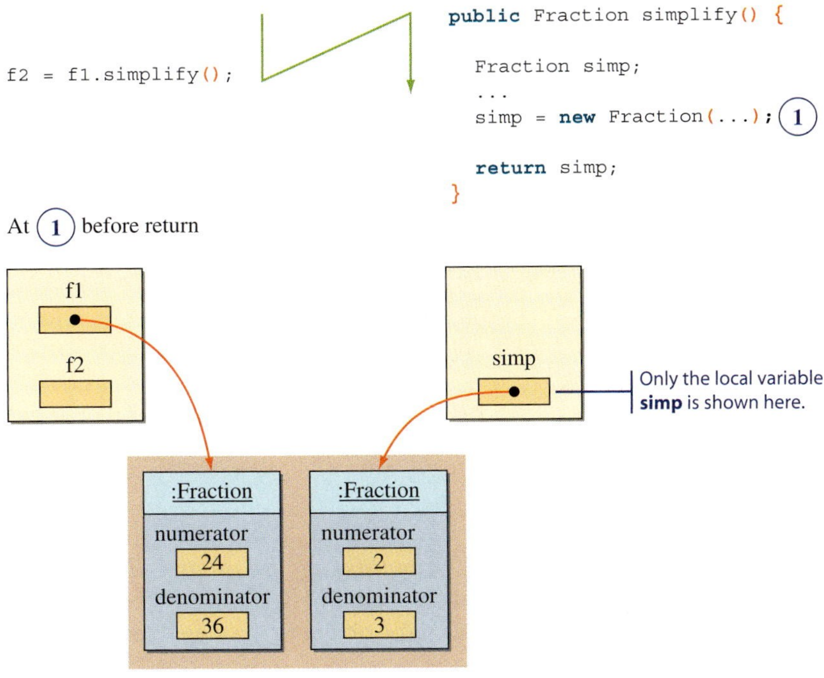

Figure 7.1 This illustration shows the state after the **simp** object is created and assigned with the correct values.

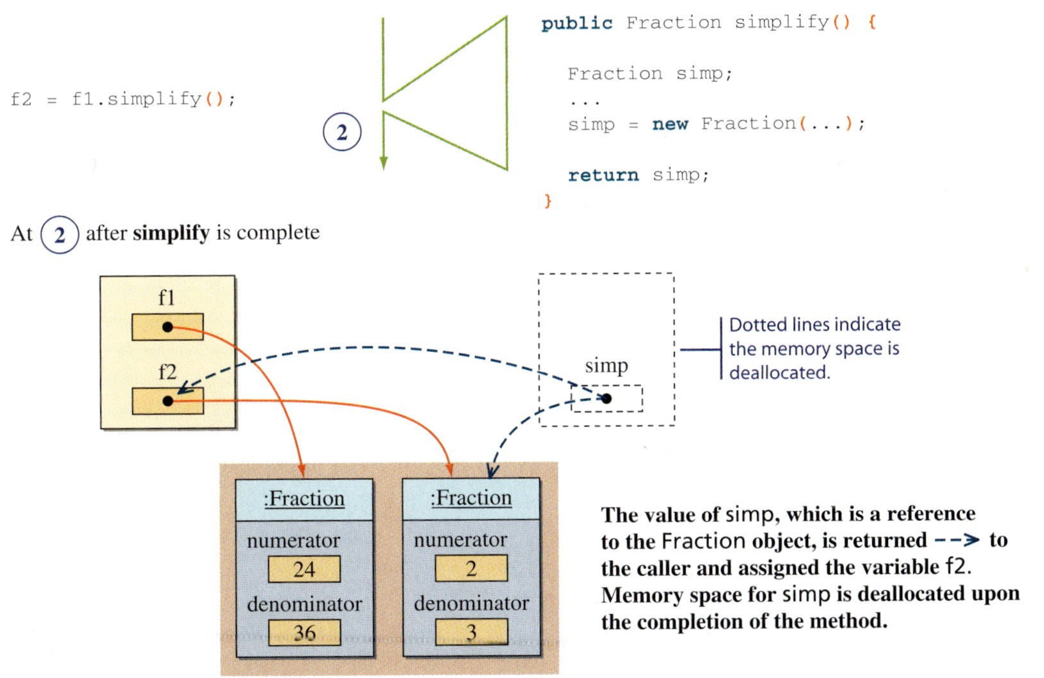

Figure 7.2 Continuation of Figure 7.1. This illustration shows how an object (actually the reference to it) is returned to the calling program.

We will be seeing more examples of object-returning methods in this and later chapters.

It is not necessary to create an object for every variable we use. Many novice programmers often make this mistake. For example, we write

```
Fraction f1, f2;
f1 = new Fraction(24, 36);
f2 = f1.simplify( );
```

We didn't write

```
Fraction f1, f2;
f1 = new Fraction(24, 36);
f2 = new Fraction(1, 1); //not necessary

f2 = f1.simplify( );
```

because it is not necessary. The ***simplify*** method returns a ***Fraction*** object, and in the calling program, all we need is a name we can use to refer to this returned ***Fraction*** object. Don't forget that the object name (variable) and the actual object instance are two separate things.

1. What's wrong with the following declaration?

```
class Question {
   Person student;

   public void getStudent( ) {

      return student;
   }

   ...
}
```

2. Define a Vehicle class. It has a data member owner of type Person. Include an accessor to retrieve the owner person and a mutator to set the owner.

7.2 The Reserved Word this

Let's continue the implementation of the Fraction class. We now consider the four arithmetic operations for fractions; see Figure 7.3. When defining the methods for the four arithmetic operations, we introduce the use of the reserved word this. The

Addition $\frac{a}{b} + \frac{c}{d} = \frac{ad + bc}{bd}$ Subtraction $\frac{a}{b} - \frac{c}{d} = \frac{ad - bc}{bd}$

Division $\frac{a}{b} \div \frac{c}{d} = \frac{ad}{bc}$ Multiplication $\frac{a}{b} \times \frac{c}{d} = \frac{ac}{bd}$

Figure 7.3 Rules for adding, subtracting, multiplying, and dividing fractions.

self-referencing pointer

reserved word this is called a ***self-referencing pointer*** because it is used to refer to the receiving object of a message from within this object's method.

Let's start with the add method that adds two fractions:

Explicit use of the reserved word **this**

```
public Fraction add( Fraction frac) {

    int a, b, c, d;

    Fraction sum;

    a = this.getNumerator();     //get the receiving
    b = this.getDenominator();   //object's num and denom

    c = frac.getNumerator();    //get frac's num
    d = frac.getDenominator(); //and denom

    sum = new Fraction(a*d + b*c, b*d);

    return sum;

}
```

Let's first look at how this add method is used. The following code adds two fractions f1 and f2 and assigns the sum to f3:

```
Fraction f1, f2, f3;

f1 = new Fraction(1, 2);
f2 = new Fraction(1, 4);

f3 = f1.add(f2);

System.out.println("Sum of " + f1.toString() + " and " +
                               f2.toString() + " is " +
                               f3.toString());
```

This code, when executed, will produce the following output:

```
Sum of 1/2 and 1/4 is 6/8
```

Not simplified because the **simplify** method is not called.

In the statement

```
f3 = f1.add(f2);
```

we are calling the add method of f1 and passing the argument f2. So in this case, the receiving object is f1. Figure 7.4 shows the state of memory at the point where the add method of f1 is called. Notice that the self-referencing pointer this is referring to f1 because it is the receiving object.

Because f2 is also a Fraction object, we can write the statement as

```
f3 = f2.add(f1);
```

and get the same result (since the operation is addition). In this case, the receiving object is f2, and the argument is f1. Figure 7.5 shows the state of memory at the point where the add method of f2 is called. Notice how the objects referenced by frac and this are swapped. This time the self-referencing pointer this is referring to f2.

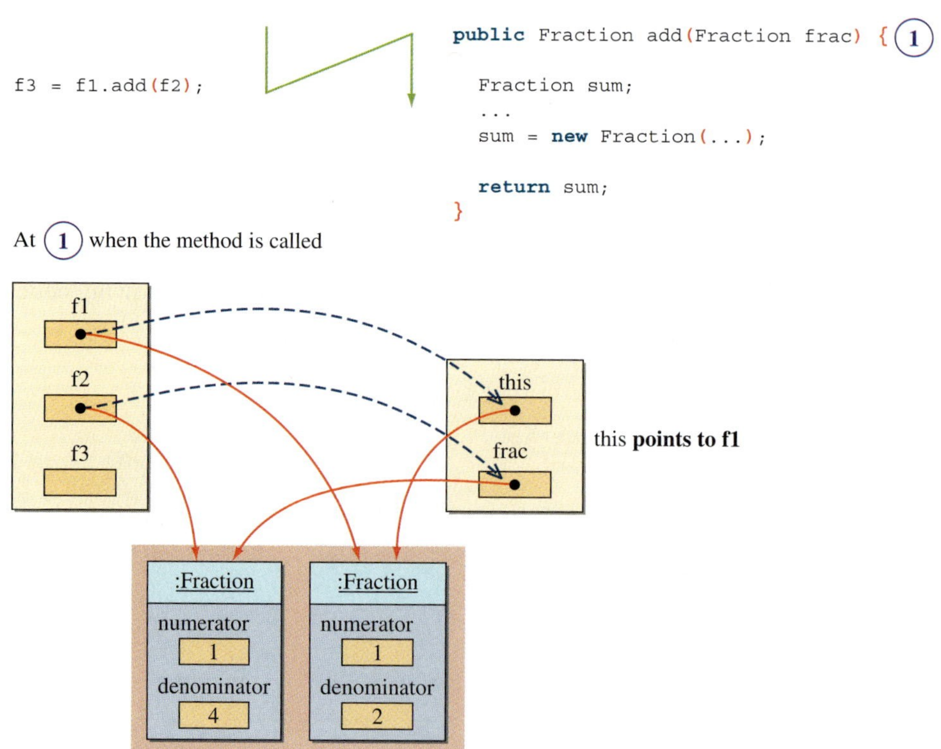

Figure 7.4 This illustration shows the state of memory for **f1.add(f2).**

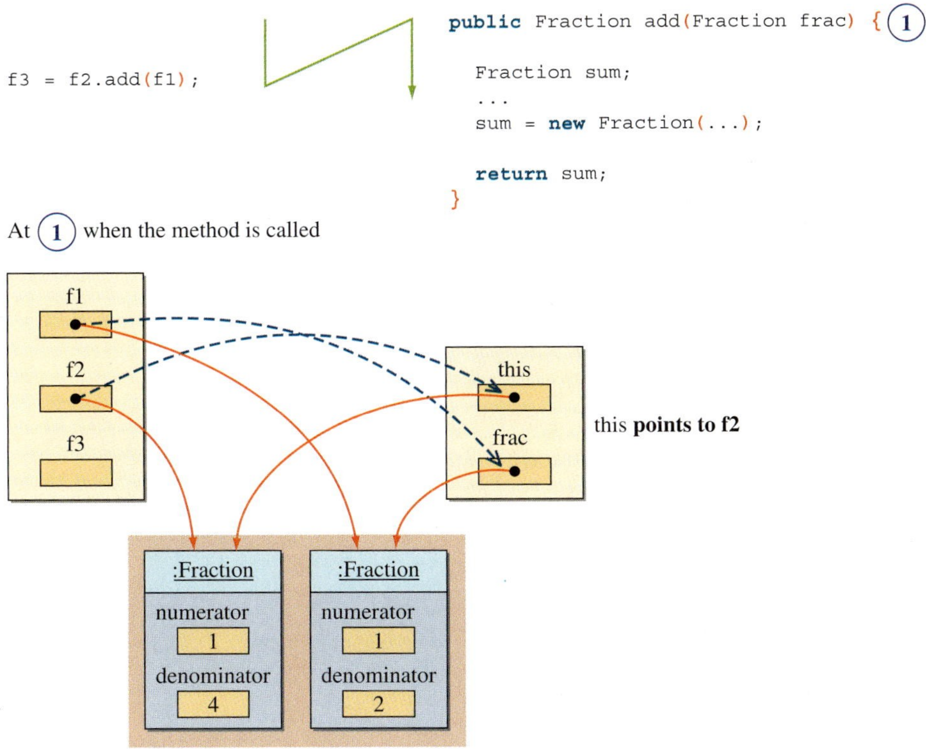

Figure 7.5 This illustration shows the state of memory for **f2.add(f1).**

The add method computes the sum of the receiving Fraction object and the argument Fraction object. We used the identifier frac for the parameter, so

```
c = frac.getNumerator();
d = frac.getDenominator();
```

will retrieve the numerator and the denominator of the argument Fraction object.

To retrieve the numerator and the denominator of the receiving Fraction object, we write

```
a = this.getNumerator();
b = this.getDenominator();
```

because the reserved word this refers to the receiving object.

The use of the reserved word this is actually optional. If we do not include it explicitly, then the compiler will insert the reserved word for us. For example, if we write

```
class Sample {

   public void m1( ) {
      ...
   }

   public void m2( ) {
      m1();
   }
}
```

then the compiler will interpret the definition as

```
class Sample [

   public void m1( ) {
      ...
   }

   public void m2( ) {

      this.m1();
   }
}
```

The reserved word **this** is added by the compiler.

This is the reason why we were able to call a method from another method of the same class without the use of dot notation. In fact, it was dot notation with the reserved word this. We will discuss the use of this when referring to data members of class at the end of this section.

The methods for the other three arithmetic operations are defined in a similar manner:

```
public Fraction divide(Fraction frac) {
    int a, b, c, d;

    Fraction quotient;

    a = this.getNumerator();
    b = this.getDenominator();
    c = frac.getNumerator();
    d = frac.getDenominator();

    quotient = new Fraction(a*d, b*c);

    return quotient;
}
```

```
public Fraction multiply(Fraction frac) {
    int a, b, c, d;

    Fraction product;

    a = this.getNumerator();
    b = this.getDenominator();
    c = frac.getNumerator();
    d = frac.getDenominator();

    product = new Fraction(a*c, b*d);

    return product;
}

public Fraction subtract(Fraction frac) {
    int a, b, c, d;

    Fraction diff;

    a = this.getNumerator();
    b = this.getDenominator();
    c = frac.getNumerator();
    d = frac.getDenominator();

    diff = new Fraction(a*d - b*c, b*d);

    return diff;
}
```

We could have defined the four arithmetic methods as void methods, instead of returning the result as a Fraction object. But doing so will severely limit the flexibility. Because the methods are object-returning methods, we can write a statement such as

```
f3 = f1.add(f2);
```

that reflects the mathematical expression

```
f3 = f1 + f2
```

naturally. Moreover, because the add method returns a Fraction object as the sum, we can compose the calls to implement multiple additions. For example, the mathematical expression

```
f4 = f1 + f2 + f3
```

can be written as

```
f4 = f1.add( f2.add(f3) );
```

where the sum of f2 and f3 is passed as an argument to the add method of f1. We can also write the expression as

```
f4 = f1.add(f2).add(f3);
```

because f1.add(f2) refers to a (unnamed) Fraction object, and we can call this unnamed object's add method with f3 as an argument.

Another Use of this

Consider the following class declaration:

```
class MusicCD {

   private String   artist;
   private String   title;

   private String   id;

   public MusicCD(String name1, String name2) {

      artist = name1;
      title  = name2;
      id     = artist.substring(0,2) + "-" +
               title.substring(0,9);

   }
   ...
}
```

The constructor has two String parameters, one for the artist and another for the title. An id for a MusicCD object is set to be the first two letters of the artist name followed by a hyphen and the first nine letters of the title.

Now, consider what happens if we include (say, inadvertently) a local declaration for the identifier id like this:

Local declaration for **id.**

This **id** is now a local variable.

```
public MusicCD(String name1, String name2) {
   String id;

   artist = name1;
   title  = name2;
   id     = artist.substring(0,2) + "-" +
            title.substring(0,9);
}
```

Bad Version

Because there is a matching local declaration for id, the identifier refers to the local variable, not to the third data member anymore. When an identifier is encountered in a method, the following rules are applied to determine the association.

Things to Remember

Rules for associating an identifier to a local variable, a parameter, and a data member

1. *If there's a matching local variable declaration or a parameter, then the identifier refers to the local variable or the parameter.*
2. *Otherwise, if there's a matching data member declaration, then the identifier refers to the data member.*
3. *Otherwise, it is an error because there's no matching declaration.*

Why does the Java compiler not catch such an error? When would anyone want to use the same identifier for both the data member and the local variable or parameter? It is true that we strongly recommend to always use an identifier different from any data member in declaring a local variable. But there is a situation in which we may want to use the same identifier for a parameter and a data member. In the MusicCD constructor, we declared the parameters name1 and name2 to avoid naming conflict. It would actually be more meaningful to use the conflicting identifiers artist and title. To do so, we rewrite the method by using the reserved word this as follows.

```
public MusicCD(String artist, String title) {

   this.artist = artist;
   this.title  = title;
   id      = artist.substring(0,2) + "-" +
                title.substring(0,9);
}
```

This refers to the data member. (this.artist)

This refers to the parameter. (artist)

Following the stated rules, the identifier artist refers to the parameter. To refer to the data member artist from within this constructor, we prefix the identifier artist with the reserved word this, using dot notation, as this.artist. In the modified constructor, we did not use the reserved word this to refer to the data member id because it was not necessary. Its use is optional, so we could have written

```
this.id = artist.substring(0,2) + "-" +
             title.substring(0,9);
```

to make the code look more consistent. The reserved word this can always be used to refer to the receiving object's data members, whether there is a naming conflict or not.

Things to Remember

Optionally, dot notation with the reserved **this** *can be used to refer to an object's data member from the object's methods and constructors.*

In general, following the common practice, we do not use dot notation (with the reserved word this) to refer to an object's data members from the object's methods unless it is necessary.

Note that we can also avoid the naming conflict and still use a meaningful name for a parameter by prefixing an article to the parameter. For example, we could use the identifiers anArtist and aTitle instead of name1 and name2. This naming will not conflict with the data members, so the use of the reserved word this is not necessary in the constructor. As long as you use meaningful identifiers, which technique you adopt to avoid naming conflict is more of a personal preference.

1. Write a single statement to express the following operations on fractions, using the methods from the Fraction class.

```
f5 = (f1 + f2) / (f3 - f4)
```

2. If the add method is defined thus

```
public void add(Fraction frac) {

    int a, b, c, d;

    a = this.getNumerator();    //get this fraction's
    b = this.getDenominator();  //num and denom

    c = frac.getNumerator();    //get frac's num
    d = frac.getDenominator();  //and denom

    setNumerator(a*b + c*b);  //updates this
    setDenominator(b*d);     //fraction's num and denom
}
```

why is it wrong to call the method as follows?

```
f3 = f1.add(f2);
```

3. Write statements to assign the sum of fractions f1 and f2 to fraction f3, using the add method defined in question 2.

7.3 Overloaded Methods and Constructors

Let's continue to improve the Fraction class. Given the Fraction class in its current form, how can a client programmer express the following mathematical expression?

```
f3 = 2/3 + 9
```

One way is to convert the integer 9 to a fraction 9/1 and then use the add method.

```
Fraction f1, f2, f3;

f1 = new Fraction(2, 3);
f2 = new Fraction(9, 1);

f3 = f1.add(f2);
```

This is not bad, but it would be nicer if we could write something like this:

```
Fraction f1, f3;

f1 = new Fraction(2, 3);

f3 = f1.add(9);
```

In other words, instead of passing a Fraction object, we want to pass a simple integer value. Of course, with the current Fraction class, the statement

```
f3 = f1.add(9);
```

will result in an error because no matching method is defined in the class. So what we want here is two versions of addition, one that accepts a Fraction object and another that accepts an integer. Here are the two definitions:

```
//Version 1
public Fraction add(Fraction frac) {

   //same as before

}

//Version 2
public Fraction add(int number) {

   Fraction sum;
   int a, b, c, d;

   a = getNumerator();
   b = getDenominator();
   c = number;
   d = 1;

   sum = new Fraction(a*d + c*b, b*d);
   return sum;
}
```

Including **d** here is redundant because its value is **1.** We include it here anyway for the sake of clarity.

overloaded methods

With the second add method, we now have two methods in the class that have the same name. This is not a problem as long as certain rules are met. The methods having the same name are called ***overloaded methods***.

Multiple methods can share the same name as long as one of the following rules is met:

1. They have a different number of parameters.
2. The parameters are of different data types when the number of parameters is the same.

The two add methods of the Fraction class satisfy the second rule. The following is an example in which two methods satisfy the first rule:

```
public void myMethod(int x, int y) { ... }

public void myMethod(int x) { ... }
```

method signature

More formally, we say two methods can be overloaded if they do not have the same signature. The ***method signature*** refers to the name of the method and the number and types of its parameters. The two myMethod methods have different signatures because the data types of the second parameter are different.

Two methods cannot be overloaded just by the different return types because two such methods would have the same signature. For example, the following two methods cannot be defined in the same class:

Bad Version

```
public double getInfo(String item) { ... }
public int    getInfo(String item) { ... }
```

Now, let's look at the second add method again. Instead of defining it as we have, we can define it by calling the first add method. Here's how:

```
//More concise Version 2

public Fraction add(int number) {

   Fraction frac = new Fraction(number, 1);

   Fraction sum = add(frac); //calls the first add method

   return sum;
}
```

In defining overloaded methods, it is common for one of them to call another. Such implemenation indicates their relationship clearly—that they are different versions of the same logical operation. It also makes the modification easier because we need to change the code in only one method. Other methods calling this method require no changes. We can define the overloaded methods for the other three arithmetic operations in a similar manner.

Overloading Constructors

Up until now, our programmer-defined classes included exactly one constructor. But a constructor is also a method, so it, too, can be overloaded. Indeed, it is much

multiple constructors

more common to define ***multiple constructors*** in a programmer-defined class. The same rules for overloaded methods apply. Defining multiple constructors for a class gives the client programmer flexibility in creating instances. The client programmer can pick one of the several constructors that is suitable for her needs at hand. Let's define multiple constructors for the Fraction class. Here are the four constructors (including the one already defined before at the bottom):

```
public Fraction( ) { //creates 0/1
    setNumerator(0);
    setDenominator(1);
}

public Fraction(int number) { //creates number/1
    setNumerator(number);
    setDenominator(1);
}

public Fraction(Fraction frac) { //copy constructor
    setNumerator(frac.getNumerator());
    setDenominator(frac.getDenominator());
}

public Fraction(int num, int denom) {
    setNumerator(num);
    setDenominator(denom);
}
```

copy constructor

The third constructor that accepts a Fraction object and creates a copy of the passed Fraction object is called a ***copy constructor***. A copy constructor can be quite handy when we need to create instances of a class that includes many data members. Often we want to create a copy before changing the values of or experimenting with the original object.

As another example, here's a Bicycle class with two constructors that initialize the two data members:

```
class Bicycle {

   // Data Members

   private String id;

   private String ownerName;

   // Constructors
   public Bicycle( ) {

      id = "XXXX-XXXX";
      ownerName = "Unassigned";
   }
```

```
    public Bicycle(String tagNo, String name) {

        id = tagNo;
        ownerName = name;
    }

    //the rest of the class
    . . .
}
```

Calling a Constructor From Another Constructor by Using this

The last use of the reserved word this is to call a constructor from another constructor of the same class. Here's how we can rewrite the four constructors of the Fraction class by using the reserved word this:

```
public Fraction( ) { //creates 0/1
    this(0, 1);
}

public Fraction(int number) { //creates number/1
    this(number, 1);
}

public Fraction(Fraction frac) { //copy constructor
    this( frac.getNumerator(),
          frac.getDenominator() );
}

public Fraction(int num, int denom) {
     setNumerator(num);
     setDenominator(denom);
}
```

This constructor is called by the other three constructors.

The syntax for calling a constructor from another constructor of the same class is

```
this( <parameter-list> );
```

The constructor that matches the parameter list will be called. We can add more statements after the this statement in a constructor, but not before it. In other words, the call to this in a constructor must be the first statement of the constructor.

Things to Remember

*When you use **this** to call a constructor from another constructor of the same class, the **this** statement must be the first statement in the constructor.*

1. Are there any conflicts in the following three constructors for ClassX to be valid?

```
public ClassX( int X ) {

    ...
}

public ClassX( float X ) {

    ...
}

public ClassX( int Y ) {

    ...
}
```

2. Define a Student class. A Student has a name. Define two constructors, one with no argument and another with the name as its argument. Initialize the name to a default value Unknown for the zero-argument constructor.
3. Rewrite the following constructors, so the first one calls the second one.

```
public ClassOne(int alpha) {
   this.alpha = alpha;
   this.beat  = 0;
}

public ClassOne(int alpha, int beta) {

   this.alpha = alpha;
   this.beta  = beta;
}
```

7.4 Class Variables and Methods

We introduced the concepts of class methods, class variables, and class constants in Chapter 1. We saw how class constants are declared in the actual Java statements in Chapter 4. We complete our study of class components in this section by describing how class methods and class variables are used in Java programs. Let's begin with the class methods.

The Math class includes a class method called min to compare two numbers. We use this class method as follows:

```
int i, j, smaller;

i = ...;
j = ...;

smaller = Math.min(i, j);
```

Now suppose we want to have a method to find the smaller of two Fraction objects. Where do we define such a method? The logical place is, of course, the Fraction class. But will this method be an instance method? No, a class method, which follows the pattern of the min method of the Math class, is most appropriate. We can define a class method called min that accepts two Fraction objects as arguments and returns the smaller fraction. Here's how we define the min method:

```
class Fraction {

   ...

   public static Fraction min(Fraction f1, Fraction f2) {

      //convert to decimals and then compare

      double f1_dec = f1.decimal();
      double f2_dec = f2.decimal();

      if ( f1_dec <= f2_dec) {

         return f1;

      } else {

         return f2;
      }
   }

   private double decimal( ) {
      //returns the decimal equivalent
      return (double) getNumerator() / getDenominator();
   }

   ...
}
```

The reserved word static indicates that the min method is a class method. A class method is called by using dot notation with the class name. Here's a sample use:

```
Fraction f1, f2, smaller;

f1 = new Fraction(1, 6);
f2 = new Fraction(4, 5);

smaller = Fraction.min(f1, f2);
```

Remember, in Chapter 6 we discussed the need for finding the greatest common divisor of two integers to simplify a given fraction. Following the logic of the min method, we can define the gcd method as a class method. Here's how:

```
public static int gcd(int m, int n) {

   //the code implementing the Euclidean algorithm

}
```

Notice that the arguments to this method are two integers. When this method is called from another method of the Fraction class, the numerator and the denominator are passed as the arguments. We declare this method public so the client programmers of the Fraction class can use it also. If this is not necessary, then we can declare it private. (*Note:* Logically, the gcd method should be a class method, but there will be no serious consequences if we define it as an instance method.)

In a manner similar to the min and gcd methods, we can define the methods for arithmetic operations as class methods. For example, here's how:

```
public static Fraction add(Fraction f1, Fraction f2) {

   int a, b, c, d;

   Fraction sum;

   a = f1.getNumerator();
   b = f1.getDenominator();
   c = f2.getNumerator();
   d = f2.getDenominator();

   sum = new Fraction(a*d + b*c, b*d);

   return sum;
}
```

To use this class method, we write something like this:

```
Fraction x = new Fraction(1, 8);
Fraction y = new Fraction(4, 9);

Fraction sum = Fraction.add(x, y);
```

The class method add, however, becomes awkward when we try to compose additions. To add three fractions x, y, and z, for example, we have to write

```
Fraction sum = Fraction.add(Fraction.add(x,y), z);
```

The instance method add, as we defined at the beginning of the chapter, allows a lot more natural and flexible use.

Now let's look at an example of class variables (we have been using class constants since Chap. 4). Suppose we want to assign a tag number automatically when a new instance of the Bicycle class is created. We want the tag numbers to be ABC-101, ABC-102, ABC-103, and so forth. What we need to define in the Bicycle class is a counter that counts up from 101. Only one counter is necessary for the whole class, so it is logical to define this counter as a class variable.

First, we declare and initialize the class variable counter:

```
class Bicycle {

   private static int counter = 101;

   ...
}
```

Then we adjust the constructor, so the id of a bicycle is assigned correctly. Here's how:

```
public Bicycle( ) {

   id = "ABC-" + counter;
   ...
   counter++;

}
```

Static Initializer

There are cases in which we may need to do more than a simple assignment to initialize a class variable. For example, we may be required to read the starting value for the class variable counter of the Bicycle class from a file. If we need to perform more than a simple assignment to initialize a class variable, then we define a static initializer. A ***static initializer*** is a code that gets executed when a class is loaded into the Java system. It is defined in the following manner:

static initializer

```
class XYZ {

   ...

   static {

       //code to initialize
       //class variables and perform
       //other tasks

   }

   ...

}
```

As an illustration, here's how we define the static initializer for the Bicycle class to set the starting value of counter to 101:

```
class Bicycle {

    private static int counter;

    ...

    static {

        counter = 101;

    }

    ...

}
```

We conclude this section with important reminders.

Things to Remember

1. *Class methods can access only the class variables and the class constants of the class.*
2. *Instance methods, including constructors, can access all types of data members.*
3. *Class methods cannot call instance methods of the same class.*
4. *Instance methods can call all other methods of the same class.*

7.5 Call-by-Value Parameter Passing

We will provide more detailed coverage on how arguments are passed to a method. Let's first review some key facts. Local variables are used for temporary purposes, such as storing intermediate results of a computation. While the data members of a class are accessible from all instance methods of the class, local variables and parameters are accessible only from the method in which they are declared, and they are available only while the method is being executed. Memory space for local variables and parameters is allocated upon declaration and at the beginning of the method, respectively, and erased upon exiting from the method.

call-by-value scheme

When a method is called, the value of the argument is passed to the matching parameter, and separate memory space is allocated to store this value. This way of passing the value of arguments is called a *pass-by-value* or ***call-by-value scheme***. Since separate memory space is allocated for each parameter during the execution of the method, the parameter is local to the method, and therefore changes made to the parameter will not affect the value of the corresponding argument.

Consider the following myMethod method of the Tester class. The method does not do anything meaningful. We use it here to illustrate how the call-by-value scheme works.

```
class Tester {

   public void myMethod(int one, double two ) {

      one = 25;
      two = 35.4;
   }
}
```

What will be the output from the following code?

```
Tester tester;
int x, y;

tester = new Tester();
x = 10;
y = 20;

tester.myMethod( x, y );

System.out.println( x + "     " + y );
```

The output will be

```
10    20
```

because with the pass-by-value scheme, the values of arguments are passed to the parameters, but changes made to the parameters are not passed back to the arguments. Figure 7.6 shows how the pass-by-value scheme works.

Notice that the arguments are matched against the parameters in the left-to-right order; that is, the value of the leftmost argument is passed to the leftmost parameter, the value of the second-leftmost argument is passed to the second-leftmost parameter, and so forth. The number of arguments in the method call must match the number of parameters in the method definition. For example, the following calls to myMethod of the Tester class are all invalid because the number of arguments and number of parameters do not match.

```
tester.myMethod( 12 );
tester.myMethod( x, y, 24.5);
```

Since we are assigning the value of an argument to the matching parameter, the data type of an argument must be assignment-compatible with the data type of the matching parameter. For example, we can pass an integer argument to a float parameter, but not vice versa. In the following, the first call is valid, but the second one is invalid:

```
tester.myMethod( 12, 25 );
tester.myMethod( 23.0, 34.5 );
```

The name of the parameter and the name of the argument can be the same. Keep in mind, however, that the values of arguments are still passed to a method by the pass-by-value scheme; that is, local copies are made whether the argument and the parameter share the same name or not.

Things to Remember

Remember these key points about arguments and parameters:

1. *Arguments are passed to a method by using the pass-by- value scheme.*
2. *Arguments are matched to the parameters from left to right. The data type of an argument must be assignment-compatible with the data type of the matching parameter.*
3. *The number of arguments in the method call must match the number of parameters in the method definition.*
4. *Parameters and arguments do not have to have the same name.*
5. *Local copies, which are distinct from arguments, are created even if the parameters and arguments share the same name.*
6. *Parameters are input to a method, and they are local to the method. Changes made to the parameters will not affect the value of corresponding arguments.*

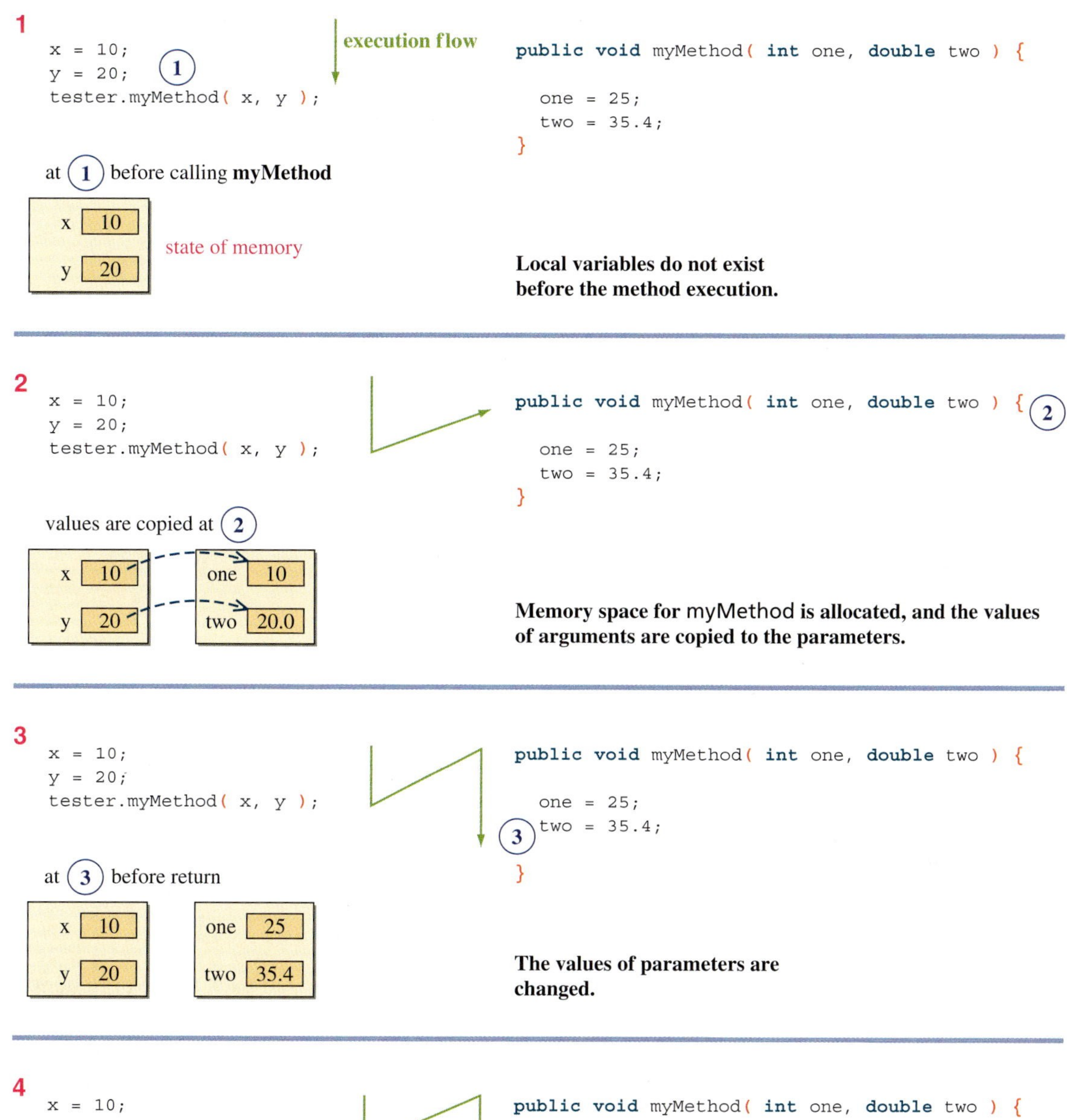

Figure 7.6 How memory space for the parameters is allocated and deallocated.

Now let's look at a similar example again, but this time with objects. Consider the following class:

```
class ObjectTester {

   public void swap(Fraction f1, Fraction f2) {

      Fraction temp;

      temp = f1; //swap the two fractions
      f1   = f2;
      f2   = temp;
   }
}
```

What will be the output from the following code?

```
ObjectTester tester;
Fraction     x, y;

tester = new ObjectTester();

x = new Fraction(1, 2);

y = new Fraction(3, 4);

tester.swap(x, y);

System.out.println("x = " + x.toString());
System.out.println("y = " + y.toString());
```

The output will be

```
x = 1/2
y = 3/4
```

because the changes made to the parameters are not passed back to the arguments. It does not matter whether we are passing primitive data values or objects (actually, references to the objects). Figure 7.7 shows the effect of calling the swap method.

Changes made to the parameters are not passed back to the arguments, but when we are passing objects to a method, then the changes made to the object itself are reflected back to the caller because the calling side still has the same reference to the object. Let's look at an example. Consider the following class:

```
class ObjectTester2 {

   public void change(Fraction f1) {

      f1.setNumerator(10);
   }
}
```

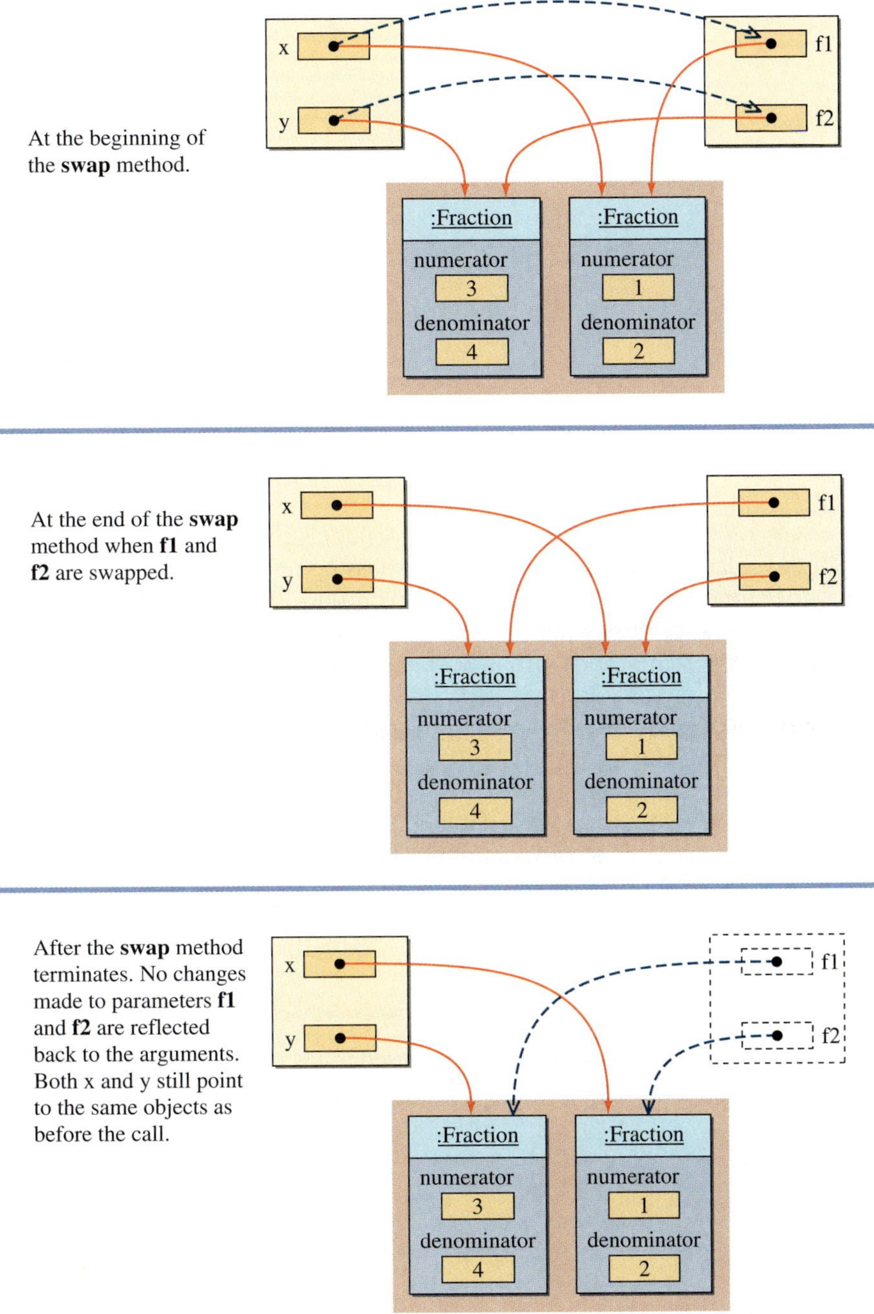

At the beginning of the **swap** method.
x
y
f1
f2
:Fraction
numerator
3
denominator
4
:Fraction
numerator
1
denominator
2
At the end of the **swap** method when **f1** and **f2** are swapped.
After the **swap** method terminates. No changes made to parameters **f1** and **f2** are reflected back to the arguments. Both x and y still point to the same objects as before the call.

Figure 7.7 This illustration shows the effect of calling the **swap** method.

What will be the output from the following code?

```
ObjectTester2 tester;
Fraction      x;

tester = new ObjectTester();

x = new Fraction(1, 2);

tester.change(x);
System.out.println("x = " + x.toString());
```

The output will be

```
x = 10/2
```

Figure 7.8 shows the effect of calling the change method. Notice that the variable x continues to point to the same object, but the object itself has been modified.

You Might Want to Know

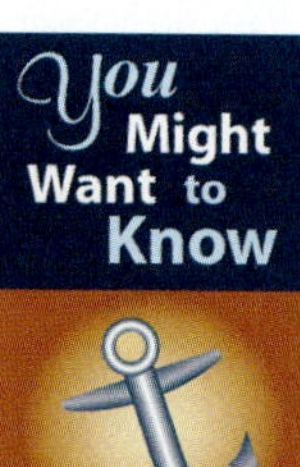

Pass-by-value (also known as call-by-value) is the *only* parameter passing mechanism Java supports. Because we are passing references when objects are passed to methods, many people with background in other programming languages use the term *pass by reference* (or *call by reference*) when referring to the passing of objects to methods. This is *wrong.* Pass by reference means an address (or reference) of a variable is passed, whereas pass by value means the content of a variable is passed (and copied into a parameter). In Java, the content of a variable is either a value of primitive data type or a reference to an object (this is the source of confusion). But it doesn't matter what the content of a variable is; as long as the content of a variable is passed and copied into a parameter, it is a call by value. If a programming language supports the pass-by-reference mechanism, then it is possible, for example, to swap the values of two arguments in a single method call. No such thing is possible in Java.

Quick CHECK

1. What is the name of the scheme used in Java to pass arguments to a method?
2. What is the output from the following code?

```
class Question {
   private int one;

   public void myMethod( int one ) {
      this.one = one;
      one = 12;
   }
}

class Test {

   public static void main(String[] arg) {
      int one = 30;
```

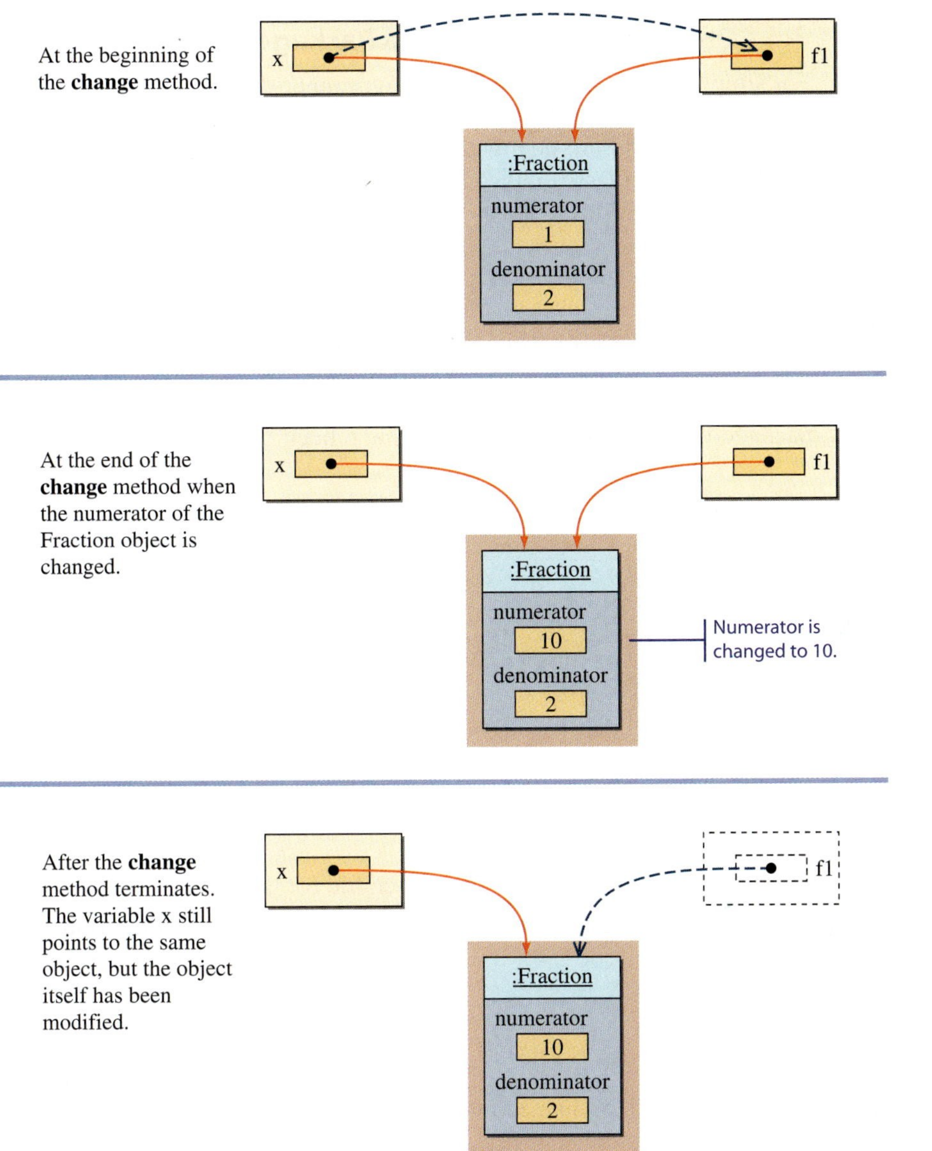

Figure 7.8 This illustration shows the effect of calling the **change** method.

```
            Question q = new Question();
            q.myMethod(one);

            System.out.println(one);
        }
    }
```

7.6 Organizing Classes into a Package

For simplicity, we have placed all programmer-defined classes of a program in the same folder since Chapter 4. This approach works fine while we are learning programming and do not deal with many classes. But in a more real-life context, we need to manage classes more effectively. For example, following the approach, we have to copy the Fraction class to multiple folders if we want to use this class in different programs.

The correct approach to reusing programmer-defined classes is to organize them into packages, just as the standard classes are organized into packages. We illustrate the process by using the Fraction class. Let's name the package to place the Fraction class myutil. It is a Java convention to name the package with all lowercase letters. Once this package is set up correctly, we can use the classes in the package by importing it, just as we have been doing with the standard packages.

```
import myutil.*;

class MyClient {
   Fraction f1;
   ...
}
```

programmer-defined packages

To set up the ***programmer-defined packages*** for general reuse, not just use by the programs in the same folder, we have to perform the following tasks:

1. Include the statement

   ```
   package myutil;
   ```

   as the first statement of the source file for the Fraction class.
2. The class declaration must include the visibility modifier public as

   ```
   public class Fraction {
      ...
   }
   ```

3. Create a folder named myutil, the same name as the package name. In Java, the package must have a one-to-one correspondence with the folder.
4. Place the modified Fraction class into the myutil folder and compile it.
5. Modify the CLASSPATH environment variable to include the folder that contains the myutil folder. See below.

Step 5 is the most troublesome step for those new to Java. Since the exact steps to change the CLASSPATH environment variable are different from each platform (Windows, Unix, Mac) and Java IDE (Eclipse, NetBeans, jGRASP, BlueJ, etc.), we will describe only the general idea for the Windows platform here. Suppose we have a folder named JavaPrograms under the C: drive, and the myutil package (folder) is placed inside this JavaPrograms folder. Then to use the classes in the myutil package, the classpath environment should make a reference to the JavaPrograms folder (not to the package myutil itself):

```
set classpath=.;c:\JavaPrograms
```

The period after the equals symbol refers to the current folder (the folder where the client program we are trying to execute is located). Without this reference to the current folder, the client program will not recognize other classes in the same folder.

Things to Remember

*To make the programmer-defined packages accessible to all client programs, the **CLASSPATH** environment variable must be set up correctly.*

7.7 Using Javadoc Comments for Class Documentation

javadoc comments

We mentioned in Chapter 2 that there are three styles of comments in Java. We have been using the two of them. We introduce the third style called *javadoc comments* in this section. Many of the programmer-defined classes we design are intended to be used by other programmers. It is, therefore, very important to provide meaningful documentation to the client programmers so they can understand how to use our classes correctly. By adding javadoc comments to the classes we design, we can provide a consistent style of documenting the classes. Once the javadoc comments are added to a class, we can use a special program (comes as a part of Java 2 SDK) to generate HTML files for documentation. (*Note:* An HTML file is a specially marked file intended for a Web browser.) We mentioned in Chapter 2 that the documentation for the standard classes can be found at **http://java.sun.com/j2se/1.5/docs/api/index.html.**

This documentation is derived from the javadoc comments embedded in the standard classes.

We will describe how to use javadoc comments and generate the corresponding-HTML documentation files. Before we get into the details, we first show the end result so you can visualize where the process is leading. Figure 7.9 shows a portion of the HTML documentation for the Fraction class displayed in a browser.

A javadoc comment is used as header comment for a class, a data member, or a method. Let's begin with the class header comment for the Fraction class in the javadoc format:

```
/**
 * An instance of this class represents a fraction.
 *
 * @author Dr. Caffeine
 *
 */
class Fraction {
    ...
}
```

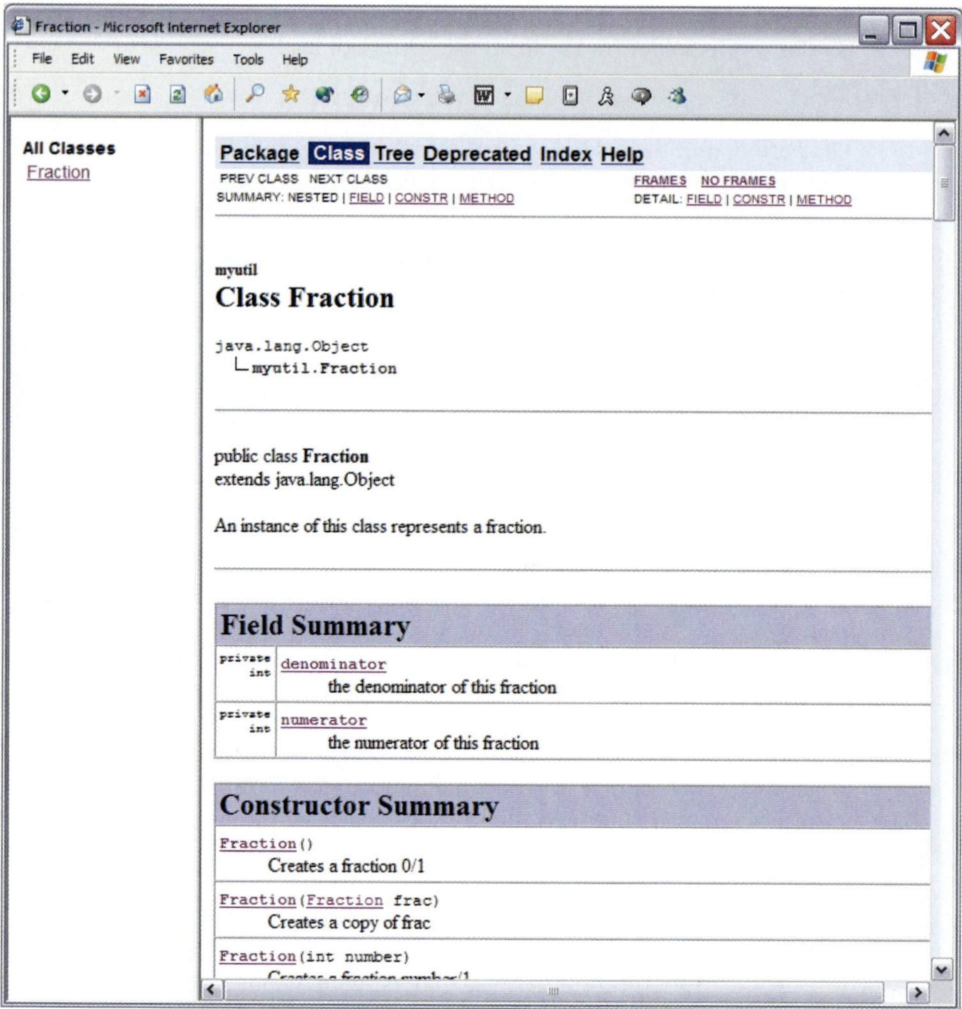

Figure 7.9 A browser showing the HTML documentation file derived from the javadoc comments for the **Fraction** class.

The javadoc comments begin with the marker /** and end with the marker */. The asterisks on the lines between the first and the last markers have no significance; they are there to provide a visual aid to highlight the comments in the program. It is an accepted standard to use the asterisks in this manner for the javadoc comments.

javadoc tags

@**author** tag

Inside the javadoc comments, we can use a number of ***javadoc tags***, special markers that begin with the @ mark. In this example, we see one javadoc tag @author, which we use to list the authors of the class.

Here's how we comment a data member in javadoc:

```
/**
* The numerator portion of this fraction
*/
private int numerator;
```

When the length of a comment is short and fits in a single line, then we can write the javadoc comment as

```
/** The numerator portion of this fraction */
private int numerator;
```

The javadoc comment for a method is similar to the one for the class header comment. It will include a number of javadoc tags in addition to a general description. Here's how a method is commented by using javadoc:

```
/**
 * Returns the sum of this Fraction
 * and the parameter frac. The sum
 * returned is NOT simplified.
 *
 * @param frac the Fraction to add to this
 *             Fraction
 *
 * @return the sum of this and frac
 */
public Fraction add(Fraction frac) {
    ...
}
```

@param tag

The purpose of the method header comment is to record the method's purpose, list of parameters passed to the method, and value returned from the method. This method receives one parameter, so there is one @param ***tag***. We attach a short description of the parameter in addition to the parameter's name. The syntax for the @param javadoc tag is

```
@param <parameter name> <description>
```

@return tag

The <description> portion can go beyond one line. As this method returns a value, we add the @return ***tag***. Its syntax is

```
@return <description>
```

A javadoc comment for a constructor is defined in a manner similar to the one for a method, except there will never be an @return tag for a constructor. Figure 7.10 shows the HTML document that is generated from this javadoc comment. Notice the effect of @param and @return tags.

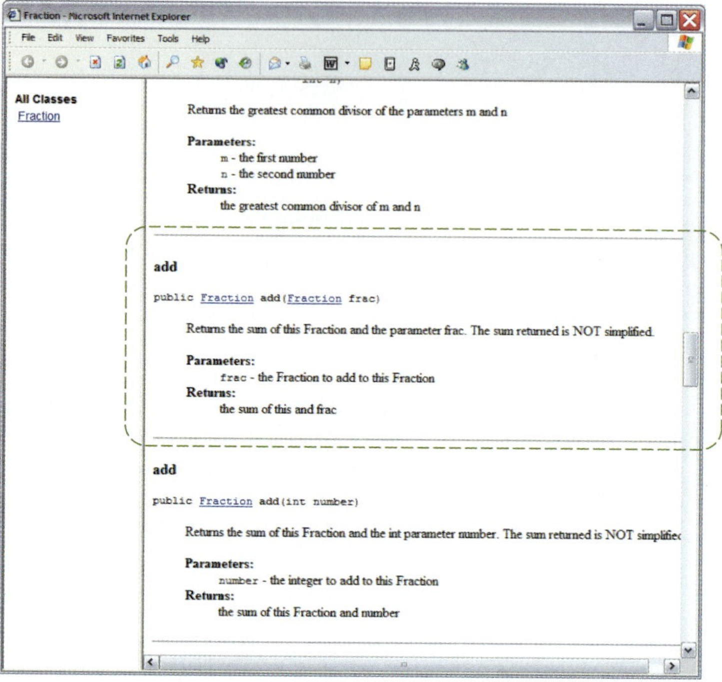

Figure 7.10 The portion of the HTML documentation file that is derived from the javadoc header comment for the **add** method.

The use of the javadoc comments does not preclude the use of other types of comments. We still need to use regular comments to describe the code as necessary. For example, we will continue to include the group comment for methods, as in

```
//-----------------------------------------
//  Public Methods:
//
//      Fraction add   ( Fraction )
//      Fraction add   ( int      )
//
//      ...
//-----------------------------------------
```

so that programmers reading the class will have a handy reference to the list of methods without referring to any online documentation. This is especially useful when the programmers are reading a hard copy of the class source file. Notice that we don't use the javadoc style for a quick reference list because javadoc comments are used only for describing the class and its data members and methods.

Once all the javadoc comments are added to a class, we are ready to generate the corresponding HTML documentation file. For easy reference, we call it the *javadoc file*. Many Java editors and IDEs include a menu option that you can use to generate javadoc files easily and quickly. Here we describe the steps you can take to generate javadoc files using the minimalist approach (see App. A). In the command prompt window, we used the commands javac and java to compile and run Java programs, respectively. Similarly, to generate javadoc files, we use the javadoc command. For example, to generate a javadoc file for the Fraction class, we enter

```
javadoc -private Fraction.java
```

We specify the -private option because we want to generate the documentation for all types of methods (so far, we have covered two of these—private and public). The -private option generates the most complete documentation. When the command is executed, status messages such as these are displayed.

```
C:\WINDOWS\System32\cmd.exe

N:\Programs\CS1ED4SamplePrograms\Chapter7>javadoc -private Fraction.java
Loading source file Fraction.java...
Constructing Javadoc information...
Standard Doclet version 1.4.2_03
Generating constant-values.html...
Building tree for all the packages and classes...
Building index for all the packages and classes...
Generating overview-tree.html...
Generating index-all.html...
Generating deprecated-list.html...
Building index for all classes...
Generating allclasses-frame.html...
Generating allclasses-noframe.html...
Generating index.html...
Generating packages.html...
Generating Fraction.html...
Generating package-list...
Generating help-doc.html...
Generating stylesheet.css...

N:\Programs\CS1ED4SamplePrograms\Chapter7>_
```

After the command is executed successfully, there will actually be a collection of HTML files, not just the expected Fraction.html. You can view the content shown in Figure 7.9 by opening the file index.html and clicking the Fraction link. Open the Fraction.html directly from your browser and see the difference. We encourage you to open other HTML files to see how these files are related. The generated HTML files are located in the same directory where the source file Fraction.java is located. You can change the directory by setting the -d option and specifying the directory to store the generated HTML files (alternatively, you can move the files using an operating system's file manager). We ordinarily do not generate javadoc files one class at a time. Rather, it is more common to generate a complete set of javadoc files for all classes in a single package at once, as in

```
javadoc -private *.java
```

We will refer you to websites for a more complete discussion of javadoc.

Things to Remember

General information on javadoc is located at
http://java.sun.com/j2se/javadoc
Detailed reference on how to use javadoc on Windows is located at
http://java.sun.com/j2se/1.5/docs/tooldocs/windows/javadoc.html

Is it really important to use javadoc comments? It's true that we have to learn a few extra items to use javadoc comments, but the benefits warrant a little extra effort. First, by using javadoc comments, we can easily produce the standard online documentation. Even if we don't have an immediate need to produce an online documentation, we can use javadoc comments because they are really not that different from other styles of commenting, and their use gives us an option to produce an online documentation later. Second, since javadoc is a standard, other programmers will have an easier time reading your code with javadoc comments than reading code with a nonstandard style of comments.

1. Add javadoc comments to the following class.

```
class Instructor {
   private String name;

   public void setName(String name) {
      this.name = name;
   }

   public String getName( ) {
      return name;
   }
}
```

2. What is the purpose of @author tag?

7.8 The Complete Fraction Class

In this section, we will list a complete definition for the myutil.Fraction class. In the final version of the class, we will include improvements to one of the constructors and the simplify method. Earlier in the chapter, we presented the fourth constructor as follows:

```
public Fraction(int num, int denom) {

   setNumerator(num);
   setDenominator(denom);
}
```

For this constructor to function properly, we made an assumption that the values for both parameters are nonnegative. Let's remove this assumption and make the necessary modifications to the constructor.

Consider the following two statements:

```
Fraction f1 = new Fraction(-2, 9);
Fraction f2 = new Fraction(2, -9);
```

Both represent the same value, namely, $-\frac{2}{9}$. With the given constructor, f1 will have the values -2 and 9 for its data members numerator and denominator, respectively. And f2 will have the values 2 and -9 for its data members numerator and denominator, respectively. This means that we have two distinct ways to represent the same value. It is always preferable to maintain a consistent representation because multiple representations for the same value would lead to a more complex code for handling different representations correctly. We will improve this constructor so that a negative fraction is always represented by a negative value for numerator and a positive value for denominator.

Now, consider the following two statements:

```
Fraction f3 = new Fraction(2, 9);
Fraction f4 = new Fraction(-2, -9);
```

Both objects represent the same positive fraction $\frac{2}{9}$. Again, to maintain consistent representation, a positive fraction is always represented by positive values for both numerator and denominator.

Finally, consider the following two statements:

```
Fraction f3 = new Fraction(0, 9);
Fraction f4 = new Fraction(0, -5);
```

Both objects represent the numerical value of 0. We will always represent the numerical value of 0 by storing 0 in the data member numerator and 1 in denominator.

Here's the modified constructor:

```
public Fraction(int num, int denom) {

   if (denom < 0) {
      num   = -num;
      denom = -denom;
   }

   if (num == 0) {
      denom = 1;
   }

   setNumerator(num);
   setDenominator(denom);
}
```

We will also make a modification to the simplify method. The original simplify method fails when someone tries to simplify a zero fraction (i.e., a fraction with numerical value of 0). To reduce a fraction to its simplified form, we find the greatest common divisor of its numerator and denominator and divide them by the greatest common divisor. What happens when the numerator is 0? The greatest common divisor of 0 and any other value is 0. So we would end up dividing the numerator and denominator by 0! Here's the new simplify method that avoids this problem:

```
public Fraction simplify( ) {

    int num   = getNumerator();
    int denom = getDenominator();

    int divisor = 1;

    if (num != 0) {
       divisor  = gcd(Math.abs(num), denom);
    }

    return new Fraction(num/divisor, denom/divisor);
}
```

```
package myutil;
/**
 * An instance of this class represents a fraction.
 *
 *
 */
public class Fraction {

   /** the numerator of this fraction */
   private int numerator;

   /** the denominator of this fraction */
   private int denominator;

//----------------------------------------
// Constructors
//----------------------------------------
   /**
    * Creates a fraction 0/1
    */
   public Fraction( ) {
       this(0, 1);
   }
```

Data Members

Constructors

```
    /**
     * Creates a fraction number/1
     *
     * @param number the numerator
     */
    public Fraction(int number) {
        this(number, 1);
    }

    /**
     * Creates a copy of frac
     *
     * @param frac a copy of this parameter is created
     */
    public Fraction(Fraction frac) {
        this(frac.getNumerator(), frac.getDenominator());
    }

    /**
     * Creates a fraction num/denom. Create a negative
     * fraction as -num and denom. If negative values
     * are specified for both num and denom, the fraction
     * is converted to a positive. If num is positive and
     * denom is negative, the fraction will be converted to
     * have negative num and positive denom.
     * When the num is zero, denom is set to 1. Zero is
     * always represented as 0/1
     *
     * @param num   the numerator
     * @param denom the denominator
     */
    public Fraction(int num, int denom) {

        if (denom < 0) {
            num   = -num;
            denom = -denom;
        }

        if (num == 0) {
            denom = 1;
        }

        setNumerator(num);
        setDenominator(denom);
    }

//------------------------------------------
// Class Methods
//
//------------------------------------------
```

```
/**
 * Returns the greatest common divisor of
 * the parameters m and n
 *
 * @param m the first number
 * @param n the second number
 *
 * @return the greatest common divisor of m and n
 */
public static int gcd(int m, int n) {

    int r = n % m;

    while (r !=0) {

        n = m;

        m = r;

        r = n % m;

    }

    return m;

}

/**
 * Returns the smaller of the two parameters f1 and f2
 *
 * @param f1 the first fraction to compare
 * @param f2 the second fraction to compare
 *
 * @return the smaller of the two parameters
*/
public static Fraction min(Fraction f1, Fraction f2) {

   //convert to decimals and then compare
   double f1_dec = f1.decimal();
   double f2_dec = f2.decimal();

   if (f1_dec <= f2_dec) {

      return f1;

   } else {

      return f2;

   }
}
```

gcd

min

```
//-----------------------------------------
//  Public Instance Methods
//
//-----------------------------------------

    /**
     * Returns the sum of this Fraction
     * and the parameter frac. The sum
     * returned is NOT simplified.
     *
     * @param frac the Fraction to add to this
     *             Fraction
     *
     * @return the sum of this and frac
     */
    public Fraction add(Fraction frac) {
        int a, b, c, d;

        Fraction sum;

        a = this.getNumerator();
        b = this.getDenominator();
        c = frac.getNumerator();
        d = frac.getDenominator();

        sum = new Fraction(a*d + b*c, b*d);

        return sum;
    }

    /**
     * Returns the sum of this Fraction
     * and the int parameter number. The sum
     * returned is NOT simplified.
     *
     * @param number the integer to add to this
     *             Fraction
     * @return the sum of this Fraction and number
     */
    public Fraction add(int number) {

        Fraction frac = new Fraction(number, 1);

        Fraction sum = add(frac);

        return sum;

    }
```

add

add

```
/**
 * Returns the quotient of this Fraction
 * divided by the parameter frac. The quotient
 * returned is NOT simplified.
 *
 * @param frac the divisor of the division
 *
 * @return the quotient of this fraction
 *         divided by frac
 */
public Fraction divide(Fraction frac) {
    int a, b, c, d;

    Fraction quotient;

    a = this.getNumerator();
    b = this.getDenominator();
    c = frac.getNumerator();
    d = frac.getDenominator();

    quotient = new Fraction(a*d, b*c);

    return quotient;
}
```

divide

```
/**
 * Returns the quotient of this Fraction
 * divided by the int parameter number. The quotient
 * returned is NOT simplified.
 *
 * @param number the divisor
 *
 * @return the quotient of this Fraction divided by number
 */
public Fraction divide(int number) {

    Fraction frac = new Fraction(number, 1);

    Fraction quotient = divide(frac);

    return quotient;
}
```

divide

```
/**
 * Compares this fraction and the parameter frac for
 * equality. This method compares the two by first
 * reducing them to the simplest form.
 *
 * @param frac the fraction object to compare
 *
 * @return true if this Fraction object and frac are equal
 */
```

```
public boolean equals(Fraction frac) {

  Fraction f1 = simplify(); //simplify itself
  Fraction f2 = frac.simplify(); //simplify frac

  return (f1.getNumerator() == f2.getNumerator() &&
          f1.getDenominator() == f2.getDenominator());
}

 /**
  * Returns the denominator of this fraction
  *
  * @return the denominator of this fraction
  */
public int getDenominator( ) {
   return denominator;
}

 /**
  * Returns the numerator of this fraction
  *
  * @return the numerator of this fraction
  */
public int getNumerator( ) {
   return numerator;
}

 /**
  * Returns the product of this Fraction
  * and the parameter frac. The product
  * returned is NOT simplified.
  *
  * @param frac the multiplier of the multiplication
  *
  * @return the product of this fraction
  *         and the parameter frac
  */
 public Fraction multiply(Fraction frac) {
     int a, b, c, d;

     Fraction product;

     a = this.getNumerator();
     b = this.getDenominator();

     c = frac.getNumerator();
     d = frac.getDenominator();

     product = new Fraction(a*c, b*d);

     return product;
 }
```

equals

getDenominator

getNumerator

multiply

```
/**
 * Returns the product of this Fraction
 * and the int parameter number. The product
 * returned is NOT simplified.
 *
 * @param number the multiplier
 *
 * @return the product of this Fraction and number
 */

public Fraction multiply(int number) {

    Fraction frac = new Fraction(number, 1);

    Fraction product = multiply(frac);

    return product;
}

/**
 * Sets the denominator of this fraction
 *
 * @param denom the denominator of this fraction
 */
public void setDenominator(int denom) {
    if (denom == 0) {
        //Fatal error
        System.out.println("Fatal Error");
        System.exit(1);
    }
    denominator = denom;
}

/**
 * Sets the numerator of this fraction
 *
 * @param num the numerator of this fraction
 */
public void setNumerator(int num) {
    numerator = num;
}

/**
 * Returns a new Fraction object that is in
 * the simplest form of this Fraction object. If
 * this Fraction is zero, then a simple copy of
 * it is returned.
 *
 * @return a Fraction object in the simplest form
 *         of this Fraction
 */
```

multiply

setDenominator

setNumerator

```
public Fraction simplify( ) {

   int num   = getNumerator();
   int denom = getDenominator();

   int divisor = 1;

   if (num != 0) {
      divisor   = gcd(Math.abs(num), denom);
   }

   return new Fraction(num/divisor, denom/divisor);
}

/**
 * Returns the difference of this Fraction
 * and the parameter frac. The difference
 * returned is NOT simplified.
 *
 * @param frac the Fraction to subtract from
 *             this Fraction
 *
 * @return the difference of this and frac
 */
public Fraction subtract(Fraction frac) {
    int a, b, c, d;

    Fraction diff;

    a = this.getNumerator();
    b = this.getDenominator();
    c = frac.getNumerator();
    d = frac.getDenominator();

    diff = new Fraction(a*d - b*c, b*d);

    return diff;
}

/**
 * Returns the difference of this Fraction
 * and the int parameter number. The difference
 * returned is NOT simplified.
 *
 * @param number the int value to subtract
 *
 * @return the difference of this and number
 */

public Fraction subtract(int number) {

    Fraction frac = new Fraction(number, 1);

    Fraction difference = subtract(frac);

    return difference;
}
```

simplify

subtract

subtract

```
    /**
     * Returns the String representation of this Fraction
     *
     * @return the String representation of this Fraction
     */
    public String toString( ) {

        return getNumerator() + "/" + getDenominator();
    }

    //-----------------------------------------
    // Private Methods
    //
    //-----------------------------------------

    //**
     * Returns the decimal equivalent of this fraction
     *
     * @return the decimal equivalent of this fraction
     */
    private double decimal( ) {
       //returns the decimal equivalent
       return (double) getNumerator() / getDenominator();
    }
}
```

toString

decimal

7.9 Sample Development

Library Overdue Checker

How many library books are lying around in your room waiting to be returned? How much have you accrued in late charges on those overdue books? Let's write a program that computes the total charges for overdue library books. The program allows you to input the title, overdue charge per day, maximum possible charge, and due date for each book you enter. The due date is the only required input. The other three input values are optional, and when they are not provided, preset default values are used by the program. We assume that an upper limit is set for overdue charges, so your charge will not increase beyond this limit. This limit is entered as the maximum possible charge. For example, a library may set \$1.50 as the overdue charge per day and \$30 as the maximum overdue charge for a single overdue book. We enter the overdue charge per day and the maximum overdue charge for every book, because depending on the types of books, they could be different. For example, a charge for books with a 3-day loan period may be much higher than for books with a regular 2-week loan period.

After you enter information for all books, the program displays the entered book data. Then the program will allow you to enter different return dates. For each return date you enter, the program will display the total overdue charges. Being able to enter different return dates will let you make an informed decision, such as "I'll wait till tomorrow since it's raining heavily today and it costs only $2 more if I return them tomorrow." (We always encourage you to return library books promptly for the sake of fellow library users.)

A better program will warn you when there's a looming due date so you won't end up paying the overdue charges. We will discuss this and other possible extensions at the end of this section. All the possible extensions we will discuss require techniques yet to be studied. The program we develop here is implemented by the techniques we have already mastered and by using one simple helper class.

Problem Statement

Write an application that computes the total charges for the overdue library books. For each library book, the user enters the due date and (optionally) the overdue charge per day, the maximum charge, and the title. If the optional values are not entered, then the preset default values are used. A complete list of book information is displayed when the user finishes entering the input data. The user can enter different return dates to compare the overdue charges.

Overall Plan

As always, we begin our overall plan for the development with the outline of program logic. We first let the user enter the information on all books. After finishing the book data entry, we display them as a list. Then we ask repeatedly for return dates. For each return date entered, we provide the total overdue charge. We express the program flow as having three tasks:

program tasks

1. Get the information for all books.
2. Display the entered book data.
3. Ask for the return date and display the total charge. Repeat this step until the user quits.

Let's look at each task and determine objects required for handling the task. The first step sounds simple enough, but it hides the complexity of the whole program. It indicates the need for at least three types of objects. One is to carry out the actual input routines, another is to retain four pieces of information for each book, and yet another is to keep track of multiple books entered by the user. Notice that there's no limit on the number of books the user can enter, because putting such a limit will reduce the usability of the program. This means we need a class to manage a collection of book information. We have not yet learned how to manage a collection of objects (Chap. 10 covers the topic), so we will use the helper class named **BookTracker.** This class is actually very straightforward, once we learn the relevant topic. The class is written generically and does not contain much application-specific logic.

We will define a class named **LibraryBook** that keeps track of book information. An instance of this class represents a single library book. The **LibraryBook** class is the key worker bee in this program. A **LibraryBook** object keeps track of four pieces of information and is responsible for computing the overdue charge. Notice that the class is the

7.9 Sample Development—*continued*

most appropriate place to perform the computation of the overdue charge because it is where all pieces of information necessary to compute the charge are stored.

We will define another class for performing the actual input routines. An instance of this class will input the data, create a **LibraryBook** object with the input data, and add this object to a **BookTracker.** As it uses other objects, it will be the main controller of the program. We will name the class **OverdueChecker.** We will define it as an instantiable main class. For this program, we will use console input. It is a straightforward exercise to modify the **OverdueChecker** class to handle input by using **JOptionPane** or other types of GUI.

Now let's study the second task of displaying the entered book data. To be consistent with the console input, we will use console output. An **OverdueChecker** will handle the output, but the data to display come from a **BookTracker,** as it is the one maintaining the collection of **LibraryBook** objects. The **BookTracker** class has one method called **getBookList.** This method returns the book list as a single String value. The **OverdueChecker** displays the returned string on the standard output window. Notice that the **BookTracker** class is not programmed to do the output directly, because doing so will reduce its usability. By returning the book list as a **String** datum, the client of the **Book-Tracker** class retains the option of using either console output or GUI. This helps to keep the flexibility and increases the usability of a class.

For the last task, an **OverdueChecker** interacts with the user to get the return dates. For each return date entered, it asks **BookTracker** for the total charge and displays the returned value. The **BookTracker** in turn asks individual **LibraryBook** objects for their charges by calling the **computeCharge** method and computes the sum. This is the reason why we must include the method named **computeCharge** in the **LibraryBook** class that computes the overdue charge for a single book. We will discuss the details of this and other requirements in defining the **LibraryBook** class shortly.

Here's our working design document:

program classes

Design Document: Library `OverdueChecker`

Class	Purpose
`OverdueChecker`	The top-level control object that manages other objects in the program. This is an instantiable main class, as explained in Section 4.10.
`BookTracker`	The predefined helper class that keeps track of library books.
`LibraryBook`	An instance of this class represents a single library book. A library book for this program has four properties—title, charge per day, maximum charge, and due date. It is also responsible for computing the overdue charges.
`Scanner`	The standard class for handling input routines.

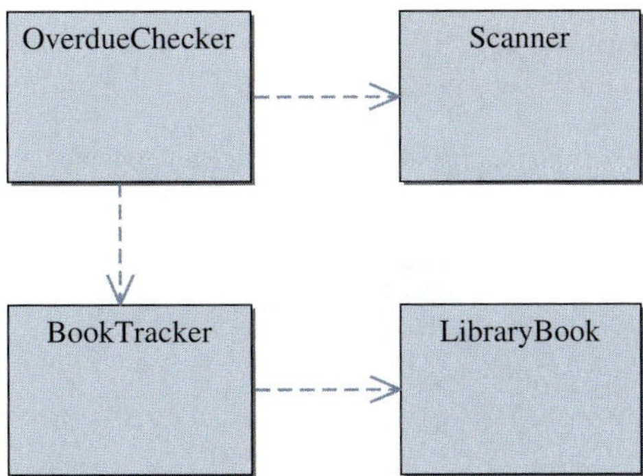

Figure 7.11 The program diagram for the **OverdueChecker** program. We will implement the **OverdueChecker** and **LibraryBook** classes. The **Scanner** class is the standard class for console input, and the **BookTracker** class is the helper class provided for this program.

Figure 7.11 is the program diagram for this program.

We will implement this program in the following five major steps:

develop-ment steps

1. Define the basic **LibraryBook** class. Use a test main class to confirm the implementation of the **LibraryBook** class.
2. Explore the given **BookTracker** class and integrate it with the **LibraryBook** class. Modify or extend the **LibraryBook** class as necessary.
3. Define the top-level **OverdueChecker** class. Implement the complete input routines. Modify or extend the **LibraryBook** class as necessary.
4. Complete the **LibraryBook** class by fully implementing the overdue charge computation.
5. Finalize the program by tying up loose ends.

Again, the development strategy we indicate here is one of the possible alternatives. We could start from the skeleton main controller class **OverdueChecker,** as we normally did in the previous sample development examples. For this program, however, we start with the **LibraryBook** class because of its importance in the program. We want to start from the most important workhorse class. Also, before we implement any elaborate input and output routines, we need to know how the **BookTracker** class works, and to explore this helper class fully, we need the **LibraryBook** class.

Step 1 Development: The Basic `LibraryBook` class

step 1 design

We begin the development with the basic **LibraryBook** class. The main purpose in step 1 is to start with the main workhorse class to establish the foundation for the development. Since this class is used by the **BookTracker** class, we need to find out the compatibility requirements so we won't define any methods that will violate the compatibility. There are two methods used by the **BookTracker** class, so we need to define them in the **LibraryBook** class. Here are the two required methods and their descriptions:

Required Methods of `LibraryBook`

`public String toString( )`
Returns the **String** representation of itself. This string is used by the **BookTracker** class to generate a complete book list.
`public double computeCharge(GregorianCalendar returnDate)`
Computes and returns the overdue charge for this book, given the return date.

The key design task for this step is to identify the data members for storing relevant information and to define their accessors and mutators as appropriate. Also, we will design multiple constructors so an instance of this class can be created in a flexible manner.

We define data members for the four pieces of required information for each book as follows:

```
private GregorianCalendar dueDate;

private String title;

private double chargePerDay;

private double maximumCharge;
```

For each of these data members, we will define the corresponding accessors and mutators.

We define four constructors. Because the due date is something that must be assigned when a new **LibraryBook** is created, every constructor requires the due date as its argument. When other optional values are not passed to the constructor, then preset default values are assigned. We define the multiple constructors using the technique we learned in this chapter. The signatures for these constructors are as follows:

```
public LibraryBook(GregorianCalendar dueDate)

public LibraryBook(GregorianCalendar dueDate,
                   double chargePerDay)

public LibraryBook(GregorianCalendar dueDate,
                   double chargePerDay,
                   double maximumCharge)

public LibraryBook(GregorianCalendar dueDate,
                   double chargePerDay,
                   double maximumCharge,
                   String title)
```

We won't be using the **BookTracker** class in this step, so we do not have to define the two required methods yet. However, we can use the **toString** method now to verify the correct operations of constructors and other methods, so we define it now. We use the formatting techniques learned in Section 6.8 to format the string we return from **toString.** Here's how we define the **toString** method:

```
public String toString( ) {

   return String.format(
          "%-30s   $%5.2f   $%7.2f   %4$tm/%4$td/%4$ty",
          getTitle(), getChargePerDay(),
          getMaxCharge(), dueDate.getTime());
}
```

A sample string returned from the method will formatted in the following manner:

```
Introduction to OOP with Java  $ 0.75  $ 50.00  07/10/06
```

Alternatively, we can format the string by using the **SimpleDateFormat** and **DecimalFormat** classes.

```
public String toString( ) {

   String tab = "\t";

   SimpleDateFormat sdf
                     = new SimpleDateFormat("MM/dd/yy");
   DecimalFormat    df = new DecimalFormat("0.00");

   return getTitle() + tab + "$ " +
            df.format(getChargePerDay()) + tab + "$ " +
            df.format(getMaxCharge()) + tab +
            sdf.format(dueDate.getTime());
}
```

step 1 code

We are now ready to implement the class. Here's the step 1 code (minus javadoc and most other comments):

```
/*
   Chapter 7 Library Overdue Checker

   Step 1 LibraryBook class

   File: LibraryBook.java
*/
```

7.9 Sample Development—*continued*

```
import java.util.*;

class LibraryBook {

    private static final double CHARGE_PER_DAY = 0.50;

    private static final double MAX_CHARGE = 50.00;

    private static final String DEFAULT_TITLE = "Title unknown";


    private GregorianCalendar dueDate;

    private String title;

    private double chargePerDay;

    private double maximumCharge;

    public LibraryBook(GregorianCalendar dueDate) {

        this(dueDate, CHARGE_PER_DAY);
    }

    public LibraryBook(GregorianCalendar dueDate,
                       double chargePerDay) {

        this(dueDate, chargePerDay, MAX_CHARGE);
    }

    public LibraryBook(GregorianCalendar dueDate,
                       double chargePerDay,
                       double maximumCharge) {

        this(dueDate, chargePerDay,
                maximumCharge, DEFAULT_TITLE);
    }

    public LibraryBook(GregorianCalendar dueDate,
                       double chargePerDay,
                       double maximumCharge,
                       String title) {

        setDueDate(dueDate);
        setChargePerDay(chargePerDay);
        setMaximumCharge(maximumCharge);
        setTitle(title);
    }

    public double getChargePerDay( ) {
        return chargePerDay;
    }
```

```
    public GregorianCalendar getDueDate( ) {
        return dueDate;
    }

    public double getMaxCharge( ) {
        return maximumCharge;
    }

    public String getTitle( ) {
        return title;
    }

    public void setChargePerDay(double charge) {
        chargePerDay = charge;
    }

    public void setDueDate(GregorianCalendar date) {
        dueDate = date;
    }

    public void setMaximumCharge(double charge) {
        maximumCharge = charge;
    }

    public void setTitle(String title) {
        this.title = title;
    }

    public String toString( ) {
        return String.format(
                        "%-30s  $%5.2f  $%7.2f  %4$tm/%4$td/%4$ty",
                        getTitle(), getChargePerDay(),
                        getMaxCharge(), dueDate.getTime());
    }
}
```

step 1 test

The purpose of step 1 testing is to verify we can create **LibraryBook** objects using different constructors. In addition, we check that the other methods are working correctly, especially the **toString** method. Here's one possible test main class:

```
/*
    Introduction to OOP with Java 4th ed., McGraw-Hill

    File: Step1/Step1Main.java
*/
```

7.9 Sample Development—*continued*

```
import java.util.*;

class Step1Main {

    public static void main( String[] args ) {

        //Create three LibraryBook objects and output them
        GregorianCalendar dueDate;
        LibraryBook book1, book2, book3, book4;

        dueDate = new GregorianCalendar(2006, Calendar.MARCH, 14);
        book1   = new LibraryBook(dueDate);

        dueDate = new GregorianCalendar(2006, Calendar.FEBRUARY, 13);
        book2   = new LibraryBook(dueDate, 0.75);
        book2.setTitle("Introduction to oop with Java");

        dueDate = new GregorianCalendar(2006, Calendar.JANUARY, 12);
        book3   = new LibraryBook(dueDate, 1.00, 100.00);
        book3.setTitle("Java for Smarties");

        dueDate = new GregorianCalendar(2006, Calendar.JANUARY, 1);
        book4   = new LibraryBook(dueDate, 1.50, 230.00,
                                               "Me and My Java");

        System.out.println(book1.toString());
        System.out.println(book2.toString());
        System.out.println(book3.toString());
        System.out.println(book4.toString());
    }
}
```

Running this program will produce the following output on the standard output window:

```
Title unknown                      $ 0.50     $  50.00      03/14/06
Introduction to OOP with Java      $ 0.75     $  50.00      02/13/06
Java for Smarties                  $ 1.00     $ 100.00      01/12/06
Me and My Java                     $ 1.50     $ 230.00      01/01/06
```

Step 2 Development: Integrate the BookTracker Class into the Program

step 2 design

In the second development step, we will bring in the helper **BookTracker** class into the program. Our main concern in this step is to understand how to interact with a **BookTracker** object correctly and adjust the **LibraryBook** class, as necessary, to make it compatible with the **BookTracker** class.

The **BookTracker** class is actually a fairly straightforward class. You are encouraged to view the source file of the class. To understand the class fully, you need to learn about an **ArrayList,** a topic covered in Chapter 10. But even without this knowledge, you should be able to understand the majority of the code when you view the source file. We will discuss the implementation of the **BookTracker** class in Chapter 10. Here's the class description:

BookTracker
An instance of this class maintains a list of **LibraryBook** objects.
`public BookTracker( )` Creates a new instance of the class.
`public void add( LibraryBook book )` Adds **book** to the book list it maintains.
`public double getCharge( )` Returns the total overdue charge for the books in the list. Uses today as the return date.
`public double getCharge( GregorianCalendar returnDate )` Returns the total overdue charge for the books in the list. The parameter is the date the book is to be returned.
`public String getList( )` Returns information on all books in the list as a single string.

As stated in step 1, the **BookTracker** class requires two specific methods in the **LibraryBook** class. We already defined the **toString** method. Since we will be implementing the full **computeCharge** method in step 4, we define a stub method for this step as

```
public double computeCharge( GregorianCalendar returnDate){

   return 1.00; //Stub method for Step 2
}
```

To check our understanding on how to interact with the **BookTracker** class, we will write a test main class. From this main class, we will create and add multiple book objects to the book tracker and experiment with the **getList** and **getCharge** methods.

step 2 code

The only change we make to the **LibraryBook** class is the addition of the stub **computeCharge** method, so the **BookTracker** class can be integrated with it. To test

7.9 Sample Development—*continued*

the **BookTracker** class, we define a test main class that checks the cases when the book list is empty and has 20 books. Here's the test main class:

```
/*
    Introduction to OOP with Java 4th ed., McGraw-Hill

    File: Step2/Step2Main.java

*/
import java.util.*;

class Step2Main {

    public static void main( String[] args ) {

        //Create 20 LibraryBook objects
        BookTracker bookTracker = new BookTracker();

        GregorianCalendar dueDate, returnDate;
        LibraryBook book;

        returnDate = new GregorianCalendar(2006, Calendar.MARCH, 15);

        //Check the error condition
        System.out.println("Error: No books added. Return code - " +
                           bookTracker.getCharge(returnDate));

        System.out.println("Output for empty book list:\n" +
                           bookTracker.getList( ));

        //Add 20 books
        System.out.println("\nAdding 20 books...\n");

        for (int i = 0; i < 20; i++) {

            dueDate = new GregorianCalendar(2006, Calendar.MARCH, i+1);

            book = new LibraryBook(dueDate);
            book.setTitle("Book Number " + (i+1));

            bookTracker.add(book);
        }

        System.out.println("Total Charge: $"
                               + bookTracker.getCharge(returnDate));
        System.out.println("\n");
        System.out.println("List: \n" + bookTracker.getList());
    }
}
```

step 2 test

We run the test main class and verify that we get the expected results. We will try other variations to increase our confidence before continuing to the next step.

Step 3 Development: Define the OverdueChecker Class

step 3 design

After the working **LibraryBook** and **BookTracker** classes, we are now ready to start implementing the top-level controller class. Besides managing a single **BookTracker** object and multiple **LibraryBook** objects, an **OverdueChecker** object's main responsibility is the handling of input and output routines. As dictated in the problem statement, we have to first input information on books and then repeatedly ask the user for return dates. Expressing this logic in pseudocode, we have

```
GregorianCalendar returnDate;

String  reply, table;
double  totalCharge;

inputBooks(); //read in all book information

table = bookTracker.getList();
System.out.println(table);

//try different return dates
do {

     returnDate = read return date ;

     totalCharge = bookTracker.getCharge(returnDate);

     displayTotalCharge(totalCharge);

     reply = prompt the user to continue or not;

} while ( reply is yes );
```

The body of the **inputBooks** method will include a loop that reads information for one book on each repetition. The method body can be expressed thus:

```
while (isContinue()) {

   title        = readString("Title         : ");
   chargePerDay = readDouble("Charge per day: ");
   maxCharge    = readDouble("Maximum charge: ");
   dueDate      = readDate  ("Due Date      : ");

   book = createBook(title, chargePerDay,
                         maxCharge, dueDate);

   bookTracker.add(book);
}
```

Notice that there are three types of input data, and we define a method for each type, namely, **readDouble, readDate,** and **readString.** These methods read input from a scanner (console input) after prompting the user.

7.9 Sample Development—*continued*

Code to handle the input of **String** and **double** values is straightforward, but the one to handle the input of the date requires some thinking. We need to decide in which format the user can enter the date. For instance, should we prompt for the year, month, and day individually? This may be acceptable if you enter the date once. When you have to input date information many times, this input routine gets tedious. For this application, we will require the user to enter the date correctly as a single string value in the **MM/dd/yyyy** format. Given a string value in this format, we use a sequence of substring methods to break it down into three pieces—month, day, and year. This operation is similar to the one we used in the Chapter 2 sample application. Then we use the **Integer.parseInt** method, introduced in Chapter 3, to convert them to **int** values. From these three **int** values, we finally create and return a **GregorianCalendar** object that represents the entered date.

After the four values are entered, a new book is created via the **createBook** method. This method handles the situation when the input value is empty. For example, the user may press only the Enter key if she wants default values for the single-day charge and maximum possible charge.

step 3 code

The other methods are straightforward, so we'll refer you to the complete class listing without further explanation. Here's the instantiable main class **OverdueChecker:**

```
/*
    Chapter 7 Library Overdue Checker

    Step 3 Implement the Main Controller

*/

import java.util.*;

class OverdueChecker {

    private static enum Response {YES, NO}

    private static final String DATE_SEPARATOR = "/";

    private Scanner scanner;

    private BookTracker  bookTracker;

//-------------------------------------------------
//    Constructors
//-------------------------------------------------

    public OverdueChecker() {

        scanner = new Scanner(System.in);
```

```
        scanner.useDelimiter(System.getProperty("line.separator"));

        bookTracker = new BookTracker();
    }

//-------------------------------------------------
//    Main Method
//-------------------------------------------------

    public static void main(String[] args) {

        OverdueChecker checker = new OverdueChecker();
        checker.start();
    }

//-------------------------------------------------
//      Public Methods
//-------------------------------------------------

    public void start( ) {

        GregorianCalendar returnDate;

        String   table;
        double   charge;
        Response response;

        inputBooks();

        table = bookTracker.getList();
        System.out.println(table);

        System.out.println("\nNow check the over due charges...\n");

        //try different return dates

        do {

            //read return date
            returnDate = readDate("\nReturn Date: ");

            charge = bookTracker.getCharge(returnDate);

            displayTotalCharge(charge);

            response = prompt("\nRun Again (yes/no)? ");

        } while (response == Response.YES);

        System.out.println(
                  "\n\nThank you for using Library Overdue Checker");
    }

//-------------------------------------------------
//      Private Methods
//-------------------------------------------------
```

7.9 Sample Development—*continued*

```
private LibraryBook createBook(String title,
                               double chargePerDay,
                               double maxCharge,
                               GregorianCalendar dueDate) {
    if (dueDate == null) {
        dueDate = new GregorianCalendar(); //set today as due date
    }

    LibraryBook book = new LibraryBook(dueDate);

    if (title.length() > 0) {
        book.setTitle(title);
    }

    if (chargePerDay > 0.0) {
        book.setChargePerDay(chargePerDay);
    }

    if (maxCharge > 0.0) {
        book.setMaximumCharge(maxCharge);
    }

    return book;
}

private void display(String text) {
    System.out.print(text);
}

private void displayTotalCharge(double charge) {

    System.out.format("\nTOTAL CHARGE:\t $%8.2f", charge);
}

private void inputBooks( ) {

    double chargePerDay, maxCharge;
    String title;

    GregorianCalendar dueDate;
    LibraryBook       book;

    //Keeps on reading input from a console
    //until stopped by the end user

    while (isContinue()) {
        System.out.println("\n");

        title        = readString("Title         : ");
        chargePerDay = readDouble("Charge per day: ");
```

```
            maxCharge     = readDouble("Maximum charge: ");
            dueDate       = readDate  ("Due Date       : ");

            book = createBook(title, chargePerDay,
                              maxCharge, dueDate);

            bookTracker.add(book);

        }
    }

    private boolean isContinue( )  {

        Response response = prompt("\nMore books to enter (y/n)?");

        return (response == Response.YES);
    }

    private Response prompt(String question) {

        String input;

        Response response = Response.NO;

        System.out.print(question + " (Yes - y; No - n): ");

        input = scanner.next();

        if (input.equals("Y") || input.equals("y")) {
            response = Response.YES;
        }

        return response;
    }

    private double readDouble(String prompt) {

        display(prompt);

        return scanner.nextDouble();
    }

    private GregorianCalendar readDate( String prompt) {

        GregorianCalendar cal;

        String yearStr, monthStr, dayStr, line;

        int    sep1, sep2;

        display(prompt);

        line = scanner.next();
```

7.9 Sample Development—*continued*

```
        if (line.length() == 0) {
            cal = null;
        } else {

            sep1 = line.indexOf(DATE_SEPARATOR);
            sep2 = line.lastIndexOf(DATE_SEPARATOR);

            monthStr = line.substring(0, sep1);
            dayStr   = line.substring(sep1 + 1, sep2);
            yearStr  = line.substring(sep2 + 1, line.length());

            cal = new GregorianCalendar(Integer.parseInt(yearStr),
                                        Integer.parseInt(monthStr)-1,
                                        Integer.parseInt(dayStr));
        }

        return cal;
    }

    private String readString(String prompt) {

        display(prompt);

        return scanner.next();
    }
}
```

step 3 test

Now we run the program multiple times, trying different input types and values. We also confirm that all control loops are implemented and working correctly. At this point, the code to compute the overdue charge is still a stub, so we will always get the same overdue charge for the same number of books. After we verify that everything is working as expected, we proceed to the next step.

Step 4 Development: Compute the Overdue Charge

step 4 design

In step 4, we complete the stub method that computes the overdue charge in the **LibraryBook** class. We have two **GregorianCalendar** objects for the due date and the return date. We first need to find out the number of days between the two. We then multiply this number by the amount of charge per day to derive the total overdue charge. If this amount is more than the maximum possible charge, then the total charge is reset to this maximum value. Also, we need to check for the situation in which the return date has not passed the due date. The logic of this process is a simple computation once we find out the number of days between the two dates. So, how can we find it?

design alternative 1

Reviewing the **GregorianCalendar** class, we see the **get** method can be used to retrieve different pieces of date information, such as year, month, and day. Using the method, we can get the month, day, and year information for two dates and compare these values. It may sound easy, but things can get tricky very quickly. Complexity arises from the facts that not every month has the same number of days and that the number of days for February can vary from year to year. This approach is doable, but not recommended.

design alternative 2

When we explore the class further, we notice there's another method, namely **getTime,** that returns a **Date** object. In Chapter 6, we used this **Date** class to compute the execution time of a loop by finding the difference between the start and end times. We can apply the same technique here. But instead of using the **getTime** method, we can actually use the **getTimeInMillis** method and bypass the **Date** class altogether. The **getTimeInMillis** method returns the time elasped since the epoch to the date in milliseconds. By subtracting this since-the-epoch milliseconds value of the due date from the same of the return date, we can find the difference between the two. If the difference is negative, then it's not past due, so there's no charge. If the difference is positive, then we convert the milliseconds to the equivalent number of days and multiply it by the per-day charge to compute the total charge. Here's a simple way to do the conversion:

```
private static final double MILLISEC_TO_DAY
                        = 1.0 / 1000 / 60 / 60 / 24;
...
dayCnt = millisec * MILLISEC_TO_DAY;
```

step 4 code

We will adopt the second approach. Here's the final **computeCharge** method of the **LibraryBook** class:

```
public double computeCharge(GregorianCalendar returnDate){

   double charge = 0.0;

   long dueTime = dueDate.getTimeInMillis();
   long returnTime = returnDate.getTimeInMillis();

   long diff = returnTime - dueTime;

   if (diff > 0) {
      charge = chargePerDay * diff * MILLISEC_TO_DAY;

      if (charge > maximumCharge) {
          charge = maximumCharge;
      }
   }

   return charge;
}
```

step 4 test

We run the program mutiple times again, possibly using the same set of input data. We enter different input variations to try out all possible cases for the **computeCharge**

7.9 Sample Development—*continued*

method. Try cases such as the return date and due date are the same, the return date occurs before the due date, the charge is beyond the maximum, and so forth. After we verify the program, we move on to the next step.

Step 5 Development: Tying Up the Loose Ends and Future Extensions

program review

As always, we will perform a critical review of the program, looking for any unfinished method, inconsistency or error in the methods, unclear or missing comments, and so forth. We should also not forget to improve the program for cleaner code and better readability. This is especially true for the input routines. Are all the possible cases handled? Are the input routines easy to use? Will it be better if we allow different formats for entering the date information?

possible extensions

We stated at the beginning of this section that it would be a better program if it warned the user, say, by popping a warning window or ringing an alarm, when the due date was approaching. Using this extended program, we enter the book data at the time we check out the book from the library. The program will store the entered information in a file, so we don't have to reenter the same data whenever we want to find out the total overdue charge. We can execute the program daily and be warned about the looming due dates. We can still run the program to find out the charges for the overdue books. Techniques necessary to implement such an extended program are covered in the later chapters of this book.

Summary

- When a method returns an object, it is actually returning a reference to this object.
- The reserved word this is used to refer to a receiving object of a message from within this object's method.
- A class may include multiple methods with the same name as long as their signatures are different. The signature of a method refers to the name of the method and the number and data types of its parameters. They are called overloaded methods.
- A class may include multiple constructors as long as their signatures are different. They are called overloaded constructors.
- A constructor can call another constructor of the same class using the reserved word this.
- Class variables and class methods are declared by using the reserved word static.
- Class methods can access only the class variables and the class constants.

- Instance methods can access all types of data members (i.e., both class and instance components).
- Arguments are passed to the methods by using the call-by-value scheme in which the value of an argument is passed. The value is the actual data in the case of a primitive data type and a reference to an object in the case of a reference data type.
- Programmer-defined classes can be grouped into a programmer-defined package.
- The javadoc comment is the third style of comments used in Java. From the javadoc comments in a class, a tool can generate its documentation in the HTML format.

Key Concepts

returning objects from methods
self referencing pointer (this)
overloaded methods
method signatures
multiple constructors
copy constructors
static initializers
call-by-value scheme
programmer-defined packages
javadoc comments

Exercises

1. Consider the following classes.

```
class Cat {
   private String name;
   private Breed  breed;
   private double weight;

   public Cat(String name, Breed breed, double weight){
      this.name = name;
      this.breed = breed;
      this.weight = weight;
   }

   public Breed getBreed() {
      return breed;
   }

   public double getWeight() {
      return weight;
   }

   //other accessors and mutators
   . . .
}
```

```
class Breed {

   private String name;
   private double averageWgt; //in lbs.

   public Breed(String name, double averageWgt){
      this.name = name;
      this.averageWgt = averageWgt;
   }

   public double getWeight( ) {
      return averageWgt;
   }

   //other accessors and mutators
   . . .
}
```

Identify the invalid statements in the following main class. For each invalid statement, state why it is invalid.

```
class Q1Main {
   public static void main(String[] args ) {

      Breed persian = new Breed("Persian", 10.0);

      Cat chacha = new Cat("Cha Cha", persian, 12.0);

      Cat bombom = new Cat("Bom Bom", "mix", 10.0);

      Cat puffpuff = new Cat("Puff Puff", chacha, 9.0);

      double diff = chacha.getWeight()
                       - persian.getWeight();

      System.out.println(
             puffpuff.getBreed().getWeight());
   }
}
```

2. Given the **Cat** and **Breed** classes from Exercise 1, what will be the output from the following code?

```
class Q2Main {
   public static void main(String[] args) {

      Cat myCat = new Cat("winky",
                     new Breed("mix", 10.5), 9.5);

      System.out.println(myCat.getWeight());
      System.out.println(myCat.getBreed().getWeight());
   }
}
```

3. Given the Fraction class from Section 7.8, draw the state-of-memory diagram at the point immediately after the last statement is executed.

```
Fraction f1, f2, f3;

f1 = new Fraction(3, 8);
f2 = new Fraction(2, 3);
f3 = f1.add(f2);
```

4. Consider the following class.

```
class Dog {
    . . .
    private double weight;
    . . .
    public boolean isBiggerThan(Dog buddy) {
        return this.getWeight() > buddy.getWeight();
    }

    public double getWeight() {
        return weight;
    }
    . . .
}
```

For each of the following codes, complete the state-of-memory diagram by filling in the arrows for this and buddy.

a.
```
Dog tuffy = new Dog(...);
Dog puffy = new Dog(...);

puffy.isBiggerThan(tuffy);
```

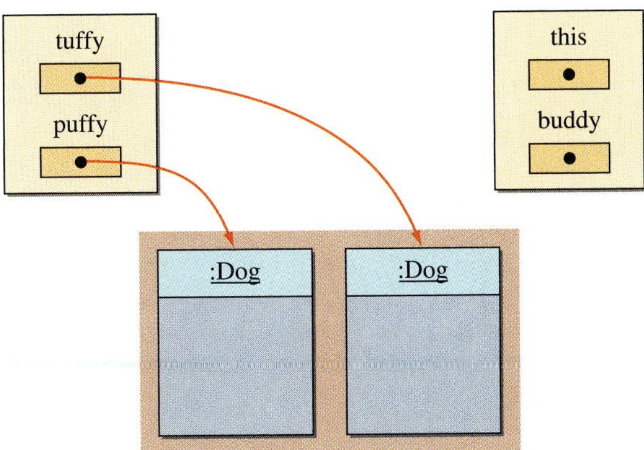

b.
```
Dog tuffy = new Dog(...);
Dog puffy = new Dog(...);

tuffy.isBiggerThan(puffy);
```

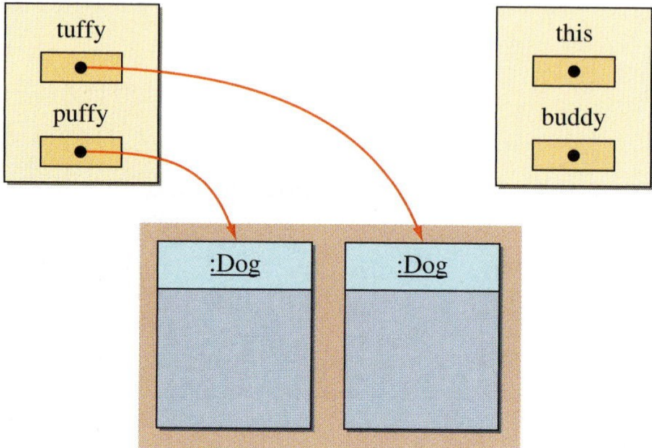

5. Complete the following constructor.

```
class Student {
   private String  name;
   private int     age;
   private Address address;

   public Student(String name, int age, Address address){

      //assign passed values to the data members
   }
```

6. Which of the following groups of overloaded constructors are valid?

a.
```
public Cat(int age) { ... }
public Cat(double wgt) { ... }
```

b.
```
public Dog(String name, double weight) { ... }
public Dog(String name, double height) { ... }
```

c.
```
public Dog(String name, double weight) { ... }
public Dog(double weight, String name) { ... }
```

d.
```
public Cat(String name) { ... }
public Cat(String name, double weight) { ... }
public Cat(double weight) { ... }
```

7. Which of the following groups of overloaded methods are valid?

a.
```
public void compute(int num) { ... }
public int  compute(double num) { ... }
```

b.
```
public void move(double length) { ... }
public void move( ) { ... }
```

c.
```
public int  adjust(double amount) { ... }
public void adjust(double amount, double charge) { ... }
```

d.
```
public void doWork( ) { ... }
public void doWork(String name) { ... }
public int  doWork(double num) { ... }
```

8. Complete the first four constructors of the following class. Each of the four constructors calls the fifth one by using the reserved word this.

```
class Cat {
   private static final String DEFAULT_NAME = "No name";
   private static final int    DEFAULT_HGT  = 6;
   private static final double DEFAULT_WGT  = 10.0;

   private String name;
   private int    height;
   private double weight;

   public Cat( ) {
      //assign defaults to all data members
   }

   public Cat(String name) {
      //assign the passed name to the data member
      //use defaults for height and weight
   }

   public Cat(String name, int height) {
      //assign passed values to name and height
      //use default for weight
   }

   public Cat(String name, double weight) {
      //assign passed values to name and weight
      //use default for height
   }

   public Cat(String name, int height, double weight){
      this.name = name;
      this.height = height;
      this.weight = weight;
   }

   ...
}
```

9. Define a class method (static) named compare to the Fraction class. The compare method accepts two Fraction objects f1 and f2. The method returns

-1	if f1 is less than f2
0	if f1 is equal to f2
+1	if f1 is greater than f2

10. Rewrite the compare method from Exercise 9 by changing it to an instance method. This method accepts a Fraction object and compares it to the receiving object. The method is declared as follows:

```
public int compare(Fraction frac) {

   //compare the Fraction objects this and frac
   //return the result of comparison
}
```

11. Discuss the pros and cons of the compare methods from Exercise 8 and Exercise 9.

12. Consider the following class.

```
class Modifier {
   public static change(int x, int y){
      x = x - 10;
      y = y + 10;
   }
}
```

What will be an output from the following code?

```
int x = 40;
int y = 20;

Modifier.change(x,y);

System.out.println("x = " + x);
System.out.println("y = " + y);
```

13. Modify the following class to make it a part of the package named myutil. In addition to adjusting the source file, what are the steps you need to take so that the class becomes usable/accessible from other classes that are outside of this myutil package?

```
class Person {

   private String name;

   public Person( ) {
      name = "Unknown";
   }

   public String getName() {
      return name;
   }

   public void setName(String name) {
      this.name = name;
   }
}
```

14. (*Optional*) Although we have not discussed the internal workings of the BookTracker class, it is not too difficult to realize the portion that handles the

generation of book list. Define a new method called getListWithCharge based on the getList method. Generate a book list as the getList method does, but include the overdue charge for each book also.

15. Design a class that keeps track of a student's food purchases at the campus cafeteria. A meal card is assigned to an individual student. When a meal card is first issued, the balance is set to the number of points. If the student does not specify the number of points, then the initial balance is set to 100 points. Points assigned to each food item are a whole number. A student can purchase additional points at any time during a semester. Every time food items are bought, points are deducted from the balance. If the balance becomes negative, the purchase of food items is not allowed. There is obviously more than one way to implement the MealCard class. Any design that supports the key functionalities is acceptable.

Development Exercises

For the following exercises, use the incremental development methodology to implement the program. For each exercise, identify the program tasks, create a design document with class descriptions, and draw the program diagram. Map out the development steps at the start. Present any design alternatives and justify your selection. Be sure to perform adequate testing at the end of each development step.

16. Write an application that plays the game of Fermi. Generate three distinct random digits between 0 and 9. These digits are assigned to positions 1, 2, and 3. The goal of the game is for the player to guess the digits in three positions correctly in the least number of tries. For each guess, the player provides three digits for positions 1, 2, and 3. The program replies with a hint consisting of Fermi, Pico, or Nano. If the digit guessed for a given position is correct, then the reply is Fermi. If the digit guessed for a given position is in a different position, the reply is Pico. If the digit guessed for a given position does not match any of the three digits, then the reply is Nano. Here are sample replies for the three secret digits 6, 5, and 8 at positions 1, 2, and 3, respectively:

Guess	Hint	Explanation
1 2 5	Nano Nano Pico	The value 5 matches but at the wrong position.
8 5 3	Pico Fermi Nano	The value 5 matches at the correct position. The value 8 matches but at the wrong position.
5 8 6	Pico Pico Pico	All match at the wrong positions.

Notice that if the hints like the above are given, the player can tell which number did not match. For example, given the hint for the second guess, we can tell that 3 is not one of the secret numbers. To avoid this, provide hints in a random order or in alphabetical order (e.g., it will be Fermi Nano Pico instead of Pico Fermi Nano for the second reply).

Play games repeatedly until the player wants to quit. After each game, display the number of guesses made.

Use javadoc comments to document the classes you design for this application.

17. Write an application that teaches children fraction arithmetic. For each training session, randomly generate 10 questions involving addition, subtraction, division, and multiplication of two fractions. At the beginning of each session, the user has the option of specifying the time limit for answering the questions. If the time limit is not specified, then use 30 s as a default time limit. After you pose a question, wait until the user answers the question. Award points based on the following rules:

Answer	Time	Points
Correct	Under limit	10
Correct	Over limit	6
Wrong	Under limit	3
Wrong	Over limit	0

After one session is over, use the console output to display the grade distribution and the total points in the following manner:

```
                       Under               Over
                       Time Limit          Time Limit

Correct Answers          4                   3

Wrong Answers            2                   1

TOTAL POINTS: 64 (40 + 18 + 6 + 0)
```

After one session is over, give the user the option to play another session.

8 Exceptions and Assertions

Objectives

After you have read and studied this chapter, you should be able to

- Improve the reliability of code by incorporating exception-handling and assertion mechanisms.
- Write methods that propagate exceptions.
- Implement the **try-catch** blocks for catching and handling the thrown exceptions.
- Write programmer-defined exception classes.
- Distinguish between the checked and unchecked, or runtime, exceptions.
- Use assertions in methods to increase the chance of detecting bugs during the development.

Introduction

When someone says his or her program is reliable, what do we expect from the program? The majority of people would probably reply correctness as the most important criterion in determining the reliability of a program. When a program is claimed to be reliable, we certainly expect the program will produce correct results for all valid input. It is hardly a reliable program if it produces correct results only for some input values. As we all know by now, writing a correct program is easier said than done. If we are not diligent and careful enough, we can easily introduce bugs in our programs. And often we fail to eradicate them. A mechanism called an ***assertion*** can be used to improve the likelihood of catching logical errors during the development. We will introduce assertions in this chapter and show how to use them effectively in our programs.

assertion

Program correctness guarantees correct results for all valid input. But what happens when the input is invalid? Another important criterion of program reliability is the robustness, which measures how well the program runs under various conditions. If a program crashes too easily when a wrong type of argument is passed to a method or an invalid input value is entered, we cannot say the program is very reliable. A mechanism called ***exception handling*** can be used to improve the program's robustness. In this chapter, we will describe how to code this exception-handling mechanism in Java to improve the program's robustness.

exception handling

8.1 Catching Exceptions

In Chapters 5 and 6 we presented two types of control flows: selection control and repetition control. Using these control structures, we alter the default sequential flow of control. We use a selection control to select and execute one block of code out of many choices, and we use a repetition control to execute a block of code repeatedly until certain conditions are met. The exception-handling mechanism can be viewed as another form of control structure. An ***exception*** represents an error condition that can occur during the normal course of program execution. When an exception occurs, the normal sequence of flow is terminated and the exception-handling routine is executed. When an exception occurs, we say an exception is *thrown.* When the matching exception-handling code is executed, we say the thrown exception is *caught*. By using exception-handling routines judiciously in our code, we can increase its robustness. In this section, we will show how the thrown exceptions can be caught and processed.

exception

We have been dealing with exceptions all along. For example, consider this code:

```
Scanner scanner = new Scanner(System.in);

System.out.print("Enter integer: ");
int number = scanner.nextInt();
```

What would happen if we entered, say, abc123, an input value that is not an int? We would get an error message like this:

```
Exception in thread "main" java.util.InputMismatchException
   at java.util.Scanner.throwFor(Scanner.java:819)
   at java.util.Scanner.next(Scanner.java:1431)
   at java.util.Scanner.nextInt(Scanner.java:2040)
   at java.util.Scanner.nextInt(Scanner.java:2000)
   at Ch8Sample1.main(Ch8Sample1.java:35)
```

This error message indicates the system has caught an exception called the InputMismatchException, an error that occurs when we try to convert a string that cannot be converted to a numerical value. Up until now, we have let the system handle the thrown exceptions. However, when we let the system handle the exceptions, a single thrown exception most likely will result in erroneous results or a program termination. Instead of depending on the system for exception handling, we can increase the program's reliability and robustness if we catch the exceptions ourselves by including error recovery routines in our program.

Let's begin with a short program to illustrate the exception-handling mechanism. We will define a service class that supports a method to input a person's age. This class is mainly for the illustrative purpose of introducing the exceptionhandling concept.We first define it without exception handling and then improve it gradually by adding exception-handling features. Because we will be defining many different versions of the class, we will name them AgeInputVer1, AgeInputVer2, and so forth. Here's the AgeInputVer1 class without exception handling:

```
/*
   Chapter 8 Sample Class: Class to input age

   File: AgeInputVer1.java
*/

import java.util.*;

class AgeInputVer1 {

    private static final String DEFAULT_MESSAGE = "Your age: ";

    private Scanner scanner;

    public AgeInputVer1( ) {
        scanner = new Scanner(System.in);
    }

    public int getAge() {
        return getAge(DEFAULT_MESSAGE);
    }
```

```
    public int getAge(String prompt) {

        System.out.print(prompt);
        int age = scanner.nextInt();

        return age;
    }
}
```

Using this service class, we can write a program that gets a person's age and replies with the year in which the person was born. Notice the program takes into consideration whether the person already had a birthday this year. Here's the program:

```
/*
   Chapter 8 Sample Program: Input a person's age

   File: Ch8AgeInputMain.java
*/

import java.util.*;

class Ch8AgeInputMain {

    public static void main(String[] args) {

        GregorianCalendar today;

        int age, thisYear, bornYr;

        String answer;

        Scanner scanner = new Scanner(System.in);

        AgeInputVer1 input = new AgeInputVer1( );
        age = input.getAge("How old are you? ");

        today    = new GregorianCalendar( );
        thisYear = today.get(Calendar.YEAR);

        bornYr   = thisYear - age;

        System.out.print("Already had your birthday this year? (Y or N)");
        answer = scanner.next();

        if (answer.equals("N") || answer.equals("n") ) {
            bornYr--;
        }

        System.out.println("\nYou are born in " + bornYr);
    }
}
```

The program works fine as long as valid input is entered. But what happens if the user spells out the age, say, nine instead of 9? An input mismatch exception is thrown because the input value nine cannot be converted to an integer by using the parseInt method. With the current implementation, the system will handle the thrown exception by displaying the error message

```
Exception in thread "main" java.util.InputMismatchException
   at java.util.Scanner.throwFor(Scanner.java:819)
   at java.util.Scanner.next(Scanner.java:1431)
   at java.util.Scanner.nextInt(Scanner.java:2040)
   at java.util.Scanner.nextInt(Scanner.java:2000)
   at AgeInputVer1.getAge(AgeInputVer1.java:48)
   at Ch8AgeInputMain.main(Ch8AgeInputMain.java:30)
```

and terminating the program. It would be a much better program if we could handle the thrown exception ourselves. Let's modify the getAge method so that it will loop until a valid input that can be converted to an integer is entered. To do this, we need to wrap the statements that can potentially throw an exception with the try-catch control statement. In this example, there's only one statement that can potentially throw an exception, namely,

try-catch

```
age = scanner.nextInt();
```

We put this statement inside the try block and the statements we want to be executed in response to the thrown exception in the matching catch block. If we just want to display an error message when the exception is thrown, then we can write the try-catch statement as follows:

```
System.out.print(prompt);

try {

    age = scanner.nextInt();

} catch (InputMismatchException e) {

    System.out.println(
        "Invalid Entry. Please enter digits only.");
}
```

A statement that could throw an exception

The type of exception to be caught

Statements in the try block are executed in sequence. When one of the statements throws an exception, then control is passed to the matching catch block and statements inside the catch block are executed. The execution next continues to the statement that follows this try block statement, ignoring any remaining statements in the try block. If no statements in the try block throw an exception, then the catch block is ignored and execution continues with the statement that follows this

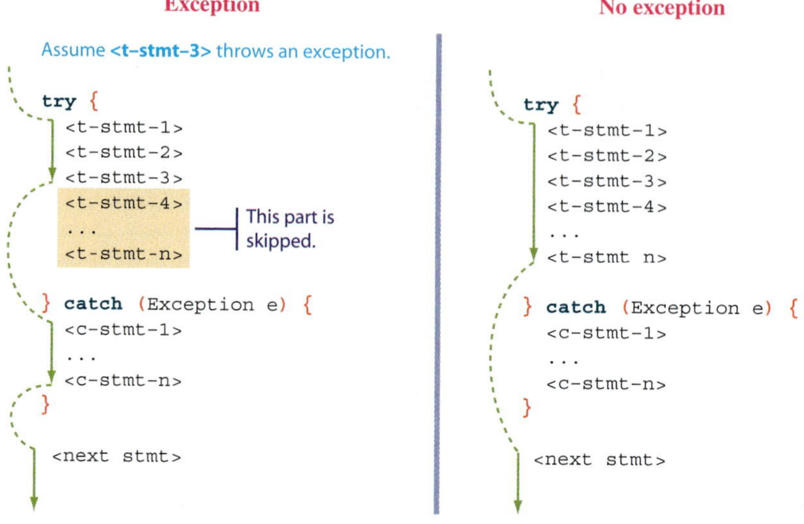

Figure 8.1 Two possible control flows of the **try-catch** statement with one **catch** block. Assume **<t-stmt-3>** throws an exception.

try-catch statement. Figure 8.1 shows the two possible control flows: one when an exception is thrown and another when no exceptions are thrown.

In the sample code, we have only one statement in the try block. If the input statement does not throw an exception, then we want to exit from the method and return the integer. If there's an exception, we display an error message inside the catch block, and repeat the input routine. To accomplish this repetition, we will put the whole try-catch statement inside a loop:

```
public int getAge(String prompt) {

   int age;
   boolean  keepGoing = true;

   while (keepGoing) {

      System.out.print(prompt);

      try {

         age = scanner.nextInt();

         keepGoing = false;

      } catch (InputMismatchException e) {

         scanner.next(); //remove the leftover garbage
                         //from the input buffer

         System.out.println(
```

This statement is executed only if no exception is thrown.

This will remove "garbage" left in the input buffer.

```
                    "Invalid Entry.Please enter digits only.");
            }
        }

        return age;
    }
```

Notice the first statement

```
scanner.next();
```

inside the catch block. It is used to remove any data that remain in the input buffer. When an exception is thrown, an input value that has caused an exception still remains in the input buffer. We need to remove this "garbage" from the input buffer, so we can process the next input value. If we don't include this statement, the code will result in an infinite loop because the nextInt method continues to process the same invalid input.

We can get rid of the boolean variable by rewriting the statement as

```
while (true) {

    System.out.print(prompt);

    try {

        age = scanner.nextInt();

        return age;

    } catch (InputMismatchException e) {

        scanner.next(); //remove the leftover garbage
                        //from the input buffer

        System.out.println(
                "Invalid Entry. Please enter digits only.");
    }
}
```

The improved class with the exception-handling getAge method is named AgeInputVer2.

There are many types of exceptions the system can throw, and we must specify which exception we are catching in the catch block's parameter list (there can be exactly one exception in the list). In the sample code, we are catching the input mismatch exception, and the parameter e represents an instance of the InputMismatchException class. In Java an exception is represented as an instance of the Throwable class or its subclasses. The Throwable class has two subclasses, Error and Exception. The Error class and its subclasses represent serious problems that should not be caught by ordinary applications, while the Exception class and its subclasses represent error conditions that should be caught. So for all practical purposes, we are only interested in the Exception class and its subclasses in our program. Later in the chapter we will learn how to define our own exception classes. We will declare these programmer-defined exception classes as subclasses of the Exception class.

There are two methods defined in the Throwable class that we can call to get some information about the thrown exception: getMessage and printStackTrace. We can call these methods inside the catch block as follows:

```
try {

   age = scanner.nextInt();

   return age;

} catch (InputMismatchException e) {

   scanner.next (); //remove the leftover garbage
                    //from the input buffer

   System.out.println(e.getMessage());
   e.printStackTrace();
}
```

With this modified code, if we enter ten as an input, then we will receive the following output:

getMessage

printStackTrace

```
null
java.util.InputMismatchException
   at java.util.Scanner.throwFor(Scanner.java:819)
   at java.util.Scanner.next(Scanner.java:1431)
   at java.util.Scanner.nextInt(Scanner.java:2040)
   at java.util.Scanner.nextInt(Scanner.java:2000)
   at AgeInputVer2.getAge(AgeInputVer2.java:54)
   at Ch8AgeInputMain.main(Ch8AgeInputMain.java:30)
```

Notice that the result we see from the printStackTrace method is the one we saw when the system handled the thrown exception. The stack trace shows the sequence of calls made from the main method of the main class to the method that throws the exception.

1. What will be displayed on the console window when the following code is executed and the user enters abc123 and 14?

```
Scanner scanner = new Scanner(System.in);
try {
   int num1 = scanner.nextInt();

   System.out.println("Input 1 accepted");

   int num2 = scanner.nextInt();

   System.out.println("Input 2 accepted");

} catch (InputMismatchException e) {

   System.out.println("Invalid Entry");
}
```

2. What is wrong with the following code? It attempts to loop until the valid input is entered.

```
Scanner scanner = new Scanner(System.in);

try {
   while (true) {
      System.out.print("Enter input: ");

      int num = scanner.nextInt();
   }

} catch (InputMismatchException e) {

      scanner.next();
      System.out.println("Invalid Entry");
}
```

8.2 Throwing Exceptions and Multiple catch Blocks

Compared to the original AgeInputVer1 class, the AgeInputVer2 class is more robust because the program does not terminate abruptly when an invalid value is entered. However, the improved class is not robust enough yet. There is still room for improvements. For example, the current implementation accepts invalid negative integers. Since negative age is not possible, let's improve the code by disallowing the input of negative integers. Notice that a negative integer is an integer, so the nextInt method will not throw an exception. We will define the third class, AgeInputVer3, to throw (and catch) an exception when the invalid input of a negative integer is detected. Here's the while loop of the modified getAge method of the AgeInputVer3 class:

Throws an exception when **age** is a negative integer.

The thrown exception is caught by this **catch** block.

```
while (true) {
   System.out.print(prompt);

   try {
      age = scanner.nextInt();

      if (age < 0) {
         throw new Exception("Negative age is invalid");
      }

      return age; //input okay so return the value & exit

   } catch (InputMismatchException e) {

      scanner.next();

      System.out.println("Input is invalid.\n" +
                         "Please enter digits only");

   } catch (Exception e) {

      System.out.println("Error: " + e.getMessage());
   }
}
```

An exception is thrown by using the throw statement. Its syntax is

```
throw <a throwable object>
```

where <a throwable object> is an instance of the Throwable class or its subclasses. As mentioned earlier, in common applications, it will be an instance of the Exception class or its subclasses. In the sample code, we threw an instance of the Exception class. When we create an instance of the Exception class, we can pass the string that describes the error. The thrown exception is caught by the corresponding catch block, and this error message is displayed.

Notice the multiple catch blocks in the sample code. When there are multiple catch blocks in a try-catch statement, they are checked in sequence, and because the exception classes form an inheritance hierarchy, it is important to check the more specialized exception classes before the more general exception classes. For example, if we reverse the order of the catch blocks to

```
try {
    ...
} catch (Exception e) {
    ...
} catch (InputMismatchException e) {
    ...
}
```

then the second catch block will never be executed because any exception object that is an instance of Exception or its subclasses will match the first catch block. When an exception is thrown, a matching catch block is executed and all other catch blocks are ignored. This is similar to the switch statement with break at the end of each case block. The execution continues to the next statement that follows the trycatch statement. When no exception is thrown, all catch blocks are ignored and the execution continues to the next statement. Figure 8.2 illustrates the control flow of the try-catch statement with multiple catch blocks.

Things to Remember

*List the **catch** blocks in the order of specialized to more general exception classes. At most one **catch** block is executed, and all other **catch** blocks are ignored.*

The sample code given at the beginning of this section illustrates how an exception can be thrown and caught by the matching catch block. Instead of catching the thrown exception immediately, it is possible to let others handle the exception. This can be achieved by not including a matching catch block. We assume in Figure 8.2 that one of the catch blocks will match the thrown exception, but it is not a requirement. It is possible that none of the catch blocks matches the thrown exception.

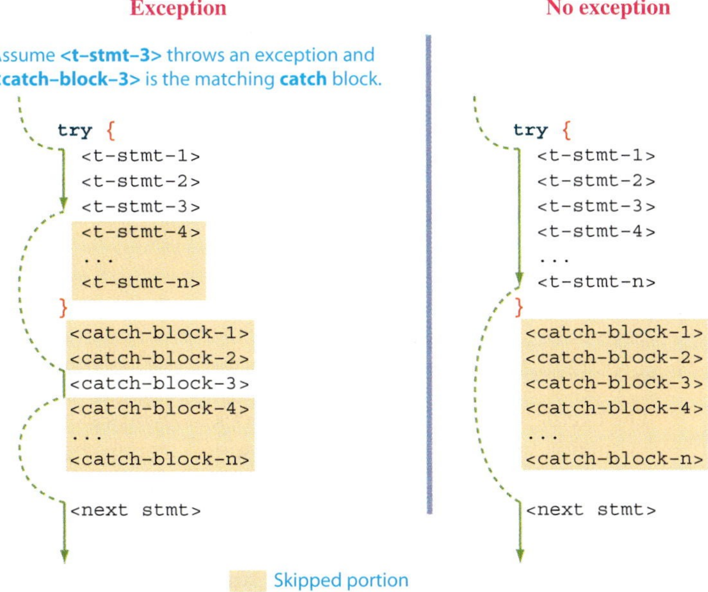

Figure 8.2 Two possible control flows of the **try-catch** statement with multiple **catch** blocks. Assume **<t-stmt-3>** throws an exception and **<catch-block-3>** is the matching **catch** block.

If there is no matching catch block, then the system will search down the stack trace for a method with a matching catch block. If none is found, then the system will handle the thrown exception. We will explain this traversing of the stack trace in greater detail in Section 8.3.

If there is a block of code that needs to be executed regardless of whether an exception is thrown, then we use the reserved word finally. Consider this code.

```
try {
    num = scanner.nextInt();

    if (num > 100) {
       throw new Exception("Out of bound");
    }

} catch (InputMismatchException e) {

    scanner.next();

    System.out.println("Not an integer");

} catch (Exception e) {

    System.out.println("Error: "+ e.getMessage());

} finally {

    System.out.println("DONE");

}
```

If there is no error in input, then no exception is thrown and the output will be

```
DONE
```

If there is an error in input, one of the two exceptions is thrown and the output will be

```
Not an integer
DONE
```

or

```
Error: Out of bound
DONE
```

The example shows that the finally block is always executed. This feature is useful in a situation where we need to execute some cleanup code after the try-catch statement. For example, suppose we open a communication channel from our Java program to a remote Web server to exchange data. If the data exchange is successfully completed in the try block, then we close the communication channel and finish the operation. If the data exchange is interrupted for some reason, an exception is thrown and the operation is aborted. In this case also, we need to close the communication channel, because leaving the channel open by one application blocks other applications from using it. Closing a channel is much like hanging up the phone. The code to close the communication channel should therefore be placed in the finally block. Figure 8.3 shows two possible control flows for the try-catch statement with the finally clause.

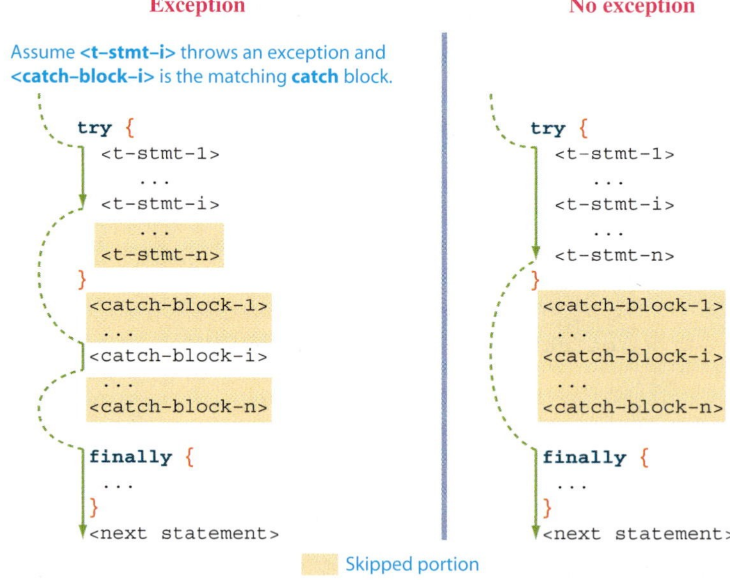

Figure 8.3 Two possible control flows of the **try-catch** statement with multiple **catch** blocks and the **finally** block. The **finally** block is always executed.

Note that even if there's a return statement inside the try block, the finally block is executed. When the return statement is encountered in the try block, statements in the finally block are executed before actually returning from the method.

1. What's wrong with the following code? Identify all errors.

```
Scanner scanner = new Scanner(System.in);

try {
   int num = scanner.nextInt();

   if (num > 100) {
     catch new Exception("Out of bound");
   }

} catch (InputMismatchException e) {

   System.out.println("Invalid Entry");

} finally(Exception e) {

   System.out.println("DONE");
}
```

2. Determine the output of the following code when the input a12 is entered.

```
Scanner scanner = new Scanner(System.in);

try {
   int num = scanner.nextInt();

   if (num < 0) {
      throw new Exception("No negative");
   }

} catch (InputMismatchException e) {

   System.out.println("Invalid Entry");

} catch (Exception e) {

   System.out.println("Error: "+ e.getMessage());

} finally {

   System.out.println("DONE");
}
```

3. Determine the output of the following code when the input a12 is entered.

```
Scanner scanner = new Scanner(System.in);

try {
   int num = scanner.nextInt();

   if (num < 0) {
      throw new Exception("No negative");
   }

} catch (Exception e) {

   System.out.println("Error: "+ e.getMessage());

} catch (InputMismatchException e) {

   System.out.println("Invalid Entry");
}
```

8.3 Propagating Exceptions

In Section 8.2 we introduced the possibility of no catch block matching the thrown exception, but we did not explain exactly how the system handles such a case. We stated only briefly that the system will search down the stack trace for a method with a matching catch block, and if no matching catch block is found, the system will handle the thrown exception. We now describe this mechanism in detail.

To present a precise description, we start with some definitions. When a method may throw an exception, either directly by including a throw statement or indirectly by calling a method that throws an exception, we call the method an ***exception thrower***. Every exception thrower must be one of the two types: catcher or propagator. An ***exception catcher*** is an exception thrower that includes a matching catch block for the thrown exception, while an ***exception propagator*** does not. For example, the getAge method of the AgeInputVer1 class is an exception propagator, while the getAge method of the AgeInputVer2 class is an exception catcher. Note that the designation of a method as being a catcher or propagator is based on a single exception. Suppose a method throws two exceptions. This method can be a catcher of the first exception and a propagator of the second exception.

exception thrower

exception catcher

exception propagator

Let's consider the sequence of method calls shown in Figure 8.4. Method A calls method B, method B in turn calls method C, and so forth. Notice the stack trace in the figure. Every time a method is executed, the method's name is placed on top of the stack. By the time method D is executed, we have A, B, C, and D in the stack. When an exception is thrown, the system searches down the stack from the top, looking for the first matching exception catcher. Method D throws an exception, but no matching catch block exists in the method, so method D is an exception propagator. The system then checks method C. This method is also an exception propagator. Finally, the system locates the matching catch block in method B, and therefore, method B is the catcher for the exception thrown by method D.

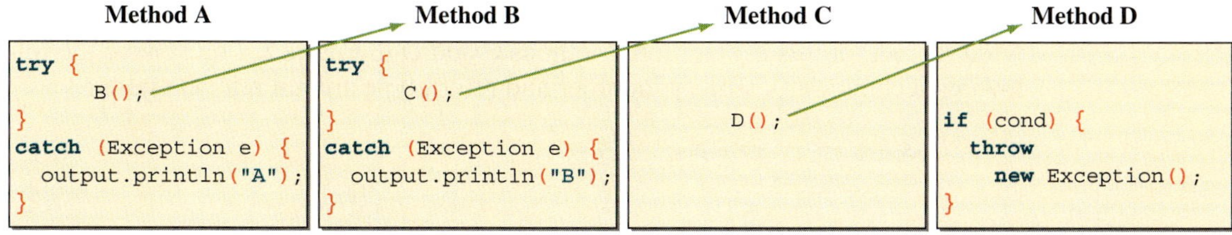

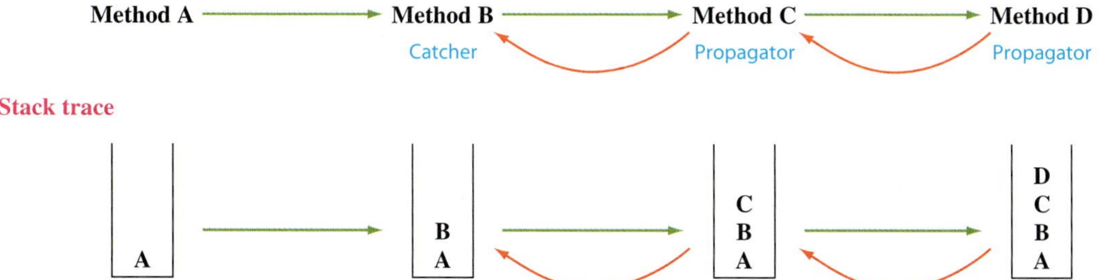

Figure 8.4 A sequence of method calls among the exception throwers. Method D throws an instance of **Exception.** The green arrows indicate the direction of calls. The red arrows show the reversing of call sequence, looking for a matching catcher. Method B is the catcher in this example. The call sequence is traced by using a stack. (*Note:* **output == System.out.**)

Method A also includes the matching catch block, but it will not be executed because the thrown exception is already caught by method B, and method B does not propagate this exception. Although the technique is not used often, an exception catcher can also be set to propagate the caught exception. For example, if we rewrite method B as

```
try {
   C();

} catch (Exception e) {
   ...          //do something here
   throw e;   //propagate the caught exception to the
                //method below this one in the trace stack
}
```

it is both a catcher and a propagator. With the modified method B, method A's matching catch block will get executed, because method B, in addition to handling the exception, throws the same exception, causing the system to look for a matching catcher down the stack.

We have one last detail to complete the description of the exception propagation mechanism. If a method is an exception propagator, we need to modify its header to declare the type of exceptions the method propagates. We use the reserved word throws for this declaration. Methods C and D in Figure 8.4 must have the following declaration (visibility modifier and return type are not relevant here):

```
void C( ) throws Exception {
    ...
}

void D( ) throws Exception {
    ...
}
```

Without the required throws Exception clause, the program will not compile. There is one exception (no pun intended) to this rule. For the exceptions of the type called *runtime exceptions,* the throws clause is optional. For example, the getAge method of AgeInputVer1 does not include the throws clause because InputMismatchException is a runtime exception. Its being optional means we can include it to explicitly state the fact if we want to. If we restate the declaration to

```
public int getAge(String prompt)

                throws InputMismatchException {
    ...
}
```

the code will compile just fine. We will explain further about different types of exceptions in Section 8.4.

Now that the exception propagation mechanism is explained, let's study how we can apply it in designing useful service classes.

First, consider the Fraction class from Chapter 7. The setDenominator method of the Fraction class was defined as follows:

```
public void setDenominator(int denom) {

    if (denom == 0) {
       System.out.println("Fatal Error");
       System.exit(1);
    }

    denominator = denom;
}
```

We stated in Chapter 7 that it is too drastic to terminate a whole program when one attempts (inadvertently or otherwise) to set the denomintor to 0. Throwing an exception is a much better approach. Here's the modified method that throws an IllegalArgumentException when the value of 0 is passed as an argument:

```
public void setDenominator(int denom)
                     throws IllegalArgumentException {
```

```
    if (denom == 0) {
        throw new IllegalArgumentException(
                    "Denominator cannot be 0");
    }
    denominator = denom;
}
```

Now let's study another example. Consider the AgeInputVer3 class. It disallows input of negative integers. When that happens, an exception is thrown. Instead of disallowing only negative integers, wouldn't it make more sense to restrict the valid input by specifying the lower and upper bounds? For example, we may want to restrict the input to an integer between 10 and 20 for one application and between 0 and 250 (e.g., entering the age of a building on the campus) for another application. To illustrate this concept, we will define the fourth class, AgeInputVer4, that allows the client programmers to specify the lower and upper bounds of acceptable input values.

The client specifies the lower and upper bounds at the time of object creation, for example,

```
AgeInputVer4 input = new AgeInputVer4(10, 20);
```

This constructor will set the lower and upper bounds to 0 and 99, respectively. The lower and upper bounds are kept as data members lowerBound and upperBound, respectively, and they are initialized in the constructor.

How should the getAge respond when it detects the input is outside the range of the client-designated lower and upper bounds? Instead of catching it, we will propagate the thrown exception to the caller of this method. Our responsibility as a provider of the service class is to tell the client by throwing an exception when a condition set by the client is violated. We will let the client handle the thrown exception. The condition is set by the client, so it is more appropriate for this client to decide what to do in case of an exception. For the number format exception, the getAge method is still the catcher because this exception is thrown when a condition not dependent on any one specific client is violated. This exception is not a client-specific exception, but a generic exception suitably handled by the service class. So the modified getAge method is a propagator of an Exception (thrown when the bounds set by the client are violated) and a catcher of an InputMismatchException (thrown when the input is not an integer). Here's the method:

```
public int getAge(String prompt) throws Exception {

    int  age;

    while (true) {
        System.out.print(prompt);

        try {
            age = scanner.nextInt();
```

Propagates an **Exception**

```
            if (age < lowerBound || age > upperBound) {
               throw new Exception("Input out of bound");
            }

            return age;

         } catch (InputMismatchException e) {

            scanner.next();

            System.out.println("Input is invalid.\n" +
                               "Please enter digits only");
         }
      }
   }
```

No catch block for **Exception**

Things to Remember

Don't catch an exception that is thrown as a result of violating the condition set by the client programmer. Instead, propagate the exception back to the client programmer's code and let him or her handle it.

The second **getAge** method that uses a default prompt calls this method, so we need to rewrite the second **getAge** method as

```
public int getAge() throws Exception {

   return getAge(DEFAULT_MESSAGE);
}
```

This call can throw an **Exception** so the method header must include the correct **throws** clause.

We have to specify the additional data members and the constructors to complete the **AgeInputVer4** class. The new data members are declared as

```
private static final int DEFAULT_LOWER_BOUND = 0;
private static final int DEFAULT_UPPER_BOUND = 99;

private int lowerBound;
private int upperBound;
```

What about the constructors? Are the following constructors acceptable?

```
public AgeInputVer4( ) {
   this(DEFAULT_LOWER_BOUND, DEFAULT_UPPER_BOUND);
}

public AgeInputVer4(int low, int high) {
   lowerBound = low;
   upperBound = high;
   scanner = new Scanner(System.in);
}
```

Yes, if we didn't know about exception handling. But now with the knowledge of exception handling, we can make the class more robust by ensuring that low is less than or equal to high. If this condition is not met, then we throw an exception. The IllegalArgumentException class is precisely the class we can use for this situation. Here's the more robust constructor:

```
public AgeInputVer4(int low, int high)
                throws IllegalArgumentException {

   if (low > high) {
      throw new IllegalArgumentException(
                      "Low (" + low + ") was " +
                      "larger than high(" + high + ")");

   } else {
      lowerBound = low;
      upperBound = high;
      scanner = new Scanner(System.in);
   }
}
```

Now, what about the default constructor? Since the default constructor calls the other two-argument constructor, which can throw an exception, this constructor must handle the exception. One approach is to propagate the exception by declaring it as

```
public AgeInputVer4( ) throws IllegalArgumentException {
   this(DEFAULT_LOWER_BOUND, DEFAULT_UPPER_BOUND);
}
```

This declaration is problematic, however, because when we use the throws clause, we are announcing that this method can potentially throw an exception. But this constructor will never throw an exception as long as the class is programmed correctly. The only time this constructor can throw an exception is when we set the value for DEFAULT_LOWER_BOUND or DEFAULT_UPPER_BOUND incorrectly. It is an internal error and must be corrected. Since this constructor should not throw an exception, we might be tempted to make this constructor an exception catcher as

Bad Version

```
public AgeInputVer4( ) {
   try {
     this(DEFAULT_LOWER_BOUND, DEFAULT_UPPER_BOUND);

   } catch (IllegalArgumentException e) {
      //never happens, so do nothing
   }
}
```

Logically, this is what we want to accomplish. But syntactically, it is an error. Java requires the call to another constructor using the reserved word this to be the first statement. In the bad version, the try statement is the first statement. To correct this problem, we can define a private method init as

```
private void init(int low, int high) {
   lowerBound = low;
   upperBound = high;
   scanner = new scanner(System.in);
}
```

and write the two constructors as

```
public AgeInputVer4( ) {
   init(DEFAULT_LOWER_BOUND, DEFAULT_UPPER_BOUND);
}

public AgeInputVer4(int low, int high)
                  throws IllegalArgumentException {

   if (low > high) {
      throw new IllegalArgumentException(
                        "Low (" + low + ") was " +
                        "larger than high(" + high + ")");

   } else {
      init(low, high);
   }
}
```

Here's the complete AgeInputVer4 class:

```
/*
   Chapter 8 Sample Class: Class to input age

   File: AgeInputVer4.java

*/

import javax.swing.*;

class AgeInputVer4 {

    private static final String DEFAULT_MESSAGE = "Your age:";
    private static final int DEFAULT_LOWER_BOUND = 0;
    private static final int DEFAULT_UPPER_BOUND = 99;

    private int lowerBound;
    private int upperBound;

    private Scanner scanner;
```

Data members

Constructors

getAge

init

```
    public AgeInputVer4( ) {
        init(DEFAULT_LOWER_BOUND, DEFAULT_UPPER_BOUND);
    }

    public AgeInputVer4(int low, int high)
                throws IllegalArgumentException {

        if (low > high) {
            throw new IllegalArgumentException(
                "Low (" + low + ") was " +
                "larger than high(" + high + ")");

        } else {
            init(low, high);
        }
    }

    public int getAge() throws Exception {

        return getAge(DEFAULT_MESSAGE);
    }

    public int getAge(String prompt) throws Exception {

        int age;

        while (true) {
            System.out.print(prompt);

            try {
                age = scanner.nextInt();

                if (age < lowerBound || age > upperBound) {
                    throw new Exception("Input out of bound");
                }

                return age; //input okay so return the value & exit

            } catch (InputMismatchException e) {

                scanner.next();

                System.out.println("Input is invalid.\n" +
                                   "Please enter digits only");
            }
        }
    }

    private void init(int low, int high) {
        lowerBound = low;
        upperBound = high;
        scanner = new Scanner(System.in);
    }
}
```

1. What's wrong with the following code?

```
public void check(int num) {
   if (num < 0) {
      throw new Exception();
   }
}
```

2. What is the difference between the reserved words throw and throws?
3. What's wrong with the following code?

```
public InputMismatchException getData( ) {

   Scanner scanner = new Scanner(System.in);

   try {
     System.out.print("Input: ");
     int num = scanner.nextInt();

     return num;
   }
}
```

8.4 Types of Exceptions

We mentioned briefly in Section 8.1 that all types of thrown errors are instances of the Throwable class or its subclasses. Serious errors that signal abnormal conditions are represented by the instances of the Error class or its subclasses. Exceptional cases that common applications are expected to handle are represented by the instances of the Exception class or its subclasses. Figure 8.5 shows a very small portion of the inheritance hierarchy rooted in the Throwable class.

checked and unchecked exception

There are two types of exceptions: checked and unchecked. A ***checked exception*** is an exception that is checked at compile time. All other exceptions are ***unchecked exceptions***, also called *runtime exceptions,* because they are unchecked at compile time and are detected only at runtime. Trying to divide a number by 0 (ArithmeticException) and trying to convert a string with letters to an integer (NumberFormatException) are two examples of runtime exceptions.

If a method is a propagator (a method that throws but does not catch an exception) of checked exceptions, then the method must have the throws clause. If a method is a propagator of runtime exceptions or errors (instances of Error or its subclasses), the throws clause is optional. When we call a method that can throw checked exceptions, then we must use the try-catch statement and place the call in the try block, or we must modify our method header to include the appropriate throws clause. When we call a method that can throw runtime exceptions or errors, then there's is no such requirement. We just make a call in our method. Figure 8.6 shows the valid callers of a method that throws checked exceptions, and Figure 8.7 shows the valid callers of a method that throws runtime, or unchecked, exceptions.

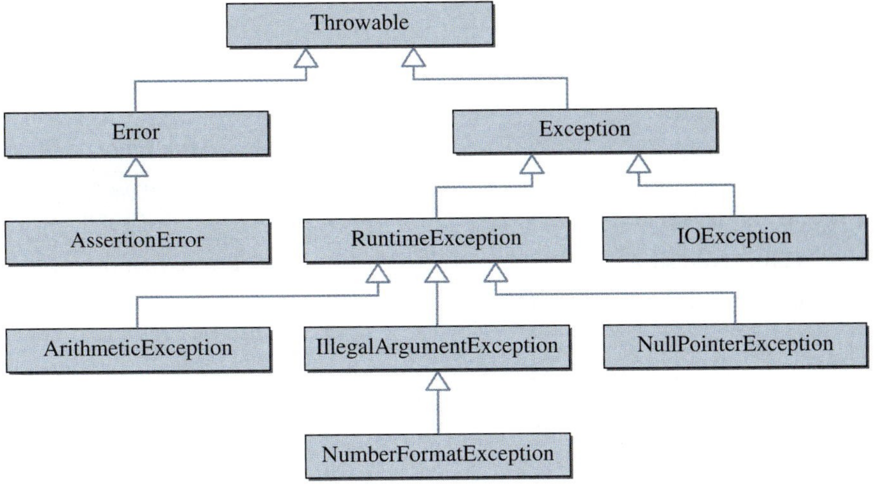

Figure 8.5 Some classes in the inheritance hierarchy from the **Throwable** class. There are over 60 classes in the hierarchy.

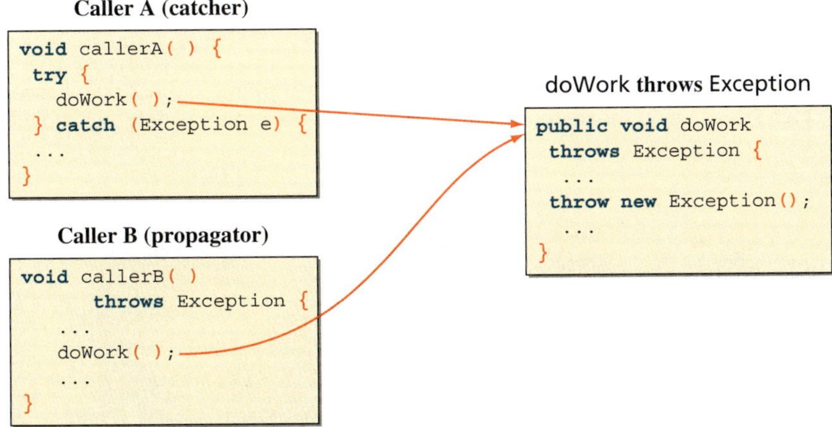

Figure 8.6 Callers of a method that can throw a checked exception must explicitly include the **try-catch** statement in the method body or the **throws** clause in the method header.

Enforcing the requirement of explicitly handling runtime exceptions means, for all methods we write, that they must either have the throws clause in the header or have the try-catch statement in the body because almost every method we call from our methods can throw runtime exceptions. This is hardly effective programming so we don't have to handle runtime exceptions explicitly in the program. For the errors of type Error and its subclasses, they indicate problems too serious for any ordinary application to handle, so we are not required to handle them explicitly. There's really nothing we can do even if we catch them, so we don't.

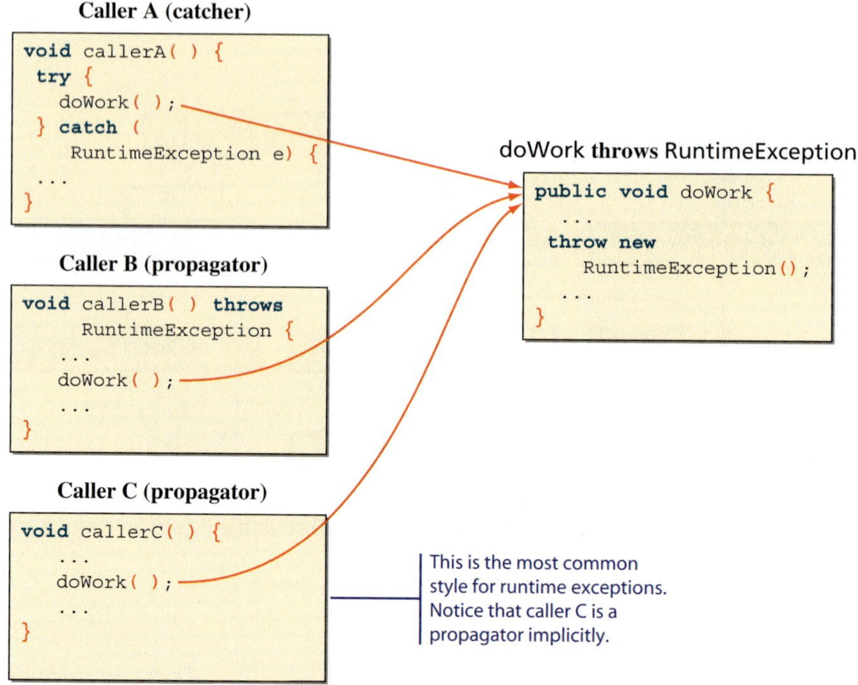

Figure 8.7 It is optional for the callers of a method that can throw runtime, or unchecked, exceptions to include the **try-catch** statement in the method body or the **throws** clause in the method header.

Things to Remember

If a method throws a checked exception, the caller of this method must explicitly include the **try-catch** *statement or the* **throws** *clause in the method header. If a method throws a runtime, or unchecked, exception, the use of the* **try-catch** *statement or the* **throws** *clause is optional.*

1. Is this code wrong?

```
public void check(int num) {
    if (num < 0) {
        throw new IllegalArgumentException();
    }
}
```

2. What is the difference between the checked and unchecked exceptions?

8.5 Programmer-Defined Exceptions

In the AgeInputVer4 class, the getAge methods throw an instance of the Exception class. The catch clause of the caller of the getAge method can use the getMessage method to retrieve the error message or use printStackTrace to display the sequence of method calls from the main method to the method that threw an exception. But there's no way for the client to get any other useful information such as the value actually entered by the user. Instead of using generic exception classes, we can define our own exception classes so we can attach useful information to the exception objects.

Let's define a class named AgeInputException as a subclass of the Exception class. To provide useful information to the client, we will define the class so the instances will carry three pieces of information: lower bound, upper bound, and the value entered by the user (in addition to the message inherited from the Exception class). We will define three public methods to access these data. Here's the class definition:

```
/*
    Chapter 8 Sample Class: Customized Exception Class

    File: AgeInputException.java
*/

class AgeInputException extends Exception {

    private static final String DEFAULT_MESSAGE = "Input out of bounds";

    private int lowerBound;
    private int upperBound;
    private int value;

    public AgeInputException(int low, int high, int input) {
        this(DEFAULT_MESSAGE, low, high, input);
    }

    public AgeInputException(String msg,
                             int low, int high, int input) {
        super(msg);

        if (low > high) {
            throw new IllegalArgumentException();
        }

        lowerBound = low;
        upperBound = high;
        value      = input;
    }
```

```
    public int lowerBound() {

        return lowerBound;
    }

    public int upperBound() {

        return upperBound;
    }

    public int value() {
        return value;
    }
}
```

The new AgeInputVer5 class is essentially the same as the AgeInputVer4 class except the getAge method of the new class throws an AgeInputException. A sample main class that uses the AgeInputVer5 is as follows:

```
/*
   Chapter 8 Sample Program: Input a person's age

   File: Ch8TestAgeInputVer5.java
*/

class Ch8TestAgeInputVer5 {

    public static void main( String[] args ) {

        int  entrantAge;

        try {

            AgeInputVer5 input = new AgeInputVer5(25, 50);

            entrantAge = input.getAge("Your Age:");

            System.out.println("Input Okay. Age = " + entrantAge);

        } catch (AgeInputException e) {
            System.out.println(
                "Error: " + e.value() + " is entered. It is " +
                "outside the valid range of [" + e.lowerBound() +
                ", " + e.upperBound() + "]");
        }
    }
}
```

e's methods are called to get info

Things to Remember

To provide useful information to the client programmers when an exception occurs, define a new exception class. Make this customized exception class a subclass of **Exception.**

Hints, & Tips, Pitfalls

When we create a new customized exception class, we should define it as a checked exception, and the most logical choice for its superclass is the **Exception** class. We should not define the customized exception class as an unchecked exception. If we did, then the client programmers would have an option of omitting the **try-catch** statement or the **throws** clause in their code. This is not a good idea. The goal of defining a customized exception class is to ensure that the client programmers handle the thrown exceptions of the customized class explicitly in their code, to increase the robustness of the whole program.

Quick CHECK

1. When do we want to define a customized exception class?
2. Should a customized exception class be a checked or unchecked exception?

8.6 Assertions

In this section we will describe a Java assertion and explain how to use it effectively in our programs. A Java assertion is a language feature we use to detect logical errors in a program. We will illustrate the key points with a very simple class that includes a logical error. Because the sample class is simple, the use of assertion may not seem so helpful. Keep in mind that this class is for illustrative purposes only. The real benefit of using the assertion feature becomes obvious when the program logic gets more complex and the number of classes in the program increases.

Here's a bank account class that allows withdrawals and deposits. There's one logical error in the class:

```
class BankAccount {
   private double balance;

   public BankAccount(double initialBalance) {
      balance = initialBalance;
   }
```

Here's a logical error. We should add the amount.

If this boolean expression results in **false,** then an **AssertionError** is thrown.

```
    public void deposit(double amount) {
        double oldBalance = balance;

        balance -= amount;

        assert balance > oldBalance;
    }
    public void withdraw(double amount) {
        double oldBalance = balance;

        balance -= amount;

        assert balance < oldBalance;
    }

    public double getBalance( ) {
        return balance;
    }
}
```

Notice the two occurences of the reserved word assert in the class definition. The syntax for the assert statement is

```
assert <boolean expression> ;
```

where <boolean expression> represents the condition that must be true if the code is working correctly. When the statement is executed, the <boolean expression> is evaluated. If it results in true, then the normal execution of the program continues. Otherwise, an AssertionError (subclass of Error) is thrown.

In this example, we want to assert that balance is more than oldBalance when we deposit and less than oldBalance when we withdraw, so we write

```
assert balance > oldBalance;
```

and

```
assert balance < oldBalance;
```

at the end of the deposit and withdraw methods, respectively.

Now let's see what happens when we use this BankAccount class in our program. Here's a simplistic main class to test the BankAccount class:

```
import javax.swing.*;

class Ch8TestAssertMain {

    public static void main(String[] args) {

        BankAccount acct = new BankAccount(200);

        acct.deposit(25);

        System.out.println(
            "Current Balance: " + acct.getBalance());
    }
}
```

To run this program with the assertion feature enabled, we must include the designation -ea as follows:

```
java -ea Ch8TestAssertMain
```

(*Note:* For most Java IDE, you specify this option in the Preference dialog. Please consult your Java IDE for details.)

If we do not provide the -ea option, then the program is executed without checking the assertions. When do we ever want to ignore the assertions we intentionally included in the program? Checking all assertions included in the program can be quite costly. By having an option of enabling or disabling the assertions, we can choose to enable the assertions while developing and testing the program and disable them once the program is fully developed and tested.

Things to Remember

To run the program with assertions enabled, use

```
java -ea <main class>
```

With the assert statements enabled, executing the Ch8TestAssertMain main class will result in the following error message:

```
Exception in thread "main" java.lang.AssertionError
        at BankAccount.deposit(BankAccount.java:13)
        at Ch8TestAssertMain.main(Ch8TestAssertMain.java:34)
```

The error message indicates an AssertionError is thrown at line 13 (the actual line number would be different if the source code included comments) of the BankAccount class, which is the assert statement

```
assert balance > oldBalance;
```

We can use the second form of the assert statement to provide a customized error message. The syntax for the second form is

```
assert <boolean expression > : <expression>;
```

where <expression> represents the value that is passed as an argument to the constructor of the AssertionError class. The value serves as the detailed message of a thrown error. For example, using the second form, we can rewrite the deposit method as

```
public void deposit(double amount) {
   double oldBalance = balance;

   balance -= amount;
```

```
    assert balance > oldBalance :
          "Serious Error -- balance becomes less" +
          "after deposit";
}
```

With this modified deposit method, the error message will be

```
Exception in thread "main" java.lang.AssertionError:
      Serious Error -- balance becomes less after deposit
      at BankAccount.deposit(BankAccount.java:14)
      at Ch8TestAssertMain.main(Ch8TestAssertMain.java:34)
```

Encountering this error message during the development, we are made aware of the existence of a bug in the program. Without the assertion feature, we may not be able to detect the bug until very late in the development, or we may not be able to detect it at all.

Again, for a small class such as BankAccount, the benefit of using assertions may not be obvious. However, in designing and building classes that solve difficult and complex problems, effective use of assertions can be an indispensable aid, especially when it is combined with a full set of testing. We will be seeing more examples of assertions (and exceptions, also) in the later sample code.

Types of Assertions

postcondition assertion

precondition assertion

control flow invariant

The type of assertion we see in the withdraw and deposit methods is called a ***postcondition assertion***. This assertion checks for a condition that must be true after a method is executed. Opposite to the postcondition assertion is a ***precondition assertion***, a checking of condition that must be true before a method is executed. The third type of assertion is called a ***control flow invariant***. Consider the following switch statement. It adds the appropriate fee to the tuition based on whether the student is a dorm resident or a dorm resident or a commuter.

```
switch (residenceType) {

   case COMMUTER:      totalFee = tuition + parkingFee;
                       break;

   case DORM_RESIDENT: totalFee = tuition + roomAndBoard;
                       break;
}
```

Now every student must be a dorm resident or a commuter, so if the variable residenceType has a value other than COMMUTER or DORM_RESIDENT, then there's a bug somewhere. To detect such bug, we can rewrite the statement as

```
switch (residenceType) {

   case COMMUTER:      totalFee = tuition + parkingFee;
                       break;
```

```
    case DORM_RESIDENT: totalFee = tuition + roomAndBoard;
                        break;

    default:            assert false:
                               "Value of residenceType " +
                               "is invalid. Value = " +
                               residenceType;
}
```

This statement documents the fact that the default case should never be executed when the program is running correctly. This is called a *control flow invariant* because the control must flow invariably to one of the two cases. Alternatively, we can place an assertion before the switch statement as

```
assert (residenceType == COMMUTER ||
        residenctType == DORM_RESIDENT) :
        "Value of residenceType is invalid. Value = " +
        residenceType;

switch (residenceType) {

    case COMMUTER:      totalFee = tuition + parkingFee;
                        break;

    case DORM_RESIDENT: totalFee = tuition + roomAndBoard;
                        break;
}
```

Differentiating Assertions and Exceptions

Because both the assertion and the exception mechanisms are intended to improve the program reliability, their use is often mixed up. For example, if we are not attentive, we could end up using the assertion feature wrongly in places where exceptionhandling routines should be used. Consider the following case. In defining the deposit and the withdraw methods, we did not bother to check the value of the parameter (for the sake of a simplified class definition). The passed amount must be greater than zero for the methods to work correctly. How shall we include such testing? One possibility (a wrong approach) is to use the assertion feature as (we only show the withdraw method).

```
public void withdraw(double amount) {

    assert amount > 0;

    double oldBalance = balance;

    balance -= amount;

    assert balance < oldBalance;
}
```

Bad Version

This is not a correct use of assertions. We should not use the assertion feature to ensure the validity of an argument. In principle, we use assertions to detect the internal programming errors, and we use exceptions to notify the client programmers of the misuse of our classes. The BankAccount class is intended as a service class used by many different programs. It is the responsibility of the client programmers to pass the valid arguments. If they don't, then we throw an exception to notify them of the misuse. Another problem is that assertions can be enabled or disabled when the program is run. But the validity checking of the arguments should never be disabled.

Things to Remember

Use assertions to detect internal errors. Use exceptions to notify the client programmers of the misuse of our class.

The correct way to implement the methods is as follows (only the withdraw method is shown here):

```
public void withdraw(double amount)
                throws IllegalArgumentException {

    if (amount <= 0) {
        throw new IllegalArgumentException(
                    "Amount must be positive");
    }

    double oldBalance = balance;

    balance -= amount;

    assert balance < oldBalance;
}
```

Quick CHECK

1. Why is the following code wrong?

```
public void doWork(int num) {
    assert num > 0;
    total += num;
}
```

2. Name three types of assertions.

8.7 Sample Development

Keyless Entry System

We will develop a program that simulates a secure keyless entry system for a dormitory. Inside the entrance hall of a dorm, there is an entry system where the dorm residents must enter their names, room numbers, and passwords. Upon entry of valid data, the system will unlock the inner door that leads to the dorm's living quarters. To implement this program, two helper classes are provided. The **Door** class simulates unlocking of the inner door. The **Dorm** class manages resident information. An instance of the **Dorm** class is capable of adding and deleting resident information, reading and saving resident information from and to a file, and retrieving information if given the resident's name. We can verify the validity of the entered data by checking them against the information kept by a **Dorm** object.

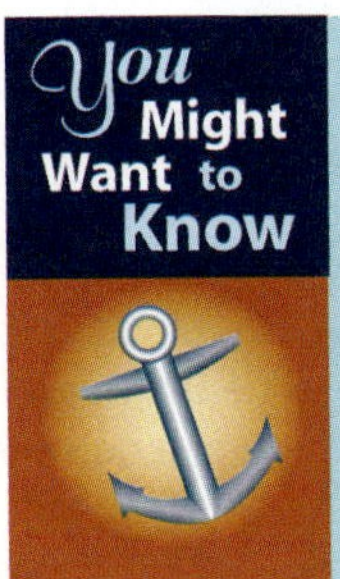

We can turn our simulation program into a real one by replacing the **Door** class with a class that actually controls the door. Java provides a mechanism called Java Native Interface (JNI) which can be used to embed a link to a low-level device driver code, so calling the **open** method actually unlocks the door.

Problem Statement

Implement a sentry program that asks for three pieces of information: resident's name, room number, and a password. A password is any sequence of characters ranging in length from 4 to 8 and is unique to an individual dorm resident. If everything matches, then the system unlocks and opens the door. We assume no two residents have the same name. Use the provided support classes **Door** *and* **Dorm.**

Overall Plan

To provide a complete system, we actually have to write two separate programs. The first one is the administrative module for adding, removing, and updating the resident information. The second is the user module that interacts with the residents. Figure 8.8 shows the program diagrams for the two modules.

In this section, we implement the user module. The administrative module is left as an exercise. To begin our development effort, we must first find out the capabilities of the **Dorm** and **Door** classes. Also, for us to implement the class correctly, we need the specification of the **Resident** class.

8.7 Sample Development—*continued*

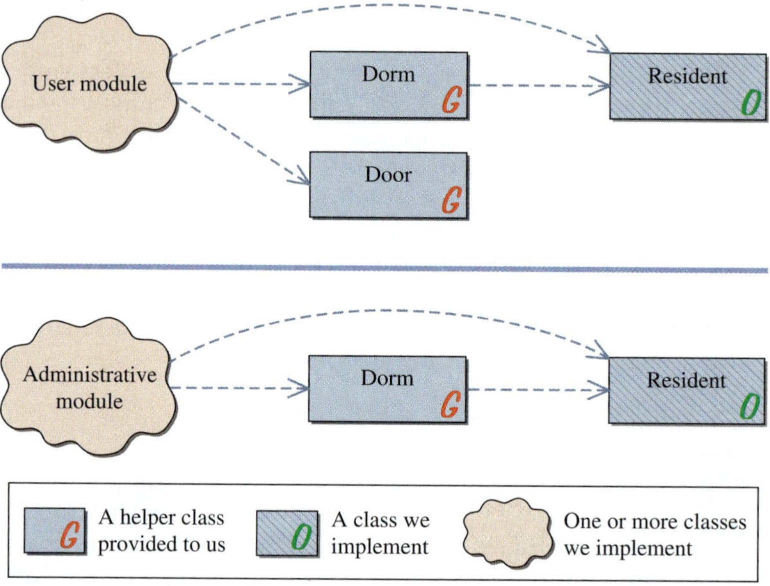

Figure 8.8 Program diagrams for the user and administrative modules. Notice the same **Dorm** and **Resident** classes are used in both programs. User and administrative modules will include one or more classes (at least one is programmer-defined).

Resident

The **Resident** class maintains information on individual dorm residents. We will be dealing with many instances of this class in the program. A password assigned to a resident must be a sequence of 4 to 8 characters. For this class to work properly with the **Dorm** class, the class must include these public methods:

Public Methods of `Resident`

`public Resident( )`
Default constructor that creates a `Resident` object with name = "unassigned", room = "000", and id = "@13&".

`public Resident(String name, String room, String password) throws IllegalArgumentException`
Creates a `Resident` object with the passed values. `IllegalArgumentException` is thrown when the given password has less than four or more than eight characters.

```
public void setName(String name)
```
Assigns the name.

```
public void setPassword(String id)
                          throws IllegalArgumentException
```
Assigns the password. `IllegalArgumentException` is thrown when the given password has less than four or more than eight characters.

```
public void setRoom(String room)
```
Assigns the room.

```
public String getName( )
```
Returns the name.

```
public String getPassWord( )
```
Returns the password.

```
public String getRoom( )
```
Returns the room number.

One important restriction to the **Resident** class is the requirement for the class to implement the **Serializable** interface. Because the **Resident** objects are saved to a file, Java requires the class definition to include the phrase **implements Serializable** as

```
import java.io.*;

class Resident implements Serializable {

    . . .

}
```

Details on the significance of the clause **implements Serializable** will be given when we discuss the file input and output in Chapter 12.

Things to Remember

For any object we need to save to a file, its class definition must include the phrase **implements Serializable.**

Dorm

The **Dorm** class is a helper class provided to us. A **Dorm** object is capable of managing a list of **Resident** objects. It allows the client to add, delete, and retrieve **Resident** objects. In addition, it is capable of saving a list to a file or reading a list from a file. By having these file input and output features, our program can work with different lists of residents much as a word processor can work with different documents (files). The class definition is as follows:

Public Methods of `Dorm`
`public Dorm( )` Default constructor that creates a `Dorm` object.
`public Dorm(String filename)` Creates a `Dorm` object with the resident list read from the file with the name `filename`. Throws `FileNotFoundException` when the designated file cannot be found and `IOException` when the file cannot be read.
`public void openFile(String filename)` Reads the resident list from the designated file. Throws `FileNotFoundException` when the designated file cannot be found and `IOException` when the file cannot be read.
`public void saveFile(String filename)` Saves the resident list to the designated file. Throws `IOException` when the file cannot be saved.
`public void add(Resident resident)` Adds the `resident` to the list. Throws `IllegalArgumentException` when a resident with the same name already exists in the list. We do not allow duplicate names. Every resident must have a unique name.
`public void delete(String name)` Deletes the designated resident from the list. If no such resident is in the list, nothing happens.
`public Resident getResident(String name)` Returns the `Resident` object with the given name. Returns `null` if no matching `Resident` is found.
`public String getResidentList( )` Returns a list of residents as a `String`. A line separator is used after each resident. For each resident, the list contains his or her name, room number, and password.

Door

The **Door** class is another helper class. It simulates the opening of the door. In a real control program, a **Door** object can have an embedded low-level device driver code, so it really opens the door. The class definition is as follows:

Public Methods of `Door`

`public Door( )`
Default constructor that creates a new `Door` object.
`public void open()`
Opens the door. For this simulator class, it displays a simple message dialog.

overall design

Now let's study the overall design of the program. In addition to the given helper classes and the **Resident** class, what other classes should we define for this program? As the number of classes gets larger, we need to plan the classes carefully. For this program, we will define a controller class named **Ch8EntranceMonitor** whose instance will manage all other objects. We will set this class as the program's main class. The user interface of the program is handled by the **InputHandler** class. Its instance is used to allow the user to enter his or her name, room number, and password. After the required input data are entered by the user, a **Ch8EntranceMonitor** checks the validity of the input data with help from a service **Dorm** object. If the **Dorm** object confirms the input data, the controller then instructs another service object, an instance of **Door,** to open the door. The following is our working design document, and Figure 8.9 is the program diagram.

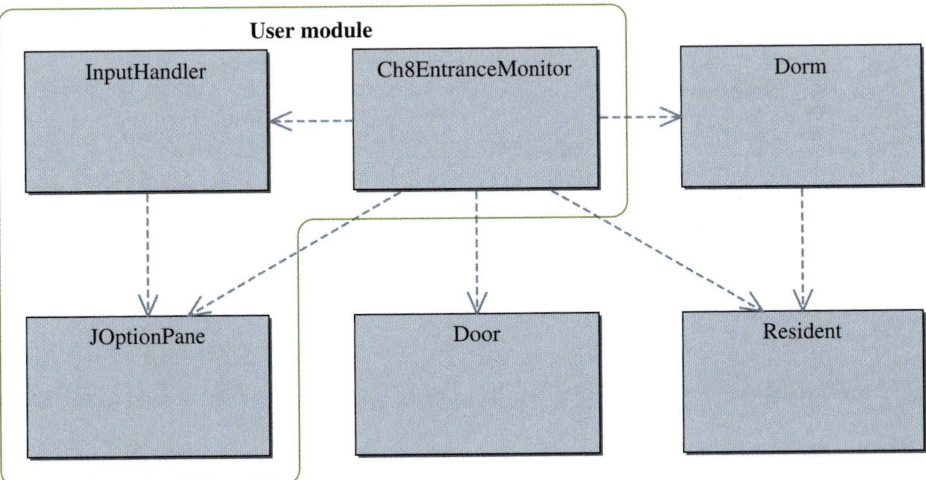

Figure 8.9 The program diagram for the **Ch8EntranceMonitor** program. There are three classes in the user module.

8.7 Sample Development—*continued*

program classes

Design Document: Ch8EntranceMonitor	
Class	**Purpose**
Ch8EntranceMonitor	The top-level control object manages other objects in the program. This is an instantiable main class.
Door	The given predefined class simulates the opening of a door.
Dorm	The given predefined class maintains a list of Resident objects.
InputHandler	The user interface class is for handling input routines.

We will implement the user module in three major steps:

develop-ment steps

1. Define the **Resident** class and explore the **Dorm** class. Start with a program skeleton to test the **Resident** class.
2. Define the user interface **InputHandler** class. Modify the top-level control class as necessary.
3. Finalize the code by making improvements and tying up loose ends.

Step 1 Development: Program Skeleton

step 1 design

Our first task is to find out about the given **Dorm** class. (The **Door** class is a very simple simulator class so there's not much to explore.) To be able to test-run the **Dorm** class, we must provide the **Resident** class, so this will be our first step. The purpose of the skeleton main class in this step is to verify the operations of the **Dorm** class.

The specification for the **Resident** class was given to us, so our task is to implement it according to the specification. No design work is necessary. When we can interact with an instance of the **Dorm** class correctly, it confirms that our implementation of the **Resident** class is working. To verify the key operations of the **Dorm** class, the top-level supervisor object **Ch8EntranceMonitor** will open a file and list the contents of the file.

step 1 code

Here's the **Resident** class:

```
/*
    Chapter 8 Sample Development: Keyless Entry System.

    File: Resident.java

*/
```

```
import java.io.*;

class Resident implements Serializable {

    private String name;
    private String room;
    private String password;

    public Resident( ) {
        this("unassigned", "000", "@13&");
    }

    public Resident(String name, String room, String pwd)
                throws IllegalArgumentException {
        setName(name);
        setRoom(room);
        setPassword(pwd);
    }

    public String getName( ) {
        return name;
    }

    public String getPassword( ) {
        return password;
    }

    public String getRoom( ) {
        return room;
    }

    public void setName(String name) {
        this.name = name;
    }

    public void setPassword(String pwd) {
        int length = pwd.length();

        if (length < 4 || length > 8) {
            throw new IllegalArgumentException();
        } else {
            this.password = pwd;
        }
    }

    public void setRoom(String room) {
        this.room = room;
    }
}
```

Data members

Constructors

Accessors

Mutators

8.7 Sample Development—*continued*

The skeleton main class is defined as follows:

```
/*
    Chapter 8 Sample Development: Keyless Entry System. (Step 1)

    File: Ch8EntranceMonitor.java
*/

import javax.swing.*;
import java.io.*;

class Ch8EntranceMonitor { //Step 1 main class

    private Dorm manager;

    private Scanner scanner;

    public Ch8EntranceMonitor( ) {

        manager = new Dorm();
        scanner = new Scanner(System.in);
    }

    public static void main(String[] args) {

        Ch8EntranceMonitor sentry = new Ch8EntranceMonitor();
        sentry.start();
    }

    public void start( ) {

        openFile( );

        String roster = manager.getResidentList();

        System.out.println(roster);
    }

    private void openFile( ) {
        String filename;

        while (true) {

            System.out.println("File to open ('x' to cancel):");
            filename = scanner.next();

            if (filename.equals("x")) {//input routine is canceled
                System.out.println("Program is canceled.");
                System.exit(0);
            }
```

start

openFile

```
            try {
                manager.openFile(filename);
                return;

            } catch (FileNotFoundException e) {

                System.out.println("No such file");

            } catch (IOException e) {

                System.out.println("Error in reading file");
            }
        }
    }
```

step 1 test

The purpose of step 1 testing is to verify that the **Dorm** class is used correctly to open a file and get the contents of the file. To test it, we need a file that contains the resident information. A sample test file can be created by executing the following program, which we can modify to create other test data files.

```
/*
    Chapter 8 Sample Development: Keyless Entry System.

    A simple class to create dummy test data.

    File: SampleCreateResidentFile.java
*/
import java.util.*;
import java.io.*;

class SampleCreateResidentFile {
    public static void main(String[] args)throws IOException {
        Resident res;
        Dorm manager = new Dorm( );

        res = new Resident("john", "1-101", "3457");
        manager.add(res);

        res = new Resident("java", "1-102", "4588");
        manager.add(res);

        res = new Resident("jill", "3-232", "8898");
        manager.add(res);
```

8.7 Sample Development—*continued*

```
            res = new Resident("jack", "3-232", "8008");
            manager.add(res);

            Scanner scanner = new Scanner(System.in);
            System.out.println("Save to which file:");
            String filename = scanner.next();

            manager.saveFile(filename);

            System.exit(0); //terminate the program
        }
    }
```

Step 2 Development: Create the User Interface

step 2 design

In the second development step, we will implement the user interface class **InputHandler,** whose task is to get three pieces of information. The main controller **Ch8EntranceMonitor** will call an **InputHandler** to get input data. An **InputHandler** will then go through a sequence of getting the three pieces of data. Once the data are entered, **Ch8EntranceMonitor** will ask the **InputHandler** for these data. The logic of **Ch8EntranceMonitor** can be expressed as follows:

```
InputHandler input = new InputHandler();

. . .

input.getInput();

String name = input.getName();
String room = input.getRoomNumber();
String pwd  = input.getPassword();
```

Given the input data, we can check for the match as

```
Dorm manager = new Dorm();

. . .

Resident res = manager.getResident(name);

if (res == null) {
   System.out.println("Invalid Entry");
```

```
} else if (res.getName().equals(name) &&
           res.getRoom().equals(room) &&
           res.getPassword().equals(password)) {

   door.open();

} else {
   System.out.println ("Invalid Entry");
}
```

The **getInput** method of the **InputHandler** class calls the scanner three times to get the name, room, and password. Each input is recorded in the corresponding data member. The accessors, such as **getName,** will simply return the value of the requested data member.

step 2 code

We will list first the **InputHandler** class and then the modified **Ch8EntranceMonitor** class. Here's the **InputHandler** class:

```
/*
   Chapter 8 Sample Development: Keyless Entry System

   File: InputHandler.java
*/

import java.util.*;
class InputHandler {

   private static final String BLANK = "";

   private String name;
   private String room;
   private String pwd;
   private Scanner scanner;

   public InputHandler( ) {

      name = BLANK;
      room = BLANK;
      pwd  = BLANK;
      scanner = new Scanner(System.in);
   }

   public void getInput( ) {

      System.out.print("Enter Name:");
      name = scanner.next();

      System.out.print("Enter Room No.:");
      room = scanner.next();

      System.out.print("Enter Password:");
      pwd  = scanner.next();
   }
```

Data members

Constructor

getInput

8.7 Sample Development—*continued*

```
    public String getName( ) {

        return name;
    }

    public String getRoom( ) {

        return room;
    }

    public String getPassword( ) {

        return pwd;
    }
}
```

Accessors

The main class is now modified to control an **InputHandler** object and to check entered information as the resident list maintained by a **Dorm** object. Here's the step 2 **Ch8EntranceMonitor** class:

```
/*
    Chapter 8 Sample Development: Keyless Entry System.

    File: Ch8EntranceMonitor.java (Step 2)
*/

import java.util.*;
import java.io.*;

class Ch8EntranceMonitor {

   private Dorm  manager;

   private Door  door;

   private InputHandler input;

   private Scanner scanner;

   public Ch8EntranceMonitor( ) {

       manager = new Dorm();
       scanner = new Scanner(System.in);
       input   = new InputHandler();
       door    = new Door();
   }
```

Data members

Constructors

```
public static void main(String[] args) {

    Ch8EntranceMonitor sentry = new Ch8EntranceMonitor();
    sentry.start();
}

public void start( ) {

    openFile( );

    String roster = manager.getResidentList(); //TEMP

    System.out.println(roster); //TEMP

    processInputData();
}

private void openFile( ) {
    String filename;

    while (true) {

        System.out.println("File to open ('x' to cancel):");
        filename = scanner.next();

        if (filename.equals("x")) {//input routine is canceled
            System.out.println("Program is canceled.");
            System.exit(0);
        }

        try {
            manager.openFile(filename);
            return;

        } catch (FileNotFoundException e) {

            System.out.println("No such file");

        } catch (IOException e) {

            System.out.println("Error in reading file");
        }
    }
}

private void processInputData( ) {

    String name, room, pwd;

    while (true) {

        input.getInput();

        name = input.getName();
        room = input.getRoom();
        pwd  = input.getPassword();
```

start

openFile

processInputData

8.7 Sample Development—*continued*

```
            validate(name, room, pwd);
        }
    }

    private void validate(String name, String room, String password) {

        Resident res = manager.getResident(name);

        if (res == null) {
            System.out.println("Invalid Entry");

        } else if (res.getName().equals(name) &&
                   res.getRoom().equals(room) &&
                   res.getPassword().equals(password)) {
            door.open();

        } else {
            System.out.println("Invalid Entry");
        }
    }
}
```

validate

Notice that the loop inside the **processInputData** method is an infinite loop. In other words, when the program starts, it will execute indefinitely. To terminate such a program, you must either close the Command window or select an appropriate menu choice (or click on a toolbar icon) in your Java IDE. We will discuss another way to terminate the program in step 3.

step 2 test

The purpose of step 2 testing is to verify the correct behavior of an **InputHandler** object. We need to test both successful and unsuccessful cases. We must verify that the door is in fact opened when valid information is entered. We must also verify that the error message is displayed when there's an error in input. We should test invalid cases such as entering nonexistent name, corrent name but wrong password, not entering all information, and so forth.

Step 3 Development: Improve and Finalize

There are several key improvements we can make to the program. The first and foremost is the improved user interface. Instead of getting three pieces of data individually by using a scanner, it would be nicer to have a frame window such as the one shown in Figure 8.10, where the user can enter all three pieces of information. We will describe how to develop such a frame window in Chapter 14.

Another improvement is to allow the administrator to terminate the program by entering special code. This is left as an exercise.

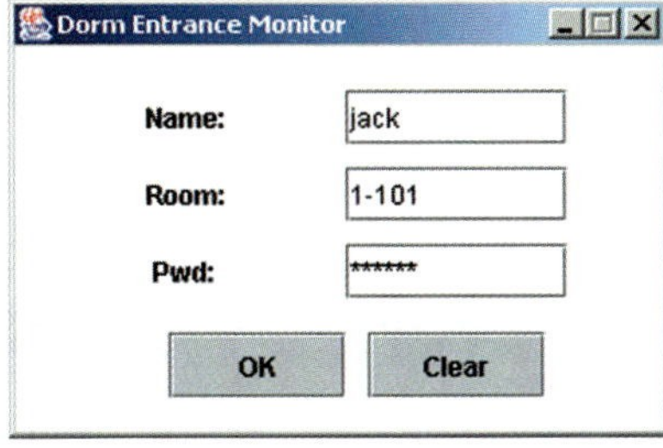

Figure 8.10 A frame window that allows the user to enter the three pieces of information together. Notice the input entered for the password is displayed back to the user as a sequence of asterisks.

Summary

- Two techniques to improve program reliability are exception handling and assertion.
- Exception handling is another type of control flow.
- An exception represents an error condition, and when it occurs, we say an exception is thrown.
- A thrown exception must be handled by either catching it or propagating it to other methods.
- If the program does include code to handle the thrown exceptions, then the system will handle them.
- A single method can be both a catcher and a propagator of an exception.
- The standard classes described or used in this chapter are

Throwable	RuntimeException
Error	IllegalArgumentException
Exception	InputMismatchException
IOException	

- The assertion feature is new to Java 2 SDK 1.4. You must use this version of the compiler to use assertions in the program.
- The assertion feature is used to detect internal logic errors.

Key Concepts

exceptions
try-catch
finally
throws
throw
exception hierarchy
programmer-defined exceptions
assertions
precondition assertions
postcondition assertions

Exercises

1. Determine the output of the following code when the input is (a) −1, (b) 0, and (c) 12XY.

```
Scanner scanner = new Scanner(System.in);

try {
   int num = scanner.nextInt();

   if (num != 0) {

       throw new Exception("Not zero");
   }

   System.out.println("I'm happy with the input.");

} catch (InputMismatchException e) {

   System.out.println("Invalid Entry");

} catch (Exception e) {

   System.out.println("Error: "+ e.getMessage());
}
```

2. Determine the output of the following code when the input is (a) −1, (b) 0, and (c) 12XY. This is the same question as Exercise 1, but the code here has the finally clause.

```
Scanner scanner = new Scanner(System.in);

try {

   int num = scanner.nextInt();

   if (num != 0) {

       throw new Exception("Not zero");
   }

   System.out.println("I'm happy with the input.");

} catch (InputMismatchException e) {

   System.out.println("Invalid Entry");
```

```
} catch (Exception e) {
   System.out.println("Error: "+ e.getMessage());
} finally {
   System.out.println("Finally Clause Executed");
}
```

3. Why is the following code not a good use of the assertion?

```
public void compute(int size) {
   assert size > 0;
   //computation code comes here
}
```

4. Modify the following code by adding the assert statement. The value of gender is either MALE or FEMALE if the program is running correctly.

```
switch (gender) {
   case MALE:        totalFee = tuition + parkingFee;
                     break;
   case FEMALE:      totalFee = tuition + roomAndBoard;
                     break;
}
```

5. Modify the following method by adding the assert statement. Assume the variable factor is a data member of the class.

```
public double compute(double value) {
   return (value * value) / factor;
}
```

6. Modify the getInput method of the InputHandler class from Section 8.7 so that the method will throw an exception when a blank string (a sequence of one or more blank spaces) is entered for the name, room, or password. Define a new exception class EmptyInputException.
7. The user module of the keyless entry system in Section 8.7 does not include any logic to terminate the program. Modify the program so it will terminate when the values Admin, X123, and $maTrix%TwO$ are entered for name, room, and password, respectively.

Development Exercises

For the following exercises, use the incremental development methodology to implement the program. For each exercise, identify the program tasks, create a design document with class descriptions, and draw the program diagram. Map out the development steps at the start. Present any design alternatives and justify your selection. Be sure to perform adequate testing at the end of each development step.

8. In the sample development, we developed the user module of the keyless entry system. For this exercise, implement the administrative module that allows the system administrator to add and delete Resident objects and modify information on existing Resident objects. The module will also allow the user to open a list from a file and save the list to a file. Is it proper to implement the administrative module by using one class? Wouldn't it be a better design if we used multiple classes with each class doing a single, well-defined task?
9. Write an application that maintains the membership lists of five social clubs in a dormitory. The five social clubs are the Computer Science Club, Biology Club, Billiard Club, No Sleep Club, and Wine Tasting Club. Use the Dorm class to manage the membership lists. Members of the social clubs are Resident objects of the dorm. Use a separate file to store the membership list for each club. Allow the user to add, delete, and modify members of each club.

9 Characters and Strings

Objectives

After you have read and studied this chapter, you should be able to

- Declare and manipulate data of the **char** type.
- Write string processing programs, using **String, StringBuilder,** and **StringBuffer** objects.
- Specify regular expressions for searching a pattern in a string.
- Differentiate the **String, StringBuilder,** and **StringBuffer** classes and use the correct class in solving a given task.
- Tell the difference between equality and equivalence testings for **String** objects.
- Use the **Pattern** and **Matcher** classes.

Introduction

Early computers in the 1940s and 1950s were more like gigantic calculators because they were used primarily for numerical computation. However, as computers have evolved to possess more computational power, our use of computers is no longer limited to numerical computation. Today we use computers for processing information of diverse types. In fact, most application software today such as Web browsers, word processors, database management systems, presentation software, and graphics design software is not intended specifically for number crunching. These programs still perform numerical computation, but their primary data are text, graphics, video, and other nonnumerical data. We have already seen examples of nonnumerical data processing. We introduced the `String` class and string processing in Chapter 2. A nonnumerical data type called `boolean` was used in Chapters 5 and 6. In this chapter, we will delve more deeply into the `String` class and present advanced string processing. We will also introduce the `char` data type for representing a single character and the `StringBuffer` class for an efficient operation on a certain type of string processing.

9.1 Characters

char

In Java single characters are represented by using the data type **char**. Character constants are written as symbols enclosed in single quotes, for example, 'a', 'X', and '5'. Just as we use different formats to represent integers and real numbers using 0s and 1s in computer memory, we use special codes of 0s and 1s to represent single characters. For example, we may assign 1 to represent 'A' and 2 to represent 'B'. We can assign codes similarly to lowercase letters, punctuation marks, digits, and other special symbols. In the early days of computing, different computers used not only different coding schemes but also different character sets. For example, one computer could represent the symbol ¼, while other computers could not. Individualized coding schemes did not allow computers to share information. Documents created by using one scheme are complete gibberish if we try to read these documents by using another scheme. To avoid this problem, U.S. computer manufacturers devised several coding schemes. One of the coding schemes widely used today is ***ASCII*** (American Standard Code for Information Interchange). We pronounce ASCII "ăs kē." Table 9.1 shows the 128 standard ASCII codes.

ASCII

Adding the row and column indexes gives you the ASCII code for a given character. For example, the value 87 is the ASCII code for the character 'W'. Not all characters in the table are printable. ASCII codes 0 through 31 and 127 are nonprintable control characters. For example, ASCII code 7 is the bell (the computer beeps when you send this character to output), and code 9 is the tab.

When we use a word processor to create a document, the file that contains the document includes not only the contents but also the formatting information. Since each software company uses its own coding scheme for storing this information, we have to use the same word processor to open the document. Often it is even worse. We cannot open a document created by a newer version of the same word processor with an older version. If we just want to exchange the text of a document, then we can convert it to ASCII format. Any word processor can open and save ASCII files. If we would like to retain the formatting information also, we can convert the document, using software such as Adobe Acrobat. This software converts a document (including text, formatting, images, etc.) created by different word processors to a format called PDF. Anybody with a free Acrobat Reader can open a PDF file. Many of the documents available from our website are in this PDF format.

To represent all 128 ASCII codes, we need 7 bits ranging from 000 0000 (0) to 111 1111 (127). Although 7 bits is enough, ASCII codes occupy 1 byte (8 bits) because the byte is the smallest unit of memory you can access. Computer manufacturers use the extra bit for other nonstandard symbols (e.g., lines and boxes). Using 8 bits, we can represent 256 symbols in total—128 standard ASCII codes and 128 nonstandard symbols.

Table 9.1 ASCII codes

	0	1	2	3	4	5	6	7	8	9
0	nul	soh	stx	etx	eot	enq	ack	bel	bs	ht
10	lf	vt	ff	cr	so	si	dle	dc1	dc2	dc3
20	cd4	nak	syn	etb	can	em	sub	esc	fs	gs
30	rs	us	sp	!	"	#	$	%	&	'
40	(	)	*	+	,	-	.	/	0	1
50	2	3	4	5	6	7	8	9	:	;
60	<	=	>	?	@	A	B	C	D	E
70	F	G	H	I	J	K	L	M	N	O
80	P	Q	R	S	T	U	V	W	X	Y
90	Z	[	\	]	^	_	`	a	b	c
100	d	e	f	g	h	i	j	k	l	m
110	n	o	p	q	r	s	t	u	v	w
120	x	y	z	{	|	}	~	del		

The standard ASCII codes work just fine as long as we are dealing with the English language because all letters and punctuation marks used in English are included in the ASCII codes. We cannot say the same for other languages. For languages such as French and German, the additional 128 codes may be used to represent character symbols not available in standard ASCII. But what about different currency symbols? What about non-European languages? Chinese, Japanese, and Korean all use different coding schemes to represent their character sets. Eight bits is not enough to represent thousands of ideographs. If we try to read Japanese characters by using ASCII, we will see only meaningless symbols.

Unicode

To accommodate the character symbols of non-English languages, the Unicode Consortium established the *Unicode Worldwide Character Standard,* commonly known simply as ***Unicode***, to support the interchange, processing, and display of the written texts of diverse languages. The standard currently contains 34,168 distinct characters, which cover the major languages of the Americas, Europe, the Middle East, Africa, India, Asia, and Pacifica. To accommodate such a large number of distinct character symbols, Unicode characters occupy 2 bytes. Unicode codes for the character set shown in Table 9.1 are the same as ASCII codes.

Java, being a language for the Internet, uses the Unicode standard for representing char constants. Although Java uses the Unicode standard internally to store characters, to use foreign characters for input and output in our programs, the operating system and the development tool we use for Java programs must be capable of handling the foreign characters.

Characters are declared and used in a manner similar to data of other types. The declaration

```
char ch1, ch2 = 'X';
```

declares two char variables ch1 and ch2 with ch2 initialized to 'X'. We can display the ASCII code of a character by converting it to an integer. For example, we can execute

```
System.out.println("ASCII code of character X is "
                     + (int)'X' );
```

Conversely, we can see a character by converting its ASCII code to the char data type, for example,

```
System.out.println(
        "Character with ASCII code 88 is " + (char)88 );
```

Because the characters have numerical ASCII values, we can compare characters just as we compare integers and real numbers. For example, the comparison

```
'A' < 'c'
```

returns true because the ASCII value of 'A' is 65 while that of 'c' is 99.

1. Determine the output of the following statements.

   a. `System.out.println( (char) 65 );`
   b. `System.out.println( (int) 'C' );`
   c. `System.out.println( 'Y' );`
   d.
   ```
   if ( 'A' < '?' )
      System.out.println( 'A' );
   else
      System.out.println( '?' );
   ```

2. How many distinct characters can you represent by using 8 bits?

9.2 Strings

String

A *string* is a sequence of characters that is treated as a single value. Instances of the **String** class are used to represent strings in Java. Rudimentary string processing was already presented in Chapter 2, using methods such as substring, length, and indexOf. In this section we will learn more advanced string processing, using other methods of the String class.

To introduce additional methods of the String class, we will go through a number of common string processing routines. The first is to process a string looking for a certain character or characters. Let's say we want to input a person's name and determine the number of vowels that the name contains. The basic idea is very simple:

```
for each character ch in the string {
   if (ch is a vowel) {
      increment the counter
   }
}
```

There are two details we need to know before being able to translate that into actual code. First, we need to know how to refer to an individual character in the string. Second, we need to know how to determine the size of the string, that is, the number of characters the string contains, so we can write the boolean expression to stop the loop correctly. We know from Chapter 2 that the second task is done by using the length method. For the first task, we use charAt.

charAt

We access individual characters of a string by calling the **charAt** method of the String object. For example, to display the individual characters of the string Sumatra one at a time, we can write

```
String name = "Sumatra";
int    size = name.length( );

for (int i = 0; i < size; i++) {
   System.out.println(name.charAt(i));
}
```

Each character in a string has an index that we use to access the character. We use zero-based indexing; that is, the first character has index 0, the second character

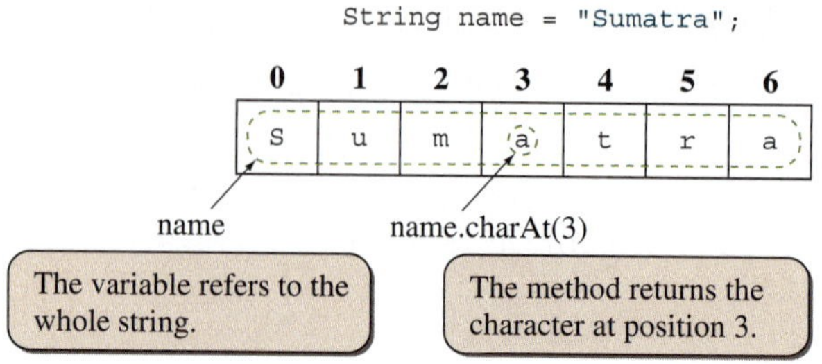

Figure 9.1 An indexed expression is used to refer to individual characters in a string.

has index 1, the third character has index 2, and so forth. To refer to the first character of name, for example, we say

```
name.charAt(0)
```

Since the characters are indexed from 0 to size-1, we could express the preceding for loop as

```
for (int i = 0; i <= size - 1; i++)
```

However, we will use the first style almost exclusively to be consistent.

Figure 9.1 illustrates how the charAt method works. Notice that name refers to a String object, and we are calling its charAt method that returns a value of primitive data type char. Strictly speaking, we must say "name is a variable of type String whose value is a reference to an instance of String." However, when the value of a variable X is a reference to an instance of class Y, we usually say "X is an instance of Y" or "X is a Y object."

Things to Remember

*If the value of a variable **X** is a reference to an object of class **Y**, then we say "**X** is a **Y** object" or "**X** is an instance of **Y**."*

Since String is a class, we can create an instance of a class by using the new method. The statements we have been using so far, such as

```
String name1 = "Kona";

String name2;
name2 = "Espresso";
```

work as a shorthand for

```
String name1 = new String("Kona");

String name2;
name2 = new String("Espresso");
```

Be aware that this shorthand works for the String class only. Moreover, although the difference will not be critical in almost all situations, they are not exactly the same. We will discuss the subtle difference between the two in Section 9.5.

Here is the code for counting the number of vowels:

```
/*
    Chapter 9 Sample Program: Count the number of vowels
                              in a given string

    File: Ch9CountVowels.java
*/

import java.util.*;

class Ch9CountVowels {

    public static void main (String[] args) {

        Scanner scanner = new Scanner(System.in);
        scanner.useDelimiter(System.getProperty("line.separator"));

        String name;

        int     numberOfCharacters,
                vowelCount = 0;

        char    letter;

        System.out.print("What is your name?");
        name = scanner.next( );

        numberOfCharacters = name.length( );

        for (int i = 0; i < numberOfCharacters; i++) {

            letter = name.charAt(i);

            if (letter == 'a' || letter == 'A' ||
                letter == 'e' || letter == 'E' ||
                letter == 'i' || letter == 'I' ||
                letter == 'o' || letter == 'O' ||
                letter == 'u' || letter == 'U'     ) {

                vowelCount++;
            }
        }

        System.out.println(name + ", your name has " +
                                vowelCount + " vowels");
    }
}
```

We can shorten the boolean expression in the if statement by using the toUpperCase method of the String class. This method converts every character in a string to uppercase. Here's the rewritten code:

```
/*
    Chapter 9 Sample Program: Count the number of vowels
                              in a given string using toUpperCase

    File: Ch9CountVowels2.java
*/

import java.util.*;

class Ch9CountVowels2 {

    public static void main (String[] args) {

        Scanner scanner = new Scanner(System.in);
        scanner.useDelimiter(System.getProperty("line.separator?"));

        String    name, nameUpper;

        int       numberOfCharacters,
                  vowelCount = 0;

        char      letter;

        System.out.print("What is your name?");
        name = scanner.next( );

        numberOfCharacters = name.length( );
        nameUpper = name.toUpperCase( );

        for (int i = 0; i < numberOfCharacters; i++) {

            letter = nameUpper.charAt(i);

            if (letter == 'A' ||
                letter == 'E' ||
                letter == 'I' ||
                letter == 'O' ||
                letter == 'U'    ) {

                vowelCount++;
            }
        }

        (name + ", your name has " +
        vowelCount + " vowels");
    }
}
```

toUpperCase

Notice that the original string name is unchanged. A new, converted string is returned from the **toUpperCase** method and assigned to the second String variable nameUpper.

Let's try another example. This time we read in a string and count how many words the string contains. For this example we consider a word as a sequence of characters separated, or delimited, by blank spaces. We treat punctuation marks and other symbols as part of a word. Expressing the task in pseudocode, we have the following:

```
read in a sentence;

while (there are more characters in the sentence) {

    look for the beginning of the next word;

    now look for the end of this word;

    increment the word counter;
}
```

We use a while loop here instead of do–while to handle the case when the input sentence contains no characters, that is, when it is an empty string. Let's implement the routine. Here's our first attempt:

```
//Attempt No. 1

static final char BLANK = ' ';

Scanner scanner = new Scanner(System.in);
scanner.useDelimiter(System.getProperty("line.separator "));

int     index, wordCount, numberOfCharacters;

System.out.println("Enter a sentence: ");
String sentence = scanner.next( );

numberOfCharacters = sentence.length();
index     = 0;
wordCount = 0;

while (index < numberOfCharacters ) {

   //ignore blank spaces
   while (sentence.charAt(index) == BLANK) {
      index++;
   }

   //now locate the end of the word
   while (sentence.charAt(index) != BLANK) {
      index++;
   }

   //another word has been found, so increment the counter
   wordCount++;
}
```

Skip blank spaces until a character that is not a blank space is encountered. This is the beginning of a word.

Once the beginning of a word is detected, we skip nonblank characters until a blank space is encountered. This is the end of the word.

Bad Version

Bad Version

This implementation has a problem. The counter variable index is incremented inside the two inner while loops, and this index could become equal to numberOfCharacters, which is an error, because the position of the last character is numberOfCharacters – 1. We need to modify the two while loops so that index will not become larger than numberOfCharacters –1. Here's the modified code:

```
/*
    Chapter 9 Sample Program: Count the number of words
                              in a given string

    File: Ch9CountWords.java (Attempt 2)
*/

import java.util.*;

class Ch9CountWords { //Attempt 2

    private static final char BLANK = ' ';

    public static void main (String[] args) {

        Scanner scanner = new Scanner(System.in);
        scanner.useDelimiter(System.getProperty("line.separator "));

        int     index, wordCount, numberOfCharacters;

        System.out.println("Enter a sentence: ");
        String sentence = scanner.next( );

        numberOfCharacters = sentence.length( );
        index              = 0;
        wordCount          = 0;

        while ( index < numberOfCharacters ) {

            //ignore blank spaces
            while (index < numberOfCharacters &&
                   sentence.charAt(index) == BLANK) {

                index++;
            }

            //now locate the end of the word
            while (index < numberOfCharacters &&
                   sentence.charAt(index) != BLANK) {

                index++;
            }

            //another word is found, so increment the counter
            wordCount++;

        }
```

```
        //display the result
        System.out.println( "\n input sentence: " + sentence );
        System.out.println( "       Word count: " + wordCount + " words" );

    }
}
```

Notice that the order of comparisons in the boolean expression

```
index < numberOfCharacters
            && sentence.charAt(index) == BLANK
```

is critical. If we switch the order to

```
sentence.charAt(index) == BLANK
            && index < numberOfCharacters
```

out-of-bound exception

and if the last character in the string is a space, then an ***out-of-bound exception*** will occur because the value of index is a position that does not exist in the string sentence. By putting the expression correctly as

```
index < numberOfCharacters && sentence.charAt(index) != ' '
```

we will not get an out-of-bound exception because the boolean operator && is a shortcircuit operator. If the relation index < numberOfCharacters is false, then the second half of the expression sentence.charAT(index) != BLANK will not get evaluated.

There is still a problem with the attempt 2 code. If the sentence ends with one or more blank spaces, then the value for wordCount will be 1 more than the actual number of words in the sentence. It is left as an exercise to correct this bug (see Exercise 15 at the end of the chapter).

Our third example counts the number of times the word Java occurs in the input. The repetition stops when the word STOP is read. Lowercase and uppercase letters are not distinguished when an input word is compared to Java, but the word STOP for terminating the loop must be in all uppercase letters. Here's the pseudocode:

```
javaCount = 0;

while (true) {
   read in next word;

   if (word is "STOP") {
      break;
```

```
        } else if (word is "Java" ignoring cases) {
            javaCount++;
        }
    }
```

And here's the actual code. Pay close attention to how the strings are compared.

```
/*
    Chapter 9 Sample Program:

        Count the number of times the word 'java' occurs
        in input. Case-insensitive comparison is used here.
        The program terminates when the word STOP (case-sensitive)
        is entered.

    File: Ch9CountJava.java
*/

import java.util.*;

class Ch9CountJava {

    public static void main (String[] args) {

        Scanner scanner = new Scanner(System.in);

        int     javaCount = 0;

        String  word;

        while (true) {

            System.out.print("Next word: ");
            word = scanner.next( );

            if (word.equals("STOP") )  {
                break;

            } else if (word.equalsIgnoreCase("Java") ) {
                javaCount++;
            }
        }

        System.out.println("'Java' count: " + javaCount );
    }
}
```

String comparison is done by two methods—equals and equalsIgnoreCase—whose meanings should be clear from the example. Another comparison method is compareTo. This method compares two String objects str1 and str2 as in

compareTo

```
str1.compareTo( str2 );
```

and returns 0 if they are equal, a negative integer if str1 is less than str2, and a positive integer if str1 is greater than str2. The comparison is based on the lexicographic order of Unicode. For example, caffeine is less than latte. Also, the string jaVa is less than the string java because the Unicode value of V is smaller than the Unicode value of v. (See the ASCII table, Table 9.1.)

Some of you may be wondering why we don't say

```
if ( word == "STOP" )
```

We can, in fact, use the equality comparison symbol == to compare two String objects, but the result is different from the result of the method equals. We will explain the difference in Section 9.5.

Let's try another example, using the substring method we introduced in Chapter 2. To refresh our memory, here's how the method works. If str is a String object, then the expression

```
str.substring ( beginIndex, endIndex )
```

returns a new string that is a substring of str from position beginIndex to endIndex – 1. The value of beginIndex must be between 0 and str.length() – 1, and the value of endIndex must be between 0 and str.length(). In addition, the value of beginIndex must be less than or equal to the value of endIndex. Passing invalid values for beginIndex or endIndex will result in a runtime error.

In this example, we print out the words from a given sentence, using one line per word. For example, given an input sentence

```
I want to be a Java programmer
```

the code will print out

```
I
want
to
be
a
Java
programmer
```

This sample code is similar to the previous one that counts the number of words in a given sentence. Instead of just counting the words, we need to extract the word from the sentence and print it out. Here's how we write the code:

```
/*
    Chapter 9 Sample Program:

            Extract the words in a given sentence and
            print them, using one line per word.

    File: Ch9ExtractWords.java
*/

import java.util.*;

class Ch9ExtractWords {

    private static final char BLANK = ' ';

    public static void main (String[] args) {

        Scanner scanner = new Scanner(System.in);
        scanner.useDelimiter(System.getProperty("line.separator"));

        int     index,   numberOfCharacters,
                beginIdx, endIdx;

        String word, sentence;
        System.out.print("Input: ");
        Sentence = scanner.next( );

        numberOfCharacters = sentence.length();
        index = 0;

        while (index < numberOfCharacters) {

            //ignore leading blank spaces
            while (index < numberOfCharacters &&
                   sentence.charAt(index) == BLANK) {

                index++;
            }

            beginIdx = index;

            //now locate the end of the word
            while (index < numberOfCharacters &&
                   sentence.charAt(index) != BLANK) {

                index++;
            }
```

```
                endIdx = index;

                if (beginIdx != endIdx) {

                    //another word is found, extract it from the
                    //sentence and print it out

                        word = sentence.substring( beginIdx, endIdx );

                        System.out.println(word);
                }
            }
        }
    }
```

Notice the signficance of the test

```
if (beginIdx != endIdx)
```

in the code. For what kinds of input sentences will the variables beginIdx and endIdx be equal? We'll leave this as an exercise (see Exercise 16 at the end of the chapter).

1. Determine the output of the following code.

   a.
   ```
   String str = "Programming";
   for (int i = 0; i < 9; i+=2) {
       System.out.print( str.charAt( i ) );
   }
   ```

   b.
   ```
   String str = "World Wide Web";
   for (int i = 0; i < 10; i ++ ) {
      if ( str.charAt(i) == 'W') {
         System.out.println( 'M' );
      } else {
         System.out.print( str.charAt(i) );
      }
   }
   ```

2. Write a loop that prints out a string in reverse. If the string is Hello, then the code outputs olleH.

3. Assume two String objects str1 and str2 are initialized as follows:

```
String str1 = "programming";
String str2 = "language";
```

Determine the value of each of the following expressions if they are valid. If they are not valid, state the reason why.

a. `str1.compareTo( str2 )`
b. `str2.compareTo( str2 )`
c. `str2.substring( 1, 1 )`
d. `str2.substring( 0, 7 )`
e. `str2.charAt( 11 )`
f. `str1.length( ) + str2.length( )`

4. What is the difference between the two String methods equals and equalsIgnoreCase?

9.3 Pattern Matching and Regular Expression

pattern matching

One sample code from Section 9.2 searched for the word Java in a given string. This sample code illustrated a very simplified version of a well-known problem called ***pattern matching***. Word processor features such as finding a text and replacing a text with another text are two specialized cases of a pattern-matching problem.

The matches Method

Let's begin with the matches method from the String class. In its simplest form, it looks very similar to the equals method. For example, given a string str, the two statements

```
str.equals("Hello");

str.matches("Hello");
```

both evaluate to true if str is the string Hello. However, they are not truly equivalent, because, unlike equals, the argument to the matches method can be a pattern, a feature that brings great flexibility and power to the matches method.

Suppose we assign a three-digit code to all incoming students. The first digit represents the major, and 5 stands for the computer science major. The second digit represents the home state: 1 is for in-state students, 2 is for out-of-state students, and 3 is for foreign students. And the third digit represents the residence of the student. On-campus dormitories are represented by digits from 1 through 7. Students living off campus are represented by digit 8. For example, the valid encodings for students majoring in computer science and living off campus are 518, 528, and 538. The valid three-digit code for computer science majors living in one of the on-campus dormitories can be expressed succinctly as

```
5[123][1-7]
```

and here's how we interpret the pattern:

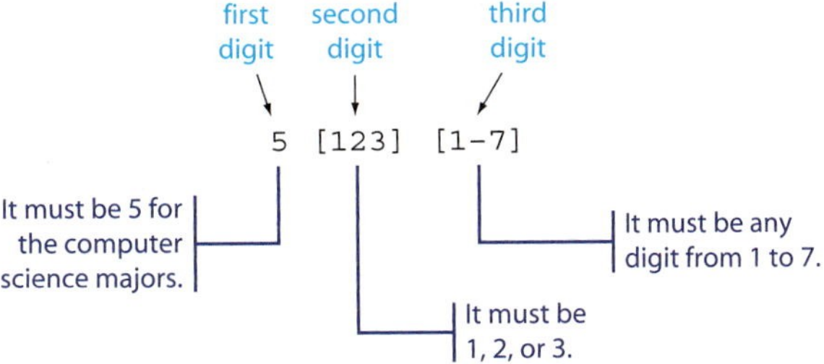

regular expression

The pattern is called a ***regular expression*** that allows us to denote a large (often infinite) set of words succinctly. The "word" is composed of any sequence of symbols and is not limited to alphabets. The brackets [ ] are used here to represent choices, so [123] means 1, 2, or 3. We can use the notation for alphabets also. For example, [aBc] means a, B, or c. Notice the notation is case-sensitive. The hyphen in the brackets shows the range, so [1-7] means any digit from 1 to 7. If we want to allow any lowercase letter, then the regular expression will be [a-z]. The hat symbol ^ is used for negation. For example, [^abc] means any character except a, b, or c. Notice that this expression does not restrict the character to lowercase letters; it can be any character including digits and symbols. To refer to all lowercase letters except a, b, or c, the correct expression is [a-z&&[^abc]]. The double ampersand represents an intersection. Here are more examples:

Expression	Description
`[013]`	A single digit 0, 1, or 3.
`[0-9][0-9]`	Any two-digit number from 00 to 99.
`A[0-4]b[05]`	A string that consists of four characters. The first character is A. The second character is 0, 1, 2, 3, or 4. The third character is b. And the last character is either 0 or 5.
`[0-9&&[^4567]]`	A single digit that is 0, 1, 2, 3, 8, or 9.
`[a-z0-9]`	A single character that is either a lowercase letter or a digit.

We can use repetition symbols * or + to designate a sequence of unbounded length. The symbol * means 0 or more times, and the symbol + means 1 or more times. Let's try an example using a repetition symbol. Remember the definition for a valid Java identifier? We define it as a seqence of alphanumeric characters, underscores, and dollar signs, with the first character being an alphabet. In regular expression, we can state this definition as

```
[a-zA-Z][a-zA-Z0-9_$]*
```

Let's write a short program that will input a word and determine whether it is a valid Java identifier. The program stops when the word entered is **STOP**. Here's the program:

```
/*
    Chapter 9 Sample Program: Checks whether the input
            string is a valid identifier.

    File: Ch9MatchJavaIdentifier.java
*/

import java.util.*;

class Ch9MatchJavaIdentifier {

    private static final String STOP    = "STOP";
    private static final String VALID   = "Valid Java identifier";
    private static final String INVALID = "Not a valid Java identifier";

    private static final String VALID_IDENTIFIER_PATTERN
                            = "[a-zA-Z][a-zA-Z0-9_$]*";

    public static void main (String[] args) {

        Scanner scanner = new Scanner (System.in);

        String str, reply;

        while (true) {

            System.out.print ("Identifier: ");
            str = scanner.next( );

            if (str.equals(STOP)) break;

            if (str.matches(VALID_IDENTIFIER_PATTERN)) {
                reply = VALID;

            } else {
                reply = INVALID;
            }

            System.out.println(str + ": " + reply + "\n");
        }
    }
}
```

It is also possible to designate a sequence of fixed length. For example, to specify four-digit numbers, we write **[0-9]{4}**. The number in the braces { and } denotes the number of repetitions. We can specify the minimum and maximum numbers of repetitions also. Here are the rules:

Expression	Description
X{N}	Repeat X exactly N times, where X is a regular expression for a single character.
X{N,}	Repeat X at least N times.
X{N,M}	Repeat X at least N but no more than M times.

Here's an example of using a sequence of fixed length. Suppose we want to determine whether the input string represents a valid phone number that follows the pattern of

```
xxx-xxx-xxxx
```

where x is a single digit from 0 through 9. The following is a program that inputs a string continually and replies whether the input string conforms to the pattern. The program terminates when a single digit 0 is entered. Structurally this program is identical to the Ch9MatchJavaIdentifier class. Here's the program:

```
/*
    Chapter 9 Sample Program: Checks whether the input
            string conforms to the phone number
            pattern xxx-xxx-xxxx.

    File: Ch9MatchPhoneNumber.java
*/

import java.util.*;

class Ch9MatchPhoneNumber {

    private static final String STOP    = "0";
    private static final String VALID   = "Valid phone number";
    private static final String INVALID = "Not a valid phone number";

    private static final String VALID_PHONE_PATTERN
                    = "[0-9]{3}-[0-9]{3}-[0-9]{4}";

    public static void main (String[] args) {

        Scanner scanner = new Scanner (System.in);

        String phoneStr, reply;

        while (true) {

            System.out.print ("Phone#: ");
            phoneStr = scanner.next( );
```

```
            if (phoneStr.equals(STOP)) break;

            if (phoneStr.matches(VALID_PHONE_PATTERN)) {
                reply = VALID;

            } else {
                reply = INVALID;
            }

            System.out.println(phoneStr + ": " + reply + "\n");
        }
    }
}
```

Suppose, with the proliferation of cell phones, the number of digits used for a prefix increases from three to four in major cities. (In fact, Tokyo now uses a four-digit prefix. Phenomenal growth in the use of fax machines in both offices and homes caused the increase from three to four digits.) The valid format for phone numbers then becomes

```
xxx-xxx-xxxx    or    xxx-xxxx-xxxx
```

This change can be handled effortlessly by defining VALID_PHONE_PATTERN as

```
private static final String VALID_PHONE_PATTERN
        = "[0-9]{3}-[0-9]{3,4}-[0-9]{4}";
```

This is the power of regular expression and pattern-matching methods. All we need to do is to make one simple adjustment to the regular expression. No other changes are made to the program. Had we written the program without using the pattern-matching technique (i.e., written the program using repetition control to test the first to the last character individually), changing the code to handle both a three-digit and a four-digit prefix requires substantially greater effort.

The period symbol (.) is used to match any character except a line terminator such as \n or \r. (By using the Pattern class, we can make it match a line terminator also. We discuss more details on the Pattern class later.) We can use the period symbol with the zero-or-more-times notation * to check if a given string contains a sequence of characters we are looking for. For example, suppose a String object document holds the content of some document, and we want to check if the phrase "zen of objects" is in it. We can do it as follows:

```
String document;

document = ...; //assign text to 'document'

if (document.matches(".*zen of objects.*") {

   System.out.println("Found");
```

```
} else {

   System.out.println("Not found");

}
```

The brackets [and] are used for expressing a range of choices for a single character. If we need to express a range of choices for multiple characters, then we use the parentheses and the vertical bar. For example, if we search for the word *maximum* or *minimum,* we express the pattern as

```
(max|min)imum
```

Here are some more examples:

Expression	Description
`[wb](ad|eed)`	Matches `wad`, `weed`, `bad`, and `beed`.
`(pro|anti)-OO?`	Matches `pro-OOP` and `anti-OOP`.
`(AZ|CA|CO)[0-9]{4}`	Matches AZxxxx, CAxxxx, and COxxxx, where x is a single digit.

The replaceAll Method

Using the replaceAll method, we can replace all occurrences of a substring that matches a given regular expression with a given replacement string. For example, here's how to replace all vowels in the string with the @ symbol:

```
String originalText, modifiedText;
originalText = ...; //assign string to 'originalText'

modifiedText = originalText.replaceAll("[aeiou]", "@");
```

Notice the original text is unchanged. The replaceAll method returns a modified text as a separate string. Here are more examples:

Expression	Description
`str.replaceAll("OOP", "object-oriented programming")`	Replace all occurrences of `OOP` with `object-oriented programming`.
`str.replaceAll( "[0-9]{3}-[0-9]{2}-[0-9]{4}", "xxx-xx-xxxx")`	Replace all social security numbers with `xxx-xx-xxxx`.
`str.replaceAll("o{2,}", "oo")`	Replace all occurrences of a sequence that has two or more of letter `o` with `oo`.

If we want to match only the whole word, we have to use the \b symbol to designate the word boundary. Suppose we write

```
str.replaceAll("temp", "temporary");
```

expecting to replace all occurrences of the abbreviated word temp by temporary. We will get a surprising result. All occurrences of the sequence of characters temp will be replaced; so, for example, words such as attempt or tempting would be replaced by attemporaryt or temporaryting, respectively. To designate the sequence temp as a whole word, we place the word boundary symbol \b in the front and end of the sequence.

```
str.replaceAll("\\btemp\\b", "temporary");
```

Notice the use of two backslashes. The symbol we use in the regular expression is \b. However, we must write this regular expression in a String representation. And remember that the backslash symbol in a string represents a control character such as \n, \t, and \r. To specify the regular expression symbol with a backslash, we must use additional backslash, so the system will not interpret it as some kind of control character. The regular expression we want here is

```
\btemp\b
```

To put it in a String representation, we write

```
"\\btemp\\b"
```

Here are the common backslash symbols used in regular expressions:

Expression	String Representation	Description
`\d`	`"\\d"`	A single digit. Equivalent to `[0-9]`.
`\D`	`"\\D"`	A single nondigit. Equivalent to `[^0-9]`.
`\s`	`"\\s"`	A white space character, such as space, tab, new line, etc.
`\S`	`"\\S"`	A non-white-space character.
`\w`	`"\\w"`	A word character. Equivalent to `[a-zA-Z_0-9]`.
`\W`	`"\\W"`	A nonword character.
`\b`	`"\\b"`	A word boundary (such as a white space and punctuation mark).
`\B`	`"\\B"`	A nonword boundary.

We also use the backslash if we want to search for a command character. For example, the plus symbol designates one or more repetitions. If we want to search for the plus symbol in the text, we use the backslash as \+ and to express it as a string, we write "\\+". Here's an example. To replace all occurrences of C and C++ (not necessarily a whole word) with Java, we write

```
str.replaceAll("(C|C\\+\\+)", "Java");
```

1. Describe the string that the following regular expressions match.
   a. `a*b`
   b. `b[aiu]d`
   c. `[Oo]bject(s| )`
2. Write a regular expression for a state vehicle license number whose format is a single capital letter, followed by three digits and four lowercase letters.
3. Which of the following regular expressions are invalid?
   a. `(a-z)*+`
   b. `[a|ab]xyz`
   c. `abe-14`
   d. `[a-z&&^a^b]`
   e. `[//one]two`

9.4 The Pattern and Matcher Classes

The matches and replaceAll methods of the String class are shorthand for using the Pattern and Matcher classes from the java.util.regex package. We will describe how to use these two classes for more efficient pattern matching.

The statement

```
str.matches(regex);
```

where str and regex are String objects is equivalent to

```
Pattern.matches(regex, str);
```

which in turn is equivalent to

```
Pattern pattern = Pattern.compile(regex);
Matcher matcher = pattern.matcher(str);
matcher.matches();
```

Similarly, the statement

```
str.replaceAll(regex, replacement);
```

where replacement is a replacement text is equivalent to

```
Pattern pattern = Pattern.compile(regex);
Matcher matcher = pattern.matcher(str);
matcher.replaceAll(replacement);
```

Explicit creation of Pattern and Matcher objects gives us more options and greater efficiency. We specify regular expressions as strings, but for the system to actually carry out the pattern-matching operation, the stated regular expression must first be converted to an internal format. This is done by the compile method of the Pattern class. When we use the matches method of the String or Pattern class, this conversion into the internal format is carried out every time the matches method is executed. So if we use the same pattern multiple times, then it is more efficient to convert just once, instead of repeating the same conversion, as was the case for the Ch9MatchJavaIdentifier and Ch9MatchPhoneNumber classes. The following is Ch9MatchJavaIdentifierPM, a more efficient version of Ch9MatchJavaIdentifier:

```
/*
    Chapter 9 Sample Program: Checks whether the input
            string is a valid identifier. This version
            uses the Matcher and Pattern classes.

    File: Ch9MatchJavaIdentifierPM.java
*/

import java.util.*;
import java.util.regex.*;

class Ch9MatchJavaIdentifierPM {

    private static final String STOP    = "STOP";
    private static final String VALID   = "Valid Java identifier";
    private static final String INVALID = "Not a valid Java identifier";

    private static final String VALID_IDENTIFIER_PATTERN
                    = "[a-zA-Z][a-zA-Z0-9_$]*";

    public static void main (String[] args) {

        Scanner scanner = new Scanner(System.in);

        String  str, reply;
        Matcher matcher;
        Pattern pattern
                    = Pattern.compile(VALID_IDENTIFIER_PATTERN);

        while (true) {

            System.out.print("Identifier: ");
            str = Scanner.next();

            if (str.equals(STOP)) break;

            matcher = pattern.matcher(str);

            if (matcher.matches()) {
                reply = VALID;
```

```
            } else {
                reply = INVALID;
            }

            System.out.println(str + ": " + reply + "\n");
        }
    }
}
```

We have a number of options when the **Pattern** compiles into an internal format. For example, by default, the period symbol does not match the line terminator character. We can override this default by passing **DOTALL** as the second argument as

```
Pattern pattern = Pattern.compile(regex, Pattern.DOTALL);
```

To enable case-insensitive matching, we pass the **CASE_INSENSITIVE** constant.

The **find** method is another powerful method of the **Matcher** class. This method searches for the next sequence in a string that matches the pattern. The method returns **true** if the patten is found. We can call the method repeatedly until it returns **false** to find all matches. Here's an example that counts the number of times the word **java** occurs in a given document. We will search for the word in a case-insensitive manner.

```
/*
    Chapter 9 Sample Program:

            Count the number of times the word 'java' occurs
            in input sentence using pattern matching.

    File: Ch9CountJavaPM.java
*/

import java.util.*;
import java.util.regex.*;

class Ch9CountJavaPM {

    public static void main (String[] args) {

        Scanner scanner = new Scanner(System.in);
        scanner.useDelimiter(System.getProperty("line.separator"));

        String   document;
        int      javaCount;

        Matcher  matcher;
        Pattern  pattern = Pattern.compile("java",
                                           Pattern.CASE_INSENSITIVE);
```

```
        System.out.println("Sentence: ");
        document = scanner.next();

        javaCount = 0;
        matcher   = pattern.matcher(document);

        while (matcher.find()) {

            javaCount++;
        }

        System.out.println("The word 'java' occurred " +
                            javaCount + " times.");
    }
}
```

When a matcher finds a matching sequence of characters, we can query the location of the sequence by using the start and end methods. The start method returns the position in the string where the first character of the pattern is found, and the end method returns the value 1 more than the position in the string where the last character of the pattern is found. Here's the code that prints out the matching sequences and their locations in the string when searching for the word java in a case-insensitive manner.

```
/*
    Chapter 9 Sample Program:

            Displays the positions of the word 'java'
            in a given string using pattern-matching technique.

    File: Ch9LocateJavaPM.java
*/

import javax.swing.*;
import java.util.regex.*;

class Ch9LocateJavaPM {

    public static void main (String[] args) {

        Scanner scanner = new Scanner(System.in);
        scanner.useDelimiter(System.getProperty("line.separator"));

        String  document;

        Matcher matcher;
        Pattern pattern = Pattern.compile("java",
                                          Pattern.CASE_INSENSITIVE);
```

```
            System.out.println("Sentence: ");
            document = scanner.next();

            matcher  = pattern.matcher(document);

            while (matcher.find()) {

                System.out.println(document.substring(matcher.start(),
                                                      matcher.end())
                                   + " found at position "
                                   + matcher.start());
            }
        }
    }
```

1. Replace the following statements with the equivalent ones using the Pattern and Matcher classes.

   a. `str.replaceAll("1", "one");`
   b. `str.matches("alpha");`

2. Using the find method of the Matcher class, check if the given string document contains the whole word Java.

9.5 Comparing Strings

We already discussed how objects are compared in Chapter 5. The same rule applies for the string, but we have to be careful in certain situations because of the difference in the way a new String object is created. First, we will review how the objects are compared. The difference between

== versus equals

```
String word1, word2;
...
if ( word1 == word2 ) ...
```

and

```
if ( word1.equals(word2) ) ...
```

is illustrated in Figure 9.2. The equality test == is true if the contents of variables are the same. For a primitive data type, the contents are values themselves; but for a reference data type, the contents are addresses. So for a reference data type, the equality test is true if both variables refer to the same object, because they both contain the same address. The equals method, on the other hand, is true if the String objects to which the two variables refer contain the same string value. To distinguish the two types of comparisons, we will use the term ***equivalence test*** for the equals method.

equivalence test

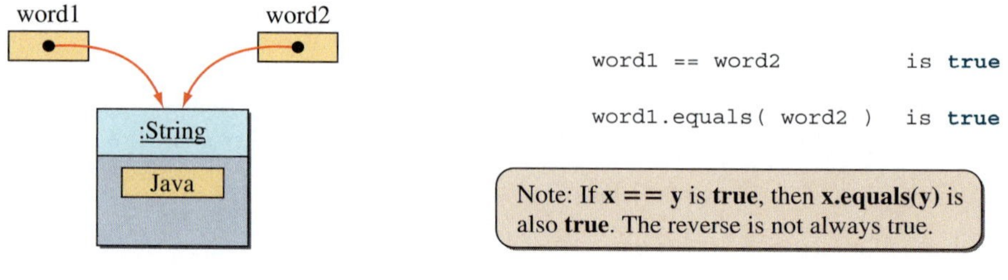
Case A: Referring to the same object.
word1
word2
:String
Java
word1 == word2 is true
word1.equals(word2) is true
Note: If x == y is true, then x.equals(y) is also true. The reverse is not always true.

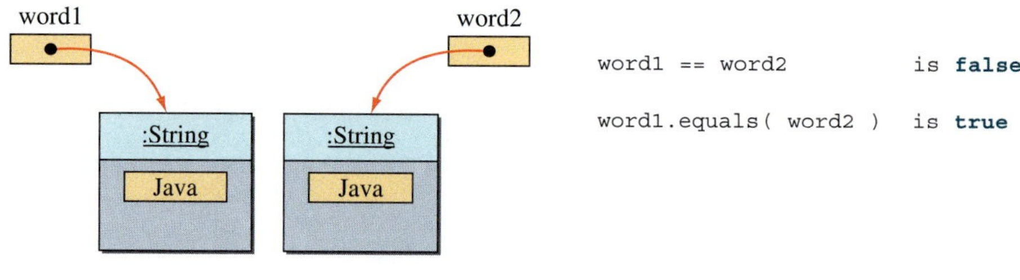
Case B: Referring to different objects having identical string values.
word1
word2
:String
Java
:String
Java
word1 == word2 is false
word1.equals(word2) is true

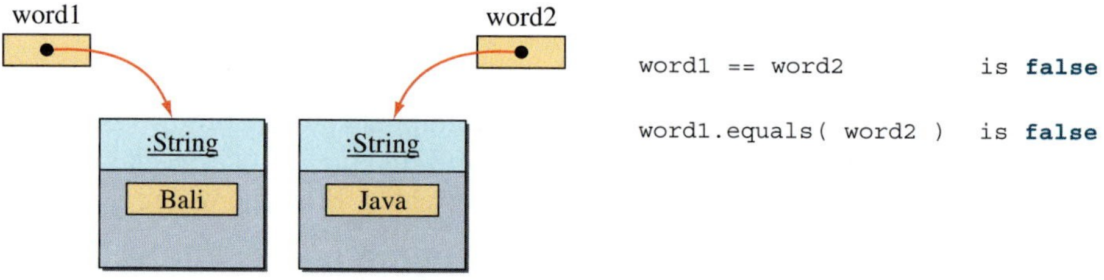
Case C: Referring to different objects having different string values.
word1
word2
:String
Bali
:String
Java
word1 == word2 is false
word1.equals(word2) is false

Figure 9.2 The difference between the equality test and the **equals** method.

As long as we create a new String object as

```
String str = new String("Java");
```

using the new operator, the rule for comparing objects applies to comparing strings. However, when the new operator is not used, for example, in

```
String str = "Java";
```

we have to be careful. Figure 9.3 shows the difference in assigning a String object to a variable. If we do not use the new operator, then string data are treated as if they

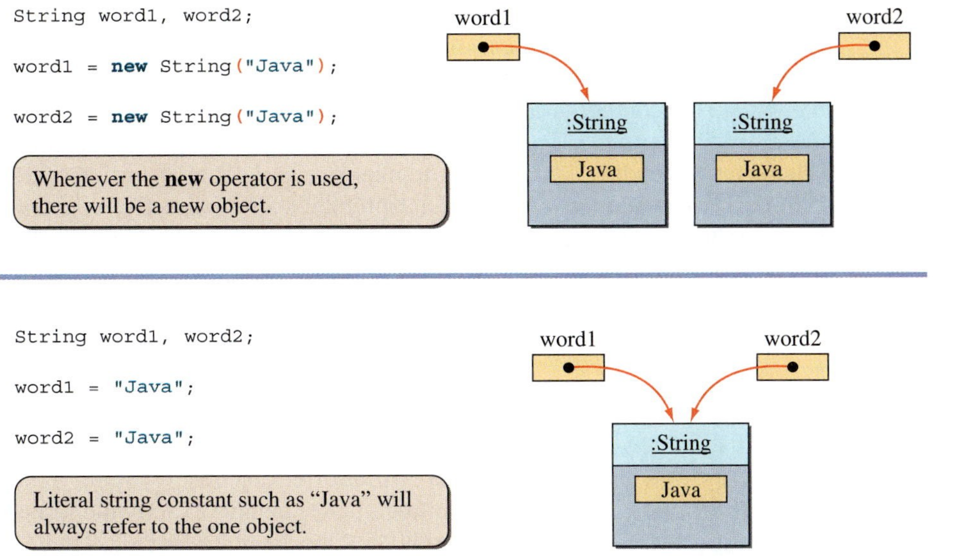
String word1, word2;
word1 = new String("Java");
word2 = new String("Java");
Whenever the new operator is used, there will be a new object.
word1
word2
:String
Java
:String
Java
String word1, word2;
word1 = "Java";
word2 = "Java";
Literal string constant such as "Java" will always refer to the one object.
word1
word2
:String
Java

Figure 9.3 Difference between using and not using the **new** operator for **String.**

are primitive data type. When we use the same literal String constants in a program, there will be exactly one String object.

Quick
CHECK

1. Show the state of memory after the following statements are executed.

```
String str1, str2, str3;
str1 = "Jasmine";
str2 = "Oolong";
str3 = str2;
str2 = str1;
```

9.6 StringBuffer and StringBuilder

A String object is immutable, which means that once a String object is created, we cannot change it. In other words, we can read individual characters in a string, but we cannot add, delete, or modify characters of a String object. Remember that the methods of the String class, such as replaceAll and substring, do not modify the original string; they return a new string. Java adopts this immutability restriction to implement an efficient memory allocation scheme for managing String objects. The immutability is the reason why we can treat the string data much as a primitive data type.

Creating a new string from the old one will work for most cases, but sometimes manipulating the content of a string directly is more convenient. When we need to compose a long string from a number of words, for example, being able to manipulate the content of a string directly is much more convenient than creating a new copy of a string. ***String manipulation*** here means operations such as replacing a character, appending a string with another string, deleting a portion of a string, and so forth. If we need to manipulate the content of a string directly, we must use either the StringBuffer or the StringBuilder class. Here's a simple example of modifying the string Java to Diva using a StringBuffer object:

string manipulation

```
StringBuffer word = new StringBuffer( "Java" );
word.setCharAt(0, 'D');
word.setCharAt(1, 'i');
```

Notice that no new string is created, the original string Java is modified. Also, we must use the new method to create a StringBuffer object.

The StringBuffer and StringBuilder classes behave exactly the same (i.e., they support the same set of public methods), but the StringBuilder class in general has a better performance. The StringBuilder class is new to Java 2 SDK version 1.5, so it cannot be used with the older versions of Java SDK. There are advanced cases where you have to use the StringBuffer class, but for the sample string processing programs in this book, we can use either one of them. Of course, to use the StringBuilder class, we must be using version 1.5 SDK. We can also continue to use the StringBuffer class with version 1.5.

Because the StringBuffer class can be used with all versions of Java SDK, and the string processing performance in not our major concern here, we will be using the StringBuffer class exclusively in this book. If the string processing performance is a concern, then all we have to do is to replace all occurrences of the word StringBuffer to StringBuilder in the program and run it with version 1.5 SDK.

StringBuffer

Let's look at some examples using **StringBuffer** objects. The first example reads a sentence and replaces all vowels in the sentence with the character X.

```
/*
    Chapter 9 Sample Program: Replace every vowel in a given sentence
                              with 'X' using StringBuffer.

    File: Ch9ReplaceVowelsWithX.java
*/

import java.util.*;

class Ch9ReplaceVowelsWithX {

    public static void main (String[] args) {

        Scanner scanner = new Scanner(System.in);
        scanner.useDelimiter(System.getProperty("line.separator"));
```

```
        StringBuffer tempStringBuffer;
        String       inSentence;

        int          numberOfCharacters;
        char         letter;

        System.out.println("Sentence: ");
        inSentence = scanner.next();

        tempStringBuffer   = new StringBuffer(inSentence);

        numberOfCharacters = tempStringBuffer.length();

        for (int index = 0; index < numberOfCharacters; index++) {

          letter = tempStringBuffer.charAt(index);

          if (letter == 'a' || letter == 'A' ||
              letter == 'e' || letter == 'E' ||
              letter == 'i' || letter == 'I' ||
              letter == 'o' || letter == 'O' ||
              letter == 'u' || letter == 'U'   ) {

            tempStringBuffer.setCharAt(index,'X');
          }
        }

        System.out.println("Input:  " + inSentence);
        System.out.println("Output: " + tempStringBuffer);
    }
}
```

Notice how the input routine is done. We are reading in a String object and converting it to a StringBuffer object, because we cannot simply assign a String object to a StringBuffer variable. For example, the following code is invalid:

Bad Version

```
StringBuffer strBuffer = scanner.next();
```

We are required to create a StringBuffer object from a String object as in

```
String       str    = "Hello";
StringBuffer strBuf = new StringBuffer( str );
```

Things to Remember

*We cannot input **StringBuffer** objects. We have to input **String** objects and convert them to **StringBuffer** objects.*

Our next example constructs a new sentence from input words that have an even number of letters. The program stops when the word **STOP** is read. Let's begin with the pseudocode:

```
set tempStringBuffer to empty string;

repeat = true;

while ( repeat ) {

   read in next word;

   if (word is "STOP") {

      repeat = false;

   } else if (word has even number of letters) {

      append word to tempStringBuffer;
   }
}
```

And here's the actual code:

```
/*
   Chapter 9 Sample Program: Constructs a new sentence from
                             input words that have an even number of letters.

   File: Ch9EvenLetterWords.java
*/

import javax.swing.*;

class Ch9EvenLetterWords {

   public static void main (String[] args) {

      Scanner scanner = new Scanner(System.in);

      boolean repeat = true;

      String  word;

      StringBuffer tempStringBuffer = new StringBuffer("");

      while (repeat) {

         System.out.print("Next word: ");
         word = scanner.next( );

         if (word.equals("STOP")) {

           repeat = false;

         } else if (word.length() % 2 == 0) {

           tempStringBuffer.append(word + " ");
         }
      }
```

Create **StringBuffer** object with an empty string.

Append **word** and a space to **tempStringBuffer.**

```
        System.out.println("Output: " + tempStringBuffer);

    }
}
```

We use the append method to append a String or a StringBuffer object to the end of a StringBuffer object. The method append also can take an argument of the primitive data type. For example, all the following statements are valid:

```
int    i  = 12;
float  x  = 12.4f;
char   ch = 'W';

StringBuffer str = new StringBuffer("");

str.append(i);
str.append(x);
str.append(ch);
```

Any primitive data type argument is converted to a string before it is appended to a StringBuffer object.

Notice that we can write the second example using only String objects. Here's how:

```
boolean repeat = true;
String word, newSentence;

newSentence = ""; //empty string
while (repeat) {

   System.out.print("Next word: ");
   word = scanner.next();

   if (word.equals("STOP")) {
      repeat = false;

   } else if (word.length() % 2 == 0) {
        newSentence = newSentence + word;
                                       //string concatenation
   }
}
```

Although this code does not explicitly use any StringBuffer object, the Java compiler may use StringBuffer when compiling the string concatenation operator. For example, the expression

```
newSentence + word
```

can be compiled as if the expression were

```
new StringBuffer().append(word).toString()
```

Using the append method of StringBuffer is preferable to using the string concatenation operator + because we can avoid creating temporary string objects by using StringBuffer.

In addition to appending a string at the end of StringBuffer, we can insert a string at a specified position by using the insert method. The syntax for this method is

```
<StringBuffer> . insert ( <insertIndex>, <value> ) ;
```

where <insertIndex> must be greater than or equal to 0 and less than or equal to the length of <StringBuffer> and the <value> is an object or a value of the primitive data type. For example, to change the string

```
Java is great
```

to

```
Java is really great
```

we can execute

```
StringBuffer str = new StringBuffer("Java is great");
str.insert(8, "really ");
```

1. Determine the value of str after the following statements are executed.

   a.
   ```
   StringBuffer str
            = new StringBuffer( "Caffeine" );
   str.insert(0, "Dr. ");
   ```
   b.
   ```
   String       str  = "Caffeine";
   StringBuffer str1 =
      new StringBuffer( str.substring(1, 3) );
   str1.append('e');
   str = "De" + str1;
   ```
   c.
   ```
   String       str  = "Caffeine";
   StringBuffer str  =
      new StringBuffer( str.substring(4, 8);
   str1.insert ( 3,'f');
   str = "De" + str1
   ```

2. Assume a String object str is assigned as a string value. Write a code segment to replace all occurrences of lowercase vowels in a given string to the letter C by using String and StringBuffer objects.

3. Find the errors in the following code.

```
String       str   = "Caffeine";
StringBuffer str1  = str.substring(1, 3);
str1.append('e');
System.out(str1);
str1 = str1 + str;
```

9.7 Sample Development

Building Word Concordance

word concordance

One technique to analyze a historical document or literature is to track word occurrences. A basic form of ***word concordance*** is a list of all words in a document and the number of times each word appears in the document. Word concordance is useful in revealing the writing style of an author. For example, given a word concordance of a document, we can scan the list and count the numbers of nouns, verbs, prepositions, and so forth. If the ratios of these grammatical elements differ significantly between the two documents, there is a high probability that they are not written by the same person. Another application of word concordance is seen in the indexing of a document, which, for each word, lists the page numbers or line numbers where it appears in the document. In this sample development, we will build a word concordance of a given document, utilizing the string-processing technique we learned in this chapter.

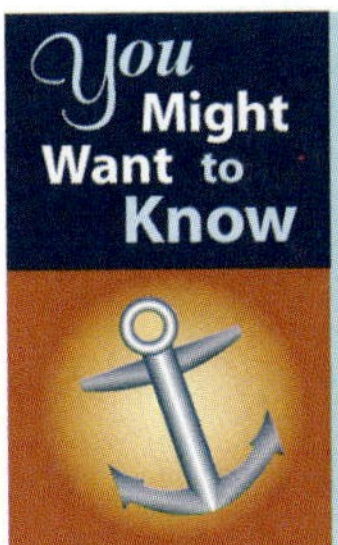

One of the most popular search engine websites on the Internet today is Google (**www.google.com**). At the core of their innovative technology is a concordance of all Web pages on the Internet. Every month the company's Web crawler software visits 3 billion (and steadily growing) Web pages, and from these visits, a concordance is built. When the user enters a query, the Google servers search the concordance for a list of matching Web pages and return the list in the order of relevance.

Problem Statement

Write an application that will build a word concordance of a document. The output from the application is an alphabetical list of all words in the given document and the number of times they occur in the document. The documents are a text file (contents of the file are ASCII characters), and the output of the program is saved as an ASCII file also.

Overall Plan

As usual, let's begin the program development by first identifying the major tasks of the program. The first task is to get a text document from a designated file. We will use a helper class called **FileManager** to do this task. File processing techniques to implement the **FileManager** class will be presented in Chapter 12. The whole content of an ASCII file is represented in the program as a single **String** object. Using a pattern-matching technique, we extract individual words from the document. For each distinct word in the document, we associate a counter and increment it every time the word is repeated. We will use the second helper class called **WordList** for maintaining a word list. An entry in this list has two components—a word and how many times this word occurs in the document.

9.7 Sample Development—*continued*

A **WordList** object can handle an unbounded number of entries. Entries in the list are arranged in alphabetical order. We will learn how to implement the **WordList** class in Chapter 10.

We can express the program logic in pseudocode as

program tasks

```
while ( the user wants to process another file ) {

    Task 1: read the file;

    Task 2: build the word list;

    Task 3: save the word list to a file;
}
```

Let's look at the three tasks and determine objects that will be responsible for handling the tasks. For the first task, we will use the helper class **FileManager.** For the second task of building a word list, we will define the **Ch9WordConcordance** class, whose instance will use the **Pattern** and **Matcher** classes for word extraction, and another helper class **WordList** for maintaining the word list. The last task of saving the result is done by the **FileManager** class also.

Finally, we will define a top-level control object that manages all other objects. We will call this class **Ch9WordConcordanceMain.** This will be our instantiable main class. Here's our working design document:

program classes

Design Document: Ch9WordConcordanceMain	
Class	**Purpose**
Ch9WordConcordanceMain	The instantiable main class of the program that implements the top-level program control.
Ch9WordConcordance	The key class of the program. An instance of this class manages other objects to build the word list.
FileManager	A helper class for opening a file and saving the result to a file. Details of this class can be found in Chapter 12.
WordList	Another helper class for maintaining a word list. Details of this class can be found in Chapter 10.
Pattern/Matcher	Classes for pattern-matching operations.

Figure 9.4 is the working program diagram.

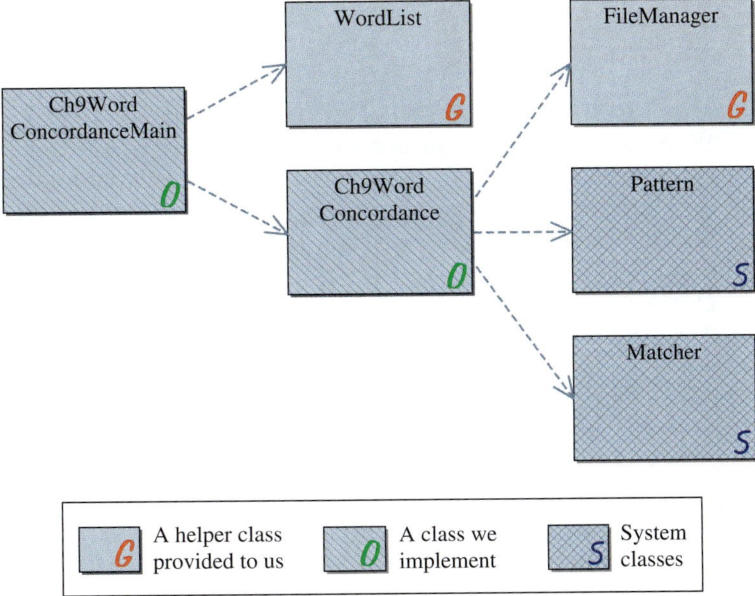

Figure 9.4 The program diagram for the **Ch9WordConcordanceMain** program. Base system classes such as **String** and **JOptionPane** are not shown.

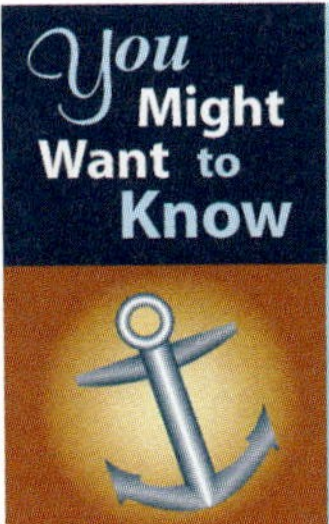

In lieu of the **Pattern** and **Matcher** classes, we could use the **StringTokenizer** class. This class is fairly straightforward to use if the white space (tab, return, blank, etc.) is a word delimiter. However, using this class becomes a little more complicated if we need to include punctuation marks and others as a word delimiter also. Overall, the **Pattern** and **Matcher** classes are more powerful and useful in many types of applications than the **StringTokenizer** class.

development steps

We will implement this program in four major steps:

1. Start with a program skeleton. Define the main class with data members. To test the main class, we will also define a skeleton **Ch9WordConcordance** class with just a default constructor.
2. Add code to open a file and save the result. Extend the step 1 classes as necessary.
3. Complete the implementation of the **Ch9WordConcordance** class.
4. Finalize the code by removing temporary statements and tying up loose ends.

9.7 Sample Development—*continued*

Step 1 Development: Skeleton

step 1 design

The design of **Ch9WordConcordanceMain** is straightforward, as its structure is very similar to that of other main classes. We will make this an instantiable main class and define the **start** method that implements the top-level control logic. We will define a default constructor to create instances of other classes. A skeleton **Ch9WordConcordance** class is also defined in this step so we can compile and run the main class. The skeleton **Ch9WordConcordance** class only has an empty default constructor. The working design document for the **Ch9WordConcordanceMain** class is as follows:

Design Document: The `Ch9WordConcordanceMain` Class		
Method	**Visibility**	**Purpose**
`<constructor>`	`public`	Creates the instances of other classes in the program.
`start`	`private`	Implements the top-level control logic of the program.

step 1 code

For the skeleton, the **start** method loops (doing nothing inside the loop in this step) until the user selects No on the confirmation dialog. Here's the skeleton:

```
/*
    Chapter 9 Sample Development: Word Concordance

    File: Step1/Ch9WordConcordanceMain.java
*/

import java.util.*;

class Ch9WordConcordanceMain {

    private static enum Response {YES, NO}

    private FileManager fileManager;
    private Ch9WordConcordance builder;
    private Scanner scanner;

    //----------------------------------
    //      Main method
    //----------------------------------
    public static void main(String[] args) {
        Ch9WordConcordanceMain main = new Ch9WordConcordanceMain();
        main.start();
    }
```

```
    public Ch9WordConcordanceMain() {

        fileManager = new FileManager( );
        builder     = new Ch9WordConcordance( );

        scanner     = new Scanner(System.in);
    }

    private void start( ) {

        Response userReply;

        while (true) {

            userReply = prompt("Run the program?");

            if (userReply == Response.NO) {
                break;
            }
        }

        System.out.println("Thank you for using the program. Good-Bye");
    }

    private Response prompt(String question) {

        String input;

        Response response = Response.NO;

        System.out.print(question + " (Yes - y; No - n): ");

        input = scanner.next();

        if (input.equals("Y") || input.equals("y")) {
            response = Response.YES;
        }

        return response;
    }
}
```

The skeleton **Ch9WordConcordance** class has only an empty default constructor. Here's the skeleton class:

```
class Ch9WordConcordance {

    public Ch9WordConcordance() {

    }
}
```

9.7 Sample Development—*continued*

step 1 test

We run the program and verify that the constructor is executed correctly, and the repetition control in the **start** method works as expected.

Step 2 Development: Open and Save Files

step 2 design

In the second development step, we add routines to handle input and output. The tasks of opening and saving a file are delegated to the service class **FileManager.** We will learn the implementation details of the **FileManager** class in Chapter 12. Our responsibility right now is to use the class correctly. The class provides two key methods: one to open a file and another to save a file. So that we can create and view the content easily, the **FileManager** class deals only with text files. To open a text file, we call its **openFile** method. There are two versions. With the first version, we pass the filename. For example, the code

```
FileManager fm  = new FileManager();
String      doc = ...; //assign string data

fm.saveFile("output1.txt", doc);
```

will save the string data **doc** to a file named **output1.txt.** With the second version, we will let the end user select a file, using the standard file dialog. A sample file dialog is shown in Figure 9.5. With the second version, we pass only the string data to be saved as

```
fm.saveFile(doc);
```

When there's an error in saving a file, an **IOException** is thrown.

To open a text file, we use one of the two versions of the **openFile** method. The distinction is identical to the one for the **saveFile** methods. The first version requires the

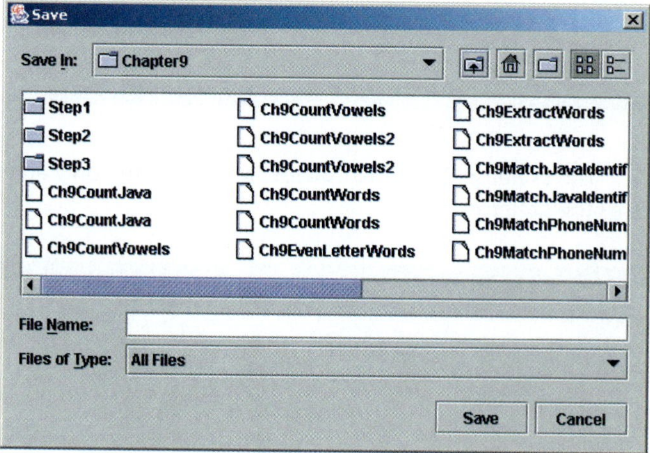

Figure 9.5 A sample file dialog for opening a file.

filename to open. The second version allows the end user to select a file to save the data, so we pass no parameter. The **openFile** method will throw a **FileNotFoundException** when the designated file cannot be found and an **IOException** when the designated file cannot be opened correctly.

Here's the summary of the **FileManager** class:

Public Methods of `FileManager`

```
public String openFile(String filename)
              throws FileNotFoundException, IOException
```
Opens the text file `filename` and returns the content as a `String`.

```
public String openFile( )
              throws FileNotFoundException, IOException
```
Opens the text file selected by the end user, using the standard file open dialog, and returns the content as a `String`.

```
public String saveFile(String filename, String data)
                  throws IOException
```
Save the string `data` to `filename`.

```
public String saveFile(String data) throws IOException
```
Saves the string `data` to a file selected by the end user, using the standard file save dialog.

We modify the **start** method to open a file, create a word concordance, and then save the generated word concordance to a file. The method is defined as follows:

```
private void start( ) {

   Response userReply;

   String document, wordList;

   while (true) {

      userReply = prompt("Run the program?");

      if (userReply == Response.NO) {
          break;
      }

      document = inputFile(); //open file

      wordList = build(document); //build concordance

      saveFile(wordList); //save the generated concordance
   }
   ... //'Good-bye' message dialog
}
```

Added portion

9.7 Sample Development—*continued*

The **inputFile** method is defined as follows:

```
private String inputFile( ) {
   String doc = "";

   try {
      doc = fileManager.openFile( );

   } catch ( FileNotFoundException e) {
      System.out.println("File not found.");

   } catch ( IOException e) {
      System.out.println("Error in opening file: "
                               + e.getMessage());
   }

   System.out.println("Input Document:\n" + doc); //TEMP

   return doc;
}
```

with a temporary output to verify the input routine. Because the **openFile** method of **FileManager** throws exceptions, we handle them here with the **try-catch** block.

The **saveFile** method is defined as follows:

```
private void saveFile(String list) {

   try {
      fileManager.saveFile(list);

   } catch (IOException e) {
      System.out.println("Error in saving file: "
                               + e.getMessage());
   }
}
```

The method is very simple as the hard work of actually saving the text data is done by our **FileManager** helper object.

Finally, the **build** method is defined as

```
private String build(String document) {

   String concordance;

   concordance = builder.build(document);

   return concordance;
}
```

The **Ch9WordConcordanceMain** class is now complete. To run and test this class, we will define a stub **build** method for the **Ch9WordConcordance** class. The method is temporarily defined as

```
public String build(String document) {

    //TEMP
    String list
            = "one 14\ntwo 3\nthree 3\nfour 5\nfive 92\n";

    return list;

    //TEMP
}
```

We will implement the method fully in the next step.

step 2 code

Here's the final **Ch9WordConcordanceMain** class:

```
/*
    Chapter 9 Sample Development: Word Concordance

    File: Step2/Ch9WordConcordanceMain.java
*/
import java.io.*;
import java.util.*;

class Ch9WordConcordanceMain {

    . . .

    private String build(String document) {

        String concordance;

        concordance = builder.build(document);

        return concordance;
    }

    private String inputFile( ) {
        String doc = "";

        try {
            doc = fileManager.openFile( );

        } catch (FileNotFoundException e) {
            System.out.println("File not found.");

        } catch (IOException e) {
          System.out.println("Error in opening file: " + e.getMessage());
        }
```

build

inputFile

```
        System.out.println("Input Document:\n" + doc); //TEMP

        return doc;
    }

    private void saveFile(String list) {

        try {
            fileManager.saveFile(list);

        } catch (IOException e) {
          System.out.println("Error in saving file: " + e.getMessage());
        }
    }

    private void start( ) {
        while (true) {
            ...
            document = inputFile();

            wordList = build(document);

            saveFile(wordList);
        }
        ...
    }
}
```

saveFile

start

The temporary **Ch9WordConcordance** class now has the stub **build** method:

```
class Ch9WordConcordance {
    ...
    public String build(String document) {

        //TEMP
        String list = "one 14\ntwo 3\nthree 3\nfour 5\nfive 92\n";

        return list;
        //TEMP
    }
}
```

step 2 test

We are ready to run the program. The step 2 directory contains several sample input files. We will open them and verify the file contents are read correctly by checking the temporary echo print output to **System.out.** To verify the output routine, we save to the output (the temporary output created by the **build** method of **Ch9WordConcordance**) and verify its content. Since the output is a text file, we can use any word processor or text editor to view its contents. (*Note:* If we use NotePad on the Windows platform to view the file, it may not appear correctly. See the box below on how to avoid this problem.)

Hints, & Tips, Pitfalls

The control characters used for a line separator are not the same for each platform (Windows, Mac, Unix, etc.) . One platform may use **\n** for a line separator while another platform may use **\r\n** for a line separator. Even on the same platform, different software may not interpret the control characters in the same way. To make our Java code work correctly across all platforms, we do, for example,

```
String newline
  = System.getProperties().getProperty("line.separator");

String output = "line 1" + newline + "line 2" + newline;
```

instead of

```
String output = "line 1\nline 2\n";
```

Step 3 Development: Generate Word Concordance

step 3 design

In the third development step, we finish the program by implementing the **Ch9WordConcordance** class, specifically, its **build** method. Since we are using another helper class in this step, first we must find out how to use this helper class. The **WordList** class supports the maintenance of a word list. Every time we extract a new word from the document, we enter this word into a word list. If the word is already in the list, its count is incremented by 1. If the word occurs for the first time in the document, then the word is added to the list with its count initialized to 1. When we are done processing the document, we can get the word concordance from a **WordList** by calling its **getConcordance** method. The method returns the list as a single **String** with each line containing a word and its count in the following format:

```
2  Chapter
1  Early
1  However
2  In
1  already
1  also
1  an
```

9.7 Sample Development—*continued*

```
7  and
1  are
2  as
1  because
```

Because a single **WordList** object handles multiple documents, there's a method called **reset** to clear the word list before processing the next document. Here's the method summary:

Public Methods of `WordList`
`public void add(String word)` Increments the count for the given word. If the word is already in the list, its count is incremented by 1. If the word does not exist in the list, then it is added to the list with its count set to 1.
`public String getConcordance( )` Returns the word concordance in alphabetical order of words as a single string. Each line consists of a word and its count.
`public void reset( )` Clears the internal data structure so a new word list can be constructed. This method must be called every time before a new document is processed.

The general idea behind the **build** method of the **Ch9WordConcordance** class is straightforward. We need to keep extracting a word from the document, and for every word found, we add it to the word list. Expressed in pseudocode, we have

```
while (document has more words) {

   word = next word in the document;
   wordList.add(word);
}

String concordance = wordList.getConcordance();
```

The most difficult part here is how to extract words from a document. We can write our own homemade routine to extract words, based on the technique presented in Section 9.2. However, this is too much work to get the task done. Writing a code that detects various kinds of word terminators (in addition to space, punctuation mark, control characters such as tab, new line, etc., all satisfy as the word terminator) is not that easy. Conceptually, it is not that hard, but it can be quite tedious to iron out all the details. Instead, we can use the pattern-matching technique provided by the **Pattern** and **Matcher** classes for a reliable and efficient solution.

The pattern for finding a word can be stated in a regular expression as

```
\w+
```

Putting it in a string format results in

```
"\\w+"
```

The **Pattern** and **Matcher** objects are thus created as

```
Pattern pattern = Pattern.compile("\\w+");
Matcher matcher = pattern.matcher(document);
```

and the control loop to find and extract words is

```
wordList.reset();
while (matcher.find( )) {
    wordList.add(document.substring(matcher.start(),
                                    matcher.end()));
}
```

step 3 code

Here's the final **Ch9WordConcordance** class:

```
/*
    Chapter 9 Sample Development: Word Concordance

    File: Step3/Ch9WordConcordance.java
*/

import java.util.regex.*;

class Ch9WordConcordance {
    private static final String WORD = "\\w+";
    private WordList wordList;
    private Pattern pattern;

    public Ch9WordConcordance() {
        wordList = new WordList();
        pattern = Pattern.compile(WORD); //pattern is compiled only once
    }

    public String build(String document) {

        Matcher matcher = pattern.matcher(document);

        wordList.reset();

        while (matcher.find()){
            wordList.add(document.substring(matcher.start(),
                                            matcher.end()));
        }

        return wordList.getConcordance();
    }
}
```

build

9.7 Sample Development—*continued*

Notice how short the class is, thanks to the power of pattern matching and the helper **WordList** class.

step 3 test

We run the program against varying types of input text files. We can use a long document such as the term paper for the last term's economy class (don't forget to save it as a text file before testing). We should also use some specially created files for testing purposes. One file may contain only one word repeated 7 times, for example. Another file may contain no words at all. We verify that the program works correctly for all types of input files.

Step 4 Development: Finalize

program review

As always, we finalize the program in the last step. We perform a critical review to find any inconsistency or error in the methods, any incomplete methods, places to add more comments, and so forth.

In addition, we may consider possible extensions. One is an integrated user interface where the end user can view both the input document files and the output word list files. Another is the generation of different types of list. In the sample development, we count the number of occurrences of each word. Instead, we can generate a list of positions where each word appears in the document. The **WordList** class itself needs to be modified for such extension.

Summary

- The char data type represents a single character.
- The char constant is denoted by a single quotation mark, for example, 'a'.
- The character coding scheme used widely today is ASCII (American Standard Code for Information Exchange).
- Java uses Unicode, which is capable of representing characters of diverse languages. ASCII is compatible with Unicode.
- A string is a sequence of characters, and in Java, strings are represented by String objects.
- The Pattern and Matcher classes are introduced in Java 2 SDK 1.4. They provide support for pattern-matching applications.
- Regular expression is used to represent a pattern to match (search) in a given text.
- The String objects are immutable. Once they are created, they cannot be changed.
- To manipulate mutable strings, use StringBuffer.

- Strings are objects in Java, and the rules for comparing objects apply when comparing strings.
- Only one String object is created for the same literal String constants.
- The standard classes described or used in this chapter are

String	Pattern
StringBuffer	Matcher
StringBuilder	

Key Concepts

characters
strings
string processing
regular expression
pattern matching
character encoding
String comparison

Exercises

1. What is the difference between 'a' and "a"?
2. Discuss the difference between

```
str = str + word; //string concatenation
```

and

```
tempStringBuffer.append(word)
```

where str is a String object and tempStringBuffer is a StringBuffer object.

3. Show that if x and y are String objects and x == y is true, then x.equals(y) is also true, but the reverse is not necessarily true.
4. What will be the output from the following code?

```
StringBuffer word1, word2;
word1 = new StringBuffer("Lisa");
word2 = word1;
word2.insert(0, "Mona ");
System.out.println(word1);
```

5. Show the state of memory after the execution of each statement in the following code.

```
String word1, word2;
word1 = "Hello";
word2 = word1;
word1 = "Java";
```

6. Using a state-of-memory diagram, illustrate the difference between a null string and an empty string—a string that has no characters in it. Show the state-of-memory diagram for the following code. Variable word1 is a null string, while word2 is an empty string.

```
String word1, word2;
word1 = null;
word2 = "";
```

7. Draw a state-of-memory diagram for each of the following groups of statements.

```
String word1, word2;

word1 = "French Roast";
word2 = word1;
```

```
String word1, word2;

word1 = "French Roast";
word2 = "French Roast";
```

8. Write an application that reads in a character and displays the character's ASCII. The getText method of the JTextField class returns a String object, so you need to extract a char value, as in

```
String inputString = inputField.getText();
char character = inputString.charAt(0);
```

   Display an error message if more than one character is entered.

9. Write a method that returns the number of uppercase letters in a String object passed to the method as an argument. Use the class method isUpperCase of the Character class, which returns true if the passed parameter of type char is an uppercase letter. You need to explore the Character class from the java.lang package on your own.

10. Redo Exercise 9 without using the Character class. *Hint:* The ASCII of any uppercase letter will fall between 65 (code for 'A') and 90 (code for 'Z').

11. Write a program that reads a sentence and prints out the sentence with all uppercase letters changed to lowercase and all lowercase letters changed to uppercase.

12. Write a program that reads a sentence and prints out the sentence in reverse order. For example, the method will display

```
?uoy era woH
```

   for the input

```
How are you?
```

13. Write a method that transposes words in a given sentence. For example, given an input sentence

```
The gate to Java nirvana is near
```

   the method outputs

```
ehT etag ot avaJ anavrin si raen
```

To simplify the problem, you may assume the input sentence contains no punctuation marks. You may also assume that the input sentence starts with a nonblank character and that there is exactly one blank space between the words.

14. Improve the method in Exercise 13 by removing the assumptions. For example, an input sentence could be

```
Hello, how are you? I use JDK 1.2.2.   Bye-bye.
```

An input sentence may contain punctuation marks and more than one blank space between two words. Transposing the above will result in

```
olleH, woh era uoy? I esu KDJ 1.2.2. eyB-eyb.
```

Notice the position of punctuation marks does not change and only one blank space is inserted between the transposed words.

15. The Ch9CountWords program that counts the number of words in a given sentence has a bug. If the input sentence has one or more blank spaces at the end, the value for wordCount will be 1 more than the actual number of words in the sentence. Correct this bug in two ways: one with the trim method of the String class and another without using this method.

16. The Ch9ExtractWords program for extracting words in a given sentence includes the test

```
if (beginIdx != endIdx) ...
```

Describe the type of input sentences that will result in the variables beginIdx and endIdx becoming equal.

17. Write an application that reads in a sentence and displays the count of individual vowels in the sentence. Use any output routine of your choice to display the result in this format. Count only the lowercase vowels.

```
Vowel counts for the sentence

        Mary had a little lamb.

# of 'a' : 4
# of 'e' : 1
# of 'i' : 1
# of 'o' : 0
# of 'u' : 0
```

18. Write an application that determines if an input word is a palindrome. A palindrome is a string that reads the same forward and backward, for example, *noon* and *madam*. Ignore the case of the letter. So, for example, *maDaM, MadAm,* and *mAdaM* are all palindromes.

19. Write an application that determines if an input sentence is a palindrome, for example, *A man, a plan, a canal, Panama!* You ignore the punctuation marks, blanks, and case of the letters.

Development Exercises

For the following exercises, use the incremental development methodology to implement the program. For each exercise, identify the program tasks, create a design document with class descriptions, and draw the program diagram. Map out the development steps at the start. Present any design alternatives and justify your selection. Be sure to perform adequate testing at the end of each development step.

20. Write an Eggy-Peggy program. Given a string, convert it to a new string by placing egg in front of every vowel. For example, the string

```
I Love Java
```

becomes

```
eggI Leegoveege Jeegaveega
```

21. Write a variation of the Eggy-Peggy program. Implement the following four variations:

- Sha — Add sha to the beginning of every word.
- Na — Add na to the end of every word.
- Sha Na Na — Add sha to the beginning and na na to the end of every word.
- Ava — Move the first letter to the end of the word and add ava to it.

Allow the user to select one of four possible variations.

22. Write a word guessing game. The game is played by two players, each taking a turn in guessing the secret word entered by the other player. Ask the first player to enter a secret word. After a secret word is entered, display a hint that consists of a row of dashes, one for each letter in the secret word. Then ask the second player to guess a letter in the secret word. If the letter is in the secret word, replace the dashes in the hint with the letter at all positions where this letter occurs in the word. If the letter does not appear in the word, the number of incorrect guesses is incremented by 1. The second player keeps guessing letters until either

- The player guesses all the letters in the word. or
- The player makes 10 incorrect guesses.

Here's a sample interaction with blue indicating the letter entered by the player:

```
- - - -
S
- - - -
```

```
A
- A - A
V
- A V A
D
- A V A
J
J A V A
Bingo! You won.
```

Support the following features:

- Accept an input in either lowercase or uppercase.
- If the player enters something other than a single letter (a digit, special character, multiple letters, etc.), display an error message. The number of incorrect guesses is not incremented.
- If the player enters the same correct letter more than once, reply with the previous hint.
- Entering an incorrect letter the second time is counted as another wrong guess. For example, suppose the letter W is not in the secret word. Every time the player enters W as a guess, the number of incorrect guesses is incremented by 1.

After a game is over, switch the role of players and continue with another game. When it is the first player's turn to enter a secret word, give an option to the players to stop playing. Keep the tally and announce the winner at the end of the program. The tally will include for each player the number of wins and the total number of incorrect guesses made for all games. The player with more wins is the winner. In the case where both players have the same number of wins, the one with the lower number of total incorrect guesses is the winner. If the total numbers of incorrect guesses for both players are the same also, then it is a draw.

23. Write another word guessing game similar to the one described in Exercise 22. For this word game, instead of using a row of dashes for a secret word, a hint is provided by displaying the letters in the secret word in random order. For example, if the secret word is COMPUTER, then a possible hint is MPTUREOC. The player has only one chance to enter a guess. The player wins if he guessed the word correctly. Time how long the player took to guess the secret word. After a guess is entered, display whether the guess is correct or not. If correct, display the amount of time in minutes and seconds used by the player.

The tally will include for each player the number of wins and the total amount of time taken for guessing the secret words correctly (amount of time used for incorrect guesses is not tallied). The player with more wins is the winner. In the case where both players have the same number of wins, the one who used the lesser amount of time for correct guesses is the winner. If the total time used by both players is the same also, then it is a draw.

24. The word game Eggy-Peggy is an example of encryption. Encryption has been used since ancient times to communicate messages secretly. One of the many techniques used for encryption is called a *Caesar cipher*. With this technique, each character in the original message is shifted *N* positions. For example, if $N = 1$, then the message

```
I drink only decaf
```

becomes

```
J!esjol!pomz!efdbg
```

The encrypted message is decrypted to the original message by shifting back every character *N* positions. Shifting *N* positions forward and backward is achieved by converting the character to ASCII and adding or subtracting *N*. Write an application that reads in the original text and the value for *N* and displays the encrypted text. Make sure the ASCII value resulting from encryption falls between 32 and 126. For example, if you add 8 (value of *N*) to 122 (ASCII code for 'z'), you should "wrap around" and get 35.

Write another application that reads the encrypted text and the value for *N* and displays the original text by using the Caesar cipher technique. Design a suitable user interface.

25. Another encryption technique is called a *Vignere cipher*. This technique is similar to a Caesar cipher in that a key is applied cyclically to the original message. For this exercise a key is composed of uppercase letters only. Encryption is done by adding the code values of the key's characters to the code values of the characters in the original message. Code values for the key characters are assigned as follows: 0 for A, 1 for B, 2 for C, . . . , and 25 for Z. Let's say the key is COFFEE and the original message is I drink only decaf. Encryption works as follows:

Decryption reverses the process to generate the original message. Write an application that reads in a text and displays the encrypted text. Make sure the ASCII value resulting from encryption or decryption falls between 32 and 126. You can get the code for key characters by `(int) keyChar - 65`.

Write another application that reads the encrypted text and displays the original text, using the Vignere cipher technique.

26. A public-key cryptography allows anyone to encode messages while only people with a secret key can decipher them. In 1977, Ronald Rivest, Adi Shamir, and Leonard Adleman developed a form of public-key cryptography called the *RSA system*.

To encode a message using the RSA system, one needs n and e. The value n is a product of any two prime numbers p and q. The value e is any number less than n that cannot be evenly divided into y (that is, $y \div e$ would have a remainder), where $y = (p - 1) \times (q - 1)$. The values n and e can be published in a newspaper or posted on the Internet, so anybody can encrypt messages. The original character is encoded to a numerical value c by using the formula

$$c = m^e \bmod n$$

where m is a numerical representation of the original character (for example, 1 for A, 2 for B, and so forth).

Now, to decode a message, one needs d. The value d is a number that satisfies the formula

$$e \cdot d \bmod y = 1$$

where e and y are the values defined in the encoding step. The original character m can be derived from the encrypted character c by using the formula

$$m = c^d \bmod n$$

Write a program that encodes and decodes messages using the RSA system. Use large prime numbers for p and q in computing the value for n, because when p and q are small, it is not that difficult to find the value of d. When p and q are very large, however, it becomes practically impossible to determine the value of d. Use the ASCII values as appropriate for the numerical representation of characters. Visit http://www.rsasecurity.com for more information on how the RSA system is applied in the real world.

10 Arrays and Collections

Objectives

After you have read and studied this chapter, you should be able to

- Manipulate a collection of data values, using an array.
- Declare and use an array of primitive data types in writing a program.
- Declare and use an array of objects in writing a program.
- Define a method that accepts an array as its parameter and a method that returns an array.
- Describe how a two-dimensional array is implemented as an array of arrays.
- Manipulate a collection of objects, using lists and maps.

Introduction

People collect all sorts of items from bottle caps to exotic cars. For proof, just go to eBay (www.ebay.com) and see millions and millions of collectibles up for auction. Now with computers, people amass intangible items such as music files. Exactly how many MP3 files do you have on your computer? Probably in the hundreds and you lost track of exactly how many. You may want to develop a custom software, so you can store the information you want in the format you like, to keep track of all MP3 files downloaded from the Web.

When we write a program to deal with a collection of items, say, 500 Student objects, 200 integers, 300 MP3 files, and so forth, simple variables will not work. It is just not practical or feasible to use 500 variables to process 500 Student objects. In theory, you can, but honestly, do you want to type in identifiers for 500 variables (student1, student2, . . .)? A feature supported by programming languages to manipulate a collection of values is an array.

In this chapter we will learn about Java arrays. We will learn the basics of array manipulation and how to use different types of arrays properly and effectively. In addition, we will study several collection classes from the java.util package that provide more advanced data management features not found in the basic Java arrays.

10.1 Array Basics

Suppose we want to compute the annual average rainfall from 12 monthly averages. We can use three variables and compute the annual average as follows (in this and other code fragment examples, we assume scanner is a properly declared and created Scanner object):

```
double sum, rainfall, annualAverage;

sum = 0.0;

for (int i = 0; i < 12; i++) {

    System.out.print("Rainfall for month " + (i+1) + ": ");
    rainfall = scanner.nextDouble();

    sum += rainfall;
}

annualAverage = sum / 12.0;
```

Now suppose we want to compute the difference between the annual and monthly averages for every month and display a table with three columns, similar to the one shown in Figure 10.1.

Annual Average Rainfall: 15.03 mm

Month	Average	Variation
1	13.3	1.73
2	14.9	0.13
3	14.7	0.33
4	23.0	7.97
5	25.8	10.77
6	27.7	12.67
7	12.3	2.73
8	10.0	5.03
9	9.8	5.23
10	8.7	6.33
11	8.0	7.03
12	12.2	2.83

Figure 10.1 Monthly rainfall figures and their variation from the annual average.

To compute the difference between the annual and monthly averages, we need to remember the 12 monthly rainfall averages. Without remembering the 12 monthly averages, we won't be able to derive the monthly variations after the annual average is computed. Instead of using 12 variables januaryRainfall, februaryRainfall, and so forth to solve this problem, we use an array.

array

An *array* is a collection of data values of the same type. For example, we may declare an array consisting of double, but not an array consisting of both int and double. The following declares an array of double:

```
double[] rainfall;
```

array declaration

The square brackets indicate the *array declaration*. The brackets may be attached to a variable instead of the data type. For example, the declaration

```
double rainfall[];
```

is equivalent to the previous declaration. In Java, an array is a reference data type. Unlike the primitive data type, the amount of memory allocated to store an array varies, depending on the number and type of values in the array. We use the new operator to allocate the memory to store the values in an array. Although we use the same reserved word new for the array memory allocation as for the creation of a new instance of a class, strictly speaking, an array is not an object.

Things to Remember

In Java, an array is a reference data type. We use the ***new*** *operator to allocate the memory to store the values in an array.*

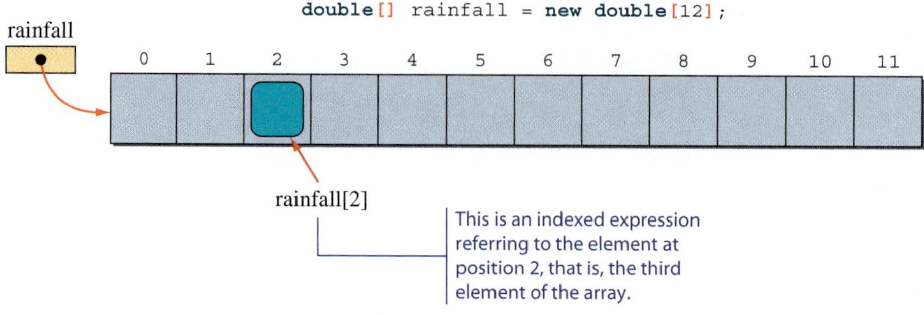
double[] rainfall = new double[12];
rainfall
0 1 2 3 4 5 6 7 8 9 10 11
rainfall[2]
This is an indexed expression referring to the element at position 2, that is, the third element of the array.

Figure 10.2 An array of 12 **double** values.

The following statement allocates the memory to store 12 double values and associates the identifier rainfall to it.

```
rainfall = new double[12]; //create an array of size 12
```

Figure 10.2 shows this array.

We can also declare and allocate memory for an array in one statement, as in

```
double[] rainfall = new double[12];
```

indexed expression

array element

The number 12 designates the size of the array—the number of values the array contains. We use a single identifier to refer to the whole collection and use an ***indexed expression*** to refer to the individual values of the collection. An individual value in an array is called an ***array element***. Zero-based indexing is used to indicate the positions of an element in the array. They are numbered 0, 1, 2, . . . , and size – 1, where size is the size of an array. For example, to refer to the third element of the rainfall array, we use the indexed expression

```
rainfall[2]
```

Instead of a literal constant such as 2, we can use an expression such as

```
rainfall[i+3]
```

Notice that the index for the first position in an array is zero. As for a String object, Java uses zero-based indexing for an array.

Things to Remember

The index of the first position in an array is 0.

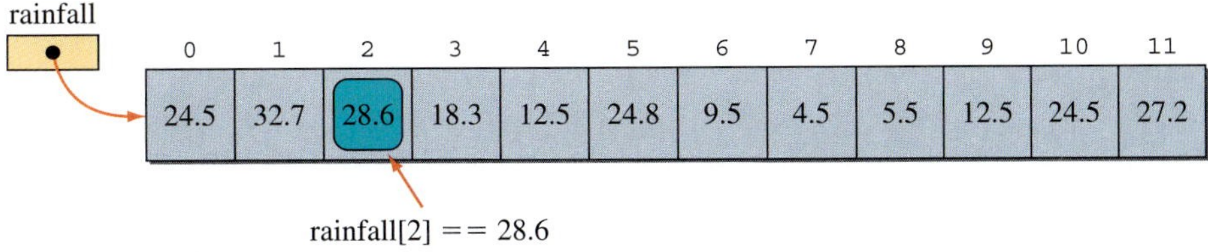

Figure 10.3 An array of 12 **double** values after all 12 are assigned values.

Using the rainfall array, we can input 12 monthly averages and compute the annual average as

```
double[] rainfall = new double[12];
double   annualAverage,
         sum = 0.0;

for (int i = 0; i < 12; i++) {

   System.out.print("Rainfall for month " + (i+1) + ": ");
   rainfall[i] = scanner.nextDouble();

   sum += rainfall[i];
}

annualAverage = sum / 12.0;
```

Can also be declared as
```
double rainfall[]
   = new double[12];
```

Figure 10.3 shows how the array will appear after all 12 values are entered.

After the 12 monthly averages are stored in the array, we can print out the table (alignment of the columns is not done here, but will be in the complete program listing).

```
double difference;

for (int i = 0; i < 12; i++) {
   System.out.print(i+1); //month #

   //average rainfall for the month
   System.out.print(" " + rainfall[i]);

   //difference between the monthly and annual averages
   difference = Math.abs( rainfall[i] - annualAverage );
   System.out.println(" " + difference);
}
```

Here's the complete program:

```
/*
   Chapter 10 Sample Program: Compute the annual average rainfall
                              and the variation from monthly average.

   File: Ch10Rainfall.java
*/
```

```
import java.util.*;

class Ch10Rainfall {

    public static void main (String[] args) {

        Scanner scanner = new Scanner (System.in);

        double[] rainfall = new double[12];

        double   annualAverage,
                 sum,
                 difference;

        sum = 0.0;

        for (int i = 0; i < 12; i++) {

            System.out.print("Rainfall for month " + (i+1) + ": ");
            rainfall[i] = scanner.nextDouble();

            sum += rainfall[i];
        }

        annualAverage = sum / 12.0;

        System.out.format("Annual Average Rainfall:%5.2f\n\n",
                                annualAverage);

        for (int i = 0; i < 12; i++) {

            System.out.format("%3d", i+1); //month #

            //average rainfall for the month
            System.out.format("%15.2f", rainfall[i]);

            //difference between the monthly and annual averages
            difference = Math.abs( rainfall[i] - annualAverage );
            System.out.format("%15.2f\n", difference);
        }
    }
}
```

Notice that the values displayed in the columns are aligned by using the formatting string.

length

An array has a public constant length for the size of an array. Using this constant, we can rewrite the for loop as

```
for (int i = 0; i < rainfall.length; i++) {
    ...
}
```

This for loop is more general since we do not have to modify the loop statement when the size of an array is changed. Also, the use of length is necessary when the size of an array is not known in advance. This happens, for example, when we write a method with an array as its parameter. We will provide an example of such a method in Section 10.3.

Notice the prompts for getting the values in the previous example are Rainfall for month 1, Rainfall for month 2, and so forth. A better prompt will spell out the month name, for example, Rainfall for January, Rainfall for February, and so forth. We can easily achieve a better prompt by using an array of strings. Here's how:

```
double[] rainfall = new double[12];  //an array of double

String[] monthName = new String[12]; //an array of String
double   annualAverage,
         sum = 0.0;

monthName[0]  = "January";
monthName[1]  = "February";
monthName[2]  = "March";
monthName[3]  = "April";
monthName[4]  = "May";
monthName[5]  = "June";
monthName[6]  = "July";
monthName[7]  = "August";
monthName[8]  = "September";
monthName[9]  = "October";
monthName[10] = "November";
monthName[11] = "December";

for (int i = 0; i < rainfall.length; i++) {

   System.out.print("Rainfall for month" +
                         monthName[i] + ": ");
   rainfall[i] = scanner.nextDouble();

   sum += rainfall[i];
}

annualAverage = sum / 12.0;
```

It is very easy to mix up the **length** value of an array and the **length** method of a **String** object. The **length** is a method for a **String** object, so we use the syntax for calling a method.

```
String str = "This is a string";
int    size = str.length();
```

But for an array, which is not an object but a reference data type, we do not use the syntax of method calling. We refer to the **length** value as

```
int size = rainfall.length;
```

Instead of assigning array elements individually, we can initialize the array at the time of declaration. We can, for example, initialize the monthName array by

No size is specified.

```
String[] monthName = { "January", "February", "March",
                       "April", "May", "June", "July",
                       "August", "September", "October",
                       "November", "December" };
```

Notice that we do not specify the size of an array if the array elements are initialized at the time of declaration. The size of an array is determined by the number of values in the list. In the above example, there are 12 values in the list, so the size of the array monthName is set to 12.

Let's try some more examples. We assume the rainfall array is declared, and all 12 values are read in. The following code computes the average rainfall for the odd months (January, March, . . .) and the even months (February, April, . . .).

```
double  oddMonthSum, oddMonthAverage,
        evenMonthSum, evenMonthAverage;

oddMonthSum  = 0.0;
evenMonthSum = 0.0;

//compute the average for the odd months
for (int i = 0; i < rainfall.length; i += 2) {
   oddMonthSum += rainfall[i];
}
oddMonthAverage = oddMonthSum / 6.0;

//compute the average for the even months
for (int i = 1; i < rainfall.length; i += 2) {
   evenMonthSum += rainfall[i];
}
evenMonthAverage = evenMonthSum / 6.0;
```

We can compute the same result by using one for loop.

```
for (int i = 0; i < rainfall.length; i += 2 ) {
   oddMonthSum  += rainfall[i];
   evenMonthSum += rainfall[i+1];
}

oddMonthAverage  = oddMonthSum / 6.0;
evenMonthAverage = evenMonthSum / 6.0;
```

To compute the average for each quarter (quarter 1 has January, February, and March; quarter 2 has April, May, and June; and so forth), we can write

```
for (int i = 0; i < 3; i++ ) {
   quarter1Sum += rainfall[i];
   quarter2Sum += rainfall[i+3];
   quarter3Sum += rainfall[i+6];
   quarter4Sum += rainfall[i+9];
}
```

```
quarter1Average = quarter1Sum / 3.0;
quarter2Average = quarter2Sum / 3.0;
quarter3Average = quarter3Sum / 3.0;
quarter4Average = quarter4Sum / 3.0;
```

We can use another array to store the quarter averages instead of using four variables:

```
double[] quarterAverage = new double[4];

for (int i = 0; i < 4; i++) {

   sum = 0;

   for (int j = 0; j < 3; j++) { //compute the sum of
      sum += rainfall[3*i + j];   //one quarter
   }

   quarterAverage[i] = sum / 3.0;//average for quarter i+1
}
```

Notice how the inner for loop is used to compute the sum of one quarter. The following table illustrates how the values for the variables i and j and the expression 3*i + j change.

i	j	3*i + j
0	0	0
	1	1
	2	2
1	0	3
	1	4
	2	5
2	0	6
	1	7
	2	8
3	0	9
	1	10
	2	11

Here's the complete program:

```
/*
    Chapter 10 Sample Program: Compute different statistics
                               from monthly rainfall averages.

    File: Ch10RainfallStat.java
*/
```

```
import java.util.*;

class Ch10RainfallStat {

    public static void main(String[] args) {

        Scanner scanner = new Scanner(System.in);

        String[] monthName = { "January", "February", "March",
                               "April", "May", "June", "July",
                               "August", "September", "October",
                               "November", "December" };

        double[]  rainfall = new double[12];

        double[]  quarterAverage = new double[4];

        double    annualAverage,
                  sum,
                  difference;

        double    oddMonthSum, oddMonthAverage,
                  evenMonthSum, evenMonthAverage;

        sum = 0.0;

        for (int i = 0; i < rainfall.length; i++) {

            System.out.print("Rainfall for month " + monthName[i] + ": ");
            rainfall[i] = scanner.nextDouble();

            sum += rainfall[i];
        }

        annualAverage = sum / 12.0;

        System.out.format( "Annual Average Rainfall:%6.2f\n\n",
                                                    annualAverage );

        oddMonthSum  = 0.0;
        evenMonthSum = 0.0;

        ///////////// Odd and Even Month Averages //////////////////

        //compute the average for the odd months
        for (int i = 0; i < rainfall.length; i += 2) {

            oddMonthSum += rainfall[i];
        }

        oddMonthAverage = oddMonthSum / 6.0;

        //compute the average for the even months
        for (int i = 1; i < rainfall.length; i += 2) {

            evenMonthSum += rainfall[i];
        }
```

```
        evenMonthAverage = evenMonthSum / 6.0;

        System.out.format("Odd Month Rainfall Average: %6.2f\n",
                                                  oddMonthAverage );

        System.out.format("Even Month Rainfall Average:%6.2f\n\n",
                                                  evenMonthAverage );

        /////////////////// Quarter Averages //////////////////////

        for (int i = 0; i < 4; i++) {

            sum = 0;

            for (int j = 0; j < 3; j++) {    //compute the sum of
                sum += rainfall[3*i + j];    //one quarter
            }

            quarterAverage[i] = sum / 3.0;   //average for quarter i+1

            System.out.format("Rainfall Average Qtr.%3d:%6.2f\n",
                                  i+1, quarterAverage[i] );

        }
    }
}
```

In the previous examples, we used a constant to specify the size of an array, such as the literal constant 12 in the following declaration:

```
double[] rainfall = new double[12];
```

fixed-size array declaration

Using constants to declare array sizes does not always lead to efficient space usage. We call the declaration of arrays with constants a ***fixed-size array declaration***. There are two potential problems with fixed-size array declarations. Suppose, for example, we declare an integer array of size 100:

```
int[] number = new int[100];
```

The first problem is that the program can process only up to 100 numbers. What if we need to process 101 numbers? We have to modify the program and compile it again. The second problem is a possible underutilization of space. The above declaration allocates 100 spaces whether they are used or not. Suppose the program on average processes 20 numbers. Then the program's average space usage is only 20 percent of the allocated space. With Java, we are not limited to fixed-size array declaration. We can declare an array of different size every time we run the program. The following code prompts the user for the size of an array and declares an array of designated size:

```
int    size;
int[]  number;

System.out.print("Size of an array: ");
size = scanner.nextInt();

number = new int[size];
```

With this approach, every time the program is executed, only the needed amount of space is allocated for the array. Any valid integer arithmetic expression is allowed for size specification, for example,

```
System.out.print("Enter int: ");
size = scanner.nextInt();

number = new int[size*size + 2* size + 5];
```

variable-size array creation

We call the creation of arrays with nonconstant values a ***variable-size array creation***. This capability comes very handy, for example, when an array runs out of space and we need to create a new, larger array. Suppose we start with an array of 20 elements. What would happen when we had to add the 21st element? We can create a new, larger array, say, twice as large as the original array. We then copy the values from the original array to the new array and finally add the 21st element to the new array. We will show you a concrete example of this scenario in Section 10.7.

Hints, Tips, & Pitfalls

Notice the first index position of an array is 0. Java adopted this feature from the programming language C. Using the zero-based indexing, the index value of an element indicates the number of elements in front of the element. For example, an index value of 0 for the first element indicates that there are zero elements in front of it; an index value of 4 for the fifth element indicates that there are four elements in front of it. Zero-based indexing allows a simpler formula to compute the actual memory address of array elements.

Quick CHECK

1. Which of the following statements are invalid?

   a. `float    number[23];`

   b. `float    number = { 1.0f, 2.0f, 3.0f };`

   c. `int      number;`
      `number = new Array[23];`

   d. `int[]  number = [ 1, 2, 3, 4 ];`

2. Write a code fragment to compute the sum of all positive real numbers stored in the following array.

```
double[] number = new double[25];
```

3. Describe the difference between the following two code fragments.

```
//code fragment 1
for (int i = 0; i < number.length; i++) {
   if ( i % 2 == 0 ) {
      System.out.println( number[i] );
   }
}

//code fragment 2
for (int i = 0; i < number.length; i++) {
   if ( number[i] % 2 == 0 ) {
      System.out.println( number[i] );
   }
}
```

10.2 Arrays of Objects

Array elements are not limited to primitive data types. Indeed, since a String is an object, we actually have seen an example of an array of objects in Section 10.1. In this section we will explore arrays of objects. To illustrate the processing of an array of objects, we will use the Person class in the following examples. We will define this Person class later in the chapter to introduce additional object-oriented concepts. Here's the portion of the Person class definition we will use in this section:

Public Methods of the `Person` Class
`public int getAge ( )` Returns the age of a person. Default age of a person is set to 0.
`public char getGender( )` Returns the gender of a person. The character `F` stands for female and `M` for male. Default gender of a person is set to the character `U` for unknown.
`public String getName ( )` Returns the name of a person. Default name of a person is set to `Not Given`.
`public void setAge ( int age )` Sets the age of a person.
`public void setGender( char gender )` Sets the gender of a person to the argument `gender`. The character `F` stands for female and `M` for male. The character `U` designates unknown gender.
`public void setName ( String name )` Sets the name of a person to the argument `name`.

The following code creates a Person object:

```
Person latte;

latte = new Person( );
latte.setName("Ms. Latte");
latte.setAge(20);
latte.setGender('F');

System.out.println( "Name: " + latte.getName()   );
System.out.println( "Age : " + latte.getAge()    );
System.out.println( "Sex : " + latte.getGender() );
```

Now let's study how we can create and manipulate an array of Person objects. An array of objects is declared and created just as an array of primitive data types is. The following are a declaration and a creation of an array of Person objects.

```
Person[] person;              //declare the person array
person = new Person[20];      //and then create it
```

Execution of the above code will result in a state shown in Figure 10.4.

Notice that the elements, that is, Person objects, are not yet created; only the array is created. Array elements are initially null. Since each individual element is an object, it also must be created. To create a Person object and set it as the array's first element, we write

```
person[0] = new Person( );
```

Figure 10.5 shows the state after the first Person object is added to the array.

Notice that no data values are assigned to the object yet. The object has default values at this point. To assign data values to this object, we can execute

```
person[0].setName   ( "Ms. Latte" );
person[0].setAge    ( 20 );
person[0].setGender( 'F' );
```

The indexed expression

```
person[0]
```

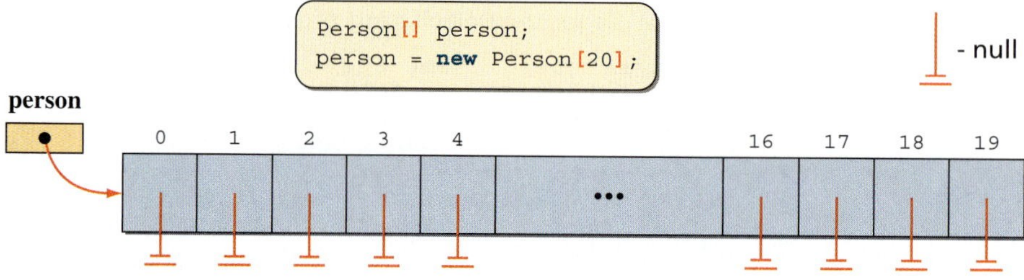

Figure 10.4 An array of **Person** objects after the array is created.

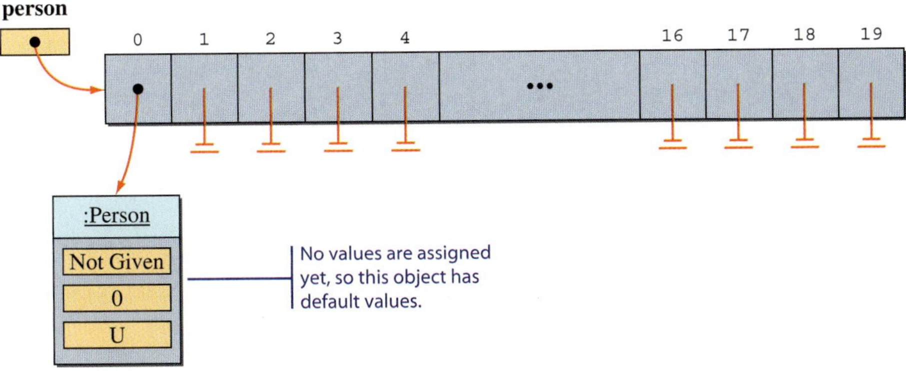

Figure 10.5 The **person** array with one **Person** object added to it.

refers to the first object in the person array. Since this expression refers to an object, we write

```
person[0].setAge( 20 );
```

to call this Person object's setAge method, for example. This is the syntax we use to call an object's method. We are just using an indexed expression to refer to an object instead of a simple variable.

Let's go through typical array processing to illustrate the basic operations. The first is to create Person objects and set up the person array. We assume that the person array is already declared and created.

```
String    name, inpStr;
int       age;
char      gender;

for (int i = 0; i < person.length; i++) {

   //read in data values
   System.out.print("Enter name: ");
   name = scanner.next();

   System.out.print("Enter age: ");
   age = scanner.nextInt();

   System.out.print("Enter gender: ");
   inpStr = scanner.next();
   gender = inpStr.charAt(0);

   //create a new Person and assign values
   person[i] = new Person( );

   person[i].setName   ( name    );
   person[i].setAge    (  age    );
   person[i].setGender( gender );
}
```

Note: To focus on array processing, we used the most simplistic input routine. For instance, we did not perform any input error checking, but this is not to say that input error checking is unimportant. We simply want to focus on array processing here.

To find the average age, we execute

find the average age

```
double sum = 0, averageAge;

for (int i = 0; i < person.length; i++) {
   sum += person[i].getAge();
}

averageAge = sum / person.length;
```

To print out the name and age of the youngest and the oldest persons, we can execute

find the youngest and the oldest persons

```
String nameOfYoungest, nameOfOldest;
int    min, max, age;

nameOfYoungest = nameOfOldest = person[0].getName();
min = max = person[0].getAge();

for (int i = 1; i < person.length; i++) {
   age = person[i].getAge();

   if (age < min) {     //found a younger person
      min            = age;
      nameOfYoungest = person[i].getName();

   }else if (age > max) { //found an older person
      max          = age;
      nameOfOldest = person[i].getName();
   }
}
System.out.println("Oldest   : " + nameOfOldest + " is "
                                 + max + " years old.");

System.out.println("Youngest: " + nameOfYoungest + " is "
                                 + min + " years old.");
```

Instead of using separate String and int variables, we can use the index to the youngest and the oldest persons. Here's the code:

```
int  minIdx,     //index to the youngest person
     maxIdx;     //index to the oldest person

minIdx = maxIdx = 0;

for (int i = 1; i < person.length; i++) {

   if (person[i].getAge() < person[minIdx].getAge()) {
      //found a younger person
      minIdx    = i;
```

```
        }else if (person[i].getAge() > person[maxIdx.getAge()){
            //found an older person
            maxIdx     = i;
        }
    }

    System.out.println("Oldest   : " + person[maxIdx].getName()
                                     + " is "
                                     + person[maxIdx].getAge()
                                     + " years old.");

    System.out.println("Youngest: " + person[minIdx].getName()
                                     + " is "
                                     + person[minIdx].getAge()
                                     + " years old.");
```

Yet another approach is to use variables for **Person** objects. Figure 10.6 shows how the **Person** variables **oldest** and **youngest** point to objects in the **person** array. Here's the code using **Person** variables:

```
Person   youngest,    //points to the youngest person
         oldest;      //points to the oldest person

youngest = oldest = person[0];

for (int i = 1; i < person.length; i++) {

    if (person[i].getAge() < youngest.getAge()) {
        //found a younger person
        youngest  = person[i];
    }
```

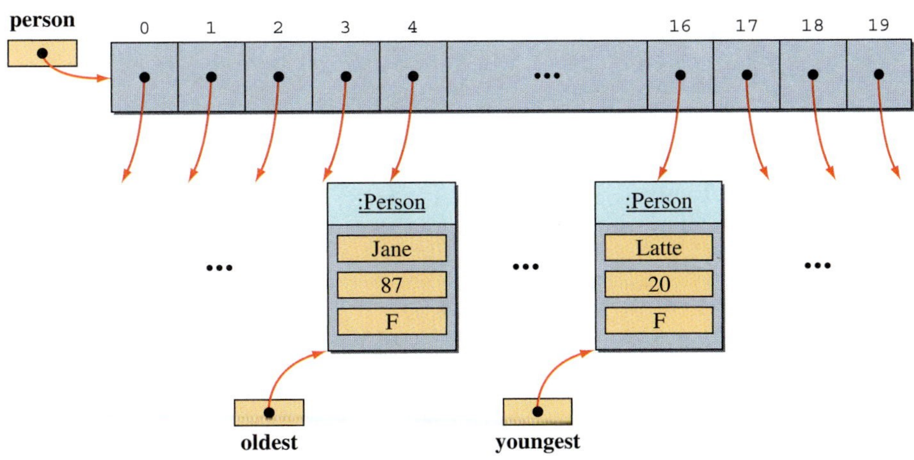

Figure 10.6 An array of **Person** objects with two **Person** variables.

```
        else if (person[i].getAge() > oldest.getAge()) {
            //found an older person
            oldest = person[i];
        }
    }

    System.out.println("Oldest  : " + oldest.getName()
              + " is " +  oldest.getAge() + " years old.");

    System.out.println("Youngest: " + youngest.getName()
              + " is " + youngest.getAge() + " years old.");
```

find a particular person

Our next example is to search for a particular person. We can scan through the array until the desired person is found. Suppose we want to search for a person whose name is Latte. If we assume the person is in the array, then we can write

```
int i = 0;
while (!person[i].getName().equals("Latte")) {
    i++;
}

System.out.println("Found Ms. Latte at position " + i);
```

The expression

```
person[i].getName().equals("Latte")
```

is evaluated left to right and is equivalent to

```
Person p   =  person[i];
String str=  p.getName();

str.equals("Latte");
```

In this example, we assume that the person for whom we are searching is in the array. If we cannot assume this, then we need to rewrite the terminating condition to take care of the case when the person is not in the array. Here's how:

```
int i = 0;

while (i < person.length &&//still more persons to search
        !person[i].getName().equals("Latte")) {
    i++;
}

if (i == person.length) {
    //not found - unsuccessful search
    System.out.println("Ms. Latte was not in the array");

} else {
    //found - successful search
    System.out.println("Found Ms. Latte at position " + i);
}
```

Here's the complete program that summarizes the topics covered so far in this section:

```
/*
   Chapter 10 Sample Program: Illustrate the processing
                              of an array of Person objects

   File: Ch10ProcessPersonArray.java
*/

import java.util.*;

class Ch10ProcessPersonArray {

    public static void main (String[] args) {

        Person[]   person;           //declare the person array
        person = new Person[5];     //and then create it

        //----------- Create person Array -------------------//

        String      name, inpStr;
        int         age;
        char        gender;

        for (int i = 0; i < person.length; i++) {

            //read in data values
            System.out.print("Enter name: ");
            name = scanner.next();

            System.out.print("Enter age: ");
            age = scanner.nextInt();

            System.out.print("Enter gender: ");
            inpStr = scanner.next();
            gender = inpStr.charAt(0);

            //create a new Person and assign values
            person[i] = new Person( );

            person[i].setName   ( name   );
            person[i].setAge    ( age    );
            person[i].setGender( gender );
        }

        //-------------- Compute Average Age --------------//

        float sum = 0, averageAge;

        for (int i = 0; i < person.length; i++) {

            sum += person[i].getAge();
        }
```

```
        averageAge = sum / (float) person.length;

        System.out.println("Average age: " + averageAge);
        System.out.println("\n");

        //------ Find the youngest and oldest persons ----------//
        //------ Approach No. 3: Using person reference --------//

        Person    youngest,        //points to the youngest person
                  oldest;          //points to the oldest person

        youngest = oldest = person[0];

        for (int i = 1; i < person.length; i++) {

            if (person[i].getAge() < youngest.getAge()) {
                //found a younger person
                youngest = person[i];
            }
            else if (person[i].getAge() > oldest.getAge()) {
                 //found an older person
                 oldest = person[i];
            }
        }

        System.out.println("Oldest : " + oldest.getName()
                    + " is " +   oldest.getAge() + " years old.");

        System.out.println("Youngest: " + youngest.getName()
                    + " is " + youngest.getAge() + " years old.");

        //----------- Search for a particular person ------------//

        System.out.print("Name to search: ");
        String searchName = scanner.next();

        int i = 0;

        while (i < person.length &&      //still more persons to search
                !person[i].getName().equals(searchName)) {
            i++;
        }

        if (i == person.length) {
             //not found - unsuccessful search
             System.out.println( searchName + " was not in the array" );

        } else {
            //found - successful search
          System.out.println("Found " + searchName + " at position " + i);
        }
    }
}
```

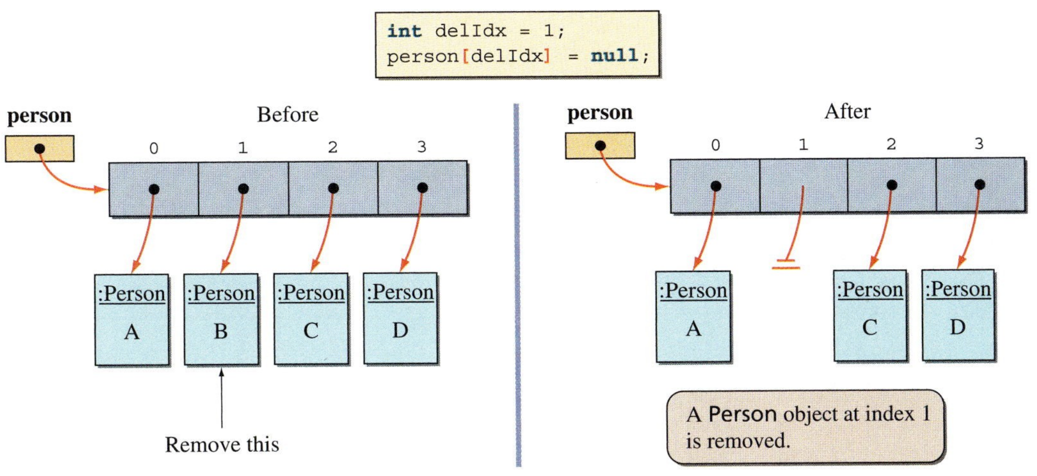

Figure 10.7 Approach 1 deletion: setting a reference to **null.** The array length is 4.

delete a particular person

Now let's consider the deletion operation. The deletion operation requires some kind of a search routine to locate the Person object to be removed. To concentrate on the deletion operation, we will assume there's a search method that returns the index of the Person object in the array to be removed. There are two possible ways to remove an object from the array. The first approach is to reset the array element to null. Remember that each element in an array of objects is a reference to an object, so removing an object from an array could be accomplished by setting the reference to null. Figure 10.7 illustrates how the object at position 1 is deleted by using approach 1.

Since any index position can be set to null, there can be "holes," that is, null references, anywhere in the array. Instead of intermixing real and null references, the second approach will pack the elements so that the real references occur at the beginning and the null references at the end:

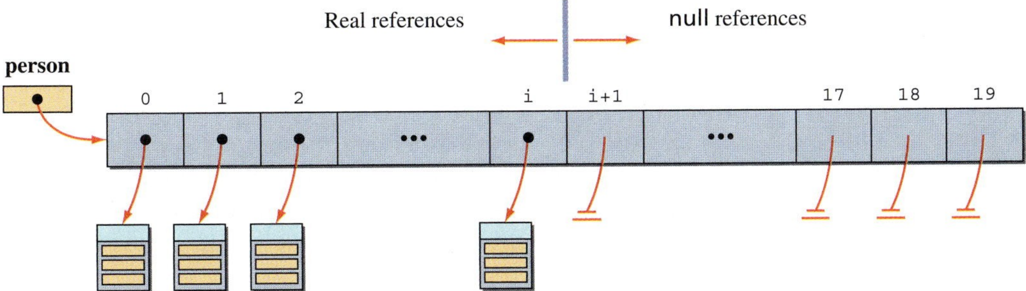

With approach 2, we must fill the hole. There are two possible solutions. The first solution is to pack the elements. If an object at position J is removed (i.e., this position is set to null), then elements from position J+1 up to the last non-null reference are shifted one position lower. And, finally, the last non-null reference is set to null. The second solution is to replace the removed element by the last element in the

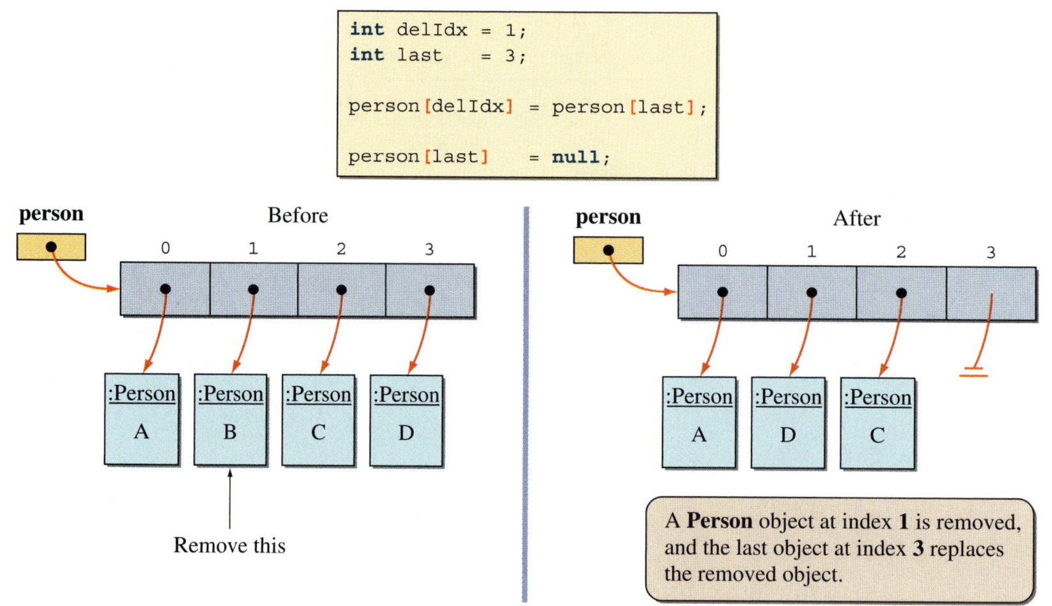

Figure 10.8 Approach 2 deletion: replace the removed element with the last element in the array. The array length is 4.

array. The first solution is necessary if the Person objects are arranged in some order (e.g., in ascending order of age). The second solution is a better one if the Person objects are not arranged in any order. Since we are not arranging them in any order, we will use the second solution. Figure 10.8 illustrates how the object at position 1 is replaced by the last element.

The search routine we presented earlier in this section assumes the full array; that is, all elements are non-null references. With the deletion routine, either approach 1 or 2, given above, an array element could be a null. The search routine must therefore be modified to skip the null references (for approach 1) or to stop the search when the first null reference is encountered (for approach 2).

In both Figures 10.7 and 10.8, we removed the icon for Person B in the diagrams when the array element was set to null as though the object were erased from the memory. Eventually, the object will indeed be erased, but the operation of assigning null to the array element will not erase the object by itself. The operation simply initiates a chain reaction that will eventually erase the object from the memory.

As we have shown several times already, a single object can have multiple references pointing to it. For example, the following code will result in two references pointing to a single Person object:

```
Person p1, p2;

p1 = new Person();
p2 = p1;
```

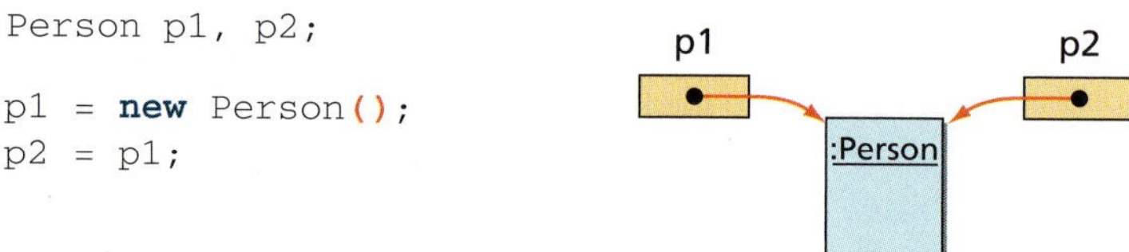

When an object has no references pointing to it, then the system will erase the object and make the memory space available for other uses. We call the erasing of an object *deallocation* of memory, and the process of deallocating memory is called ***garbage collection***. Unlike in other programming languages, garbage collection is automatically done in Java, so we do not have to be conscious of it when developing Java programs.

garbage collection

1. Which of these statements are invalid?

   a. `Person[25] person;`
   b. `Person[ ] person;`
   c. `Person person[] = new Person[25];`
   d. `Person person[25] = new Person[25];`

2. Write a code fragment to print out the names of those who are older than 20. Assume the following declaration and that the array is already set up correctly.

```
Person[ ]  friend = new Person[100];
```

10.3 The For-Each Loop

In Chapter 6, we mentioned a new form of the for loop that is introduced in Java 5.0. There is no official name to this for loop, but the term *for-each* is used most often. The term *enhanced for loop* is also used by many to refer to this for loop. We will use both terms interchangeably in this book.

We will show here how to use the for-each loop in processing an array. We will show how to use it in processing a collection in Section 10.5. Let's assume number is an int array of 100 integers. Using the standard for loop, we compute the sum of all elements in the number array as follows:

```
int sum = 0;

for (int i = 0; i < number.length; i++) {

   sum = sum + number[i];
}
```

We can also compute the sum by using a for-each loop as follows:

```
int sum = 0;

for (int value : number) {

   sum = sum + value;
}
```

The loop iterates over every element in the number array, and the loop body is executed for each iteration. The variable value refers to each element in the array during the iteration. So we can interpret this loop as saying something like "For each value in number, execute the following loop body."

The general syntax for the for-each loop is

```
for ( <type> <variable> : <array> )

    <loop body>
```

where <type> is the data type of <variable>, <array> the name of the array, and <loop body> is a sequence of 0 or more statements (the left and right braces are required if there is more than one statement in the loop body).

Let's look at another example. This time we use an array of objects. Suppose we have an array of 100 Person objects called person:

```
Person[] person = new Person[100];
```

The Person class is defined in Section 10.2. Assuming that 100 Person objects are created and assigned to person[0] to person[99], we can list the name of every person in the array by using the following for-each loop:

```
for (Person p : person) {

   System.out.println(p.getName());
}
```

Contrast this to the standard for loop:

```
for (int i = 0; i < person.length; i++) {

   System.out.println(person[i].getName());
}
```

The for-each loop is, in general, cleaner and easier to read.

There are several restrictions on using the for-each loop. First, you cannot change an element in the array during the iteration. The following code does not reset the array elements to 0:

```
int [] number = {10, 20, 30, 40, 50};

for (int value : number){

   value = 0;
}

for (int value : number) {

   System.out.println(value);
}
```

This loop has no effect.

The first for-each loop has no effect, so the output from this code will be

```
10
20
30
40
50
```

We can characterize the for-each loop as a read-only iteration of the elements.

The for-each loop only allows access to the elements. The elements cannot be changed.

For an array of objects, an element is actually a reference to an object, so the following for-each loop is ineffective. Specifically, it does not reset the elements to null.

```
Person[] person = new Person[100];

for (int i = 0; i < person.length; i++) {
   person[i] = ...; //code to create a new Person object
}

for (Person p : person) {
   p = null;
}
```

This loop has no effect.

Although we cannot change the elements of an array, we can change the content of an object if the element is a reference to an object. For example, the following for-each loop will reset the names of all objects to Java:

```
Person[] person = new Person[100];

for (int i = 0; i < person.length; i++) {
   person[i] = ...; //code to create a new Person object
}

for (Person p : person) {
   p.setName("Java");
}
```

This loop is effective. The name of every **Person** object is set to **Java.**

Notice that we are not changing the elements (references to objects) themselves, but the content of the objects referenced by these elements. Thus, the code is effective.

The second restriction is that we cannot access more than one array using a single for-each loop. Suppose we have two integer arrays num1 and num2 of length 200 and want to create a third array num3 whose elements are sum of the corresponding elements in num1 and num2. Here's the standard for loop:

```
int[] num1 = new int[200];
int[] num2 = new int[200];
int[] num3 = new int[200];

//code to assign values to the elements of num1 and num2

//compute the sums
for (int i = 0; i < num3.length; i++) {
   num3[i] = num1[i] + num2[i];
}
```

Such a loop cannot be written with a for-each loop.

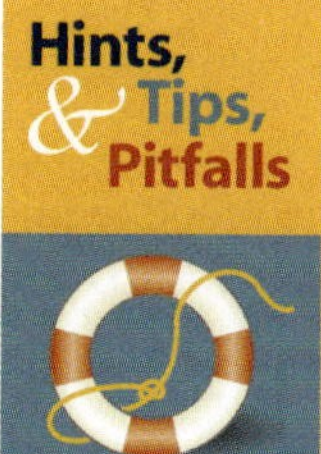

The for-each loop allows access to only a single array.

The third restriction is that we must access all elements in an array from the first to the last element. We cannot, for example, access only the first half or the last half of the array. We cannot access elements in reverse order either.

The for-each loop iterates over every element of an array from the first to the last element. We cannot use the for-each loop to access only a portion of an array or to access the elements in reverse order.

This restriction complicates the matter when we try to access elements in an array of objects. Consider the following code:

```
Person[] person = new Person[100];

for (int i = 0; i < 50; i++) {
   person[i] = ...; //code to create a new Person object
}
```

```
for (Person p : person) {
    System.out.println(
            p.getName());
}
```

This loop will result in a **NullPointerException** error.

This code will crash when the variable p is set to the 51st element (i.e., an element at index position 50), because the element is null. Notice that only the first 50 elements actually point to Person objects. The elements in the second half of the array are all null.

1. Rewrite the following for loop by using a for-each loop.

```
for (int i = 0; i < number.length; i++) {

    System.out.println(number[i]);
}
```

2. Rewrite the following for loop by using the standard for loop.

```
for (Person p : person) {
    System.out.println(p.getName());
}
```

3. Why can't the following for loop be expressed as a for-each loop?

```
for (int i = 0; i < number.length; i++) {

    number[i] = number[i] + 50;
}
```

10.4 Passing Arrays to Methods

We discussed the passing of an object to a method by using String objects as illustrations in Chapter 4. Since both an array and an object are a reference data type, the rules for passing an object to a method and returning an object from the method apply to arrays also. However, there are some additional rules we need to remember in passing an array to a method and returning it from a method. We will cover these topics in this section.

Let's define a method that returns the index of the smallest element in an array of real numbers. The array to search for the smallest element is passed to the method. Here's the method:

```
public int searchMinimum(double[] number) {

    int indexOfMinimum = 0;

    for (int i = 1; i < number.length; i++) {
        if (number[i] < number[indexOfMinimum]) { //found a
```

```
                indexOfMinimum = i;          //smaller element
            }
        }

        return indexOfMinimum;
    }
```

Notice that we use the square brackets to designate that number is an array. The square brackets may also be attached to the parameter, as in

```
public int searchMinimum(double number[])
```

To call this method (from a method of the same class), we write something like this:

```
double[] arrayOne, arrayTwo;

//create and assign values to arrayOne and arrayTwo
...
//get the index of the smallest element of arrayOne
int minOne = searchMinimum( arrayOne );

//get the index of the smallest element of arrayTwo
int minTwo = searchMinimum( arrayTwo );

//output the result
System.out.print("Minimum value in Array One is ");
System.out.print(arrayOne[minOne] +" at position "
                                        + minOne);

System.out.print("\n\n");

System.out.print("Minimum value in Array Two is ");
System.out.print(arrayTwo[minTwo] + " at position "
                                        + minTwo);
```

Just like other objects, an array is a reference data type, so we are passing the reference to an array, not the whole array, when we call the searchMinimum method. For example, when the method is called with arrayOne as its argument, the states of memory illustrated in Figures 10.9 and 10.10 will result. There are two references to the same array. The method does not create a separate copy of the array.

Things to Remember

*When an array is passed to a method, only its reference is passed. A copy of the array is **not** created in the method.*

Now let's try another example in which we return an array (actually the reference to the array) from a method. Suppose we want to define a method that inputs

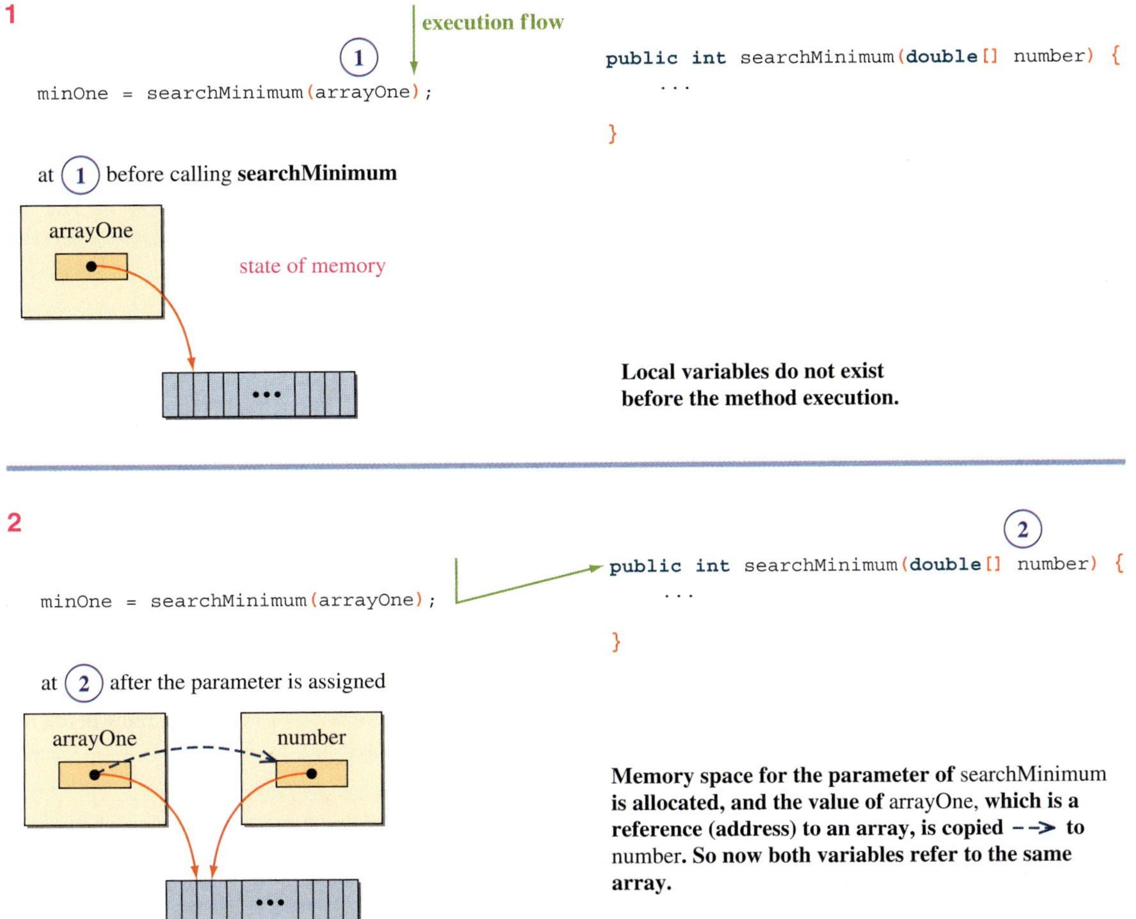

Figure 10.9 Passing an array to a method means we are passing a reference to an array. We are not passing the whole array.

double values and returns the values as an array of double. We can define the method as follows:

```
public double[] readDoubles() {
   double[] number;
   System.out.print("How many input values? ");
   int N = scanner.nextInt();

   number = new double[N];

   for (int i = 0; i < N; i++) {
      System.out.print("Number " + i + ": ");
      number[i] = scanner.nextDouble();
   }

   return number;
}
```

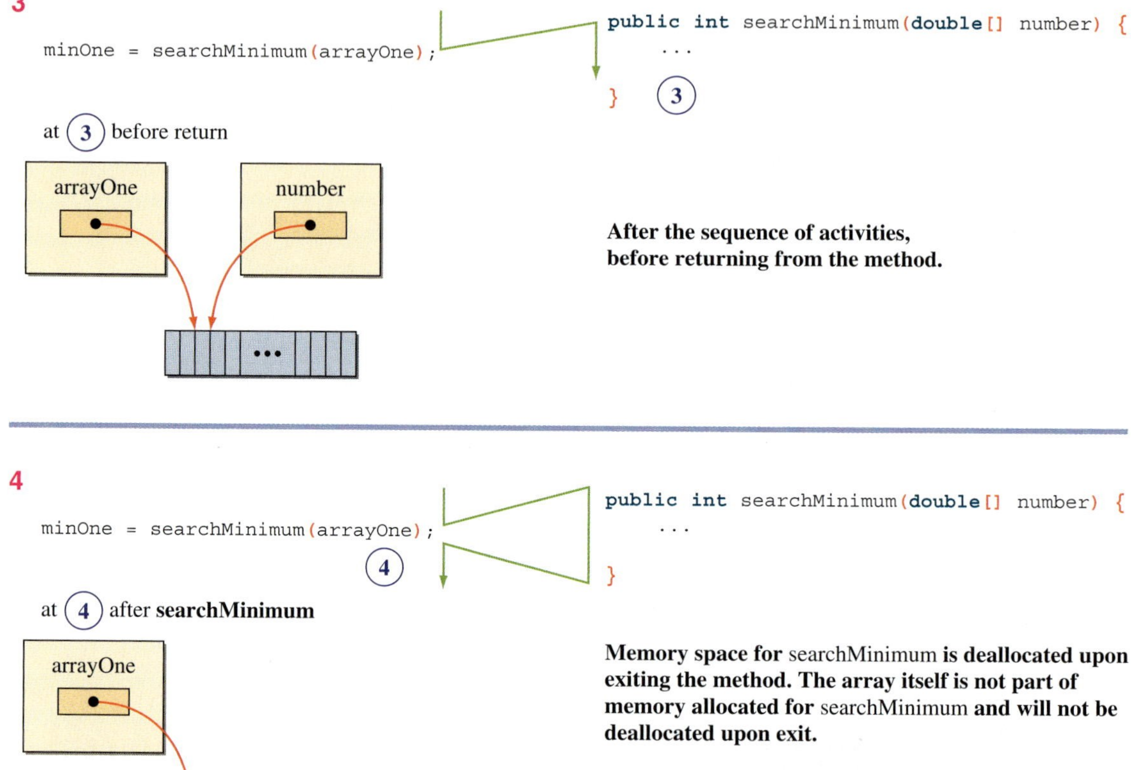

Figure 10.10 Continuation of Figure 10.9.

The square brackets beside the method return type double indicate that the method returns an array of double. Because an array is a reference data type, when we say "returns an array of double," we are really saying "returns the reference to an array of double." We will use the shorter expression in general and use the longer expression only when we need to be precise.

The readDoubles method is called in this manner:

```
double[] arrayOne, arrayTwo;

//assign values to arrayOne and arrayTwo
arrayOne = readDoubles();

arrayTwo = readDoubles();
```

Since a new array is created by the method, we do not have to create an array from the calling side. In other words, we don't have to do this:

```
double[] arrayOne, arrayTwo;

arrayOne = new double[30]; //this is NOT necessary

arrayOne = readDoubles();
```

It won't cause an error if we create an array from the calling side, but we are doing a very wasteful operation. First, it takes up extra memory space. Second, it slows down the whole operation because the computer must garbage-collect the extra memory space that is not being used.

Let's try an alternative approach. This time, instead of creating an array inside the method and returning the array, the calling side creates an array and passes this array to the method:

```
int[] myIntArray = new int[50];

readIntegers(myIntArray);
```

The method readIntegers fills the passed array with integers. The method is defined as follows:

```
public void readIntegers(int[] number) {
   for (int i = 0; i < number.length; i++) {
      System.out.print("Number " + i + ": ");
      number[i] = scanner.nextDouble();
   }
}
```

Notice the return type of readIntegers is void because we are not returning an array. The method modifies the array that is passed to it.

Be careful not to mix the two alternative approaches. The following method will not work:

```
public void badMethod( double[] number ) {
   System.out.print("How many input values? ");
   int N = scanner.nextInt();
   number = new double[N];

   for (int i = 0; i < N; i++) {
      System.out.print("Number " + i + ": ");
      number[i] = scanner.nextDouble();
   }
}
```

Bad Version

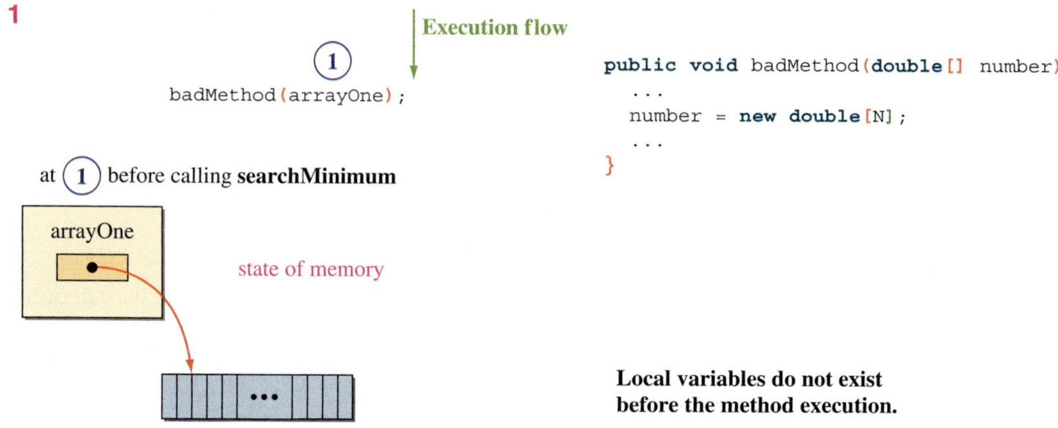

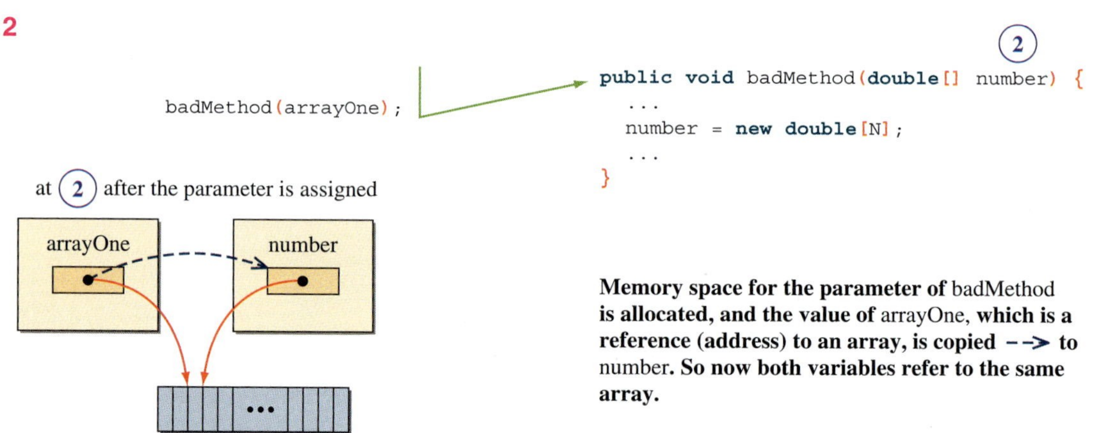

Figure 10.11 Effect of creating a local array and not returning it.

Code such as

```
double[] arrayOne = new double[30];

badMethod( arrayOne );
```

will leave arrayOne unchanged. Figures 10.11 and 10.12 show the effect of creating a local array in badMethod and not returning it. (*Note:* The return type of badMethod is void.)

1. What will be an output from the following code?

```
int[] list = {10, 20, 30, 40 };
myMethod(list);
System.out.println(list[1]);
```

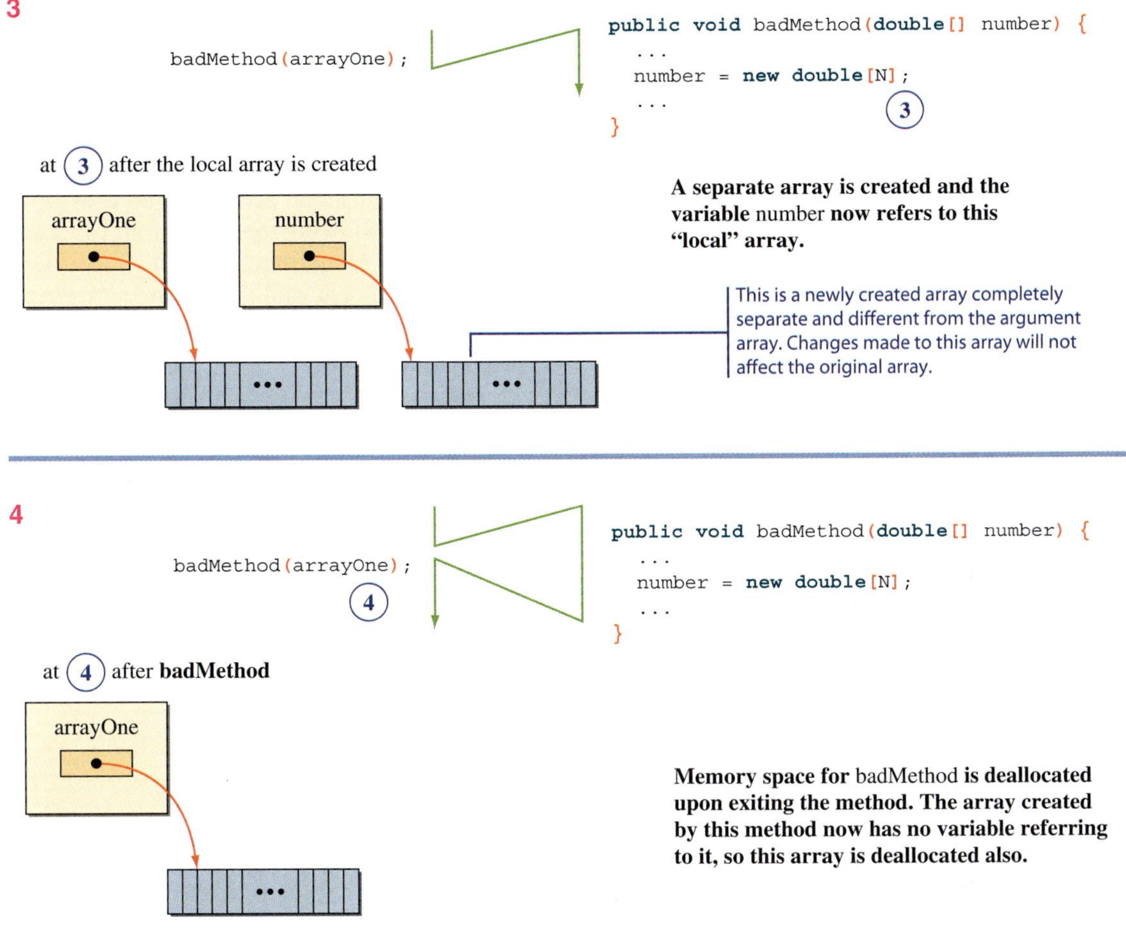

Figure 10.12 Continuation of Figure 10.11.

```
System.out.println(list[3]);

...
public void myMethod(int[] intArray) {
    for (int i = 0; i < intArray.length; i+=2) {
       intArray[i] = i;
    }
}
```

2. If we replace myMethod of question 1 with the following, what will be an output?

```
public void myMethod(int[] intArray)
{
    int[] local = intArray;
    for (int i = 0; i < local.length; i+=2) {
       local[i] = i;
    }
}
```

10.5 Two-Dimensional Arrays

two-dimensional array

A table organized in rows and columns is a very effective means for communicating many different types of information. Figure 10.13 shows sample data displayed in a tabular format. In Java, we represent tables as ***two-dimensional arrays***. The arrays we have discussed so far are *one-dimensional arrays* because they have only one index. In this section, we describe how two-dimensional arrays are used in Java.

Let's begin with an example. Consider the following table with four rows and five columns. The table contains the hourly rate of programmers based on their skill level. The rows (horizontal) represent the grade levels, and the columns (vertical)

Distance Table (in miles)

	Los Angeles	San Francisco	San Jose	San Diego	Monterey
Los Angeles	—	600	500	150	450
San Francisco	600	—	100	750	150
San Jose	500	100	—	650	50
San Diego	150	750	650	—	600
Monterey	450	150	50	600	—

Multiplication Table

	1	2	3	4	5	6	7	8	9
1	1	2	3	4	5	6	7	8	9
2	2	4	6	8	10	12	14	16	18
3	3	6	9	12	15	18	21	24	27
4	4	8	12	16	20	24	28	32	36
5	5	10	15	20	25	30	35	40	45
6	6	12	18	24	30	36	42	48	54
7	7	14	21	28	35	42	49	56	63
8	8	16	24	32	40	48	56	64	72
9	9	18	27	36	45	54	63	72	81

Tuition Table

	Day Students	Boarding Students
Grades 1–6	$16,000.00	$28,000.00
Grades 7–8	$19,000.00	$31,000.00
Grades 9–12	$22,500.00	$34,500.00

Figure 10.13 Examples of information represented as tables.

represent the steps within a grade level. Reading the table, we know a programmer with skill grade level 2, step 1 earns $36.50 per hour.

		Step				
		0	**1**	**2**	**3**	**4**
Grade	**0**	10.50	12.00	14.50	16.75	18.00
	1	20.50	22.25	24.00	26.25	28.00
	2	34.00	36.50	38.00	40.35	43.00
	3	50.00	60.00	70.00	80.00	99.99

We declare the pay scale table as

```
double[][] payScaleTable;
```

or

```
double payScaleTable[][];
```

and create the array as

```
payScaleTable = new double[4][5];
```

The payScaleTable array is a *two-dimensional array* because two indices—one for the row and another for the column—are used to refer to an array element. For example, to refer to the element at the second column (column 1) of the third row (row 2), we say

```
payScaleTable[2][1]
```

Figure 10.14 illustrates how the two indices are used to access an array element of a two-dimensional array.

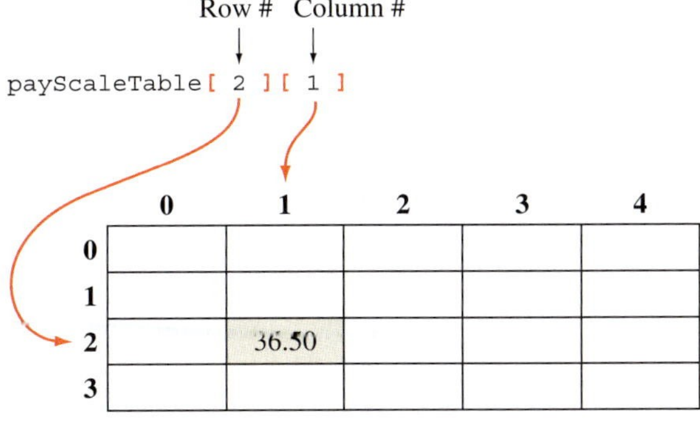

Figure 10.14 Accessing an element of a two-dimensional array.

Let's go over some examples to see how the elements of two-dimensional arrays are manipulated. This code finds the average pay of the grade 2 programmers.

```
double average, sum = 0.0;

for (int j = 0; j < 5; j++) {
   sum += payScaleTable[2][j];
}

average = sum / 5;
```

The next example prints out the pay difference between the lowest and highest steps for each grade level.

```
double difference;

for (int i = 0; i < 4; i++) {
   difference = payScaleTable[i][4] - payScaleTable[i][0];
   System.out.println("Pay difference at Grade Level " +
                           i + " is " + difference);
}
```

This code adds $1.50 to every skill level.

```
for (int i = 0; i < 4; i++) {
   for (int j = 0; j < 5; j++) {
       payScaleTable[i][j] += 1.50;
   }
}
```

In the previous examples, we used literal constants such as 5 and 4 to keep them simple. For real programs, we need to write a loop that will work for two-dimensional arrays of any size, not just with the one with four rows and five columns. We can use the length field of an array to write such a loop. Using the length field, we can rewrite the third example as

```
for (int i = 0; i < payScaleTable.length; i++) {
   for (int j = 0; j < payScaleTable[i].length; j++) {
      payScaleTable[i][j] += 1.50;
   }
}
```

Do you notice a subtle difference in the code? Let's examine the difference between the expressions

```
payScaleTable.length
```

and

```
payScaleTable[i].length
```

First, there is actually no explicit structure called *two-dimensional array* in Java. We only have one-dimensional arrays in Java. However, we can have an array of arrays, and this is how the conceptual two-dimensional array is implemented in Java. The sample array creation

```
payScaleTable = new double[4][5];
```

is really a shorthand for

```
payScaleTable = new double[4][ ];

payScaleTable[0] = new double[5];
payScaleTable[1] = new double[5];
payScaleTable[2] = new double[5];
payScaleTable[3] = new double[5];
```

which is equivalent to

```
payScaleTable = new double[4][ ];

for (int i = 0; i < 4; i++) {
   payScaleTable[i] = new double[5];
}
```

Figure 10.15 shows the effect of executing the five statements. The expression

```
payScaleTable.length
```

refers to the length of the payScaleTable array itself.

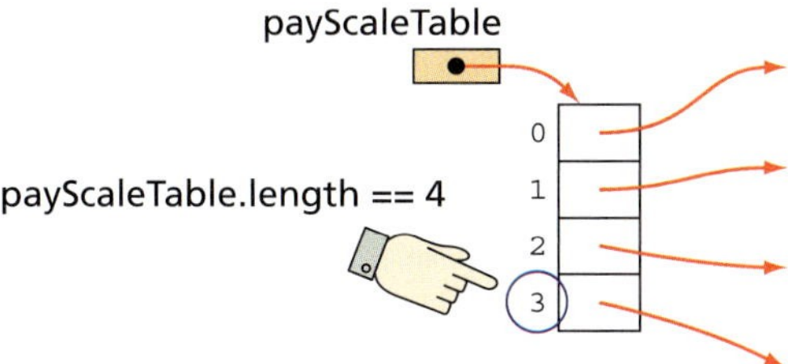

And the expression

```
payScaleTable[1].length
```

refers to the length of an array stored at row 1 of payScaleTable.

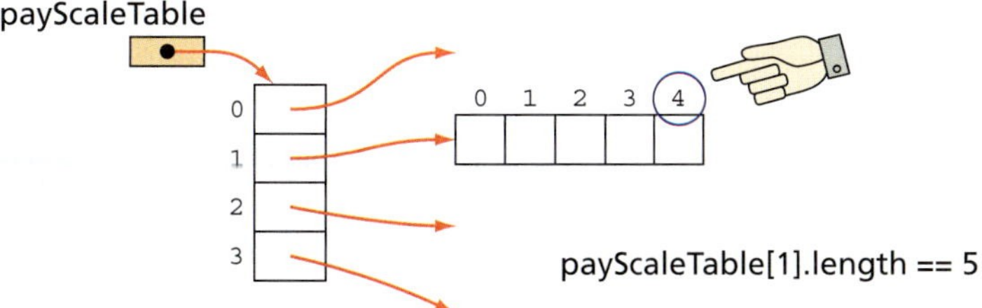

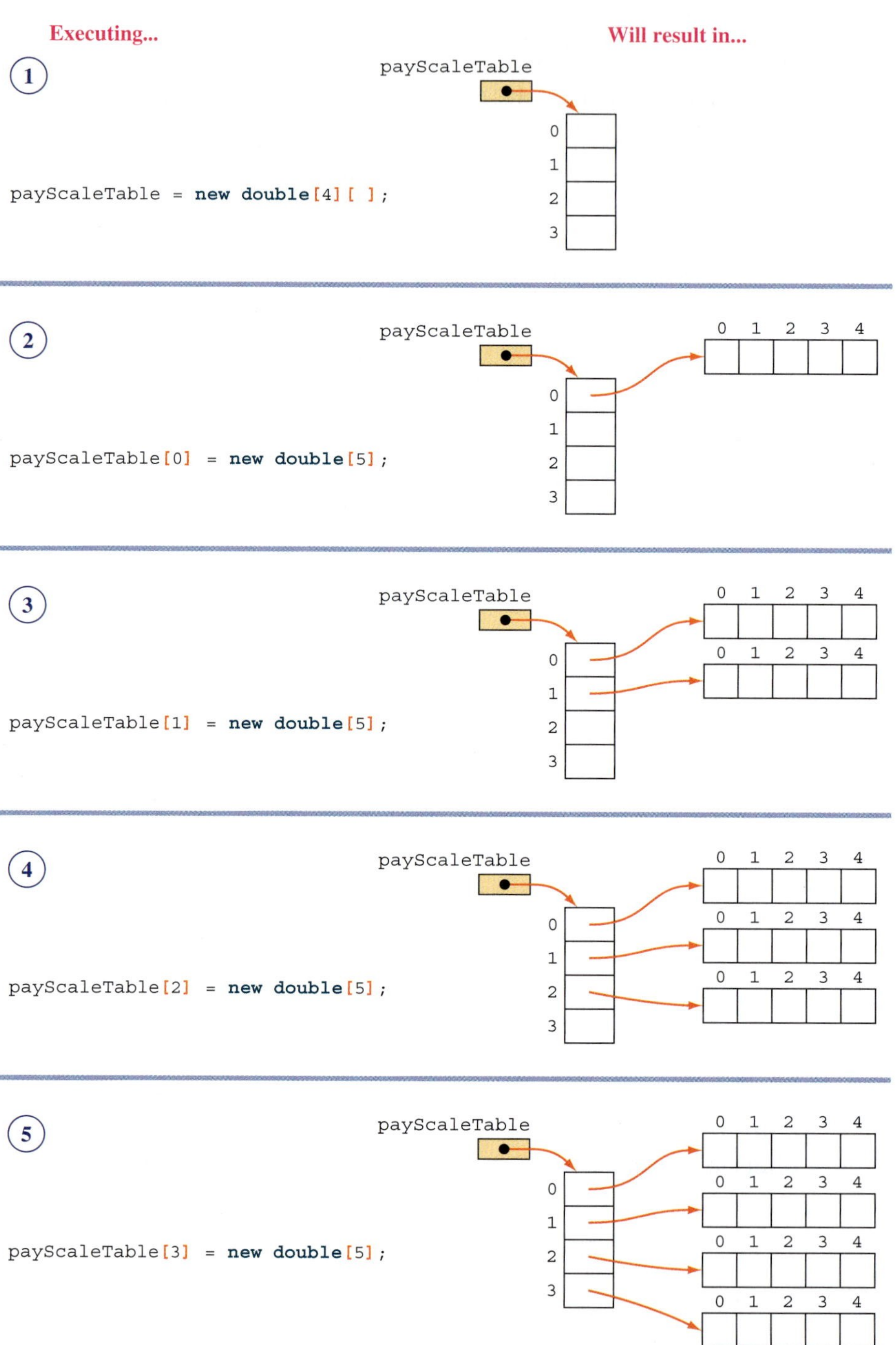

Figure 10.15 Executing the statements on the left in sequence will create the array of arrays shown on the right.

We call an array that is part of another a *subarray*. The payScaleTable has four subarrays of the same length. Since we allocate the subarrays individually, we can create subarrays of different lengths. The following code creates a triangular array whose subarray triangularArray[i] has length i.

```
triangularArray = new double[4][ ];

for (int i = 0; i < 4; i++)
   triangularArray[i] = new double[i+1];
```

The resulting triangularArray looks like this:

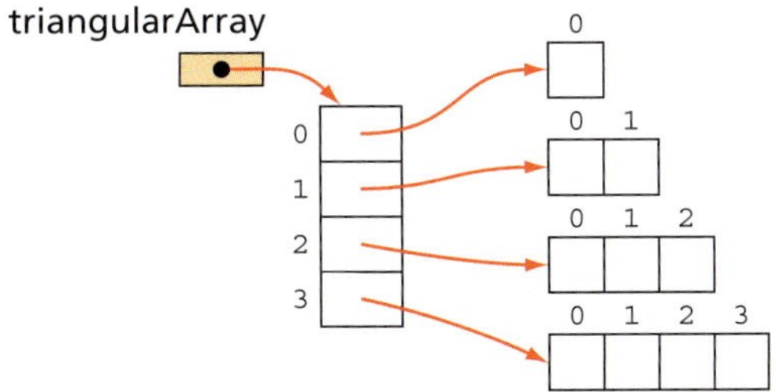

An array of arrays can be initialized at the time of declaration. The following declaration initializes the payScaleTable array:

```
double[][] payScaleTable
         = { {10.50, 12.00, 14.50, 16.75, 18.00},
             {20.50, 22.25, 24.00, 26.25, 28.00},
             {34.00, 36.50, 38.00, 40.35, 43.00},
             {50.00, 60.00, 70.00, 80.00, 99.99} };
```

Here's the complete sample program:

```
/*

    Chapter 10 Sample Program: Sample program for processing
                               2-D array of double.

    File: Ch10PayScaleTable.java
*/

class Ch10PayScaleTable {
    public static void main (String[] args) {

        double[][] payScaleTable
                      = {  {10.50, 12.00, 14.50, 16.75, 18.00},
                           {20.50, 22.25, 24.00, 26.25, 28.00},
                           {34.00, 36.50, 38.00, 40.35, 43.00},
                           {50.00, 60.00, 70.00, 80.00, 99.99}  };
```

```
        //Find the average pay of level 2 employees
        double sum = 0.0, average;

        for (int j = 0; j < 5; j++) {
            sum += payScaleTable[2][j];
        }

        average = sum / 5;

        System.out.println(" Average of Level 2 Employees: " + average );
        System.out.println("\n");

        //Display the pay difference at each grade level
        double difference;

        for (int i = 0; i < 4; i++) {
            difference = payScaleTable[i][4] - payScaleTable[i][0];
            System.out.println("Pay difference at Grade Level " +
                                         i + " is " + difference);
        }

        //Print out the pay scale table
        System.out.println("\n");

        for (int i = 0; i < payScaleTable.length; i++) {

            for (int j = 0; j < payScaleTable[i].length; j++) {

                System.out.print( payScaleTable[i][j] + "     " );
            }

            System.out.println("");
        }

        //Increase the pay by 1.50 for every level/step
        //and display the resulting table
        System.out.println("\n");

        for (int i = 0; i < payScaleTable.length; i++) {

            for (int j = 0; j < payScaleTable[i].length; j++) {

                payScaleTable[i][j] += 1.50;

                System.out.print(payScaleTable[i][j] + "     ");
            }

            System.out.println("");
        }
    }
}
```

We can nest for-each loops to process a two-dimensional array. Remember that the two-dimensional array is structurally an array of arrays (as illustrated in Figure 10.15), and the nested for-each loops will make this fact explict. To print out the pay scale table, for example, we write

```
for (double[] row : payScaleTable) {

   for (double pay : row) {

      System.out.print(pay + "      ");
   }

   System.out.println("");
}
```

The outer loop iterates over the rows in the payScaleTable two-dimensional array. Each row is one-dimensional array of double, so the type is declared as double[]. And the inner loop iterates over the elements in each row. Notice that we cannot rewrite the other loop statements in the Ch10PayScaleTable program by using the for-each loop.

There is no limit to the number of dimensions an array can have. We can declare three-dimensional, four-dimensional, and higher-dimensional arrays. However, arrays with a dimension higher than 2 are not frequently used in object-oriented languages. For example, data that were represented as a three-dimensional array in a non-object-oriented language can be represented more naturally as a one-dimensional array of objects with each object containing an array or some other form of data structure (see Exercise 12 on page 615).

1. Write a code fragment to compute the average pay of the pays stored in the payScaleTable array.
2. Write a code fragment that finds the largest integer in this two-dimensional array.

   ```
   int[][] table = new int[10][10];
   ```

3. What is an output from this code?

   ```
   int[][] table = new int[10][5];

   System.out.println(table.length);
   System.out.println(table[4].length);
   ```

10.6 Lists and Maps

Once an array is created, its capacity cannot be changed. For example, if we create an array of 20 elements, then we are limited to store at most 20 elements in using this array. If we need to add elements, then we have to create a new array. (*Note:* We will learn how to do this in Section 10.7.) We call the condition in which an array does not have any unused position left to add another element an ***array overflow***.

array overflow

Whenever we use arrays in an application, we need to consider the possibility of an array overflow. We can usually avoid an array overflow by declaring its capacity to be a large number. However, if we declare the capacity of an array too large, we may avoid an array overflow but end up underutilizing the space (e.g., using only 20 positions in an array with the capacity of 500). If we do not want our application to be limited to some fixed capacity, we need to write code that handles an array overflow by allocating a larger array.

If we need to handle an array overflow for multiple arrays we use in an application, we can define a class that handles the array overflow so we don't have to implement an overflow-handling code for individual arrays. We might call the new class ExpandableArray. By using this class, we can keep adding new elements without worrying about the overflow condition, because the class handles the overflow condition automatically.

java.util

It turns out there's no need for us to write such an ExpandableArray class because the Java standard library **java.util** already includes various classes and (interfaces) for maintaining a collection of objects. They are collectively referred as the *Java Collection Framework,* or ***JCF***. We will study the basic ones in this section.

JCF

interface

abstract method

The first is the List interface. Like a class, an ***interface*** is a reference data type; but unlike a class, an interface includes only constants and abstract methods. An ***abstract method*** has only the method header (or, more formally, the *method prototype*); that is, it has no method body. The abstract methods of an interface define a behavior. For example, the List interface includes 25 abstract methods that collectively define a behavior of a linear list, such as adding an element, removing an element, and so forth.

We cannot create an instance of a Java interface. (*Note:* To differentiate a user interface from a reference data type interface, we will use the term *Java interface* to refer to the latter.) For example, the following will result in a compile-time error:

Bad Version

```
List myList = new List ( );
```

To create an instance that will support a List behavior, we need a class that implements the List interface. We say a class implements an interface if it provides the method body to all the abstract methods defined in the Java interface.

There are two classes in JCF that implement the List interface: ArrayList and LinkedList. Because they implement the same interface, they behave exactly the same. That is, there's no difference in using them (as long as we use the methods defined in the List interface). They differ in the internal data structure they use to implement the interface. The ArrayList class uses an array, and the LinkedList class uses a technique called *linked-node representation*. We choose one over the other depending on the nature of application (e.g., choose LinkedList if the application requires frequent insertions and deletions of elements but occasional searching for elements in the list). It is beyond our scope to provide an in-depth comparative analysis here. In most situations, the ArrayList class would be preferable so we will use it for the examples in this chapter. We will provide more detailed coverage and analysis on the array versus linked-node representation in Chapters 16 and 18.

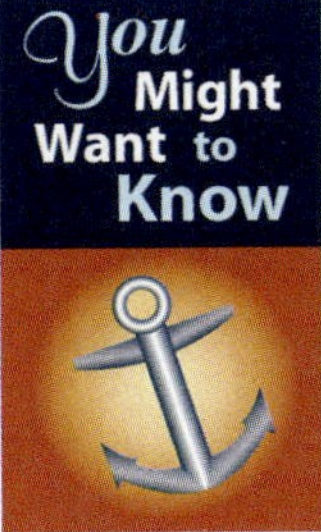

There is another "expandable array" in the JCF called **Vector.** The **Vector** class predates the JCF classes, but from Java 2 SDK 1.2, the class was modified to implement the **List** interface. Because it was designed before the JCF classes, it includes many methods in addition to the **List** methods. In general, the **ArrayList** class is recommended for most situations.

Let's study how we can use the methods of the List interface. First we need to declare and create an instance of a class that implements the List interface. Let's use the ArrayList class. From what we have learned so far about declaring and creating an instance of a class, we would write something like

```
ArrayList myList;
...
myList = new ArrayList();
```

Not recommended

if the class is ArrayList. This would work (you'll get only a compiler warning), but it is not a recommended style of programming. There are two improvements we should make. The first is to declare the variable as the Java interface and to assign an instance of the class that implements the interface. Applying this improvement will result in

```
List myList;
...
myList = new ArrayList();
```

myList is declared as type **List**

Basically this style of declaration improves the ease of program modification. Suppose, for example, there are many methods that accept a list object

```
public void myMethod(ArrayList aList)
```

With this declaration, we can only pass an instance of ArrayList. Now suppose at a later time we decide to use LinkedList to improve performances for certain types of operations. We have to go back and make changes to all those method headers. But what if we declare the method from the beginning as follows?

```
public void myMethod(List aList)
```

Since we can pass an instance of either ArrayList or LinkedList (or an instance of any class that implements the List interface), no changes are required. We will study the Java interface in greater detail in Chapter 13.

The second improvement is specific to Java 5.0 JCF classes. If we declare a list object as

```
List myList = new ArrayList();
```

there are no restrictions on the type of objects we can add to the list. For example, we can add String objects, Person objects, Vehicle objects, and so forth to this myList.

heterogeneous list

homogeneous list

We call such list a ***heterogeneous list***. In most applications, there is no need to maintain such heterogeneous lists. What we need is a ***homogeneous list***, where the elements are restricted to a specific type such as a list of Person objects, a list of String objects, a list of Book objects, and so forth. Specifying the element type improves the program reliability because an error such as trying to add a wrong type of object to a list can be caught during the compile time. It is strongly recommended to use homogeneous lists.

To specify a homogeneous list, we must include the type of elements in the declaration and creation statements. Here's an example that declares and creates a list of Person objects:

```
List<Person> friends;
...
friends = new ArrayList<Person>( );
```

The general syntax for the declaration is

interface-or-class-name < *element-type* > *identifier*;

And the general syntax for the creation is

identifier = **new** *class-name* < *element-type* > (*parameters*) ;

We can combine the two into a single statement as

interface-or-class-name < *element-type* > *identifier*
    = **new** *class-name* <*element-type*> (*parameters*) ;

for example,

```
List<Person> friends = new ArrayList<Person>{ );
```

add

Now we are ready to study the basic operations of the List interface. Once a list is created properly, we can start adding elements. In the following example, we create a list named friends and **add** four Person objects to the list:

```
List<Person> friends = new ArrayList<Person>{ );
Person person;

person = new Person("Jane", 10, 'F');
friends.add(person);

person = new Person("Jack", 16, 'M');
friends.add(person);

person = new Person("Jill", 8, 'F');
friends.add(person);

person = new Person("John", 12, 'M');
friends.add(person);
```

size

To find out the number of elements in a list, we use its **size** method. The following code will print out 3:

```
List<String> sample = new ArrayList<String>( );

sample.add("One Java");
sample.add("One Java");
sample.add("One Java");

System.out.println(sample.size());
```

get

We can access objects in a list by giving their index position in the list, much as we did with the array. We use the **get** method to access an object at index position i. For example, to access the Person object at position 3 (*note:* the first element is at position 0) in the friends list, we write

```
Person p = friends.get(3);
```

An invalid argument, such as a negative value or a value greater than size() – 1, will result in an IndexOutOfBoundsException error.

traversal

One of the most common operations we perform on a list is ***traversal***. This operation, also called *scanning* or *iteration*, accesses all elements in a list. To traverse a list from the first to the last element, we can use the for-each loop. Here's how we can print out the names of all those in the friends list by using the for-each loop:

```
for (Person p : friends) {

   System.out.println(p.getName());
}
```

iterator

This for-each loop, new to Java 5.0, is actually a shortcut for using an iterator pattern. When we call the **iterator** method of a list, it returns an Iterator object (an instance of a class that implements the Iterator interface) that supports the two methods hasNext and next. Here's the code to print out the names of all those in the friends list by using an iterator:

```
Person p;

Iterator<Person> itr = friends.iterator();

while (itr.hasNext()) {

   p = itr.next();

   System.out.println(p.getName());
}
```

Again, the for-each loop is built on top of the iterator pattern as a syntactical shortcut, and wherever the iterator pattern is available, we can (and should) use the cleaner and less error-prone for-each loop.

The traversal operation is necessary to search a list for elements that meet some criterion. Let's say we want to print out the names of those in the friends list who are older than 10. Here's the code:

```
for (Person p : friends) {

   if (p.age() > 10) {
      System.out.println(p.getName());
   }
}
```

Instead of simply printing out their names, we could create another list to keep track of those who are older than 10:

```
List<Person> olderThan10List = new ArrayList<Person>();

for (Person p : friends) {

   if (p.age() > 10) {
      olderThan10List.add(p);
   }
}
```

The original friends list remains unchanged; that is, no objects are removed from the list. We simply have a second list that points to a subset of elements in the friends list. The situation can be illustrated as follows (two Person objects are older than 10):

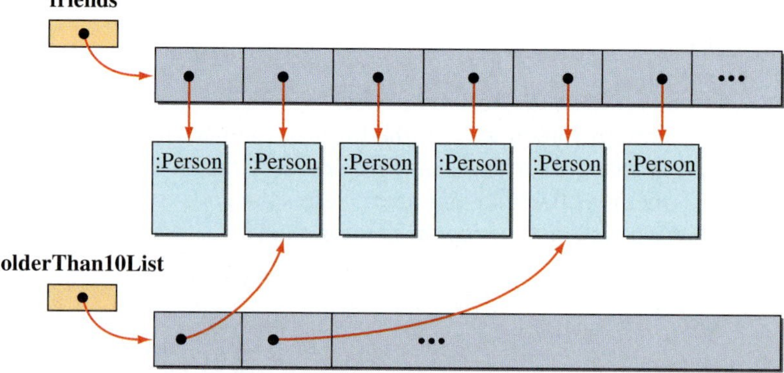

remove

To remove an element from a list, we use the **remove** method. There are two versions: one specifies the index position of the object to remove, and the other specifies the object itself (i.e., the reference to this object). If we use the first version, here's how we remove the Person object at index position 2 in the friends list:

```
friends.remove(2);
```

The second version of the remove method requires a reference to an object. One way to acquire a reference to an object we want to remove is via traversal.

Here's the code that traverses the friends list and removes all Person objects who are older than 10:

```
List<Person> tempList = new ArrayList<Person>();

//first we collect those we want to remove from the
//friends list in a separate list
for (Person p : friends) {

   if (p.age() > 10) {
      tempList.add(p);
   }
}

//then we remove every element in tempList
//from the friends list
for (Person p : tempList) {

   friends.add(p);
}
```

Some of you might have thought about the following code:

```
for (Person p : friends) {

   if (p.age() > 10) {
      friends.remove(p);
   }
}
```

Bad Version

This is an invalid operation. We are not allowed to modify the list we are traversing. The for-each loop (and the underlying iterator pattern) is a read-only traversal.

Hints, & Tips, Pitfalls

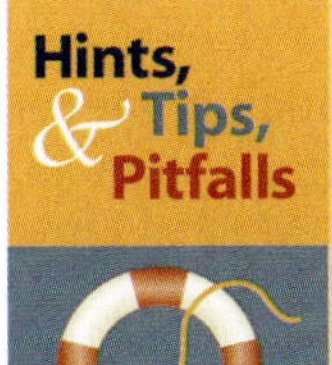

No changes can be made to a list while traversing it with an iterator or a for-each loop.

Lists and Primitive Data Types

With an array, we can store either primitive data values (int, double, etc.) or objects. With a list, we can store only objects. If we need to store primitive data values in a list, then we must use wrapper classes such as Integer, Float, and Double. To add integers to a list, we have to do something like this:

```
List<Integer> intList = new ArrayList<Integer>( );

intList.add(new Integer(15));
intList.add(new Integer(30));
...
```

When we access the elements of intList, which are Integer objects, we need to use the intValue method to get the integer value. The following code computes the sum of integer values stored in intList:

```
int sum = 0;

for (Integer intObj : intList) {

   sum = sum + intObj.intValue();
}
```

Instead of this tedious way of dealing with primitive data values, Java 5.0 introduces automatic boxing and unboxing features. With Java 5.0, we can write the code as if we could store primitive data values in lists. For example, the following code is valid with Java 5.0:

```
List<Integer> intList = new ArrayList<Integer>( );

intList.add(15);
intList.add(30);
...

int sum = 0;

for (int value : intList) {

    sum = sum + value;
}
```

Keep in mind that there are no structural changes. We are still adding Integer objects to intList (see the declaration for intList). It is just a syntactical shortcut. When we write, for example,

```
intList.add(30);
```

the compiler translates it to

```
intList.add(new Integer(30));
```

This is called *auto boxing*. And when we write

```
int num = intList.get(1);
```

the compiler translates it to

```
int num = intList.get(1).intValue( );
```

This is called *auto unboxing*.

Let's conclude our discussion of the List interface with the BookTracker helper class we used in the Sample Development section of Chapter 7. The BookTracker class uses an ArrayList to keep track of library books. Here's the definition:

```
/*
   Chapter 7 Sample Development: Library Overdue Checker

   File: BookTracker.java
*/

import java.util.*;

class BookTracker {

   public static final int ERROR = -1;

   private List<LibraryBook> books;

   public BookTracker( ) {
       books = new LinkedList<LibraryBook>();
   }

   public void add(LibraryBook book) {
       books.add(book);
   }

   public double getCharge( ) {
       return getCharge(new GregorianCalendar()); //set today as due date
   }

   public double getCharge(GregorianCalendar returnDate) {

       if (books.isEmpty()) {
           return ERROR;
       } else {
          return totalCharge(returnDate);
       }
   }

   public String getList( ) {

       StringBuffer result = new StringBuffer("");

       String lineSeparator = System.getProperty("line.separator");

       for (LibraryBook book: books) {
           result.append(book.toString() + lineSeparator);
       }
```

Constructor

add

getCharge

getList

```
        return result.toString();
    }

    private double totalCharge(GregorianCalendar returnDate) {

        double totalCharge = 0.0;

        for (LibraryBook book: books) {
            totalCharge += book.computeCharge(returnDate);
        }

        return totalCharge;
    }
}
```

totalCharge

Map

Let's move on to another useful interface called Map. There are two classes that implement this interface: HashMap and TreeMap. We will describe the TreeMap class in this section because this is the class we used in implementing the helper WordList class in Chapter 9. The TreeMap class actually implements a subinterface of Map called SortedMap, where the entries in the map are sorted.

A map consists of entries, with each entry divided into two parts: key and value. No duplicate keys are allowed in the map. Both key and value can be an instance of any class. The main advantage of a map is its performance in locating an entry, given the key. Consider, for example, that we want to maintain a table of course evaluations. For each course offered on campus, we want to keep an evaluation that is summarized from the student opinion poll collected at the end of the term. The course number (e.g., CS0101) is the key, and the evaluation is the value. We would want to store the information as a map because we need to look up the evaluation of a course efficiently, as there are hundreds or thousands of courses. The search would take too long if we used other data structures.

As we know, a Java array allows only integer indices. In some situations we may want to use an array with indices other than integers. For example, a **WordList** from Chapter 9 can be viewed as an array of numbers with words (**String**) as its indices. A map can be characterized as an expandable array with instances of any class as its indices. So whenever we need an array of values with noninteger indices, a map is a possible solution.

When declaring and creating a map, we must specify the type for the key and the value. For example, to declare and create a map with String as both its key and value, we write

```
Map<String,String> table;

table = new TreeMap<String,String>( );
```

put

We use its put method to add the key-value pairs to the map as

```
table.put("CS0101", "Great course. Take it");
```

remove

where the first argument is the key and the second argument is the value. To remove an entry, we use the remove method with the key of an entry to remove from the map, for example,

```
table.remove("CS2300");
```

clear

Instead of removing individual elements, we can remove all of them at once by calling the clear method. The statement

```
table.clear( );
```

get

removes everything from the map, making it an empty map.
To retrieve the value associated to a key, we call the map's get method.

```
String courseEval = table.get("CS102");
```

contains key

We can ask the map if it contains a given key. To check, for example, whether the map contains an evaluation for course number CS0455, we write

```
boolean result = table.containsKey("CS0455");
```

entrySet

If there's no matching entry, then the value null is returned.

To traverse a map, we must first call its entrySet method to get a set of elements. The method returns an instance of a class that implements the Set interface, another interface in JCF, that models a mathematical set. Those interested in using the Set interface are referred to the Java API documentation. The methods defined in the Set interface are very similar to those defined in the List interface. If we know how to use the List interface, then it won't take long for us to understand the Set interface.

An element in a map is a key-value pair, so the entrySet method returns a set of key-value pairs. A key-value pair is an instance of a class that implements the Map.Entry interface. The dot notation indicates that the Entry interface is defined in the declaration of the Map interface. Such a nested declaration is useful in avoiding a naming conflict.

Two useful methods defined in the Map.Entry interface are the getKey and getValue, whose purpose is to retrieve the key and the value of an entry, respectively. To put it all together, here's an example that outputs the course numbers and their evaluations stored in the table map:

```
for (Map.Entry<String,String> entry : table.entrySet()) {

    System.out.println(entry.getKey() + ":\n" +
                           entry.getValue() + "\n");
}
```

Notice the type declaration for the loop variable entry is Map.Entry<String, String>. Because the key and value component of Map.Entry can be of any class, we need to indicate the actual type for the key and the value specific to this entry.

We are now ready to present the WordList class. It uses a TreeMap object to keep track of distinct words in a document and how many times they occur in the document. Notice the TreeMap class actually implements a more specialized map interface called SortedMap, a subinterface of the Map interface that adds the behavior of sorting the elements in ascending key order. This is exactly the data structure we want to use here because we want to access and display the words and their count in alphabetical order. Here's the definition:

```
/*
   Chapter 9 Sample Development: Word Concordance

   File: WordList.java
*/

import java.util.*;

class WordList {

   SortedMap<String, Integer> table;

   public WordList( ) {                                          Constructor

         table = new TreeMap<String, Integer>();
   }

   public void add(String word) {                                add

        int val;

        if (table.containsKey(word)) {

             val = table.get(word) + 1;     Auto boxing and unboxing
                                            are used in this method.
        } else {
           //word occurs for the first time
           val = 1;
      }

      table.put(word, val);
   }

   public String getConcordance( ){                              getConcordance
        String line;
        String lineTerminator
                  = System.getProperties().getProperty("line.separator");
        StringBuffer strBuf = new StringBuffer("");

        for (Map.Entry<String,Integer> entry : table.entrySet()) {
```

```
            line = entry.getValue().toString() + "\t" +
                   entry.getKey() + lineTerminator;

            strBuf.append(line);
        }

        return strBuf.toString();
    }

    public void reset( ) {
        table.clear();
    }
}
```

reset

Compared to the amount of work the class has to perform, the length of its source code is rather short. This is so because the hard part of maintaining the data structure is done by the TreeMap class. Had we tried to implement the WordList class without using the TreeMap class, the source code would have been much longer. A little effort to study the JCF classes pays handsomely when the time comes for us to implement an efficient data manager class, such as the WordList class.

1. What is the output from the following code?

```
List<String> list = new ArrayList<String>();

for(int i = 0; i < 6; i++) {
   list.add("element " + i);
   System.out.println(list.size());
}
```

2. What is the output from the following code?

```
List<String> list = new ArrayList<String>();

for(int i = 0; i < 6; i++) {
   list.add("element " + i);
}

list.remove(1);
list.remove(3);

System.out.println(list.get(2));
```

3. Identify all errors in the following code.

```
List<String> list = new ArrayList<Integer>();

List<Person> people = new List<Person>();

Map<String> table = new Map();
```

10.7 Sample Development

The Address Book

In this section, we will design a class called an **AddressBook** to maintain a collection of **Person** objects. The **AddressBook** class is implemented by using an array. We will use the **Person** class defined in Section 10.2. Through the design of the **AddressBook** class, we will reiterate the key principles of object-oriented design.

Notice that we are not developing a complete program here. We are designing only one of the many classes we need for a complete address book program. For the complete program, we need a main window, objects for doing input and output, and so forth. In this section, we will concentrate on one class that is only responsible for maintaining a collection of **Person** objects. This class will not perform, for example, input and output of **Person** objects, following the *single-task object* (STO) principle introduced in Chapter 4. We will discuss the importance of the STO principle while we develop the **AddressBook** class. One objective we have in designing the **AddressBook** class is to make the class reusable in many different programs. Many of the design decisions we will make during the development are based on implementing a reusable class.

Problem Statement

Write an **AddressBook** *class that manages a collection of* **Person** *objects. An* **AddressBook** *object will allow the programmer to add, delete, or search for a* **Person** *object in the address book.*

Overall Plan

Our first task is to come up with an overall design of the class. Let's begin by first identifying the core operations that an address book object must support. The problem statement indicated three major operations: add, delete, and search. These three operations are pretty much a standard in any collection of data values. For any kind of collections, you will always want to be able to add a new item, delete an old item, and search for an item or items. An address book is no exception as it is a collection of information about people for whom you would want to add, delete, and search data.

Our task here is to design a class that will maintain an address book by supporting these three operations. We will define three methods for the class: **add, delete,** and **search.**

Our working design document for the **AddressBook** class is therefore as follows:

Design Document: The Public Methods of the `AddressBook` Class

Method	Purpose
`AddressBook`	A constructor to initialize the object. We will include multiple constructors as necessary.
`add`	Adds a new `Person` object to the address book.
`delete`	Deletes a specified `Person` object from the address book.
`search`	Searches for a specified `Person` object in the address book and returns this person if found.

We will implement the class in this order:

development steps

1. Implement the constructor(s).
2. Implement the **add** method.
3. Implement the **search** method.
4. Implement the **delete** method.
5. Finalize the class.

This order of development follows a natural sequence. To implement any instance method of a class, we need to be able to create a properly initialized object, so we will begin the class implementation by defining a constructor. As a part of defining a constructor, we will identify necessary data members. We will add more data members as we progress through the development steps. The second step is to implement the add routine, because without being able to add a new **Person** object, we won't be able to test other operations. For the third step, we will implement the search routine. And for the fourth step, we will implement the last routine. Although we could implement the delete routine before the search routine, we need some form of searching to test the correctness of the delete routine. In other words, we delete a person and attempt to search for this person, verifying that the search will not find the deleted person. So we will implement the search routine before the delete routine.

Step 1 Development: Skeleton with Constructors

step 1 design

In step 1, we will identify the data members and define the constructor(s) to initialize them. The key data member for the class is a structure we will use to keep track of a collection of **Person** objects. We will use an array for this data structure. Our decision to use an array is based on pedagogy. Using a **List** from JCF will simplify our development effort, but it is more important to learn how to use arrays.

We will create an array of **Person** objects in the constructor. At the time we create an array, we must declare its size. Remember that the size of an array is the maximum number of elements this array can hold. The actual number of **Person** objects stored in the array will be anywhere from zero to the size of the array.

We have two possible alternatives for specifying the size of an array. First, we can let the programmer pass the size as an argument to the constructor. Second, we can set the size to a default value. Both alternatives are useful. If the programmer has a good estimate of the number of **Person** objects to manage, she can specify the size in the constructor. Otherwise, she can use the default size by not specifying the size in the constructor. We will define two constructors to support both alternatives. This will give programmers flexibility in creating an **AddressBook** object.

If we are going to provide a constructor in which the programmer can pass the size of an array, then we need to write the constructor so it won't crash when an invalid value is passed as an argument. What would be an invalid argument value? Since we are dealing with a collection of objects and the size of a collection cannot be negative, an argument value of less than zero is invalid. Also, even though a collection whose size Is zero may make sense in theory, such a collection makes no sense in practice. Therefore,

10.7 Sample Development—*continued*

we will consider zero also as an invalid argument value. We will require an argument to a constructor to be a positive integer. We will throw an **IllegalArgumentException** for an invalid value.

step 1 code

At this point, we have only one data member—an array of objects. We will call it **entry** because a **Person** object is a single entry in an address book. We will set the default size of **entry** to 25. There is no particular reason for selecting this size. We simply picked a number that is not too small or too big. We can change this value later if we need to.

We will define two constructors. The first constructor will call the second constructor with the value 25 (default size) as its argument. The second constructor creates an array of **Person** objects of the size passed as its parameter. Inside the second constructor, we include a temporary test output statement. The class is defined as follows:

```
/**
 * This class is designed to manage an address book that contains
 * Person objects. The user can specify the size of the address book
 * when it is created. If no size is specified, then the default size
 * is set to 25 Person objects.
 *
 * @author Dr. Caffeine
 *
 */
class AddressBook {

   private static final int  DEFAULT_SIZE = 25;
   private Person[]         entry;

   public AddressBook( ) {

      this( DEFAULT_SIZE );
   }

   public AddressBook(int size) {

      if (size <= 0 ) { //invalid data value, use default
         throw new IllegalArgumentException("Size must be positive.");
      }
      entry = new Person[size];

      System.out.println("array of "+ size + " is created."); //TEMP
   }
}
```

Data members

Constructors

step 1 test

To test this class, we have included a temporary output statement inside the second constructor. We will write a test program to verify that we can create an **AddressBook** object correctly. The test data are as follows:

Step 1 Test Data	
Data Value	**Purpose**
Negative numbers	Test the invalid data.
0	Test the end case of invalid data.
1	Test the end case of valid data.
>= 1	Test the normal cases.

We will use a very simple test program:

```
/*
   Chapter 10 Sample Program: A test main program for
            verifying the step 1 AddressBook class.

   File: TestAddressBook.java
*/
import java.util.*;

class TestAddressBook { //Step 1 Test Main

    public static void main(String args[]) {

        AddressBook   myBook;
        String        inputStr;
        int           size;

        Scanner scanner = new Scanner(System.in);

        while (true) {

            System.out.print("Array size: ");
            inputStr = scanner.next();

            if (inputStr.equalsIgnoreCase("stop")) {
                break;
            }

            size = Integer.parseInt(inputStr);
```

10.7 Sample Development—*continued*

```
                try {
                    myBook = new AddressBook(size);
                } catch (IllegalArgumentException e) {
                    System.out.println("Exception Thrown: size = " + size);
                }
            }
        }
    }
```

Run the program several times with a different set of test data and verify that we get the correct results.

Step 2 Development: Implement the add Method

step 2 design

In the second development step, we will implement the **add** method. We mentioned in the overall design step that this class will not do any input or output of person data. This decision is based on the STO principle. A single object doing both the input/output routines and maintaining the array will reduce its usability. For example, had the **AddressBook** class used some GUI objects to handle the input and output of person data, the use of this class would dictate or impose the style of input and output routines on the programmers. The programmer will not have an option of using the input and output objects appropriate for his or her uses.

Following the STO principle, we will let the programmer decide how she will input and output person data. The task of the **add** method is to accept a **Person** object as its parameter and add the passed **Person** object to the array. Since the array is limited in size, what should we do if there is no more space to add another **Person** object? There are two alternatives. ***Alternative design 1*** is to return **false** if a new **Person** object cannot be added to the array, that is, if the array is full. The method will return **true** otherwise. ***Alternative design 2*** is to increase the array size. Since the size of an array object cannot be changed once the object is created, we need to create another array with a larger size than that of the original if we choose to implement the second alternative.

alternative design 1

alternative design 2

Since the second alternative is more accommodating and less restrictive to the programmer, we will implement this alternative. When the array is full, we will create a new array, copy the objects from the original array to this new array, and finally set the variable **entry** to point to this new array. We will set the size of the new array to 1.5 times larger than the original array. This size increment is just an estimate. Any value between 125 and 200 percent of the old array is reasonable. You don't want to make it too small,

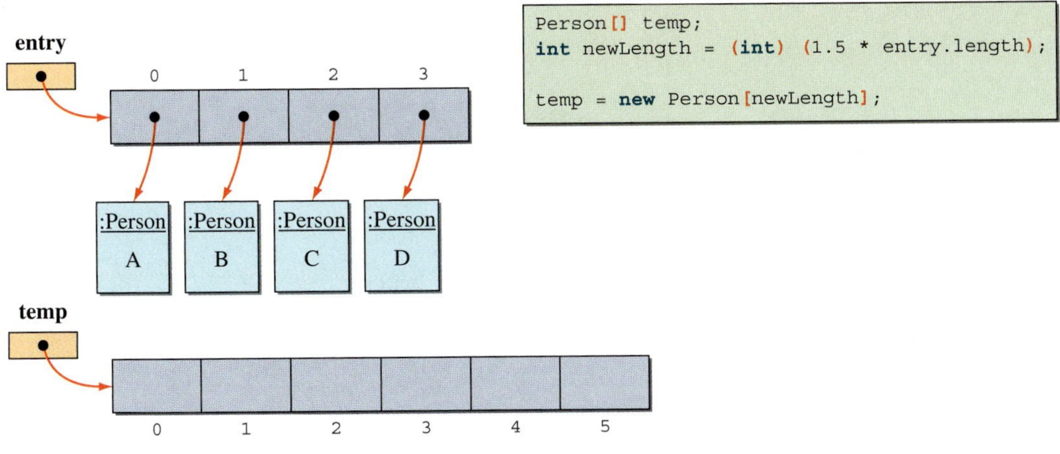

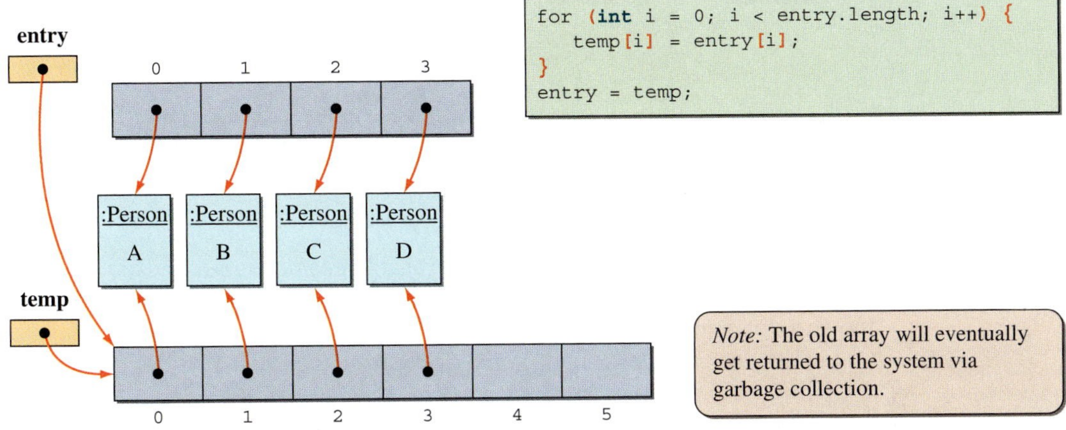

Figure 10.16 How a new array that is 150 percent of the original array is created. The size of the original array is 4.

say, 105 percent, since that will cause the **enlarge** method to be called too frequently. You don't want to make it too large either, since that will likely result in wasted space. Figure 10.16 illustrates the process of creating a larger array.

Now let's think about how to add a **Person** object to the array. To add a new object, we need to locate a position where we can insert the object. Since we are not maintaining **Person** objects in any particular order, we will add a new person at the first available position. If we fill the positions from the low to high indices (**0, 1, 2,** . . .), we can use a variable to remember the index of the next available position. Since we

10.7 Sample Development—*continued*

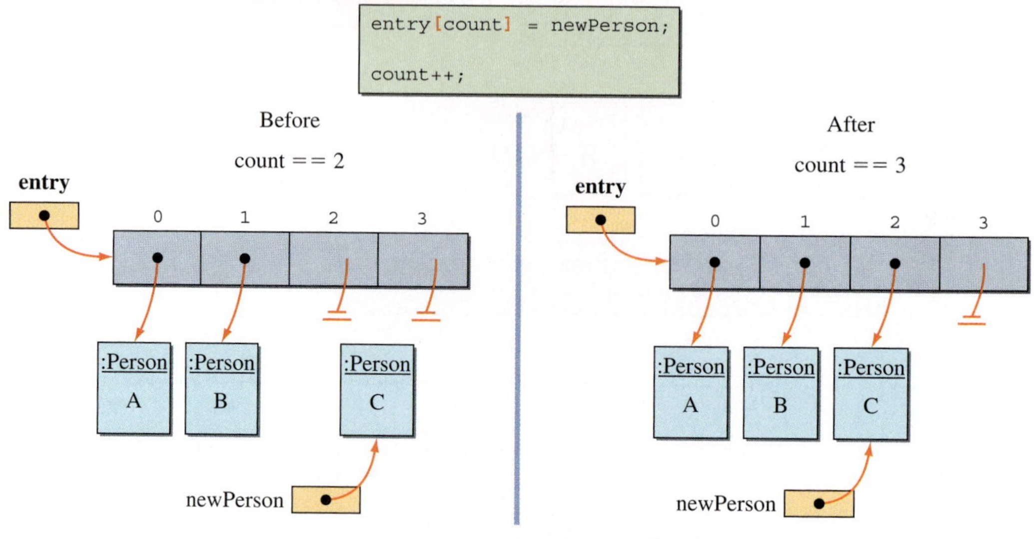

Figure 10.17 Adding a new **Person** object to the next available location. The array length is 4.

are using an array, the index of the next available position is also the number of **Person** objects currently in the array, so we will call this variable **count.** Figure 10.17 illustrates the **add** operation.

step 2 code

First we add a new instance variable **count** to the class:

```
//--------------------------
//  Data Members
//--------------------------

private int  count; //number of elements in the array,
                    //which is also the position at which to add
                    //the next Person object
```

We modify the constructor to initialize this data member:

```
public AddressBook(int size) {
    count = 0;
    //same as before
}
```

(*Note:* Because we defined the first constructor to call the second constructor, we can implement this change by rewriting only one constructor instead of two.) The **add** method is defined as follows:

```
public void add(Person newPerson) {

   assert count >=0 &&
          count <= entry.length;

   if (count == entry.length) { //no more space left,
      enlarge( );               //create a new, larger array
   }

   //at this point, entry refers to a new, larger array
   entry[count] = newPerson;
   count++;
}
```

Notice the use of the assertion feature here.

Notice the use of the assertion feature. We place the **assert** statement to make sure the value of **count** is valid. The **expand** method is a new private method that creates a new, larger array.

Design Document: The `AddressBook` Class		
Method	**Visibility**	**Purpose**
. . .	. . .	. . .
`expand`	`private`	Creates a new array that is 150 percent of the old array.

```
private void expand( ) {

   //create a new array whose size is 150% of
   //the current array
   int newLength = (int) (1.5 * entry.length);
   Person[] temp = new Person[newLength];

   //now copy the data to the new array
   for (int i = 0; i < entry.length; i++) {
      temp[i] = entry[i];
   }

   //finally set the variable entry to point to the new array
   entry = temp;

   System.out.println("Inside the method enlarge"); //TEMP
   System.out.println("Size of a new array: "
                          + entry.length); //TEMP
}
```

10.7 Sample Development—*continued*

step 2 test

We will write a test program to verify that a new **Person** object is added to the array correctly. In addition, we need to test that a new array 150 percent larger than the old one is created when there are no more spaces left in the array. The test data are as follows:

Step 2 Test Data	
Test Sequence	**Purpose**
Create the array of size 4.	Test that the array is created correctly.
Add four `Person` objects.	Test that the `Person` objects are added correctly.
Add the fifth `Person` object.	Test that the new array is created and the `Person` object is added correctly (to the new array).

The step 2 test program is as follows:

```
/*
   Chapter 10 Sample Program: A test main program for
          verifying the step 2 AddressBook class.

   File: TestAddressBook.java
*/

class TestAddressBook {

   public static void main(String[] args) {

      AddressBook   myBook;
      Person        person;

      myBook = new AddressBook(4);

      //add four Person objects
      for (int i = 0; i < 4; i++) {
         person = new Person("Ms. X" + i, 10, 'F');
         myBook.add(person);
      }

      //add the fifth person and see if
      //a new array is created
```

```
            person = new Person("fifth one", 10, 'F');
            myBook.add(person);
        }
    }
```

Run the program several times with different sizes for the address book and verify that we get the correct results.

Step 3 Development: Implement the search Method

step 3 design

In the third development step, we implement the **search** method. This method can return one or more **Person** objects that meet the search criteria. We have several options for the search criteria. Since we keep track of name, age, and gender for each person, we can use any one of these values as the search criterion. In this implementation, we will use the person's name. The search routine for the other two criteria will be left as an exercise (see Exercise 14).

To implement the **search** method, we will make an assumption that the name is unique so that there will be at most one matching **Person** object. If the name is not unique, then there are two possibilities. The **search** method can return one **Person** object (among many) that matches the given name or return all **Person** objects that match the given name. We will leave the case when the name is not unique as an exercise (see Exercise 13). Notice that the **add** method we implemented in step 2 does not check the person data. In other words, there is no mechanism to disallow the addition of a **Person** object with a duplicate name. We will leave the implementation of the modified **add** method as an exercise (see Exercise 15).

There are two possible outcomes with the **search** method—a successful or an unsuccessful search. The method has to return a value by which the programmer can verify the result of the search. We will define the **search** method so that it will return a matching **Person** object if it is found and will return **null** otherwise. The search routine will start scanning the array from the first position until the desired **Person** object is found (successful search) or until no more **Person** objects are left in the array (unsuccessful search). Expressing the search routine in pseudocode, we have

```
loc = 0;
while (loc < count &&
          name of Person at entry[loc] != searchName) {
   loc++;
}

if (loc == count) {
   foundPerson = null;
} else {
   foundPerson = entry[loc];
}
return foundPerson;
```

10.7 Sample Development—*continued*

step 3 code

Translating the pseudocode to an actual method will result in the following method:

```
public Person search(String searchName) {
    Person foundPerson;
    int    loc = 0;

    assert count >= 0 && count <= entry.length;

    while (loc < count &&
            !searchName.equals(entry[loc].getName())) {
        loc++;
    }

    if (loc == count) {
        foundPerson = null;

    } else {
        foundPerson = entry[loc];
    }

    return foundPerson;
}
```

step 3 test

To test the **search** method, we will build an address book that contains five **Person** objects. We will give names **Ms.X0, Ms.X1,** . . . , and **Ms.X4** to them. After the address book is set up, we test various cases of the search. We test for successful and unsuccessful searches. For the successful searches, we test for the end cases and normal cases. The end cases involve searching for persons stored in the first and last positions of the array. Off-by-1 error (OBOE) is very common in processing an array, so it is very important to test these end cases.

After a successful execution, we will test the class again by changing the size of the array. One test size we should not forget to test is the end case for the array size, which is 1. Also, we need to test the cases where the array is not fully filled, such as an array of size 5 containing only two **Person** objects.

The test data are as follows:

Step 3 Test Data

Test Sequence	Purpose
Create the array of size 5 and add five `Person` objects with unique names.	Test that the array is created and set up correctly. Here, we will test the case where the array is 100 percent filled.
Search for the person in the first position of the array.	Test that the successful search works correctly for the end case.

Search for the person in the last position of the array.	Test another version of the end case.
Search for a person somewhere in the middle of the array.	Test the normal case.
Search for a person not in the array.	Test for the unsuccessful search.
Repeat the above steps with an array of varying sizes, especially the array of size 1.	Test that the routine works correctly for arrays of different sizes.
Repeat the testing with the cases where the array is not fully filled, say, array length is 5 and the number of objects in the array is 0 or 3.	Test that the routine works correctly for other cases.

The step 3 test program is written as follows:

```
/*
   Chapter 10 Sample Program: A test main program for
          verifying the step 3 AddressBook class.

   File: TestAddressBook.java
*/

class TestAddressBook {

   AddressBook myBook;
   Person      person;

   public static void main(String[] args) {

      TestAddressBook tester = new TestAddressBook();
      tester.setupArray(5);
      tester.testSearch();
   }

   public void setupArray(int N) {
      myBook = new AddressBook( N );

      //add N Person objects
      for (int i = 0; i < N; i++) {
         person = new Person("Ms. X"+i, 10, 'F');
         myBook.add(person);
      }
   }

   public void testSearch( ) {
      //test for the end case
      person = myBook.search("Ms. X2");
```

10.7 Sample Development—*continued*

```
        if (person == null) {
            System.out.println
              ("Error: Didn't find the person it should");
        } else {
            System.out.println
              (person.getName() + " is found okay.");
        }
    }
}
```

Notice the **TestAddressBook** class is now an instantiable main class. Since the code for testing is getting longer, it is not practical anymore to do everything in a single **main** method. For testing, we will modify the method body of **setupArray** and **testSearch** as necessary to test all other cases described in the test data table.

Step 4 Development: Implement the delete Method

step 4 design

In the fourth development step, we implement the **delete** method. To delete a **Person** object, the programmer must somehow specify which **Person** object to remove from the address book. As we did with the **search** method, we will use the name of a person to specify which person to delete. Since we assume the name is unique, the **delete** method will remove at most one **Person** object. There are two possible outcomes: the specified person is removed from the address book (successful operation) and the specified person is not removed because he or she is not in the address book (unsuccessful operation). We will define the **delete** method so that it will return **true** if the operation is successful and **false** otherwise.

The removal of an element in an array of objects is done by setting the element to **null.** This will leave a "hole." We will fill this hole by replacing the removed element with the last element, as explained earlier (see Figure 10.8). This filling operation is necessary for other methods, specifically the **add** method, to work correctly.

To fill the hole, we need to know the location of the hole. To find this location, we write a private search method called **findIndex.** The method is very similar to the **search** method. The only difference is that the return value of **findIndex** is an index of an element in the array, whereas the return value of **search** is a **Person** object. By using this **findIndex** method, the **delete** method can be expressed as

```
boolean status;
int     loc;

loc = findIndex( searchName );
```

```
if (loc is not valid) {
   status = false;
} else { //found, pack the hole
      replace the element at index loc+1 by the last element
      at index count;

     status = true;

     count--; //decrement count,
              //since we now have one less element

     assert count is valid;
}

return status;
```

step 4 code

The private **findIndex** method will look like this:

```
private int findIndex(String searchName) {
   int loc = 0;

   assert count >=0 && count <= entry.length;

   while (loc < count &&
         !searchName.equals(entry[loc].getName())) {
      loc++;
   }

   if (loc == count) {
      loc = NOT_FOUND;
   }

   return loc;
}
```

The constant **NOT_FOUND** is set in the data member section as

```
//----------------------------
//  Data Members
//----------------------------

private static final int NOT_FOUND = -1;
```

By using this **findIndex** method, the **delete** method is defined as follows:

```
public boolean delete(String searchName) {
   boolean   status;
   int       loc;

   loc = findIndex(searchName);

   if (loc == NOT_FOUND) {
      status = false;
   } else { //found, pack the hole
```

10.7 Sample Development—*continued*

```
            entry[loc] = entry[count-1];

            status = true;
            count--;         //decrement count,
                             //since we now have one less element

            assert count >= 0 && count <= entry.length;
        }

        return status;
    }
```

step 4 test

To test the **delete** method, we will build an address book that contains five **Person** objects, as before. Test cases are to delete the first person in the array, delete the last person in the array, delete someone in the middle (normal case), and try to delete a nonexistent person.

After a successful execution, we will test the class again by changing the size of an array. One test size we should not forget to test is the end case for the array size, which is 1. Also, we need to test the cases where the array is not fully filled, such as an array of size 5 containing only two **Person** objects.

The test data are as follows:

Step 4 Test Data

Test Sequence	Purpose
Create the array of size 5 and add five `Person` objects with unique names.	Test that the array is created and set up correctly. Here, we will test the case where the array is 100 percent filled.
Search for a person to be deleted next.	Verify that the person is in the array before deletion.
Delete the person in the array.	Test that the `delete` method works correctly.
Search for the deleted person.	Test that the `delete` method works correctly by checking that the value `null` is returned by the search.
Attempt to delete a nonexistent person.	Test that the unsuccessful operation works correctly.
Repeat the above steps by deleting persons at the first and last positions.	Test that the routine works correctly for arrays of different sizes.
Repeat testing where the array is not fully filled, say, an array length is 5 and the number of objects in the array is 0 or 3.	Test that the routine works correctly for other cases.

The step 4 test program is written as follows:

```
/*
   Chapter 10 Sample Program: A test main program for
           verifying the step 4 AddressBook class.

   File: TestAddressBook.java
*/

class TestAddressBook {
   AddressBook myBook;
   Person      person;

   public static void main(String[] args) {
      TestAddressBook tester = new TestAddressBook();
      tester.setupArray( 5 );
      tester.testDelete( );
   }

   public void setupArray(int N) {
      myBook = new AddressBook( N );

      //add N Person objects
      for (int i = 0; i < N; i++) {
         person = new Person( "Ms. X" + i, 10, 'F' );
         myBook.add(person);
      }
   }

   public void testDelete( ) {
      //first make sure the person is in the array

      person = myBook.search( "Ms. X2" );

      if (person == null) {
        System.out.println("Error: Didn't find the person it should");
      } else {

        System.out.println(person.getName() + " is found okay.");

        boolean success = myBook.delete("Ms. X2");

        if (success) {

            person = myBook.search("Ms. X2");

            if (person == null) {

               System.out.println("Okay: Deletion works");
            } else {
```

10.7 Sample Development—*continued*

```
                System.out.println("Error: Person is still there");
            }
        } else {

            System.out.println("Error: Deletion has a problem");
        }
    }
  }
}
```

Modify the method body of **setupArray** and **testDelete** as necessary to test all other cases described in the step 4 test data table.

Step 5 Development: Finalize

program review

final test

As always, we finalize the program in the last step. We perform a critical ***program review*** to find any inconsistency or error in the methods, incomplete methods, places to add comments, and so forth.

Since the three operations of **add, delete,** and **search** are interrelated, it is critical to test these operations together. The test program should try out various combinations of **add, delete,** and **search** operations to verify that they work together correctly.

After we complete the class implementation and testing, we may consider improvement or extension. In addition to the several alternative designs, it is possible to add other operations. For example, we may want to add an operation to modify a **Person** object. Another common operation that is useful in manipulating a collection of objects is the traversal operation described in Section 10.6. Implementation of this operation is left as Exercise 16.

Summary

- An array is an indexed collection of data values.
- Data values in an array are called array elements.
- Individual elements in an array are accessed by the indexed expression.
- Array elements can be values of primitive data type or objects.
- In Java, an array can include only elements of the same data type.
- A Java array is a reference data type.
- A Java array is created with the new operator.
- An array can have multiple indices.

- When an array is passed to a method as an argument, only a reference to an array is passed. A copy of an array is not created. *Note:* The reference to an array we are passing is a value of an array variable, and therefore the call-by-value scheme is used here also.
- The standard classes and interfaces described or used in this chapter are

List	Iterator
ArrayList	Map
LinkedList	HashMap
	TreeMap

- The Java Collection Framework includes many data structure classes such as lists and maps.
- The List interface represents a linear ordered collection of objects.
- The ArrayList and LinkedList classes are two implementations of the List interface.
- The Map interface represents a collection of key-value pairs.
- The TreeMap and HashMap classes are two implementations of the Map interface.

Key Concepts

arrays	arrays of objects
array elements	multidimensional arrays
index expression	lists
arrays of primitive data type	maps

Exercises

1. Identify problems with this code:

```
public int searchAccount( int[25] number ) {
   number = new int[15];

   for (int i = 0; i < number.length; i++) {
      number[i] = number[i-1] + number[i+1];
   }
   return number;
}
```

2. Declare an array of double of size 365 to store daily temperatures for one year. Using this data structure, write the code to find

   - The hottest and coldest days of the year.
   - The average temperature of each month.

- The difference between the hottest and coldest days of every month.
- The temperature of any given day. The day is specified by two input values: month (1, . . . , 12) and day (1, . . . , 31). Reject invalid input values (e.g., 13 for month and 32 for day).

3. Repeat Exercise 2, using a two-dimensional array of double with 12 rows and each row having 28, 30, or 31 columns.

4. Repeat Exercise 2, using an array of Month objects with each Month object having an array of double of size 28, 30, or 31.

5. For Exercises 2 to 4, the following three data structures are used:

- One-dimensional array of double of size 365.
- Two-dimensional array of double with 12 rows. Each row has 28, 30, or 31 columns.
- An array of Month objects with each Month object having an array of double of size 28, 30, or 31.

Discuss the pros and cons of each approach.

6. Suppose you want to maintain the highest and lowest temperatures for every day of the year. What kind of data structure would you use? Describe the alternatives and list their pros and cons.

7. If a car dealer's service department wants a program to keep track of customer appointments, which data structure should they choose, an array or a list? If the number of appointments the service department accepts is fixed on any given day, which data structure is appropriate? What are the criteria you use to decide which data structure to use? Explain.

8. In Figure 10.8, the last statement

```
person[last] = null;
```

is significant. Show the state-of-memory diagram when the last statement is not executed.

9. Write an application that computes the standard deviation of *N* real numbers. The standard deviation *s* is computed according to

$$s = \sqrt{\frac{(x_1 - \bar{x})^2 + (x_2 - \bar{x})^2 + \cdots + (x_N - \bar{x})^2}{N}}$$

The variable $\bar{x}$ is the average of *N* input values x_1 through x_N. The program first prompts the user for *N* and then declares an array of size *N*.

10. Using the payScaleTable two-dimensional array from Section 10.4, write the code to find

- The average pay for every grade level
- The average pay for every step (i.e., average of every column)

11. Declare a two-dimensional array for the tuition table shown in Figure 10.13.

12. Suppose you want to maintain information on the location where a product is stored in a warehouse. Would you use a three-dimensional array such as location[i][j][k], where i is the warehouse number, j is the aisle number, and k is the bin number? Or would you define three classes Warehouse, Aisle, and Bin? Describe the alternatives and list their pros and cons.

13. The search method of the AddressBook class returns only one Person object. Modify the method so that it will return all Person objects that match the search criteria. You can use an array to return multiple Person objects.

14. Write new search routines for the AddressBook class. The search method given in the chapter finds a person with a given name. Add second and third search methods that find all persons, given an age and a gender, respectively.

15. Modify the add method of the AddressBook class. The method given in the chapter does not check for any duplicate names. Modify the method so that no Person object with a duplicate name is added to the address book.

16. Modify the AddressBook class to allow the programmer to access all Person objects in the address book. Make this modification by adding two methods: getFirstPerson and getNextPerson. The getFirstPerson method returns the first Person object in the book. The getNextPerson method returns the next Person object if there is one. If there is no next person in the book, getNextPerson returns null. The getFirstPerson method must be called before the getNextPerson method is called.

17. In addition to the List and Map interface, the third interface in the Java Collection Framework is Set. A Set is an unordered collection of objects with no duplicates. This interface models, as expected, the mathematical set. Two classes that implement the Set interface in JCF are TreeSet and HashSet. Here's a simple example of using Set:

```
Set<String> = new HashSet <String>();
set.add("ape");
set.add("bee");
set.add("ape"); //duplicate, so it won't be added
set.add("cat");
set.remove("bee");
set.remove("dog"); //not in the set, nothing happens
System.out.println("Set = " + set);
```

The output from the code will be

```
Set = [ape, cat]
```

To access the individual elements of a set, call the iterator method in the manner identical to the one we used for the List interface.

Rewrite the AddressBook class by using the HashSet instead of an array to maintain a collection of Person object.

18. Consider the following Thesaurus class:

```
class Thesaurus {
   //Returns all synonyms of the word as a Set
   //Returns null if there is no such word
   public java.util.Set<String> get (String word){...}

   //Returns all key words in this thesaurus as a Set
   //returns an empty set if there are no keys (if you
   //don't do anything, default behavior of the
   //underlying JCF class will handle it)
   public java.util.Set<String> keys(            ){...}

   //Adds 'synonym' to the synonym set of 'word'
   //Pay close attention to this method.
   public void put (String word, String synonym){...}
}
```

The get method returns a set of all synonyms of a given word. The keys method returns all key words in the thesaurus. The put method adds a new synonym to the given word. Make sure to handle the cases when the word already has a synonym list and when the word is added for the first time. Using this Thesaurus class, we can write, for example, this program:

```
class SampleMain {
   public static void main(String[] args) {
      Thesaurus t = new Thesaurus();
      t.put("fast", "speedy");
      t.put("fast", "swift");
      t.put("slow", "sluggish");

      Set<String> synonyms = t.get("fast");
      System.out.println(synonyms);
      System.out.println(t.keys());
   }
}
```

When the sample program is executed, the output will be

```
C:\WINNT\System32\cmd.exe
[speedy, swift]
[fast, slow]
Press any key to continue . . .
```

Implement the Thesaurus class, using one of the Map classes. The key is the word, and the value is the set of synonyms of this word.

Development Exercises

For the following exercises, use the incremental development methodology to implement the program. For each exercise, identify the program tasks, create a design document with class descriptions, and draw the program diagram. Map out the development steps at the start. Present any design alternatives and justify your selection. Be sure to perform adequate testing at the end of each development step.

19. Write a complete address book maintenance application. The user of the program has four options: Add a new person, delete a person, modify the data of a person, and search for a person by giving the name. Use the AddressBook class, either the original one from the chapter or the modified one from the previous exercises. You have to decide how to allow the user to enter the values for a new person, display person information, and so forth.

20. Design a currency converter class whose instance will handle conversion of all currencies. A single instance of the new currency converter class you design here will handle all currencies. Instead of having specific conversion methods such as toDollar, toYen, and so forth, the new currency converter class supports one generic conversion method called exchange. The method has three arguments: fromCurrency, toCurrency, and amount. The first two arguments are String and give the names of currencies. The third argument is float. To convert $250 to yen, we write

```
yen = converter.exchange( "dollar", "yen", 250.0 );
```

To set the exchange rate for a currency, we use the setRate method. This method takes two arguments: The first argument is the currency name, and the second argument is the rate. For example, if the exchange rate for yen is 140 yen to $1, then we write

```
converter.setRate( "yen", 140.0 );
```

Use an array to keep track of exchange rates.

21. Extend the MyJava Lo-Fat Burgers drive-through ordering system of Exercise 24 on page 294 so the program can output sales figures. For each item on the menu, the program keeps track of the sales. At closing time, the program will output the sales figure in a format similar to the following:

```
    Item              Sales Count       Total
Tofu Burger               25           $  87.25
Cajun Chicken             30           $ 137.70
  ...

    Today's Total Sales: $ 2761.20
```

22. Redo the watermelon projectile computing program of Exercise 30 on page 362 to output the average distance covered between each time interval. Use the expression

$$\sqrt{(x_2 - x_1)^2 + (y_2 - y_1)^2}$$

to compute the distance between two coordinate points (x_1, y_1) and (x_2, y_2).

23. Redo the social club program of Exercise 9 of Chapter 8. In the original program, we limit the number of clubs to 5. Remove this restriction by using an array.

24. Redo Exercise 23, but this time use one of the Java Collection Framework classes.

11 Sorting and Searching

Objectives

After you have read and studied this chapter, you should be able to

- Perform linear and binary search algorithms on arrays.
- Determine whether a linear or binary search is more effective for a given situation.
- Perform selection and bubble sort algorithms.
- Describe the heapsort algorithm and show how its performance is superior to that of the other two algorithms.
- Apply basic sorting algorithms to sort an array of objects, using the **Comparator** interface.
- Define the interface to specify common behavior and provide different versions of classes that implement the interface.

Introduction

In this chapter, we cover searching and sorting. In Chapter 10, we presented a case study of maintaining an address book and described a basic searching method to locate a student, given his or her name. In this chapter, we will present a better searching algorithm called *binary search*. To apply binary search, an array must be sorted. *Sorting* is a technique to arrange elements in some order, and it is one of the fundamental operations we study in computer science. We will cover basic sorting algorithms in this chapter and an efficient recursive sorting algorithm in Chapter 15. We will use an array of integers to illustrate searching and sorting algorithms, but all the techniques we present here are equally applicable to any array of objects as well as primitive data types. In the sample development (Section 11.4), we will extend the AddressBook class by adding the capability of sorting an array of Person objects.

11.1 Searching

Let's start with the problem statement for searching:

> *Given a value X, return the index of X in the array, if such X exists. Otherwise, return* NOT_FOUND (−1). *We assume there are no duplicate entries in the array.*

successful and unsuccessful searches

There are two possible outcomes in searching: Either we locate an *X* or we don't. We will call the first a ***successful search*** and the latter an ***unsuccessful search***. Figure 11.1 illustrates the successful and unsuccessful searches. As obvious as this may sound, it is critical to differentiate the two because it is possible for one searching algorithm to perform superbly for successful searches, but very poorly for unsuccessful searches. When we analyze the performance of a searching algorithm, we normally derive two separate performances, one for a successful search and another for an unsuccessful search.

Linear Search

linear search

The search technique we used earlier in the book is called a ***linear search*** because we search the array from the first position to the last position in a linear progression.

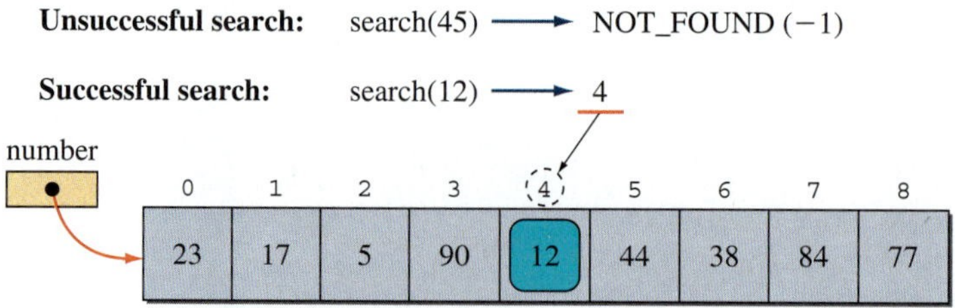

Figure 11.1 Successful and unsuccessful searches.

The linear search is also called a *sequential search*. The linear search algorithm can be expressed as

```
public int linearSearch (int[] number, int searchValue) {
   int       loc    = 0;
                         More elements
                         to search

   while ( loc < number.length &&
           number[loc] != searchValue ) {

      loc++;                            searchValue is
   }                                    not yet found.

   if ( loc == number.length) { //Not found
      return NOT_FOUND;
   } else {
      return loc;              //Found, return the position
   }
}
```

If the number of entries in the array is N, then there will be N comparisons for an unsuccessful search (i.e., you search for a value not in the array). In the case of a successful search, there will be a minimum of one comparison and a maximum of N comparisons. On average, there will be approximately $N/2$ comparisons.

Is there a way to improve the linear search? If the array is sorted, then we can improve the search routine by using the binary search technique.

Binary Search

binary search

If the values in the array are arranged in ascending or descending order, then we call the array *sorted*. In the following explanation of the binary search, we assume the array is sorted in ascending order. The crux of ***binary search*** is the winning strategy you apply for the Hi-Lo game. When you try to guess a secret number, say, between 1 and 100, your first guess will be 50. If your guess is HI, then you know the secret number is between 1 and 49. If your guess is LO, then you know the secret number is between 51 and 100. By guessing once, you eliminated one-half of the possible range of values from further consideration. This is the core idea of binary search.

Consider the following sorted array:

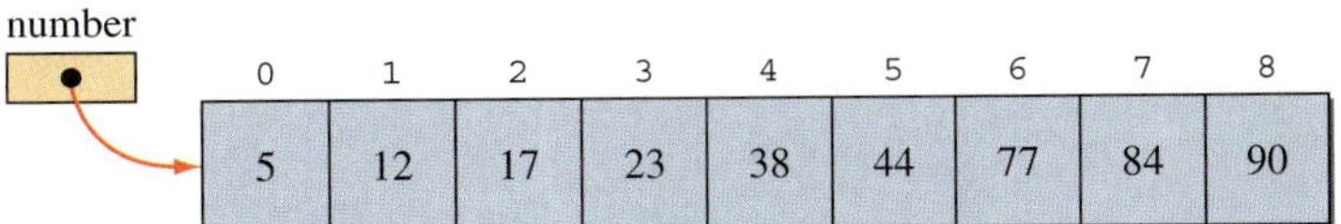

Let's suppose we are searching for 77. We first search the middle position of the array. Since this array has 9 elements, the index of the middle position is 4, so we search number[4]. The value 77 is not in this position. Since 77 is larger than 38 and

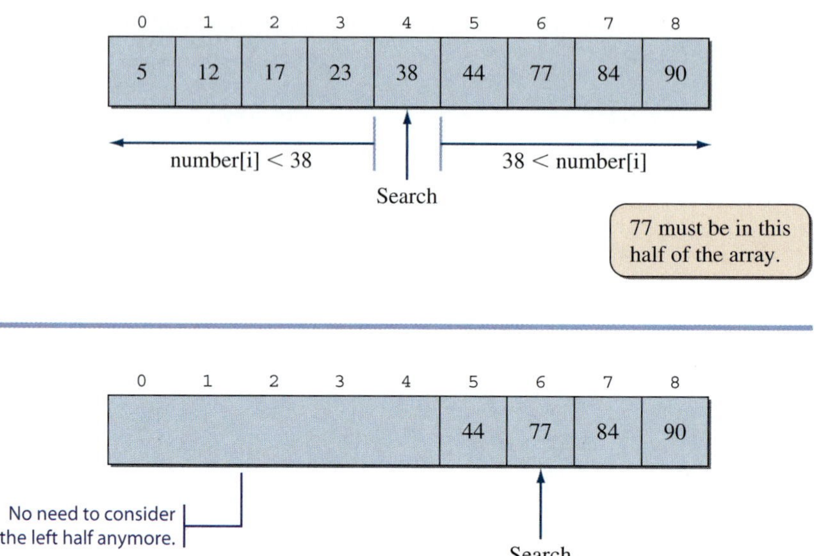

Figure 11.2 Effect of one comparison in binary search.

the array is sorted, we know that if 77 is in the array, it must be in the right half of the array. So next we search the middle position of the right half of the array, which is position 6. Figure 11.2 illustrates the effect of making one comparison in the binary search.

The search value 77 was found after two comparisons. In contrast, the linear search would take seven comparisons to locate 77. So there is a net reduction of five comparisons. How good is the binary search in general? Let's study the worst-case situation. In the binary search, after we make one comparison, we can eliminate one-half of the array from further consideration. So the number of comparisons in the worst case is the number of times you can divide the array into halves. Suppose the original size of an array is N and the value we are searching for is not in the array. Then after one comparison, we have to search the remaining $N/2$ elements. After two comparisons, we have to search $N/4$ elements, and so on. The following table shows this relationship. The left column is the number of comparisons, and the right column is the number of elements we still need to search after making K comparisons.

Number of Comparisons	Number of Elements
0	N
1	$N/2 = N/2^1$
2	$N/4 = N/2^2$
...	...
K	$N/2^K$

The maximum number of comparisons K is derived by solving the equation

$$N = 2^K$$
$$\log_2 N = K$$

This is a remarkable improvement. If the size of the original array is 2048, for example, then the unsuccessful binary search takes at most $\log_2 2048 = 11$ comparisons, while the unsuccessful linear search takes 2048 comparisons. The difference between the two algorithms gets larger and larger as the size of an array increases.

Now let's write a binary search method. The key point in the method revolves on how to stop the search. If the search value is in the array, we will eventually locate it, so the stopping condition for the successful search is easy. What about the case for an unsuccessful search? How can we detect that there are no more elements in the array to search for? Should we use some kind of a counter? We certainly can use a counter, but we can implement the method without using any counter. To compute the middle location for the next comparison, we need two indices—low and high. The low and high indices are initialized to 0 and $N - 1$, respectively. The middle location is computed as

```
mid = (low + high) / 2; //the result is truncated
```

If number[mid] is less than the search value, then low is reset to mid+1. If number[mid] is greater than the search value, then high is reset to mid−1, and the search continues. Eventually, we will locate the search value or we will run out of elements to compare. We know that there are no more elements to compare when low becomes larger than high. Figure 11.3 shows how this works.

Here's the binarySearch method:

```
public int binarySearch (int[] number, int searchValue) {
   int          low    = 0,
                high   = number.length - 1,
                mid    = (low + high) / 2;

   while (low <= high && number[mid] != searchValue) {

     if (number[mid] < searchValue) {
        low = mid + 1;

     } else { //number[mid] > searchValue
        high = mid - 1;
     }

     mid   = (low + high) / 2;
   }

   if (low > high) {
       mid = NOT_FOUND;
   }

   return mid;
}
```

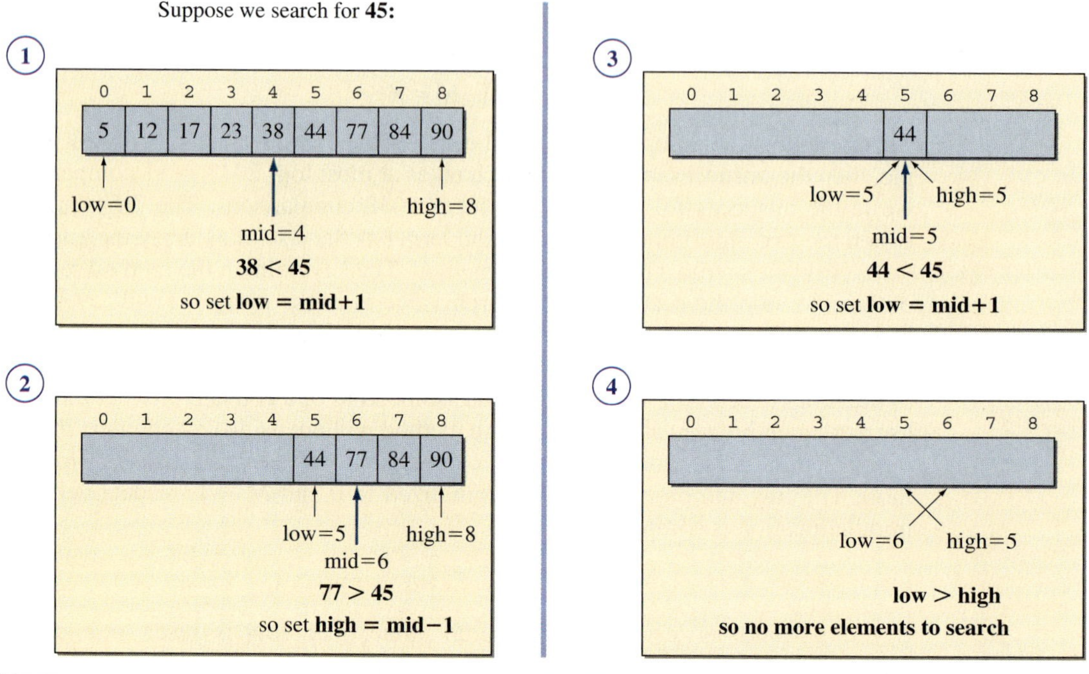

Figure 11.3 How the unsuccessful search is terminated in the binary search routine.

1. Suppose an array contains 2048 elements. What are the least and the greatest numbers of comparisons for a successful search using linear search?
2. Repeat question 1 for a binary search.

11.2 Sorting

In this section we will describe two basic sorting algorithms. A more advanced sorting algorithm will be presented in Section 11.3. Let's start with the problem statement for sorting:

Given an array of N values, arrange the values into ascending order.

Selection Sort

Given a list of integers, how would you sort them? The most natural sorting algorithm for a human looks something like this:

1. Find the smallest integer in the list.
2. Cross out the number from further consideration and copy it to a new (sorted) list.
3. Repeat steps 1 and 2 until all numbers are crossed out in the list.

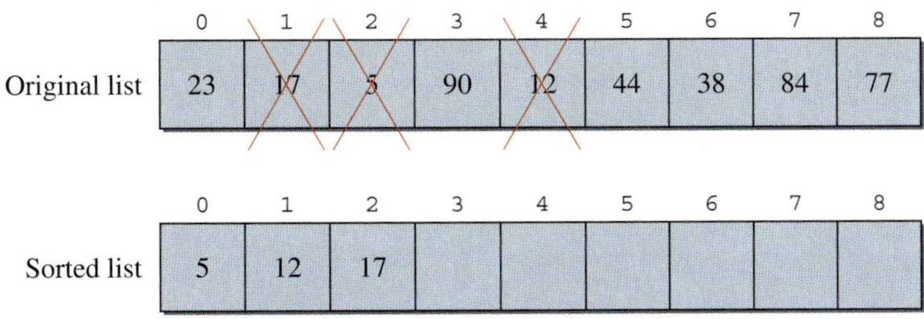

Figure 11.4 Human sorting algorithm after three numbers are moved to the sorted list.

Figure 11.4 shows this human sorting algorithm with the first three numbers being copied to the new list.

We can write a real computer program based on this sorting algorithm, but the resulting program will not be a good one. There are two problems. First, we need an extra array to keep the sorted list. This may not sound like much, but when you consider an array of, say, 10,000 elements, using a second array is very wasteful. Second, crossing out numbers is effective for humans only. We humans can see the cross marks and will not consider the numbers once they are crossed out, but in computer programs, we still have to write code to check every element to see whether it is crossed out. We can "cross out" an element by replacing it with a negative number, say, -1, if the numbers are all positive. If not, then we have to use other means to cross out an element. So crossing out the numbers does not reduce the number of comparisons in the program.

Although we do not want to implement this human sorting algorithm as is, we can derive an algorithm based on the idea of finding the smallest number in a given list and moving it to the correct position in the list. This sorting algorithm is called ***selection sort***.

selection sort

sorting passes

The selection sort is comprised of ***sorting passes***. Figure 11.5 shows the effect of the first pass on a sample array of N (= 9) elements. First we locate the smallest

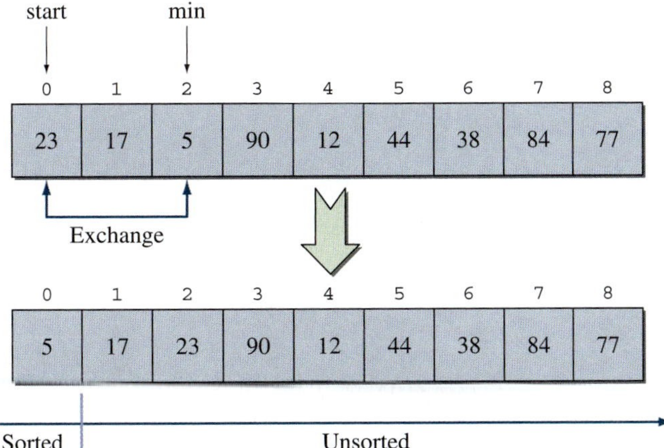

Figure 11.5 Effect of executing the first pass in the selection sort.

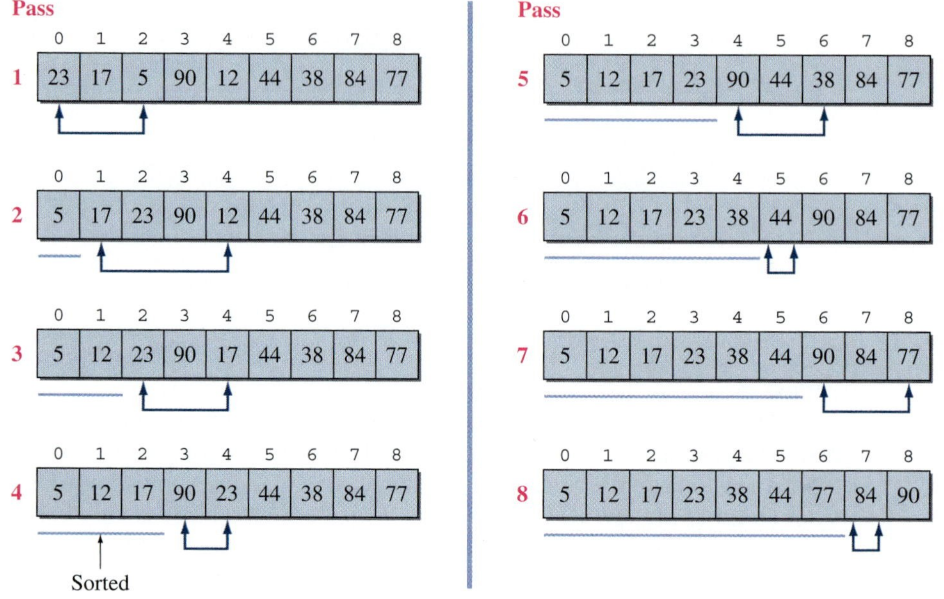

Figure 11.6 Eight passes to sort the sample array of nine elements.

element in the array and set the index min to point to this element. Then we exchange number[start] and number[min]. After the first pass, the smallest element is moved to the correct position. We increment the value of start by 1 and then execute the second pass. We start the first pass with start = 0 and end the last pass with start = N-2. Figure 11.6 shows the sequence of eight passes made to the sample array.

Here's the selectionSort method:

```
public void selectionSort(int[] number) {

   int minIndex, length, temp;
   length = number.length;

   for (int startIndex = 0; startIndex <= length-2;
   startIndex++){
       //each iteration of the for loop is one pass

       minIndex = startIndex;

       //find the smallest in this pass at
       //position minIndex
       for (int i = startIndex+1; i <= length-1; i++) {
          if (number[i] < number[minIndex]) minIndex = i;
       }
```

```
            //exchange number[startIndex] and number[minIndex]
            temp                 = number[startIndex];
            number[startIndex]   = number[minIndex];
            number[minIndex]     = temp;

            assert minStart(number, startIndex):
                   "Error: " + number[startIndex] +
                   " at position " + startIndex +
                   " is not the smallest.";
        }

        assert isSorted(number):
               "Error: the final is not sorted";
    }
```

The assertion at the end of one pass confirms that the smallest element in that pass moved to the beginning position of the pass. The minStart method is therefore written as follows:

```
    private boolean minStart(int[] number, int startIndex) {

        for (int i = startIndex+1; i < number.length; i++) {

            if (number[startIndex] > number[i]) {
                return false;
            }
        }
        return true;
    }
```

We put a second assertion at the end of the method to verify that no elements are out of place after the sorting is complete. The isSorted method is written as follows:

```
    private boolean isSorted(int[] number) {

        for (int i = 0; i < number.length-1; i++) {

            if (number[i] > number[i+1]) {
                return false;
            }
        }
        return true;
    }
```

Assertion is a very useful tool in a situation such as sorting. While developing the sorting routines, we insert a number of assertion statements to increase our confidence in the program's correctness.

Things to Remember

Be sure to run programs with assertions enabled during the development, but disable them during the actual use. Run the program with assertions enabled with

```
java -ea <main class>
```

Hints, Tips, & Pitfalls

We use assertions to find coding error. But what will happen when the code we write for assertions, such at the **minStart** method used in the selection sort routine, is wrong? How can we assert that **minStart** is correct? We do not want to write assertions for assertions! One possibility is to create a data set that is correct and to run the **minStart** method against these data to test for their validity. The use of assertions is merely an aid, not a fail-safe way to find errors.

Let's analyze the selection sort algorithm. In analyzing different sorting algorithms, we normally count two things: the number of comparisons and the number of data movements (exchanges). We will show you how to count the number of comparisons here. Counting the number of data movements is left as Exercise 4. Keep in mind that the analysis we provide in this chapter is an informal one. A detailed analysis is beyond the scope of this book, so we will give only a taste of the formal analysis.

The selection sort has one comparison (the if statement inside the nested-for loop), so we can easily count the total number of comparisons by counting the number of times the inner loop is executed. For each execution of the outer loop, the inner loop is executed length − start times. The variable start ranges from 0 to length-2. So the total number of comparisons is computed by finding the sum of the right column in the following table:

Start	Number of Comparisons (Length − Start)
0	length
1	length - 1
2	length - 2
. . .	. . .
length - 2	2

The variable length is the size of the array. If we replace length with N, the size of the array, then the sum of the right column is

$$N + (N - 1) + (N - 2) + \cdots + 2 = \sum_{i=2}^{N} i = \left(\sum_{i=1}^{N} i\right) - 1$$

$$= \frac{N(N + 1)}{2} - 1 = \frac{N^2 + N - 2}{2} \cong N^2$$

The total number of comparisons is approximately the square of the size of an array. This is a quadratic function, so the number of comparisons grows very rapidly as the size of an array increases. Is there a better sorting algorithm? The answer is yes.

Bubble Sort

The effect of one pass of the selection sort is the movement of the smallest element to its correct position. Since an array gets sorted only by moving the elements to their correct positions, the whole sorting routine will complete sooner if we increase the number of data movements. In the selection sort, we make one exchange per pass. If we could move more elements toward their correct positions in one pass, we could complete the sorting sooner than the selection sort. The bubble sort is one such algorithm that increases the number of data movements for the same number of comparisons as the selection sort makes.

The key point of the bubble sort is to make pairwise comparisons and to exchange the positions of the pair if they are out of order. Figure 11.7 shows the effect of pairwise comparisons in the first pass of the bubble sort. After the first pass, the largest element, 90, has moved to its correct position in the array. This is the guaranteed effect of one pass. In addition, we notice that many other elements have moved toward their correct positions, as bubbles move toward the water's surface.

In the worst case, the bubble sort will make $N - 1$ passes, so the worst-case performance is the same as that for the selection sort. However, in the average case, we can expect a better performance from the bubble sort. The bubble sort exhibits two properties:

- After one pass through the array, the largest element will be at the end of the array.
- During one pass, if no pair of consecutive entries is out of order, then the array is sorted.

Using these properties, we can express the bubbleSort method in pseudocode:

This **while** loop performs at most $N-1$ passes for an array with N elements. The loop will terminate when there are no exchanges in one pass.

```
bottom = number.length - 2;
exchanged = true;

while (exchanged) { //continue if the exchange is made

   //do one pass of sorting
   exchanged = false; //reset the variable
```

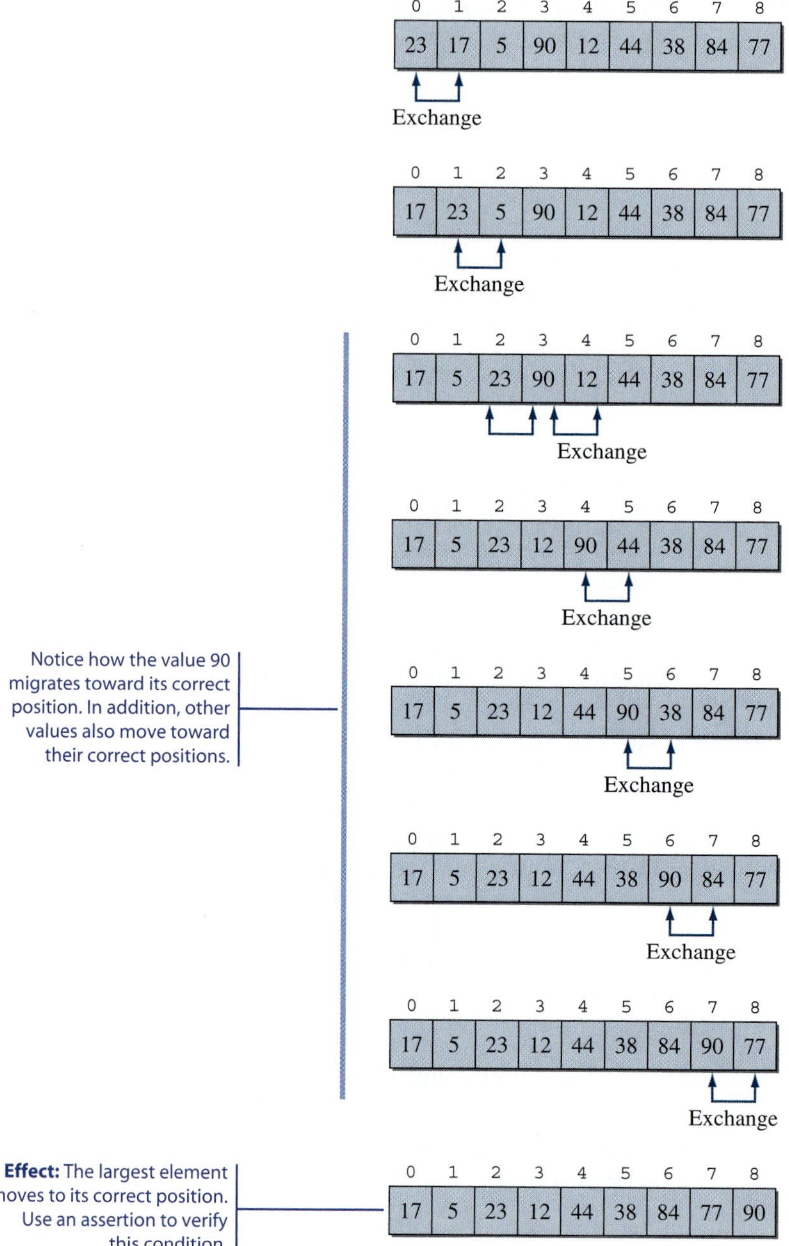

Figure 11.7 Effect of executing the first pass in the bubble sort.

One pass of bubble sort

```
    for (int i = 0; i <= bottom; i++) { //pairwise comparison
        if (number[i] > number[i+1]) {
            //the pair is out of order
            exchange them;

            exchanged = true; //an exchange is made
        }
    }
    //one pass is done, decrement the bottom index by 1
    bottom--;
}
```

Translating the pseudocode into an actual method, we have

Assert the element at position **bottom** is the largest among elements from position **0** to **bottom.**

```
public void bubbleSort(int[] number) {

    int      temp, bottom;
    boolean  exchanged = true;

    bottom = number.length - 2;

    while (exchanged) {

        exchanged = false;

        for (int i = 0; i <= bottom; i++) {
            if (number[i] > number[i+1]) {

                temp        = number[i];    //exchange
                number[i]   = number[i+1];
                number[i+1] = temp;

                exchanged   = true; //exchange is made
            }
        }

        assert maxBottom(number, bottom):
               "Error: " + number[bottom] +
               " at position " + bottom +
               " is not the largest.";

        bottom--;
    }

    assert isSorted(number):
           "Error: the final is not sorted";
}
```

The maxBottom method verifies that the largest element among elements from position 0 to bottom is at position bottom. The method is written as follows:

```
private boolean maxBottom(int[] number, int lastIndex) {

    for (int i = 0; i < lastIndex; i++) {
```

```
            if (number[lastIndex] < number[i]) {
                return false;
            }
        }
        return true;
    }
```

On average, we expect the bubble sort to finish sorting sooner than the selection sort, because there will be more data movements for the same number of comparisons, and there is a test to exit the method when the array gets sorted. The worst case of the bubble sort happens when the original array is in descending order. Notice that if the original array is already sorted, the bubble sort will perform only one pass whereas the selection sort will perform $N - 1$ passes.

1. Show the result of the second pass of bubble sort applied to the array at the bottom of Figure 11.7.
2. For an array with N elements, what is the least number of comparisons the bubble sort will execute?

11.3 Heapsort

heapsort

heap

root node

Selection and bubble sorts are two fundamental sorting algorithms that take approximately N^2 comparisons to sort an array of N elements. One interesting sorting algorithm that improves this performance to approximately $1.5N \log_2 N$ is ***heapsort***. We will describe the heapsort algorithm and analyze its performance in this section.

The heapsort algorithm uses a special data structure called a ***heap***. A heap consists of nodes, which contain data values, and edges, which link the nodes. Figure 11.8 shows a sample heap. We use integers as data values for the examples in this section. The topmost node is called the ***root node*** of a heap. Nodes in a heap

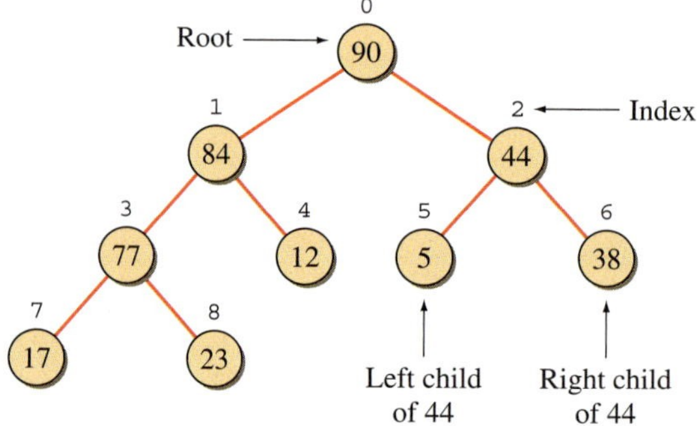

Figure 11.8 A sample heap that includes nine nodes.

left and right children

heap constraints

are indexed 0, 1, 2, and so forth in the top-to-bottom, left-to-right order, starting from the root. A node in a heap has zero, one, or two *children*. The children of a node are distinguished as the node's ***left*** and ***right children***. If a node has only one child, then it is the left child of the node.

A heap must satisfy these two constraints:

1. *Structural constraint.* Nodes in a heap with N nodes must occupy the positions numbered $0, 1, \ldots, N - 1$. Figure 11.9 shows examples of nonheaps that violate the structural constraint.
2. *Value relationship constraint.* A value stored in a node must be larger than the maximum of the values stored in its left and right children. Figure 11.10 shows examples of nonheaps that violate the value relationship constraint.

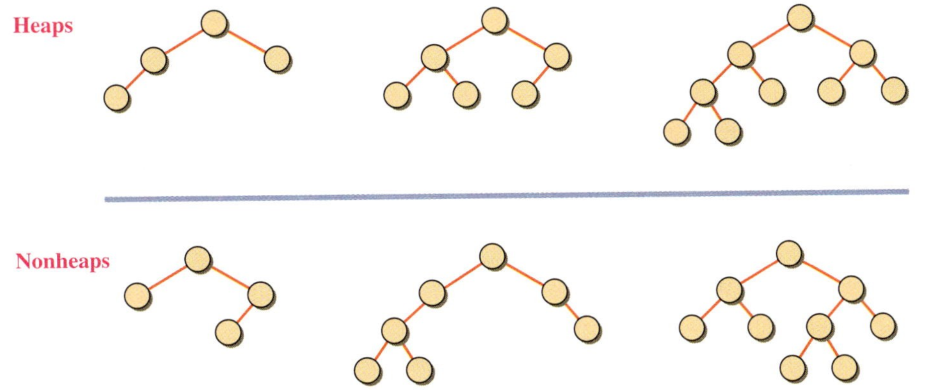

Figure 11.9 Sample heaps and nonheaps that violate the structural constraint.

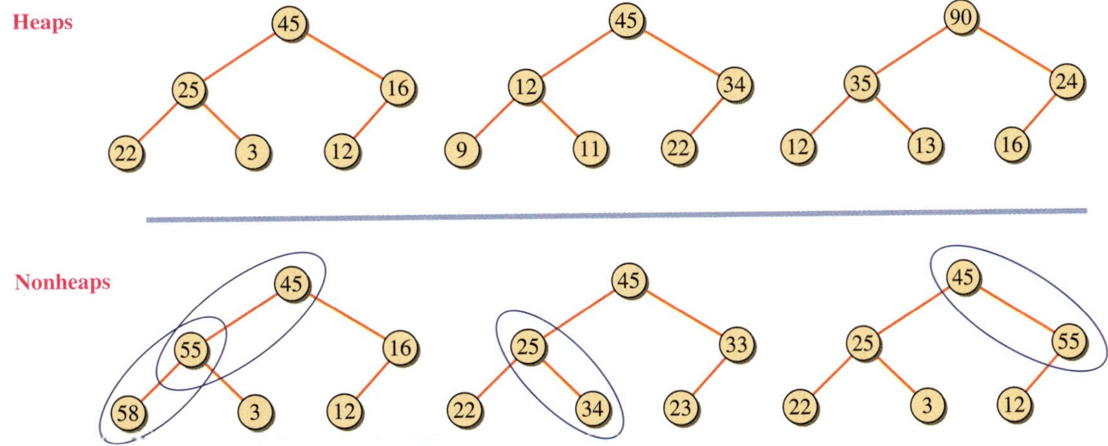

Figure 11.10 Sample heaps and nonheaps that violate the value relationship constraint. Violations are indicated by blue ellipses.

heapsort phases

How can we use the heap structure to sort *N* elements? Heapsort is carried out in two phases:

1. *Construction phase.* Construct a heap given *N* elements.
2. *Extraction phase.* Pull out the value in the root successively, creating a new heap with one less element after each extraction step.

We will begin the description of heapsort from the extraction phase. Consider the heap shown in Figure 11.8. Since every node in the heap satisfies the value relationship constraint, we can conclude that the value in the root node is the largest among the values stored in the heap. Now, after we remove the value 90 from the heap, we must create a new heap that has one less element. We can build such a heap by first moving the last element (value 23 in the figure) to the root position. With the value 23 in the root position, we have met the structural constraint for the heap with eight elements. However, the value relationship constraint is not met. The violation occurs because 23 is smaller than the larger of its two children. By swapping 84 and 23, the violation is eliminated. Since the value 23 is now at a new location, we must check again if the violation occurs at this position. It does, because 77 is larger than 23, so we swap again. We repeat the process until either there are no more children to consider or the value moved into a new position meets the value relationship constraint. We will call this process a ***rebuild step***. One rebuild step is illustrated in Figure 11.11.

rebuild step

Using a heap with *N* elements, we can sort the given *N* elements by performing the rebuild steps $N - 1$ times. Figure 11.12 illustrates the rebuild steps for the sample heap. Notice how the array for the sorted list is filled from the end. All we have to do now is to figure out how to build a heap from a given unsorted list of *N* elements. Let's study the construction phase of the algorithm.

We will illustrate the construction phase with the following unsorted nine elements:

```
23, 17, 5, 90, 12, 44, 38, 84, 77
```

If we assign the given numbers to a heap structure in ascending index order, we have the heap structure shown in Figure 11.13. This heap structure is not truly a heap because it violates the value relationship constraint. The construction phase will eliminate any violations of the value relationship constraint. The key concept for the construction phase is the rebuild step we used in the extraction phase. We will build a complete heap in a bottom-up fashion. We start out with a small heap and gradually build bigger and bigger heaps until the heap contains all *N* elements. Figure 11.14 shows the sequence of rebuild steps. The triangles indicate where the rebuild steps are applied. In the extraction step, the rebuild step is always applied to the root node. In the construction step, each rebuild step is applied successively, beginning with the node at index $\lfloor (N - 2)/2 \rfloor$ and ending with the node at index 0 (i.e., the root node).

Now let's consider how we can implement this algorithm in Java. We must first decide how to represent a heap. Among the possible alternatives, the data structure we learned in this book that can be used here very effectively is an array.

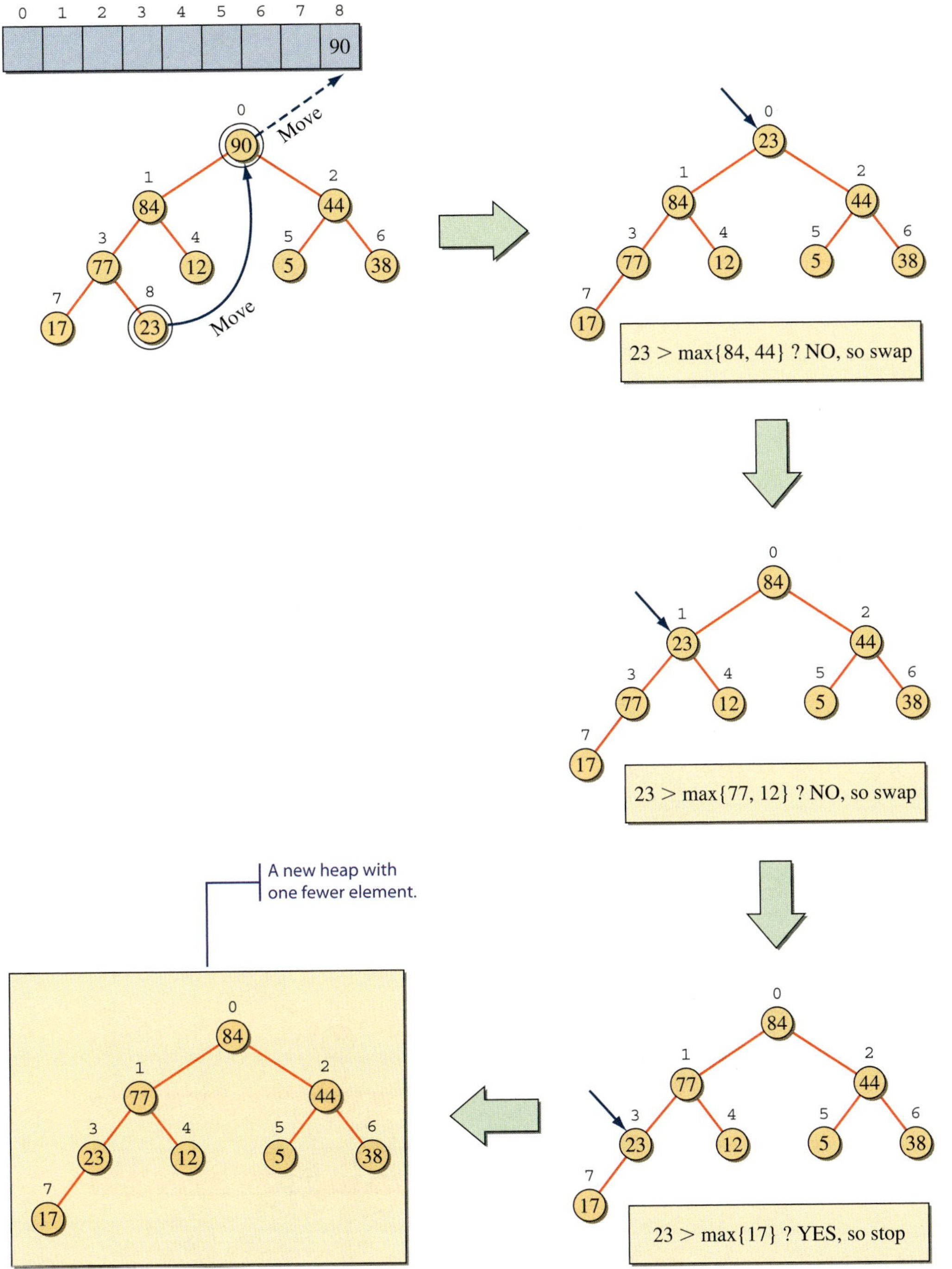

Figure 11.11 One rebuild step after the value 90 is pulled out from the heap. The net result of a single rebuild step is a new heap that contains one fewer element.

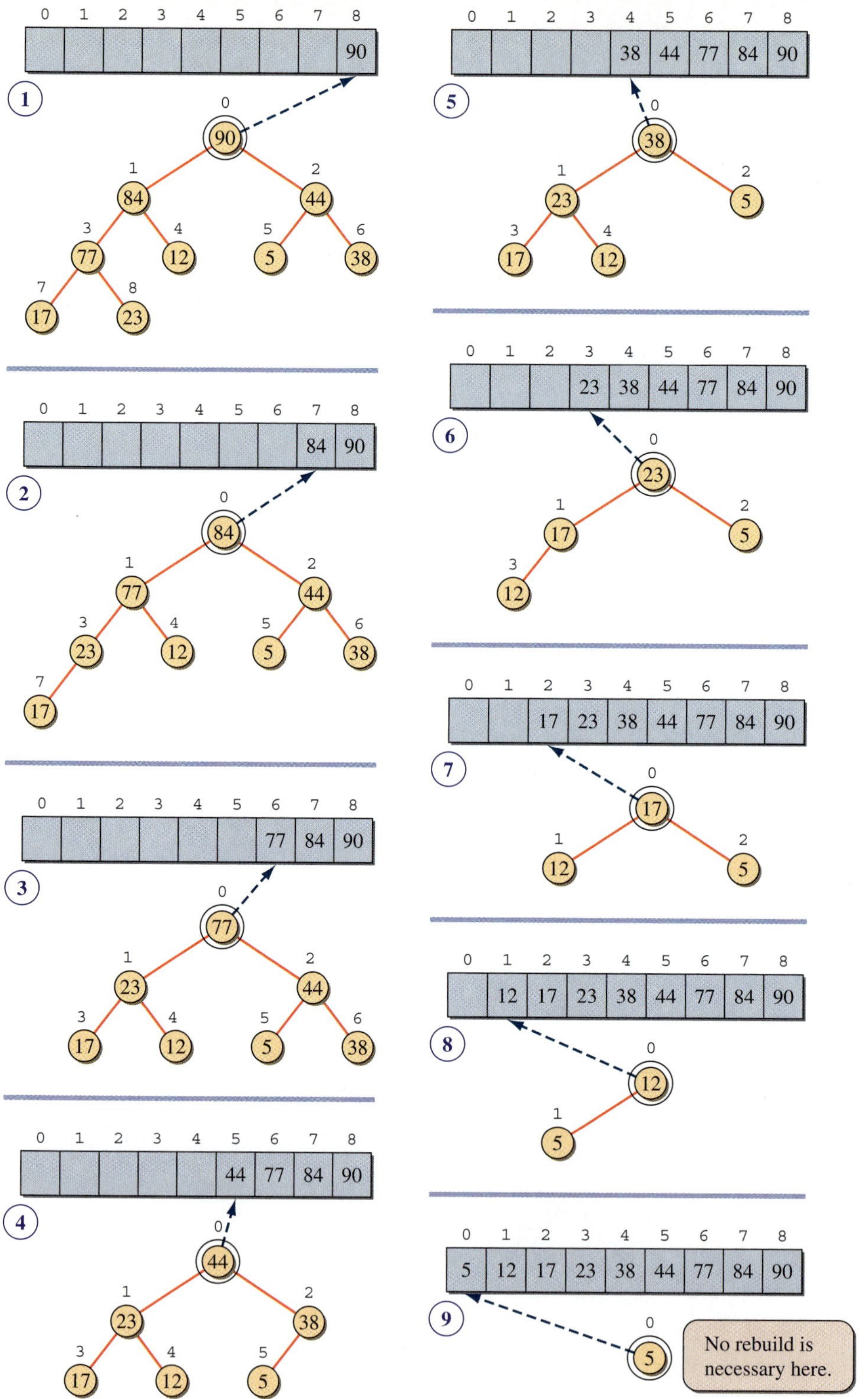

Figure 11.12 Eight rebuild steps to sort a heap with nine elements.

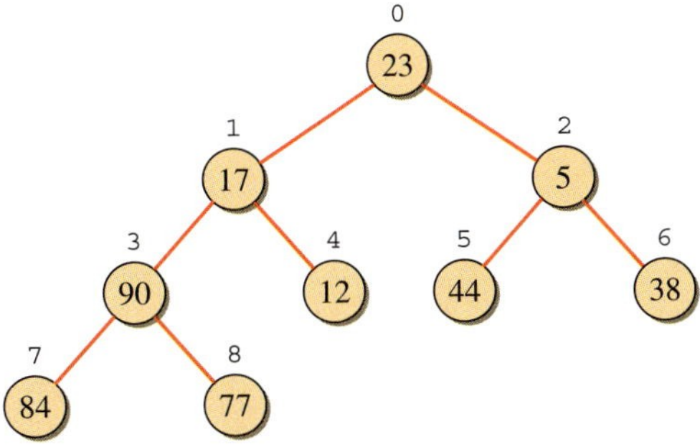

Figure 11.13 A heap structure with given numbers assigned in ascending index order.

Figure 11.15 shows the correspondence between the heap and the array representation. An important aspect in deciding which data structure to use is the ease of locating a given node's left and right children. With an array implementation, we can locate any node's left and right children easily. A node with index I has its left child at index $2I + 1$ and its right child at index $2I + 2$.

Since the heapsort algorithm is more involved than the insertion or bubble sort algorithm, we will put all the necessary code in a single class called Heap to provide a complete picture. To simplify our implementation so we can focus on the algorithm, we will allow only integers. You can modify the class to allow any objects to be sorted; see Exercise 9 at the end of this chapter. The following code illustrates how to use the Heap class:

```
int[ ] number = { 90, 44, 84, 12, 77, 23, 38, 5, 17 };
int[ ] sortedList;

Heap heap = new Heap( );

heap.setData(number);  //assign the original list

sortedList = heap.sort( );//sort the list

for (int i = 0; i < sortedList.length; i++) { //print out
   System.out.print("    " + sortedList[i]);  //the sorted
}                                             //list
```

The Heap class will include two arrays as its data members: one to implement a heap and another to store the sorted list.

```
/**
 * This class implements the heapsort algorithm. This class
 * can sort only integers.
 */
class Heap {
```

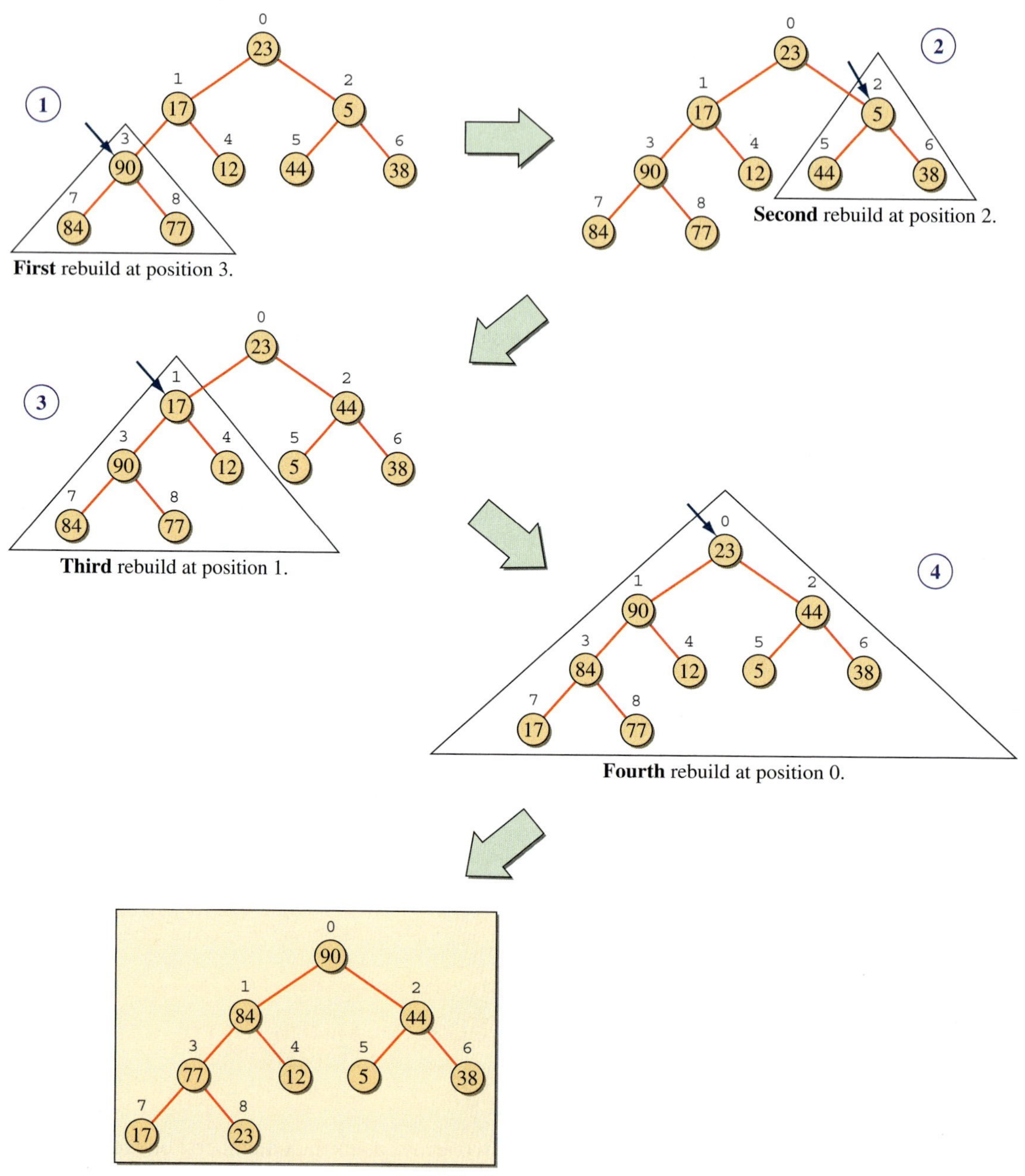

Figure 11.14 Sequence of rebuild steps applied in the construction phase. Rebuild steps are carried out at index positions 3, 2, 1, and 0.

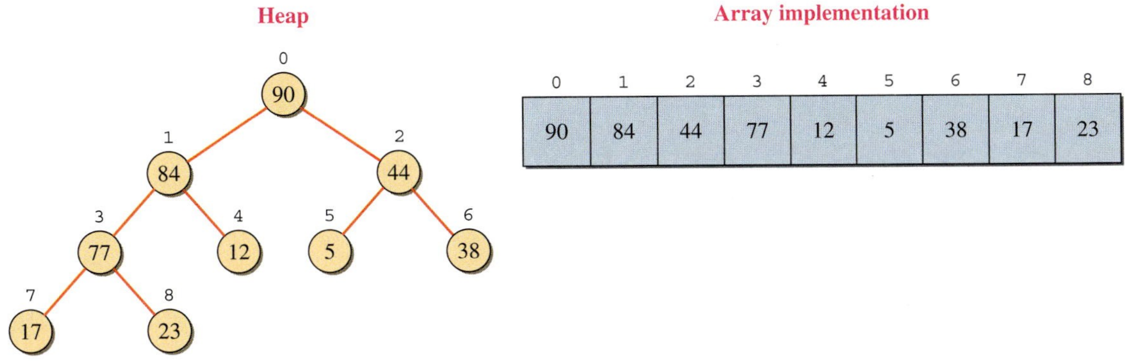

Figure 11.15 A sample heap and the corresponding array implementation.

```
    /**
     * Implements the heap
     */
    private int[ ] heap;

    /**
     * Stores the sorted list
     */
    private int[ ] sortedList;

    // methods come here
    . . .
}
```

Now let's look at the methods. The setData method initializes the two data members as follows:

```
public void setData(int[ ] data) {

    heap       = new int[data.length];
    sortedList = new int[data.length];

    for (int i = 0; i < data.length; i++) {
        heap[i] = data[i];
    }
}
```

Notice that we copy the contents of the data array to the heap array. If we simply assign the parameter to the data member heap as

```
heap = data;
```

then all we are doing is setting two names referring to the same object. Since we do not want to change the original data array, we make a separate copy.

The sort method calls two private methods that implement the two phases of the heapsort algorithm:

```
public int[ ] sort( ) {

   construct( );  //perform the construction phase

   extract( );   //perform the extraction phase

   return sortedList;
}
```

Here's the construct method:

```
private void construct( ) {

   int     current, maxChildIndex;
   boolean done;

   for (int i = (heap.length-2) / 2; i >= 0; i--) {

      current = i;
      done    = false;

      while (!done) {//perform one rebuild step
                     //with the node at index i

         if (2*current+1 > heap.length-1) {

            //current node has no children, so stop
            done = true;

         } else {
            //current node has at least one child,
            //get the index of larger child
            maxChildIndex
                = maxChild(current, heap.length-1);

            if (heap[current] < heap[maxChildIndex]) {

               //a child is larger, so swap and continue
               swap(current, maxChildIndex);
               current = maxChildIndex;

            } else { //the value relationship constraint
                    //is satisfied, so stop
               done = true;
            }
         }
      }

   assert isValidHeap(heap, i, heap.length-1):
         "Error: Construction phase is not working " +
         "correctly";
}
```

```
        testPrint(heap.length );   //TEMP
    }
```

The isValidHeap method is used to assert that elements from position start to position end form a valid heap structure. Here's the method:

```
private boolean isValidHeap(int[] heap,
                            int start, int end) {

   for (int i = start; i < end/ 2; i++) {

      if (heap[i] < Math.max(heap[2*i+1], heap[2*i+2])) {
         return false;
      }
   }

   return true;
}
```

And here's the extract method:

```
private void extract( ) {

   int     current, maxChildIndex;
   boolean done;

   for (int size = heap.length-1; size >= 0; size--) {

      //remove the root node data
      sortedList[size] = heap[0];

      //move the last node to the root
      heap[0] = heap[size];

      //rebuild the heap with one fewer element
      current = 0;
      done    = false;

      while (!done) {

         if (2*current+1 > size) {
            //current node has no children, so stop
            done = true;

         } else {
            //current node has at least one child,
            //get the index of larger child
            maxChildIndex = maxChild(current, size);

            if (heap[current] < heap[maxChildIndex]) {

               //a child is larger, so swap and continue
               swap(current, maxChildIndex);
               current = maxChildIndex;
```

```
            } else { //value relationship constraint
                      //is satisfied, so stop
               done = true;
            }
         }
      }

      assert isValidHeap(heap, i, heap.length-1):
            "Error: Construction phase is not working " +
            "correctly";
      testPrint( size ); //TEMP

   }
}
```

A number of methods are shared by both methods. The maxChild method returns the index of a node's left or right child, whichever is larger. This method is called only if a node has at least one child. The first parameter is the index of a node, and the second parameter is the index of the last node in a heap. The second parameter is necessary to determine whether a node has a right child. The method is defined as follows:

```
private int maxChild(int location, int end) {

   int result, leftChildIndex, rightChildIndex;

   rightChildIndex = 2*location + 2;
   leftChildIndex  = 2*location + 1;

   //Precondition:
   //       Node at 'location' has at least one child
   assert leftChildIndex <= end:
         "Error: node at position " + location +
         "has no children.";

   if (rightChildIndex <= end &&
         heap[leftChildIndex] < heap[rightChildIndex]) {

      result = rightChildIndex;
   } else {
      result = leftChildIndex;
   }

   return result;
}
```

The other two methods shared by the construct and extract methods are swap and testPrint. The swap method interchanges the contents of two array elements, and the testPrint method outputs the heap array for verification and debugging purposes. You can comment out the calls to testPrint from the construct and extract methods after you verify that the algorithm is implemented correctly. Here are the two methods:

```
private void swap (int loc1, int loc2) {

    int temp;

    temp = heap[loc1];
    heap[loc1] = heap[loc2];
    heap[loc2] = temp;
}

private void testPrint(int limit) {

    for (int i = 0; i < limit; i++) {
        System.out.print("  " + heap[i]);
    }

    System.out.println("     ");
}
```

There are several improvements we can make to the simple Heap class we provided here. These improvements are left as Exercise 9.

Performance

How good is the heapsort? We mentioned in Section 11.2 that the performances of both selection and bubble sort algorithms are approximately N^2 comparisons for sorting N elements. The heapsort algorithm is substantially more complex in design and implementation than the other two basic sorting algorithms. Is the extra complexity worth our effort? The answer is yes. The performance of the heapsort algorithm is approximately $1.5N \log_2 N$ comparisons for sorting N elements. This is a remarkable improvement. Consider the difference between the two performances for large N. For example, to sort 100,000 elements, the selection or bubble sort requires 10,000,000,000 comparisons, while the heapsort requires only $1.5 \cdot 100{,}000 \log_2 100{,}000 \approx 2{,}491{,}695$ comparisons. If a single comparison takes 1 microsecond (μs) (one millionth second), then the selection or bubble sort takes about 2.8 hours while the heapsort takes only about 2.492 seconds. (*Note:* The sorting operation itself may complete in a few seconds, but printing out the sorted 100,000 elements would take an enormous amount of time.)

Let's study how the performance of $1.5N \log_2 N$ comparisons is derived. What we need to count is the number of comparisons made during the rebuild steps in both the construction and extraction phases. During the extraction phase, the rebuild process is carried for $N - 1$ times. If we let K be the maximum number of comparisons required in one rebuild step, then the total number of comparisons will be $(N - 1)K$. In one rebuild step, we start comparing the value in the root node with the larger of its two children. If the value relationship constraint is not violated, the rebuild step terminates immediately. If there is a violation, we make a swap and continue. This compare-and-swap operation is carried out until either the value relationship constraint is met or there are no more nodes to compare. This means that

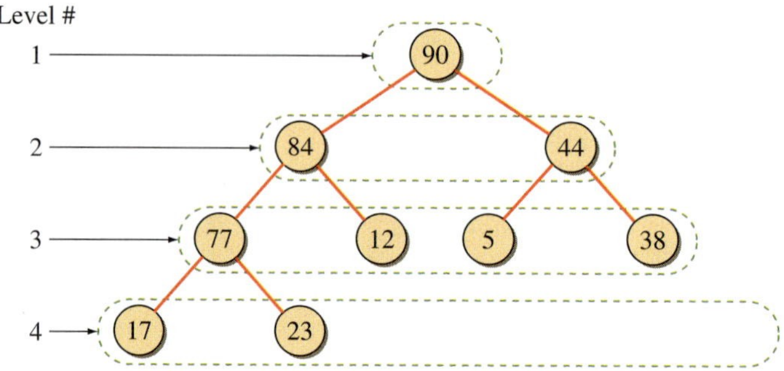

Figure 11.16 A sample heap with depth = 4, which is defined to be the largest level of all nodes in a heap.

the maximum number of comparisons K is derived by finding out how many times the value relationship constraint violation can occur before the nodes to compare are exhausted.

level

depth

Consider the heap shown in Figure 11.16. We define the ***level*** of a node in a heap to be the number of nodes in the path from the root to this node. For example, the level of node 44 in the sample heap is 3. The ***depth*** of a heap is defined to be the largest level of the nodes in the heap. The depth of the sample heap is therefore 4. Since the compare-and-swap operation starting from the root can never continue comparing beyond the largest level of the nodes, the depth of a heap is the value we seek for K. Thus, the value for K is derived by finding the depth of a heap with N elements.

At level 1, there is one node. At level 2, there are two nodes. Since a node at level i can have at most 2 children, the maximum number of nodes at level $i + 1$ is double the number of nodes at level i. Assuming the maximum number of nodes at all levels, the number of elements at level i is 2^{i-1}, so the maximum total number of nodes in a heap of depth K is

$$\sum_{i=1}^{K} 2^{i-1} = 2^K - 1$$

Because a heap must satisfy the structural constraint, we know the relationships

$$2^{K-1} - 1 < N \leq 2^K - 1$$

$$2^{K-1} < N + 1 \leq 2^K$$

will hold. By applying $\log_2$ to all terms, we have

$$K - 1 < \log_2 (N + 1) \leq K$$

so

$$K = \lceil \log_2 (N + 1) \rceil$$

Finally, the total number of comparisons for the extraction phase is

$$(N - 1)K = N \cdot \lceil \log_2(N + 1) \rceil \approx N \log_2 N$$

The construction phase will perform approximately $N/2$ rebuild steps. Each rebuild step will take no more than K comparisons, so the total number of comparisons for the construction phase is

$$\frac{N}{2} \log_2 N$$

The total number of comparisons for both phases is therefore

$$1.5N \log_2 N$$

1. The following structure violates the value relationship constraints. Use the construction phase routine of the heapsort to eliminate the violations.

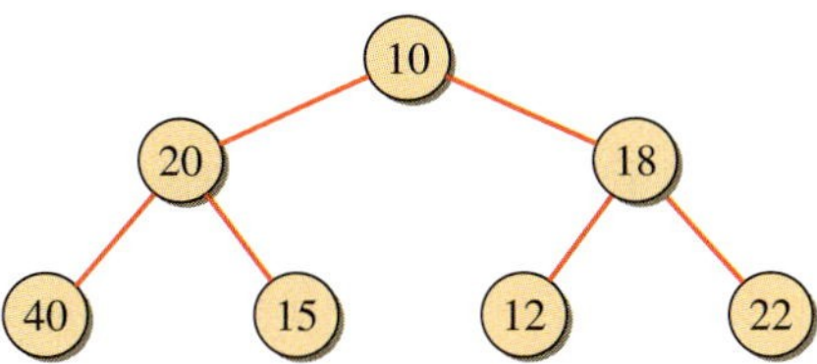

2. Identify all violations on structural and value relationship constraints in the following structure.

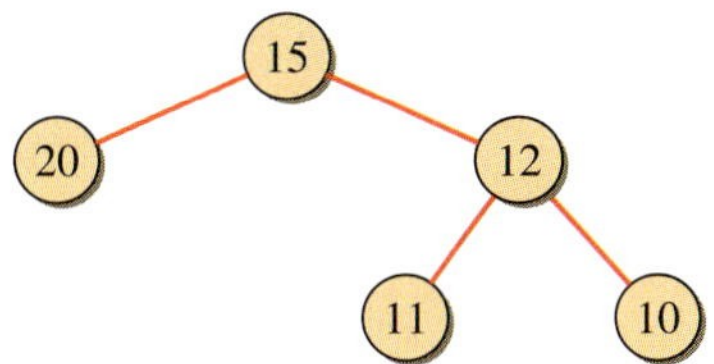

11.4 Sample Development

Sorting an AddressBook

Let's put the our basic knowledge of sorting algorithms into practice. In Chapter 10 we presented the **AddressBook** class that maintains a collection of **Person** objects. We will extend the **AddressBook** class by incorporating a sorting routine. The new **AddressBook** class will include a method that sorts the **Person** objects in alphabetical order of their names or in ascending order of their ages.

Instead of going through the development steps, we will discuss three different implementations to illustrate various techniques of Java programming. The three classes are named **AddressBookVer1, AddressBookVer2,** and **AddressBookVer3.** We will

11.4 Sample Development—*continued*

define an interface and make these three classes implement the defined interface. We have already dealt with interfaces, for example, the **List** and **Map** interfaces in Chapter 10. As we learned in that chapter, the interface defines a behavior, and if a class implements the interface, we can be certain that the instances of the class will support this behavior. Making classes implement the same interface is therefore a way to enforce consistency among the implementation classes. Because all three classes **AddressBookVer1, AddressBookVer2,** and **AddressBook3** implement the same interface, they will exhibit the same behavior, and we can therefore use them interchangeably in our programs.

The interface is named **AddressBook,** and we will include the public methods that must be supported by all versions. Collectively these public methods define the behavior common to all implementing classes. All public methods in the interface must not have any method body, only the method prototype followed by a semicolon. Here's the **AddressBook** interface:

```
/*
    Chapter 11 Sample Program: AddressBook Interface

    File: AddressBook.java
*/
interface AddressBook {

    public void       add(Person newPerson);

    public boolean    delete(String searchName);

    public Person     search(String searchName);

    public Person[ ] sort(int attribute);

}
```

The driver program to test the working of **AddressBook** is defined as follows:

```
/*
         Chapter 11 Sample Program: Test program to verify the
                  the AddressBook and Person classes

         File: TestAddressBookSorting.java
*/
```

```
import javax.swing.*;

class TestAddressBookSorting {

   public static void main(String[] args) {

        TestAddressBookSorting tester = new TestAddressBookSorting();
        tester.start();
   }

   private void start( ) {
        String[] name = {"ape", "cat", "bee", "bat", "eel",
                         "dog", "gnu", "yak", "fox", "cow",
                         "hen", "tic", "man"};
       Person p;

       AddressBook ab;

       Scanner scanner = new Scanner(System.in);

       System.out.print("Version #: ");
       int version = scanner.nextInt();

       switch (version) {
           case 1:  ab = new AddressBookVer1(); break;
           case 2:  ab = new AddressBookVer2(); break;
           case 3:  ab = new AddressBookVer3(); break;
           default: ab = new AddressBookVer1(); break;
       }

       for (int i = 0; i < name.length; i++) {
           p = new Person(name[i], random(10, 50),
                          random(0,1)==0?'M':'F');

            //note: random(0,1) == 0 ? 'M':'F'
            // means if (random(0,1) == 0) then 'M' else 'F'
               ab.add(p);
       }

       Person[] sortedlist = ab.sort(Person.AGE);

       for (int i = 0; i < sortedlist.length; i++) {
           System.out.println( sortedlist[i].toString( ));
       }

       System.out.println(" ");

       sortedlist = ab.sort(Person.NAME);

       for (int i = 0; i < sortedlist.length; i++) {
           System.out.println( sortedlist[i].toString( ));
       }
   }
```

start

11.4 Sample Development—*continued*

random

```
    private int random(int low, int high) {

        return (int) Math.floor(Math.random() * (high - low + 1))
                        + low;
    }
}
```

Version 1

In describing the basic sorting algorithms, we limit the data values to integers. This makes the comparison test easy. We write something like this:

```
if (number[i] < number[i+1]) {
   //do something...
} else {
   //do something else...
}
```

But how do we compare **Person** objects? We cannot say

```
Person p1 = new Person("Jack", 18, 'M');
Person p2 = new Person("Jill", 19, 'F');
if (p1 < p2) {
   ...
}
```

Bad Version

Cannot compare **Person** objects like this, because it does not make sense. Comparison operators other than equal (==) do not apply for objects.

because the comparison operators such as <, >, and others except the equal operator are meaningful only for comparing primitive data values. To be able to compare **Person** objects, we need to modify the class. Let's suppose that we want to compare two **Person** objects based on either their names or their ages. First we add the following two constants to the **Person** class of Chapter 10:

```
class Person {
   ...
   public static final int NAME = 0;
   public static final int AGE  = 1;
   ...
}
```

Next we add a variable to the **Person** class to set which attribute to use in comparing two objects:

```
private static int compareAttribute = NAME;
```

Notice that the variable is a class variable because this information is not specific to any individual **Person** objects, but applies to the whole class. We initialize it to **NAME** so the

Person objects will be compared on the name attribute as a default. We define a class method to let the programmer set the comparison attribute. The class method is defined as

```
public static void setCompareAttribute(int attribute) {

    compareAttribute = attribute;
}
```

Although it is not a syntax error to initialize a class variable inside a constructor, it is a logical error to do so. You cannot define a constructor that includes an initialization of the **compareAttribute** variable, as in

```
public Person( ) {

    ...
    compareAttribute = NAME;
}
```

static block

This definition is valid because the class variables can be accessed from the instance methods, but it is wrong to do so here. This constructor will set the class variable **compareAttribute** that is shared by all instances of the **Person** class every time a new **Person** object is created. This is not what we want. We need to initialize it exactly once when the class is loaded into the memory. One way to do this is to initialize at the point the class variable is declared as shown, or to use the ***static block*** we introduced in Chapter 7. Here's how:

Use the **static** block to initialize class variables.

```
class Person {
    ...

    static {
        compareAttribute = NAME;
    }
    ...
}
```

The rule to remember is never to initialize the class variables in the constructor.

Things to Remember

Do not initialize class variables in the constructor. Initialize the class variables in the **static** *block.*

Now we are ready to add a method **compareTo** that will compare the designated **Person** objects' names or ages and return the comparison result. The method is used like this:

```
//Persons p1 and p2 are defined and created already

//First set the comparison attribute to NAME
Person.setCompareAttribute(Person.NAME);
```

```
int comparisonResult = p1.compareTo(p2);

if (comparisonResult < 0) {
   //p1's name is lexicographically less than p2's name

} else if (comparisonResult == 0) {
   //p1's name is equal to p2's name

} else { //comparisonResult > 0
   //p1's name is lexicographically larger than p2's name
}
```

To compare two **Person** objects on their ages, we write

```
//Persons p1 and p2 are defined and created already

//First set the comparison attribute to AGE
Person.setCompareAttribute(Person.AGE);

int comparisonResult = p1.compareTo(p2);

if (comparisonResult < 0) {
   //p1 is younger than p2

} else if (comparisonResult == 0) {
   //p1's age is the same as p2's age

} else { //comparisonResult > 0
   //p1 is older than p2
}
```

Here's the **compareTo** method:

```
public int compareTo(Person person) {

   int comparisonResult;

   if (compareAttribute == AGE) {
      int p2age = person.getAge( );

      if (this.age < p2age) {
         comparisonResult = LESS;

      } else if (this.age == p2age) {
         comparisonResult = EQUAL;

      } else {
         assert this.age > p2age;
         comparisonResult = MORE;
      }
```

```
    } else { //compare names with String's compareTo
       String    p2name = person.getName( );
       comparisonResult = this.name.compareTo(p2name);
    }

    return comparisonResult;
}
```

The constants **LESS, EQUAL,** and **MORE** are defined in the **Person** class as

```
private static int LESS  = -1;
private static int EQUAL =  0;
private static int MORE  =  1;
```

The **compareTo** method of the **String** class behaves just as our **compareTo** method does. Indeed, our **compareTo** method is modeled after the **String** class's **compareTo** method. The wrapper classes **Integer, Float, Double,** and others also define the analogous **compareTo** method. Having consistent naming and behavior for comparing two objects of the same class allows the implementation of a more general code. See Exercise 9 at the end of the chapter.

Here's the complete **Person** class:

```
/*
    Chapter 11 Sample Program: Person class

    File: Person.java
 */

 class Person {

    public static final int NAME = 0;
    public static final int AGE = 1;

    private static final int LESS = -1;
    private static final int EQUAL = 0;
    private static final int MORE  = 1;

    private static int compareAttribute;

    private String  name;
    private int     age;
    private char    gender;

//     Static initializer
    static {
       compareAttribute = NAME;
    }

    public Person() {
        this("Not Given", 0, 'U');
    }
```

Data members

Constructors

11.4 Sample Development—*continued*

```
public Person(String name, int age, char gender) {
    this.age    = age;
    this.name   = name;
    this.gender = gender;
}

public static void setCompareAttribute(int attribute) {
    compareAttribute = attribute;
}

public int compareTo(Person person, int attribute) {
    int comparisonResult;

    if (attribute == AGE) {
        int p2age = person.getAge( );

        if (this.age < p2age) {
            comparisonResult = LESS;
        } else if (this.age == p2age) {
            comparisonResult = EQUAL;
        } else {
            assert this.age > p2age;
            comparisonResult = MORE;
        }

    } else { //compare the name using the String class's
            //compareTo method
        String   p2name = person.getName( );
        comparisonResult = this.name.compareTo(p2name);
    }

    return comparisonResult;
}

public int compareTo(Person person) {
    return compareTo(person, compareAttribute);
}

public int getAge( ) {
    return age;
}

public char getGender( ) {
    return gender;
}

public String getName( ) {
    return name;
}
```

setCompareAttribute

compareTo

Accessors

```
    public void setAge(int age) {
        this.age = age;
    }

    public void setGender(char gender) {
        this.gender = gender;
    }

    public void setName(String name) {
        this.name = name;
    }

    public String toString( ) {
        return this.name     + "\t\t" +
               this.age      + "\t\t" +
               this.gender;
    }
}
```

Mutators

toString

Now we are ready to add a sorting routine to the **AddressBook** class. The **sort** method accepts one integer parameter that specifies the attribute to compare in sorting the **Person** objects. The method returns an array of **Person** objects sorted on the designated attribute. We use the bubble sort algorithm for the method. Using the heapsort algorithm is left as Exercise 12. Here's the **sort** method.

```
public Person[ ] sort(int attribute) {

    Person[ ] sortedList = new Person[count];
    Person p1, p2, temp;

    //copy references to sortedList; see Figure 11.17
    for (int i = 0; i < count; i++) {
        sortedList[i] = entry[i];
    }

    //Set the comparison attribute
    Person.setCompareAttribute(attribute);

    //begin the bubble sort on sortedList
    int       bottom, comparisonResult;
    boolean   exchanged = true;

    bottom = sortedList.length - 2;

    while (exchanged)  {

        exchanged = false;

        for (int i = 0; i <= bottom; i++) {
            p1 = sortedList[i];
```

```
                p2 = sortedList[i+1];

                comparisonResult = p1.compareTo(p2, attribute);

                if (comparisonResult > 0) { //p1 is 'larger'
                    sortedList[i]   = p2;    //than p2,so
                    sortedList[i+1] = p1;    //exchange

                    exchanged  = true;       //exchange is made
                }
            }
            bottom--;
        }
        return sortedList;
    }
```

The **sort** method first creates a temporary array called **sortedList** and copies the references from the **entry** array into this **sortedList.** We do this so we can sort the objects on a specified attribute without affecting the order maintained in the **entry** array. Figure 11.17 illustrates how this **sortedList** array is used in sorting the **Person** objects on the **age** attribute.

Here's the **AddressBookVer1** class:

```
/*
    Chapter 11 Sample Program: Address Book Version 1

    File: AddressBookVer1.java
*/

class AddressBookVer1 implements AddressBook {

    private static final int  DEFAULT_SIZE = 25;
    private static final int  NOT_FOUND    = -1;

    private Person[]   entry;
    private int        count;

    public AddressBookVer1( ){
        this(DEFAULT_SIZE);
    }

    public AddressBookVer1(int size){
        count = 0;

        if (size <= 0) { //invalid data value, use default
```

Data members

Constructors

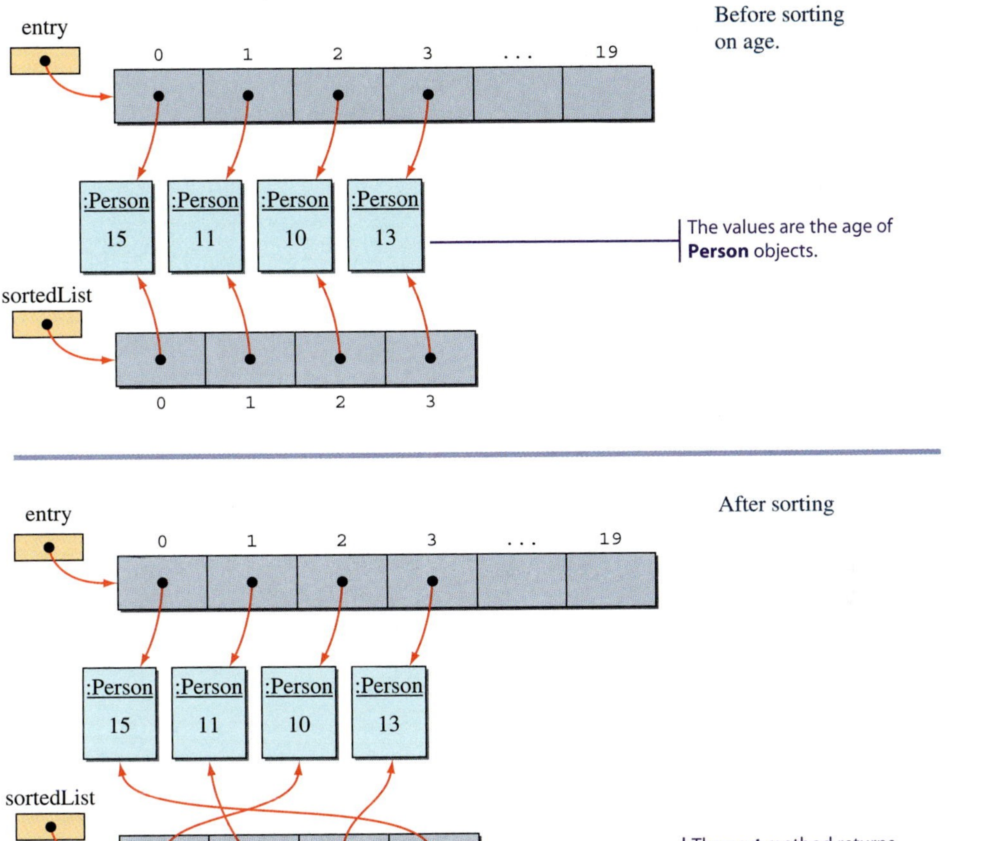

Figure 11.17 The diagram illustrates how the separate array is used in sorting. Notice that the original array is unaffected by the sorting.

```
            throw new IllegalArgumentException("Size must be positive");
        }

        entry = new Person[size];

//          System.out.println("array of "+ size + " is created."); //TEMP
    }

    public void add(Person newPerson) {

        if (count == entry.length) {    //no more space left,
            enlarge( );                 //create a new larger array
        }
```

add

11.4 Sample Development—*continued*

```
        //at this point, entry refers to a new larger array
        entry[count] = newPerson;
        count++;
    }

    public boolean delete(String searchName) {

        boolean    status;
        int        loc;

        loc = findIndex(searchName);

        if (loc == NOT_FOUND) {
            status = false;
        } else { //found, pack the hole

            entry[loc] = entry[count-1];

            status = true;
            count--;         //decrement count,
                             //since we now have one fewer element
        }

        return status;
    }

    public Person search(String searchName) {

        Person foundPerson;
        int         loc = 0;

        while (loc < count &&
                 !searchName.equals(entry[loc].getName())) {
            loc++;
        }

        if (loc == count) {

            foundPerson = null;
        } else {

            foundPerson = entry[loc];
        }

        return foundPerson;
    }

    public Person[ ] sort(int attribute) {

        Person[ ] sortedList = new Person[count];
        Person p1, p2, temp;
```

delete

search

sort

```
        //copy references to sortedList
        for (int i = 0; i < count; i++) {
            sortedList[i] = entry[i];
        }

        //set the comparison attribute
        entry[0].setCompareAttribute(attribute);

        //begin the bubble sort on sortedList
        int       bottom, comparisonResult;
        boolean   exchanged = true;

        bottom = sortedList.length - 2;

        while (exchanged) {

            exchanged = false;

            for (int i = 0; i <= bottom; i++) {
                p1 = sortedList[i];
                p2 = sortedList[i+1];
               // comparisonResult = p1.compareTo( p2, attribute );

                comparisonResult = p1.compareTo(p2);

                if (comparisonResult > 0) { //p1 is 'larger'
                                            //than p2, so
                    sortedList[i]    = p2;  //exchange
                    sortedList[i+1]  = p1;

                    exchanged = true; //exchange is made
                }
            }
            bottom--;
        }
        return sortedList;
    }

    private void enlarge( ) {
        //create a new array whose size is 150% of
        //the current array
        int newLength = (int) (1.5 * entry.length);
        Person[] temp = new Person[newLength];

        //now copy the data to the new array
        for (int i = 0; i < entry.length; i++) {
            temp[i] = entry[i];
        }

        //finally set the variable entry to point to the new array
        entry = temp;
```

enlarge

11.4 Sample Development—*continued*

```
//   System.out.println("Inside the method enlarge");              //TEMP
//   System.out.println("Size of a new array: " + entry.length); //TEMP
   }

   private int findIndex(String searchName) {
       int loc = 0;

       while (loc < count &&
              !searchName.equals(entry[loc].getName())) {
           loc++;
       }

       if (loc == count) {

           loc = NOT_FOUND;

       }

       return loc;
   }
}
```

findIndex

Version 2

In the second implementation of the **AddressBook** interface, we will use the sorting routine provided in the **java.util.Arrays** class, which includes a number of useful methods for handling arrays. To use the **sort** method of the **Arrays** class, we must pass a comparator object as its second argument. A comparator object is an instance of a class that implements the **Comparator** interface. In the first version, we relied on the comparison routines embedded in the **Person** class. We are thus limited to what's provided by the **Person** class, namely, sorting by name or sorting by age. We cannot, for example, sort on gender and then within the same gender sort on age. By providing an implementation class of the **Comparator** interface, we can sort **Person** objects (or any other types of objects) in any manner we want.

To implement the **Comparator** interface, we must implement its **compare** method. The function of the **compare** method is similar to that of the **compareTo** method in the **Person** class. Any class that implements the **Comparator** interface must specify the type of the objects it will compare. For this example, the class compares **Person** objects, so the class will implement **Comparator<Person>.** The parameters for the **compare** method must match the specified type, which in this case is **Person.** Here's the comparator class that compares two **Person** objects based on their age:

```
class AgeComparator implements Comparator <Person> {

   private final int LESS = -1;
   private final int EQUAL = 0;
   private final int MORE  = 1;

   public int compare(Person p1, Person p2) {
      int comparisonResult;

      int p1age = p1.getAge( );
      int p2age = p2.getAge( );

      if (p1age < p2age) {
         comparisonResult = LESS;
      } else if (p1age == p2age) {
         comparisonResult = EQUAL;
      } else {
         assert p1age > p2age;
         comparisonResult = MORE;
      }

      return comparisonResult;
   }
}
```

inner class

The **NameComparator** is similarly defined. The **AgeComparator** and **NameComparator** classes are helper classes specific to the **AddressBookVer2** class, and as such, it is appropriate to define them as the inner classes of **AddressBookVer2.** An ***inner class*** is a class whose definition is given within the definition of another class, as in

```
class Outer {

      ...

      class Inner {
         ...
      } //end of Inner

} //end of Outer
```

We can prefix the inner class definition with the visibility modifier **public** or **private.** The **public** modifier will make the inner class accessible to the client classes outside of the package while the **private** modifier will make the inner class inaccessible to all other classes. Just as the ordinary class definition, a class definition without a visibility modifier is accessible to all other classes within the same package (classes in the same directory are in the same package).

11.4 Sample Development—*continued*

As for the actual sorting task, we will use the **sort** method of the **Arrays** class instead of writing our own sorting algorithm. The **sort** method of the **AddressBookVer2** class is now defined as follows:

```
public Person[ ] sort(int attribute) {

   if (!(attribute == Person.NAME ||
         attribute == Person.AGE)) {
      throw new IllegalArgumentException( );
   }

   Person[ ] sortedList = new Person[count];

   //copy references to sortedList
   for (int i = 0; i < count; i++) {
      sortedList[i] = entry[i];
   }

   Arrays.sort(sortedList, getComparator(attribute));

   return sortedList;
}
```

Sorts the list by using the given comparator

And the private **getComparator** method is defined as follows:

```
private Comparator<String> getComparator(int attribute) {
   Comparator<String> comp = null;

   if (attribute == Person.AGE) {
      comp = new AgeComparator( );
   } else {
      assert attribute == Person.NAME:
             "Attribute not recognized for sorting";

      comp = new NameComparator( );
   }
   return comp;
}
```

The first argument to the **sort** method of the **Arrays** class is an array of objects we want to sort, and the second argument is the comparator to use in comparing array elements. For example, if we want to sort the **Person** objects by gender first and in descending order of age within the same gender, we can define the comparator as

```
class GenAgeComparator implements Comparator<Person> {

   private final int LESS = -1;
   private final int EQUAL = 0;
   private final int MORE  = 1;
```

```
public int compare(Person p1, Person p2) {
   int comparisonResult;

   int p1age = p1.getAge( );
   int p2age = p2.getAge( );

   char p1gender = p1.getGender();
   char p2gender = p2.getGender();

   if (p1gender < p2gender) {
      comparisonResult = LESS;
   } else if (p1gender == p2gender) {
      if (p2age < p1age) {
         comparisonResult = LESS;
      } else if (p2age == p1age) {
         comparisonResult = EQUAL;
      } else {
         assert p2age > p1age;
         comparisonResult = MORE;
      }

   } else {
      assert p1gender > p2gender;
      comparisonResult = MORE;
   }

   return comparisonResult;
}
}
```

Notice that we are switching the positions of **p1** and **p2** because we are sorting in descending order.

and we can call the **sort** method as

```
Arrays.sort(sortedList, new GenAgeComparator());
```

Here's the **AddressBook2** class (only the modified portions are shown):

```
/*
   Chapter 11 Sample Program: Address Book Version 2
   File: AddressBookVer2.java
*/
import java.util.*;

class AddressBookVer2 implements AddressBook {

   public AddressBookVer2( ) {
       this( DEFAULT_SIZE );
   }
```

11.4 Sample Development—*continued*

```
    public AddressBookVer2(int size) {
        ...
    }

    ...

    public Person[ ] sort(int attribute) {

        if (!(attribute == Person.NAME || attribute == Person.AGE)) {
            throw new IllegalArgumentException( );
        }

        Person[ ] sortedList = new Person[count];

        //copy references to sortedList
        for (int i = 0; i < count; i++) {
            sortedList[i] = entry[i];
        }

        Arrays.sort(sortedList, getComparator(attribute));

        return sortedList;

    }

    ...

    private Comparator<String> getComparator(int attribute) {
        Comparator<String> comp = null;

        if (attribute == Person.AGE) {
            comp = new AgeComparator( );

        } else {
            assert attribute == Person.NAME:
                    "Attribute not recognized for sorting";

            comp = new NameComparator( );
        }
        return comp;
    }

//     Inner Classes

    //Inner class for comparing age
    class AgeComparator implements Comparator<Person> {

        private final int LESS = -1;
        private final int EQUAL = 0;
        private final int MORE  = 1;
```

```
        public int compare(Person p1, Person p2) {

            int comparisonResult;

            int p1age = p1.getAge( );
            int p2age = p2.getAge( );

            if (p1age < p2age) {
                comparisonResult = LESS;
            } else if (p1age == p2age) {
                comparisonResult = EQUAL;
            } else {
                assert p1age > p2age;
                comparisonResult = MORE;
            }

            return comparisonResult;
        }
    }

    //Inner class for comparing name
    class NameComparator implements Comparator<String> {

        public int compare(Person p1, Person p2) {

            String p1name = p1.getName( );
            String p2name = p2.getName( );

            return p1name.compareTo(p2name);
        }
    }
}
```

While the main purpose of the **AddressBookVer1** class is pedagogy, the **AddressBookVer2** class, with its use of the efficient **Arrays** class **sort** method based on a high-performance sorting technique called *merge sort* and the generality provided by the **Comparator** interface, is closer to what we would really use in practice. The last version, **AddressBookVer3,** would improve further by using the map from the Java Collection Framework. This eliminates the code to maintain the array in our class.

Version 3

The third implementation of the **AddressBook** interface eliminates the use of an array altogether. Instead of maintaining the array of **Person** objects ourselves, we will rely on the service provided by the **Map** interface from the **java.util** package.

The key for the map is the person's name, and the value is the **Person** object. The **add, delete,** and **search** methods now all just make calls to the map's methods for data

11.4 Sample Development—*continued*

management. The **sort** method retrieves a collection of values in the map, converts this collection to an array, and then passes this array to the **sort** method of the **Arrays** class. Here's how we define the **sort** method:

```
public Person[ ] sort(int attribute) {

   if (!(attribute == Person.NAME ||
         attribute == Person.AGE)) {
      throw new IllegalArgumentException( );
   }

   Person[ ] sortedList = new Person[entry.size()];
   entry.values().toArray(sortedList);

   Arrays.sort(sortedList, getComparator(attribute));

   return sortedList;
}
```

Here's the **AddressBookVer3** class:

```
/*
   Chapter 11 Sample Program: Address Book Version 3

   File: AddressBookVer3.java
*/
import java.util.*;

class AddressBookVer3 implements AddressBook {

   private static final int DEFAULT_SIZE = 25;

   private Map<String, Person> entry;

   public AddressBookVer3( ) {
       this(DEFAULT_SIZE);
   }

   public AddressBookVer3(int size) {
       entry = new HashMap<String, Person> (size);
   }

   public void add(Person newPerson) {
       entry.put(newPerson.getName(), newPerson);
   }

   public boolean delete(String searchName) {

       boolean status;
       Person p = entry.remove(searchName);
```

Data members

Constructors

add

delete

```
        if (p == null) {
            status = false;
        } else {
            status = true;
        }

        return status;
    }

    public Person search(String searchName) {

        return entry.get(searchName);
    }

    public Person[ ] sort(int attribute) {

        if (!(attribute == Person.NAME || attribute == Person.AGE)) {
            throw new IllegalArgumentException( );
        }

        Person[ ] sortedList = new Person[entry.size()];
        entry.values().toArray(sortedList);

        Arrays.sort(sortedList, getComparator(attribute));

        return sortedList;
    }

    ...
}
```

search

sort

Summary

- Searching and sorting are two of the most basic nonnumeric applications of computer programs.
- Linear search looks for a value in a linear sequence.
- Binary search looks for a value by successively comparing the element in the middle of a sorted list.
- Selection sort is a basic sorting routine that runs in time proportion to N^2, where N is the size of the list to sort.
- Bubble sort is another N^2 performance algorithm, but it runs faster than the selection sort on average.
- Heapsort has a $N \log_2 N$ performance. It uses a special heap data structure to sort the elements.

- Using a class that implements the Comparator interface is convenient and flexible to dictate the manner in which objects of a class are compared.
- The Comparator interface has one method, called compare.
- The standard classes and interfaces described or used in this chapter are

  Comparator Arrays

Key Concepts

linear search
binary search
selection sort
bubble sort
heapsort
N^2 sorting algorithm
$N \log_2 N$ sorting algorithm
comparator

Exercises

1. Consider the following array of sorted integers:

0	1	2	3	4	5	6	7	8	9	10	11
10	15	25	30	33	34	46	55	78	84	96	99

   Using the binary search algorithm, search for 23. Show the sequence of array elements that are compared, and for each comparison, indicate the values for low and high.

2. We assumed all elements in an array are distinct; that is, there are no duplicate values in the array. What will be an effect on the linear search algorithm if an array contains duplicate values?
3. Will the sorting algorithms presented in this chapter work if the unsorted array contains any duplicate values?
4. In this chapter we analyzed sorting algorithms by counting the number of comparisons. Another possible method for analyzing the algorithms is to count the number of data exchanges. How many data exchanges do the selection and bubble sort make in the worst case? Regardless of the original list, the selection sort will make the same number of data exchanges. However, the number of data exchanges the bubble sort makes depends on the arrangement of elements in the original list.
5. Another simple sorting algorithm is called an *insertion sort*. Suppose we have a sorted list of N elements and we need to insert a new element X into this list to create a sorted list of $N + 1$ elements. We can insert X at the correct position in the list by comparing it with elements list[$N - 1$], list[$N - 2$], list[$N - 3$], and so forth. Every time we compare X and list[i], we shift list[i] one position to list[i + 1] if X is smaller than list[i]. When we find list[i] that is smaller than X, we put X at position $i + 1$ and stop. We can apply this logic to sort an

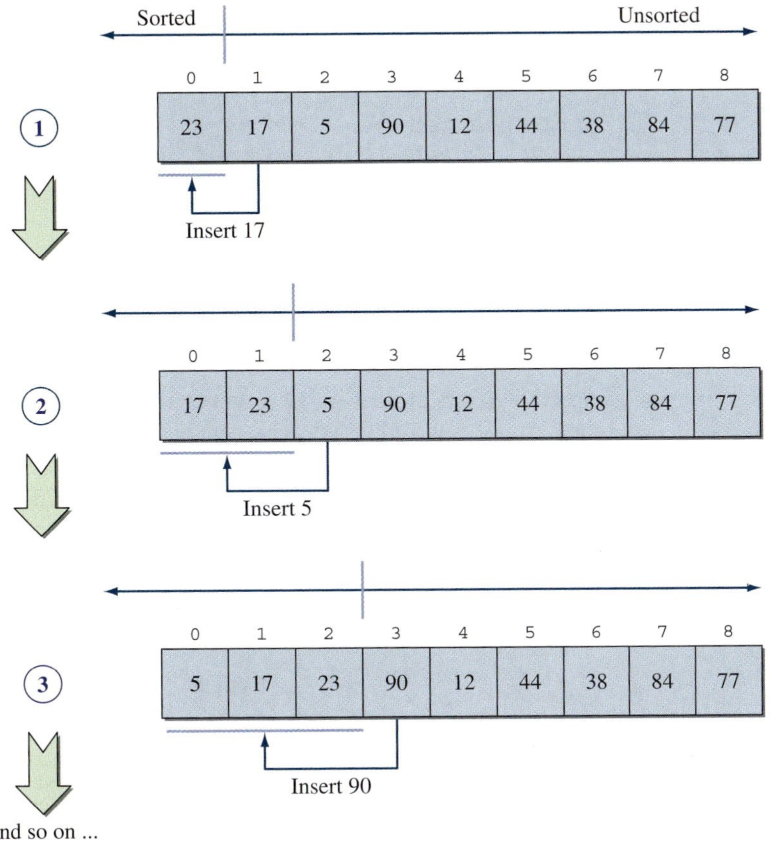

Figure 11.18 Steps in an insertion sort.

unordered list of *N* elements. We start with a sorted list of one element and insert the second element to create a sorted list of two elements. Then we add the third element to create a sorted list of three elements. Figure 11.18 illustrates the steps in the insertion sort. Write a method that implements the insertion sort algorithm. You may simplify the method by sorting only integers.

6. Analyze the insertion sort algorithm of Exercise 5 by counting the number of comparisons and data exchanges. Provide the analysis for the worst case.

7. Write a test program to compare the performances of selection sort, bubble sort, and heapsort algorithms experimentally. Use the random method from the Math class to generate 5000 integers, and sort the generated integers by using the three sorting algorithms. For each execution, record the time it took to sort the numbers. You can use the java.util.Date class to record the execution time in milliseconds, for example,

```
Date startTime, endTime;

startTime = new Date();
```

```
//sort the integers

endTime = new Date();

//record the elapsed time
double elapsedTime
            = endTime.getTime() - startTime.getTime();
```

8. Consider the following property about the bubble sort:

> *If the last exchange made in some pass occurs at the Jth and (J + 1)st positions, then all elements from the (J + 1)st to the Nth positions are in their correct location.*

Rewrite the bubble sort algorithm, using this property.

9. The Heap class given in Section 11.3 sorts only the integers. Improve the class by making it possible to sort any objects that recognize the compareTo method, which is described in Section 11.4, so the new Heap class will be able to sort Person, Integer, Double, and String objects among others. Since the elements in the internal array can be any object, declare an array of Object objects. All Java classes are automatically a subclass of Object, unless they are declared explicitly as a subclass of another class. The declaration of heap will be like this

```
private Object[ ] heap;
```

and the setData method will be like this:

```
public void setData(Object[ ] data) {
    heap       = new Object[data.length];
    sortedList = new Object[data.length];

    for (int i = 0; i < data.length; i++) {
        heap[i] = data[i];
    }
}
```

10. In the Heap class, we used two separate arrays: one for the heap and another for the sorted list. It turns out we can do everything with just one array. Notice that the heap will decrease in size by one element after every rebuild step. The unused space at the end of the heap array can be used to store the sorted list. Modify the Heap class so it will use only one array.

11. Modify the Heap class by defining a separate method called rebuild, which will be used by both the construct and extract methods.

12. In Section 11.4, we implemented the sorting routine for the AddressBook class with the bubble sort algorithm. Modify the sorting routine by using the Heap class of Exercise 9.

13. Instead of maintaining an unsorted list and returning the sorted list when the sort method is called, modify the AddressBook class so that it maintains the sorted list of Person in alphabetical order. Modify the search routine by using the binary search algorithm.

12 File Input and Output

Objectives

After you have read and studied this chapter, you should be able to

- Include a **JFileChooser** object in your program to let the user specify a file.
- Write bytes to a file and read them back from the file, using **FileOutputStream** and **FileInputStream.**
- Write values of primitive data types to a file and read them back from the file, using **DataOutput Stream** and **DataInputStream.**
- Write text data to a file and read them back from the file, using **PrintWriter** and **BufferedReader.**
- Read a text file using **Scanner.**
- Write objects to a file and read them back from the file, using **ObjectOutputStream** and **ObjectInputStream.**

Introduction

What is the most important action you should never forget to take while developing programs or writing documents? Saving the data, of course! It's 3 A.M., and you're in the home stretch, applying the finishing touches to the term paper due at 9 A.M. Just as you are ready to select the Print command for the final copy, it happens. The software freezes and it won't respond to your commands anymore. You forgot to turn on the Autosave feature, and you have not saved the data for the last hour. There's nothing you can do but reboot the computer.

Data not saved will be lost, and if we ever want to work on the data again, we must save the data to a file. We call the action of saving, or writing, data to a file ***file output*** and the action of reading data from a file ***file input***. A program we develop must support some form of file input and output capabilities for it to have practical uses. Suppose we develop a program that keeps track of bicycles owned by the dorm students. The program will allow the user to add, delete, and modify the bicycle information. If the program does not support the file input and output features, every time the program is started, the user must reenter the data.

file output and input

In this chapter, we will introduce the classes from the java.io and javax.swing packages that are used for file input and output operations. Also, we will show how the two helper classes from Chapters 8 and 9—Dorm and FileManager—that provided the file input and output support are implemented.

12.1 File and JFileChooser Objects

In this section we introduce two key objects for reading data from or writing data to a file. We use the term *file access* to refer to both read and write operations. If we need to be precise, we write *read access* or *write access*. (We use the terms *save* and *write* interchangeably to refer to file output, but we never say *save access*.) Suppose we want to read the contents of a file sample.data. Before we begin the actual operation of reading data from this file, we must first create a **File** object (from the java.io package) and associate it to the file. We do so by calling a File constructor:

File

```
File inFile = new File("sample.data");
```

The argument to the constructor designates the name of the file to access. The system assumes the file is located in the ***current directory***. For the following examples, we assume the directory structure shown in Figure 12.1, with Ch12 being the current directory. When you run a program whose source file is located in directory X, then the current directory is X. Please refer to Java compiler manuals for other options for designating the current directory.

current directory

It is also possible to open a file that is stored in a directory other than the current directory by providing a path name and a filename. Assuming there's a file xyz.data in the JavaPrograms directory, we can open it by executing

```
File inFile = new File("C:\\JavaPrograms", "xyz.data");
```

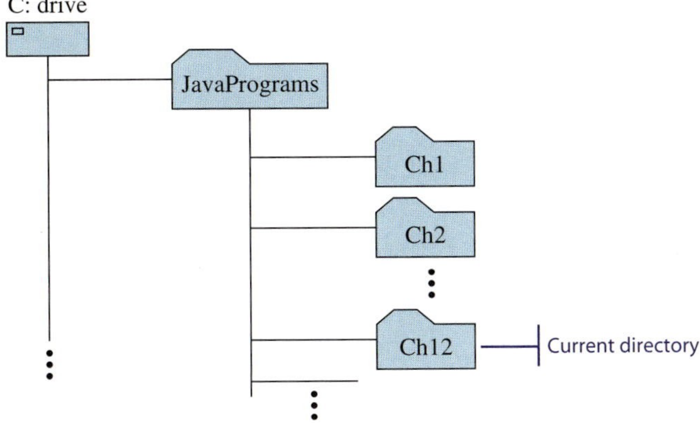

Figure 12.1 Directory structure used for the examples in this section. We assume the Windows environment.

This style of designating the path name is for the Windows platform. The actual path name we want to specify is

```
C:\JavaPrograms
```

but the backslash character is an escape character. So to specify the backslash character itself, we must use double backslashes. For the UNIX platform, we use the forward slash for a delimiter, for example,

```
"/JavaPrograms"
```

For the Mac platform, we also use a forward slash; for example, if the name of a hard disk is MacHD, then we write

```
"/MacHD/JavaPrograms"
```

To maintain the consistency across the platforms, the forward slash character is allowed for the Windows platform also, such as in

```
"C:/JavaPrograms/Ch12"
```

The path name could be absolute or relative to the current directory. The absolute path name is the full path name beginning with the disk drive name, for example,

```
"C:/JavaPrograms/Ch12"
```

The relative path name is relative to the current directory. For example, if the current directory is Ch12, then the relative path name

```
"../Ch12"
```

is equivalent to the full path name

```
"C:/JavaPrograms/Ch12"
```

where the two dots (. .) in the string mean "one directory above."

We can check if a File object is associated correctly to an existing file by calling its exists method:

```
if (inFile.exists( )) {
   // inFile is associated correctly to an existing file

} else {
   // inFile is not associated to any existing file
}
```

When a valid association is established, we say *the file is opened;* a file must be opened before we can do any input and output to the file.

Things to Remember

A file must be opened before we can execute any file access operations.

A File object can also be associated to a directory. For example, suppose we are interested in listing the content of directory Ch12. We can first create a File object and associate it to the directory. After the association is made, we can list the contents of the directory by calling the object's list method:

```
File   directory  = new File("C:/JavaPrograms/Ch12");
String filename[] = directory.list();

for (int i = 0; i < filename.length; i++) {
   System.out.println(filename[i]);
}
```

We check whether a File object is associated to a file or a directory by calling its boolean method isFile. The following code will print out I am a directory:

```
File file = new File("C:/JavaPrograms/Ch12");

if (file.isFile()) {
   System.out.println("I am a file");

} else {
   System.out.println("I am a directory");
}
```

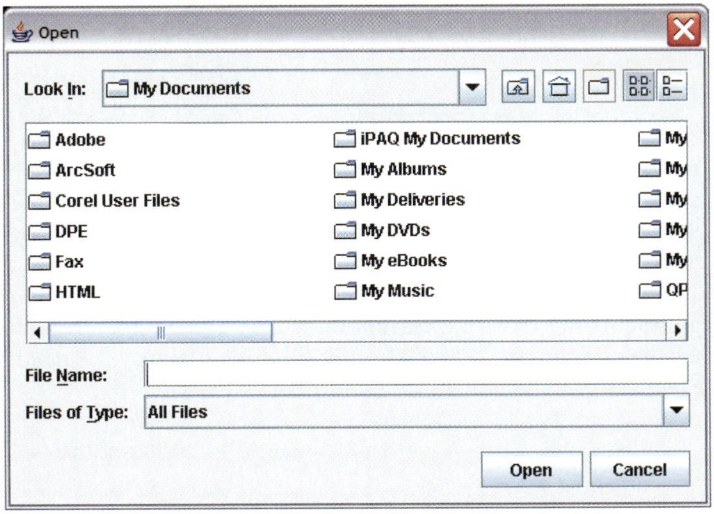

Figure 12.2 A sample **JFileChooser** object displayed with the **showOpenDialog** method. The dialog title and the okay button are labeled **Open.**

JFileChooser

We can use a javax.swing.JFileChooser object to let the user select a file. The following statement displays an open file dialog, such as the one shown in Figure 12.2 (the actual listing depends on the machine on which the program is executed):

```
JFileChooser chooser = new JFileChooser( );
...
chooser.showOpenDialog(null);
```

The null argument to the showOpenDialog indicates that there's no parent frame window, and the dialog is displayed at the center of the screen. We pass a frame window object if we want to position the file dialog at the center of the frame.

When we create an instance of JFileChooser by passing no arguments, as in this example, it will list the content of the user's home directory. For the Windows platform, the user's home directory by default is the My Documents folder. We can set the file chooser to list the contents of a desired directory when it first appears on the screen. We can do this in two ways. The first is to pass the path name of the directory as a String argument to the constructor. For example, if we want to start the listing from the C:/JavaPrograms/Ch12 directory, then we write

```
JFileChooser chooser
            = new JFileChooser("C:/JavaPrograms/Ch12");
. . .
chooser.showOpenDialog(null);
```

The second way is to use the setCurrentDirectory method as follows:

```
File startDir = new File("C:/JavaPrograms/Ch12");

chooser.setCurrentDirectory(startDir);
...
chooser.showOpenDialog(null);
```

Notice that we have to pass a File object, not a String, to the setCurrentDirectory method.

Instead of designating a fixed directory as in this example, we may wish to begin the listing from the current directory. Since the current directory is different when the program is executed from a different directory, we need a general approach. We can achieve the generality by writing

```
String current = System.getProperty("user.dir");

JFileChooser chooser
                 = new JFileChooser(current);
...
```

or equivalently

```
String current = System.getProperty("user.dir");

JFileChooser chooser
                 = new JFileChooser( );

chooser.setCurrentDirectory(new File(current));
...
```

The content of current is the path name to the current directory.

To check whether the user has clicked on the Open or Cancel button, we test the return value from the showOpenDialog method.

```
int status = chooser.showOpenDialog(null);

if (status == JFileChooser.APPROVE_OPTION) {
   System.out.println("Open is clicked");

} else { //== JFileChooser.CANCEL_OPTION
   System.out.println("Cancel is clicked");
}
```

Once we determine the Open button is clicked, we can retrieve the selected file as

```
File selectedFile;

selectedFile = chooser.getSelectedFile();
```

and the current directory of the selected file as

```
File currentDirectory;
currentDirectory = chooser.getCurrentDirectory();
```

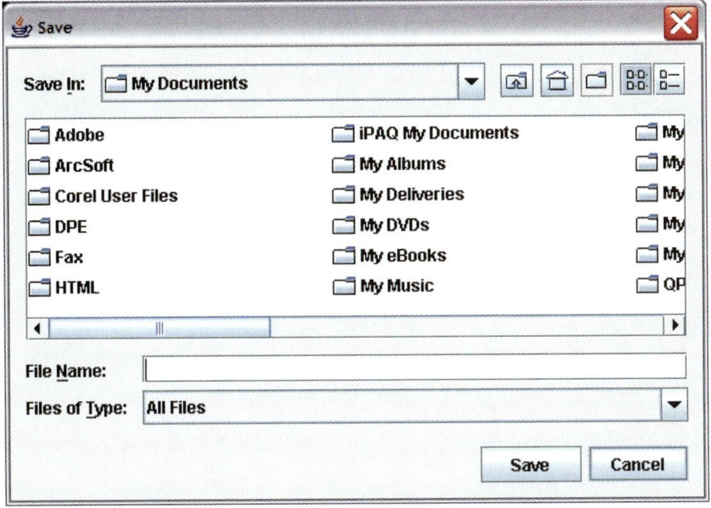

Figure 12.3 A sample **JFileChooser** object displayed with the **showCloseDialog** method. The dialog title and the okay button are labeled **Save.**

To find out the name and the full path name of a selected file, we can use the getName and getAbsolutePath methods of the File class.

```
File file = chooser.getSelectedFile();

System.out.println("Selected File: " +
                                     file.getName());
System.out.println("Full path:      " +
                                     file.getAbsolutePath());
```

To display a JFileChooser with the Save button, we write

```
chooser.showSaveDialog(null);
```

which results in a dialog shown in Figure 12.3 (the actual listing depends on the machine on which the program is executed).

The following Ch12TestJFileChooser class summarizes the methods of JFileChooser and File classes. Note this sample program does not perform actual file input or output.

```
/*
    Chapter 12 Sample Program: Illustrate the use of the
                               JFileChooser and File classes.

    File: Ch12TestJFileChooser.java
*/
```

```
import java.io.*;
import javax.swing.*;

class Ch12TestJFileChooser {
    public static void main (String[] args) {

        JFileChooser chooser;
        File         file, directory;
        int          status;

        chooser = new JFileChooser( );

        status = chooser.showOpenDialog(null);

        if (status == JFileChooser.APPROVE_OPTION) {
            file       = chooser.getSelectedFile();
            directory  = chooser.getCurrentDirectory();

            System.out.println("Directory: " +
                                directory.getName());

            System.out.println("File selected to open: " +
                                file.getName());

            System.out.println("Full path name: " +
                                file.getAbsolutePath());

        } else {
            System.out.println("Open File dialog canceled");
        }

        System.out.println("\n\n");

        status = chooser.showSaveDialog(null);

        if (status == JFileChooser.APPROVE_OPTION) {
            file       = chooser.getSelectedFile();
            directory  = chooser.getCurrentDirectory();

            System.out.println("Directory: " +
                                 directory.getName());

            System.out.println("File selected for saving data: " +
                                 file.getName());

            System.out.println("Full path name: " +
                                file.getAbsolutePath());
        } else {
            System.out.println("Save File dialog canceled");
        }
    }
}
```

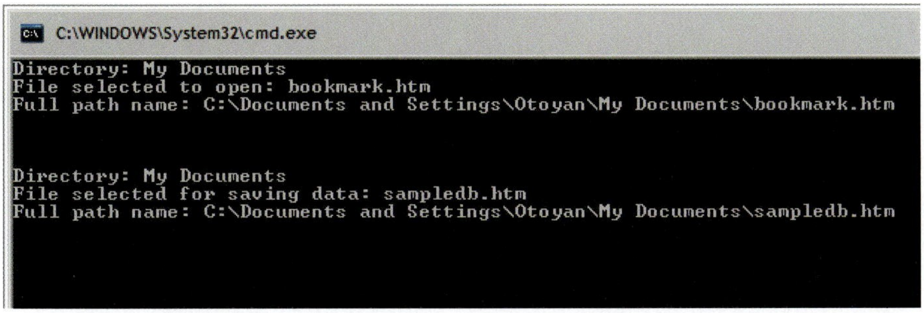

```
C:\WINDOWS\System32\cmd.exe
Directory: My Documents
File selected to open: bookmark.htm
Full path name: C:\Documents and Settings\Otoyan\My Documents\bookmark.htm


Directory: My Documents
File selected for saving data: sampledb.htm
Full path name: C:\Documents and Settings\Otoyan\My Documents\sampledb.htm
```

Figure 12.4 A sample output from running the **Ch12TestJFileChooser** program once.

Figure 12.4 shows a sample output of running the program once.

There is actually no distinction between the Open and Save dialogs created, respectively, by showOpenDialog and showCloseDialog other than the difference in the button label and the dialog title. In fact, they are really a shorthand for calling the showDialog method. Using the showDialog method, we can specify the button label and the dialog title. For example, this code will produce a JFileChooser dialog with the text Compile as its title and label for the okay button:

```
JFileChooser chooser = new JFileChooser();
chooser.showDialog(null, "Compile");
```

file filter

We can use a ***file filter*** to remove unwanted files from the list. Let's say we want to apply a filter so only the directories and the Java source files (those with the .java extension) are listed in the file chooser. To do so, we must define a subclass of the javax.swing.filechooser.FileFilter class and provide the accept and getDescription methods. The prototypes of these methods are

```
public boolean accept(File file)
public String getDescription( )
```

The accept method returns true if the parameter file is a file to be included in the list. The getDescription method returns a text that will be displayed as one of the entries for the "Files of Type:" drop-down list. Here's how the filter subclass is defined:

```
/*
    Chapter 12 Sample Program: Illustrate how to filter only
                               Java source files
                               for listing in JFileChooser

    File: JavaFilter.java
*/

import java.io.File;
import javax.swing.filechooser.*;
```

Notice that we are stating one class in the package explicitly, instead of using the more common form of **import java.io.*;** to avoid naming conflict. The **java.io** package has the interface named **FileFilter.**

```
class JavaFilter extends FileFilter {

    private static final String JAVA  = "java";
    private static final char   DOT   = '.';

    //accepts only directories and
    //files with .java extension only
    public boolean accept(File f) {

        if (f.isDirectory()) {
            return true;
        }

        if (extension(f).equalsIgnoreCase(JAVA)) {
            return true;
        } else {
            return false;
        }
    }

    //description of the filtered files
    public String getDescription( ) {
        return "Java source files (.java)";
    }

    //extracts the extension from the filename
    private String extension(File f) {

        String filename = f.getName();
        int    loc      = filename.lastIndexOf(DOT);

        if (loc > 0 && loc < filename.length() - 1) {
            //make sure the dot is not
            //at the first or the last character position
            return filename.substring(loc+1);
        } else {
            return "";
        }
    }
}
```

Data members

accept

getDescription

extension

With the filter class Java Filter in place, we can set a file chooser to list only directories and Java source files by writing

```
JFileChooser chooser = new JFileChooser( );

chooser.setFileFilter(new JavaFilter(());

int status = chooser.showOpenDialog(null);
```

1. This question is specific to the Windows platform. Suppose you want to open a file prog1.java inside the directory C:\JavaProjects\Ch11\Step4. What is the actual String value you pass in the constructor for the File class?
2. What is wrong with the following statement?

```
JFileChooser chooser
    = new JFileChooser("Run");
    chooser.showDialog(null);
```

3. Which method of the JFileChooser class do you use to get the filename of the selected file? What is returned from the method if the Cancel button is clicked?

12.2 Low-Level File I/O

stream

source

destination

Once a file is opened by properly associating a File object to it, the actual file access can commence. In this section, we will introduce basic objects for file operations. To actually read data from or write data to a file, we must create one of the Java stream objects and attach it to the file. A ***stream*** is simply a sequence of data items, usually 8 bits per item. Java has two types of streams: an input stream and an output stream. An input stream has a ***source*** from which the data items come, and an output stream has a ***destination*** to which the data items go. To read data items from a file, we attach one of the Java input stream objects to the file. Similarly, to write data items to a file, we attach one of the Java output stream objects to the file.

Java comes with a large number of stream objects for file access operations. We will cover only those that are straightforward and easy to learn for beginners. We will study two of them in this section—FileOutputStream and FileInputStream. These two objects provide low-level file access operations. In Section 12.3 we will study other stream objects.

FileOutput-Stream

Let's first study how to write data values to a file by using **FileOutputStream**. Using a FileOutputStream object, we can output only a sequence of bytes, that is, values of data type byte. In this example, we will output an array of bytes to a file named sample1.data. First we create a File object:

```
File outFile = new File("sample1.data");
```

Then we associate a new FileOutputStream object to outFile:

```
FileOutputStream outStream
                        = new FileOutputStream(outFile);
```

Now we are ready for output. Consider the following byte array:

```
byte[] byteArray = {10, 20, 30, 40, 50, 60, 70, 80};
```

We write the whole byte array at once to the file by executing

```
outStream.write(byteArray);
```

Notice that we are not dealing with the File object directly, but with outStream. It is also possible to write array elements individually, for example,

```
//output the first and fifth bytes
outStream.write(byteArray[0]);
outStream.write(byteArray[4]);
```

After the values are written to the file, we must close the stream:

```
outStream.close();
```

data caching

data buffer

If the stream object is not closed, then some data may get lost due to data caching. Because of the physical characteristics of secondary memory such as hard disks, the actual process of saving data to a file is a very time-consuming operation, whether you are saving 1 or 100 bytes. So instead of saving bytes individually, we save them in a block of, say, 500 bytes to reduce the overall time it takes to save the whole data. The operation of saving data as a block is called ***data caching***. To carry out data caching, a part of memory is reserved as a ***data buffer*** or *cache,* which is used as a temporary holding place. A typical size for a data buffer is anywhere from 1 KB to 2 KB. Data are first written to a buffer, and when the buffer becomes full, the data in the buffer are actually written to a file. If there are any remaining data in the buffer and the file is not closed, then those data will be lost. Therefore, to avoid losing any data, it is important to close the file at the end of the operations.

Things to Remember

To ensure that all data are saved to a file, close the file at the end of file access operations.

Many of the file operations, such as write and close, throw I/O exceptions, so we need to handle them. For the short sample programs, we use the propagation approach. Here's the complete program:

```
/*
    Chapter 12 Sample Program:
            A test program to save data to a file using FileOutputStream

    File: Ch12TestFileOutputStream.java
*/
import java.io.*;

class Ch12TestFileOutputStream {
   public static void main (String[] args) throws IOException {
```

Needs this clause because the file methods throw I/O exceptions.

```
        //set up file and stream
        File             outFile    = new File("sample1.data");
        FileOutputStream outStream = new FileOutputStream(outFile);

        //data to output
        byte[] byteArray = {10, 20, 30, 40, 50, 60, 70, 80};

        //write data to the stream
        outStream.write(byteArray);

        //output done, so close the stream
        outStream.close();
    }
}
```

Hints, & Tips, Pitfalls

It may seem odd at first to have both **File** and **FileStream** objects to input data from a file. Why not have just a **File** to handle everything? **File** represents a physical file that is a source of data. **Stream** objects represent the mechanism we associate to a file to perform input and output routines. **Stream** objects can also be associated to a nonfile data source such as a serial port. So separating the tasks following the STO principle resulted in more than one class to input data from a file.

Now it's true that we can make a shortcut statement such as

```
fileOutputStream outStream
     = new FileOutputStream("input.txt");
```

where we avoid the explicit creation of a **File** object. But this shortcut does not eliminate the fact that the **Stream** object is associated to a file.

FileInput-Stream

To read the data into a program, we reverse the steps in the output routine. We use the read method of **FileInputStream** to read in an array of bytes. First we create a FileInputStream object:

```
File            inFile    = new File("sample1.data");
FileInputStream inStream  = new FileInputStream(inFile);
```

Then we read the data into an array of bytes:

```
inStream.read(byteArray);
```

Before we call the read method, we must declare and create byteArray:

```
int     filesize   = (int) inFile.length();
byte[] byteArray   = new byte[filesize];
```

We use the length method of the File class to determine the size of the file, which in this case is the number of bytes in the file. We create an array of bytes whose size is the size of the file.

The following program uses FileInputStream to read in the byte array from the file sample1.data.

```
/*
   Chapter 12 Sample Program:
             A test program to read data from a file using FileInputStream

   File: Ch12TestFileInputStream.java
*/
import java.io.*;

class Ch12TestFileInputStream {
   public static void main (String[] args) throws IOException {

      //set up file and stream
      File            inFile    = new File("sample1.data");
      FileInputStream inStream  = new FileInputStream(inFile);

      //set up an array to read data in
      int fileSize = (int) inFile.length();
      byte[] byteArray = new byte[fileSize];

      //read data in and display them
      inStream.read(byteArray);
      for (int i = 0; i < fileSize; i++) {
         System.out.println(byteArray[i]);
      }

      //input done, so close the stream
      inStream.close();
   }
}
```

It is possible to output data other than bytes if we can convert (i.e., typecast) them into bytes. For example, we can output character data by typecasting them to bytes.

```
File             outFile   = new File("sample1.data");
FileOutputStream outStream = new FileOutputStream(outFile);

//data to output
byte[] byteArray = {(byte) 'J',
                    (byte) 'a',
                    (byte) 'v',
                    (byte) 'a' };
```

Typecast characters to bytes.

```
//write data to the stream
outStream.write(byteArray);

//output done, so close the stream
outStream.close();
```

To read the data back, we use the read method again. If we need to display the bytes in the original character values, we need to typecast byte to char. Without the typecasting, numerical values would be displayed. The following code illustrates the typecasting of byte to char for display.

```
File             inFile    = new File("sample1.data");
FileInputStream inStream  = new FileInputStream(inFile);

//set up an array to read data in
int    fileSize  = inFile.length();
byte[] byteArray = new byte[fileSize];

//read data in and display them
inStream.read(byteArray);

for (int i = 0; i < fileSize; i++) {

    System.out.println((char) byteArray[i]);
}

//input done, so close the stream
inStream.close();
```

Typecast bytes back to characters.

Typecasting char to byte or byte to char is simple because ASCII uses 8 bits. But what if we want to perform file I/O on numerical values such as integers and real numbers? It takes more than simple typecasting to output these numerical values to FileOutputStream and read them back from FileInputStream. An integer takes 4 bytes, so we need to break a single integer into 4 bytes and perform file I/O on this 4 bytes. Such a conversion would be too low-level and tedious. Java provides stream objects that allow us to read from or write numerical values to a file without doing any conversions ourselves. We will discuss two of them in Section 12.3.

1. What is the method you call at the end of all file I/O operations?
2. What is wrong with the following statements? Assume that outStream is a properly declared and created FileOutputStream object.

```
byte[ ]  byteArray = {(byte) 'H', (byte) 'i'};
...
outStream.print(byteArray);
...
outStream.close( );
```

12.3 High-Level File I/O

By using DataOutputStream, we can output Java primitive data type values. A DataOutputStream object will take care of the details of converting the primitive data type values to a sequence of bytes. Let's look at the complete program first. The following program writes out values of various Java primitive data types to a file. The names of the output methods (those preceded with write) should be self-explanatory.

```
/*
    Chapter 12 Sample Program:
                    A test program to save data to a file using
                    DataOutputStream for high-level I/O.

    File: Ch12TestDataOutputStream.java
*/
import java.io.*;

class Ch12TestDataOutputStream {
   public static void main (String[] args) throws IOException {

      //set up the streams
      File                  outFile       = new File("sample2.data");
      FileOutputStream      outFileStream = new FileOutputStream(outFile);
      DataOutputStream      outDataStream = new DataOutputStream
                                                (outFileStream);

      //write values of primitive data types to the stream
      outDataStream.writeInt(987654321);
      outDataStream.writeLong(11111111L);
      outDataStream.writeFloat(22222222F);
      outDataStream.writeDouble(3333333D);
      outDataStream.writeChar('A');
      outDataStream.writeBoolean(true);

      //output done, so close the stream
      outDataStream.close();
   }
}
```

Notice the sequence of statements for creating a DataOutputStream object:

```
File             outFile       = new File("sample2.data");
FileOutputStream outFileStream= new FileOutputStream(outFile);
DataOutputStream outDataStream
                          = new DataOutputStream(outFileStream);
```

```
File             outFile       = new File("sample2.data");
FileOutputStream outFileStream = new FileOutputStream(outFile);
DataOutputStream outDataStream = new DataOutputStream(outFileStream);
```

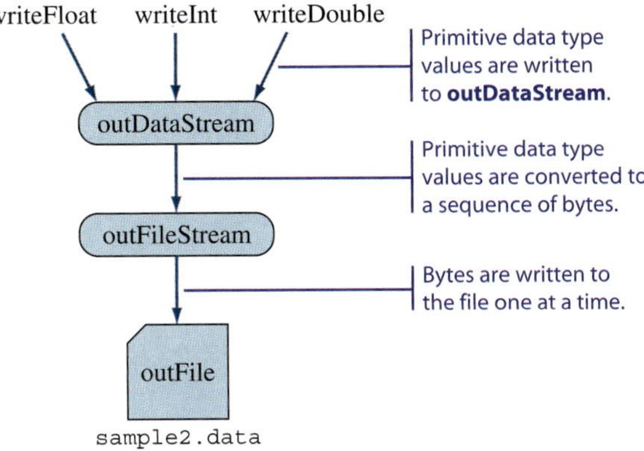

Figure 12.5 A diagram showing how the three objects **outFile, outFileStream,** and **outDataStream** are related.

DataOutput-Stream

The argument to the **DataOutputStream** constructor is a FileOutputStream object. A DataOutputStream object does not get connected to a file directly. The diagram in Figure 12.5 illustrates the relationships established among the three objects. The role of the DataOutputStream object is to provide high-level access to a file by converting a primitive data value to a sequence of bytes, which are then written to a file via a FileOutputStream object.

DataInput-Stream

To read the data back from the file, we reverse the operation. We use three objects: File, FileInputStream, and **DataInputStream**. The following program reads the data saved by the program Ch12TestDataOutputStream.

```
/*
    Chapter 12 Sample Program:
                A test program to load data from a file using
                DataInputStream for high-level I/O.

    File: Ch12TestDataInputStream.java
*/
import java.io.*;

class Ch12TestDataInputStream {
   public static void main (String[] args) throws IOException {

      //set up file and stream
      File            inFile       = new File("sample2.data");
      FileInputStream inFileStream = new FileInputStream(inFile);
      DataInputStream inDataStream = new DataInputStream(inFileStream);
```

```
        //read values back from the stream and display them
        System.out.println(inDataStream.readInt());
        System.out.println(inDataStream.readLong());
        System.out.println(inDataStream.readFloat());
        System.out.println(inDataStream.readDouble());
        System.out.println(inDataStream.readChar());
        System.out.println(inDataStream.readBoolean());

        //input done, so close the stream
        inDataStream.close();
    }
}
```

Figure 12.6 shows the relationship among the three objects. Notice that we must read the data back in the precise order. In other words, if we write data in the order of integer, float, and character, then we must read the data back in that order, as illustrated in Figure 12.7. If we don't read the data back in the correct order, the results will be unpredictable.

binary file

Both FileOutputStream and DataOutputStream objects produce a ***binary file*** in which the contents are stored in the format (called *binary format*) in which they are stored in the main memory. Instead of storing data in binary format, we can store them in ASCII format. With the ASCII format, all data are converted to string data. A file whose contents are stored in ASCII format is called a ***text file***. One major

text file

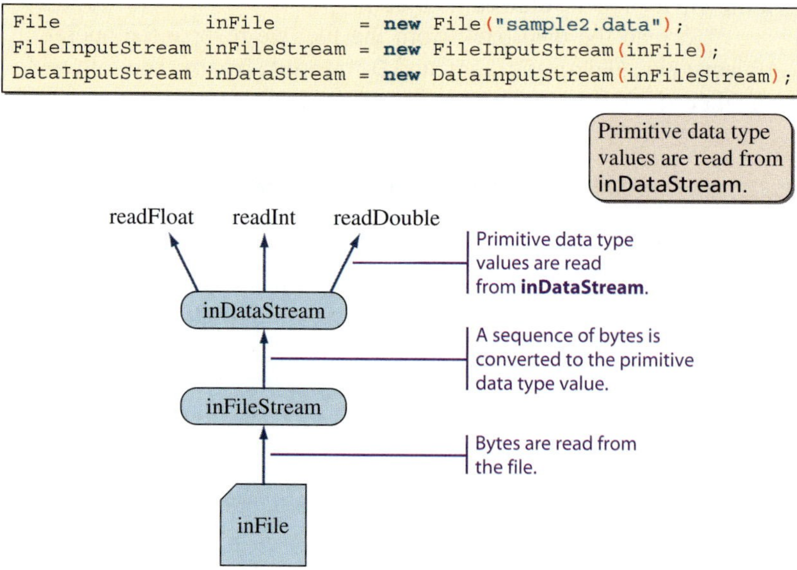
File inFile = new File("sample2.data");
FileInputStream inFileStream = new FileInputStream(inFile);
DataInputStream inDataStream = new DataInputStream(inFileStream);
Primitive data type values are read from inDataStream.
readFloat
readInt
readDouble
Primitive data type values are read from inDataStream.
inDataStream
A sequence of bytes is converted to the primitive data type value.
inFileStream
Bytes are read from the file.
inFile
sample2.data

Figure 12.6 A diagram showing how the three objects **inFile, inFileStream,** and **inDataStream** are related.

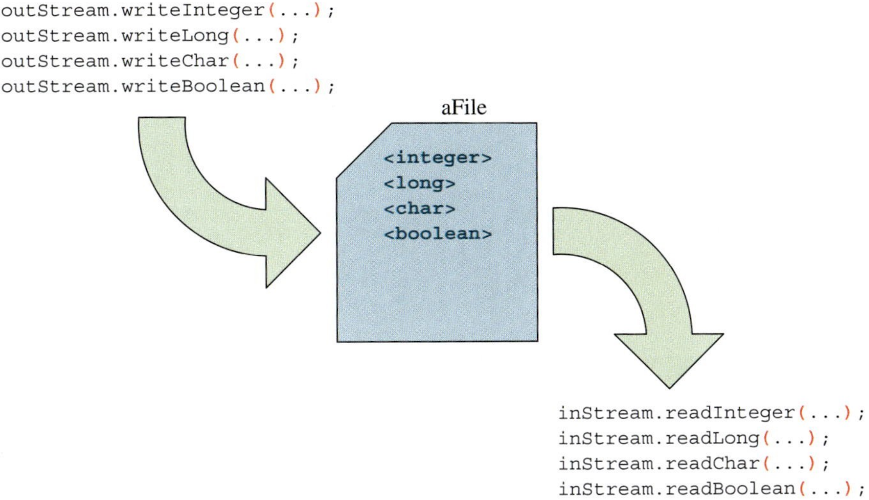
outStream.writeInteger(...);
outStream.writeLong(...);
outStream.writeChar(...);
outStream.writeBoolean(...);
aFile
<integer>
<long>
<char>
<boolean>
inStream.readInteger(...);
inStream.readLong(...);
inStream.readChar(...);
inStream.readBoolean(...);

Figure 12.7 The order of write and read operations must match to read the stored data back correctly.

benefit of a text file is that we can easily read and modify the contents of a text file by using any text editor or word processor.

PrintWriter is an object we use to generate a text file. Unlike DataOutputStream, where we have a separate write method for each individual data type, PrintWriter supports only two output methods: print and println (for print line). An argument to the methods can be any primitive data type. The methods convert the parameter to string and output this string value. The constructor of PrintWriter, similar to the one for DataOutputStream, requires an output stream as its argument. In the following program, the parameter is again an instance of FileOutputStream.

```
/*
    Chapter 12 Sample Program:
                A test program to save data to a file using
                PrintWriter for high-level I/O.

    File: Ch12TestPrintWriter.java
*/
import java.io.*;

class Ch12TestPrintWriter {
   public static void main (String[] args) throws IOException {

      //set up file and stream
      File              outFile        = new File("sample3.data");
      FileOutputStream  outFileStream  = new FileOutputStream(outFile);
      PrintWriter       outStream      = new PrintWriter(outFileStream);
```

```
        //write values of primitive data types to the stream
        outStream.println(987654321);
        outStream.println(11111111L);
        outStream.println(22222222F);
        outStream.println(33333333D);
        outStream.println('A');
        outStream.println(true);

        //output done, so close the stream
        outStream.close();
    }
}
```

We use **print** and **println** with **PrintWriter.** The **print** and **println** methods convert primitive data types to strings before writing to a file.

To read the data from a text file, we use the FileReader and BufferedReader objects. The relationship between FileReader and BufferedReader is similar to the one between FileInputStream and DataInputStream. To read data back from a text file, first we need to associate a BufferedReader object to a file. The following sequence of statements associates a BufferedReader object to a file sample3.data:

```
File           inFile     = new File("sample3.data");
FileReader     fileReader = new FileReader(inFile);
BufferedReader bufReader
                          = new BufferedReader(fileReader);
```

Then we read data, using the readLine method of BufferedReader,

```
String str = bufReader.readLine( );
```

and convert the String to a primitive data type as necessary.

Here's the program to read back from sample3.data, which was created by the program Ch12TestPrintWriter:

```
/*
    Chapter 12 Sample Program:
              A test program to load data from a file using the readLine
              method of BufferedReader for high-level String input.

    File: Ch12TestBufferedReader.java
*/
import java.io.*;

class Ch12TestBufferedReader {
    public static void main (String[] args) throws IOException {

        //set up file and stream
        File           inFile     = new File("sample3.data");
```

```
        FileReader     fileReader = new FileReader(inFile);
        BufferedReader bufReader  = new BufferedReader(fileReader);
        String str;

        //get integer
        str = bufReader.readLine();
        int i = Integer.parseInt(str);

        //get long
        str = bufReader.readLine();
        long l = Long.parseLong(str);

        //get float
        str = bufReader.readLine();
        float f = Float.parseFloat(str);

        //get double
        str = bufReader.readLine();
        double d = Double.parseDouble(str);

        //get char
        str = bufReader.readLine();
        char c = str.charAt(0);

        //get boolean
        str = bufReader.readLine();
        Boolean boolObj = new Boolean(str);
        boolean b = boolObj.booleanValue();

        System.out.println(i);
        System.out.println(l);
        System.out.println(f);
        System.out.println(d);
        System.out.println(c);
        System.out.println(b);

        //input done, so close the stream
        bufReader.close();
    }
}
```

Data are saved in ASCII format, so the conversion to the primitive data format is required.

Note: Here we only output, so there's no real need to perform data conversion. But in general we need to convert ASCII data to primitive data types to process them in the program.

Beginning with Java 5.0 (a. k. a. Java 2 SDK 1.5), we can use the Scanner class introduced in Chapter 3 to input data from a text file. Instead of associating a new Scanner object to System.in, we can associate it to a File object. For example,

```
Scanner scanner = new Scanner(
                        new File("sample3.data"));
```

will associate scanner to the file sample3.data. Once this association is made, we can use scanner methods such as nextInt, next, and others to input data from the file.

The following sample code does the same as Ch12TestBufferedReader but uses the Scanner class instead of BufferedReader. Notice that the conversion is not necessary with the Scanner class by using appropriate input methods such as nextInt and nextDouble.

```
/*
    Chapter 12 Sample Program:
                 Illustrate the use of Scanner to input text file

    File: Ch12TestScanner.java
*/

import java.util.*;
import java.io.*;

class Ch12TestScanner {

    public static void main (String args[]) throws FileNotFoundException,
                                                    IOException {

        //open the Scanner

        Scanner scanner = new Scanner(new File("sample3.data"));

        //get integer
        int i = scanner.nextInt();

        //get integer
        long l = scanner.nextLong();

        //get float
        float f = scanner.nextFloat();

        //get double
        double d = scanner.nextDouble();

        //get char
        char c = scanner.next().charAt(0);

        //get boolean
        boolean b = scanner.nextBoolean();

        System.out.println(i);
        System.out.println(l);
        System.out.println(f);
        System.out.println(d);
```

```
        System.out.println(c);
        System.out.println(b);

        //input done, so close the scanner
        scanner.close();
    }
}
```

The FileManager Class

In the Chapter 9 sample development and in Section 12.1, we used the helper class FileManager. A FileManager object provides file I/O operations for String data. To refresh our memory, here are the public methods of the class:

Public Methods of FileManager
`public String openFile(String filename) throws FileNotFoundException, IOException` Opens the text file `filename` and returns the content as a `String`.
`public String openFile( ) throws IOException` Opens the text file selected by the end user using the standard file open dialog and returns the content as a `String`.
`public String saveFile(String filename, String data) throws IOException` Saves the string `data` to `filename`.
`public String saveFile(String data) throws IOException` Saves the string `data` to a file selected by the end user using the standard file save dialog.

The class uses the BufferedReader and PrintWriter classes for text (String) output and input. Notice that all public methods throw an IOException, and only the openFile method that accepts a filename as an argument throws FileNotFoundException also. Here is the class listing:

```
/*
    Chapter 9 and Chapter 12 Helper Class

    File: FileManager.java

*/

import java.io.*;
import javax.swing.*;

class FileManager  {
```

```
private static final String EMPTY_STRING = "";
private static String lineTerminator
                            = System.getProperty("line.separator");

public FileManager( ) {
}

public String openFile( ) throws FileNotFoundException,
                           IOException {
    String filename, doc = EMPTY_STRING;

    JFileChooser chooser = new JFileChooser(
                             System.getProperty("user.dir");
    int reply = chooser.showOpenDialog(null);

    if(reply == JFileChooser.APPROVE_OPTION) {

          doc = openFile(chooser.getSelectedFile().getAbsolutePath());
    }

    return doc;
}

public String openFile(String filename)
            throws FileNotFoundException, IOException {

    String         line;
    StringBuffer   document = new StringBuffer(EMPTY_STRING);

    File           inFile     = new File(filename);
    FileReader     fileReader = new FileReader(inFile);
    BufferedReader bufReader  = new BufferedReader(fileReader);

    while (true) {
        line = bufReader.readLine();

        if (line == null) break;

        document.append(line + lineTerminator);
    }

    return document.toString();
}

public void saveFile(String data) throws IOException {
    String filename, doc = EMPTY_STRING;

    JFileChooser chooser = new JFileChooser(
                             System.getProperty("user.dir");
    int reply = chooser.showSaveDialog(null);

    if(reply == JFileChooser.APPROVE_OPTION) {

        saveFile(chooser.getSelectedFile().getAbsolutePath(),
                 data);
    }
}
```

openFile

saveFile

```
    public void saveFile(String filename, String data)
                throws IOException {

        File                outFile       = new File(filename);
        FileOutputStream    outFileStream = new FileOutputStream(outFile);
        PrintWriter         outStream     = new PrintWriter(outFileStream);

        outStream.print(data);

        outStream.close();
    }
}
```

1. Which type of files can be opened and viewed by a text editor?
2. Which class is used to save data as a text file? Which class is used to read text files?
3. Assume bufReader, a BufferedReader object, is properly declared and created. What is wrong with the following?

```
double d = bufReader.readDouble( );
```

12.4 Object I/O

We can store objects just as easily as we can store primitive data values. Older versions of Java and many other object-oriented programming languages won't allow programmers to store objects directly. In those programming languages, we must write code to store individual data members of an object separately. For example, if a Person object has data members name (String), age (int), and gender (char), then we have to store the three values individually, using the file I/O techniques explained earlier in the chapter. (*Note:* String is an object, but it can be treated much as any other primitive data types because of its immutability.) Now, if the data members of an object are all primitive data types (or a String), then storing the data members individually is a chore but not that difficult. However, if a data member is a reference to another object or to an array of objects, then storing data can become very tricky. Fortunately with Java (since version 1.1), we don't have to worry about them; we can store objects directly to a file.

ObjectOutputStream

ObjectInputStream

In this section, we will describe various approaches for storing objects. To write objects to a file, we use **ObjectOutputStream**; and to read objects from a file, we use **ObjectInputStream**. Let's see how we write Person objects to a file. First we need to modify the definition of the Person class in order for ObjectOutputStream and

ObjectInputStream to perform object I/O. We modify the definition by adding the phrase implements Serializable to it.

```
import java.io.*;
class Person implements Serializable {
   //the rest is the same
}
```

Serializable is defined in **java.io.**

Whenever we want to store an object to a file, we modify its class definition by adding the phrase implements Serializable to it. Unlike other interfaces, such as ActionListener, there are no methods for us to define in the implementation class. All we have to do is to add the phrase.

Things to Remember

If we want to perform an object I/O, then the class definition must include the phrase **implements Serializable.**

To save objects to a file, we first create an ObjectOutputStream object:

```
File               outFile
                          = new File("objects.dat");
FileOutputStream   outFileStream
                          = new FileOutputStream(outFile);
ObjectOutputStream outObjectStream
                          = new ObjectOutputStream
                                          (outFileStream);
```

To save a Person object, we write

```
Person person = new Person("Mr. Espresso", 20, 'M');

outObjectStream.writeObject(person);
```

The following sample program saves 10 Person objects to a file:

```
/*
    Chapter 12 Sample Program: Illustrate the use of ObjectOutputStream

    File: Ch12TestObjectOutputStream.java
*/

import java.io.*;
```

```
class Ch12TestObjectOutputStream {
   public static void main (String[] args) throws IOException {

        //set up the streams
        File                 outFile    = new File("objects.dat");
        FileOutputStream     outFileStream
                                        = new FileOutputStream(outFile);
        ObjectOutputStream outObjectStream
                                        = new ObjectOutputStream(outFileStream);

        //write serializable Person objects one at a time
        Person person;
        for (int i = 0; i < 10; i++) {
            person = new Person("Mr. Espresso" + i, 20+i, 'M');

            outObjectStream.writeObject(person);
        }

        //output done, so close the stream
        outObjectStream.close();
   }
}
```

It is possible to save different types of objects to a single file. Assuming the Account and Bank classes are defined properly, we can save both types of objects to a single file:

```
Account  account1, account2;
Bank     bank1, bank2;

account1 = new Account(); //create objects
account2 = new Account();
bank1    = new Bank();
bank2    = new Bank();

outObjectStream.writeObject(account1);
outObjectStream.writeObject(account2);
outObjectStream.writeObject(bank1    );
outObjectStream.writeObject(bank2    );
```

We can even mix objects and primitive data type values, for example,

```
outObjectStream.writeInt    (15       );
outObjectStream.writeObject(account1);
outObjectStream.writeChar   ('X'      );
```

To read objects from a file, we use FileInputStream and ObjectInputStream. We use the method readObject to read an object. Since we can store any types of objects to a single file, we need to typecast the object read from the file. Here's an example of reading a Person object we saved in the file objects.data.

```
File               inFile
                      = new File("objects.dat");

FileInputStream    inFileStream
                      = new FileInputStream(inFile);

ObjectInputStream inObjectStream
                      = new ObjectInputStream(inFileStream);

Person person = (Person) inObjectStream.readObject();
```

Need to typecast to the object type we are reading

ClassNot-Found-Exception

Because there is a possibility of wrong typecasting, the readObject method can throw a **ClassNotFoundException** in addition to an IOException. You can catch or propagate either or both exceptions. If you propagate both exceptions, then the declaration of a method that contains the call to readObject will look like this:

```
public void myMethod( )
              throws IOException, ClassNotFoundException {
   ...
}
```

The following sample program reads the Person objects from the objects.dat file:

```
/*
    Chapter 12 Sample Program: Illustrate the use of ObjectInputStream

    File: Ch12TestObjectInputStream.java
*/

import java.io.*;

class Ch12TestObjectInputStream {
    public static void main (String[] args) throws ClassNotFoundException,
                                                   IOException {

        //set up file and stream
        File              inFile    = new File("objects.dat");

        FileInputStream   inFileStream
                                    = new FileInputStream(inFile);

        ObjectInputStream inObjectStream
                                    = new ObjectInputStream(inFileStream);
```

```
        //read the Person objects from a file
        Person person;
        for (int i = 0; i < 10; i++) {
            person = (Person) inObjectStream.readObject();

            System.out.println(person.getName() + "      " +
                               person.getAge()  + "      " +
                               person.getGender());
        }

        //input done, so close the stream
        inObjectStream.close();
    }
}
```

If a file contains objects from different classes, we must read them in the correct order and apply the matching typecasting. For example, if the file contains two Account and two Bank objects, then we must read them in the correct order:

```
account1 = (Account) inObjectStream.readObject();
account2 = (Account) inObjectStream.readObject();
bank1    = (Bank)    inObjectStream.readObject();
bank2    = (Bank)    inObjectStream.readObject();
```

Now, consider the following array of Person objects where N represents some integer value:

```
Person[] people = new Person[N];
```

Assuming that all N Person objects are in the array, we can store them to file as

```
//save the size of an array first
outObjectStream.writeInt(people.length);

//save Person objects next
for (int i = 0; i < people.length; i++) {
   outObjectStream.writeObject(people[i]);
}
```

We store the size of an array at the beginning of the file, so we know exactly how many Person objects to read back:

```
int N = inObjectStream.readInt();

for (int i = 0; i < N; i++) {
   people[i] = (Person) inObjectStream.readObject();
}
```

We can actually store the whole array with a single writeObject method, instead of storing individual elements one at a time, that is, calling the writeObject method for each element. The whole **people** array can be stored with a single statement as

```
outObjectStream.writeObject(people);
```

and the whole array is read back with a single statement as

```
people = (Person[]) inObjectStream.readObject( );
```

Notice how the typecasting is done. We are reading an array of **Person** objects, so the typecasting is (**Person[ ]**). This approach will work with any data structure object such as a list or map.

The Dorm class

In the Chapter 8 sample development, we used the helper class **Dorm** to manage a list of **Resident** objects. A **Dorm** object is capable of saving a **Resident** list to a file and reading the list from a file. The class uses object I/O discussed in this section to perform these tasks. A list of **Resident** objects is maintained by using a **HashMap**. Instead of saving **Resident** objects individually, the whole map is saved with a single **writeObject** method and is read by a single **readObject** method. (The map data structure was explained in Chapter 10.) Here's the complete listing:

```
/*
    Chapter 8 Sample Development Helper Class

    File: Dorm.java
*/

import java.io.*;
import java.util.*;

public class Dorm {

    private Map<String,Resident> residentTable;

    public Dorm( ) {                                            // Constructors
        residentTable = new HashMap<String,Resident>();
    }

    public Dorm(String filename)
                    throws FileNotFoundException,
                           IOException {

        openFile(filename);
    }

    public void add(Resident resident)                          // add
                        throws IllegalArgumentException{

        if (residentTable.containsKey(resident.getName())) {
            throw new IllegalArgumentException(
                "Resident with the same name already exists");
```

```
        } else {
            residentTable.put(resident.getName(), resident);
        }
    }

    public void delete(String name) {

        residentTable.remove(name);
    }

    public Resident getResident(String name) {

        return residentTable.get(name);
    }

    public String getResidentList( ) {
        StringBuffer result = new StringBuffer("");

        String tab = "\t";
        String lineSeparator = System.getProperty("line.separator");

        for (Resident res: residentTable.values()) {
            result.append(res.getName()      + tab +
                          res.getRoom()      + tab +
                          res.getPassword()  + tab +
                          lineSeparator);
        }

        return result.toString();
    }

    public void openFile(String filename)
                throws FileNotFoundException,
                       IOException {

        File inFile = new File(filename);
        FileInputStream inFileStream =
                    new FileInputStream(inFile);
        ObjectInputStream inObjectStream =
                    new ObjectInputStream(inFileStream);

        try {
            residentTable = (Map<String,Resident>)
                                inObjectStream.readObject();
        } catch (ClassNotFoundException e) {
            throw new IOException(
                        "Unrecognized data in the designated file");
        }

        inObjectStream.close();
    }

    public void saveFile(String filename)
                throws IOException {
```

delete

getResident

getResidentList

openFile

saveFile

```
        File outFile = new File(filename);
        FileOutputStream outFileStream =
                new FileOutputStream(outFile);
        ObjectOutputStream outObjectStream =
                new ObjectOutputStream(outFileStream);

        outObjectStream.writeObject(residentTable);

        outObjectStream.close();
    }
}
```

1. When do you have to include the clause implements Serializable to a class definition?
2. You cannot save the whole array at once—you must save the array elements individually, true or false?

12.5 Sample Development

Saving an AddressBook Object

As an illustration of object I/O, we will write a class that handles the storage of an **AddressBook** object. The class will provide methods to write an **AddressBook** object to a file and to read the object back from the file.

Problem Statement

Write a class that manages file I/O of an **AddressBook** *object.*

Overall Plan

Before we begin to design the class, we must modify the definition of the class that implements the **AddressBook** interface by adding the phrase **implements Serializable,** such as

```
import java.io.*;
class AddressBookVer1 implements AddressBook,
                                 Serializable {
   //same as before
}
```

In the following discussion, we will use the implementation class **AddressBookVers1.** This modification allows us to store instances of the AddressBookVer1 class. We will use the expression "an **AddressBook** object" to refer to an instance of any class that implements the **AddressBook** interface.

Since the class handles the file I/O operations, we will call the class **AddressBookStorage.** Following the STO (single-task object) principle, this class will be responsible solely for file I/O of an **AddressBook** object. The class will not perform, for instance, any operations that deal with a user interface.

What kinds of core operations should this class support? Since the class handles the file I/O, the class should support two public methods to write and read an **AddressBook** object. Let's call the methods **write** and **read.** The argument will be an **AddressBook** object we want to write or read. If **filer** is an **AddressBookStorage** object, then the calls should be something like

```
filer.write(addressBook);
```

and

```
addressBook = filer.read( );
```

For an **AddressBookStorage** to actually store an **AddressBook** object, it must know the file to which an address book is written or from which it is read. How should we let the programmer specify this file? One possibility is to let the programmer pass the filename to a constructor, such as

```
AddressBookStorage filer
          = new AddressBookStorage("book.data");
```

Another possibility is to define a method to set the file, say, **setFile,** which is called as

```
filer.setFile("book.data");
```

Instead of choosing one over the other, we will support both. If we don't provide the **setFile** method, **filer** can input and output to a single file only. By using the **setFile** method, the programmer can change the file if she or he needs to. As for the constructor, we do not want to define a constructor with no argument because we do not want the programmer to create an **AddressBookStorage** object without specifying a filename. Yes, he or she can call the **setFile** method later, but as the **AddressBookStorage** class designer, we cannot ensure the programmer will call the **setFile** method. If the programmer doesn't call the method, then the subsequent calls to the **write** or **read** method will fail. Some may consider assigning a default filename in a no-argument constructor. But what will be the default filename? No matter which filename we choose, there's a possibility that a file with this filename already exists, which will cause the file to be erased. To make our class reliable, we will not provide a no-argument constructor.

We will implement the class in the following order:

development steps

1. Implement the constructor and the **setFile** method.
2. Implement the **write** method.
3. Implement the **read** method.
4. Finalize the class.

12.5 Sample Development—*continued*

This order of development follows a natural sequence. We begin with the constructor as usual. Since the constructor and the **setFile** method carry out similar operations, we will implement them together. We will identify necessary data members in this step. The second step is to implement the file output routine, because without being able to write an **AddressBook** object, we won't be able to test the file input routine. For the third step, we will implement the file input routine.

Step 1 Development: Constructor and setFile

step 1 design

In step 1, we will identify the data members and define a constructor to initialize them. We will also implement the **setFile** method, which should be very similar to the constructor.

We need **File, FileInputStream, FileOutputStream, ObjectInputStream,** and **ObjectOutputStream** objects to do object I/O. Should we define a data member for each type of object? This is certainly a possibility, but we should not use any unnecessary data members. We need **ObjectInputStream** and **ObjectOutputStream** objects only at the time the actual read and write operations take place. We can create these objects in the **read** and **write** methods, only when they are needed. Had we used data members for all those objects, we would need to create and assign objects every time the **setFile** method was called. But calling the **setFile** method does not necessarily mean the actual file I/O will take place. Consider the case where the user changes the filename before actually saving an address book to a file. This will result in calling the **setFile** method twice before doing the actual file I/O. To avoid this type of unnecessary repetition, we will use one data member only, a **String** variable **filename** to keep the filename. The **setFile** method simply assigns the parameter to this variable. The constructor can do the same by calling this **setFile** method.

step 1 code

At this point, we have only one data member:

```
//---------------------------
//  Data Members
//---------------------------

private  String  filename; //name of the file to store
                           //an AddressBook object
```

The **setFile** method assigns the parameter to the data member. The class is defined as follows:

```
/*
   Chapter 12 Sample Program: Address Book Storage

   File: AddressBookStorage.java
*/
class AddressBookStorage {
```

```
    private String filename;

    public AddressBookStorage (String filename) {
        setFile(filename);
    }

    public void setFile(String filename) {
        this.filename = filename;
        System.out.println("Inside setFile. Filename is " + filename);
                                                                 //TEMP
    }
}
```

step 1 test

To test this class, we have included a temporary output statement inside the **setFile** method. We will write a test program to verify that we can create an **AddressBookStorage** object and use the **setFile** method correctly:

```
/*
    Chapter 12 Sample Program: Driver class to test
                               the skeleton AddressBookStorage

    File: TestAddressBookStorage.java (Step 1)
*/

class TestAddressBookStorage {

    public static void main (String[] args) {

        AddressBookStorage fileManager;

        fileManager = new AddressBookStorage("one.data");
        fileManager.setFile("two.data");
        fileManager.setFile("three.data");
    }
}
```

Step 2 Development: Implement the write Method

step 2 design

In the second development step, we will implement the **write** method. From the data member **filename,** we will create an **ObjectOutputStream** object and write the parameter **AddressBook** object to it. A sequence of method calls to create an **ObjectOutputStream** object can throw an **IOException,** so we must either propagate it or handle it.

12.5 Sample Development—*continued*

Following the STO principle, the method will propagate the thrown exception. The responsibility of an **AddressBookStorage** object is to take care of file I/O for others. When there's an exception, the object will inform the caller about the exception and let the caller decide what to do about it.

step 2 code

Here's the step 2 code with the **write** method:

```
/*
    Chapter 12 Sample Program: The class that provides the
                               file I/O for AddressBook

    File: AddressBookStorage.java
*/

import java.io.*;

class AddressBookStorage {

   ...

   public void write(AddressBook book) throws IOException {
      //first create an ObjectOutputStream
      File outFile = new File(filename);
      FileOutputStream outFileStream =
               new FileOutputStream(outFile);
      ObjectOutputStream outObjectStream =
               new ObjectOutputStream(outFileStream);

      //save the data to it
      outObjectStream.writeObject(book);

      //and close it
      outObjectStream.close();
   }
}
```

step 2 test

We will write a test program to verify that the data are saved to a file. Since we do not have a method to read the file contents yet, we can only verify at this point that the file is created and that this file has something in it. To do so, we run the following step 2 test program first. Then we use whatever tool is available (e.g., Windows Explorer, DOS command **dir,** UNIX command **ls,** etc.) and check that the specified file exists and that the file size is greater than zero.

The step 2 test program is as follows (**TestAddressBookWrite** is now an instantiable main class):

```
/*
    Chapter 12 Sample Program: Test the write method

    File: TestAddressBookWrite.java
*/

import java.io.*;

class TestAddressBookWrite {

    AddressBook          myBook;
    AddressBookStorage   fileManager;

   public static void main(String[] args) throws IOException {
      TestAddressBookWrite tester = new TestAddressBookWrite(15);

      tester.write("book.data");
   }

    public TestAddressBookWrite(int N) {
        myBook = new AddressBookVer1(N);

        for (int i = 0; i < N; i++) {
           Person person = new Person("Ms. X" + i, 10, 'F');
           myBook.add(person);
        }
    }

    public void write(String filename) {
         fileManager = new AddressBookStorage(filename);

         try {
            fileManager.write(myBook);
         }
         catch (IOException e) {
            System.out.println("Error: IOException is thrown.");
         }
    }
}
```

We run the program several times with different sizes for the address book and verify that the resulting files have different sizes. Notice that we can verify only that the file is created to store an **AddressBook** object. We cannot verify that the object is saved properly until we are able to read the data back, which we will do in the next step.

12.5 Sample Development—*continued*

Step 3 Development: Implement the read Method

step 3 design

In the third development step, we will implement the **read** method. The method reads the **AddressBook** object saved in the file and returns this object to the caller. As with the **write** method, if there's an exception, this method will propagate it back to the caller and let the caller decide what to do to the thrown exception.

step 3 code

Here's the step 3 code with the **read** method:

```
/*
    Chapter 12 Sample Program: The class that provides the
                               file I/O for AddressBook

    File: AddressBookStorage.java
*/

import java.io.*;

class AddressBookStorage {
    ...

    public AddressBook read() throws IOException {
        AddressBook book;

        //first create an ObjectInputStream
        File inFile = new File(filename);
        FileInputStream inFileStream =
                 new FileInputStream(inFile);
        ObjectInputStream inObjectStream =
                 new ObjectInputStream(inFileStream);

        try {
           //read the data from it
           book = (AddressBook) inObjectStream.readObject();
        }
        catch (ClassNotFoundException e) {
           book = null;
           System.out.println("Error: AddressBook class not found");
        }

        //and close it
        inObjectStream.close();

        //and return the object
        return book;
    }
    ...
}
```

step 3 test

We will write a test program to verify that the data can be read back correctly from a file. To test the read operation, the file to read the data from must already exist. Instead of copying the data file created in step 2 to the step 3 folder, we will make this test program to save the data first by using the **TestAddressBookWrite** class. The step 3 test program is as follows:

```
/*
   Chapter 12 Sample Program: Test the read (and write) method

   File: TestAddressBookRead.java
*/

import java.io.*;

class TestAddressBookRead {
    AddressBook         myBook;
    AddressBookStorage  fileManager;

    public static void main(String[] args) throws IOException {
        TestAddressBookWrite writer = new TestAddressBookWrite(15);
        TestAddressBookRead  reader = new TestAddressBookRead( );

        writer.write("book.data");
        reader.read("book.data");

        reader.search("Ms. X5");
    }

    public void search(String name) {
        Person person;

        person = myBook.search(name);

        if (person != null) {
           System.out.print(person.getName() + "    ");
           System.out.print(person.getAge()  + "    ");
           System.out.println(person.getGender() + "\n");
        }

        else {
           System.out.println("Error: object not found");
        }
    }

    public void read(String filename) {
        fileManager = new AddressBookStorage(filename);

        try {
           myBook = fileManager.read();
        }
```

12.5 Sample Development—*continued*

```
            catch (IOException e) {
                System.out.println("Error: IOException is thrown.");
            }
        }
    }
```

We run the program several times, changing the method body of **printout** to access different **Person** objects in the address book as necessary, and we verify that we can read the **Person** object in the file correctly. If you did Exercise 16 on page 615, then use the **getFirstPerson** and **getNextPerson** methods to access all **Person** objects in the address book.

Step 4 Development: Finalize

program review

final test

We finalize the program in the last step. We perform a critical review for finding any inconsistency or error in the methods, incomplete methods, places to add more comments, and so forth. And, as always, we will carry out the final test. As the result of the critical review and final testing, we may identify and wish to implement any additional features.

Summary

- A File object represents a file or a directory.
- An instance of the JFileChooser class is a file dialog that lets the user select a file to read data from or save data to.
- Various input and output stream classes are defined in the java.io package.
- Low-level file input and output read and write data 1 byte at a time.
- FileInputStream and FileOutputStream classes are used for low-level file I/O.
- High-level file input and output read and write data of primitive data type.
- DataInputStream and DataOutputStream classes are used for high-level file I/O.
- With text I/O, data are read and saved as strings.
- PrinterWriter and BufferedReader classes are used for text I/O.
- The Scanner class can be used to input data from a text file.
- With object I/O, data are read and saved as objects.
- ObjectInputStream and ObjectOutputStream are used for object I/O.
- To be able to save objects to a file, the class they belong to must implement the Serializable interface.

- The standard classes described or used in this chapter are

File	FileReader
JFileChooser	BufferedReader
FileOutputStream	Scanner
FileInputStream	Serializable
DataOutputStream	ObjectOutputStream
DataInputStream	ObjectInputStream
PrintWriter	

Key Concepts

file
directory
file dialog
streams
binary files
text files
low-level I/O (bytes)
high-level I/O (primitive data types)
text I/O (strings)
object I/O (objects)
Serializable interface

Exercises

1. What will happen if you forget to close a file?
2. What is the difference between binary files and text files?
3. Using the try–catch block, write code that opens a file default.dat when an attempt to open a user-designated file raises an exception.
4. Using a File object, write code to display files in a user-specified directory.
5. Write code to store and read the contents of the payScaleTable two-dimensional array from Section 10.5 in the following two file formats:
   - A file of double values
   - A file of two-dimensional array
6. Write an application that reads a text file and converts its content to an Eggy-Peggy text (see Exercise 20 of Chapter 8). Save the converted text to another text file. Use JFileChooser to let the user specify the input and output files. Create the input file by using a text editor.
7. Write an application that randomly generates N integers and stores them in a binary file integers.dat. The value for N is input by the user. Open the file with a text editor and see what the contents of a binary file look like.
8. Write an application that reads the data from the file integers.dat generated in Exercise 7. After the data are read, display the smallest, the largest, and the average.
9. Repeat Exercise 7, but this time, store the numbers in a text file integers.txt. Open this file with a text editor and verify that you can read the contents.

10. Repeat Exercise 8 with the text file integers.txt generated in Exercise 9.
11. Extend the AddressBookStorage class by adding import and export capabilities. Add a method exportFile that stores the contents of AddressBook to a text file. Add a second method importFile that reads the text file back and constructs an AddressBook. This type of import/export feature is a convenient means to move data from one application to another.
12. Extend the encryption application of Exercise 25 of Chapter 9 so that the original text is read from a user-specified text file and the encrypted text is stored to another user-specified text file.
13. Extend the watermelon projectile computation program of Exercise 30 on page 362 so the output is saved to a file. Which file format would you use for the program, a binary file or a text file? Or would you consider using an array to keep the (x, y) coordinates and save this array by using an object I/O?
14. Write a program that inputs a document from a text file and saves the modified version to another text file. Modify the original document by replacing all occurrences of the word designated by the user with the text <BLACKED OUT>. Use JFileChooser to select the input and output text file and Scanner to input the word to replace from the user. For the text replacement operation, consider using the pattern matching techniques discussed in Chapter 9.

Development Exercises

For Exercises 15 through 19, use the incremental development methodology to implement the program. For each exercise, identify the program tasks, create a design document with class descriptions, and draw the program diagram. Map out the development steps at the start. Present any design alternatives and justify your selection. Be sure to perform adequate testing at the end of each development step.

15. Write a currency converter application. Allow the user to specify the from and to currencies and the amount to exchange. Use the interface of your choice to input these three values. When the application starts, read the exchange rates from a text file rate.txt. Use a text editor to create this text file. By using a text file, you can easily update the exchange rates. The format for the text file is

```
<name of currency> <units per dollar>
```

For example, the following shows how much $1 is worth in five foreign currencies:

```
French franc                 5.95
Indonesian rupiah        12900.0
Japanese yen               123.91
Mexican peso                 9.18
Papua New Guinea kina        2.381
```

You can get the exchange rates from various websites, one of which is http://www.oanda.com.

16. Extend any application you have written before by adding a quote-of-the-day dialog. When the user starts the application, a quote of the day is displayed. Save the quotes in a text file. Use a random number generator to select the quote to display. Notice the quotes can be about any information (many commercial applications start with a dialog that shows tips on using the software).

17. In Exercise 23 of Chapter 5 you wrote a drive-through ordering system for MyJava Lo-Carb Gourmet Sandwich (the company has since changed its name to reflect the current trend in the food industry). You are hired again as a freelance computer consultant to make extensions to the program.

Instead of having a fixed number of menu categories and a fixed number of menu items per category, you will input this information from a text file. The data in the input file have the following format:

#menu category

menu item $price
menu item $price
...

#menu category

menu item $price

Each menu category is preceded by the pound symbol (#). A list of menu items that belong to this menu category follows it. Each menu item includes its name and price. The price is preceded by the dollar sign. Here's a sample input file:

#Entree

Tofu Burger $3.99
Chili Burger $2.99
Chef Salad $6.99

#Drink

Oolong Tea $0.79
Latte $3.29
House Wine $4.99
Chai Latte $2.50

#Side

Freedom Fries $0.99

#Appetizer

Onion Bloom $4.05
Calamari $3.50

You may assume that that input file contains at least one menu category and each menu category has at least one menu item. Also, you may assume that all input lines conform to the given format; that is, there will be no invalid input lines. Finally, there will be at most 20 menu categories and 25 menu items per menu category.

After the input file data are read into a program, the operation mode begins, where you continually process the customer orders. For each item on the menu, keep track of the sales. At the closing time, the store manager keys in a special code to shut down the program. Before stopping the program, output the sales figure in a format similar to the following:

```
Item                 Sales Count          Total
Tofu Burger              25             $  87.25
Cajun Chicken            30             $ 137.70
   ...

Today's Total Sales:  $ 2761.20
```

Place enough space between columns so the output is easy to read. You are not required to align the decimal points of the dollar figures. Output the sales figure to the standard output. Save the sales figure to a text file.

18. Write an application that removes extra spaces from a text file. In the days of the typewriter, it was common practice to leave two spaces after periods. We shouldn't be doing that anymore with the computer, but many people still do. Read an original text file and output an edited version to another text file. The edited version should replace two or more consecutive spaces with one space.

19. Write a mail merge application. You use two files for this program. The first is a text file that contains a template letter in the following style:

```
Dear <<N>>,

Because you are <<A>> years old and <<G>>, we have a
free gift for you. You have absolutely nothing to buy;
just pay the shipping and handling charge of $9.99. To
claim your gift, call us immediately.

Thank you,
Office of Claims Department
```

The tags <<N>>, <<A>>, and <<G>> are placeholders for the person's name, age, and gender. The second file contains the name, age, and gender information of people to whom you want to send a letter. Use whatever format you wish for the second file. Read two files and print out the letter with the placeholders replaced by the actual values from the second file. Run the program multiple times, each time using a different template file. For this program, output the personalized letter to a customized frame. Add menus to this frame so the user can save personalized letters to files (one personalized letter to a file).

13 Inheritance and Polymorphism

Objectives

After you have read and studied this chapter, you should be able to

- Write programs that are easily extensible and modifiable by applying polymorphism in program design.
- Define reusable classes based on inheritance and abstract classes and abstract methods.
- Differentiate the abstract classes and Java interface.
- Define methods, using the **protected** modifier.
- Parse strings, using a **StringTokenizer** object.

Introduction

In this chapter, we will describe two important and powerful features in object-oriented programming—inheritance and polymorphism. The inheritance feature of object-oriented programming was introduced in Chapter 1. We will provide a more detailed explanation and examples of inheritance in this chapter.

polymorphism

The second major topic we cover in this chapter is ***polymorphism***, another indispensable feature in object-oriented programming, which allows programmers to send the same message to objects from different classes. Consider the statement

```
account.computeMonthlyFee();
```

where account could be either a SavingsAccount or a CheckingAccount object. If account is a SavingsAccount object, then the method computeMonthlyFee defined for the SavingsAccount class is executed. Likewise, if account is a CheckingAccount object, then the method computeMonthlyFee defined for the CheckingAccount class is executed. Sending the same message therefore could result in executing different methods. The message computeMonthlyFee is called a ***polymorphic message*** because depending on the receiver object, different methods are executed. Polymorphism helps us write code that is easy to modify and extend. We will explain polymorphism in this chapter.

polymorphic message

13.1 A Simple Example

Before we get into details, we start with a simple example of inheritance and polymorphism to give a taste of what's coming. Let's begin with a class that models a bank account. We will purposely keep the class very simplistic (e.g., we're not including any constructor) to focus on inheritance mechanism. Here's the definition:

```
class Pet {
    private String name;

    public String getName( ) {
        return name;
    }

    public void setName(String petName) {
        name = petName;
    }

    public String speak( ) {
        return "I'm your cuddly little pet.";
    }
}
```

And here's a sample code that uses the class:

```
Pet myPet = new Pet( );
System.out.println(myPet.speak());
```

There are many different types of pets, so we really can't expect one class to be capable of modeling them all. We all know how different dogs, cats, and reptiles are, for example. Let's define the individual Cat and Dog classes to model them a little more precisely than the generic Pet class. Now, instead of defining the two new classes independently, we will define them based on the Pet class. Although they are different, they share common traits of being a pet, so it makes sense to derive the two classes from the Pet class. This is inheritance. We'll make the Dog and Cat classes inherit the data members and methods of the Pet class.

Let's see how we might define the Cat class by using inheritance:

This indicates **Cat** is a subclass of **Pet**

```
class Cat extends Pet {

    public String speak( ) {
        return "Don't give me orders.\n" +
               "I speak only when I want to.";
    }
}
```

subclass
superclass

We call the Cat class the ***subclass*** or *derived* class and the Pet class the ***superclass*** or *base* class. We use the reserved word extends to define a subclass. Data members and methods of a superclass are inherited by its subclasses. So, for example, the following code is valid:

```
Cat myCat = new Cat( );
myCat.setName("Cha Cha");

System.out.println("Hi, my name is " + myCat.getName( ));
```

overrides

In the Cat class, we see that the body of the speak method is different. We say the Cat class ***overrides*** the speak method. For example, the code

```
Cat myCat = new Cat( );
myCat.setName("Puff Puff");

System.out.println(myCat.getName( ) + " says: ");
System.out.println(myCat.speak( ));
```

will result in

```
Puff Puff says:
Don't give me orders. I speak only when I want to.
```

We can also define additional methods and data members to a subclass. The following Dog class defines an additional method named fetch:

```
class Dog extends Pet {

    public String fetch( ) {
        return "Yes, master. Fetch I will.";
    }
}
```

In addition to using all the inherited methods, we can call the fetch method if it is a dog:

```
Dog myDog = new Dog( );
myDog.setName("Fifi");

System.out.println(myCat.getName( ) + " says: ");
System.out.println(myDog.speak( ));
System.out.println(myDog.fetch( ));
```

```
Fifi says:
I'my your cuddly little pet.
Yes, master. Fetch I will.
```

Now, consider the following code:

```
Pet petOne = new Dog( );
Pet petTwo = new Cat( );
```

Will it work? The answer is yes. When a variable (such as petOne) is declared to be of class S (such as Pet), the variable can reference an instance of S or any of its subclasses (such as Dog and Cat). The inverse is not valid, for example:

```
Dog myDog = new Pet( );  ←— INVALID
```

The fact that the same variable can be referring to an instance of a different class results in polymorphism. The following two output statements will produce different results, depending on whether p is a Dog or a Cat:

```
Pet p;

p = new Dog( );
System.out.println(p.speak( ));

p = new Cat( );
System.out.println(p.speak( ));
```

polymorphic method

The speak method is called a ***polymorphic method***.

If a variable is declared of type S and is referring to an instance of a subclass of S, then we must typecast the variable to the subclass when calling noninherited methods of the subclass. For example, the fetch method is defined in the Dog class only. So code such as

```
Pet p;

p = new Dog( );
System.out.println(p.fetch( ));  ←— INVALID
```

is invalid. We must typecast p to Dog, as in

```
Pet p;

p = new Dog( );
System.out.println( ((Dog)p).fetch( ) );
```

Whenever we need to call a method unique to a subclass, we must typecast the variable to the subclass if the variable's declared type is the superclass.

To use inheritance and polymorphism effectively in our programs, we need to master many rules associated with them. We will present these rules in the remainder of the chapter.

1. Define the Reptile class as a subclass of the Pet class. The speak method returns an empty string.
2. Which one of the following statements is valid?

```
Pet p = new Cat();

Cat c = new Pet();
```

3. Is the following code valid?

```
Pet p = new Dog();
System.out.println(p.fetch( ));
```

13.2 Defining Classes with Inheritance

Suppose we want to maintain a class roster for a class whose enrolled students include both undergraduate and graduate students. For each student, we record her or his name, three test scores, and the final course grade. The final course grade, either pass or no pass, is determined by the following formula:

Type of Student	Grading Scheme
Undergraduate	Pass if (test1 + test2 + test3)/3 >= 70
Graduate	Pass if (test1 + test2 + test3)/3 >= 80

What kind of objects should we use to model undergraduate and graduate students? There are basically two broad ways to design the classes to model them. The first way is to define two unrelated classes, one for undergraduate students and another for graduate students. We call the two classes *unrelated classes* if they are not connected in an inheritance relationship, that is, if neither one is an ancestor

unrelated classes

or descendant class of the other and they do not share a common ancestor.[1] The second way is to model undergraduate and graduate students by using classes that are related in an inheritance hierarchy.

Defining two unrelated classes for entities that share common data or behavior would make class definition ineffective because we would end up duplicating code common to both classes. Although different, graduate and undergraduate students do share many common data and behaviors, so we will design these two classes by using inheritance.

We will actually define three classes. The first is the Student class to incorporate behavior and data common to both graduate and undergraduate students. The second and third classes are the GraduateStudent class to incorporate behavior specific to graduate students and the UndergraduateStudent class to incorporate behavior specific to undergraduate students. The Student class is defined as

```
/*
    Chapter 13 Sample Program: Student

    File: Student.java

*/

class Student {

    protected final static int NUM_OF_TESTS = 3;

    protected String name;
    protected int[]  test;
    protected String courseGrade;

    public Student( ) {
        this("No Name");
    }

    public Student(String studentName) {
        name = studentName;
        test = new int[NUM_OF_TESTS];
        courseGrade = "****";
    }

    public String getCourseGrade( ) {
      return courseGrade;
    }
```

Protected fields are visible to the descendant objects.

[1]In Java, the class Object is automatically set to be the superclass of a class if the class definition does not include the keyword extends. To be technically precise, we must say that two classes are unrelated if they do not share a common ancestor besides Object.

```
    public String getName( ) {
      return name;
    }

    public int getTestScore(int testNumber) {
      return test[testNumber-1];
    }

    public void setName(String newName) {
      name = newName;
    }

    public void setTestScore(int testNumber, int testScore) {
      test[testNumber-1] = testScore;
    }
}
```

Notice that the modifier for the instance variables is protected, making them visible and accessible to the instances of the class and the descendant classes. If you declare a data member of a class private, then this data member is accessible only to the instances of the class. If you declare a data member public, this data member is accessible to everybody. We declare them protected so they become accessible only to the instances of the class and the descendant classes. We will explore further the protected modifier later in the chapter.

extends

We define the classes UndergraduateStudent and GraduateStudent as subclasses of the Student class. In Java, we say a subclass ***extends*** its superclass. The difference between the classes GraduateStudent and UndergraduateStudent lies in the way their final course grades are computed. The two subclasses are defined as follows:

```
class GraduateStudent extends Student {

   public void computeCourseGrade() {

      int total = 0;
      for (int i = 0; i < NUM_OF_TESTS; i++) {
         total += test[i];
      }

      if (total/NUM_OF_TESTS >= 80) {
         courseGrade = "Pass";
      } else {
         courseGrade = "No Pass";
      }
   }
}
```

```
class UndergraduateStudent extends Student {

   public void computeCourseGrade() {

      int total = 0;
      for (int i = 0; i < NUM_OF_TESTS; i++) {
         total += test[i];
      }

      if (total/NUM_OF_TESTS >= 70) {
         courseGrade = "Pass";
      } else {
         courseGrade = "No Pass";
      }
   }
}
```

Figure 13.1 shows the class diagram relating the three classes. Notice the use of the pound symbol (#) for the protected modifier. Notice also that we do not show inherited data members and methods in the subclasses. By seeing an inheritance arrow connecting a subclass to its superclass, we know that data members and methods indicated on the superclass are applicable to the subclasses also. We attach methods and data members to the subclasses only if they are defined in the subclasses or if they are overridden in the subclasses (we will discuss overriding in detail later in the chapter). In Figure 13.1, both subclasses have the method computeCourseGrade attached to them because the method is defined in the subclasses.

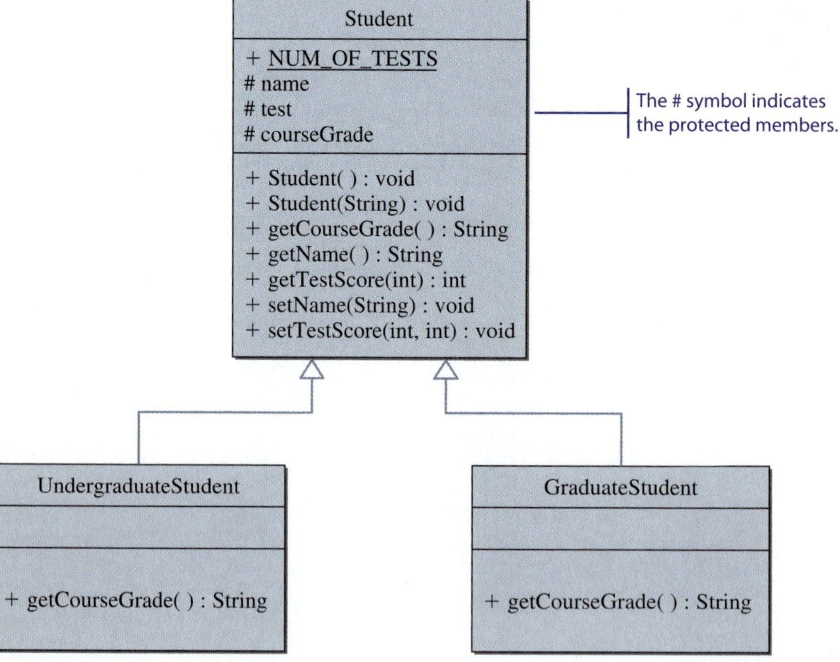

Figure 13.1 A superclass **Student** and its subclasses **GraduateStudent** and **UndergraduateStudent.**

1. Which is the subclass and which is the superclass in this declaration?

```
class X extends Y { ... }
```

2. Which visibility modifier allows the data members of a superclass to be accessible to the instances of subclasses?

13.3 Using Classes Effectively with Polymorphism

Now let's see how the Student class and its subclasses can be used effectively in the class roster program. Since both undergraduate and graduate students are enrolled in a class, should we declare the two arrays shown below to maintain the class roster?

```
GraduateStudent          gradRoster[20];
UndergraduateStudent     undergradRoster[20];
```

We mentioned in Chapter 10 that an array must contain elements of the same data type. For example, we cannot store integers and real numbers in the same array. To follow this rule, it seems necessary for us to declare two separate arrays, one for graduate students and another for undergraduate students. This rule, however, does not apply when the array elements are objects. We only need to declare a single array, for example,

```
Student roster[40];
```

Elements of the roster array can be instances of either the Student class or any of its descendant GraduateStudent or UndergraduateStudent classes. Figure 13.2 illustrates the array with both types of students as array elements.

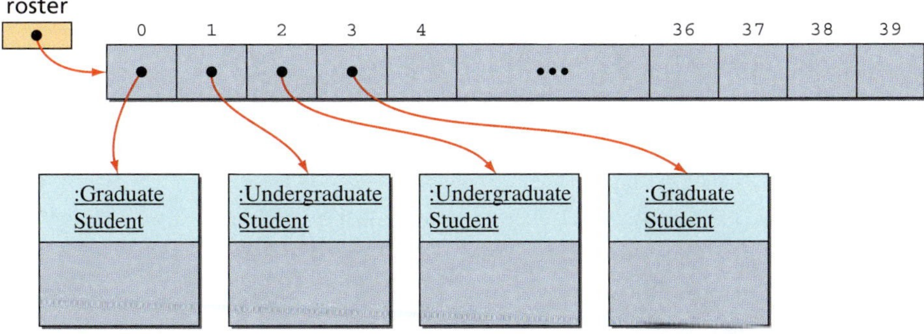

Figure 13.2 The **roster** array with elements referring to instances of **GraduateStudent** or **UndergraduateStudent** classes.

Before showing how this array is used in the program, we will explain the concept of polymorphism. In its simplest form, polymorphism allows a single variable to refer to objects from different classes. Consider, for example, the declaration

```
Student student;
```

With this declaration, we can say not only

```
student = new Student( );
```

but also

```
student = new GraduateStudent( );
```

or

```
student = new UndergraduateStudent( );
```

In other words, the single variable student is not limited to referring to an object from the Student class but can refer to any object from the descendant classes of Student. In a similar manner we can say something like

```
roster[0] = new GraduateStudent( );
roster[1] = new UndergraduateStudent( );
roster[2] = new UndergraduateStudent( );
roster[3] = new GraduateStudent( );
...
```

sibling classes

However, you cannot make a variable of class X refer to an object from the superclass or sibling classes of X. ***Sibling classes*** are those that share the common ancestor class. For example, the following assignment statements are both invalid.

```
GraduateStudent grad1, grad2;

grad1 = new Student( );
grad2 = new UndergraduateStudent( );
```

✘ NOT VALID →

Now, to compute the course grade using the roster array, we execute

```
for (int i = 0; i < numberOfStudents; i++) {
    roster[i].computeCourseGrade();
}
```

If roster[i] refers to a GraduateStudent, then the computeCourseGrade method of the GraduateStudent class is executed; and if it refers to an UndergraduateStudent, then the computeCourseGrade method of UndergraduateStudent is executed. We call the message computeCourseGrade *polymorphic* because the message refers to methods from different classes depending on the object referenced by roster[i]. Polymorphism allows us to maintain the class roster with one array instead of maintaining a separate array for each type of student, and this simplifies the processing tremendously.

benefits of polymorphism

Polymorphism makes possible smooth and easy extension and modification of a program. Suppose, for example, we have to add a third type of student, say, audit student, to the class roster program. If we have to define a separate array for each type of student, this extension forces us to define a new class and a third array for audit students. But with polymorphism, we only have to define a new subclass of Student. And as long as this new subclass includes the correct computeCourseGrade method, the for loop to compute the course grade for students remains the same. Without polymorphism, not only do we have to add the new code, but also we have to rewrite existing code to accommodate the change. With polymorphism, on the other hand, we don't have to touch the existing code. Modifying existing code is a tedious and error-prone activity. A slight change to existing code could cause a program to stop working correctly. To be certain that a change in one portion of existing code won't affect other portions of existing code adversely, we must understand the existing code completely. And understanding code, especially one that is long and/or written by somebody else, is a very time-consuming task.

An element of the roster array is a reference to an instance of either the GraduateStudent or the UndergraduateStudent class. Most of the time, we do not have to know which is which. There are times, however, when we need to know the class of a referenced object. For example, we may want to find out the number of undergraduate students who passed the course. To determine the class of an object, we use the instanceof operator. We use this operator as follows:

```
Student x = new UndergraduateStudent( );

if ( x instanceof UndergraduateStudent ) {
   System.out.println("Mr. X is an undergraduate student");
} else {
   System.out.println("Mr. X is a graduate student");
}
```

This will print out Mr. X is an undergraduate student. The following code counts the number of undergraduate students in the roster array.

```
int undergradCount = 0;
for (int i = 0; i < numberOfStudents; i++) {
   if ( roster[i] instanceof UndergraduateStudent ) {
      undergradCount++;
   }
}
```

1. Suppose Truck and Motorcycle are subclasses of Vehicle. Which of these declarations are invalid?

```
Truck        t = new Vehicle();
Vehicle      v = new Truck();
Motorcycle m1 = new Vehicle();
Motorcycle m2 = new Truck();
```

2. What is the purpose of the instanceof operator?

13.4 Inheritance and Member Accessibility

We will describe the rules of inheritance in this section and Sections 13.5 and 13.6. In this section, we will explain which members (variables and methods) of a superclass are inherited by a subclass and how these members are accessed. In addition to declaring members private and public, we can declare them protected. The protected modifier is meaningful only if used with inheritance. Consider the following declarations:

```
class Super {

   public    int   public_Super_Field;
   protected int   protected_Super_Field;
   private   int   private_Super_Field;

   public Super() {
      public_Super_Field     = 10;
      protected_Super_Field  = 20;
      private_Super_Field    = 30;
   }
   ...
}

class Sub extends Super {
   public    int    public_Sub_Field;
   protected int    protected_Sub_Field;
   private   int    private_Sub_Field;

   public Sub() {
      public_Sub_Field    = 100;
      protected_Sub_Field = 200;
      private_Sub_Field   = 300;
   }
   ...
}
```

super is a reserved word, so don't use it.

We use instance variables for illustration, but the rules we describe here are equally applicable to other types of members (class variables, class methods, and instance methods). We use the graphical representation shown in Figure 13.3 for the three modifiers.

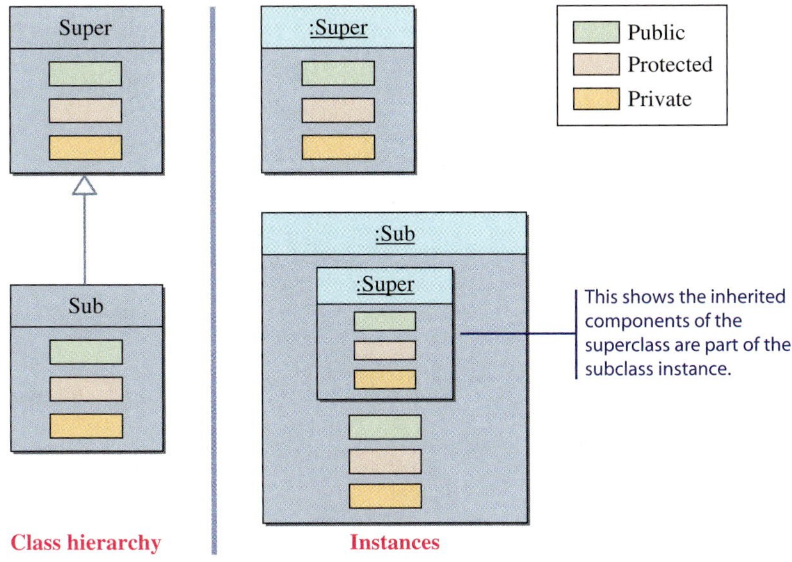

Figure 13.3 A graphical representation of superclasses and subclasses with **public, private,** and **protected** members. (*Note:* This representation is for illustration purposes only and is not a formal UML diagram.)

You already know the difference between the public and private modifiers. A public member is accessible to any method, but a private member is accessible only to the methods that belong to the same class. Let's illustrate this point. Consider a class that is unrelated to the classes Super and Sub:

```
class Client {
   public void test() {
      Super  mySuper = new Super();
      Sub    mySub = new Sub();

      int i = mySuper.public_Super_Field;

      int j = mySub.public_Super_Field; //inherited
                                        //by mySub

      int k = mySub.public_Sub_Field;
   }
}
```

✓ VALID →

Public members of a class, whether they are inherited or not, are accessible from any object or class. Private members of a class, on the other hand, are never accessible from any outside object or class. The following statements, if placed in the test method of the Client class, are therefore all invalid:

```
int l = mySuper.private_Super_Field;

int m = mySub.private_Sub_Field;

int n = mySub.private_Super_Field;
```

✗ NOT VALID →

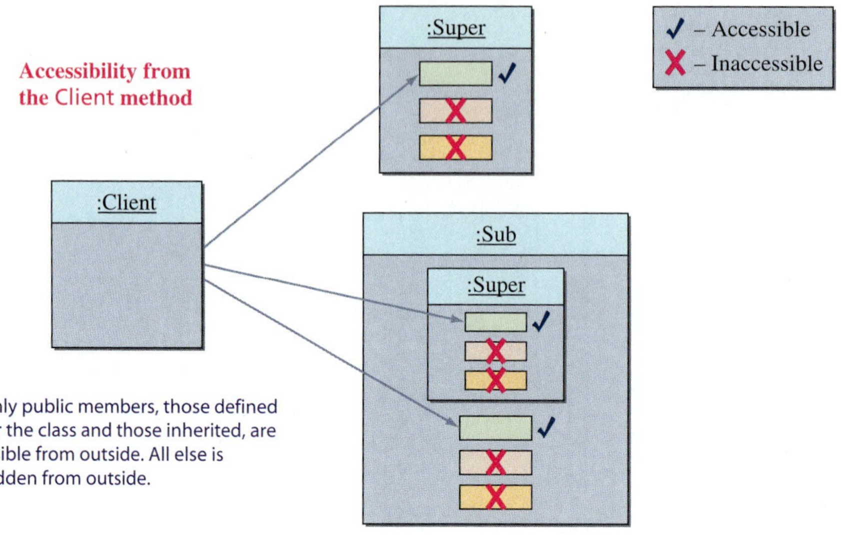

Figure 13.4 The difference between **public, private,** and **protected** modifiers. Only public members are visible from outside.

A protected member is accessible only to the methods that belong to the same class or to the descendant classes. It is inaccessible to the methods of an unrelated class. The following statements, if placed in the test method of the Client class, are all invalid:

X NOT VALID →

```
int o = mySuper.protected_Super_Field;

int p = mySub.protected_Sub_Field;

int q = mySub.protected_Super_Field;
```

Figure 13.4 summarizes the accessibility of class members from a method of an unrelated class.

Now let's study the accessibility of class members from the methods of a Sub object. A method in the Sub object can access both the protected and public members of Super, but not the private members of Super. Figure 13.5 summarizes the accessibility of members from a method of a Sub object.

Figure 13.5 shows the case where a method of a Sub object is accessing members of itself. Everything except the private members of the Super class is accessible from a method of the Sub class.

What about accessing the members of an object from another object that belongs to the same class? If a member X, whether inherited or defined in a class, is accessible from an instance of the class, then X is also accessible from all instances of the same class. Figure 13.6 illustrates that an instance can access members of other instances of the same class.

Accessibility from a method of the Sub class

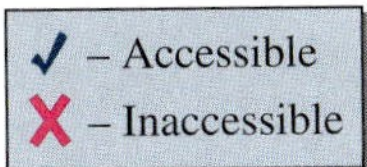

From a method of Sub, everything is visible except the private members of its superclass.

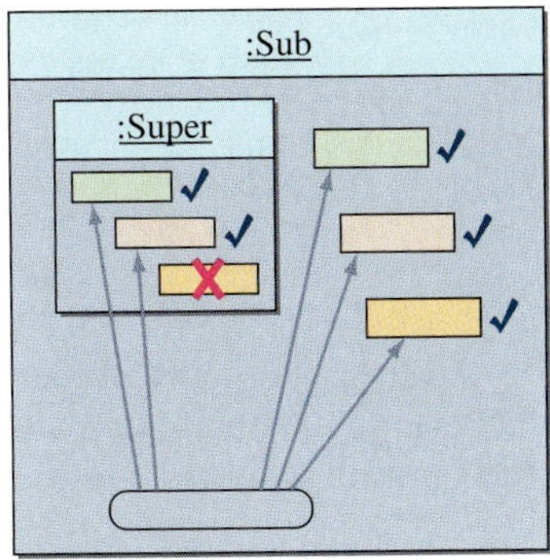

Figure 13.5 The difference between **public, private,** and **protected** modifiers. Everything except the **private** members of the **Super** class is visible from a method of the **Sub** class.

If a data member is accessible from anInstance, that data member is also accessible from anotherInstance.

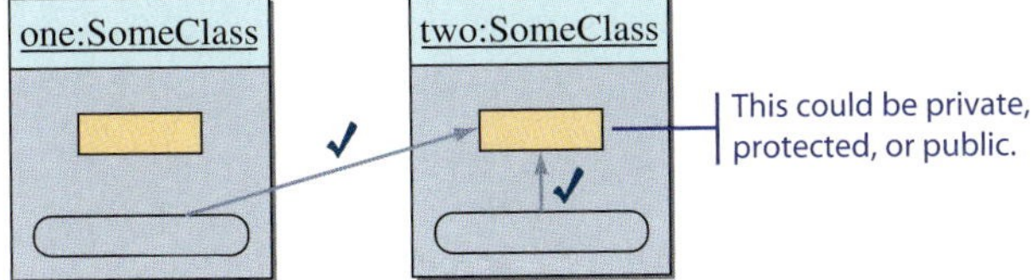

Figure 13.6 Data members accessible from an instance are also accessible from other instances of the same class.

Consider the following two classes:

✓ VALID →

```
class Super {
   ...
   public void superToSuper( Super anotherSuper){

      int i = anotherSuper.public_Super_Field;
      int j = anotherSuper.protected_Super_Field;
      int l = anotherSuper.private_Super_Field;
   }
   ...
}

class Sub extends Super {

   ...
   public void subToSub( Sub anotherSub){

      int i = anotherSub.public_Sub_Field;
      int j = anotherSub.protected_Sub_Field;
      int k = anotherSub.private_Sub_Field;
```

✓ VALID →

```
✓ VALID →        int l = anotherSub.public_Super_Field;     //inherited
                 int m = anotherSub.protected_Super_Field;  //members
✗ NOT VALID →    int n = anotherSub.private_Super_Field;
              }
              ...
          }
```

All the statements in the two methods, except the last one in subToSub, are valid because members accessible to an object are also accessible from other objects of the same class. Now, consider the following two classes:

```
          class Super {
              ...
              public void superToSub(Sub sub){
✓ VALID →         int i = sub.public_Sub_Field;
✗ NOT VALID →     int j = sub.protected_Sub_Field;
                  int k = sub.private_Sub_Field;
              }
              ...
          }

          class Sub extends Super {

              ...
              public void subToSuper(Super mySuper){
✓ VALID →         int i = mySuper.public_Super_Field;
✗ NOT VALID →     int j = mySuper.protected_Super_Field;
                  int k = mySuper.private_Super_Field;
              }
              ...
          }
```

The two methods show that only the public members of an object are accessible from another object if the two objects belong to different classes. Whether one class is a subclass of the other class is irrelevant here.

In addition to the **private, protected,** and **public** modifiers, Java supports the fourth visibility modifier, called *package visibility*. If no explicit modifier (**public, private,** and **protected**) is included in the declaration, then the component is package-visible, which means the component is accessible from any method of a class that belongs to the same package as the component's class. Package visibility is not as critical as the other three visibility modifiers, and therefore, we do not discuss it in the text.

1. If X is a private member of the Super class, is X accessible from a subclass of Super?
2. If X is a protected member of the Super class, is X of one instance accessible from another instance of Super? What about from the instances of a subclass of Super?

13.5 Inheritance and Constructors

In this section, we explain how the constructors of a class are affected by inheritance. Unlike other members of a superclass, constructors of a superclass are not inherited by its subclasses. This means that you must define a constructor for a class or use the default constructor added by the compiler. As we mentioned in Chapter 4, a default constructor is added to a class if you do not declare any constructor for the class. A class definition such as

```
class Person {
   public void sayHello( ) {
      System.out.println("Well, hello.");
   }
}
```

is equivalent to

```
class Person {
   public Person( ) {
      super();
   }
   public void sayHello( ) {
      System.out.println("Well, hello.");
   }
}
```

Automatically added to the class by the compiler

This statement calls the superclass's constructor.

The statement

```
super();
```

calls the superclass's constructor. Every class has a superclass. If the class declaration does not explicitly designate the superclass with the extends clause, then the class's superclass is the Object class.

If you declare a constructor, then no default constructor is added to the class. For example, if you define a class as

```
class MyClass {
   public MyClass(int x) {
      ...
   }
}
```

then a statement such as

```
MyClass test = new MyClass();
```

is invalid because MyClass has no matching constructor.

If the constructor you define does not contain an explicit call to a superclass constructor, then the compiler adds the statement

```
super();
```

as the first statement of the constructor. For example, if you define a constructor as

```
class MyClass {
   private int myInt;
   public MyClass() {
      myInt = 10;
   }
}
```

then the compiler will rewrite the constructor to

```
public MyClass() {
   super();
   myInt = 10;
}
```

Let's look at another example. Consider the following class definitions:

```
class Vehicle {
   private String vin;
   public Vehicle(String vehicleIdNumber) {
      vin = vehicleIdNumber;
   }
```

```
      public String getVIN() {
         return vin;
      }
   }
```

Since the class has a constructor, no default constructor is added to the class. This means a statement such as

```
Vehicle myCar = new Vehicle();
```

causes a compilation error because the class does not have a matching constructor. This is actually what we want because we do not want to create an instance of Vehicle without a vehicle identification number. Now let's consider a subclass definition for trucks. A Truck object has one additional instance variable called cargoWeightLimit that refers to a maximum weight of cargo the truck can carry. We assume the truck's weight limit for cargo can vary (say, depending on how much the owner pays in fees). Here's our first attempt:

```
class Truck extends Vehicle {
   private int cargoWeightLimit;
   public void setWeightLimit(int newLimit) {
      cargoWeightLimit = newLimit;
   }
   public int getWeightLimit() {
      return cargoWeightLimit;
   }
}
```

Bad Version

If we compile this definition, we will get a compiler error. Since no constructor is defined for the class, the compiler adds a default constructor

```
public void Truck() {
   super();
}
```

This constructor calls the superclass's constructor with no arguments, but there's no matching constructor in the superclass. Thus, the compilation error results. Here's a correct definition:

You need to make this call. Otherwise, the compiler will add **super()**, which will result in an error because there is no matching constructor in **Vehicle.**

```
class Truck extends Vehicle {
   private int cargoWeightLimit;
   public Truck(int weightLimit, String vin) {
      super(vin);
      cargoWeightLimit = weightLimit;
   }
   public void setWeightLimit(int newLimit) {
```

```
      cargoWeightLimit = newLimit;
   }

   public int getWeightLimit() {

      return cargoWeightLimit;
   }
}
```

Now let's apply this knowledge to the design of the UndergraduateStudent and GraduateStudent classes. If we want a constructor that accepts the name, then we need to define such a constructor in both classes because the constructor defined for the Student class is not inherited by these classes. Notice that we can create instances of these classes by

```
student1 = new UndergraduateStudent( );
student2 = new GraduateStudent( );
```

because the default constructor is added by the compiler, not because the one defined in the Student class is inherited by the subclasses. Remember that constructors of a superclass are not inherited by its subclasses.

Here are a rule and a guideline to remember for a subclass constructor:

Things to Remember

If a class has a superclass that is not the ***Object*** *class, then a constructor of the class should make an explicit call to a constructor of the superclass.*

Design Guidelines

Always provide a constructor for every class you define. Don't rely on default constructors.

1. How do you call the superclass's constructor from its subclass?
2. What statement will be added to a constructor of a subclass if it is not included in the constructor explicitly by the programmer?
3. Modify the definition of GraduateStudent and UndergraduateStudent in Section 13.1 so we can create their instances in this way:

```
student1 = new UndergraduateStudent();
student2 = new UndergraduateStudent("Mr. Espresso");
student3 = new GraduateStudent();
student4 = new GraduateStudent("Ms. Latte");
```

13.6 Abstract Superclasses and Abstract Methods

When we define a superclass, we often do not need to create any instances of the superclass. In Section 13.5, we defined the Student superclass and its two subclasses GraduateStudent and UndergraduateStudent. We gave examples of creating instances of GraduateStudent and UndergraduateStudent, but not of creating instances of Student. Does it make sense to create an instance of the Student class? Depending on whether we need to create instances of Student, we must define the class differently. We will describe different ways of defining a superclass in this section.

Even though we can create an instance of Student if we want to (because of the way the class is currently defined), is there a need to create an instance of Student? If a student can be only a graduate or an undergraduate student, then there is no need to create an instance of Student. In fact, because of the way the class is defined, had we created an instance of Student and stored it in the roster array, the program would crash. Why? Because the Student class does not have a computeCourseGrade method.

In the following discussion, we will consider two cases. In the first case, we assume that a student must be either a graduate or an undergraduate student. In the second case, we assume that a student does not have to be a graduate or an undergraduate student (e.g., the student could be a nonmatriculated auditing student).

Case 1: Student Must Be Undergraduate or Graduate

For the case where a student must be a graduate or an undergraduate student, we only need instances of GraduateStudent and UndergraduateStudent. So we must define the Student class in such a way that no instances of it can be created. One way is to define Student as an abstract class. An ***abstract class*** is a class defined with the modifier abstract, and no instances can be created from an abstract class. Let's see how the abstract Student class is defined.

abstract class

The keyword **abstract** here denotes an abstract class.

```
abstract class Student {

   protected final static int NUM_OF_TESTS = 3;

   protected String   name;
   protected int[]    test;
   protected String   courseGrade;

   public Student() {

      this("No name");
   }

   public Student(String studentName) {

      name        = studentName;
      test        = new int[NUM_OF_TESTS];
      courseGrade = "****";
   }

   abstract public void computeCourseGrade();
```

The keyword **abstract** here denotes an abstract method.

Abstract method has no method body, just a semicolon.

```
        public String getCourseGrade() {
           return courseGrade;
        }

        public String getName() {
           return name;
        }

        public int getTestScore(int testNumber) {
           return test[testNumber-1];
        }

        public void setName(String newName) {
           name = newName;
        }

        public void setTestScore(int testNumber,int testScore){
           test[testNumber-1] = testScore;
        }
     }
```

abstract method

implementing a method

An ***abstract method*** is a method with the keyword abstract, and it ends with a semicolon instead of a method body. A class is *abstract* if the class contains an abstract method or does not provide an implementation of an inherited abstract method. We say a method is ***implemented*** if it has a method body. If a subclass has no abstract methods and no unimplemented inherited abstract methods (and does not include the keyword abstract in its class definition), then the subclass is no longer abstract, and thus its instances can be created.

abstract superclass

An abstract class must include the keyword abstract in its definition. Notice that the abstract class Student has an incomplete definition because the class includes the abstract method computeCourseGrade that does not have a method body. The intent is to let its subclasses provide the implementation of the computeCourseGrade method. If a subclass does not provide an implementation of the inherited abstract method, the subclass is also an abstract class, and therefore, no instances of the subclass can be created. Since an abstract class can only make sense when it is a superclass, we frequently use the term ***abstract superclass***.

Is the **Math** class an abstract class? It is true that we cannot create an instance of the **Math** class, but it is not an abstract class. If a class is abstract, then you cannot create an instance of the class, but not being able to create an instance does not necessarily imply that the class is abstract. The intent of an abstract class is to define code common to all its subclasses and leave some portions, that is, abstract methods, to be completed by the individual subclasses. We classify the **Math** class as a noninstantiable class, a class for which we cannot create an instance. Notice that an abstract class is a noninstantiable class by definition, but the reverse is not always true. There are noninstantiable classes, for example, the **Math** class, that are not abstract. If you want define a noninstantiable class, then simply declare a private constructor with no arguments and declare no other constructors for the class.

In a program diagram, we represent an abstract class by using the keyword abstract. The Student abstract superclass is drawn as

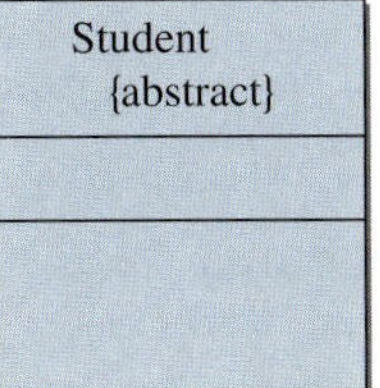

Case 2: Student Does Not Have to Be Undergraduate or Graduate

For the second case, where a student does not have to be a graduate or an undergraduate student, we can design classes in two different ways. The first approach is to make the Student class instantiable. The second approach is to leave the Student class abstract and add a third subclass, say, OtherStudent, to handle a student who is neither a graduate nor an undergraduate student. Let's call students who are neither graduate nor undergraduate students *nonregular students*. Let's assume further that the nonregular student will receive a pass grade if her or his average test score is greater than or equal to 50. With the first approach, we define the Student class as

Not an abstract class anymore →

```
class Student {

   protected final static int NUM_OF_TESTS = 3;
   protected String           name;
   protected int[]            test;
   protected String           courseGrade;

   public Student( ) {

      this("No name");
   }

   public Student(String studentName) {

      name         = studentName;
      test         = new int[NUM_OF_TESTS];
      courseGrade = "****";
   }

   public void computeCourseGrade() {

      int total = 0;
      for (int i = 0; i < NUM_OF_TESTS; i++) {
         total += test[i];
      }

      if (total/NUM_OF_TESTS >= 50) {
         courseGrade = "Pass";
      } else {
```

Not an abstract method anymore → (points to `public void computeCourseGrade()`)

```
            courseGrade = "No Pass";
         }
      }

      public String getCourseGrade() {
         return courseGrade;
      }

      public String getName() {
         return name;
      }

      public int getTestScore(int testNumber) {
         return test[testNumber-1];
      }

      public void setName(String newName) {
         name = newName;
      }

      public void setTestScore(int testNumber,int testScore){
         test[testNumber-1] = testScore;
      }
   }
```

The class is no longer abstract, and we can create an instance of **Student** to represent a nonregular student.

With the second approach, we leave the **Student** class abstract. To represent nonregular students, we define a third subclass called **OtherStudent** as follows:

```
class OtherStudent extends Student {

   public void computeCourseGrade() {

      int total = 0;
      for (int i = 0; i < NUM_OF_TESTS; i++) {
         total += test[i];
      }

      if (total/NUM_OF_TESTS >= 50) {
         courseGrade = "Pass";
      } else {
         courseGrade = "No Pass";
      }
   }
}
```

Figure 13.7 is a program diagram that includes the third subclass.

Which approach is better? There's no easy answer. It all depends on a given situation. To determine which approach is better for a given situation, we can ask ourselves which approach allows easier modification and extension. Consider, for

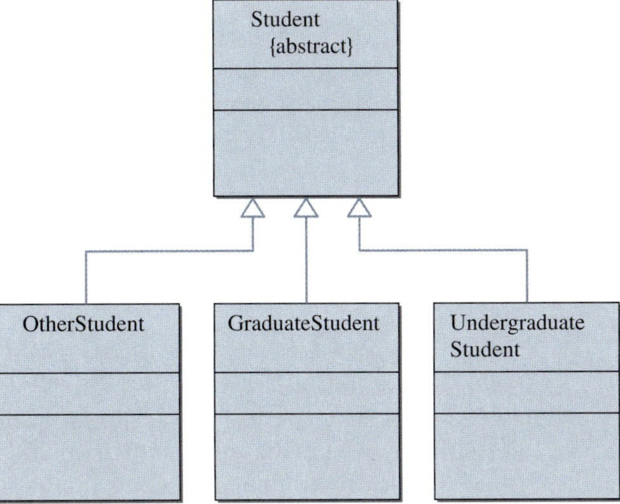

Figure 13.7 A program diagram of the abstract superclass **Student** and its three subclasses.

example, which approach will facilitate easier modification if we have to add a new type of student, say, scholarship students. Or consider the case where the rule for assigning a course grade for the undergraduate and graduate students is modified; say, they become the same.

Finally, not all methods can be declared abstract.

Things to Remember

The following types of methods cannot be declared as `abstract`:

- *Private methods*
- *Static methods*

Quick CHECK

1. Can you create an instance of an abstract class?
2. Must an abstract class include an abstract method?
3. What is wrong with the following declaration?

```
class Vehicle {
   abstract public getVIN();
   . . .
}
```

13.7 Inheritance versus Interface

Java interface and inheritance are language features used to support object-oriented modeling. They are similar because they are both used to model an IS-A relationship. Consider, for example, the following class definitions:

```
class AddressBookVer1 implements AddressBook {
    . . .
}

class SavingsAccount extends Account {
    . . .
}
```

We say "AddressBookVer1 is an AddressBook" and "SavingsAccount is an Account." Because of this similarity, beginning programmers often have some difficulty in differentiating the two clearly. Although they are similar, their intended uses are quite different.

We use the Java interface to share common behavior (defined by its abstract methods) among the instances of unrelated classes. And one class can implement multiple interfaces. For example, we can define a single Person class that implements multiple interfaces such as Driver, Commuter, and Biker.

We use inheritance, on the other hand, to share common code (including both data members and methods) among the instances of related classes. And a single subclass can extend at most one superclass. For example, the GraduateStudent and UndergraduateStudent classes are subclasses of the Student class, the Truck and Motorcycle classes are subclasses of the Vehicle class, and so forth. The superclasses include data members and/or methods that are shared by the subclasses. The IS-A relationship that exists between a subclass and its superclass is a specialization, as Truck is a specialized Vehicle. Such a specialization relationship does not exist with the Java interface.

Design Guidelines

Use the Java interface to share common behavior. Use the inheritance to share common code.

Design Guidelines

If an entity A is a specialized form of another entity B, then model them by using inheritance. Declare A as a subclass of B.

We must be careful not to mix up the use of service class and inheritance. Beginners often make this mistake. Suppose you want to define a class that maintains a list of music CDs. Which of the following two definitions is a better design?

```
class CDManager extends java.util.ArrayList {
    ...
}

class CDManager {

    private List list;
    ..
}
```

The first version uses inheritance and defines a subclass of ArrayList. The second version defines a data member of type ArrayList. The first version is a misuse of inheritance. When we define a subclass A of superclass B, we must ask ourselves, Is A a B? Can we say CDManager is an ArrayList? No. The CDManager is not a specialized version of the ArrayList. The CDManager class simply needs to reuse the service provided by the ArrayList class. Thus, the second version is the proper design. We call this type of code reuse ***code reuse by composition***.

code reuse by composition

Beyond the conceptual problem, defining the CDManager class as a subclass of ArrayList has practical weaknesses. Because it is a subclass, the client of the CDManager class can call any methods defined in the superclass ArrayList. But does it make sense for the client to call the method such as ensureCapacity? Another weakness is the difficulty in changing the implementation of the CDManager class. Suppose we need to modify the data structure class from ArrayList to HashMap for better performance. With the inheritance approach, any client that uses the inherited methods of ArrayList needs to be rewritten. With the composition approach, the client that uses only the methods defined for the CDManager class will continue to work without change. The change made from the ArrayList class to the HashMap class is encapsulated in the CDManager class and does not affect the clients.

13.8 Sample Development

Computing Course Grades

Let's develop a program that illustrates the use of **Student** and its subclasses **GraduateStudent** and **UndergraduateStudent.** The program will input student data from a user-designated text file, compute the course grades, and display the results. We assume the input text file is created by using a text editor or another application. For example, a teacher may have kept his student grades in a notebook. Instead of manually computing the grades with a pencil and calculator, he enters data into a text file and uses this program to compute the course grades. Another possible scenario is that the teacher uses some kind of application software that allows him to maintain student records. Suppose this application does not allow the teacher to use different formulas for computing the course grades of undergraduate and graduate students. In such a case, the teacher can export data to a text file and use our program to compute the course grades for undergraduate and graduate students using the different formulas. Using text files to transfer data from one application to another application is a very common technique in software applications.

To focus on the use of inheritance and polymorphism, we will adopt the basic input and output routines. It is left as exercises to implement them differently. Exercise 4 asks you to save the data to an object file and Exercise 5 asks you to use the **Scanner** class for input.

Problem Statement

Write an application that reads in a text file organized in the manner shown below and displays the final course grades. The course grades are computed differently for the undergraduate and graduate students based on the formulas listed on page 717. The input text file format is as follows:

- *A single line is used for information on one student.*
- *Each line uses the format*

  <Type> <Name> <Test 1> <Test 2> <Test 3>

  where <Type> *designates either a graduate or an undergraduate student,* <Name> *designates the student's first and last name, and* <Test i> *designates the* ith *test score.*
- *End of input is designated by the word* END. *The case of the letters is insignificant.*

Figure 13.8 shows a sample input text file.

Overall Plan

We will implement a class that will

1. Read an input text file.
2. Compute the course grades.
3. Print out the result.

<Type>	<Name>	<Test 1>	<Test 2>	<Test 3>
U	John Doe	87	78	90
G	Jill Jones	90	95	87
G	Jack Smith	67	77	68
U	Mary Hines	80	85	80
U	Mick Taylor	76	69	79
END				

Figure 13.8 A sample text file containing student names and test scores. **U** at the beginning of a line designates an undergraduate student, and **G** designates a graduate student.

To read a text file, we will use the standard file I/O objects **File, FileReader,** and **BufferedReader.** To compute the course grades, we will use the **Student, Undergraduate,** and **Graduate** classes defined earlier in the chapter. The formulas for calculating the course grades are defined in their respective **computeCourseGrades** methods. Since the input file is a text file, we must create either a **Graduate** or an **Undergraduate** object for each line of input, so we will be able to call its **computeCourseGrades** method. To store the created student objects (instances of either **Graduate** or **Undergraduate**), we will use an array of **Student** to gain more practice on using arrays.

To focus on the inheritance and polymorphism topics, we will use two helper classes. The first is the **OutputBox** class which we use to display the course grades and save the result back to a text file. We use its **print** and **println** methods for output and its **saveToFile** method to save the data to a text file. The **saveToFile** method saves the complete text in an **OutputBox** to a designated file. If the file already exists, then the original contents of the file will be replaced by the text currently shown in the **OutputBox.** Often, we need the capability to save the text in different format. For example, assuming the student information includes the student ID number, the teacher may want to save only the last four digits of the ID numbers and the final course grades so the results can be posted. If we wish to save the text in a different format, then we have to implement our own method with such capability.

The second helper class is the **MainWindow** class. We will name our main class **ComputeGrades,** and as another example of inheritance, we make it a subclass of **MainWindow.** The **MainWindow** is itself a subclass of **JFrame** and has the functionality of positioning itself at the center of the screen (among other features). We cover the details of subclassing the **JFrame** class in Chapter 14.

Here's our working design document:

program classes

Design Document: `ComputeGrades`

Class	**Purpose**
`ComputeGrades`	The top-level control object manages other objects in the program. The class is a subclass of the helper class `MainWindow`. This class is the instantiable main class.
`OutputBox`	An `OutputBox` object is used to display the input data and computed course grades.
`Student, Under-graduateStudent, GraduateStudent`	These are application logic objects for students. The `Student` class is an abstract superclass.
`File, FileReader, BufferedReader`	These are objects necessary for reading data from a text file.

13.8 Sample Development—*continued*

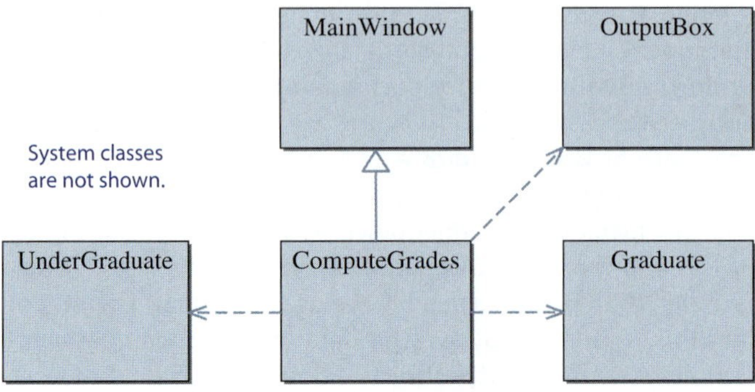

Figure 13.9 An object diagram of the **ComputeGrades** program.

Figure 13.9 is the program diagram.

Now let's think about the methods of **ComputeGrades.** What kinds of public methods should the class support? Since a **ComputeGrades** object is a top-level controller object, we need a single public method to initiate the operations. Let's define a method called **processData** that will carry out the three main tasks. The **main** method of **ComputeGrades** will call this method.

```
public static void main(String[] args) {
   ComputeGrades gradeComputer = new ComputeGrades();
   gradeComputer.processData();
}
```

The **processData** method will look something like this:

```
this.setVisible(true); //make this main window
outputBox.setVisible(true);//and an outputBox visible

boolean success = readData();

if (success) {
   computeGrade();
   printResult();
} else {
   print error message "File Input Error";
}
```

The **readData** method returns **true** if the input data are read in correctly from a text file and the array of **Student** objects is properly created. Our working design document for the **ComputeGrades** class is as follows:

Design Document: The ComputeGrades Class		
Method	**Visibility**	**Purpose**
`<constructor>`	`public`	Creates and initializes the objects used by a `ComputeGrades` object.
`processData`	`public`	Displays itself and carries out three main tasks.
`readData`	`private`	Opens and reads data from a text file and creates an array of `Student` objects from the input data. If the operation is successful, returns `true`.
`computeGrade`	`private`	Scans through the array of `Student` objects and computes the course grades.
`printResult`	`private`	Prints out the student information along with the computed grades to an `OutputBox`.

We will develop the program in five incremental steps:

1. Start with the program skeleton. Define the skeleton **ComputeGrades** classes.
2. Implement the **printResult** method. Define any other methods necessary to implement **printResult.**
3. Implement the **computeGrade** method. Define any other methods necessary to implement **computeGrade.**
4. Implement the **readData** method. Define any other methods necessary to implement **readData.**
5. Finalize and look for improvements.

We defer the implementation of the hardest method, **readData,** until the last. Some programmers prefer to deal with the hardest aspect of the program first, and there's no strict rule for ordering the implementation steps. You should order the steps in a way with which you are most comfortable. However, this does not mean you can implement the methods at random. You must always plan the implementation steps carefully so the steps follow a logical sequence. For this program, we start with the output routine so we can use the final output routine for testing other methods, instead of defining a temporary output routine for testing purposes.

Step 1 Development: Program Skeleton

step 1 design

Let's begin with the data members and the constructors for the **ComputeGrades** class. We will start with the following data members:

```
private   OutputBox     outputBox;   //for output
private   Student[ ]    roster;      //for maintaining
                                     //student info
```

13.8 Sample Development—*continued*

It is a straightforward operation to create the first four objects, but we need to think a little about the **roster** array. How big should the array be? There are several possibilities:

1. Create an array of an arbitrary size, say, 25.
2. Let the programmer pass the size in the constructor.
3. Do not create it in the constructor. Modify the input text file to include the size of an array in the first line.

Option 3 is not attractive because it will require a change in the problem specification. Moreover, requiring the size information in the input file will put a lot of burden on the user who must go over the text file and count the number of lines the file contains. Such a burdensome task should be left to a computer. So we will implement options 1 and 2. If the data cannot fit into an array of a predesignated size, then we will use the technique discussed in Chapter 9 to expand the array.

We declare a constant

```
private static final int   DEFAULT_SIZE = 25;
```

and declare the two constructors as

```
public ComputeGrades( ) {
   this(DEFAULT_SIZE);
}

public ComputeGrades(int arraySize) {
   super();  //an explicit call to the superclass constructor
   outputBox = new OutputBox(this);
   roster = new Student[arraySize];
}
```

Notice that we can't create **inFile, fileReader,** and **bufReader** until we know the actual file to open. We will create these objects in one of the methods we define later.

step 1 code

For the skeleton program, we include temporary output statements in the private methods to verify that they are called correctly in the right order. Here's the skeleton:

```
/*
    Chapter 13 Sample Development: Compute Grades for Undergraduate
                                   and Graduate Students
    File: ComputeGrades.java
*/
```

```
//---------------------- STEP 1 ----------------------//
class ComputeGrades extends MainWindow {

    private static final int DEFAULT_SIZE = 25;

    private OutputBox outputBox;

    private Student[] roster;

    public ComputeGrades() {
       this (DEFAULT_SIZE);
    }

    public ComputeGrades(int arraySize) {
        super();   // an explicit call to the superclass constructor

        outputBox    = new OutputBox(this);

        roster       = new Student[arraySize];
    }

//-------------------------------
// Main
//-------------------------------
    public static void main(String[] args) {
      ComputeGrades gradeComputer = new ComputeGrades();
      gradeComputer.processData();
    }

    public void processData() {
         this.setVisible(true);
         outputBox.setVisible(true);

         boolean success = readData();

         if (success) {
            computeGrade();
            printResult();
         } else {
            outputBox.println("File Input Error");
         }
    }

    private void computeGrade() {

        outputBox.println("Inside computeGrade");  //TEMP
    }

    private void printResult() {

        outputBox.println("Inside printResult");  //TEMP
    }
```

```
    private boolean readData() {

        outputBox.pristln("Inside readData");   //TEMP
        return true;
    }
}
```

step 1 test

We execute the skeleton main class **ComputeGrades** for verification. When it is executed, we will see the top-level frame window (**ComputeGrades**) and an **OutputBox** appearing on the screen and the following messages in the **OutputBox:**

```
Inside readData
Inside computeGrade
Inside printResult
```

Step 2 Development: Implement the printResult Method

step 2 design

In the second development step, we add a routine that places the result in an **outputBox.** To implement and test this method, we need to create the **roster** array. We will include temporary code inside the **readData** method to build a test **roster** array. We can use **for** loops as in

The first half of the array is undergraduate students.

The second half of the array is graduate students.

```
for (int i = 0; i < 15; i++) {
    roster[i] = new UndergraduateStudent( );
    roster[i].setName( "Undergrad # " + i );

    roster[i].setTestScore(1, 70 + i);
    roster[i].setTestScore(2, 75 + i);
    roster[i].setTestScore(3, 80 + i);
}

for (int i = 15; i < DEFAULT_SIZE; i++) {
    roster[i] = new GraduateStudent( );
    roster[i].setName( "Grad # " + i );

    roster[i].setTestScore(1, 80 + i);
    roster[i].setTestScore(2, 85 + i);
    roster[i].setTestScore(3, 90 + i);
}
```

to create a temporary **roster** for testing purposes.

Now, let's design the **printResult** method. When this method is called, we have the **roster** array built. The method scans through the array and retrieves the student data, using the **getName, getCourseGrade,** and **getTestScore** methods. Expressed in pseudocode, we have the following:

```
for each element i in the roster array {

   output the name of roster[i];

   output the test scores of roster[i];

   output the course grade of roster[i];

   skip to the next line;
}
```

How should we terminate the loop? We should realize first that the **roster** array may or may not be full. For example, its default size is 25, but the actual number of elements may be less than 25, so using the value of **roster.length** will not work. Since **roster** is an array of objects, one possible way to express the loop is as follows:

```
while (roster[i] != null) {

   //output roster[i] information
}
```

One problem with this **while** loop is that we must have at least one empty slot in the array for the loop to terminate correctly. We can improve it by using the **length** value as

```
while (i < roster.length && roster[i] != null) {
   ...
}
```

Another possibility is to keep the count, which we set in the **readData** method. This count will be a data member of type **int.** Let's call this count variable **studentCount.** Then the processing loop becomes

```
for (int i = 0; i < studentCount; i++) {

   //output roster[i] information
}
```

We will adopt this approach because having this count information is useful for other purposes. For example, if we want to compute the percentage of students passing the course, we can use **studentCount** to compute it. If we don't have this variable, then every time we need to compute the percentage, we have to find out the number of students in the **roster** array.

Finally, to print out student information so the data will align properly, we will output the control character **\t** (for tab). For a simple output like this, sending tabs to

13.8 Sample Development—*continued*

output will work fine. For a more elaborate output, we can use the formatting technique discussed in Chapter 6.

step 2 code

Here's the step 2 code. Notice we add the declaration for a new data member **studentCount,** and this data member is initialized to 0 in the constructor.

```
/*
   Chapter 13 Sample Development: Compute Grades for Undergraduate
                                  and Graduate Students

   File: ComputeGrades.java

*/

//--------------------- STEP 2 -------------------------//
class ComputeGrades extends MainWindow {

    ...
    private int studentCount;

    ...
    public ComputeGrades(int arraySize) {
        ...
        studentCount = 0;
    }
    ...

    private void printResult() {

        for (int i = 0; i < studentCount; i++) {

            //print one student
            outputBox.print (roster[i].getName());

            for (int testNum = 1; testNum <= Student.NUM_OF_TESTS;
                                                    testNum++) {

                outputBox.print("\t" + roster[i].getTestScore (testNum));
            }

            outputBox.println("\t" + roster[i].getCourseGrade());
        }
    }

    private boolean readData() {
        outputBox.println("Inside readData");   //TEMP
```

```
        //TEMP
        //      Create a temporary roster array to
        //      test the printResult method.
        //
        for (int i = 0; i < 15; i++) {
            roster[i] = new UndergraduateStudent();
            roster[i].setName("Undergrad # " + i);

            roster[i].setTestScore(1, 70 + i);
            roster[i].setTestScore(2, 80 + i);
            roster[i].setTestScore(3, 90 + i);

        }
        for (int i = 15; i < DEFAULT_SIZE; i++) {
            roster[i] = new GraduateStudent();
            roster[i].setName("Grad # " + i);

            roster[i].setTestScore(1, 80 + i);
            roster[i].setTestScore(2, 85 + i);
            roster[i].setTestScore(3, 90 + i);

        }

        studentCount = DEFAULT_SIZE;

        return true;
    }
}
```

step 2 test

We verify two items in this step. First, the temporary **readData** method includes creating student objects and calling their methods. Correct execution will verify that we are including the correct student classes and using their methods properly. Second, the **printResult** method should display the output as intended. Since we have not implemented the **computeGrade** method, we will see four asterisks for the course grades. We have to run the program several times and adjust the display format. Also, it is important to try different values for names and test scores before moving to the next step.

Step 3 Development: Implement the computeGrade Method

step 3 design

The functionality of computing the course grades is embedded inside the student classes, specifically, inside the respective **computeCourseGrade** methods of the **GraduateStudent** and **UndergraduateStudent** classes. Therefore, all we need to do in the **computeGrade** method is to scan through the **roster** array and call the element's **computeCourseGrade** method. This simplicity is a direct result of polymorphism.

13.8 Sample Development—*continued*

step 3 code

Here's the listing. The only addition is the **computeGrade** method.

```
/*
    Chapter 13 Sample Development: Compute Grades for Undergraduate
                                     and Graduate Students

    File: ComputeGrades.java
*/

//----------------------  STEP 3  ----------------------//
class ComputeGrades extends MainWindow {

    ...

    private void computeGrade() {

        for (int i = 0; i < studentCount; i++) {
            roster[i].computeCourseGrade();
        }
    }
   ...
}
```

step 3 test

We repeat the same testing routines of step 2. Instead of seeing four asterisks for the course grades, we should be seeing correct values. To make the verification easy, we can set the fixed test scores for all students. Make sure you assign test scores that will result in students both passing and not passing. Don't forget to try out end cases such as zero for all three test scores. What about negative test scores? Will the Student classes handle them correctly? If we identify serious problems with the **Student** classes at this point, we may have to suspend our development until we correct the **Student** class.

Step 4 Development: Implement the readData Method

step 4 design

We will now design the core function of the class, the **readData** method. We can express the overall logic of the method in pseudocode as

```
get the filename from the user;

if (the filename is provided)
   read in data and build the roster array;
```

```
else
   output an error message;
```

We will use a **JFileChooser** object from the standard **javax.swing** package to let the user specify the file. If the user cancels this dialog, then **null** is returned. In this case, we print out an error message and stop. If the user specifies a file, then we pass this information to a private method **buildRoster,** which will read data from the designated file and build the **roster** array.

The **buildRoster** method will read one line of data from the designated file at a time, and for each line of data, it creates an appropriate student object (an instance of **GraduateStudent** if the type is **G** and an instance of **UndergraduateStudent** if the type is **U**). The counter **studentCount** is incremented by 1 after each line is processed. When the line contains the terminator **END,** the method completes its execution. If the data in a line do not conform to the designated format, then the line is ignored. The method, expressed in pseudocode, is as follows:

```
try {
   set bufReader for input;

   while (!done) {
      line = get next line;

      if (line is END) {
         done = true;
      } else {
         student = createStudent(line);

         if (student != null) {
            roster[studentCount] = student;
                                                //add to roster
            studentCount++;
         }
      }
   }
}
catch (IOException e) {
   output an error message;
}
```

createStudent will return **null** if **line** does not conform to the designated format.

We use the **try–catch** block because the creation of the **BufferedReader** object **bufReader** from a given filename could result in an exception. We can use the **Scanner** class instead of the **FileReader** and **BufferedReader** classes. The **createStudent** method accepts a **String** argument, which is one line of the input file, and returns an instance of either **GraduateStudent** or **UndergraduateStudent** depending on the type specified in the line. If there's an error in the input line, then **createStudent** returns **null.** Instead of terminating the whole program, we will simply ignore the lines that do not conform to the specified format.

13.8 Sample Development—*continued*

In a very simplified form, the **createStudent** method looks like this:

```
type = first element of inputLine;

if (type.equals(UNDER_GRAD) || type.equals(GRAD)) {
   student = newStudentWithData( inputLine );
} else { //invalid type is encountered
   student = null;
}
return student;
```

newStudentWithData will return **null** if **inputLine** contains invalid data.

The top statement requires us to extract the first item in the input line (**String**). How should we do it? The **newStudentWithData** method, which creates an instance of **GraduateStudent** or **UndergraduateStudent** and assigns data to it, also requires an operation to extract individual elements of data from a single line. We can write our own string processing routine to parse a given line and extract data on type, name, and test scores, but there's a better solution. We can use a standard class called **StringTokenizer** from the **java.util** package. We will take a quick detour to explain this class. Instead of using the **StringTokenizer** class, we could use the pattern-matching techniques with the **Pattern** and **Matcher** classes. The **StringTokenizer** class, however, is suitable for a case such as this, where we want to extract tokens from a given string.

String-Tokenizer

A **StringTokenizer** object is used to extract tokens from a given string. A *token* is a string of characters separated by *delimiter characters*, or simply *delimiters*. Any character can be designated as a delimiter, but space is the most commonly used delimiter. By default, a **StringTokenizer** object uses a white space (blank, tab, new line, or return) as its delimiter. Here's an example. The following code

```
String inputString
         = "I drink   100 cups of coffee every morning.";

StringTokenizer parser = new StringTokenizer(inputString);

while (parser.hasMoreTokens())  {
    System.out.println(parser.nextToken());
}
```

will print out

```
I
drink
100
cups
of
```

```
coffee
every
morning.
```

The **hasMoreTokens** method returns **true** if there are more tokens remaining in **parser,** and the **nextToken** method returns the next token in **parser.** The **nextToken** method throws a **NoSuchElementException** if there is no token to return. Please refer to a **java.util** reference manual for more information on **StringTokenizer.**

Hints, & Tips, Pitfalls

It's great if you already know about **StringTokenizer,** but if you don't, you're out of luck. You would end up programming the functionality of **StringTokenizer** yourself, redoing something that has been done already. That's always a challenge for everybody, not just for beginners. Whenever you encounter a situtation that seems to call for a common programming task, first look up the Java API reference manuals. You also can ask your classmates, teaching assistant, or instructor for guidance. They may know something. You should also make a habit of browsing the Java API reference manuals so you will have general knowledge about the standard classes. The key is always to look for the existing classes to reuse.

Now let's get back to the design. Using a **StringTokenizer** object, we can express the **createStudent** method as

```
StringTokenizer parser = new StringTokenizer(line);
String          type;

try {
   type = parser.nextToken();

   if (type.equals(UNDER_GRAD) || type.equals(GRAD)) {
      student = newStudentWithData(type, parser);
   } else  { //invalid type is encountered
      student = null;
   }

} catch (NoSuchElementException e) { //no token
   student = null;
}
return student;
```

A private **newStudentWithData** method accepts a **String** that specifies the type of student and a **StringTokenizer** object. The method creates an instance of

13.8 Sample Development—*continued*

UndergraduateStudent or **GraduateStudent** and assigns data to the object by calling the **StringTokenizer** object's **nextToken** method repeatedly:

```
//type and parser are the parameters
try {
   if (type.equals(UNDER_GRAD)) {
      student = new UndergraduateStudent();
   } else {
      student = new GraduateStudent();
   }

   set the student name //use parser.nextToken() to
                        //extract data from a line

   set the student test scores

} catch (Exception e) { //thrown by parser.nextToken() or
   student = null;      //Integer.parseInt(...)
}

return student;
```

Our design document for the **ComputeGrades** class now includes three more private methods:

Design Document: The `ComputeGrades` Class

Method	Visibility	Purpose
. . .	. . .	. . .
`buildRoster`	`private`	Reads one line of data from the designated file at a time; and for each line of data, creates an appropriate student object. If the data in a line do not conform to the designated format, then the line is ignored.
`createStudent`	`private`	Creates a student object by calling `newStudentWithData` if the type in the input line is `U` or `G`. If successful, returns the created student; otherwise, returns `null`.
`newStudentWithData`	`private`	Creates an instance of `UndergraduateStudent` or `GraduateStudent` and assigns data to the object by calling the `StringTokenizer` object's `nextToken` method repeatedly.

step 4 code

Here's the complete step 4 code:

```
/*
    Chapter 13 Sample Development: Compute Grades for Undergraduate
                                   and Graduate Students

    File: ComputeGrades.java

*/

import java.io.*;
import java.util.*;
import javax.swing.*;

//------------------------ STEP 4 ---------------------------//
class ComputeGrades extends MainWindow {

    private static final int DEFAULT_SIZE = 25;

    private static final String UNDER_GRAD = "U";
    private static final String GRAD = "G";
    private static final String END_OF_FILE_STR = "END";

    private OutputBox   outputBox;
    private Student[]   roster;
    private int         studentCount;

    public ComputeGrades() {
        this (DEFAULT_SIZE);
    }

    public ComputeGrades(int arraySize) {
        super();   // an explicit call to the superclass constructor

        outputBox = new OutputBox(this);

        roster    = new Student[arraySize];

        studentCount = 0;
    }

//-----------------------------------
// Main
//-----------------------------------
    public static void main(String[] args) {
      ComputeGrades gradeComputer = new ComputeGrades();
      gradeComputer.processData();
    }

    public void processData() {
        setVisible(true);
        outputBox.setVisible(true);
```

13.8 Sample Development—*continued*

```
        boolean success = readData();

        if (success) {
           computeGrade();
           printResult();
        } else {
           outputBox.println("File Input Error");
        }
    }

    private boolean buildRoster(String filename) {
        String inputLine;
        Student student;

        File              inFile;
        FileReader        fileReader;
        BufferedReader    bufReader;

        boolean status    = true;
        boolean done      = false;

        try {
          inFile = new File(filename);
          fileReader = new FileReader(inFile);
          bufReader  = new BufferedReader(fileReader);

           while (!done) {

              inputLine = bufReader.readLine(); //read one line

              if (inputLine.equalsIgnoreCase(END_OF_FILE_STR)) {
                 done = true;
              }
              else {
                 student = createStudent(inputLine);

                 if (student != null) {
                    roster[studentCount] = student;
                    studentCount++;
                 }
              }
           } // while

           bufReader.close();
        }
        catch (IOException e) {
            status = false;
        }
```

```
    return status;
}

private void computeGrade() {
    for (int i = 0; i < studentCount; i++) {
        roster[i].computeCourseGrade();
    }
}

private Student createStudent(String line) {
    Student         student;
    StringTokenizer parser = new StringTokenizer(line);
    String          type;

    try {
        type = parser.nextToken();

        if (type.equals(UNDER_GRAD) || type.equals(GRAD)) {

            student = newStudentWithData(type, parser);

        } else {

            student = null;
        }
    } catch (NoSuchElementException e) { //no token
        student = null;
    }

    return student;
}

private Student newStudentWithData(String type,
                                   StringTokenizer parser) {
    Student student;

    try {
        if (type.equals(UNDER_GRAD)) {

            student = new UndergraduateStudent();

        } else {

            student = new GraduateStudent();
        }

        //set the student name
        String  firstName   = parser.nextToken();
        String  lastName    = parser.nextToken();

        student.setName(firstName + " " + lastName);

        //set the student test scores
        for (int testNum = 1; testNum <= Student.NUM_OF_TESTS;
                                                  testNum++) {
```

13.8 Sample Development—*continued*

```
                student.setTestScore(testNum, Integer.parseInt(
                                            parser.nextToken()));
            }

        } catch (Exception e) { //either parser.nextToken() or
                                //Integer.parseInt(...) thrown exception
            student = null;
        }

        return student;
    }

    private void printResult() {

        for (int i = 0; i < studentCount; i++) (

          //print one student
          outputBox.print (roster[i].getName());

          for (int testNum = 1; testNum <= Student.NUM_OF_TESTS;
                                                  testNum++) {

             outputBox.print("\t" + roster[i].getTestScore (testNum));
          }

          outputBox.println("\t" + roster[i].getCourseGrade());
       }
    }

    private boolean readData() {
       //get file to open
        JFileChooser fileChooser = new JFileChooser(".");
                            //start the listing from the current directory

        int returnVal = fileChooser.showOpenDialog(this);

        boolean result = false;

        if(returnVal == JFileChooser.APPROVE_OPTION) {
           String filename
                   = fileChooser.getSelectedFile().getAbsolutePath();

           if (filename != null) {

               result = buildRoster(filename);
           }
        }

        return result;
    }
}
```

step 4 test

We run through a more complete testing routine in this step. We need to run the program for various types of input files. Some of the possible file contents are as follows:

Step 4 Test Data	
Test File	**Purpose**
File with 5 to 20 entries of student information with all lines in correct format	Test the normal case.
File with 5 to 20 entries of student information with some lines in incorrect format	Test that readData and supporting methods handle the error case properly.
File with no entries	Test that buildRoster method handles the error case properly.
File with more than 25 entries	Test that readData and supporting methods handle the case where the number of entries is larger than the default size for the roster array.

Step 5 Development: Finalize and Improve

program review

As always, we will finalize the program by correcting any remaining errors, inconsistency, or unfinished methods. We also look for improvement in the last step. One improvement we can always look for relates to the length of the methods. Although there are no hard rules for the length, a method should not be any longer than a single page. The **buildRoster** and **newStudentWithData** methods are close to the maximum. If we notice the method is getting longer in the coding stage, we may want to rethink our design. For example, if the **buildRoster** method becomes too big, then we can define a new method that takes care of a portion of the method, such as moving the **if–then–else** statement in the method to a new method.

One problem that remains (which would have been identified in step 4 testing) is the missing method for expanding the **roster** array when the input file includes more student entries than the set default size of 25. We leave this method as Exercise 3. We also leave some of the possible improvements as exercises.

Summary

- Inheritance and polymorphism are powerful language features to develop extensible and modifiable code.
- Inheritance mechanism is used to share common code among the related classes.
- Inheritance is different from the Java interface, which is used to share common behavior among unrelated classes.

- The third visibility modifier is the protected modifier.
- If no instances are created from a superclass, then define the superclass as an abstract class.
- Polymorphic messages tell us that the method executed in response to the message will vary according to the class to which the object belongs.
- The first statement in a constructor of a subclass must be a call to a constructor of the superclass. If the required statement is not made explicitly, then the statement to call the default constructor of the superclass is inserted automatically by the Java compiler.
- The standard class described or used in this chapter is StringTokenizer.

Key Concepts

superclass and subclass
inheritance
inheritance and constructors
inheritance and visibility modifiers
abstract superclass
abstract methods
polymorphism
inheritance versus interface

Exercises

1. Consider the following class definitions. Identify invalid statements.

```
class Car {
   public    String   make;
   protected int      weight;
   private   String   color;

   ...
}

class ElectricCar extends Car {
   private   int   rechargeHour;

   public ElectricCar() {
      ...
   }

   //copy constructor
   public ElectricCar (ElectricCar car) {
      this.make         = car.make;
      this.weight       = car.weight;
      this.color        = new String(car.color);
      this.rechargeHour= car.rechargeHour;
   }

   ...
}
```

```
class TestMain {
   public static void main (String[] args) {
      Car         myCar;
      ElectricCar myElecCar;

      myCar = new Car();
      myCar.make = "Chevy";
      myCar.weight = 1000;
      myCar.color = "Red";

      myElecCar = new ElectricCar();
      myCar.make = "Chevy";
      myCar.weight = 500;
      myCar.color = "Silver";
   }
}
```

2. Consider the following class definitions. Identify which calls to the constructor are invalid.

```
class Car {
   public    String    make;
   protected int       weight;
   private   String    color;

   private Car (String make, int weight, String color) {
      this.make   = make;
      this.weight = weight;
      this.color  = color;
   }

   public Car () {
      this("unknown", -1, "white");
   }

class ElectricCar extends Car {
   private   int   rechargeHour;

   public ElectricCar() {
      this(10);
   }

   private ElectricCar(int charge) {
      super();
      rechargeHour = charge;
   }
}

class TestMain {
   public static void main (String[] args) {

      Car         myCar1,  myCar2;
      ElectricCar myElec1, myElec2;
```

```
        myCar1  = new Car();
        myCar2  = new Car("Ford", 1200, "Green");

        myElec1 = new ElectricCar();
        myElec2 = new ElectricCar(15);
    }
}
```

3. In the ComputeGrades sample program, we set the default size of the roster array to 25. Modify the program so the size of the array will be increased if the input file contains more than 25 students. You need to add a method that expands the array, say by 50 percent. The technique to expand an array was discussed in Chapter 10.
4. Extend the ComputeGrades sample program by storing the roster array using ObjectOutputStream. Give an option to the user to read the data from a text file (this is how the original ComputeGrades works) or an object file. Similarly, give an option to the user to save the data to a textfile or an object file.
5. Modify the ComputeGrades sample program to input the data from a text file using the Scanner class instead of the FileReader and BufferedReader classes. Use the tab character (\t) as the delimiter.
6. How would you modify the ComputeGrades sample program if the formula for computing the course grade were different for freshman, sophomore, junior, and senior undergraduate students? Would you design four subclasses of UndergraduateStudent? Or would you modify the body of the computeCourseGrade method of UndergraduateStudent? Discuss the pros and cons of each approach.
7. In the Chapter 5 sample development, we defined the DrawableShape class that includes a method to draw one of the three possible shapes—rectangle, rounded rectangle, or ellipse. Modify the DrawableShape class as a super class of the three subclasses Rectangle, RoundedRectangle, and Ellipse. The actual drawing of a shape is done by the drawShape method defined in each of the three subclasses. Using the DrawingBoard helper class from Chapter 5 and the four classes defined in this exercise, write a screensaver program that draws 10 rectangles, 15 rounded rectangles, and 20 ellipses of various sizes. All shapes will move smoothly across the screen.

Development Exercises

For the following exercises, use the incremental development methodology to implement the program. For each exercise, identify the program tasks, create a design document with class descriptions, and draw the program diagram. Map out the development steps at the start. Present any design alternatives and justify your selection. Be sure to perform adequate testing at the end of each development step.

8. Write a personal finance manager program that maintains information on your bank accounts. Incorporate these rules:

    - For the savings accounts, you can make a maximum of three withdrawals in a month without incurring a fee. The bank charges $1.00 for every withdrawal after the third.
    - For the checking accounts, the bank charges $0.50 for every check you write for the first 20 checks (i.e., withdrawals) in a month. After that, there will be no charge.

    You should be able to open and save account information to a file. You should be able to list all transactions of a given account or of all accounts. Include appropriate menus to select the options supported by the program. Consider using the Date class to record the date of transactions. The Date class is from the java.util package. Please refer to a java.util reference manual for information on this class.

9. Extend the address book sample development from Chapter 10. Instead of managing a single type of Person, incorporate additional types of persons such as PersonalFriend and BusinessAssociate. Define these classes as a subclass of Person. Design carefully to decide whether the Person class will be an abstract class.

10. Consider an asset-tracking program that will track four types of assets: electronic appliances, automobiles, furniture, and compact disks. What classes would you design for the program? Would you define four unrelated classes or one superclass and four subclasses? If you design a superclass, will it be an abstract superclass?

11. Implement the asset-tracking program of Exercise 10. Allow the user to add, modify, and delete electronic appliances, automobiles, furniture, and compact disks. Allow the user to list the assets by category and search for an asset by its serial number.

12. Extend the asset-tracking program of Exercise 11 by adding an object I/O capability.

13. Write an application that reads daily temperatures for 12 months and allows the user to get statistics. Support at least three options: monthly average of a given month, yearly average, and lowest and highest temperatures of a given month. Use a text file to store temperatures. A line in the text file contains daily temperatures for one month. The first line in the text file contains temperatures for January; the second line, those for February; and so forth. Use StringTokenizer to parse a line into temperatures of type float. For a data structure, consider using either an array of Month or a two-dimensional array of float. Month is a class you define yourself.

14 GUI and Event-Driven Programming

Objectives

After you have read and studied this chapter, you should be able to

- Define a subclass of the **JFrame** class using inheritance.
- Write event-driven programs using Java's delegation-based event model.
- Arrange GUI objects on a window using layout managers and nested panels.
- Write GUI application programs using **JButton, JLabel, ImageIcon, JTextField, JTextArea, JCheckBox, JRadioButton, JComboBox, JList,** and **JSlider** objects from the **javax.swing** package.
- Write GUI application programs with menus using **menu** objects from the **javax.swing** package.
- Write GUI application programs that process mouse events.

Introduction

The sample programs we have written so far used standard classes such as Scanner, PrintStream (System.out is an instance of PrintStream), and others for handling user interface. These standard classes are convenient and adequate for a basic program that does not require any elaborate user interface. For example, when we need to input a single integer value, calling the nextInt method of Scanner once to read that input is appropriate and effective. However, when we need to input, say, 10 values for a Student object (e.g., name, age, address, phone number, GPA), then using the Scanner class can be problematic because there is no simple and elegant way to allow the user to reenter any one of the values after all 10 input values are entered. So, instead of using the standard console input, it is a much better user interface to employ a single customized window that allows the user to enter all 10 values. We will learn how to build such a customized user interface in this chapter. As a part of building of a customized user interface, we will also learn how to detect mouse movements and clicking of mouse buttons.

When we write a program for our own use, then we may choose to use the standard console input to enter 10 values. When we write a program for others, however, an effective user interface becomes of paramount importance. Next to the program correctness, the user interface of a program is often the most important criterion for the users to select one program over another, so it is critical for the success of the program to include the user interface that is logical, easy to use, and visually appealing.

graphical user interface

The type of user interface we cover in this chapter is called a ***graphical user interface*** (GUI). In contrast, the user interface that uses System.in and System.out exclusively is the called the *non-GUI,* or *console user interface*. In Java, GUI-based programs are implemented by using the classes from the standard javax.swing and java.awt packages. We will refer to them collectively as *GUI classes.* When we need to differentiate them, we will refer to the classes from javax.swing as ***Swing classes*** and those from java.awt as ***AWT classes***. Some of the GUI objects from the javax.swing package are shown in Figure 14.1.

Swing and AWT classes

Before Java 2 SDK 1.2, we had only AWT classes to build GUI-based programs. Many of the AWT classes are now superseded by their counterpart Swing classes (e.g., AWT Button class is superseded by Swing JButton class). AWT classes are still available, but it is generally preferable to use Swing classes. There are two main advantages in using the Swing classes over the AWT classes.

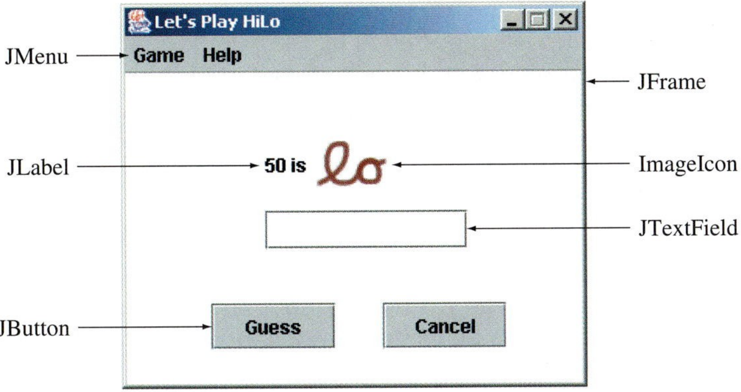

Figure 14.1 Various GUI objects from the **javax.swing** package.

First, the Swing classes provide greater compatibility across different operating systems. The Swing classes are implemented fully in Java, and they behave the same on different operating systems. The AWT classes, on the other hand, are implemented by using the native GUI objects. For example, an AWT Button is implemented by using the Windows button object for the Windows operating system, the Macintosh button object for the Mac operating system, and so forth. Because the behaviors of underlying platform-specific GUI objects are not necessarily identical, an application that uses AWT classes may not behave the same on the different operating systems. To characterize the difference in implementation, the Swing classes are called *lightweight classes* and the AWT classes *heavyweight classes*.

Second, the Swing classes support many new functionalities not supported by the AWT counterparts. For example, we can easily display an image inside a button in addition to a text by using a Swing JButton, but only text can be displayed inside a button with an AWT Button.

We discuss the Swing classes exclusively. We use the AWT classes only when there are no counterpart Swing classes. One thing we must be careful of in using them is not to mix the counterparts in the same program because of their differences in implementation. For example, we should not mix Swing buttons and AWT buttons or Swing menus and AWT menus. If an AWT class has no counterpart Swing class, for example, the AWT Graphics class, then using it with other Swing classes poses no problem.

Things to Remember

The Swing classes are called lightweight classes and the AWT classes heavyweight classes. As a general rule, because they are implemented differently, it is best not to mix the counterparts (e.g., Swing ***JButton*** *and AWT* ***Button****) in the same program.*

You Might Want to Know

Many AWT classes are superseded by the Swing counterpart classes, but they are still available in the newer versions of Java SDK. Why? For example, if the Swing **JButton** class is a better version of the AWT **Button** class, then why don't we get rid of the **Button** class? The first reason is the backward compatibility, which means programs written for older Java SDKs will continue to run under newer SDKs. Had a newer Java SDK dropped the superceded AWT classes, then old programs that use those AWT classes would not run under the newer version of Java. The second reason is the availability of compatible Java interpreters. When you write a program using Swing classes, then the users of your program must have a compatible Java interpreter installed on their machines. If your users employ a Java interpreter that recognizes only AWT classes, then you have no option but to write the program using only the AWT classes. For instance, the micro edition of Java for the Pocket PC PDA does not recognize Swing classes. So if you want to write programs for the Pocket PC PDA, then you must use only the AWT classes.

event-driven programming

To build an effective graphical user interface using objects from the javax.swing and java.awt packages, we must learn a new style of program control called ***event-driven programming***. An *event* occurs when the user interacts with a GUI object. For example, when you move the cursor, click on a button, or select a menu choice, an event occurs. In event-driven programs, we program objects to respond to these events by defining event-handling methods. In this chapter we will learn the fundamentals of event-driven programming. Almost all modern GUI-based application software is event-driven, so it is very important to learn this programming style well.

Since the main objective for this chapter is to teach the fundamentals of GUI and event-driven programming and not to provide an exhaustive coverage of the Swing classes, we will cover only the most common GUI objects.

14.1 Simple GUI I/O with JOptionPane

One of the easiest ways to provide a simple GUI-based input and output is by using the JOptionPane class. For example, when we execute the statement

```
JOptionPane.showMessageDialog(null, "I Love Java");
```

the dialog shown in Figure 14.2 appears on the center of the screen.

In a GUI environment, there are basically two types of windows: a *general-purpose frame* and a *special-purpose dialog*. In Java, we use a JFrame object for a frame window and a JDialog object for a dialog. The first argument to the showMessageDialog method is a frame object that controls this dialog, and the second argument is the text to display. In the example statement, we pass null, a reserved word, meaning there is no frame object. If we pass null as the first argument, the dialog appears on the center of the screen. If we pass a frame object, then

Figure 14.2 A simple "message" dialog created by the **showMessageDialog** method by using the **JOptionPane** class.

the dialog is positioned at the center of the frame. Run the Ch14ShowMessageDialog class and confirm this behavior.

Ch14ShowMessageDialog

```
/*
    Chapter 14 Sample Program: Shows a Message Dialog

    File: Ch14ShowMessageDialog.java
*/

import javax.swing.*;

class Ch14ShowMessageDialog {

    public static void main(String[] args) {

        JFrame jFrame;

        jFrame = new JFrame();
        jFrame.setSize(400,300);
        jFrame.setVisible(true);

        JOptionPane.showMessageDialog(jFrame, "How are you?");

        JOptionPane.showMessageDialog(null, "Good Bye");
    }
}
```

Notice that we are not creating an instance of the JDialog class directly by ourselves. However, when we call the showMessageDialog method, the JOptionPane class is actually creating an instance of JDialog internally. Notice that showMessageDialog is a class method, and therefore we are not creating a JOptionPane object. If we need a more complex dialog, then we create an instance of JDialog. But for a simple display of text, calling the showMessageDialog class method of JOptionPane would suffice.

If we want to display multiple lines of text, we can use a special character sequence \n to separate the lines, as in

```
JOptionPane.showMessageDialog(null, "one\ntwo\nthree");
```

which will result in a dialog shown in Figure 14.3.

We can also use the JOptionPane class for input by using its showInputDialog method. For example, when we execute

```
JOptionPane.showInputDialog(null, "Enter text:");
```

the dialog shown in Figure 14.4 appears on the screen. To assign the name input to an input string, we write

```
String  input;

input = JOptionPane.showInputDialog(null, "Enter text:");
```

Unlike the Scanner class that supports different input methods for specific data types, that is, nextInt and nextDouble, the JOptionPane supports only a string

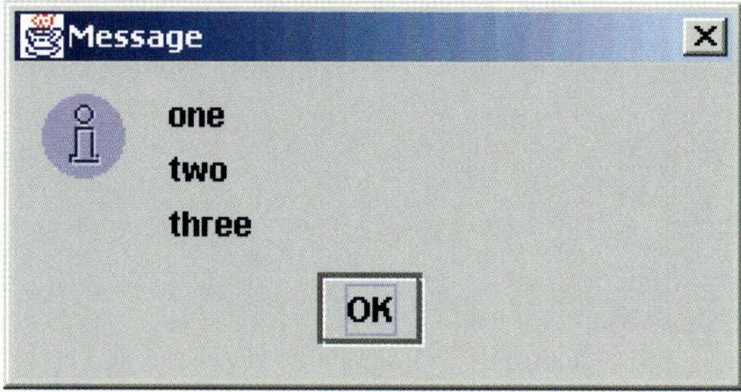

Figure 14.3 A dialog with multiple lines of text.

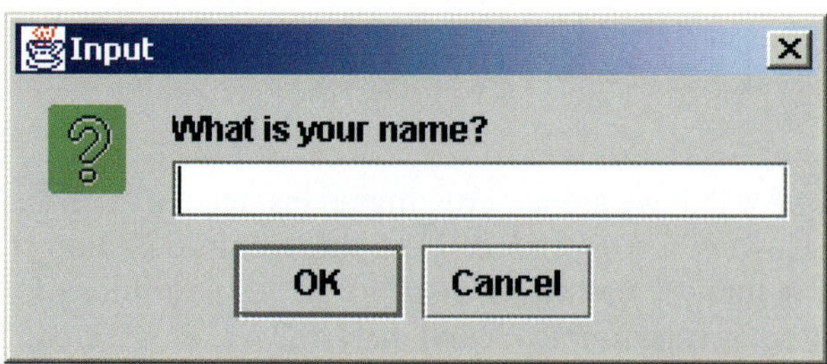

Figure 14.4 An input dialog that appears as a result of calling the **showInputDialog** class method of the **JOptionPane** class with "What is your name?" as the method's second argument.

Table 14.1 Common wrapper classes and their conversion methods.

Class	Method	Example
Integer	parseInt	Integer.parseInt("25") → 25 Integer.parseInt("25.3") → error
Long	parseLong	Long.parseLong("25") → 25L Long.parseLong("25.3") → error
Float	parseFloat	Float.parseFloat("25.3") → 25.3F Float.parseFloat("ab3") → error
Double	parseDouble	Double.parseDouble("25") → 25.0 Double.parseDouble("ab3") → error

input. To input a numerical value, we need to perform the string conversion ourselves. To input an integer value, say, age, we can write the code as follows:

```
String str
        = JOptionPane.showInputDialog(null, "Enter age:");

int age = Integer.parseInt(str);
```

If the user enters a string that cannot be converted to an int, for example, 12.34 or abc123, a NumberFormatException error will result. We use corresponding wrapper classes to convert the string input to other numerical data values.

Table 14.1 lists common wrapper classes and their corresponding conversion methods.

1. Display the message I Love Java by using JOptionPane.
2. Using JOptionPane input dialog, write a statement to input the person's first name.
3. Using JOptionPane input dialog, write a statement to input the person's age (integer).

14.2 Customizing Frame Windows

To create a customized user interface, we often define a subclass of the JFrame class. The helper class MainWindow we used in the Sample Development section of Chapter 13, for example, is a subclass of the JFrame class. The JFrame class contains the most rudimentary functionalities to support features found in any frame window, such as minimizing the window, moving the window, and resizing the window.

In writing practical programs, we normally do not create an instance of the JFrame class because a JFrame object is not capable of doing anything meaningful. For example, if we want to use a frame window for a word processor, we need a frame window capable of allowing the user to enter, cut, and paste text; change font; print text; and so forth. To design such a frame window, we would define a subclass of the JFrame class and add methods and data members to implement the needed functionalities.

Before we show sample subclasses of JFrame, let's first look at the following program which displays a default JFrame object on the screen:

```
/*
   Chapter 14 Sample Program: Displays a default JFrame window

   File: Ch14DefaultJFrame.java

*/

import javax.swing.*;

class Ch14DefaultJFrame {

    public static void main(String[] args) {

        JFrame defaultJFrame;

        defaultJFrame = new JFrame();

        defaultJFrame.setVisible(true);
    }
}
```

When this program is executed, a default JFrame object, shown in Figure 14.5, appears on the screen. Since no methods (other than setVisible) to set the properties of the JFrame object (such as its title, location, and size) are called, a very small default JFrame object appears at the top left corner of the screen.

You may not notice this frame window on the screen at first because it is so small. Look carefully at the top left corner of the screen.

Figure 14.5 A default **JFrame** window appears at the top left corner of the screen.

Now let's define a subclass of the JFrame class and add some default characteristics. To define a subclass of another class, we declare the subclass with the reserved word **extends**. So, to define a class named Ch14JFrameSubclass1 as a subclass of JFrame, we declare the subclass as

extends

```
class Ch14JFrameSubclass1 extends JFrame {

    . . .
}
```

For the Ch14JFrameSubclass1 class, we will add the following default characteristics:

- The title is set to My First Subclass.
- The program terminates when the Close box is clicked.[1]
- The size of the frame is set to 300 pixels wide and 200 pixels high.
- The frame is positioned at screen coordinate (150, 250).

The effect of these properties is illustrated in Figure 14.6.

All these properties are set inside the default constructor. To set the frame's title, we pass the title to the setTitle method. To set the frame's size, we pass its width and height to the setSize method. To position the frame's top left corner to the coordinate (x, y), we pass the values x and y to the setLocation method. Finally, to terminate

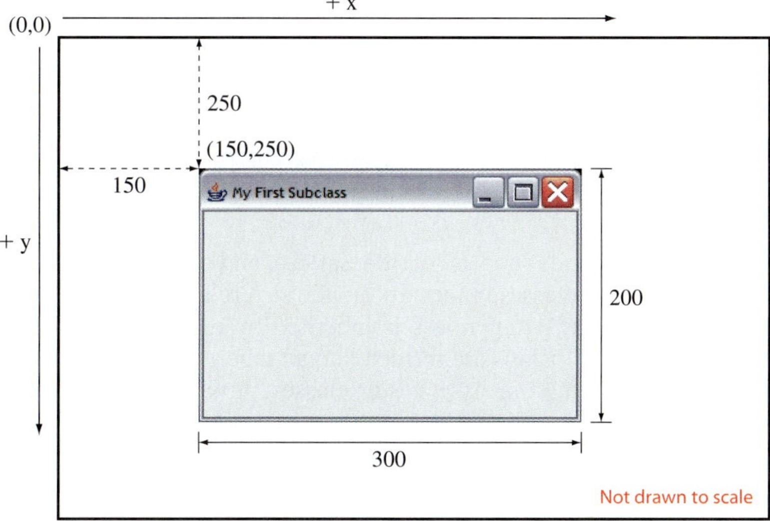

Figure 14.6 How an instance of **Ch14JFrameSubclass1** will appear on the screen.

[1]If we don't add this functionality, the window will close, but the program does not terminate. In a normal environment, we can still terminate the program by closing the command window, the one with the black background on the Windows platform.

the program when the frame is closed, we call the setDefaultCloseOperation with the class constant EXIT_ON_CLOSE as an argument. The Ch14JFrameSubclass1 class is declared as follows:

```
/*
    Chapter 14 Sample Program: A simple subclass of JFrame

    File: Ch14JFrameSubclass1.java
*/

import javax.swing.*;

class Ch14JFrameSubclass1 extends JFrame {

    private static final int FRAME_WIDTH    = 300;
    private static final int FRAME_HEIGHT   = 200;
    private static final int FRAME_X_ORIGIN = 150;
    private static final int FRAME_Y_ORIGIN = 250;

    public Ch14JFrameSubclass1 ( ) {

        //set the frame default properties
        setTitle     ("My First Subclass");
        setSize      (FRAME_WIDTH, FRAME_HEIGHT);
        setLocation  (FRAME_X_ORIGIN, FRAME_Y_ORIGIN);

        //register 'Exit upon closing' as a default close operation
                    setDefaultCloseOperation( EXIT_ON_CLOSE );
    }
}
```

Calls the inherited methods.

Notice the methods such as setTitle, setSize, and others are all defined in the JFrame and its ancestor classes (ancestors are the superclasses in the inheritance hierarchy). Every method of a superclass is inherited by its subclass. Because the subclass-superclass relationships are formed into an inheritance hierarchy, a subclass inherits all methods defined in its ancestor classes. And we can call an inherited method from the method of a subclass in the manner identical to calling a method defined in the subclass, that is, without using dot notation or by using dot notation with the reserved word this.

Things to Remember

Inherited methods are called from the method of a subclass without using dot notation or by using dot notation with the reserved word **this.**

Here's the main class to test the Ch14JFrameSubclass1 class:

```
/*
    Chapter 14 Sample Program: Displays a default Ch14JFrameSubclass window

    File: Ch14TestJFrameSubclass.java
*/

class Ch14TestJFrameSubclass {

    public static void main(String[] args) {

        Ch14JFrameSubclass1 myFrame;

        myFrame = new Ch14JFrameSubclass1();

        myFrame.setVisible(true);
    }
}
```

When it is executed, an instance of Ch14JFrameSubclass1 appears on the screen, as illustrated in Figure 14.6. Notice this main class is identical to Ch14DefaultJFrame except for the creation of a Ch14JFrameSubclass1 instance instead of a JFrame instance. Also notice that there's no need to import the javax.swing package because the main class does not make any direct reference to the classes in this package.

content pane

Since we did not set the background color for Ch14JFrameSubclass1, the default white was used as the frame's background color. (*Note:* If you use Java2 SDK 1.4 or earlier, the default background color is gray.) Let's define another subclass named Ch14JFrameSubclass2 that has a blue background color instead. We will define this class as an instantiable main class so we don't have to define a separate main class. To make the background appear in blue, we need to access the content pane of a frame. A frame's ***content pane*** designates the area of the frame that excludes the title and menu bars and the border. It is the area we can use to display the content (text, image, etc.). We access the content pane of a frame by calling the frame's getContentPane method. And to change the background color to blue, we call the content pane's setBackground method. We carry out these operations in the private changeBkColor method of Ch14JFrameSubclass2. Here's the class definition:

```
/*
    Chapter 14 Sample Program: A simple subclass of JFrame
                               that changes the background
                               color to white.
```

```
    File: Ch14JFrameSubclass2.java
*/

import javax.swing.*;
import java.awt.*;

class Ch14JFrameSubclass2 extends JFrame {

    private static final int FRAME_WIDTH    = 300;
    private static final int FRAME_HEIGHT   = 200;
    private static final int FRAME_X_ORIGIN = 150;
    private static final int FRAME_Y_ORIGIN = 250;

    public static void main(String[] args) {
        Ch14JFrameSubclass2 frame = new Ch14JFrameSubclass2();
        frame.setVisible(true);
    }

    public Ch14JFrameSubclass2() {

        //set the frame default properties
        setTitle    ("Blue Background JFrame Subclass");
        setSize     (FRAME_WIDTH, FRAME_HEIGHT);
        setLocation (FRAME_X_ORIGIN, FRAME_Y_ORIGIN);

        //register 'Exit upon closing' as a default close operation
        setDefaultCloseOperation(EXIT_ON_CLOSE);

        changeBkColor();
    }

    private void changeBkColor() {
        Container contentPane = getContentPane();
        contentPane.setBackground(Color.BLUE);
    }
}
```

Running the program will result in the frame shown in Figure 14.7 appearing on the screen. Notice that we declare the variable contentPane in the changeBkColor method as Container. We do *not* have a class named ContentPane. By declaring the variable contentPane as Container, we can make it refer to any instance of the Container class or the descendant classes of Container. This makes our code more general because we are not tying the variable contentPane to any one specific class. By default, the getContentPane method of JFrame in fact returns the descendant class of Container called JPanel. We will describe the JPanel class in Section 14.5.

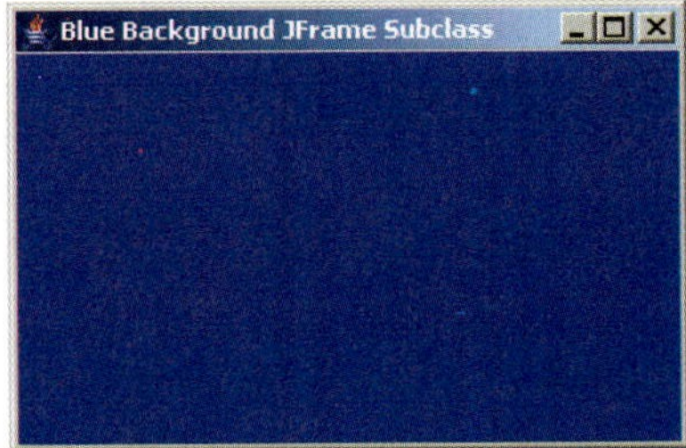

Figure 14.7 An instance of **Ch14JFrameSubclass2** that has blue background.

14.3 GUI Programming Basics

In this section, we will develop a sample frame window that illustrates the fundamentals of GUI programming. The sample frame window has two buttons labeled CANCEL and OK. When you click the CANCEL button, the window's title is changed to You clicked CANCEL. Likewise, when you click the OK button, the window's title is changed to You clicked OK. Figure 14.8 shows the window when it is first opened and after the CANCEL button is clicked.

There are two key aspects involved in GUI programming. One is the placement of GUI objects on the content pane of a frame, and the other is the handling of events generated by these GUI objects. We will develop the sample program in two steps. First we will define a JFrame subclass called Ch14JButtonFrame to show how the two buttons labeled OK and CANCEL are placed on the frame. Then we will implement another subclass called Ch14JButtonEvents to show how the button events are processed to change the frame's title.

Button Placement

pushbutton

The type of button we use here is called a ***pushbutton***. Since we discuss the pushbuttons only in this chapter, we will simply call them buttons. To use a button in a

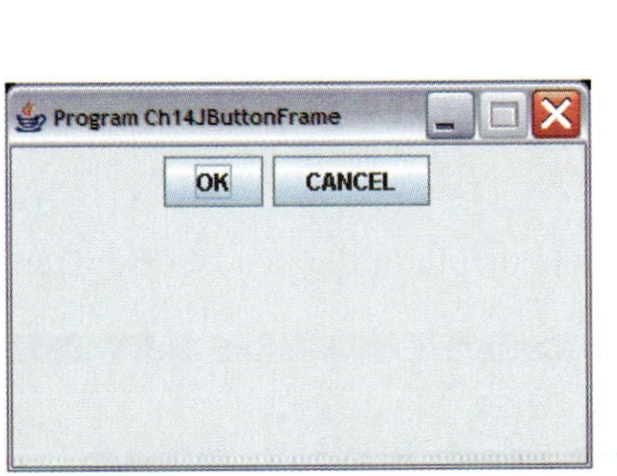

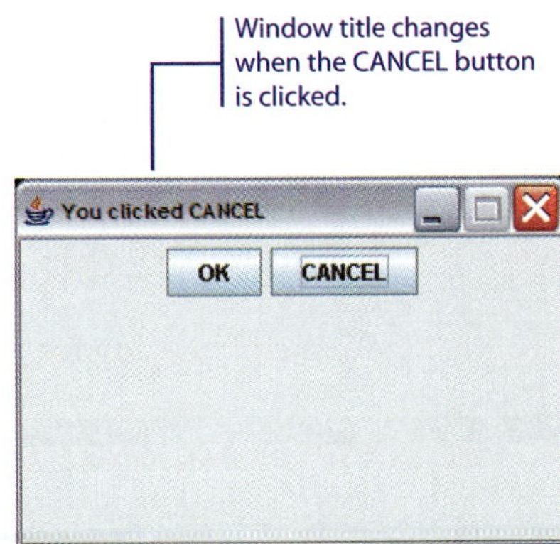

Figure 14.8 A sample window when it is first opened and after the **CANCEL** button is clicked.

program, we create an instance of the javax.swing.JButton class. We will create two buttons and place them on the frame's content pane in the constructor. Let's name the two buttons cancelButton and okButton. We declare and create these buttons in the following manner:

```
import javax.swing.*;

...
JButton cancelButton, okButton;

cancelButton = new JButton("CANCEL");
okButton     = new JButton("OK");
```

The text we pass to the constructor is the label of a button. After the buttons are created, we must place them on frame's content pane.

There are two general approaches to placing buttons (and other types of GUI objects) on a frame's content pane, one that uses a layout manager and another that does not. The ***layout manager*** for a container is an object that controls the placement of the GUI objects. For example, the simplest layout manager called FlowLayout places GUI objects in the top-to-bottom, left-to-right order. If we do not use any layout manager, then we place GUI objects by explicitly specifying their position and size on the content pane. We call this approach ***absolute positioning***. In this section, we will use FlowLayout. We will discuss other common layout managers and absolute positioning in Section 14.4.

layout manager

absolute positioning

To use the flow layout, we set the layout manager of a frame's content pane by passing an instance of FlowLayout to the setLayout method:

```
contentPane.setLayout(new FlowLayout());
```

After the layout manager is set, we add the two buttons to the content pane, so they become visible when the frame is displayed on the screen:

```
contentPane.add(okButton);
contentPane.add(cancelButton);
```

Because the default size of a button depends on the number of characters in the button's label, the sizes of the two buttons will be different. We can override the default by calling the setSize method. For example, we can set their width to 80 pixels and height to 30 pixels by writing

```
okButton.setSize(80, 30);
cancelButton.setSize(80, 30);
```

We are now ready for the complete listing of the Ch14JButtonFrame class:

```
/*
    Chapter 14 Sample Program: Displays a frame with two buttons

    File: Ch14JButtonFrame.java
*/
```

```
import javax.swing.*;
import java.awt.*;

class Ch14JButtonFrame extends JFrame {

    private static final int FRAME_WIDTH    = 300;
    private static final int FRAME_HEIGHT   = 200;
    private static final int FRAME_X_ORIGIN = 150;
    private static final int FRAME_Y_ORIGIN = 250;

    private static final int BUTTON_WIDTH  = 80;
    private static final int BUTTON_HEIGHT = 30;

    private JButton cancelButton;
    private JButton okButton;

    public static void main(String[] args) {
        Ch14JButtonFrame frame = new Ch14JButtonFrame();
        frame.setVisible(true);
    }

    public Ch14JButtonFrame() {

        Container contentPane = getContentPane( );

        //set the frame properties
        setSize     (FRAME_WIDTH, FRAME_HEIGHT);
        setResizable(false);
        setTitle    ("Program Ch14JButtonFrame");
        setLocation (FRAME_X_ORIGIN, FRAME_Y_ORIGIN);

        //set the layout manager
        contentPane.setLayout(new FlowLayout());

        //create and place two buttons on the frame's content pane
        okButton = new JButton("OK");
        okButton.setSize(BUTTON_WIDTH, BUTTON_HEIGHT);
        contentPane.add(okButton);

        cancelButton = new JButton("CANCEL");
        cancelButton.setSize(BUTTON_WIDTH, BUTTON_HEIGHT);
        contentPane.add(cancelButton);

        //register 'Exit upon closing' as a default close operation
        setDefaultCloseOperation(EXIT_ON_CLOSE);
    }
}
```

When we run the program, we see two buttons appear on the frame. We can click the buttons, but nothing happens, of course, because the code to handle the button clicks is not yet added to the class. We'll add the required code next.

Handling Button Events

event

delegation-based event model

event source

event listener

action event

Now let's study how we process the button clicks. An action such as clicking a button is called an ***event***, and the mechanism to process the events *event handling*. The event-handling model of Java is based on the concept known as the ***delegation based event model***. With this model, event handling is implemented by two types of objects: event source objects and event listener objects.

A GUI object, such as a button, where the event occurs is called an *event,* or simply, the ***event source***. We say an event source *generates* events. So, for example, when the user clicks on a button, the corresponding JButton object will generate an action event. When an event is generated, the system notifies the relevant event listener objects. An *event listener object,* or simply an ***event listener***, is an object that includes a method that gets executed in response to generated events. It is possible for a single object to be both an event source and an event listener.

Among the many different types of events, the most common one is called an ***action event***. For example, when a button is clicked or a menu item is selected, an event source will generate an action event. For the generated events to be processed, we must associate, or register, event listeners to the event sources. If the event sources have no registered listeners, then generated events are simply ignored (this is what happened in the Ch14JButtonFrame program). For each type of event, we have a corresponding listener. For example, we have action listeners for action events, window listeners for window events, mouse listeners for mouse events, and so forth. Event types other than action events are discussed later in this chapter. If we wish to process the action events generated by a button, then we must associate an action listener to the button.

An object that can be registered as an action listener must be an instance of a class that is declared specifically for the purpose. We call such class an *action listener class*. For this sample program, let's name the action listener class ButtonHandler. We will describe how to define the ButtonHandler class shortly. But first we will show the step to register an instance of ButtonHandler as the action listener of the two action event sources—okButton and cancelButton—of the sample frame window.

An action listener is associated to an action event source by calling the event source's addActionListener method with this action listener as its argument. For example, to register an instance of ButtonHandler as an action listener of okButton and cancelButton, we can execute the following code:

```
ButtonHandler handler = new ButtonHandler( );

    okButton.addActionListener(handler);
cancelButton.addActionListener(handler);
```

Notice that we are associating a single ButtonHandler object as an action listener of both buttons, because, although we can, it is not necessary to associate two separate listeners, one for the OK button and another for the CANCEL button. A single listener can be associated to multiple event sources. Likewise, although not frequently used, multiple listeners can be associated to a single event source.

Things to Remember

A single listener can be associated to multiple event sources, and multiple listeners can be associated to a single event source.

When an event source generates an event, the system checks for matching registered listeners (e.g., for action events the system looks for registered action listeners, for window events the system looks for registered window listeners, and so forth). If there is no matching listener, the event is ignored. If there is a matching listener, the system notifies the listener by calling the listener's corresponding method. In case of action events, this method is actionPerformed. To ensure that the programmer includes the necessary actionPerformed method in the action listener class, the class must implement the ActionListener interface. The ButtonHandler class, for example, must be defined in the following way:

```
import java.awt.event.*;

class ButtonHandler implements ActionListener {
   ...
}
```

ActionListener is defined in this package.

Remember that, unlike a class, a Java interface includes only constants and abstract methods. The java.awt.event.ActionListener, for instance, is defined as

```
interface ActionListener {

   public void actionPerformed(ActionEvent evt);
}
```

There's no method body, only the method header.

The ButtonHandler class is defined as follows:

```
class ButtonHandler implements ActionListener {

   //data members and constructors come here

   public void actionPerformed(ActionEvent evt) {

      //event-handling statements come here
   }
}
```

An argument to the actionPerformed method is an ActionEvent object that represents an action event, and the ActionEvent class includes methods to access the properties of a generated event.

We want to change the title of a frame to You clicked OK or You clicked CANCEL depending on which button is clicked. This is done inside the actionPerformed method. The general idea of the method is as follows:

```
public void actionPerformed(ActionEvent evt) {

   String buttonText
             = get the text of the event source;

   JFrame frame
             = the frame that contains this event source;

   frame.setTitle("You clicked " + buttonText);
}
```

The first statement retrieves the text of the event source (the text of the okButton is the string OK and the text of the cancelButton is the string CANCEL). We can do this in two ways. The first way is to use the getActionCommand method of the action event object evt. Using this method, we can retrieve the text of the clicked button as

```
String buttonText = evt.getActionCommand();
```

The second way is to use the getSource method of the action event object evt. Using this method, we can retrieve the text of the clicked button as

Notice the typecast to an appropriate class is necessary.

```
JButton clickedButton = (JButton) evt.getSource();
String  buttonText    = clickedButton.getText();
```

Notice the typecasting of an object returned by the getSource method to JButton. The object returned by the getSource method can be an instance of any class, so we need to typecast the returned object to a proper class in order to use the desired method.

Now, to find the frame that contains the event source, we proceed in two steps. First, we get the root pane to which this event source belongs. Second, we get the frame that contains this root pane. Here's the necessary sequence of statements to access the frame that contains the event source:

```
JRootPane rootPane = clickedButton.getRootPane( );
Frame     frame    =  (JFrame) rootPane.getParent();
```

Typecasting is necessary here, too.

A frame window contains nested layers of panes (the content pane in which we place GUI objects is one of them). The topmost pane is called the *root pane* (an instance of JRootPane). We can access the root pane of a frame by calling the GUI object's getRootPane method. From the root pane, we can access the frame object by calling the root pane's getParent method. Because a root pane can be contained by different types of containers (frames, dialogs, etc.), we need to typecast the returned object to JFrame in this example.

Here's the complete ButtonHandler class:

```
/*
    Chapter 14 Sample Program: Event listener for button click events

    File: ButtonHandler.java
*/

import javax.swing.*;
import java.awt.*;
import java.awt.event.*;

class ButtonHandler implements ActionListener {

    public ButtonHandler() {

    }

    public void actionPerformed(ActionEvent event) {

        JButton clickedButton = (JButton) event.getSource();

        JRootPane rootPane = clickedButton.getRootPane();
        Frame     frame    = (JFrame) rootPane.getParent();

        String  buttonText = clickedButton.getText();

        frame.setTitle("You clicked " + buttonText);
    }
}
```

And here's the complete Ch14JButtonEvents class (notice that this class is essentially the same as the Ch14JButtonFrame class except for the portion that deals with the registration of a ButtonHandler to two event sources):

```
/*
    Chapter 14 Sample Program: Displays a frame with two buttons
                               and associates an instance of
                               ButtonHandler to the two buttons

    File: Ch14JButtonEvents.java
*/

import javax.swing.*;
import java.awt.*;

class Ch14JButtonEvents extends JFrame {

    private static final int FRAME_WIDTH  = 300;
    private static final int FRAME_HEIGHT = 200;
```

```
    private static final int FRAME_X_ORIGIN = 150;
    private static final int FRAME_Y_ORIGIN = 250;

    private static final int BUTTON_WIDTH  = 80;
    private static final int BUTTON_HEIGHT = 30;

    private JButton cancelButton;
    private JButton okButton;

    public static void main(String[] args) {
        Ch14JButtonEvents frame = new Ch14JButtonEvents();
        frame.setVisible(true);
    }

    public Ch14JButtonEvents() {

        Container contentPane = getContentPane( );

        //set the frame properties
        setSize       (FRAME_WIDTH, FRAME_HEIGHT);
        setResizable (false);
        setTitle      ("Program Ch14JButtonFrame");
        setLocation   (FRAME_X_ORIGIN, FRAME_Y_ORIGIN);

        //set the layout manager
        contentPane.setLayout(new FlowLayout());

        //create and place two buttons on the frame's content pane
        okButton = new JButton("OK");
        okButton.setSize(BUTTON_WIDTH, BUTTON_HEIGHT);
        contentPane.add(okButton);

        cancelButton = new JButton("CANCEL");
        cancelButton.setSize(BUTTON_WIDTH, BUTTON_HEIGHT);
        contentPane.add(cancelButton);

        //registering a ButtonHandler as an action listener of the
        //two buttons
        ButtonHandler handler = new ButtonHandler();
        cancelButton.addActionListener(handler);
        okButton.addActionListener(handler);

        //register 'Exit upon closing' as a default close operation
        setDefaultCloseOperation(EXIT_ON_CLOSE);
    }
}
```

Making a Frame the Event Listener

Instead of creating a separate event listener class such as ButtonHandler, it is actually more common to let a frame be the event listener of the GUI objects it contains. We stated earlier that any class can implement the ActionListener interface. We can declare a subclass of JFrame that implements the ActionListener interface. As an illustration of this technique, let's define a subclass of JFrame called Ch14JButton-FrameHandler. This class combines the functionalities of the Ch14JButtonEvents and ButtonHandler classes.

Here's the class:

```
/*
    Chapter 14 Sample Program: Displays a frame with two buttons
                                and handles the button events

    File: Ch14JButtonFrameHandler.java
*/

import javax.swing.*;
import java.awt.*;
import java.awt.event.*;

class Ch14JButtonFrameHandler extends JFrame implements ActionListener {

    private static final int FRAME_WIDTH    = 300;
    private static final int FRAME_HEIGHT   = 200;
    private static final int FRAME_X_ORIGIN = 150;
    private static final int FRAME_Y_ORIGIN = 250;

    private static final int BUTTON_WIDTH  = 80;
    private static final int BUTTON_HEIGHT = 30;

    private JButton cancelButton;
    private JButton okButton;

    public static void main(String[] args) {
        Ch14JButtonFrameHandler frame = new Ch14JButtonFrameHandler();
        frame.setVisible(true);
    }

    public Ch14JButtonFrameHandler() {

        Container contentPane = getContentPane( );

        //set the frame properties
        setSize      (FRAME_WIDTH, FRAME_HEIGHT);
        setResizable(false);
        setTitle     ("Program Ch14JButtonFrameHandler");
        setLocation  (FRAME_X_ORIGIN, FRAME_Y_ORIGIN);

        //set the layout manager
        contentPane.setLayout(new FlowLayout());

        //create and place two buttons on the frame's content pane
        okButton = new JButton("OK");
```

```
        okButton.setSize(BUTTON_WIDTH, BUTTON_HEIGHT);
        contentPane.add(okButton);

        cancelButton = new JButton("CANCEL");
        cancelButton.setSize(BUTTON_WIDTH, BUTTON_HEIGHT);
        contentPane.add(cancelButton);

        //register this frame as an action listener of the two buttons
        cancelButton.addActionListener(this);
        okButton.addActionListener(this);

        //register 'Exit upon closing' as a default close operation
        setDefaultCloseOperation(EXIT_ON_CLOSE);

    }

    public void actionPerformed(ActionEvent event) {
        JButton clickedButton = (JButton) event.getSource();

        String buttonText = clickedButton.getText();

        setTitle("You clicked " + buttonText);
    }
}
```

Calls the **setTitle** method of this frame object.

Notice how we call the addActionListener method of cancelButton and okButton. This frame object is the action event listener, so we pass it as an argument to the method as

```
cancelButton.addActionListener(this);
    okButton.addActionListener(this);
```

Likewise, because the actionPerformed method now belongs to this frame class itself, we can call other methods of the frame class from the actionPerformed method without dot notation. So the statement to change the title is simply

```
setTitle("You clicked " + buttonText);
```

1. What is the purpose of a layout manager?
2. Which object generates events? Which object processes events?
3. A class that implements the ActionListener interface must implement which method?
4. What does the getActionCommand method of the ActionEvent class return?

14.4 Text-Related GUI Components

In this section we will introduce three Swing GUI classes—JLabel, JTextField, and JTextArea—that deal with text. The first two deal with a single line of text. A TextField object allows the user to enter a single line of text, while a JLabel object is for displaying uneditable text. A JTextArea object allows the user to enter multiple lines of text. It can also be used for displaying multiple lines of uneditable text.

Like a JButton object, an instance of JTextField generates an action event. A TextField object generates an action event when the user presses the Enter key while the object is active (it is active when you see the vertical blinking line in it). JLabel, on the other hand, does not generate any event. A JTextArea object also generates events, specifically the types of events called *text events* and *document events*. Handling of these events is more involved than handling action events, so to keep the discussion manageable, we won't be processing the JTextArea events.

We will describe the JTextField class first. We set a JTextField object's size and position and register its action listener in the same way as we did for the JButton class. To illustrate its use, we will modify the Ch14JButtonFrameHandler by adding a single JTextField object. We will call the new class Ch14TextFrame1. The effect of clicking the buttons CANCEL and OK is the same as before. If the user presses the Enter key while the JTextField object is active, then we will change the title to whatever text is entered in this JTextField object. In the data declaration part, we add

```
JTextField inputLine;
```

and in the constructor we create a JTextField object and register the frame as its action listener:

```
public Ch14TextFrame1 {
    ...
    inputLine = new JTextField();
    inputLine.setColumns(22);
    add(inputLine);

    inputLine.addActionListener(this);
    ...
}
```

Notice the use of setColumns method instead of setSize in the earlier examples. We do not use the setSize method to set the size of a text field. The number we pass to the setColumns method does not necessarily mean the number of characters visible on the text field because the default font may be a variable-pitch font. If we set the font to a fixed-pitch font as in

```
...
inputLine.setColumns(20);
inputLine.setFont(new Font("Courier", Font.PLAIN, 14));
```

then 20 characters will be visible. Also, notice that the setColumns method affects the number of characters visible by setting the size of the text field. It does not affect the number of characters we can enter in the text field. There is no fixed bound on the number of characters we can enter. When we enter more than the visible number of characters, then the text will scroll to the left.

instanceof

Now we need to modify the actionPerformed method to handle both the button click events and the Enter key events. We have three event sources (two buttons and one text field), so the first thing we must do in the actionPerformed method is to determine the source. We will use the **instanceof** operator to determine the class to which the event source belongs. Here's the general idea:

```
if (event.getSource() instanceof JButton) {
   //event source is either cancelButton
   //or okButton
   ...
} else { //event source must be inputLine
   ...
}
```

We use the getText method of JTextField to retrieve the text that the user has entered. The complete method is written as

```
public void actionPerformed(ActionEvent event) {

   if (event.getSource() instanceof JButton) {
      JButton clickedButton = (JButton) event.getSource();

      String buttonText = clickedButton.getText();

      setTitle("You clicked " + buttonText);

   } else { //the event source is inputLine
      setTitle("You entered '" +
                             inputLine.getText() + "'");
   }
}
```

Notice that we can—but did not—write the else part as

```
JTextField textField = (JTextField) event.getSource();
setTitle("You entered '" + textField.getText() + "'");
```

because we know that the event source is inputLine in the else part. So we wrote it more succinctly as

```
setTitle("You entered '" + inputLine.getText() + "'");
```

Another approach to event handling is to associate a ButtonHandler (defined in Section 14.3) to the two button event sources and a TextHandler (need to add this new class) to the text field event source. This approach is left as an exercise.

Here's the complete Ch14TextFrame1 class:

```
/*
    Chapter 14 Sample Program: Displays a frame with two buttons
                               and one text field

    File: Ch14TextFrame1.java
*/

import javax.swing.*;
import java.awt.*;
import java.awt.event.*;

class Ch14TextFrame1 extends JFrame implements ActionListener {

    private static final int FRAME_WIDTH    = 300;
    private static final int FRAME_HEIGHT   = 200;
    private static final int FRAME_X_ORIGIN = 150;
    private static final int FRAME_Y_ORIGIN = 250;

    private static final int BUTTON_WIDTH  = 80;
    private static final int BUTTON_HEIGHT = 30;

    private JButton cancelButton;
    private JButton okButton;

    private JTextField inputLine;

    public static void main(String[] args) {
        Ch14TextFrame1 frame = new Ch14TextFrame1();
        frame.setVisible(true);
    }

    public Ch14TextFrame1() {
        Container contentPane;

        //set the frame properties
        setSize     (FRAME_WIDTH, FRAME_HEIGHT);
        setResizable(false);
        setTitle    ("Program Ch14SecondJFrame");
        setLocation (FRAME_X_ORIGIN, FRAME_Y_ORIGIN);

        contentPane = getContentPane();
        contentPane.setLayout( new FlowLayout());

        inputLine = new JTextField( );
        inputLine.setColumns(22);
        contentPane.add(inputLine);

        inputLine.addActionListener(this);
```

Adding the **inputLine** text field.

```
        //create and place two buttons on the frame
        okButton = new JButton ("OK");
        okButton.setSize(BUTTON_WIDTH, BUTTON_HEIGHT);
        contentPane.add(okButton);

        cancelButton = new JButton ("CANCEL");
        cancelButton.setSize(BUTTON_WIDTH, BUTTON_HEIGHT);
        contentPane.add(cancelButton);

        //register this frame as an action listener of the two buttons
        cancelButton.addActionListener(this);
        okButton.addActionListener(this);

        //register 'Exit upon closing' as a default close operation
        setDefaultCloseOperation(EXIT_ON_CLOSE);
    }

    public void actionPerformed(ActionEvent event) {

        if (event.getSource() instanceof JButton) {
            JButton clickedButton = (JButton) event.getSource();

            String buttonText = clickedButton.getText();

            setTitle("You clicked " + buttonText);

        } else { //the event source is inputLine
            setTitle("You entered '" + inputLine.getText() + "'");
        }
    }
}
```

Now, let's add a JLabel object to the frame. In the Ch14TextFrame1 class, we have one text field without any indication of what this text field is for. A JLabel object is useful in displaying a label that explains the purpose of the text field. Let's modify the Ch14TextFrame1 class by placing the label Please enter your name above the inputLine text field. We will call the modified class Ch14TextFrame2. We add the data member declaration

```
private JLabel prompt;
```

and create the object and position it in the constructor as

```
public Ch14TextFrame2 {
   ...
   prompt = new JLabel( );
   prompt.setText("Please enter your name");
```

```
        prompt.setSize(150, 25);
        contentPane.add(prompt);
        ...
    }
```

We can also set the text at the time of object creation as

```
    prompt = new JLabel("Please enter your name");
```

ImageIcon

The JLabel class is not limited to the display of text. We can also use it to displayan image. To display an image, we pass an ImageIcon object when we create a JLabel object instead of a string. To create this ImageIcon object, we must specify the filename of an image. Notice that the program we are running, Ch14TextFrame2, and the image file are placed in the same directory. We can place the image file anywhere we want, but the way we write the code here requires the image file to be placed in the same directory. We keep it this way to keep the code simple. We add the data member declaration

```
    private JLabel image;
```

and then create it in the constructor as

```
    public Ch14TextFrame2 {
        ...
        image = new JLabel(new ImageIcon("cat.gif"));
        image.setSize(50, 50);
        contentPane.add(image);
        ...
    }
```

Figure 14.9 shows the frame that appears on the screen when the program is executed. As the sample code shows, it is a simple matter to replace the image. All we have to do is to put the image we want in the right directory and refer to this image file correctly when creating a new ImageIcon object. When we use a different image, we have to be careful, however, to adjust the width and height values in the setBounds method so the values will be large enough to display the complete image.

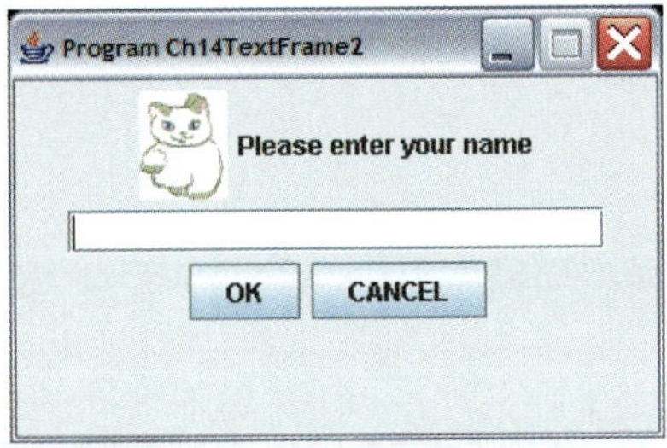

Figure 14.9 The **Ch14TextFrame2** window with one text **JLabel,** one image **JLabel,** one **JTextField,** and two **JButton** objects.

Here's the Ch14TextFrame2 class (only the portion that is different from Ch14TextFrame1 is listed here):

```
/*
    Chapter 14 Sample Program: Displays a frame with two buttons,
                               one text field and one label

    File: Ch14TextFrame2.java
*/

import javax.swing.*;
import java.awt.*;
import java.awt.event.*;

class Ch14TextFrame2 extends JFrame implements ActionListener {

    ...

    private JLabel prompt;
    private JLabel image;

    public static void main(String[] args) {
        Ch14TextFrame2 frame = new Ch14TextFrame2();
        frame.setVisible(true);
    }

    public Ch14TextFrame2() {
        ...

        image = new JLabel(new ImageIcon("cat.gif"));
        image.setSize(50, 50);
        contentPane.add(image);

        prompt = new JLabel();
        prompt.setText("Please enter your name");
        prompt.setSize(150, 25);
        contentPane.add(prompt);

        ...
    }

    ...
}
```

Now let's create the third example by using a JTextArea object. We will call the sample class Ch14TextFrame3. In this sample program, we will add two buttons labeled ADD and CLEAR, one text field, and one text area to a frame. When a text is

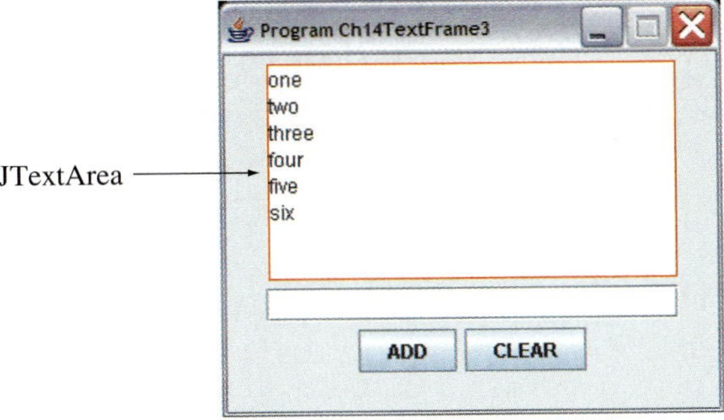

Figure 14.10 The state of a **Ch14TextFrame3** window after six words are entered.

entered in the text field and the Enter (Return) key is pressed or the ADD button is clicked, the entered text is added to the list shown in the text area. Figure 14.10 shows the state of this frame after six words are entered.

We declare a JTextArea object textArea in the data member section as

```
private JTextArea textArea;
```

and add the statements to create it inside the constructor as

```
textArea = new JTextArea();
textArea.setColumns(22);
textArea.setRows(8);
textArea.setBorder(
                BorderFactory.createLineBorder(Color.RED));
textArea.setEditable(false);
contentPane.add(textArea);
```

By default, unlike the single-line JTextField, the rectangle that indicates the boundary of a JTextArea object is not displayed on the frame. We need to create the border for a JTextArea object explicitly. The easiest way to do so is to call one of the class methods of the BorderFactory class. In the example, we called the createLineBorder method with a Color object as its argument. We passed Color.RED so the red rectangle is displayed, as shown in Figure 14.10. The createLineBorder method returns a properly created Border object, and we pass this Border object to the setBorder method of the text area object. There are other interesting borders you might want to try. Table 14.2 lists other border types and the methods to create them. The API documentation of the BorderFactory class records more options and variations.

In the sample frame, we do not want the user to edit the text displayed in the text area, so we disable editing by the statement

```
textArea.setEditable(false);
```

Table 14.2 Border-creating methods of the `javax.swing.BorderFactory` class. The listed methods are all class methods.

Some Class Methods of `javax.swing.BorderFactory`
`public static Border createEtchedBorder (java.awt.Color lineColor, java.awt.Color shadowColor)` Creates an etched border with `lineColor` as line color and `shadowColor` as shadow color.
`public static Border createLoweredBevelBorder()` Creates a border with a lowered beveled edge with a bright shade of the GUI object's current background color for line and dark shading for shadow. This border is effective when you change the background color of the GUI object.
`public static Border createRaisedBevelBorder()` Creates a border with a raised beveled edge with a bright shade of the GUI object's current background color for line and dark shading for shadow. This border is effective when you change the background color of the GUI object.
`public static Border createTitledBorder(String title)` Creates a default (etched) border with `title` displayed at the left corner of the border.

To add a text to the text area, we use the append method. Notice that we cannot use the setText method of JTextArea here because it will replace the old content with the new text. What we want here is to add new text to the current content. Also, since we need to add new text on a separate line, we need to output the new-line control character \n. Here's the basic idea for adding new text to the text area object textArea:

```
String enteredText = inputLine.getText();

textArea.append(enteredText + "\n");
```

Because the actual sequence of characters to separate lines is dependent on the operating systems, if we want to maintain consistent behavior across all operating systems, it is best to not use a fixed character such as \n. Instead, we should call the getProperty method of the System class, passing the string line.separator as an argument, to get the actual sequence of characters used by the operating system on which the program is being executed. We can define a class constant as

```
private static final String NEWLINE
            = System.getProperty("line.separator");
```

and use it in the program as

```
textArea.append(enteredText + NEWLINE);
```

Here's the Ch14TextFrame3 class:

```
/*
    Chapter 14 Sample Program: Displays a frame with two buttons,
                               one text field, and one text area

    File: Ch14TextFrame3.java
*/

import javax.swing.*;
import java.awt.*;
import java.awt.event.*;

class Ch14TextFrame3 extends JFrame implements ActionListener {

    private static final int FRAME_WIDTH    = 300;
    private static final int FRAME_HEIGHT   = 250;
    private static final int FRAME_X_ORIGIN = 150;
    private static final int FRAME_Y_ORIGIN = 250;

    private static final int BUTTON_WIDTH  = 80;
    private static final int BUTTON_HEIGHT = 30;

    private static final String EMPTY_STRING = "";
    private static final String NEWLINE
                            = System.getProperty("line.separator");

    private JButton    clearButton;
    private JButton    addButton;
    private JTextField inputLine;
    private JTextArea  textArea;

    public static void main(String[] args) {
        Ch14TextFrame3 frame = new Ch14TextFrame3();
        frame.setVisible(true);
    }

    public Ch14TextFrame3() {
        Container contentPane;

        //set the frame properties
        setSize      (FRAME_WIDTH, FRAME_HEIGHT);
        setResizable(false);
        setTitle     ("Program Ch14TextFrame3");
        setLocation (FRAME_X_ORIGIN, FRAME_Y_ORIGIN);

        contentPane = getContentPane();
        contentPane.setLayout(new FlowLayout ());

        textArea = new JTextArea();
        textArea.setColumns(22);
        textArea.setRows(8);
        textArea.setBorder(BorderFactory.createLineBorder(Color.RED));
```

```
        textArea.setEditable(false);
        contentPane.add(textArea);

        inputLine = new JTextField();
        inputLine.setColumns(22);
        contentPane.add(inputLine);

        inputLine.addActionListener(this);

        //create and place two buttons on the frame
        addButton = new JButton ("ADD");
        addButton.setSize(BUTTON_WIDTH, BUTTON_HEIGHT);
        contentPane.add(addButton);

        clearButton = new JButton ("CLEAR");
        clearButton.setSize(BUTTON_WIDTH, BUTTON_HEIGHT);
        contentPane.add(clearButton);

        //register this frame as an action listener of the two buttons
        clearButton.addActionListener(this);
        addButton.addActionListener(this);

        //register 'Exit upon closing' as a default close operation
        setDefaultCloseOperation(EXIT_ON_CLOSE);
    }

    public void actionPerformed(ActionEvent event) {

        if (event.getSource() instanceof JButton) {
            JButton clickedButton = (JButton) event.getSource();

            if (clickedButton == addButton) {
                addText(inputLine.getText());

            } else {
                clearText();
            }

        } else { //the event source is inputLine
            addText(inputLine.getText());
        }
    }

    private void addText(String newline) {
        textArea.append(newline + NEWLINE);
        inputLine.setText("");
    }

    private void clearText() {
        textArea.setText(EMPTY_STRING);
        inputLine.setText(EMPTY_STRING);
    }
}
```

Using a JScrollPane to Add Scroll Bars Automatically

When we run the Ch14TextFrame3 class and add more rows (lines) of text than the number of rows set by calling the setRows method, what happens? The height of the text area gets taller. Likewise, the text area expands horizontally when we enter a line longer than the specified width. This is not a desired behavior. The easiest way to handle the situation is to wrap the text area with an instance of javax.swing.JScrollPane that adds the vertical and horizontal scroll bars when necessary.

JScrollPane

In the original Ch14TextFrame3 class, this is what we did to create and set the JTextArea object:

```
textArea = new JTextArea();
textArea.setColumns(22);
textArea.setRows(8);
textArea.setBorder(
            BorderFactory.createLineBorder(Color.RED));
textArea.setEditable(false);
contentPane.add(textArea);
```

To add scroll bars that will appear automatically when needed, we replace the code with the following:

The scroll pane "wraps around" the text area.

```
textArea = new JTextArea();
textArea.setColumns(22);
textArea.setRows(8);
textArea.setEditable(false);
JScrollPane scrollText= new JScrollPane(textArea);
scrollText.setSize(200, 135);
scrollText.setBorder(
            BorderFactory.createLineBorder(Color.RED));
contentPane.add(scrollText);
```

Notice that the properties, such as the border and bounds, of the JScrollPane object are set, no longer the properties of the JTextArea. Figure 14.11 shows a sample Ch14TextFrame3 object when the JScrollPane class is used.

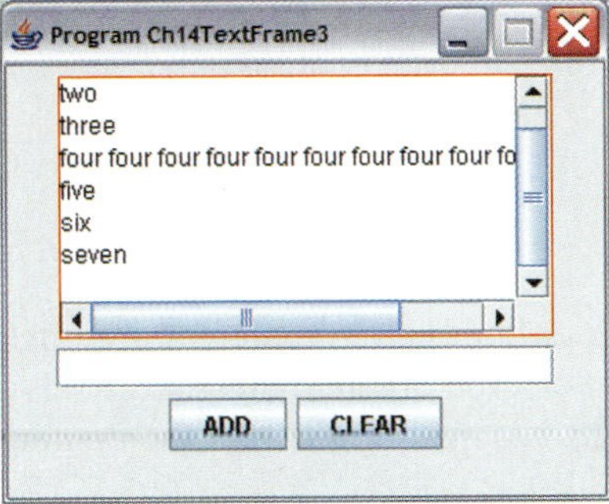

Figure 14.11 A sample **Ch14TextFrame3** window when the **JScrollPane** GUI object is used.

1. What is the purpose of the instanceof operator?
2. What user action will result in a JTextField object generating an action event?
3. Does a JLabel object generate an event?
4. What is the difference between textArea.setText ("Hello") and textArea.append ("Hello")?

14.5 Layout Managers

We showed only a very simplistic use of FlowLayout manager in Section 14.3. In this section, we will explain the use of layout managers in greater detail by discussing three commonly used layout managers. In addition, we will describe absolute positioning at the end of the section.

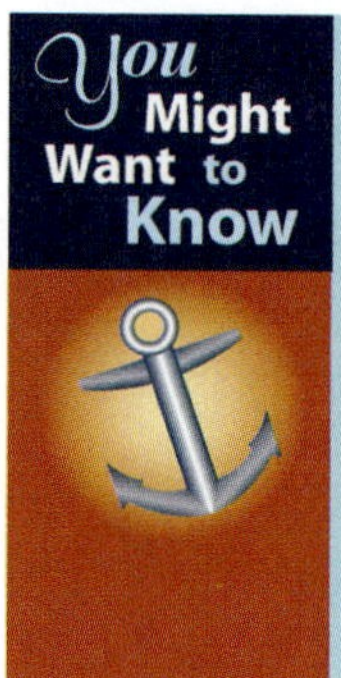

A benefit of using a layout manager is the automatic adjustment of GUI objects when their container (frame, dialog, applet, etc.) is resized. For example, if we place a **JButton** at the center of the container by using some layout manager, then this **JButton** will still be positioned at the center when the size of the container is changed. This automatic adjustment is important also when we consider running our program on different platforms, because by using a layout manager effectively we will get a more consistent look to our frames and dialogs across different platforms. With absolute positioning, a frame that looks nice on one platform may not appear as nice on another platform.

FlowLayout

The most basic layout is java.awt.FlowLayout. In using this layout, GUI components are placed in left-to-right order. When the component does not fit on the same line, left-to-right placement continues on the next line. As a default, components on each line are centered. When the frame containing the component is resized, the placement of components is adjusted accordingly. Figure 14.12 shows the placement of five buttons by using FlowLayout.

Before we add any components, first we assign the desired layout manager to the container, in this case the content pane of a frame, in the frame's constructor.

```
Container contentPane = getContentPane();
...
contentPane.setLayout(new FlowLayout());
```

A container has a default layout manager assigned to it, but it is always safer to explicitly assign the desired layout manager ourselves. After the layout manager is set, we create five buttons and add them to the content pane.

```
JButton button1, button2, button3, button4, button5;
...
```

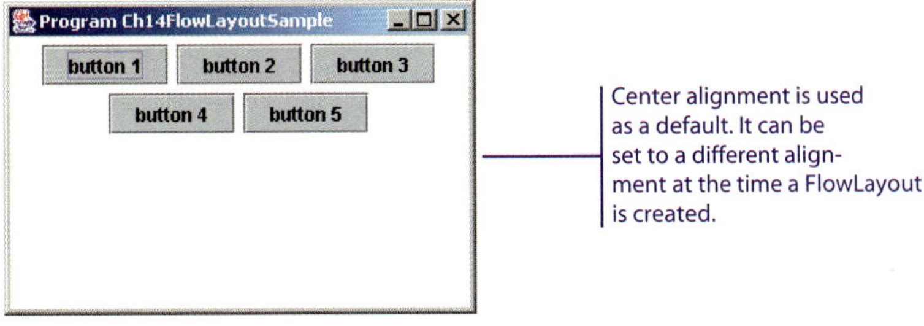

Center alignment is used as a default. It can be set to a different alignment at the time a FlowLayout is created.

When the frame first appears on the screen.

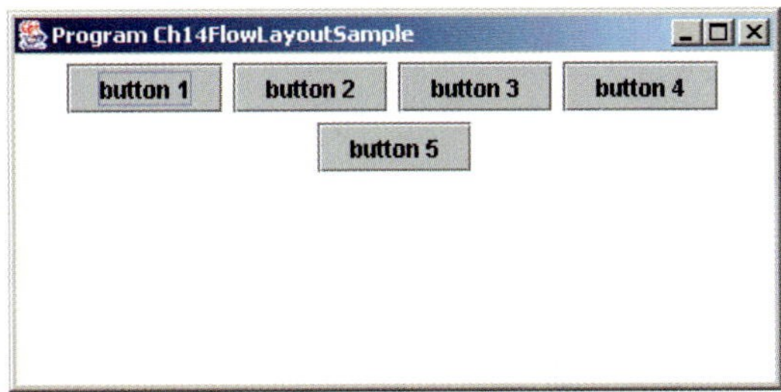

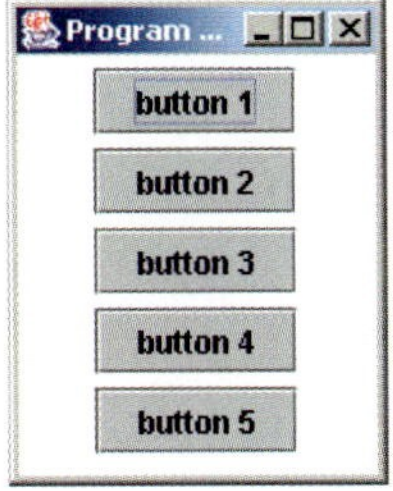

After the frame's width is widened and shortened.

Figure 14.12 Placement of five buttons by using **FlowLayout** when the frame is first opened and after the frame is resized.

```
button1 = new JButton("button1");
//do the same for other buttons

contentPane.add(button1);
contentPane.add(button2);
//and so forth
```

Notice the default is center alignment. We can change it to left or right alignment as

```
contentPane.setLayout(new FlowLayout(FlowLayout.LEFT));
```

or

```
contentPane.setLayout(new FlowLayout(FlowLayout.RIGHT));
```

Here's the complete sample code:

```
/*
    Chapter 14 Sample Program: Illustrates the use of FlowLayout

    File: Ch14FlowLayoutSample.java
*/
```

```
import javax.swing.*;
import java.awt.*;

class Ch14FlowLayoutSample extends JFrame {

    private static final int FRAME_WIDTH    = 300;
    private static final int FRAME_HEIGHT   = 200;
    private static final int FRAME_X_ORIGIN = 150;
    private static final int FRAME_Y_ORIGIN = 250;

//----------------------------------
//      Main method
//----------------------------------
    public static void main(String[] args) {
        Ch14FlowLayoutSample frame = new Ch14FlowLayoutSample();
        frame.setVisible(true);
    }

    public Ch14FlowLayoutSample() {
        Container contentPane;
        JButton   button1, button2, button3, button4, button5;

        //set the frame properties
        setSize    (FRAME_WIDTH, FRAME_HEIGHT);
        setTitle   ("Program Ch14FlowLayoutSample");
        setLocation(FRAME_X_ORIGIN, FRAME_Y_ORIGIN);

        contentPane = getContentPane( );
        contentPane.setBackground(Color.WHITE);
        contentPane.setLayout(new FlowLayout());

        //create and place four buttons on the content pane
        button1 = new JButton("button 1");
        button2 = new JButton("button 2");
        button3 = new JButton("button 3");
        button4 = new JButton("button 4");
        button5 = new JButton("button 5");

        contentPane.add(button1);
        contentPane.add(button2);
        contentPane.add(button3);
        contentPane.add(button4);
        contentPane.add(button5);

        //register 'Exit upon closing' as a default close operation
        setDefaultCloseOperation(EXIT_ON_CLOSE);
    }
}
```

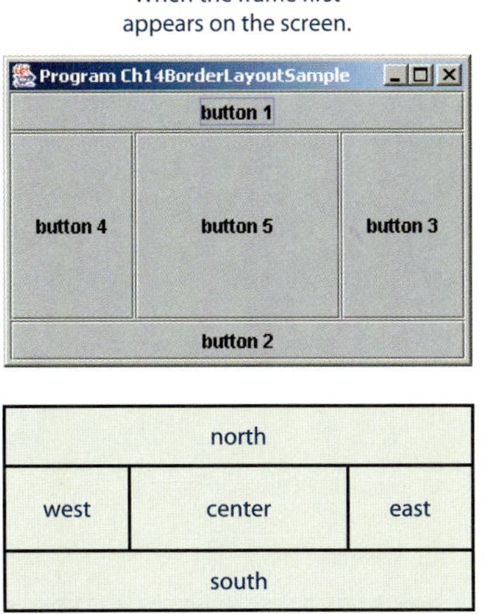

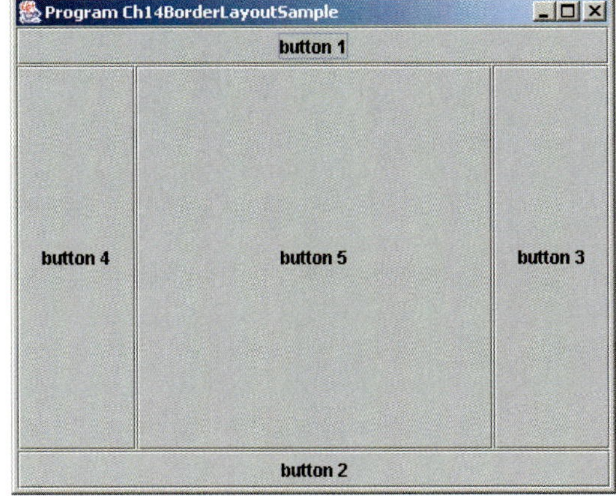

Figure 14.13 Placement of five buttons by using **BorderLayout** when the frame is first opened and after the frame is resized.

BorderLayout

The second layout manager is java.awt.BorderLayout. This layout manager divides the container into five regions: center, north, south, east, and west. Figure 14.13 shows five buttons placed in these five regions. The right frame in the figure is the state after it is resized. The north and south regions expand or shrink in height only, the east and west regions expand or shrink in width only, and the center region expands or shrinks on both height and width. Not all regions have to be occupied. Figure 14.14 shows the frame with only the center and east regions occupied with buttons.

We set the BorderLayout analogously as

```
contentPane.setLayout(new BorderLayout());
```

and then we place the GUI components, in this case, buttons, with the second argument specifying the region.

```
contentPane.add(button1, BorderLayout.NORTH);
contentPane.add(button2, BorderLayout.SOUTH);
contentPane.add(button3, BorderLayout.EAST);
contentPane.add(button4, BorderLayout.WEST);
contentPane.add(button5, BorderLayout.CENTER);
```

The BorderLayout used in Figures 14.13 and 14.14 has no gaps between the regions, which is the default. We can specify the amount of vertical and horizontal gaps between the regions in pixels. For example, to leave 10-pixel-wide gaps and 20-pixel-high gaps between the regions, we create a BorderLayout object by passing these values as arguments to the constructor.

```
contentPane.setLayout(new BorderLayout(10, 20));
```

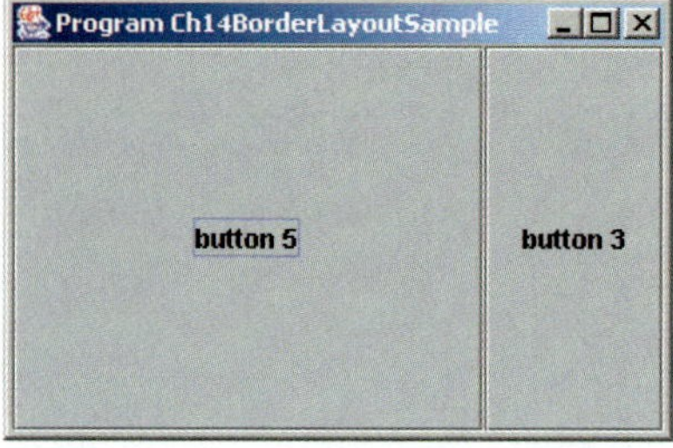

Figure 14.14 Placement of two buttons by using **BorderLayout.** Buttons are placed on the center and east regions.

Here's the complete sample program:

```
/*
    Chapter 14 Sample Program: Illustrates the use of BorderLayout

    File: Ch14BorderLayoutSample.java
*/

import javax.swing.*;
import java.awt.*;

class Ch14BorderLayoutSample extends JFrame {

    private static final int FRAME_WIDTH    = 300;
    private static final int FRAME_HEIGHT   = 200;
    private static final int FRAME_X_ORIGIN = 150;
    private static final int FRAME_Y_ORIGIN = 250;

//----------------------------------
//      Main method
//----------------------------------
    public static void main(String[] args) {
        Ch14BorderLayoutSample frame = new Ch14BorderLayoutSample();
        frame.setVisible(true);
    }

    public Ch14BorderLayoutSample() {
        Container contentPane;
        JButton   button1, button2, button3, button4, button5;

        //set the frame properties
        setSize    (FRAME_WIDTH, FRAME_HEIGHT);
        setTitle   ("Program Ch14BorderLayoutSample");
        setLocation(FRAME_X_ORIGIN, FRAME_Y_ORIGIN);
```

```
        contentPane = getContentPane( );
        contentPane.setBackground(Color.WHITE);
        contentPane.setLayout(new BorderLayout());

        //contentPane.setLayout(new BorderLayout(/*hgap*/10, /*vgap*/10));

        //create and place four buttons on the content pane
        button1 = new JButton("button 1");
        button2 = new JButton("button 2");
        button3 = new JButton("button 3");
        button4 = new JButton("button 4");
        button5 = new JButton("button 5");

        contentPane.add(button1, BorderLayout.NORTH);
        contentPane.add(button2, BorderLayout.SOUTH);
        contentPane.add(button3, BorderLayout.EAST);
        contentPane.add(button4, BorderLayout.WEST);
        contentPane.add(button5, BorderLayout.CENTER);

        //register 'Exit upon closing' as a default close operation
        setDefaultCloseOperation( EXIT_ON_CLOSE );
    }
}
```

GridLayout

The third layout manager is java.awt.GridLayout. This layout manager places GUI components on equal-size $N \times M$ grids. Figure 14.15 shows five buttons placed on 2×3 grids. Components are placed in top-to-bottom, left-to-right order. The frame on the right in Figure 14.15 is the state after it is resized. Notice the number of rows and columns remains the same, but the width and height of each region are changed.

To create a GridLayout object, we pass two arguments: number of rows and number of columns.

```
contentPane.setLayout(new GridLayout(2, 3));
```

We then place GUI components in the manner analogous to the one used for FlowLayout. If the value provided for the number of rows is nonzero, then the value we specify for the number of columns is actually irrelevant. The layout will create the designated number of rows and adjust the number of columns so that all components will fit in the designated number of rows. For example, placing the five buttons with any one of the following three statements will result in the same layout, namely, two rows of grids:

```
contentPane.setLayout(new GridLayout(2, 0));
contentPane.setLayout(new GridLayout(2, 1));
contentPane.setLayout(new GridLayout(2, 5));
```

When the frame first appears on the screen.

After the frame is resized.

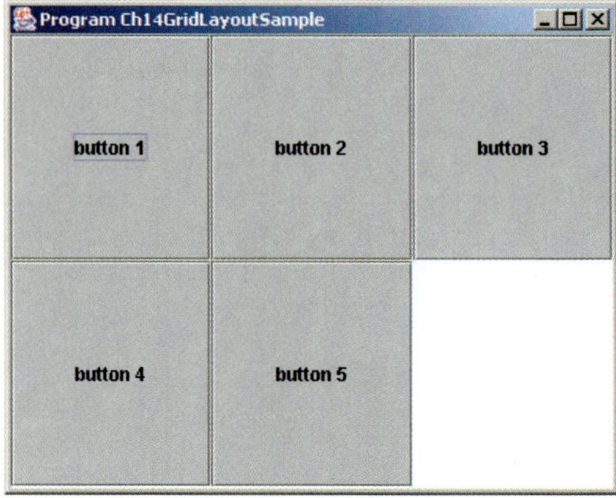

Figure 14.15 Placement of five buttons by using **GridLayout** of two rows and three columns when the frame is first opened and after the frame is resized.

Here's the complete program listing for Ch14GridLayoutSample:

```
/*
    Chapter 14 Sample Program: Illustrates the use of GridLayout

    File: Ch14GridLayoutSample.java
*/

import javax.swing.*;
import java.awt.*;

class Ch14GridLayoutSample extends JFrame {

    private static final int FRAME_WIDTH    = 300;
    private static final int FRAME_HEIGHT   = 200;
    private static final int FRAME_X_ORIGIN = 150;
    private static final int FRAME_Y_ORIGIN = 250;

//---------------------------------
//      Main method
//---------------------------------
    public static void main(String[] args) {
        Ch14GridLayoutSample frame = new Ch14GridLayoutSample();
        frame.setVisible(true);
    }
```

```
    public Ch14GridLayoutSample() {
        Container contentPane;
        JButton   button1, button2, button3, button4, button5;

        //set the frame properties
        setSize     (FRAME_WIDTH, FRAME_HEIGHT);
        setTitle    ("Program Ch14GridLayoutSample");
        setLocation(FRAME_X_ORIGIN, FRAME_Y_ORIGIN);

        contentPane = getContentPane( );
        contentPane.setBackground( Color.WHITE );
        contentPane.setLayout(new GridLayout(2,3));

        //create and place four buttons on the content pane
        button1 = new JButton("button 1");
        button2 = new JButton("button 2");
        button3 = new JButton("button 3");
        button4 = new JButton("button 4");
        button5 = new JButton("button 5");

        contentPane.add(button1);
        contentPane.add(button2);
        contentPane.add(button3);
        contentPane.add(button4);
        contentPane.add(button5);

        //register 'Exit upon closing' as a default close operation
        setDefaultCloseOperation( EXIT_ON_CLOSE );
    }
}
```

absolute positioning

It is possible not to use any layout manager. If we do not use one, then we place GUI objects on the frame's content pane by explicitly specifying their position and size. We call this approach ***absolute positioning***. Although layout managers are very useful in practical applications, knowing various layout managers is not indispensable for learning object-oriented and event-driven programming. So using absolute positioning is acceptable while learning object-oriented and event-driven programming. Keep in mind, however, that to build practical GUI-based Java programs, we must learn how to use layout managers effectively.

To use absolute positioning, we set the layout manager of a frame's content pane to none by passing null to the setLayout method:

```
contentPane.setLayout(null);
```

After the layout manager is set to null, we place two buttons at the position and in the size we want by calling the button's setBounds method as in

```
okButton.setBounds(75, 125, 80, 30);
```

```
Container contentPane = getContentPane();
JButton   okButton    = new JButton("OK");

contentPane.setLayout(null);
okButton.setBounds(70, 125, 80, 30);

contentPane.add(okButton);
```

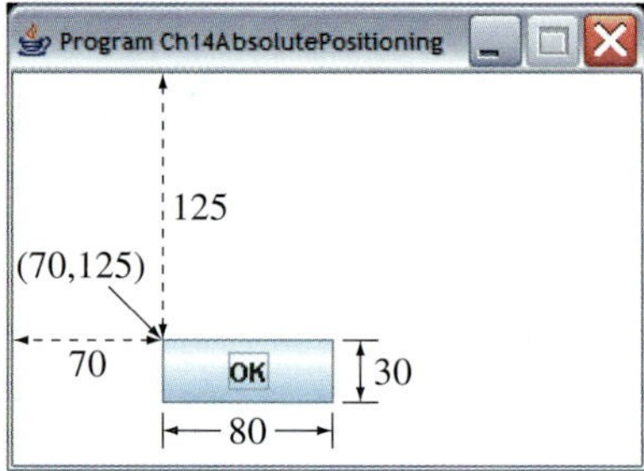

Figure 14.16 This diagram illustrates the process of creating a button and placing it on a frame.

where the first two arguments specify the position of the button and the last two arguments specify the width and height of the button. Finally, to make a button appear on the frame, we need to add it to the content pane by calling the add method. For example, to add okButton, we call

```
contentPane.add(okButton);
```

Figure 14.16 illustrates the process.

Here's the program listing for Ch14AbsolutePositioning:

```
/*
    Chapter 14 Sample Program: Shows how the absolute position works

    File: Ch14AbsolutePositioning.java
*/

import javax.swing.*;
import java.awt.*;

class Ch14AbsolutePositioning extends JFrame {

    private static final int FRAME_WIDTH    = 300;
    private static final int FRAME_HEIGHT   = 220;
    private static final int FRAME_X_ORIGIN = 150;
    private static final int FRAME_Y_ORIGIN = 250;
```

```
    private static final int BUTTON_WIDTH  = 80;
    private static final int BUTTON_HEIGHT = 30;

    private JButton cancelButton;
    private JButton okButton;

//----------------------------------
//      Main method
//----------------------------------
    public static void main(String[] args) {
        Ch14AbsolutePositioning frame = new Ch14AbsolutePositioning();
        frame.setVisible(true);
    }

    public Ch14AbsolutePositioning() {

        Container contentPane = getContentPane();

        //set the frame properties
        setSize     (FRAME_WIDTH, FRAME_HEIGHT);
        setResizable(false);
        setTitle    ("Program Ch14AbsolutePositioning");
        setLocation (FRAME_X_ORIGIN, FRAME_Y_ORIGIN);

        //set the content pane properties
        contentPane.setLayout(null);
        contentPane.setBackground(Color.WHITE);

        //create and place two buttons on the frame's content pane
        okButton = new JButton("OK");
        okButton.setBounds(70, 125, BUTTON_WIDTH, BUTTON_HEIGHT);
        contentPane.add(okButton);

        cancelButton = new JButton("CANCEL");
        cancelButton.setBounds(160, 125, BUTTON_WIDTH, BUTTON_HEIGHT);
        contentPane.add(cancelButton);

        //register 'Exit upon closing' as a default close operation
        setDefaultCloseOperation(EXIT_ON_CLOSE);
    }
}
```

1. How does the flow layout place the components?
2. Which layout manager divides the container into grids of equal size?
3. Write a statement to create a border layout with 20-pixel gaps in both horizontal and vertical directions.

14.6 Effective Use of Nested Panels

In this section, we will discuss how to nest panels effectively to get a desired layout of GUI components. It is possible, but very difficult, to place all GUI components on a single JPanel or other types of containers. A better approach is to use multiple panels, placing panels inside other panels. To illustrate this technique, we will create two sample frames that contain nested panels. The first sample, shown in Figure 14.17, provides the user interface for playing Tic Tac Toe. And the second sample, shown in Figure 14.18, provides the user interface for playing HiLo. Note that we only illustrate the visual layout using nested panels. The sample frames do not include any code for actually playing the games.

The frame shown in Figure 14.17 has four panels. The topmost JPanel, the content pane of the frame, has a border layout. The content pane's center region is

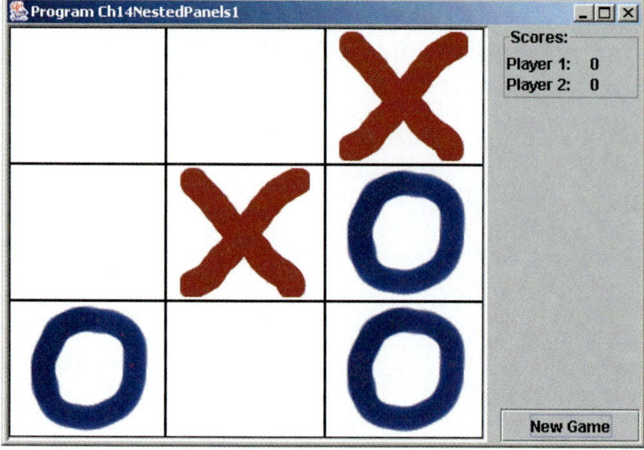

Figure 14.17 A sample frame that contains nested panels. Four **JPanel** objects are used in this frame.

Figure 14.18 Another sample frame that contains nested panels. Five **JPanel** objects are used in this frame.

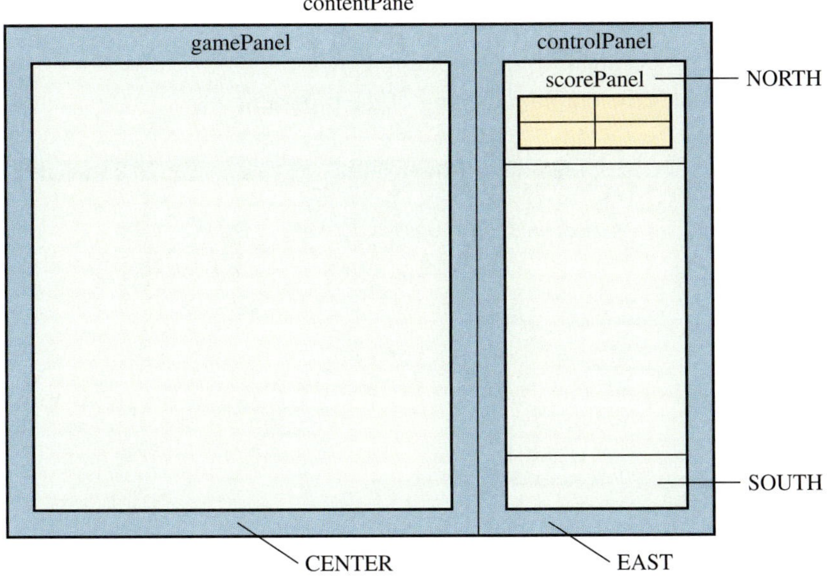

Figure 14.19 This diagram shows how the panels of the frame in Figure 14.17 are nested. There are four **JPanel** objects. We associate a border layout to both **contentPane** and **controlPanel** and a grid layout to **scorePanel.** The **gamePanel** is a specialized **JPanel** (it's a subclass of **JPanel**) that uses a grid layout.

occupied by an instance of Ch14TicTacToePanel named gamePanel. Ch14TicTacToePanel is itself a nested panel. We will design and implement this panel at the end of this section. The content pane's east region is occupied by an instance of another JPanel named controlPanel. A border layout is used for this panel. The north region of controlPanel is occupied by another JPanel named scorePanel, and the south region is occupied by a JButton. The layout for scorePanel is set to a grid layout with four grids, each occupied by a JLabel object. The nesting relationship is shown in Figure 14.19.

When we nest panels, it is often very useful to mark their borders. In this sample frame, we use a titled border for scorePanel and a lowered bevel border for gamePanel. A titled border draws a rectangle around the panel and displays a designated title. We create a titled border by calling the class method createTitledBorder of the BorderFactory class and assign to a panel by calling the setBorder method. Here's the statement:

```
scorePanel.setBorder(
            BorderFactory.createTitledBorder("Scores:"));
```

A lowered bevel border gives an illusion of the panel being recessed into the frame. Here's the statement to create and set the lowered bevel border to gamePanel:

```
gamePanel.setBorder (
            BorderFactory.createLoweredBevelBorder());
```

Additional types of borders, such as line border, matte border, and raised bevel border, are available. For more information, please consult the documentation for the BorderFactory class.

Here's the complete listing of the program:

```
/*
    Chapter 14 Sample Program: Illustrates the use of
                               nested panels

    File: Ch14NestedPanels1.java
*/

import javax.swing.*;
import java.awt.*;

class Ch14NestedPanels1 extends JFrame {

    private static final int FRAME_WIDTH    = 500;
    private static final int FRAME_HEIGHT   = 350;
    private static final int FRAME_X_ORIGIN = 150;
    private static final int FRAME_Y_ORIGIN = 250;

    public static void main(String[] args) {
        Ch14NestedPanels1 frame = new Ch14NestedPanels1();
        frame.setVisible(true);
    }

    public Ch14NestedPanels1() {
        Container         contentPane;
        Ch14TicTacToePanel gamePanel;
        JPanel            controlPanel;
        JPanel            scorePanel;

        //set the frame properties
        setSize    (FRAME_WIDTH, FRAME_HEIGHT);
        setTitle   ("Program Ch14NestedPanels1");
        setLocation(FRAME_X_ORIGIN, FRAME_Y_ORIGIN);

        contentPane = getContentPane( );
        contentPane.setLayout(new BorderLayout(10, 0));

        gamePanel = new Ch14TicTacToePanel();
        gamePanel.setBorder(BorderFactory.createLoweredBevelBorder());
        controlPanel = new JPanel();
        controlPanel.setLayout(new BorderLayout( ));

        contentPane.add(gamePanel, BorderLayout.CENTER);
        contentPane.add(controlPanel, BorderLayout.EAST);

        scorePanel = new JPanel();
        scorePanel.setBorder(BorderFactory.createTitledBorder("Scores:"));
```

```
        scorePanel.setLayout(new GridLayout(2, 2));
        scorePanel.add(new JLabel("Player 1:"));
        scorePanel.add(new JLabel("      0"));
        scorePanel.add(new JLabel("Player 2:"));
        scorePanel.add(new JLabel("      0"));

        controlPanel.add(scorePanel,BorderLayout.NORTH);
        controlPanel.add(new JButton("New Game"), BorderLayout.SOUTH);

        //register 'Exit upon closing' as a default close operation
        setDefaultCloseOperation(EXIT_ON_CLOSE);
    }
}
```

Remember that this class illustrates only the visual aspect of the program. There is no code for handling events or actually playing the game.

Now let's move on to the second sample frame. For this frame, we will use nested panels shown in Figure 14.20. Notice the panel that has a BorderLayout. This panel seems extra, but without it, the buttons will appear away from the bottom, closer to the response label. We feel it is more appealing visually when the buttons are placed at the bottom.

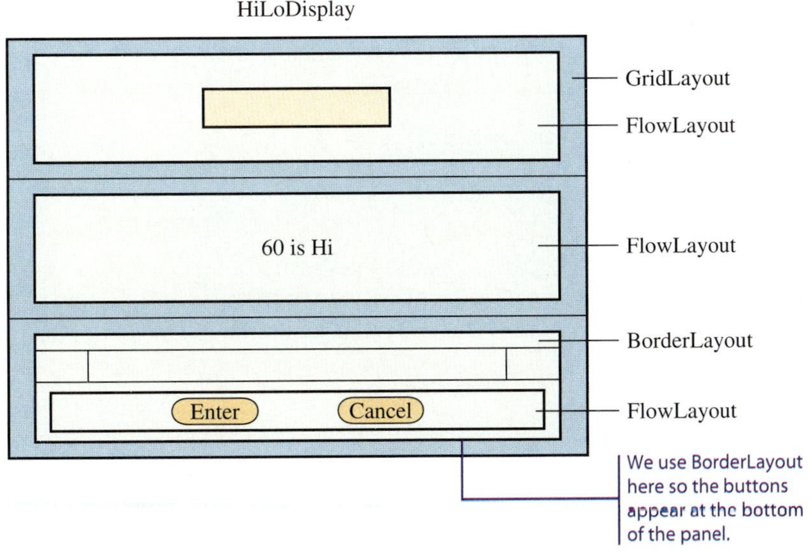

Figure 14.20 The nested panels and associated layout managers for **HiLoDisplay.**

Here's the Ch14NestedPanels2 class:

```
/*
    Chapter 14 Sample Program: Illustration of Nested Panels

    File: Ch14NestedPanels2.java
*/

import javax.swing.*;
import java.awt.*;

class Ch14NestedPanels2 extends JFrame {

    private static final int FRAME_WIDTH    = 250;
    private static final int FRAME_HEIGHT   = 270;
    private static final int FRAME_X_ORIGIN = 150;
    private static final int FRAME_Y_ORIGIN = 250;

    private final String ENTER  = "Enter";
    private final String CANCEL = "Cancel";
    private final String BLANK  = "";

    private JTextField guessEntry;
    private JLabel     hint;

    public static void main(String[] args) {
        Ch14NestedPanels2 frame = new Ch14NestedPanels2();
        frame.setVisible(true);
    }

    public Ch14NestedPanels2() {
        JPanel  guessPanel, hintPanel,
                controlPanel, buttonPanel;

        JButton enterBtn, cancelBtn;

        Container contentPane;

        //set the frame properties
        setSize    (FRAME_WIDTH, FRAME_HEIGHT);
        setTitle   ("Program Ch14NestedPanels2");
        setLocation(FRAME_X_ORIGIN, FRAME_Y_ORIGIN);

        contentPane = getContentPane();

        contentPane.setLayout(new GridLayout(3, 1));

        guessPanel = new JPanel();
        guessPanel.setBorder(BorderFactory.createTitledBorder(
                                                        "Your Guess"));
        guessPanel.add(guessEntry = new JTextField(10));
```

```
        hintPanel = new JPanel();
        hintPanel.setBorder(BorderFactory.createTitledBorder("Hint"));
        hintPanel.add(hint = new JLabel("Let's Play HiLo"));

        controlPanel = new JPanel(new BorderLayout());
        buttonPanel  = new JPanel();
        buttonPanel.add(enterBtn = new JButton(ENTER));
        buttonPanel.add(cancelBtn = new JButton(CANCEL));
        controlPanel.add(buttonPanel, BorderLayout.SOUTH);

        contentPane.add(guessPanel);
        contentPane.add(hintPanel);
        contentPane.add(controlPanel);
    }
}
```

Tic Tac Toe Panel

As promised, let's design and implement a panel specialized in displaying the Tic Tac Toe board of $N \times N = N^2$ cells (default is $3 \times 3 = 9$ cells). Figure 14.17 shows this Tic Tac Toe panel placed on a frame. The panel handles the mouse click events, so every time the player clicks on the cell, the circle or cross is displayed. However, this code for handling mouse click events is only for demonstration. There's no logic of actually playing the game of Tic Tac Toe. For instance, when we click on the cell that already has a cross or circle, a new mark replaces the current one. In the real game, this should not happen. The demonstration code simply alternates between the cross and circle. When we click the panel for the first time, the circle is placed, then the cross, then the circle, and so forth.

How shall we implement this panel? There are two approaches. The first approach is to compute the origin point—the top left corner—of each cell based on the dimension of the panel and the number of cells in the panel. When we know the origin point of a cell, then we can draw a circle or cross by using the drawLine and drawOval methods. Figure 14.21 illustrates how this is done. When a cell is clicked, we get the x and y coordinates of the mouse click location and determine in which cell the mouse click event has occurred. Once we know the cell, we use its origin point to draw a circle or cross at the correct position and size. This approach requires a fair amount of coding to determine the cell and the correct position to draw lines and circles. We can avoid all these computations by using the second approach.

The second approach, the one which we will adopt here, uses the nested panels. We will define two classes—Ch14TicTacToePanel and Ch14TicTacToeCell—both subclasses of JPanel. An instance of Ch14TicTacToePanel will contain N^2 instances of Ch14TicTacToeCell, each instance representing a single cell in the Tic Tac Toe board. A Ch14TicTacToeCell object contains one component, namely, an instance of JLabel. Instead of a text, we assign an image icon to this JLabel object. We have three image files: the first one for the circle, the second for the cross, and the last one

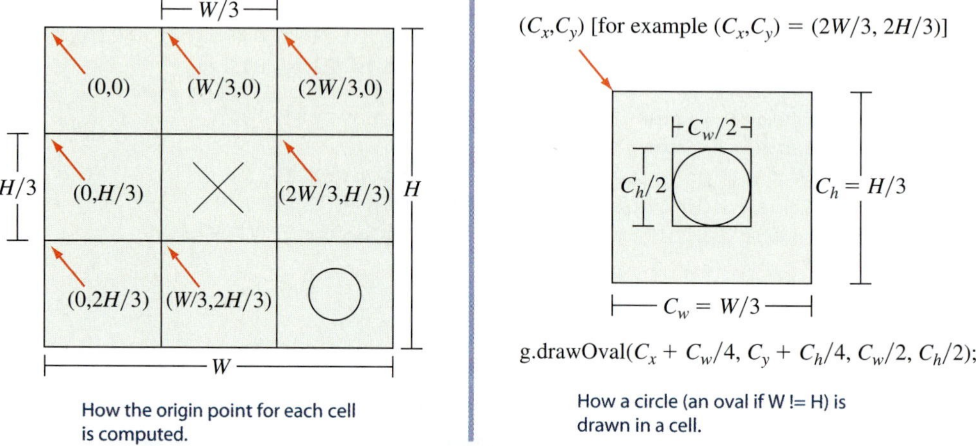

Figure 14.21 The approach not adopted here. This approach is left as Exercise 14. The panel is divided into equal-size cells. A circle or cross can be drawn by using the **drawOval** or **drawLine** method at the position slightly offset from the origin point of the cell.

for a blank cell. These files are named circle.gif, cross.gif, and blank.gif, respectively. All three images have a transparent background so the background color of the Ch14TicTacToeCell will be visible. Notice that these image files must be put in the same folder as the class files Ch14TicTacToePanel.class and Ch14TicTacToeCell.class. Initially, all cells are assigned the blank.gif image. And we set a line border for each cell so the boundary lines are visible. Without such boundary lines, we wouldn't be able to tell how many cells the board had and where each cell began and ended. When a cell is clicked, Ch14TicTacToePanel will set it to a cross or a circle by calling the cell's setContent method.

The class includes one data member called location, a Point object, to record the cell's position on the Tic Tac Toe board. This information is not used in this sample. We need to process the location information when we develop the complete Tic Tac Toe playing program.

Here's the complete listing of the Ch14TicTacToeCell class:

```
/*
   Chapter 14 Sample Program: Tic Tac Toe

   File: Ch14TicTacToeCell.java
*/

import java.awt.*;
import javax.swing.*;

public class Ch14TicTacToeCell extends JPanel {

    public static enum Image {BLANK,CIRCLE,CROSS}
```

```
    private static final String CROSS_IMAGE_FILE  = "cross.gif";
    private static final String CIRCLE_IMAGE_FILE = "circle.gif";
    private static final String BLANK_IMAGE_FILE  = "blank.gif";

    private JLabel content;
    private Point location;

    public Ch14TicTacToeCell() {
        this(null);
    }

    public Ch14TicTacToeCell(Point pt) {

        ImageIcon initImage = new ImageIcon("blank.gif");

        setLayout(new BorderLayout());
        setBackground(Color.white);
        setBorder(BorderFactory.createLineBorder(Color.BLACK));

        content = new JLabel(initImage);
        add(content);

        location = pt;
    }

    public Point getPosition( ) {
        return location;
    }

    public void setContent(Image image) {

        switch (image) {

            case CIRCLE: content.setIcon(new ImageIcon(CIRCLE_IMAGE_FILE));
                         break;

            case CROSS:  content.setIcon(new ImageIcon(CROSS_IMAGE_FILE));
                         break;

            default:     //do nothing
                         break;
        }
    }
}
```

The main tasks for the Ch14TicTacToePanel to handle are the layout of N^2 Ch14TicTacToeCell objects and the mouse click events. Since the board is divided into equal-size cells, the grid layout is the perfect layout manager to use here. By using the grid layout manager, the images will stay at the center of the cells even when the panel is resized.

Each cell is the source of mouse events, and the container of these cells, that is, an instance of Ch14TicTacToePanel, is designated as the listener of the mouse events. Again, the event-handling code for this class is temporary. We will set an image of a circle or a cross to the clicked cell. There's no logic here to actually play the game, for example, to determine the winner. The code for the actual game-playing logic is available from www.drcaffeine.com. Here's the complete listing of the Ch14TicTacToePanel class:

```
/*
   Chapter 14 Sample Program: Tic Tac Toe Board

   File: Ch14TicTacToePanel.java
*/

import java.awt.*;
import javax.swing.*;
import java.awt.event.*;

public class Ch14TicTacToePanel extends JPanel implements MouseListener {

    private boolean circle;

    public Ch14TicTacToePanel() {
        this(3);
    }

    public Ch14TicTacToePanel(int size) {

        Ch14TicTacToeCell cell;

        setLayout(new GridLayout(size, size));

        for (int row = 0; row < size; row++) {
            for (int col = 0; col < size; col++) {
                cell = new Ch14TicTacToeCell( );

                cell.addMouseListener(this);
                add(cell);
            }
        }

        circle = true;
    }

    public void mouseClicked(MouseEvent event) {

        Ch14TicTacToeCell cell = (Ch14TicTacToeCell) event.getSource();

        if (circle) {
            cell.setContent(Ch14TicTacToeCell.Image.CIRCLE);
        } else {
            cell.setContent(Ch14TicTacToeCell.Image.CROSS);
        }
```

```
        circle = !circle;
    }

    public void mouseEntered (MouseEvent event) { }
    public void mouseExited  (MouseEvent event) { }
    public void mousePressed (MouseEvent event) { }
    public void mouseReleased(MouseEvent event) { }
}
```

14.7 Other GUI Components

We will introduce other useful Swing components in this section. Please keep in mind that we limit the discussion to the most basic use of these components. They are actually far more capable than what we present here. However, the materials presented in this section should be enough to let you use them in most common situations and should serve as a good starting point from which you can explore more advanced uses of these components on your own.

JCheckBox

The JButton class represents a type of button called a *pushbutton*. Two other common types of buttons are called *check-box* and *radio buttons*. We will explain the check-box buttons in this subsection and the radio buttons in the next subsection.

The JCheckBox class is used to represent check-box buttons. Figure 14.22 shows a frame with four check-box buttons and one pushbutton. Check-box buttons are useful in presenting a collection of binary (yes/no, true/false) options. The frame shown in Figure 14.22 gives the user the option to select the programming languages he or she can program with by clicking on the appropriate check-box button.

We deal with the JCheckBox class in a manner very similar to that for the JButton class. To create a check-box button with a text Java, we write

```
JCheckBox cbBtn = new JCheckBox("Java");
```

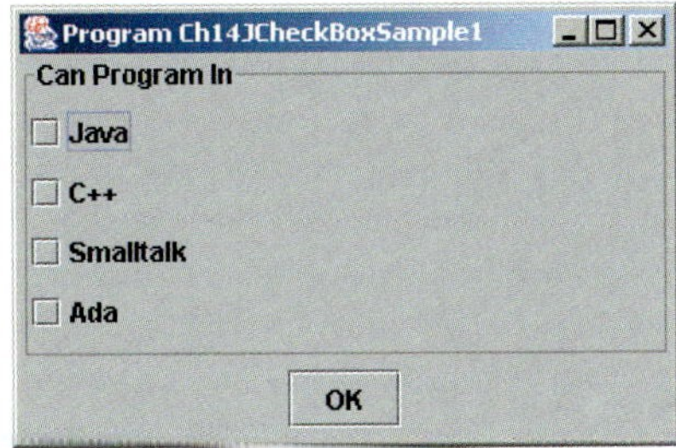

The state when the frame first appeared on the screen.

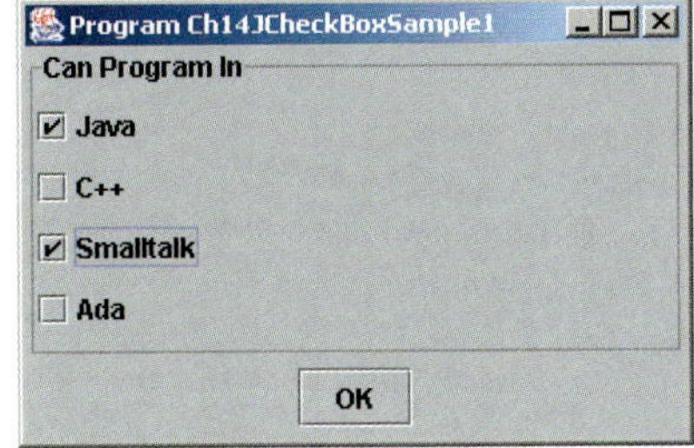

The state after the two check-box buttons are clicked.

Figure 14.22 A frame with four check-box buttons and one pushbutton.

To check if a check-box button is selected (i.e., has a check mark) or deselected, we call its isSelected method. For example,

```
if (cbBtn.isSelected()) {
   System.out.println("You can program in"
                           + cbBtn.getText());

} else {
   System.out.println("You cannot program in "
                          + cbBtn.getText ());
}
```

Just as with a pushbutton, we can retrieve the text associated to a check-box button by calling its getText method. We can use the corresponding setText method to change the button text.

The following Ch14JCheckBoxSample1 class displays the frame shown in Figure 14.22. When the OK pushbutton is clicked, we respond by opening a message dialog with a list of selected programming languages. In the program, notice the use of an array of string btnText in creating an array of JCheckBox buttons. We can easily list any number of names by simply including all names when btnText is initialized, for example,

```
String[] btnText = {"Java", "C++", "Smalltalk", "Ada",
                    "COBOL", "Algol", "Pascal", "BASIC"};
```

There's no need to modify the program code. The ease of achieving this generality is a direct benefit of using panels and layout managers instead of absolute positioning. (You still can do it, but it would be a lot more tedious work to code the same capability with absolute positioning.)

Here's the class:

```
/*
   Chapter 14 Sample Program: Illustrates the use of JCheckBox

   File: Ch14JCheckBoxSample1.java
*/

import javax.swing.*;
import java.awt.*;
import java.awt.event.*;

class Ch14JCheckBoxSample1 extends JFrame implements ActionListener {

    private static final int FRAME_WIDTH    = 300;
    private static final int FRAME_HEIGHT   = 200;
    private static final int FRAME_X_ORIGIN = 150;
    private static final int FRAME_Y_ORIGIN = 250;
```

```
private JCheckBox[] checkBox;

public static void main(String[] args) {
    Ch14JCheckBoxSample1 frame = new Ch14JCheckBoxSample1();
    frame.setVisible(true);
}

public Ch14JCheckBoxSample1() {
    Container contentPane;
    JPanel    checkPanel, okPanel;

    JButton   okButton;
    String[]  btnText = {"Java", "C++", "Smalltalk", "Ada"};

    //set the frame properties
    setSize     (FRAME_WIDTH, FRAME_HEIGHT);
    setTitle    ("Program Ch14JCheckBoxSample1");
    setLocation(FRAME_X_ORIGIN, FRAME_Y_ORIGIN);

    contentPane = getContentPane( );
    contentPane.setBackground(Color.WHITE);
    contentPane.setLayout(new BorderLayout());

    //create and place four check boxes
    checkPanel = new JPanel(new GridLayout(0,1));
    checkPanel.setBorder(BorderFactory.createTitledBorder(
                                                "Can Program In"));
    checkBox = new JCheckBox[btnText.length];

    for (int i = 0; i < checkBox.length; i++) {
        checkBox[i] = new JCheckBox(btnText[i]);
        checkPanel.add(checkBox[i]);
    }

    //create and place the OK button
    okPanel = new JPanel(new FlowLayout());
    okButton = new JButton("OK");
    okButton.addActionListener(this);
    okPanel.add(okButton);

    contentPane.add(checkPanel, BorderLayout.CENTER);
    contentPane.add(okPanel, BorderLayout.SOUTH);

    //register 'Exit upon closing' as a default close operation
    setDefaultCloseOperation(EXIT_ON_CLOSE);
}

public void actionPerformed(ActionEvent event) {

    StringBuffer skill = new StringBuffer("You can program in\n");
    for (int i = 0; i < checkBox.length; i++) {
```

```
            if (checkBox[i].isSelected()) {
                skill.append(checkBox[i].getText() + "\n ");
            }
        }

        JOptionPane.showMessageDialog(this, skill.toString());
    }
}
```

item events

Although we did not process them in the Ch14JCheckBoxSample1 program, a JCheckBox object generates action events just as any other buttons do. So we can associate an action listener to JCheckBox objects, but it is not that common to process action events generated by JCheckBox objects. In addition, a JCheckBox object generates another type of event called ***item events***. An item event is generated when the state (selected or deselected) of a check-box button changes. We can register an instance of a class that implements the ItemListener interface as an item listener of a JCheckBox object. When an item event is generated, its itemStateChanged method is called. Inside the method, we can check the state of change by calling the getStateChange method. Here's a sample itemStateChanged method:

```
public void itemStateChanged(ItemEvent event) {

    if (event.getStateChange() == ItemEvent.SELECTED) {
        System.out.println("You checked the box");
    } else {
        System.out.println("You unchecked the box");
    }
}
```

Here's the Ch14JCheckBoxSample2 class that adds the item event handling to the Ch14JCheckBoxSample1 class:

```
/*
   Chapter 14 Sample Program: Illustrates the use of JCheckBox

   File: Ch14JCheckBoxSample2.java
*/

import javax.swing.*;
import java.awt.*;
import java.awt.event.*;

class Ch14JCheckBoxSample2 extends JFrame
                           implements ActionListener,
                                      ItemListener    {
```

```
private static final int FRAME_WIDTH    = 300;
private static final int FRAME_HEIGHT   = 200;
private static final int FRAME_X_ORIGIN = 150;
private static final int FRAME_Y_ORIGIN = 250;

private JCheckBox[] checkBox;

public static void main(String[] args) {
    Ch14JCheckBoxSample2 frame = new Ch14JCheckBoxSample2();
    frame.setVisible(true);
}

public Ch14JCheckBoxSample2() {
    Container contentPane;
    JPanel    checkPanel, okPanel;

    JButton   okButton;
    String[]  btnText = {"Java", "C++", "Smalltalk", "Ada"};

    //set the frame properties
    setSize    (FRAME_WIDTH, FRAME_HEIGHT);
    setTitle   ("Program Ch14JCheckBoxSample2");
    setLocation(FRAME_X_ORIGIN, FRAME_Y_ORIGIN);

    contentPane = getContentPane( );
    contentPane.setBackground(Color.WHITE);
    contentPane.setLayout(new BorderLayout());

    //create and place four check boxes
    checkPanel = new JPanel(new GridLayout(0,1));
    checkPanel.setBorder(BorderFactory.createTitledBorder(
                                       "Can Program In"));

    checkBox = new JCheckBox[btnText.length];

    for (int i = 0; i < checkBox.length; i++) {
       checkBox[i] = new JCheckBox(btnText[i]);
       checkPanel.add(checkBox[i]);

       checkBox[i].addItemListener(this);
    }

    //create and place the OK button
    okPanel = new JPanel(new FlowLayout());
    okButton = new JButton("OK");
    okButton.addActionListener(this);
    okPanel.add(okButton);

    contentPane.add(checkPanel, BorderLayout.CENTER);
    contentPane.add(okPanel, BorderLayout.SOUTH);

    //register 'Exit upon closing' as a default close operation
    setDefaultCloseOperation(EXIT_ON_CLOSE);
}
```

```
    public void actionPerformed(ActionEvent event) {

        StringBuffer skill = new StringBuffer("You can program in\n");

        for (int i = 0; i < checkBox.length; i++) {

            if (checkBox[i].isSelected()) {
                skill.append(checkBox[i].getText() + "\n ");
            }
        }

        JOptionPane.showMessageDialog(this, skill.toString());
    }

    public void itemStateChanged(ItemEvent event) {

        JCheckBox source = (JCheckBox) event.getSource();

        String state;

        if (event.getStateChange() == ItemEvent.SELECTED) {
            state = "is selected";
        } else {
            state = "is deselected";
        }

        JOptionPane.showMessageDialog(this, "JCheckBox '" +
                                            source.getText() +
                                            "' " + state);

    }
}
```

JRadioButton

The JRadioButton class is used to represent a type of button called a *radio button*. Similar to a check-box button, you can select or deselect a radio button. But unlike with a check-box button, you can only select one of the radio buttons that belong to the same group. Figure 14.23 shows a frame with four radio buttons and one push-button. We can select exactly one of the four radio buttons at a time because they belong to the same group. When we select a new one, then the currently selected radio button will get deselected. Radio buttons are useful in allowing the user to select one from a list of possible choices. The sample frame in Figure 14.23 allows the user to select the favorite programming language.

We can use the JRadioButton class in almost an identical manner as that for the JCheckBox class. Like JCheckBox, JRadioButton generates both action events and item events. The key difference is the requirement to add JRadioButton objects to a button group, in addition to adding them to a container. Notice that the addition of radio buttons to a group is a logical operation (only one radio button in a group can be selected at a time), and the addition of radio buttons to a container is a visual

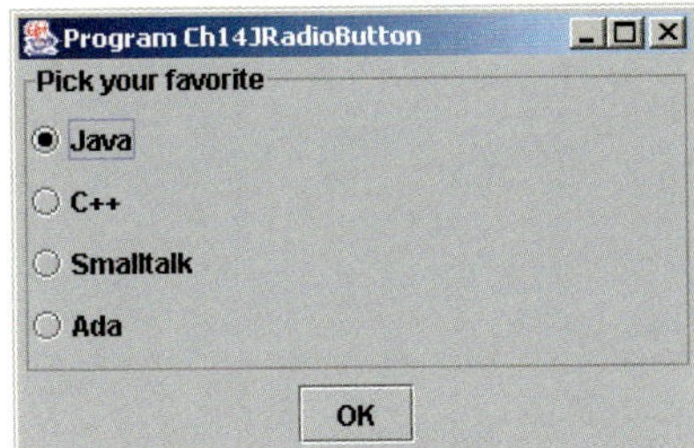

The state when the frame first appeared on the screen.

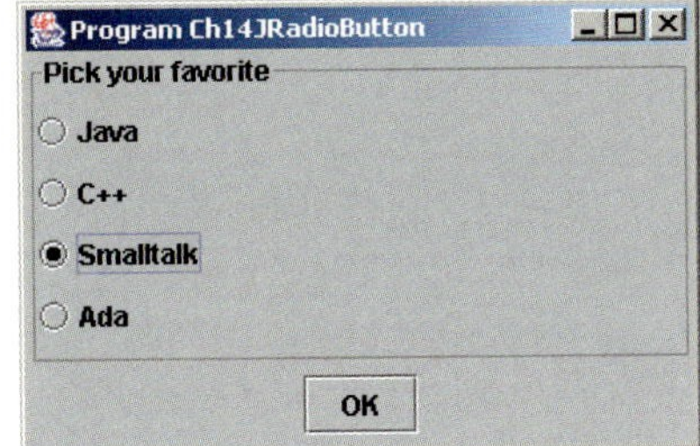

The state after the third radio button is clicked. Previous selection gets deselected.

Figure 14.23 A frame with four radio buttons and one pushbutton.

layout operation. Here's a portion that creates radio buttons and adds them to a group (an instance of a ButtonGroup) and a container (an instance of a JPanel):

```
ButtonGroup languageGroup = new ButtonGroup( );
JPanel      radioPanel    = new JPanel(...);

for (int i = 0; i < radioButton.length; i++) {
   radioButton[i] = new JRadioButton(...);
   ...
   languageGroup.add(radioButton[i]);
   radioPanel.add(radioButton[i]);
}
```

(Three dots . . . represent a piece of actual code not directly relevant here.)

Here's the Ch14JRadioButtonSample class:

```
/*
   Chapter 14 Sample Program: Illustrates the use of JRadioButton

   File: Ch14JRadioButtonSample.java
*/

import javax.swing.*;
import java.awt.*;
import java.awt.event.*;

class Ch14JRadioButtonSample extends JFrame
                             implements ActionListener,
                                        ItemListener    {

    private static final int FRAME_WIDTH    = 300;
    private static final int FRAME_HEIGHT   = 200;
    private static final int FRAME_X_ORIGIN = 150;
    private static final int FRAME_Y_ORIGIN = 250;
```

```
    private JRadioButton[] radioButton;

    public static void main(String[] args) {
        Ch14JRadioButtonSample frame = new Ch14JRadioButtonSample();
        frame.setVisible(true);
    }

    public Ch14JRadioButtonSample() {
        Container   contentPane;
        JPanel      radioPanel, okPanel;
        ButtonGroup languageGroup;

        JButton     okButton;
        String[]    btnText = {"Java", "C++", "Smalltalk", "Ada"};

        //set the frame properties
        setSize     (FRAME_WIDTH, FRAME_HEIGHT);
        setTitle    ("Program Ch14JRadioButton");
        setLocation(FRAME_X_ORIGIN, FRAME_Y_ORIGIN);

        contentPane = getContentPane( );
        contentPane.setBackground(Color.WHITE);
        contentPane.setLayout(new BorderLayout());

        //create and place four radio buttons
        radioPanel = new JPanel(new GridLayout(0,1));
        radioPanel.setBorder(BorderFactory.createTitledBorder(
                                            "Pick your favorite"));

        languageGroup = new ButtonGroup();
        radioButton   = new JRadioButton[btnText.length];

        for (int i = 0; i < radioButton.length; i++) {
            radioButton[i] = new JRadioButton(btnText[i]);
            radioButton[i].addItemListener(this);
            languageGroup.add(radioButton[i]);
            radioPanel.add(radioButton[i]);
        }

        radioButton[0].setSelected(true); //selects the first choice

        //create and place the OK button
        okPanel = new JPanel(new FlowLayout());
        okButton = new JButton("OK");
        okButton.addActionListener(this);
        okPanel.add(okButton);

        contentPane.add(radioPanel, BorderLayout.CENTER);
        contentPane.add(okPanel, BorderLayout.SOUTH);

        //register 'Exit upon closing' as a default close operation
        setDefaultCloseOperation(EXIT_ON_CLOSE);
    }
```

```
    public void actionPerformed(ActionEvent event) {

        String favorite = null;

        int i = 0;
        while (favorite == null) {
            if (radioButton[i].isSelected()) {
                favorite = radioButton[i].getText();
            }

            i++;
        }

        JOptionPane.showMessageDialog(this, "Your favorite language is "
                                            + favorite);
    }

    public void itemStateChanged(ItemEvent event) {

        JRadioButton source = (JRadioButton) event.getSource();

        String state;

        if (event.getStateChange() == ItemEvent.SELECTED) {
            state = "is selected";
        } else {
            state = "is deselected";
        }

        JOptionPane.showMessageDialog(this, "JRadioButton '" +
                                       source.getText() +
                                       "' " + state);

    }
}
```

Every time a radio button is selected, the itemStateChanged method is called twice. The first time is for the deselection of the currently selected item, and the second is for the selection of the new item. Also notice the statement

```
radioButton[0].setSelected(true);
```

in the constructor. If we don't include this statement, then no item will be selected when the frame is first opened. For radio buttons, it is more common to start with one preselected when they first appear on the screen.

JComboBox

The JComboBox class presents a combo box. This class is similar to the JRadioButton class in that it also allows the user to select one item from a list of possible choices. The

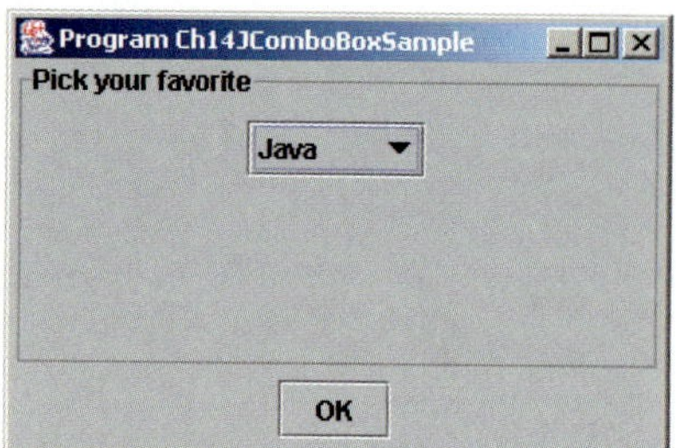

The state when the frame first appeared on the screen.

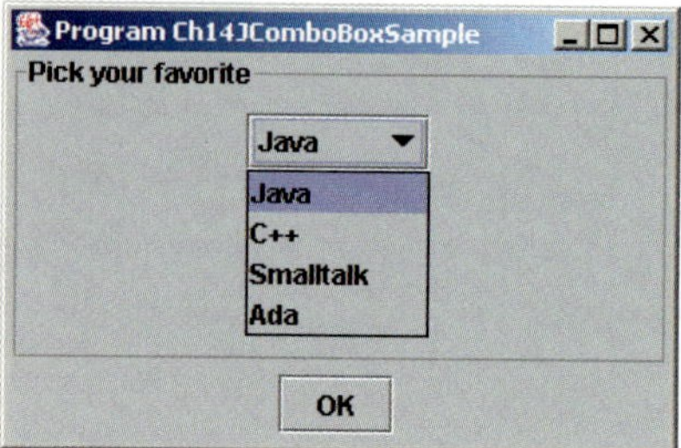

The state after the items in the combo box are revealed by clicking on the down arrow.

Figure 14.24 A frame with one combo box (drop-down list) and one pushbutton.

difference between the two lies in how the choices are presented to the user. Another name for a combo box is a *drop-down list,* which is more descriptive of its interaction style. Figure 14.24 shows a frame with one combo box and one pushbutton.

We can construct a new JComboBox by passing an array of String objects, for example,

```
String[] comboBoxItem
            = {"Java", "C++", "Smalltalk", "Ada"};

JComboBox comboBox = new JComboBox(comboBoxItem);
```

A JComboBox object generates both action events and item events. An action event is generated every time a JComboBox is clicked (note it is not that common to process action events of JComboBox). Every time an item different from the currently selected item is selected, an item event is generated and the itemStateChanged method is called twice. The first time is for the deselection of the currently selected item, and the second is for the selection of the new item. Notice that when the same item is selected again, no item event is generated.

To find out the currently selected item, we call the getSelectedItem method of JComboBox. Because the return type of this method is Object, we must typecast to the correct type. For this example, items are String objects, so we write

```
String selection = (String) comboBox.getSelectedItem();
```

Also, we can call the getSelectedIndex method to retrieve the position of the selected item. The first item in the list is at position 0.

Here's the Ch14JComboBoxSample class:

```
/*
   Chapter 14 Sample Program: Illustrates the use of JComboBox

   File: Ch14JComboBoxSample.java
*/
```

```
import javax.swing.*;
import java.awt.*;
import java.awt.event.*;

class Ch14JComboBoxSample extends JFrame
                          implements ActionListener,
                                     ItemListener    {

    private static final int FRAME_WIDTH    = 300;
    private static final int FRAME_HEIGHT   = 200;
    private static final int FRAME_X_ORIGIN = 150;
    private static final int FRAME_Y_ORIGIN = 250;

    private JComboBox comboBox;

    public static void main(String[] args) {
        Ch14JComboBoxSample frame = new Ch14JComboBoxSample();
        frame.setVisible(true);
    }

    public Ch14JComboBoxSample() {
        Container contentPane;
        JPanel    comboPanel, okPanel;

        JButton   okButton;
        String[]  comboBoxItem = {"Java", "C++", "Smalltalk", "Ada"};

        //set the frame properties
        setSize    (FRAME_WIDTH, FRAME_HEIGHT);
        setTitle   ("Program Ch14JComboBoxSample");
        setLocation(FRAME_X_ORIGIN, FRAME_Y_ORIGIN);

        contentPane = getContentPane( );
        contentPane.setBackground(Color.WHITE);
        contentPane.setLayout(new BorderLayout());

        //create and place a combo box
        comboPanel = new JPanel(new FlowLayout());
        comboPanel.setBorder(BorderFactory.createTitledBorder(
                                          "Pick your favorite"));

        comboBox = new JComboBox(comboBoxItem);
        comboBox.addItemListener(this);
        comboPanel.add(comboBox);

        //create and place the OK button
        okPanel = new JPanel(new FlowLayout());
        okButton = new JButton("OK");
        okButton.addActionListener(this);
        okPanel.add(okButton);

        contentPane.add(comboPanel, BorderLayout.CENTER);
        contentPane.add(okPanel, BorderLayout.SOUTH);
```

```
        //register 'Exit upon closing' as a default close operation
        setDefaultCloseOperation(EXIT_ON_CLOSE);
    }

    public void actionPerformed(ActionEvent event) {

        String favorite;
        int    loc;

        favorite = (String) comboBox.getSelectedItem();
        loc      = comboBox.getSelectedIndex();

        JOptionPane.showMessageDialog(this, "Currently selected item '" +
                              favorite + "' is at index position " + loc);
    }

    public void itemStateChanged(ItemEvent event) {

        String state;

        if (event.getStateChange() == ItemEvent.SELECTED) {
            state = "is selected ";
        } else {
            state = "is deselected ";
        }

        JOptionPane.showMessageDialog(this, "JComboBox Item '" +
                                            event.getItem() +
                                            "' " + state);
    }
}
```

JList

The JList class is useful when we need to display a list of items, for example, a list of students, a list of files, and so forth. Figure 14.25 shows a frame with one JList listing animals with three-letter names and one pushbutton.

We can construct a JList object in a manner identical to the way we construct a JComboBox object, that is, by passing an array of String, such as

```
String[] names = {"Ape", "Bat", "Bee", "Cat",
                  "Dog", "Eel", "Fox", "Gnu",
                  "Hen", "Man", "Sow", "Yak"};
JList list = new JList (names);
```

With JList, we have an option of specifying one of the three selection modes: single-selection, single-interval, and multiple-interval. The single-selection mode allows the user to select only one item at a time. The single-interval mode allows the user to select a single contiguous interval. And the multiple-interval mode allows

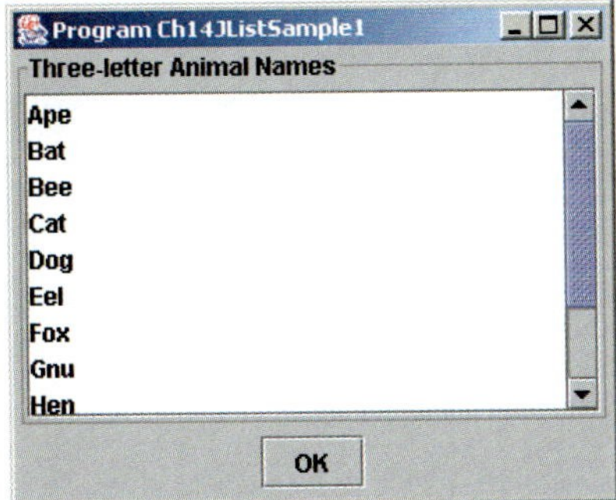

The state when the frame first appeared on the screen.

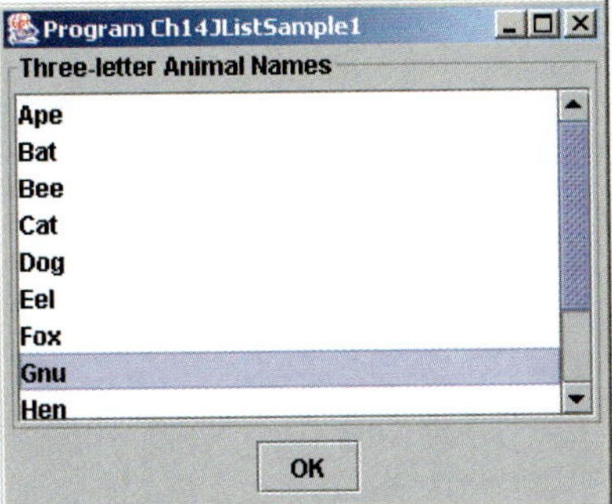

The state after the item Gnu is selected.

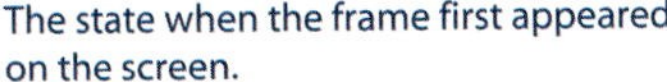

Figure 14.25 A frame with one list and one pushbutton.

the user to select multiple contiguous intervals (each interval will include one or more items). The multiple-interval mode is the default mode. The following three statements show how to set the three selection modes:

```
list.setSelectionMode(
          ListSelectionModel.SINGLE_SELECTION);

list.setSelectionMode(
          ListSelectionModel.SINGLE_INTERVAL_SELECTION);

list.setSelectionMode(
          ListSelectionModel.MULTIPLE_INTERVAL_SELECTION);
```

Because multiple items can be selected, we use getSelectedValues and getSelectedIndices to retrieve an array of selected items and an array of the indices of the selected items, respectively. The following code will display the selected items and their index positions:

```
Object[] name;
int[]    loc;

name = list.getSelectedValues();
loc  = list.getSelectedIndices();

for (int i = 0; i < name.length; i++) {
   System.out.println((String)name[i] +
                       " at position " + loc[i]);
}
```

Notice the return type of getSelectedValues is an array of Object, so we typecast the items in the name array to String before printing it on System.out. If we know the selection mode is single selection, then we can use getSelectedValue and getSelectedIndex instead. Also notice in the code that we are not adding a JList object directly to a panel. Instead, we wrap it in a JScrollPane and add this JScrollPane to a panel because JList itself does not include scroll bars.

Here's the Ch14JListSample class:

```
/*
    Chapter 14 Sample Program: Illustrates the use of JList

    File: Ch14JListSample.java
*/

import javax.swing.*;
import java.awt.*;
import java.awt.event.*;

class Ch14JListSample extends JFrame
                             implements ActionListener {

    private static final int FRAME_WIDTH    = 300;
    private static final int FRAME_HEIGHT   = 250;
    private static final int FRAME_X_ORIGIN = 150;
    private static final int FRAME_Y_ORIGIN = 250;

    private JList list;

    public static void main(String[] args) {
        Ch14JListSample frame = new Ch14JListSample();
        frame.setVisible(true);
    }

    public Ch14JListSample() {
        Container contentPane;
        JPanel    listPanel, okPanel;

        JButton   okButton;
        String[]  names = {"Ape", "Bat", "Bee", "Cat",
                           "Dog", "Eel", "Fox", "Gnu",
                           "Hen", "Man", "Sow", "Yak"};

        //set the frame properties
        setSize    (FRAME_WIDTH, FRAME_HEIGHT);
        setTitle   ("Program Ch14JListSample2");
        setLocation(FRAME_X_ORIGIN, FRAME_Y_ORIGIN);

        contentPane = getContentPane( );
        contentPane.setBackground(Color.WHITE);
        contentPane.setLayout(new BorderLayout());

        //create and place a JList
        listPanel = new JPanel(new GridLayout(0,1));
        listPanel.setBorder(BorderFactory.createTitledBorder(
                                     "Three-letter Animal Names"));

        list = new JList(names);
        listPanel.add(new JScrollPane(list));
```

```
        list.setSelectionMode(
                        ListSelectionModel.MULTIPLE_INTERVAL_SELECTION);
            //this is default, so the explicit call is not necessary

        //create and place the OK button
        okPanel  = new JPanel(new FlowLayout());
        okButton = new JButton("OK");
        okButton.addActionListener(this);
        okPanel.add(okButton);

        contentPane.add(listPanel, BorderLayout.CENTER);
        contentPane.add(okPanel, BorderLayout.SOUTH);

        //register 'Exit upon closing' as a default close operation
        setDefaultCloseOperation(EXIT_ON_CLOSE);
    }

    public void actionPerformed(ActionEvent event) {

        Object[] name;
        int[]    loc;

        name = list.getSelectedValues();
        loc  = list.getSelectedIndices();

        System.out.println("Currently selected animal names are");
        for (int i = 0; i < name.length; i++) {
            System.out.println((String)name[i] + " at position " + loc[i]);
        }
    }
}
```

JSlider

The JSlider class represents a slider in which the user can move a nob to a desired position. The position of the nob on a slider determines the selected value. Figure 14.26 shows a frame with three sliders. This is a classic example of sliders where the user moves the three nobs to set the red, green, blue (RGB) value in selecting a color. Values for the R, G, and B range from 0 to 255, inclusive. Some of properties we can set for a JSlider object are the minimum and maximum range of values, whether to display the tick marks, the spacing of major and minor tick marks, whether to display the label for the major tick marks, and the placement orientation (either vertical or horizontal).

The sliders in the sample program are created and initialized in the following manner:

```
JSlider slider = new JSlider();

slider.setOrientation(JSlider.VERTICAL);
slider.setPaintLabels(true); //show tick mark labels
slider.setPaintTicks(true);  //show tick marks
```

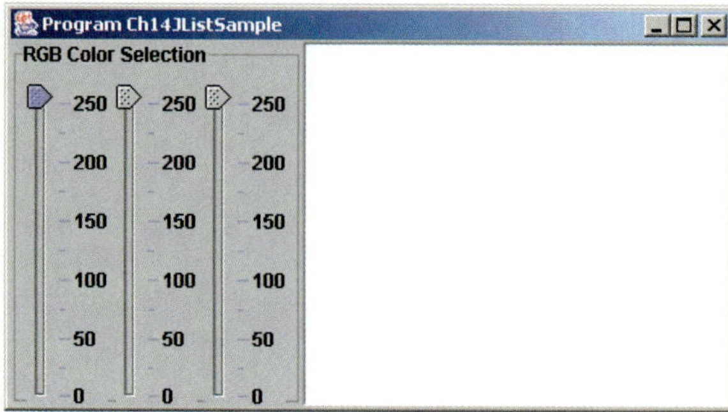

The state when the frame first appeared on the screen.

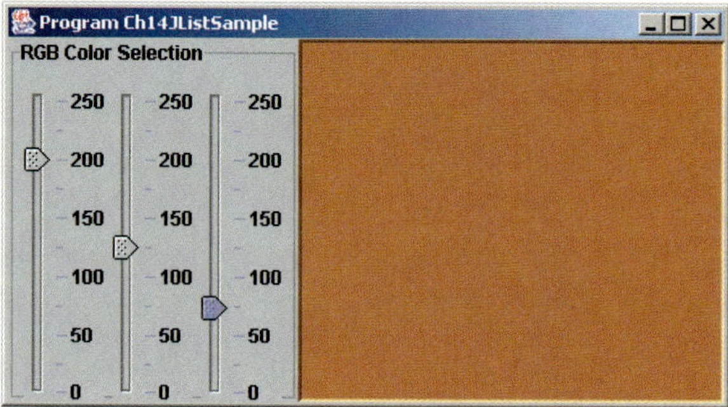

The state after three nobs are moved.

Figure 14.26 A frame with three vertical sliders for setting an RGB value.

```
slider.setMinimum(MIN_COLOR);
slider.setMaximum(MAX_COLOR);
slider.setValue(MAX_COLOR); //initial position of a nob
slider.setMajorTickSpacing(50);
slider.setMinorTickSpacing(25);
```

When a nob is moved, a JSlider object generates a change event (this event occurs when there's a change in the event source, such as the nob is moved). To process change events, we must register change event listeners to a JSlider event source object. The class that implements the ChangeListener interface must define a method called stateChanged, whose parameter is an instance of ChangeEvent. For this program, whenever a change event is generated, we read the value from each slider and set the background of a panel to a designated color. Here's the body of the stateChanged method:

```
int R, G, B;

R = redSlider.getValue();
G = greenSlider.getValue();
B = blueSlider.getValue();

colorPanel.setBackground(new Color (R, G, B));
```

Here's the Ch14JSliderSample class:

```
/*
   Chapter 14 Sample Program: Illustrates the use of JSlider

   File: Ch14JSliderSample.java
*/

import javax.swing.event.*;
import javax.swing.*;
import java.awt.*;

class Ch14JSliderSample extends JFrame
                                implements ChangeListener {

    private static final int FRAME_WIDTH    = 450;
    private static final int FRAME_HEIGHT   = 250;
    private static final int FRAME_X_ORIGIN = 150;
    private static final int FRAME_Y_ORIGIN = 250;

    private static final int MIN_COLOR = 0;
    private static final int MAX_COLOR = 255;

    private JSlider redSlider;
    private JSlider greenSlider;
    private JSlider blueSlider;

    private JPanel colorPanel;

    public static void main(String[] args) {
        Ch14JSliderSample frame = new Ch14JSliderSample();
        frame.setVisible(true);
    }

    public Ch14JSliderSample( ) {
        Container contentPane;
        JPanel    sliderPanel;

        //set the frame properties
        setSize    (FRAME_WIDTH, FRAME_HEIGHT);
        setTitle   ("Program Ch14JListSample");
        setLocation(FRAME_X_ORIGIN, FRAME_Y_ORIGIN);

        contentPane = getContentPane();
        contentPane.setBackground(Color.WHITE);
        contentPane.setLayout(new BorderLayout());

        //create and place a JList
        sliderPanel = new JPanel(new FlowLayout());
```

```
        sliderPanel.setBorder(BorderFactory.createTitledBorder(
                                          "RGB Color Selection"));

        redSlider = createSlider(MAX_COLOR);
        greenSlider = createSlider(MAX_COLOR);
        blueSlider = createSlider(MAX_COLOR);

        sliderPanel.add(redSlider);
        sliderPanel.add(greenSlider);
        sliderPanel.add(blueSlider);

        colorPanel = new JPanel( );
        colorPanel.setBackground(Color.white);
        colorPanel.setBorder(BorderFactory.createLoweredBevelBorder());
        contentPane.add(colorPanel, BorderLayout.CENTER);
        contentPane.add(sliderPanel, BorderLayout.WEST);

        //register 'Exit upon closing' as a default close operation
        setDefaultCloseOperation(EXIT_ON_CLOSE);
    }

    public void stateChanged(ChangeEvent event) {

        int R, G, B;

        R = redSlider.getValue();
        G = greenSlider.getValue();
        B = blueSlider.getValue();

        colorPanel.setBackground(new Color(R, G, B));
    }

    private JSlider createSlider(int value) {

        JSlider slider = new JSlider();

        slider.setOrientation(JSlider.VERTICAL);
        slider.setPaintLabels(true);
        slider.setPaintTicks(true);
        slider.setMinimum(MIN_COLOR);
        slider.setMaximum(MAX_COLOR);
        slider.setValue(value);
        slider.setMajorTickSpacing(50);
        slider.setMinorTickSpacing(25);

        slider.addChangeListener(this);

        return slider;
    }
}
```

14.8 Menus

Practical programs with a graphical user interface will almost always support menus. In this section we will describe how to display menus and process menu events by using JMenu, JMenuItem, and JMenuBar from the javax.swing package. Let's write a sample code to illustrate the display of menus and the processing of menu item selections. We will create two menus, File and Edit, with the following menu items:

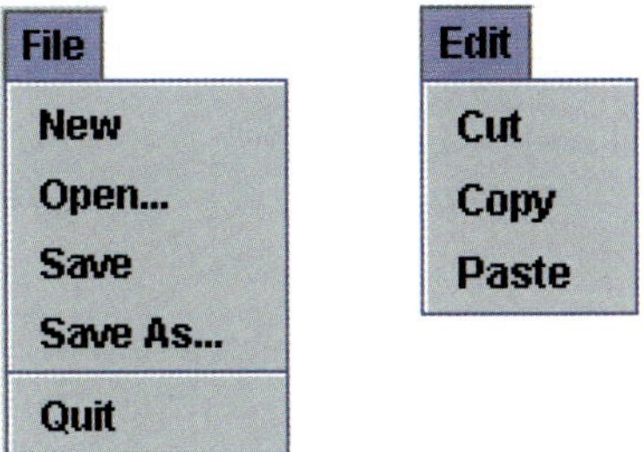

If the menu item Quit is selected, then we terminate the program. When a menu item other than Quit is selected, we print a message that identifies the selected menu item, for example,

```
Menu item 'New' is selected
```

Figure 14.27 shows a Ch14JMenuFrame when it is first opened and after the menu choice Save is selected.

One possible sequence of steps to create and add menus is this:

1. Create a JMenuBar object and attach it to a frame.
2. Create a JMenu object.
3. Create JMenuItem objects and add them to the JMenu object.
4. Attach the JMenu object to the JMenuBar object.

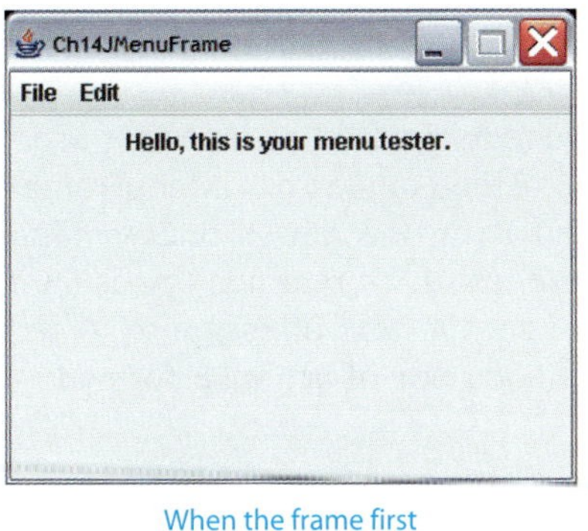

When the frame first appears on the screen.

After the menu item **Save** is selected.

Figure 14.27 **Ch14JMenuFrame** window when it is first opened and after the menu item **Save** is selected.

We will create two JMenu objects: fileMenu and editMenu. We create a fileMenu object as

```
fileMenu = new JMenu("File");
```

The argument to the JMenu constructor is the name of the menu. After the menu is created, we add a menu item to it. A menu item is the event source of menu selection, so we need to register an action listener to every menu item we add to the menu. In this sample code, we will let a Ch14JMenuFrame object be the action listener of all menu items. To create and add a menu item New to fileMenu, we execute

```
item = new JMenuItem("New");     //New
item.addActionListener(this);
fileMenu.add(item);
```

We repeat this sequence for all other menu items. Menu items are placed from the top in the order they are added to the menu. We can also include a horizontal line as a separator between menu items by calling the menu's addSeparator method.

```
fileMenu.addSeparator();
```

After the menus and their menu items are created, we attach them to a menu bar. In the constructor, we create a JMenuBar object, attach it to the frame by calling the frame's setMenuBar method, and add these two JMenu objects to the menu bar.

```
JMenuBar menuBar = new JMenuBar();
setMenuBar(menuBar);                //attach it to the frame
menuBar.add(fileMenu);
menuBar.add(editMenu);
```

To display which menu item was selected, we use a JLabel object response. We add response to the frame by

```
response = new JLabel("Hello, this is your menu tester.");
response.setSize(250, 50);
contentPane.add(response);
```

When a menu item is selected, the registered action listener's actionPerformed method is called. The actionPerformed method of the Ch14JMenuFrame is defined as follows: If an event source is a menu item, the getActionCommand method of ActionEvent returns the menu's text. We test if the returned text is Quit. If it is, we terminate the program. Otherwise, we set the text of response to indicate which menu item was selected. Here's the method body of actionPerformed:

```
String menuName;

menuName = event.getActionCommand();

if (menuName.equals("Quit")) {
   System.exit(0);
```

```
            } else {
               response.setText("Menu item '" + menuName +
                                      "' is selected");
            }
```

Here's the complete Ch14JMenuFrame program:

```
/*
    Chapter 14 Sample Program: Displays a frame with two menus

    File: Ch14JMenuFrame.java
*/

import javax.swing.*;
import java.awt.*;
import java.awt.event.*;

class Ch14JMenuFrame extends JFrame implements ActionListener {

    private static final int FRAME_WIDTH    = 300;
    private static final int FRAME_HEIGHT   = 250;
    private static final int FRAME_X_ORIGIN = 150;
    private static final int FRAME_Y_ORIGIN = 250;

    private JLabel response;
    private JMenu  fileMenu;
    private JMenu  editMenu;

//----------------------------------
//      Main method
//----------------------------------
    public static void main(String[] args) {
        Ch14JMenuFrame frame = new Ch14JMenuFrame();
        frame.setVisible(true);
    }

    public Ch14JMenuFrame(){
        Container contentPane;

        //set the frame properties
        setTitle     ("Ch14JMenuFrame");
        setSize      (FRAME_WIDTH, FRAME_HEIGHT);
        setResizable(false);
        setLocation (FRAME_X_ORIGIN, FRAME_Y_ORIGIN);

        contentPane = getContentPane( );
        contentPane.setLayout(new FlowLayout());

        //create two menus and their menu items
        createFileMenu();
        createEditMenu();
```

```
        //and add them to the menu bar
        JMenuBar menuBar = new JMenuBar();
        setJMenuBar(menuBar);
        menuBar.add(fileMenu);
        menuBar.add(editMenu);

        //create and position response label
        response = new JLabel("Hello, this is your menu tester.");
        response.setSize(250, 50);
        contentPane.add(response);

        setDefaultCloseOperation(EXIT_ON_CLOSE);
    }

    public void actionPerformed(ActionEvent event) {
        String menuName;

        menuName = event.getActionCommand();

        if (menuName.equals("Quit")) {
            System.exit(0);

        } else {
            response.setText("Menu Item '" + menuName + "' is selected.");
        }
    }

    private void createFileMenu( ) {
        JMenuItem item;

        fileMenu = new JMenu("File");

        item = new JMenuItem("New");        //New
        item.addActionListener(this);
        fileMenu.add(item);

        item = new JMenuItem("Open");       //Open...
        item.addActionListener(this);
        fileMenu.add(item);

        item = new JMenuItem("Save");       //Save
        item.addActionListener(this);
        fileMenu.add(item);

        item = new JMenuItem("Save As..."); //Save As...
        item.addActionListener(this);
        fileMenu.add(item);

        fileMenu.addSeparator();         //add a horizontal separator line

        item = new JMenuItem("Quit");       //Quit
        item.addActionListener(this);
        fileMenu.add(item);
    }
```

```
    private void createEditMenu() {
        JMenuItem item;

        editMenu = new JMenu("Edit");

        item = new JMenuItem("Cut");          //Cut
        item.addActionListener(this);
        editMenu.add(item);

        item = new JMenuItem("Copy");         //Copy
        item.addActionListener(this);
        editMenu.add(item);

        item = new JMenuItem("Paste");        //Paste
        item.addActionListener(this);
        editMenu.add(item);
    }
}
```

If the size of text for the response label is too small, then we can make it bigger by including the following statement in the constructor:

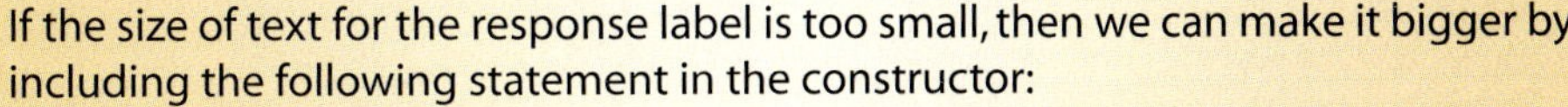

```
response.setFont( new Font("Helvetica", /*font name*/
                           Font.BOLD,   /*font style*/
                           16 ) );      /*font size*/
```

1. To which object do we register as an action listener— JMenu, JMenuItem, or JMenuBar?
2. How do we get the text of a selected menu item in the actionPerformed method?
3. How do we place a horizontal bar between two menu items?

14.9 Handling Mouse Events

In this section we describe the handling of mouse events. Mouse events include such user interactions as moving the mouse, dragging the mouse (i.e., moving the mouse while the mouse button is being pressed), and clicking the mouse buttons.

Let's look at an example in which we display the *x* and *y* pixel coordinates of a location where a mouse button is pressed. We will define a subclass of JFrame, named Ch14TrackMouseFrame, that handles the left mouse button click events, and we will use System.out to print out the location of mouse clicks. *Note:* For a system with a one-button mouse, we treat this button as the left mouse button.

A Ch14TrackMouseFrame object is an event source of mouse events. We will let this object be a mouse event listener also. For a Ch14TrackMouseFrame object to be a mouse event listener, its class must implement MouseListener. This interface has five abstract methods: mouseClicked, mouseEntered, mouseExited, mousePressed, and mouseReleased. The argument to all five methods is an instance of MouseEvent.

The class declaration for Ch14TrackMouseFrame will look like this:

```
class Ch14TrackMouseFrame extends Frame
                          implements MouseListener {
   ...
}
```

In the constructor we set the frame properties and register this frame as a mouse event listener of itself. The constructor is defined as

```
public Ch14TrackMouseFrame {
   //set the frame properties
   ...

   //set the output for printing out
   //the mouse click points
   output = System.out;

   //register itself as its mouse event listener
   addMouseListener(this);
}
```

When the left mouse button is clicked, the mouseClicked method of its mouse event listener is called. In this method, we want to find out the *x* and *y* coordinates of the mouse click point and print out these values in output. To find the *x* and *y* coordinate values, we use the getX and getY methods of MouseEvent. So the mouseClicked method of Ch14TrackMouseFrame is defined as

```
public void mouseClicked( MouseEvent event ) {
   int x, y;

   x = event.getX(); //return the x and y coordinates
   y = event.getY(); //of a mouse click point

   output.println("[" + x + "," + y + "]");
}
```

This method is called every time the left mouse button is clicked, that is, the mouse button is pressed down and released. If we want to detect the mouse button press and release separately, then we can provide a method body to the mousePressed and mouseReleased methods. For example, if we define these methods as

```
public void mousePressed(MouseEvent event) {
   output.println("Down");
}
```

and

```
public void mouseReleased(MouseEvent event) {
   output.println("Up");
}
```

instead of empty method bodies, then we will see something like

```
Down
Up
[200,120]
```

when we click a mouse button.

Before we present the complete program, let's extend the mouseClicked method so that when the left mouse button is double-clicked, we will terminate the program. We check the number of button clicks by calling the getClickCount method of MouseEvent. Here's the method that terminates the program when a double-click occurs (a single mouse click will print out the location of a mouse click, as before):

```
private static final int DOUBLE_CLICK = 2;

public void mouseClicked(MouseEvent event) {

   if (event.getClickCount() == DOUBLE_CLICK) {
      System.exit (0);

   } else {              //print out mouse click location
      int x, y;

      x = event.getX();
      y = event.getY();

      output.println("[" + x + "," + y + "]");
   }
}
```

Because a double-click is a sequence of two single clicks, this method is called twice when you double-click. The getClickCount method returns 1 for the first call and returns 2 for the second call.

Here's the complete program listing:

```
/*
   Chapter 14 Sample Program: Tracks the mouse movement

   File: Ch14TrackMouseFrame.java
*/

import javax.swing.*;
import java.awt.event.*;
import java.io.*;

class Ch14TrackMouseFrame extends JFrame implements MouseListener {

    private static final int FRAME_WIDTH    = 450;
    private static final int FRAME_HEIGHT   = 300;
    private static final int FRAME_X_ORIGIN = 150;
    private static final int FRAME_Y_ORIGIN = 250;
    private static final int DOUBLE_CLICK   = 2;

    private PrintStream output;

//----------------------------------
//     Main method
//----------------------------------
    public static void main(String[] args) {
        Ch14TrackMouseFrame frame = new Ch14TrackMouseFrame();
        frame.setVisible(true);
    }

    public Ch14TrackMouseFrame() {
        //set frame properties
        setTitle     ("TrackMouseFrame");
        setSize      (FRAME_WIDTH, FRAME_HEIGHT);
        setResizable(false);
        setLocation (FRAME_X_ORIGIN, FRAME_Y_ORIGIN);

        setDefaultCloseOperation(EXIT_ON_CLOSE);

        //create an output for printing out
        //the mouse click points
        output = System.out;

        //register self as a mouse event listener
        addMouseListener(this);
    }

    public void mouseClicked(MouseEvent event) {
        if (event.getClickCount() == DOUBLE_CLICK) {
           System.exit(0);
```

```
        } else {
           int x, y;

           x = event.getX(); //get the x and y coordinates of
           y = event.getY(); //the mouse click point

           output.println("[" + x + "," + y + "]");
        }
    }

    public void mouseEntered (MouseEvent event) { }
    public void mouseExited  (MouseEvent event) { }
    public void mousePressed (MouseEvent event) {
        output.println("Down");
    }

    public void mouseReleased(MouseEvent event) {
        output.println ("Up");
    }
}
```

SketchPad

Let's try another example. The basic idea of this program is to keep track of three events:

1. The left mouse button is pressed down.
2. The right mouse button is pressed down.
3. The mouse is dragged.

Notice that we are processing mouse button presses, not clicks. (*Note:* For the Mac platform, a mouse button press is treated as the left button press, and the Command press is treated as the right button press. For a platform that supports three mouse buttons, the middle mouse button is also treated as the left mouse button.)

To implement this class, we will declare Ch14SketchPad to implement two interfaces: MouseListener and MouseMotionListener. Since we want a Ch14SketchPad frame to process mouse button clicks, we must implement the MouseListener interface. In addition, we need to implement the MouseMotionListener interface to track the mouse dragging. The MouseMotionListener interface includes two abstract methods: mouseDragged and mouseMoved. The argument to both methods is an instance of MouseEvent.

When a mouse button, either the left or right button, is pressed, the event listener's mousePressed is called. Let's study how we should implement this method. If the right mouse button is pressed, then we have to erase the current drawing. If the left mouse button is pressed, then it is the start of a new mouse drag, so we have to remember the location where the left button is pressed. To determine which mouse button is pressed inside the mousePressed method, we call the isMetaDown method of MouseEvent as

```
if (event.isMetaDown()) {
   //the right button is pressed
   ...
}
```

The isMetaDown method returns true if the right button is pressed. We don't have a method such as isRightButtonPress in MouseEvent because not all platforms support the right mouse button. The Mac platform, for example, has only one mouse button, and for the Mac, the Command press is treated as the right mouse button press.

The code to erase the contents of the window is

```
if (event.isMetaDown()) {
   //the right button is pressed
   //so erase the contents
   Graphics  g = getGraphics();
   Rectangle r = getBounds();
   g.clearRect(0, 0, r.width, r.height);
   g.dispose();
}
```

We erase the contents by drawing a filled rectangle as big as the window itself with the rectangle filled in the background color. The getBounds method returns the size of a window.

If it is not a right mouse button press, then it is a left button press, so we remember the first position to draw a line.

last_x and **last_y** are instance variables.

```
if (event.isMetaDown()) {
   //the right button is pressed
   ...
} else {
   //remember the starting point of a new mouse drag
   last_x = x;
   last_y = y;
}
```

The position (*x*, *y*) is computed at the beginning of the mousePressed method as

```
int x = event.getX();
int y = event.getY();
```

The getX and getY methods of the MouseEvent class return the *x* and *y* coordinates, respectively, of the point where the mouse button is pressed.

Now, to process the mouse drag event, we need to define the mouseDragged method. From the argument object MouseEvent, we get a new position (*x*, *y*) and draw a line from the previous position to this new position, using the Graphics object g as follows:

```
g.drawLine(last_x, last_y, x, y);
```

After the drawing is done, we reset the variables.

```
last_x = x;
last_y = y;
```

Similar to the mousePressed method, the mouseDragged method is called whether the mouse was dragged with the left or right button. So we need to include the if test

```
if (!event.isMetaDown()) {
   //it's a left mouse button drag,
   //so draw a line
   ...
}
```

inside the method so the drawing will occur only for the left mouse button drag.

Here's a complete listing of the program:

```
/*
   Chapter 14 Sample Program: My SketchPad

   File: Ch14SketchPad.java
*/

import javax.swing.*;
import java.awt.*;
import java.awt.event.*;

class Ch14SketchPad extends JFrame
                        implements MouseListener, MouseMotionListener {

    private static final int FRAME_WIDTH    = 450;
    private static final int FRAME_HEIGHT   = 300;
    private static final int FRAME_X_ORIGIN = 150;
    private static final int FRAME_Y_ORIGIN = 250;

    private int last_x;
    private int last_y;

//----------------------------------
//    Main method
//----------------------------------
    public static void main(String[] args) {
        Ch14SketchPad frame = new Ch14SketchPad();
        frame.setVisible(true);
    }

    public Ch14SketchPad() {
        //set frame properties
        setTitle    ("Chapter 14 SketchPad");
```

```
        setSize      (FRAME_WIDTH, FRAME_HEIGHT);
        setResizable(false);
        setLocation (FRAME_X_ORIGIN, FRAME_Y_ORIGIN);

        setDefaultCloseOperation(EXIT_ON_CLOSE);

        last_x = last_y = 0;

        addMouseListener(this);       //adds itself as mouse and
        addMouseMotionListener(this); //mouse motion listener
    }

//----------------------------------
//  Mouse Event Handling
//----------------------------------

    public void mousePressed(MouseEvent event) {
        int x = event.getX();
        int y = event.getY();

        if (event.isMetaDown()) {
           //the right mouse button is pressed, so erase the contents
           Graphics    g = getGraphics();
           Rectangle   r = getBounds();
           g.clearRect(0, 0, r.width, r.height);
           g.dispose();

        } else {
            //the left mouse button is pressed,
            //remember the starting point of a new mouse drag
            last_x = x;
            last_y = y;
        }
    }

    public void mouseClicked (MouseEvent event) { }
    public void mouseEntered (MouseEvent event) { }
    public void mouseExited  (MouseEvent event) { }
    public void mouseReleased(MouseEvent event) { }

//----------------------------------
//  Mouse Motion Event Handling
//----------------------------------

    public void mouseDragged(MouseEvent event) {
        int x = event.getX();
        int y = event.getY();

        if (!event.isMetaDown()) {
            //don't process the right button drag
            Graphics g = getGraphics();

            g.drawLine(last_x, last_y, x, y);
            g.dispose();
```

```
            last_x = x;
            last_y = y;
        }
    }

    public void mouseMoved (MouseEvent event) { }
}
```

1. Which listener object listens to mouse movements? Which listener object listens to mouse button presses and clicks?
2. What is the purpose of the isMetaDown method?
3. What is the difference between mouseClicked and mousePressed?

Summary

- The type of user interface covered in this chapter is called a *graphical user interface* (GUI).
- GUI objects in the javax.swing package are collectively called *Swing classes.*
- To program the customized user interface effectively, we must learn a new style of programming control called *event-driven programming*
- The GUI and related classes and interfaces introduced in this chapter are

ActionEvent	JButton
ActionListener	JCheckBox
BorderFactory	JComboBox
BorderLayout	JFrame
ButtonGroup	JLabel
ChangeEvent	JList
ChangeListener	JMenu
Container	JMenuBar
FlowLayout	JMenuItem
GridLayout	JOptionPane
ImageIcon	JPanel
ItemEvent	JRadioButton
ItemListener	JScrollPane
JTextArea	JSlider
JTextField	MouseListener
MouseEvent	MouseMotionListener

- The JOptionPane class is used for a simple GUI input and output.
- GUI objects such as buttons and text fields are placed on the content pane of a frame window.
- The layout manager determines the placement of the GUI objects.
- The FlowLayout manager places components in left-to-right, top-to-bottom order.
- The BorderLayout manager places components in one of the five regions: north, south, east, west, and center.
- The GridLayout manager places components in one of the equal-size $N \times M$ grids.
- GUI objects can be placed on the content pane without using any layout manager. Such placement is called *absolute positioning*.
- Effective layout of GUI components is achieved by nesting panels and applying different layout managers to the panels.
- JPanel is a container for GUI components. JPanel itself is a GUI component, and therefore, we can nest JPanel objects.
- Event handling is divided into event sources and event listeners. Event sources generate events, and event listeners include a method that gets executed in response to the generated events.
- The most common event type is called an *action event*.
- ActionListener handles the action events.
- We use an instance of JButton to represent a pushbutton on a frame. JButton objects generate action events.
- GUI objects dealing with text are JLabel, JTextfield, and JTextArea. The JTextField objects generate action events.
- A JLabel object can include an image of type ImageIcon.
- The JCheckBox class is used for check-box buttons. An instance of the class generates action and item events.
- ItemEvent is generated when the state (selected/deselected) of an item changes.
- ItemEvent is handled by an instance of a class that implements the ItemListener interface.
- The JRadioButton class is used for radio buttons. An instance of the class generates action and item events.
- The JComboBox class is used for combo boxes, also known as drop-down lists. An instance of the class generates action and item events.
- The JList class is used for displaying a list of items. (*Note:* A JList object generates action and list events. To keep the examples brief and at the introductory level, we did not give any sample code that deals with events generated by a JList object.)

- The JSlider class is used for sliders. An instance of the class generates change events.
- ChangeEvent is handled by an instance of a class that implements the ChangeListener interface.
- We can find out the class to which an object belongs by using the instanceof operator.
- A frame has one JMenuBar object. A single JMenuBar can have many JMenu objects with many JMenuItem objects associated to a single JMenu object.
- JMenuItem objects generate action events.
- User actions such as moving or dragging the mouse and clicking the mouse buttons will result in the generation of mouse events.
- MouseListener handles the button actions, and MouseMotionListener handles the mouse movements.

Key Concepts

graphical user interface
Swing classes
content pane
absolute positioning
events
event-driven programming
event sources
event listeners
instanceof operator
buttons
menus
mouse events
mouse listeners
item events
item listeners
change events
change listeners
layout managers
nested panels
radio and check-box buttons
combo boxes (drop-down lists)
lists
sliders

Exercises

1. Define a subclass of JFrame and name it Ch14Q1Frame. Set the subclass so its instances will be 400 pixels wide and 450 pixels high and will have a blue background. The program terminates when the Close box is clicked.
2. Define a JFrame subclass that has four vertically aligned buttons. The labels for the four buttons are Senior, Junior, Sophomore, and Freshman.

This is one possible layout:

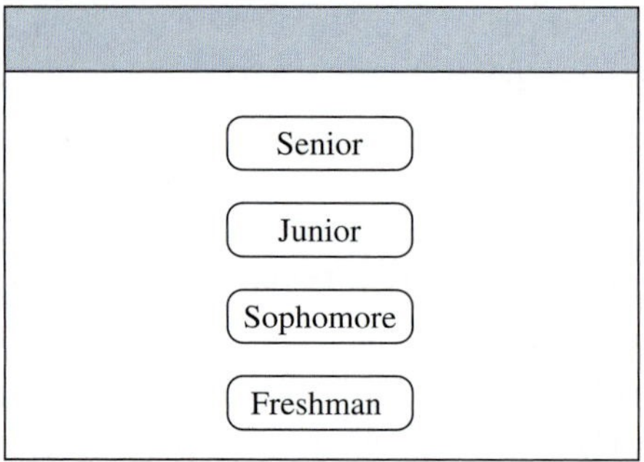

When a button is clicked, display a message that identifies which button is clicked, using JOptionPane.

3. In the Ch14TextFrame1 class, event handling was done with this class. Modify the class so the button events are handled by a ButtonHandler and the text events are handled by a TextHandler. You can use the ButtonHandler class defined in the chapter, but you need to define your own TextHandler class.

4. Using the frame layout shown, write a program that displays *N* prime numbers, where *N* is a value entered in the text field. A *prime number* is an integer greater than 1 and divisible by only itself and 1.

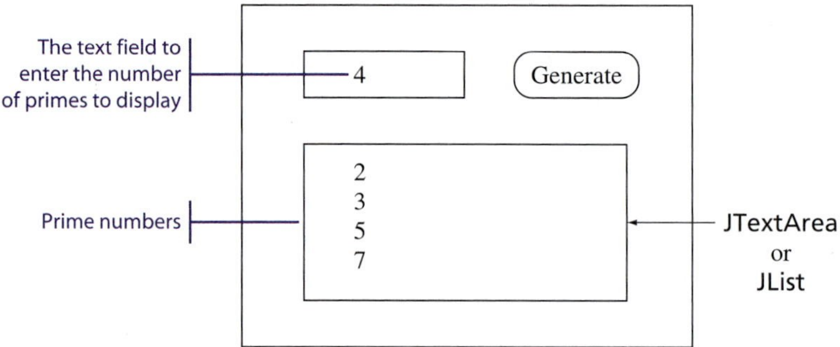

5. Define an OutputBox class as a subclass of JFrame. The OutputBox class provides the functionality of System.out (PrintStream) by supporting these methods:

```
public void println(String line)
public void print(String text)
```

The OutputBox class contains one JTextArea object. Do not use absolute positioning. Use the default layout and add a JScrollPane that wraps the JTextArea object to the content pane.

6. Redo Exercise 19 on page 358, but this time use the OutputBox class created in Exercise 5 for output.
7. A slugging percentage of a baseball player is computed by dividing the total bases of all hits by the total times at bat (single = 1 base, double = 2 bases, triple = 3 bases, and home run = 4 bases). Write an application that computes the slugging percentage. Create a customized frame and use JTextField objects to accept five input values: number of singles, number of doubles, number of triples, number of home runs, and number of times at bat. When the user clicks the Compute button, display the slugging percentage, using JLabel.
8. Write a graphical user interface for the slot machine program in Exercise 31 on page 362. Use three JLabel objects for displaying bells, grapes, and cherries. Add a button that simulates the motion of pulling down the handle.
9. Add images to the Exercise 8 solution. Create three gif files, one each for the bell, grape, and cherry. Use JLabel objects with ImageIcon to display these images on the frame.
10. Write a MyMenuFrame class with these menu choices.

File	Edit	Color
Quit	Erase	Red Green Blue Pink Black

When the user selects Quit, stop the program. When the user selects one of the colors, change the background of the frame (i.e., change the background color of the frame's content pane) to the selected color. When the user selects Erase, reset the background color to white.

11. Write a program that draws a selected geometric shape in random color and at a random location. The menu choices for the program are

Shape
Circle Rectangle Square

12. Write an application that draws a circle every time the mouse button is clicked. The position where the mouse is clicked will become the center of the circle. Set the radius of the circle to 100 pixels.
13. Extend Exercise 12 by adding the following menu to let the user select the shape to draw every time the mouse button is clicked. The clicked point will

be the center of the selected shape. Choose appropriate values for the dimensions of the three shapes.

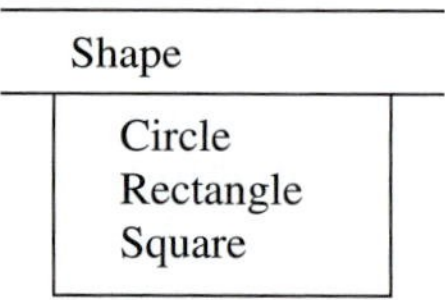

14. Rewrite the Ch14TicTacToePanel class by using the approach illustrated in Figure 14.21.

Development Exercises

For Exercises 15 through 28, use the incremental development methodology to implement the program. Design a visually appealing GUI with Swing components and layout managers. For each exercise, identify the program tasks, create a design document with class descriptions, and draw the program diagram. Map out the development steps at the start. Present any design alternatives and justify your selection. Be sure to perform adequate testing at the end of each development step.

15. Write a TeachArithmeticFrame class that teaches children arithmetic. The frame uses a JLabel for a problem and a JTextField for the user answer. When the user presses the Enter key (while the JTextField object is active) or clicks the OK button, display a message stating whether the user's answer is correct. When the Next button is clicked, display a new problem. The numbers are limited to two digits.

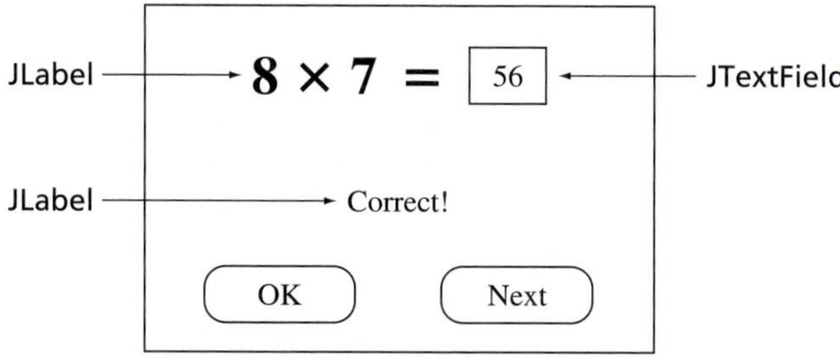

Consider using a larger font for the JLabel and JTextField text. You can change the color of text by calling the setForeground method, for example.

```
questionLbl.setForeground(Color.red);
```

Define a helper class that generates problems.

16. Extend the TeachArithmeticFrame class so that the numbers of correct and incorrect answers are kept. Display these two numbers somewhere on the frame. Add the third button labeled Reset. When this button is clicked, the counters for correct and incorrect answers are reset to zero.

17. Modify the mortgage table program of Exercise 30 in Chapter 6. Add this menu

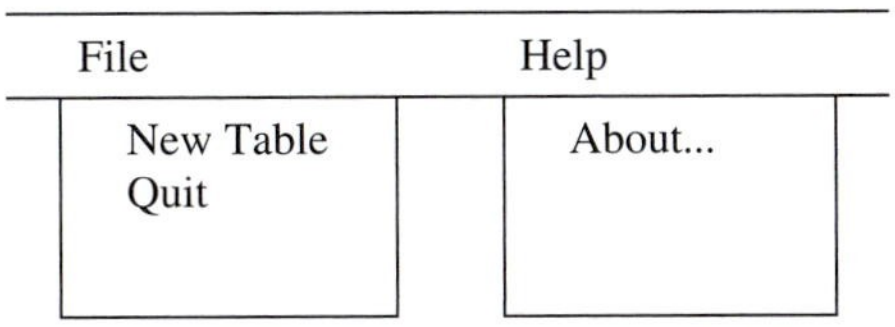

File	Help
New Table Quit	About...

to the program. When the user selects the menu choice New Table, the program opens another frame in which the user can enter three input values. The input frame should look something like this:

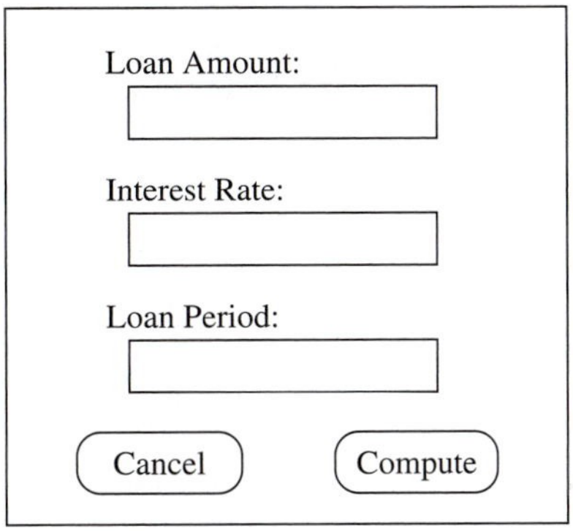

Loan Amount:

Interest Rate:

Loan Period:

Cancel Compute

If the user clicks on the Compute button and the three input values are valid, generate a mortgage table. Use the OutputBox class from Exercise 5 to display the mortgage table. If the input values are invalid, then print out an appropriate error message. Decide on the range of valid values for the loan amount, interest rate, and loan period. When the user selects the menu choice About . . . , describe the purpose of the program by using another frame. You should create only one input frame, but may decide to use more than one OutputBox frame so you can see multiple loan tables at once.

18. Redo Exercise 17 with a new user interface. The left side of a frame is used to enter the loan amount, interest rate, and loan period. The right side of a frame displays the mortgage table for given input values. The following layout is merely a suggestion. Feel free to use other GUI components as you see fit. For example, consider using JComboBox for entering interest rates and loan periods.

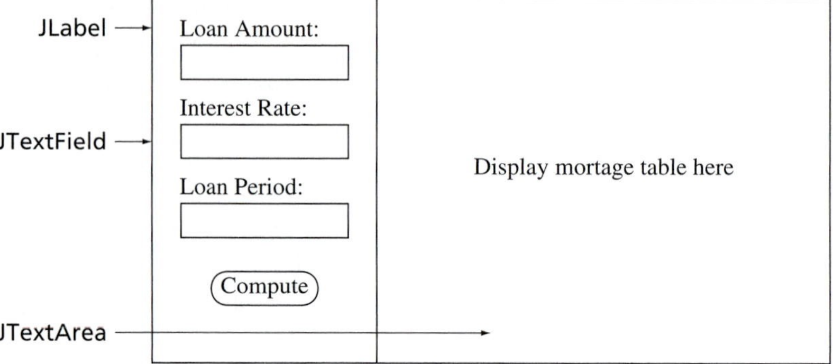

19. (Challenge) Write a class that implements a calculator with the layout similar to this:

The user enters a number, using digit buttons only. Some of the issues you need to consider include

- How to determine whether the user is entering a left operand or a right operand.
- How to handle the entering of multiple decimal points. A typical calculator accepts the first decimal point and ignores the rest. For example, if you press `1 . 4 . 3 .`, the number entered is `1.43`.
- When the display is 0 and the user enters 0, the display will not change. However, if the display is nonzero and the user enters 0, the 0 is appended to the number currently displayed.

- How to handle the operator precedence. For example, what will be the result if the user enters 4 + 3 × 2? Will it be 14 or 10? It is easier to treat all operators as having equal precedence and process them from left to right.

Study any real four-function calculator and try to implement a software calculator that simulates the real calculator as faithfully as possible, but feel free to make any reasonable changes.

20. Extend the calculator of Exercise 19 to allow the user to enter a number by using the keyboard. The class needs to implement the KeyListener interface and define the keyTyped method. You have to find information on KeyListener and KeyEvent from a Java API reference manual.

21. Latte Gallery in Carmel, California, is a small gallery that specializes in selling contemporary fine art, especially lithographs and photographs. All items sold in the gallery are signed and numbered. Write an application that keeps track of

    - Customers and their art purchases.
    - Artists and their works that have appeared in the gallery.
    - Current inventory.

    Allow the user to add, delete, or modify the customer, artist, and artwork information. An inventory will include the purchase price of the artwork and the selling price when sold. Give the user an option to list all customers or one customer. The user will specify the customer to display by entering the customer's last name and phone number.

    Define at least four data members for each type of information. For customers, include the name, phone number, address, and artwork and artist preferences. For artists, include the name, speciality, whether alive or deceased, and price ranges of artwork. For artwork, include the title, date purchased, date sold, and artist. Feel free to add more data members as you see fit.

    Design appropriate GUI for entering and editing customers, artists, and artwork.

22. Improve the Latte Gallery information manager application by adding the following capabilities:

    - List all customers who bought artwork by a given artist.
    - List all artists who are still alive (so you can buy their artwork while the price is still reasonable).
    - List all artwork in the inventory that did not sell for over 3 months. (This requires the use of the Date class from the java.util package.)

    Adjust the GUI accordingly.

23. Improve the Latte Gallery information manager application by adding a feature that allows the user to select a customer from the list of all customers by clicking on the customer that he or she wants to see. The listing of all

customers will include their names. When the user clicks on a name, the full information of the selected customer will appear on the right side of the frame.

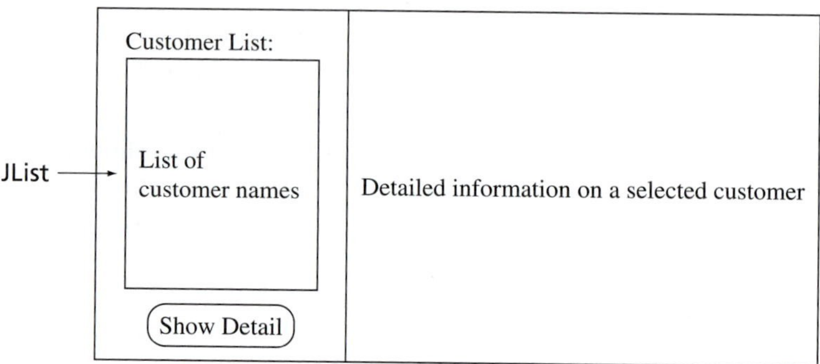

24. Write a program that plays the game of Fermi. The program generates three distinct random digits between 0 and 9. These digits are assigned to positions 1, 2, and 3. The goal of the game is for the player to guess the digits in three positions correctly in the least number of tries. For each guess, the player provides three digits for positions 1, 2, and 3. The program replies with a hint consisting of Fermi, Pico, or Nano. If the digit guessed for a given position is correct, then the reply is Fermi. If the digit guessed for a given position is in a different position, the reply is Pico. If the digit guessed for a given position does not match any of the three digits, then the reply is Nano. Here are sample replies for the three secret digits 6, 5, and 8 at positions 1, 2, and 3, respectively.

Guess	Hint	Explanation
1 2 5	Nano Nano Pico	The value 5 matches but at the wrong position.
8 5 3	Pico Fermi Nano	The value 5 matches at the correct position. The value 8 matches but at the wrong position.
5 8 6	Pico Pico Pico	All match at the wrong positions.

Notice that if the hints like the above are given, the player can tell which number did not match. For example, given the hint for the second guess, we can tell that 3 is not one of the secret numbers. To avoid this, provide hints in a random order or in alphabetical order (e.g., it will be Fermi Nano Pico instead of Pico Fermi Nano for the second reply). Implement the program with an attractive and elegant GUI.

25. Extend the Fermi playing program by allowing the player to

- Select the number of secret digits.
- Select alphabets instead of digits.
- Include duplicate secret digits.

Adjust the GUI accordingly.

26. Write a personal scheduler application. Each entry in the scheduler is an appointment, a to-do item, or a memo. Each entry has the date and the time it is entered. An entry can be locked, and if it is locked, the user cannot modify it. For an appointment entry, include the person and the place of meeting. For a to-do entry, include a short description of a task and the due date. For a memo, include a text. Implement the program with an attractive and elegant GUI.

27. Write a rental point-tracking system for an up-and-coming Espresso's Dynamo Mopeds in Monterey, California. To compete against Ms. Latte's Mopeds R Us, Espresso's Dynamo Mopeds decided to install an automated point-tracking system. When a customer first rents a moped, his or her information is entered into a database. For each rental, a customer receives points, and when the total points reach 100, the customer can rent a moped free for 3 hours or redeem a free movie rental coupon from Espresso's Majestic Movies. The points are earned in the following scheme:

Renter	Type	Points
College student	50cc Moppi	15
	150cc Magnum	20
Adult	50cc Moppi	10
	150cc Magnum	15
Senior	50cc Moppi	20
	150cc Magnum	30

In addition to the basic operations of updating the point information for every rental, include an operation to list all customers who earned over 100 points. Also, support an operation to edit the customer information. Implement the program with an attractive and elegant GUI.

28. Update the rental point-tracking system to support a new rental system and point-awarding rules for Espresso's Dynamo Mopeds. Now the customers can rent only on an hourly basis, and the points are awarded accordingly. Upon rental, the customer will state the number of hours he or she will rent in increments of 1 hour with a maximum of 10 hours. The rental fee is based on the following formula:

Renter	Type	Total Rental ≤ 5 hours	Total Rental > 5 hours
College student	50cc Moppi	\$3.50 per hour	\$2.50 per hour
	150cc Magnum	\$4.50 per hour	\$3.50 per hour
Adult	50cc Moppi	\$5.00 per hour	\$4.00 per hour
	150cc Magnum	\$6.50 per hour	\$5.00 per hour
Senior	50cc Moppi	\$4.00 per hour	\$3.00 per hour
	150cc Magnum	\$5.25 per hour	\$4.00 per hour

15 Recursive Algorithms

Objectives

After you have read and studied this chapter, you should be able to

- Write recursive algorithms for mathematical functions and nonnumerical operations.
- Decide when to use recursion and when not to.
- Describe the recursive quicksort algorithm and explain how its performance is better than that of selection and bubble sort algorithms.

Introduction

We introduced recursion in Chapter 6 and showed how to write recursive methods to implement mathematical functions. We used mathematical functions in Chapter 6 because it is easier to see how the recursion works with mathematical functions. However, recursive methods are not limited to implementing mathematical functions, and we will present several nonnumerical recursive algorithms in this chapter. We will also discuss some criteria for deciding when to use recursion and when not to. All the recursive algorithms we provide in this chapter, other than those we use for explanation, are algorithms that should be written recursively.

15.1 Basic Elements of Recursion

recursive method

A ***recursive method*** is a method that contains a statement (or statements) that makes a call to itself. In Chapter 6, we implemented three mathematical functions using recursion. In this chapter, we will present recursive algorithms for nonnumerical operations. But before we introduce new examples, let's review one of the recursive algorithms we presented in Chapter 6.

The *factorial* of *N* is the product of the first *N* positive integers, denoted mathematically as

```
N! = N * (N-1) * (N-2) * ... * 2 * 1
```

We can define the factorial of *N* recursively as

$$\text{factorial(N)} = \begin{cases} 1 & \text{if N = 1} \\ \text{N * factorial(N-1)} & \text{otherwise} \end{cases}$$

We mentioned in Chapter 6 that any recursive method will include the following three basic elements:

1. A test to stop or continue the recursion.
2. An end case that terminates the recursion.
3. A recursive call(s) that continues the recursion.

These three elements are included in the following recursive factorial method.

```
public int factorial(int N)
{
    if (N == 1) {     <------ Test to stop or continue.
        return 1;     <------ End case: recursion stops.
    }
```

```
    else {

        return N * factorial(N-1);
    }
}
```

Recursive case: recursion continues with a recursive call.

15.2 Directory Listing

Let's try some recursive algorithms for nonnumerical applications. A first nonnumerical recursive algorithm will list the filename of all files in a given directory (or folder) of a hard disk and its subdirectories. We will use a File object from the java.io package to implement the method. Assuming a Windows platform, we create a File object by passing the name of a file or a directory, as in

```
File file = new File("D:/Java/Projects");
```

Notice that we pass the full path name. If a File object represents a directory, then the boolean method isDirectory returns true. To get an array of names of files and subdirectories in a directory, we use the list method.

```
String[] fileList = file.list();
```

Let's call the method directoryListing. The argument to the method will be a File object that represents a directory. The basic idea can be expressed as follows:

```
public void directoryListing(File dir) {

    //assumption: dir represents a directory

    fileList = an array of names of files and
               subdirectories in the directory dir;

    for (each element in fileList) {

        if (an element is a file) {
            output the element's filename; //end case: it's
                                           //a file.
        } else { //recursive case: it's a directory
            call directoryListing with element as
            an argument;
        }
    }
}
```

The complete method is as follows:

```
public void directoryListing(File dir) {

    //assumption: dir represents a directory

    String[] fileList = dir.list(); //get the contents
    String dirPath = dir.getAbsolutePath();
```

```
        for (int i = 0; i < fileList.length; i++) {

           File file = new File(dirPath + "/" + fileList[i]);

Test ────────► if (file.isFile()) {     //it's a file

End case ────────► System.out.println( file.getName() );
           } else {

Recursive case ────────► directoryListing(file); //it's a directory
           }                             //so make a recursive call
        }
     }
```

Notice the argument we pass to create a new File object inside the for loop is

```
File file = new File(dirPath + File.separator
                        + fileList[i] );
```

where dirPath is set as

```
String dirPath  = dir.getAbsolutePath();
```

and File.separator is a class constant for the system-dependent character used as the file separator.

The getAbsolutePath method returns the full path name for the directory, and we need to prepend it to the name (fileList[i]) of a file or a subdirectory in this directory in order to make the testing

```
if (file.isFile()) ...
```

work correctly.

To give you more practice in reading recursive methods, we will remove the assumption that the argument File represents a directory and rewrite the method. If the argument File object to directoryListing can be either a file or a directory, then we need to check this first. If the argument object is a file, then we list its filename and stop the recursion. If the argument object is a directory, then we get the list of contents in the directory and make recursive calls. Here's the second version:

```
public void directoryListing(File file) {
   //'file' may be a directory or a file

   String[] fileList;
   String   pathname = file.getAbsolutePath();

Test ────────► if (file.isFile()) {
                                          //it's a file so
End case ────────► System.out.println(file.getName()); //print it out

   } else { //it's a directory, so make a recursive call
```

```
    fileList = file.list();
    for (int i = 0; i < fileList.length; i++) {
      File nextFile = new File(pathname+ File.separator
                                   + fileList[i]);
      directoryListing(nextFile); //recursive call
    }
  }
}
```

Recursive case

15.3 Anagram

anagram

Our second example of a nonnumerical recursive method is to derive all anagrams of a given word. An ***anagram*** is a word or phrase formed by reordering the letters of another word or phrase. If the word is CAT, for example, then its anagrams are

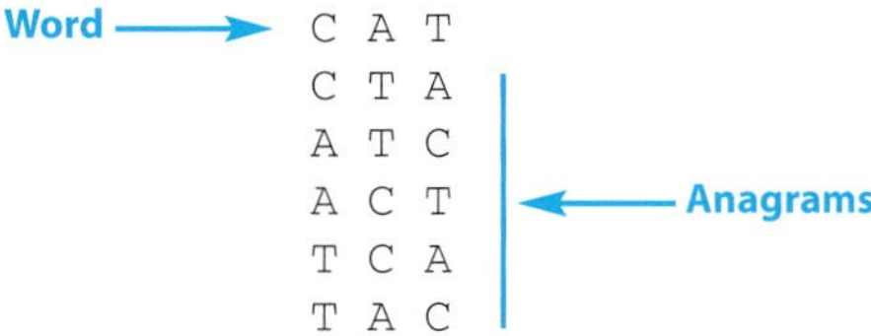

Figure 15.1 illustrates the basic idea of using recursion to list all anagrams of a word.

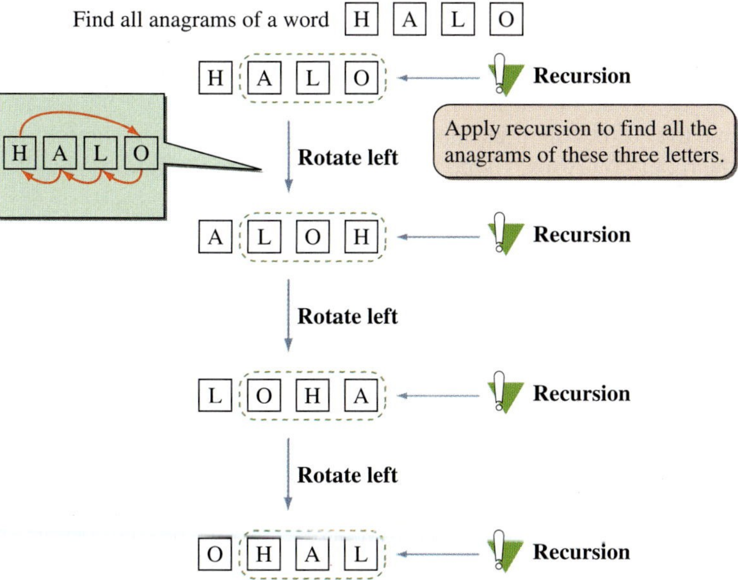

Figure 15.1 How to generate all the anagrams of a word by using recursion.

Expressing the basic idea, we have something like this:

```
public void anagram(String word) {
   int numOfChars = word.length();

   if (numOfChars == 1) {
      //End case: there's only one character left,
      //          so we can't make a recursive call
   } else {
      for (int i = 1; i <= numOfChars; i++) {

         char firstLetter = word.charAt(0);

         suffix = word.substring(1, numOfChars);

         anagram(suffix); //make a recursive call with
                             the remaining
                           //letters in the word

         //rotate left
         word = suffix + firstLetter;
      }
   }
}
```

This **for** loop is illustrated in Figure 15.1.

To derive the real method that executes correctly, we must finalize a number of things. First, what will we do when the recursion stops? Hitting upon the end case means that we have found one anagram, so we will print it out. Now, this is the tricky part. When we call the method recursively, we are passing a word that has the first letter chopped off. This means the words being passed to successive recursive calls are getting shorter and shorter. But we need to access all letters in a word to print it out. We can solve this problem by passing two parameters: the prefix and the suffix of a word. In each successive call, the prefix becomes one letter more and the suffix becomes one letter less. When the suffix becomes one letter only, then the recursion stops. Using this idea, we see the method now looks like this:

```
public void anagram(String prefix, String suffix) {
   int numOfChars = suffix.length();

   if (numOfChars == 1) {
      //End case: print out one anagram
      System.out.println(prefix + suffix);
   } else {
      ...
   }
}
```

and this method is initially set with an empty prefix and the word being the suffix, as in

```
anagram("", "HALO");
```

Now, by using the two parameters prefix and suffix, the for loop is written as

```
for (int i = 1; i <=numOfChars; i++) {

   newSuffix = suffix.substring(1, numOfChars);
   newPrefix = prefix + suffix.charAt(0);

   anagram(newPrefix, newSuffix); //recursive case

   //rotate left to create a rearranged suffix
   suffix = newSuffix + suffix.charAt(0);
}
```

Putting everything together, we have the final anagram method:

```
public void anagram(String prefix, String suffix) {
   String newPrefix, newSuffix;
   int numOfChars = suffix.length();

   if (numOfChars == 1) {
      //End case: print out one anagram
      System.out.println(prefix + suffix);
   } else {
      for (int i = 1; i <= numOfChars; i++) {
         newSuffix = suffix.substring(1, numOfChars);
         newPrefix = prefix + suffix.charAt(0);

         anagram(newPrefix, newSuffix);
                                       //recursive call

         //rotate left to create a rearranged suffix
         suffix = newSuffix + suffix.charAt(0);
      }
   }
}
```

Test → (the if test); End case → (the System.out.println statement); Recursive case → (the for loop in the else block)

Because the ending condition for recursion is tricky, let's study carefully the test to stop the recursion. We set the test to

```
if (numOfChars == 1) ...
```

Is there any assumption we must make about the parameters so that this method will work correctly? We mentioned earlier that the initial call to the recursive method is something like

```
anagram("", "HALO");
```

What would happen if we made the call initially like

```
String str = inputBox.getString();
anagram("", str);
```

and the user entered an empty string? This is left as Exercise 8.

1. Determine the output of these calls without actually running the method.

   a. `anagram("", "DOG");`
   b. `anagram("", "CAFE");`

15.4 Towers of Hanoi

The objective of a puzzle called the *Towers of Hanoi* is deceptively simple, but finding a solution is another matter. The goal of the puzzle is to move *N* disks from peg 1 to peg 3 by moving one disk at a time and never placing a larger disk on top of a smaller disk. See Figure 15.2.

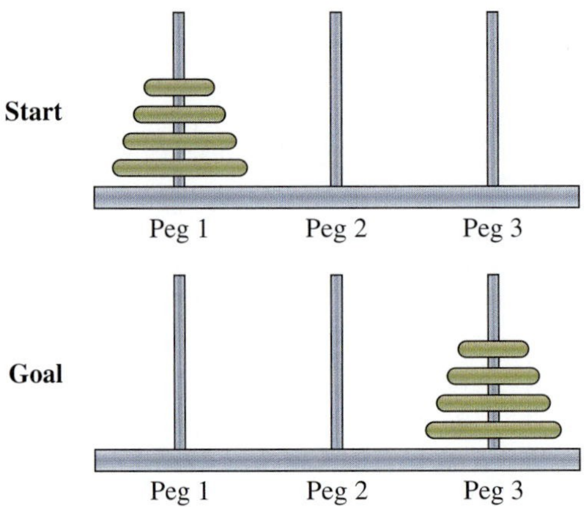

Figure 15.2 Towers of Hanoi with $N = 4$ disks.

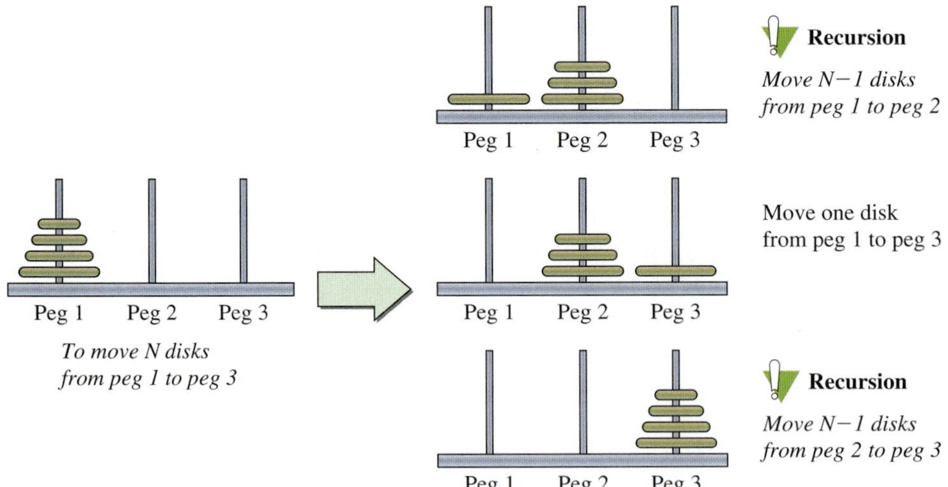

Figure 15.3 Recursive solution to the Towers of Hanoi puzzle.

The Towers of Hanoi puzzle can be solved very nicely by using recursion. The Aha! moment to this puzzle occurs when you realize that you can solve the puzzle if somehow you can move the top $N - 1$ disks to peg 2. After the top $N - 1$ disks are moved to peg 2 temporarily, you move the largest disk from peg 1 to peg 3 and finally move the $N - 1$ disks from peg 2 to peg 3. Figure 15.3 illustrates these three steps. The first and the third steps are, of course, the same puzzle with one fewer disk and the destination peg changed. So you apply the same logic recursively to the first and third steps. When the number of disks becomes 1, then the recursion stops. Applying this recursive thinking, we can write the method as

```
public void towersOfHanoi(int N,      //number of disks
                          int from,   //origin peg
                          int to,     //destination peg
                          int spare) //"middle" peg
{
   if (N == 1) {
      moveOne(from, to);
   } else {
      towersOfHanoi(N-1, from, spare, to);

      moveOne(from, to);

      towersOfHanoi(N-1, spare, to, from);
   }
}
```

The moveOne is the method that actually moves the disk. Here we will define the method to print out the move, using System.out.

```
private void moveOne(int from, int to) {
   System.out.println(from + " ---> " + to);
}
```

When we run this method with $N = 4$, we get the following output:

```
1 ---> 2
1 ---> 3
2 ---> 3
1 ---> 2
3 ---> 1
3 ---> 2
1 ---> 2
1 ---> 3
2 ---> 3
2 ---> 1
3 ---> 1
2 ---> 3
1 ---> 2
1 ---> 3
2 ---> 3
```

The output is very difficult to read. We can improve the output considerably by padding a varying number of blank spaces to show the level of recursion. We can change the output to

```
          1 ---> 2
          1 ---> 3
          2 ---> 3
        1 ---> 2
          3 ---> 1
          3 ---> 2
          1 ---> 2
      1 ---> 3
          2 ---> 3
          2 ---> 1
          3 ---> 1
        2 ---> 3
          1 ---> 2
          1 ---> 3
          2 ---> 3
```

These steps are for moving 3 disks from peg 1 to peg 2.

by rewriting the methods as follows:

```
public void towersOfHanoi(int N,     //number of disks
                          int from,  //origin peg
                          int to,    //destination peg
                          int spare, //"middle" peg
                          int indent)//# of leading spaces
{
   if (N == 1) {
      moveOne(from, to, indent);
   } else {
      towersOfHanoi(N-1, from, spare, to, indent+2);

      moveOne(from, to, indent+2);

      towersOfHanoi(N-1, spare, to, from, indent+2);
   }
}

private void moveOne(int from, int to, int indent) {
   System.out.format("%" + (indent+8) + "s\n",
                     from + " ---> " + to);
}
```

15.5 Quicksort

We will present a sorting algorithm that uses recursion in this section. This sorting algorithm is called *quicksort,* and we will compare the performance of quicksort against that of the previous two sorting algorithms at the end of this section, to verify that quicksort deserves its name.

Any element can be used as a pivot. For simplicity, we use number[low] as pivot **p**.

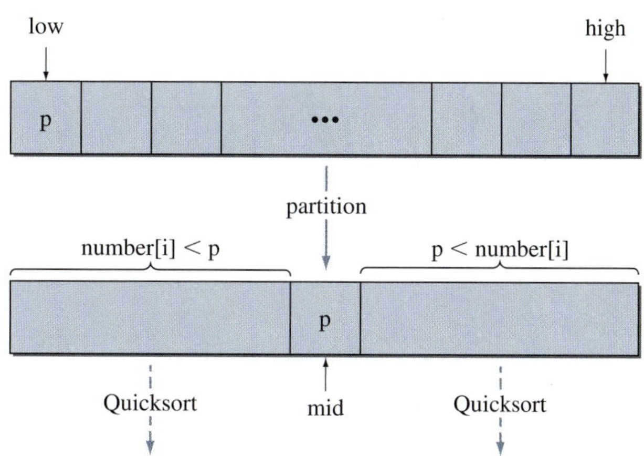

Figure 15.4 The core idea of the quicksort algorithm.

Figure 15.4 illustrates the core thinking of quicksort. To sort an array from index low to high, we first select a pivot element p. We can select any element in the array as a pivot, but for simplicity, we choose number[low] as the pivot. Using p as the pivot, we scan through the array and move all elements smaller than p to the lower half (left half in the figure) and all elements larger than p to the upper half. Then we sort the lower and upper halves recursively, using quicksort. The variable mid points to the position where the pivot is placed. So the lower half of the array is from index low to mid-1, and the upper half of the array is from index mid+1 to high. The recursion stops when the condition low >= high becomes true.

Here's the quicksort algorithm:

```
public void quickSort(int[] number, int low, int high) {
   if (low < high) {

      int mid = partition(number, low, high);

      quickSort(number,    low, mid-1);
      quickSort(number, mid+1, high);
   }
}
```

The partition method splits the array elements number[low] to number[high] into two halves, as shown in Figure 15.4. We use number[low] as the pivot element. The method returns the position where the pivot element is placed. Figure 15.5 shows the result of partitioning the array by using the element 23 as a pivot.

We first set the pivot to number[low]. Then we start looking for a number smaller than the pivot from position high, high-1, and so forth. Let's say the number is found at position J. Since this number is smaller than the pivot, we move it to position low. Now we start looking for a number larger than the pivot from low+1, low+2, and so forth. Let's say the number is found at position I. We move it to position J. We then repeat the process, this time looking for a number smaller than the pivot from J-1, J-2, and so forth. Figure 15.6 shows the details of the partitioning process.

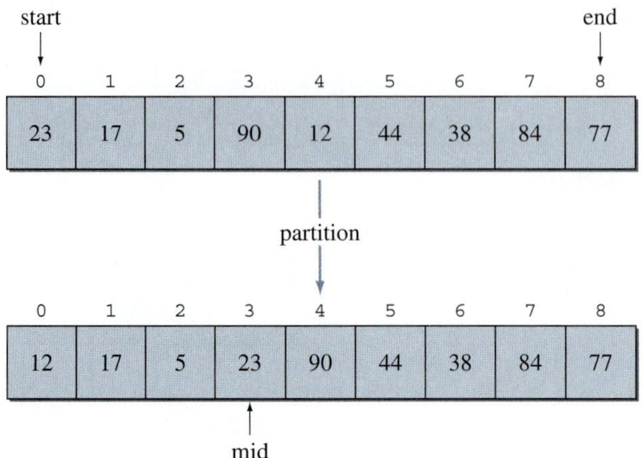

Figure 15.5 Result of partitioning using **23** as a pivot.

Here's the partition method:

```
private int partition(int[] number, int start, int end) {
    //set the pivot
    int pivot = number[start];

    do {
        //look for a number smaller than pivot from the end
        while (start < end && number[end] >= pivot) {
            end--;
        }

        if (start < end) { //found a smaller number
            number[start] = number[end];

            //now find a number larger than pivot
            //from the start
            while (start < end && number[start] <= pivot) {
                start++;
            }

            if (start < end) { //found a larger number
                number[end] = number[start];
            }
        }

    } while (start < end);

    //done, move the pivot back to the array
    number[start] = pivot;

    return start;
}
```

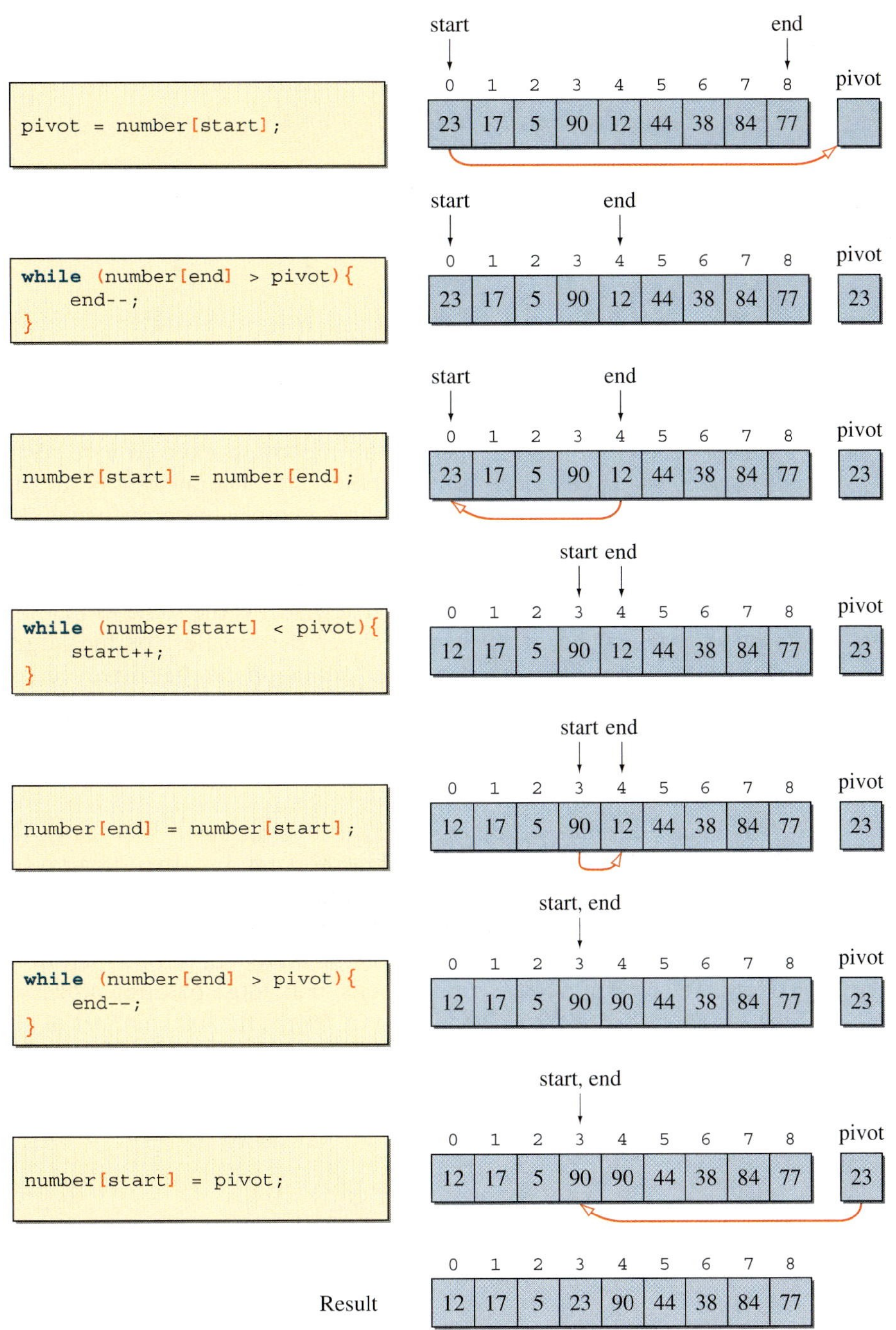

Figure 15.6 Details of one partitioning.

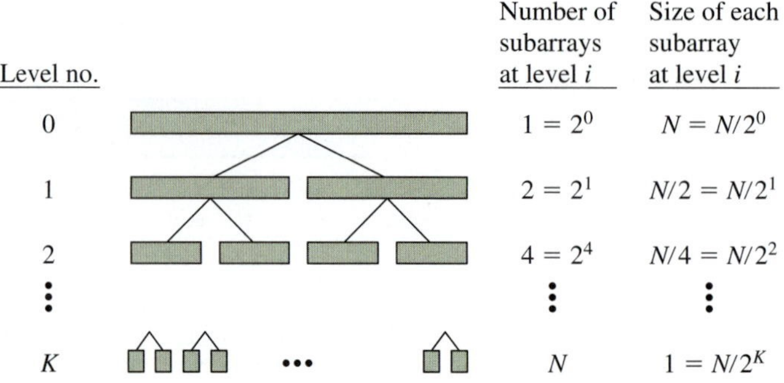

Figure 15.7 A hierarchy of partitioning an array into smaller and smaller arrays in the quicksort.

How good is quicksort? Does the algorithm execute a fewer number of comparisons than the selection or bubble sort? The answer is no in the worst case. Quicksort executes roughly the same number of comparisons as the selection sort and bubble sort in the worst case. When the original list is either already sorted or in descending order, then after a partition process, either the lower half or the upper half has $N - 1$ elements. The effect is the same as that of the previous two sorting algorithms; that is, either the smallest or the largest number moves to its correct position. The worst situation can be improved somewhat if we select the median of three numbers, say, number[low], number[high], and number[(low+high)/2], as the pivot element. Even with this improvement, the number of comparisons in the worst case is still approximately the square of the size of the array.

Is the name quicksort a kind of false advertisement? Not really. On average, we can expect a partition process to split the array into two subarrays of roughly equal size. Figure 15.7 shows how the original array is partitioned into smaller subarrays. When the size of all subarrays becomes 1, then the array becomes sorted. At level i, there are 2^i subarrays of size $N/2^i$. So there will be $N/2^i$ partition processes at level i. The total number of comparisons of all those partition processes at level i is therefore $2^i \cdot N/2^i = N$. Since there are K levels, the total number of comparisons for sorting the whole array is

$$K \cdot N$$

but

$$N = 2^K$$

$$\log_2 N = K$$

so

$$KN = N \log_2 N$$

The total number of comparisons is proportional to $N \log_2 N$, which is a great improvement over N^2. A more rigorous mathematical analysis will show that the quicksort on average requires approximately $2N \log_2 N$ comparisons.

1. Partition the following arrays, using the partition method.

   a.

0	1	2	3	4	5	6	7	8
18	19	5	77	12	14	13	84	45

   b.

0	1	2	3	4	5	6	7	8
98	19	15	86	12	44	13	24	45

15.6 When Not to Use Recursion

Recursion is a powerful tool to express complex algorithms succinctly. For example, writing a nonrecursive algorithm for the Towers of Hanoi is unexpectedly difficult. Likewise, a recursive quicksort algorithm is easier to understand than its nonrecursive counterpart. For both problems, we prefer recursive algorithms because recursion is the most natural way to express their solution. However, just being natural is not the criterion for selecting a recursive solution over a nonrecursive one.

Consider a solution for computing the *N*th Fibonacci number. A Fibonacci number is defined recursively as

```
                    ⎧ 1                      if N = 0 or N = 1
fibonacci(N)   =    ⎨
                    ⎩ fibonacci(N-1)
                       + fibonacci(N-2)      otherwise
```

Because the function is defined recursively, it is natural to implement the function by using a recursive method.

```
public int fibonacci(int N) {
   if (N == 0 || N == 1) {

      return 1;        //end case

   } else {//recursive case

      return fibonacci(N-1) + fibonacci(N-2);
   }
}
```

This recursive method is succinct, easy to understand, and elegant. But is this the way to implement it? The answer is no, because the recursive method is grossly inefficient and a nonrecursive version is just as easy to understand. The method is inefficient because the same value is computed over and over. Figure 15.8 shows the recursive calls for computing the fifth Fibonacci number. Notice that the same value, for example, fibonacci(2), is computed repeatedly.

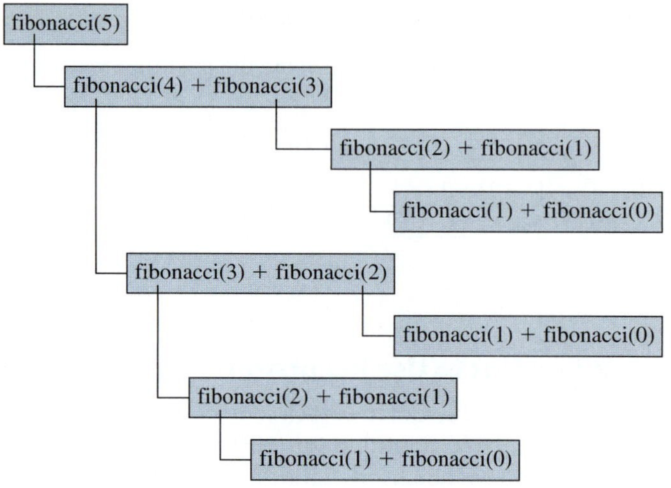

Figure 15.8 Recursive calls to compute **fibonacci(5).**

The *N*th Fibonacci number can be computed by using a nonrecursive method.

```
public int fibonacci(int N) {

   int fibN, fibN1, fibN2, cnt;

   if (N == 0 || N == 1) {
      return 1;
   } else {

      fibN1 = fibN2 = 1;
      cnt = 2;

      while (cnt <= N) {
        fibN = fibN1 + fibN2; //get the next fib no.

        fibN1 = fibN2;
        fibN2 = fibN;

        cnt ++;
      }
      return fibN;
   }
}
```

F_0		F_1		F_2
1	+	1	=	2
F_1		F_2		F_3
1	+	2	=	3
F_2		F_3		F_4
2	+	3	=	5

The nonrecursive method is not as succinct as the recursive version, but at the same time, it is not that difficult to understand. The nonrecursive version is much more efficient, and it is the one that should be used. This nonrecursive version is written in such a way that its structure parallels the structure of the recursive version, so we can compare the two easily. It is possible to rewrite the nonrecursive version with a simple for loop as

```
public int fibonacci(int N)  {

   int fibN1, fibN2, fibN;

   fibN = fibN1 = fibN2 = 1;

   for (int i = 1; i < N; i++) {

      fibN = fibN1 + fibN2;

      fibN1 = fibN2;
      fibN2 = fibN;
   }

   return fibN;
}
```

There is no clear-cut rule to determine whether a routine should be implemented recursively or nonrecursively. In general, we should always search for a nonrecursive solution first. We should use recursion only when a recursive solution is more natural and easier to understand and the resulting method is not too inefficient. We repeat the guideline for using recursive methods we mentioned in Chapter 6.

Design Guidelines

Use recursion if

1. *A recursive solution is natural and easy to understand.*
2. *A recursive solution does not result in excessive duplicate computation.*
3. *The equivalent iterative solution is too complex.*

Summary

- Recursion is a special type of repetition control.
- A recursive method is a method that calls itself.
- A recursive method consists of a test to stop the recursion, the end case that gets executed at the end of recursion, and the recursive case that makes a recursive call to continue the recursion.
- The use of recursion should be avoided if a suitable nonrecursive looping statement can be developed.

Key Concepts

recursive methods
end cases
recursive cases

Exercises

1. Write a recursive method to find the smallest element in an array. *Note:* This is strictly an exercise. You should not write the real method recursively.
2. Write a recursive method to compute the average of the elements in an array. *Note:* This is strictly an exercise. You should not write the real method recursively.
3. Write a recursive method to determine whether a given string is a palindrome. A string is a palindrome if it reads the same both forward and backward. Ignore the case of the letters and punctuation marks.
4. Write a recursive binary search method. Should this method be written recursively or nonrecursively in practice?
5. Write a recursive method to reverse a given string. The method accepts a string as an argument and returns the reverse of the argument. For example, if the argument is Java, then the method returns avaJ. Show this method be written recursively or nonrecursively in practice?
6. In Chapter 6, we gave the nonrecursive and recursive solutions for finding the greatest common divisor of two given integers. Which version is the one you should use in practice?
7. The partition method of quicksort selects the first element as its pivot. Improve the method by using the median of the values in the first, the middle, and the last elements of an array. If an array number to partition has 8 elements indexed from 0 to 7, then the first element is number[0], the middle element is number[4], and the last element is number[7]. If these elements are 55, 34, and 89, for example, then the median is 55.
8. What would happen if the anagram method were called initially by passing an empty string as the second parameter as

   ```
   anagram("", "");
   ```

   Will the method work? Why or why not? If not, correct the problem. If yes, then would it be logical to leave it as is or should the method be corrected to make it more logical?
9. Another recursive sorting algorithm is called *merge sort*. The merge sort divides the array into two halves, sorts the two halves recursively using mergesort, and finally merges the two sorted halves into a sorted list. In a

diagram, the process of merge sort looks like this:

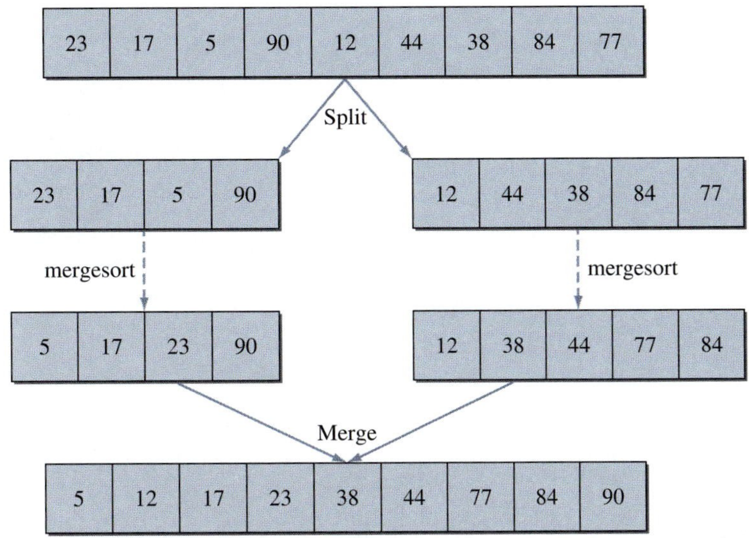

Write the `mergesort` method.

10. You can visualize the growth of a tree recursively. First you start with a trunk of a set length:

From this trunk, two branches grow out:

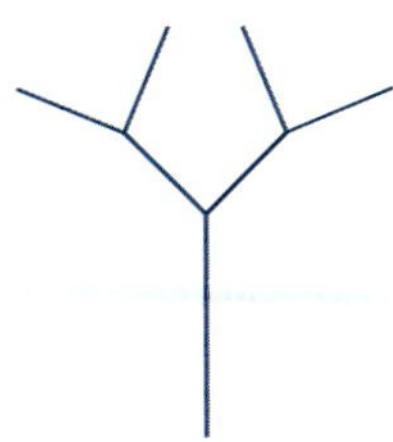

Now if you consider the two branches as the trunks of their respective subtrees, you have another growth, resulting in

Continue this recursive growth, and you will end up with a tree that looks something like this:

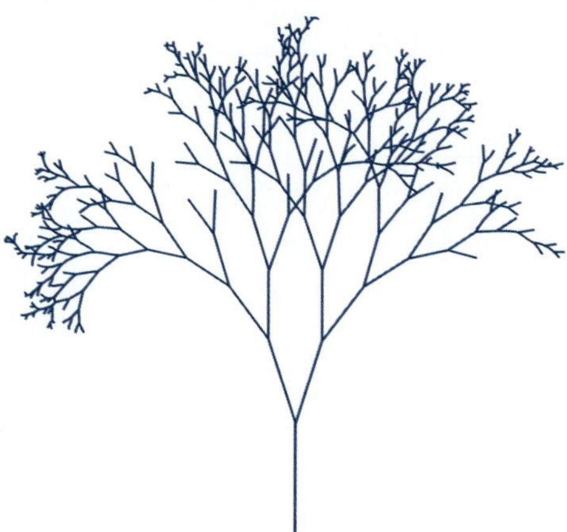

The length of the branch will get shorter and shorter. Once the length becomes shorter than some preset value, the recursion stops. Also, as you can see from the tree above, you should use some form of probability whether the branch will continue to grow or not. Try first the fixed probability of 0.9. Experiment with others, such as the probability of growth as a function based on the length of the branch.

16 Memory Allocation Schemes and Linked Data Structures

Objectives

After you have read and studied this chapter, you should be able to

- Describe continguous and noncontinguous memory allocation schemes
- List the pros and cons of the two memory allocation schemes
- Manipulate linked lists of primitive data
- Manipulate linked lists of objects

Introduction

When our program manipulates a collection of data, such as a list of Person objects or an array of integers, memory space must be allocated to store these data. We will study two memory allocation schemes in this chapter. Understanding them is helpful when we study different types of data structures in the following chapters.

In Java, whenever we execute the new operator, memory space is allocated. Suppose we need to write a program that requires up to 500 integers. We can declare and allocate an array of 500 integers as follows:

```
int[] num = new int[500];
```

contiguous memory allocation (CMA)

memory cell

This will allocate a single, contiguous block of memory that is large enough to store 5000 integers. We characterize this memory allocation scheme as ***contiguous memory allocation (CMA)*** because data are stored in contiguous memory addresses. Figure 16.1 illustrates the allocation of a single memory block for 500 integers. In the illustration, we depict computer memory as a linear sequence of memory cells. Each ***memory cell*** is associated with an address and has the fixed size. We assume here the common size of 1 byte for a single memory cell.

Another approach is to allocate a number of smaller memory blocks. For example, instead of allocating a single memory block for 500 integers, we can allocate 10 memory blocks, with each block having the capacity of 50 integers. We call

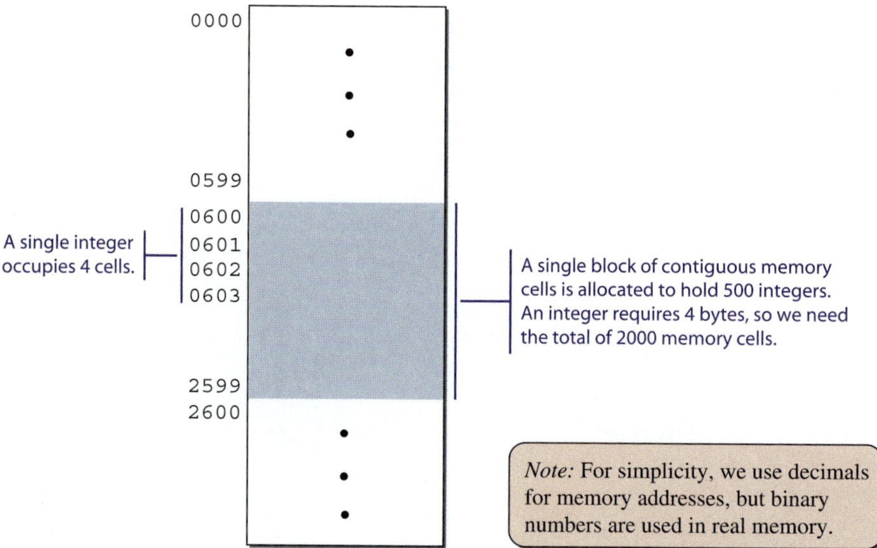
0000
0599
0600
0601
0602
0603
2599
2600
A single integer occupies 4 cells.
A single block of contiguous memory cells is allocated to hold 500 integers. An integer requires 4 bytes, so we need the total of 2000 memory cells.
Note: For simplicity, we use decimals for memory addresses, but binary numbers are used in real memory.

Figure 16.1 This diagram illustrates the contiguous memory allocation. A single memory block that is capable of holding 5000 integers is allocated. We assume each cell holds 1 byte. This illustration shows that the address of the first cell in block is 600.

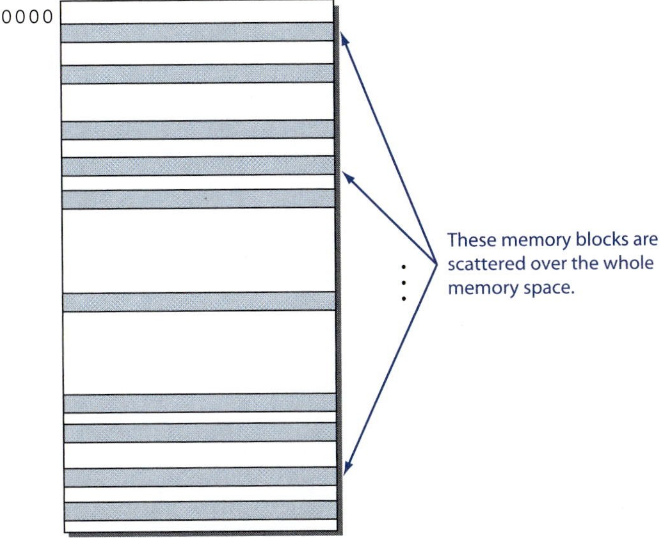

Figure 16.2 This diagram illustrates the noncontiguous memory allocation. Instead of allocating a single block for 500 integers, 10 blocks of 50-integer capacity are allocated.

noncontiguous memory allocation (NMA)

this allocation scheme ***noncontiguous memory allocation (NMA)*** because memory blocks are not allocated at contiguous memory addresses. Figure 16.2 illustrates how 10 blocks, each holding 50 integers, might be allocated.

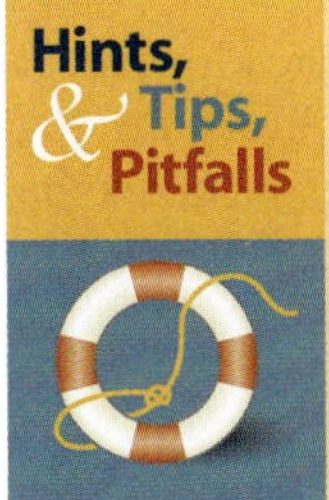

The acronyms *CMA* and *NMA* are not standard terminology in computer science. They are used in this chapter as a shorthand to refer to two memory allocation schemes.

In this chapter we will study the two allocation schemes in detail and explore their advantages and disadvantages. In addition, we will learn how to manipulate a collection of data in Java by using a data management technique called a ***linked data structure***. We will see that a noncontiguous memory allocation scheme is essential in implementing linked data structures.

16.1 Contiguous Memory Allocation Scheme

When a memory space is allocated for an array, the contiguous memory allocation scheme is used. Let's study how the use of CMA affects the data manipulation in arrays. We will use an array of int as an illustration.

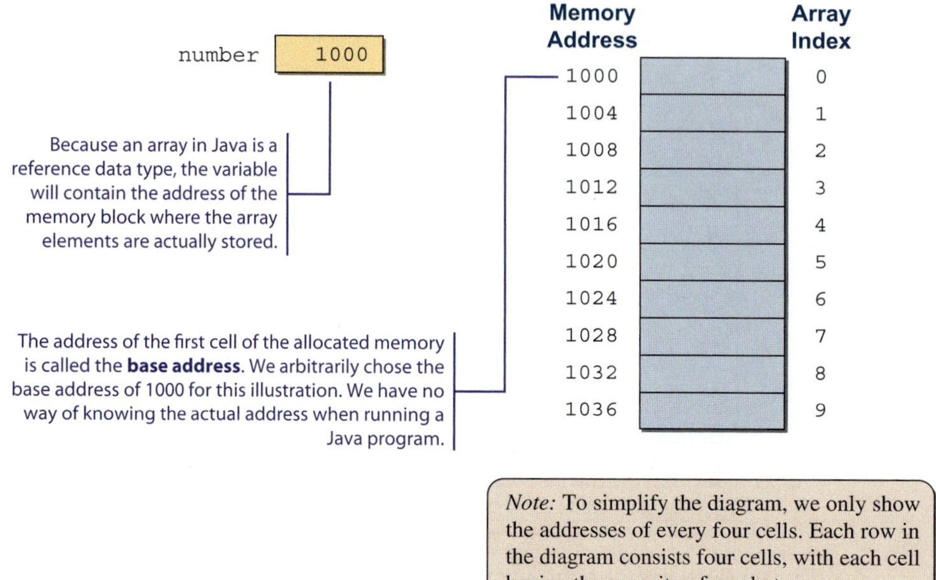
number
1000
Because an array in Java is a reference data type, the variable will contain the address of the memory block where the array elements are actually stored.
The address of the first cell of the allocated memory is called the **base address**. We arbitrarily chose the base address of 1000 for this illustration. We have no way of knowing the actual address when running a Java program.
Memory Address
Array Index
1000 0
1004 1
1008 2
1012 3
1016 4
1020 5
1024 6
1028 7
1032 8
1036 9
Note: To simplify the diagram, we only show the addresses of every four cells. Each row in the diagram consists four cells, with each cell having the capacity of one byte.

Figure 16.3 This diagram illustrates the contiguous memory allocation for an array of int.

Consider the declaration and creation of an array of 10 integers:

```
int[] number = new int[10];
```

When the statement is executed, a contiguous memory block 40 bytes long is allocated in memory (4 bytes per integer × 10 integers = 40 bytes). Figure 16.3 shows the contiguous memory allocation for the array and the correspondence between the actual address and the array index.

We access individual elements by using the indexed expression

```
<array name> [ <index> ]
```

where <array name> is the name of the array and <index> is the position of an element in the array. The valid value for <index> ranges from 0 to array size −1. The index value of 0 refers to the first element in the array. For example, the expression

```
number[5]
```

refers to the element at index position 5 in the array, which is the sixth element in the array. In Figure 16.3 we see that number[5] is located at address 1020. Let's see how the address is computed, given the index position.

Address Computation

Given the index position of an element, say *I*, we can easily compute the address where this element is stored. The address computation requires two components.

base address

offset

First is the ***base address***, which is the address where the first element is stored in the memory. Second is the ***offset***, which is the total number of bytes allocated for the elements at index positions 0 to *I*-1. To determine the offset, we need to know the number of bytes used for each element. An int value, for example, uses 4 bytes and a double value uses 8 bytes. We can compute the address of an element with the following formula:

```
address of index I = base address + I * B
```

where I is the index value and B is the number of bytes per element. The value I * B is the offset. Using this formula, we see that address of number[5] is 1020:

```
address of index 5 = 1000 + 5 * 4 = 1020
```

The key point to remember here that this simple and quick address computation is made possible by storing array elements in contiguous memory cells, with each element requiring the same amount of memory.

Things to Remember

Array elements are stored in contiguous memory cells. This enables very efficient address computation.

The price we pay for the simple and efficient access includes potentially very costly update operations, such as adding an element to or removing it from an array. Let's study the main disadvantages of the CMA scheme.

Overflow

When we create an array, we must designate its size. For example, when we create an array as

```
new int[20];
```

overflow

we are allocating a single memory block to store 20 int values. What will happen when this amount of space is not enough? In other words, what will happen if there is 21st integer we need to store? The condition is characterized as an ***overflow*** condition. When there's an overflow, we must allocate a new, larger block of memory cells and copy the values from the old block to the new block. Here's the code to handle the overflow condition:

```
//Step 1:
//     Allocate a new block of memory that is 200%
//     of the overflowing block of memory
int[] temp = new int [num.length * 2];
```

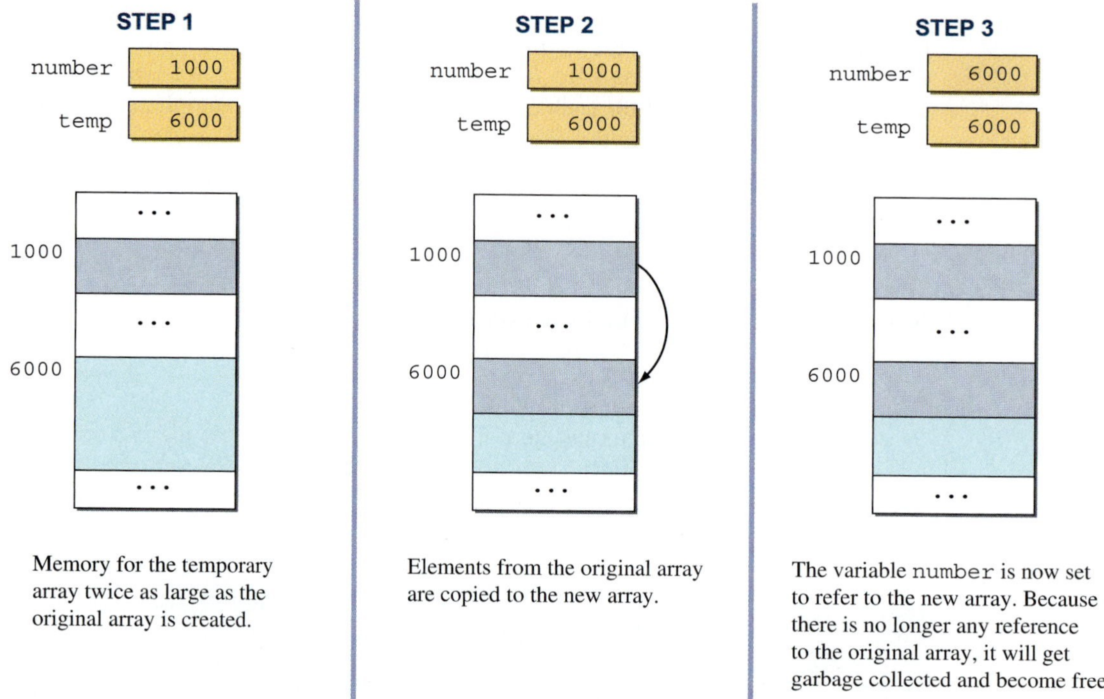

Figure 16.4 Handling overflow by allocating a new, larger block of memory.

```
//Step 2:
//      Copy elements from the old block to the new block
for (int i = 0; i < num.length; i++) {
   temp[i] = num[i];
}

//Step 3:
//      Set num to point to this new block of memory
num = temp;
```

We presented this technique for handling overflow in Chapter 10. Figure 16.4 illustrates the handling of an overflow condition. In the sample code, we set the new block of memory to be twice as large as the old block. This is an arbitrary decision. We can handle the overflow by allocating a new block of memory that is just large enough to store one additional element. However, it is not a good idea to do so, because the chance of overflowing again is high. When we allocate a new block of memory, we want to allocate an amount large enough to reduce the chance of immediate recurrence of overflow condition.

Underutilization

Because we have to allocate a whole block of memory at once, we always run a risk of underutilizing the allocated amount of memory. If we allocate space for an array of 1000 int values, for example, but actually store only 20 int values in the array, then we are wasting 98 percent of the allocated space. On the other hand, if the allocation amount is too small, we run the risk of overflow. If the amount of memory use varies widely every time the program is executed, then allocating just the right amount of memory to reduce the chances of underutilization and overflow may prove to be difficult.

Costly Update Operations

Suppose we have an array that contains ages (int), and the ages are sorted in ascending order. We can then use the efficient binary search, explained in Chapter 11, to locate a specific age in the array. Notice the ability to use the binary search here is the direct benefit of the CMA scheme. To maintain the sorted order, we must add a new element to the array at the right position. Similarly, when we remove an existing age from the array, a "hole" results in the array, and we must fill this hole by shifting the elements in the array. The cost of adding an element to and removing an element from an array is, therefore, proportional to the size of memory.

You Might Want to Know

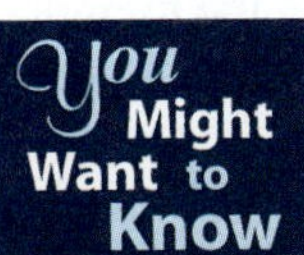

Dynamic Versus Static Memory Allocation

dynamic memory allocation

Dynamic memory allocation means the amount of memory for storing data can be specified at runtime, that is, while the program is being executed. In contrast, *static memory allocation* means the amount of memory for storing data must be specified at compile time. With static memory allocation the amount of memory a program uses is therefore known before the program is executed. And the amount of memory allocated for the program cannot be changed during the runtime.

static memory allocation

One advantage of dynamic allocation is the ability to customize the size of an array to the user's request. We can prompt the user to enter the size of an array she wants and then allocate the space accordingly, for example:

```
int[] number;

int size = getInput(); //ask the user for the array size

number = new int[size]; //allocate the size the user wants
```

heap memory

Older programming languages, such as Fortran, support only the static allocation, while more modern programming languages, such as Java, support the dynamic allocation also. Java uses dynamic memory allocation for the reference data types. The Java system reserves a portion of memory called *heap memory* for dynamically allocated data.

Quick CHECK

1. If the base address of an int array number is 2030, then what is the address of number[6]?
2. Name the possible disadvantages of CMA.

16.2 Noncontiguous Memory Allocation Scheme

One of the disadvantages of the CMA scheme is a possible underutilization of allocated space because the program may not always utilize all the allocated space. To achieve more efficient usage of allocated space, the NMA scheme allocates a number of smaller blocks piecemeal. For example, instead of allocating a single memory block of 500 integers, we can allocate 10 memory blocks, with each block having the capacity for 50 integers. We allocate these 50-integer memory blocks not all at once, but over the course of execution as the need arises. For example, if the program processed 200 integers in one execution, then we would allocate only 4 blocks. If the program processed 70 integers in another execution, then we would allocate 2 blocks.

If the memory blocks are not allocated at once but in piecemeal fashion, then we cannot expect them to be allocated at contiguous memory addresses because, by the time a request for a next block is made, it is very likely the space that immediately follows the previously allocated block is already allocated and used for other purposes. So the space for the next block must be found somewhere else in the memory. This will result in allocated blocks being scattered over the memory, as illustrated in Figure 16.2. Since the allocated memory blocks are not contiguous, the NMA scheme "links" the blocks into a chain so we can access the data in these blocks.

Figure 16.5 shows the state where three blocks are allocated. A block can be declared to store any type and number of data items. For example, we can declare a block to hold 1000 integers, 20 characters, 500 doubles, and so forth. For this discussion, we do not care about the actual contents of the blocks, so we will simply

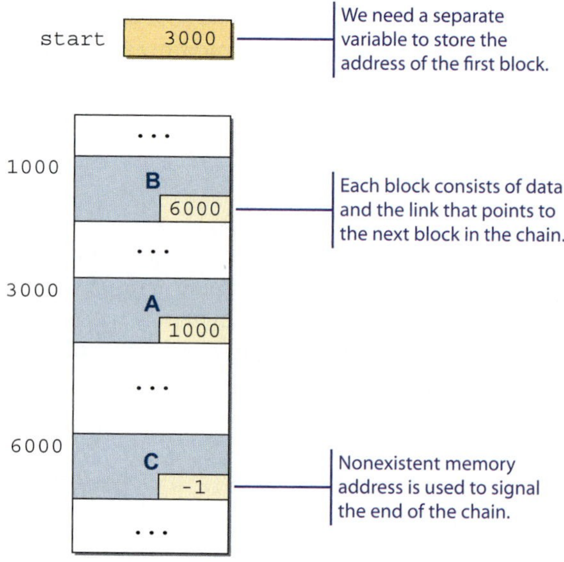

Figure 16.5 Three separate blocks of memory are allocated, with each block containing the address of the next block in the chain. Following the links from **start,** we visit blocks in the order of A, B, and C.

label them with alphabets. We label the first block A, the second block B, and so forth. To be able to access the blocks in a chain, we link them by appending each block with the address of the next block that follows it. Because memory addresses are positive values, we place a negative number, such as −1, to signal the end of the chain. The addresses we place in the blocks are called ***links*** or ***pointers***. The end-of-chain marker is called a ***null link***. Notice that the addresses of the blocks have no relation whatsoever to the relative order of the blocks in the chain. In other words, the address of a block does not have to be lower than those of the blocks that follow it in the chain. For example, block A comes before block B in the chain, but the address of block A is higher than the address of block B.

links, pointers

null link

Adding to or removing a block from a chain is a matter of simply adjusting the link values. To remove a block from a chain, all we have to do is to reset one link. Figure 16.6 shows an example where we remove block B from the chain. All we do is to change the link value in block A from 1000 to 6000. Block B becomes "garbage" and eventually gets marked as usable by the garbage collection process.

Adding a new block to a chain is equally easy. We first locate the space large enough for the block and allocate it. Then we adjust the link values. Figure 16.7 shows an example of adding a new block at the end of a chain.

In the illustrations up to now, we showed hypothetical addresses for allocated blocks. In reality, a programmer (using a high-level programming language such as Java) does not have a means to know the actual addresses where the blocks are allocated. As such, it is more convenient for us to draw a conceptual picture of linked blocks. Figure 16.8 redraws Figure 16.5 as a conceptual diagram that does not include any memory addresses. For the remainder of this book, we will use only the conceptual diagrams.

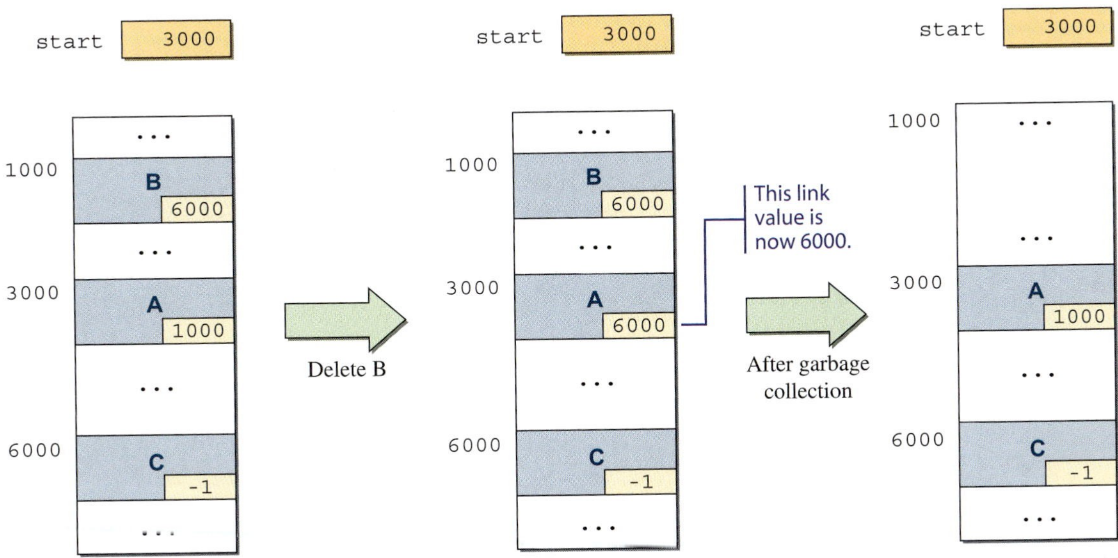

Figure 16.6 This diagram illustrates the removal of a block from a chain. We remove a block from a chain by resetting the link value of the previous block to point to the block that follows the block we're removing.

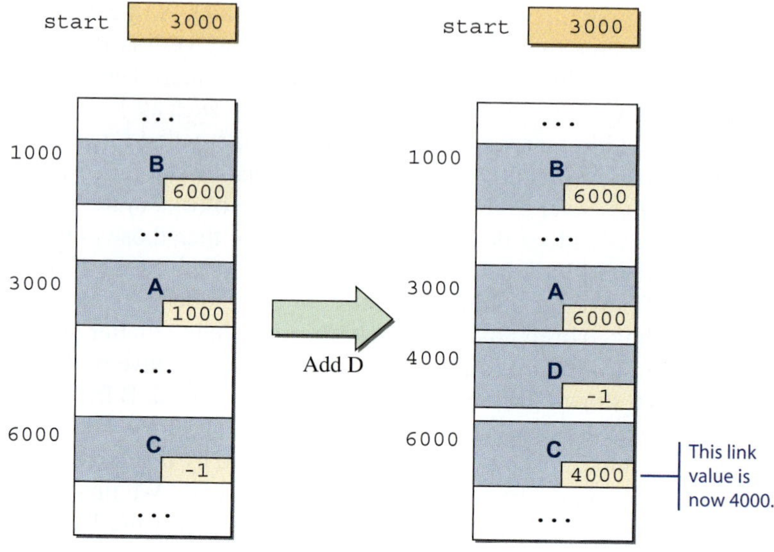

Figure 16.7 This diagram illustrates the addition of a new block to a chain. Here the new block is added as the last block of the chain.

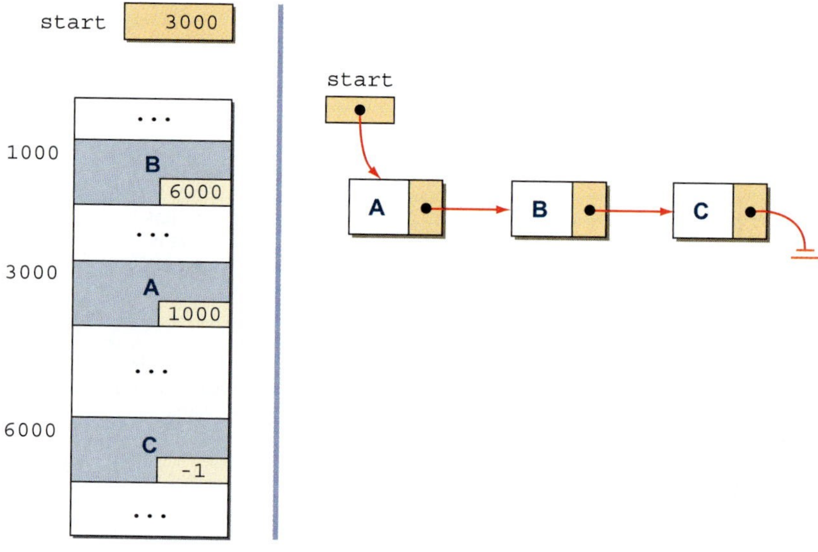

Figure 16.8 Two types of diagrams for depicting a chain of memory blocks. Because we do not care about the actual addresses of the blocks, we use arrows in the conceptual diagram.

Finer Control of Space Usage

With CMA, we often end up not fully utilizing the allocated memory space. But with NMA, we allocate only the necessary amount of memory when it is needed, so we have a finer control of space usage that will eliminate the kind of space waste we see in CMA. Notice, however, that for each allocated block in NMA, we use extra space for the links. For the most part, the extra space we need for a link (most commonly, 4 bytes) is negligible compared to the total size of a block.

Faster Update Operations

With CMA, when we insert an item, we may have to shift items so we can place the added item in a correct position to maintain some order (e.g., descending order of age values). Similarly, when we remove an item, we have to fill the vacated position with another item. We described such update operations for CMA (an array) in Chapter 10. With NMA, adding to and removing a block from a chain are just a matter of updating the link field. We will see exactly how the update operations are done in Section 16.3.

Slower Traversing of Elements

One of the main advantages of CMA is the fast access to an item by using the simple address computation with indexing. Such fast access is not possible with NMA. We have to traverse the links starting from the first block. When the number of blocks increases, the time to locate the desired item grows proportionally. The access time of CMA, on the other hand, remains the same regardless of the size of the allocated block.

1. Redraw the following memory diagram as a conceptual diagram:

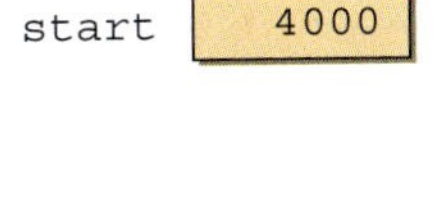

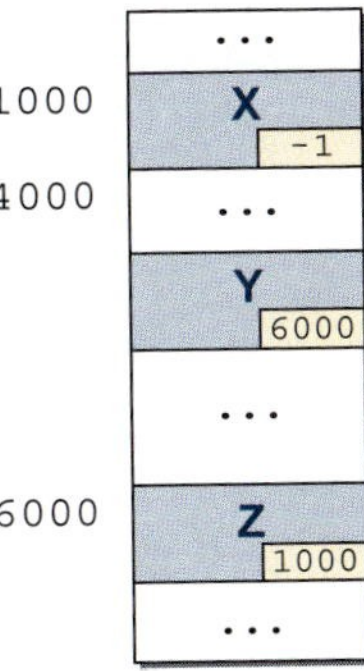

2. Name the key disadvantage of CMA.

16.3 Manipulating Linked Lists

linked list

nodes

data field

link field

When we create and manipulate arrays in our program, we are effectively using the CMA. In this section, we will learn how to define a class that uses the NMA. Let's begin by introducing a couple of new terms when using the NMA in a program. It is more common to refer to a chain of blocks as the ***linked list*** and the blocks in the chain as the ***nodes***. To keep our discussion simple, we will use a node that contains only a single integer (more complex cases will be presented in Section 16.4 and the later chapters). A single node in a linked list, therefore, has two components: a single integer and a link. The single integer is the data we store in a node, and the link points to a node that follows this node (or a null link if this node is the last node in the list). These components in a node are often called the ***data field*** and the ***link field***.

To realize this node structure, we define a class with two data members. We will call the class Node and its two data members item and next:

```
class Node {

   private int item;

   private Node next;

   ...
}
```

Notice the data type for the data member next. It is declared as Node, which may look peculiar at first, but it makes a perfect sense if you think about it a little. The next field of a node points to the next node, so the value we store in the next data member must be a reference to the next node, which is another instance of the Node class. Thus, the data type of the data member next is declared as Node. We store a null reference in the link field when there's no next node. After adding the constructors, the accessors, and the mutators, we have the complete definition:

Node

```
class Node {

   private int item;

   private Node next;

   public Node( ) {
      this(0, null);
   }

   public Node(int data, Node node) {
      setItem(data);
      setNext(node);
   }
```

```
    public int getItem( ) {
        return item;
    }

    public Node getNext( ) {
        return next;
    }

    public void setItem(int data) {
        item = data;
    }

    public void setNext(Node node) {
        next = node;
    }
}
```

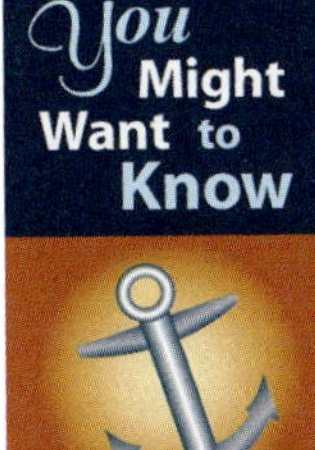

Diagram for Linked Nodes

If we used the standard icon adopted in this textbook for drawing an object, then we would have drawn an instance of the **Node** class as

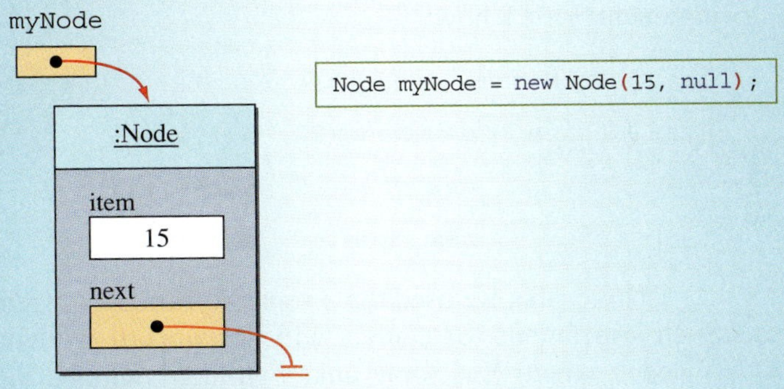

However, a linked node structure is traditionally drawn as

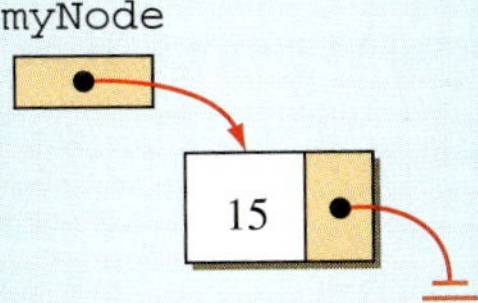

We will use the traditional notation in this textbook when drawing linked lists.

Adding Nodes to a Linked List

Let's go through a number of examples to illustrate how we might use **Node** objects in building a linked list. In the first example, we will create a linked list of three integers 45, 98, and 23. Here's the code:

```
Node one, two, three;

one   = new Node(45, null); //create the first node

two   = new Node(98, null); //the second node, and

three = new Node(23, null); //the third node

one.setNext(two);           //link them

two.setNext(three);
```

Executing this code will result in the following state:

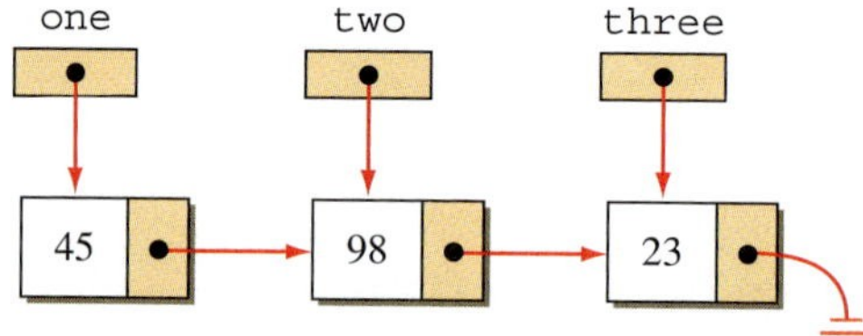

We can achieve the same result without calling the **setNext** method. When creating a new node, we can pass a reference to the next node as the second argument. Here's how:

```
Node one, two, three;

three = new Node(23, null);

two   = new Node(98, three);

one   = new Node(45, two);
```

Notice that we used three separate variables to refer to three individual nodes. Such a technique, of course, will not work if we have to create a linked list of *N* nodes, where *N* is some unknown large number. Say, for example, we need to create a linked list of positive integers entered by the user. We repeatedly ask the user for the next positive integer and stop the repetition when a zero or a negative number is entered. We can create such a list by using only three variables. We will go through several variations. Here's the first one:

```
/* Variation 1: Creating a linked list of N nodes
                using three variables 'start', 'tail',
                and 'next'
*/

Scanner scanner = new Scanner(System.in);

Node start, tail, next;
```

```
    start = null;

    int number = scanner.nextInt();

    if (number > 0) {

       start = new Node(number, null); //create the first node

       tail = start;

       //get more numbers
       while (true) {
          number = scanner.nextInt();

          if (number <= 0) break;

          next = new Node(number, null); //create a new node

          tail.setNext(next); //link the node as the last node

          tail = next; //set tail point to the new last node
       }
    }
```

This code handles the case of empty list properly. When the first number entered is not a positive value, the variable start is set to null. If there is one or more positive integers, then the variables start and tail point to the first node and the last node, respectively. Figure 16.9 shows the sequence of creating a linked list of four positive integers, and Figure 16.10 shows the three steps involved in adding a new node to a list.

In the next variation, we will accomplish the same task by using only two variables start and tail. Instead of using a separate variable next to refer to a new node, we can directly link the new node to the current last node by updating the next field of the tail node (i.e., the node which tail is pointing at). Here's how:

```
/* Variation 2: Creating a linked list of N nodes
                using only two variables 'start' and 'tail'
*/

Scanner scanner = new Scanner(System.in);

Node start, tail;

start = null;

int number = scanner.nextInt();

if (number > 0) {

   start = new Node(number, null); //create the first node

   tail = start;

   //get more numbers
   while (true) {
      number = scanner.nextInt();

      if (number <= 0) break;
```

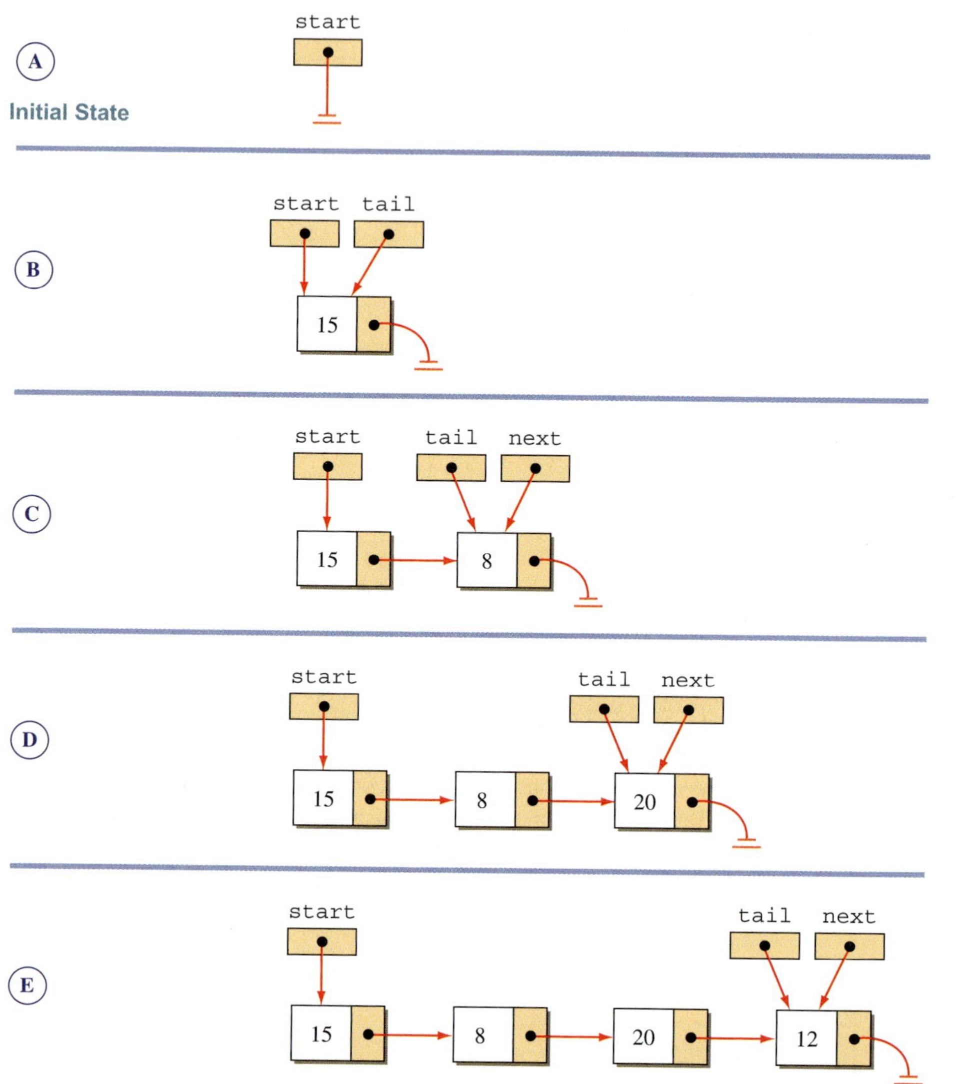

Figure 16.9 A linked list of four positive integers is created by using three variables.

```
            tail.setNext(new Node(number, null));
                              //create a new node and link
                              //the current last node to it

            tail = tail.getNext(); //move tail to the new last node
        }
    }
```

Notice that the while loop in the code requires that the variable tail point to a node. To ensure this, we input the first value before the while loop. If the first input

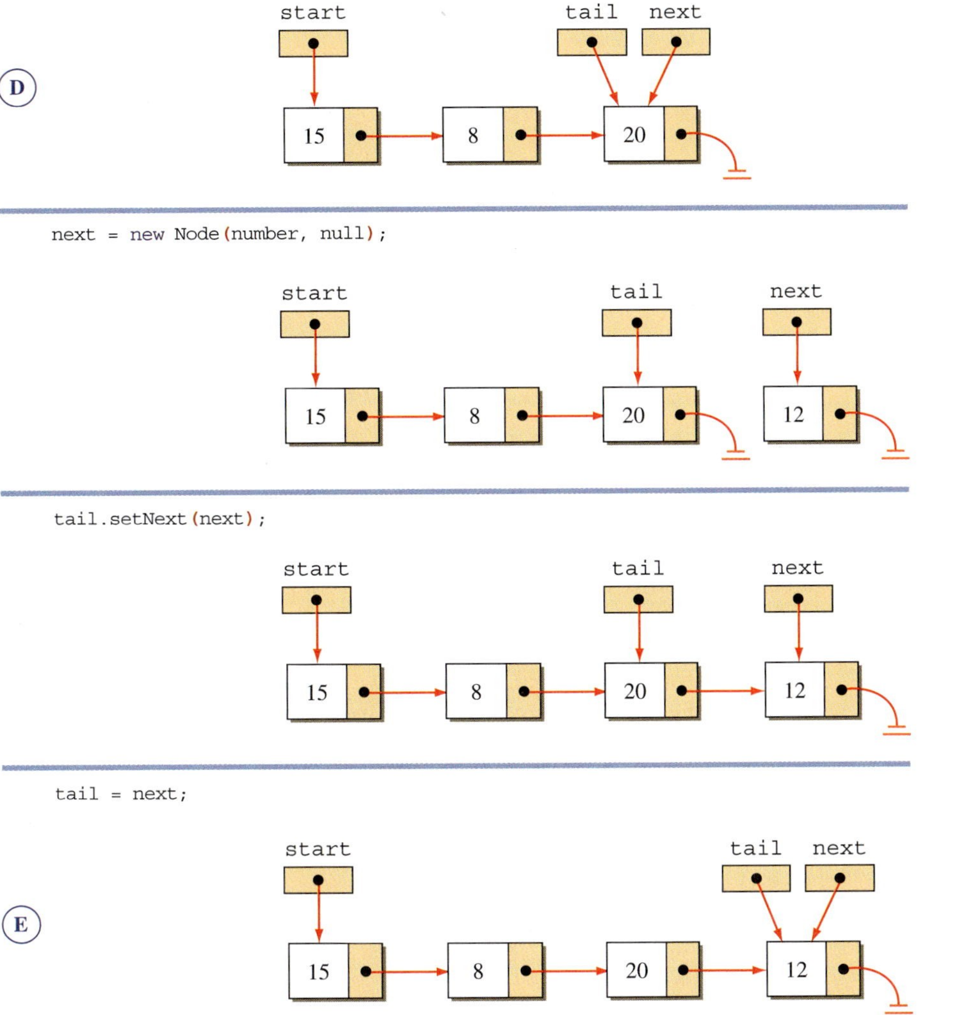

Figure 16.10 Steps for adding a node to a list. This shows the detailed steps of the transition from state D to state E of Figure 16.9.

value is positive, then tail is set to point to the first node and the while loop is executed to input the subsequent values. If the first input value is not positive, the whole routine terminates and start remains equal to null, indicating correctly that the list is empty.

In the third variation, we eliminate this special handling of the first input value by using a temporary dummy node. Here's the code:

```
/* Variation 3: Creating a linked list of N nodes
               using a temporary dummy first node
*/

Scanner scanner = new Scanner(System.in);
```

```
Node start, tail;

start = new Node(0, null); //create a dummy first node
tail  = start;

//input numbers
while (true) {
   int number = scanner.nextInt();

   if (number <= 0) break;

   tail.setNext(new Node(number, null));
                    //create a new node and link
                    //the current last node to it

   tail = tail.getNext(); //move tail to the new last node
}

start = start.getNext(); //make start point to the real
                         //first node
```

For all three variations, when the list is empty, the value of start is null. The value of tail, however, is undefined in the first two variations and is a reference to the dummy node in the third variation. It is left as an exercise to set the value of tail to null for all variations when the list is empty.

In the fourth, and final, variation, we will add new nodes to the front of a list, whereas in the previous three variations we added new nodes to the end of a list. In this variation, we do not have a pointer that points to the last node (notice that the last node in the list is the first input value entered by the user). It is left as an exercise to set a variable tail to point to the last node. Here's the code that adds new nodes to the front of a list:

```
/* Variation 4: Creating a linked list of N nodes
                by adding new nodes to the front
                of the list
*/

Scanner scanner = new Scanner(System.in);

Node start, temp;

start = null;

//input numbers
while (true) {

   int number = scanner.nextInt();

   if (number <= 0) break;

   temp = start; //remember the current front

   start = new Node(number, temp); //add the new front
                                   //node and set its link
                                   //point to the old front
}
```

We use the variable temp for clarity, but it can be eliminated by replacing the last two statements inside the while loop with the following:

```
start = new Node(number, start);
```

Figure 16.11 shows a sample list created by the variation 4 code, and Figure 16.12 shows the detailed steps of adding a new node to a list.

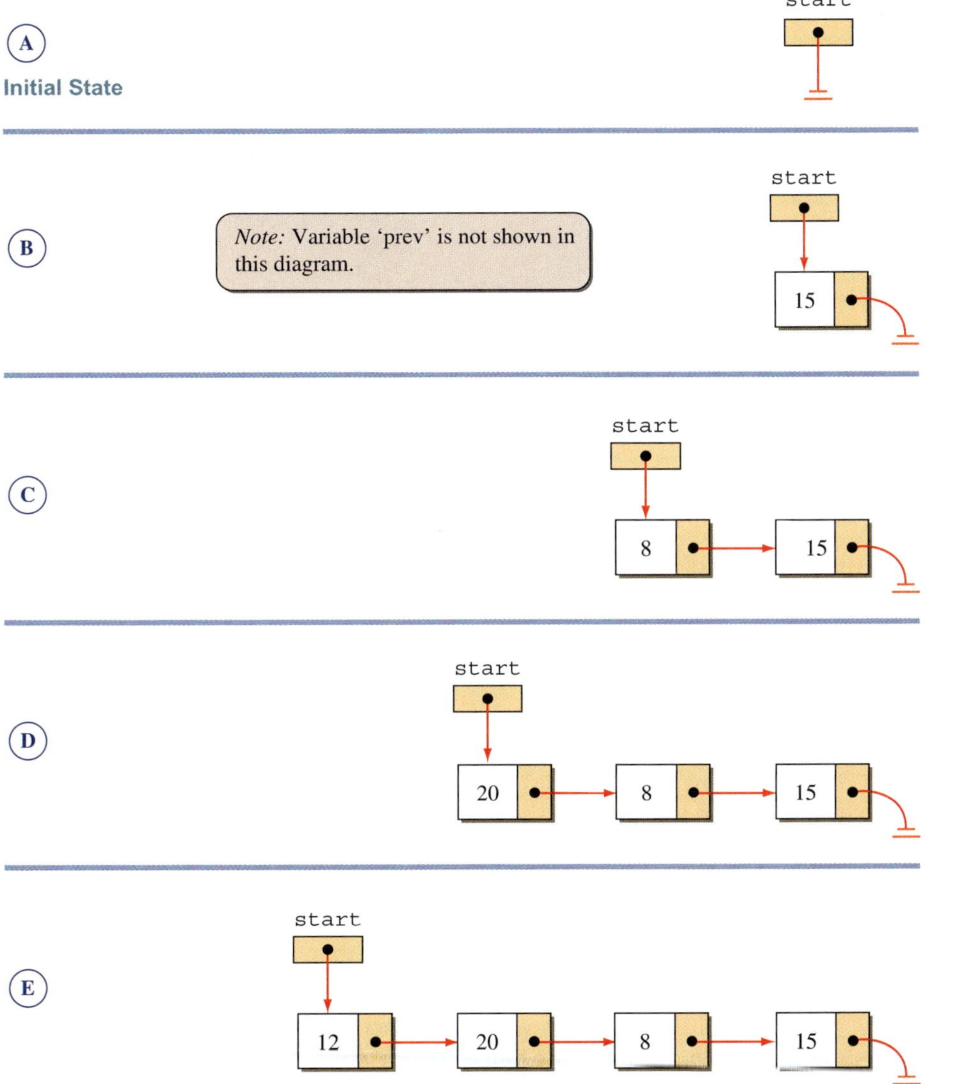

Figure 16.11 The variation 4 code for creating a linked list. Nodes are added to the front of a list. This shows the result of adding 15, 8, 20, and 12.

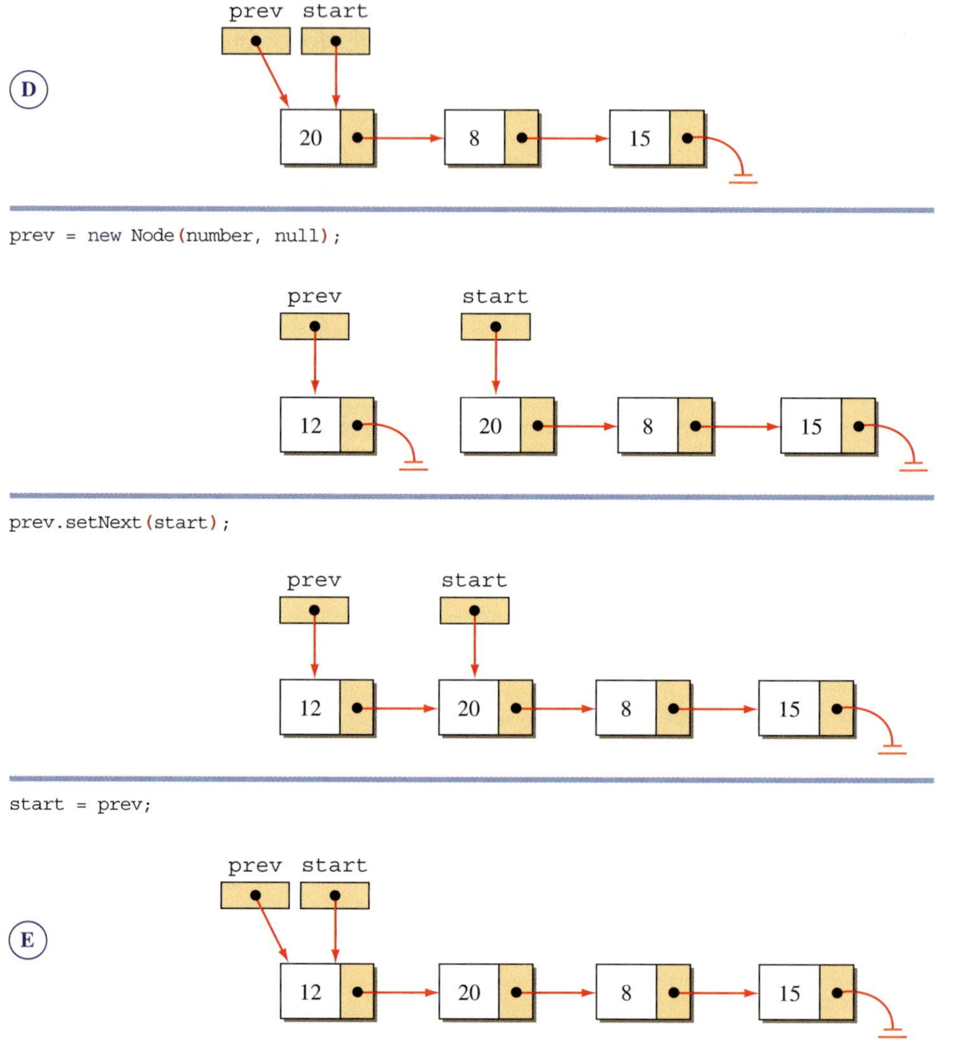

Figure 16.12 Steps for adding a node to a list by using variation 4. This shows the detailed steps of the transition from state D to state E of Figure 16.11.

Searching Nodes in Linked Lists

searching

When we maintain a collection of data, one of the key operations we need is the ability to search for desired information. For example, we might want to locate the node with the largest value. An operation to locate a desired information is called ***searching***. There are two different ways to search for an item in a collection. The first is a search by position, and the second is a search by value. Let's assume we already have a linked list with the variable start pointing at the first node. We will present the search by value here and leave the search by position as an exercise.

Given a linked list start, the following code prints out Found if the searched number is in the list and Not Found otherwise. If start is an empty list, we will print out Not Found.

```
Scanner scanner = new Scanner(System.in);

Node p;

int number = scanner.nextInt();

p = start;   //'start' points to a linked list

while (p != null) {

    if (p.getItem() == number) { //found the node
        break;
    }

    p = p.getNext(); //move p to the next node
}

if (p != null) {

    System.out.println("Found");

} else {

    System.out.println("Not Found");
}
```

The while loop

```
while (p != null) {

    ...

    p = p.getNext(); //move p to the next node
}
```

follows the standard pattern of traversing the nodes in a linked list. We use this processing pattern frequently. For example, the following code counts the number of nodes in a given linked list.

```
Node p;
int cnt = 0;

p = start; //we assume start points to a linked list

while (p != null) {

    cnt++;

    p = p.getNext(); //move p to the next node
}

System.out.println("Size of a list is " + cnt);
```

When the loop includes an if test that breaks out of the loop, we can include the test in the while condition. In other words, instead of writing

```
while (p != null) {

   if (p.getItem() == number) { //found the node
      break;
   }

   p = p.getNext(); //move p to the next node
}
```

we can write

```
while (p != null && p.getItem() != number) {

    p = p.getNext();
}
```

But we must be very careful because we cannot write it as

```
While (p.getItem() != number && p != null) {

   p = p.getNext ()
}
```

Bad Version

Can you tell why not?

Removing Nodes from Linked Lists

Let's study how we can remove a node from a linked list. Consider the following linked list:

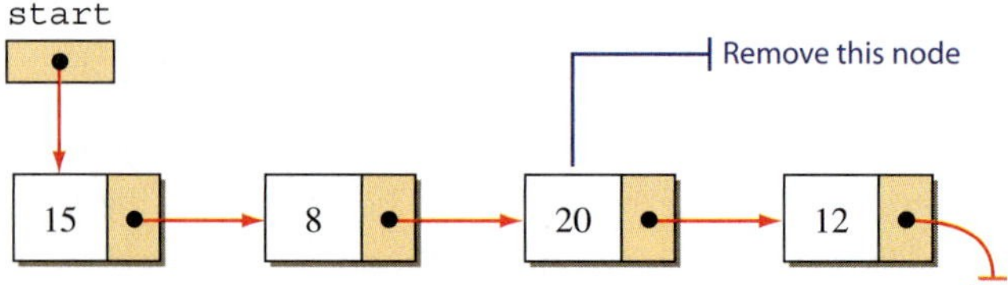

Suppose we want to remove the 20 node (i.e., the node whose content is 20) from the linked list. We remove the designated node by detaching it from the linked list; that is, we reset the next field of the 8 node to point to the 12 node as follows:

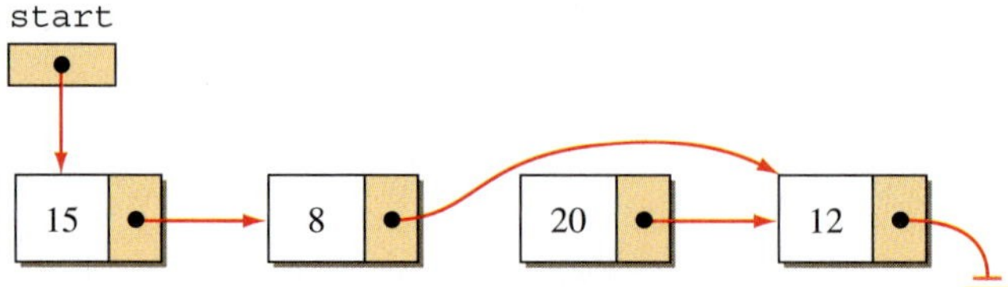

Since no links are now pointing to the **20** node any longer, the garbage collection will eventually deallocate memory occupied by this node.

To remove a node, we need a pointer to the node that precedes the node to be removed. For this example, we need a pointer to the **8** node to remove the **20** node. We assume the node to be removed is identified by its value. Here's the code to remove the specified node:

```
Scanner scanner = new Scanner(System.in);

Node prev, del; //del points to the node to remove
                //prev points to the previous node

int number = scanner.nextInt();

del  = start; //we assume start points to a linked list
prev = null;

while (del != null && number != del.getItem()) {

   prev = del;       //move the two pointers forward
    del = del.getNext();
}

if (del == null) {

   System.out.println("Delete Node Not Found");

} else {

   if (del == start) {

      start = start.getNext(); //remove the first node

   } else {

      prev.setNext(del.getNext());
                  //sets the next field of prev to
                  //the next field of del
   }
}
```

Figure 16.13 illustrates the two cases when removing a node. In case 1, we remove the first node. We achieve this by updating the variable **start** to point to the second node, which will become the first node in the new linked list. In case 2, we remove a node other than the first node. We reset the **next** field of the previous node to point to the node that follows the removed node. Notice that in both cases, even though the removed node is detached from the linked list, the variable **del** still points to it in the diagram. As long as there's a variable that is pointing to a node, it does not get deallocated. If **del** is declared as a local variable (which is most likely the case), then it is erased when the execution of the method is complete. So the removed node will eventually have no variables

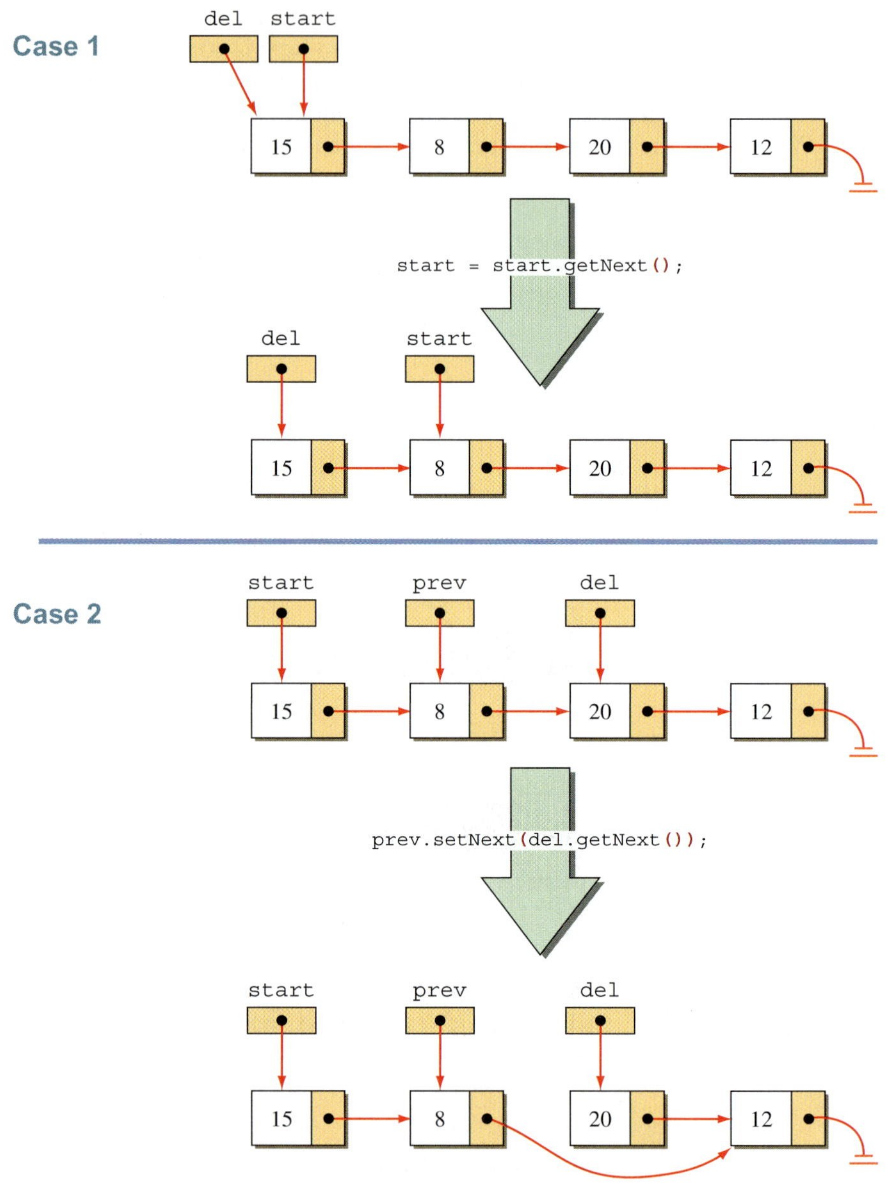

Figure 16.13 Two cases of deleting a node from a linked list. The first is the removal of the first node. The second is the general case of removing a node other than the first node.

pointing at it and get deallocated. Even if the del variable is not a local (it could be a data member of some class, for example), in a subsequent removal operation, it will get reset to point to another node. So either way, the removed node will get deallocated eventually.

1. Draw a diagram that shows the result of running the following code:

```
Node one = new Node(10, null);
Node two = new Node(20, one);
```

2. Given a linked list start, write a code that counts the number of nodes in the list.
3. Given a linked list start, write a code that sets the second pointer tail to point to the last node in the list. You must scan the list from the first node to locate the last node (the one with the null link field).

16.4 Linked Lists of Objects

As we can declare arrays of primitive data types and arrays of objects, we can define both linked lists of primitive data types and objects. In Section 16.3, we presented a linked list of primitive data type. To complete our study of the basic linked data structure, we will describe a linked list of objects in this section. We will use the simple Bicycle class introduced in Chapter 4 with a slight modification. Here's the definition of the Bicycle class we use in this section:

```
class Bicycle {

   private String ownerName;

   public Bicycle(String name) {
      setOwnerName(name);
   }

   public String getOwnerName( ) {
      return ownerName;
   }

   public void setOwnerName(String name) {
      ownerName = name;
   }
}
```

First we define the node structure. To avoid confusion, we will name this node structure BNode. Here's the definition:

BNode

```
class BNode {

   private Bicycle item;

   private BNode next;
```

```
    public BNode( ) {
       this(null, null);
    }

    public BNode(Bicycle data, BNode node) {
       setItem(data);
       setNext(node);
    }

    public Bicycle getItem( ) {
       return item;
    }

    public BNode getNext( ) {
       return next;
    }

    public void setItem(Bicycle data) {
       item = data;
    }

    public void setNext(BNode node) {
       next = node;
    }
}
```

Notice the similarity between the BNode and Node classes. They are basically identical except for the difference in the data types of the item field. We will examine the possibility of defining a generic node structure that will be able to store any type of data item in Chapter 17.

The data type of the item field in the BNode structure is declared as Bicycle. This means the value we store in the item field is a reference to a Bicycle object. The following diagram illustrates a linked list of three BNode nodes with the item field of each node pointing at a Bicycle object:

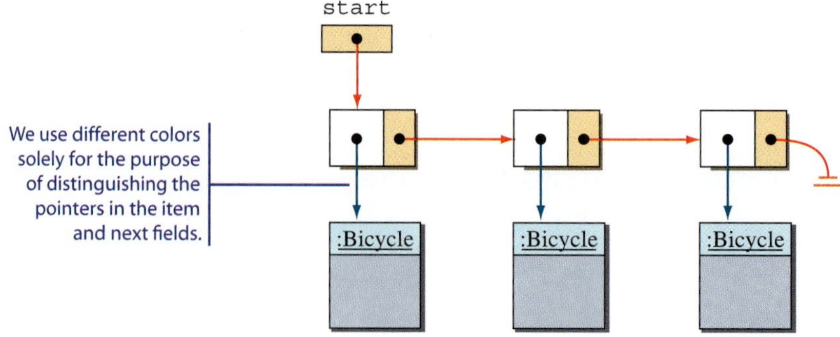
start
We use different colors solely for the purpose of distinguishing the pointers in the item and next fields.
:Bicycle
:Bicycle
:Bicycle

Adding Nodes to Linked Lists of Objects

Let's go through a number of examples, similar to those described in the previous section, to illustrate how we manipulate BNode objects. In the first example, we will create a linked list of *N* Bicycle objects. We repeatedly ask the user for the owner name of a Bicycle object and stop the repetition when the string QUIT is entered. Here's one way to create a linked list of *N* Bicycle objects:

```
Scanner scanner = new Scanner(System.in);

BNode start, tail, next;

start = null;

String name = scanner.next();

if (!name.equalsIgnoreCase("QUIT")) {

   start = new BNode(new Bicycle(name), null);
                                  //create the first node

   tail = start;

   //get more names
   while (true) {
      name = scanner.next();

      if (name.equalsIgnoreCase("QUIT")) break;

      next = new BNode(new Bicycle(name), null);
                                  //create a new node

      tail.setNext(next); //link the node as the last node

      tail = next; //set tail to point to the new last node
   }
}
```

Searching Nodes in Linked Lists of Objects

Now let's see how we can search for a specific Bicycle object. We search for a Bicycle object by specifying its owner name. We will return the first Bicycle object that matches the given owner name. If the names are distinct, then the object found is the only Bicycle object that matches the search criteria. We assume here that we already have a linked list with the variable start pointing at the first node. Given a linked list start (i.e., a linked list whose first node is pointed by the variable start), the following code prints out Found if the search name is located in the list and Not Found otherwise. If start is an empty list, we will print out Not Found.

```
Scanner scanner = new Scanner(System.in);

BNode p;

String searchName = scanner.next();

p = start;   //we assume start points to a linked list
```

```
while (p != null) {

   String name = p.getItem().getOwnerName();

   if (name.equals(searchName)) {  //found the node
      break;
   }

   p = p.getNext(); //move p to the next node
}

if (p != null) {

   System.out.println("Found");

} else {

   System.out.println("Not Found");
}
```

Notice the general pattern of the search routine is basically identical to the one we've seen for searching a linked list of integers. The key, and critical, difference is in the way we retrieve the data item. In the code, the expression

```
p.getItem()
```

will return a Bicycle object (specifically, a reference to a Bicycle object). We are interested in the owner's name of this Bicycle object, so we write

```
String name = p.getItem().getOwnerName();
```

Then we compare it against the search name as

```
if (name.equals(searchName)) {
```

We can break the statement that retrieves the owner's name of a Bicycle object into two statements as

```
Bicycle bike = p.getItem();
String name  = bike.getOwnerName();
```

A separate variable such as bike is useful when we need to access more than one data member value or call other methods of an object. We do not have such a need in this example, so we combine the two statements into one.

Removing Nodes from Linked Lists of Objects

The code to remove a BNode from a list is identical to the one seen in the previous section. The only difference is in how we compare the item and the search value. The content of the item field is a reference to a Bicycle object. We retrieve its owner name and compare this to the search value as

```
del.getItem().getOwnerName().equals(searchName)
```

We will list the almost identical code to remove the searched node for completeness:

```
Scanner scanner = new Scanner(System.in);

BNode prev, del; //del points to the node to remove
                 //prev points to the previous node

String searchName = scanner.next();

del = start; //we assume start points to a linked list
prev = null;

while (del != null) {

   if (del.getItem().getOwnerName().equals(searchName)) {
       break; //found the node
   }

   prev = del;       //move the two pointers forward

   del = del.getNext();
}

if (del == null) {

   System.out.println("Delete Node Not Found");

} else {

   if (del == start) {

      start = start.getNext(); //remove the first node

   } else {

      prev.setNext(del.getNext());
                        //sets the next field of prev to
                        //the next field of del
   }
}
```

1. Draw a diagram that shows the result of running the following code:

```
BNode one = new BNode(new Bicycle("John"), null);
BNode two = new BNode(new Bicycle("Jack"), one);
```

2. Given a linked list start, write a code that prints out the owner name of all Bicycle objects in the list.

16.5 Sample Development

HumongousInteger

Let's study how we can use the linked node structure in implementing a useful class. If you look inside the **java.math** package, you will find a class named **BigInteger.** The primitive data type **int** uses 4 bytes to store an integer value and is limited to the maximum value of $2^{32} - 1$. However, in many applications, such as cryptography, we need to deal with integer values much larger than the **int** data type can hold. A **BigInteger** object has no limits on the size of a value it can store. In this section, we will implement a very simplified version of the **BigInteger** class by using a linked list.

Problem Statement

Design a class that implements a simplified version of **java.math.BigInteger.** *The class supports four basic arithmetic operations along with appropriate constructors and utility methods. Use the linked node structure for implementation.*

Overall Plan

Public Interface

To avoid the naming conflict with the **java.math.BigInteger** class, we will name our class **HumongousInteger.** We have two major tasks to complete in the overall development plan. The first task is to decide the ***public interface*** of the class, that is, its public methods, including the constructor. We will model our design after the **BigInteger** class. The second task is to decide the data representation, including details such as how many digits we store in a node and how we are going to distinguish positive and negative humongous integers.

We will define one method for each of the four basic arithmetic operations. We define these methods in the style of the **Fraction** class from Chapter 7:

```
HumongousInteger hi1, hi2, hi3, hi4, hi5, hi6, hi7;
...
h3 = h1.add(h2);   //add h2 to h1
h4 = h1.sub(h2);   //subtract h2 from h1
h5 = h1.mult(h2);  //multiply h2 to h1
h6 = h1.div(h2);   //divide h1 by h2
```

We will implement these operations as nondestructive methods so both the receiver object **h1** and the argument object **h2** remain the same. The result of an operation is returned as a new **HumongousInteger** object.

For the constructors, we allow the client programmer to create a new instance of **HumongousInteger** by passing either a string or a **long** as an argument. For example, we can create an instance as

```
HumongousInteger hi
        = new HumongousInteger("12345678901234567890");
```

or

```
HumongousInteger hi
        = new HumongousInteger(1234567890);
```

The second constructor takes an integer value (data type **long**) as an argument. By setting the data type to **long,** we can accept any integer data type (**byte, short, int,** and **long**). Following the convention, we will include a zero-argument constructor, that initializes the new created **HumongousInteger** object to 0, as the third constructor.

We will provide one comparison method named **compareTo** that returns a negative, zero, or positive value when the receiving object is less than, equal to, or greater than the argument object, respectively. Finally, we will define the standard **toString** method that returns the string representation of a **HumongousInteger** object. For this implementation, we will not include any grouping character, such as the comma, that separates a group of three digits. The **toString** method that includes a grouping character is left as an exercise.

Here's the draft class definition:

```
class HumongousInteger {
    ...
    public HumongousInteger( ) { ... }
    public HumongousInteger(long value) { ... }
    public HumongousInteger(String value) { ... }

    public HumongousInteger add(HumongousInteger hi) {...}
    public HumongousInteger sub(HumongousInteger hi) {...}
    public HumongousInteger mult(HumongousInteger hi) {...}
    public HumongousInteger div(HumongousInteger hi) {...}

    public int compareTo(HumongousInteger hi) {...}

    public String toString( ) {...}
}
```

Data Representation

Our second task is to decide the data structure to represent a humongous integer. Since each **HumongousInteger** object has a varying number of digits and there is no fixed upper bound on the number of digits a **HumongousInteger** object can have, using a linked list to store the digits is a logical choice. To determine the exact data structure, let's review the process involved in adding two numbers. Consider the following addition:

```
        1 1    <---- carry
2 3 4 0 3 9 8
    + 9 0 4 3
-------------
2 3 4 9 4 4 1
```

We start adding the numbers from the least significant digits and carry 1 over to the next significant digit when the sum of digits is larger than 10. To support this process of

16.5 Sample Development—*continued*

adding digits, we want the link fields to point in the direction from the least to the most significant digits. If we put a single digit in a node, then the value **9043,** for example, can be represented as

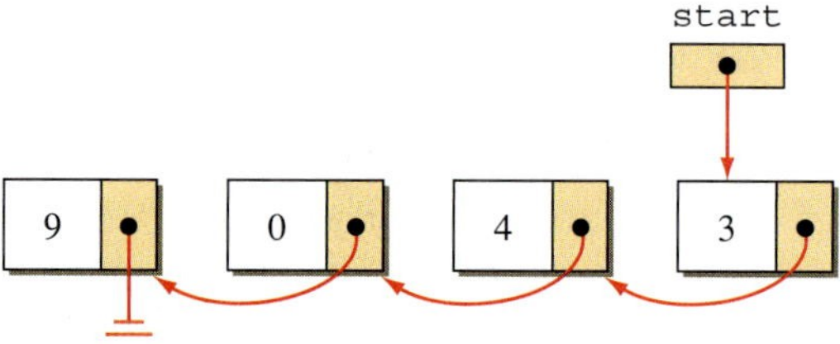

It is common to draw the link field to the right of the **item** field, but it's not a rule, so we can draw the same information as follows:

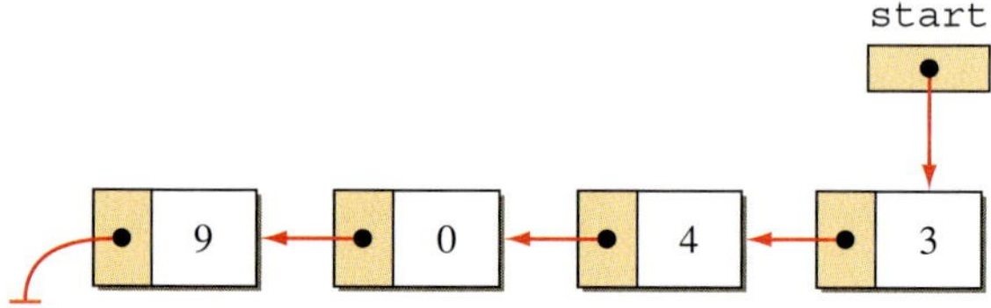

And, of course, we can reverse the direction of the links and draw the linked list in a more conventional way as

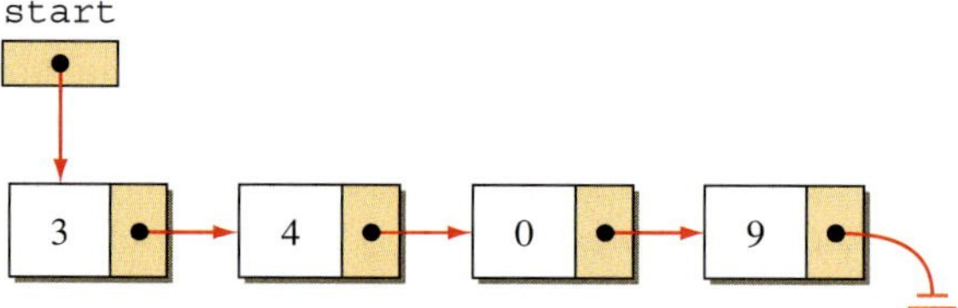

We will be using either the second or the third type of drawing, whichever is more appropriate to the discussion on hand.

Storing one digit per node, as shown in the illustrations here, is a viable option, but it is not the only option. We can pack each node with more digits so the overall length of a linked list is shortened. For example, to represent an integer with 100 digits, we need 100 single-digit nodes, but only 20 five-digit nodes (i.e., each node stores five digits). What would be an ideal number of digits to store in a single node? To facilitate some experiments later to determine the effects of the size of the **item** field, let's implement the class in such a way that we can vary the number of digits we store in a node with a simple modification of the source code. For the base implementation, we will store 3 digits per node. Using 3-digit nodes, the number **2340398,** for example, is represented as

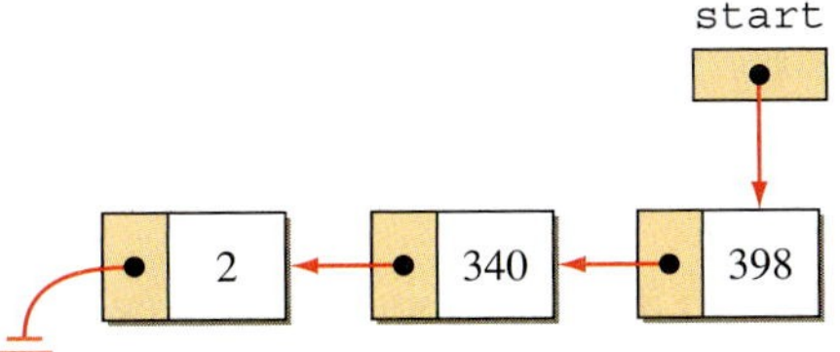

Notice that the carry from adding the values of two nodes is no more than 1 regardless of the number of digits stored in a single node.

There is one more detail to consider. How shall we represent negative humongous integers? We will adopt the signed representation by reserving a data member to store the sign of a number. This data member will hold −1 for a negative number and +1 for a positive number. A **HumongousInteger** object therefore needs (at least) two data members: one is the sign field and the other is the pointer to the first node of a linked list. Figure 16.14 shows how two humongous integers, one positive and the other negative, can be represented using this structure.

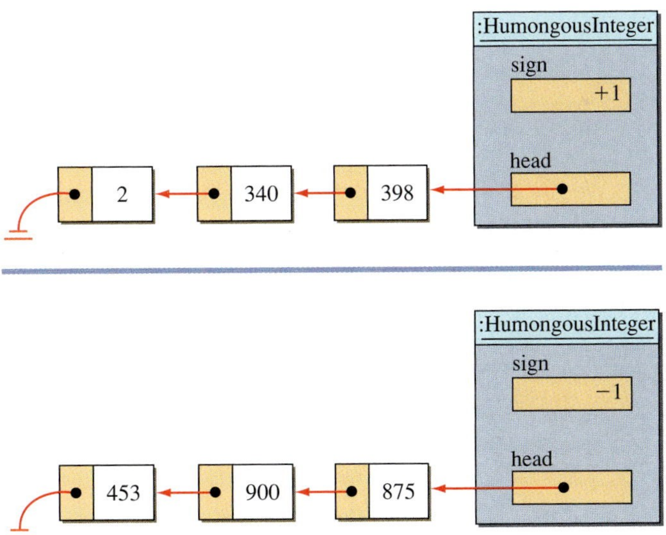

Figure 16.14 The diagrams illustrate the internal data structure for **HumongousInteger** objects. The top one represents **2340398** and the bottom one **−453900875.**

16.5 Sample Development—*continued*

Let's first review the addition and subtraction of signed numbers. When adding two integers, we must consider their signs. The four possible cases are

```
 A  +   B
 A  +  -B
-A  +   B
-A  +  -B
```

where **A** and **B** are positive values. Likewise, when we subtract an integer from another integer, we must consider their signs. There are also four possible cases for subtraction:

```
 A  -   B
 A  -  -B
-A  -   B
-A  -  -B
```

Instead of trying to solve the eight cases individually, we will organize them into a smaller number of cases via algebraic simplification as follows:

```
 A  +   B  →    A + B
 A  +  -B  →    A - B
-A  +   B  →    B - A
-A  +  -B  →  -(A + B)
 A  -   B  →    A - B
 A  -  -B  →    A + B
-A  -   B  →  -(A + B)
-A  -  -B  →    B - A
```

We can solve all eight different cases by solving only two cases. They are addition and subtraction of two positive integers:

```
A  +  B
```

and

```
A  -  B
```

For the subtraction, we assume **A** is greater than or equal to **B.** If not, we solve

```
-(B - A)
```

Once we can add and subtract two positive integers, we can implement the full addition and subtraction methods in a very straightforward manner.

Development Steps

We will develop the class in six steps:

1. Define the node data structure. Implement the constructor and the **toString** method.
2. Implement the addition of two positive integers.
3. Implement the subtraction of two positive integers.
4. Implement the full addition and subtraction.
5. Implement the multiplication (left as an exercise).
6. Implement the division (left as an exercise).

Step 1: Implement the Constructors and the toString Method

Step 1 Design

We have three constructors to implement. The first two can be implemented simply by calling the third constructor as follows:

```
public HumongousInteger( ) {
   this("0");
}

public HumongousInteger(long number) {
   this("" + number);
}
```

The third constructor accepts a **String** value and converts it to a linked list representation. To simply the implementation, we will only consider a valid input (see Exercise 13 on page 938). We define the valid format as follows:

```
[<minus sign>]<digit>+
```

where the brackets [and] signal the optional component and the plus sign + specifies one or more repetitions. The formula states an input string has one or more digits optionally preceded by the negative sign. We do not consider an invalid case such as

```
HumongousInteger num = new HumongousInteger("9x00912-2");
```

Notice that an argument string with leading zeros such as

```
"0000345"
```

is valid. The conversion process should ignore the leading zeros; so, for example, given this **String** value, the result will be

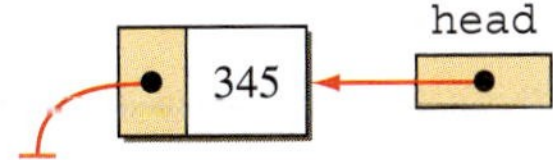

not

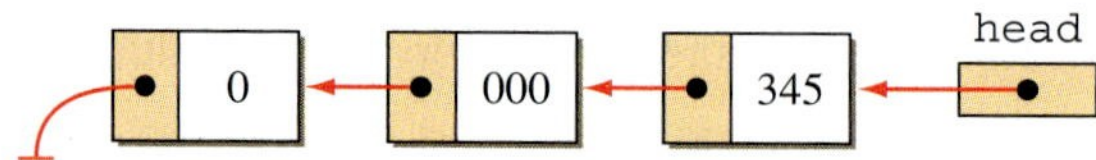

How shall we convert a given **String** value to the corresponding linked list structure? The basic idea is to repeatedly extract *N* characters from the least significant digits until there are no more characters to extract, where *N* is the number of digits to store in a single node. Here we set *N* to 3. For each extraction, we create a new **Node** and store the value in it. Figure 16.15 illustrates the extraction process.

Handling of leading zeroes is a little tricky. For example, if the argument string is

```
"000000876"
```

then we can stop the processing when we first hit three zeros. However, seeing three zeros while processing the string does not always mean we encounter the leading zeros. For example, consider the following string:

```
"5000000876"
```

Instead of trying to handle leading zeros in the extraction process, we will preprocess the input string and eliminate leading zeros. After any leading zeros are removed from the argument string, we apply the extraction process illustrated in Figure 16.15. This preprocessing keeps the extraction process simple. Here's the overall control flow for the conversion:

1. Check the first character. If it is the minus sign, remove it and set the sign field to −1. Otherwise, set the sign field to +1.
2. Eliminate any leading zeros.
3. Apply the extraction process.

Another potential pitfall we must watch out for is the handling of different **String** values that represent the numerical value of zero. The following **String** values all represent zero:

```
"0"
"0000"
"-00"
```

We will have exactly one internal representation for zero, so the implementation of arithmetic operations that involve zero as their operand is streamlined. Internally, zero will

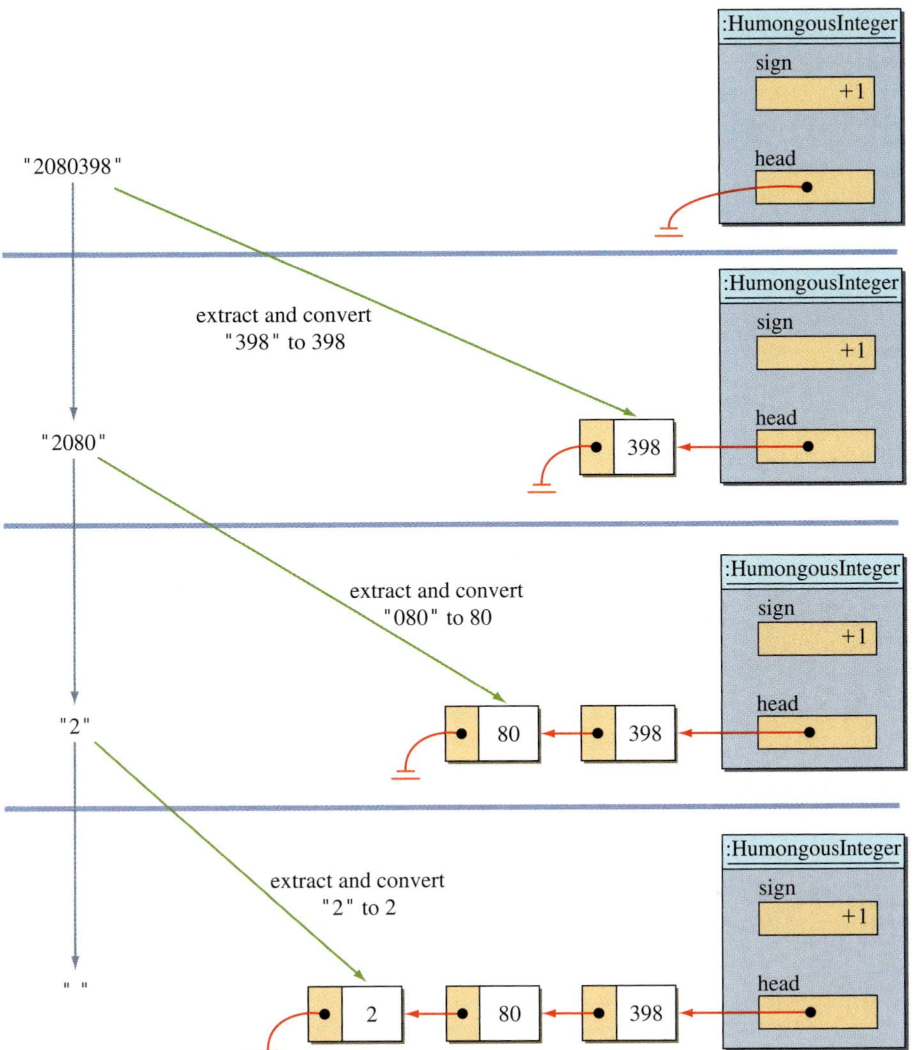

Figure 16.15 This shows the process of converting a given string representation of a humongous integer to an internal linked list representation. We continue extracting three characters from the least significant digits.

always be represented as a positive value, that is, +0. For example, even if one passes **"−0"** or **"−000"** to the constructor, internally the numerical value zero will always be represented as +0.

The **toString** method is basically the reverse of the constructors. We perform the reverse of the extraction process of the constructor by scanning through the linked list and appending the digits to the front of the string. Figure 16.16 illustrates this process.

16.5 Sample Development—*continued*

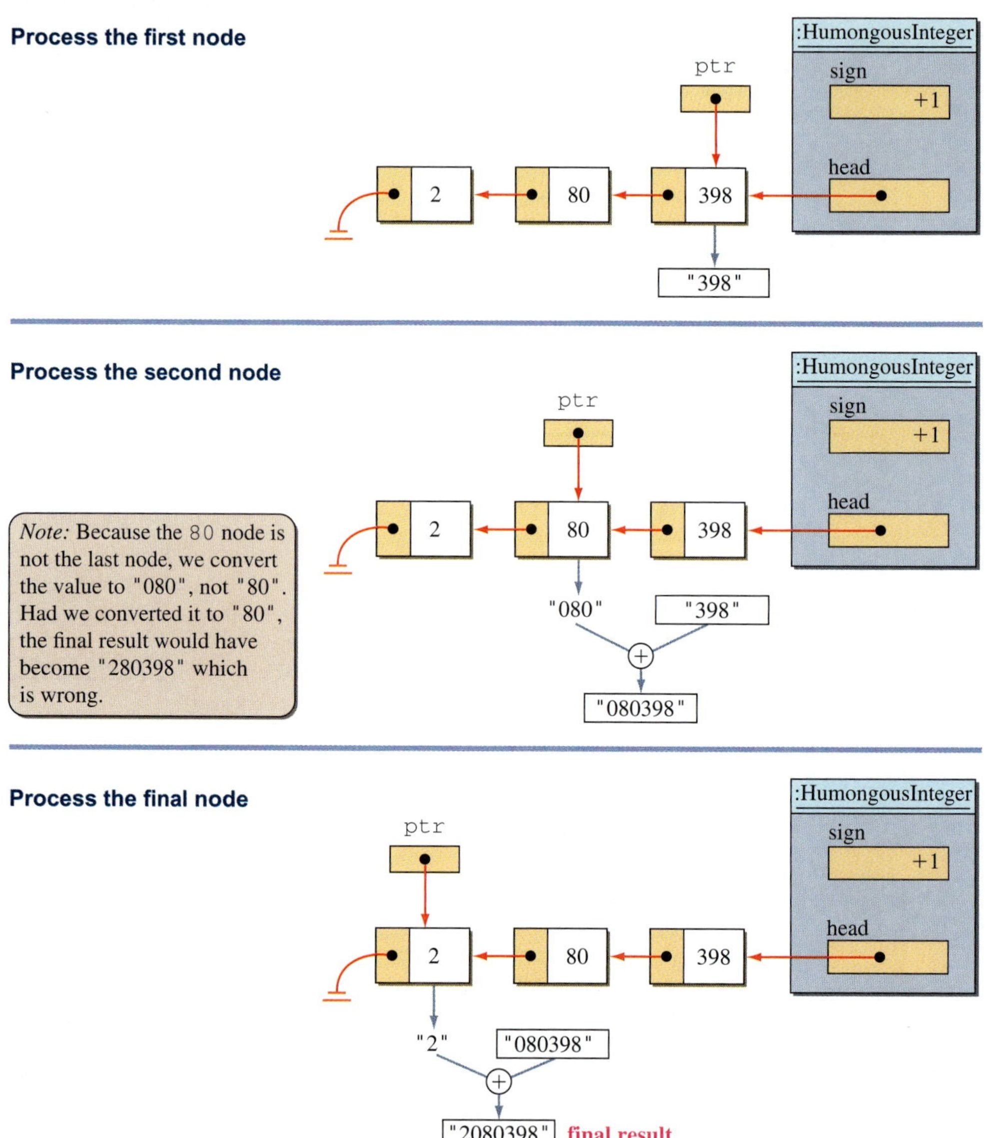

Figure 16.16 This shows the process of converting a linked list representation of **HumongousInteger** to a string.

As shown in the figure, we have to be careful when the content of a node has less than the maximum number of digits the node can hold. In the illustration, we convert the numerical value of 80 to the string value **"080"** to maintain the correct magnitude of the number.

Step 1 Code

Here's the step 1 code. Notice how the **Node** class is defined as the inner class of **HumongousInteger.** This class is used strictly by the **HumongousInteger** class so it is most natural to define it as the inner class. We define two class constants **MAX_DIGITS** and **VALUE_RANGE,** respectively, for the maximum number of digits we store in a node and the range of possible values we can store in a node. Because the data member **value** is declared as **short, MAX_DIGITS** can range from **1** to **4.** The actual value we store in the **value** data member ranges from 0 to **VALUE_RANGE − 1.**

HumongousInteger (Step 1)

```
class HumongousInteger {

   private static final char MINUS = '-';

   private Node head;

   private byte sign;

   public HumongousInteger( ) {
        this("0");
   }

   public HumongousInteger(long number) {
      this("" + number);
   }

   public HumongousInteger(String number) {

      //no error checking; assume the parameter has a valid format

      number.trim();

      sign = +1;

      if (number.charAt(0) == MINUS) {

         sign = -1;

         number = number.substring(1); //remove the first character

      }

      number = trimLeadingZero(number);

      if (number.equals("0")) {
         sign = +1;            //input pattern \-0+ or \+0+ gets convert to
                               //+0 internally
      }
```

Constructors

16.5 Sample Development—*continued*

```
        head = new Node(); //uses a dummy head node

        Node tail = head;

        String digits;

        while (!number.equals("")) {

            int loc = Math.max(number.length() - Node.MAX_DIGITS, 0);

            digits = number.substring(loc); //chop off the last 3 digits
                                            //chop off all if < 3 digits

            number = number.substring(0,loc);
                                    //if loc == 0, number becomes ""

            Node block = new Node(digits);

            tail.next = block;
            tail = block;
        }

        head = head.next; //remove the dummy node
    }

    public String toString( ) {

        StringBuffer strBuf = new StringBuffer("");

        String format = "%0" + Node.MAX_DIGITS + "d";

        Node p = head;

        while (p.next != null) {

            strBuf.insert(0, String.format(format, p.value));
                        //pad leading 0s if the digits are
                        //in the middle of the number

            p = p.next;
        }

        strBuf.insert(0, p.value); //process the most significant node
                                   //don't pad leading 0s for this node

        if (sign < 0) {
            strBuf.insert(0, "-");
        }

        return strBuf.toString();
    }

    private static String trimLeadingZero(String str) {

        StringBuffer strBuf = new StringBuffer(str);
```

toString

trimLeadingZero

```
        int length = strBuf.length();

        for (int i = 0; i < length; i++) {

            if (strBuf.charAt(0) == '0') {
                strBuf.deleteCharAt(0);
            }
        }

        if (strBuf.length() == 0) {
            strBuf.append('0');
        }

        return strBuf.toString();
    }

//-------------------------------
// Inner Class: Node
//-------------------------------

    class Node {

        /** Number of digits to store in a block */
        private static final short MAX_DIGITS = 3;

        private short value; //ranges from 0 to VALUE_RANGE - 1

        private Node next;

        private Node( ) {

            this("0");
        }

        private Node(String str) {

            this(Short.parseShort(str));
        }

        private Node(short val) {
            value = val;
            next = null;
        }
    }
}
```

Node

Step 1 Test

We need to test that all three constructors and the **toString** method work correctly. Here's one possible test sequence:

```
HumongousInteger[] hi = new HumongousInteger[7];

hi[0] = new HumongousInteger(123456789);
hi[1] = new HumongousInteger(-45);
```

```
hi[2] = new HumongousInteger("123456789012344");
hi[3] = new HumongousInteger("-0004000000");
hi[4] = new HumongousInteger(-3458);
hi[5] = new HumongousInteger(-0000);
hi[6] = new HumongousInteger();

for (int i = 0; i < hi.length; i++) {

   System.out.println(i + ": " + hi[i].toString( ));
}
```

Running this test should result in the following output:

```
0: 123456789
1: -45
2: 123456789012344
3: -4000000
4: -3458
5: 0
6: 0
```

Step 2: Implement the Basic Addition

Step 2 Design

In this step, we will implement the addition operation of two positive numbers. And in the next step, we will implement the subtraction operation of two positive numbers. We need these two operations in order to implement the full addition and subtraction operations for signed numbers.

The basic idea for adding two positive humongous integers is simple. We have two linked lists, each representing a single humongous integer. We need to create a new linked list that represents the sum of the two linked lists. To compute the sum, we scan through the two linked lists and add the corresponding pairs, starting with the least significant nodes of the two linked lists. When the addition of two nodes results in a carry, we include this carry in the next addition. When no more nodes remain in one of the linked lists (e.g., if the first list contains five nodes and the second list contains nine nodes, then no more nodes remain in the first list after the five pairwise additions), we move the remaining nodes from the other list to the result list, adding the carry as necessary.

Step 2 Code

Here's the step 2 code.

HumongousInteger (Step 2)

```
class HumongousInteger {

   ...

   private HumongousInteger(Node head) {
```

Constructors

```
        this.head = head;
        this.sign = +1;
    }

    ...

    public HumongousInteger add(HumongousInteger num) {

        return this.addPos(num); //TEMP -- add only two positive values
    }

    private HumongousInteger addPos(HumongousInteger num) {

        Node p, q, r, t;

        p = this.head;
        q = num.head;

        t = new Node(); //dummy head node
        r = t;

        short carry = 0;

        while (p != null && q != null) {

            short sum = (short) (carry + p.value + q.value);

            r.next = new Node();
            r = r.next;

            r.value = (short) (sum % Node.MAX_VALUE);
            carry   = (short) (sum / Node.MAX_VALUE);

            p = p.next;
            q = q.next;
        }

        p = (p == null) ? q : p; //reset p to point to the remaining blocks

        while (p != null) {

            r.next = new Node();
            r = r.next;

            r.value = (short) ((p.value + carry) % Node.MAX_VALUE);
            carry   = (short) ((p.value + carry) / Node.MAX_VALUE);

            p = p.next;
        }

        if (carry > 0) { //overflow, final carry
            r.next = new Node((short) carry);
        }

        return new HumongousInteger(t.next); //remove the dummy head node
    }

    ...
```

addPos

16.5 Sample Development—*continued*

```
    class Node {
        ...
        /** The range of values stored in a Block */
        private static final short MAX_VALUE = 1000;
        ...
    }
}
```

Node

Step 2 Test

The testing procedure for step 2 is more complex than that for step 1. When we add two humongous integers, how can we check that the result is correct? We can certainly do it manually, but that would be too tedious. What we can do is to compare the result with the result of adding two **BigInteger** values. Here's how:

```
HumongousInteger h1, h2, hsum;
BigInteger       b1, b2, bsum;

h1  = new HumongousInteger("123450006789");
h2  = new HumongousInteger("987654321");
hsum = h1.add(h2);

b1  = new BigInteger("123450006789");
b2  = new BigInteger("987654321");
bsum = b1.add(b2);

if (bsum.compareTo(new BigInteger(hsum.toString())) == 0){
    System.out.println("Okay");
} else {
    System.out.println("Not Okay");
}
```

We can modify the code to repeatedly accept input values (**String**) when creating **HumongousInteger** and **BigInteger** objects to test the operation by using different values. If we wanted to test the operation numerous times, this interactive approach would become cumbersome. A better approach is to use an array to store values and test the addition of all pairs as follows:

```
String strArray[] = {"100005000",
                     "9182734738218170000000072817",
                     "8000",
                     "3283748300000",
                     "7",
```

```
                                "100005000",
                                "2147483646",
                                "2147480000",
                                "1000000000000000000000000000000000",
                                };

HumongousInteger hi1;
HumongousInteger hi2;
HumongousInteger hi3;

BigInteger bi1;
BigInteger bi2;
BigInteger bi3;

int errorCnt = 0;

for (int i =0; i < strArray.length; i++) {

    for (int j =0; j < strArray.length; j++) {

        hi1 = new HumongousInteger(strArray[i]);
        hi2 = new HumongousInteger(strArray[j]);

        bi1 = new BigInteger(strArray[i]);
        bi2 = new BigInteger(strArray[j]);

        System.out.println("\n");
        System.out.println("For number pairs: i= " + i + " j= " + j);
        System.out.print  ("hi1: " + hi1.toString() + "  ");
        System.out.println("hi2: " + hi2.toString() + "  ");

        //---------- A D D      P O S I T I V E ----------------//
        hi3 = hi1.add(hi2);
        bi3 = bi1.add(bi2);

        System.out.print("Result: " + hi3.toString( ) + "         ");

        if (bi3.compareTo(new BigInteger (hi3.toString())) != 0) {
            errorCnt++;
            System.out.println("Addition Failed");
        }
    }
}

System.out.println("\n\nTest Result: " + (errorCnt == 0 ?
                                              "Success!" :
                                              errorCnt + " errors"));
```

We can easily increase or decrease the number of values in the array. If there are no errors, the message **Success!** is displayed. Otherwise, the message **<N> errors** is displayed where **<N>** is replaced by the actual number of errors.

16.5 Sample Development—*continued*

Step 3: Implement the Basic Subtraction

Step 3 Design

We are now ready to implement the subtraction of two positive humongous integers. To implement this operation, we must first be able to compare two humongous integers so that we can always subtract the smaller number from the larger one. Suppose we want to subtract a humongous integer **R** from **L.** If **L** is greater than or equal to **R,** then we compute

```
L - R
```

If, however, **L** is smaller than **R,** then we compute

```
-(R - L)
```

For example, if we want to subtract 5 from 8 (8 − 5), we compute

```
8 - 5 ==> 3
```

If we want to subtract 8 from 5 (5 − 8), then we compute the result by subtracting the smaller number from the larger one and negating the difference as

```
- (8 - 5) ==> -3
```

So, to implement the basic subtraction method, we must be able to compare two humongous integers. We have already identified a method called **compareTo** that compares two humongous integers. We will implement this method in this step so the basic subtraction method can use it. (Notice that the **compareTo** method we implement here is capable of comparing both positive and negative numbers.)

Suppose **L** and **R** are humongous integers. The **compareTo** method is called in the following manner:

```
L.compareTo(R)
```

We need to return a negative value **(int)** if **L** is less than **R,** zero if **L** and **R** are equal, and a positive value if **L** is greater than **R.** There are three cases to consider:

Case 1. The signs of **L** and **R** are different.

Case 2. The signs of **L** and **R** are the same, but the lengths of their respective linked lists are different.

Case 3. The signs of **L** and **R** are the same and the lengths of their respective linked lists are the same.

For case 1, we can easily determine the result by just checking their signs. For example, if **L** is negative and **R** is positive, the result is negative. For case 2, we can count the number of nodes in their linked lists. If both **L** and **R** are positive, the one with a longer list is the larger of the two. Otherwise, the one with a shorter list is larger. For case 3, we can scan the linked lists from the most to the least significant nodes and compare their values.

Unfortunately this scanning order is not trivial to implement because the direction of the links is from the least to the most significant nodes. We can implement this approach by temporarily reversing the links, but it is pretty complicated. This approach is left as an exercise.

Let's consider another approach that uses string comparison. Suppose, for example, we want to compare two humongous integers **345000179** and **443456579**. We can convert them to strings and perform a string comparison. We know that

```
"345000179" < "443456579"
```

based on lexicographic ordering (that is, **"0"** < **"1"** < · · · < **"8"** < **"9"**). When using a string comparison to compare numerical values, we have to watch out for the case when the respective lengths of the two strings are different. For example, 6 < 50, but **"6"** > **"50"**. Here's the basic idea of how the method can be written:

```
HumongousInteger L = ...;
HumongousInteger R = ...;

if (L is positive and R is negative) {
   return +1; //L is larger
}

if (L is negative and R is positive) {
   return -1; //R is larger
}

//L and R have the same sign
String Lstr = L.toString();
String Rstr = R.toString();

int result;

if (Lstr == Rstr) {
   result = Lstr.compareTo(Rstr);
} else {
   result = Lstr.length() < Rstr.length() ? -1 : +1;
}

return L.sign * result;
```

Notice that we multiply **L.sign** to **result** to get the final result. Consider, for example, **L** is −41 and **R** is −50. The comparison should return a positive value because −41 is larger than −50, but **"−41".compareTo("−50")** will return a negative value. By multiplying the sign of **L,** we can get the final (correct) result.

Now we are ready to tackle the design of the basic subtraction. Assume we are subtracting a smaller integer **R** from a larger integer **L.** We proceed from the least to most significant digits and repeat the pairwise subtraction, that is, subtracting the content of an **R** node from the corresponding **L** node. When we perform a pairwise subtraction, we first check if there was a borrow in the previous pairwise subtraction. If there was, then we subtract the borrowed amount from the content of the **L** node. Then we check

16.5 Sample Development—*continued*

if a borrow is necessary for this pairwise subtraction. If it is necessary, then we add the borrowed amount to the content of the current **L** node and subtract the content of the corresponding **R** node from it. We remember if there is a borrow, so this borrow is correctly reflected in the next pairwise subtraction.

Similar to the addition operation, when there are no more nodes left to process in one of the lists, we copy the contents of the remaining nodes in the other list to the corresponding nodes in the result list, with an appropriate adjustment if there's any borrow.

When we perform a pairwise subtraction, the result could be 0. This means the content of the corresponding node in the result list will be 0. After the complete subtraction is done, it is possible that leading nodes contain only zeros. Consider for example, subtracting **555444330** from **555444300.** The result should be 30, not **000000030.** We must adjust the internal data structure so that leading zeros are eliminated. We will define a method called **removeLeadingZero** for this purpose. Notice that we now have two methods with the same name **removeLeadingZero.** The first method is a utility method that removes leading zeros in a given string. The second method that we're adding here removes leading nodes of a linked list that contains the value of zero. The second method is implemented by using the first method.

Step 3 Code

Here's the step 3 code.

HumongousInteger (Step 3)

```
class HumongousInteger {

   . . .

      private HumongousInteger(Node head) {

         this.head = head;
         this.sign = +1;
      }

      public int compareTo(HumongousInteger num) {

         HumongousInteger L = this;
         HumongousInteger R = num;

         if (L.isPositive() && R.isNegative()) {
            return +1;
         }

         if (L.isNegative() && R.isPositive()) {
            return -1;
         }
```

Constructor

compareTo

```
        //L and R have the same sign, so we compare them.
        //We will use a trick here by converting L and R
        //back to String and use String compareTo

        String Lstr = L.toString();
        String Rstr = R.toString();

        int result;

        int lengthL = Lstr.length();
        int lengthR = Rstr.length();

        //check the magnitude first
        if (lengthL == lengthR) {

            result = Lstr.compareTo(Rstr);

        } else {

            result = (lengthL < lengthR) ? -1 : +1;
        }

        //now check the sign of two HI
        return L.sign * result; // Note: Because the String compareTo
                          //could return values other than +1, 0, or -1,
                          //so does this method as the consequence
    }

    public HumongousInteger sub(HumongousInteger num) {

        return this.subPos(num);
                        //TEMP - subtraction of two positive HI
    }

    private HumongousInteger trimLeadingZero( ) {

        String numStr = this.toString();

        String result = trimLeadingZero(numStr);

        if (result.equals("0")) {

            return new HumongousInteger(0);

        } else if (result.length() < numStr.length()) {

            return new HumongousInteger(result);

        } else {
            return this;
        }
    }

    . . .
```

sub

trimLeadingZero

16.5 Sample Development—*continued*

isPositive

isNegative

negate

subPos

```
private boolean isPositive( ) {

    return sign > 0;
}

private boolean isNegative( ) {

    return sign < 0;
}

private HumongousInteger negate( ) {

    sign = (byte) -sign; // -sign is int so typecast is necessary

    return this;
}

private HumongousInteger subPos(HumongousInteger num) {

    Node p, q, r, t;

    boolean isNegative = false;

    //always subtract smaller from the larger.
    //if num is larger, then the result is negative
    if (this.compareTo(num) >= 0) { // this - num
        p = this.head;
        q = num.head;

    } else {                          //-(num - this)
        p = num.head;
        q = this.head; isNegative = true;
    }

    t = new Node(); //dummy head node
    r = t;

    short borrow = 0, minuend; //for L is a minuend

    while (p != null && q != null) {

        r.next = new Node();
        r = r.next;

        minuend = (short) (p.value - borrow);

        if (minuend < q.value) { //need to borrow
           r.value = (short) (Node.MAX_VALUE + minuend
                                                - q.value);
           borrow = 1;
```

```
            } else { //no borrow
                r.value = (short) (minuend - q.value);
                borrow = 0;
            }

            p = p.next;
            q = q.next;
        }

        p = (p == null) ? q : p; //reset p to point to the remaining blocks

        while (p != null) {

            r.next = new Node();
            r = r.next;

            r.value = (short) (p.value - borrow);

            if (r.value < 0) {

                r.value += Node.MAX_VALUE;
                borrow = 1;

            } else {
                borrow = 0;
            }

            p = p.next;
        }

        HumongousInteger result = new HumongousInteger(t.next);
                              //remove the dummy head node
        result = result.trimLeadingZero();

        if (isNegative) result.negate();

        return result;
    }

    . . .
}
```

Step 3 Test

We perform the testing routine of step 3 with the addition operation replaced by the subtraction operation. We replace the code

```
//---------- A D D     P O S I T I V E ----------------//
        hi3 = hi1.add(hi2);
        bi3 = bi1.add(bi2);
```

16.5 Sample Development—*continued*

with

```
//-------- S U B T R A C T   P O S I T I V E -----------//
      hi3 = hi1.sub(hi2);
      bi3 = bi1.subtract(bi2);
```

All the other parts of the step 2 test code remain the same.

Step 4: Implement the Full Addition and Subtraction

Step 4 Design

Once we have the methods for adding and subtracting two positive integers, we can implement the full addition and subtraction operations by using the arithmetic rules stated earlier:

```
 A  +   B  →    A + B
 A  +  -B  →    A - B
-A  +   B  →    B - A
-A  +  -B  →  -(A + B)

 A  -   B  →    A - B
 A  -  -B  →    A + B
-A  -   B  →  -(A + B)
-A  -  -B  →    B - A
```

Here **A** and **B** represent positive humongous integers. The right-hand side of the arrow indicates either the addition or the subtraction of positive integers. Let's consider the case

```
-A  -   B  →  -(A + B)
```

Assume two humongous integers **L** and **R.** The value of **L** could be **A** or **-A,** and the value of **R** could be **B** or **-B.** We have this case when **L** is negative (**-A**) and **R** is positive (**B**). We can implement this case as follows:

```
HumongousInteger temp, result;

temp = L.negate().addPos(R); //-L + R == -(-A) + B == A + B
result = temp.negate();      //-(A + B)
```

or more succintly as

```
HumongousInteger result = L.negate().addPos(R).negate();
```

The other eight cases can be implemented in a similar manner.

Step 4 Code

Here's the step 4 code.

HumongousInteger (Step 4)

```
class HumongousInteger {

    . . .

    /**
     * Copy constructor
     */
    public HumongousInteger(HumongousInteger num) {

        this.sign = num.sign;

        this.head = new Node( ); //dummy head node

        Node p = head;

        Node q = num.head;

        while (q != null) {

            p.next = new Node(q.value);
            p = p.next;
            q = q.next;
        }

        this.head = this.head.next; //remove the dummy head node
    }

    public HumongousInteger add(HumongousInteger num) {

        /* We need to consider four cases, and for each
         * of the four cases, we convert the operation
         * in terms of addPos and subPos.
         *
         * We solve the four cases as follows
         *
         *            A +  B   --->     A + B
         *            A + -B   --->     A - B
         *           -A +  B   --->     B - A
         *           -A + -B   --->   -(A + B)
         */
        HumongousInteger L = new HumongousInteger(this);
        HumongousInteger R = new HumongousInteger(num);

        if (L.isPositive() && R.isPositive()) {

            return L.addPos(R);
        }

        if (L.isPositive() && R.isNegative()) {

            return L.subPos(R.negate());
        }
```

Constructor

add

16.5 Sample Development—*continued*

```
        if (L.isNegative() && R.isPositive()) {

            return R.subPos(L.negate());
        }

        //both negative
        return L.negate().addPos(R.negate()).negate();
    }

    . . .

    public HumongousInteger sub(HumongousInteger num) {

        /* We need to consider four cases, and for each
         * of the four cases, we convert the operation
         * in terms of addAbs and subAbs.
         *
         * We solve the four cases as follows:
         *
         *           A -  B  --->    A - B
         *           A - -B  --->    A + B
         *          -A -  B  --->  -(A + B)
         *          -A - -B  --->    B - A
         */
        HumongousInteger L = new HumongousInteger(this);
        HumongousInteger R = new HumongousInteger(num);

        if (L.isPositive() && R.isPositive()) {

            return L.subPos(R);
        }

        if (L.isPositive() && R.isNegative()) {

            return L.addPos(R.negate());
        }

        if (L.isNegative() && R.isPositive()) {

            return L.negate().addPos(R).negate();
        }

        //both negative
        return R.negate().subPos(L.negate());
    }

    . . .
}
```

sub

Step 4 Test

We now test both the full addition and subtraction operations using a mixture of positive and negative humongous integers. Here's the test code:

```
String strArray[] =
        {"100005000",
         "918273473821817000000072817",
         "8000",
         "10",
         "3283748300000",
         "7",
         "100005000",
         "-4000",
         "2147483646",
         "-4500",
         "2147480000",
         "-2147483646",
         "1000000000000000000000000000000000000",
         };

HumongousInteger hi1;
HumongousInteger hi2;
HumongousInteger hi3;

BigInteger bi1;
BigInteger bi2;
BigInteger bi3;

int addErrorCnt = 0, subErrorCnt = 0;

for (int i =0; i < strArray.length; i++) {

    for (int j =0; j < strArray.length; j++) {

        hi1 = new HumongousInteger(strArray[i]);
        hi2 = new HumongousInteger(strArray[j]);

        bi1 = new BigInteger(strArray[i]);
        bi2 = new BigInteger(strArray[j]);

        System.out.println("\n");
        System.out.println("For number pairs: i= " + i + " j= " + j);
        System.out.print  ("hi1: " + hi1.toString() + "    ");
        System.out.println("hi2: " + hi2.toString() + "    ");

        //----------- A D D --------------------//
        hi3 = hi1.add(hi2);
        bi3 = bi1.add(bi2);

        System.out.print("Result: " + hi3.toString( ) + "         ");

        if (bi3.compareTo(new BigInteger (hi3.toString())) != 0
                || !bi3.toString().equals(hi3.toString())) {
```

```
                addErrorCnt++;
                System.out.println("Addition Failed");
            }

            //----------- S U B T R A C T ---------//
            hi3 = hi1.sub(hi2);
            bi3 = bi1.subtract(bi2);

            System.out.print("Result: " + hi3.toString( ) + "         ");

            if (bi3.compareTo(new BigInteger (hi3.toString())) != 0
                    || !bi3.toString().equals(hi3.toString())) {
                subErrorCnt++;
                System.out.println("Subtraction Failed");
            }
        }
    }

    System.out.println("\n\nTest Result: " +
            (addErrorCnt == 0 && subErrorCnt == 0 ?
                    "Success!" : "Error somewhere"));
}
```

Step 5: Implement the Multiplication Operation

There are two ways the multiplication operation can be implemented. A simplistic implementation computes the product of two humongous integers **L** and **R** by adding **L** to the result **R** times. For example, to derive the product of 8 and 3, we compute

```
8 + 8 + 8
```

A better implementation, with a much better performance, computes the product by carrying out the long multiplication algorithm we learned in elementary school. It is left as exercises to implement both solutions.

Step 6: Implement the Division Operation

Similar to the multiplication operation, we have two possible implementations for the division operation. To compute the result of **L** divided by **R,** a simplistic implementation continually subtracts **R** from **L** until the remainder becomes smaller than **R.** We initialize the result (quotient) to 0 and increment it by 1 for every subtraction. Remember that we are implementing an integer division. A better implementation computes the result by carring out the long division algorithm. Here again, it is left as exercises to implement both solutions.

Summary

- Each memory cell is associated with an address.
- Contiguous memory allocation (CMA) scheme allocates a single, contiguous block of memory.
- Noncontiguous memory allocation (NMA) scheme allocates multiple blocks of memory at noncontiguous memory locations.
- The key advantage of CMA is its fast search. Data in CMA can be located very efficiently by the address computation. The search performance is independent of the size of the block.
- Disadvantages of CMA are overflow, underutilization, and costly update operations.
- Blocks in NMA are linked into a chain.
- NMA supports a finer control of space usage.
- Advantages of NMA are finer control of space usage and faster update operations.
- A disadvantage of NMA is its slower search. The time to locate data in NMA is proportional to the number of nodes in the chain.
- A linked list is a chain of nodes, with each node having a link that points to the node that follows it.
- A node in a linked list contains two fields: `data` and `link`. The content of a `data` field can be primitive data or an object (i.e., a reference to the object).

Key Concepts

contiguous memory allocation
noncontiguous memory allocation
linked list
linked list traversal
memory cell
memory address computation
memory overflow
node

Exercises

1. Compare the CMA and NMA schemes. List their advantages and disadvantages.
2. If your program uses exactly 1000 integers every time it is executed, which allocation scheme would you prefer? Do you use an array of 1000 integers or a linked list with each node containing one integer?
3. If your program used the minimum of 10 and the maximum of 1000 integers when it executed, which allocation scheme would you prefer? Do you use an array of 1000 integers or a linked list with each node containing one integer?

4. In Section 16.3, we provided three variations of creating a linked list by adding a new node at the end of the list. All three variations set the value of the pointer start to null correctly when the list is empty. The value of the other pointer tail, however, is undefined in the first two variations and is a reference to the dummy node in the third variation. Modify the code for all three variations, so the value of tail is null when the list is empty.
5. In the code for creating a linked list by adding a new node to the front of the list, we only keep the pointer start that points to the first node in the list Modify the code by adding another pointer tail that points to the last node.
6. The search routine we presented in Section 16.3 searches the desired node by specifying the value. Write the search-by-position routine that locates the node, given its position in the list. Set the pointer ptr to the desired node. The position of the first node is 0, and the last node is $N - 1$, where N is the total number of nodes in the list. If the position given is less than 0 or larger than $N - 1$, set ptr to null.
7. Consider a linked list of Bicycle objects, as illustrated in Section 16.4. Write a code that locates all Bicycle objects with the specified owner name. Assume the variable start points to the first node in the list. For each bicycle found, print out its position in the list. For example, if the search name is John and there are three matching Bicycle objects at positions 0, 4, and 8, the output will be

```
Bicycle with the owner John found at
   position 0
   position 4
   position 8
```

8. Consider the following Person class:

```
class Person {

  private String name;
  private int    age;

  public Person(String name) {
     setName(name);
  }

  public int getAge( ) {
     return age;
  }

  public String getName( ) {
     return name;
  }
  public void setAge(int age) {
     this.age = age;
  }
```

```
    public void setName(String name) {
        this.name = name;
    }
}
```

Define a PNode class similar to the BNode class. The data field of PNode points to a Person object, and the link field points to the next PNode in the list.

9. Using the PNode defined in Exercise 8, write a code that builds a linked list of Person objects. Prompt the user for a person's name and age. Add this person to the end of a list. Repeat the process until the input value DONE is entered for the name. At the end of the routine, the variable start points to the first node. If no input is given, set start to null.

10. Assume a linked list of Person objects created in Exercise 9. Given the pointer start, write a code that prints out the name of the oldest person. If the list is empty (start == null), then print out an appropriate message.

11. The following code attempts to create a linked list of Bicycle objects. Identify the problem.

```
Scanner scanner = new Scanner(System.in);

BNode start, tail, next;

Bicycle bike = new Bicycle("No Name");

start = null;

String name = scanner.next();

if (!name.equalsIgnoreCase("QUIT")) {

   bike.setName(name);

   start = new BNode(bike, null); //create the first node

   tail = start;

   //get more names
   while (true) {
      name = scanner.next();

      if (!name.equalsIgnoreCase("QUIT")) break;

      bike.setName(name);

      next = new BNode(bike, null);

      tail.setNext(next); //link the node as the last node

      tail = next; //set tail to point to the new last node
   }
}
```

12. Write a code that reverses the links in a given linked list. Assume the Node class.

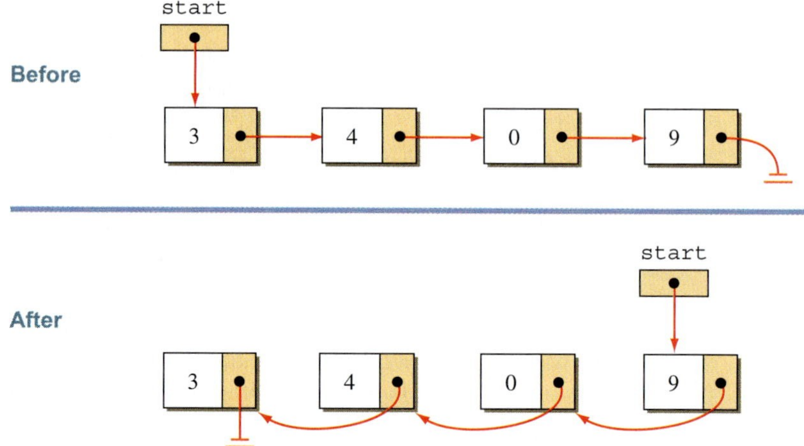

13. The constructor of the HumongousInteger class that accepts a String argument assumes the format of the string is valid. Extend the constructor so that it will throw an IllegalArgumentException if the format of the argument string is invalid.

14. The toString method we implemented for the HumongousInteger class does not use any grouping character such as a comma. Define the second toString method that accepts a grouping character and place it every three digits (counting from the least significant digits). The method accepts the grouping character as an argument to support different locales. In the United States, we use commas to separate groups (say, 1,234,567), but some European nations use a period, for example. The signature for the second toString method is

```
public String toString(String separator)
```

Notice that with this toString method implemented, we can rewrite the first toString method simply as

```
public String toString( ) {
   return toString("");
}
```

15. Incrementing a counter by 1 is a frequently used operation, and we would like to support such operation for the HumonguousInteger class also. We can certainly implement the increment operation by using the add method as

```
HumongousInteger counter = new HumongousInteger("0");
HumongousInteger one     = new HumongousInteger("1");

...

counter.add(one);
```

but this would be too costly. Going through the full addition routine just to increment a counter by 1 is not efficient. Implement a method called incr in the HumonguousInteger class that increments a humongous integer by 1. The signature of the method will be as follows

```
public void incr( )
```

To increment a humongous integer by 1 efficiently, add 1 to the least significant node. If it does not generate a carry, then stop. If it does, then move to the next node and add the carry. Repeat this process until either no carry is generated or no more node is left. In the latter case, create a new most significant node whose value is 1 (the value of the final carry).

16. Analogous to the incr method of the HumongousInteger class, implement the decr method that decrements a humongous integer by 1.

17. Implement a simplistic multiplication solution for the HumongousInteger class. We can compute the product of two humongous integers L and R by adding L to the result R times. For example, to derive the product of 8 and 3, we compute

```
8 + 8 + 8
```

The pseudocode for computing the product of L and R is as follows:

```
//assume the absolute value of L is larger than or
//equal to the absolute value of R
counter = 0;

limit = Math.abs(R);
term  = Math.abs(L);

product = 0;

while (counter < limit) {

   product += term;

   counter++;
}

if (product == 0 || sign of L == sign of R)
   sign of product = +1; //positive
else
   sign of product = -1; //negative
```

Notice that we're assuming the absolute value of L is greater than or equal to the absolute value of R to minimize the number of times the while loop is executed. In the algorithm we increment the variable counter by 1 in the while loop. Because the variable counter is a humongous integer, we cannot actually use the increment operation ++. Use the incr method of Exercise 15.

Test the multiplication operation with the testing pattern used in Section 16.5. But decrease the magnitude of the values we use, for example,

```
String strArray[] = {"1000005",
                     "8000",
                     "10",
                     "7",
                     "0",
                     "-4000",
                     "2147496",
                     "-4500",
                     "-000",
                     };
```

Since the simplistic multiplication algorithm results in a very long execution time, we do not want to test it with large values.

18. The simplistic multiplication method for the HumonguousInteger class from Exercise 17 is not efficient. A more complicated, but much faster approach is to implement the long multiplication technique we learned in elementary school. Implement the multiplication method by using the long multiplication technique.

19. Implement a simplistic division solution for the HumongousInteger class. Suppose we want to divide L by R. Suppose both L and R are positive. We compute the result by repeatedly subtracting R from L until the remainder becomes smaller than R. Remember that the division here is an integer division. We initialize the quotient to 0 and increment it by 1 for every subtraction.

If both L and R are negative, we change the signs of L and R and compute the quotient (say, $-8 / -2 \rightarrow 8 / 2 \rightarrow 4$). If the signs of L and R are different, we change the sign of one of them so both become positive. We compute the quotient and get the final result by negating the quotient (say, $-8 / 2 \rightarrow 8 / 2 \rightarrow 4 \rightarrow -4$). If the quotient is zero, then we set its sign to $+1$ so the value is represented correctly as $+0$. Finally, since the division by zero is not allowed, we will throw an ArithmeticException when the divisor R is zero.

Here's the algorithm:

```
if (R == 0) {
   throw new ArithmeticException();
}

quotient = 0;
remainder = positive L;
divisor = positive R;

while (remainder >= divisor) {

   remainder = remainder - divisor;
```

```
      quotient++;
   }
   if (quotient == 0 || sign of L == sign of R)
      sign of quotient = +1; //positive
   else
      sign of quotient = -1; //negative
```

Test the division operation using the same testing pattern from Section 16.5. The only structural difference this time is the use of the try–catch block to catch the divide-by-zero exception:

```
try {
   hi3 = hi1.div(hi2);
   bi3 = bi1.divide(bi2);

   System.out.print("Result: " + hi3.toString( )
                      + "       ");

   if (bi3.compareTo(new BigInteger (hi3.toString())) != 0
                                  ||
      !bi3.toString().equals(hi3.toString())) {

      errorCnt++;
      System.out.println("Division Failed");
   }
} catch (ArithmeticException e) {

   System.out.println("Exception: " + e.getMessage());
}
```

20. The simplistic division method for the HumongousInteger class from Exercise 19 is not efficient. A more complicated, but much faster approach is to implement the long division technique we learned in elementary school. Implement the division method by using the long division technique. The technique to reverse the direction of the links becomes handy to solve this problem (see Exercise 12).

21. The linked nodes we introduced in this chapter contain only one link field. It is possible to define a node that includes two links. For example, we can set the first link to point to the previous node and the second link to point to the next node.

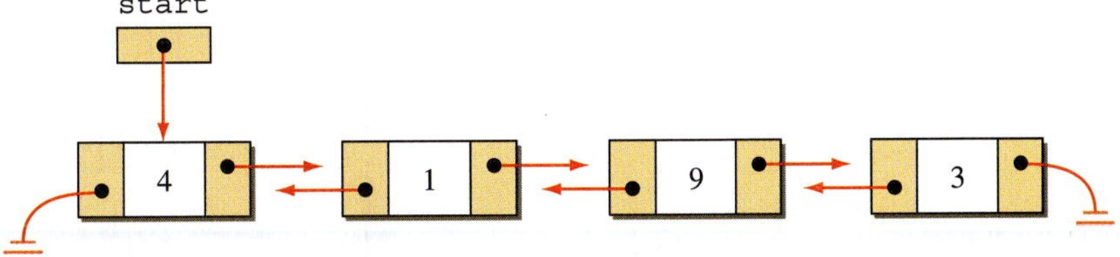

Provide a class definition for such *doubly linked list.* Assume the type for the data field is int. Call the class DNode.

22. Using the DNode class defined in Exercise 21, write a code that builds a doubly linked list. Repeatedly prompt the user for an integer, and add a new node to the beginning of the list. Stop the routine when −1 is entered. The sample doubly linked list of Exercise 21 results when the integers are entered in the order of 3, 9, 1, and 4.

23. Write a code that deletes the node pointed by ptr from a doubly linked list by adjusting the pointers of the adjacent nodes.

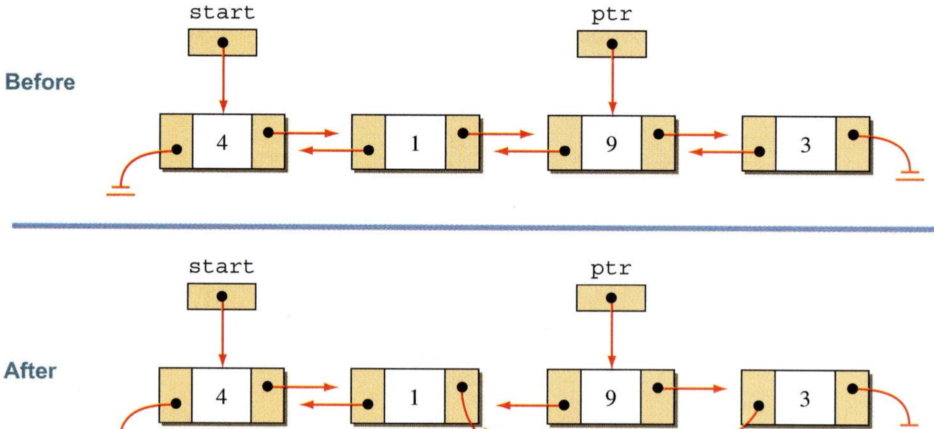

Notice the 9 node will be garbage collected eventually. Make sure the code works correctly when ptr points to the first or the last node.

24. In Chapter 11, we presented the heapsort algorithm and described how a heap structure is implemented by using an array. The DNode class defined in Exercise 21 can be used to implement a heap also.

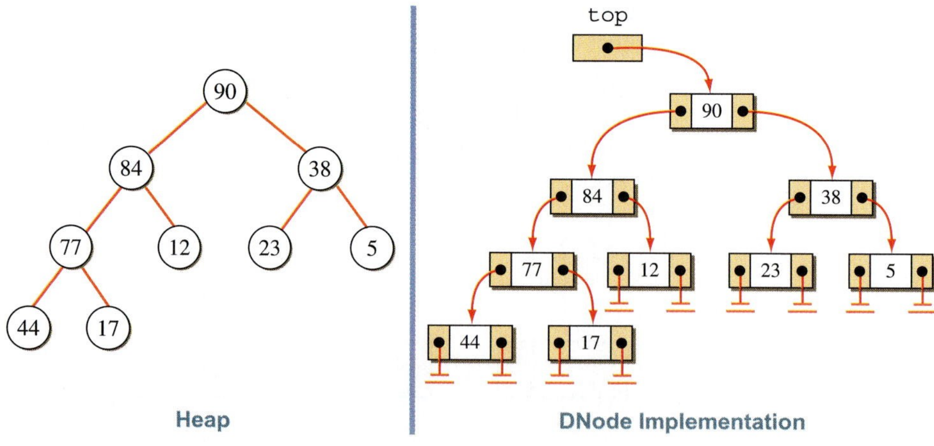

Rewrite the heapsort algorithm using the DNode implementation. Is there any advantage of the DNode implementation over the array implementation?

25. Another variation of the basic linked list is a circular linked list. Instead of the `link` field of the last node being a `null`, it points to the first node in the list. Here's an example:

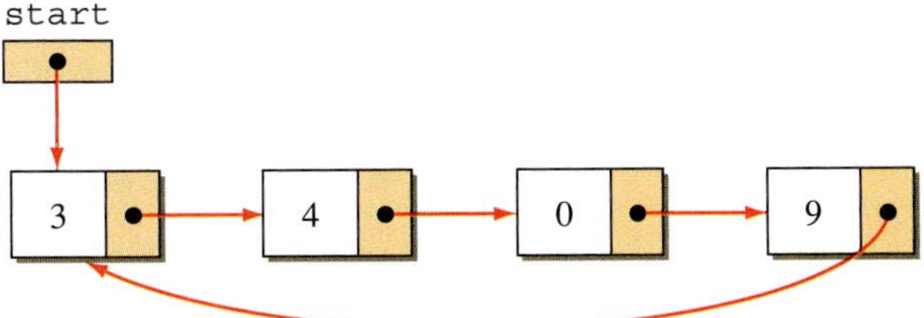

Using a circular list, implement a solution to the Josephus problem. The problem is stated as follows: Arrange `M` students in a circle. Represent each student by the numbers `1` through `M` and set `ptr` to the first student.

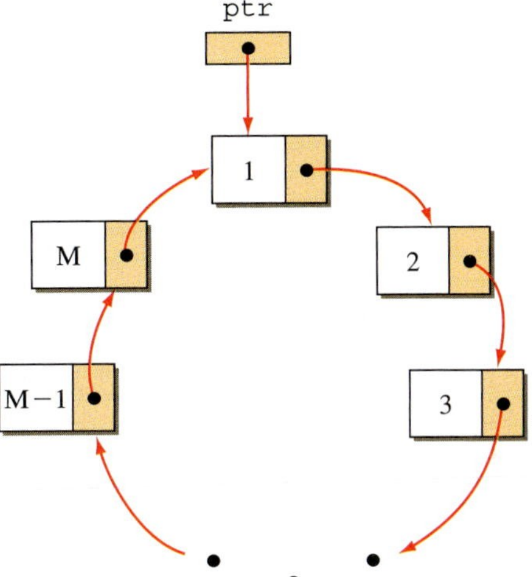

Starting from `ptr`, remove every *N*th student from the list. If $N = 3$, for example, then you remove students 3, 6, 9, 12, and so forth. Continue the process until only one student is left. Display this student's number and stop. The values for `M` and `N` are input to the program. (The original Josephus problem, named after a Jewish historian Josephus Flavius, placed 41 soldiers in a circle and killed every third soldier. Soldiers chose death over surrender to the Romans.)

17 Generics and Type Safety

After you have read and studied this chapter, you should be able to

- Define generic classes
- Define classes by using generics, intheritance, and interfaces
- Instantiate type-safe Java Collections Framework classes
- Describe how the generics mechanism supports type safety
- Define a simple linked list with a generic node

Introduction

One of the new features strongly requested by Java programmers is generics, which is finally included in the language from Java 5.0. The biggest advantage of adding generics to Java is the improvement in using Java Collections Framework classes such as ArrayList. Prior to Java 5.0, these collections could include any type of objects. For example, if you have a list (either ArrayList or LinkedList), there are no restrictions on the types of objects you can add to the list. In other words, we can add objects from Integer, String, Person, Vehicle, and other classes to a single list. In practice, however, we rarely need such heterogeneous collections in which the elements are of different types. What we need most in practice is a homogeneous collection in which the elements are of the same type, such as a list of Vehicle objects, a set of Person objects, and so forth. But prior to Java 5.0, we could not declare such homogeneous collections. It is therefore up to the programmers to ensure that only the valid objects are added to a collection. If the programmers make a mistake and inadvertently write an erroneous code that adds objects of invalid types to a collections, a runtime error most likely will result. Addition of the generics mechanism allows the programmers to declare homogeneous collections, and any attempt in the code to add invalid objects will be caught at compile time. Detecting errors at compile time is considered far superior to detecting errors at runtime.

We've already seen simple examples of the generics mechanism when defining a homogeneous collection in Chapter 10. In this chapter, we provide a more in-depth coverage of generics, such as defining our own generic classes. We begin with the basics and gradually introduce variations and details. We show how to define a simple generic linked list class by adding the generics to the linked node structure we learned in Chapter 16. We conclude the chapter with a discussion of advanced topics and common errors.

17.1 Generic Classes

Let's begin with a very simple case of defining a generic class. Suppose we wish to design a class to model a Harry Potter locker that will adjust its dimensions so we can put any single item in it. An item can be as mundane as a book or as exciting as a Nimbus 2000 broomstick. When you request a locker, you specify the type of item you put in it. Once the type is specified, you can only put an item of the designated type. Here's how we might define such a magical locker:

```
class Locker<T> {

    private T content;

    public Locker( ) {
        store(null);
    }
```

```
        public T retrieve( ) {
            return content;
        }

        public void store(T item) {
            content = item;
        }
    }
```

type parameter

generic class

Notice the use of the identifier T and its appearance next to the class name as Locker<T>. The identifier T is called a ***type parameter*** and the class Locker a ***generic class***. Any valid Java identifier (except reserved words, of course) can be used for the type parameter, but it is more common to use a single identifier such as T or E. When we declare and create an instance of a generic class, we must replace the type parameter with an actual class type (or an array type, with restriction). Here are examples:

```
Locker<String> lockerOne; //content is set to string
Locker<Integer> lockerTwo; //content is set to Integer

lockerOne = new Locker<String>( ); //create lockers
lockerTwo = new Locker<Integer>( );
```

(*Note:* We are using the standard classes String and Integer in these examples instead of more interesting classes such as Book and Broomstick to keep our first examples as small as possible. At the end of the chapter, Exercise 1 asks you to store Book and Broomstick objects in a locker.) We have created two Locker objects. The first locker is designated and restricted to store a String object, and the second locker an Integer object. Because we need to "plug in" the actual type to create an instance, we might characterize the generic class as a *pluggable class*. Another common name used for a generic class is a *parameterized class*.

When we interact with a Locker object, we must do so in the manner consistent with the declaration, for example,

```
lockerOne.store("Hello");              //store an appropriate
lockerTwo.store(new Integer(100)); //content

String str     = lockerOne.retrieve( ); //fetch content
Integer intObj = lockerTwo.retrieve( );
```

It will result in a compile time error if we attempt to store or retrieve content whose data type is inconsistent with the declaration, such as

```
lockerOne.store(new Double()); <----- INVALID

String str = lockerTwo.retrieve();
```

In the definition of the Locker generic class, we see there are four references to the type parameter T. With the class declaration

```
class Locker<T>
```

we are indicating that this generic class includes one type parameter in the class definition. This type parameter T is a placeholder for an actual type that needs to be specified when we are declaring or creating a Locker object. Every occurrence of the type parameter T in the class definition refers to the actual type, such as String, Integer, Book, Broomstick, and so forth. For example, the declaration

```
private T content;
```

states that the actual type of the data member content is the one specified at the time of object declaration and creation. We know that T is not the name of an actual class but is a type parameter, because it appears in the angle brackets next to the class name. The same interpretation applies to the occurrences of T in the two methods

```
public T retrieve( ) {
   return content;
}

public void store(T item) {
   content = item;
}
```

To help us understand the use of type parameters, we can compare the definition of a generic class against those that specify the actual types. In Figure 17.1, we see two different definitions of a locker. The first definition is restricted to an Integer object, and the second definition is restricted to a String object. To define a Locker that can store an object of any type, we parameterize the type and derive the generic Locker class, shown at the bottom of the figure. Notice how the structure of the three class definitions is identical.

The declarations

```
Locker<String>  lockerOne;
Locker<Integer> lockerTwo;
```

may seem to indicate there are two distinct classes based on the generic Locker<T> class. This is not the case. There is no Locker<String> or Locker<Integer> class. There is exactly one Locker class, and no derivative classes are ever created. Both lockerOne and lockerTwo are instances of the Locker class. We can confirm this with the following code:

```
Locker<String> lockerOne = new Locker<String>();
Locker<Integer> lockerTwo = new Locker<Integer>();

System.out.println("Class of lockerOne is " +
                    lockerOne.getClass().getName());

System.out.println("Class of lockerTwo is " +
                    lockerTwo.getClass().getName());
```

Definition 1:
This `Locker` holds an `Integer` object only.

```
class Locker {

    private Integer content;

    public Locker( ) {
        store(null);
    }

    public Integer retrieve( ) {
        return content;
    }

    public void store( Integer item){
        content = item;
    }
}
```

Definition 2:
This `Locker` holds a `String` object only.

```
class Locker {

    private String content;

    public Locker( ) {
        store(null);
    }

    public String retrieve( ) {
        return content;
    }

    public void store( String item){
        content = item;
    }
}
```

This `Locker` holds an object of any type.

```
class Locker <T> {

    private T content;

    public Locker( ) {
        store(null);
    }

    public T retrieve( ) {
        return content;
    }

    public void store( T item ){
        content = item;
    }
}
```

Without this identifier T in the angle brackets here, the compiler will not know that the identifier T in the class definition is a type parameter. If <T> is missing from here, then the compiler will assume the identifier T is referring to an actual class inside the `Locker` class body.

The constructor does not include the angle brackets.

Figure 17.1 This illustrates the basic idea behind generic classes. Generics allow you to define type-pluggable classes. Notice how the references to the actual types **Integer** and **String** in the top two classes are replaced by the type parameter T in the generic class at the bottom.

The output will be

```
Class of lockerOne is Locker
Class of lockerTwo is Locker
```

Although both lockerOne and lockerTwo are instances of the same class, we cannot use them interchangeably, because their actual types for the type parameter T are different. For example, the assignment in the following code is invalid:

```
Locker<String> lockerOne  = new Locker<String>();
```

```
Locker<Integer> lockerTwo = new Locker<Integer>();

lockerOne = lockerTwo;  <------ INVALID
```

For the same reason, the following is also invalid:

```
Locker<String> lockerOne;

lockerOne = new Locker<Double>();  <------ INVALID
```

Generics in Java are similar to C++ templates, but they are not identical.

Hints, & Tips, Pitfalls

Generics are new to Java 5.0. You must use JDK 1.5 in order to use generics in your programs.

1. Declare and create a Locker object whose actual type for the type parameter is Double.
2. What is wrong with the following code?

```
Locker<String> locker = new Locker<Integer>( );
```

Generic Classes with More Than One Type Parameter

The number of type parameters we can include in a generic class is not limited to 1. If there are multiple type parameters for a generic class, we separate them by commas in the angle brackets. Let's look at an example. We will modify the Locker class by allowing it to hold a pair of items of any type. Here's how we might define such a generic class:

```
class SecondLocker<T1, T2> {

    private T1 content1;
    private T2 content2;
```

```
        public SecondLocker( ) {
            this(null, null);
        }

        public SecondLocker(T1 item1, T2 item2) {
            storeFirstItem(item1);
            storeSecondItem(item2);
        }

        public T1 retrieveFirstItem( ) {
            return content1;
        }

        public void storeFirstItem(T1 item) {
            content1 = item;
        }

        public T2 retrieveSecondItem( ) {
            return content2;
        }

        public void storeSecondItem(T2 item) {
            content2 = item;
        }
    }
```

We add this two-argument constructor for convenience.

We create and use the SecondLocker class as follows:

```
SecondLocker<String, Integer> myLocker =
        new SecondLocker<String, Integer>("Hello",
                                          new Integer(20));

        String str     = myLocker.retrieveFirstItem( );
        Integer intObj = myLocker.retrieveSecondItem( );
```

Since there are no restrictions on T1 and T2, we can store two items of the same type, such as

```
SecondLocker<String, String> myLocker =
        new SecondLocker<String, String>("Hello", "Java");
```

If we want to restrict the two items to be of the same type, then we need only one type parameter. Such a class can be defined as follows:

```
class ThirdLocker<T> {

    private T content1;
    private T content2;

    public ThirdLocker( ) {
        this(null, null);
    }
```

```
        public ThirdLocker(T item1, T item2) {
            storeFirstItem(item1);
            storeSecondItem(item2);
        }

        public T retrieveFirstItem( ) {
            return content1;
        }

        public void storeFirstItem(T item) {
            content1 = item;
        }

        public T retrieveSecondItem( ) {
            return content2;
        }

        public void storeSecondItem(T item) {
            content2 = item;
        }
    }
```

And here's an example of how we might instantiate it:

```
ThirdLocker<String> myLocker1 = new ThirdLocker<String>( );

ThirdLocker<String> myLocker2
            = new ThirdLocker<String>("Hello", "Java");
```

1. Create an instance of SecondLocker whose contents are both Integer objects. Set their values to 20 and 40.
2. What is wrong with the following code?

```
SecondLocker<String, Integer> locker
            = new SecondLocker<Integer, String>( );
```

Type Safety

At this point, a keen observer might argue, "What's the big deal with the generic classes?" If storing any kind of object in a locker is a goal, then one might propose defining the following class:

```
class NonGenLocker {

    private Object content;

    public NonGenLocker( ) {
        store(null);
    }
```

```
    public Object retrieve( ) {
        return content;
    }

    public void store(Object item) {
        content = item;
    }
}
```

Since every class in Java is a subclass of Object, by defining the class in this way we can easily store String and Integer objects as

```
NonGenLocker one = new NonGenLocker( );
NonGenLocker two = new NonGenLocker( );

one.store(new String("Hello"));
two.store(new Integer(10));
```

The danger with this definition is a possible runtime error. Consider the following example:

```
NonGenLocker locker = new NonGenLocker( );

locker.store("Hello");

Integer intObj = (Integer) locker.retrieve( );
```

typing error

This is obviously wrong because one cannot typecast a String object to an Integer object. We call such a logical error in incompatible types a ***typing error***. The sample logical error cannot be detected until runtime, at which time one will get a ClassCastException error. It is much safer and more reliable to detect logical errors such as the typing error at compile time than at runtime. By using the generic class, such code is detected at compile time:

```
Locker<String> lockerOne;

lockerOne = new Locker<Integer>( );
```

type safety

We say the generics mechanism provides ***type safety*** because typing errors are detected at compile time. Type safety is the greatest benefit that generics provide to Java programmers.

Hints, Tips, & Pitfalls

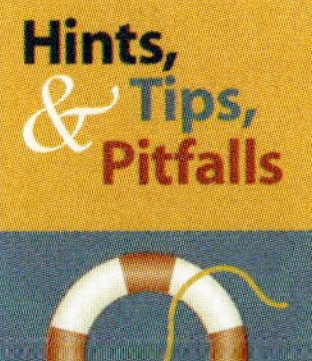

The greatest benefit that generics provide to the Java programmers is type safety.

Also notice that the typecasting is no longer necessary with the generic classes because the specific type is known, so there is no ambiguity. Compare this code fragment without generics

```
NonGenLocker locker = new NonGenLocker( );
locker.store("Hello");
String str =(String) locker.retrieve( );
```

to the one with generics:

```
Locker<String> locker = new Locker<String>( );
locker.store("Hello");
String str = locker.retrieve( );
```

1. Which is considered superior, catching logical errors at compile time or at runtime?
2. Why is typecasting not necessary with the generic classes?

Bounded Types

bounded types

With the `Locker` class, we can store an instance of any class. Instead of allowing one to store just any type of objects, it may make more sense to restrict the types of objects we can store in a locker. It is possible to restrict the actual types that can substitute for the parameterized types. Such restricted parameterized types are called ***bounded types***.

For example, if we want to limit an object we can store in a locker to strictly a number, then we can define the class as follows:

```
class FourthLocker<T extends Number> {

    private Object content;

    public FourthLocker( ) {
        this(null);
    }

    public FourthLocker(T item) {
        store(item);
    }

    public T retrieve( ) {
        return content;
    }

    public void store(T item) {
        content = item;
    }
}
```

This class is essentially the same as the Locker class except for the bounded type parameter and the second constructor.

The Number class is a superclass of Double, Integer, and other classes that represent a numerical value. So, with this generic class, declarations such as

```
FourthLocker<Double>  doubleLocker;
FourthLocker<Integer> intLocker;
FourthLocker<Number>  numLocker;
```

are valid, but the declaration

INVALID →
```
FourthLocker<String> strLocker;
```

is now invalid. As expected, instances can be created as

```
doubleLocker = new FourthLocker<Double>(new Double(2.0));
intLocker    = new FourthLocker<Integer>(new Integer(12));
```

But the following is invalid because the Number class is an abstract class.

```
numLocker = new FourthLocker<Number>( );
```

INVALID →
```
numLocker.store(new Number(20));
```

Although we cannot store an instance of Number (because we cannot create it), we can store an instance of any (nonabstract) subclass of Number, such as

```
numLocker.store(new Double(3.5));
```

It is interesting to note that the following statement is invalid:

INVALID →
```
FourthLocker<Number> locker = new FourthLocker<Double>( );
```

This is somewhat unexpected because Double is a subclass of Number. What we need to remember here is that there is exactly one class named FourthLocker so FourthLocker<Number> and FourthLocker<Double> are not distinct classes, and therefore they cannot have a superclass/subclass relationship. We explore the relationships between inheritance and generic classes and also present common pitfalls and restrictions in using generics later in the chapter.

1. Identify the invalid statements.

```
FourthLocker<Double> locker1
          = new FourthLocker<Double>( );

FourthLocker<Number> locker2 =
          new FourthLocker<Number>( );

locker1.store(new Integer(2));
locker2.store(new Number(3));
```

2. Identify the invalid statements.

```
FourthLocker<Number> locker1 =
                        new FourthLocker<Double>( );

FourthLocker<Double> locker2 =
                        new FourthLocker<Integer>( );

FourthLocker<Number> locker3 =
                        new FourthLocker<Number>( );
```

Wildcard Types

wildcard type

Let's extend the FourthLocker class so we can compare the values stored in the lockers. We call this new class FifthLocker, and we add a method called isSameValue that returns true if the numerical value stored in the argument FifthLocker object is the same as the value stored in the receiving FifthLocker object. To define such a method, we need to use a ***wildcard type***. Here's how we can define the class with a wildcard type:

```
class FifthLocker<T extends Number> {

   private T content;

   public FifthLocker( ) {
      this(null);
   }

   public FifthLocker(T item) {
      store(item);
   }

   public T retrieve( ) {
      return content;
   }

   public void store(T item) {
      content = item;
   }

   public boolean isSameValue(FifthLocker<?> item) {

      return this.retrieve().doubleValue() ==
             item.retrieve().doubleValue();
   }
}
```

The ? symbol is the wildcard designation.

Here's how we might use the FifthLocker class:

```
FifthLocker<Double> locker1 =
                new FifthLocker<Double>(new Double(3.0));

FifthLocker<Integer> locker2 =
                new FifthLocker<Integer>(new Integer(3));
```

```
System.out.println("Values in locker1 and locker2 " +
                   "are the same: " +
                   locker1.isSameValue(locker2));
```

The data type for the parameter to the isSameValue method is designated as FifthLocker<?>. The question mark indicates a wildcard that matches any type. Since the class declaration FifthLocker<T extends Number> limits the actual type for the type parameter T to Number or any of its subclasses, FifthLocker<?> matches FifthLocker<Double>, FifthLocker<Integer>, and so forth. Thus, we can pass any valid FifthLocker object as an argument to the isSameValue method.

At first, the use of wildcard type may not be obvious. It may seem that the following definition would work fine as well:

```
class FifthLocker2<T extends Number> {

   public FifthLocker2( ) {
       this(null);
   }

   public FifthLocker2(T item) {
       store(item);
   }

   public T retrieve( ) {
       return content;
   }

   public void store(T item) {
       content = item;
   }

   public boolean isSameValue(FifthLocker2<T> item) {

       return this.retrieve().doubleValue() ==
              item.retrieve().doubleValue();
   }
}
```

Instead of a wildcard, we indicate the same type parameter T.

This definition is not what we want because with this definition the argument object we can pass to the isSameValue method must be the same as the concrete type we use in the substitution. For example, the statements

```
FifthLocker2<Double> locker1 =
            new FifthLocker2<Double>(new Double(3.0));

FifthLocker2<Double> locker2 =
            new FifthLocker2<Double>(new Double(3));

System.out.println("Are values in locker1 and " +
                   "locker2 the same: " +
                    locker1.isSameValue(locker2));
```

are valid because the actual type is Double for both locker1 and locker2. But the statements

```
FifthLocker2<Double> locker1 =
            new FifthLocker2<Double>(new Double(3.0));

FifthLocker2<Integer> locker2 =
            new FifthLocker2<Integer>(new Integer(3));

System.out.println("Are values in locker1 and " +
                  "locker2 the same: " +
INVALID ──→        locker1.isSameValue(locker2));
```

are invalid (compile time error) because the actual types for T in locker1 and locker2 are different. The way FifthLocker2 is declared, to call the isSameValue method of locker1, we must pass an object of type FifthLocker2<Double> as an argument. Thus, passing a Locker<Integer> object, as in this example, is wrong.

As a side note, some of you may be wondering why we did not name the method equals? It may seem more conventional to name the method equals than isSameValue. We did not name the method equals because the equals method is defined in the Object class. This will lead us to a very insidious error if we do not specify the type for the parameter correctly. Had we defined the equals method correctly as

```
public boolean equals(FifthLocker<?> item) {
   ...
}
```

then everything would have been fine. However, if we declare it erroneously as

```
public boolean equals(FifthLocker<T> item) {
   ...
}
```

and write a code such as

```
FifthLocker<Double> locker1 =
            new FifthLocker<Double>(new Double(3.0));

FifthLocker<Integer> locker2 =
            new FifthLocker<Integer>(new Integer(3));

System.out.println("Are values in locker1 and " +
                  "locker2 the same: " +
                   locker1.equals(locker2));
```

then no compile time or runtime error is raised! Because FifthLocker is a subclass of Object, the equals method of the Object class is actually called, and the result of false is returned. Because the code runs but produces a wrong result, it would the most difficult kind of error to detect.

1. If we declare a generic class as

```
class GenClass<Y> {
   public boolean check(GenClass<Y> param) {
      return this == param;
   }
}
```

why is the following code invalid?

```
GenClass<String> genOne = new GenClass<String>();
GenClass<Double> genTwo = new GenClass<Double>();

boolean result = genOne.check(genTwo);
```

2. The following class declaration is wrong. Why?

```
class MyClass<?> {...}
```

Restrictions

Before we conclude the basics of defining a generic class, we list a couple of restrictions. First, we are not allowed to create an instance of a type parameter inside a generic class. Here's an illegal generic class:

```
class NoGoodLocker<T> {

   private T content;

   public NoGoodLocker( ) {

      content = new T(); <------ INVALID
   }

   ...
}
```

The reason is due to the way generics are implemented in Java 5.0. Basically, the technique called *erasure* is used, and at the bytecode level, the type parameter information is erased and replaced by the actual type. There is no class T in the bytecode, so the system won't be able to create it. It may seem that the statement

```
content = new T();
```

can be substituted with

```
content = new String();
```

or

```
content = new Integer();
```

or whatever the actual type that is plugged in for the type parameter T. Alas, this is not how the generics are implemented in Java. There is exactly one generic class G, not multiple classes of G<Integer>, G<String>, etc., for all different possible actual types. Since there is exactly one generic class, it is not possible to insert different versions of

```
content = new T( );
```

with the type parameter T substituted by the actual type.

Hints, & Tips, Pitfalls

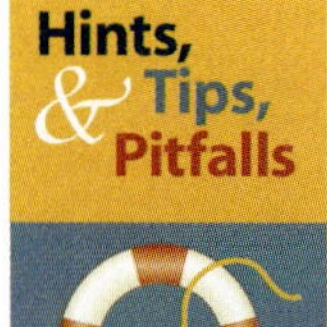

An instance of a type parameter cannot be created inside a generic class.

Another restriction disallows the use of a type parameter with the static components of a generic class. Consider the following invalid generic class definition:

```
class NoGoodGenClass {

           private static T item;  <---- INVALID

INVALID ----> public static T getItem( ) {

              return item;  <---- INVALID
           }
}
```

Type parameters cannot be used with the static data members and methods because the type parameter is substituted by the actual type at the time an instance is created. Without an instance, the system will not know what the type parameter T actually stands for, and therefore, static data members and methods cannot be declared with type parameters.

Type parameters cannot be used with the static data members and methods of a generic class.

17.2 Generics and Collections

One of the main reasons for adding generics to Java is to improve the usability and reliability of Java Collections Framework (JCF) classes. We've seen simple examples of creating homogeneous lists in Chapter 10. Let's review the benefits of generics with an ArrayList, a very commonly used JCF class. Prior to Java 5.0, here's how we use it. Suppose we want to maintain a list of Book objects in which the Book class is defined as follows:

```
class Book {

   private String author;

   public Book(String name) {
       setAuthor(name);
   }

   public String getAuthor( ) {
       return author;
   }

   public void setAuthor(String author) {
       this.author = author;
   }
}
```

Here's a sample code fragment that adds Book objects to a list:

```
import java.util.*;
...
List bookList = new ArrayList();

bookList.add(new Book("Jane Austin"));
bookList.add(new Book("Charles Dickens"));
bookList.add(new Book("Henry James"));

//and so forth ...
```

To display author information in booklist, we use an iterator.

```
Iterator itr = bookList.iterator();

while (itr.hasNext()) {

   Book book = (Book) itr.next();

   System.out.println(book.getAuthor());
}
```

Typecast is required.

Notice the required typecasting of an object retrieved from the iterator to the Book type. Although we know booklist contains nothing but Book objects, typecasting is necessary here because an instance of any class can be added to the bookList.

In other words, ArrayList and other JCF collection classes maintain a heterogeneous collection of objects. So, whether written intentionally or not, the statement

```
bookList.add(new String("Java"));
```

would execute fine. Of course, the previous iterator loop will fail if bookList contains an object other than a Book. What we want here is a way to specify a homogeneous collection of objects; that is, every object in a collection is drawn from the same class. This improves the type safety.

All JCF collection classes are retrofitted with the generics mechanism in Java 5.0 to allow the specification of a homogeneous collection of objects. The class declaration for the ArrayList class in the java.util package is as follows:

```
public class ArrayList<E> extends ...
```

where the identifier E is the type parameter (E is used here instead of T to signify that the type parameter is for the elements in the collection). By specifying the actual type for E, we can create a homogeneous ArrayList that contains only Book objects:

```
import java.util.*;

ArrayList<Book> booklist = new ArrayList<Book>();

booklist.add(new Book("Jane Austin"));
booklist.add(new Book("Charles Dickens"));
booklist.add(new Book("Henry James"));
...
```

This can be declared as List<Book>. We'll discuss it more in Section 17.3.

Unlike a nongeneric list, the elements of this booklist are limited to Book objects, so the following would result in a compile time error:

```
booklist.add(new String("Java"));   <----- INVALID
```

An iterator prior to Java 5.0 is a heterogeneous collection also, so we were required to typecast to a proper class when accessing elements. Since an iterator from Java 5.0 is a generic collection, we need to specify the actual type when declaring an iterator. Here's how we access the elements of booklist via an iterator:

```
Iterator<Book> itr = booklist.iterator();

while (itr.hasNext()) {

   Book book = itr.next();   <----- No typecasting is necessary here.

   System.out.println(book.getAuthor());
}
```

Typecasting is no longer necessary when an element is accessed from the iterator because the iterator can contain only Book objects.

Even simpler approach of scanning a list is done by using the for-each loop. Using a for-each loop, we can access the elements in booklist very concisely as follows:

```
for (Book book : booklist) {

   System.out.println(book.getAuthor());
}
```

Nested Generic Class Declaration

Let's study another example. This time, we will create an ArrayList of Locker objects. To create an ArrayList, we must plug in a real type for the type parameter E, and to create a Locker object, we must plug in a real type for the type parameter T. Here's how we create such a list:

```
ArrayList<Locker<Book>> bookLockerList =
                 new ArrayList<Locker<Book>>( );

Locker<Book>bookLocker = new Locker<Book>( );
bookLocker.store(new Book("Jane"));
bookLockerList.add(bookLocker);
. . .

for (Locker<Book> locker : bookLockerList) {
   System.out.println(locker.retrieve().getAuthor());
}
```

Notice the data type for the for-each loop variable is Locker<Book>, not Locker.

Defining a Simple Generic Linked List

In Chapter 16, we introduced the linked node structure and defined several different node classes (e.g., Node and BNode). The only difference among the different node classes is the data type of the item we put in a node. If that is the case, using the generics will eliminate the need to create a customized node class for each type of item. We can define such generic Node class as follows:

Node

```
class Node<E> {

   private E item;

   private Node next;

   public Node( ) {
      this(null, null);
   }
```

```
    public Node(E data, Node node) {
        setItem(data);
        setNext(node);
    }

    public E getItem( ) {
        return item;
    }

    public Node<E> getNext( ) {
        return next;
    }

    public void setItem(E data) {
        item = data;
    }

    public void setNext(Node<E> node) {
        next = node;
    }
}
```

Here's one example of creating a linked list of three nodes with each node having String as its data item:

```
Node<String> one, two, three;

three = new Node<String>("trois", null);
two   = new Node<String>("deux", three);
one   = new Node<String>("un", two);
```

Notice that the link field can only point to a node of the same actual type. For example, the link field of Node<String> can only point to Node<String>. This guarantees that every node in a linked list will be of the same actual type. In other words, the linked list will be homogeneous.

By defining the node class generic, we achieve the goal of allowing only a homogeneous list. From the design standpoint, however, it is more natural and easier to use if we define a generic linked list class. The fact that we are using nodes is really not the concern of the client programmer. We will be discussing the list and different implementations further in Chapter 18. Here we limit our discussion on how to define a homogeneous linked list class.

When we use the generic node class, we are required to specify the actual type whenever we create a new instance of a node. This is tedious for the client programmer. When a programmer wants to use a homogeneous list, it would be more convenient if she is only required to specify the actual type of the items in the list just once. To allow this, we can define a generic linked list class. Let's study how we can define such a generic linked list class. We will keep this class very simplistic so we can concentrate on generics. We will delve deeper into a more elaborate and full implementation in Chapter 18.

The SimpleLinkedList class we define here consists of only four public methods. The first is the add method that adds a new item to the end of the list. The second is the get method that returns the *i*th item in the list. The method will throw a NoSuchElementException if the specified position is invalid. The first item in the list is at position 0. The third is the setEmpty method that empties the list. And the fourth is the isEmpty method that returns true if the list is empty. We keep two pointers head and tail that points to the first and the last node in a list. If the list is empty, they are both equal to null. The node class is defined as its inner class and hidden from the client programmer. Here's the definition:

SimpleLinkedList

```
import java.util.NoSuchElementException;

    class SimpleLinkedList<E> {

    private Node head;

    private Node tail;

    public SimpleLinkedList( ){

        setEmpty();
    }

    public void add(E item) {

        Node node = new Node(item, null);

        if (isEmpty()) {

            head = tail = node;

        } else {

            tail.setNext(node);
            tail = node;
        }
    }

    public E get(int index) throws NoSuchElementException {

        if (index < 0) {
            throw new NoSuchElementException();
        }

        int loc = 0;

        Node p = head;
```

```
        while (loc < index) {
            p = p.getNext();

            if (p == null) {
                throw new NoSuchElementException();
            }

            loc++;
        }

        return p.getItem();
    }

    public boolean isEmpty( ) {

        if (head == null && tail == null) {
            return true;
        } else {

            return false;
        }
    }

    public void setEmpty( ) {

        head = tail = null;
    }

    class Node {

        private E item;

        private Node next;

        public Node( ) {
            this(null, null);
        }

        public Node(E data, Node node) {
            setItem(data);
            setNext(node);
        }

        public E getItem( ) {
            return item;
        }

        public Node getNext( ) {
            return next;
        }

        public void setItem(E data) {
            item = data;
        }
```

```
        public void setNext(Node node) {
            next = node;
        }
    }
}
```

Notice the Node class is defined as the inner class of SimpleLinkedList. It still refers to the type parameter E in its methods, but the class itself is not a generic class anymore. After we create a SimpleLinkedList, for example, as

```
SimpleLinkedList<Bicyle> myList
            = new SimpleLinkedList<Bicycle>( );
```

we will only be able to pass a Bicycle object to the add method of myList, thus making the list homogeneous. And we only have to specify the actual type of items once when we create a list, not every time we create a node.

We close this section with examples of using the SimpleLinkedList class. Let's first generate 1000 random integers and put them in a list:

```
import java.util.Random;
...
Random generator = new Random();

SimpleLinkedList<Integer> list =
                    new SimpleLinkedList<Integer>();

for (int i = 0; i < 1000; i++) {
   list.add(new Integer(generator.nextInt()));
}
```

Once we have a list, we can traverse the list by calling its get method. For example, we can find out the number of negative integers in the list by the following code:

```
int negCnt = 0;

for (int i = 0; i < 1000; i++) {

   Integer num = list.get(i);

   if (num.intValue() < 0) {
      negCnt++;
   }
}

System.out.println("Number of negative integers = "
                       + negCnt);
```

We purposely made the use of the Integer class explicit to illustrate the generics feature clearly. If we use the autoboxing/unboxing feature of Java 5.0, then we rewrite the two statements for adding and getting an item as

```
list.add(generator.nextInt());
...
int num = list.get(i);
```

We use the for loop to get the items in the list because we know the size of the list. We still can iterate over the items without knowing the size of a list by catching an exception thrown by the get method. Here's how:

```
int i = 0, negCnt = 0;

while (true) {

   try {
      int num = list.get(i);

      if (num < 0) {
         negCnt++;
      }

      i++;

   } catch (NoSuchElementException e) {

      break; //jump out from the while loop
   }
}
```

Calling the get method repeatedly with an increasing index value to traverse is inefficient because each call of the get method will restart the search from the head node. This is the reason why the full-blown collection classes from java.util support an iterator as an efficient way of traversing items in a list. We will be discussing these issues in Chapter 18 when we cover lists in greater detail.

1. The HashMap class is declared as

```
public class HashMap<K, V> ...
```

where K is the key and V is the value of a map entry. Declare and create a new HashMap with Integer as the key and String as the value.

2. Identify the invalid statements.

```
ArrayList<Locker> list;

list = new ArrayList<Locker<Book>>( );
```

```
for (Locker locker : list) {
   System.out.println(
         locker.retrieve().getAuthor());
}
```

3. Draw a diagram showing the linked list after the following code is executed:

```
Node<String> one, two, three;

three = new Node<String>("trois", null);
two   = new Node<String>("deux", three);
one   = new Node<String>("un", two);
```

17.3 Generics, Inheritance, and Java Interface

Generic classes can be organized into a class hierarchy just as any other nongeneric classes can. A subclass of a generic superclass must also be generic, but we can define a generic subclass of a nongeneric superclass. Similarly, we can define a class that implements a generic interface. We study different cases in this section.

A Subclass of a Generic Superclass

When we define a subclass of a generic superclass, we must include the type parameter of the superclass in the subclass, because if we do not, then the compiler cannot resolve the type parameter specified in the generic superclass. Since a subclass of a generic superclass must include the type parameter, it must also be a generic class. Let's define a subclass of the Locker class. This subclass has an additional data member that stores a unique integer value as its identification number. Here's how we define a subclass LockerSub. (The Locker class is repeated here for easy reference.)

```
class Locker<T> {

    private T content;

    public Locker( ) {
        store(null);
    }

    public T retrieve( ) {
        return content;
    }

    public void store(T item) {
        content = item;
    }
}

public class LockerSub<T> extends Locker<T> {

    private int id;
```

```
        private static int idCounter = 100;

        public LockerSub( ) {
            this(null);
        }

        public LockerSub(T item) {

            super();

            id = idCounter++;

            store(item);
        }

        public int showID() {
            return id;
        }
    }
```

The compiler will insert this call to the superclass constructor if not explicitly stated as here.

Here's a sample code that creates a number of LockerSub objects:

```
LockerSub<String> subLockOne;
LockerSub<Integer> subLockTwo;

subLockOne = new LockerSub<String>("Hello");
subLockTwo = new LockerSub<Integer>( ); //null object will
                                        //be stored

System.out.println(subLockOne.showID() + ": " +
                   subLockOne.retrieve());

System.out.println(subLockTwo.showID() + ": " +
                   subLockTwo.retrieve());
```

The output will be

```
100: Hello
101: null
```

Notice that the statement such as

```
Locker<String> lock = new LockerSub<String>("Hello");
```

is valid, following the same rule for nongeneric classes. A variable can be declared as class C and point to an instance of a subclass of C. This is how polymorphism is applied in writing a flexible code. Note, however, that you cannot call any method unique to the subclass without typecasting. For an example, consider these statements:

```
        Locker<String> lock = new LockerSub<String>("Java Rules");
INVALID System.out.println(lock.showID());
VALID   System.out.println( ((LockerSub<String>) lock).showID());
```

Our next example defines a subclass that includes a type parameter in addition to the one inherited from the superclass. Let's define the second subclass of the Locker class named LockerSubTwo. This subclass includes two type parameters. The first one is inherited from the Locker superclass, and the second one is the type parameter specific to this subclass for storing the renter object. Here's the definition:

```
class LockerSubTwo<T, R> extends Locker<T> {

    private R renter;

    public LockerSubTwo( ) {
        this(null, null);
    }

    public LockerSubTwo(T item, R renter) {

        super( );

        store(item);
        setRenter(renter);
    }

    public R getRenter( ) {
        return renter;
    }

    public void setRenter(R renter) {
        this.renter = renter;
    }
```

And here's a sample declaration for LockerSubTwo objects:

```
LockerSubTwo<String, Person> lockerOne;
LockerSubTwo<Integer, Company> lockerTwo;
```

A Generic Subclass of a Nongeneric Superclass

Actually we have been defining a subclass of a nongeneric superclass all along because every class we define in Java is a subclass of the Object class, whether implicitly or explicitly specified. Here's a small example of defining a generic subclass of a nongeneric superclass (that is not Object):

```
class Box {

    private static int idCounter = 100;

    private int id;

    public Box( ) {
        id = idCounter++;
    }
```

```
    public int showID( ) {
        return id;
    }
}

class MagicBox<T> extends Box {

    private T content;

    public MagicBox( ) {
        super(); //assigns ID number
        store(null);
    }

    public T retrieve( ) {
        return content;
    }

    public void store(T item) {
        content = item;
    }
}
```

Generic Interfaces and Their Implementing Classes

generic interface

In addition to defining generic classes, we can define the ***generic interface***. Here's an example of a generic interface that specifies the behavior of storing and retrieving objects:

```
interface MagicContainer<T> {

    public T retrieve( );

    public void store(T item);
}
```

A class that implements a generic interface must repeat the type parameters indicated in the generic interface. Here's a sample class that implements MagicContainer:

```
class MagicTrunk<T> implements MagicContainer<T> {

    private T content;

    public MagicTrunk( ) {
        store(null);
    }

    public T retrieve( ) {
        return content;
    }

    public void store(T item) {
        content = item;
    }
}
```

The type parameters in the class declaration may be bounded, as in

```
interface MagicContainer<T> {...}

class MagicTrunk<T extends Number>
      implements MagicContainer<T> {...}
```

If the type parameter in the interface is bounded, then we must repeat the bounded expression in the class declaration also (somewhat unexpected) as in

```
interface MagicContainer<T extends Number> {...}

class MagicTrunk<T extends Number>
      implements MagicContainger<T> {...}
```

This has to be <T> not <T extends Number>.

It is also possible to implement a class without the type parameter if we provide the actual type in the interface. For example, we can define a MagicTrunk that stores with String objects only as follows:

```
class StringTrunk implements MagicContainer<String> {

    private String content;

    public StringTrunk( ) {
        store(null);
    }

    public String retrieve( ) {
        return content;
    }

    public void store(String item) {
        content = item;
    }
}
```

Actual type is specified here.

Notice that the type parameter T is completely removed from the class and replaced by the actual type String.

We can declare the interface as the data type of a variable and make the variable refer to an instance of a class that implements this interface. This is how we normally declare and create an instance of a JCF class prior to Java 5.0:

```
List myList = new ArrayList( );
```

The same rule applies with generic interfaces, so we can write, for example,

```
MagicContainer<String> myTrunk
                       = new MagicTrunk<String>( );

List<String> myList = new ArrayList<String>( );
```

instead of

```
MagicTrunk<String> myTrunk2 = new MagicTrunk<String>( );
ArrayList<String> myList2 = new ArrayList<String>( );
```

It is preferable to specify the interface for the data type of a variable so that it can refer to an instance of any class that implements the interface.

17.4 Additional Topics and Pitfalls

In this section, we cover additional topics and some common pitfalls of using generics in Java.

Raw Types

Consider the following statements:

```
Locker locker = new Locker();
locker.store(new Integer(4));
```

Will these work? From our understanding of the generic class so far, we would most reasonably say no. Actually, the statements do work. When we compile them, we get the warning

```
unchecked or unsafe operations.
Note: Recompile with-Xlint:unchecked for details
```

raw type

but we still can execute them without error. If we don't specify the actual type for the type parameter when creating an instance of a generic class, a ***raw type*** is created. With the raw type variable, the type restriction is removed. For example, if we write

```
Locker<String> strLocker = new Locker<String>( );
```

the compiler will restrict us to storing a String object. A compile time error is generated when we try to store an object other than a String. This is the type safety provided by the use of generics. With the raw type of Locker, for example, there's no restriction, so the following statements are all valid (only the compile time warning is generated):

```
Locker myLocker = new Locker( );
myLocker.store("Hello");
myLocker.store(new Integer(10));
myLocker.store(new Book("Anne Bronte");
```

The Locker class is defined as

```
class Locker<T> {...}
```

and when a raw type Locker is created, it essentially substitutes T with Object. This means an instance of the Object class or any of its subclasses can be stored in a raw-type Locker. Now, the FourthLocker is defined with a bounded type as

```
class FourthLocker<T extends Number> {...}
```

In this case, we can store an instance of the Number class or any of it subclasses in a raw-type FourthLocker.

Because the type restriction is removed from the raw type, the following assignment statements are valid (but very dangerous):

```
Locker rawLocker = new Locker( );
Locker<String>  strLocker = new Locker<String>( );
Locker<Integer> intLocker = new Locker<Integer>( );

rawLocker = intLocker; //valid, not even a warning

strLocker = rawLocker; //valid, only a compile time warning
```

This is dangerous from the type safety standpoint because we can write statements such as these.

```
intLocker.store(new Integer(10));

rawLocker = intLocker;

strLocker = rawLocker; //only a compile time warning here

String str = strLocker.retrieve();
```

INVALID → (points to `String str = strLocker.retrieve();`)

The last statement is invalid and logically wrong, of course; but through the two hideous assignments, strLocker is set to refer to a Locker object that holds an Integer. The compiler cannot catch this error. Not even a warning is generated.

As stated, the use of raw types removes the type safety. But this does not make sense because the goal of generics is type safety. Why allow something that nullifies the goal? The answer is backward compatibility.

Hints, & Tips, Pitfalls

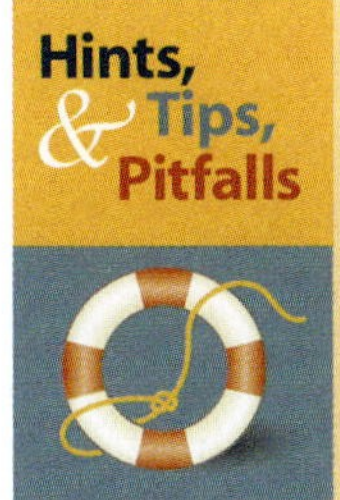

Raw types are allowed in Java 5.0 to maintain the backward compatibility.

Consider the following statement:

```
List myList = new ArrayList( );
```

If the raw types were not allowed in Java 5.0, the statement would not compile. Thus, without raw types Java programs that use JCF classes and are written prior to Java 5.0 will not run with Java 5.0. Backward compatibility that allows older Java programs to be executed with a newer version of Java is considered sacred in the Java community. To maintain backward compatibility with the tons of legacy Java code, raw types are permitted. However, whenever you develop a new program with Java 5.0, avoid using raw types at all cost so that the intended type safety is not lost.

Do not use raw types even if they are permitted in Java 5.0.

Generics and Arrays

Generics can be used with arrays, but their use can be tricky. We describe how generics and arrays are used together and identify some common pitfalls. The most surprising (and annoying) is that you are not allowed to create an array whose elements are instances of a type-specified generic class. For example, the second statement in the pair

```
Locker<String>[] lockers;
lockers = new Locker<String>[25];
```

INVALID → (second statement)

will not compile. Java simply does not allow this for the reason of not being able to ensure type safety if it had been allowed. Notice that the declaration

```
Locker<String>[] lockers;
```

itself is valid because we can create lockers as follows:

```
lockers = new Locker[25]; //raw type lockers
```

An array of type-specified generic class is disallowed, but an array of raw type generic class or a wildcard generic class is allowed. The following creations are both valid:

```
Locker[] rawLockers = new Locker[25];
Locker<?>[] wildLockers = new Locker<?>[25];
```

These are type-unsafe operations, but the compiler will generate a compile time warning. The easiest way to handle this situation is to forget about using arrays with generics altogether. Use either an ArrayList or LinkedList instead.

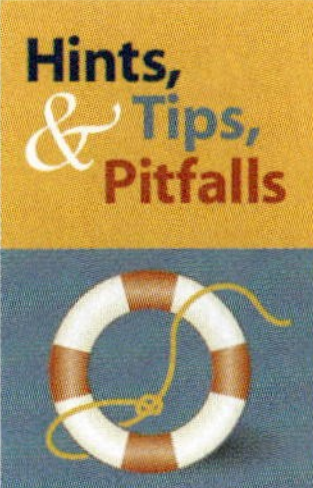

Do not use arrays with generics. Use either an ArrayList or a LinkedList instead.

Summary

- Generics are a new feature from Java 5.0 that provides type safety.
- The definition of a generic class includes one or more type parameters surrounded by angle brackets.
- A concrete type must be provided when one is declaring and creating an instance of a generic class.
- Type parameters can be bounded, or restricted, to subclasses of a specified class.
- A wildcard type can be used for the type parameter to designate "free-ranging" type.
- The static data members and methods cannot include any reference to the type parameter.
- From Java 5.0, Java Collections Framework (JCF) classes, such as ArrayList and HashMap, include type parameters. They are now generic classes.
- The new for-each loop allows a simple and clean way to access elements in JCF collection classes or arrays.
- A subclass of a generic class can be defined. This subclass must also be a generic class.
- A generic subclass of a nongeneric superclass can be defined.
- A class that implements a generic interface must be a generic class.
- A raw-type instance of the generic class is created when it is created without specifying the actual type for the type parameter.
- An array of a type-specified generic class is not allowed. But an array of a raw-type or wildcard generic class is allowed.

Key Concepts

generic class
generic interface
type safety
type parameter
typing error
bounded type
wildcard type
for-each loop
raw type

Exercises

1. Here are the class definitions for Book and Broomstick:

```
class Book {

    private String author;

    public Book( ) {
        this("Unknown");
    }

    public Book(String author) {
      setAuthor(author);
    }

    public String getAuthor( ) {
        return author;
    }

    public void setAuthor(String author) {
        this.author = author;
    }
}

class Broomstick {

    private double value;

    public Broomstick( ) {
        this(0.0);
    }

    public Broomstick(double value) {
        setValue(value);
    }

    public double getValue( ) {
        return value;
    }

    public void setValue(double value) {
        this.value = value;
    }
}
```

Determine the output from the following code:

```
Locker<Book>       lock1, lock2;
Locker<Broomstick> lock3;

lock1 = new Locker<Book>( );
lock2 = new Locker<Book>( );
lock3 = new Locker<Broomstick>( );

lock1.store(new Book("Edgar Allan Poe");
lock3.store(new Broomstick());

System.out.println(lock1.retrieve());
System.out.println(lock2.retrieve().getAuthor());
System.out.println(lock3.retrieve().getValue());
```

2. Given the Book and Broomstick classes from Exercise 1, identify the invalid statements in the following code fragment. For each statement, indicate whether it causes a compile time warning, compile time error, or runtime error.

```
Locker<Book>       lock1, lock2;
Locker<Broomstick> lock3, lock4;

lock1 = new Locker<Book>( );
lock2 = new Locker( );

lock1 = lock2;
lock2 = lock1;

lock3 = new Locker<Broomstick>( );
lock4 = lock3;
lock3 = lock2;

System.out.println(lock3.retrieve().getAuthor());
```

3. Given the Locker and LockerSub classes, which of the following statements are invalid?

```
Locker<Book>    locker;
LockerSub<Book> lockerSub;

locker  = new LockerSub<Book>();

locker  = lockerSub;

lockerSub = locker;
```

4. Explain why it is not allowed to add the following two constructors.

```
class SecondLocker<T1, T2> {

    ...

    public SecondLocker(T1 item) {
       setFirstItem(item);
    }
```

```
        public SecondLocker(T2 item) {
            setSecondItem(item);
        }

        ...
    }
```

5. Which statements will result in a compile time warning or error in the following code fragment?

```
Locker<Integer>[] lockers1;
Locker<Integer>[] lockers2;
Locker[]          lockers3;

lockers1 = new Locker<Integer>[34];

lockers2 = new Locker[23];

lockers3 = new Locker<String>[20];
```

6. Declare and create an ArrayList of Locker<String> objects and add 100 lockers to the list. Use simple string values such as data0, data1, . . . , data99.
7. Repeat Exercise 6, but this time, add 100 Locker<Book> objects. Use the Book class defined in Exercise 1. For the author names, use author0, author1, . . . , author99.
8. Using the SimpleLinkedList class from Section 17.2, write a program that plays fortune telling. First, input *N* fortunes. Each fortune is a String. The value for *N* is entered by the user. You may assume that input *N* is always positive. Next, repeatedly prompt the user to display a fortune. If the reply is yes, display a fortune randomly chosen from the list. If the reply is no, then stop the program.
9. Here's a generic interface:

```
interface Storable<T> {
    public T remove( );

    public void put(T stuff);
}
```

   Define a class named Bin that implements the Storable interface.
10. Define a generic class named AddressBook whose type parameter T can be subtituted by the Person class or any of its subclasses. The AddressBook object maintains a homogeneous collection of T objects. Include the add method, which adds a new T object to the collection, and the delete method, which removes all T objects that match the given name. Assume the Person class (and its subclasses) has the method getName that returns the name of a person. Use an array to implement the AddressBook class.
11. Repeat Exercise 10, but this time use a linked list to implement the AddressBook class.

18 List ADT

After you have read and studied this chapter, you should be able to

- Describe the key features of the List ADT.
- Implement the List ADT using an array and linked list.
- Describe and implement the iterator pattern.
- Explain the key differences between the array and linked implementations of the List ADT.

Introduction

We introduced the concept of linked lists in Chapter 16 and provided the fundamentals of manipulating links. And, in Chapter 17, we introduced the generics feature of Java 5.0 and used it in defining the SimpleLinkedList class that provides a higher-level abtraction to the client programmers. Using a SimpleLinkedList, the client programmers do not have to deal directly with the linked nodes. Instead, they deal strictly with list objects. The fact that the linked nodes are used in implementation is hidden from the client programmers. This embodies the software engineering principle of information hiding. In this chapter, we will expand this concept further by introducing an abstract data type (ADT). ADTs are reusable software components that support reliable and flexible software construction.

abstract data type (ADT)

An ***abstract data type (ADT)*** is a mathematical specification of a set of data and the corresponding set of operations performed on those data. The key point is that an ADT does not specify how the set of data is actually represented in memory or how the set of operations is implemented. Nice examples of ADTs can be found in the Java Collections Framework. When we look in the java.util package, for example, we see the Java interface List and two classes that implement the List interface. The List interface represents the List ADT, and the two classes—ArrayList and LinkedList—implement the List ADT. The ArrayList uses an array, and the LinkedList uses linked nodes to implement the List ADT, respectively.

To study how the ADT is defined and implemented, we will create our own List ADT and provide two implementations in this chapter which we model after the java.util.List interface and its two implementations. Ours is a much simplified version of those in the java.util package. In Chapters 19 and 20, we will study the Stack and Queue ADTs, respectively.

18.1 The List ADT

list ADT

A ***list*** is a linearly ordered collection of elements. Figure 18.1 shows a sample list, named sampleList, with five elements and another list, named myList, with five three-letter animal names (String objects). Mathematically, we can designate sampleList as

$$\text{sampleList} = (L_0, L_1, L_2, L_3, L_4)$$

linear ordering

duplicate elements

Elements in a list are said to be ***linearly ordered***. This means L_0 comes before L_1 and L_1 comes before L_2, and so forth. For the sample list myList, the first element is L_0 and the last element is L_4. Note that we are using the zero-based indexing. Elements in a list do not have to be distinct; i.e., ***duplicate elements*** are

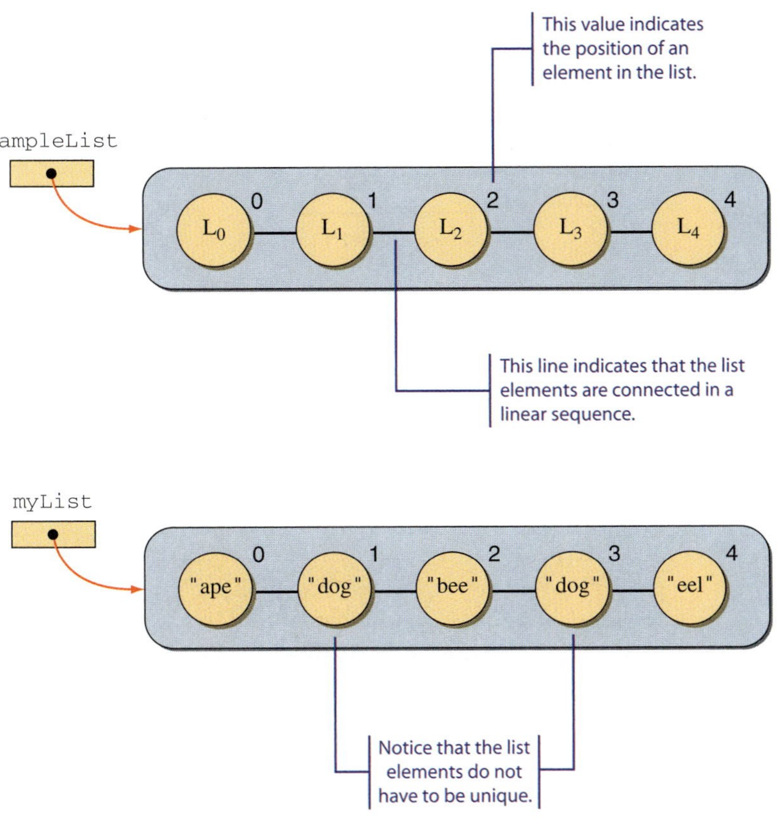
This value indicates the position of an element in the list.
sampleList
0
1
2
3
4
L0
L1
L2
L3
L4
This line indicates that the list elements are connected in a linear sequence.
myList
"ape"
"dog"
"bee"
"dog"
"eel"
Notice that the list elements do not have to be unique.

Figure 18.1 A generic list named **sampleList** with five elements and a list of three-letter animals, named **myList.**

allowed. Two objects o1 and o2 are considered duplicates if o1.equals(o2) is true. In the sample list myList, we see that L_1 and L_3 are duplicates. A list also allows multiple null ***elements***. We will discuss more about the impact of duplicate and null elements in the implementation sections.

null elements

In the remainder of this section, we will describe the operations of the List ADT.

add

The add operation adds a new element to a list. There are two versions: The first one adds a new element at the end of the list. The second one adds a new element at the designated position in the list.

For the second version, all elements in that and higher positions will be shifted to a position one index higher; that is, an element at position i will be shifted to position $i + 1$. If the given position is a negative value, or larger than the current size of the list, then the index out-of-bound exception will be thrown. Figure 18.2 illustrates the second version of the add operation.

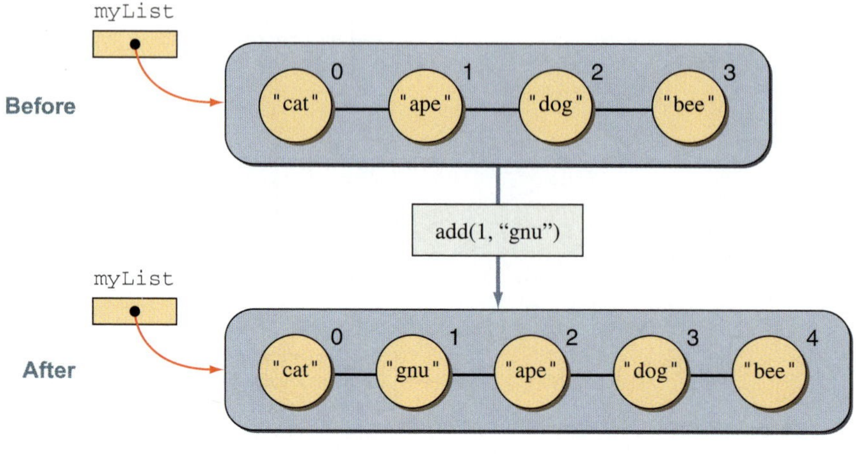

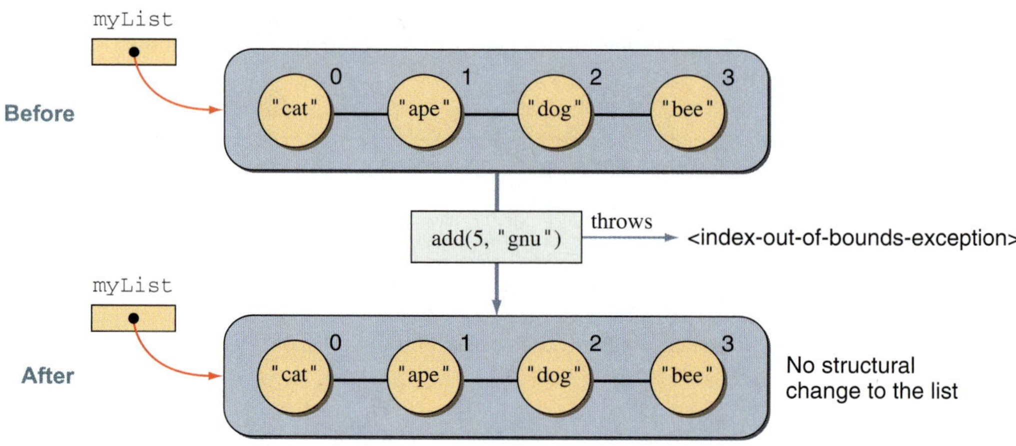

Figure 18.2 Sample version 2 **add** operations on **myList.**

clear

The clear operation removes all elements in the list, which results in an empty list. Figure 18.3 illustrates the clear operation.

contains

The contains operation returns true if a specified element is included in the list. Otherwise, false is returned. Notice that there could be duplicate objects. The search will stop immediately after the first match, and true is returned. Figure 18.4 illustrates the contains operation.

get

The get operation returns the element stored at the designated position. If the given position is outside of a valid range—less than 0 or greater than or equal to the size of the list—an index out-of-bound exception is thrown. The get operation is a read-only operation. It does not remove the element, so the list remains the same after the get operation. Figure 18.5 illustrates the get operation.

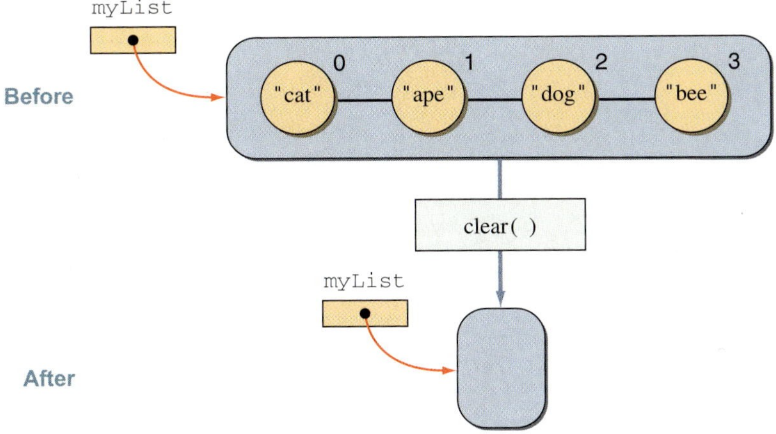

Figure 18.3 The effect of the **clear** operation on the **myList** list.

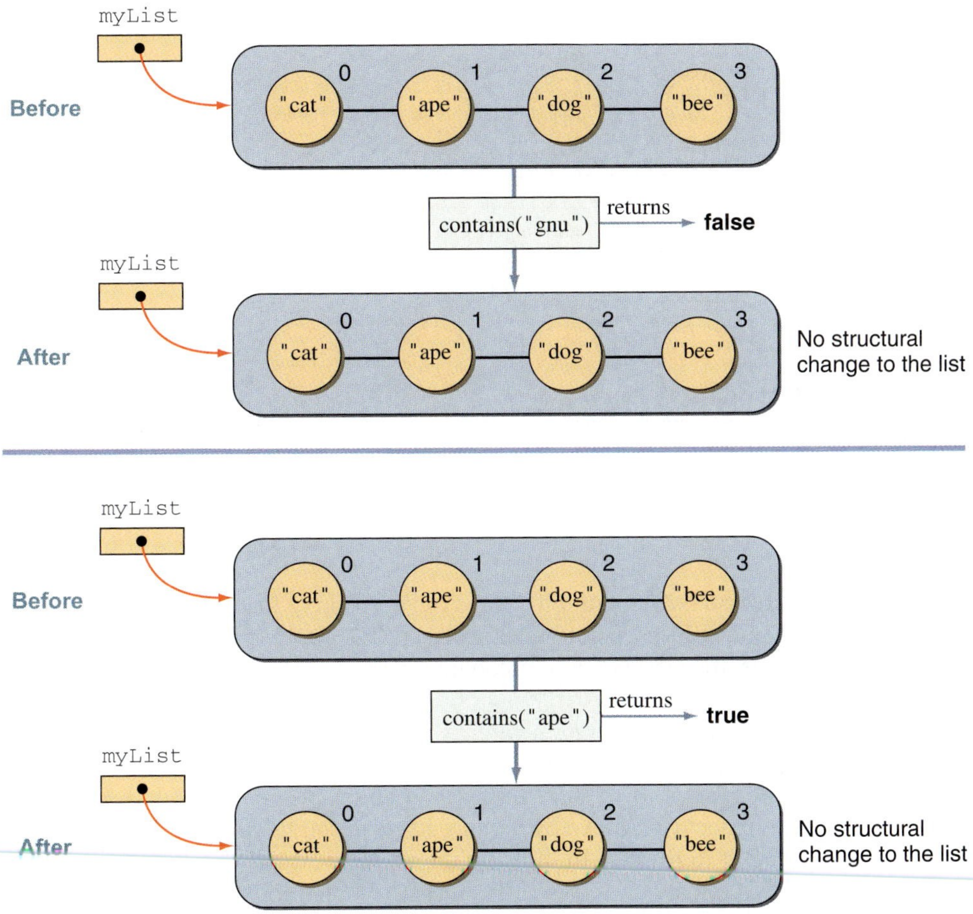

myList
Before
"cat" "ape" "dog" "bee"
0 1 2 3
contains("gnu") returns **false**
myList
After
"cat" "ape" "dog" "bee"
0 1 2 3
No structural change to the list

myList
Before
"cat" "ape" "dog" "bee"
0 1 2 3
contains("ape") returns **true**
myList
After
"cat" "ape" "dog" "bee"
0 1 2 3
No structural change to the list

Figure 18.4 Sample **contains** operations on the **myList** list.

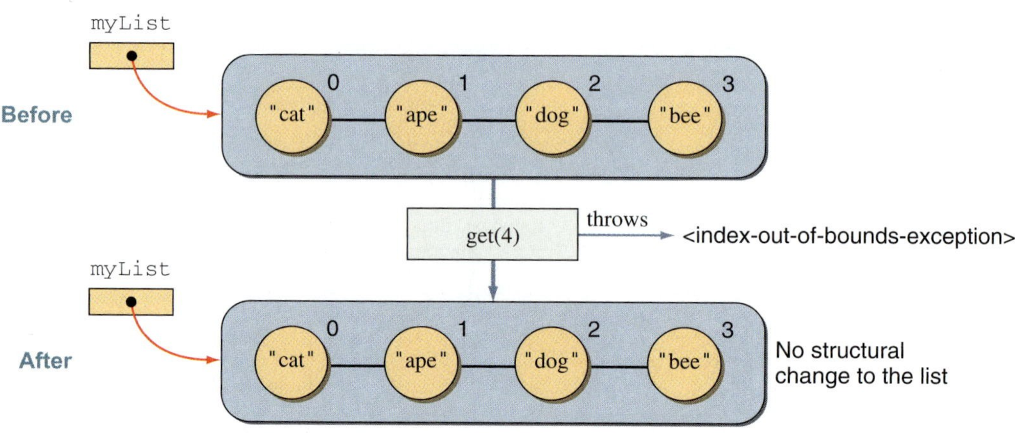

Figure 18.5 Sample **get** operations on the **myList** list.

indexOf

The indexOf operation returns the position of the specified object in the list. If the specified object is not in the list, then NOT_FOUND (−1) is returned. If there are duplicates, then the position of the first match is returned. Figure 18.6 illustrates the indexOf operation.

isEmpty

The isEmpty operation returns true if the list is empty. Otherwise, false is returned. Figure 18.7 illustrates the isEmpty operation.

remove

There are two versions of the remove operation. In the first version, we specify the element to remove by passing its position; in the second version, we specify the element to remove by passing the element itself. The first version returns the element removed from the list. It throws an index out-of-bound exception if the index i is outside the valid range of 0 and the size of the list minus 1, that is, $0 \le i \le$ size $-$ 1.

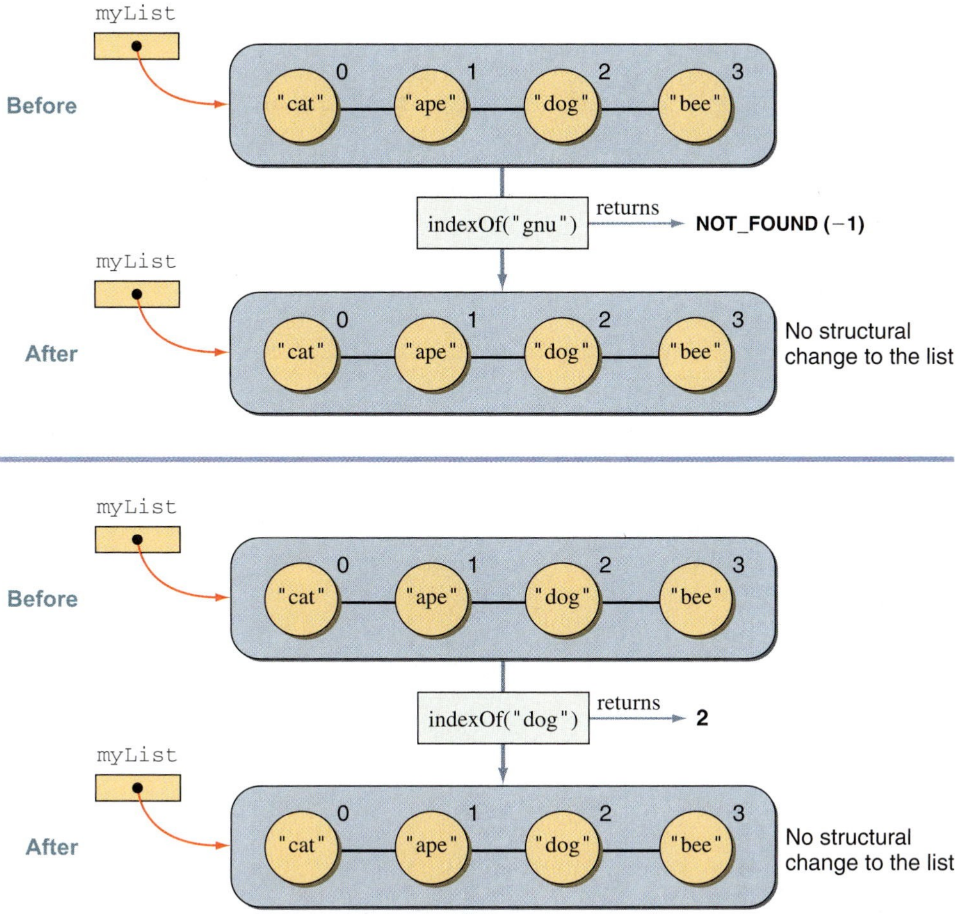

Figure 18.6 Sample **indexOf** operations on the **myList** list.

The second version removes the element and returns `true`. If the designated element is not found, then the list remains the same and `false` is returned. If any duplicates exist, then the first element in the list is removed. In both versions, if an element is successfully removed, then all elements in the position higher than the position of the removed element will be shifted to a position one index lower; that is, elements at position i will be shifted to position $i - 1$. Figure 18.8 illustrates both types of removal operations.

set

The set operation replaces the element at the designated position with the given element. If the operation is successful, then the operation returns the element previously stored in the designated position. If the designated position is outside of a valid range, then an index out-of-bound exception is thrown. Figure 18.9 illustrates the set operations.

size

The size operation returns the size of the list. Figure 18.10 illustrates the size operation.

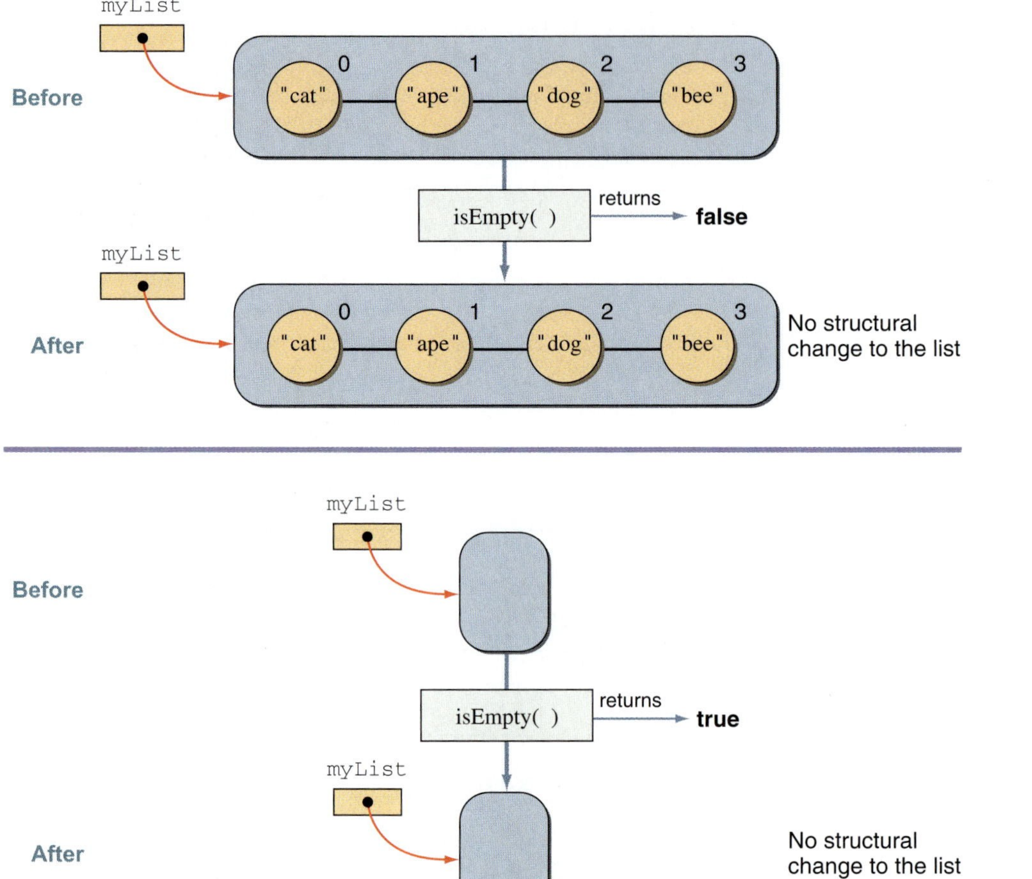

Figure 18.7 Sample **isEmpty** operations on the **myList** list.

18.2 The List Interface

We will use a Java interface to define the List ADT. To avoid confusion with the java.util classes, we will prefix the name of the interfaces and classes we define here with NPS (NPS stands for the author's affiliation, Naval Postgraduate School, in Monterey, California). In the NPSList interface definition, we use the generics feature introduced in Chapter 17. Formalizing what we have presented in Section 18.1, we have the following definition, and Table 18.1 summarizes the methods:

NPSList

```
package edu.nps.util;

interface NPSList<E> {

    public void add(E item);

    public void add(int index, E item) throws IndexOutOfBoundsException;
```

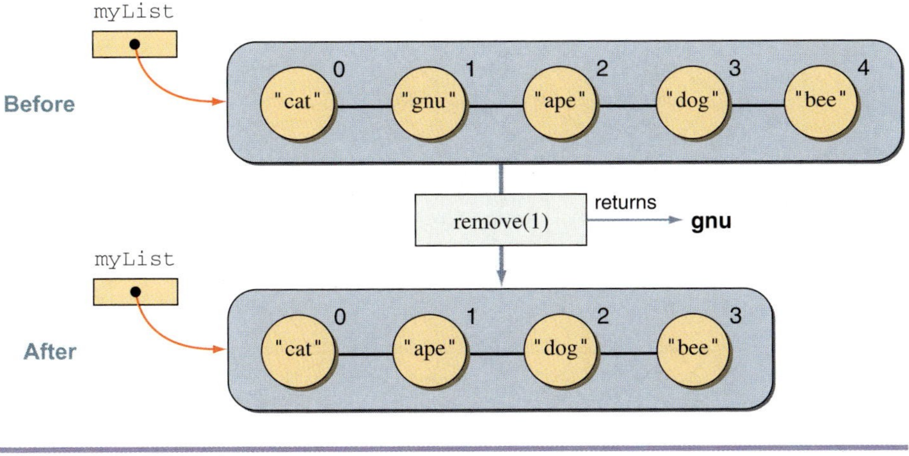

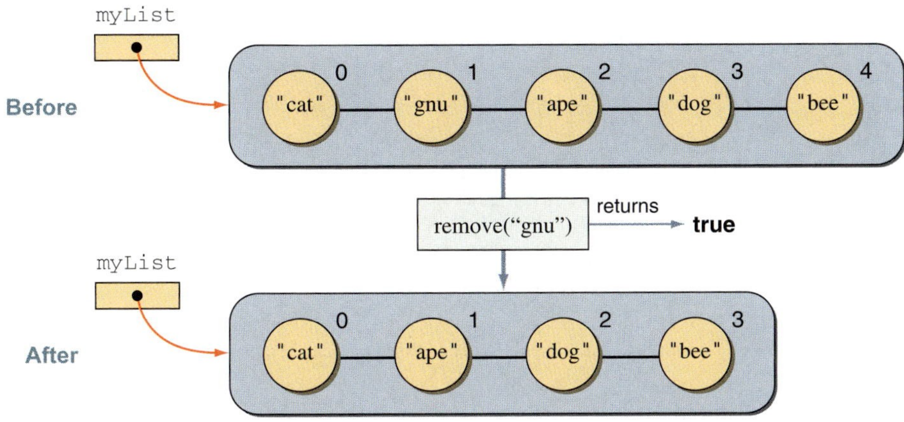

Figure 18.8 Sample **remove** operations on the **myList** list.

```
    public void clear( );
    public boolean contains(E item);
    public E get(int index) throws IndexOutOfBoundsException;
    public int indexOf(E item);
    public boolean isEmpty( );
    public E remove(int index)throws IndexOutOfBoundsException;
    public boolean remove(E item);
    public E set(int index, E item) throws IndexOutOfBoundsException;
    public int size( );
}
```

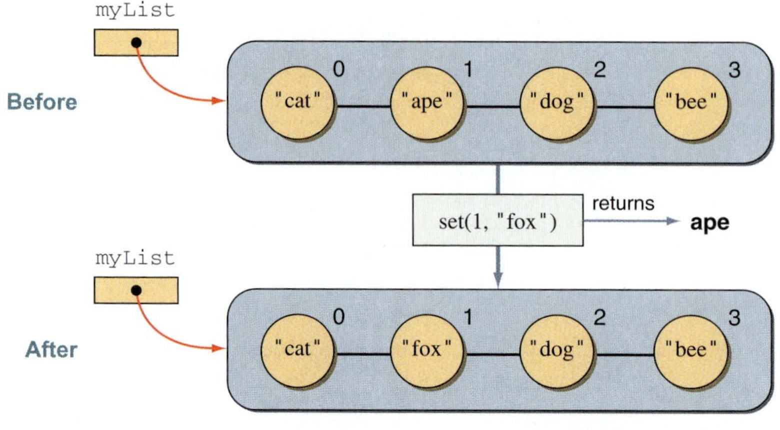

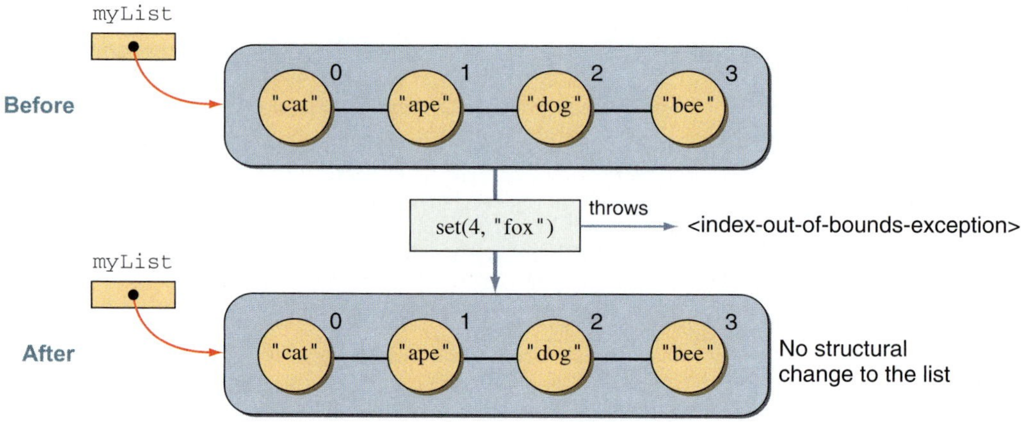

Figure 18.9 Sample **set** operations on the **myList** list.

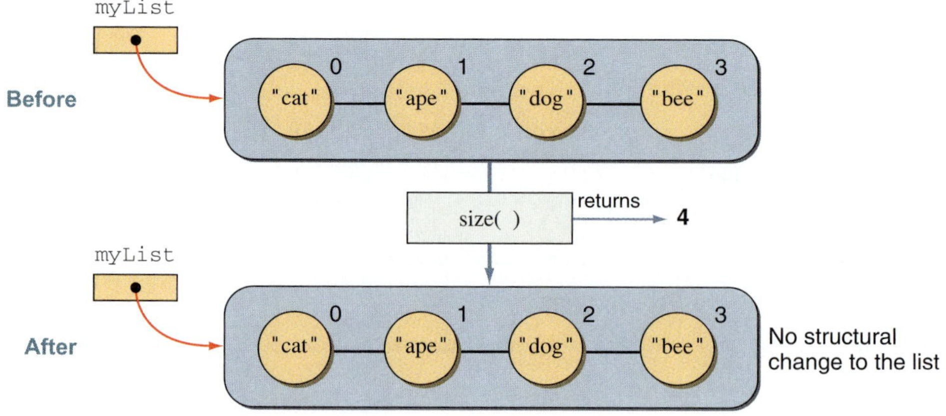

Figure 18.10 A sample **size** operation on the **myList** list.

Table 18.1 The `public` methods of the list interface. The identifier `E` is the parameterized type that will be replaced by the actual type such as `String` and `Person`

Interface: `NPSList`	
`void`	`add( E item )` Adds the item to the end of the list.
`void`	`add( int index, E item ) throws IndexOutOfBoundsException` Adds the item at the specified index position. If the value for `index` is less than 0 or larger than the size of the list, an `IndexOutOfBoundsException` is thrown.
`void`	`clear( )` Empties the list. After the `clear` method is called, the method `isEmpty` will return `true`.
`boolean`	`contains( E item )` Returns `true` if the item is in the list. Otherwise, returns `false`. If the list is empty, the result is `false`.
`E`	`get( int index ) throws IndexOutOfBoundsException` Returns the item at the specified index position. Notice that the item is not removed from the list.
`int`	`indexOf( E item )` Returns the index position of the specified item in the list. The value `NOT_FOUND` `(-1)` is returned when the item is not in the list.
`boolean`	`isEmpty( )` Returns `true` if the list is empty. Otherwise, returns `false`.
`E`	`remove( int index ) throws IndexOutOfBoundsException` Removes the item at the index position from the list. If the specified index value is less than `0` or greater than `size( )-1`, an `IndexOutOfBoundsException` is thrown.
`boolean`	`remove( E item )` Removes the item from the list and returns `true`. Returns `false` if the item is not found.
`void`	`set( int index, E item ) throws IndexOutOfBoundsException` Replaces the item at the index position with the passed item. If the index is less than `0` or greater than `size( ) -1`, an `IndexOutOfBoundsException` is thrown.
`int`	`size( )` Returns the number of items in the list.

We will define two classes—NPSArrayList and NPSLinkedList—in Sections 18.3 and 18.4. A typical way to declare and create an NPSList object is as follows:

```
NPSList<Person> personList = new NPSArrayList<Person>( );
NPSList<String> stringList = new NPSLinkedList<String>( );
```

The first is a (homogeneous) list of Person objects, and the second is a list of String objects.

18.3 The Array Implementation of the List ADT

There are two basic approaches in implementing the List ADT—array and linked-list implementions. In this section, we will implement the list interface by using an array. The linked-list implementation is presented in Section 18.4. For all our implementations, we will use the generics feature so the list members will be homogeneous. To illustrate the list operations with concrete examples, we will use String objects as list members in the following discussion. Figure 18.11 illustrates the array implementation of a list.

The NPSArrayList Class

We use an array to store the elements and an int variable to keep track of the number of elements currently in the list. These members are declared as

```
private E[] element;
private int count;
```

and initialized as

```
element = (E[]) new Object[DEFAULT_SIZE];
count   = 0;
```

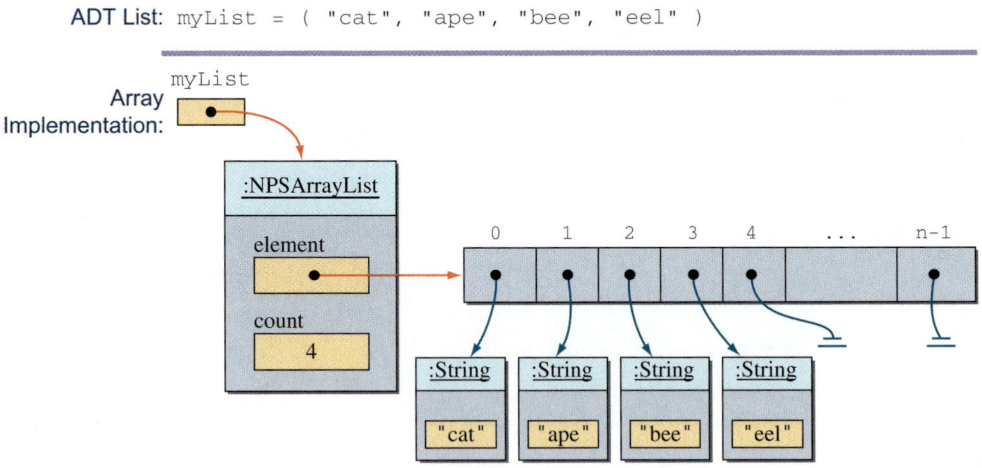

ADT List: myList = ("cat", "ape", "bee", "eel")

myList
Array Implementation:
:NPSArrayList
element
count
4
0 1 2 3 4 . . . n-1
:String :String :String :String
"cat" "ape" "bee" "eel"

Figure 18.11 An array implementation of the list **myList.**

in a constructor. We assume the class constant DEFAULT_SIZE is assigned some arbitrary integer. Notice that we first create an array of Object and then typecast it to an array of E, the type parameter. This is necessary because it is not allowed to create an array of generic type.

add

Adding an element at the end of the list can be achieved very easily. We add a new element at the count position and increment the count by 1. The only complication is the overflow condition. The expand method is used to handle the overflow condition. We detect the overflow condition when the value for count is equal to the length of the element array. Here's the version 1 add method:

```
public void add(E item) {

    if (count == element.length) {

        expand( );
    }

    element[count] = item;
    count++;
}
```

See the full source code listing at the end of this section for the **expand** method.

Instead of implementing the first add method explicitly as shown, we can implement it by simply calling the second add method as

```
public void add(E item) {

    add(count, item);
}
```

because the value of count is also the index position of the next available slot in the array, i.e., the end of the list, to add an item.

Now, let's see how we can implement the second version of the add method. To insert an element at position i, we must shift current elements at positions i to count-1 one position to the right to positions i+1, . . . , count, respectively. If an invalid value is given for the position, then an index out-of-bound exception is thrown. Here's the method:

```
public void add(int index, E item)
                    throws IndexOutOfBoundsException {

    checkInsertPosition(index, size());

    if (count == element.length) {
        expand( );
    }

    //shift one position to the right
    for (int i = count; i > index; i--) {
        element[i] = element[i-1];
    }

    element[index] = item;
    count++;
}
```

The private method checkInsertPosition verifies the validity of index. If it is outside the valid range, an IndexOutOfBoundsException is thrown. The method is defined as follows:

```
private void checkInsertPosition(int index) {

   if (index < 0) {

      throw new IndexOutOfBoundsException(
               "Negative index of " + index +
                " is invalid");

   } else if (index > size()) {

      throw new IndexOutOfBoundsException(index +
               " is larger than valid upper bound" +
               size());
   }
}
```

The size method returns the number of elements in the list (the method is defined at the end of this section).

clear

We will set element[i] to null, where i = 0, . . ., count-1, so the objects referenced by element[i] will be garbage-collected. We will then reset the count variable to 0.

```
public void clear( ) {

   for (int i = 0; i < count; i++) {
      element[i] = null;
   }

   count = 0;
}
```

contains

We implement this method by using the indexOf method. If the indexOf method returns a value other than NOT_FOUND (-1), then the specified object is in the list, so the contains method returns true. If the indexOf method returns NOT_FOUND, then the contains method returns false.

```
public boolean contains(E item) {

   boolean result = true;

   int loc = indexOf(item);

   if (loc == NOT_FOUND) {
      result = false;
   }

   return result;
}
```

NOT_FOUND is a class constant.

get

Because we are using an array, this method is straightforward. All we have to do is to return an object at position index of the element array, after confirming that the value for index is valid. Here's the method:

```
public E get(int index) throws IndexOutOfBoundsException {
   checkAccessPosition(index);
   return element[index];
}
```

The private method checkAccessPosition ensures that the given index specifies a valid position for accessing an element. If it is outside the valid range, an IndexOutOfBoundsException is thrown. Here's the method:

```
private void checkAccessPosition(int index) {
   if (size() == 0) {
      throw new IndexOutOfBoundsException(
       "Index " + index + " is invalid. List is empty.");
   } else if (index < 0) {
      throw new IndexOutOfBoundsException(
            "Negative index of " + index +
             " is invalid");
   } else if (index > size()-1) {
      throw new IndexOutOfBoundsException(index +
            " is larger than valid upper bound" +
            (size()-1));
   }
}
```

indexOf

This method scans the list from the beginning and stops when the first match is located. If the specified object is not in the list, then NOT_FOUND (-1) is returned. For this method to work properly, the elements in the list must support the equals method, which we will use to locate the matching element.

```
public int indexOf(E item) {
   int loc = 0;
   while (loc < count && !element[loc].equals(item)) {
      loc++;
   }
   if (loc == count) {
      loc = NOT_FOUND;
   }
   return loc;
}
```

isEmpty

This method is also straightforward. We just check the value of the count variable.

```
public boolean isEmpty( ) {

   return (count == 0);
}
```

remove

After the element at position i is removed, we must shift current elements at positions i+1 to count one position to the left, to positions i, . . . , count-1, respectively. And, we decrement the count variable by 1.

```
public E remove(int index)
              throws IndexOutOfBoundsException {

   checkAccessPosition(index);

   E item = element[index];

   //shift one position to the left
   for (int i = index; i < count; i++) {
      element[i] = element[i+1];
   }

   element[count] = null;
   count--;

   return item;
}
```

The second version of remove requires a routine to find the index of the item to be removed. Once we get the index of an object to remove, we call the first remove method to remove it. If there are any duplicates, then only the first match is removed. If the passed item is not found, then nothing happens.

```
public boolean remove(E item) {

   int loc = indexOf(item);

   if (loc == NOT_FOUND) {

      return false;

   } else {

      remove(loc);

      return true;
   }
}
```

set

The set method replaces an object at the specified index position with the passed object. If the index is invalid, an index out-of-bound error is thrown. If the operation is successful, then the method returns the previous object in the index position.

```
public E set(int index, E item)
        throws IndexOutOfBoundsException {

    checkAccessPosition(index);

    E old = element[index];

    element[index] = item;

    return old;
}
```

size

This method is straightforward. We simply return the value of the count variable.

```
public int size( ) {

    return count;
}
```

We are now ready to list the complete NPSArrayList class. In the source code listing, we do not show any javadoc comments in order to keep the listing to a manageable size. The actual source code includes the full javadoc comments.

NPSArrayList

```
package edu.nps.util;

public class NPSArrayList<E> implements NPSList<E> {

    public static final int DEFAULT_SIZE = 25;

    public static final int NOT_FOUND = -1;

    private E[] element;

    private int count;

    public NPSArrayList( ) {
        this(DEFAULT_SIZE);
    }

    public NPSArrayList(int size) {

        if (size <= 0) {
            throw new IllegalArgumentException(
                            "Initial capacity must be positive" );
        }

        element = (E[]) new Object[size];
        count   = 0;
    }
```

Constructors

```
public void add(E item) {

    if (count == element.length) {
        expand( );
    }

    element[count] = item;
    count++;
}

public void add(int index, E item) throws IndexOutOfBoundsException {

    checkInsertPosition(index);

    if (count == element.length) {
        expand( );
    }

    //shift one position to the right
    for (int i = count; i > index; i--) {
        element[i] = element[i-1];
    }

    element[index] = item;
    count++;
}

public void clear( ) {

    for(int i = 0; i < count; i++) {
        element[i] = null;
    }

    count = 0;
}

public boolean contains(E item) {

    boolean result = true;

    int loc = indexOf(item);

    if (loc == NOT_FOUND) {
        result = false;
    }

    return result;
}

public E get(int index) throws IndexOutOfBoundsException {

    checkAccessPosition(index);

    return element[index];
}
```

add

add

clear

contains

get

```
public int indexOf(E item) {

    int loc = 0;

    while (loc < count && !element[loc].equals(item)) {
        loc++;
    }

    if (loc == count) {
        loc = NOT_FOUND;
    }

    return loc;
}

public boolean isEmpty( ) {

    return (count == 0);
}

public E remove(int index) throws IndexOutOfBoundsException {

    checkAccessPosition(index);

    E item = element[index];

    //shift one position to the left
    for (int i = index; i < count; i++) {
        element[i] = element[i+1];
    }

    element[count] = null;
    count--;

    return item;
}

public boolean remove(E item) {

    int loc = indexOf(item);

    if (loc == NOT_FOUND) {

        return false;

    } else {

        remove(loc);

        return true;
    }
}

public E set(int index, E item) throws IndexOutOfBoundsException {

    checkAccessPosition(index);
```

indexOf

isEmpty

remove

remove

set

```
        E old = element[index];

        element[index] = item;

        return old;
    }

    public int size( ) {

        return count;
    }

    private void checkAccessPosition(int index) {

       if (size() == 0) {

        throw new IndexOutOfBoundsException(
          "Index " + index + " is invalid. List is empty.");

       } else if (index < 0) {

          throw new IndexOutOfBoundsException("Negative index of" + index +
                                              "is invalid");

       } else if (index > size()-1) {

          throw new IndexOutOfBoundsException(index +
                                          "is larger than valid upper bound" +
                                          (size()-1));
       }
    }

    private void checkInsertPosition(int index) {

        if (index < 0) {

            throw new IndexOutOfBoundsException(
                        "Negative index of " + index + " is invalid");

        } else if (index > size()) {

            throw new IndexOutOfBoundsException(index +
                        " is larger than valid upper bound" + size());
        }
    }

    private void expand( ) {

        //create a new array whose size is 150% of
        //the current array
        int newLength = (int) (1.5 * element.length);
        E[] temp = (E[]) new Object[newLength];
```

size

checkAccessPosition

checkInsertPosition

expand

```
            //now copy the data to the new array
            for (int i = 0; i < element.length; i++) {
                temp[i] = element[i];
            }

            //finally set the variable entry to point to the new array
            element = temp;
        }
    }
```

18.4 The Linked-List Implementation of the List ADT

With the array implementation, a whole block of memory is allocated at once. When an overflow condition occurs, a new larger block of memory is allocated and the contents of the original array are copied to the new array. The original array will eventually get garbage-collected when the data member **element** is set to refer to the new array. Instead of allocating a large block of memory, the linked implementation allocates a small amount of memory that is just large enough for a single element. In general, this finer granularity of memory allocation leads to a more efficient use of memory. These points were discussed in detail in Chapter 16. In this section, we will describe how the linked-list implementation works. Figure 18.12 illustrates the linked implementation of a list.

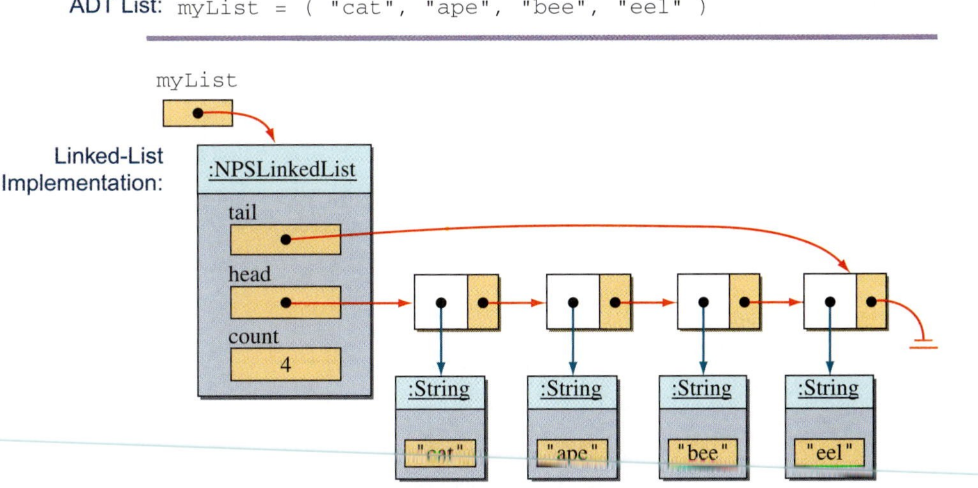

Figure 18.12 A linked-list implementation of the list **myList.**

The ListNode Class

Figure 18.13 compares the array implementation and the linked implementation. With the array implementation, these references are grouped together, occupying the contiguous memory location. Each reference is accessed by the index value of the array position. As detailed in Chapter 16, with the linked-list implementation, they are individually allocated. Since they do not occupy any contiguous memory locations, they must be linked to form a chain for us to be able access them.

We define a class named ListNode to represent the pair of references. We often use the term *link* or *pointer* for the second reference that points to another list node. To distinguish the two different types of references, we use a blue arrow for the first reference and a red arrow for the link. Each node will be represented by a single ListNode object. The ListNode class has two data members, and the class is declared as follows (the generic parameter E is declared in the NPSLinkedList class):

```
class ListNode {

   private E item;

   private ListNode next;

   public ListNode(E item) {
      this.item = item;
      this.next = null;
   }
}
```

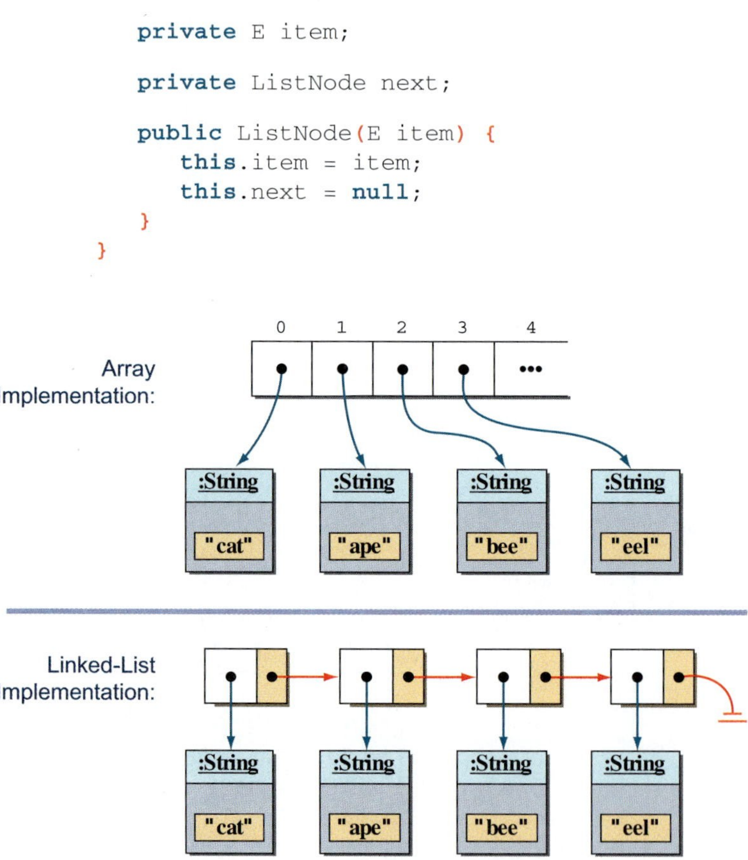

Figure 18.13 The structural difference between the array and linked-list implementations.

The NPSLinkedList Class

Similar to the NPSArrayList class, we need an int variable to keep track of the number of elements currently in the list. In addition, we use two references: one points to the first node, and the other points to the last node. The reference to the last node allows us to add a new node at the end of the list quickly. Without it, we have to traverse the links from the head to locate the last node. These data members are declared as

```
private ListNode head;
private ListNode tail;
private int      count;
```

and initialized as

```
head = null;
tail = null;

count = 0;
```

in a constructor (the actual constructor calls the clear method, which resets the list as an empty list by executing the above three statements).

add

Let's start with the first version. There are two cases we need to consider when adding an element at the end of the list. The first case involves adding an element to an empty list. Figure 18.14 illustrates this case. Both head and tail are null when the list is empty. When a node is added to an empty list, this node is both the first and last node of the list, so both head and tail are set to point to this newly added node. This is the end case.

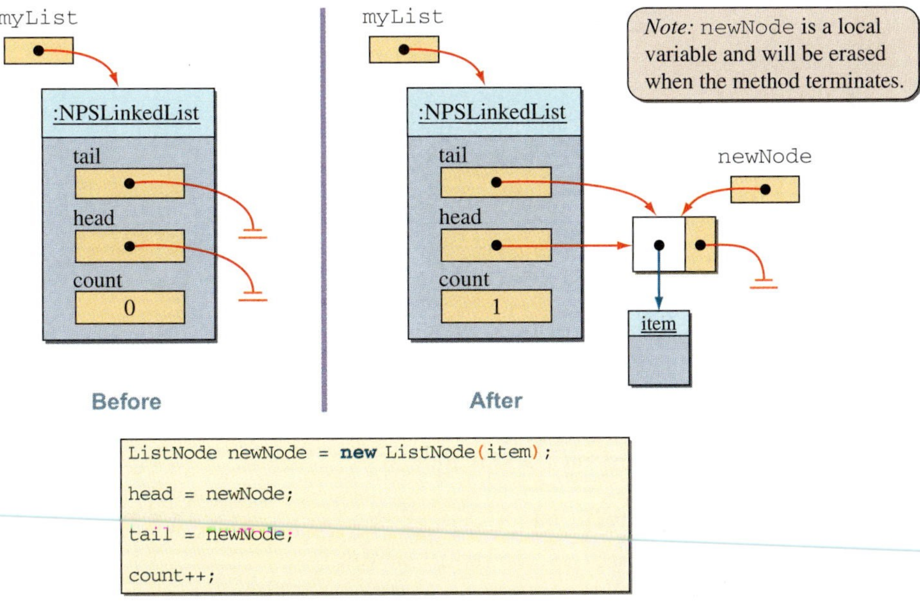

Figure 18.14 Adding an element at the end of an empty list.

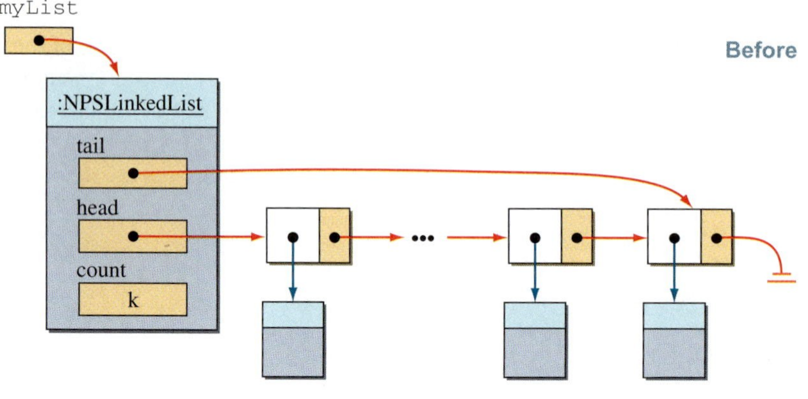

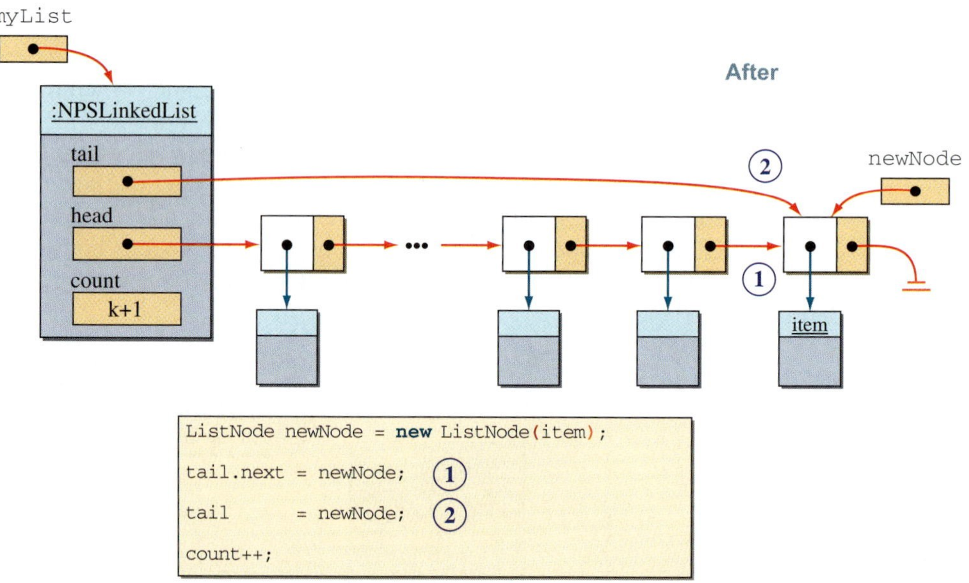

Figure 18.15 The general case of adding an element at the end of a list.

In the general case, where the list has one or more nodes, a newly added node is added at the end, so this new added node becomes the new tail node of the list. The pointer from the tail node before the addition is set to point to the new tail node after the addition. Figure 18.15 illustrates the general case.

Here's the version 1 add method:

```
public void add(E item) {

    //creates a new ListNode
    ListNode newNode = new ListNode(item);

    if (isEmpty()) {

        head = tail = newNode;
```

```
        } else {

            tail.next = newNode;
            tail = newNode;
        }

        count++;
    }
```

As was the case with the NPSArrayList class, we implemented the method explicitly to illustrate clearly the thinking process behind the operation, but we can actually implement it succinctly by calling the second version as follows:

```
public void add(E item) {

    add(count, item);
}
```

Now, let's see how we can implement the second version of the add method. Again, we have to handle the two cases separately. The end case occurs when the new node is added as the first element, that is, index == 0. In this case we have to adjust the head to point to the newly added node and the link field of this new node to point to the node that was the first node before the addition. Figure 18.16 illustrates this case.

In the general case, we must locate the position to insert the new node as the ith node. Unlike the array implementation, where we can locate an element at position i by simply using an indexed expression, in the case of linked implementation we must traverse the pointers in the linked fields. To insert a new node as the ith node in the list (the first node being the 0 node), we need a pointer to the i-1st node. Once we locate this node, the rest is a matter of adjusting two link fields. Figure 18.17 illustrates the general case.

Here's the complete definition for the second version of the add method:

```
public void add(int index, E item)
        throws IndexOutOfBoundsException {

    checkInsertPosition(index);

    ListNode ptr = head;

    ListNode newNode = new ListNode(item);

    if (index == 0) { //adding the new node as
                      // the first node

        newNode.next = head;
        head = newNode;

    } else {
        for (int i = 1; i < index; i++) {
            ptr = ptr.next;
        }

        newNode.next = ptr.next;
        ptr.next     = newNode;
    }
```

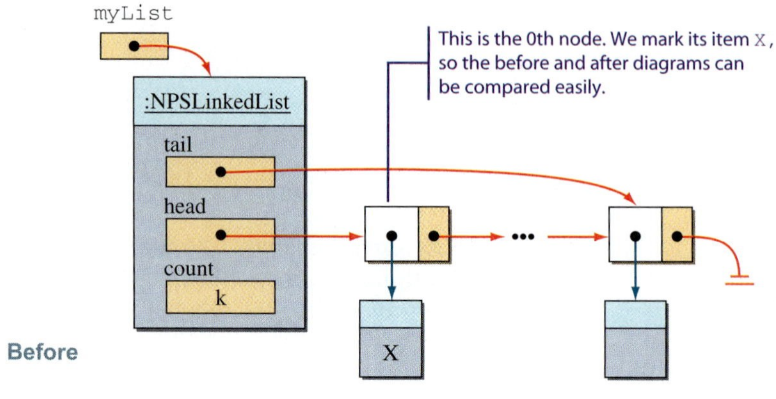

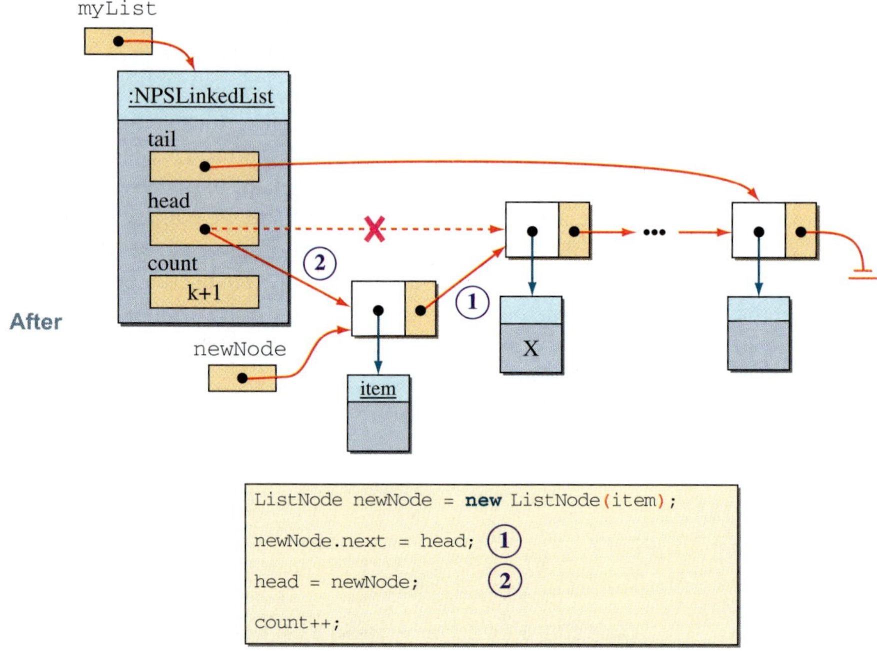

Figure 18.16 The second version of **add** with **index == 0,** i.e., adding an element as the first node in a list.

```
        //adjust tail if the new node added is
        //the last node in the list
        if (index == count) {
            tail = newNode;
        }

        count++;
    }
```

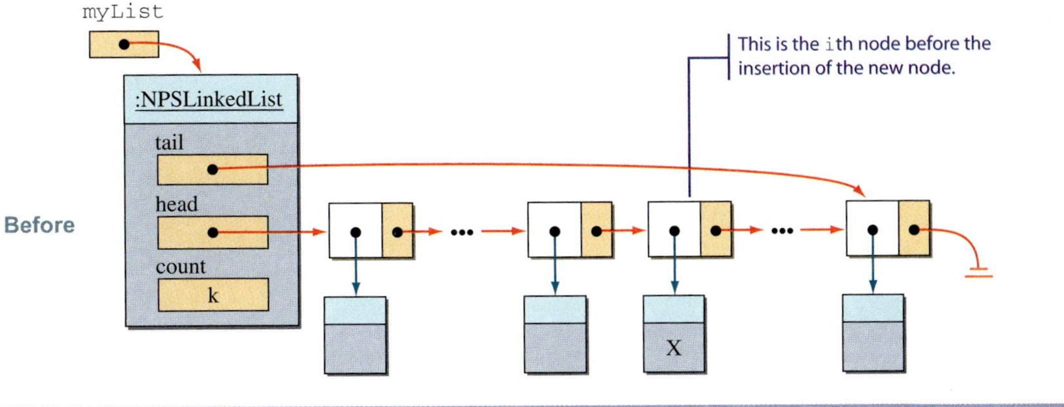

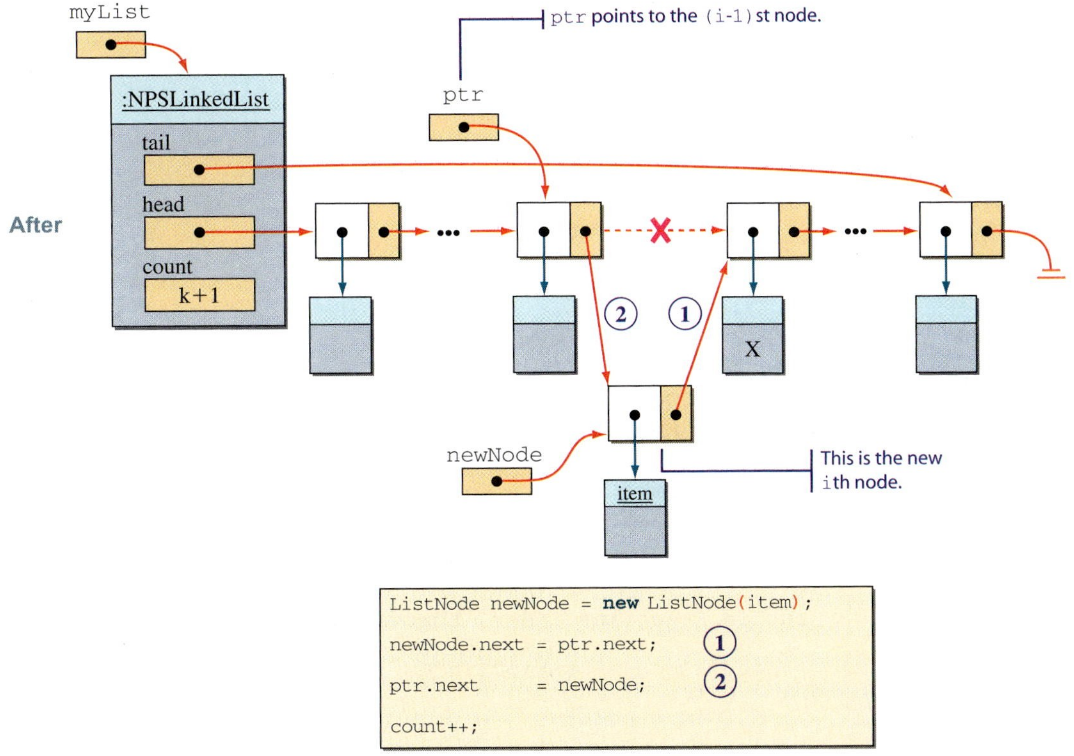

Figure 18.17 The general case of adding a new node as the **i**th node.

Notice the last if statement in the method. If the newly added node is the last node after the insertion, then we must adjust the tail pointer. We know that the newly added node is the last node if its index is equal to count. If the test is true, then we set tail to point to the new node.

clear

The clear method empties the list; that is, it resets the list as an empty list. Its implementation is straightforward. We reset head and tail to null and count to 0. By setting head to null, all the nodes in the list will eventually get garbage-collected. Here's the method:

```
public void clear( ) {

   head = tail = null;

   count = 0;
}
```

contains

The contains method is implemented by using the indexOf method. If the indexOf method returns a value other than NOT_FOUND (-1), then the specified object is in the list, so the contains method returns true. If the indexOf method returns NOT_FOUND, then the contains method returns false.

```
public boolean contains(E item) {

   boolean result = true;

   int loc = indexOf(item);

   if (loc == NOT_FOUND) {
      result = false;
   }

   return result;
}
```

get

The get method for the linked implementation requires the traversing of link fields to locate the desired node. After checking that the passed index value is valid, the method traverses the pointers. The traversing is essentially the same as we did for the second version of the add method. The only difference is that we are setting the pointer ptr to point to the index node, not to the index-1st node, as was the case with the add method. Here's the method:

This loop traverses the list by following the link field for *index* times.

```
public E get(int index) throws IndexOutOfBoundsException {

   checkAccessPosition(index);

   E item = null;

   ListNode ptr = head;

   for (int i = 0; i < index; i++) {
      ptr = ptr.next;
   }

   item = ptr.item;

   return item;
}
```

indexOf

The indexOf method traverses the pointers from head and stops when the first match is located. The counter loc is incremented every time the next node is visited. If the specified object is not in the list, then NOT_FOUND (-1) is returned.

```
public int indexOf(E item) {

   int loc = 0;

   ListNode ptr = head;

   while (loc < count && !ptr.item.equals(item)) {
      loc++;
      ptr = ptr.next;
   }

   if (loc == count) {
      loc = NOT_FOUND;
   }

   return loc;
}
```

Be careful that the order of operands in the while test is critical. We cannot write it as

INVALID ⟶
```
while (!ptr.item.equals(item) && loc < count) {
```

because doing so would result in a NullPointerException error in the case where the searched item is not found (i.e., when loc becomes equal to count, ptr is null).

isEmpty

The isEmpty method is simple. We just check the value of the count variable.

```
public boolean isEmpty( ) {

   return (count == 0);
}
```

remove

For the first version of remove, we must locate the i-1st node. Once this node is located, all that is left to do is to adjust this node's next field. Unlike in the array implementation, no shifting is necessary. This is one advantage of the linked implementation. On the other hand, with the array implementation, there's no search is involved, while the linked implemention requires the traversal of links to locate the i-1st node. Figure 18.18 illustrates the operation for the general case. There are end cases we need to watch out for: First, when the node we are removing is the last node in the list, we must adjust the tail pointer to point to the new last node after the removal. Second, when the node we are removing is the first node, then we must adjust the head pointer. If this first node is the only node in the list, then we must also adjust the tail pointer. If we are removing the

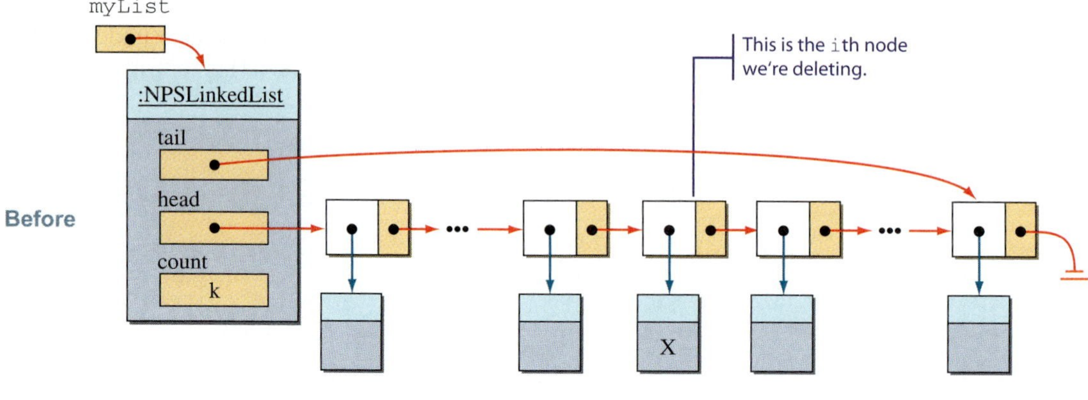

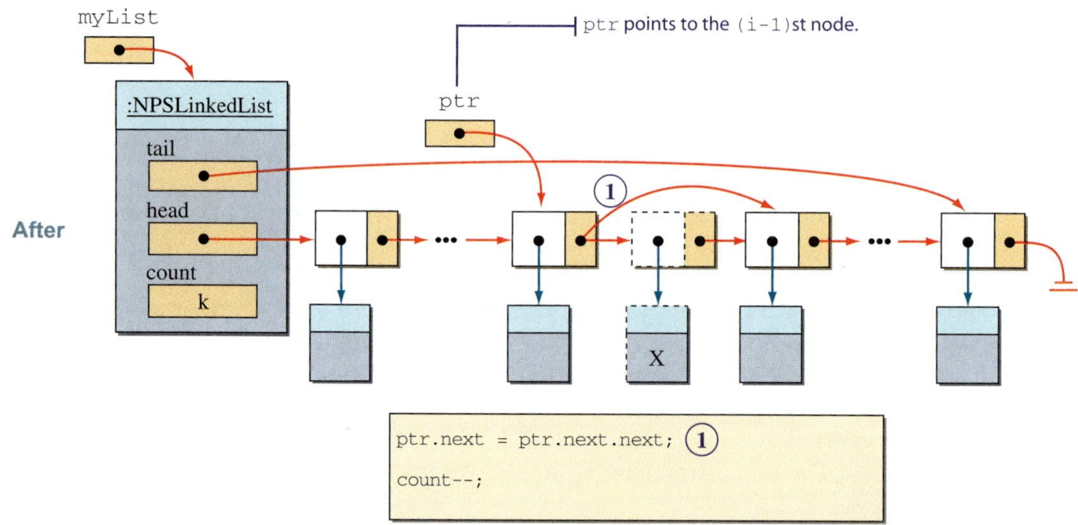

Figure 18.18 The first version of the **remove** operation. Remove the **i**th node given the value **i.**

only node in the list (both head and tail point to this node), the net result is that both head and tail become null.

```
public E remove(int index)
                    throws IndexOutOfBoundsException {

    checkAccessPosition(index);

    ListNode deleteNode;

    ListNode ptr = head;

    if (index == 0) { //removing the first node

        deleteNode = ptr;

        head = head.next;
```

```
            if (head == null) { //the first node is
                                //the only node

               tail = null;
            }

         } else {

            for (int i = 1; i < index; i++) {
               ptr = ptr.next;
            }

            deleteNode = ptr.next;

            ptr.next = deleteNode.next;

            if (ptr.next == null) { //very last node was removed
               tail = ptr;          //we have a new last node
            }
         }

         count--;

         return deleteNode.item;
      }
```

The second version of remove requires a traversal to locate the node to be removed. If there are duplicates, then the first match is removed. If the passed item is not found, then nothing happens. To locate the desired node, we use two pointers: ptr and trail. The ptr will point to the node to be removed, and the trail will point to the node one before the ptr node. In other words, the following relationship holds between the two:

```
trail.next == ptr
```

As with the first version, we must watch out for the end cases of removing the first node, the last node, or the only node. Here's the second remove method:

```
public boolean remove(E item) {

   boolean result = false;

   ListNode ptr = head;
   ListNode trail = null;

   while (ptr != null && !ptr.item.equals(item)) {

      trail = ptr;
      ptr   = ptr.next;
   }

   if (ptr != null) { //found item

      if (trail == null) { //removing the first node

         head = head.next;
```

```
            if (head == null) { //the first node is
                                //the only node
               tail = null;
            }

         } else {

            trail.next = ptr.next;

            if (trail.next == null) { //very last node was
               tail = trail;          //removed, so set tail to
                                      //point to a new last node
            }
         }

         count--;

         result=true;
      }

         return result;
   }
```

set

After checking that the passed index value is valid, the set method traverses the list index times and sets the pointer ptr to the node to be modified. Once this node is located, its data field is set to refer to the passed item.

```
public E set(int index, E item) {

   checkAccessPosition(index);

   ListNode ptr = head;

   for (int i = 0; i < index; i++) {
      ptr = ptr.next;
   }

   E old = ptr.item;

   ptr.item = item;

   return old;
}
```

size

This method is easy (for a change). We simply return the value of the count variable.

```
public int size( ) {

   return count;
}
```

We are now ready to list the complete NPSLinkedList class. In the source code listing, we do not show any javadoc comments, to keep the listing to a manageable size. The actual source code includes the full javadoc comments.

NPSLinkedList

```
package edu.nps.util;

public class NPSLinkedList<E> implements NPSList<E> {

   public static final int NOT_FOUND = -1;

   private ListNode head;

   private ListNode tail;

   private int count;

   public NPSLinkedList( ) {                                    Constructor

      clear( );
   }

   public void add(E item) {                                    add

      //creates a new ListNode
      ListNode newNode = new ListNode(item);

      if (count == 0) {

         head = tail = newNode;

      } else {

         tail.next = newNode;
         tail = newNode;
      }

      count++;
   }

   public void add(int index, E item) throws IndexOutOfBoundsException {

      checkInsertPosition(index);                               add

      ListNode ptr = head;

      ListNode newNode = new ListNode(item);

      if (index == 0) { //adding the new node as the first node

         newNode.next = head;
         head = newNode;

      } else {
```

```
            for (int i = 1; i < index; i++) {
                ptr = ptr.next;
            }

            newNode.next = ptr.next;
            ptr.next     = newNode;
        }

        //adjust tail if the new node added is
        //the last node in the list
        if (index == count) {
            tail = newNode;
        }

        count++;
    }

    public void clear( ) {

        head  = tail = null;

        count = 0;
    }

    public boolean contains(E item) {

        boolean result = true;

        int loc = indexOf(item);

        if (loc == NOT_FOUND) {
            result = false;
        }

        return result;
    }

    public E get(int index) throws IndexOutOfBoundsException {

        checkAccessPosition(index);

        E item = null;

        ListNode ptr = head;

        for (int i = 0; i < index; i++) {
           ptr = ptr.next;
        }

        item = ptr.item;

        return item;
    }

    public int indexOf(E item) {

        int loc = 0;
```

clear

contains

get

indexOf

```
        ListNode ptr = head;

        while (loc < count && !ptr.item.equals(item)) {

            loc++;
            ptr = ptr.next;
        }

        if (loc == count) {
            loc = NOT_FOUND;
        }

        return loc;
    }

    public boolean isEmpty( ) {

        return (count == 0);
    }

    public E remove(int index) throws IndexOutOfBoundsException {

        checkAccessPosition(index);

        ListNode deleteNode;

        ListNode ptr = head;

        if (index == 0) { //removing the first node

            deleteNode = ptr;

            head = head.next;

            if (head == null) { //the first node is the only node
                tail = null;
            }

        } else {

            for (int i = 1; i < index; i++) {
                ptr = ptr.next;
            }

            deleteNode = ptr.next;

            ptr.next = deleteNode.next;

            if (ptr.next == null) { //very last node was removed
                tail = ptr;         //we have a new last node
            }
        }

        count--;

        return deleteNode.item;
    }
```

isEmpty

remove

remove

```
public boolean remove(E item) {

    boolean result = false;

    ListNode ptr = head;
    ListNode trail = null;

    while (ptr != null && !ptr.item.equals(item)) {

        trail = ptr;
        ptr   = ptr.next;
    }

    if (ptr != null) { //found item

        if (trail == null) { //removing the first node

            head = head.next;

            if (head == null) { //the first node is the only node
                tail = null;
            }

        } else {

            trail.next = ptr.next;

            if (trail.next == null) { //very last node was removed, so
                tail = trail;         //set tail to point to a new
                                        last node
            }
        }

        count--;

        result = true;
    }

    return result;
}
```

set

```
public E set(int index, E item) {

    checkAcessPosition(index);

    ListNode ptr = head;

    for (int i = 0; i < index; i++) {
        ptr = ptr.next;
    }

    E old = ptr.item;

    ptr.item = item;

    return old;
}
```

```
    public int size( ) {
        return count;
    }

    private void checkAccessPosition(int index) {
        if (size() == 0) {
            throw new IndexOutOfBoundsException(
            "Index " + index + " is invalid. List is empty.");
        } else if (index < 0) {
            throw new IndexOutOfBoundsException("Negative index of " + index +
                                                " is invalid");
        } else if (index > size()-1) {
            throw new IndexOutOfBoundsException(index +
                                            " is larger than valid upper bound" +
                                            (size()-1));
        }
    }

    private void checkInsertPosition(int index) {
        if (index < 0) {
            throw new IndexOutOfBoundsException(
                        "Negative index of " + index + " is invalid");
        } else if (index > size()) {
            throw new IndexOutOfBoundsException(index +
                        " is larger than valid upper bound" + size());
        }
    }

    // Inner Class: ListNode
    class ListNode {
        private E  item;
        private ListNode next;
        public ListNode(E item) {
            this.item = item;
            this.next = null;
        }
    }
}
```

size

checkAccessPosition

checkInsertPosition

ListNode

18.5 The Linked Implementation with the Head Node

end cases

In both versions of the add and remove methods of the linked implementation, we have to include a test to determine the special case of removing the first node because we need to treat the removal of the first node differently from the other general cases. The special cases are also called ***end cases*** or ***boundary cases.*** Consider the case of removal: If we are dealing with a large list, we do not expect the removal of the first node to happen frequently in ordinary applications. Yet, every time we remove a node we must test if it is the removal of the first node. It is not efficient to check every time for something that rarely occurs. Can we do something about it? Is there a way to eliminate this testing?

The technique we can use to eliminate the testing of the end case is to insert one extra "dummy" node at the head of a list. By including this head node, one set of code can be used to handle both the end and general cases. Figure 18.19 shows the lists with the head node.

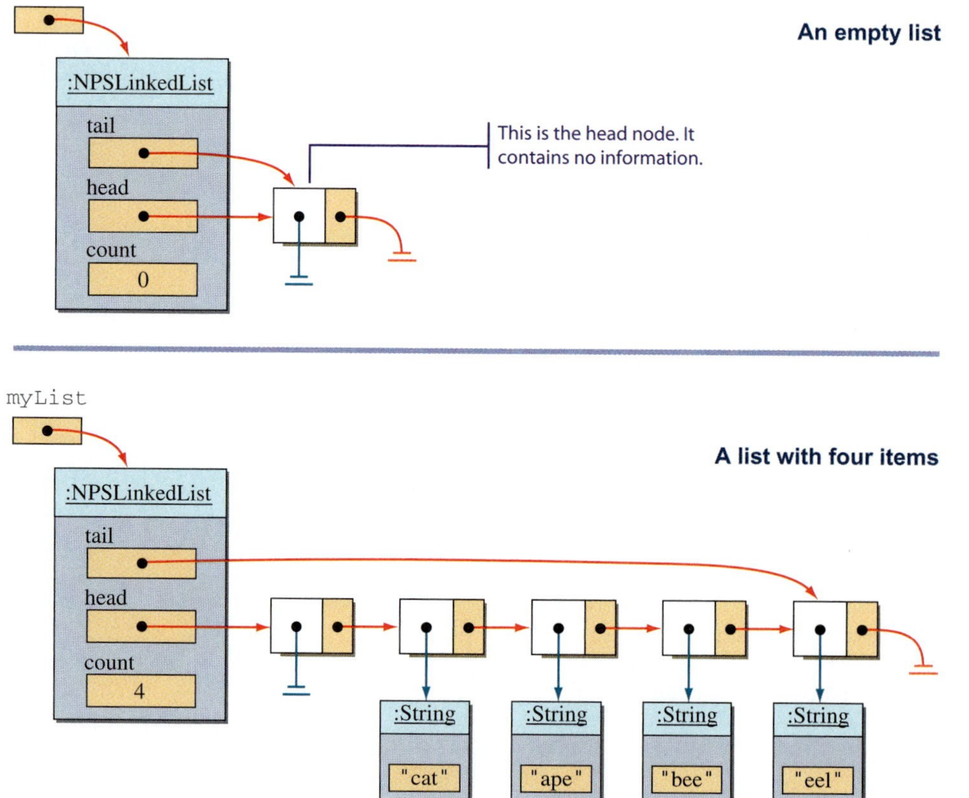

Figure 18.19 Sample linked lists with the head node.

With the head node in a list, version 1 remove can be written as follows:

```
public E remove(int index)
                    throws IndexOutOfBoundsException {

   checkAccessPosition(index);

   ListNode deleteNode;

   ListNode trail = head;

   for (int i = 0; i <= index; i++) {
      trail = trail.next;
   }

   deleteNode = trail.next;
   trail.next = deleteNode.next;

   if (deleteNode.next == null) { //very last node was
      tail = trail;               //removed so set tail
                                  //to the new last node
   }

   count--;

   return deleteNode.item;
}
```

Compare this remove to the corresponding method of the NPSLinkedList class. The other remove method and the two versions of the add method can be improved in a similar manner. Here is the NPSLinkedListWithHeader class (the methods that remain the same as those in NPSLinkedList are not listed here).

NPSLinkedListWithHeader

```
package edu.nps.util;

public class NPSLinkedListWithHeader<E> implements NPSList<E> {

    public static final int NOT_FOUND = -1;

    private ListNode head;

    private ListNode tail;

    private int count;

    public NPSLinkedListWithHeader( ) {

        ListNode headNode = new ListNode(null);

        head  = headNode;
        tail  = headNode;

        count = 0;
    }
```

Note:
The methods that remain the same as those in **NPSLinkedList** are not listed here.

Constructor

```
public void add(E item) {

    //creates a new ListNode
    ListNode newNode = new ListNode(item);

    tail.next = newNode;
    tail = newNode;

    count++;
}
```

add

```
public void add(int index, E item) throws IndexOutOfBoundsException {

    checkInsertPosition(index);

    ListNode ptr = head;

    ListNode newNode = new ListNode(item);

    for (int i = 0; i < index; i++) {
        ptr = ptr.next;
    }

    newNode.next = ptr.next;
    ptr.next     = newNode;

    //adjust tail if the new node added is
    //the last node in the list
    if (index == count) {
        tail = newNode;
    }

    count++;
}
```

add

```
public void clear( ) {

    head.next = null; //don't remove the dummy head node
    tail = head;

    count = 0;
}
```

clear

```
public E get(int index) {

    checkAccessPosition(index);

    ListNode ptr = head.next;

    for (int i = 0; i < index; i++) {
        ptr = ptr.next;
    }

    return ptr.item;
}
```

get

```
public int indexOf(E item) {

    int loc = 0;

    ListNode ptr = head.next;

    while (loc < count && !ptr.item.equals(item)) {
        loc++;
        ptr = ptr.next;
    }

    if (loc == count) {
        loc = NOT_FOUND;
    }

    return loc;
}

public E remove(int index) throws IndexOutOfBoundsException {

    checkAcessPosition(index);

    ListNode deleteNode;

    ListNode trail = head;

    for (int i = 0; i <= index; i++) {
       trail = trail.next;
    }

    deleteNode = trail.next;
    trail.next = deleteNode.next;

    if (deleteNode.next == null) { //very last node was
       tail = trail;               //removed so set tail
                                 //to the new last node

    }

    count--;

    return deleteNode.item;
}

public boolean remove(E item) {

    boolean result = false;

    ListNode ptr   = head.next;
    ListNode trail = head;

    while (ptr != null && !ptr.item.equals(item)) {

        trail = ptr;
        ptr   = ptr.next;
    }
```

indexOf

remove

remove

```
        if (ptr != null) {
            trail.next = ptr.next;

            if (trail.next == null) { //very last node was removed
                 tail = trail;          //we have a new last node
            }

            Count--;

            result = true;
        }

        return result;
    }

    public E set(int index, E item) {

        checkAccessPosition(index);

        ListNode ptr = head.next;

        for (int i = 0; i < index; i++) {
            ptr = ptr.next;
        }

        E old = ptr.item;

        ptr.item = item;

        return old;
    }

    . . .
}
```

set

18.6 The Iterator Design Pattern

traversal

One of the most common operations we perform on a data structure, including the linear list, is a ***traversal***. Traversing a data structure means visiting, or accessing, every element in the data structure. For example, if a data structure contains Person objects and we want to find out their average age, we have to visit every Person object in the data structure to derive the sum of their ages and then divide the sum by the total number of elements.

Traversing a complex data structure can be complicated because there could be many different ways to visit elements. For a simpler data structure, such as the linear list, however, traversal is straightforward. We visit the elements in sequence: visit the first element, the second element, and so forth. Here's a sample code for traversing Person objects in a list to compute their average:

```
NPSList<Person> personList;

//Assume personList is created and includes
//Person objects; for simplicity we assume
//the list includes at least one element

double ageSum, avgAge;

ageSum = 0;

for (int i = 0; i < personList.size(); i++) {

   Person p = personList.get(i);

   ageSum += p.getAge();
}

avgAge = ageSum / personList.size();
```

What would be the cost of such a traversal operation? It depends on the implementation. With the array implementation, the cost of accessing every element in the list is N, but with the linked-list implementation, the cost is $(N^2 + N)/2$. Let's see why there is such an order-of-magnitude difference. The cost of the get method in the array implementation is the same regardless of the location of an element, because any element in an array can be accessed by applying the same address computation formula. How about the get method of the linked implementation? To access the ith element, we must traverse the links i times, starting from the head node, so the cost is i. Assuming that the cost of following a link and the cost of address computation are the same, we can derive the total cost for scanning as follows: $\sum_{i=1}^{N} 1 = N$ for the array implementation and $\sum_{i=1}^{N} i = (N^2 + N)/2$ for the linked implementation.

Since traversal is a frequently used operation, it is worth the effort to improve its performance. We would like to improve the performance of the linked-list implementation to the level of the array implementation, that is, from $(N^2 + N)/2$ to N. We can do so by applying the technique known as the iterator design pattern. An *iterator* is a design pattern that supports a consistent way to access the elements stored in a data structure. We define an iterator as an ADT that supports two operations—the first to prompt if there are more elements to visit and the second to retrieve the next element to visit. Here's the interface definition for the ADT:

iterator

NPSIterator

```
package edu.nps.util;

interface NPSIterator<E> {

    public boolean hasNext( );

    public E next( ) throws NPSNoSuchElementException;
}
```

The hasNext method returns true if there are more elements in the iterator. The next method returns the next object in the iterator if there is one. Otherwise, it throws an NPSNoSuchElementException. This exception class is patterned after the NoSuchElementException class in the java.util package. We avoid using classes and interfaces from the java.util package in our edu.nps.util package to make it self-contained. We do not want to require client programmers to import the java.util package also when using the edu.nps.util package.

We add a method, named iterator, to the NPSList interface that returns an iterator. With the iterator method, we can compute the average age of Person objects in a list as follows:

```
NPSList<Person> personList;

//Assume personList is created and includes
//Person objects; for simplicity we assume
//the list includes at least one element

double ageSum, avgAge;

ageSum = 0;

NPSIterator itr = personList.iterator();

while (itr.hasNext()) {

   Person p = itr.next();

   ageSum += p.getAge();
}

avgAge = ageSum / personList.size();
```

Let's first modify the NPSLinkedList class to include the iterator method. Notice that NPSIterator is an interface, so the iterator method must return an instance of a class that implements this interface. The best way to achieve this is to define an inner class that implements the NPSIterator interface inside the NPSLinkedList class. In this inner class, we keep a data member current that keeps track of the node whose item value we return when the next method is called. Every time the next method is called, we update the current pointer to the next node in the list. When the next method is called and the current points to the last node in the list, the updated current becomes null, and the next time the hasNext method is called, it returns false.

Here's how we define the modified class:

NPSLinkedList (final version)

```
package edu.nps.util;

public class NPSLinkedList<E> implements NPSList<E> {

    ...
```

```
    public NPSIterator iterator( ) {

        return new MyIterator(head);
    }

    . . .

    //-----Inner Class: MyIterator -------------//
    private class MyIterator implements NPSIterator<E> {

        private ListNode current;

        public MyIterator(ListNode node) {

            current = node;
        }

        public boolean hasNext( ) {

            return current != null;
        }

        public E next( ) throws NPSNoSuchElementException {

            if (current == null) {
                throw new NPSNoSuchElementException("No more element");
            }

            Object item = current.item;

            current = current.next;

            return item;
        }
    }
}
```

Notice that the type parameter is not specified for the inner class MyIterator. It is invalid to declare the inner class as

INVALID

```
private class MyIterator<E> implements NPSIterator<E> {
```

Doing so would conflict with the type parameter of the outer class NPSLinkedList. With this invalid declaration, E in the inner class and E in the outer class would be viewed as referring to two different actual types. By not associating any type parameter to MyIterator, the generic type E in the inner and outer classes refers to the same actual type.

The NPSNoSuchElementException class is a very simple class. Here's the definition:

NPSNoSuchElementException

```
package edu.nps.util;

public class NPSNoSuchElementException extends RuntimeException {

    public NPSNoSuchElementException( ) {

        this("Requested element does not exist in the data structure");
    }

    public NPSNoSuchElementException(String message) {

        super(message);
    }
}
```

Now let's look at how we can implement the iterator method for the NPSArrayList class. We should realize that we are not gaining any performance improvement in doing this, because the cost of calling the get method *N* times, once for each node in the list, to scan the elements in a list is *O*(*N*). But defining the iterator method to the NPSArrayList class gives us a consistent and easy-to-use manner of traversing elements in all types of diverse data structures.

We follow the same approach used in the iterator inner class of NPSLinkedList. This time, however, instead of the current pointer, we maintain an int data member current that keeps track of the index of the current node. We initialize current to 0. The hasNext method returns true if the value of current is less than or equal to the maximum possible index value, i.e., the size of the list minus 1. When the next method is called and the value of current is not less than the size of the list, it throws an exception. Otherwise, the method returns the current element and increments current by 1 so it will point to the next element.

The modified NPSArrayList is defined as follows:

NPSArrayList (final version)

```
package edu.nps.util;

public class NPSArrayList<E> implements NPSList<E> {

    ...

    public NPSIterator iterator( ) {

       return new MyIterator(0);
    }
```

```
        ////---------- Inner Class : MyIterator -------------////
        private class MyIterator implements NPSIterator<E> {

            private int current;

            public MyIterator( ) {
                current = 0;
            }

            public boolean hasNext( ) {

            if (current < size()-1) {
                return true;
            } else {
                return false;
            }
        }

        public E next( ) throws NPSNoSuchElementException {

            if (current >= size()) {
                throw new NPSNoSuchElementException();

            } else {
                int idx = current;     //these three statements can be written
                current++;             //succinctly in a single statement as
                return element[idx]; //return element[current++]
            }
        }
    }
}
```

18.7 Sample Development

Fortune Cookies

Let's write a simple application that illustrates the use of a list. The program will display a fortune cookie, a short text message, when requested by the user. Since each fortune cookie is a string, we maintain a database of fortune cookies using a list ADT.

Problem Statement

Write a program that displays a fortune cookie (text message) every time the user wishes it. Repeatedly prompt the user if he or she wishes to read another fortune cookie. If the reply is yes, display it. If the reply is no, terminate the program. Assume there is a text file named fortune.txt that contains text messages. Each line of text represents a single fortune cookie.

18.7 Sample Development—*continued*

Overall Design

Let's begin by identifying the core objects and their tasks. First, we need an object to handle the user interaction. This object can serve as the top-level controller of the program. Second, we need an object to maintain a list of fortune cookies. This object will return a random fortune cookie when requested. And third, we need an object to input fortune cookies from the designated text file.

design document

Design Document: `FortuneCookie`

Class	Purpose
`FortuneCookieMain`	The top-level control object handles the user interaction. This is the instantiable main class.
`FortuneCookieFile`	This class handles the input of text messages for fortune cookies from the designated text file fortune.txt.
`FortuneCookieManager`	This is the core class for this application. It maintains the database of fortune cookies.

Among the several different possibilities, we will establish the class dependencies as follows:

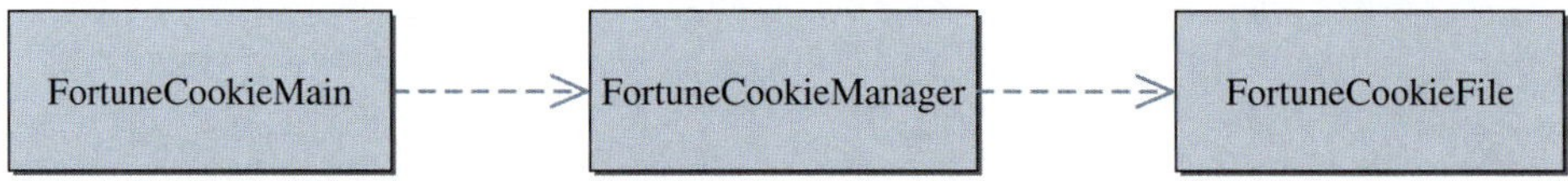

We will implement this program in the following three major steps:

development steps

1. Implement the **FortuneCookieMain** main class. Use a stub **FortuneCookieManager** class.
2. Implement the **FortuneCookieManager** main class. Use a stub **FortuneCookieFile** class.
3. Implement the **FortuneCookieFile** class and finalize the program.

We will present some design ideas for steps 1 and 3, but the actual implementations are left as exercises. These two steps are straightforward, and the related topics are discussed in previous chapters. Our focus for this sample development is step 2.

Step 1 Development: Implement the FortuneCookieMain Class

This step is left as an exercise. You may choose a simplistic console-based user interface or a GUI. In either case, you need to call a method of **FortuneCookieManager** to retrieve the next fortune cookie. We can use a stub for this method. Here's how we could define a temporary **FortuneCookieManager** class.

```
class FortuneCookieManager {

   public FortuneCookieManager( ) {

   }

   public String nextFortune( ) {

      return "Here's your fortune"; //STUB - TEMP
   }
}
```

The interaction from the main class to the manager class is limited to the creation of a manager instance and the repeated calling of the **nextFortune** method.

Step 2 Development: Implement the FortuneCookieManager Class

Step 2 Design

We now replace the temporary **FortuneCookieManager** class with the real one. The manager class will be assisted by the file class **FortuneCookieFile** in reading fortune cookies. This file class will hide all the gory details of file input. The manager class simply needs to call the method **getList** to get a list of strings. Each string in the list represents a single fortune cookie. We set **NPSList** as the return type of this method. We return **null** from the method if there's any problem reading a file. Here's a sample code to retrieve a list:

```
NPSList list;
FortuneCookieFile inputFile;

inputFile = new FortuneCookieFile();

list = inputFile.getList();
```

The temporary **FortuneCookieFile** class can be defined as follows:

```
import edu.nps.util.*;

public class FortuneCookieFile {

    public FortuneCookieFile() {

    }

    public NPSList<String> getList( ) {

        NPSList<String> list = new NPSArrayList<String>();

        list.add("You will lead a happy life");
        list.add("Patience is virtue");
        list.add("Your talent is unbounded and will be" +
                      " rewarded with happiness");
```

```
            list.add("You will live to a ripe old age.");
            list.add("You will graduate with distinction");

            return list;
        }
    }
```

Implementation of the **FortuneCookieManager** class is remarkably simple, thanks to the use of a list. All the hard work is taken care of by the list. We just need one method that returns a fortune cookie and a constructor. Here's the design document:

Design Document: The `FortuneCookieManager` Class		
Method	**Visibility**	**Purpose**
`<constructor>`	`public`	Creates and initializes the data members. Throws an `IOException` when the fortune cookie list cannot be created. This happens, for example, when the specified file is not found or is corrupted.
`nextFortune`	`public`	Returns a randomly selected fortune cookie from the list.

step 2 code

Here's the full code listing:

FortuneCookieManager

```
import java.io.IOException;
import java.util.Random;
import edu.nps.util.NPSList;

public class FortuneCookieManager {

    private NPSList<String> fortunes;

    private Random random;

    private int listSize;

    public FortuneCookieManager( ) throws IOException {

        FortuneCookieFile fortuneFile = new FortuneCookieFile();
        fortunes = fortuneFile.getList();

        if (fortunes == null) {
            throw new IOException();
        }
```

```
        random = new Random();

        listSize = fortunes.size();
    }

    public String nextFortune( ) {

        return fortunes.get(random.nextInt(listSize));
    }
}
```

step 2 test

We run the same main class from step 1 with the fully implemented **FortuneCookie-Manager** class and confirm that the random fortune cookies are displayed before proceeding to the final step.

Step 3 Development: Implement the FortuneCookieFile Class

In this final step, we implement the file class that handles the input of fortune cookies from the designated text file. This step is left as an exercise. The name of the text file is set to *fortune.txt*. To add flexibility to the program, we can pass the name of the text file to open when we create an instance of **FortuneCookieFile.** We also leave this option as an exercise.

Summary

- An abstract data type (ADT) is a mathematical specification of a set of data and the corresponding set of operations performed on those data.
- A list is a linearly ordered collection of elements.
- An array and a linked list are two possible implementations of a List ADT.
- The linked-list implementation with a dummy head node eliminates the testing for the boundary cases.
- The traversal of list members is a very common operation.
- The iterator pattern supports a very efficient traversal operation.
- The use of a list ADT simplifies the program development remarkably as illustrated in the Fortune Cookies sample development.

Key Concepts

abstract data type (ADT)
List ADT
array implementation
linked-list implementation
header node
iterator pattern

Exercises

1. Both NPSArrayList and NPSLinkedList implement the NPSList interface so they behave exactly the same. However, since their implementations are different, the performances of their methods are different. Compare the performances of their add and remove methods. Contrast the amount of time required to locate the position to add or remove the item and the amount of time required to update the structure (shifting the items for the array implementation and chaining of links for the linked implementation).

2. Suppose p1, p2, and p3 are unique instances of the Person class. What would be an output from the following code?

```
Person p1, p2, p3;
p1 = ...;
p2 = ...;
p3 = ...;

NPSList list = new NPSArrayList();

list.add(p1);
list.add(p2);
list.add(p3);
list.add(p2);

System.out.prinlnt("Size of list: " + list.size());
```

3. Add a new method called removeRange

```
public void removeRange(int fromIndex, int toIndex)
```

   that removes elements in the index positions from fromIndex, inclusive, to toIndex, exclusive. Throw an IndexOutOfBoundsException if either fromIndex or toIndex is less than 0 or greater than size( ). Do nothing if fromIndex is greater than or equal to toIndex.

4. Write a method returns a union of two given lists. Assume the two lists contain String objects. There are no duplicates in each of the two input lists. If the two input lists are, for example,

```
("one", "two", "three", "four", "five")
```

   and

```
("one", "five", "zero", "four", "eight")
```

   then their union is

```
("one", "two", "three", "four", "five", "zero", "eight")
```

   The method prototype is as follows:

```
public NPSList<String> union(NPSList<String> list1,
                             NPSList<String> list2)
```

5. Repeat Exercise 4, but this time the method returns the intersection of the two given lists. If the two input lists are, for example,

```
("one", "two", "three", "four", "five")
```

and

```
("one", "five", "zero", "four", "eight")
```

then their intersection is

```
("one", "four", "five")
```

The method prototype is as follows:

```
public NPSList<String> intersect(NPSList<String> list1,
                                 NPSList<String> list2)
```

6. Repeat Exercise 4, but this time the method returns the difference of the two given lists. If the two input lists are, for example,

```
("one", "two", "three", "four", "five")
```

and

```
("one", "five", "zero", "four", "eight")
```

then their intersection is

```
("two", "three", "four")
```

The method prototype is as follows:

```
public NPSList<String> difference (NPSList<String> list1,
                                   NPSList<String> list2)
```

7. Draw a state-of-memory diagram for the list after the following code is executed:

```
NPSList<Integer> list = new NPSLinkedList<Integer>( );

Integer intObj = new Integer(10);

list.add(intObj);
list.add(intObj);
list.add(intObj);
```

8. Write a subclass of NPSLinkedList that does not allow any duplicates in the list. Call this subclass NPSNoDupLinkedList. Elements e1 and e2 are duplicates if e1.equals(e2) is true. Implement the subclass by overriding the two add methods. The modified add methods disallow the insertion of a duplicate. The methods do nothing when a duplicate is passed to them.

9. Repeat Exercise 8, but this time write a subclass of NPSArrayList. Call this subclass NPSNoDupArrayList.

10. Elements in the NPSList are unordered. Define a new interface NPSOrderedList where elements are ordered in ascending order. Elements we add to an

ordered list must be instances of a class that implements the Comparable interface so they can be compared. The methods for the NPSOrderedList interface are essentially the same as those for the NPSList interface, except for the add method that specifies the index position of a newly added element. With the NPSOrderedList interface, there is only one add method that adds an element to the correct position, so the resulting list is ordered. Duplicates are not allowed in the ordered list. Throw an IllegalArgumentException when one attempts to add a duplicate. An element e1 is a duplicate if there is an e2 in the list such that e1.compareTo(e2) == 0. Define only the interface in this exercise. You will be asked to implement the interface in Exercises 11 and 12.

11. Implement the NPSOrderedList interface (see Exercise 10) by using an array. Name this class NPSOrderedArrayList.

12. Implement the NPSOrderedList interface (see Exercise 10) by using a linked list. Name this class NPSOrderedLinkedList.

13. The Iterator interface we presented in the chapter allows you to move in one direction. Define a new interface called TwoWayIterator that allows you to move both forward and backward. When you try to go beyond the first or the last element, throw an NPSNoSuchElementException. You only need to define the interface here. You will define classes that implement this interface in the next two exercises. (Note: This TwoWayIterator interface is inspired by the ListIterator interface in the java.util package.)

14. Add an inner class that implements the TwoWayIterator interface to the NPSArrayList class.

15. Add an inner class that implements the TwoWayIterator interface to the NPSLinkedList class.

16. Implement step 1 of the fortune cookie sample development.

17. Implement step 3 of the fortune cookie sample development.

18. Modify the base implementation of the FortuneCookieFile class done in Exercise 17 so the modified class can input data from any text file. The file name of the text file to open is passed as an argument to the constructor.

19. Extend the fortune cookie sample development program so that the administrator can add and delete fortunes from the list. The administrator enters a password when the program prompts whether to display the next fortune. This will bring the program into an administrative mode. In this mode, you can add new fortunes and delete existing fortunes. A new fortune is added to the end of the list. You can delete existing fortunes in two ways. With the first way, you specify the index position of the fortune in the list. With the second way, the program will list all fortunes in the list one by one. For each fortune listed, you can enter D to delete it, K to keep it, or X to stop the listing.

20. In Section 16.5, we implemented the HumongousInteger class using linked nodes. We defined the inner Node class and manipulated links ourselves. Reimplement the HumongousInteger class by using an NPSList instead. Is there any clear benefit in using an NPSList?

19 Stack ADT

Objectives

After you have read and studied this chapter, you should be able to

- Describe the key features of the Stack ADT.
- Develop applications using stacks.
- Implement the Stack ADT by using an array.
- Implement the Stack ADT by using a linked list.
- Explain the key differences between the array and linked implementations of the Stack ADT.

Introduction

We continue our study of ADTs with the Stack ADT in this chapter. As we did in Chapter 18, we start with the definition of the Stack ADT and present two different implementations. We conclude the chapter with sample applications of the Stack ADT.

The Stack ADT is modeled after a physical stack of items, such as a stack of pancakes or a stack of plates. If you were asked to remove any plate from a stack of plates, which one would you remove? The topmost one, of course. Similarly, the most effortless place to add a new plate is at the top of the stack. Like its physical counterpart, the defining feature of the Stack ADT is its restrictive insertion and removal operations. An item can only be added to the top of the stack, and only the topmost item of the stack can be removed. Because of this restriction, the Stack ADT is quite simple. And consequently, its implementations are relatively straightforward, compared to the List ADT. As simple as it may be, the Stack ADT is remarkably versatile and useful in many diverse types of applications.

19.1 The Stack ADT

stack

top of stack

LIFO

A ***stack*** is a linearly ordered collection of elements where elements, or items, are added to and removed from the collection at the one end called the ***top of stack***. This restriction will ensure that the last element added to a stack is the first to be removed next. For this reason, a stack is characterized as a ***last-in, first-out (LIFO)*** list. Figure 19.1 shows a sample generic stack named sampleStack with five elements and another stack named myStack with five three-letter animal names.

Items in a stack are said to be *linearly ordered* because the order in which the items are added and removed follows the strict linear sequence. In other words, the item at the *i*th position below the top of the stack moves to the $(i - 1)$st position when the topmost item is removed. Similarly, the item at the *i*th position below the top of the stack moves to the $(i + 1)$st position when a new item is added to the top of the stack.

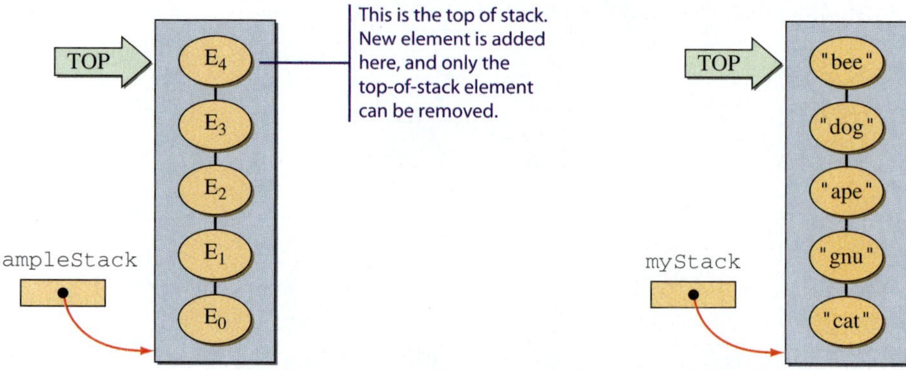

Figure 19.1 A generic stack **sampleStack** with five elements and a stack **myStack** with three-letter animal names.

Because the addition and removal operations are restricted, the methods defined for the Stack ADT are much simpler than those defined for the List ADT. The add operation named *push* adds a new item to the top of the stack. The remove operation named *pop* removes the topmost item. The get operation named *peek* returns the topmost item, without actually removing it. There are two query operations named *size* and *isEmpty*. The size method returns the number of items in the stack, and the isEmpty method returns true if the size of the stack is 0. The update operation named *clear* empties the stack.

push

The push operation will add the designated element to the top of the stack. The current elements in the stack are pushed down one position. The stack does not have any size restriction. It will grow without bound. Of course, the computer memory is not limitless, so there will be a hardware limitation on how big a stack can grow, but there will be no size restriction at the ADT level. Also, there is no restriction on the elements. You can add duplicates, for instance. Figure 19.2 illustrates the push operation.

pop

The pop operation is the reverse of the push operation. It will remove the topmost element from the stack if there is any. If the stack is empty, then the operation will throw an exception. There are a number of possible Java exceptions that the operation can throw, and we will discuss them in Section 19.2. For now, we'll just say that the operation will throw some kind of exception. Figure 19.3 illustrates the pop operation on nonempty and empty stacks.

peek

The peek operation is just like the pop operation except that the top element is not removed from the stack. Figure 19.4 illustrates the peek operation on non-empty and empty stacks.

clear

The clear operation removes all elements in the stack. It causes no problem to call the clear operation on an empty stack. This operation becomes handy, for example, when you want to clear the stack before reusing it for processing the next batch of input data. See Figures 19.5 and 19.6.

size

The size operation returns the number of elements in the stack. This operation is not as commonly used on the stacks as the isEmpty operation, but we will include it in the specification as it is not costly to implement this operation. Including this operation maintains the consistent set of methods available on all types of collection objects.

isEmpty

The isEmpty operation tests whether the stack is empty. If it is, then true is returned. Otherwise, false is returned. See Figure 19.7.

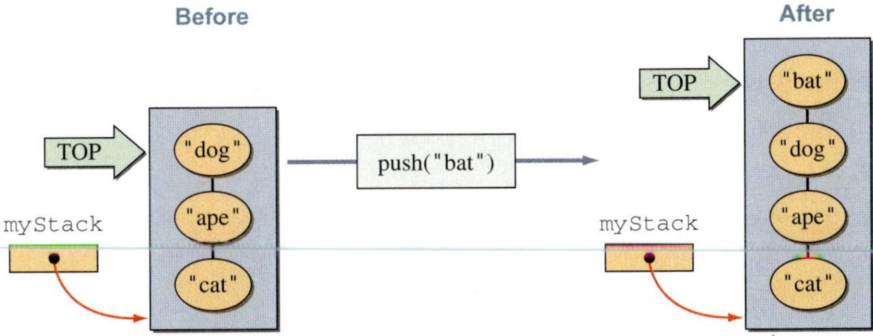

Figure 19.2 A sample **push** operation on the **myStack** stack.

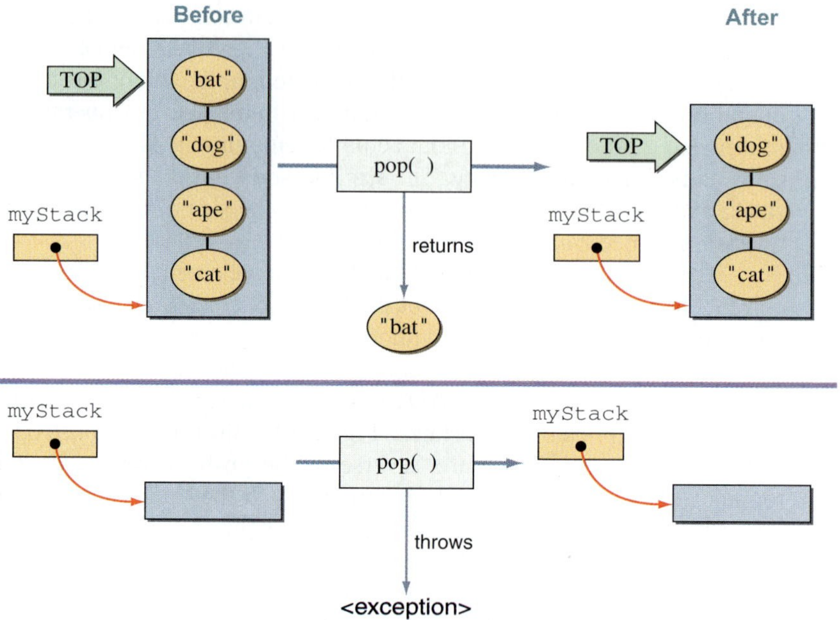

Figure 19.3 Sample **pop** operations on the **myStack** stack.

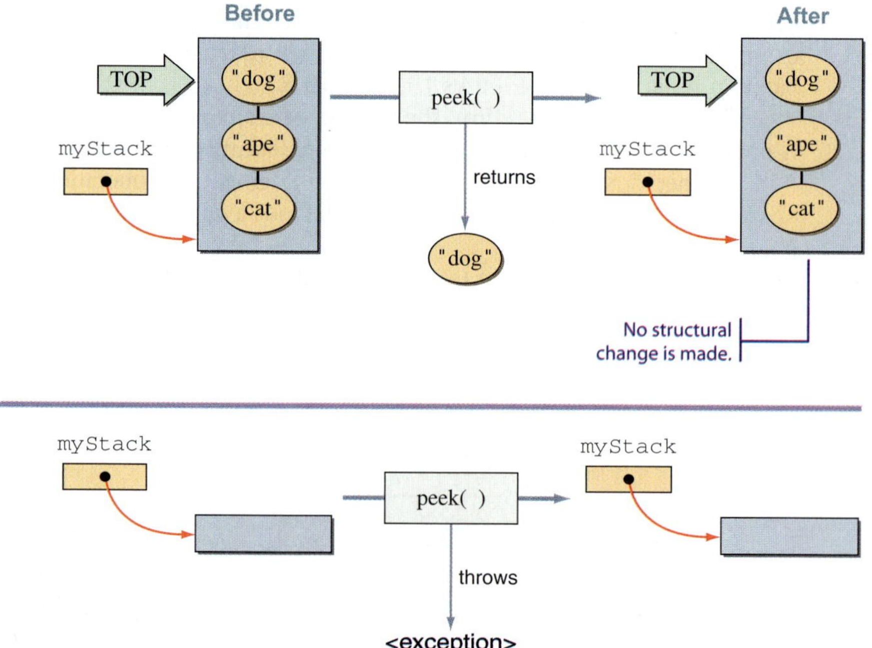

Figure 19.4 Sample **peek** operations on the **myStack** stack.

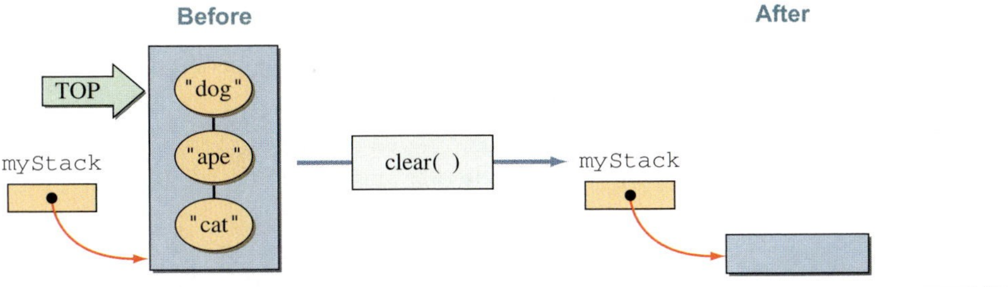

Figure 19.5 A sample **clear** operation on the **myStack** stack.

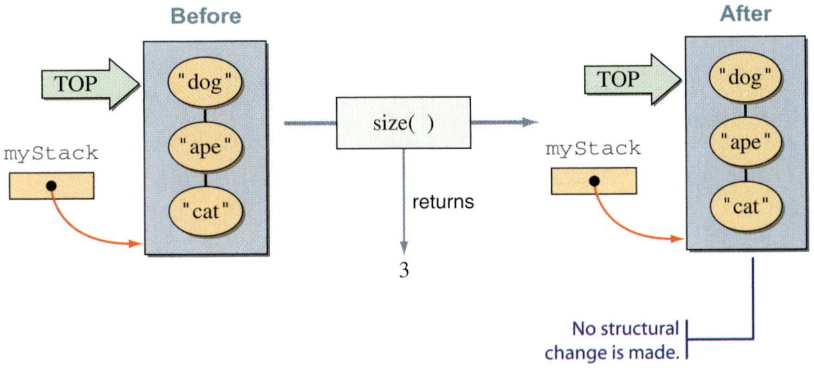

Figure 19.6 A sample **clear** operation on the **myStack** stack.

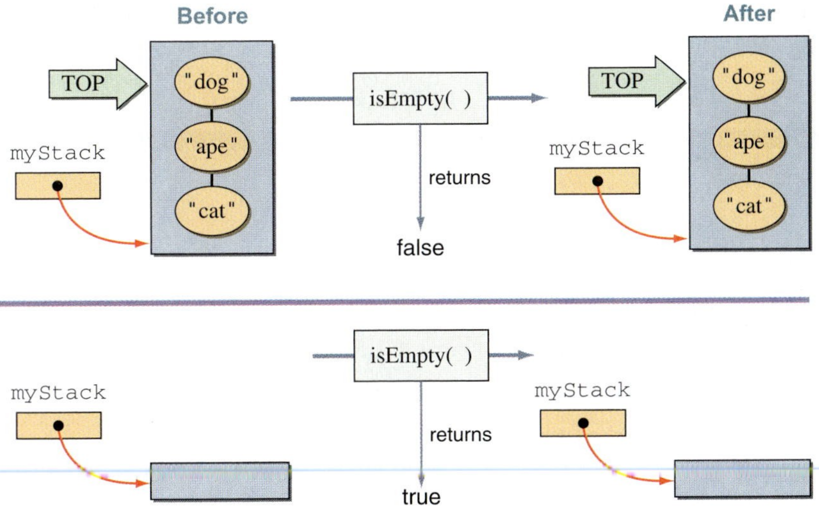

Figure 19.7 Sample **isEmpty** operations on the **myStack** stack.

1. Draw the stack after executing the following operations, starting with an empty stack called myStack.

```
String bee = new String("bee");
String cat = new String("cat");

myStack.clear( );
myStack.push(bee);
myStack.push(cat);
myStack.pop( );
```

2. Repeat Question 1 with the following statements:

```
String bee = new String("bee");
String cat = new String("cat");
String dog = new String("dog");

petStack.push(bee);
petStack.push(cat);
petStack.push(dog);
petStack.peek( );
petStack.pop( );
petStack.pop( );
petStack.push(dog);
```

19.2 The Stack Interface

As we did for the List ADT, we will use a Java interface to define the Stack ADT. We will continue to prefix our interfaces and classes with NPS. (There are no conflicts because no interface named Stack and no classes named ArrayStack and LinkedStack exist in the java.util packages; but for consistency, we will prefix all of our interfaces and classes with NPS.) Formalizing what we have presented in Section 19.1, we have the following definition:

NPSStack

```
package edu.nps.util;

public interface NPSStack<E> {

    public void clear( );

    public boolean isEmpty( );

    public E peek( ) throws NPSStackEmptyException;

    public E pop( ) throws NPSStackEmptyException;

    public void push(E element);

    public int size( );
}
```

TABLE 19.1 The NPSStack interface

Interface: NPSStack	
void	clear( ) Removes all elements from the stack.
boolean	isEmpty( ) Determines whether the stack is empty. Returns true if it is empty; false otherwise.
E	peek( ) throws NPSStackEmptyException Returns the top-of-stack element without removing it from the stack. Throws an exception when the stack is empty.
E	pop( ) throws NPSStackEmptyException Removes the top-of-stack element and returns it. Throws an exception when the stack is empty.
void	push(E element) Adds an element to the stack. This element becomes the new top-of-stack element.
int	size( ) Returns the number of elements in the stack.

Table 19.1 summarizes the methods of the NPSStack interface.

The peek and pop methods are defined to throw an NPSStackEmptyException. We could have thrown an NPSNoSuchElementException because there is no such (top-of-stack) element when you attempt to pop or peek an empty stack. However, NPSNoSuchElementException is equally applicable, for example, when you search for an element that is not in a data structure. It is preferable to use an exception that identifies the error condition as precisely as possible, instead of using a generic exception. Because the specific error condition that would result in an exception for the pop and peek operations is an empty stack, we chose to throw an exception specifically defined for this purpose. The NPSNoSuchElementException class is a very simple class. Here's the definition:

NPSNoSuchElementException

```
package edu.nps.util;
public class NPSStackEmptyException extends RuntimeException {
    public NPSStackEmptyException( ) {
        this("Stack is empty");
    }
    public NPSStackEmptyException(String message) {
        super(message);
    }
}
```

19.3 The Array Implementation

In this section, we will implement the NPSStack interface by using an array to store the stack elements. Figure 19.8 illustrates the array implementation of the Stack ADT.

The NPSArrayStack Definition

The NPSArrayStack class implements the NPSStack interface, and its class declaration is as follows:

```
package edu.nps.util;

public class NPSArrayStack<E> implements NPSStack<E> {

    //class body comes here

}
```

We use an array element to store the stack elements and an int variable count to keep track of the number of elements currently in the stack. Since the Java array uses zero-based indexing, the value of count is also the index of the array where we add the next element. We will also define a constant for the default size we use when creating the array in the zero-argument constructor. These data members are declared as

```
private static final int DEFAULT_SIZE = 25;
private E[ ] element;
private int  count;
```

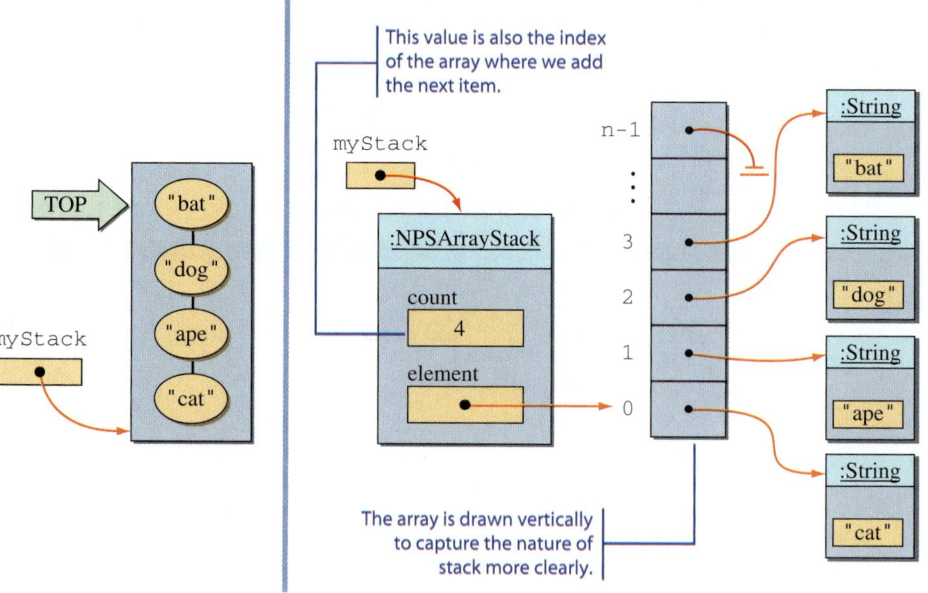

Figure 19.8 An array implementation of the Stack ADT.

We will define two constructors: one takes no argument and another takes one argument that specifies the initial size of the array. They are defined as follows:

```
public NPSArrayStack( ) {
   this(DEFAULT_SIZE);
}

public NPSArrayStack(int size) {
   if (size <= 0) {
       throw new IllegalArgumentException(
                    "Initial capacity must be positive");
   }

   element = (E[]) new Object[size];
   count   = 0;
}
```

Notice that we first create an array of Object and then typecast it to an array of E, the type parameter. This is necessary because it is not allowed to create an array of generic type in Java.

clear

We will set element[i] to null, where i = 0, . . . , count-1, so the objects referenced by element[i] will be garbage-collected. We will then reset the count variable to 0.

```
public void clear( ) {

   for (int i = 0; i < count; i++) {
      element[i] = null;
   }

   count = 0;
}
```

isEmpty

This operation is straightforward. If the value of count is 0, then the stack is empty. Otherwise, the stack is not empty.

```
public boolean isEmpty( ) {

   return (count == 0);
}
```

peek

This is one of the two operations that can potentially throw an NPSStackEmptyException. We throw an NPSStackEmptyException when the stack is empty. Otherwise, we return the top-of-stack element.

```
public E peek() throws NPSStackEmptyException {

   if (isEmpty( )) {

      throw new NPSStackEmptyException( );

   } else {

      return element[count-1];
   }
}
```

Be careful! The current top of stack is at the **(count-1)** index position.

pop

The pop operation removes the top-of-stack element. If the stack is not empty, we adjust the count data member and remove the topmost element by setting the value of the corresponding index position to null. Here's the method:

```
public E pop() throws NPSStackEmptyException {

   if (isEmpty( )) {

      throw new NPSStackEmptyException( );

   } else {

      count--;

      E item = element[count];
      element[count] = null;

      return item;
   }
}
```

push

Adding a new item to the top of a stack and updating the count data member can be expressed easily and concisely as

```
element[count] = item;
count++;
```

Can be combined into one statement as **element[count++] = item;**

The complication will arise when the array is fully occupied. When the array is full, we need to enlarge it to accommodate more items. We will define a private method called expand to create a new array that is 1.5 times larger than the current array. This is the same technique we used in the NPSArrayList class. Here's the method:

```
private void expand( ) {

   // create a new array whose size is 150% of
   // the current array
   int newLength = (int) (1.5 * element.length);
   E[] temp = (E[]) new Object[newLength];

   // now copy the data to the new array
   for (int i = 0; i < element.length; i++) {
      temp[i] = element[i];
   }

   element = temp;
}
```

The push method is defined as follows:

```
public void push(E item) {

   if (count == element.length) {
       expand( );
   }

   element[count++] = item;
}
```

size

The last method is straightforward. We simply return the value of the count data member.

```
public int size ( ) {

    return count;
}
```

Here's the complete source code (for brevity, javadoc and most other comments in the actual source file are removed here):

NPSArrayStack

```
package edu.nps.util;

public class NPSArrayStack<E> implements NPSStack<E> {

    private static final int DEFAULT_SIZE = 25;

    private E[ ] element;

    private int count;

    public NPSArrayStack( ) {
        this(DEFAULT_SIZE);
    }

    public NPSArrayStack(int size) {
        if (size <= 0) {
            throw new IllegalArgumentException(
                                        "Initial capacity must be positive");

        }

        element = (E[]) new Object[size];
        count   = 0;
    }

    public void clear() {

        for(int i = 0; i < count; i++) {
            element[i] = null;
        }

        count = 0;
    }

    public boolean isEmpty() {

        return count == 0;
    }

    public E peek( ) throws NPSStackEmptyException {

        if (isEmpty( )) {
```

Constructor

clear

isEmpty

peek

```
            throw new NPSStackEmptyException( );

        } else {

            return element[count-1];
        }
    }

    public E pop() throws NPSStackEmptyException {

        if (isEmpty( )) {

            throw new NPSStackEmptyException( );

        } else {

            count--;

            E item = element[count];
            element[count] = null;

            return item;
        }
    }

    public void push(E item) {

        if (count == element.length) {
            expand( );
        }

        element[count++] = item;
    }

    public int size( ) {

        return count;
    }

    private void expand( ) {

        int newLength = (int) (1.5 * element.length);
        E[] temp = (E[]) new Object[newLength];

        for (int i = 0; i < element.length; i++) {
            temp[i] = element[i];
        }

        element = temp;
    }
}
```

pop

push

size

expand

1. Draw the array stack (like the right-hand side diagram in Figure 19.8) after executing thc following operations, starting with an empty stack called myStack.

```
String bee = new String("bee");
String cat = new String("cat");

myStack.clear();
myStack.push(cat);
myStack.push(bee);
```

2. What is the purpose of the enlarge method?
3. What will happen if you replace the statement inside the else block of the pop method with the following?

```
return element[count--];
```

19.4 The Linked-List Implementation

The linked-list implementation of the Stack ADT follows the same implementation pattern for the List ADT in Chapter 18. Figure 19.9 illustrates the linked-list implementation of the Stack ADT.

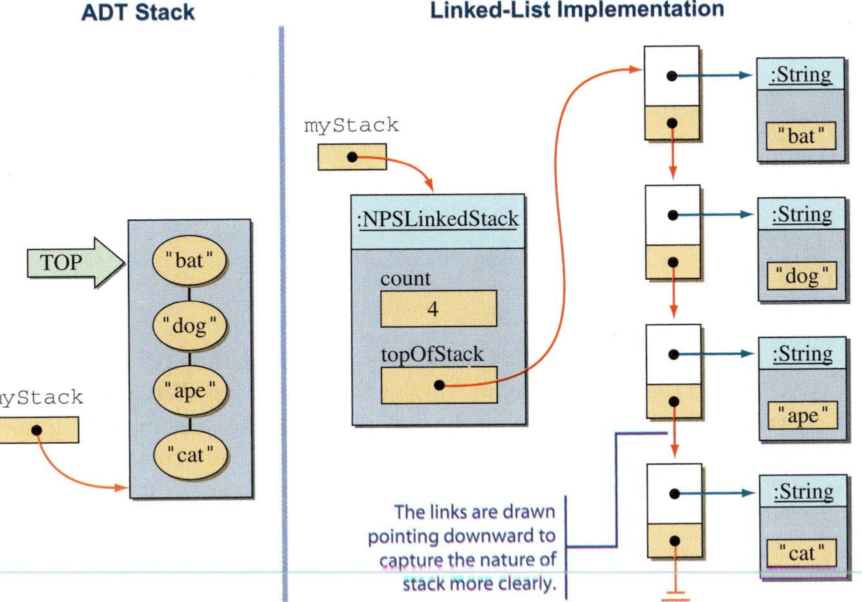

Figure 19.9 A linked-list implementation of the stack **myStack.**

The StackNode Class

The linked node structure for the stack is exactly the same as the one for the list. The StackNode class is defined as the inner class of the NPSLinkedStack class. Here's the class definition:

```
class StackNode {

   private E item;

   private StackNode next;

   public StackNode(E item) {
      this.item = item;
      this.next = null;
   }
}
```

The NPSLinkedStack Class

We keep two data members in the class. The first data member is a reference variable topOfStack that points to the top-of-stack element. We adjust its value every time we pop an item from or push an item onto the stack. The second data member is an int variable count that keeps track of the number of elements currently in the stack. Their declarations are as follows:

```
private StackNode topOfStack;

Private int       count;
```

We define only a single constructor that takes no arguments and sets the stack to its initial state, which is an empty stack. The constructor is defined as follows:

```
public NPSLinkedStack( ) {
   clear( );
}
```

When we reset the topOfStack pointer to null, the topmost node will get garbage-collected (because no pointers point to it any more). When this topmost node gets garbage-collected, the node below no longer has a pointer pointing to it, which causes this node to be garbage-collected also. This ripple effect will eventually cause all nodes to be garbage-collected. Here's the clear method:

clear

```
public void clear( ) {
   topOfStack = null;
   count = 0;
}
```

isEmpty

The isEmpty method is implemented easily by checking the value of the data member count:

```
public boolean isEmpty( ) {
   return count == 0;
}
```

peek

If the stack is empty, we throw an NPSstackEmptyException. Otherwise, we return the top-of-stack node (without actually removing it). Here's the method:

```
public E peek( ) throws NPSStackEmptyException {

   if (isEmpty( )) {

      throw new NPSStackEmptyException( );

   } else {

      return topOfStack.item;
   }
}
```

pop

If the stack is empty, we throw an NPSStackEmptyException. Otherwise, we set a temp pointer to the topmost item, update the topOfStack pointer, and return the topmost item. Here's the method:

```
public E pop( ) throws NPSStackEmptyException {

   if (isEmpty( )) {

      throw new NPSStackEmptyException( );

   } else {

      count--;
      E temp = topOfStack.item;

      topOfStack = topOfStack.link;

      return temp;
   }
}
```

push

Adding a new element to a link-based stack is simpler than adding to an array-based stack because we do not have to worry about the overflow condition. All we need to do is to allocate a new node, adjust the topOfStack pointer, and increment the counter. The method is defined as follows:

```
public void push(E element) {

   StackNode newTop = new StackNode(element);

   newTop.link = topOfStack; //add the new node to top

   topOfStack = newTop;      //set new node as top-of-stack

   count++;
}
```

size

The size method simply return the value of the data member count:

```
public int size( ) {
   return count;
}
```

We are now ready to list the complete NPSLinkedStack class. In the source code listing, we do not show any javadoc comments, to keep the listing to a manageable size. The actual source code includes the full javadoc comments.

NPSLinkedStack

```
package edu.nps.util;

public class NPSLinkedStack<E> implements NPSStack<E> {

    private StackNode topOfStack;

    private int count;

    public NPSLinkedStack( ) {                                    // Constructor
        clear( );
    }

    public void clear( ) {                                        // clear

        topOfStack = null;

        count = 0;
    }

    public boolean isEmpty( ) {                                   // isEmpty

        return (count == 0);
    }

    public E peek( ) throws NPSStackEmptyException {              // peek

        if (isEmpty( )) {

            throw new NPSStackEmptyException( );

        } else {

            return topOfStack.item;
        }
    }

    public E pop( ) throws NPSStackEmptyException {               // pop

        if (isEmpty( )) {

            throw new NPSStackEmptyException( );

        } else {

            count--;
            E temp = topOfStack.item;
```

```
            topOfStack = topOfStack.link;

            return temp;
        }
    }

    public void push(E element) {

        StackNode newTop = new StackNode(element);

        newTop.link = topOfStack;

        topOfStack = newTop;

        count++;
    }

    public int size( ) {

        return count;
    }

    class StackNode {

        private E item;

        private StackNode link; //points to the element
                                //one position below this node

        public StackNode(E item) {

            this.item = item;
            this.link = null;
        }
    }
}
```

push

size

StackNode

1. Draw the linked stack (like the right-hand side diagram in Figure 19.9) after executing the following operations, starting with an empty stack called myStack.

```
String bee = new String("bee");
String cat = new String("cat");

myStack.clear();
myStack.push(cat);
myStack.push(bee);
```

2. Instead of using count == 0 to check for an empty stack, can we use topOfStack == null?

19.5 Implementation Using NPSList

At the beginning of this chapter, we wrote that a stack can be characterized as a special kind of a list called a LIFO list. A stack is a LIFO list because the last item to be added to a stack is the first item to be removed from the stack next. We can in fact implement the Stack ADT by using a list. Consider the following NPSListStack class:

NPSListStack

```
package edu.nps.util;

public class NPSListStack<E> implements NPSStack<E> {

    private static final int FRONT = 0;

    private NPSList<E> list;

    public NPSListStack( ) {
        list = new NPSLinkedList<E>();
    }

    public void clear( ) {
        list.clear();
    }

    public boolean isEmpty( ) {
        return list.isEmpty();
    }

    public E peek( ) throws NPSStackEmptyException {
       if (isEmpty( )) {

           throw new NPSStackEmptyException( );

       } else {

           return list.get(FRONT);
       }
    }

    public E pop( ) throws NPSStackEmptyException {
        if (isEmpty( )) {

            throw new NPSStackEmptyException( );

        } else {

            return list.remove(FRONT);
        }
    }

    public void push(E element) {
        list.add(FRONT, element);
    }
```

```
    public int size( ) {

        return list.size();
    }
}
```

See how easily and succinctly the whole class can be implemented. Notice that in this implementation, we treat the first item in the linked list as the top-of-stack item. Do you know why? Instead of the NPSLinkedList class, we can use the NPSArrayList class. But with the NPSArrayList class, we should treat the last item in the list as the top-of-stack element to avoid the shifting of items when a new item is added.

19.6 Sample Application

Matching HTML Tags

The use of the Stack ADT is quite common in many different applications. In this section we will illustrate a typical use of a stack. We will write a program that checks the correctness of a given HTML document. An HTML, which stands for Hyper Text Markup Language, is a markup language designed for creating a web page. HTML uses a set of predefined tags to describe the structure of a document. The tags are used, for example, to specify the title, different levels of headings, numbered lists, and tables in a document. XML, or eXtended Markup Language, is another markup language that is used widely in today's computing world.

It is not necessary to understand HTML fully to appreciate the use of a stack in checking the syntax of an HTML document. We only need to know how the HTML tags are organized in a document. The following is a very small (and valid) HTML document:

```
<html>
<head>
<title>A sample HTML page</title>
</head>
<body>
<h1>Sample HTML</h1>
<p>See how the tags are matched in pairs?</p>
<h4>This is a table</h4>
<table border="2">
  <tr>
    <td>row 1 column 1</td>
    <td>row 1 column 2</td>
  </tr>
</table>
</body>
</html>
```

19.6 Sample Application—*continued*

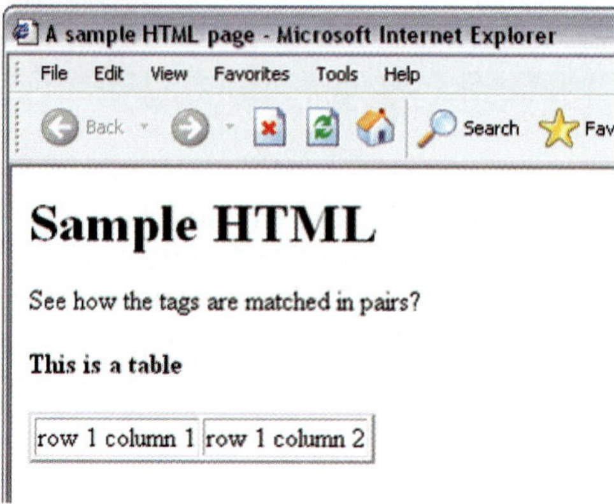

Figure 19.10 A Web browser displaying the sample HTML document.

Figure 19.10 shows how this HTML document is displayed in a Web browser. The Web browser interprets the tags in the given HTML document and renders the page accordingly.

The key characteristic of HTML tags is that the tags come in pairs: the opening and matching closing tags. There's an exception to this rule, but we will ignore it for the sake of simplicity in the following discussion (see Exercise 11). For example, the opening tag for the title is

```
<title>
```

and its matching closing tag is

```
</title>
```

The closing tag includes the forward slash (/) before the tag name. The tag names are case-insensitive, so it doesn't matter, for example, if we specify the opening tag for the title as

```
<title>
```

or as

```
<TITLE>
```

The tags in the example HTML document are displayed in blue for easy viewing. The text in black is the content that gets displayed in the Web browser. If we strip the content,

this is what we get (tags are indented to show the structure clearly):

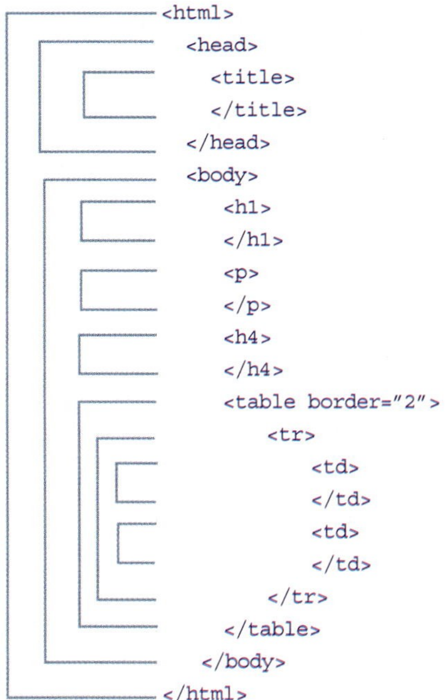

Notice how the matching tags are nested. We will never encounter a situation in which the matching tags cross over. In other words, in a valid HTML document, we will never face a situation like this:

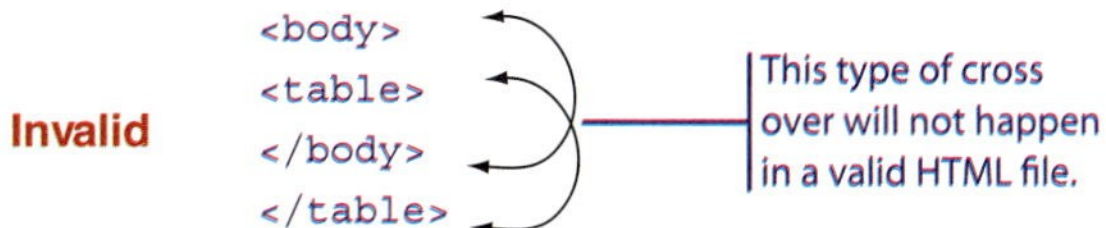

We can characterize the formulation of tags in a valid HTML document as follows:

1. All opening tags have matching closing tags.
2. When a closing tag is encountered in the document, its corresponding opening tag was already encountered. That is, opening tags always come before the closing tags.
3. Tags can be nested, but they never overlap.

19.6 Sample Application—*continued*

These characteristics call for a stack to check the validity of a given HTML document. Here's the pseudocode for the syntax checker:

```
NPSStack tagStack = new NPSArrayStack( );

boolean hasError = false, done = false;

while (!done) {

   if (no more tags in a file) {
      done = true;
      if (!tagStack.isEmpty( )) {
         hasError = true;
      }
   } else {
      nextTag = get next tag from the file;

      if (nextTag is an opening tag) {

         tagStack.push(nextTag); //every opening tag gets
                                 //stacked exactly once
      } else { //it's a closing tag

         topTag = tagStack.pop( );

         if (topTag does not match nextTag) {
            done     = true;
            hasError = true;
         }
      }
   }
}

if (hasError) {
   //Invalid HTML
} else {
   //Valid HTML
}
```

If all tags are processed and yet the stack is not empty, then it means there were opening tags with no matching closing tags.

If the next incoming tag is a closing tag, its corresponding opening tag must be the current top-of-stack element because of the properly nested characteristic.

To concentrate on the stack processing, we assume the two helper classes—**HTMLTagRetriever** and **HTMLTag.** An **HTMLTagRetriever** object handles the retrieval of HTML tags from the specified file. An **HTMLTag** object represents a single HTML tag. Implementation of these classes is left as an exercise. Table 19.2 lists the methods of **HTMLTagRetriever,** and Table 19.3 lists the method of **HTMLTag.**

Now we are ready to implement the pseudocode. Let's define a class named **HTMLTagChecker.** The major portion of the logic expressed in the pseudocode is implemented in the key method called **isValid.** This method returns **true** if the tags in the designated

Table 19.2 The `HTMLTagRetriever` class

Class: `HTMLTagRetriever`	
	`HTMLTagRetriever( String filename ) throws IOException` Constructs a new `HTMLTagRetriever` object and associates it to the file with the name `filename`. Throws an `IOException` if the said file cannot be opened.
`void`	`reset( )` Resets this object so the processing of the tags can be repeated from the beginning.
`void`	`reset( String filename ) throws IOException` Same as the `reset` method with no parameter. This method, however, associates the object to the new file. Throws an `IOException` if said file cannot be opened.
`boolean`	`hasMoreTags( )` Returns `true` if there are more tags in the file. Otherwise, returns `false`.
`HTMLTag`	`nextTag( ) throws NoSuchElementException` Returns the next `HTMLTag` object in the file. If there are no more tags, then the `NoSuchElementException` exception is thrown.

file are syntactically correct. Otherwise, it returns **false.** The name of the file to process is passed to the constructor of **HTMLTagChecker.** Here's the class:

HTMLTagChecker

```
import edu.nps.util.*;
import java.io.IOException;
public class HTMLTagChecker {
    private NPSStack<HTMLTag> tagStack;
    private HTMLTagRetriever tagRetriever;
    public HTMLTagChecker(String filename) throws IOException {
        tagStack = new NPSArrayStack<HTMLTag>( );
        tagRetriever = new HTMLTagRetriever(filename);
    }
```

19.6 Sample Application—*continued*

Table 19.3 The `HTMLTag` class

Class: `HTMLTag`
`HTMLTag(String text)` Creates a new `HTMLTag` object. The parameter `text` is the actual string, such as `<body>` and `<title>`, for the tag.
`boolean match(HTMLTag tag)` Compares the parameter `tag` with this `HTMLTag` object in a case-insensitive manner. The `tag` object can represent either the opening or the closing tag. The method will make the appropriate checking. For example, if this `HTMLTag` object represents `<HEAD>` and the argument tag object represents `</HEAD>`, then it is a match. Likewise, if this `HTMLTag` object represents `</HEAD>` and the argument tag object represents `<HEAD>`, then it is a match also. If there is a match, the method returns true. Otherwise, it returns `false`. The opening `HTMLTag` object can contain attribute values. For example, in the tag `<TABLE border="2">` the border attribute specifies the width of the table border. This method correctly matches the opening tag that includes attributes with its closing tag.
`boolean isOpeningTag( )` Returns `true` if this object represents an opening tag. Otherwise, returns `false`.
`boolean isClosingTag( )` Returns `true` if this object represents a closing tag. Otherwise, returns `false`.

```
public boolean isValid( ) {

    HTMLTag nextTag = null,
            topTag  = null;

    tagStack.clear( );

    boolean hasError = false,
            done     = false;

    while (!done) {

        if (!tagRetriever.hasMoreTags( )) { //no more tags

            done = true;
```

```
                if (!tagStack.isEmpty( )) { //there are some
                                             //leftover opening tags
                    hasError = true;       //with no matching closing tags

                    done = true;
                }

            } else {

                nextTag = tagRetriever.nextTag( );

                if (nextTag.isOpeningTag( )) {

                    tagStack.push(nextTag);

                } else { //it's a closing tag

                    topTag = tagStack.pop( );

                    if (!topTag.match(nextTag)) {

                        done     = true;
                        hasError = true;
                    }
                }
            }
        }

        return hasError;
    }

    ///------------ M A I N  m e t h o d ---------------------//
    public static void main(String[] arg) {

        try {

            HTMLTagChecker checker = new HTMLTagChecker("index.html");

            if (checker.isValid()) {
                System.out.println("Input HTML file is valid");
            } else {
                System.out.println("Input HTML file is NOT valid");
            }

        } catch (IOException e) {
            System.out.println("Error opening the designated file");
        }
    }
}
```

19.7 Sample Application

Solving a Maze with Backtracking

backtracking

Many computer problems can be solved by the technique called ***backtracking***. The name characterizes how the solution to a problem is found. Consider a maze problem. We define a maze to be a two-dimensional array of cells. Each cell has four sides with at most three sides having a wall. You can move from one cell to an adjacent cell if there is no wall between the two cells. Two special cells are indentified as the entry and exit cells. The problem is to find a path that takes you from the entry cell to the exit cell of a given maze. Figure 19.11 shows a sample 5-by-5 maze. For humans, finding a solution path for a such small maze is almost immediate. But when the maze gets larger, say, 100 by100, finding a solution is not an easy matter anymore. (We're talking here about a human finding a solution for a maze drawn on a sheet of paper, and not about finding solution for a real-life maze or labyrinth.)

What kind of a computer solution can we devise to find a solution path? We assume here that a given maze includes at least one solution path. A maze is represented by a **Maze** object that consists of *N*-by-*M* cells. A cell is represented by a **MazeCell** object. The **Maze** and **MazeCell** classes are described in Tables 19.4 and 19.5, respectively. It is left as an exercise to implement these two classes.

One brute-force solution is to visit cells randomly, starting from the entry cell. This is akin to a human walking blindly around the maze. This simplistic approach can be expressed in the following manner:

```
public void solveRandom(Maze maze) {

   MazeCell current = maze.getEntryCell();
   MazeCell exit    = maze.getExitCell();
```

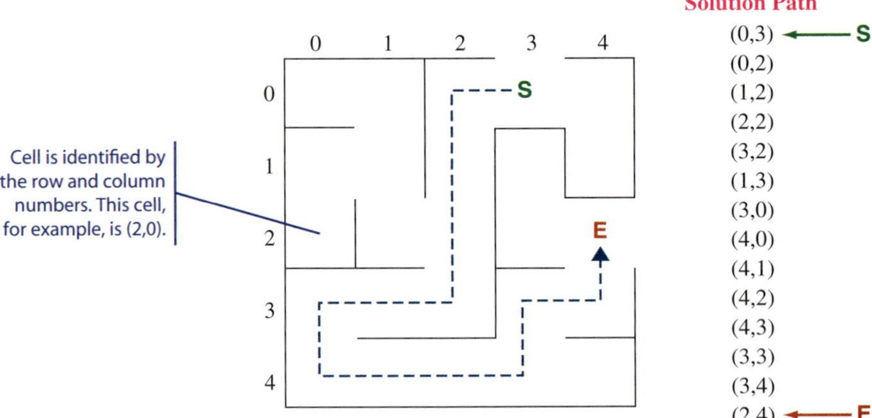

Figure 19.11 A sample maze with 5-by-5 cells. The entry cell is marked with S and the exit cell with E. The dotted line shows the solution path from S to E. For this maze, there's exactly one solution path.

Table 19.4 The `Maze` class

Class: `Maze`	
	`Maze( int rowSize, int columnSize )` Creates a new `rowSize`-by-`columnSize` maze. In its initial state, all cells are marked unvisited. One cell is designated as the entry cell and another cell as the exit cell. The entry and exit cells border one of the outer boundaries.
`void`	`clear( )` Resets the maze to its initial state.
`int`	`getColumnCount( )` Returns the number of columns of this maze.
`int`	`getRowCount( )` Returns the number of rows of this maze.
`MazeCell`	`getEntryCell( )` Returns the entry cell.
`MazeCell`	`getExitCell( )` Returns the exit cell.
`MazeCell`	`getNextCell( MazeCell currentCell )` Returns a visitable cell adjacent to `currentCell`. Returns `null` if there is no visitable adjacent cell.
`MazeCell`	`getNextRandomCell( MazeCell currentCell )` Randomly selects and returns a cell adjacent to `currentCell`. The state of cell (visitable or not) is ignored by this method.

```
    while (current != exit) {

        //move to a random adjacent cell
        current = maze.getNextRandomCell(current);

    }

    System.out.println("Solution Path Found");
}
```

Since the method does not keep track of the cells visited, all it does is to output the message **Solution Path Found** when the exit cell is reached. It does not (cannot) print out the solution path.

A much more elegant solution would be backtracking. Here's how it works. Mark the entry cell visited. Visit an adjacent cell that is not yet visited. Mark this cell visited (so we won't visit this cell again). Repeat this visit-and-mark-visited routine until either the exit cell is visited or there is no adjacent cell to visit from the current cell. If the exit cell is visited, then we found the solution. If there are no more adjacent cells to visit from the

19.7 Sample Application—*continued*

Table 19.5 The MazeCell class

Class: MazeCell	
	`MazeCell( int rowNum, int columnNum )` Creates a new cell. Each cell is identified by its row number and column number, the position it occupies in a maze. In its initial state, all four walls are up.
`int`	`getColumnNumber( )` Returns the column number of this cell.
`int`	`getRowNumber( )` Returns the row number of this cell.
`boolean`	`isVisited( )` Returns `true` if the cell is not visited yet (i.e., it is visitable) and `false` if the cell is visited.
`boolean`	`isWallUp( int side )` Returns `true` if the wall of the specified side of this cell is up. Possible values for the parameter are `MazeCell.NORTH`, `MazeCell.SOUTH`, `MazeCell.EAST`, and `MazeCell.WEST`.
`void`	`putWallDown( int side )` Knocks down the wall of the specified side of this cell. Possible values for the parameter are `MazeCell.NORTH`, `MazeCell.SOUTH`, `MazeCell.EAST`, and `MazeCell.WEST`.
`void`	`setVisited( boolean state )` Sets the state of this cell. The value of `true` means the cell is visited and `false` means not visited.

current node, we backtrack to the cell before the current cell and repeat the process again from that cell. Figure 19.12 illustrates two backtracking steps.

The key aspect of implementing this backtracking algorithm is to remember the cell to backtrack to. The ADT that goes hand in hand with backtracking is a stack. When we visit a cell, we push it onto a stack. The current cell is at the top of stack, and the adjacent cell we visit next from the current cell will be the new top of stack (and it will be the current cell in the next iteration). When we backtrack from a cell, we simply pop a stack. The new top of stack is the cell we're backtracking to. Figure 19.13 shows the correspondence between the path and the stack content.

We use the **setVisited** method of the **MazeCell** class to mark a visited cell. The **getNextCell** method of the **Maze** class returns a next visitable cell (a cell that is not yet

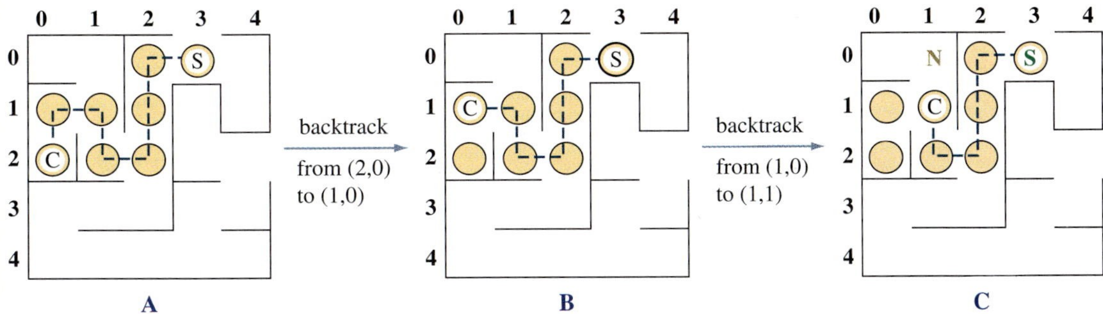

Figure 19.12 This illustrates how the backtracking works. Visited cells are marked with a red circle. **Diagram A:** There are no more adjacent cells to visit from the current cell (C), so we backtrack to cell (1,0). **Diagram B:** Again, there are no more adjacent from the current cell, so we backtrack. **Diagram C:** From the current cell, we can visit cell (0,1), so we visit it next (N).

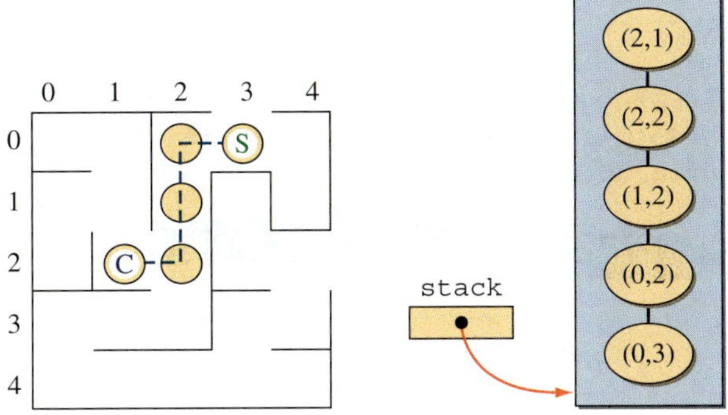

Figure 19.13 The stack content shows the order of visiting cells in the path currently under consideration.

visited) from a given cell. If there are no more visitable cells from a given cell, the method returns **null.** Here's the method that finds a solution path by backtracking:

```
public void solveBacktracking(Maze maze) {

  MazeCell current = maze.getEntryCell();
  MazeCell exit    = maze.getExitCell();

  NPSStack<MazeCell> stack
                     = new NPSArrayStack<MazeCell>( );
  stack.push(current);

  while (current != exit) {

     current = maze.getNextCell(current);
```

19.7 Sample Application—*continued*

```
        if (current != null) {

            current.setVisited(true); //mark it visited
            stack.push(current);

        } else { //no more visitable cells from the
                 //top-of-stack cell, so backtrack

            current = stack.pop();
        }
    }

    System.out.println("Solution Path:");

    while (stack.isEmpty()) {         //print out the solution
        System.out.println(stack.pop()); //path backward
    }
}
```

Because we are using a stack, the solution path found is printed backward from the exit cell to the entry cell. It is more natural to print out the path forward from the entry cell to the exit cell. This is left as an exercise.

Summary

- A stack is a linearly ordered last-in, first-out (LIFO) collection of elements.
- An item can be added to only the top of a stack, and only the top item of a stack can be removed.
- An array and a linked-list are two possible implementations of the Stack ADT.
- The Stack ADT can be implemented easily by using a list (an instance of a class that implements the List ADT).
- Base implementation of the Stack ADT does not support any traversal operation.
- The use of the Stack ADT is illustrated in two sample applications: an HTML syntax checker and a maze solver.
- Backtracking is a technique used in finding a solution for a search problem. The Stack ADT is used in implementing the backtracking algorithm.

Key Concepts

Stack ADT

array implementation of Stack ADT

linked-list implementation of Stack ADT

backtracking

Exercises

1. Draw a state-of-memory diagram that shows the effect of the pop operation on a NPSLinkedStack. Use the state where there are four items in the stack before the pop operation.
2. Draw a state-of-memory diagram that shows the effect of the push operation on a NPSLinkedStack. Use the state where there are three items in the stack before the push operation.
3. Draw a state-of-memory diagram that shows the result of executing each of the following two sets of code.

   a.
   ```
   NPSStack stack = new NPSLinkedStack( );

   Person p = new Person(...);

   stack.push(p);
   stack.push(p);
   ```

   b.
   ```
   NPSStack stack = new NPSLinkedStack( );

   Person p1 = new Person(...);
   Person p2 = new Person(...);

   stack.push(p1);
   stack.push(p2);
   ```

4. Add a new method toArray to the NPSStack interface and implement the method in both NPSArrayStack and NPSLinkedStack. The toArray method will return an array with the bottommost element at position 0, element 1 above the bottom at position 1, and so forth. For a mathematically pure Stack ADT, we do not define such conversion operation. But in the actual use of stacks, we often need to access every element in the stack. For example, in the maze sample application, if the toArray method is available, we can easily print out the solution path in the forward direction (from the entry cell to the exit cell) instead of the backward direction that we printed in the solveBacktracking method.
5. Adding the toArray method is one way to provide access to all elements in a stack. Another way is to include the iterator method to the NPSStack interface that returns an iterator. Implement the iterator method in both NPSArrayStack and NPSLinkedStack. The iterator will access the items in the stack from top to bottom.

6. Code a new implementation class for the Stack interface called NoDupStack that does not allow a duplicate of the existing element to be pushed onto the stack. We define an element e2 to be a duplicate of e1 if e1.equals(e2) is true. Define a new exception class called NPSDuplicateException and throw this exception from the push method when an attempt is made to push a duplicate. Use an array for this implementation.
7. Repeat Exercise 6, but this time use the linked nodes instead of an array.
8. In the NPSLinkStack class, the data member list is an instance of NPSLinkedList we use to maintain the stack elements. If a stack is a LIFO list (i.e., a stack *IS-A* a list), shouldn't we define it as a subclass of the NPSLinkedList class? Why is it wrong to so?
9. When implementing the NPSListStack class, we treat the first item in a list as the top-of-stack item. Modify the class so the last item in the linked list is treated as the top-of-stack item. Which implementation is more efficient? Why?
10. Implement the NPSListStack class using the NPSArrayList class.
11. Implement the HTMLTagRetriever class. There are some HTML tags that do not have the matching closing tags. For this exercise, assume such tags are <br>, <hr>, and <img> tags. The nextTag method must ignore these tags.
12. Implement the HTMLTag class. Pay close attention to the match method. Some opening tags, such as the <table> tag, can contain attributes in addition to the tag name. For example, the <table> tag can be

    ```
    <table>
    ```

    or

    ```
    <table border="2">
    ```

    When you match the opening and closing tags, you have to ignore the attributes in the opening tags.
13. In this chapter, we assumed that a given maze has at least one solution path. Modify the solveBacktracking method so it will handle the case when a given maze does not have any solution. Terminate the method after displaying the message No Solution Path if there is no solution path.
14. The solveBacktracking method prints out the solution path backward. Modify the method so the solution path is printed forward from the entry cell to the exit cell. Assume the original definition of the NPSStack interface. Specifically, you cannot use the toArray method (see Exercise 4). *Hint*: Use another stack.
15. Implement the Maze and MazeCell classes. Their public methods are described in Tables 19.4 and 19.5, respectively. The most difficult aspect of this exercise is the creation of a maze, which is carried out in the constructor of the Maze class. Here's one way to create a maze that has exactly one solution path from the entry cell to the exit cell:
    1. Start with all four walls up for every cell in the maze.
    2. Knock down the walls to create paths.

3. Randomly select the entry and exit cells. Make sure these are selected from the boundary cells (those that face the boundary of the maze).

The basic idea of the algorithm for step 2 goes like this: Start from a random cell. Remember this cell in a list. Mark this cell as visited. (You will visit every cell in the maze exactly once.) Set this cell as current. Find an adjacent cell of the current cell that is not yet visited. Knock down the walls between this cell and the current cell. Set this cell as the current cell and repeat the process. If there are no more visitable cells from the current cell, remove a random cell from the list and repeat the process. Stop the routine when all cells in the maze are visited. Expressing this basic idea in a more "formal" pseudocode, we have the following:

```
mark all cells as 'not visited';

currentCell = pick a random cell;

list.add(currentCell);

while (there are unvisited cells) {

   currentCell = list.get(random location);

   while (currentCell has a 'not visited' adjacent cell) {

      if (currentCell has more than 1
              'not visited' adjacent cell) {

         list.add(currentCell); //put it back in the list
      }                         //so other adjacent cells are
                                //considered later

      previousCell = currentCell;
      currentCell = getNextCell(previousCell);

      mark currentCell as 'visited';

      knock down the wall between
         previousCell and currentCell;

      list.add(currentCell);
   }
}
```

To support some of the operations expressed in the pseudocode, you may have to define additional methods in the MazeCell class.

16. Write a program that checks if the input arithmetic expression is syntactically correct. Assume the arithmetic expressions include only integer constants, four arithmetic operators, and parentheses. Nested parentheses are allowed. Here are examples of valid arithmetic expressions:

```
4 + 5
48 * (2 + 7)
(23 / (3 - 4)) / 8
12
```

And here are examples of invalid arithmetic expressions:

```
3 + - 8
9 * (4 + 2))
) 4 + 3 (
```

17. Forth is a unique and interesting programming language. It can be characterized as a *stack-oriented programming language* where programs are written in postfix notation. If we write arithmetic expressions using postfix notation, we write them as

```
<leftOperand> <rightOperand> <operator>
```

For example, instead of writing

```
45 + 9
```

we write

```
45 9 +
```

in postfix notation. The ordinary way we write arithmetic expressions uses the notation called *infix*. Here are some examples that compare the infix and postfix expressions:

Infix	Postfix
4 + 8 − 5	4 8 + 5 −
4 + (8 − 5)	4 8 5 − +
4 * 8 + 5	4 8 * 5 +
4 * (8 + 5)	4 8 5 + *

Notice that postfix expressions do not include parentheses because they are not necessary. Write a program that evaluates a given postfix arithmetic expression that consists of integer constants and four arithmetic operators +, −, /, and *. You use a stack to remember the operands. Whenever you encounter an operand in the input postfix expression, stack it. When you encounter an operator in the input postfix expression, its left and right operands are in the stack. Pop the stack twice to get the left and right operands, compute the result, and push the result back to the stack. When there are no more operators left in the expression, the top-of-stack element in the stack is the result of the whole expression. You may assume the input postfix expression is syntactically correct, so you do not have to do any error checking.

20 Queue ADT

Objectives

After you have read and studied this chapter, you should be able to

- Describe the key features of the Queue ADT.
- Implement the Queue ADT by using an array.
- Implement the Queue ADT by using a linked list.
- Explain the key differences between the array and linked implementations of the Queue ADT.
- Implement a special type of queue called a priority queue.

Introduction

Our study of the fundamental ADTs concludes with the Queue ADT in this chapter. Just as the Stack ADT is natural and intuitive because stacks are ubiquitous in our everyday, physical world, so is the Queue ADT. The Queue ADT is almost identical to the Stack ADT except for the one key difference, and often it is treated as an inseparable sibling of the Stack ADT.

The Queue ADT models a line of objects, such as people or vehicles, waiting to be serviced. Students waiting in line to pay for food at the cashier in the student union cafeteria, moviegoers waiting in line to enter the 16-screen cineplex, and vehicles waiting in line at the signal-controlled freeway on-ramp are all examples of queues. The defining feature of a queue is that the object at the front of the queue is the next to be serviced (imagine the ensuing chaos and havoc at Disney's Space Mountain if you randomly picked people in line for the next ride) and a new object is added to the end, or tail, of the queue.

As in the previous chapters, we begin with the definition of the Queue ADT and then provide two different implementations based on the array and the linked list. We will conclude the chapter with a special variation of a queue called a priority queue.

20.1 The Queue ADT

queue

tail

front

A ***queue*** is a linearly ordered collection of elements in which elements, or items, are added to a list at one end, called the ***tail***, and removed from the other end, called the ***front***. This restriction will ensure that the first element added to a list is the first to be removed next. For this reason, a queue is characterized as a *first-in, first-out (FIFO)* list. Figure 20.1 shows a sample generic queue named sampleQueue with five elements and another queue named myQueue with five three-letter animal names.

The operations we support in the Queue ADT are almost identical to those in the Stack ADT. The clear, isEmpty, peek, and size operations behave the same as those of the Stack ADT. The *clear* operation empties a queue. The *isEmpty* operation returns true if the queue contains no items. The *peek* operation returns the front item, without actually removing it. The *size* operation rereturns the number of items in the queue. The update operations for the queue are called *add* and *remove*. They are also called *enqueue* and *dequeue*, respectively. The *add* operation adds an item to the tail of a queue, and the *remove* operation removes the item at the front of a queue. We will describe these operations in greater detail.

add

The add operation will add the designated element to the tail of the queue. The queue does not have any size restriction, so it will grow without bound, just as the stack does. There is no restriction on the elements, so you can add duplicates. Figure 20.2 illustrates the add operation.

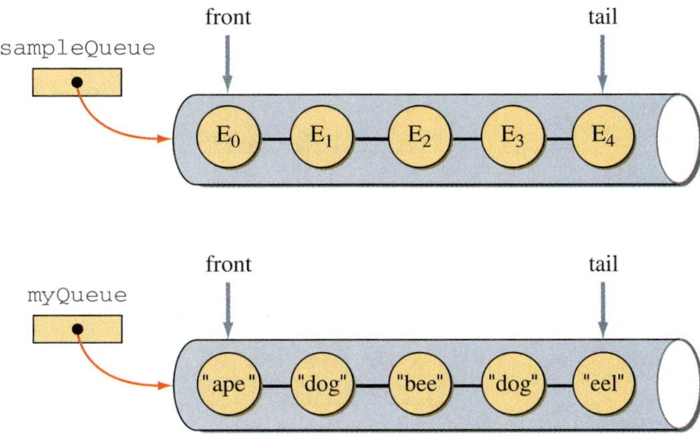

Figure 20.1 A generic stack **sampleQueue** with five elements and a stack **myQueue** with three-letter animal names.

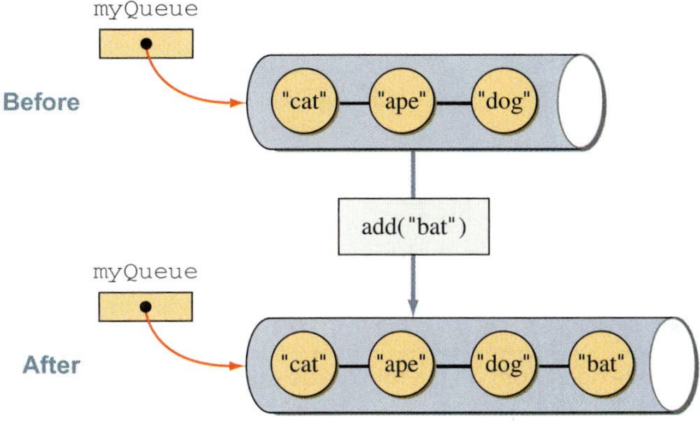

Figure 20.2 A sample **add** operation on the **myQueue** queue.

remove

The remove operation removes the front element from the queue if there is any. If the queue is empty, then the operation will throw an exception. Figure 20.3 illustrates the remove operation on nonempty and empty stacks.

peek

The peek operation is just like the remove operation except that the front element is not removed from the queue. If the queue is empty, then the operation will throw an exception.

clear

The clear operation removes all elements in the queue. It causes no problem to call the clear operation on an empty queue. This operation is useful when you want to reuse a queue. Before you reuse the queue for another purpose, you need to flush out any remaining items in the queue, and you can do it by calling the clear

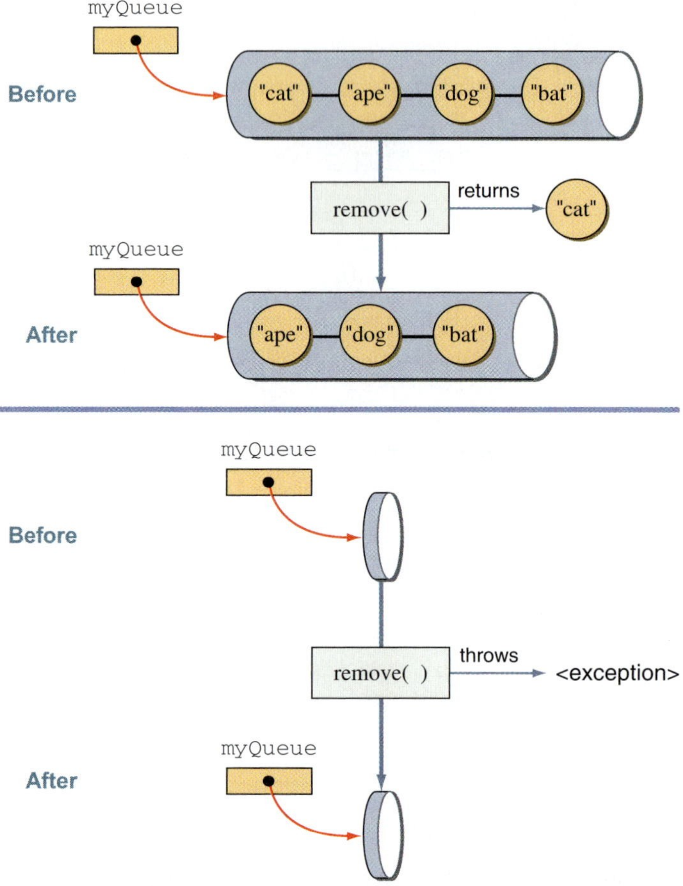

Figure 20.3 Sample **remove** operations on the **myQueue** queue.

operation, instead of removing items individually by calling the remove method repeatedly.

size

The size operation returns the number of elements in the queue.

isEmpty

The isEmpty operation tests whether the queue is empty. If it is, then true is returned. Otherwise, false is returned.

1. Draw the queue after executing the following operations, starting with an empty queue called myQueue.

```
String bee = new String("bee");
String cat = new String("cat");
```

```
myQueue.clear( );
myQueue.add(bee);
myQueue.add(cat);
myQueue.remove( );
```

2. Repeat Question 1 with the following statements:

```
String bee = new String("bee");
String cat = new String("cat");
String dog = new String("dog");

myQueue.add(bee);
myQueue.add(cat);
myQueue.add(dog);
myQueue.peek( );
myQueue.remove( );
myQueue.remove( );
myQueue.add(dog);
```

20.2 The Queue Interface

As we did for the List and Stack ADTs, we will use a Java interface to define the Queue ADT. We will continue to prefix our interfaces and classes with NPS. Here's the NSPQueue interface:

NPSQueue

```
package edu.nps.util;

public interface NPSSQueue<E> {

   public void add(E element);

   public void clear( );

   public boolean isEmpty( );

   public E peek( ) throws NPSQueueEmptyException;

   public E remove( ) throws NPSQueueEmptyException;

   public int size( );
}
```

Table 20.1 The `NPSQueue` interface

Interface: `NPSStack`	
`void`	`add( E element )` Adds an element to the queue. The element is added to the tail of the queue.
`void`	`clear( )` Removes all elements from the queue.
`boolean`	`isEmpty( )` Determines whether the queue is empty. Returns `true` if it is empty; `false` otherwise.
`E`	`peek( ) throws NPSQueueEmptyException` Returns the front element without removing it from the queue. Throws an exception when the queue is empty.
`E`	`remove( ) throws NPSQueueEmptyException` Removes the front element and returns it. Throws an exception when the queue is empty.
`int`	`size( )` Returns the number of elements in the queue.

Table 20.1 summarizes the methods of the NPSQueue interface.

Analogous to the implementation of the Stack ADT, the peek and remove methods are defined to throw an NPSQueueEmptyException. It is based on our design philosophy to use an exception that identifies the error condition as precisely as possible, instead of using a generic exception. Here's the definition:

NPSQueueEmptyException

```
package edu.nps.util;

public class NPSQueueEmptyException extends RuntimeException {

    public NPSQueueEmptyException( ) {

        this("Queue is empty");
    }

    public NPSQueueEmptyException(String message) {

        super(message);
    }
}
```

20.3 The Array Implementation

In this section, we will implement the NPSQueue interface by using an array to store the queue elements. Figure 20.4 illustrates the array implementation of the Queue ADT.

The NPSArrayQueue Definition

The NPSArrayQueue class implements the NPSStack interface, and its class declaration is as follows:

```
package edu.nps.util;

public class NPSArrayQueue<E> implements NPSQueue<E> {

    //class body comes here
}
```

We use an array element to store the queue elements and an int variable count to keep track of the number of elements currently in the queue. In addition, we use two int variables front and tail to keep track of the index positions of the element array to remove an item from and add an item to the queue. These data members are declared as

```
private static final int DEFAULT_SIZE = 25;
private E[ ] element;
```

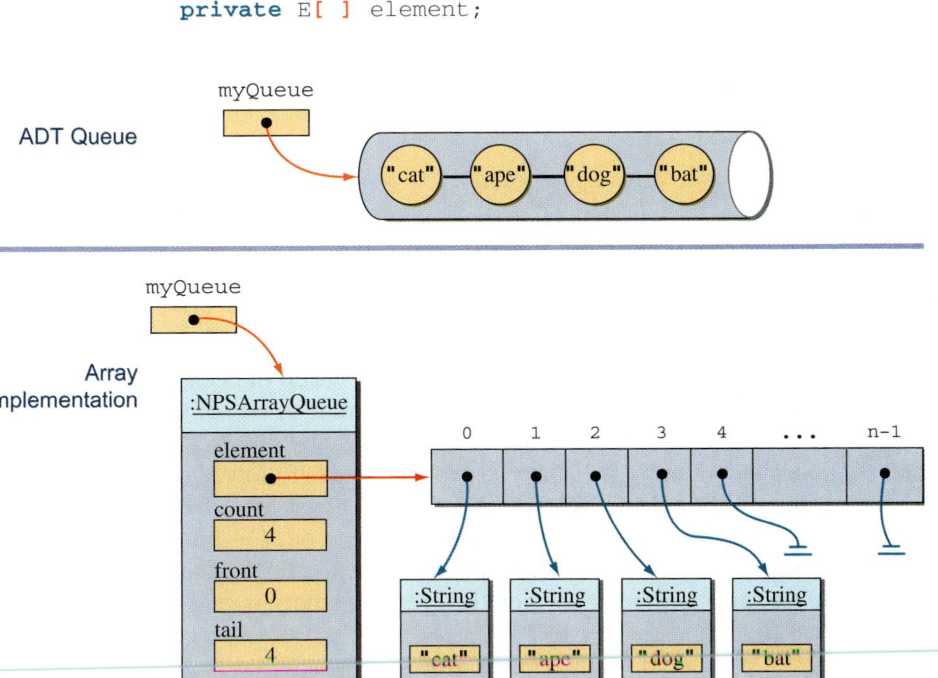

Figure 20.4 An array implementation of the Queue ADT.

```
private int count; //number of items in the queue
private int front; //position of the item to remove
private int tail; //position to add the next item
```

We will define two constructors: one takes no argument and another takes one argument that specifies the initial size of the array. They are defined as follows:

```
public NPSArrayQueue( ) {
    this(DEFAULT_SIZE);
}

public NPSArrayQueue(int size) {
   if (size <= 0) {
            throw new IllegalArgumentException(
                       "Initial capacity must be positive");
   }

    element = (E[]) new Object[size];
    clear( );
}
```

We create an array of Object and typecast it to an array of E, the type parameter, because it is not allowed to create an array of generic type in Java.

add

We maintain the data member tail to keep track of the index position of the element array to add an item. So we might think that the code

```
element[tail] = item;
tail++;
```

would suffice (provided, of course, that the overflow condition is handled by creating a new, larger array, as we did with the expand method in the NPSArrayList and NPSArrayStack classes). But this clean and straightforward solution would not work for the queue. Why?

The code does not work because we cannot increment the value of tail beyond element.length-1. Doing so would result in an IndexOutOfBoundsException. Easy, just create a new, larger array when the current value of tail becomes equal to element.length? It is not appropriate to do so because the condition does not indicate the array is full. Consider the following scenario. Suppose the size of the element array is N and you execute N adds followed by N removes. Since every time we remove the front item we need to increment front so it points to the new front item, the values of front and tail would be $N - 1$ and N, respectively. Do you want to create a new, larger array at this point? No, the queue is actually empty. Creating a larger array when the queue is empty is grossly inefficient. What shall we do?

We should create a larger array only when the array is full, and we detect this condition when the variable count is equal to element.length. The trick here to avoid the value of counters becoming larger than element.length-1 is to view the

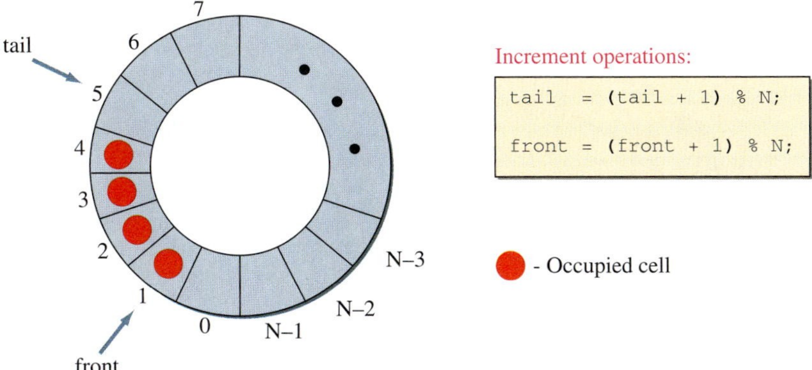

Figure 20.5 This illustrates viewing an array as if it were circular. The index counters move in a clockwise fashion. By using modulo arithmetic, the value of the index counters never gets beyond $N - 1$. After $N - 1$, the counters are reset to **0.**

element array as a circular array. Figure 20.5 illustrates a circular array with four items. We treat an array as if it is circular by using the modulo arithmetic when incrementing the index counters

```
tail  = (tail + 1) % N;

front = (front + 1) % N;
```

where N is the size (length) of the array. For example, when tail is equal to $N - 1$, incrementing it will result in tail having the value 0. By using this modulo arithmetic, the counters move round and round in clockwise fashion.

The add method is defined as follows:

```
public void add(E item) {

   //check if full
   if (count == element.length) {
       expand( );
   }

   element[tail] = item;

   tail = (tail + 1) % element.length;

   count++;
}
```

The expand method for the NPSArrayQueue class is a lot more complex than the corresponding method in the NPSArrayList and the NPSArrayStack classes because the array is "circular" in NPSArrayQueue. It is no longer a simple matter of copying elements at index position I in one array to the same index position I of

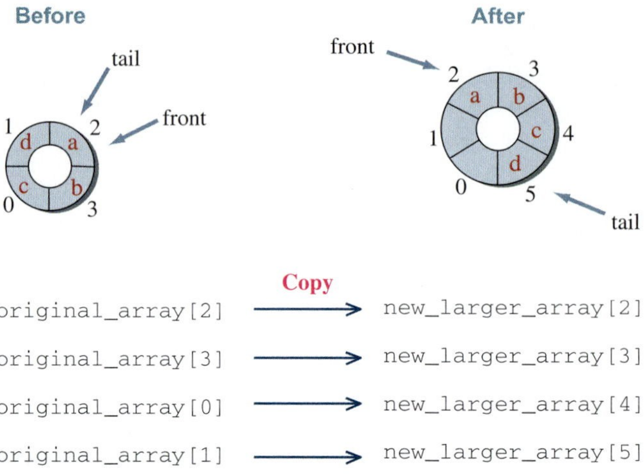

Figure 20.6 This illustrates how the **expand** method works for the circular array. The length of the original array is 4, and the front of the queue is stored at index position 2. Notice how the items are copied to the expanded array. The value of **front** remains the same, but the value of **tail** needs to be adjusted as shown.

the expanded array. Consider the example shown in Figure 20.6. The length of the original array is 4. The front item of the queue is stored at index position 2. When the overflow occurs, the condition front == tail is true. We create a new array that is 1.5 times larger than the original array, so the length of the new array is 6. Then we start copying the elements from the original array to the new larger array, starting from the front item. Because both arrays are circular, we cannot simply write something like

```
for (int i = front; i < tail; i++) {          <—— INVALID
   new_larger_array[i] = original_array[i];
}
```

Although conceptually this is what we want to do, the actual indices we need here must be incremented cyclically. Here's the correct procedure to copy items from a circular array element to a new and larger circular array temp:

```
int e_idx = front;
int t_idx = front;

for (int i = 0; i < count; i++) {  //count - # of items
                                   //         in queue
   temp[t_idx] = element[e_idx];
   t_idx = (t_idx + 1) % temp.length;
   e_idx = (e_idx + 1) % element.length;
}

tail = t_idx;
```

remove

This operation removes the front element from the queue. If the queue is not empty, we adjust the count data member and remove the topmost element by setting the value of the corresponding index position to null. Here's the method:

```
public E remove() throws NPSQueueEmptyException {

   E item;
   if (isEmpty( )) {

      throw new NPSQueueEmptyException( );

   } else {

      item = element[front];
      element[front] = null;
      front = (front + 1) % element.length;
      count--;
   }

   return item;
}
```

clear

We set element[i] to null, where i = 0, . . . , count-1, so the objects referenced by element[i] will be garbage-collected. We then reset the three variables to 0 to reflect the empty state.

```
public void clear( ) {

   for (int i = 0; i < count; i++) {
      element[i] = null;
   }

   front = tail = count = 0;
}
```

isEmpty

This operation is straightforward. If the value of count is 0, then the stack is empty. Otherwise, the stack is not empty.

```
public boolean isEmpty( ) {

   return (count == 0);
}
```

peek

We throw an NPSQueueEmptyException when the queue is empty. Otherwise, we return the front item.

```
public E peek() throws NPSQueueEmptyException {

   if (isEmpty( )) {

      throw new NPSQueueEmptyException( );

   } else {
```

```
            return element[front];
        }
    }
```

size

The last method is straightforward. We simply return the value of the count data member.

```
public int size ( ) {

    return count;
}
```

Here's the complete source code (for brevity, javadoc and most other comments in the actual source file are removed here):

NPSArrayQueue

```
package edu.nps.util;

public class NPSArrayQueue<E> implements NPSQueue<E> {

    private static final int DEFAULT_SIZE = 25;

    private E[ ] element;

    private int count;

    private int front;

    private int tail;

    public NPSArrayQueue( ) {

        this(DEFAULT_SIZE);
    }

    public NPSArrayQueue(int size) {

        if (size <= 0) {
            throw new IllegalArgumentException(
                                "Initial capacity must be positive");
        }

        element = (E[]) new Object[size];
        count = 0;
    }

    public void add(E item) {

        if (count == element.length) {
            expand( );
        }
```

Constructor

add

```
    tail = (tail + 1) % element.length;
    count++;
}

public void clear() {

    for (int i = 0; i < count; i++) {
        element[i] = null;
    }

    front = tail = count = 0;
}

public boolean isEmpty() {

    return count == 0;
}

public E peek( ) throws NPSQueueEmptyException {

    if (isEmpty( )) {

        throw new NPSQueueEmptyException( );

    } else {

        return element[front];
    }
}

public E remove() throws NPSQueueEmptyException {

   E item;

   if (isEmpty( )) {

        throw new NPSQueueEmptyException( );

    } else {

        item = element[front];
        element[front] = null;
        front = (front + 1) % element.length;
        count--;
    }

    return item;
}

public int size( ) {

    return count;
}
```

clear

isEmpty

peek

remove

size

```
    private void expand( ) {

        E[] temp = (E[]) new Object[(int)(1.5 * element.length)];

        int e_idx = front;
        int t_idx = front;

        for (int i = 0; i < count; i++) {

            temp[t_idx] = element[e_idx];

            t_idx = (t_idx + 1) % temp.length;
            e_idx = (e_idx + 1) % element.length;
        }

        tail = t_idx;

        element = temp;
    }
}
```

expand

1. Draw the array queue (like the diagram in Figure 20.4) after executing the following operations, starting with an empty queue called myQueue.

```
String bee = new String("bee");
String cat = new String("cat");

myQueue.clear();
myQueue.add(cat);
myQueue.add(bee);
```

2. Can we use the test front == tail to detect the empty queue?

20.4 The Linked-List Implementation

Compared to the array implementation of the List and Stack ADTs, the array implementation of the Queue ADT has an increased complexity of dealing with the circular array. Fortunately, the linked-list implementation of the Queue ADT does not incur any additional complexity. Its implementation is rather straightfoward. Figure 20.7 illustrates the linked-list implementation of the Queue ADT.

The QueueNode Class

The linked node structure for the queue is exactly the same as the one for the list and the stack. The QueueNode class is defined as the inner class of the NPSLinkedQueue

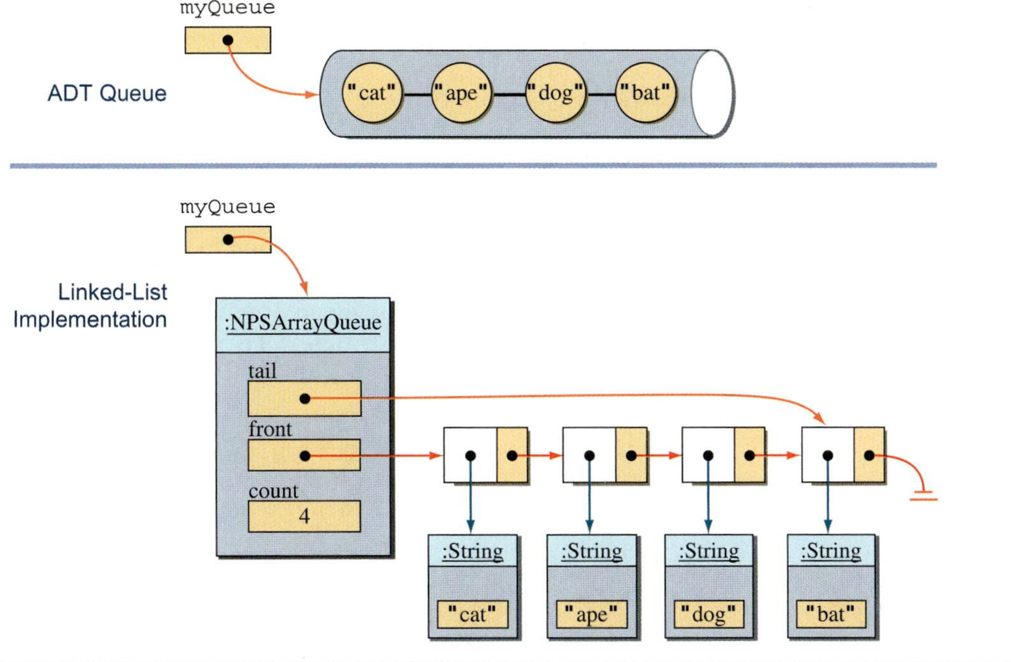

Figure 20.7 A linked-list implementation of the stack **myQueue.**

class. It's class definition is as follows:

```
class QueueNode {

   private E item;

   private QueueNode next;

   public QueueNode(E item) {
      this.item = item;
      this.next = null;
   }
}
```

The NPSLinkedQueue Class

We keep three data members in the class. As always, we have one data member to keep track of the number of items currently in the queue. The other two data members—front and tail—are reference variables that point to the front and tail elements. Their declarations are

```
private QueueNode front;

private QueueNode tail;

private int       count;
```

We define only a single constructor that takes no arguments and sets the stack to its initial state, which is an empty queue. The constructor is defined as follows:

```
public NPSLinkedQueue( ) {
   clear( );
}
```

add

There are two cases to consider when adding a new item. In the first case, the queue is empty. In this case, we set both front and tail to the new item. In the second case, the queue is not empty. In this case, we append the new item as the last node in the linked list and need to adjust the tail pointer only. In both cases, we increment the counter variable count by 1. Here's the method:

```
public void add(E item) {

   QueueNode newNode = new QueueNode(item);

   if (isEmpty()) {

       front = tail = newNode;

   } else {

      tail.next = newNode;
      tail = newNode;
   }

   count++;
}
```

clear

We reset the two pointers front and tail to null and the counter count to 0. By setting front and tail to null, all nodes in the linked list will get garbage-collected eventually. Here's the clear method:

```
public void clear( ) {

   front = tail = null;
   count = 0;
}
```

isEmpty

We detect the queue is empty when the value of count is 0:

```
public boolean isEmpty( ) {
   return count == 0;
}
```

peek

If the queue is empty, we throw an NPSQueueEmptyException. Otherwise, we return the front item (without actually removing it). Here's the method:

```
public E peek( ) throws NPSQueueEmptyException {

   if (isEmpty( )) {
```

```
            throw new NPSQueueEmptyException( );

        } else {

            return front.item;
        }
    }
```

remove

If the queue is empty, we throw an NPSQueueEmptyException. Otherwise, we set a temp pointer to the topmost item, update the topOfStack pointer, and return the topmost item. Here's the method:

```
    public E remove( ) throws NPSQueueEmptyException {

        E item;

        if (isEmpty( )) {

            throw new NPSQueueEmptyException( );

        } else {

            item = front.item;

            front = front.next;

            count--;
        }

        return item;
    }
```

size

The size method simply returns the value of the data member count:

```
    public int size( ) {
        return count;
    }
```

Here's the complete source code listing of the NPSLinkedQueue class (as usual, javadoc comments are omitted for brevity):

NPSLinkedQueue

```
package edu.nps.util;

public class NPSLinkedQueue<E> implements NPSQueue<E> {

    private QueueNode front;

    private QueueNode tail;

    private int count;
```

```
public NPSLinkedQueue( ) {
    clear( );
}
```

Constructor

```
public void add(E item) {

   QueueNode newNode = new QueueNode(item);

   if (isEmpty()) {

      front = tail = newNode;

   } else {

      tail.next = newNode;
      tail = newNode;
   }

   count++;
}
```

add

```
public void clear( ) {

    front = tail = null;

    count = 0;
}
```

clear

```
public boolean isEmpty( ) {

    return (count == 0);
}
```

isEmpty

```
public E peek( ) throws NPSQueueEmptyException {

    if (isEmpty( )) {

        throw new NPSQueueEmptyException( );

    } else {

        return front.item;
    }
}
```

peek

```
public E remove( ) throws NPSQueueEmptyException {

   E item;

   if (isEmpty( )) {

      throw new NPSQueueEmptyException( );
```

remove

```
        } else {

            item = front.item;

            front = front.next;

            count--;
        }

        return item;
    }

    public int size( ) {

        return count;
    }

    class QueueNode {

        private E item;

        private Queue next;

        public QueueNode(E item) {

            this.item = item;
            this.next = null;
        }
    }
}
```

size

QueueNode

1. Draw the linked stack (like the right-hand side diagram in Figure 20.7) after executing the following operations, starting with an empty stack called myQueue.

```
String bee = new String("bee");
String cat = new String("cat");

myQueue.clear();
myQueue.push(cat);
myQueue.push(bee);
```

2. Instead of using count == 0 to check for an empty stack, can we use front == null or tail == null?

20.5 Implementation Using NPSList

Analogous to the **NPSListStack** class, we can define a class that implements the **NPSQueue** interface easily by using an **NPSList**. Here's the **NPSListQueue** class:

NPSListQueue

```
package edu.nps.util;

public class NPSListQueue<E> implements NPSQueue<E> {

    private static final int FRONT = 0;

    private NPSList<E> list;

    public NPSListQueue( ) {
        list = new NPSLinkedList<E>();
    }

    public void add(E element) {
        list.add(list.size(), element);
    }

    public void clear( ) {
        list.clear();
    }

    public boolean isEmpty( ) {
        return list.isEmpty();
    }

    public E peek( ) throws NPSQueueEmptyException {

        if (isEmpty( )) {

            throw new NPSQueueEmptyException( );

        } else {

            return list.get(FRONT);
        }
    }

    public E remove( ) throws NPSQueueEmptyException {

        if (isEmpty( )) {

            throw new NPSQueueEmptyException( );

        } else {

            return list.remove(FRONT);
        }
    }
```

Constructor

add

clear

isEmpty

peek

remove

```
    public int size( ) {
        return list.size();
    }
}
```

size

The class is implemented cleanly and elegantly by using a list. Since a queue is a FIFO list, we add a new item at the end of the list and remove only the first (front) item of the list.

20.6 Priority Queue

With a queue, items are treated fairly and equally. An item that arrives first in line is the first to be served next. In real life, queues do not always follow this egalitarian rule. Travelers are routinely moved up to the front of the security line at the airport when their flights are departing soon. Partygoers who know the right people never wait in line to get into the hottest nightclub in town. In many situations, we have legitimate reasons to prioritize items in the queue so the highest-priority item is served next. See Exercise 9 for a computer-related example.

priority queue

A ***priority queue*** is a queue in which items are prioritized so that the item with the highest priority is placed at the front of the queue. Every time a new item is added, the queue is rearranged so the highest-priority item will always be at the front. In this section, we describe how such a priority queue can be implemented very effectively by using the heap structure we introduced in Chapter 11.

We will call the class NPSPriorityQueue that realizes the priority queue. It is a queue so we set the class to implement the NPSQueue interface:

```
public class NPSPriorityQueue<E extends Comparable>
                                implements NPSQueue<E>
```

We will use the heap structure to maintain the priority queue (see Section 11.3). When we add an item, we place it as the last node of the heap and go through the construction process so the highest-priority item will move to the root of the heap. Remember that the construction process includes approximately $N/2$ rebuilding processes (see Figure 11.14). The remove method will remove the root of the heap. After the removal, we need to rebuild the heap with one fewer item. We do this by moving (temporarily) the last node of the heap to the root position and going through the rebuilding process once (see Figure 11.11).

To be able to move around items in the heap, we need to decide how to compare the priorities of items. First, we dictate that the type parameter E implement the Comparable interface; that is, E must include the method compareTo. Second, the compareTo method must defined in the following manner:

```
e1.compareTo(e2) < 0    e1 has higher priority than e2
e1.compareTo(e2) == 0   e1 and e2 has the same priority
e1.compareTo(e2) > 0    e1 has lower priority than e2
```

Remember that we used an array to implement the heap structure in Chapter 11. We will use the same technique here to implement the heap structure we need for the NPSPriorityQueue class. Implementation of the NPSPriorityQueue class is basically a combination of the code that appeared in the NPSArrayQueue class and the Heap class (from Chapter 11) with some necessary modifications. As such, we will just go ahead and list the complete class now, skipping the explanation of the methods that are essentially identical to those we've seen already.

NPSPriorityQueue

```
package edu.nps.util;

public class NPSPriorityQueue<E> implements NPSQueue<E> {

    private static final int DEFAULT_SIZE = 25;

    private static final int ROOT = 0;

    private E[] heap;

    private int count;

    public NPSPriorityQueue( ) {

        this(DEFAULT_SIZE);
    }

    public NPSPriorityQueue(int size) {

        if (size <= 0) {
            throw new IllegalArgumentException(
                        "Initial capacity must be positive");
        }

        heap = (E[])new Object[size];

        clear();
    }

    public void add(E item) {

        if (count == heap.length) {
            expand( );
        }

        heap[count] = item;

        construct();

        count++;
    }
```

Constructors

add

```
public void clear() {

    for (int i = 0; i < count; i++) {
         heap[i] = null;
    }

    count = 0;
}

public boolean isEmpty( ) {
    return count == 0;
}

public E peek() throws NPSQueueEmptyException {

    if (isEmpty()) {

        throw new NPSQueueEmptyException( );

    } else {

        return (E) heap[ROOT];
    }
}

public E remove() throws NPSQueueEmptyException {

    E item;

    if (isEmpty()) {

        throw new NPSQueueEmptyException( );

    } else {

        item = heap[ROOT];

        heap[ROOT] = heap[count-1];

        count--;

        rebuild(ROOT);
    }

    return item;
}

public int size( ) {

    return count;
}

private void construct( ) {

    for (int i = (count-2) / 2; i >= 0; i--) {
```

clear

isEmpty

peek

remove

size

construct

```
            rebuild(i);
        }
    }

    private void expand( ) {

        E[] temp = (E[])new Object[(int) (heap.length * 1.5)];

        for (int i = 0; i < heap.length; i++) {
            temp[i] = heap[i];
        }

        heap = temp;
    }

    private int higherPriorityChild(int location, int end) {

        int result, leftChildIndex, rightChildIndex;

        rightChildIndex = 2*location + 2;
        leftChildIndex  = 2*location + 1;

        if ( rightChildIndex <= end &&
            ((Comparable<E>)heap[leftChildIndex]).
                compareTo(heap[rightChildIndex]) < 0) {

            result = leftChildIndex;

        } else {

            result = rightChildIndex;
        }

        return result;
    }

    private void rebuild(int root) {

        int current = root;

        boolean done = false;

        while (!done) {

            if (2*current+1 > count-1) {
                //current node has no children, so stop
                done = true;

            } else {

                //current node has at least one child,
                //get the index of higher-priority child
                int hiChildIndex = higherPriorityChild(current, count-1);
```

expand

higherPriorityChild

rebuild

```
                if ((Comparable<E>)heap[hiChildIndex]).
                        compareTo(heap[current]) < 0) {

                    swap(current, hiChildIndex);
                    current = hiChildIndex;

                } else { //value relationship constraint
                       //is satisfied, so stop
                    done = true;
                }
            }
        }
    }

    private void swap(int loc1, int loc2) {

        E temp;

        temp = heap[loc1];
        heap[loc1] = heap[loc2];
        heap[loc2] = temp;
    }
}
```

swap

Here's a short sample code that illustrates the use of NPSPriorityQueue. The program adds 100 random integers (ranges from 0 to 999, inclusive) and removes them one by one from the priority. The output list will display integers in ascending order.

```
import java.util.*;

import edu.nps.util.*;

class TestPriorityQueue {

    public static void main(String[] args) {

        NPSQueue<Integer> pq =
                    new NPSPriorityQueue<Integer>();

        Random random = new Random();

        for (int i = 0; i < 100; i++) {

            pq.add(random.nextInt(1000));
        }

        for (int j = 0; j < 100; j++) {

            System.out.println(pq.remove());
        }
    }
}
```

Summary

- A queue is a linearly ordered first-in, first-out (FIFO) collection of elements.
- An item can be added to only the end of a queue, and only the first item of a queue can be removed.
- The last item is called the *tail* of a queue, and the first item is called the *front*.
- An array and a linked list are two possible implementations of the Queue ADT.
- The Queue ADT can be implemented easily by using a list (an instance of a class that implements the List ADT).
- Base implementation of the Queue ADT does not support any traversal operation.
- A priority queue is a special type of queue that moves the highest-priority item to the front of the queue.

Key Concepts

queue ADT
array implementation of Queue ADT
linked-list implementation of Queue ADT
priority queue

Exercises

1. Draw a state-of-memory diagram that shows the result of executing each of the following sets of code. Do not forget to show the values of `front` and `tail`.

a.

```
NPSQueue queue = new NPSArrayQueue(5);

queue.add("one");
queue.add("two");
queue.add("three");
queue.add("four");

queue.remove( );
queue.remove( );
```

b.

```
NPSQueue queue = new NPSLinkedQueue( );

queue.add("one");
queue.add("two");
queue.add("three");
queue.add("four");

queue.remove( );
queue.remove( );
```

2. Add a new method toArray to the NPSQueue interface and implement the method in both NPSArrayQueue and NPSLinkedQueue. The toArray method will return an array with the front element at position 0, the element after the front at position 1, and so forth.
3. Add a new method iterator to the NPSQueue interface that returns an iterator. Implement the iterator method in the NPSArrayQueue and NPSLinkedQueue classes.
4. Although the use of the count data member makes the implementation of the NPSArrayQueue class cleaner and slightly easier, its use is not a strict requirement. You can implement the class without it. Rewrite the NPSArrayQueue class with the count data member removed. You have to find out the number of items in the queue from the values of front and tail data members. Because the array is circular, you cannot simply use the expression

```
tail - front
```

to determine the number of items in the queue. Also, you have to be very careful in detecting the array is full. *Hint:* If the length of an array is N, occupy at most $N - 1$ positions. Treat the array is full when $N - 1$ positions are filled.
5. Redo Exercise 4 with the NPSLinkedQueue class. Without the count data member, you must traverse the linked list to find out how many items are in the queue.
6. Write a program that sorts input strings in lexicographic order by using the NPSPriorityQueue class. Continually prompt for the next input word until the end marker −1 is entered. Terminate the program after printing out the input words in lexicographic order, one word per line. Notice that the String class already implements the Comparable interface so no additional effort is necessary for you to add String objects to an NPSPriorityQueue. The priority queue treats a string that comes earlier in lexicographic order as having a higher priority. For example, the word cat has a higher priority than dog.
7. Repeat Exercise 6, but this time output the words in reverse lexicographic order. You are not allowed to change the implementation of the NPSPriorityQueue class. Although the source code of NPSPriorityQueue is available to you, treat it as if it is a part of some standard API.
8. Write a bank ATM simulation program. The purpose of this simulation is to find out the average waiting time for customers using the ATMs. There are three inputs to the program: M is the number of minutes to simulate, P is the probability of a customer arriving at each minute, and N is the number of ATMs. For example, if the input values for M, P, and N are 60, 0.5, and 4, respectively, then we are simulating 4 ATMs during a 60-minute period with 50 percent chance that a customer arrives at each minute. When a customer arrives, randomly assign a number between 1 minute and 5 minutes, inclusive, as this customer's transaction time, the time it takes for this

customer to finish using the ATM. Each ATM has its own queue, and an arriving customer will move to the shortest queue. An ATM is either available (open) or not available (currently used by another customer). When a customer completes his or her transaction, an ATM becomes available immediately. And if there's a customer waiting in the queue, the ATM will service this customer immediately (and becomes unavailable).

Each minute is treated as a discrete event, so the top-level simulation control can be expressed as a for loop:

```
for (int min = 0; min < M; min++) {

    //process incoming customer
    if (a new customer arrives) {
       assign him/her to the shortest queue
    }

    //process ATMs
    for (int i = 0; i < N; i++) {

       if (ATM[i] is in use) {

           decrement the transaction time of
            its customer by 1;

           if (the remaining time of the customer == 0) {
              //this customer is done
              set the status of ATM[i] to available
           }
       }

        if (ATM[i] is available) {
            //pick the next customer from
            //the queue if there's one
            if (ATM[i] has customer in its queue) {
                   remove the customer form the queue,
                   set his/her waiting time, and
                   assign him/her to ATM[i]
            }
        }
    }
}
```

At the end of simulation, output the average waiting time along with the input values. Run the program multiple times. Experiment with different values for *P* and *N* to see the effect. For instance, you should expect to see an increase in average waiting times if you keep the values for *M* and *P* the same, but decrease the value for *N*, say, from 4 to 1.

Notice that when the outer for loop [for (int min = 0; min < M; min++)] exits, it is possible that the queues may still contain customers. There are two possible ways to handle the situation. The first way is to assume that all those waiting customers will be served immediately (you can say that the bank will open up as many ATMs as necessary to serve immediately). The second way is to continue the simulation loop until all queues are empty. For this exercise, you may choose either solution.

9. Write a job scheduling simulation program. In good old days, well before the PC revolution, computer science students wrote programs by using keypunch machines and ran them on the mainframe computers. A program is recorded on a stack of punch cards, one statement per punch card. To run their programs, students must submit the program (the stack of cards) to the computer operator. A submitted program is called a *job*. Students taking a computer course are assigned a certain number of units (kind of a virtual money) and charged *N* units to run a program. The actual amount charged is determined by the priority the students assign to their programs. For this exercise, assume that the priorities range from 1 to 5, with 1 being the highest.

Write a program that simulates the job scheduling. Inputs to the program are *M*, which is the number of minutes to simulate, and *N*, which is the number of jobs that the computer can run concurrently. Treat each minute as a discrete event. Assume that a single job arrives at each minute. When a job arrives, randomly assign its priority and the number of minutes it needs to be executed. Choose any integer between 1 minute and 10 minutes, inclusive, for the execution time. An arriving job is placed in a priority queue. At every discrete event, if the number of jobs assigned to the computer is below the maximum number of jobs the computer can handle, remove jobs from the priority queue and assign them to the computer.

At the end of the simulation, output the average waiting time and the maximum waiting time for each priority level. See Exercise 8 on how to handle the situation in which the queue is not empty at the end of simulated minutes.

Appendix A
How to Run Java Programs

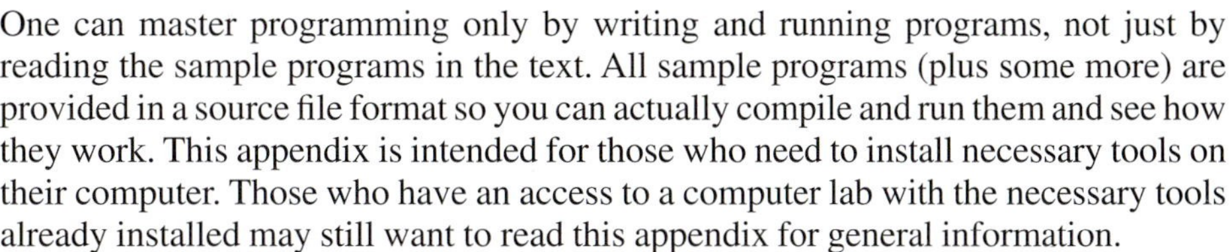

One can master programming only by writing and running programs, not just by reading the sample programs in the text. All sample programs (plus some more) are provided in a source file format so you can actually compile and run them and see how they work. This appendix is intended for those who need to install necessary tools on their computer. Those who have an access to a computer lab with the necessary tools already installed may still want to read this appendix for general information.

In this appendix, we will explain a number of different ways of running Java programs. They can be divided broadly into three categories: minimalist, enhanced editor, and full *integrated development environment* (IDE). For the beginning programmers, we recommend the enhanced editor approach. You can find additional information, such as detailed step-by-step instructions, on using some of the tools mentioned in this appendix from our website at www.drcaffeine.com.

Things to Remember

Please read Chapter 2 before this appendix.

At the end of this appendix, we will describe how to use classes from programmer-defined packages, such as the author-provided javabook package, in running your programs.

The Minimalist Approach

In this approach we use the absolute minimum to compile and run Java programs. We need to download a necessary compiler and other tools for compiling and running Java programs from the Sun Microsystems website at http://java.sun.com. A collection of tools for compiling and running Java programs is called a *Java 2 SDK (Software Development Kit)*. Sun also uses the term JDK instead of SDK. JDK stands for Java Development Kit. Sun Microsystems provides three versions for SDK: enterprise edition (J2EE SDK), standard edition (J2SE SDK), and micro edition (J2ME SDK). The one you need to download is the standard edition. We describe the steps for the MS Windows platform here.

1. **Installation**

   Download the most recent version J2SE JDK 5.0 for MS Windows. At the time of this writing (October, 2006), the most recent version is JDK 5.0 Update 9. The website for downloading J2SE JDK 5.0 is

   http://java.sun.com/javase/downloads/index.jsp.

   Please be aware that website addresses change frequently. If the given address does not work, you can search for the correct page starting from the Java homepage at http://java.sun.com. Click the Download button next to the heading **JDK 5.0 Update 9.** Click the Accept radio button to accept the license agreement and then click the link "Windows Offline Installation, Multi-language." This will download the file titled jdk-1_5_0_09-windows-i586-p.exe. Once the file is downloaded, double-click the file to begin the installation. You may choose any directory for installation. In this example, we assume the tools are installed in the directory

   ```
   C:\jdk1.5.0
   ```

   You may change it to any name and location you like. When the installation completes successfully, you will see a number of subdirectories, such as bin and lib, under the installation directory.

2. **Create a Program**

   We are now ready to create a program. Using Notepad (or any other text editor, but don't use a word processor that saves special markers with a document), create the following program:

   ```
   import javax.swing.*;
   class MyFirstProgram {
      public static void main(String[] arg) {
         JOptionPane.showMessageDialog(null, "It works!");
         System.exit(0);
      }
   }
   ```

   Type in the program exactly as shown, making sure the uppercase and lowercase letters are entered correctly. Note: A simple text editor, such as Notepad, will display the code in black only.

3. **Save the Program**

   Before we compile and run the program, let's save the program. First create a folder. (*Note:* We use the words *folder* and *directory* synonymously.) For this example, we will create a folder named JavaPrograms under the C: drive.

   ```
   C:\JavaPrograms
   ```

   Save the program by selecting the menu choice File/Save of Notepad and giving the name MyFirstProgram.java. Put this file in the C:\JavaPrograms folder. The name of the class is MyFirstProgram, so we save it as MyFirstProgram.java. If you name the program XYZ, then save it as XYZ.java. Note that it is case-sensitive. When you use Notepad, be careful that the file is not saved as MyFirstProgram.java.txt. Make sure there's no txt suffix appended to the filename. To avoid the automatic appending of the txt suffix, don't forget to set the value for Save as type to All Files.

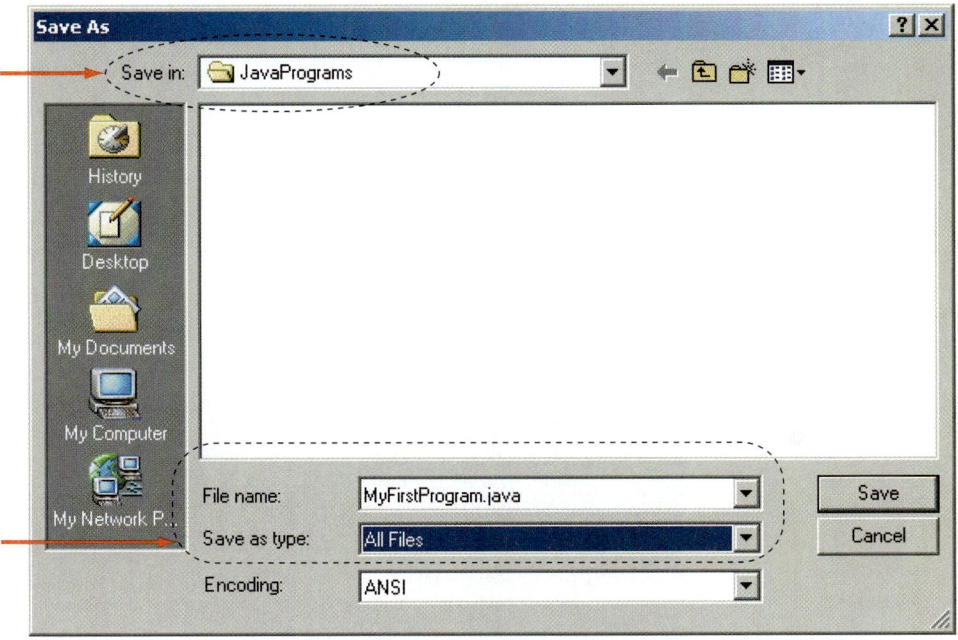

4. **Open a Command Prompt Window**
   After the source file is created and saved properly, we are ready to compile and run it. We use a command prompt window to enter the commands for compiling and running Java programs. Open a command prompt window by selecting the Start/Run... option

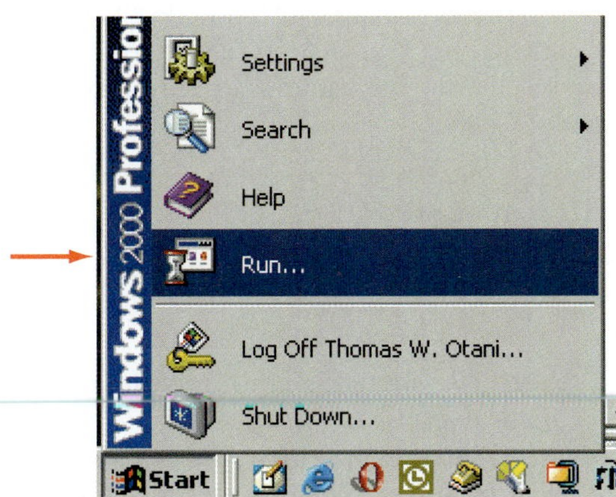

and entering the text cmd in the text field of the Run dialog box (if cmd does not work, try command):

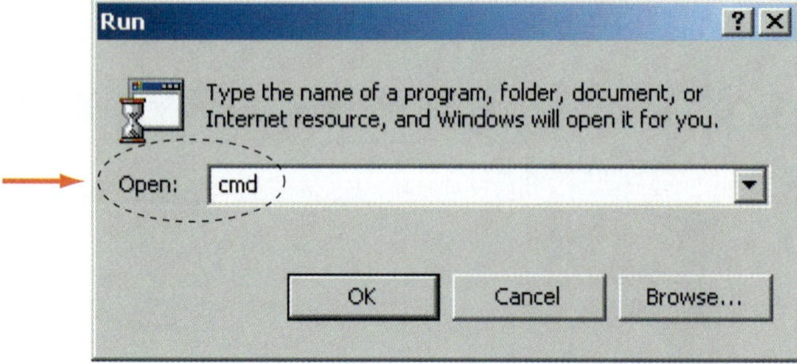

Click the OK button. A command prompt window appears on the screen:

```
C:\WINNT\System32\cmd.exe
Microsoft Windows 2000 [Version 5.00.2195]
(C) Copyright 1985-2000 Microsoft Corp.

C:\>_
```

From this point on, all commands are entered in this window.

5. **Set the Environment**
   Before we can actually compile and run the program, we must set the environment. First change to the JavaPrograms directory where the source file is stored by entering the command cd JavaPrograms (and pressing the Enter key):

```
C:\> cd \JavaPrograms
C:\JavaPrograms>
```

Note: The text we enter is shown in blue. The prompt displayed by the computer is shown in black.
Note: It is beyond the scope of this appendix to explain DOS commands. Please consult other sources if you need to learn DOS commands.

Enter the following two commands in sequence to set the environment:

```
C:\JavaPrograms>set path=C:\jdk1.5.0\bin
C:\JavaPrograms>set classpath=.
C:\JavaPrograms>
```

Enter the commands exactly as shown. Do not introduce any spaces between the equals symbols (=), for example. The first command sets the PATH environment variable so we can refer to the executable files in the bin subdirectory of C:\jdk1.5.0. The second command tells the Java compiler and interpreter where to find the source files. The period (.) indicates the current directory. You need to enter the two commands only once.

6. **Compile the Program**
Finally we are ready to compile the program. To compile a Java source file, use the javac command followed by the filename of the source file. Enter the following command exactly, that is, in a case-sensitive manner:

```
C:\JavaPrograms>javac MyFirstProgram.java
```

After a moment of pause, when there's no error in the program, the prompt to enter the next command appears. An error message will appear if there's an error. If that happens, go back to Notepad and check the program. Make any necessary changes and save it again. Then enter the javac command again. As explained in Chapter 2, successful compilation will result in a creation of a bytecode file.

7. **Run the Program**
After the successful compilation of the program, we are finally ready to run the program by executing its bytecode file. To run the program, we use the java command followed by the name of the bytecode file (with no suffix). Enter the following command and press the Enter key:

```
C:\JavaPrograms> java MyFirstProgram
```

The program starts and a message dialog appears on the screen:

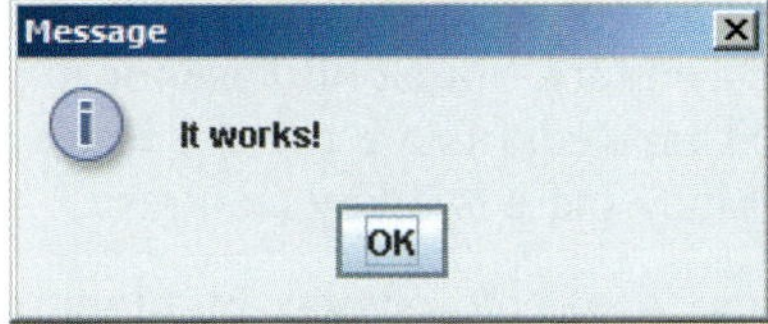

Close this message dialog by clicking its OK button.
Congratulations! You have successfully executed your first Java program.

The Significance of the System.exit Statement

The last statement of the sample program was

```
System.exit(0);
```

which caused the program to terminate. If you adopt the minimalist approach of using Notepad (or another simple text editor) and a command prompt window, you must include the exit statement to terminate the sample MyFirstProgram program. If you don't, then the program will not terminate. The message dialog disappears from the screen when you click its OK button, but the program is still active. When this happens, you will not get another prompt in the command prompt window. And, of course, without getting a command prompt, you can't enter another command anymore. Not all programs behave in this way. Specifically, a program that uses console-based standard input and output does not require the exit statement, while a program that uses GUI-based input and output (such as MyFirstProgram that uses the GUI-based JOptionPane for output) requires the exit statement. When you are using the minimalist approach, the easiest thing to do is to include the exit statement for all programs.

The Enhanced Editor Approach

For a very simple program, the minimalist approach may be an acceptable alternative. However, when the programs we develop become larger, the minimalist approach becomes cumbersome. Unlike with the minimalist approach in which we have to deal with separate tools for editing (Notepad) and running (command prompt) programs, with the enhanced editor approach, we interact with a single tool that will let us edit, compile, and run Java programs. For the beginning programmers, we recommend the enhanced editor approach.

There are a number of good software tools that fall under this category. Some of the more well-known ones are

- TextPad (www.textpad.com)
- jEdit (www.jedit.org)
- JCreator (www.jcreator.com)
- BlueJ (www.bluej.org)
- jGrasp (www.eng.auburn.edu/grasp)

You can look for other enhanced editors by visiting Google and entering the search text "Java editors." Most of these tools are available free or for a nominal fee. The enhanced Java editors are diverse in user interface style and the options they support, but they share two key features:

1. **Support of color syntax highlighting.** Different portions of the code are displayed in different colors (reserved words in blue, comments in green, string constants in cyan, and so forth).

2. Use of Java 2 SDK. The enhanced editors provide us with an environment where we can enter, compile, and run Java programs, but the actual compilation and execution of programs are done by Java 2 SDK tools (javac, java, etc.). In other words, instead of dealing with Java 2 SDK tools directly by entering commands in the command prompt window, we deal with them by selecting corresponding menu choices of the enhanced editor.

Since we cannot describe the enhanced editors adequately in a limited space, we refer you to their respective websites for instructions on how to use them. Also, brief how-to documents on most of the enhanced editors listed here can be found at our website (www.drcaffeine.com).

The IDE Approach

Tools in the IDE approach are geared toward serious programmers developing large-scale programs. Borland JBuilder, Eclipse, Metrowerks CodeWarrior, and NetBeans are some of the well-known full IDEs. In addition to many features, they typically include a visual editor that lets programmers design the user interface of a program visually by dragging and dropping GUI objects from the component palettes. They are complicated, and it takes time to master and use the various features supported by them properly. For this reason, this approach is not recommend for beginning programmers.

Using Programmer-Defined Packages

When we are using classes from the system packages such as javax.swing, java.util, and others, all we do is to include appropriate import statements in the program. This is not enough when we are using classes from programmer-defined packages. We must also set the environment correctly. How we set the environment is dependent on the development tools we use. We will describe how to set the environment to use programmer-defined packages with the minimalist approach. Please visit our website (www.drcaffeine.com) for information on using programmer-defined packages with the enhanced editor approach.

We will use the author-provided javabook package as an example to illustrate the procedure. You can download this package and its documentation from the textbook website. We assume you have downloaded and installed the javabook classes under the C:\JavaPrograms\javabook directory. Notice that the name of the package is javabook, and the directory that contains the classes in this package is also named javabook. This is the requirement. The classes in the package xyz must be placed in the directory named xyz. The directory xyz, however, can be placed anywhere you want. In this example, we put the javabook directory under C:\JavaPrograms. When the installation is done correctly, you should see the source and bytecode files of the javabook classes such as MainWindow.java, MainWindow.class, OutputBox.java, OutputBox.class, and others in the C:\JavaPrograms\javabook directory.

Things to Remember

For this example, we assume that the classes from the author-provided **javabook** *package are placed in the directory.*

```
C:\JavaPrograms\javabook
```

All you have to do is to change the setting for the class path as follows:

```
set classpath=.;c:\JavaPrograms
```

Notice that we specify the directory that contains the javabook directory. We do specify the full path name to the javabook directory itself.

Things to Remember

To use the **javabook** *classes stored in the directory* **C:\Javaprograms\javabook,** *set the class path by entering the command.*

```
set classpath=.;c:\JavaPrograms
```

Appendix B

Sample Programs

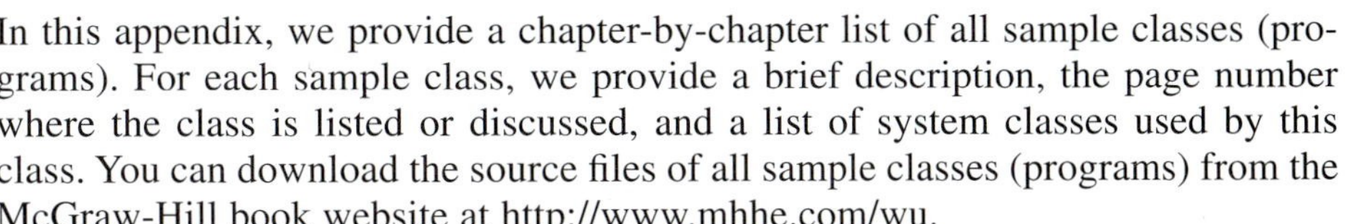

In this appendix, we provide a chapter-by-chapter list of all sample classes (programs). For each sample class, we provide a brief description, the page number where the class is listed or discussed, and a list of system classes used by this class. You can download the source files of all sample classes (programs) from the McGraw-Hill book website at http://www.mhhe.com/wu.

Chapter-by-Chapter List

The single asterisk means only the fragment of the program is listed in the main text. The double asterisks mean the program is not listed in the main text. Such programs are provided as additional examples or variations on the programs listed in the main text.

<chapter #>		
Name	**Page #**	**Standard Classes**
<class name>	<page # where the class is listed>	<list of standard classes or interfaces used or referred to in the class> *Note:* Unless the **String** class is the major focus of a program, it will not be listed in this column. Also, **System** will not be listed.
<A brief description of the class>		
<class used in the sample development>		

CHAPTER 2		
Class Name	**Page #**	**Standard Classes**
`Ch2Sample1`	31	`JFrame`
This program opens a simple **JFrame** window.		
`Ch2StringProcessing`	59	`String`
Illustrates string processing with the **substring, indexof,** and **length** methods of the **String** class.		

Chapter 2 *(Continued)*

Class Name	Page #	Standard Classes
Ch2DateDisplay	62	Date SimpleDateFormat
Creates and displays today's date in two different styles: one in the format **10/15/06 9:25AM** and another in the format **Sunday October 15, 2006.**		
Ch2Greetings*	64	String Scanner
Accepts a name as a string input and replies with a greeting.		
Ch2StringProcessing2**	N/A	Scanner
Same as **Ch2StringProcessing** but accepts input by using the **Scanner** class.		
Ch2Monogram	70, 73	String Scanner
A class in the Chapter 2 sample development program that accepts a full name as a string input and displays the monogram of the input name.		

CHAPTER 3

Class Name	Page #	Standard Classes
Ch3Circle	100	String
Assigns a value to a radius and displays the circle's area and circumference.		
Ch3Circle2**	N/A	String DecimalFormat
Same as **Ch3Circle,** but restricts the fractional values to three decimal places when displaying the area and circumference. Formatting of the **double** values is done by using the **DecimalFormat** class.		
Ch3Circle3	102	String DecimalFormat
Same as **Ch3Circle2** but with additional formatting with control characters.		
Ch3Circle4	108	Scanner
Same as **Ch2Circle3** but inputs a value for the radius using the **Scanner** class.		
Ch3PoleHeight	112	DecimalFormat Math Scanner
Computes the height of a given pole. Illustrates mathematical computation using the class methods of the **Math** class.		

Chapter 3 *(Continued)*

Class Name	Page #	Standard Classes
`Ch3SelectWinner`	114	`Scanner`
This program selects a random number between M and M+N, where M and N are inputs to the program. The program uses the **Math.random** method.		
`Ch3SelectWinner2**`	N/A	`Scanner`
Same as **Ch3SelectWinner** but uses the **Random** class instead of the **Math.random** method.		
`Ch3TestCalendar`	117	`GregorianCalendar`
Illustrates how to use the **GregorianCalendar** class for date manipulation.		
`Ch3IndependenceDay`	118	`GregorianCalendar` `SimpleDateFormat`
This program displays the day of the week of a designed date (in this example, we chose Independence Day). The date is specified in the program by changing the arguments in the **GregorianCalendar** constructor.		

`Ch3FindDayOfWeek`	118	`GregorianCalendar`
		`SimpleDateFormat`
		`Scanner`

Same as **Ch3IndependenceDay** but this program accepts year, month, and day as input and displays the day of the week of the given date.		

`Ch3LoanCalculator`	123, 125,
	127, 129
		`DecimalFormat`
		`Math`
		`Scanner`

Computes and displays the monthly and total payments for a given loan amount, loan period, and interest rate.		

CHAPTER 4

Class Name	Page #	Standard Classes
`BicycleRegistration`	146	
This is a sample main class that uses two **Bicycle** objects.		
`Bicycle`	147	
A sample programmer-defined class that models a bicycle.		
`SecondMain`	157	
This sample program shows the use of two programmer-defined classes **Bicycle** and **Account.**		
`Account`	158	
This is the second sample programmer-defined class. It models a bank account.		

Chapter 4 *(Continued)*		
Class Name	**Page #**	**Standard Classes**
`Student`	162	
This programmer-defined class models a student.		
`LibraryCard`	163	
This programmer-defined class models a library card.		
`Librarian`	165	
This main class shows the sample usage of the **Student** and **LibraryCard** classes.		
`AccountVer2`	169	
A version of the **Account** class that includes a constructor with two parameters.		
`AccountVer3`	175	
Another version of the **Account** class. This version illustrates the use of a class constant that represents a fee charged for withdrawals.		
`DeductionWithFee`	176	`DecimalFormat`
A sample main class that uses the **AccountVer3** class.		
`Die`	178	`Math`
A programmer-defined class that models a die. The class shows how a random number between 1 and 6 is generated by using the **random** method of the **Math** class.		
`RollDice`	179	
This is a main class that shows the sample usage of the **Die** class.		
`LotteryCard`	180	`Math`
A programmer-defined class that models a lottery card. Each card is randomly assigned a number between 10 and 15 and one of the three possible colors—red, green, or blue.		
`RoomWinner`	181	
This is a main class that shows the sample usage of the **LotteryCard** class.		
`AccountVer4`	186	
This is the fourth version of the **Account** class. This version shows the use of a private method.		
`DieVer2`	187	`Math`
This version of the **Die** class illustrates the calling of a private method from the constructor.		
`Bicycle`	189	
This version of the **Bicycle** class includes the main method. This version is stored in a separate subfolder to avoid the naming conflict with the original class.		

Chapter 4 *(Continued)*

Class Name	Page #	Standard Classes
`LoanCalculator`	195, 198, 201	
The top-level controller class for the loan program. This class is defined as an instantiable main class.		
`Loan`	196, 199, 202, 203	`Math`
An instance of this class maintains three pieces of loan information: amount, period, and interest rate.		

CHAPTER 5

Class Name	Page #	Standard Classes
`Ch5Circle`	221	
This class illustrates the use of **if** statements. An instance of this class can compute the area and circumference of a circle, given the radius.		
`Ch5Sample1`	223	
A program to test the operations of the **Ch5Circle** class.		
`Ch5Account`	230	
This version of the **Account** class shows the use of selection control in the **add** and **deduct** methods.		
`Ch5AccountVer2`	237	
This is an improved version of the **Ch5Account** class. This version includes a boolean data member **active** that records the state of an account—active or inactive.		
`Fraction*`	241	
A programmer-defined class that illustrates how objects are compared.		
`Ch5SampleGraphics`	249	`JFrame` `Graphics`
This class illustrates how a **Graphics** object is used by drawing a rectangle and filled rectangle on a frame window.		

`Ch5SampleGraphics2**`	N/A	`JFrame`
		`Graphics`
		`Color`

This class is the same as the **Ch5SampleGraphics** class, but draws the rectangles in blue and red.		

`Ch5RoomWinner`	256	`JFrame`
		`Graphics`
		`Color`

This is the graphical version of RoomWinner from Chapter 4.		
`GraphicLotteryCard`	257	
This class adds the graphics drawing capability to LotteryCard from Chapter 4.		

Chapter 5 *(Continued)*

Class Name	Page #	Standard Classes

`Ch5DrawShape`	269, 272, 276, 281, 283	`Point`
		`Dimension`
		`Scanner`

This is the instantiable main class of the sample development program.		

`DrawableShape`	271, 278, 282	`Point`
		`Dimension`
		`Color`
		`Graphics`

The class encapsulates the functionalities of a shape that can be drawn.		
`DrawingBoard`	N/A	
This is a helper class given to you as support for implementing this application.		

CHAPTER 6

Class Name	Page #	Standard Classes
`Ch6SleepStatistics`	301	`DecimalFormat` `Scanner`
This program computes the average sleeping time of dorm residents. This program uses a **while** loop.		
`Ch6GCD*`	304	`Math`
This class shows a number of different ways for finding the greatest common divisor of two given integers.		
`Ch6DroppingWaterMelon`	321	`Math` `Scanner`
This program inputs the initial height and computes the position of a watermelon every second until it touches the ground. This program illustrates the use of the **for** loop.		
`Ch6ComplexForLoops*`	322	`Math`
This program illustrates the use of complex **for** loops.		
`Ch6CarpetPriceTable*`	324	
This program illustrates the use of nested **for** loops. The program outputs the price of a carpet ranging in size from 5 by 11 to 25 by 20.		
`Ch6CarpetPriceTable-withFormat`	330	
This class modifies the **Ch6CarpetPriceTable** class by formatting the output values. The format is done by using **Ch6Format.**		

Chapter 6 *(Continued)*

Class Name	Page #	Standard Classes
`Ch6TimeGcd`	335	`Date` `Scanner`
This program illustrates the technique of timing the execution by using the **Date** class.		
`Ch6HiLo`	346, 349, 352	
A sample development program that plays the HiLo game.		

CHAPTER 7

Class Name	Page #	Standard Classes
`Fraction`	402	
This sample class models a fraction. The class definition includes almost all the fundamental object-oriented concepts covered in Chapters 4 and 7. The class is placed in the package named **myutil.**		
`Ch7Fraction_Test1**`	N/A	
A simple test class that adds two **Fraction** objects.		
`Ch7Fraction_Test2**`	N/A	
Another main class to test the operations of the **Fraction** class.		
`LibraryBook`	415	
This class models a library card.		
`Step1Main`	418	`GregorianCalendar`
The main class to test the step 1 **LibraryBook** class.		
`Step2Main`	420	`GregorianCalendar` `Scanner`
The step 2 main class to test the operations of the helper class **BookTracker.**		
`OverDueChecker`	422	`GregorianCalendar` `Scanner`
The main class of the sample development program.		

CHAPTER 8

Class Name	Page #	Standard Classes
`Ch8Sample1*`	438	`Scanner`
This sample program illustrates the throwing of **InputMismatchException** when an input is not an **int.**		

Chapter 8 *(Continued)*

Class Name	Page #	Standard Classes
AgeInputVer1	439	Scanner

This is the first version of a class that provides methods to input ages. This class includes no exception handling routines; i.e., the system will handle any thrown exceptions.

Class Name	Page #	Standard Classes
Ch8AgeInputMain	440	GregorianCalendar Scanner

A test program to illustrate the behavior of different versions of the age input class. The program asks for the user's age and replies with the year in which the user was born.

Class Name	Page #	Standard Classes
AgeInputVer2*	443	Scanner

The second version of the age input class with the **try-catch** exception handling. Its **getAge** method will not return until a valid integer is entered. The method includes a **while** loop that repeats until a valid integer is entered. The loop continues while there's a number format exception.

Class Name	Page #	Standard Classes
AgeInputVer3*	445	Scanner

The third version of the age input class that improves the second version by throwing an exception when the input is a negative integer.

Class Name	Page #	Standard Classes
AgeInputVer4	456	Scanner

In this fourth version of the age input class, a client programmer can set the lower and upper bounds of the acceptable input age values. An exception is thrown if the input value is not an integer (as in previous versions) or violates the specified bounds.

Class Name	Page #	Standard Classes
Ch8TestAgeInputVer4**	N/A	

This driver program tests the behavior of the **AgeInputVer4** class.

Class Name	Page #	Standard Classes
AgeInputException	461	

This is a programmer-defined exception class that includes the designated lower and upper bounds and the input value that violates the specified bounds.

Class Name	Page #	Standard Classes
AgeInputVer5**	N/A	Scanner

The fifth version of the age input class is similar to the fourth version. The key difference is the throwing of programmer-defined exception **AgeInputException** when the input value is outside the range of specified bounds.

Class Name	Page #	Standard Classes
Ch8TestAgeInputVer5	462	

This driver program tests the behavior of the **AgeInputVer5** class

Class Name	Page #	Standard Classes
BankAccount	463	

A sample class that specifies assertions in the **deposit** and **withdraw** methods.

Class Name	Page #	Standard Classes
Ch8TestAssertMain	464	Scanner

A driver program to test the behavior of the **BankAccount** class.

Chapter 8 *(Continued)*		
Class Name	**Page #**	**Standard Classes**
`Resident`	475	
An instance of this class represents a dorm resident. A **Resident** object has name, room number, and password.		
`Door`	N/A	
This helper class models the entrance door of a dorm.		
`Dorm`	N/A	
This helper class models a dorm. A **Dorm** object maintains a list of **Resident** objects.		
`Ch8EntranceMonitor`	476, 480	
The main class of the program.		
`SampleCreateResidentFile`	477	
A simple (self-contained) program to create sample test data for the **Ch8EntranceMonitor** program.		
`InputHandler`	479	
The user interface of the application that accepts the name, room number, and password.		

CHAPTER 9		
Class Name	**Page #**	**Standard Classes**
`Ch9TestChar*`	490	
A simple illustration of conversion between **char** and **int.**		
`Ch9CountVowels`	493	`Scanner` `String`
Illustrates basic string processing. The program counts the number of vowels in a given string.		
`Ch9CountVowels2`	494	`Scanner` `String`
Same as **Ch9CountVowels** but uses the **toUpperCase** method to simply the testing.		
`Ch9CountWords`	496	`Scanner` `String`
The program counts the number of words in a given string. This program has a minor bug of counting one more than the actual number of words if there is one or more spaces at the end.		

Chapter 9 *(Continued)*

Class Name	Page #	Standard Classes
`Ch9CountJava`	498	`Scanner` `String`
This program inputs words (one word at a time) and counts the number of times the word **java** occurs in input (case-insensitive comparison). The program terminates when the word **STOP** (case-sensitive) is entered.		
`Ch9ExtractWords`	500	`Scanner` `String`
This programs extracts words from a given string and displays them one word per line.		
`Ch9PatternMatch1**`	N/A	`Scanner` `String`
A simple illustration of the **matches** method, a pattern-matching method of the **String** class.		
`Ch9MatchJavaIdentifier`	504	`Scanner` `String`
This program illustrates the basic pattern-matching technique by showing how to determine whether a given input word is a valid Java identifier.		
`Ch9MatchPhoneNumber`	505	`Scanner` `String`
This program illustrates the basic pattern-matching technique by showing how to determine whether a given input is a valid phone number.		

`Ch9MatchPhonePM**`	N/A	`Scanner`
		`String`
		`Matcher`
		`Pattern`

Performs the same task as **Ch9MatchPhoneNumber** but uses the **Matcher** and **Pattern** classes.		

`Ch9MatchJavaIdentifierPM`	510	`Scanner`
		`String`
		`Matcher`
		`Pattern`

Performs the same task as **Ch9MatchJavaIdentifier** but uses the **Matcher** and **Pattern** classes.		

`Ch9CountJavaPM`	511	`Scanner`
		`String`
		`Matcher`
		`Pattern`

Performs the same task as **Ch9CountJava** but uses the pattern-matching technique with the **Matcher** and **Pattern** classes.		

Chapter 9 *(Continued)*

Class Name	Page #	Standard Classes
`Ch9LocateJavaPM`	512	
Similar to **Ch9PMCountJava** but instead of counting the number of occurrences, this program displays the locations in the string where the word **java** is found.		

`Ch9ReplaceVowelWithX`	516	`Scanner`
		`String`
		`StringBuffer`

This program illustrates the use of the **StringBuffer** class by showing how the vowels in a given string are replaced by character **X.**		

`Ch9EvenLetterWords`	518	`Scanner`
		`String`
		`StringBuffer`

Another sample program illustrating the use of the **StringBuffer** class. This program extracts words with an even number of letters from a given string and creates a new string with these words.		
`FileManager`	N/A	
This is a helper class for reading from and saving data to a text file.		
`WordList`	N/A	
This is a helper class for maintaining a word list.		

`Ch9WordConcordanceMain`	524, 529	`Scanner`
		`String`
		`FileNotFoundException`
		`IOException`

The instantiable main class of the program.		
`Ch9WordConcordance`	525, 530, 533	`Matcher` `Pattern`
This class creates a word concordance for a given document. For each word in the document, the number of times the word occurs in the document is kept.		

CHAPTER 10

Class Name	Page #	Standard Classes
`Ch10RainFall`	548	`Scanner`
The first sample program that illustrates the use of one-dimensional array of numbers. The program computes the annual average rainfall and the variation from the monthly averages.		

Chapter 10 *(Continued)*

Class Name	Page #	Standard Classes
Ch10RainFall2*	549	Scanner
The variation of **Ch10RainFall** that uses an array of **String** so the month name is used to prompt the user when inputting monthly rainfall averages. The original **Ch10RainFall** uses month number (1, 2, etc.) instead of month names (January, February, etc.).		
Ch10RainFallStat	552	Scanner
More examples of using arrays by showing how to compute various statistics from given monthly rainfall averages.		
Person**	N/A	
A simple class used by **Ch10ProcessPersonArray** to illustrate how an array of objects is processed.		
Ch10ProcessPersonArray	561	Scanner
This class illustrates the processing of an array of **Person** objects.		
Ch10TestArrayParameter*	570	Scanner
This class is a collection of methods to show how an array is passed to a method.		
Ch10PayScaleTable	581	
This sample program maintains a pay scale table by using a two-dimensional array of **double.**		
Ch10FriendsList*	586	List ArrayList
A simple program to show how a list of **Person** objects can be manipulated with an **ArrayList.**		
BookTracker	591	List LinkedList
The helper class for the Chapter 7 sample development program. This class maintains a list of library books.		
WordList	594	SortedMap TreeMap
The helper class for the Chapter 9 sample development program. This class maintains a word list to track the number of times each word in the list occurs in a given document.		
Person**	N/A	
A logical class that represents a person. This class is the same as the **Person** class used in the regular sample programs.		
AddressBook	598, 603, 606, 609	
This class implements functionalities of an address book for keeping track of persons. The class supports insertion, deletion, and search operations. Assertion statements are used in this class.		
TestAddressBook	599, 604, 607, 611	
A test program to check the operations of **AddressBook.**		

CHAPTER 11		
Class Name	**Page #**	**Standard Classes**
SearchRoutines*	621,623	
The class defines two search methods—linear and binary search.		
Ch11TestLinearSearch**	N/A	
A driver program to test the linear search method defined in **SearchRoutines.**		
Ch11TestBinarySearch**	N/A	System
A driver program to test the binary search method defined in **SearchRoutines.**		
SortingRoutines*	626,631	
The class defines two sorting methods—selection and bubble sort.		
Ch11TestSelectionSort**	N/A	
A driver program to test the selection sort method defined in **SortingRoutines.**		
Ch11TestBubbleSort**	N/A	
A driver program to test the bubble sort method defined in **SortingRoutines.**		
Heap*	640,641,642	
This class implements the heapsort sorting method.		
Ch11TestHeapSort**	N/A	
A driver program to test the sorting method defined in **Heap.**		
Person	651	
A logical class that represents a person. The class includes methods to compare its instances.		
AddressBook (interface)	646	
This interface defines the behavior of an address book that maintains a collection of **Person** objects. An address book is capable of adding and removing objects and sorting objects by their name or age.		
AddressBookVer1	654	
This class implement the **AddressBook** interface by using an array of **Person** objects. Bubble sort is used to sort the objects.		
AddressBookVer2	661	Arrays
This class implements the **AddressBook** interface by using an array of **Person** objects. For sorting, it uses the generic sorting method included in the **Arrays** class.		
AddressBookVer3	664	Map HashMap Arrays
This class implements the **AddressBook** interface by using an array of **Person** objects. The **HashMap** class is used for managing **Person** objects and the **Arrays** class for sorting **Person** objects.		

Chapter 11 *(Continued)*

Class Name	Page #	Standard Classes
AgeComparator (inner class)	662	
The inner class of **AddressBookVer2** and **AddressBookVer3** that compares two **Person** objects on their ages.		
NameComparator (inner class)	663	
The inner class of **AddressBookVer2** and **AddressBookVer3** that compares two **Person** objects on their names.		
TestAddressBookSorting	647	
A driver program to test the sorting routine of the address book.		

CHAPTER 12

Class Name	Page #	Standard Classes
Ch12TestJFileChooser	676	JFileChooser File
A simple program that shows how to use **JFileChooser** and **File** classes.		
JavaFilter	677	FileFilter File
A simple program to illustrate the use of file filter to list only Java source files in a **JFileChooser.**		
Ch12TestFileOutputStream	680	IOException File FileOutputStream
A test program to save data to a file using **FileOutputStream.**		
Ch12TestFileInputStream	682	IOException File FileInputStream
A test program to read data from a file using **FileInputStream.**		
Ch12TestDataOutputStream	684	IOException File FileOutputStream DataOutputStream
A test program to save data to a file using **DataOutputStream.**		

Chapter 12 *(Continued)*

Class Name	Page #	Standard Classes
Ch12TestDataInputStream	685	IOException File FileInputStream DataInputStream
A test program to read data from a file using **DataInputStream.**		
Ch12TestPrintWriter	687	IOException File FileOutputStream PrintWriter
A test program to save data to a text file using **PrintWriter.**		
Ch12TestBufferedReader	688	IOException File FileReader BufferedReader
A test program to read text data from a text file using **BufferedReader.**		
Ch12TestScanner	690	FileNotFoundException IOException File Scanner
A test program to read text data from a text file using **Scanner.**		
FileManager (Ch 9 Helper class)	691	FileNotFoundException, IOException, File, FileReader, BufferedReader, FileOutputStream, PrintWriter, JFileChooser
The helper class for **Ch9WordConcordance** program used for saving to and reading data from a text file.		
Ch12TestObjectOutputStream	695	IOException File FileOutputStream ObjectOutputStream
A test program to save objects to a file using **ObjectOutputStream.**		
Ch13TestObjectInputStream	696	ClassNotFoundException, File, FileInputStream, ObjectInputStream
A test program to read objects from a file using **ObjectInputStream.**		

Chapter 12 *(Continued)*

Class Name	Page #	Standard Classes
`Dorm` (Ch 8 Helper Class)	698	`FileNotFoundException, IOException, IllegalArgumentException, ClassNotFoundException, File, FileInputStream, ObjectInputStream, FileOutputStream, ObjectOutputStream, StringBuffer`
This helper class for Chapter 8 Sample Development maintains a list of **Resident** objects. In addition, the class supports file input and output operations.		
`Ch12JavaViewer**`	N/A	`JFileChooser File`
This program displays the content of a Java source file.		
`Person**`	N/A	`Serializable`
The same class from Chapter 11, but modified to implement the **Serializable** interface so its instances can be saved to a file.		
`AddressBook (interface)`	646	
The same interface from Chapter 11.		
`AddressBookVer1**`	N/A	
The same class from Chapter 11.		
`AddressBookStorage`	703, 704, 706	`IOException, File, FileOutputStream, ObjectOutputStream, FileInputStream, ObjectInputStream`
This class provides file input and output services to save to and read **AddressBook** objects from a file.		
`TestAddressBookWrite`	705	`IOException`
This class tests the write operation.		
`TestAddressBookRead`	707	`IOException`
This class tests the read and search operations.		
`TestAddressBookFinal**`	N/A	`IOException`
This class tests the read and write operations.		

CHAPTER 13		
Class Name	**Page #**	**Standard Classes**
Pet	714	
This is a superclass of both **Cat** and **Dog.**		
Cat	715	
This class models a cat. The class is a subclass of **Pet.**		
Dog	715	
This class models a dog. The class is a subclass of **Pet.**		
Ch13TestCatAndDog*	716	
A sample program that illustrates the use of the **Cat** and **Dog** classes.		
Student	718	
This class models a student entity.		
GraduateStudent	719	
A subclass of **Student** to model a graduate student entity.		
UndergraduateStudent	720	
A subclass of **Student** to model an undergraduate student entity.		
Student**	N/A	
A slightly different version of the **Student** class used in the sample development program. This version is declared as an abstract class.		
GraduateStudent**	N/A	
A slightly different version of the **GraduateStudent** subclass used in the sample development program.		
UndergraduateStudent**	N/A	
A slightly different version of the **UndergraduateStudent** subclass used in the sample development program.		
OutputWindow**	N/A	
This is a helper class that supports a dialog window for displaying text output.		
MainWindow**	N/A	
This is a helper class that models a frame window. The frame window appears at the center of the screen.		
ComputeGrades	745, 748, 750, 755	File, FileReader, BufferedReader, StringTokenizer, JFileChooser
The main class of the grading program that determines the course grade for graduate and undergraduate students using a different formula. To illustrate inheritance, this class is defined as the subclass of **MainWindow.**		

CHAPTER 14

Class Name	Page #	Standard Classes
Ch14ShowMessageDialog	769	JOptionPane
A sample program that illustrates the use of **JOptionPane** for displaying a text in a dialog window.		
Ch14DefaultJFrame	772	JFrame
A test program to check the default properties of a **JFrame** object.		
Ch14JFrameSubclass1	774	JFrame
A simple subclass of **JFrame** to illustrate the basics of inheritance.		
Ch14TestJFrameSubclass	775	
A test main class that creates an instance of **Ch14JFrameSubclass1.**		
Ch14JFrameSubclass2	776	JFrame
Same as the **Ch7JFrameSubclass1** but this class sets the background of a frame to white.		
Ch14JButtonFrame	779	JFrame JButton
A subclass of **JFrame** with two **JButton** objects. This class only does the layout; no events are processed.		
ButtonHandler	783	JRootPane JButton ActionListener
An instance of this class is registered as an action event listener for two buttons in the **Ch7JButtonEvents** frame.		
Ch14JButtonEvents	783	JFrame JButton
This class is an extension of **Ch7JButtonFrame** by adding event-handling routines. The event handler is an instance of **ButtonHandler** (see below).		
Ch14JButtonFrameHandler	785	JFrame JButton ActionListener
This class places two **JButton** objects on its frame and handles the action events of the buttons. This class combines the functionalities of **Ch14ButtonEvents** and **ButtonHandler.**		
Ch14TextFrame1	789	JFrame JButton JTextField ActionListener
This class places two buttons (**JButton**) and one text field (**JTextField**) and handles actions events generated by these three GUI components.		

Chapter 14 *(Continued)*

Class Name	Page #	Standard Classes
Ch14TextFrame2	792	JFrame, JLabel, JButton, JTextField, ImageIcon, ActionListener
Similar to **Ch14TextFrame1,** but adds **JLabel** objects. How an image is added to a **JLabel** is demonstrated in this class.		
Ch14TextFrame3	795	JFrame, JButton, JTextField, JTextArea, BorderFactory, ActionListener.
This class places two buttons, one text field, and one text area. String data entered in the text field are added to the strings in the text area when an action event is generated.		
Ch14FlowLayoutSample	800	JFrame FlowLayout JButton
A sample frame to illustrate the placing of GUI objects with the **FlowLayout** manager.		
Ch14BorderLayoutSample	802	JFrame BorderLayout JButton
A sample frame to illustrate the placing of GUI objects with the **BorderLayout** manager.		
Ch14GridLayoutSample	804	JFrame BorderLayout JButton
A sample frame to illustrate the placing of GUI objects with the **GridLayout** manager.		
Ch14AbsolutePositioning	806	JFrame JButton
A sample frame to illustrate the placing of GUI objects with no layout manager, i.e., using absolute positioning.		
Ch14NestedPanels1	810	JFrame, JPanel, BorderFactory, GridLayout, BorderLayout, JButton
A sample frame to illustrate the placing of nested panels with each panel having a different layout manager.		
Ch14NestedPanels2	812	JFrame, JPanel, BorderFactory, GridLayout, BorderLayout, JButton, JTextField, JLabel
A redesigned GUI for the HiLo game using nested panels.		

Chapter 14 *(Continued)*		
Class Name	**Page #**	**Standard Classes**
`Ch14TicTacToeCell`	814	`JPanel, JLabel, ImageIcon, BorderLayout, BorderFactory, Point`
An instance of this class represents a single cell in the Tic Tac Toe game board. A standard game is 3 X 3 so there are 9 cells.		
`Ch14TicTacToePanel`	816	`JPanel MouseListener`
A panel for displaying the Tic Tac Toe game board. This sample class illustrates the use of nested panels.		
`Ch14JCheckBoxSample1`	818	`JFrame, ActionListener, ActionEvent, JPanel, JButton, BorderLayout, GridLayout, FlowLayout, BorderFactory, JCheckBox`
A sample frame to illustrate the use of **JCheckBox.**		
`Ch14JCheckBoxSample2`	820	`JFrame, ActionListener, ActionEvent, ItemListener, ItemAction, JPanel, JButton, BorderLayout, GridLayout, FlowLayout, BorderFactory, JCheckBox`
This is an extended version of **Ch14JCheckBoxSample1** that process item events in addition to action events.		
`Ch14JRadioButtonSample`	823	`JFrame, ActionListener, ActionEvent, ItemListener, ItemAction, JPanel, JButton, BorderLayout, GridLayout, FlowLayout, BorderFactory, JRadioButton`
A sample frame to illustrate the use of **JRadioButton.**		
`Ch14JComboBoxSample`	827	`JFrame, ActionListener, ActionEvent, ItemListener, ItemAction, JPanel, JButton, BorderLayout, GridLayout, BorderFactory, JRadioButton`
A sample frame to illustrate the use of **JComboBox.**		

Chapter 14 *(Continued)*

Class Name	Page #	Standard Classes
Ch14JListSample	830	JFrame, ActionListener, ActionEvent, JPanel, JButton, BorderLayout, GridLayout, FlowLayout, BorderFactory, JScrollPane, JList
A sample frame to illustrate the use of **JList.**		
Ch14JSliderSample	833	JFrame, ChangeListener, ChangeEvent, JPanel, JButton, BorderLayout, BorderFactory, JSlider
A sample frame to illustrate the use of **JSlider.**		
Ch14JMenuFrame	837	JFrame, JMenuBar, JMenu, JMenuItem, ActionListener
A frame class with menus that illustrates the menu action processing.		
Ch14TrackMouseFrame	842	JFrame MouseListener System
This program tracks the mouse click events. When a mouse button is clicked, the location where the mouse button is clicked is displayed.		
Ch14SketchPad	845	JFrame MouseListener MouseMotionListener
This program provides a freehand drawing by tracing the mouse movements.		

CHAPTER 15

Class Name	Page #	Standard Classes
Ch15Algorithms*	862, 865, 867, 869, 870, 873	
This class includes a collection of recursive algorithms discussed in Chapter 15.		
TestCh15Algorithms**	N/A	
A driver program for testing algorithms in **Ch15Algorithms.**		

CHAPTER 16		
Name	**Page #**	**Standard Classes**
`Node`	890	
This class provides the basic definition for a node in a linked list.		
`CreateListVariation1*`	892	
This program creates a linked list by using three variables **start, tail,** and **next.**		
`CreateListVariation2*`	893	
This variation creates a linked list by using only two variables **start** and **tail.**		
`CreateListVariation3*`	895	
This variation creates a linked list by using a temporary dummy first node.		
`CreateListVariation4*`	896	
This variation creates a linked list by adding new nodes to the front of the list.		
`SearchList*`	899	
This program illustrates how the search is carried out in a linked list of integers.		
`RemoveNodeFromList*`	901	
This program shows how a node is removed from a linked list of integers.		
`Bicycle`	903	
A simple class used in illustrating operations on a linked list of objects.		
`BNode`	904	
The data item of this node is a reference to a **Bicycle** object.		
`CreateBicycleList*`	905	
This program creates a linked list of **Bicycle** objects.		
`SearchBicycleList*`	906	
This program shows how the search is carried out in a linked list of **Bicycle** objects.		
`RemoveNodeFromBicycleList*`	907	
This program shows how a node is removed from a linked list of **Bicycle** objects.		
`HumongousInteger`	917, 921, 926, 931	
This class implements a very simplified version of **java.math.BigInteger** by using a linked list.		
`TestStep1HumongousInteger*`	920	
A test program to check the step 1 **HumongousInteger** class.		

Chapter 16 *(Continued)*

Name	Page #	Standard Classes
`TestStep2HumongousInteger*`	923	
A test program to check the step 2 **HumongousInteger** class.		
`TestStep3HumongousInteger*`	930	
A test program to check the step 3 **HumongousInteger** class.		
`TestStep4HumongousInteger*`	933	
A test program to check the step 4 **HumongousInteger** class.		

CHAPTER 17

Name	Page #	Standard Classes
`Locker`	946	
This is a very simple class that illustrates the basic use of the Java generics.		
`LockerDemo*`	947	
A sample program that shows how the generic **Locker** class is used.		
`SecondLocker`	950	
A sample generic class with two type parameters.		
`ThirdLockder`	951	
The third sample generic class that shows two data members are of the same generic type.		
`NonGenLocker`	952	
A sample class that does not use generics to illustrate the benefits of defining a generic class.		
`FourthLocker`	954	
The fourth generic **Locker** class that illustrates the use of bounded types.		
`FifthLocker`	956	
The fourth generic **Locker** class that illustrates the use of wildcard types.		
`Book`	961	
A simple class used in illustrating operations on a generic linked list.		

Chapter 17 *(Continued)*

Name	Page #	Standard Classes
`BookListDemo*`	961	
A demo class for showing the use of generics and Java collection class **ArrayList.**		
`Node`	963	
A simple class to illustrate a generic node in a linked list.		
`SimpleLinkedList`	965	
This generic class shows how the Java generics can be used to maintain a homogeneous list of objects.		
`UseSimpleLinkedList*`	967	
A simple program that illustrates the use of the **SimpleLinkedList** class.		
`LockerSub`	969	
This class illustrates how a subclass of a generic class is defined.		
`LockerSubTwo`	971	
Another example of defining a subclass of a generic class.		
`Box`	971	
A simple class used in an example to illustrate how a generic subclass can be defined from a nongeneric superclass.		
`MagicBox`	972	
This class illustrates the definition of a generic subclass of a nongeneric superclass **Box.**		
`MagicContainer`	972	
This example illustrates a simple generic Java interface.		
`MagicTrunk`	972	
The first example of defining a class that implements a generic Java interface.		
`StringTrunk`	973	
The second example of defining a class that implements a generic Java interface.		

CHAPTER 18

Name	Page #	Standard Classes
`NPSList`	988	
A generic Java interface for defining the **List ADT.**		
`NPSArrayList`	997, 1026	
This class implements the **NPSList** interface by using an array.		

Chapter 18 *(Continued)*

Name	Page #	Standard Classes
NPSLinkedList	1013, 1024	
This class implements the **NPSList** interface by using linked nodes.		
NPSLinkedListWithHeader	1019	
This is a variation of **NPSLinkedList** by using a dummy head node.		
NPSIterator	1023	
This Java interface specifies the iterator design pattern.		
NPSNoSuchElementException	1026	
A customized exception class for the **NPS** collection classes to indicate an exception when the requested item does not exist in the collection.		
FortuneCookieMain**	N/A	
The main class of a program that displays fortunes. Implementation of this class is left as an exercise.		
FortuneCookieManager	1030	
The core class of the program that maintains the database of fortune cookies.		
FortuneCookieFile**	N/A	
This class handles the input of text messages for fortune cookies from the designated text file **fortune.txt.** Implementation of this class is left as an exercise.		

CHAPTER 19

Name	Page #	Standard Classes
NPSStack	1040	
A generic Java interface for defining the **Stack ADT.**		
NPSStackEmptyException	1041	
A customized exception to signal a stack empty error.		
NPSArrayStack	1045	
This class implements the **NPSStack** interface by using an array.		
NPSLinkedStack	1050	
This class implements the **NPSStack** interface by using linked nodes.		
NPSListStack	1052	
This class implements the **NPSStack** interface by the **NPSLinkedList** class.		
HTMLTag**	N/A	
This class models the HTML tag. Full implementation of the class is left as an exercise.		

Chapter 19 *(Continued)*

Name	Page #	Standard Classes
`HTMLTagChecker`	1057	
This program checks whether a given HTML file has the matching opening and closing HTML tags.		
`HTMLTagRetriever**`	N/A	
This class handles the retrieval of HTML tags from a specified HTML file. Full implementation of the class is left as an exercise.		

CHAPTER 20

Name	Page #	Standard Classes
`NPSQueue`	1073	
A generic Java interface for defining the **Queue ADT.**		
`NPSQueueEmptyException`	1074	
A customized exception to signal a queue empty error.		
`NPSArrayQueue`	1080	
This class implements the **NPSQueue** interface by using an array.		
`NPSLinkedQueue`	1085	
This class implements the **NPSQueue** interface by using linked nodes.		
`NPSListQueue`	1088	
This class implements the **NPSQueue** interface by the **NPSLinkedList** class.		
`NPSPriorityQueue`	1090	
This class implements the priority queue.		
`TestNPSPriorityQueue`	1093	
A simple program that illustrates the use of the **NPSPriorityQueue** class.		

Appendix C
Standard Classes and Interfaces

In this appendix, we provide a list of standard Java classes and interfaces used in the textbook's sample programs. Many of these classes and interfaces are discussed fully in the book and used extensively in the sample programs, while some are mentioned briefly and used only in a few sample programs. For a subset of these classes and interfaces, we provide a brief summary and a list of key methods.

Alphabetical List

Standard Java classes and interfaces mentioned in this book are listed alphabetically. The interfaces are shown in italic font.

Alphabetical List		
ActionEvent	Double	InputStreamReader
ActionListener	Exception	Integer
ArrayList	File	IOException
Arrays	FileFilter	ItemEvent
BorderFactory	FileInputStream	*ItemListener*
BorderLayout	FileNotFoundException	JButton
BufferedReader	FileOutputStream	JCheckBox
ChangeEvent	FileReader	JFileChooser
ChangeListener	Float	JFrame
ClassNotFoundException	FlowLayout	JLabel
Color	Graphics	JList
DataInputStream	GregorianCalendar	JMenu
DataOutputStream	GridLayout	JMenuBar
Date	HashMap	JMenuItem
DecimalFormat	IllegalArgumentException	JOptionPane
Dimension	ImageIcon	JPanel

Alphabetical List *(Continued)*		
JPasswordField	Matcher	PrintWriter
JRadioButton	Math	*SerializableScanner*
JRootPane	MouseEvent	SimpleDateFormat
JScrollPane	*MouseListener*	*SortedMap*
JSlider	*MouseMotionListener*	StringBuffer
JTextArea	NumberFormatException	String
JTextField	ObjectInputStream	StringTokenizer
LinkedList	ObjectOutputStream	System
List	Pattern	TreeMap
Long	Point	
Map	PrintStream	

Logical List

The following list organizes the standard classes and interfaces from the alphabetical list in logical groups.

Logical List		
	Drawing	
Color	Dimension	Graphics
Point		
	Events	
ActionEvent	*ActionListener*	ChangeEvent
ChangeListener	ItemEvent	*ItemListener*
MouseEvent	*MouseListener*	*MouseMotionListener*
	Exceptions	
ClassNotFoundException	Exception	FileNotFoundException
IllegalArgumentException	IOException	NumberFormatException
	File Input and Output	
BufferedReader	DataInputStream	DataOutputStream
File	FileFilter	FileInputStream

Logical List *(Continued)*

`FileOutputStream`	`FileReader`	`InputStreamReader`
`ObjectInputStream`	`ObjectOutputStream`	`PrintStream`
`PrintWriter`	*`Serializable`*	
	GUI	
`BorderFactory`	`BorderLayout`	`FlowLayout`
`GridLayout`	`ImageIcon`	`JButton`
`JCheckBox`	`JFileChooser`	`JFrame`
`JLabel`	`JList`	`JMenu`
`JMenuBar`	`JMenuItem`	`JOptionPane`
`JPanel`	`JPasswordField`	`JRadioButton`
`JRootPane`	`JScrollPane`	`JSlider`
`JTextArea`	`JTextField`	
	Java Collection Framework	
`ArrayList`	`HashMap`	`LinkedList`
`List`	*`Map`*	*`SortedMap`*
`TreeMap`		
	Utility	
`Arrays`	`Date`	`DecimalFormat`
`GregorianCalendar`	`Matcher`	`Math`
`Pattern`	`ScannerSimpleDateFormat`	`StringBuffer`
`String`	`StringTokenizer`	`System`
	Wrapper	
`Double`	`Float`	`Integer`
`Long`		

Class Hierarchy for Swing Components

Many of the methods we use for various Swing-based components are defined in the common superclass. Instead of repeating the same information in individual classes, we will list the methods in the class in which they are defined. Here is the inheritance hierarchy for the Swing components mentioned in the book (classes summarized in the next section are shown in blue):

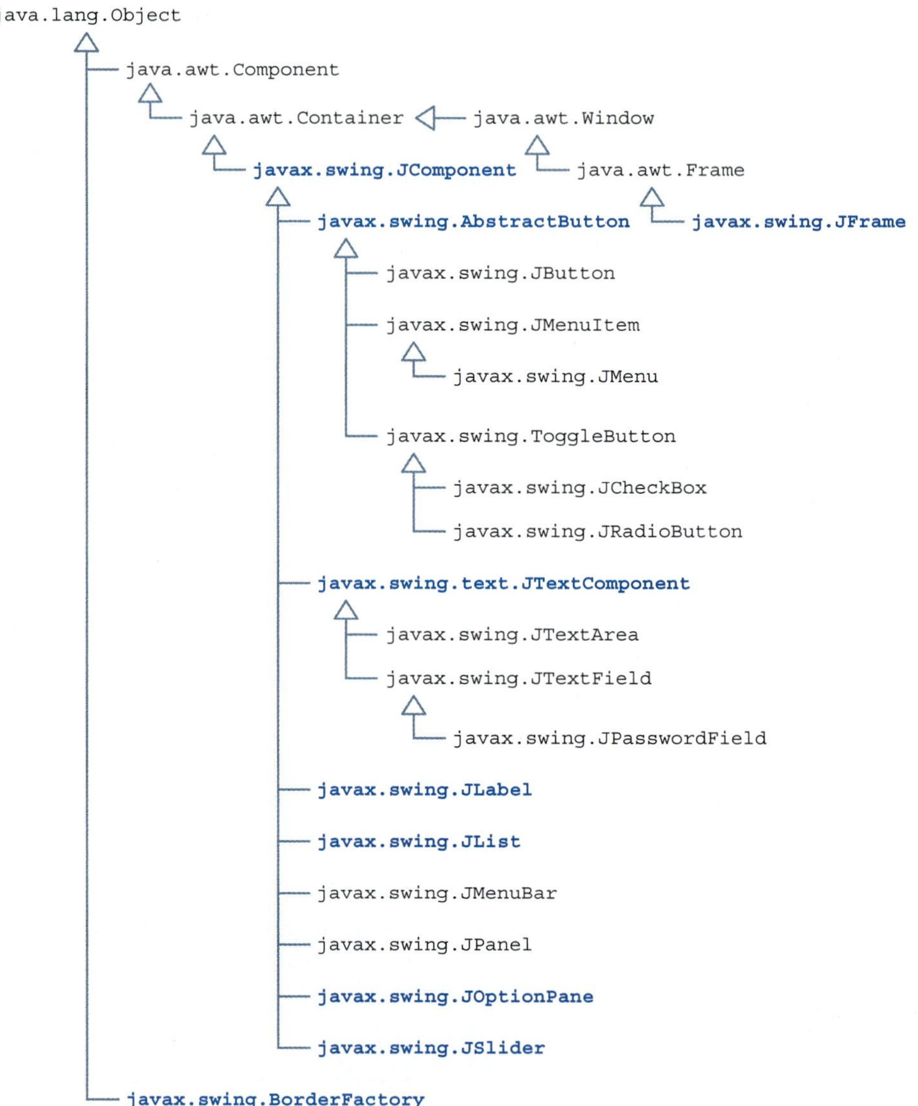

Summary of Selected Classes and Interfaces

In this section, we summarize a subset of standard classes and interfaces mentioned in the book. The classes and interfaces are listed in alphabetical order. For each class and interface we summarize, we include a brief description and some of its methods. The summary is intended as a quick reference. It is not a substitute for the API documentation. For a complete list of methods and full description, please consult the API documentation.

Class: `javax.swing.`**`AbstractButton`**

Purpose: This is the base class of button and menu objects. Methods defined here are applicable to all subclasses.

Hierarchy: `java.lang.Object` ◁— `java.awt.Component` ◁— `java.awt.Container` ◁— `javax.swing.JComponent` ◁— `javax.swing.AbstractButton`

Subclasses: `JButton, JCheckBox, JRadioButton, JMenuItem, JMenu`

Public Methods:

`void ActionListener (ActionListener listener)`

Adds `listener` as an action listener of this button.

`String getText ( )`

Returns the text of this button.

`void setText (string text)`

Sets the text of this button.

Class: `java.awt.event.`**`ActionEvent`**

Purpose: An instance of this class represents an action event such as clicking a pushbutton or pressing the `Enter` key while the text field has a focus.

Hierarchy: `java.lang.Object` ◁— `java.util.EventObject` ◁— `java.awt.AWTEvent` ◁— `java.awt.event.ActionEvent`

Public Methods:

`String getActionCommand( )`

Returns a string associated with the event source.

`Object getSource( )`

Returns the source object that generated an action event.

Interface: java.awt.event.**ActionListener**

Purpose: An instance of this class represents an action event such as clicking a pushbutton or pressing the `Enter` key while the text field has a focus.

Hierarchy: `java.util.EventListener ◁— java.awt.event.ActionListener`

Public Methods:

```
void actionPerformed(ActionEvent event)
```

This method is called when the event source generates an action event. A class that implements this interface must define the `actionPerformed` method.

Class: javax.swing.**BorderFactory**

Purpose: This factory class produces various types of borders for GUI components

Hierarchy: `java.lang.Object ◁— javax.swing.BorderFactory`

Public Methods:

```
static Border createBevelBorder (int type, Color highlight,
                                 Color shadow)
```

Creates a beveled border object of a specified type and colors for highlighting and shadowing. The value for `type` can be either `BevelBorder.LOWERED` or `BevelBorder.RAISED`.

```
static Border createEtchedBorder (int type, Color highlight,
                                  Color shadow)
```

Creates an etched border object of a specified type and colors for highlighting and shadowing. The value for `type` can be either `EtchedBorder.LOWERED` or `EtchedBorder.RAISED`.

```
static Border createLineBorder (Color color)
```

Creates a line border object in a specified color and default line thickness.

```
static Border createLineBorder (Color color, int thickness)
```

Creates a line border object in a specified color and line thickness.

Class: `java.util.Date`

Purpose: This class represents a specific instance in time with millisecond precision.

Hierarchy: `java.lang.Object <- java.util.Date`

Constructors:

`Date ( )`

Creates a new `Date` whose value is set to the time instance when it is created.

Public Methods:

`boolean after (Date date)`

Returns `true` if this date is after the argument `date`.

`boolean before (Date date)`

Returns `true` if this date is before the argument `date`.

`long getTime ( )`

Returns the elapsed time in milliseconds since the epoch, which is designated as January 1, 1970, 00:00:00 GMT.

Class: `java.text.DecimalFormat`

Purpose: This class is used to format decimal numbers.

Hierarchy: `java.lang.Object <- java.text.Format <- java.text.NumberFormat <- java.text.DecimalFormat`

Constructors:

`DecimalFormat (String pattern)`

Creates a new `DecimalFormat` initialized to a given `pattern`.

Public Methods:

`String format (long number)`
`String format (double number)`

Return the formatted string of a given `number`.

Class: `java.io.File`

Purpose: An instance of this class represents a file or a directory.

Hierarchy: `java.lang.Object` ← `java.io.File`

Public Constants:

`String pathSeparator`

This system-dependent path separator symbol is represented as a string. A path separator for Windows is the semicolon. This value can be retrieved by the statement `System.getProperty("path.separator")` also.

`String separator`

This system-dependent file separator symbol is represented as a string. A file separator for Windows is the backslash. This value can be retrieved by the statement `System.getProperty("file.separator")` also.

Constructors:

`File (String filename)`

Creates a `File` object for a given filename. The filename can be a full path name or a name relative to the current directory.

Public Methods:

`String getAbsolutePath( )`

Returns the full path name of this file.

`boolean isDirectory( )`

Returns `true` if this `File` object represents a directory.

`boolean isFile( )`

Returns `true` if this `File` object represents a file.

`String[] list( )`

Returns an array of file and subdirectory names of this `File` object representing a directory.

Class: `java.util.Formatter`

Purpose: This class is used to format the numerical and text output with justification and alignment. See Section 6.8 for sample usage.

Hierarchy: `java.lang.Object` ← `java.util.Formatter`

Class: `java.util.Formatter` *(Continued)*

Constructors:

`Formatter ( outputStream out )`

Creates a Formatter for the specified output stream. Example:

```
Formatter formatter = new Formatter(System.out);
```

Public methods:

`Formatter format (String format, Object... expressions)`

Formats the given **expressions** using the formatting pattern **format** and outputs the result to the associated output stream. Expressions can be numerical, sttring, **GregorianCalendar,** and other types of data. The formatting pattern is explained in Section 6.8.

Note: From Java 5.0 (SDK 1.5) **System.out (PrintStream** object) and **String** both support a new method named **format** that does the formatting. The **format** method of the **String** class is a class method that returns the formatted string.

Class: `java.awt.Graphics`

Purpose: This class supports drawing functionality.

Hierarchy: `java.lang.Object` ⇽ `java.awt.Graphics`

Public Methods:

`void drawLine(int x1, int y1, int x2, int y2)`

Draws a line between (`x1, y1`) and (`x2, y2`).

`void drawOval(int x, int y, int width, int height)`

Draws an oval.

`void drawRect(int x, int y, int width, int height)`

Draws a rectangle.

```
void drawRoundRect(int x, int y, int width, int height,
                   int arcWidth, int arcHeight)
```

Draws a rectangle with rounded corners

Class: `java.awt.`**`Graphics`** *(Continued)*

```
void drawString(String text, int x, int y)
```

Draws a given text at position (*x*, *y*).

```
void fillOval(int x, int y, int width, int height)
```

Draws a filled oval.

```
void fillRect(int x, int y, int width, int height)
```

Draws a filled rectangle.

```
void fillRoundRect(int x, int y, int width, int height,
                   int arcWidth, int arcHeight)
```

Draws a filled rectangle with rounded corners.

```
void setColor(Color  color)
```

Sets the pen color to `color`.

```
void setFont(Font font)
```

Sets the font to `font`.

Class: `java.util.`**`GregorianCalendar`**

Purpose: This class represents a specific instance in time using the Gregorian calendar.

Hierarchy: `java.lang.Object` ◁— `java.util.Calendar` ◁— `java.util.GregorianCalendar`

Public Constants: A partial list of constants defined in the `Calendar` class.

```
int DAY_OF_MONTH
int DAY_OF_WEEK
int DAY_OF_WEEK_IN_MONTH
int DAY_OF_YEAR
int HOUR
int HOUR_OF_DAY
int MINUTE
int SECOND
```

See the `Ch3TestCalendar` class for the sample uses of these constants.

Class: `java.util.`**`GregorianCalendar`** *(Continued)*

Constructors:

```
GregorianCalendar ( )
```

Creates a new `GregorianCalendar` set to the time and date of the system clock when this object is created.

```
GregorianCalendar (int year, int month, int day)
```

Creates a new `GregorianCalendar` set to the argument year, month, and day. Notice the month ranges from 0 to 11.

```
GregorianCalendar (int year, int month, int day,
                   int hour, int minute)
```

Creates a new `GregorianCalendar` set to the argument values.

```
GregorianCalendar (int year, int month, int day,
                   int hour, int minute, int second)
```

Creates a new `GregorianCalendar` set to the argument values.

Public Methods:

```
int get (int field)
```

Returns the specified field's value. See the class constants for the possible fields.

```
Date getTime ( )
```

Returns this object represented as a `Date`.

```
long getTime ( )
```

Returns the elapsed time in milliseconds since the epoch, which is designated as January 1, 1970, 00:00:00 GMT.

Class: `javax.swing.`**`JComponent`**

Purpose: This is the base class of all Swing GUI components such as buttons, text fields, menus, and others. Methods defined here are applicable to all subclasses.

Hierarchy: `java.lang.Object` <— `java.awt.Component` <— `java.awt.Container` <— `javax.swing.JComponent`

Class: `javax.swing.JComponent` *(Continued)*

Public Methods:

`JRootPane getRootPane ( )`

Returns the root pane that contains this component.

`void setBackground (Color color)`

Sets the background of this component to `color`.

`void setBorder (Border border)`

Sets the border of this component to `border`.

`void setEnabled (boolean state)`

Enables this component if `state` is `true` and disables it if `state` is `false`.

`void setFont (Font font)`

Sets the font used for this component to `font`.

`void setForeground (Color color)`

Sets the foreground of this component to `color`. This is how you change the text color of a component.

`void setVisible (boolean state)`

Makes this component visible if `state` is `true` and invisible if `state` is `false`.

Class: `javax.swing.JFrame`

Purpose: This class is the extended version of `java.awt.Frame` that works as a container for Swing GUI components.

Hierarchy: `java.lang.Object` ⊲— `java.awt.Component` ⊲— `java.awt.Container` ⊲— `java.awt.Window` ⊲— `java.awt.Frame` ⊲— `javax.swing.JFrame`

Class: `javax.swing.JFrame` *(Continued)*

Constructors:

`JFrame (  )`

Creates a new `JFrame` initialized to default properties.

`JFrame (String title)`

Creates a new `JFrame` with a specified title and default values for other properties.

Public Methods:

`Container getContentPane (  )`

Returns the content pane of this frame.

`void resizable (boolean state)`

Enables the resizing of this frame if `state` is `true` and disables the resizing if `state` is `false`.

`void setContentPane (Container pane)`

Sets the content pane of this frame. You can pass an instance of `JPanel` as an argument.

`void setJMenuBar (JMenuBar menubar)`

Sets the menu bar of this frame.

`void setBounds (int x, int y, int width, int height)`

Sets the origin point of this frame to (*x*, *y*), width to `width`, and height to `height`.

`void setLocation (int x, int y)`

Sets the origin point of this frame to (x, y).

`void setSize (int width, int height)`

Sets the width to `width` and height to `height`.

`void setTitle (String title)`

Sets the title of this frame.

`void setVisible (boolean state)`

Makes this frame visible if `state` is `true` and invisible if `state` is `false`.

Class: `javax.swing.`**`JLabel`**

Purpose: An instance of this class is used to display uneditable text or image (or both).

Hierarchy: `java.lang.Object` ◁— `java.awt.Component` ◁— `java.awt.Container` ◁— `javax.swing.JComponent` ◁— `javax.swing.JLabel`

Constructors:

`JLabel ( )`

Creates a new `JLabel` initialized to an empty image and text.

`JLabel (Icon icon)`

Creates a new `JLabel` with the specified image. Note that `Icon` is an interface, and the `ImageIcon` class implements this interface, so you can pass an `ImageIcon` object as an argument.

`JLabel (String text)`

Creates a new `JLabel` with the specified text.

Public Methods:

`Icon getIcon ( )`

Returns the icon of this label.

`String getText ( )`

Returns the text of this label.

`void setIcon (Icon icon)`

Sets the icon of this label.

`void setText (String text)`

Sets the text of this label. The argument should be a single line of text. Any text after the new-line character is ignored.

Class: `javax.swing.`**`JList`**

Purpose: This component represents a list box.

Hierarchy: `java.lang.Object` ◁— `java.awt.Component` ◁— `java.awt.Container` ◁— `javax.swing.JComponent` ◁— `javax.swing.JList`

Class: `javax.swing.`**`JList`** *(Continued)*

Constructors:

`JList (Object[] list)`

Creates a new `JList` with its items set to the passed array elements.

Public Methods:

`int getSelectedIndex ( )`

Returns the index of the first selected items. If no item is selected, then -1 is returned.

`int[] getSelectedIndices ( )`

Returns an array of indices of all selected items.

`void setSelectionMode (int mode)`

Sets the selection mode of this list to `mode`. The three possible values for mode are `ListSelectionModel.SINGLE_SELECTION`, `ListSelectionModel.SINGLE_INTERVAL_SELECTION`, and `ListSelectionModel.MULTIPLE_INTERVAL_SELECTION`. The default mode is `ListSelectionModel.MULTIPLE_INTERVAL_SELECTION`.

Class: `javax.swing.`**`JOptionPane`**

Purpose: This is a convenience class that supports a quick and easy way to deal with a standard dialog box for displaying short messages or getting an input value.

Hierarchy: `java.lang.Object` ⟵ `java.awt.Component` ⟵ `java.awt.Container` ⟵ `javax.swing.JComponent` ⟵ `javax.swing.JOptionPane`

Public Constants: This is a partial list.

`int YES_OPTION`
`int NO_OPTION`
`int CANCEL_OPTION`
`int OK_OPTION`
`int YES_NO_CANCEL_OPTION`

Public Methods: Note the listed methods are all class methods.

`static int showConfirmDialog (Component parent, Object message)`

Displays a standard confirmation dialog and returns the value to indicate which button (`Yes`, `No`, or `Cancel`) is clicked.

Class: `javax.swing.JOptionPane` *(Continued)*

```
static int showConfirmDialog (Component parent, Object message,
                              String title, int optionType)
```

Displays a confirmation dialog with `message` as its prompt and `title` as the dialog title. The value of `optionType` determines which buttons are shown in the dialog.

```
static String showInputDialog (Component parent, Object message)
```

Displays a standard input dialog and returns the entered value as a `String`.

```
static void showMessageDialog (Component parent, Object message)
```

Displays a standard message dialog with the text `message`.

Class: `javax.swing.JSlider`

Purpose: This component represents a slider.

Hierarchy: `java.lang.Object` ◁— `java.awt.Component` ◁— `java.awt.Container` ◁— `javax.swing.JComponent` ◁— `javax.swing.JSlider`

Constructors:

```
JSlider ( )
```

Creates a new horizontal slider ranging from `0` to `100`. The initial position of the slider knob is set to `50`.

```
JSlider (int min, int max)
```

Creates a new horizontal slider ranging from `min` to `max`. The initial position of the slider knob is set to the average of `min` and `max`.

```
JSlider (int orientation, int min, int max, int value)
```

Creates a new slider ranging in values from `min` to `max`. The initial position of the slider knob is set to `value`, and the orientation to `orientation` (`JSlider.VERTICAL` or `JSlider.HORIZONTAL`).

Public Methods:

```
int getValue ( )
```

Returns the current value of this slider.

Class: `javax.swing.JSlider` *(Continued)*

`void setMajorTickSpacing (int spacing)`

Sets the major tick spacing to `spacing`.

`void setMaximum (int max)`

Sets the maximum to `max`.

`void setMinimum (int min)`

Sets the minimum to `min`.

`void setMinorTickSpacing (int spacing)`

Sets the minor tick spacing to `spacing`.

`void setPaintLabels (boolean state)`

Draws the labels if `state` is `true`.

`void setPaintTicks (boolean state)`

Draws the tick marks if `state` is `true`.

`void setValue (int value)`

Sets the current value of this slider to `value`.

Class: `javax.swing.JTextComponent`

Purpose: An instance of this class is used to display uneditable text or image (or both).

Hierarchy: `java.lang.Object` ⇽ `java.awt.Component` ⇽ `java.awt.Container` ⇽ `javax.swing.JComponent` ⇽ `javax.swing.JTextComponent`

Constructors: They use the constructors of the subclasses `JTextArea` and `JTextField`.

Public Methods:

`String getSelectedText ( )`

Returns the selected text of this text component.

`String getText ( )`

Returns the text of this text component.

Class: `javax.swing.JTextComponent` *(Continued)*
`void setEditable (boolean state)`
Makes this text component editable if `state` is `true` and an editable if `state` is `false`.
`void setText (String str)`
Sets the text of this text component to a specified `str`.

Class: `java.lang.Math`	
Purpose:	This class supports mathematical functions.
Hierarchy:	`java.lang.Object <— java.awt.Graphics`
Public Constants:	
`double PI`	
The value of pi.	
`double E`	
The value of natural number *e*.	
Public Methods:	Please refer to Table 3.6 for a list of methods.

Class: `java.util.Scanner`	
Purpose:	An object to input data from an input stream.
Hierarchy:	`java.lang.Object <— java.util.Scanner`
Constructors:	
`Scanner ( InputStream source )`	
Creates a new **Scanner** with input values coming from the **source.** Example: `Scanner scanner = new Scanner(System.in);`	
Public methods:	
`byte nextByte( )`	
Returns the next input value as a **byte.**	

Class: `java.util.Scanner` *(Continued)*

`double nextDouble( )`

Returns the next input value as a **double.**

`float nextFloat( )`

Returns the next input value as a **float.**

`int nextInt( )`

Returns the next input value as a **int.**

`long nextLong( )`

Returns the next input value as a **long.**

`short nextShort( )`

Returns the next input value as a **short.**

`String next( )`

Returns the next input value as a **String.**

`void useDelimeter(String marker)`

Sets **marker** as a marker to separate the input values. Useful when reading a text that contains spaces. Example: To set the tab as the separator, write `scanner.useDelimeter("\t");`

Class: `java.text.SimpleDateFormat`

Purpose: This class is used to format dates.

Hierarchy: `java.lang.Object` ⇽ `java.text.Format` ⇽ `java.text.DateFormat` ⇽ `java.text.SimpleDateFormat`

Constructors:

`SimpleDateFormat (    )`

Creates a new `SimpleDateFormat` initialized to a default format.

`SimpleDateFormat (String format)`

Creates a new `SimpleDateFormat` initialized to the specified format. See Table 2.1 for the symbols you can use to specify the format.

Class: `java.text.`**`SimpleDateFormat`** *(Continued)*

Public Methods:

`String format (Date date)`

Returns the formatted string of a given `date`.

Class: `java.lang.`**`String`**

Purpose: This class represents an immutable sequence of characters.

Hierarchy: `java.lang.Object` ◁— `java.lang.String`

Constructors:

`String ( )`

Creates a new empty `String`.

`String (String str)`

Creates a new `String` from a given `str`.

Public Methods:

`char chatAt (int index)`

Returns a character at position `index`. The first character in a string is at position 0.

`String concat(String str)`

Returns a new string that is a concatenation of this string and the argument `str`. The concatenation operator + is equivalent to this method.

`boolean equals(String str)`

Returns `true` if this string has the same sequence of characters as the argument `str`. Comparison is done in a case-sensitive manner.

`boolean equalsIgnoreCase(String str)`

Is the same as `equals` but in a case-insensitive manner.

Class: `java.lang.`**`String`** *(Continued)*

`static String format(String format, Object... expressions)`

Formats the given `expressions` following the formatting pattern `format` and returns the formatted string.

`int length()`

Returns the number of characters in this string.

`boolean matches(String regex)`

Returns `true` if this string matches the given regular expression `regex`.

`String substring(int start)`

Returns a substring of this string from index position `start` to the last character of this string.

`String substring(int start, int end)`

Returns a substring of this string from index position `start` to `end-1`.

`String toLowerCase(    )`

Converts this string to all lowercase characters.

`String toUpperCase(    )`

Converts this string to all uppercase characters.

`String trim(    )`

Removes the leading and trailing whitespaces (e.g., blank spaces, tabs, new lines).

Class: `java.lang.`**`StringBuffer`**

Purpose: This class represents a mutable sequence of characters.

Hierarchy: `java.lang.Object` <— `java.lang.StringBuffer`

Constructors:

`StringBuffer ( )`

Creates a new empty `StringBuffer` with the initial capacity of 16 characters.

Class: `java.lang.StringBuffer` *(Continued)*

`StringBuffer (String str)`

Creates a new `StringBuffer` whose content is initialized to a given `str`.

Public Methods:

`StringBuffer append (char ch)`
`StringBuffer append (String str)`

Appends an argument to this string buffer.

`char charAt(int index)`

Returns a character at position `index`. The first character in a string is at position `0`.

`StringBuffer deleteCharAt(int index)`

Removes the character at position `index` from this string buffer.

`StringBuffer insert (int index, char ch)`
`StringBuffer insert (int index,  String str)`

Inserts an argument to this string buffer at position `index`.

`int length()`

Returns the number of characters in this string.

`StringBuffer reverse(    )`

Reverses this string buffer.

`String substring(int start)`

Returns a substring of this string buffer from index position `start` to the last character of this string.

`String substring(int start, int end)`

Returns a substring of this string buffer from index position `start` to `end-1`.

Appendix D

UML Diagrams

What is UML?

The unified modeling language (UML) provides graphical notation that can be used to model computer systems developed using object-oriented software engineering (OOSE). The focus of OOSE is identifying the problem elements that produce or consume information and describing the relationships among these elements. In OOSE, objects are defined to represent these elements during the system analysis and design process. UML diagrams allow software engineers to indicate the relationships among the objects used to define the system. Most of these objects will need to be implemented using software in the final system. UML is particularly useful when the plan is to implement the system in an object-oriented language like Java.

Software engineers use several types of models during the analysis and design phases of the software development process. Data models describe object attributes and relationships with each other. Functional models show how data is transformed as it flows through the system. Behavioral models depict the actions taken by the system in response to events. Architectural diagrams show the relationships among the hardware and software components needed to implement the complete system. UML provides several types of diagrams to support the modeling needs of software engineers. The author has made use of a subset of the UML class diagram notation to describe class content throughout this text.

This appendix will describe the use of UML diagrams to model the attributes, behavior, and architecture of a simple vending machine. This vending machine accepts a single coin and dispenses a single product. The machine does not give change. If a bad coin is inserted, or if the machine has no product to dispense, the coin will be returned to the customer. A merchant owns the machine and adds products to it. The merchant also removes the coins from the coin box.

Class Diagram

Class diagrams were introduced in the first two chapters of this text. Class diagrams are one of the most important UML diagrams used by software engineers. Class diagrams are used to create logical models of computer-based systems. A class diagram shows class structure, contents, and the static relationships among the classes used to model a system. These relationships are known as associations and are drawn as lines connecting the related graph nodes. Each node in a class diagram is

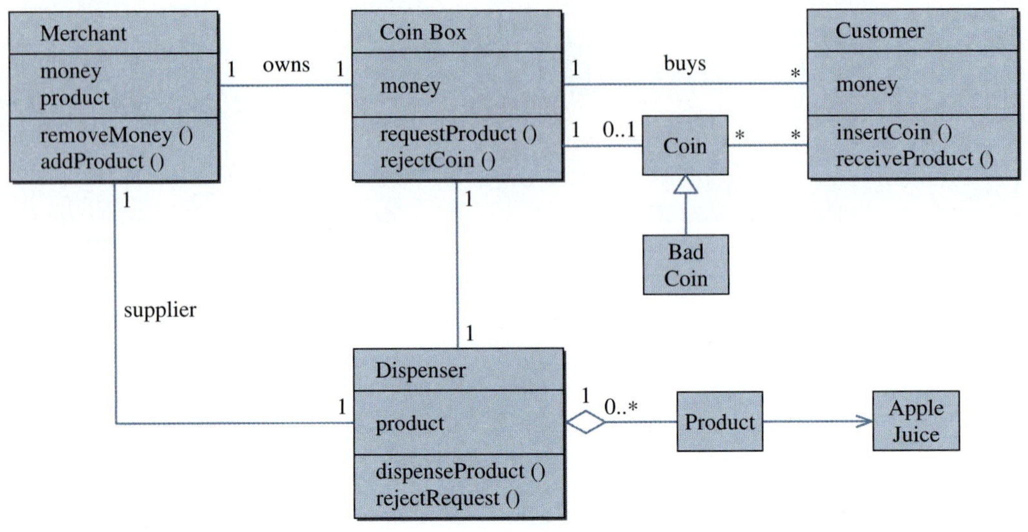

Figure 1 Class diagram.

labeled with its class name. The class node may also contain lists of data attributes and method prototypes. The visibility of attributes or methods can be indicated by prefixing their names with a + (public) or − (private).

An association line indicates that there is a linkage between two classes. Some associations may be labeled with a string indicating the type of relationship between the classes. Each end of the association is labeled with a number, *, or range to describe the multiplicity of the link (e.g., 1..* designates a multiplicity that ranges from 1 to many). Part whole relationships (known as aggregations in UML) are indicated using an open diamond at one end of the link. Inheritance relationships (known as generalizations in UML) are indicated using an open triangle to point to the appropriate super class. Class instances are shown drawing an arrowhead pointing to a class instance node.

Use Case Diagram

Use case diagrams are used to model system functional requirements. These diagrams show how users interact with the system. They are drawn to be independent of the specific user interface design that will be used in the final system. Use cases summarize several scenarios for a user task or goal. A scenario is an instance of an instance of use case for a particular actor, at a specific time, with specific data. Each scenario would be described using text description and shown graphically with a sequence diagram. Use case diagrams assist software engineers to develop test cases.

Users are called actors and are represented in use case diagrams by labeled stick figures. Use case nodes are labeled with user goals or tasks. Actors are connected to the appropriate nodes using lines. Links may be labeled with the string

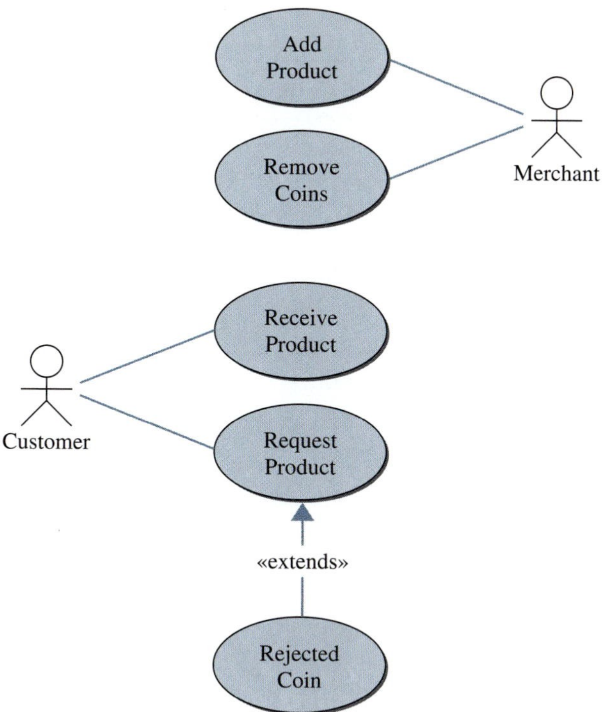

Figure 2 Use case diagram.

«extends» to show explicitly optional actor interactions or handling of exceptional uses. The string «uses» may be used to label links to existing use cases being used as subsystems in the current use case. Each path through a use case diagram represents a separate use case.

Sequence Diagram

Sequence diagrams model system behavior for use cases by showing the necessary class interactions. Sequence diagrams depict workflow from a use case graphically. They show the temporal sequence of message exchanges among a collection of objects as they communicate to achieve a specific task. In particular they show how the user (actor) interacts with a system to get work done (i.e., what messages get sent and when are they sent). The events modeled in sequence diagrams are external events initiated by an actor.

The actors and objects are arranged horizontally across the top of the diagram. The vertical dimension represents time. A vertical line called a lifeline is attached to each actor or object. The lifeline becomes an activation box to show the live activation period of the object or actor. A message is represented using an arrow labeled with a message. The message label may contain an argument list and a return type. Dashed arrows may be used to indicate object flow. If an object's

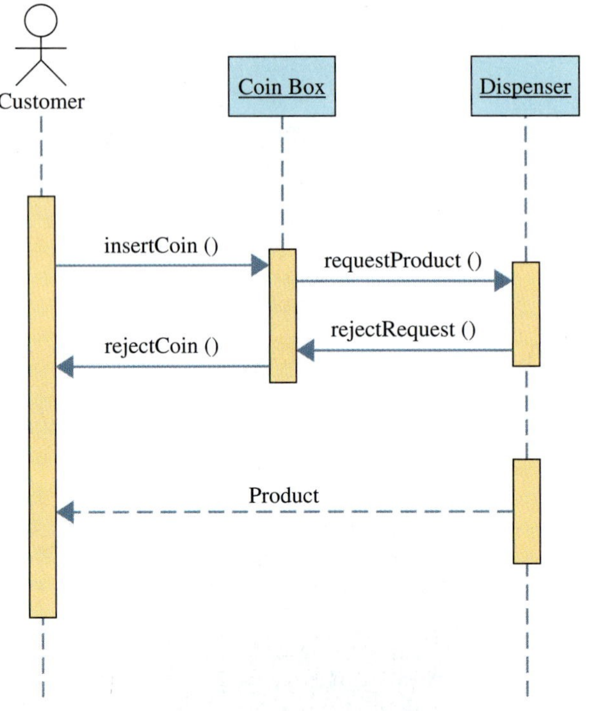

Figure 3 Sequence diagram.

life ends during the execution of the use case an X is placed at the bottom of its lifeline.

Collaboration Diagram

Collaboration diagrams show the message passing structure of the system. The focus is on the roles of the objects as they interact to realize a system function. They can be used to represent portions of a design pattern and are useful for validating class diagrams.

A collaboration diagram is a directed graph with the objects and actors as vertices. Directional links are used to indicate communication between objects. These

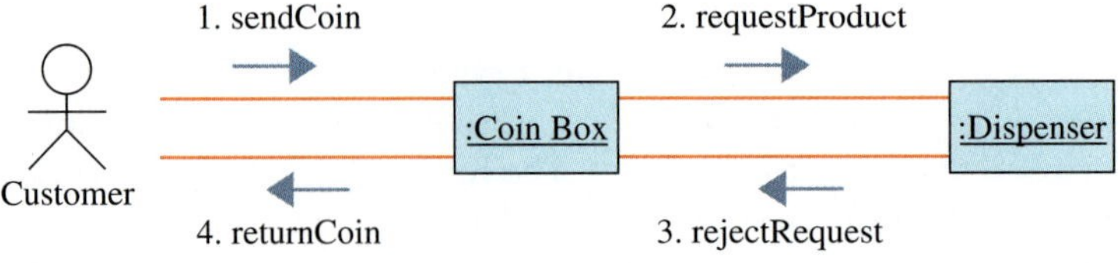

Figure 4 Return coin collaboration diagram.

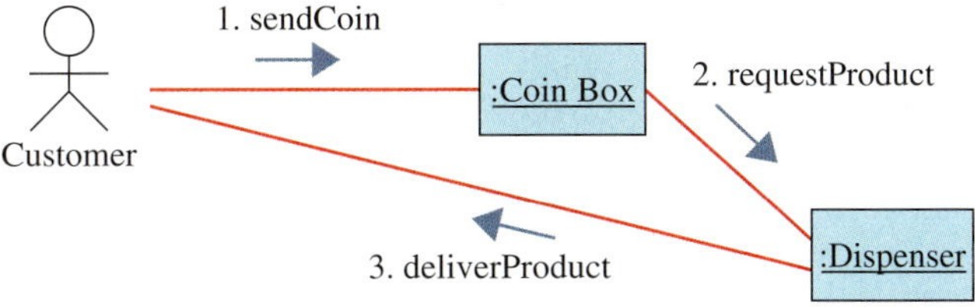

Figure 5 Product delivery collaboration diagram.

links are labeled using appropriate messages. Each message is prefixed with a sequence number to indicate the time ordering required to complete the system function. As you can see in Figure 5, not every collaboration diagram can be drawn horizontally or vertically.

State Diagram

State diagrams describe the behavior of a system, subsystem, or an individual object. The system state is determined by the values assigned to object attributes. A system is assumed to remain in its current state until some new event occurs. State diagrams show changes in system state or object attributes in response to external

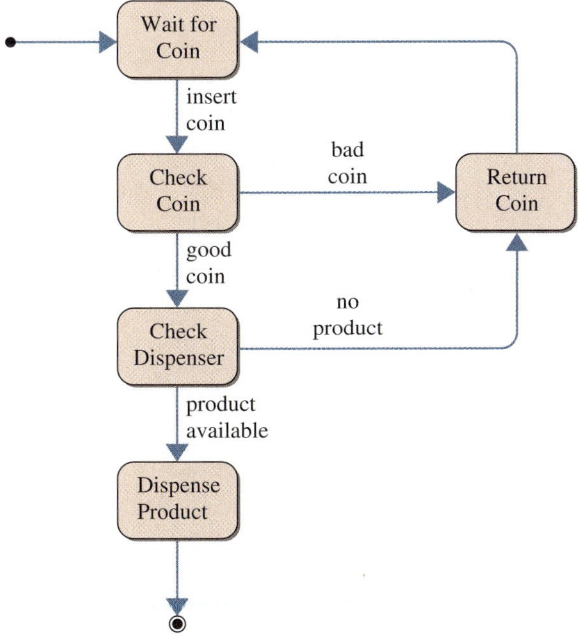

Figure 6 State diagram.

events or triggers. They can display the sequence of states an object goes through in response to potential triggers.

A state diagram is a directed graph whose nodes are labeled with state names. The nodes in a state diagram are drawn as rectangles with rounded corners. The links between the nodes are called transitions and are labeled with the name of the triggering event. A small black circle is used to represent the start state. A small black circle with a ring around it is used to represent the end state. Enclosing a group of nodes in the state diagram with a rectangle having rounded corners can be done to identify a substate.

Activity Diagram

Activity diagrams show the workflow that an object or system component performs. They can show both data flow (information exchange) and control flow (operation ordering). Activities are states representing the execution of a set of operations or thread needed to realize a system function. The transitions to new activities are triggered by the completion of the current activity. Activity diagrams are similar to

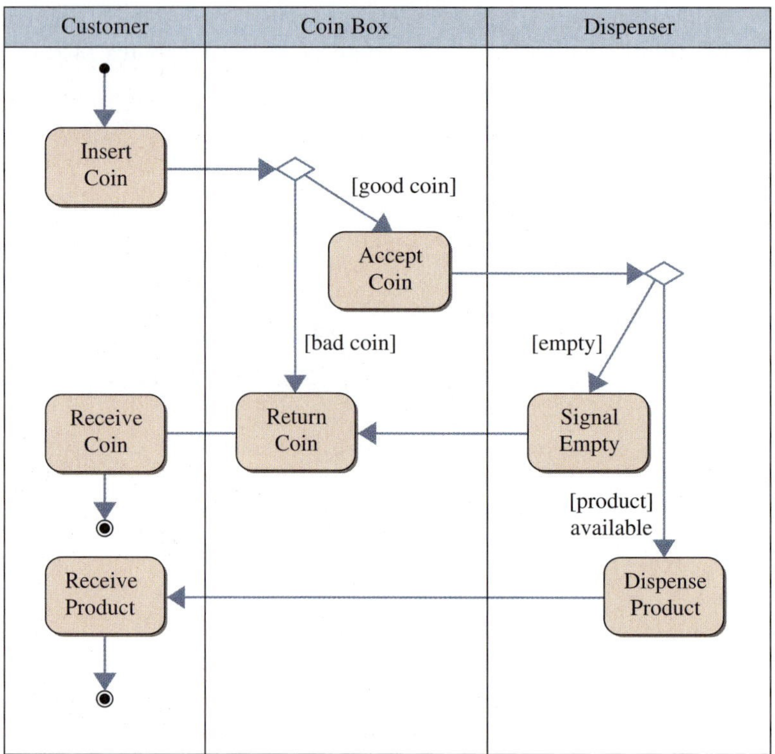

Figure 7 Activity diagram.

state diagrams except that transitions are triggered by internal events. Internal events are not visible to the system user. Activity diagrams can be used to visualize the interrelations and interactions between different use cases. Activity diagrams are usually associated with several classes.

Object responsibilities can be shown in an activity diagram by drawing swim lanes labeled with object names. Activity nodes are drawn using rectangles having semicircles on each end. The start and end state symbols are the same as those used in state diagrams. Links may be labeled with conditions that are the result of completing an activity. Decision points may be represented using unlabeled diamonds. Activity diagrams can be used to show concurrent operations like fork, join, and rendezvous.

Component Diagram

The component diagram shows the relationships (i.e. dependencies, communication, location, and interfaces) among the software building blocks or components in a system. The component diagram might be described as a physical analog of the system class diagram. It is typically made up of several classes and shows the high level code structure of the system.

Each system component is represented as a rectangle with tabs. A component interface is represented using a small round circle connected to a component by a line. An interface describes a group of operations used or created by a component. Arrows can be used to show the direction of information flow. Dashed lines can be used to indicate dependencies among components.

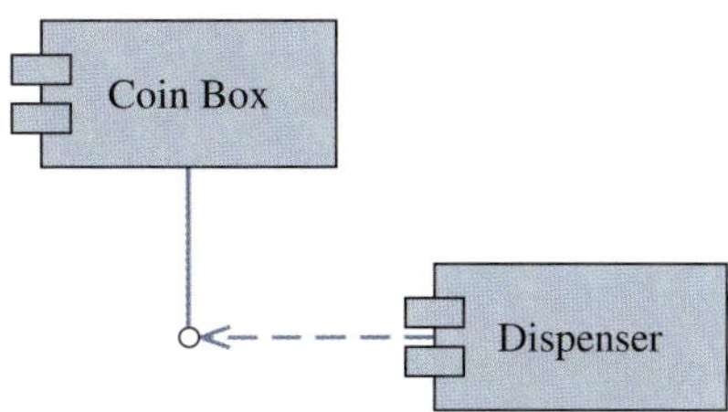

Figure 8 Component diagram.

Deployment Diagram

Deployment diagrams depict the physical resources for a system including nodes, components, and connections. Deployment diagrams show the relationships among both hardware and software components. They can also show the configuration or deployment of run-time elements, software components, processes, and objects. Often component diagrams are combined in a single system deployment diagram.

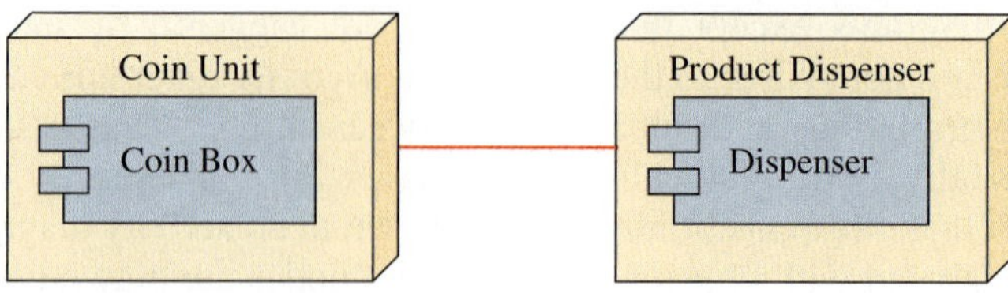

Figure 9 Deployment diagram.

Nodes in a deployment diagram are typically capable of executing code components and are represented by 3D drawings of boxes. Associations between two nodes are drawn as lines to represent physical connections (e.g., Ethernet) between the nodes.

Index

A

C

D

E

F

G

H

J

K

L

M

N

O